CW01369188

THE BUILDINGS OF SCOTLAND

FOUNDING EDITORS:
NIKOLAUS PEVSNER & COLIN MCWILLIAM

PERTH AND KINROSS

JOHN GIFFORD

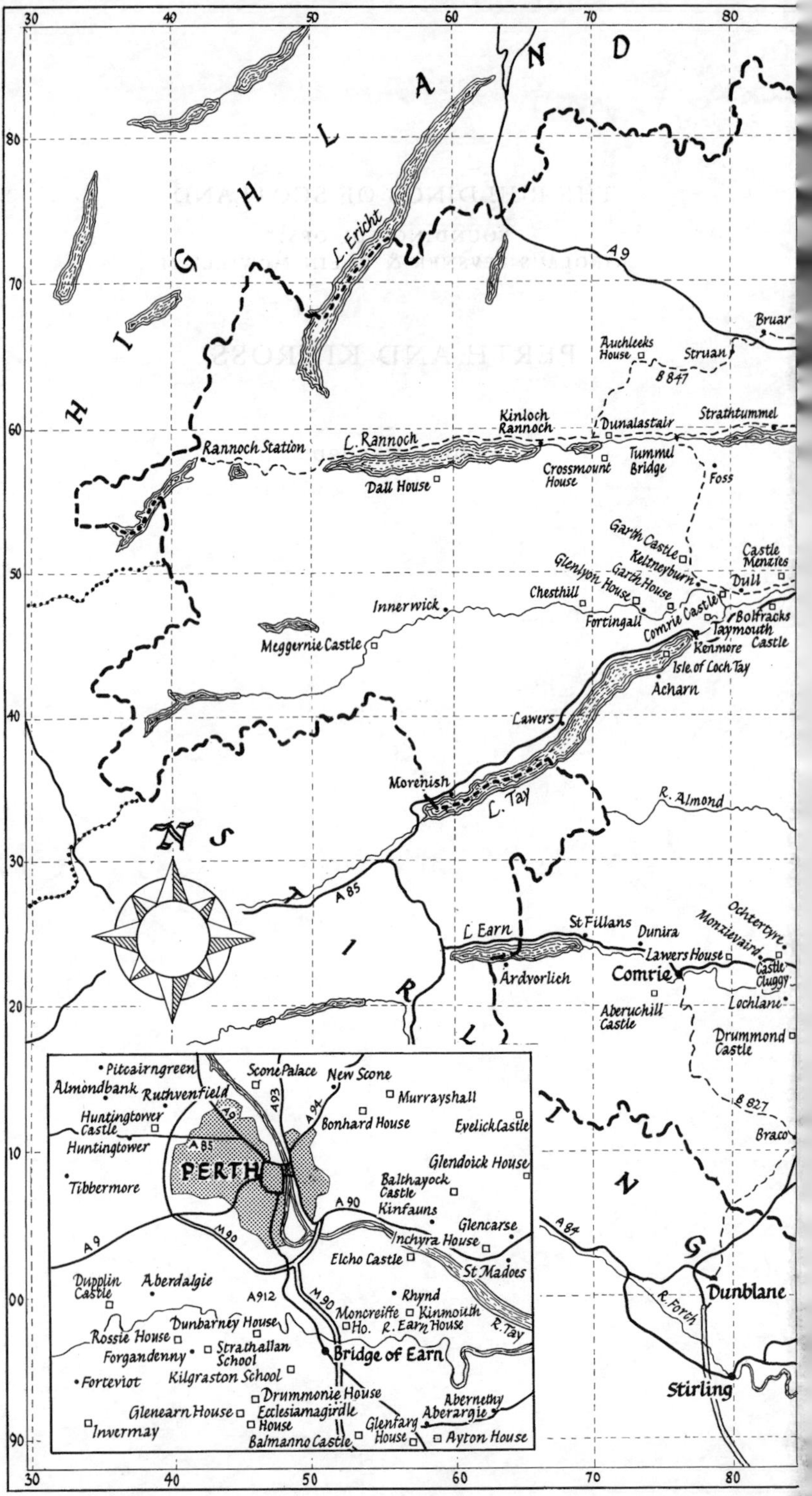

PERTH and KINROSS
Motorways
'A' Roads
'B' Roads
Rivers and lochs
Boundary of Perth and Kinross
ANGUS
FIFE
90
00
10
20
30
40
80
70
60
50
40
30
20
10
00
90
0 5 10 15 km
0 5 10 miles
Dalmunzie House
Spittal of Glenshee
A93
Dalnaglar Castle
Cray
Whitefield Castle
Ashintully Castle
Straloch
A924
Balnakeilly
Kirkmichael
B951
R. Isla
Blair Castle
Lude House
Blair Atholl
Old Fincastle
Tenandry
Faskally House
Glenfincastle
Bonskeid House
Pitlochry
Edradour
Dunfallandy
Pitnacree House
Ballinluig
Tulliemet House
Ballintuim
Blackcraig Castle
Bridge of Cally
Bamff
Inverquiech Castle
Findynate Ho.
Derculich
Strathtay
Grandtully
Clochfoldich
Weem
Logierait
Kinnaird House
Craighall Rattray
Alyth
Aberfeldy
Dalguise House
Dowally
Glasclune Castle
Balhary
Balendoch
A94
Jordanstone
Drumkilbo
Cardney House
A923
Forneth House
Kinloch
Blairgowrie
Meigle
Kinvaird House
Loch of Clunie
Clunie Castle
Bardmony Ho.
Kings of Kinloch
Belmont Castle
Arthurstone
A826
Dunkeld
Birnam
Lethendy
Tower of Lethendy
Bendochy
Ardler
The Hermitage
Inver
Glendelvine Ho.
Caputh
Spittalfield
Meikleour
Coupar Angus
A822
Rohallion Lodge
Murthly
Kinclaven
Cargill
Keithick
Kettins
Hallyburton House
Amulree
Ballathie House
Woodside
Burrelton
Pitcur Castle
Bankfoot
Stobhall
Wolfhill
Balledgarno
Tullybelton House
Stanley
A93
Dunsinnan House
Collace
Rossie Priory
Cambusmichael
Kinrossie
Knapp
Invergowrie
Chapelhill
Battleby
St Martins
Balbeggie
Abernyte
Glenalmond House
Moneydie
Luncarty
Moncur Cas.
Ballindean
Longforgan
Redgorton
Stormontfield
Kinnaird
Castle Huntly
Glenalmond College
Inchture
Rait
Inchmartine House
Keillour Castle
A94
Kilspindie
Hosh
Monzie
Fowlis Wester
A85
Methven
Megginch Castle
Gilmerton
Inchaffray Abbey
A90
Cultoquhey Ho.
PERTH
Errol
Woodend
to Tay Bridge
Crieff
Abercairney
Madderty
Findo Gask
Innerpeffray
Millearne
Kinkell
Gask Ho.
R. Earn
Muthill
Trinity Gask
Colquhalzie
Auchterarder Ho.
Duncrub Park
Culdees
Strathallan Castle
Garvock Ho.
Tullibardine
Dunning
Aberuthven
Kippen House
A91
Cupar
Auchterarder
Cloan
Keltie Castle
M90
Rossie Ochil
Balvaird Castle
Gleneagles Hotel
Kincardine Castle
Fordel House
Orchil House
Glenfarg
Blackford
Gleneagles House
A9
B934
Arlary House
A823
Milnathort
Tullibole Castle
Glendevon
Burleigh Castle
Kinnesswood
A91
Scotlandwell
L. Leven
Kinross
A911
Lendrick Muir
Lochleven Castle
Arnot Tower
Glenrothes
Rumbling Bridge
Crook of Devon
St Serf's Priory
Briglands
House of Aldie
Cleish
A91
Blairingone
Dowhill
Blair Adam
Solsgirth House
A92
Alloa
M90
Kirkcaldy

PEVSNER ARCHITECTURAL GUIDES

The Buildings of Scotland was founded by
Sir Nikolaus Pevsner (1902–83) and
Colin McWilliam (1928–89) as a companion series
to *The Buildings of England*. Between 1979 and
2001 it was published by Penguin Books.

THE BUILDINGS OF SCOTLAND TRUST

The Buildings of Scotland Trust is a charitable trust,
founded in 1991, which manages and finances the research
programme needed to sustain the Buildings of Scotland series.
The Trust is sponsored by Historic Scotland (on behalf of
Scottish Ministers), The National Trust for Scotland and the
Royal Commission on the Ancient and Historical Monuments
of Scotland. The Buildings of Scotland Trust is grateful for and
wishes to acknowledge the support of the many individuals,
charitable trusts and foundations, companies and local
authorities who have given financial help to its work. Without
that support it would not be possible to look forward to the
completion of the research programme for the series. In
particular the Trust wishes to record its thanks to the National
Trust for Scotland, which carried the financial responsibility
for this work over a considerable period before the new
trust was set up.

The trustees wish to acknowledge the generous support of
H.M. The Queen and H.R.H. The Prince of Wales.

Special thanks are due to the following donors:

Aberbrothock Charitable Trust
Binks Trust, Dulverton Trust
Esmée Fairbairn Charitable Trust
Marc Fitch Fund
Gordon Fraser Charitable Trust
Gargunnock Estate Trust
A. S. and Miss M. I. Henderson Trust
Historic Scotland, Imlay Foundation Inc.
Sir Peter Leslie, Leverhulme Trust
MacRoberts Trusts
Colin McWilliam Memorial Fund
Nancie Massey Charitable Trust
Merchants House of Glasgow
National Trust for Scotland, Pilgrim Trust
Radcliffe Trust, Joseph Rank Benevolent Trust
Royal Bank of Scotland plc, Russell Trust
Walter Scott
VisitScotland
James Wood Bequest Fund

and
The Paul Mellon Centre for Studies in British Art for a
grant towards the cost of illustrations

Perth and Kinross

BY

JOHN GIFFORD

THE BUILDINGS OF SCOTLAND

YALE UNIVERSITY PRESS
NEW HAVEN AND LONDON

YALE UNIVERSITY PRESS
NEW HAVEN AND LONDON
302 Temple Street, New Haven CT 06511
47 Bedford Square, London WC1B 3DP
www.pevsner.co.uk
www.yalebooks.co.uk
www.yalebooks.com

Published by Yale University Press 2007
2 4 6 8 10 9 7 5 3 1

ISBN 978 0 300 10922 1

© John Gifford, 2007

Printed in China
through World Print
Set in Monotype Plantin

All rights reserved.
This book may not be reproduced
in whole or in part, in any form (beyond that
copying permitted by Sections 107 and 108 of the
U.S. Copyright Law and except by reviewers
for the public press), without written
permission from the publishers

For
ANDREW AND CHARLOTTE
THEIR CATTLE, CHICKENS AND CHILDREN

ACCESS TO BUILDINGS

Many of the buildings described in this book are public places, and in some obvious cases their interiors (at least the public sections of them) can be seen without formality. But it must be emphasized that the mention of buildings or lands does not imply any rights of public access to them, or the existence of any arrangements for visiting them.

Some churches are open within regular hours, and it is usually possible to see the interiors of others by arrangement with the minister or church officer. Particulars of admission to Ancient Monuments and other buildings in the care of Scottish Ministers (free to the Friends of Historic Scotland) are available from Historic Scotland, Longmore House, Salisbury Place, Edinburgh EH9 1SH or its website, www.historic-scotland.gov.uk. Details of access to properties of the National Trust for Scotland are available from the Trust's head office at 28 Charlotte Square, Edinburgh, EH2 4ET or via its website, www.nts.org.uk. Admission is free to members, on whose subscriptions and donations the Trust's work depends.

Scotland's Gardens Scheme, 42a Castle Street, Edinburgh EH2 3BN, provides a list of gardens open to visitors, also available on the National Gardens Scheme website (www.gardensofscotland.org), Scotland's Churches Scheme (www.churchesinscotland.co.uk), Dunedin, Holehouse Road, Eaglesham, Glasgow G76 0JF, publishes an annual directory of churches open to visitors while *Hudson's Historic Houses, Castles and Gardens Open to the Public* includes many private houses.

Local tourist offices can advise the visitor on what properties in each area are open to the public and will usually give helpful directions as to how to get to them.

CONTENTS

LIST OF TEXT FIGURES AND MAPS — x
MAP REFERENCES — xiii
ACKNOWLEDGEMENTS FOR ILLUSTRATIONS — xiv
FOREWORD — xv

INTRODUCTION — 1
GEOLOGY, TOPOGRAPHY AND BUILDING MATERIALS — 1
PREHISTORIC PERTH AND KINROSS — 4
THE ROMANS IN PERTH AND KINROSS — 16
PICTISH PERTH AND KINROSS — 22
MEDIEVAL CHURCHES — 30
POST-REFORMATION CHURCHES — 39
MAUSOLEA, MONUMENTS, GRAVEYARDS AND STATUES — 55
MOTTES, CASTLES, TOWERS AND LAIRDS' HOUSES — 62
PALACES, MANSIONS AND COUNTRY HOUSES — 72
ROADS, RAILWAYS AND HARBOURS — 91
BURGHS AND VILLAGES — 99
RURAL MANSES, FARMHOUSES AND STEADINGS — 121
INDUSTRIAL BUILDINGS — 126

PERTH AND KINROSS — 133

GLOSSARY — 747
INDEX OF ARTISTS — 775
INDEX OF PLACES — 789

LIST OF TEXT FIGURES AND MAPS

Kettins, Pitcur, souterrain. Plan (RCAHMS, *South-East Perth an archaeological landscape*, 1994)	12
Alyth, Barry Hill, fort. Site plan (RCAHMS, *North-East Perth an archaeological landscape*, 1990)	14
Spittalfield, Inchtuthil, Roman fortress. Plan (Society for the Promotion of Roman Studies, *Inchtuthil Roman Fort*, 1985)	19
Abernethy Round Tower. Engraving, 1802, after view by Thomas Girtin, *c.* 1785 (RCAHMS)	26
Dunkeld Cathedral. Engraving from J. Slezer, *Theatrum Scotiae*, 1693 (RCAHMS)	32
Dron Parish Church. East elevation by William Stirling I, 1824 (National Library of Scotland)	44
Scone Palace, Mausoleum. West elevation probably by William Atkinson, 1807 (The Earl of Mansfield)	56
Castle Huntly. Perspective (R. W. Billings, *The Baronial and Ecclesiastical Antiquities of Scotland*, 1845–52)	66
Elcho Castle. Perspective (R. W. Billings, *The Baronial and Ecclesiastical Antiquities of Scotland*, 1845–52)	69
Taymouth Castle. Elevation of south front in 1856 (RCAHMS)	79
Rossie Priory. Perspective of south front from J. P. Neale, *Views of Seats*, 2nd ser., ii, 1825 (RCAHMS)	81
Blair Castle. Watercolour perspective of east front by David Bryce, 1869 (RCAHMS)	84
Dull, Nether Camserney, longhouse. Axonometric view (RCAHMS)	125
Aberfeldy, Tay Bridge. Elevation by William Adam, *c.* 1733 (W. Adam, *Vitruvius Scoticus*, 1811)	137
Ballindean House. Perspective sketch, by David Walker, *c.* 1965 (David Walker)	178
Balvaird Castle. Ground-floor plan (RCAHMS)	186
Blair Castle. Elevation of east front, *c.* 1750 (The Blair Trust)	212
Blair Castle. Perspective of east front, *c.* 1840 (The Blair Trust)	213
Blair Castle. Reconstruction of plans in *c.* 1760 (RCAHMS)	216
Briglands. Perspective and ground-floor plan (V. D. Horsburgh), *c.* 1907 (Peter Savage)	247

LIST OF TEXT FIGURES AND MAPS

Burleigh Castle. Ground-floor plan (RCAHMS)	250
Castle Menzies. First-floor plan (RCAHMS)	265
Collace, Dunsinane Hill, fort. Site plan (RCAHMS, *South-East Perth an archaeological landscape*, 1994)	275
Culdees Castle. Sketch reconstruction of elevations and principal floor plan in *c.* 1810 (RCAHMS)	307
Dowhill Castle. Ground-floor plan (RCAHMS)	314
Dron Parish Church. Sections by William Stirling I, 1824 (National Library of Scotland)	317
Drummond Castle. Site plan (RCAHMS)	320
Dunfallandy Stone (J. Stuart, *Sculptured Stones of Scotland*, i, 1856)	331
Dunkeld. View of town from J. Slezer, *Theatrum Scotiae*, 1693 (RCAHMS)	332
Dunkeld Cathedral. Plan (RCAHMS)	335
Dunning, St Serf's Church, Dupplin Cross (J. Stuart, *Sculptured Stones of Scotland*, ii, 1867)	351
Elcho Castle. Plans (RCAHMS)	360
Glasclune Castle. Ground-floor plan (RCAHMS)	383
Glenalmond College. Perspective of original design (*The Builder*, ix, January 11, 1851)	384
Gleneagles House. Drawing of north front, by David Walker, *c.* 1967 (David Walker)	398
The Hermitage. Engraving after a pastel by George Walker, from James Cririe, *Scottish Scenery*, 1807 (RCAHMS)	411
Huntingtower Castle. Plans (RCAHMS)	417
Kinfauns Castle, Gallery. Engraving after a painting by Robert Gibb, *c.* 1827, from J. P. Neale, *Views of the Seats*, 2nd. ser., iv, 1828 (RCAHMS)	462
Kinross House. Reconstruction of site plan of *c.* 1685 (RCAHMS)	485
Kinross House. Plans of house in *c.* 1700 (RCAHMS)	491
Lochleven Castle. Ground-floor plan (RCAHMS)	502
Meigle Museum, Pictish stone (Meigle 11) (RCAHMS, *South-East Perth an archaeological landscape*, 1994)	520
Murthly Castle. Plans of development (RCAHMS)	546
Perth. View of city from J. Slezer, *Theatrum Scotiae*, 1693 (RCAHMS)	565
Perth. Map of city, *c.* 1850 (RCAHMS)	569
Perth, St John's Kirk of Perth. Engraved perspective of south elevation in 1775 after an etching by Archibald Rutherford (*Sconiana*, 1807)	572
Perth, St John's Kirk of Perth. Plan (RCAHMS)	574
Perth, Old Council Chambers. Perspective (*The Builder*, xxxiii, September 25, 1880)	603
Perth Prison. Bird's-eye view, by J. D. Collinson, *c.* 1810 (RCAHMS)	606
Rossie Priory, Mausoleum, cross-slab (RCAHMS, *South-East Perth an archaeological landscape*, 1994)	682
Scone Palace. East elevation by William Atkinson, 1803 (The Earl of Mansfield)	689

Scone Palace, Long Gallery. Painting by Robert Gibb,
 c. 1827 (The Earl of Mansfield) 692
Stobhall. Block-plan (RCAHMS) 705
Taymouth Castle. First-floor plan (RCAHMS) 722
Tulliebole Castle. Plans (RCAHMS) 737

MAPS
Aberfeldy 136
Alyth 150
Auchterarder 165
Blairgowrie 225
Comrie 276
Coupar Angus 282
Crieff 291
Dunkeld 343
Kinross 475
New Scone 558
Perth: City Centre 571
Perth: Suburbs 644
Perth: Barnhill, Bridgend and Gannochy 646
Pitlochry 673

MAP REFERENCES

The numbers printed in italic type in the margin against the place names in the gazetteer indicate the position of the place in question on the area map (pages ii–iii), which is divided into sections by the 10-kilometre reference lines of the National Grid. The reference given here omits the two initial letters (formerly numbers) which in a full grid reference refer to the 100-kilometre squares into which the country is divided. The first two numbers indicate the *western* boundary, and the last two the *southern* boundary, of the 10-kilometre square in which the place is situated. For example, Innerpeffray, reference 9010, will be found in the 10-kilometre square bounded by grid lines 90 (on the *west*) and 00, and 10 (on the *south*) and 20; Tullybelton House, reference 0030, in the square bounded by grid lines 00 (on the *west*) and 10, and 30 (on the *south*) and 40.

ACKNOWLEDGEMENTS FOR ILLUSTRATIONS

Royal Commission on the Ancient and Historical Monuments of Scotland

We are deeply indebted to Heather Stoddart of the Royal Commission on the Ancient and Historical Monuments of Scotland (RCAHMS) who redrew measured drawings and plans for this volume and to Angus Lamb and Jim Mackie who specially took the majority of the colour photographs.

Photographs are copyright of the RCAHMS with the exception of the following:

Alamy: 89
David Barbour/BDP: 122
Historic Scotland: 12, 23, 54, 55, 56, 57, 63
Perth Museum and Art Gallery: 4, 27
Scone Palace: 79, 80
Visit Scotland, Perthshire: 1

The plates are indexed in the indexes of names and places, and references to them are given by numbers in the margin of the text.

FOREWORD

Perth and Kinross is the tenth volume of *The Buildings of Scotland* series. The project began about thirty-five years ago when Sir Nikolaus Pevsner, having almost completed *The Buildings of England* (many of its volumes now in revised editions), gave the task of overseeing a similar series for Scotland to Colin McWilliam. Colin himself was author or co-author of the first two Scottish volumes, *Lothian* and *Edinburgh*, and had carried out preliminary work on *Dumfries and Galloway* before his death in 1989. From the start he had intended that the different regions of Scotland should be covered by a number of authors who shared his respect for scholarship, catholicity of taste and lack of antiquarian or narrowly nationalistic prejudice. It is a tribute to Colin's influence on his colleagues and disciples that something at least of what he intended for the series has been achieved in the published volumes.

The Buildings of Scotland, whilst conscious of kinship with the other *Buildings of . . .* series covering England, Ireland and Wales, has claimed and largely enjoyed a certain autonomy, if not full independence. The series' individuality stems partly from the political, religious, social and economic history of Scotland, which has given the country its own mixture of building types and sometimes distinctive architecture, but also from Colin McWilliam's acceptance of the value of buildings of all periods, the pleasure he found in those too easily dismissed as second- or third-rate and his delight in the quirky and even the ugly. Some differences from *The Buildings of England* are readily understood. In the Gazetteer entries churches have been arranged not according to some supposed hierarchy of denominations but alphabetically under the names they presently enjoy (if in use) or under their original names (if disused or secularized). So too have public buildings. More personally attributable to Colin McWilliam are a few peculiarities of the series. He was insistent that the C19 and C20 stained glass in which Scotland is exceptionally rich should be fully covered and the subjects of windows mentioned. Pipe organs (Colin's grandfather and brother were organists) are routinely noted and so too, if they can be associated with buildings, are monkey-puzzle trees – sadly, the inhabitants of Perth and Kinross have often preferred larches.

At the outset of work on *The Buildings of Scotland* Colin McWilliam decided that the volumes should be researched thoroughly. I was employed as one of the first researchers and spent some years extracting all references to Scottish buildings from C19 and C20 architectural and building journals (*The Builder*, *The*

Building News, The Architect, etc.) which supplemented greatly the information already published in the Government's List of Buildings of Special Architectural or Historic Interest and the Inventories of the Royal Commission on the Ancient and Historical Monuments of Scotland, these last covering only part of Scotland. The Commission's earlier volumes were restricted to buildings erected before 1707; later volumes extended the cut-off date to 1840. A starting point for many of the earlier buildings in areas not covered by the Inventories was provided by the magisterial volumes of David MacGibbon and Thomas Ross, *The Castellated and Domestic Architecture of Scotland* (5 vols, 1887–92) and *The Ecclesiastical Architecture of Scotland* (3 vols, 1896–7) and by Howard Colvin's *A Biographical Dictionary of British Architects, 1600–1840* (3rd edn, 1995). The recent (on-line) publication of David Walker's *Dictionary of Scottish Architects, 1840–1940* (www.scottisharchitects.org.uk) has increased enormously the information available on C19 and C20 architects and their works.

For Perth and Kinross the task of arranging material culled from these sources and of looking through a great number of local histories and guidebooks was largely undertaken by Alexandra Jones and Siobhan Marples who also waded through ecclesiastical records and the Registers of Improvements on Entailed Estates now held in the National Archives of Scotland. I myself spent many weeks of research in the National Archives, mostly working on family and estate papers deposited there, most time-consumingly but profitably on those relating to Drummond, Murthly and Taymouth Castles. The staff have been consistently cheering and helpful. Just as welcoming have been Stephen Connelly and his colleagues at the Perth and Kinross Council Archive, repository of many of the building control records for the region, as well as of the minute books of local councils and school boards and much other material. My account of the history of Blair Castle could not have been written without the enthusiastic assistance of Jane Anderson, the castle's archivist, who gave me access to the Atholl papers, of which her knowledge is immense, helped me on my visits to the building and was a most efficient facilitator of the photography of the castle's interiors which was carried out for this book. Her dog's watchful supervision deterred me from theft or vandalism. Much work has been done in libraries, especially the National Library of Scotland, the Edinburgh Central Public Library (notably the Scottish and Fine Arts Departments) and the A. K. Bell Library at Perth where Jeremy Duncan and other members of the Local Services Department showed both the courtesy for which Perth is renowned and an exemplary dedication to the history of the area. Most frequent have been my visits to the National Monuments Record of Scotland, now almost my second, though not weekend, home where the research notes for *Perth and Kinross* will be deposited, as have those of other published volumes in the series.

Information on individual buildings has been given by owners, clergy and members of their congregations. The staff of Perth and Kinross Council, most notably Gordon McFarlane, have taken time to answer my queries about recent buildings. Many historians and architects have contributed much, either by answering specific questions or by discussing the buildings and architecture of the area more generally. Thanks are especially due to David Breeze, Howard Colvin, Kitty Cruft, Ali Darragh, Christopher Dingwall, Andrew Driver, John Dunbar, Richard Fawcett, Ian Fisher, Miles Glendinning, Ian Gow, Abigail Grater, Fergus Harris, Bob Heath, Yvonne Hillyard, Tom Davidson Kelly, Aonghus MacKechnie, Allan Maclean, Debbie Mays, Sean O'Reilly, Matthew Pease, Helen Smailes, Geoffrey Stell, Margaret Stewart, David Walker, Mark Watson and Diane Watters. Owners and custodians of buildings have, with very few exceptions, been welcoming although occasionally surprised that these could be of interest. I hope that my trespasses on their time and, not infrequently, their property may be excused.

The book's Editor at Yale University Press, Charles O'Brien, read the whole text. Most of his suggested alterations have been adopted or adapted and very few caused real irritation. Bernard Dod has acted as copy editor and Charley Chapman as proof reader. Among the Yale team the co-ordination of the text has been undertaken by Emily Winter and illustrations were commissioned and co-ordinated by Emily Wraith. I prepared the index of Artists and Judith Wardman the index of Places. Maps of the general area have been drawn by Reg and Marjorie Piggott. The town maps are by Alan Fagan.

The Royal Commission on the Ancient and Historical Monuments of Scotland has given immense help with the illustrations. Heather Stoddart prepared the plans of buildings, in some cases having to use mutually inconsistent sources and suffer my changes of mind as to what should be shown. She remained outwardly calm. Most of the photographs were taken specially by the Commission's photographers, principally Angus Lamb and Jim Mackie, and scanned by Claire Brockley and Tahra Duncan. Responsibility for ordering and transmitting the photographs was undertaken by Kristina Watson and Diane Watters whose commitment to the task has given me hope that I might be engaged in an enterprise of some worth.

Shelter, drink and food have been given me by various inhabitants of Perth and Kinross, most abundantly by my brother and sister-in-law. On several visits I have been accompanied by David Bassett who, more than anyone else, has supported and suffered me during the writing of this book.

Research and travelling costs for *The Buildings of Scotland* were, for many years, underwritten by the National Trust for Scotland. In 1991 the ongoing task of raising money for these was taken over by The Buildings of Scotland Trust. Peter Wordie, its first Chairman, showed himself a determined supporter of the series. Just as determined and hugely generous of his time and energy in working for the Trust and a great help to me personally has been David Connelly, Secretary of the Trust from 1991 to 2003. Ian Riches, the Trust's present Secretary, continues the tradition.

Finally I shall be grateful for corrections to any errors or omissions in this volume.

INTRODUCTION

GEOLOGY, TOPOGRAPHY AND BUILDING MATERIALS

Topographically and geologically Perth and Kinross resembles an untidily constructed multi-deck sandwich, the layers tilted in a SW–NE direction. At the N, like a heavy slice of bread, is the band of the Grampian Mountains, inhospitable moorland consistently over 300 m. above sea level and, on the region's N boundary, over 600 m. but without any dramatic peak. The Moine metamorphic rocks here are the oldest in the region, formed from sedimentary deposits of sand laid down in an ocean over 1,000 million years ago and compressed and folded into mountains during the Grenvillian and Caledonian Orogenies (mountain-building periods when continents collided) of about 1,000 million and 470 million years ago. In these orogenies intense heat metamorphosed the sandstone, predominantly into a hard granular quartz (psammitic granulite) liable to split into flags along the original bedding surfaces of the sand. At the W end of this layer, under Rannoch Moor, and at the NE, on the N side of Glen Tilt, are large intrusions of granite formed about 550–400 million years ago from molten silicate cooling below the earth's surface to form rock which, because of its relative lightness, then thrust up through the Moine rocks and now forms two of the highest peaks in this part of the region, of over 1,000 m. at Beinn Dearg, near Blair Atholl, and 784 m. at Beinn Pharlagain, near Rannoch Station.

The next and much broader layer to the S has an irregular N boundary running SE from Glen Tilt to Loch Tummel, then N to Loch Errochty from where it passes SW to cross the E end of Loch Rannoch and down to Glen Lyon, its almost straight S boundary that of the Highland Boundary Fault running SW from Alyth to beyond Comrie. Again it is covered mostly with moorland but the underlying rocks are Dalradian, formed from mudstone or shale marine sediments laid down over 550 million years ago but compressed, folded and metamorphosed to mountains of schists, quartzite and marble during the Caledonian Orogeny. A sizeable intrusion of granite erupts N of Comrie. The greater variety of the metamorphosed rocks has led to more strongly differentiated subsequent erosion of these former mountains than in the area to the N, with two of the region's highest peaks, Schiehallion (1,083 m.) to the SE of Kinloch Rannoch and Carn Mairg (1,042 m.) to its SW topped by summits of hard quartzite which have protected the schists below from erosion. The calcareous schists of the highest peak, Ben Lawers (1,214 m.) have produced a calcium-rich soil favourable to the growth of the Alpine-Arctic plants for which it is noted.

By the end of the Caledonian mountain-building period the geological masses of Moine and Dalradian rocks formed high mountains, their appearance much closer to that of the Himalayas than anything found in Scotland today. However, these, still bare of vegetation, were quickly eroded by rivers flooding down their sides. The heavier boulders, cobbles and gravels washed down by these were deposited below in fan-shaped spreads, these depositions gradually cementing together to form a narrow band of coarse-grained conglomerate rocks, as found immediately N of Blairgowrie. Finer particles of sand were carried further away to form alluvial plains where they cemented together as sandstone (Old Red Sandstone) or, if deposited in shallow lakes, mudstone. Old Red Sandstone extends S from Strathmore to the region's S boundary. However, at about the same time as it was formed, volcanic eruptions produced a range of hills (the Sidlaws and Ochils, with the Lomond Hills serving as an outlier on the E side of Kinross-shire) cutting across the sandstone band. The lavas of these volcanoes cooled to form rocks, principally of fine-grained andesite and basalt. Further earth movements about 380 million years ago formed large folds in the sedimentary rocks, the largest being the creation of a rift valley under the originally single volcanic mass which then divided into the present Sidlaw and Ochil Hills. Further erosion followed when rivers flowing to the E deposited conglomerates and sand to form the New Red Sandstone which underlies SW Kinross-shire and the Carse of Gowrie from which it extends to a little W of Bridge of Earn.

The whole of the landscape of Perth and Kinross was modified during the ice ages of the Pleistocene period of 2 million–10,000 years ago, the last and most important glaciation taking place c. 27,000–14,000 years ago when ice, accumulated in great quantity in the basin of Rannoch Moor, advanced E. During its progress the ice scoured, broadened and deepened existing valleys in which it deposited till and formed the deep depressions of Lochs Rannoch, Tay, Earn and Tummel and the Firth of Tay. The weight of the ice also pushed down the height of the land surface. When the climate gradually turned warmer again, the rocks in the uplands of the area, freed from the ice covering, were exposed, as they still are, to shattering by frost which produced scree, that untidy scattering of rock fragments which makes them unwelcoming visually and physically to the casual stroller. In this early warming active glaciers occupied the sides of the valleys, their eventual melting leaving behind pockets of ice which formed kettle holes or depressions, some now appearing as lochs, e.g. the chain of small lochs (Clunie, Butterstone, etc.) E of Dunkeld and the large Loch Leven underlain by two kettle holes. Melting of the ice also led to a rise in the level of the sea which advanced over the lower valley of the Tay and Strathearn and covered completely the Carse of Gowrie. The land, freed from the weight of ice, then rose again and these underwater areas, now covered with glacio-marine clays and marine deposits, were again exposed.

The extensive geological development of the region has left a varied landscape with, at the N, mountainous terrain cut through by deep narrow valleys and lochs and, to the S of the Highland Boundary Fault, the broad plains of Strathmore, Strathearn, the Carse of Gowrie and S Kinross-shire bisected by the hill ranges of the Sidlaws and Ochils. Soil is equally varied. In Strathmore, the Carse of Gowrie and Strathearn the underlying rocks are covered with clays and sands which, if well drained, provide some of the best pastoral and agricultural land in Scotland, suitable for the growing of crops and fruit (sadly often now in plastic tunnels). The upland glens generally contain narrow strips of potentially fertile land, when drained, lying beside the river beds and on the alluvial deltas which extend from the ends of some lochs but, on the hillsides behind, pasture usually gives way quickly to moorland. Much of this, if below *c.* 300m., was formerly covered in forest, predominantly of oak, Scots pine and birch, which was later cleared for agriculture, sheepwalks and deer forests (despite the name, usually devoid of trees). Reforestation, begun in the late C18 by improving landowners such as the fourth Duke of Atholl who planted extensive stands of larch (especially lush where placed above marble rock formations) on his estates round Blair Atholl and Dunkeld, was continued in the mid and late C20 on a large scale and often with non-native species by the Forestry Commission.

The region's underlying rocks have been extensively quarried for BUILDING STONE, especially since the later C18. Not surprisingly, given the geological structure, the stone extracted has been predominantly SANDSTONE. Many quarries served only their immediate localities although Huntingtower stone was much used for buildings in Perth, and stone from Kingoodie, near Invergowrie, for the Late Georgian mansions of Pitfour Castle, Kinfauns Castle and Rossie Priory. The durability and colour of the sandstone varies. Disappointingly, much of it weathers to a khaki colour and muddy texture but some much more attractive red-coloured sandstone is found. Most appealing, perhaps, is that quarried at Birnam, which was used in the construction of Dunkeld Cathedral. WHINSTONE, the popular name (i.e. stone on which only whin (gorse) would grow) for many of the very hard igneous rocks of the volcanic formations in the area, has been quarried for building purposes along the edges of the Sidlaw and Ochil Hills but is too intractable to be used for dressed work, which has usually been executed in sandstone. SLATE, found among the Dalradian rocks, has been quarried for roofs (e.g. at Craiglea, near Methven, at Newtyle, near Caputh, and in the neighbourhood of Comrie) but many buildings until the C19 were covered with turf or, more durably, heather or reeds, these last grown along the River Tay in considerable quantity. MARBLE from near Blair Atholl was quarried primarily to be exported from the region for the manufacture of chimneypieces. The clays of the Carse of Gowrie and near Perth were exploited by the C18 for making bricks and tiles, with commercial brickworks established at Redgorton and St Madoes by the early C19.

Local timber was presumably used for most buildings until the C17 but thereafter most wood to be used in the construction of larger buildings was imported from the Baltic. The development of the railway network from the mid C19 facilitated the importation of many more building materials. Local slate was largely supplanted by West Highland slate from Easdale and Ballachulish in Argyll. At Perth in the 1880s and 1890s, Craigie Church was built of Ballochmyle stone from Ayrshire, the (demolished) Wilson United Presbyterian Church of Eastlawbridge stone from Dumfriesshire. Dumfriesshire stone, from Corsehill, was used also at the Middle Free Church, Tay Street, Perth and, in Invergowrie, at All Souls' Episcopal Church. Steel framing and concrete became ubiquitous in the C20 although often discreetly covered in harling, render or a veneer of stone. The eighth Duke of Atholl's promotion in the 1920s of steel as a walling material for houses proved neither a popular nor a financial success.

PREHISTORIC PERTH AND KINROSS

Prehistoric remains standing above ground are fairly few for the size of the region and generally unspectacular. As elsewhere in Scotland, protracted habitation or agricultural activity in many areas has covered up, damaged or destroyed much of the evidence of early human activity in Perth and Kinross. Aerial photography during the last fifty years has produced cropmark evidence of many possible prehistoric sites but hardly any of these have been excavated and deductions made from the photographic evidence alone must be treated with caution. Archaeological dating, even with the aid of radiocarbon techniques, remains often approximate and, although broad dates can be given for the introduction of new techniques (e.g. for the manufacture of bronze implements and weapons from the later third millennium B.C.), it is much harder to evaluate how generally such technologies were adopted, and substantial differences may have co-existed within geographically quite small areas for long periods.

Scotland's first inhabitants arrived, in tiny numbers, by the beginning of the seventh millennium B.C., after the ending of the last Ice Age. These MESOLITHIC folk were hunter-gatherers, living on the flesh of animals, birds and fish which they trapped or killed and on shellfish, plants and nuts which they picked. What tools they possessed (e.g. scrapers, blades, awls and corers) were made of flint, bone or horn. Their dwellings, if other than caves, must have been primitive and their sites probably used only seasonally. Evidence from Stirling and Central Scotland, Fife and Angus suggests that they had reached the Firths of Forth and Tay to the W, SW and E of Perth and Kinross by the sixth millennium B.C. That they had penetrated along the Tay estuary W of Dundee by that time is likely but physical remains have been buried under river silt. A possible Mesolithic log-boat was, however, retrieved from Friarton Quarry on the edge of Perth in the C19 and scatters of worked flints have been found in the Sidlaw Hills between the Carse of Gowrie and Strathmore and along the Lunan Burn S of Blairgowrie. Further pointers to early habitation in Perthshire have come from pollen analysis and it seems likely that most of the region had been explored by the end of the fifth millennium B.C.

From about 4000 B.C. NEOLITHIC culture spread across Perth and Kinross, as throughout Scotland, the new ideas and techniques perhaps brought or accompanied by immigration from both E and W. Substantial growth in population over the next centuries was accompanied by clearance of forest, the domestication of animals and the cultivation of cereal crops, although hunting, fishing and the harvesting of wild crops doubtless remained important. Substantial funeral and ritual monuments were erected, a number of which have survived above ground.

EARTHWORKS (CURSUS MONUMENTS) consisting of roughly straight banks or ditches are perhaps the most enigmatic of Neolithic monuments. Visually they must have appeared as boundaries but they did not enclose or cut off areas of land. Rather than defences they were, perhaps, indications of places of special, perhaps ritual, significance. The three examples in Perth and Kinross (two known only from cropmarks) are all sited on low-lying level ground at the W end of Strathmore. One, at Milton of Rattray, near Blairgowrie, is traceable for 120 m. and consisted of two lines, *c.* 4 m. from each other. Comparable in size has been a *c.* 190 m.-long ditch at Blairhall, near Stormontfield, its width averaging 24 m. but with its E third slightly broader than the rest and set at a slight angle, probably the result of different stages of construction. Evidence of constructional phases has been found by excavation of the easily visible and far longer (2.3 km.) Cleaven Dyke, near Meikleour, a bank of sand and gravel revetted with turf, which stands up to 1.8 m. high and is generally 8 m.–10 m. broad but thickens at the W end to a breadth of *c.* 16 m. The bank is flanked by berms or platforms, each *c.* 20 m. broad, whose outer sides are bounded by *c.* 4 m.-broad ditches. The earthwork as a whole has been dated by radiocarbon testing to *c.* 4000 B.C. The size alone suggests that the Cleaven Dyke marked a meeting place of more than local significance.

Funerary Monuments: Tombs and Cairns

The earliest of the FUNERARY STRUCTURES may have been of wood. Excavation of an oval cairn at Pitnacree, near Strathtay, has revealed that the first building on the site had been erected *c.* 3500 B.C. and consisted of a rectangular burial enclosure, *c.* 2.7 m. by 2.4 m., and presumably intended for communal interments, each end wall formed by a massive halved tree trunk which stood to a height of up to 4m., the side walls perhaps of wickerwork. Similar structures may have preceded other burial cairns visible in the region.

The largest of burial cairns are the few LONG CAIRNS found in W Perthshire. All belong to the 'Clyde' group of tombs, most commonly found in Argyll, which, although cut off from Perth and Kinross by barren and mountainous terrain, was presumably the source of the design if not of the builders themselves of the Perthshire examples. All are sited on hillsides but close to valley floors and the three most prominent examples of the four or five in the region appear to have developed in a similar manner. At each of these, Kindrochet, near St Fillans, and Rottenreoch, near Crieff, both on the upper reaches of the River Earn, and Clach na Tiompan in the Almond valley, near Amulree, there was set up, probably in the fourth millennium B.C., an E–W line of three or more CHAMBERED TOMBS set *c.* 6m.–12m. apart, each tomb comprising a low irregular oblong structure, generally *c.* 2.7m. long (but less than 1.5m. at the known example at Rottenreoch), narrowing in width from *c.* 1m. to *c.* 0.7m., and *c.* 0.9m. high, the walls and roof constructed of stone slabs.

The space within these tombs was usually divided by slab partitions into an ante-chamber and one or two inner chambers intended to house several corpses (the bones perhaps later removed to make way for new arrivals). Tall upright slabs marked the outer entrance and, stretching forward from these, an arrangement of diminishing slabs delineated a forecourt or roofless passage. The placing of the external entrances at the E or S ends allowed the sun to penetrate the chambers in midsummer, a time perhaps associated with some ritual of ancestor worship. Each tomb was covered originally by its own round or oval cairn composed of small stones. Later, probably in the third millennium B.C., the separate tombs of each group were unified under a single cairn mound, the mound at Rottenreoch originally *c.* 49 m. long, those at Kindrochet and Clach na Tiompan 58m. long, all three tapering from a width of *c.* 11–14m. at the E end to as little as 4m. at the W. At the relatively undisturbed mound of Clach na Tiompan the E–W taper is accompanied by a fall in height from *c.* 1.5m. at the E to ground level at the W. The stones of this cairn include significant quantities of quartz whose sparkle must have given the mound, when clear of vegetation, yet more prominence in the landscape.

The substitution at each group of a single long cairn in place of individual cairns over the adjacent chambered tombs probably resulted from social and/or religious changes, perhaps a shift from a society of individual farming families, apparently cooperating with their neighbours but each possessing its own focus for ancestor worship, to a more hierarchical structure in which a group of families was united under a single chieftain and venerated a supposedly common ancestor.

ROUND AND OVAL CAIRNS are common further E. Although most probably date from the Early Bronze Age of *c.* 2500–*c.* 1500 B.C., they may, like the oval cairn at Pitnacree, stand on much earlier sites. At Pitnacree, after the posts of the wooden burial enclosure had eventually rotted, a stone structure was put up, perhaps early in the third millennium. This comprised a bank-surrounded oval enclosure, perhaps roofed with timber and turf, to form a chambered tomb, *c.* 6 m. by 2 m., approached from the E by a stone-roofed passage *c.* 1.5 m. high. Either at the same time or soon after, all this was covered with turf and stones to form a mound of *c.* 20 m. by 23 m., its edge defined by a drystone kerb, originally probably *c.* 0.5 m. high, faced with a blocking of water-worn and rounded stones and pebbles.

The size of the cairn mound at Pitnacree is far from exceptional. Not far away, although on higher ground, are or were the (demolished) White Cairn in Glen Cochill, near Amulree, of 18.3 m. diameter, also with a boulder-kerb round the edge, an oval cairn (also largely demolished) at Margmore, near Aberfeldy, of *c.* 12 m. by 18 m., and the cairn at Monzie, near Blair Atholl, of *c.* 24 m. diameter. Further E and S are the riverside cairn, 15.5 m. in diameter and *c.* 3 m. high, at Balchrochan, near Kirkmichael, the hillside Grey Cairn (*c.* 29 m. in diameter, its former height of over 7 m. now reduced to 1 m.) at Balnabroich, near Ballintuim, both in Strathardle, and the large hilltop cairns in the Sidlaws at Pole Hill, near Evelick Castle, and Shien Hill, near New Scone, respectively 19.5 m. and over 30 m. in diameter and 2.2 m. and 4 m. high, and, on lower ground, cairns of 30 m. diameter and 2.5 m. height at Kinloch. The cairns at Pole Hill and Shien Hill, the one with a double-stepped profile, the other composed of two distinct layers (of sandy and of stony soil), seem to be of two or three stages of construction. Probably also of two stages is the low-lying cairn (now *c.* 17 m. in diameter and 1.5 m. high) at Glendelvine House, near Spittalfield, which was excavated in 1901.

The earliest phases of at least some of these cairns are probably Neolithic. Some may have begun as ring cairns (i.e. circular or oval banks of cairn material enclosing roofless centres) and later had their centres filled in, a process discovered by excavation at the (now destroyed) third-millennium large round cairn (40 m. in diameter and 5.5 m. high) which stood at North Mains (of Strathallan), near Kinkell.

Generally sited in relatively discreet positions, the region's surviving unmodified RING CAIRNS are mostly low (*c.* 0.3 m. in height) and small (e.g. the two examples at Balnabroich, near Ballintuim, of *c.* 6.5 m. and 6.8–7.5 m. in diameter, or the even smaller cairn of 4 m. diameter at Middleton Muir, near Bridge of Cally), but the cairn at Lair, near Cray, is 15 m. in diameter. Probably all had kerbs of boulders or slabs to define the outer and inner edges of the ring-banks, the outer kerb surviving almost intact at Lair, the kerbstones often graded in height with the tallest frequently in the SW segment, a feature shared with the similar third-millennium Clava Group cairns of Inverness-shire and Argyll.

All cairns contained interments, whether in the communal chambers of the chambered tombs of the fifth and fourth millennia or in much smaller cists intended to contain one or two bodies or, by the second millennium, cremations, and seem to have been intended to mark graves of some importance. Other interments, apparently without individual markers, took place in GRAVEYARD ENCLOSURES. An early example (of c. 4000 B.C.) of these, at Inchtuthil, has been excavated and shown to consist of an oblong enclosure (54m. by 9m.) surrounded by a trench, probably for the base of a palisade. Elsewhere, cist burials took place apparently without either marker or enclosure, as seems to have been the case at Gairney Bank, near Kinross, where five cists have been found within a 50m.-long area but without evidence of any boundary feature. Many more such burials have been destroyed by ploughing but probably most of the region's prehistoric inhabitants, like their successors, were interred without benefit of coffin, cist or grave marker.

ROCK CARVINGS, pecked with stone axes and probably of Neolithic date, are found widely through Perthshire but concentrated in certain areas such as the Sidlaw Hills, the gently rising ground between Stormontfield and St Martins, the moorland NE of Dunkeld and along the upper Tay valley, although absence from others may be, at least in part, the result of clearance of stones from arable areas during agricultural improvement in the C18. The carvings, found on boulders and rock outcrops, generally occur on only one face of a stone, suggesting that most of these were laid flat. The repetitive designs are cup-marks (circular shallow scoops) or cup-and-ring marks (cup marks surrounded by circles); some also have 'dumb-bell' markings or straight grooves, usually radiating from the cup marks. The number of marks found on an individual stone ranges from a single mark (e.g. on a standing stone in the ruinous stone circle at Colen, near Stormontfield) to more than 130 on one face of a standing stone at East Cult, near Caputh. Unusually, the exceptionally large standing stone ('Macbeth's Stone') at Belmont Castle bears cup marks on each face, with twenty-four on the W and forty on the E. The significance of these carved stones is obscure. Most probably they were territorial markers although a quasi-religious meaning (not necessarily incompatible with a territorial function) may be suggested by the use or reuse of some in settings of stones.

Standing Stones

STANDING STONES (slabs or boulders which have been stood on end) are found, singly, in alignments of two or more or in rectangular, circular or oval arrangements throughout the region. The more ambitious arrangements almost certainly served as sites for religious rituals. Some have been preceded by wooden structures or settings of posts. Excavation of the stone circle at Croftmoraig, near Kenmore, has revealed that the first structure on the site, dating probably from the third millennium B.C., was an irregular horseshoe or pennanular shape of about fourteeen posts enclosing an area of c. 7m. by 7.92 m., small enough to have been covered by a roof and perhaps the shelter for an altar, as suggested by the flat boulder in its centre; just outside its SE arc, a pair of post-holes had held the bases of six further posts which, if they carried a roof, would have formed the sides of a porch-like projection, although the entrance to the main structure seems to have been at its other side. Excavation in 1974, preparatory to construction of the M90, of the site of a stone circle (the stones now re-erected nearby) close to Moncreiffe House disclosed that, before the stones were erected, there had been a circle (*c.* 6.5 m. in diameter) of pits, which may have served as post-holes for timber uprights, surrounded by a horseshoe-shaped ditch crossed by a causeway.

The STONE CIRCLES AND OVALS of Perth and Kinross, their stones all probably placed in position during the third or second millennium B.C., varied considerably in size, height and complexity. The vast majority consisted of single settings but in a few cases, as at Airlich, Meikle Findowie, near Amulree, and Croftmoraig, there are two, apparently erected at different periods, the outer and probably later circle or oval with taller stones. Diameter ranged from 7 m. or less (e.g. the oval setting at Machuim, near Lawers, or the circle at New Scone) to 16 m. at Carse, near Dull. At a small circle (now destroyed) in the policies of Taymouth Castle the stones stood less than 1 m. above ground and at the much larger double circle (also destroyed) on the slopes of Craig Formal, near Aberfeldy, less than 0.5 m. high, but the tallest stones of the circles at Croftmoraig and Moncreiffe House were well over 2 m. high. Often the stones are graded in height, with the lowest and highest in opposing arcs of the circle or oval. The stones of some circles are widely spaced; at others they form an almost unbroken kerb. At Croftmoraig's outer circle the intervals between its widely spaced principal stones are filled with small kerbstones. In kerb circles, their design clearly related to the Clava-type kerb cairns of Inverness-shire and Argyll, the stones are almost always graded in height and, sometimes, one end of the axis thus delineated across the circle is provided by a reused cup-marked stone, as in the circle at Monzie Castle whose tallest (W) kerbstone is faced directly by a cup-marked stone. At the E of the two adjacent circles at Fowlis Wester a cup-marked stone was placed at the SW end of the SW–NE axis but below ground level as if its significance was an esoteric secret.

The axes produced by the grading of stones seem to relate to astronomical phenomena, being aligned variously on midsummer, equinoctial and midwinter risings and settings of the sun and moon, possibly indicating that the social or religious group responsible for a particular stone setting had placed itself under the special protection of a particular astronomical event, rather as the dedication of a church is sometimes seen as giving its congregation a special relationship to the tutelary saint. As the choice of particular saints for church dedications has been subject to changing fashions, so may have been the choice of astronomical alignments for stone circles – the erection of the E circle at Fowlis Wester, aligned on the midwinter moonrise, blocked the equinoctial solar alignment of the presumably earlier W circle. At each of the Fowlis Wester circles is an outlying stone. The E circle's outlier stands on the axis formed by the grading of the kerb but such a relationship of an outlier to a circle's axis is uncommon – the axis of the Fowlis Wester W circle is WSW–ENE but its outlier stands due W; at Monzie Castle's circle the kerb is graded with an E–W axis (aligned on the midwinter sunset) but an outlier, a cup-and-ring-marked boulder, lies SW of the circle to which it is joined by a causeway of small stones whose presence suggests that the position of the outlier is not accidental. A similar disregard of the axis of a graded kerb is shown at Croftmoraig's outer circle whose gradation provides a NNE–SSW axis (perhaps aligned on midsummer sunset) but whose outliers, a pair of unusually massive stones, stand outside the circle's SE arc.

A variant on the circular or oval settings of standing stones is provided by the 'FOUR-POSTERS' concentrated in Glen Shee and the upper reaches of the Tay. Standing generally on hill-terraces, these settings are rough squares or oblongs defined by stones, usually less than 1 m. high, at the four 'corners', the short sides of the oblongs c. 2.5 m.–4.3 m. in length and the long sides 3 m.–6 m. These settings are placed diagonally to the cardinal points of the compass, with two sides running SW–NE and the other two SE–NW, possibly so that the corner stones of their NE and SW sides could frame respectively the rising of the sun in midsummer and its setting in midwinter. Pottery containing cremations found at those whose sites have been excavated suggests a mid-second millennium date for their erection and that they had a funerary function, although not necessarily to the exclusion of others.

In or near the valleys of the Tay and Earn and in Strathardle and with one isolated example at Orwell, near Milnathort, are PAIRED STANDING STONES, their broad faces either looking outwards in the same direction or fronting one another. All were probably erected in the second millennium. Most of these stones are 1.3 m.–2.5. high, 0.9 m.–1.8 m. broad and less, sometimes considerably less, than 1 m. thick. The great majority of pairs have their stones placed 1.5 m.–4.5 m. apart, the 0.15 m. separation at Gellybanks, near Luncarty, and the 10.7 m. distance between the stones at East Cult, near Caputh, both quite exceptional. Most pairs have stones of similar height and thickness although the height of two (fallen) stones at Thorn, near Fowlis Wester, differed by more than 1 m. and the thickness of the stones at East Cult by the same amount. Considerable care must have been taken to select the stones at Tullybannocher, near Comrie, their height (1.3 m.) identical, their breadth and width differing by only 0.2 m. and 0.3 m., the attention to detail almost pernickety since they stand almost 6 m. apart. At most pairs the stones are aligned, at least approximately, E–W but at a few (e.g. the pair of outliers at the Croftmoraig stone circle, the exceptionally closely spaced pair at Gellybanks or the pair at Newtyle, near Dunkeld) they stand N–S. Both the E–W and N–S alignments preclude these paired stones having been intended to frame solar or lunar risings or settings. Some pairs seem to have marked graves. The socket-hole of the E stone of the pair at Orwell was found by excavation in 1972 to have contained cremation deposits and another such deposit was found near the W stone; the outlying pair at Croftmoraig was closely accompanied by what seem to be grave pits, each for a single body.

SINGLE STANDING STONES, the majority erected probably in the second millennium, are found throughout the region, the largest being the heavily cup-marked 'Macbeth's Stone' at Belmont Castle. Some may be surviving elements of circles, 'four-posters' or pairs. Others, such as the stone erected on top of the cairn at Pitnacree above an inserted second-millennium cremation, marked graves and probably sites of local ritual importance.

Prehistoric Dwellings

Evidence (mostly from cropmarks) of HOUSES OF THE LATE BRONZE AND IRON AGES in E Perthshire, the best-studied part of the region, is plentiful, especially in those upland areas which have been least affected by post-medieval agricultural techniques. Precise dating is scarce but radiocarbon testing has provided dates from the end of the second millennium to the middle of the first millennium B.C. for house sites at Tulloch Field, near Straloch, in Strathardle. The sites identified in the heather moorlands of Glen Shee and Strathardle are placed remarkably high, many up to 450 m. OD and five on a SW spur of Creag Bhreac, near Spittal of Glenshee, at c. 500 m. These probably date from shortly before the climatic deterioration which set in by 750 B.C. These buildings in Perth and Kinross were usually circular, the lack of corners obviating the need for dressed stone, often dug into the slope of a hillside but occasionally placed on artificial platforms. Although the diameter of the houses varied from as little as 3.5 m. at Craigend, near Clunie, to 18 m. at Wester Drumatherty, near Spittalfield, most were of c. 7 m.–11 m. Some (e.g. on sites at Dunsinane Hill, near Collace, or Pole Hill, near Kilspindie) were constructed of timber, others of drystone or drystone and turf. Of about 850 sites of stone houses noted in NE Perthshire about one-fifth were built with double walls. At some houses the walls were fairly closely spaced and concentric, the gap of c. 2 m. probably used for storage or sleeping quarters, at others the two walls were further apart and eccentric, the space between perhaps used as animal pens, as may well have been the case with one example at Pitcarmick, near Kirkmichael, whose outer wall defined a curved enclosure of c. 16 m. by 10 m. with its own external entrance. These double-walled houses showed some sophistication, the inner faces of the inner walls often constructed of stone slabs and with slabs used also at their entrances.

Many of these Late Bronze or Iron Age dwellings stood in ENCLOSURES whose boundaries were formed by narrow ditches, the majority probably serving as trenches for palisades whose purpose was to pen livestock and protect them from wild animals

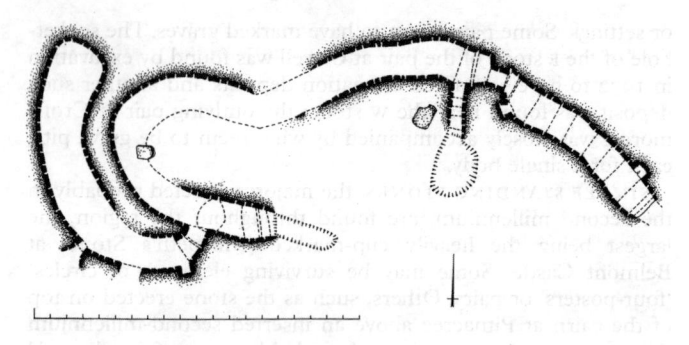

Kettins, Pitcur, souterrain.
Plan

rather than as defence against human enemies. Most enclosures were circular, *c.* 20 m.–30 m. in diameter, containing areas of 0.03–0.1 ha. Considerably larger than the average is one of two enclosures on the summit of a hill at Stralochy, near Spittalfield, which was of *c.* 40 m. in diameter and, unusually for the area, surrounded by two concentric palisades *c.* 4 m. apart, although these may represent two phases of enclosure of the site. Larger still were enclosures of *c.* 52 m. by 42 m. (0.18 ha.) at Old Mains of Rattray, near Blairgowrie, and of *c.* 62 m. diameter (0.3 ha.) at Upper Gothens, near Lethendy.

Some houses were accompanied by SOUTERRAINS, probably all constructed in the later first millennium B.C. and found (often by cropmarks) on sites with free-draining soil in the arable lands of Strathmore and the Carse of Gowrie. These underground curved passage-like stores, usually *c.* 2 m.–3 m. broad but perhaps sometimes considerably less and *c.* 1.5 m.–2 m. high, were constructed by the digging of *c.* 3 m.-deep trenches which were then faced with boulders or slabs (backed by rubble in the case of an excavated souterrain at Glencarse), the walls corbelled inwards at the top to support roofing slabs on which was placed *c.* 1 m. of soil. The length of souterrains ranged from *c.* 10 m. to over 30 m. Exposed by excavation at Pitcur, near Kettins, is a complex of three interconnected boulder-faced souterrains with a combined length of at least 66 m. and a height of up to 2 m., the massive roof slabs still in place at the E end. The central and W souterrains of the Pitcur complex had side entrances, presumably leading from houses, and cupboards in the walls; at the entrances from the central souterrain into its E and W counterparts are jambs rebated for doors. Excavation in 1840 of a souterrain at Lintrose, also near Kettins, discovered a paved floor. The joining up of the Pitcur souterrains was exceptional but close proximity of several souterrains and their associated dwelling houses may not have been uncommon. At Glencarse, *c.* 60 m. from the excavated souterrain are cropmarks of another and, a further 100 m. away, cropmarks of a third. At Pitroddie Farm, near Kilspindie, there are cropmarks of two complexes of souterrains less than *c.* 180 m. apart and of a single souterrain *c.* 150 m. beyond the second complex. Cropmarks in the grounds of Rossie Priory suggest that seven or eight souterrains formed a rough line *c.* 250 m. long in the S slope of Rossie Hill.

CRANNOGS, wholly or partly artificial islands constructed close to the shores of lochs, were formed well into the medieval period by which time they seem to have been constructed largely of boulders. The earliest, however, date probably from the first millennium B.C. when bronze-working was well established, iron-working had been introduced and climatic deterioration made high ground unsuitable for cultivation. Seventeen crannog sites have been identified in Loch Tay (fourteen of these within the boundaries of Perth and Kinross) and the relative paucity elsewhere may result from the obliteration of many by the drainage of lochs. Excavation of one of the Loch Tay sites at Oakbank, Fearnan, near Fortingall, has provided radiocarbon dates in the earlier first millennium B.C. and testing of another, off Firbush Point, near Killin (Stirling and Central Scotland), has given a date towards the end of that millennium. The Oakbank crannog (a reconstruction now standing at the Scottish Crannog Centre, near Kenmore) originally consisted of a wooden framework whose uprights stood on the loch floor and rose above the water to support a platform, presumably surmounted by a wooden round-house and linked to the shore by an oak causeway. Among the timbers the excavators found a large quantity of sheep dung, evidence that the crannog's first inhabitants raised livestock as well as exploiting the abundance of salmon in the loch. A second phase in this crannog's development, after a period of abandonment, took place probably in the C5 B.C. when the original wooden framework was covered with boulders and a new wooden structure erected above.

Fortifications

Crannogs and palisaded homesteads may have provided a modicum of security from attack for many of the region's inhabitants. Much more purposefully defensive are the dry-stone-walled fortifications of the area. In NW Perthshire, sited in uplands near the valleys of the Tummel and Lyon, is a scattering of DUNS (e.g. at Ceann na Coille, near Foss, Roromore, near Innerwick, or Balnacraig, near Fortingall), probably all dating from the late first millennium B.C. or early in the first millennium A.D. and built by incomers from Argyll. These are round or oval houses, generally of 15 m.–16 m. in internal diameter (comparable in size to the larger round-houses elsewhere), with walls *c.* 3 m.–3.6 m. thick. Probably each contained living accommodation for a single family. A similar stone-walled round-house is sited on Little Dunsinane (or Black) Hill, near Collace, but its relatively small (12 m.) diameter distinguishes it from the duns further W, as does the 5 m. thickness of its wall which suggests that this contained an internal passage at the upper level and that

14   INTRODUCTION

the building should be classed as a BROCH, a house type more generally associated with N Scotland and the Northern Isles, perhaps the abode of some immigrant from those parts.

FORTS, enclosures defended by substantial earth or stone ramparts and broad ditches, are widespread in the region. They suggest that, from the first millennium B.C., there had developed a social stratification with chieftains of varying importance con-

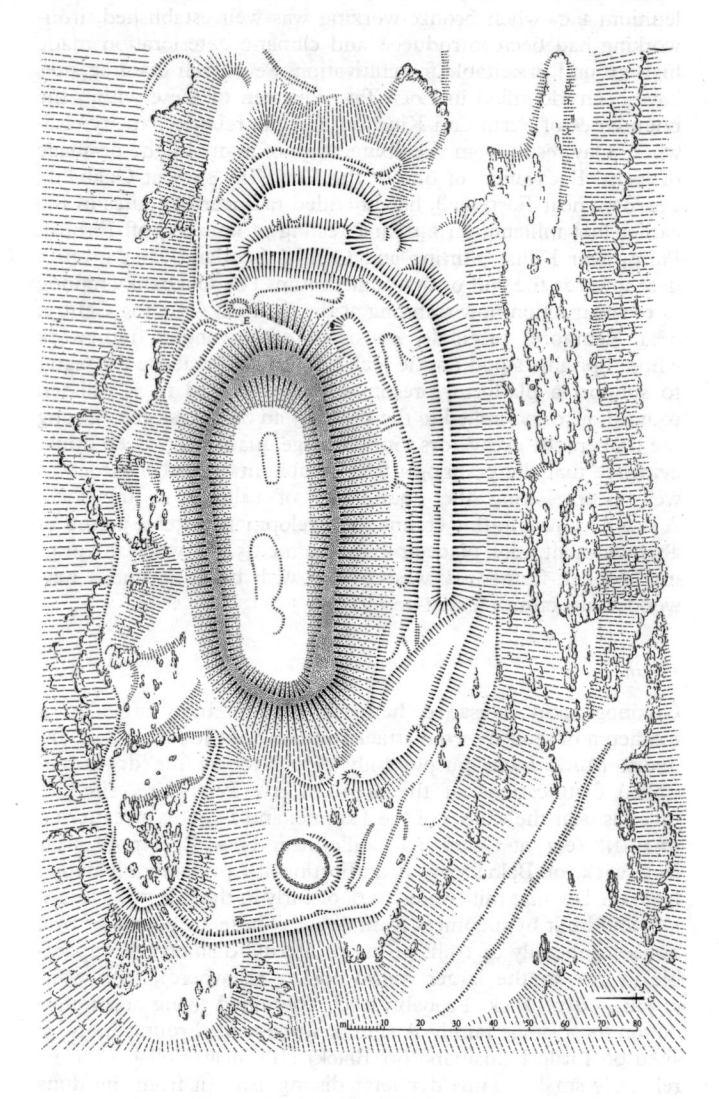

Alyth, Barry Hill, fort.
Site plan

trolling local areas and their inhabitants whose labour was used to provide fortified residences for their lords. The forts vary hugely in size, the area of the enclosures inside the defences ranging from less than 0.1 ha. (e.g. at Castle Law, near Abernethy, or The Dun at Tyndrum, near Aberfeldy) to over 2 ha. at Rossie Law, near Dunning, Dunsinane Hill, near Collace, and Barry Hill, near Alyth. All, however occupied naturally defensible sites although these too ranged from promontories or the ends of hill ridges to outcrop knolls on hillsides and hilltops themselves. Many sites were low-lying, placed close to rivers (e.g. the sites shown by cropmarks at The Welton, near Blairgowrie, Gold Castle, near Stormontfield, or Rosemount, near St Martins), and may well have been of primarily local significance. Others, however, appear strategically and sometimes prominently placed, commanding routes through hills into the fertile straths. The fort on Castle Law, near Abernethy, is placed at the junction of land routes from the S along Abernethy Glen and Glen Farg into the plain at the confluence of the Rivers Tay and Earn. The forts on Dunsinane Hill, Pole Hill, near Evelick Castle, and Law Hill, Arnbathie, near New Scone, control passes through the Sidlaw Hills between the Carse of Gowrie and Strathmore. A similar line of forts stands on the N side of the Ochil Hills overlooking Strathearn, e.g. at Culteuchar Hill, near Forgandenny, on Rossie Law, near Dunning, and on Ogle Hill, near Auchterarder. The fort of Dun Mac Tual on Drummond Hill, near Keltneyburn, is placed at the confluence of the River Lyon with the River Tay and that of King's Seat, near Dunkeld, at the confluence of the River Braan with the Tay. At the E end of the region the fort on Barry Hill lords it over Strathmore and it, like the fort on Dunsinane Hill, seems an assertion of the status of its lord.

Most forts seem to have been occupied for long periods, sometimes interspersed with periods of abandonment. Some may have begun as simple palisaded enclosures. The forts at The Welton and Inchtuthil, near Spittalfield, both occupy low promontory-like ridges whose ends seem to have been cut off by curved palisades supplemented, perhaps a little later, by ditches. Afterwards, the enclosures were extended outwards and provided with new and much stronger defences, those at Inchtuthil consisting of close-set ramparts and ditches. Evidence of palisades at other forts may have been lost under later defences.

Major artificial defences were usually provided only where necessary. The neighbouring forts of Ogle Hill and Ben Effery, near Auchterarder, and the fort of Dumglow, near Cleish, are placed on hilltops approachable from only one direction and defended only by ramparts cutting across the approach. The fort of Dun Mac Tual occupies a rocky knoll which is surrounded by a stone wall but this defence is supplemented by a curved wall enclosing an annexe beside the relatively easy NE approach and two additional ramparts at the most vulnerable W side. The defences of several forts show evidence of more than one stage of construction and perhaps of occupation. The fort on Pole Hill has ramparts to the N and W but the outer N rampart blocks the original entrance and must postdate those behind. Some forts contain a central citadel surrounded by an outer enclosure, e.g. the forts at Castle Law, near Forgandenny, King's Seat, Barry Hill and Dunsinane Hill. At each of the two last the citadel belongs to a second phase of work, the outer walls of the Dunsinane Hill fort probably robbed of stone for its construction.

The forts' defences, whether constructed of earth or stone, have been impressive displays of strength. The approach to the fort on Pole Hill in its final form was cut across by five close-set ramparts and ditches with a total width of *c.* 35 m., a width found also at the arc of ditches which defended the fort at Rosemount, near St Martins. The ramparts themselves were massive. The main stone walls enclosing the hilltop forts of The Dun and Castle Dow, near Logierait, are each *c.* 4.5 m. thick, those of Castle Law, near Abernethy, up to 6.6 m. thick. Some of these stone walls were laced with timber beams of which evidence is given by vitrified stone (the vitrefaction caused by the timbers having been set on fire) at Barry Hill and Dunsinane Hill. At Castle Law, near Abernethy, the fort's walls contained sockets for wooden beams running horizontally through and along their interiors. This fort's main wall still stands over 2 m. tall; the main wall of Dun Mac Tual, only 2.75 m. thick, was calculated in the C19 to have stood originally to a height of between 3.7 m. and 4.6 m. The organization and manpower required to construct such defences is persuasive evidence of a structured, if warlike, society.

THE ROMANS IN PERTH AND KINROSS

Much of Britain formed part of the Roman Empire for a period of over 360 years after the initial invasion in 43 A.D. but the imperial army was present in Perth and Kinross for less than a tenth of that time and only intermittently. What is remarkable is the extent of physical evidence, although much of it buried, of that army's brief periods of campaigning and residence in the region. Perhaps as noteworthy is the paucity of evidence that the Romans had any but inconsequential effects on the way of life of the native tribes.

After his accession in 68 A.D. the Emperor Vespasian pursued a forward policy in Britain to bring the territory of the Brigantes between the Humber and the Tyne–Tees isthmus under Roman control. A legionary fortress was constructed at York in 71 and the conquest of Brigantia accomplished soon after, with roads and forts built through the area. In 79,[*] the same year that Vespasian was succeeded by his son Titus, a further Roman advance

---

[*] Or, less probably, 80. In this account I have assumed it was 79.

was undertaken by the new governor of Britain, Gnaeus Julius Agricola, who, with a force of about 20,000 men, gained control of the lands occupied by the Selgovae in the Borders and Lothian and carried out a reconnaissance, a processional display of martial strength, as far N as the Tay, passing through the territory of the Vericones between the Forth and Strathearn and bordering on the lands of the Caledonii to the N. The next year Agricola constructed a line of military bases along the Forth–Clyde isthmus to mark the new northern frontier of Roman Britain of which his son-in-law and biographer Tacitus wrote wistfully that 'if the valour of the army and the glory of Rome had allowed it, a halting place would have been found within the island'. However, in 82 Agricola undertook an advance of the frontier beyond this 'halting place' by campaigning in Perthshire, Angus and northern Scotland as far as Nairnshire and probably the Spey valley. The next year he resumed operations, again taking his army to the NE where he inflicted a crushing defeat on the Caledonii at the battle of Mons Graupius.

Physical evidence, sometimes of cropmarks revealed by aerial photography, for the Agricolan campaigns of 79 and 82–3 in Perth and Kinross shows some of the army's MARCHING CAMPS which were occupied for no more than three nights, by when the food in the area would have been eaten and the water supply fouled. Each camp was formed by a single stake-topped rampart constructed of earth dug out of a surrounding ditch. Inside the camp the soldiers were housed in eight-person leather tents. Two of these camps, at Dunning and at Carey, near Abernethy, occupy 46-ha. sites and perhaps date from the 'reconnaissance' of 79. The others, to the W and NE, are of 9–14 ha. and probably of 82–3. Their disposition suggests that the army may have advanced from W to E in two columns, one moving from Dunblane (Stirling and Central Scotland) by way of Ardoch, near Braco, and Dornock in Strathearn, the other taking a more northerly route from Lake of Menteith (Stirling and Central Scotland) to Dalginross at Comrie and then along the N side of the Earn, the two columns perhaps uniting near Perth before crossing the Tay and moving into Strathmore and then up the coastal plain of Angus to NE Scotland. The camps of the putative second line are of conventional oblong shape but two, those at Lake of Menteith and Dalginross, share a peculiarity with the camp at Stracathro (Angus) in having an entrance guarded by two external projections of the rampart, one curved, the other straight, to form a claw-shaped funnel (*clavicula*) suggesting that they were designed by the same engineer who had worked also at Castledykes near Carstairs (Lanarkshire).

Agricola's tenure of the governorship ended in late 83, and although he may have planned and even begun PERMANENT FORTIFICATIONS along a new northern frontier, it was probably his unknown successor who was chiefly responsible for execution of the work in the next few years. This entailed the construction of a gravelled road which ran from Camelon at Falkirk (Stirling and Central Scotland) to Ardoch and then along the Gask Ridge to Bertha just N of Perth where it crossed the Tay and continued to Cargill and was probably intended to continue to Stracathro. Along this road stood a line of forts and fortlets beginning with a fort of 1.4 ha. at Barochan Hill near Houston (Renfrewshire), a small fort (0.4 ha.) at Mollins (Lanarkshire), large forts (2.4 ha. and 2.6 ha.) at Camelon and Doune (both Stirling and Central Scotland), a fortlet at Glenbank SW of Braco, another large fort (3.5 ha.) at Ardoch, a fortlet at Kaims Castle NE of Braco, a small fort (1.77 ha.) at Strageath near Innerpeffray, a large fort (3.8 ha.) at Bertha, a fortlet at Cargill and two large forts (both over 3.2 ha.) at Cardean, near Meigle, and Stracathro, perhaps with an undiscovered intervening small fort. Beside the road E of Strageath stood a line of watch towers, usually less than one Roman mile (1.48 km.) apart, whose garrisons of perhaps half-a-dozen men could monitor activity in the frontier zone each side of the road.

A second line of forts, probably built c. 84–6, formed a roughly parallel line to the NW, running from Drumquhassle near Drymen via Malling at the W end of Lake of Menteith to Bochastle at Callander (all Stirling and Central Scotland), Dalginross, Fendoch at the mouth of the Sma' Glen, a legionary fortress at Inchtuthil near Spittalfield and ending with a fort at Inverquharity, near Cortachy (Angus). Unlike the forts to the SE they were not linked by a road, although one may have been intended, and each stood at the mouth of one or more glens leading into the foothills of the Grampians. They may have been intended to guard against attack from the glens or as springboards for a Roman advance up them, the two functions not necessarily incompatible.

These late C1 fortifications established a frontier line not only for the Romans in Britain but for the Roman Empire. That Britain was part of a much larger imperial whole was made clear immediately after 85 when severe defeats and significant loss of forces on the Danube, the empire's NE frontier, led to the withdrawal of perhaps a quarter of the Roman army in Britain, including the *legio II Adiutrix*, to reinforce the Danubian frontier, and retrenchment by the remaining forces. Work on the uncompleted fortress at Inchtuthil was halted and the NW line of forts abandoned, their buildings systematically destroyed. It is not unlikely that, at the same time, some or all of the forts on the SE line from Barochan Hill to Stracathro were altered to hold smaller numbers of troops. Probably at the same time, a new fort of c. 2 ha., superseding the fortlet 0.3 km. to the W, was built at Cargill, now deprived of the forward defence of the nearby fortress at Inchtuthil. However, by c. 90 all the Roman forces had withdrawn to the Forth–Clyde isthmus and by the end of the C1 to the Tyne–Solway line from which Agricola's advance had been launched twenty-one years before.

In 139 the Emperor Antoninus Pius, who had succeeded Hadrian the year before, began preparations for a new advance into Scotland. Victory was formally celebrated in 142. By that date the main frontier had been re-established on the Forth–

THE ROMANS IN PERTH AND KINROSS

Clyde line with a turf wall (the Antonine Wall), forts and fortlets built across the isthmus. N of that line, Perth and Kinross' SE line of C1 forts from Ardoch to Bertha were brought back into commission, apparently with garrisons of the same size as those they had contained in the early 80s. The Antonine occupation of southern and midland Scotland lasted only one generation. In the early 160s the Roman forces were withdrawn to Hadrian's Wall with only the forts at Newstead (Borders) and Birrens (Dumfries and Galloway) garrisoned as Scottish outposts for another twenty years, a relatively peaceful co-existence between the Roman provinces and the tribes to its N probably maintained by treaties and bribery.

The Roman FORTRESSES, FORTS and FORTLETS of the C1 and C2 provided defensible accommodation for soldiers whose main purpose was to campaign or patrol in the surrounding area or further afield. The fortress of Inchtuthil was designed to accommodate a legion of about 5,000–6,000 men, mostly infantry, the large forts held auxiliary cohorts, possibly accom-

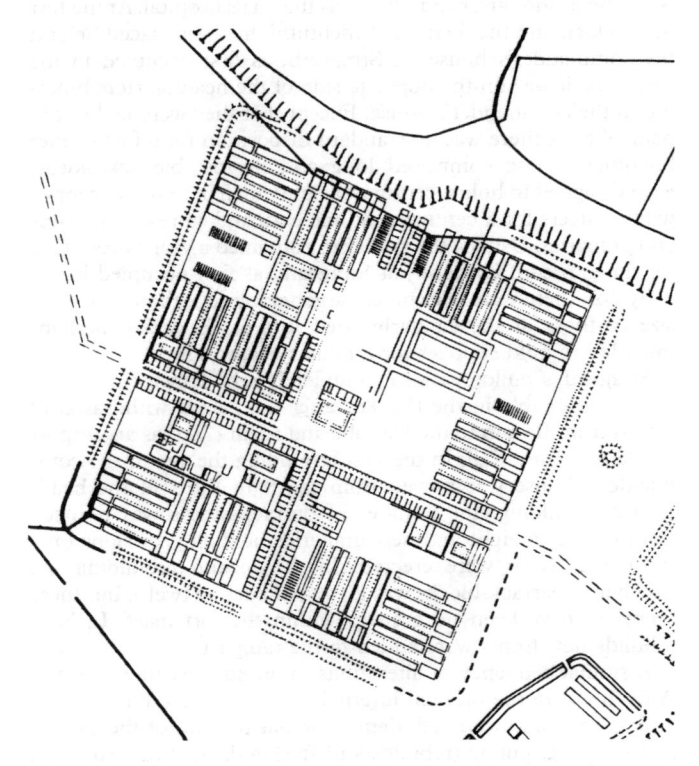

Spittalfield, Inchtuthil, Roman fortress.
Plan

panied by legionary detachments, totalling between 600 and 1,000, the small forts perhaps a few hundred. Despite varying in size from under *c.* 1.4 ha. to over 3.2 ha., the forts were generally similar. Oblong in shape, each was surrounded by one or two ditches (three at Cargill) and an inner rampart of turf, occasionally faced with stone. Roughly in the centre of each side was an entrance defended by a pair of flanking towers or a single tower over it. Inside, there was an encircling street (the *intervallum*) following the line of the rampart and a cross of streets running from the entrances to the centre and dividing the interior into four sections. At the centre stood the fort's headquarters building. This consisted of a courtyard entered through a screen wall on one side. On the sides flanking the entrance were probably stores or armouries. The principal range faced the entrance and was fronted by a hall occupying the full length of the range and serving as a courtroom and public hall. Behind the hall and opening off it were rooms, usually five, of varying sizes. The end rooms were offices, the larger centre room a shrine in which were placed an effigy of the emperor and regimental standards. Standing by itself to one side of the headquarters building was the commander's house, also built round a courtyard. Near the headquarters building was the fort's hospital. At the fort of Fendoch and the fortress of Inchtuthil this was placed behind the commander's house, at Strageath, as first occupied in the early 80s, it was on the opposite side of the headquarters building to the commander's house. Except that they were laid out in parallel rows there was no standard disposition for a fort's other buildings. These comprised long and narrow barrack-blocks, each designed to hold a century of eighty men in ten-man rooms, with quarters for a centurion at one end, and stores, workshops and granaries. Usually the granaries contained a year's provisions for the garrison. However, at Strageath, as first occupied in the early 80s, there were very much larger granaries (about twice the size of those at the similarly sized fort of Fendoch), perhaps intended to hold supplies for a military campaign.

Strageath's buildings were completely rebuilt twice in the C1 and C2, probably in the late 80s after the partial withdrawal of troops from Britain to the Danube and again *c.* 130 as an outpost to the Antonine Wall. In the first rebuilding the site of the commander's house was moved from the N to the S of the headquarters building, the number of barrack-blocks was reduced from twelve to eight and new granaries holding provisions only for the garrison were erected. In the second rebuilding the number of barrack-blocks was increased back to twelve but there seems to have been no granary within the fort itself. In both rebuilds new fronts were added to the rampart.

A similar sequence of alterations to an 80s fort took place at Ardoch where the original internal structures were rebuilt soon after it was first occupied, demolished at the end of the C1 and new buildings put up (rebuilt soon after) in the mid C2. However, at Ardoch the C2 fort, as first reoccupied, was given a new earth rampart, revetted with turf and occupying a slightly smaller area than its predecessor, the space between the C1 pair of ditches and the new rampart filled by additional ditches. The second C2 rebuilding produced a still smaller fort, considerably contracted at the N end where further ditches were dug, and with a new stone-faced rampart. Its earthworks still provide a powerful symbol of strength although the multiplication of ditches may in reality have subtracted from its defensibility since they placed the ground outside beyond javelin-throwing range and provided cover for an attacking force.

The C1 and C2 buildings inside these forts were all single-storey and timber-framed, the posts placed in trenches in the first phase of construction and in post-holes in later rebuildings. Walls were of wattle-and-daub and the roofs covered with thatch or wooden slats. The barrack-blocks were fronted by verandas and the courtyards of the headquarters buildings and commanders' houses surrounded by colonnaded loggias giving some protection from Scottish rain but perhaps erected in the dogged belief that an Italian sun shone over the furthest parts of the Roman Empire.

Outside most of the forts are annexes, roughly rectangular areas, each surrounded by a ditch and rampart. These may have had various uses, as camps during the construction or reconstruction of a fort, as corrals for the horses of cavalry units, for stores or workshops, or as exercise and training grounds.

Fortlets were miniature versions of forts, less than 0.5 ha. in size and designed to hold no more than one century (eighty men) at most, housed in one or more barrack-blocks. Like the forts, they were surrounded by a single or double ditch and rampart but with only a single entrance defended by a wooden tower. The two late C1 fortlets at Kaims Castle and Glenbank each had two ditches, the ditches of Kaims Castle curved although the rampart is the usual rectangle. These fortlets' garrisons probably manned some of the nearby WATCH TOWERS beside the road along the Gask Ridge. Each was defended by a ditch and rampart, usually with an outer counterscarp, and approached through a single entrance. Inside the enclosure stood a square wooden tower, the post-holes of several towers discovered by excavation.

A postscript to the Roman activity in Perth and Kinross is provided by the campaigns undertaken in 208–c. 212 by the Emperor Septimius Severus and his sons, Geta and Caracalla, probably in response to Caledonian raids as far S as Hadrian's Wall. In these campaigns the Roman forces advanced through Perth and Kinross from Ardoch through Gowrie and Strathmore and thence to NE Scotland. Probably at the end of three years of campaigning a fortress was built at Carpow on the S bank of the Tay near Abernethy and with easy contact by sea to the fortress at Cramond (Edinburgh) beside the Forth. The Carpow fortress was of c. 12 ha., defended by the usual double ditch and rampart, with an entrance in each side, a stone from the E gate (now in the McManus Galleries, Dundee) carved with a relief of 'Victory', a goat and horses (emblems of the *legio II Augusta* which was presumably responsible for construction of the fortress). Excavation has shown that the fortress's central headquarters building was large, its shrine containing a stone altar and flanked by eight side rooms. It was of half-timbered construction with wattle-and-daub walls and roofed with tiles bearing the stamp of the *legio II Victrix Britannica*. The commander's house to the S was built of stone and surrounded a courtyard bisected by a columned screen. In its W range was a bath house heated by a hypocaust. N of the headquarters building was a granary, also built of stone or of wood on stone foundations. The barrack-blocks were of timber. Although abandoned soon after its construction, the fortress at Carpow was clearly designed to be more than a temporary base, but was it intended as a solitary sea-supplied forward position from which punitive attacks could be launched against the northern tribes or to stand at the SE end of a new frontier which would, perhaps, have extended up the W bank of the Tay to Bertha and then along the C1 Gask Ridge frontier? Whatever the intention there is no evidence of an attempt to bring the earlier forts back into use.

The Roman army withdrew to the Tyne–Tees frontier of Hadrian's wall by *c.* 215 and from Britain altogether in 410. The impact of the empire on Perth and Kinross had been predominantly military. Some finds of Roman pottery and coins suggest a limited amount of trade but no significant impact on the culture of the inhabitants of the region.

PICTISH PERTH AND KINROSS

The inhabitants of Perth and Kinross encountered by the Romans in the C1–C4 were known by 279 as Picts, a term applied generally until the C9 to the inhabitants of Scotland N of the Forth–Clyde isthmus except for those of Argyll and the British kingdom of Strathclyde with its stronghold of Dumbarton. These Picts, all speakers of a form of P-Celtic,* must have been descendants of the several tribes noted *c.* 150 on Ptolemy's map of Great Britain as occupying Scotland N of the Forth–Clyde isthmus. By *c.* 200 these had grouped into two confederations, noted by Dio Cassius as the Maeatae occupying land near the Antonine Wall and the Caledonii to the N; by the mid C4 they were known to Ammianus Marcellinus as the Verturiones and the Dicalydones (clearly the Caledonii) and to Bede writing (in the C8) of events in the C6 as the northern and southern Picts, but by the late C7 they seem to have formed a single confederation under the overlordship of the king of Fortriu.

Within the one or two confederations of the Picts were individual kingdoms. Those in Perth and Kinross by the mid C6 seem to have been Fortriu comprising Fife, Kinross, Strathearn and

---

* Derived from Gallo-Brythonic and distinct from Q-Celtic from which developed Gaelic.

Menteith, a kingdom of Gowrie and Angus, and the kingdom of Atholl. The Pictish kingdoms of Fortriu and Atholl were separated by Drumalban, the SW range of the Grampians, from Argyll which, by the C5 and probably earlier, was occupied by the Scottish (i.e. Irish) confederation of Dál Riata, a grouping of Gaelic-speaking kingdoms. SW of Fortriu was the British kingdom of Strathclyde with the rock of Dumbarton (Stirling and Central Scotland) its chief fortress. S of the Forth was another British kingdom, that of the Gododdin in Lothian which fell under the control of the Angles of Northumbria in the C7. The Picts, the Scots of Dál Riata, the Britons of Strathclyde and Lothian and the Northumbrians were regarded as distinct *gentes* or peoples, each with its own language or dialect. Early medieval annals, mostly from Irish sources, record warfare between them but these conflicts should, perhaps, be seen as exceptional, extended periods of peace not thought worth note by the annalists. There is strong evidence of intermarriage, at least among the royal families. The late C6 Pictish overlord, Gartnait, may have been the son of Áedán mac Gabhráin, overlord of Dál Riata, three overlords of the Picts between 631 and 653 seem to have been of British descent and were followed by Talorcan, the son of Eanfrith, king of Northumbria, and a Pictish mother, after whose death Oswy, king of Northumbria 'subdued the greater part of the Picts' in 658. This Northumbrian overlordship ended in 685 with the defeat of the Angles at the battle of Nechtansmere (or Dunnichen) by the Pictish king, Brudei son of Bili, who was probably the son of a king of Strathclyde and raised at the Northumbrian court.

Oengus son of Fergus, the Gaelic-named king of Fortriu, was also overlord of Dál Riata in 741–50, and Constantine son of Fergus, king of Fortriu, and his successors also held the overlordship of both Pictland and Dál Riata from 811 until the death of Eóganán son of Óengus together with 'men of Fortriu beyond counting' in battle with Norse raiders in 839. Perhaps as a result of ensuing chaos in Fortriu Kenneth mac Alpin (Cináed mac Alpín), a Dál Riatan adventurer but probably of royal descent, gained acceptance as overlord of Dál Riata, probably in 841, and of Pictland in 843, apparently taking up residence in Fortriu where he died in his *palacium* at Forteviot fifteen years later. Except for a brief period in the C11 the overlordship of Picts and Scots continued in the hands of Kenneth mac Alpin's descendants (kings of Alba or of Scots) who, by the end of the C10, had extended their hegemony to all of present-day Scotland except the Norse territories of Caithness, Sutherland and the Western and Northern Isles. In Perth and Kinross, as elsewhere, the Pictish language was replaced by Gaelic and the predominance of Gaelic place-names may indicate a considerable influx of Gaelic settlers.

Description of the social structure of Pictish Perth and Kinross must be speculative but it is likely that, below the kings, was an aristocracy whose members, like the later *toiseachs* (leaders of hundreds) or *mormaers* (predominant *toiseachs*), were lords of extensive areas which were divided into *petts* (portions), each with its own minor lord holding a substantial farm worked perhaps by slaves.

The kings of Pictland were presumably, like medieval kings of Scots, peripatetic, making regular progresses through their dominions to collect *cain* (payments in kind) and enjoy *conveth* (hospitality rent), perhaps presiding over feasts intended to inspire loyalty in their subjects. However, as with medieval kings, they seem to have possessed specifically ROYAL RESIDENCES. In Fortriu at least two hill-forts appear to have been royal strongholds. Dundurn, near St Fillans where passes from the Clyde Valley and Argyll meet at the W entrance to Strathearn, was of sufficient importance for a siege there in 683 to be recorded in the *Annals of Ulster* and, according to another source, to have been where Giric, king of Scots and nephew of Kenneth mac Alpin, died in 889. Clatchard Craig (Fife) just E of Abernethy commanded the E entry to Strathearn from Fife. Each was a craggy hill (Clatchard Craig now destroyed by quarrying) rising abruptly from a valley floor and fortified (Clatchard Craig refortified, partly using Iron Age defences) apparently early in the C7, with a crowning citadel surrounded by enclosures, all defended by drystone ramparts. Clearly these strongholds were intended to impress both as dramatic features in the landscape and as large complexes housing the royal retinue, a visitor having to pass through one court after another to reach the citadel itself. Something similar is present at the fort of Carnac on Moncreiffe Hill near Bridge of Earn although here the outer defences may be all of the late first millennium B.C. and only the citadel itself, a massive circular rampart enclosing the sites of round houses, of the early historic period.

Other hill-forts, all sited close to good arable land but modest in size (usually less than 0.75 ha. in total size and with a living area of less than 0.25 ha.), comprise a single court enclosed by at least three ramparts, their line sometimes stopped short of an impregnable cliff on one side. Many of these may be Iron Age but were probably occupied or reoccupied in the first millennium A.D. by Pictish aristocrats. Occupying the projecting corner of the plateau on which had been constructed the Roman fortress of Inchtuthil is a fort defended by five ditches and ramparts, the inner rampart partly built of stones quarried from Gourdie and presumably reused from the Roman work. One of the most dramatically sited of these is the fort surrounding the Baird Monument on the top of Tom a' Chaisteil near Monzievaird, although its size precludes it having been a stronghold of more than local importance.

From the C8 there seems to have been a shift away from hill-forts down to the valleys. A royal palace (*palacium*) at Forteviot near the confluence of the Water of May and the River Earn is recorded as a seat of Óengus I or Óengus II in the C8 or early C9 and where Kenneth mac Alpin died in 858. The low Moot Hill at Scone appears as the inauguration site of kings by the C9 and both Dunkeld and Abernethy seem to have served as royal as well as ecclesiastical centres. Of royal palaces there survives only the large fragment of an arch-stone from Forteviot (see below). A similar shift to more easily accessible, though less defensive, sites is likely to have occurred among the aristocracy. Aerial photography has disclosed the existence of rectangular wooden buildings, probably halls, scattered through Stathmore, Gowrie and Strathearn. It would be surprising if some were not early historic.

Minor lords were primarily farmers. In NW Perthshire a sizeable number of 'RING FORTS' or HOMESTEADS, at least one datable to c. 1000, provides evidence of their residences in this upland area. Typically these are sited on the edge of pasture land and often at the entrance to glens. Each consists of a massive (c. 3 m. thick) drystone wall up to 1.5 m. high and pierced by a single entrance which encloses a circular space of 15 m.–30 m. in diameter, the only defence provided by the wall itself. One of the better-preserved is at Litigan, near Keltneyburn, which contained a central hearth surrounded by two concentric rings of post-holes for substantial timber uprights, suggesting that it was covered by a conical roof. All were probably at least partly roofed and probably provided accommodation for both people and livestock. Another type of homestead, datable from radiocarbon testing to the C8 or C9, is found in the upland areas of Strathardle and Strathbraan in NE Perthshire. Known from the farm where they were first identified as 'Pitcarmick'-type houses, these are rough oblongs (c. 17 m.–28 m. by c. 7 m.) with fairly straight long sides constructed of clay or turf but with stone-built curved ends. Inside several of these a substantial part of the floor was sunken, perhaps as storage, and the unsunk area contained a hearth. On lower and more fertile ground oval or round-houses, often with a partly sunk floor, seem to have been usual, their sites usually without defences although some were surrounded by palisades as at Upper Gothens, near Lethendy, or Dalpatrick, near Innerpeffray, or by ditches as at Dunbarney, near Bridge of Earn, where three round-houses and a rectangular enclosure (probably a corral) were surrounded by an oval ditch.

CHRISTIANITY was established in Ireland and Galloway in the C5 and in Lothian, Strathclyde and Dál Riata by the earlier C6. In 635, at the request of Oswald, king of Northumbria, St Aidan was sent from Iona to Northumbria to establish Christianity there and in 681, during the period of Northumbrian overlordship over Pictland, a bishopric for the Picts was set up at Abercorn (Lothian). Although this bishopric was abandoned after the Northumbrian defeat at Nechtansmere four years later, the Picts, apparently instructed by missionaries from Iona, seem to have adopted Christianity at about this time. Certainly this must have been before 710 when Nechtan, king of Fortriu, wrote to Ceolfrith, abbot of Monkwearmouth and Jarrow, requesting instruction in the arguments for adopting, as had the Northumbrian Church, the Roman rather than Celtic observances of calculating the date of Easter and form of clerical tonsure. Nechtan also 'asked that architects be sent him to build a stone church in his nation after the Roman manner' (*architectos sibi mitti petiit, qui iuxta morem Romanorum ecclesiam de lapide in gente ipsius facerent*).

Endowments for bishoprics and monasteries could have been provided only by kings or nobles. Nechtan himself may well have established a bishopric (apparently short-lived) at Abernethy in the early C8. About 815 Constantine son of Fergus, king of Fortriu, founded a monastery at Dunkeld to which Kenneth mac Alpin brought relics of St Columba from Iona in 849 and whose abbot, Tuathal son of Argus, was described as 'prim-escop' (chief bishop) of Fortriu in 865. Other monasteries or colleges of priests were established at Abernethy, St Serf's Isle, Methven, Inchaffray and Muthill, some containing communities of *Céli Dé* ('vassals of God') inspired by Irish monastic reforms of the C8 and C9 which stressed religious observance and the position of bishops. Clergy seem to have been grouped in relatively few religious centres, each serving a large territorial area.

Of ECCLESIASTICAL BUILDINGS of the early historic period hardly anything survives. Now in the National Museum of Scotland is a large fragment of the arch-stone of a round- or segmental-headed door or narrow chancel arch, perhaps of the C9, which was discovered in the Water of May at Forteviot and presumably came from the palace chapel. It is carved with a (mutilated) central cross and animal, perhaps a lamb (the *Agnus Dei*). On one side of the cross and beast is the large figure of an

Abernethy Round Tower.
Engraving, 1802, after view by Thomas Girtin, *c.* 1785

elaborately coiffed and moustachioed man holding a staff or scabbarded sword, his feet resting on an animal; on the other side, smaller figures of hooded men holding staffs. These may represent an overlord and subject kings, all subject to the Cross of Christ. In the Meigle Museum is a broken stone (Meigle 22) which seems to be a fragment from an architectural frieze, carved with a pair of long-clawed fantastic beasts and a seated siren (symbol of temptation) which may have come from a church. The only complete ecclesiastical structure and one which may be of the late C11 is the *c.* 27.6 m.-high free-standing round tower 99 in the churchyard at Abernethy. Its general form and the placing of the door above ground level are derived from Irish examples, the door from late Anglo-Saxon work and the belfry openings from Norman work.

The most distinctive and aesthetically most enjoyable products of early historic Perth and Kinross are its SCULPTURED SLABS. Some of the slabs marked graves but others seem to have had a more public function, perhaps identifying possession of a particular tract of land, standing at the entry to monasteries or graveyards or denoting meeting places, possibly for worship. Most bear symbols which are found only in a few isolated cases outside Pictland but are common in Scotland N of the Tay. Some symbols seem to be abstract geometrical shapes (e.g. the 'disc', the 'double-disc', the 'rectangle') or possibly stylized representations, some perhaps jewellery designs; others (e.g. the salmon, the goose, the serpent) are clearly representational. Not infrequently a variant symbol is created by the addition of a 'V-rod' or 'Z-rod', respectively representations of a broken arrow and spear or possibly sceptre. Usually the symbols are paired, with one directly above the other. Between twenty and thirty symbols (i.e. not decorative motifs) have been identified, most with a wide geographical distribution which seems to preclude them having been identifying signs of particular tribes or families. The likeliest explanation of their meaning is that each represents a name and their paired groupings consist of the names of a man and his father (X son of Y), the general form of naming individuals in contemporary annals and found in the Latin inscription on the early C9 Dupplin Cross, now in St Serf's Church, Dunning. *p. 351*

The simplest of these carved stones probably date from the C6 and C7. These are undressed slabs or pillars whose sparing decoration consists only of incised symbols such as the stones at Peterhead, near Blackford, and Bruceton, near Alyth, each bearing a single pair of symbols (goose and 'rectangle'; horseshoe and 'Pictish beast'), but a slab found in the parkland of Inchyra House (now in the Perth Museum and Art Gallery) bears no fewer than three pairs of symbols ('double-disc' and salmon; 'tuning-fork' (perhaps a double-bladed sword) and 'mirror'; salmon and serpent), two carved on one face and one on the other. The pillar stone at High Keillor, near Kettins, has a trio of symbols (wolf, 'double-disc-and-Z-rod' and 'mirror-and-comb'), perhaps for X son of Y son of Z. The most accomplished of this class of stone in Perth and Kinross is beside the round tower in Abernethy churchyard. Its paired symbols ('tuning-fork' and 'crescent-and-V-rod') are both embellished with curvilinear decoration. Flanking them are a hammer and anvil or perhaps a crucible, probably to represent the trade, a highly skilled and valued one if he were a goldsmith, of the man commemorated here.

A variant on this first class of Pictish stone is to be found in the porch of Alyth Parish Church. This is an undressed slab, one face incised with the 'double-disc-and-Z-rod' symbol but the other bearing a cross, also incised, decorated with interlacing and with coiled rope motifs between the arms. This must date from after the conversion of the Picts to Christianity but probably not by long and was carved perhaps late in the C7. A much more sophisticated but perhaps also early Christian stone with incised carving, found at Gellyburn, near Murthly, and now in the Perth Museum and Art Gallery, is a pillar whose surfaces have been dressed. On one face is displayed a cross with ringed and pierced armpits, the arms and shaft with interlacing and a spiral of ropework which ends in animal heads. On the other side, a circle contains interlacing and the round holes of the cross's armpits; below are the paired symbols of a 'crescent-and-V-rod' and a 'Pictish beast'.

The largest category of EARLY CHRISTIAN SCULPTURE in Perth and Kinross, dating probably from the C8 and C9, ranges in size from stones less than 1 m. high, probably intended to mark graves, to what must have been public monuments, one (now in Fowlis Wester Parish Church) over 3 m. tall, consists of dressed slabs carved in relief, their sculptured motifs including crosses and Pictish 'symbols'. Most have a cross carved only on one face but a couple (the 'Bore Stone', now at Moncreiffe House, and the slab in the mausoleum at Rossie Priory) have crosses on both. On these two slabs one or both of their crosses have ringed heads, a motif found also at Meigle 2 in the Meigle Museum and a slab from St Madoes (now in Perth Museum and Art Gallery). The crosses of Meigle 6, Meigle 7 and the larger slab in Fowlis Wester Parish Church have rectangular notches at the armpits but most have rounded hollows, some (e.g. Meigle 1 and Meigle 5) filled with rings. All the crosses are decorated with interlacing, usually of a continuous pattern on each limb but sometimes (e.g. the Dunfallandy Stone or the slab from St Madoes) in panels, each containing a different design. On a couple of slabs (at Fowlis Wester Parish Church and the slab from St Madoes) the central panel of the cross head is decorated with bosses, as may have been the weathered central panel of the Dunfallandy Stone whose limbs' panels contain bosses. Unusually, one of the slabs at Fowlis Wester has on the cross a badly worn panel carved with fantastic beasts.

Quite exceptional among these slabs is the cross on one face of the slab at Rossie Priory whose shaft has a relief of three horsemen, a continuation of the hunting scene which fills the space to the r. of the cross. The cross on this slab's other face is flanked by fantastic beasts as is the cross of Meigle 1. More naturalistic are the hounds which flank the cross on the slab from St Madoes. The panels bordering the cross on the Dunfallandy Stone are filled with a mixture of fantastic beasts, naturalistic animals and a couple of angels. Similar medleys of the fantastic and the naturalistic flank the crosses on the two faces of the 'Bore Stone' at Moncreiffe House but here one face also bears a hunting scene and a pair of symbols and the other has hagiographical and Biblical scenes (St Antony of Egypt and a Centaur, Wrestling Jacob (?) and David Killing a Lion). A depiction of St Paul the Hermit and St Antony of Egypt (exemplars of the eremitical and monastic life) appears on the back of the Dunfallandy Stone together with the apparently quite unconnected and secular depiction of a horseman, paired symbols and a smith's tools, all within a border of two fantastic snakes devouring a man. The backs of other slabs display only secular scenes, horsemen on the slab from St Madoes and the fragmentary stones at Logierait and Meigle 3–6, a hunting scene and the depiction of warriors following a cow at Fowlis Wester, a crowded assortment of a hunting scene, a fantastic beast, a camel and an angel on Meigle 1, all with symbols.

A third category of carved slabs, characterized by an absence of symbols and perhaps of the c9, is represented by a few slabs. One, Meigle 2, has on the front a ringed cross flanked by fantastic beasts. The cross's head and ring are studded with bosses, the shaft carved with fantastic beasts. On the back is a tier of seemingly unrelated scenes, a hunting party and angel, Daniel in the Lions' Den, a centaur, and a dog baiting an ox watched by a man holding a club. The front of another, in Fowlis Wester Parish Church, is carved with a richly interlaced ringed cross flanked by the seated figures of St Paul and St Antony. This is sophisticated sculpture. By contrast, a slab (the 'Apostles' Stone') in Dunkeld Cathedral seems incompetent folk art. Without either symbols or a cross, it is carved with reliefs. On the lower part of one face is a depiction of Daniel in the Lions' Den. Above is what looks like the scene after a battle with an array of corpses surmounted by warriors, all shown in profile and some mounted. The scene is continued across one of the slab's edges which bears another horseman and, perhaps, also on the back which displays bearded heads, possibly an allusion to decapitated foes, and a shield. On the lower part of the back and edge are forward-facing cloaked figures, seemingly beardless. Could these possibly be clerics and represent the bishop and clergy of Dunkeld? Allied to this category of slabs is the most impressive sculptured monument in Perth and Kinross, the Dupplin Cross, now in St Serf's Church, Dunning, but which formerly stood on a hillside looking over the palace of Forteviot to a second cross near Invermay on the other side of the valley of the River Earn. The design of the Dupplin Cross, erected by or to commemorate Constantine son of Fergus, overlord of Pictland and Dál Riata, in the early c9, shows influence from Ireland, Iona and Northumberland but is distinctively Pictish, the panels carved with scenes celebrating royal power, either directly (depictions of warriors of varying status) or by Biblical allusion (Scenes from the Life of King David) interspersed with interlace motifs.

A few Pictish GRAVE-SLABS survive at Meigle. The top of each has a slot in which may have been fixed a cross. Otherwise, their relief decoration combines animals, some fantastic, interlacing and bosses. On one side of the largest (Meigle 11) is a scene of huntsmen followed by a human figure with an animal head and holding snakes. On one side of Meigle 12 are depicted battling bulls. Among the reliefs on the top of Meigle 26 is a pair of dancing seahorses. Incised at the end of this slab is a naked man looking nervously over his shoulder at a manticore, the man-eating beast of Aristotelian 'zoology', a reminder that the inhabitants of Dark Age Perth and Kinross were not ignorant of the classical world. More austere are the late c10 hogback recumbent gravestones, probably produced under Norse influence and resembling miniature houses with pitched roofs carved with 'tiles'. A weathered example stands in the graveyard near Tulliebole Castle. Much better preserved is Meigle 25, its ridge sloping towards one end and covered with a long eel-like creature with a fishtail and benign animal head.

MEDIEVAL CHURCHES

From the late c11 the Scottish Church was modernized and reformed, a process vigorously encouraged by Malcolm III and his queen, St Margaret (both †1093), and their sons, Edgar (†1107), Alexander I (†1124) and most notably, David I (†1153).

Monastic and Cathedral Buildings

One of this reform movement's defining features was the introduction to Scotland of international religious orders, themselves mostly newly formed. Margaret herself founded a Benedictine priory at Dunfermline (Fife) c. 1070 and Edgar a second Benedictine house at Coldingham (Borders) c. 1100. In Perth and Kinross, Alexander I founded an Augustinian priory at Scone c. 1120, its first canons brought from Nostell Priory (Yorkshire), and in 1145 David I converted a monastic establishment of *Céli Dé* on St Serf's Island in Loch Leven into an Augustinian priory (St Serf's Priory) under the superiority of the priory of that order which he had established at St Andrews (Fife). Scone Priory was raised to the status of an abbey in 1164, just after David I's grandson and successor, Malcolm IV, had founded a Cistercian abbey at Coupar Angus, its first monks imported from David I's foundation of Melrose Abbey (Borders) which had itself been colonized from Rievaulx Abbey (Yorkshire). In 1200 Gilbert, Earl of Strathearn, whose lands encompassed most of the former Pictish kingdom of Fortriu, founded an Augustinian priory (an abbey from c. 1220) at Inchaffray, its first canons brought from Scone to replace or subsume an existing establishment of *Céli*

Dé. About thirty or forty years later Sir David Lindsay, a Justiciar of Scotland, and his mother, Lady Marjory, a member of the royal house, established a Cistercian nunnery at Elcho. To these monastic foundations were added houses of friars, a Dominican friary being erected in Perth with an endowment largely provided by Alexander II, *c.* 1235, and a Carmelite friary at Tullylumb just outside the same burgh's medieval boundary in 1262, its chapel granted to the friars by Robert, Bishop of Dunkeld, each of these houses apparently providing accommodation for its royal or episcopal patron and his successors as required. Two further friaries, both in Perth, were founded in the C15, the Charterhouse of the Carthusians by James I in 1426 and a Franciscan house *c.* 1490.

The three Augustinian and Cistercian abbeys in Perth and Kinross were sizeable, each containing between sixteen and twenty-five canons or monks at the Reformation. The other religious houses were smaller, the Charterhouse with its complement of a prior and twelve friars probably the largest. The layout of the monastic and friary buildings was standardized. At each these surrounded a square cloister, the church or chapel generally on the N side with a chancel projecting E of the cloister, an E range containing a chapter house and dormitory, a S range containing the refectory and, in the W range, a guesthouse or, in the case of Cistercian monasteries before that order's reform in the C15, accommodation for lay brothers. Outside the conventual buildings was an area of ground (the precinct) enclosed by a wall. At the friaries this may have comprised little more than a graveyard but at Scone Abbey the precinct extended to 4.8ha. The cloister of Inchaffray Abbey was *c.* 27m. square internally and the chancel of its church projected 28m. to the E. Scone Abbey and Coupar Angus Abbey must have been of similar size. The nunnery at Elcho was probably about half the size of these, its church's nave, partly revealed in an excavation of 1968–73, having been 7m. wide. Also much smaller than the abbeys were St Serf's Priory, the nave of its 13.1m.-long church 6.1m. wide and its chancel only 3.66m. wide, and the friaries, although the Perth Charterhouse was described by John Knox in the mid C16 as 'a buylding of a wonderouse coast and greatness'.

In Perth and Kinross the Protestant Reformation of the mid C16 was exceptionally destructive of monastic buildings. The abbeys of Scone and Coupar Angus, the nunnery at Elcho and the friaries in and near Perth were all wrecked in 1559. Almost all their buildings seem to have been demolished by the early C17, although the C15 porch of the Perth Charterhouse was re-erected at St John's Kirk of Perth where it stood until it was removed *c.* 1800. Inchaffray Abbey was taken over by James Drummond (later, Lord Maderty) who allowed the monastic buildings to be quarried for building stone and seems to have reconstructed the abbey guesthouse as a mansion house for himself. Otherwise, the only building to remain in mutilated form is Coupar Angus Abbey's precinct gatehouse, probably of the C15, with a round-headed pend. A few architectural fragments from Scone Abbey survive in the grounds of Scone Palace and other fragments from Coupar Angus Abbey are in and immediately outside the present Abbey Church at Coupar Angus and in the walled garden of Arthurstone.

Dioceses with defined territorial boundaries* had probably been established in Scotland by the C10. However, all of the bishoprics except that of St Andrews seem to have been left vacant during the C11 and the diocesan structure was not fully revived until the mid C12. Perth and Kinross was divided between three dioceses, Kinross-shire, the area round Perth and Gowrie (the SE part of Perthshire) belonging to St Andrews, Strathearn and SW Perthshire to Dunblane, and N Perthshire forming the diocese of Dunkeld, the only one of the three with its cathedral church inside the region. After the bishopric of Dunkeld was filled in the early C12 the cathedral church may have been served initially by an existing community of *Céli Dé* but seems to have had only two priests by the middle of the century. It was not until *c.* 1230 that the cathedral was equipped with a regularly organized chapter of dignitaries and canons numbering about ten, its constitution based on that of Salisbury Cathedral. This was followed, apparently swiftly, by the beginning of the construction of a new cathedral, its layout with a long unaisled chancel projecting from a fully aisled nave, very similar to that of the approximately contemporary Dunblane Cathedral (Stirling and Central Scotland), probably fixed from the start. The choir seems to have been built in the mid C14, its walls pierced by a single tier of large pointed windows. Inside,

---

*But within the general bounds of a particular diocese were 'peculiars', parishes which fell under the jurisdiction of the bishop of another diocese.

Dunkeld Cathedral.
Engraving from J. Slezer, *Theatrum Scotiae*, 1693

stone blind arcading along the N wall may have backed the stalls of the canons and choristers; a triple sedilia, perhaps an early C14 insertion, provided seating for the celebrant and assistants during celebrations of the Mass. The nave followed in 1406–64, its aisle windows' reticulated and curvilinear tracery characteristic of the C15, its clearstorey windows small and with unadventurous detail. The interior is reminiscent of Romanesque churches, the elevations' three storeys divided by the horizontals of the columns' capitals and string courses, with sturdy round columns carrying the not very tall (pointed) arches and with round-headed openings to the triforium. A final phase of medieval work at the cathedral in 1469–c. 1500 consisted of the construction of a huge NW bell-tower and a remodelling of the W front, its new and elaborately traceried off-centre great window weirdly positioned in relation to the entrance below and the even more markedly off-centre roundel above.

Parish Churches

By the early C12 Scotland was divided territorially into parishes, each served usually by one priest and covering a defined area in which tiends (tithes) were levied on the inhabitants' annual agricultural and piscatorial produce for the support of the Church. Most parish churches in Perth and Kinross were appropriated to bishoprics, cathedrals or monasteries who enjoyed the right to appoint the parish priest (vicar) and to receive the 'garbal' tiend levied on crops, the vicar being supported by the 'lesser' tiends from livestock, milk and cheese. It was the responsibility of the parishioners to maintain or rebuild the nave of a parish church but the rector (generally an appropriator) was responsible for the chancel. The more important and richer landowners often had close connections with a monastery or cathedral (e.g. the Earls of Strathearn with Inchaffray Abbey which they had founded and where they were buried) and relatively little interest in parish churches, and the rectors were more concerned with the cathedrals or monasteries where they lived and worshipped. Moreover, masons and wrights capable of more than basic construction seem to have been in short supply and expensive to employ. Unsurprisingly, most medieval parish churches in Perth and Kinross appear to have been humble rubble-walled rectangular structures, without aisles and generally quite narrow. Some (e.g. St Kattan's Church, Aberuthven, probably of the C13, or the late medieval former parish churches at Cambusmichael, Invergowrie and Kinfauns) were single-cell with no structural break between the nave and chancel, the division presumably marked formerly by a wooden rood screen. At others (e.g. the former Rossie Parish Church (now mausoleum) in the grounds of Rossie Priory or Inchmartin Church near Kinnaird) the division into nave and chancel was marked internally by a cross wall pierced by an arch. The surviving architectural detail of these rural churches is very simple, the decoration generally restricted to mouldings of no great elaboration at the openings of doors, windows and chancel arches. The chevron-carved head of a door or window, probably of the C12, now built into the S wall of Forgandenny Parish Church, is exceptional.

13   A handful of churches stood out from the unambitious norm. St Serf's Church at Dunning of *c.* 1200 and the slightly earlier Muthill Old Church, the one built probably by Gilbert, Earl of Strathearn, and the other by his younger brother, have tall saddle-backed W towers with, at the belfry stage, round-headed recesses containing pairs of round-headed openings with central cushion-capitalled columns or piers, a motif perhaps borrowed from the C12 tower of Dunblane Cathedral (Stirling and Central Scotland). The tower of Muthill Old Church, perhaps originally free-standing, has only a plain entrance into the present nave but at St Serf's, Dunning, the tower's entrance from the nave is through a steeply pointed and expensively carved arch carried on semicircular responds with scalloped capitals. The much altered unaisled nave and originally narrower and lower chancel of St Serf's have survived but with only some wall-head corbels intended to carry parapets, fragments of carved work incorporated in the rebuilt S wall and one door (now missing its nook-shafts) to hint at its former elaboration of detail. Muthill Old Church was rebuilt or heavily remodelled in the C15 with a fully aisled nave and a narrower unaisled chancel. Michael Ochiltree, Dean (later Bishop) of Dunblane, is said to have been responsible for the work, and the nave windows are reminiscent of those of the N clearstorey windows of the choir of Dunblane Cathedral. The pointed arches of the nave arcades spring directly from octagonal piers without the interruption of capitals. Also probably of the C15 was the addition of a chapel on the N side of the chancel and aisles to the nave of the former Alyth Parish Church, the surviving N arcade also with octagonal piers but with capitals and carrying round-headed arches.

The C15 aisles at Muthill Old Church and the former Alyth Parish Church were probably intended to house altars endowed by local families for the saying of votive or requiem masses which had become a common part of late medieval worship. Certainly the housing of such altars must have been a major factor in the
15   planning of St John's Kirk of Perth when it was rebuilt, *c.* 1440–*c.* 1500, on a cruciform plan, the nave and choir both flanked by aisles, and with a tower over the crossing and a show-off two-storey N porch. By the Reformation it contained more than thirty altars, all, except the high altar, endowed by local families or trade incorporations. As befitted a town of the importance of
p. 572 Perth its burgh church was, in both size and architectural ambition, by far the most important in the region (roughly three times the size of Muthill Old Church) and would have been even more so had the nave aisles been completed to their originally intended full height and the size of the W window not curtailed. The windows of the choir, presumably executed before the cost-cutting evident at the nave, provide an exuberant display of late medieval tracery (much restored) with swirling mouchettes and reticulation, and similar tracery seems to have occupied the five-

light upper window of the N porch, the principal entrance to the church. The crossing tower proclaimed the civic and religious status of the building placed at the centre of the region's chief burgh. The interior was carefully considered, the detailing of the arcades increasing in elaboration from the nave to the choir to the presbytery, the crossing surmounted by a ribbed stone vault carried on massive piers.

For the richest families an alternative to the endowment of an altar in a parish church for the saying of votive and requiem masses was the foundation of a chantry chapel or collegiate church whose clergy could devote themselves to the spiritual needs in this life and the afterlife of the members of a particular family. Some COLLEGIATE CHURCHES, staffed by colleges of chaplains or canons and with their endowment charters specifying that masses were to be offered for the souls of the king and queen and the founders' families, were established by conversion of an existing church. At Abernethy, *c.* 1330, John Stewart, Earl of Angus and husband of a co-heiress of Sir Alexander Abernethy, transformed an Augustinian priory, itself formed from a community of *Céli Dé*, into a collegiate church staffed in the early C16 by a provost, five canons and three choristers. In 1433 Walter Stewart, Earl of Atholl, took over the existing parish church at Methven for a college consisting of a provost, five canons and five choirboys, the establishment augmented in 1510–16 by the endowment of nine prebends, one founded by James IV. At Innerpeffray an earlier chapel was rebuilt by John, Lord Drummond, *c.* 1507, when he endowed four chaplainries there, the establishment soon after acquiring collegiate status.

Among these collegiate foundations may be included the church at Tullibardine, strictly a chantry chapel but probably intended to be a collegiate church, founded in 1446 by Sir David Murray of Tullibardine and enlarged by his great-grandson *c.* 1500. The medieval Abernethy Church was demolished at the beginning of the C19. Of the former Methven Church, apparently cruciform, there remains only the N transept (the Methven Aisle), probably an early C16 addition, its large crowsteps with gableted heads, its N window containing reticulated tracery and flanked by an image niche and the royal coat-of-arms, presumably in honour of James IV's endowment of a prebend here. The church at Innerpeffray is a rubble-walled and rectangular-windowed oblong, externally almost unadorned except by an image niche on the E gable and the Drummond coat-of-arms carved on the door lintels. Inside, it was divided into a W vestibule opening through a round-headed arch into a short nave which was separated from the canons' choir by a rood screen. Much more assertive is the church at Tullibardine, which was probably begun as a straightforward rectangle but extended W and given transepts and a squat tower in the enlargement of *c.* 1507, the windows of the new work containing uncusped loop tracery. A generous provision of tracery proclaims the church's possession by the Murray family.

The surviving medieval churches of Perth and Kinross have been stripped of their MEDIEVAL FURNISHINGS and usually of their plaster, leaving them as jewel boxes without their contents. Some effort to visualize what has been lost is necessary if they are to be understood.

Each contained a high altar placed at or near the E end of the chancel as still stands the stone high altar (deprived of its top slab) of the collegiate church at Innerpeffray. Most contained one or more other altars dedicated in honour of particular saints (the Virgin Mary, etc.) or aspects of Christ's Passion (the Holy Blood, the Holy Rood, etc.). The church at Innerpeffray contained four altars in 1507, St John's Kirk of Perth more than thirty by the time of the Reformation. These subsidiary altars might be placed against the walls or screen either side of a chancel arch, at the E end of aisles or against pillars of nave arcades. Sometimes they occupied distinct chapels like the chapel on the N side of the chancel of the former Alyth Parish Church or the likely chapel in the NW corner of Muthill Old Church. At Dunkeld Cathedral slots in the piers of the nave's S arcade show that its two E bays were screened off as a chapel (St Ninian's Chapel) whose altar had been endowed by Bishop Robert Cardeny and whose tomb stood here. Grooves in this chapel's E wall may have been intended as fixings for a reredos above the altar. The same cathedral's high altar reredos was painted in the C15 with depictions of twenty-four miracles associated with St Columba, whose relics had been brought here by Kenneth mac Alpin in 849.

The chancel of any church was marked off from the nave by a screen surmounted by a platform (the rood loft) on which stood a great crucifix and perhaps also an altar. In abbey churches there was usually a second screen (the pulpitum or choir screen) to the E closing off the W end of the monastic choir. Slits in the E responds of the nave arcades of Dunkeld Cathedral and corbels in the side walls of the collegiate church at Innerpeffray and at the W arch of the crossing at St John's Kirk of Perth provided seatings for wooden rood lofts.

Reservation of a host (wafer) consecrated at the Mass to be used for veneration or to give communion to the dying was universal. Commonly in late medieval Scotland the host was reserved in a sacrament house or aumbry at the E end of the N wall of the chancel or in its E wall, to the N of the high altar. A couple of plain probable sacrament houses survive at Alyth Old Church and Cambusmichael Church. Another is at Fowlis Wester Parish Church, its lintel carved with the names of Jesus ('ihs') and Mary ('ma[ria]'). At Bendochy Parish Church, but not *in situ,* is a weathered but more elaborate sacrament house bearing the relief of a chalice above the aumbry opening and, below, the coat-of-arms and initials of William Turnbull, Abbot of Coupar Angus, who presumably presented it to the church in the early C16. Other aumbries were routinely provided for the storage of altar plate. Piscinae (sinks for the washing of the celebrant's hands and the sacred vessels during Mass) were also standard features, usually placed in the wall S of an altar but sometimes in an E wall like the piscina in the chapel at the E end of the S nave aisle of Dunkeld Cathedral or the ogee-arched C15 example in the choir of St John's Kirk of Perth.

For the ceremonies of Holy Week each church required an Easter Sepulchre in which, on Good Friday, were 'buried' a consecrated host and a crucifix, both 'rising again' early on Easter Sunday. The Easter Sepulchre, placed on the N side of the chancel, was usually a movable wooden structure but might be a permanent stone canopied recess, often serving also as the tomb of some notable. Such may have been the late medieval tomb recess standing in the position expected of an Easter Sepulchre in the former Kinfauns Parish Church, its elliptical arch covered with a crocketed hoodmould.

Seating for clergy during Mass was provided by sedilia on the S side of the chancel. Probably most were of wood but some were of stone and built into the wall. Well preserved early C14 triple sedilia with cusped and hoodmoulded arches survive in the choir of Dunkeld Cathedral. Of the choir stalls erected in that cathedral by Bishop Thomas Lauder in the later C15 and whose canopies were painted in the early C16 there is now no trace nor is there of the stalls which must have been present in monastic and collegiate churches. One medieval lectern is documented in Perth and Kinross, that given to Dunkeld Cathedral by Bishop George Brown *c.* 1500. It was of brass, the stem formed by a statue of Moses, the superstructure consisting of four desks, apparently for the four gospels, and with a brass candelabrum.

Fonts stood usually at the W end of churches near their principal entrance, a position symbolic of Baptism as the entry to the Church. Many were simple stone bowls placed on pedestals. However, Perth and Kinross contains two of some elaboration. In Meigle Parish Church is a font bowl of *c.* 1500. It is octagonal, each face carved with an ogee-arched panel, two of these bearing reliefs of the Crucifixion and Resurrection of Our Lord, the others emblems of his Passion, the subject of much late medieval devotion but also recalling that the believer was baptized into the death as well as the resurrection of Our Lord. At Longforgan Parish Church fragments of a roughly contemporary font bowl display scenes from the Passion and death of Our Lord. Also to hold holy water were stoups placed beside the entrances to churches so that worshippers could dip fingers in the water and cross themselves on entering. Stoups were routinely destroyed at the Reformation, their former position sometimes marked by disturbance in the masonry, but one survives at the late medieval former Kinfauns Parish Church where it is set in an ogee-arched recess.

The rubble walling of medieval churches was generally plastered or rendered and then lime-washed, the lime wash also covering ashlar masonry. In some churches at least the lime wash was painted with decoration, either patterns or figurative scenes. Very little of this has survived in Scotland but fragmentary remains of what seems to have been a complete scheme of *c.* 1500 are visible in the ground-floor room of the bell-tower of Dunkeld Cathedral. This was used as a courtroom and the walls were painted with biblical scenes of judicial or quasi-judicial proceedings, the Judgment of Solomon and the Woman Taken in Adultery still discernible. At the collegiate church of Innerpeffray consecration crosses are painted on the walls.

MEDIEVAL STAINED GLASS in Perth and Kinross is known only from documentary sources. Alexander Myln's C16 *Vitae Dunkeldensis Ecclesiae Episcoporum* recounts the gifts of glass to Dunkeld Cathedral by successive bishops, the great E window decorated with *diversis ymaginibus* (diverse images) erected by Bishop John de Peblys in the late C14, the other windows of the choir a few years later, the window beside the Lady Altar at the E end of the N nave aisle given in the 1430s by Bishop Donald Macnachtane and embellished with his coat of arms, and the other nave windows filled by Bishop Thomas Lauder later in the C15. According to Myln Bishop Lauder also built the choir of the former Caputh Parish Church and decorated it with glass windows, probably a reference to stained glass.

Church towers were intended to house bells. Bishop George Brown hung two bells in the tower of Dunkeld Cathedral *c.* 1500. Still in St John's Kirk of Perth is a collection of bells of the C14 and early C16, all probably Flemish, one (cast by *Peter Waghevens* in 1506) bearing decorative panels and a relief of St John the Baptist, patron saint of the church.

Burial in churches was probably reserved for major benefactors, lay or clerical. Often there seems to have been a desire among those enjoying this privilege to be interred near the high altar or an altar endowed by them. At Dunkeld Cathedral the tomb of Bishop William Sinclair †1337 was originally in the centre of the choir, the tomb of Alexander Stewart, Earl of Buchan, †1394 was also in the choir, and the tomb of Bishop Robert Cardeny †1437 was placed in St Ninian's Chapel, apparently intended as his own chantry chapel, at the E end of the S nave aisle. GRAVE-SLABS could mark the burial place of those of middling means. Some are incised. A badly worn slab of *c.* 1260 in the former Rossie Church (now mausoleum) at Rossie Priory is incised with the figures of a knight and his lady set in a pair of arches. Much better preserved is the early C14 slab in Longforgan Parish Church commemorating John de Galychtly and his wife, Mariota, incised with a portrait of the pair, their heads turned so that they gaze into each others' eyes and with a diminutive armour-clad figure, perhaps their son, standing in front of Mariota. That incised decoration continued into the C16 is shown by the grave-slab of Alexander Douglas, Rector of Moneydie, in Dunkeld Cathedral, the priest portrayed in mass vestments but with a tasselled cloth on his head. Relief carving appears in Aberdalgie Parish Church where a grave-slab, probably of the 1360s, depicts a knight in a canopied recess, and at the Abbey Church in Coupar Angus where the grave-slab of Abbot John Schanwel †1506 shows the ecclesiastic in cope and mitre.

Much grander and more expensive were TOMBS, their sarcophagus bases usually surmounted by effigies. Some effigies have survived divorced from their original setting, like the now headless alabaster c14 figure of Bishop William Sinclair in Dunkeld Cathedral or the late medieval double effigy of a knight and his lady in Muthill Old Church. However, in Dunkeld Cathedral the mid-c15 mitred effigy of Bishop Robert Cardeny still reposes on a stone sarcophagus contained in a segmental-arched recess covered with a crocketed ogee-arched hoodmould. This sarcophagus front's carved angels and human figures are conventional emblems of piety. Much livelier are the panels of c. 1400, probably from the sarcophagus of a tomb, in the Abbey Church at Coupar Angus, carved in relief with the naturalistically posed figures of knights, malefactors and an executioner. Of about the same date and naturalistic are the sculpted knights in the canopied niches on the sides of the sarcophagus of Alexander Stewart, Earl of Buchan. The surmounting recumbent effigy depicts the Earl with hands joined in prayer but dressed in full armour as if in contented rest after his destruction of Elgin Cathedral four years before his death.

POST-REFORMATION CHURCHES

The city of Perth was at the heart of the Scottish Reformation. In May, 1559, a few days after returning from Calvinist Geneva, John Knox preached in St John's Kirk against idolatry. This provoked a riot in which the mob destroyed statues and furnishings in that church and sacked the religious houses of the city and its suburbs. In August of the following year Parliament forbade celebration of the Mass according to Catholic usage, proscribed acceptance of papal authority and adopted a Calvinist Confession of Faith. Monastic and religious houses were dissolved. From 1633 until 1925 responsibility for the maintenance and, if necessary, rebuilding of parish churches passed to the heritors (landowners) of each parish. Forms of church government (presbyterian, episcopal and combinations of the two) varied, as did doctrinal understanding, until the Presbyterian settlement of 1690. But the established Church of Scotland's worship was, despite Charles I's attempts in the 1630s to introduce permanent communion tables and a more eucharistically centred liturgy, strongly Protestant in ethos, the starkness of its forms of worship and their surroundings only lessened from the later c19 by the introduction of 'Scoto-Catholic' innovations. Prayer and preaching in vernacular language, comprehensible and audible to the whole congregation, were the chief constituents of most services, celebrations of the sacrament of Holy Communion held only occasionally.

Most medieval parish churches were fairly small and could be adapted quite easily, if not conveniently, for reformed worship by the removal of the stone altar and rood screen or beam, the provision of a pulpit, often placed at the centre of one side of the nave, and of some form of seating. The only really large medieval churches of Perth and Kinross to continue in use after the Reformation were Dunkeld Cathedral and St John's Kirk of Perth. The cathedral's nave was abandoned and unroofed but its choir was fitted up as a parish church *c.* 1600. St John's Kirk, probably big enough to house all its parishioners (the population of the city of Perth), was too large for them all to hear the preaching and praying of one minister. Consequently, they were divided into two congregations or parishes in 1598 and three in 1715, these divisions followed by alterations to the building to provide each congregation with its own walled-off space.

The first LATE SIXTEENTH AND EARLY SEVENTEENTH-CENTURY CHURCHES built after the Reformation apparently stood on the foundations of their predecessors, e.g. the relatively long and narrow parish churches of Bendochy, St Bean's at Kinkell, and Monzievaird and Strowan of *c.* 1600 and Weem (now the Menzies Mausoleum) of 1609–14. St Bride's Kirk, Old Blair, near Blair Atholl, perhaps rebuilt a little earlier, had its accommodation increased by the addition of a transeptal 'aisle', just as was proposed although probably not executed at Kilspindie in 1634. The proposal to build an 'aisle' at Kilspindie was certainly a response to a growth in population of that parish but the 'aisle' at Murthly Castle's chapel of *c.* 1600 contained a gallery for the laird. At St Serf's Church, Dunning, the medieval chancel, no longer required for an altar, was taken over by the Rollos of Duncrub for their use during services.

Architecturally, the new churches and 'aisles' of the late C16 and C17 seem generally to have been unambitious. Decorative detail at Weem is restricted to carved heraldic panels and a birdcage bellcote. However, St Bride's Kirk, Old Blair, had a W tower and a tower was also provided in the mid C17 at the former Auchterarder Parish Church, its belfry stage pierced by pointed openings. More ambitious and displaying classical influence is the W tower added in 1690 by Patrick, Earl of Strathmore, to Longforgan Parish Church, the wall head surmounted by a balustrade, the sides containing round windows and dummy oculi under the rectangular belfry openings.

A fair number of EIGHTEENTH-CENTURY PARISH CHURCHES were built in the region, most beside or on the sites of their predecessors. The former Blackford Parish Church of 1738–9, like late C16 and C17 post-Reformation churches, is long and narrow, probably because it stands on medieval foundations. However, most of these new churches, usually simple oblongs or T-plan, had main blocks which were relatively broad in proportion to their length so as to seat the congregations as close as possible to the pulpits. When Abernyte Parish Church was rebuilt in 1736–7 the length was shortened by *c.* 3.7 m. In 1754 the chancel of the medieval Cargill Parish Church (since demolished) was removed and the nave widened by *c.* 6 m. The usual position of the pulpit in the centre of the S side was sometimes marked by tall flanking windows, e.g. at Aberdalgie of 1773, Kirkmichael of 1791–2, Little Dunkeld at Birnam of 1797–8 and, in the opening years of the C19, at Abernethy of 1801–3 and Scone

Old Parish Church, New Scone, of 1804. At Kettins Parish Church of 1767–8 the pulpit's flanking windows were surmounted by oculi. At Blackford and at Longforgan of 1794–5, a door for the minister's use was placed directly behind the pulpit, the imposts and lintel of the door at Blackford inscribed with the initials of the minister and of his son who had been appointed his assistant and successor. Several churches contained galleries, usually placed at the ends and sometimes opposite the pulpit, in a jamb if the building were T-shaped. Originally, these were often reached from external stone forestairs, most removed as hazardous in the C19 but a few surviving, e.g. at St Serf's Church, Dunning. At Findo Gask the gallery stair built in 1800–1 is housed in a bow projecting from the E gable. The end galleries of the churches of Aberdalgie, St Madoes and Kinfauns of 1788–9, Kirkmichael and Scone Old were lit by Venetian windows, those of Scone Old with pointed lights. Gothic windows appear also at other churches from the 1790s, e.g. at Longforgan, Kilspindie and Rait Parish Church of 1795, Fossoway St Serf's and Devonside at Crook of Devon, of 1805–6 and St Anne's, Dowally, of 1818.

A bellcote on one gable of the main block was a standard accoutrement of any parish church. Most are of simple birdcage design but the bulbous baluster piers and obelisk finials of the bellcote added to Dull Parish Church in 1717 form an engaging if inept exhibition of a mason's skills. More accomplished and much later are the Tuscan and Roman Doric columns of the bellcotes at St Madoes and Kinfauns and Scone Old Parish Churches. At Little Dunkeld Parish Church *John Stewart* balanced the two-stage balustered bellcote of the W gable with swagged urns at the E and, at Logierait Parish Church in 1804–6, he gave swagged urns to both gables as well as a bellcote (since replaced) at the W, and he provided yet more urns in 1811–13 on the corners of Auchtergaven Parish Church at Bankfoot.

A few churches of the C18 and first decade of the C19 stand out from the seemly but generally thrifty norm. Kenmore Parish Church, built for the third Earl of Breadalbane in 1760, was cruciform (one limb containing the earl's gallery) and with a battlemented W tower whose sides were pierced by circular windows. Another battlemented tower but placed in the centre of the S side behind the pulpit dignifies the former Crieff Parish Church of 1786. For the former Comrie Parish (now The White) Church of 1803–5, *John Stewart* designed a W steeple with an octagonal top stage and stone spire. At Aberdalgie Parish Church in 1773, the ninth Earl of Kinnoull provided not only Venetian windows for parishioners sitting in the galleries but Diocletian windows for those below and, for his own gallery in the N 'aisle', a fireplace whose chimney rises above an open-pedimented gablet which adorns the W side visible on the approach. Suavest of all is St Paul's Church in Perth designed by *John Paterson c.* 1800 and built by the city council to provide both additional ecclesiastical accommodation for the expanding burgh and an architectural ornament to encourage further development. This battlemented tall Gothic octagon, fronted by an elegant steeple, is an exemplar of urban elegance but now abandoned.

The INTERIORS of parish churches remodelled or rebuilt in the first two and a half centuries after the Reformation seem to have been largely unadorned. Some were uncomfortable. Moulin Parish Church at Pitlochry (later replaced) was not given a plaster ceiling until 1787; at Rhynd, the parish church on the eve of its rebuilding in 1839 had an earth floor. The tunnel-vaulted wooden ceiling, its boards painted with stylized foliage, in the chapel of c. 1600 at Murthly Castle is exceptional, its existence probably a consequence of the building's primary function being to serve the spiritual welfare of one landed family rather than of the community as a whole. Exceptional too were the plaster vaults erected in St Paul's Church at Perth and, in 1820, at Dunkeld Cathedral. Besides its ceiling, the Murthly Castle chapel contains part of the front of a contemporary Ionic pilastered laird's loft or gallery. Even more sumptuous as a display of status is the Stormont Pew of 1616 in Scone Old Parish Church, the exuberant and expensive setting for the public attendance at worship of Lord Scone and his family. At Dunkeld Cathedral in the C18 the Dukes of Atholl occupied a private pew placed on the N side of the choir, facing the pulpit and backed by the family mausoleum which had been formed in the medieval chapter house. In 1820 this pew was replaced by a roomy enclosure, some of the woodwork of its Gothic screen designed by *Archibald Elliot* now in St Anne's Church at Dowally.

Most lairds' galleries and pews (e.g. the Breadalbane Gallery at Kenmore and the Atholl Pew at Dunkeld) were removed in C19 and C20 reordering of churches. Lost too have been many more utilitarian galleries which had been erected, often on an *ad hoc* basis, in the C16, C17 and C18 to accommodate ordinary parishioners. Surviving galleries generally have simple panelled fronts, e.g. the late C18 galleries in St Madoes and Kinfauns Parish Church. Unusually smart are the surviving fronts of the galleries of c. 1800 which belonged to the guild incorporations of wrights and procurators in St John's Kirk of Perth and are decorated in best Adamesque fashion. Seating seems to have been utilitarian and pulpits simple. Tables for Holy Communion were generally erected only for the services themselves and then taken away. At Dunkeld in the late C18 these infrequent services were conducted not in the parish church formed from the cathedral choir but in a tent set up in the roofless nave, and something similar may have occurred in other parishes.

Probably as the result of a combination of increased agricultural prosperity and wider education and cultural aspirations among landlords, farming tenants and parish ministers, new PARISH CHURCHES OF THE 1820s AND 1830s are abundant in the region, usually built quite expensively although eschewing frivolous extravagance. Their designs were by architects rather than by masons or wrights and have a seriousness of purpose which sometimes leaves the visitor yearning for a touch of artisanal ineptitude. Classicism is rare but in his remodelling of Methven and Logiealmond Parish Church in 1825–6 *W. M. Mackenzie* gave the s front a three-bay centrepiece, its pediment broken by a central bay which breaks forward to support its own pediment surmounted by a pilastered and stone-spired steeple. Ten years later he provided Perth with St Leonard's Church whose front is crowned by a version of the Choragic Monument of Lysicrates. Romanesque of an unarchaeological variety was employed by *James Gillespie Graham* in 1830–3 for most of the detail of Errol Parish Church although the large s window contains Late Gothic tracery and the height of the not especially Romanesque tall Greek cross shape is emphasized by the crocket-finialled pinnacles of the corner buttresses and tower parapet. Similar but taking advantage of a more prominent position is *Thomas Hamilton*'s Alyth Parish Church of 1836–9 whose generally Romanesque manner is lightened by pinnacles and touches of Late Gothic detail. More Italianate than Romanesque in feeling is Rattray Parish Church at Blairgowrie, by *William Stirling I*, 1820, its slender tower finished with a bellcast-eaved pyramidal roof.

Gothic, usually of a Perpendicular or Tudor variety, was the most popular dress for these new churches of the earlier C19. Most were simple oblongs on plan but often dominated by an end tower containing the principal entrance or the vestry. At Moneydie Parish Church of 1813–14, probably designed by the local landowner and architectural connoisseur, *Lt-Gen. Sir Thomas Graham* of Balgowan, the walls of the piend-roofed box of the church itself are pierced by acutely pointed windows but the battlemented tower is Tudor Gothic. Battlements rising from the wall-heads of towers appear also at Dron Parish Church (by *William Stirling I*, 1824) and, with the addition of pinnacles, at the churches designed in 1825 by *James Gillespie Graham* at Muthill and in 1839 by *W. M. Mackenzie* at Clunie and Rhynd. Corner buttresses were provided at the towers of Collace Parish Church of 1812–13, where they are pinnacled and, with turreted tops linked by latticed stone parapets, at Kinross Parish Church of 1831–2, designed by *George Angus* as a near-identical version of his Fife churches of Kettle (Kingskettle) and Tulliallan (Kincardine-on-Forth). The tower parapet at Crieff West Church of 1837–8 forms a gablet at each face. Much more delicate is the pagoda-like s tower of 1824 at the former Blairgowrie Parish Church. Bellcotes, where they appear on churches of this period, are much more forceful than their C18 predecessors. At St Martins (by *Andrew Heiton Sen.*, 1842) the bellcote is of birdcage type but very tall and stands not on one end of the church but surmounting the gabled centrepiece of its s side. At Kinnoull, Perth (by *William Burn*, 1824–6), Monzie (by *William Stirling I*, 1830–1) and Inchture (by *David Mackenzie*, 1834–5) the bellcotes are spired octagons, Inchture's spire rising from within a battlement.

The finishing of the interiors of these early C19 parish churches was more than utilitarian. Large plaster ceiling roses, variously

Dron Parish Church.
East elevation by William Stirling I, 1824

of a sort of Romanesque, Perpendicular and Tudor, are found at Errol, Muthill and Clunie. At Burn's cruciform Kinnoull Parish Church there is a saucer dome over the crossing and pointed plaster tunnel vaults over the limbs. Galleries were usual, the front of the U-plan gallery at Muthill decorated with blind arcading. Usually these were carried along both sides and one end and, at cruciform churches, filled the arms of the cross but at Rattray a semi-hexagonal gallery runs along both ends and the N side. Here and at Methven and Logiealmond Parish Church the pulpit is placed in standard C18 fashion in the centre of the S wall but it was now more usual to find the pulpit at one end, sometimes, as in the churches at Alyth and Errol, occupying the 'chancel' of a cruciform building. The pulpits themselves (many replaced

later) could be showy. At Clunie the pulpit's back continues the
Tudor Gothic of the rest of the building; at St Martins its Gothic
canopy is finished with crocketed and foliaged finials. Showiest
is Muthill Parish Church's pulpit surmounted by a crown-spired
canopy.

CHURCHES OF OTHER DENOMINATIONS were put up in the
C18 and early C19. By far the most numerous category (over forty
in the region) was of churches or chapels built for members of
the various and fissiparous Secession groups which split from the
established Church, often because of the unpopular appointment
of a new minister, during this period. Most of these buildings,
especially in rural areas were humble, reflecting the financial and
often numerical poverty of their congregations. They usually consisted of simple oblong structures, perhaps containing galleries
but without bellcotes or towers. The former ANTIBURGHER
CHURCHES of the 1790s at Kinkell and Kinross are typical, only
the round-headed windows in their sides giving a hint of architectural pretension. Hardly more ambitious is the former Old
Light Antiburgher Chapel of 1821 in Perth, a piend-roofed box
with pointed windows. Contemporary but larger and relatively
expensive is the former Burgher Church at Milnathort, designed
by *James Milne* of Edinburgh with pedimented gables, one
pediment containing a cinquefoil enclosed in a dummy oculus,
the other surmounting the tall round-headed windows which
flanked the pulpit. A few INDEPENDENT (CONGREGATIONAL),
BAPTIST AND METHODIST CHAPELS were erected in the early
C19. The earliest and still standing is the former Congregational
Church built at Dunkeld in 1800, an unassuming harled box.
Slightly more pretentious are the former Methodist and Baptist
chapels of 1816 and 1830 at Nos. 170–178 and Nos. 151–157
South Street, Perth, both placed above shops but distinguished
by pointed windows.

It was only after the repeal of the early C18 penal laws in 1792–3
that Episcopalians and Roman Catholics were permitted to build
churches. One of the first of the few EPISCOPALIAN churches
built in the region before the 1840s was St Adamnan-
Kilmaveonaig at Blair Atholl in 1794. Before Victorian remodelling it was externally indistinguishable from a contemporary
Presbyterian rural parish church, a rubble-walled oblong with a
birdcage bellcote on the W gable and round-headed S windows
flanking the pulpit. The interior contained galleries along the N
side and at the ends (the E a laird's loft). Only the presence of a
small wooden communion table in front of the pulpit marked out
the church's denominational identity. The Church of England
chapel built at Perth in 1796–1800 was 'a neat structure, but very
unecclesiastical in its architectural features'. Except for its communion table housed in a short chancel, the Gothic St James'
Episcopal Church at Muthill, designed by *R. & R. Dickson* in
1835, might just as well have been one of the more up-to-date
Presbyterian churches of the same time. Also of the 1830s is St
John the Baptist's Church constructed by the ROMAN CATHOLICS
in Perth and originally plain ('Gothic with little architectural

ornament'), although an advance in terms of aesthetics and comfort on the converted barn at Park, near Cargill, in which its congregation had previously worshipped.

In the Disruption of 1843, two-fifths of its ministers, generally those of Evangelical persuasion, left the established Church of Scotland to form the FREE CHURCH OF SCOTLAND. This was intended not as a sect but as a replacement for the established Church and one of the Free Church's first aims, almost completely achieved within a few years, was to provide a Free church, manse and school in each parish. In Perth and Kinross, as elsewhere, the early Free churches were inexpensive. Typical were the Free churches of 1843 at Alyth and Comrie, simple boxes with pointed windows and birdcage bellcotes. The church at Comrie had, as a further small decorative touch, a quatrefoil panel inscribed with the date of its erection, and the contemporary Lethendy and Kinloch Free Church had quatrefoil lights in the gables. Rather more ambitious were the Free churches of Auchterarder, Errol and Collace (at Kinrossie), all with squat end towers, the detail of Auchterarder's tower Romanesque but of a Georgian variety. The front gable of Coupar Angus Free Church, also of 1843, was flanked by a pair of low towers. Taller is the battlemented tower of the otherwise demolished Braco Free Church.

CHURCHES AFTER 1850. Four years after the Disruption, the United Secession and Relief Churches, the two principal groupings into which the Secessionist sects had coalesced, came together to form the United Presbyterian Church of Scotland. From then, until the unions of 1900 between the Free and United Presbyterian Churches to form the United Free Church and of 1929 when the United Free Church joined or, according to one school of thought, was joined by the Church of Scotland, Scottish Presbyterians were divided into three competing denominations of not hugely different size, although the United Presbyterians were relatively weak in Perth and Kinross. PRESBYTERIAN CHURCHES of the C19 and beginning of the c20 were built in some quantity to serve these denominations. A few were erected to serve new or growing centres of population, e.g. Blairgowrie South Free Church of 1858 or the established (Church of Scotland) churches in the villages of St Fillans (Dundurn Parish Church of 1878–9), Aberfeldy, Ardler and Pitlochry in 1883 and Craigie of 1894–6 in a new suburb of Perth, but most were replacements of earlier buildings. The United Presbyterians, now enjoying greater prosperity and the self-confidence of belonging to a sizeable denomination, rebuilt several churches, especially urban ones, on a considerably larger scale than before between 1855 and 1870, e.g. at Crieff, Abernethy, Alyth, Comrie, Coupar Angus, Perth, Methven and Milnathort. They followed in the 1880s and 1890s with new churches at Bankfoot, Kinross, Perth and Crieff.

The Free Church replaced several churches which had been thrown up in haste immediately after the Disruption with more dignified and sometimes imposing examples of architectural worth, e.g. the churches at Pitlochry, Fortingall, Blackford, Dunkeld, Perth, St Stephen's, the present St Matthew's and Comrie in the 1860s and 1870s and, in the 1880s and 1890s, at Crieff, Forgandenny, Kirkmichael, Muthill, New Scone and Pitcairngreen. The Church of Scotland replaced its parish churches at Blackford and Coupar Angus in the 1850s, at Kinfauns and Meigle in the 1860s, at Crieff in 1880-2 and at Auchterarder in 1904-5, almost exactly contemporary with new United Free Churches at Blairgowrie and Almondbank. Other parish churches were remodelled, frequently with drastic change of their internal character, or extended. A steeple was added to Kettins Parish Church in 1893 and a tower to the chancel of Cleish Parish Church four years later.

Many of these rebuildings and remodellings are innocently intended expressions of the pride of a congregation or of its more forceful members in their place of worship and of a growing expectation that a church should be more than a utilitarian meeting house. In some places, however, it is hard to avoid suspecting interdenominational battles for architectural dominance. At Blackford, the Parish Church of 1858-9 by *David MacGibbon* and the Free Church designed by *William Henderson* in 1865 both stand on the main thoroughfare of Moray Street and flaunt steeples. Their construction costs of £1,420 and c. £1,000 were sizeable for this not very prosperous village and surrounding parish. At Crieff the tower of the Church of Scotland's West Church of 1837-8 is dwarfed by the c. 36.5 m.-high steeple of Crieff Free Church built just to its E in 1881-2. Elsewhere in this town, the tall steeples of Crieff Parish Church and Crieff United Presbyterian Church glare sidelong at each other across Strathearn Terrace. The Parish Church was completed in 1882 at a cost of £4,500, the United Presbyterian, begun the next year, nearly £1,500 more.

Although there is no evidence that the Presbyterians regarded it as morally or religiously superior to other styles, GOTHIC was generally preferred for these later C19 churches. The parish churches of Coupar Angus and Meigle, rebuilt in 1859-60 and 1869-70, were both designed, not very imaginatively, by *John Carver* but their Gothic makes a determined attempt to disguise the fact that, essentially, they are standard Georgian preaching boxes, the one an oblong but provided with a tower at one corner, the other T-plan with a tower in an inner angle. Buttressing at the Coupar Angus church's front gable suggests (falsely) that the interior is divided into a nave and aisles. A similar suggestion is made by the broach-spired steeple of Milnathort United Presbyterian Church (by *William Ingram*, 1867-9). Designs of more convincingly archaeological Gothic plan were produced in the 1880s for the large St Matthew's (originally West Free) Church at Perth and the Parish, Free and United Presbyterian churches of Crieff, all with nave aisles and transepts. At St Matthew's, Perth, there is an end recess for the pulpit, at Crieff Parish Church a small apsidal chancel and a chapel off one transept. The style of all these is derived from C13 Gothic, some of Crieff

Free Church's details culled from Dunblane Cathedral. Much sturdier although also Early Gothic in manner is *Honeyman, Keppie & Mackintosh*'s Auchterarder Parish Church of 1904–5, the broad nave ending in a chancel and accompanied by a single aisle and octagonal-spired low tower. Late Gothic of a distinctively Scottish variety was used by *J. J. Stevenson* in his design of 1882 for St Leonard's-in-the-Fields and Trinity (originally St Leonard's Free) Church dominating the South Inch at Perth. Its aisled nave also ends with an apse (derived from the C15 apse of the Church of the Holy Rude at Stirling) and, projecting from the nave's E (liturgical W) end is a massive tower surmounted by a crown spire clearly inspired by that of St Giles' Cathedral in Edinburgh. Scots Late Gothic appears memorably also at *Sydney Mitchell & Wilson*'s red sandstone Scone New (originally Scone Free) Church of 1886–7, its battlemented tall tower surmounted by a crowstep-gabled caphouse. Less consciously revivalist is the use of Scots Gothic on a small scale by *W. Dunn & R. Watson* in 1901–2 for their rebuilding of Fortingall Parish Church as a very simple harled and crowstep-gabled nave and chancel, a replica of the previous church's C18 birdcage bellcote on the W end, a looptraceried E window lighting the chancel.

Although Gothic was dominant for these churches, OTHER STYLES appear. At Perth the York Place United Presbyterian Church (now Trinity Church of the Nazarene) was designed by *Andrew Heiton Jun.* in 1858 in a thinly detailed Romanesque manner. More forceful Romanesque was employed in 1883–4 by *C. & L. Ower* for Pitlochry Parish Church. *T. L. Watson*'s North (former North United Presbyterian) Church in Perth of 1878–80 is also Romanesque but of Italian rather than North European derivation and its interior contains pendentived domes over the side aisles and a tunnel vault (all these of plaster) covering the nave. A studiedly simple use of round-headed openings is found at the diminutive Braes of Rannoch Church, near Bridge of Gaur, designed in 1907 by *P. Macgregor Chalmers*, whose Early Christian manner evokes the supposed purity of the Columban Church.

The internal layout and planning of many Victorian Presbyterian churches differed little from that of their Georgian predecessors although FURNISHINGS were often designed with more seriousness and at greater cost. The interior of the T-plan Meigle Parish Church of 1869–70 contains a Gothic pulpit at the centre of the main block's long S wall, galleries at the ends and in the jamb, their fronts' boards arranged in herringbone patterns, and pitch-pine pews. The nave arcades of *John Honeyman*'s St Matthew's, Perth, of 1869–71 are formed by cast-iron columns and the aisles and E end filled with galleries, the pulpit standing at the W end as the focal point. The same galleried arrangement, although with the arcades' cast-iron columns supporting stone arches, was provided by *J. J. Stevenson* at the same city's St Leonard's-in-the Fields and Trinity Church. Elaboration was sometimes exhibited in roofs and ceilings. The plaster ceiling of Meigle Parish Church is compartmented in standard up-market Late Georgian fashion but with sacred symbols decorating the bosses. Show-off displays of the carpenter's craft appear elsewhere. The nave of St Matthew's, Perth, has a hammerbeam roof. In his remodelling of Moulin Parish Church at Pitlochry in 1874–5 *James C. Walker* introduced a new roof whose queenposts are carved as Neo-Jacobean barley-sugar columns rising from pendants. At the same town's Pitlochry Parish Church of 1883–4 the roof was an over-ambitious exhibition of bracing which soon required to be strengthened by the introduction of columns.

The foundation of the Aberdeen (later Scottish) Ecclesiological Society in 1886 marked the advent of a new approach to the planning and use of Presbyterian churches. The Society's members, many of them antiquarian-minded and scholarly ministers, argued that the architecture of church buildings was part of worship which should express the unity of Word and Sacrament advocated by c16 Reformers. They looked for inspiration to medieval buildings but advocated simplicity in the arrangement of furnishings, although not for money to be skimped on the design and execution of the communion table, pulpit and font. The communion table was to be the focal point placed, if possible, in a short chancel on one side of whose entrance was to stand the pulpit and, on the other, a lectern or the font if that were not at the church's (liturgical) W end. The ecclesiologists disliked galleries, especially lairds' lofts, except at the W end, and wished the congregation to be seated in low pews without social distinction. Reordering of one 1830s church along ecclesiological lines was carried out in 1894 at Monzie by *H.B.W. Steele & Balfour* who removed the side galleries and formed a 'chancel' containing the communion table at the N end, a new pulpit being erected on one side of the chancel. Similar was the reordering of the 1790s Longforgan Parish Church five years later when galleries were removed from the N side and E end and the position of the pulpit shifted from the centre of the S wall to one side of the arch into the chancel which had been added to house the communion table.

The early c20 churches of Fortingall and Braes of Rannoch were both arranged along ecclesiological lines, the communion table at Fortingall backed by a reredos. This, like the church itself, was designed by *W. Dunn & R. Watson* who were also employed in 1908 to restore the choir (parish church) of Dunkeld Cathedral. Here they replaced the Georgian plaster vault with a wooden ceiling, took out the Georgian galleries and seating, the removal of the Atholl Pew acclaimed by the leading ecclesiologist, Professor James Cooper, as showing that 'there is no longer any flaunting of earthly greatness in the House of Him before Whom all are equal', and provided new pews of uniform design. An organ and choir gallery was erected at the W end with a new stone font placed in front of it. An open wooden screen, the pulpit projecting from one corner, divided off the cathedral's E bay which now formed a sanctuary in which stood the holy table.

The building of VICTORIAN ROMAN CATHOLIC CHURCHES kicked off in triumphalist vein at Murthly Castle with the Chapel of St Anthony the Eremite which was added in 1845–6 by *James Gillespie Graham* to the existing chapel of c. 1600, henceforth relegated to the status of a mausoleum. The new chapel was a piece of Romanesque Catholic bravado, its great w tower containing a clock whose bell rang the *Angelus* thrice daily. Despite its size, larger than that of most rural parish churches, this was decidedly the private chapel of the Stewarts of Grandtully, the completely tiled floor empty of seating except for a bench round the walls. The family pew was provided by the tower's first-floor room from which they could look to the depiction of the Conversion of Constantine (perhaps an allusion to Sir William George Drummond Stewart's own conversion to Catholicism) painted above the arch which opened into the old chapel behind but contained organ pipes above the altar and reredos. The chapel's hammerbeam roof was decorated with gold stars on a blue ground, its walls painted with figures of saints, the windows filled with stained glass. The region's other large Roman Catholic church was also a chapel, that of St Mary's Monastery (now Pastoral and Retreat Centre) on the edge of Perth, designed by *Andrew Heiton Jun.* in 1867. It is a Gothic cruciform, the external austerity relieved by statues of saints in tabernacled niches. More statues are placed inside, on the reredoses over the high altar and the altars of the aisle chapels dedicated to the Sacred Heart and St Alfonso de Liguori, founder of the Redemptorist order to which the monastery belonged. Other Roman Catholic churches in the region were few, small and cheap, St Fillan's at Crieff, with a large rose window in the bellcoted front gable, the most ambitious architecturally.

VICTORIAN EPISCOPALIAN CHURCHES showed much greater confidence. By the 1840s the Scottish Episcopal Church had grown in confidence, numbers and wealth, aided by the adherence of a good number of landowners, often encouraged by devout English spouses. It was strongly influenced by the doctrinal and ecclesiological teaching of the English Tractarians, such as Newman, Keble and Pusey. To give a specifically Anglican and Episcopalian, indeed Anglo-Catholic, emphasis to the education of Episcopalian ordinands Glenalmond College was founded in the 1840s, when the divinity faculties of the Scottish universities were controlled by the Presbyterian Church of Scotland. Glenalmond was to serve both as a theological college and as a school for the children of Episcopalian lairds and professionals. The College's chapel, intended to be linked to the dormitory and teaching blocks by a cloister, was given a major place whose importance would have been further emphasized had the proposed steeple over its entrance been executed. Its design by *John Henderson*, architect of all the 1840s buildings at Genalmond, was unashamedly cribbed from the C13 chapel of Merton College, Oxford, to form one of the most faithful reproductions of the Decorated Gothic style advocated by ecclesiologically minded Tractarians for churches. The interior, a single space but originally divided by an organ screen into a three-bay ante-chapel and four-bay chapel, its pews arranged in collegiate fashion to face each other, was focused inexorably on the stone altar.

Contemporary with the building of Glenalmond College was the first phase of construction of St Ninian's Cathedral in Perth. This project, promoted by two aristocratic Tractarian laymen, was intended both to provide a setting for the daily worship of the diocesan bishop and a team of clergy, and to be an advertisement of the resurgence of the Episcopal Church to visitors to Scotland for whom Perth, at the nexus of the railway system, was often a necessary port of call. The appointment as architect of *William Butterfield* (succeeded by *F. L. Pearson* for completion of the cathedral fifty years later) showed a determination to have a building designed in accord with the ecclesiological principles advocated by Tractarian ideologists. Consequently, the style was Decorated and the plan cruciform, with a long chancel to contain the choir and clergy stalls and, at its E end, the sanctuary housing the altar. Unfortunately, Butterfield's intended great W tower (a revision of his original proposal for twin towers) was unexecuted because of structural problems and the site, on the corner of two streets, unsuitable for what should have appeared as an ecclesiastical enclave of cathedral, bishop's palace and canons' houses.

The model for ordinary Episcopalian churches advocated by the highly influential Tractarian *Ecclesiologist* was of a village church, its style Decorated or Flamboyant (a more Scottish medieval style but eschewed by C19 architects), with a distinct nave and chancel and placed in a tree-shaded churchyard. One of the first Victorian churches in Perth and Kinross was the small St Catherine's at Blairgowrie of 1842–3, whose nave and chancel conformed to the model but whose lancet windows marked an economical deviation from the preferred style and which was set in a street rather than a churchyard. Perhaps unsurprisingly, the building did not prelude a notable architectural career for its designer, *J. B. Henderson*, the teenage stepson of the incumbent clergyman. Much larger, Decorated in style and with a prominent steeple is St John the Baptist, Perth, designed by *J., W. H. & J. M. Hay* in 1850, but its very broad nave, the galleries in the transepts and the short chancel (little more than an 'altar recess') place it at some distance from the Tractarian ideal, the more so since its intractably urban setting is hardly that of the country church which it aims to be. Much more satisfactory village sites were provided for St Mary's, Birnam (Geometric, by *William Slater*) and Holy Trinity, Pitlochry (Decorated, by *Charles Buckeridge*), both opened in 1858.

Stylistically, quite a number of churches deviated from ecclesiological principles. Romanesque was used by *James Gillespie Graham* for the chapel built at Gask House in 1845–6 by the Oliphants, perhaps an Episcopalian riposte to the Roman Catholic pretensions of the Stewarts of Grandtully at Murthly Castle, and also by *David Bryce* in 1857 for St Ninian's, Alyth. Simple lancet-windowed Gothic appears at St Paul's, Kinross, designed by *John Lessels* in 1872. All Saints', Glencarse, by *Duncan D. Stewart*, 1878, of white-painted concrete with applied half-timbering and a red-tiled roof, is enjoyably picturesque but Gothic detail is confined to cusped lights in the rectangular window openings. Similarly detailed windows are used at the tiny granite and whinstone-walled St Michael and All Angels, Ballintuim, of 1899, its picturesqueness produced by bargeboards. Standing apart from the village church ideal is the huge All Soul's, Invergowrie, designed by *Hippolyte J. Blanc* and erected in 1890–6 by Frances, Lady Kinnaird, as a memorial to her husband whose Episcopalian chapel at Rossie Priory had been closed by his Presbyterian brother and heir. All Soul's is an Early English cruciform edifice, constructed of red sandstone, whose crossing tower surmounted by an octagonal stone spire rises high above its surroundings and makes an unmissable landmark on the road (now by-passed) from Rossie Priory to Dundee. The interior is that of an Anglo-Catholic shrine, the walls bearing reliefs of the Stations of the Cross, the high altar of black marble inlaid with alabaster and surmounted by a reredos whose giant alabaster crucifix stands out from a background of painted cloth. Such a single-minded affirmation of Catholic-inspired Episcopalian doctrine and practice is unique in the area. Furnishings which might be condemned as 'Popish' by Presbyterians and even some Anglicans are not rare in Episcopalian churches. The high altar of St Ninian's Cathedral, Perth, is sheltered by a mosaic-clad early C20 baldacchino decorated with sculptures of the Crucifixion and the patron saints of Great Britain and Ireland. British and Irish saints preaching the Gospel appear on reliefs on the cathedral's pulpit erected in 1901. The stone pulpit of St John's, Perth, was given marble reliefs of Scenes in the Life of St John the Baptist in 1872 and the oak pulpit of 1897 at St Mary's, Birnam, bears reliefs of Scenes in the Life of Our Lord. The altar (a replacement of 1901) in the chapel of Glenalmond College, of rose-coloured alabaster, the front decoarated with mosaics of the Good Shepherd and angels, could hardly be mistaken for a Protestant communion table. At Holy Trinity, Pitlochry, a richly carved and coloured reredos by *J. Ninian Comper* was erected in 1893 and a more sombre late Gothic reredos of oak, designed by *Robert S. Lorimer*, its central crucifix flanked by angels holding chalices, was installed in St Adamnan-Kilmaveonaig at Blair Atholl in 1908.

Reordering of Presbyterian CHURCHES IN THE 1920S AND 1930S along generally 'ecclesiological' lines continued, with more galleries removed and more 'chancels' formed. Permanent communion tables became standard furnishings. In 1927 *J. Jeffrey Waddell* refitted the E end of the much altered medieval Fowlis Wester Parish Church as a chancel containing an oak communion table and choir stalls, the entrance to the chancel flanked by a pulpit and lectern, the new furnishings decorated with touches of Neo-Celtic carving. The next year Waddell provided new furnishings, displaying Early Christian motifs, in the panelled 'chancel' he formed within the Georgian Logierait Parish Church.

The most far-reaching scheme of this period was *Robert S. Lorimer*'s restoration in 1923–6 of St John's Kirk of Perth as a single church, the work carried out as a memorial to the inhabitants of that city and county killed in the First World War.

Lorimer reconstructed the exterior of the nave in a unified late medieval manner, restored an upper storey (but its design taken from St Michael's, Linlithgow) to the medieval N porch and added the Shrine (War Memorial) Chapel on the site of a medieval chapel, this new chapel and the main W front adorned with sculptured stone beasts. The internal work largely consisted of a restoration of medieval fabric but over the nave and transepts Lorimer erected wooden pointed tunnel vaults embellished with carved and painted panels depicting Scenes from the Life of Our Lord and Christian symbols. A new pulpit was installed under the crossing. Richly but decorously carved choir stalls and an organ case were placed in the two W bays of the chancel. In the next bay E stood an oak communion table, its front carved with a relief of the Last Supper, backed by an open reredos-screen which divided off the chancel's two E bays (the supposed medieval presbytery) as the John Knox Chapel in honour, presumably unironic, of the Reformer's sermon against idolatry preached in the church in 1559.

A large donation to the work on St John's Kirk was given by the first Lord Forteviot who also financed *Lorimer & Matthew*'s reordering in 1926–8 of Aberdalgie Parish Church, an expensive but unostentatious scheme which gave the building a compartmented ceiling, dado and pews of Austrian oak. The pilastered proscenium arch framing the laird's gallery in the jamb is a pardonable expression of proprietorial status.

New churches of the 1920s and 1930s are few but at Birnam in 1932 *Reginald Fairlie* designed St Columba's R.C. Church, a memorably simple harled structure with round-headed windows. CHURCHES SINCE 1950 are also scarce and small. Among the handful built in Perth are the octagonal Craigend-Moncreiffe Church, by *Carvell & Partners*, 1974–5, its roof surmounted by a lead spire, and *James F. Stephen*'s Riverside Church of 2002, with ribbed metal roofs dominating the pale brick walls. Discreetly sited but worth discovery outside the city is the chapel of Kilgraston School, by *Gillespie, Kidd & Coia*, 1961, a flat-roofed rectangle pierced by horizontal clearstorey windows.

STAINED GLASS, now plentiful, was frowned on by Presbyterians until the late C19, although in the 1830s the windows of St Leonard's Church in Perth were filled with glass decorated with coloured patterns. Roman Catholics and Episcopalians were less inhibited. In the 1840s, the Edinburgh firm of *Ballantine & Allan* supplied brightly coloured glass including depictions of angels for the windows of the chapel at Murthly Castle and, in the 1850s, the English firm of *James Powell & Sons* provided patterned glass for the side windows of Glenalmond College Chapel whose great E and W windows were given glass depicting Old and New Testament Scenes (the W window by *Henry Hughes*). Just after the church was opened in 1857, the chancel windows of St Ninian's, Alyth, were provided with glass by *O'Connor* showing the Good Shepherd flanked by St Martha and St Mary Magdalene. Scenes from the Life of Our Lord adorned the windows erected *c.* 1866 in the chapel at Rossie Priory.

The first significant introduction of stained glass to a Presbyterian church in Perth and Kinross was in 1867 when the great s window of Errol Parish Church was filled with glass containing small Biblical scenes set among brightly coloured patterns, the work designed by *J. Murray Drummond* of Megginch and executed by *James Ballantine & Son*. Much more prominent figures are displayed in the scenes from parables on the w window designed by *J. E. Millais* and executed by *Lavers, Barraud & Westlake* in 1870 at Kinnoull Parish Church, Perth. Seven years later St Ninian's Cathedral, Perth, belatedly filled its E window with strongly coloured archaic glass (Christ in Glory) by *Alexander Gibbs* carrying out a design by *William Butterfield*.

From the 1880s stained glass proliferated in churches of all denominations, although until the C20 Presbyterians generally confined their subject matter to Scriptural scenes whilst Episcopalians and Roman Catholics were happy to depict non-Biblical saints. Much was by the *Ballantine* firm (successively, *James Ballantine & Son*, *A. Ballantine & Gardiner* and *A. Ballantine & Son*) of Edinburgh, competent but uninspired. Also competent but lacking excitement are the windows by *Burlison & Grylls* in St Ninian's Cathedral, Perth, and Dunkeld Cathedral. More satisfying are the clearly drawn and well-coloured windows by *Clayton & Bell* and *C. E. Kempe* in the Episcopalian churches at Alyth, Blair Atholl, Coupar Angus, Kinross and Pitlochry and in Longforgan Parish Church. Much lusher is the work of *Morris & Co.* in St Mary's, Birnam, St Serf's, Comrie, and Monzie Parish Church, and by *Henry Holiday* in Alyth Parish Church.

Artists working from *c.* 1920 until the later C20 are widely represented in the region although seldom by more than one or two windows in any church. *J. Ninian Comper* produced a memorial window for Glenalmond College Chapel in 1923, *Henry Holiday* a late work at Kenmore Parish Church in 1947. *Margaret Chilton* provided depictions of saints in St Adamnan-Kilmaveonaig, Blair Atholl, and Longforgan Parish Church in 1925 and 1956, and *Gordon Webster* strongly coloured lights at St Anne's, Coupar Angus, and the former Crieff United Presbyterian Church in 1962–71. There are examples of the work of *Douglas Strachan*, at his best when working with small panes of thick glass, at Auchterarder Parish Church, the former Crieff Free Church and (almost certainly) Kinclaven Parish Church. Characteristic examples of *William Wilson*'s stylized and sometimes expressionist realism are found in the parish churches of Abernethy and Dron, Alyth, Crieff and Kenmore and at St Serf's Episcopal Church at Comrie. St John's Kirk of Perth is a showcase of C20 stained glass, mostly by Scottish artists, with no fewer than six windows by *Herbert Hendrie*, three by *Margaret Chilton* and *Marjorie Kemp*, two by *Douglas Strachan* and one each by *William Meikle & Sons*, *Morris Meredith Williams*, *J. & W. Guthrie & Andrew Wells Ltd*, *Louis Davis* and *Isobel Goudie*. The latest window erected here (in 1975), worthy of its setting and its companions, is by the American *Harvey Salvin*.

MAUSOLEA, MONUMENTS, GRAVEYARDS AND STATUES

The post-Reformation reordering of churches for Protestant worship deprived chancels of their specific liturgical function. Often they were taken over by local landowners who erected in them their own pews or galleries and formed family BURIAL VAULTS below. In Perth and Kinross the chancel of the medieval Alyth Parish Church became the burial place of the Ramsays of Bamff, the chancel of St Serf's Church, Dunning, that of the Rollos of Duncrub, the chancel of Caputh Parish Church that of the Mackenzies of Delvine and the chancel of St Mary's, Grandtully, that of the Stewarts of Grandtully. The Earls (later, Dukes) of Atholl constructed their burial vault under the chapter house of Dunkeld Cathedral. At other churches lairds built transeptal 'AISLES', also containing pews or galleries above burial vaults, e.g. the Charteris Aisle added to the former Kinfauns Parish Church in 1598, the early C17 'aisles' erected by the Earl of Kinnoull at the former Kinnoull Parish Church, Perth, and by Lord Scone at the former Scone Parish Church in the grounds of Scone Palace, or the Bruce Aisle of c. 1680 at the former Kinross Parish Church.

When churches were rebuilt on new sites these 'aisles' were left as MAUSOLEA, used solely for burials. At Kinfauns, after the building of a new church, the arch which had opened from the Charteris Aisle into the former church was infilled. At Kinnoull, the s gable of the Kinnoull Aisle, which, presumably, had contained an opening into the church, was rebuilt. Work was more drastic, however, at the 'aisle' of the former Scone Parish Church. In 1807 *William Atkinson* remodelled this in Late Gothic dress. It now looks like a temple standing on a knoll in the park. At Caputh the surviving medieval chancel of the former church was given a pyramidal roof c. 1800 and then, in 1879, recast in Romanesque form.

Some mausolea were new structures. In 1736 *William Adam* designed a mausoleum for the Dukes of Montrose at Aberuthven after St Kattan's Church there had been abandoned for worship and partly demolished. The Dukes had previously taken over the chancel of St Kattan's as their 'aisle' and the new mausoleum occupied the same site but extended also to its s. It is a square ashlar-walled (now rendered) building, the pyramid roof surmounted by a stone urn, Adam's round-headed entrance replaced by a Venetian door in 1785. *James Playfair* produced a starkly powerful French Neoclassical mausoleum for Thomas Graham of Balgowan (later, Lord Lynedoch) at Methven in 1793. Also classical but idiosyncratic, with round-headed panels on the walls, is the mausoleum put up for the Stuarts of Rait at Kilspindie in 1822. Heavy-handed Perpendicular Gothic was used for the design (by *C. H. Tatham*) of the Murray Mausoleum at Ochtertyre in 1809 and Romanesque for the Kinloch Mausoleum, near Meigle, in 1861. Also of the 1860s was the ninth Lord Kinnaird's restoration (by *T. S. Robertson*) of the medieval

Scone Palace, Mausoleum.
West elevation probably by William Atkinson, 1807

Rossie Church in the grounds of Rossie Priory as his family's mausoleum. Cheaper than mausolea and often utilitarian are the walled but roofless family BURIAL ENCLOSURES found in many churchyards. Unusually smart is the early C20 enclosure of the Lyles of Glendelvine at Caputh, the ball-finialled piers designed in an Early Georgian manner. It is the setting for *E. Cole*'s bronze statue of Elizabeth Moir Lyle accompanied by a pair of naked children.

MONUMENTS IN MAUSOLEA AND CHURCHES abound but, sadly, few are more than politely detailed and worded marble inscription tablets. The region's earliest post-Reformation monuments, however, promised better. One, erected in Dunkeld Cathedral's chapter house to John Stewart, Earl of Atholl, †1603, is a classicizing version of an empty medieval tomb recess, the arch framed by superimposed pilasters, the entablature surmounted by a scroll-flanked panel under a pediment carved with the Earl's coat of arms.

The general concept of a tomb recess set in a classical surround appears also at two slightly later and much larger monuments. One, of 1616 in the former Weem Parish Church, was

MAUSOLEA, MONUMENTS, GRAVEYARDS

erected by Sir Alexander Menzies of Weem to commemorate himself and his wife, the other, in the mausoleum at Scone Palace, was made by *Maximilian Colt* in 1618–19 for the first Lord Scone. The monument at Weem is still medieval in feeling although the elaborate detail is all classical of a sort, with pilasters at the sarcophagus' frame and attached columns carrying the arch of the recess. The rectangular outer framework is aedicular but with statues of Faith and Charity in place of columns. On the entablature are praying figures of Menzies and his wife and, in the centre, trumpeting angels perched on the sides of a broken pediment which contains an heraldic achievement and is surmounted by a panel carved with a relief of God the Father. The monument at Scone, executed in coloured marbles, is much more confidently classical, the sarcophagus topped by the armour-clad figure of Lord Scone at prayer. The framework is a triumphal arch, the place of the columns taken by armoured knights under smaller statues of Justice and Peace, the spandrels of the round-headed arch carved with reliefs of angels. Above the entablature is a display of heraldry crowned by the small figure of an angel.

The same components of a sarcophagus under a classical superstructure surmounted by heraldry appear at the more vertically proportioned monument to the first Earl of Kinnoull †1634 erected in his family 'aisle' at the former Kinnoull Parish Church, Perth. Here, however, the sarcophagus, decorated with trophies and a strapworked inscription panel, forms the base of a bipartite superstructure whose variously carved columns (copied from the frontispiece of Sir Walter Raleigh's *History of the World*, published in 1614) serve as the portico to a high-relief depiction of the Earl, dressed in his robes of Lord Chancellor of Scotland, standing beside a cloth-draped table on which is propped the purse containing the Great Seal, formerly accompanied by a skull, with an angel hovering above. A still brightly coloured monument of *c.* 1600 at St Martin's Parish Church marks the burial place of the Drummonds of Gairdrum. This is a Corinthianish aedicule, the open pediment bearing a coat of arms and flanked by reliefs of the sun and moon. Also aedicular but with an Ionic order and a curvaceous pediment is the monument to Apollonia Kichlais in Longforgan Parish Church, which is carved with reliefs of reminders of mortality under the inscription. Similar emblems decorate the pedestals under the paired columns of the much larger Corinthian aedicule commemorating Sir Thomas Stewart of Grandtully †1688 in the chapel of Murthly Castle. Above the entablature flaming urns flank the swan-neck pediment, its sides bearing figures of trumpeting angels. On the inscription panel is a relief portrait of Sir Thomas. More disciplined is Dunkeld Cathedral's monument of 1704–5 to the first Marquess of Atholl. Designed by *Alexander Edward*, it is another Corinthian aedicule, the columns adorned with oval panels carved in relief with portraits of the Marquess and his wife. Flaming urns stand on the ends of the open pediment which encloses a carved and painted heraldic achievement. Also carved and painted are the paired coats-of-arms that flank the inscription panel which is placed above and below reliefs of trophies, skulls and bones.

Restrained classicism characterizes most later monuments erected in the C18 and early C19, perhaps the most elegant that in white and grey marble to Henrietta, Viscountess Stormont, †1766 in the mausoleum at Scone Palace. At Dunkeld Cathedral, the monument by *John Ternouth* to Lord Charles Murray †1821 is carved with a broken bow and an urn bearing the relief of a sheep. More assertive and with little hint of sorrow is Ternouth's monument of 1835, also in Dunkeld Cathedral, to Murray's father, the fourth Duke of Atholl, a white marble statue of the deceased dressed as a Knight of the Order of the Thistle and striding confidently forward. The same cathedral's Black Watch monument of 1872 by *John Steell*, however, is calculated to bring tears. It depicts an officer searching a heap of corpses for the body of a companion. A calm reminder of the piety of a faithful Christian is given by the bronze figure (by *George Frampton*) of Bishop George Howard Wilkinson at prayer which was placed in an arch between the choir and Lady Chapel of St Ninian's Cathedral, Perth, in 1911.

Most burials have been in GRAVEYARDS. Until the provision of private or municipal cemeteries from the mid C19 these usually surrounded parish churches or chapels, although at Perth the site of the demolished Franciscan (Greyfriars) friary was taken over as the city's graveyard in 1580. Earlier interments are almost always found s of the churches, i.e. on the usual approach to their entrance. Most, until the mid or later C19, were in unmarked graves, sometimes used temporarily until the flesh had rotted away and the bones could be reinterred in communal ossuary pits. For an individual or family to have the right in perpetuity to a particular burial plot generally required payment to the parish fund for poor relief. Ownership of a private plot was, thus, a mark of status, usually emphasized by the erection of a monument, grave-slab or headstone to commemorate the plot's occupants.

GRAVEYARD MONUMENTS outside burial enclosures are fairly few until the C19 when free-standing monuments, usually of routine classical or Gothic form or sentimental figures of mourning angels, became common. Among the few early examples are the sarcophagi erected in the C17 at Errol to commemorate two ministers of that parish, Alexander Omay †1639 and William Bell †1665, the sides of both carved with emblems of death. Omay's monument also boasts depictions of human figures, Father Time and angels who trumpet news of the Resurrection. On the w wall of the same churchyard was placed *c.* 1700 a monument in the form of a Roman Doric portico sheltering a slab which displayed heraldry under a pair of angels who held a crown of life, in a restrained display of classicism. No such restraint is shown by the large graveyard wall monument (now moved to within the church for preservation) at Innerpeffray erected by James Faichney, probably a master mason, to commemorate his wife, Joanna Murray †1707. It is an aedicule, the pilasters formed from superimposed figures of their children, the ends of the cornice topped by standing figures. Over the centre of the cornice is a panel carved with portraits of James Faichney and Joanna Murray and surmounted by the bust of a woman. The inscription panel displays heraldry and symbols of death and the Resurrection (trumpeting angels).

The combination of reminders of mortality (skulls, crossbones, hourglasses, etc.) with symbols of the Resurrection (angels' heads (souls) or trumpeting angels) was typical of the grave-slabs and headstones erected in churchyards until the mid C19. After the Reformation, GRAVE-SLABS continued to be placed over interments but became rare after the late C17. One C16 example, now fixed to a wall inside Longforgan Parish Church, is that of James Fyf †1588. As with medieval predecessors, the (Latin) inscription forms a border. Inside this are panels, one carved with a skull and bone, a second with a cross as symbol of redemption, a third with a coat-of-arms. Coats-of-arms also appear prominently on a couple of C17 slabs commemorating the Campbells of Laginrech and Monzie in Monzie Parish Churchyard. More explicitly religious is the ambitious but inept mid-C17 slab to John Shioch in Greyfriars Burial Ground at Perth on which figures of Faith, Hope and Charity are displayed among a welter of symbolic figures and scenes together with the tailor's tools of Shioch's trade. Another mid-C17 grave-slab in the same burial ground, that of a butcher, Thomas Anderson, is more disciplined although well supplied with emblems of death (a skull, crossbones and Father Time). The angel's head symbol of the Resurrection surmounts a shield carved with the scene of a butcher slaughtering an ox whose head is gripped by a dog. A similar scene but with the addition of a border of onlooking sheeps' heads is portrayed on a headstone erected by a butcher at Abernyte in the early C18. This is framed by a pedimented aedicule.

A fair number of the region's HEADSTONES are aedicular. One of the earliest, that of Dugal Wright †1699 at Ecclesiamagirdle, has Ionic pilasters but with upside-down volutes, and the classicism of many others (e.g. the early C18 stones in Portmoak Churchyard, near Scotlandwell) is more approximate than correct, the work apparently of local masons with little opportunity to study or execute 'polite' architecture. What these works lack in aesthetic quality is, however, recompensed by the exuberance of their carving. Some show Scriptural scenes, like three headstones of the 1780s at Kinfauns and Logierait depicting the Fall of Adam and Eve or the contemporary stone to James Thomson at St Mary's, Grandtully, which shows Abraham about to sacrifice Isaac. These may have been copied from woodcuts. Many others bear emblems of the trade of the deceased or of the relative who commissioned the stone (e.g. the crowned hammer of a smith, the tools of a mason or wright or a weaver's shuttle). The importance of fishing in the region is attested by stones showing bird's-eye views of boats containing salmon, e.g. the headstone of John Buist †1761 at Kinfauns.

An almost comprehensive list of the trades practised at Perth in the C18 can be assembled from the headstones in Greyfriars

Burial Ground. Memorable among them are those of the 1760s and 1770s to the Peters family of carriers, with the relief of a horse-drawn cart, to the barber and wigmaker, Alexander Bisset, its shield carved with razors, a comb and wigstand, and to the leather-worker, Andrew Kippen, which displays his tools together with pairs of breeches and gloves. More macabre is the headstone of 1791 erected by the weaver, Alexander Ferrier, in memory of his children, with a shield bearing three heads, their mouths filled with shuttles. Of recent headstones, one which has something of the same vigour is that erected in Longforgan Parish Churchyard in 2001 to Alberto Morrocco and carved by *Vincent Butler* with a depiction of the Annunciation.

On the edge, often at the entrance, of several churchyards (e.g. at Milnathort, St Martins and Redgorton) are SESSION HOUSES, simple detached one-room buildings put up, usually in the early C19, to house meetings of the parish kirk sessions. Similar are HEARSE HOUSES, constructed to accommodate the parish hearse and sexton's tools. The hearse house of 1832 at Redgorton is quite plain except for an oculus above the door but at Crook of Devon the hearse house has a pointed window and door. Slightly more elaborate are the region's few remaining WATCH HOUSES intended to be occupied by those guarding newly occupied graves against 'resurrectionists' who stole corpses for sale to university medical schools. The watch house of 1829 in the middle of the graveyard of Coupar Angus Abbey Church is an octagon, that of 1851-3 on the edge of Kinross's Old Parish Churchyard a battlemented square tower.

CHURCHYARD GATEWAYS are generally simple but at Fowlis Wester is a round-headed arch, perhaps of 1644, the date on the pediment (now replaced) which surmounted it. A mid-C18 gateway into the former parish church's graveyard at Blackford has recesses in its side walls, perhaps to shelter elders of the kirk session who collected money for relief of the poor from arriving worshippers. Decorative and usually of commemorative intention are the few LYCHGATES. The Edwardian lychgates at Kettins (a memorial to Mrs Graham Menzies of Hallyburton) and Kenmore (a memorial to Queen Victoria) are wooden structures covered with red-tiled roofs. Those at Kilspindie and Kinclaven are First World War memorials, the first with bargeboards, the other (by *Reginald Fairlie*) a smoother round-arched essay in ashlar masonry carved with Christian symbols.

WAR MEMORIALS were put up in almost all parishes after 1918. Many are routinely detailed granite crosses but the Lorimerian crosses at Crieff and Auchterarder (by *John Stewart*, 1921) display greater originality, as does the blocky cross at Longforgan. Notable for its size and position at the centre of the town and very like a market cross but with its finial carved as a Pelican in Piety is the memorial at Blairgowrie designed in 1920 by *Reginald Fairlie*. In front stands the bronze statue of a mourning soldier by *Alexander Carrick*. Powerfully simple is the roughly shaped boulder erected in 1924 at Blair Atholl. At Aberfeldy, a memorial gateway (by *W. Erskine Thomson*, 1922) is carved with the targes and claymores of an earlier generation of Highland warriors.

STATUES AND MONUMENTS OUTSIDE CHURCHYARDS commemorate the illustrious. In Perth the Victorians erected stone statues of Sir Walter Scott in 1845, the laboured effort of a local carver ('the sculpture is wonderful, considering the inexperience of the artist', proclaimed the *Perthshire Courier*) and of the Prince Consort, a more accomplished effort, by *William Brodie*, in 1864. Almost a century after his death, a statue of Major-General David Stewart by *H. S. Gamley* was erected in 1924 at Keltneyburn to honour this historian of the Highland clans and regiments. The exploits of one of these regiments are celebrated by *W. Birnie Rhind*'s Black Watch Memorial of 1887 at Aberfeldy, the large rock pedestal carved with the names of the regiment's battle honours and the relief of a Victorian soldier, the monument's surmounting figure the giant stone statue of a soldier in C18 dress. It seems calculated to appeal to tourists. Unpleasantly sentimental is *Alan B. Heriot*'s 51st Highland Division Monument erected in 1995 on the North Inch at Perth, a bronze of a girl handing a rose to a military piper. Obelisks crown a few hills. One, the Melville Monument on Dunmore Hill, near Comrie, commemorates the Tory politician, Henry Dundas, Viscount Melville. It was erected in 1812 by public subscription. The cost of the granite obelisk erected in 1832 to General Sir David Baird on Tom a' Chaisteal, near Monzievaird, was met by the general's widow. Monuments of a sort, although commemorating only the taste of their owners, are two hilltop towers overlooking the Carse of Gowrie, the battlemented square observatory tower on Binn Hill, near Kinfauns, built by the fourteenth Lord Gray *c.* 1815, and the round tower on Kinnoull Hill, near Perth, put up by the tenth Earl of Kinnoull in 1829.

Some FOUNTAINS were erected to commemorate people or significant events. At Dunkeld in 1866 *Charles S. Robertson* designed a French Gothic fountain of Eleanor Cross type as a memorial to the sixth Duke of Atholl. It is lavishly embellished with carving by *John Rhind*. A canopied fountain was set up in Aberfeldy by Gavin, Marquess of Breadalbane, ostensibly as a memento of his and his wife's visit to the town in 1886 but its coronet finial suggests that it may also have marked his promotion in the peerage at the same time. The figure of a heron stands on the bowl. Statuary but of sportive dolphins surrounds the domed top of the fountain, by *William Mossman*, 1893–4, erected at Crieff in recognition of the benefits conferred on the burgh by the Murrays of Ochtertyre. Apparently an assertion of (unwarranted) burgh status is the market cross which surmounts the fountain put up in Errol in 1899 to mark Queen Victoria's Diamond Jubilee of two years before.

PUBLIC SCULPTURE OF THE LATE TWENTIETH AND EARLY TWENTY-FIRST CENTURIES has been commissioned in pleasing quantity and quality for Perth itself. Progress along the pedestrianized High Street is punctuated by a couple of bronzes of the 1990s, by *Graham Ibbeson* and *David Annand*. Three more sculptures, of 2002–3, by *Shona Kinloch*, *David Annand* and, a curvaceous depiction of leaping salmon, by *Lee Brewster* stand along the E side of Tay Street overlooking the river. A disciplined octagon of slabs (by *Frances Pelly*, 1991) is placed on the North Inch in front of Rose Terrace. In the South Inch's car park is the stylized bronze of 'Fish with a Boy' by *Doug Cocker*, 1995. N of this is *J. D. Fergusson*'s 'Torse de Femme', modelled in 1914 but not cast in bronze until 1994, which stands outside the gallery named in honour of its sculptor.

MOTTES, CASTLES, TOWERS AND LAIRDS' HOUSES

In the C12 much of Perth and Kinross was held by a handful of magnates. Chief among these were the Kings of Scots whose demesne lands included much of Gowrie and Kinross-shire. Strathearn and Atholl were both earldoms, the latter held by descendants of Maelmuir, younger brother of Malcolm III. In the course of this century successive Kings of Scots equipped themselves with a well-armoured mounted military force, often drawn from Anglo-Norman incomers who had been granted fiefs on demesne lands in return for providing the service of one or more fully equipped knights or paying for part of the cost of a knight. This granting of fiefs in return for knight service, begun in southern Scotland by David I, took place in Perth and Kinross during the reign of David's grandson, William the Lion in the later C12 and early C13. He granted the lands of Kinnaird to Ralph Ruffus (ancestor of the Kinnaird family) and Cargill to Richard de Montfiquet, each for one knight's service, and Errol to William de la Hay for the service of two knights. Feudalism extended also to the earldom of Strathearn where Earl Gilbert granted the lands of Comrie, Muthill, Blackford and Dunning to his brother, Malise, for one knight's service. Earl Gilbert himself held the fief of Meikleour and Lethendy of the Crown, also for the service of one knight.

Connected with this introduction of feudal holdings was the construction of a new type of fortification, the MOTTE. This was a scarped earth mound, roughly in the shape of a truncated cone, of wholly or partially artificial construction, often surrounded by a ditch and always surmounted by a wooden tower. The surviving motte of the Hays at Law Knowe, Mains of Murie, near Errol, is a simple rounded mound, 8 m. high, with a summit area of 13 m. by 11 m. That of the earls of Strathearn at Meikleour is *c.* 5 m. high, its roughly circular summit *c.* 22 m. in diameter. The motte of Barton Hill at Kinnaird, probably formed by Ralph Ruffus in the 1170s, is a volcanic plug with a ditch cut round its base and whose roughly oval summit (24.7 m. by 18.4 m.) has been artificially dished and apparently enclosed with a palisaded turf rampart within which stood a rectangular wooden tower of *c.* 6.2 m. by 6.8 m. These stood alone but the motte (now almost destroyed by quarrying) of Castle of Rattray, near Blairgowrie, was accompanied by two baileys or outer enclosures, each surrounded by a bank and ditch. At Cargill the Montfiquets erected a RINGWORK castle, defending the landward side of a steep promontory beside the River Tay with a massive bank. Other naturally defensive promontory sites were cut off by ditches, as at Inchbervis Castle in the grounds of Stanley House where a promontory seems to have been fortified in the C13 when the lands were held by Robert de Oghtergeven.

Stone-walled CASTLES or houses, their construction expensive and requiring the employment of skilled craftsmen, are rare before the C15. The royal castles of Inverquiech and Kinclaven built in the late C12 or early C13 occupy naturally defensive sites. The steeply sloping promontory (c. 40 m. by 85 m.) of Inverquiech, bounded by the Burn of Quiech and a bend of the River Isla, may have been entirely enclosed by a curtain wall (parts of the N and E ranges surviving) which followed the contours of the site. Kinclaven is a low hill surrounded by a ditch, the c. 40 m. square summit enclosed by a rectangular curtain which had a tower at each corner. Round towers survive at the corners of the less regular oblong (c. 33.5 m. by 25.9 m.) of Moulin Castle at Pitlochry which was built on an island site by the Earls of Atholl in the C13.

Inside these castles, living accommodation was provided in stone or wooden buildings. Almost all have been demolished or subsumed in later work but at Blair Castle, probably originally a castle of enclosure of c. 1269, the lower part of Cumming's Tower may comprise a simple rectangular stone building of two or three storeys which served as that castle's keep or lord's lodging in the C13. Vestiges of a similar simple tower survive at Clunie Castle constructed from the 1140s on a natural hillock as a royal hunting lodge defended by a stone curtain wall. The combination of a castle of enclosure and a keep is much more impressively displayed at the well-preserved Lochleven Castle, its curtain wall of roughly cubical masonry probably constructed c. 1300, its rubble-built keep or tower house some forty years later. This house was a self-contained residence for the keeper of the royal castle. Externally, it is a plain oblong block with a corbelled parapet which breaks into angle rounds at three of the corners and is carried up as a caphouse at the fourth. The only entrance, a round-headed doorway reached by a wooden stair, was placed at second-floor level, too high for a battering-ram easily to be used against it. The interior was well appointed, the two vaulted lower floors containing a store and kitchen, the upper floors each with a single room, most of the windows provided with stone seats and with the turnpike stair and garderobes contained in the thickness of the walls.

During the C14, C15 and C16 the lands of Perth and Kinross were divided into estates which continued, for the most part, as recognizable entities into the C20. This subdivision of some of the greatest lordships of the earlier medieval period was partly the result of a desire or need to provide for younger sons, partly of a failure to produce male heirs and the consequent partitioning of land among co-heiresses and, by the early C16, of the granting of Crown and Church lands in feu ferme (i.e. in return for a capital sum and fixed annual cash payment, its value quickly eroded by the massive price inflation of the C16). Each of these estates had the residence of a laird as its administrative and usually judicial centre. Most of these residences probably occupied earlier sites but the very visible expression of thuggish force given by mottes was exchanged for a quieter assertion of status, although defence was not forgotten. The Kinnairds abandoned their motte on Barton Hill for the adjacent promontory site of Kinnaird Castle, the Hays their motte of Law Knowe for a site on or near that of the present Errol Park, and the Drummonds, successors to the Montfiquets in the barony of Cargill, moved from the ringwork of Cargill to another promontory at Stobhall. These new or reused sites often enjoyed natural strength, like those of Ardblair Castle which was formerly surrounded by a loch, Dowhill Castle's hillock rising out of marshy ground or the cliff edge of Balthayock Castle. The supplementary earthworks or palisaded defences and wooden towers characteristic of mottes and ringworks were, from the end of the C14, replaced by walls and towers of stone, although most subsidiary buildings were still of timber construction.

Generally, these nobles' and lairds' residences consisted of steading-like complexes (hall, laird's lodging, kitchen, etc.) standing in walled enclosures known as BARMKINS set among ploughed field strips. Changes in agriculture and garden fashion in the C18 brought about the removal of most of these buildings and their barmkins. Surviving tower houses now often stand among lawns and shrubs. Vestiges of barmkins, although not of medieval agriculture, survive in fragmentary fashion at several towers (e.g. Balthayock Castle, Gleneagles Castle and Kinnaird Castle), in more substantial form at Arnot Tower, Burleigh Castle, Dowhill Castle, complete in outline at Balvaird Castle and almost intact though much repaired at Stobhall. The areas enclosed by barmkins were generally about half the size of those of castles of enclosure and the walls thinner and of undressed rubble. Nevertheless, these walls afforded some protection at least against robbers and hostile neighbours. Sometimes they were reinforced with protruding corner towers, each affording a line of fire to cover two sides of a rectangular enclosure, such as survive at the corners of the former barmkins of the mid-C16 Elcho Castle and Dowhill Castle of *c.* 1600, both equipped with shot-holes for handguns. More purposeful displays of murderous intent are found at Lochleven Castle's mid-C16 Glassin Tower with its plentiful provision of gunloops and shot-holes and at Burleigh Castle's SW tower of *c.* 1582, still equipped with wooden mountings for cannon.

Any barmkin had, of necessity, an entrance. Most may have been no more demonstrative than the simple round-headed gateway, perhaps of *c.* 1300, at the entrance to Lochleven Castle. However, at Huntingtower Castle the present E tower incorporates a much altered two-storey former gatehouse of perhaps *c.* 1400, with round-headed entrances at the ends of a tunnel-vaulted transe. At Balvaird Castle the gatehouse of 1567 also has round-headed entrances to its vaulted transe but the outer face displays a powerful gunloop and the moulded frame of a heraldic panel, both expresssions of baronial status. Heraldry has also been prominent at the gatehouse (w) range of 1582 at Burleigh Castle, the early C17 gatehouses of Stobhall and Drummond Castle and the mid-C17 gateways of Ecclesiamagirdle House and Ardblair Castle, the coats-of-arms at Stobhall and Ardblair Castle both framed in aedicules.

With the exception of the tower houses which housed the lairds, very few of the buildings which stood inside barmkins have survived. Some (e.g. kitchens) were replaced by the later C17 by additions to the tower houses, others (e.g. barns and stables) were rebuilt from the C18 at a distance from the houses and yet others (e.g. halls), redundant through social change, demolished. The detached kitchen, probably of the 1570s, at Stobhall still stands. So also at Stobhall does the contemporary hall but the former existence of the hall at Huntingtower Castle is now revealed only by a roof raggle in the w tower.

From the end of the C14 TOWER HOUSES formed the principal structures of barmkins, always placed at one corner of the enclosure. Probably the earliest in Perth and Kinross is Garth Castle, apparently built for Alexander Stewart, Earl of Buchan, at the end of the C14. Standing as a sentinel guarding the approach to Strathearn from the N, this is a simple four-storey oblong (*c.* 12.9 m. by 8.8 m.), the entrance perhaps originally placed some way above ground level and opening onto the stair which is contained in the 1.9 m. thickness of one wall. Originally, the two lowest storeys at least were vaulted. The ground floor contained storage, each upper floor a single room, the first-floor hall provided with stone seats in the window embrasures. Considerably larger (*c.* 16 m. by 12 m.) is Balthayock Castle of *c.* 1400. It is also an oblong, with the round-headed entrance at first-floor level and the stairs contained in the thickness of one wall. As at Garth Castle, the vaulted ground floor contained storage, each of the upper floors a single room, the first-floor hall covered by a high tunnel vault. The C15 Gleneagles Castle is of similar size (*c.* 17.1 m. by 11.9 m.) but other oblong towers built in the region by *c.* 1500 were smaller: Arnot Tower, the original tower of Dowhill Castle and the N tower of Burleigh Castle are all *c.* 10 m. by 8 m. At Arnot Tower and Burleigh Castle vaulting covered only the ground-floor storage. At Gleneagles Castle and Dowhill Castle a tall vault covered both the ground-floor stores and a wooden entresol floor above. Each of these last houses boasted the baronial status symbol of a pit prison hollowed out in the wall thickness of one corner and entered from a hatch in the floor of the first-floor hall. The wall-heads of all these towers were probably finished with battlements or parapets whose moulded corbels survive at Arnot Tower and Burleigh Castle. At Burleigh Castle the corbelling carried angle rounds at three corners and a cap-house over the stair at the fourth.

Castle Huntly.
Perspective

One variant of the C15 oblong tower house is found at Kinnaird Castle of *c.* 1500. This is a straightforward four-storey rectangle (*c.* 11.7m. by 8.3m.), the wall head surmounted by a corbelled parapet which breaks out into bartizans at the corners and a box machicolation above the round-headed entrance. The interior is unusual for the date in that only the ends of the ground-floor store are vaulted, the centre of its ceiling being flat and of wooden construction with beams supported on corbels. Just as idiosyncratic is the jamb which projects from the house's NW corner. Taller than the main block, this is only 1.8m. square. Each of its two top storeys contains a room, only *c.* 1.5m. by

1 m., too small to be of practical use, entered off the stair which rises within the thickness of the main block's NW corner. At the first floor of the jamb a passage from the stair leads to a door which opened onto the top of the N wall of the house's barmkin. Perhaps the jamb was intended as a decorative expression of baronial status.

Another variant on the oblong tower and, like Kinnaird Castle, exceptional among houses of the date is the keep of Drummond Castle, built *c.* 1490. The main block is a standard three-storey rectangle, quite large at *c.* 13.1 m. by 11.3 m., the pointed-arch entrance placed a little above ground level. The internal arrangement and accommodation with a vaulted store on the ground floor, a first-floor hall, also vaulted, and an upper hall above, is very like that of Balthayock Castle. Projecting for *c.* 1.5 m. from the centre of the S side, however, is a rectangular jamb, *c.* 4 m. broad. Containing most of a turnpike stair (its N segment notched out of the wall thickness of the main block), this serves a more obviously practical purpose than the jamb of Kinnaird Castle but the stair, only 1.5 m. in diameter, could have been accommodated wholly within the wall thickness of the main block and this jamb also seems to have a decorative or symbolic function, asserting the status of the house's owner.

A major departure from the simple oblong tower house appeared in Perth and Kinross in the 1450s with the construction by the first Lord Gray of Castle Huntly. Dramatically perched on the edge of a cliff, this is L-plan and exceptionally large, the main block *c.* 18.9 m. by 11.6 m., the jamb *c.* 7 m. by 9.1 m. The stair or stairs were contained in the wall thickness of the main block. As usual, the ground floor was filled with vaulted cellars. At each upper floor was a hall, that of the first floor exceptionally tall (its height allowing the insertion of another floor in the late C17) which opened directly into a room in the jamb. The same planning, although in a slightly later basically L-plan house of more conventional size (the main block *c.* 11 m. by 8.2 m., the jamb *c.* 6.4 m. square) is found in the early C16 house built in the SW corner of the barmkin of Huntingtower Castle, although its jamb projects both W and S of the main block's SW corner and the stair occupies a tight tower at the NW corner. Slightly larger and a massive presence on its hilltop site, Balvaird Castle of *c.* 1500 is also L-plan. Here, however, the inner angle of the L is partly filled by a rectangular tower containing a broad turnpike stair (*c.* 3 m. in diameter) surmounted by a caphouse around which is carried a continuation of the corbelled battlement of the main block and jamb. Balvaird Castle's exterior is a bullying display of strength, the battlement forming rounds at the corners and at the centres of the gunloop-pierced outer faces of the main block. The house was a self-contained lodging, with a vaulted kitchen on the ground floor of the jamb, apparently the first in the region to form an integral part of a tower house. The main block's tunnel-vaulted lowest storey, divided by an entresol floor, probably contained a retainers' hall above storage. On each of the main block's two upper floors was a hall, that of the first floor with a crocketed aumbry and a large fireplace whose corniced lintel is supported on bundled shafts. As at Castle Huntly, the jamb contained a room on each of its upper floors, all comfortably equipped with fireplaces and window seats, but here there is no direct communication from the rooms in the main block to those in the jamb.

Stone-built tower houses multiplied from the end of the C15, many built for lairds who had acquired land in feu ferme from the Crown or Church. This burgeoning building activity was apparently accompanied by a development in the skills of masons able to construct buildings with thinner walls, more varied plan types and comfortable staircases. In almost all these TOWER HOUSES OF THE SIXTEENTH AND EARLY SEVENTEENTH CENTURY vaulted stores and sometimes, as at Balvaird, a kitchen, occupied the ground floor from which, as at Whitefield Castle, a service stair, as well as the main stair, might rise to the first floor. The principal (often the only) room on the first floor was a hall, apparently combining the functions of the great hall and more private laird's hall or chamber of dais of earlier castles. The simplest arrangement, showing no advance on C15 precedents, is found at House of Aldie. As built in about 1520, this was a simple oblong, with the stair contained in the wall thickness, a hall occupying the whole of the first floor and an upper hall or inner chamber on the second. Almost as simple and also with one room on each floor is Prince Charlie's Tower at Murthly Castle but its stair, rising the full height of the house, is contained in a tower which projects minimally from one corner. At the larger and later Tower of Lethendy (of *c.* 1600) a more spacious stair in a bolder jamb also rises the full height but the hall and inner chamber were both placed on the first floor. The lower part of the jamb of some L-plan houses (e.g. the early C16 Ardblair Castle and the later houses of Ashintully Castle, Comrie Castle and Whitefield Castle) accommodated a comfortably proportioned stair which rose only to the first-floor hall, allowing rooms to be placed on the jamb's upper floors. At Ardblair Castle and Comrie Castle a corbelled-out turret stair gave access from the hall to the floor above which contained an upper hall or inner chamber off which opened a room, probably the laird's bedchamber, in the jamb. Another house whose principal stair rises only to first-floor level is Tulliebole Castle of 1608 but this stair is contained in the jamb which forms the tail of the T-plan E section of the house whose first-floor hall opens onto an en suite inner chamber. At another, more regularly composed and earlier, T-plan house, Pitcur Castle of *c.* 1500, the stair was placed in the inner angle of the main block and jamb whose ground floor was occupied by the kitchen and its first and second floors by chambers opening off the W side of the hall and upper hall.

This housing of the principal stair in a tower occupying the inner angle of a jamb and the main block, pioneered in the region by Balvaird Castle, was adopted by several L-plan houses of the mid or later C16 and early C17. At all these, unlike Balvaird Castle but as at Pitcur Castle, the rooms on each floor of the main block and jamb communicated directly. In the 1570s tower of Stobhall Castle each upper floor of the main block was occupied by a hall and the jamb by a chamber. The larger Innerpeffray Castle and Balmanno Castle both contain a dog-leg suite of three rooms (hall, inner chamber and bedchamber) on both first and second floors of both the main block and jamb. The first floor of Evelick Castle had a hall occupying the whole of the main block and a chamber in the jamb but the second floor contained three rooms.

The grandest of the region's houses built between *c.* 1550 and *c.* 1600 were Z-plan with jambs at opposed corners of the main block. One of the simpler and latest (of *c.* 1600) is the three-storey Moncur Castle. Its NE jamb is rectangular, the SW round. The main stair, in the NE jamb, rises to the first floor where the main block was filled by a hall and chamber off which was a bed-chamber in the SW jamb. Grandtully Castle, originally an oblong house of *c.* 1500, was converted to a Z by the addition of square jambs about sixty years later. The stair in the inner angle of the main block and SE jamb opened onto a first-floor hall in the main block from which was entered a chamber in the NW jamb. A room in the SE jamb, entered off the stair and with no direct communication with the hall, may have served originally as a guest chamber. A similar absence of direct communication between a jamb and the main block appears to have obtained at Glasclune Castle whose SW jamb's two first-floor rooms opened off the stair. Even more marked a separation is found at Castle Menzies where the rooms in the SW jamb are not only entered from the stair but also placed at different levels from the first and second floors of the main block, each of which contains a hall and chamber off which opens a bedchamber in the NE jamb.

The most elaborate of these houses is Elcho Castle built for the Wemysses of Wemyss in the mid C16. The shape is basically a Z with a large square jamb at the SW corner and a smaller round jamb at the NE. However, there are also a square NW jamb, smaller than the SW, and a rounded stair-tower on the N side of the main block. The principal stair in the SW jamb rises to the first floor where the main block is occupied by a hall and chamber off which is a closet in the NE jamb. The NW jamb's vaulted first-floor room, perhaps a charter room, was entered from a screens passage at the W end of the hall. The principal access to the second and third floors of the main block was by the N stair off the first-floor hall's E end. On each of these floors were two suites of rooms, the E consisting of a chamber with a closet in the NE jamb, the W of two rooms. The rooms on the upper floors of the two W jambs contained chambers reached from stairs in the jambs' inner angles with the main block. The rooms in the SW jamb, well equipped with fireplaces, cupboards and garderobes, may have been intended as guest chambers.

63, p. 70

The external appearance of these tower houses, large or small, built in the C16 and the opening years of the C17 was largely dictated by their plan forms. All are of three or four storeys, rubble-built and often harled, their windows usually with roll-and-hollow-moulded or chamfered surrounds, their gables crow-

Elcho Castle.
Perspective

stepped. Most give an impression of solid worth rather than opulence although the size alone of a house such as Castle Menzies asserts the importance of its owner. The towers of Huntingtower Castle are finished with corbelled battlements, the verticality of the W tower further emphasized by its attic doocot, but such wallhead defences were generally eschewed. Swagger is not entirely absent. At Elcho Castle, the jambs and N stair projection are all given a strongly tower-like air, two topped by corbelled-out top storeys and one finished with a parapet from which project stone spouts and angle rounds. The W end of Tulliebole Castle is carried up as a tower, its proclamation of the house as the seat of a feudal baron reinforced by the turreted treatment of the jamb containing the entrance. The not especially big house of Grandtully Castle was given a disproportionate importance by the heightening of its stair-tower, topped by an ogee roof, in 1626. More modest claims to status are made by the conical-roofed turrets that adorn the corners of Castle Menzies and Aberuchill Castle and the square turrets of Meggernie Castle. At Castle Menzies the turrets combine with aedicular dormer windows to suggest a battlement.

C15 tower houses relied for defence primarily on their very thick walls, pierced at the ground floor only by slits, and the battlements surmounting their wall-heads. However, in the jamb of Kinnaird Castle are keyhole gunloops, and inverted keyhole gunloops appear at the ground floor of Gleneagles Castle and the second floor of the main block and at the jamb of Drummond Castle. To what extent these were intended for serious defence rather than as fashionable assertions of status is debatable. Also questionable may be the primarily defensive purpose of the gunloops provided as a matter of course at most houses built after 1500. At Pitcur Castle they are of keyhole form and at Balvaird Castle and Huntingtower Castle inverted keyholes. The early C17 s range of House of Aldie boasts a mixture of inverted keyhole and oval gunloops, and oval gunloops pierce the walls of other houses, e.g. Castle Menzies and Moncur Castle. The most fearsome displays of gunloops are at Huntingtower Castle where they pierce all three outer faces of the sw jamb and the w front of the main block, at Evelick Castle where they bristle from the upper floors and at Glasclune Castle whose s wing's window breasts are all equipped with shot-holes. That their purpose might be more than symbolic is suggested by the ledges for mounting weapons provided inside the plentiful gunloops around the ground floor of Elcho Castle.

Gunloops placed beside the entrance to a house could provide some defence of the building's most vulnerable feature but they also marked the status of its owner. At Balvaird Castle, the tower house's entrance is covered by a gunloop but hardly less assertive is the three-tiered display of heraldic panels above. Heraldry over the doors of tower houses is common. Some armorial panels, like the one over the C16 entrance to Castle Menzies, relied for effect only on their display of carved and originally painted heraldic bearings. The (missing) panel at Evelick Castle was set in a simple moulded frame. Much showier frames of classical inspiration are found at Ashintully Castle and Ecclesiamagirdle House, the one with baluster shafts supporting a cornice, the other a Doric aedicule. Doorways themselves are usually simple. The entrance to the tower house of Ardblair Castle is exceptional, the moulded surround with a rope-carved cornice from which hangs a pendant corbel, all flanked by baluster columns. The panel frame above, weirdly decorated with high-relief figures of men and beasts, is probably an embellishment brought from elsewhere.

The INTERIORS of most C16 and early C17 houses were probably plain, furnishings and hangings providing whatever sense of luxury they enjoyed. Fireplace surrounds are usually simply moulded. In the first-floor hall of the late C16 tower at Stobhall, however, is a stone chimneypiece elaborately carved with human faces, flowers and foliage which almost eclipse the importance of the central heraldic achievement. Also in this tower is late C16 painted decoration, with ceiling beams patterned with coloured foliage designs. Probably rather earlier is the ceiling in the first-floor hall of the E tower of Huntingtower Castle, the boards and joists all with painted patterns, some of the beams below the joists bearing panels of foliage and flowers and the central beam with panels which contain foliage, dragons' heads and a hound. On this room's walls survive fragments of painted plaster, including pictures of animals and a naked man appealing for mercy to an angel, all set among foliage and grapes. The region's most striking painted scheme is that on the ceiling of the chapel (the former great hall) at Stobhall, its panels painted in the early C17 with portraits of animals, birds and full-length portraits of the monarchs of Europe. At Stobhall, in the early C17 Dower House, is a plaster stair ceiling enriched with flowers, foliage, cherubs' heads and emblems of the Stewart monarchy. Of the same period but much more fragmentary is the plaster frieze displaying symbols of the kingdoms united under James VI and I in the first-floor chamber of Elcho Castle, a reminder of the feudal overlord from whom all rights to land and baronial status derived.

PALACES, MANSIONS AND COUNTRY HOUSES

From the C15 to the early C17 royal PALACES in Scotland (e.g. Linlithgow, Holyroodhouse, Falkland and Stirling Castle) were rebuilt with the principal rooms ranged round quadrangles. Defensive display was confined to outer works, the hall, chapel and lodging ranges designed to house a civilized Renaissance monarchy. In Perth and Kinross one such palace was constructed in the later years of the C16 and the beginning of the C17, not by the Crown but by the two families who held successively the former lands of Scone Abbey – the Ruthvens, Earls of Gowrie, and the Murrays, Lords Scone and Viscounts Stormont (from the C18 Earls of Mansfield). Scone Palace, as completed in the early C17, was built round two courtyards, the principal E and S ranges each consisting of a two-storey main block from which projected a taller centrepiece and ends, the E range's centrepiece containing the principal entrance and surmounted by a birdcage bellcote. Except for crowstepped gables, ornament seems to have been sparing, and the palace impressed by its size, the E front's length of *c.* 64 m. comparable to that of the S range of Falkland Palace and considerably longer than any elevation of Linlithgow Palace. Inside was a long gallery of *c.* 46 m. by 5.5 m., the panels of its tunnel-vaulted wooden ceiling painted with hunting scenes, heraldry and decorative motifs. The main dining room or hall contained a marble chimneypiece, its overmantel carved with the Royal Arms above those of the Murrays, and some rooms in the S range seem to have formed a suite intended for the King's occupation and were covered by the C18 with enriched plaster ceilings, conceivably original although perhaps embellishments of the later C17.

A few LAIRDS' HOUSES OF THE EARLIER SEVENTEENTH CENTURY also eschewed martial display. The simplest, perhaps because designed as a jointure or dower house, is the Dower House of Stobhall Castle, a two-storey and attic crowstep-gabled oblong, its only external display a pedimented heraldic dormer-head on the rear elevation but with an exuberantly modelled plaster ceiling above the straight staircase which bisects the interior. Ecclesiamagirdle House and Old House of Gask, both probably built in the 1630s or 1640s, are of three storeys and T-plan, Ecclesiamagirdle House with a stair-turret in one inner angle, Old House of Gask's S range with scrolled dormerheads. The sculpture on the dormerheads of the similar but L-plan Monzie Castle of 1634 affirms both its owners' status and their piety.

COUNTRY HOUSES AFTER 1660. The civil wars of 1639–51 and the subsequent Cromwellian military occupation of Scotland were not conducive to the building or remodelling of houses. The restoration of the monarchy in 1660, however, was accompanied, coincidentally, in Perth and Kinross by Patrick, third Earl of Kinghorne (later, Earl of Strathmore and Kinghorne), taking up residence in Castle Huntly which he proceeded to repair and remodel. Much of the work on the house itself undertaken in 1660–70 was internal, the principal alteration being removal of the vault over the C15 hall and division of this room by the insertion of a floor. On the approach to the house, the Earl constructed a succession of walled enclosures so that the visitor reached its entrance only after passing through seven gateways. Similar though fewer courts were formed on the approach to Murthly Castle as part of the work undertaken there in the 1660s and 1670s by Sir Thomas Stewart of Grandtully who also built large but low-key additions to the house, their main feature a crowstep-gabled tower at the centre of the remodelled and extended s range.

Much more ambitious architecturally were a number of houses put up from the 1670s. The design of Methven Castle, built in 1678–81 for a merchant and moneylender, Patrick Smyth, exploits the concept of a basically U-plan house, its open centre filled with a balustraded and flat-roofed block containing the entrance. This concept had been used in the design of a number of Scottish houses (e.g. Panmure House in Angus or Balcaskie House in Fife) from the 1660s. At Methven Castle, however, the massing is unusually vertical and a large round tower projects from each corner. Further evidence of Smyth's desire that his house be regarded as a castle and he as a feudal baron is given by the tier of (decorative) shot-holes which pierce the building's E side. Much less if any attempt to suggest a castle was made at other new houses put up in the 1670s and 1680s. Dunkeld House (demolished), built for the first Marquess of Atholl, was a sizeable piend-roofed mansion of three storeys above a basement, with small windows to the second floor and an aediculed door at the centre of the front. Although it seems to have incorporated a round tower from an earlier house, the three-storey piend-roofed main block of Dupplin Castle (demolished) erected by Thomas, Viscount Dupplin (later, sixth Earl of Kinnoull), was firmly classical, the front's centrepiece a columned and pedimented aedicule containing pedimented first-floor windows. Inside, Dupplin Castle's ground floor contained the family rooms, the first floor a six-room state apartment intended, at least symbolically, for the King and described in 1723 as 'extreamly well furnish'd, and Wainscotted with Oak, adorn'd with carved Work...'

The PLANNING of new mansions to contain two main suites of rooms, often one above the other, for family occupation and for a state apartment, had become general in Scotland since the

1660s. Such planning, derived from that of royal palaces, was promoted most effectively by the politician, arbiter of taste and architect (though incompetent draughtsman) *Sir William Bruce*, who had used such a layout at his own house of Balcaskie (Fife) in 1668, and in the remodelling from 1670 of Thirlestane Castle (Borders) for the Duke of Lauderdale. Between 1679 and 1684 on his estate of Kinross, acquired as a replacement for Balcaskie, Bruce laid out parkland and gardens and constructed a new mansion house, the most accomplished work of architecture in C17 Scotland. Externally, Kinross is a two-storey and basement oblong faced with polished ashlar, channelled at the basement, the front's ends slightly advanced between single pilasters, a motif probably derived from Bernini, the tall roof surmounted by a cupola. Detail is restrained except at the central doors of the entrance and garden fronts which are placed behind porticoes of coupled Ionic columns, the stonework above carved with exuberant reliefs of trophies and fruits. The interior was planned with the family rooms on the ground floor and overlooking the garden. Behind the entrance hall was the Garden Hall (dining room) off which opened a suite of drawing room, family bedchamber, closet and dressing room. Off the Garden Hall's other end was a second suite of bedchamber, closet and dressing room. The state apartment, reached from the Great Stair off the entrance hall's NW corner, was intended to occupy much of the first floor. From a saloon above the entrance hall would have opened the State Drawing Room in the centre of the house's E side and, to its S, a procession of ante-room, state bedchamber and closet. Only the ground-floor rooms and Great Stair were finished during Bruce's lifetime and the quality of their restrained but rich woodwork and curvaceous chimneypieces makes especially regrettable the failure to complete the work, presumably in richer fashion, on the floor above.

The mansion at Kinross, however, was only one part of an extraordinarily grand scheme which embraced also the landscape and gardens to celebrate Sir William Bruce's position, taste and loyalty to the Stewart dynasty. A great gateway from the town of Kinross opened onto an avenue running through the parkland to an outer and inner court in front of the house. From the inner court a broad flight of steps rose to the house's entrance whence there was a view through the house and its partly glazed garden door to the parterre behind which lay Loch Leven with the main tower of Lochleven Castle on the axis. Although Bruce's state apartment provided the same axial view from the saloon through the State Drawing Room, that apartment could, at least in fine weather, be by-passed in favour of a processional route through the ground floor of the house (entrance hall and Garden Hall) into the parterre whose central path ended at the elaborately sculpted Fish Gate opening onto a small harbour scooped out of the shore of the loch. In the harbour was moored a ceremonial barge to carry the favoured visitor to Lochleven Castle, scene of the imprisonment of Mary, Queen of Scots, ancestor of the martyred Charles I and his sons, successive kings of the monarchy

PALACES, MANSIONS AND COUNTRY HOUSES

which had been restored in 1660 and of which Bruce was the loyal servant.

Bruce's political views were regarded with suspicion or hostility by governments after the deposition of James VII in 1689 but his architectural predilection for restrained classicism was widely accepted and developed during much of the c18. In Perth and Kinross in the 1720s *James Smith* extended Dupplin Castle by the addition of a pair of large piend-roofed office pavilions forming two sides of a forecourt in front of the house. Service wings or pavilions were provided during the next twenty years for the new mansion of Meikleour House, and for *William Adam*'s rebuilding or remodelling of Lawers House and Taymouth Castle. Meikleour House was restrained, its front dignified by a segmental pediment over the centrepiece and Venetian windows at the wings. At Lawers House the pedimented centrepiece contained segmental-headed ground-floor windows flanking the segmental-pedimented entrance and, above, round-arched windows whose height denoted the presence behind of the principal floor's cove-ceilinged and grandly finished saloon. Unusually in a house designed by William Adam, the state rooms did not form a processional sequence, the drawing room being behind and the bedchamber to one side of the saloon.

At Murthly Castle, alterations and additions of the 1730s for which Adam's rival, *John Douglas*, was the contractor and almost certainly the architect apparently provided the conventional succession from state dining room to state drawing room to state bedchamber and closet in the remodelled c17 w range. Onto that range's front was added a Palladian-inspired and pedimented block containing a first-floor hall to serve the state apartment, the new block's entrance reached from an external horseshoe-shaped double stair. Similar detailing appears at Douglas's much more extensive scheme of 1736 for a remodelling of Blair Castle in classical dress. Here, an external stair would have given access to a first-floor entrance hall behind which were placed a private dining room, the first of a sequence of family rooms (drawing room, library, bedchamber and dressing rooms and closets for the Duke and Duchess of Atholl). Off one side of the entrance hall would have been the state stair to the even grander second-floor state rooms, a billiard room above the entrance hall giving access to the Great Dining Room from which led the procession of ante-chamber, drawing room, bedchamber, dressing room and Great Closet. This was unexecuted, as was a scheme of 1743 by *James Winter*, internally very similar but with the proposed new front elevation's central pediment flanked by scooped parapets. Instead, in 1743–4, the third Duke of Atholl began construction of what must have been intended as a vast new house just s of the existing. Of this was built one wing containing a suite of interconnecting family rooms embellished with stucco decoration by *Thomas Clayton*, the ceiling of the Star Chamber (probably the Duke's dressing room) displaying the star of the Order of the Thistle. Presumably the remainder of this intended house would have consisted of a main block containing a grand entrance hall and saloon and, extending from it, a second wing containing the state apartment.

Building work at Blair Castle was halted by the Jacobite rising of 1745–6 and when it began again, with *John Douglas* as the principal and *Thomas Winter* as executant architect and *Abraham Swan* providing designs for some internal detail, it had been decided to extend the new wing to join to the existing house which was to be comprehensively recast and remodelled. The new exterior, shorn of C16 and C17 upper works, was disappointingly barracks-like without even achieving symmetry. The interior, however, completed in 1758, is the most stunning Rococo ensemble in Scotland, the stucco work all by Clayton. Remarkable for its quality of decoration, this is also a key historical artefact, evidence of a shift in the Scottish nobility's understanding of itself and of its relationship with the Crown. From the Restoration almost every major house built or remodelled in Scotland had included or been intended to include a state apartment, supposedly to receive the King from whom the house's owner held his lands, and a state apartment had been a major element in the schemes of 1736 and 1743 for Blair Castle. Now, however, the Duke of Atholl undertook a magnificent reconstruction of his principal seat but without a royal state apartment, the grandest of the house's new rooms asserting the wealth and position of the Duke himself. Two processional routes were provided to the Great Dining Room on the first floor. One, for the Duke and his retinue, led from the private wing of 1743–4 to the Picture Staircase, its sumptuous stucco work framing portraits of the Atholl family. This stair led to the private drawing room from which was entered the Duchess's Bedchamber. Off this, a closet gave access to the S end of the Great Dining Room. The second processional route, for those invited or commanded to attend on the Duke, began at the main block's ground-floor entrance hall off which rose the Great Staircase. From this stair's first-floor landing was entered an ante-room which opened into the N end of the Great Dining Room facing the door through which the Duke would make his entrance. From the Great Dining Room the company could then process, presumably led by the Duke, up the Great Staircase to the Great Drawing Room above, the largest and most spectacularly finished room in the house. Approached through a mean ante-room off the Great Drawing Room was the Tapestry Bedroom in which had been placed the state bed, but this bedchamber is at the N and not the S end of the Great Drawing Room, so there is no processional route to it through that room to which it appears little more than an appended curiosity.

FEW LAIRDS' HOUSES OF THE EARLY AND MID EIGHTEENTH CENTURY survive, most having been rebuilt or converted to service wings for larger new houses. Those which remain are family houses, not bothering to pretend that the King might some day command lodging in them. The main block of Old Fincastle, built in 1702, was a straightforward rubble-walled oblong, its front openings symmetrically disposed, the tall first-floor windows denoting the principal floor. Inside, its two principal rooms were recast in the 1750s when the ground-floor parlour was given panelling and a sideboard recess and the first-floor drawing room was also panelled but further dressed up with an enriched ceiling whose boldly modelled stucco work, with a head of Apollo at the centre, is surprisingly grand for such a house and perhaps the work of craftsmen employed at the time at the nearby Blair Castle. Also of two storeys is the harled and piend-roofed Lochlane of 1710, its front displaying rather more ambition, with a pedimented doorpiece squeezed between two windows and the wall head's centre crowned with a stone gablet carved with scrolls and the owner's coat-of-arms. The front of Arlary House, as built in the earlier C18, had a slightly advanced two-bay centrepiece. Also of the earlier C18 but grander in conception was the design of the new Gleneagles House. This would have comprised a main block flanked by two-storey pavilions (the W containing the kitchen) but the main block was not built and the existing C17 house abutting the E pavilion enlarged instead. Inside the E pavilion is a ground-floor parlour, panelled and with a stucco trophy above the fireplace, the stucco work perhaps commissioned for the unexecuted main block. Gleneagles House, if completed, might have been a minor mansion.

p. 398

Glendoick House, built *c.* 1750 by an advocate (later judge), Robert Craigie, has something of the character of villas put up on the edge of Edinburgh by lawyers and nobles at the same time. Externally, it is a simple harled oblong without pavilions but the front's advanced centre is pedimented and contains a doorpiece derived from a design by Batty Langley. The interior has no state apartment but the family's principal rooms, all on the ground floor and panelled, are exceptionally well finished, the entrance hall fireplace's overmantel painting in a lavishly decorated and pedimented stucco surround, the drawing room ceiling a Rococo display of the stuccoist's skill. Villa-like CLASSICAL LAIRDS' HOUSES continued to be built through the late C18 and into the early C19. For Glencarse House in 1790 *R. & J. Adam* produced an austere piend-roofed main block with a columned screen fronting the entrance and a full-height bow at the back. At each end was a low service pavilion (housing the kitchen and brew-house) with a three-light window to the front; unusually for this firm, the pavilions directly abutted the main block. As at Glendoick House, the principal rooms (dining room, drawing room, study and family bedchamber) were arranged on the ground floor round a central stair hall. Similar, both in external appearance (although with pedimented centrepieces at their entrance fronts) and in the internal disposition of their principal rooms, were the grandly sited mansion house of Ochtertyre designed by *James McLeran* in 1785 and St Martin's Abbey of 1791–5.

In 1801–5 was built Gask House, an essay in Robert Adam's classical manner. The architect was *Richard Crichton*, who *c.* 1815 enlarged the main block of Lawers House, its centrepiece previously remodelled and given an Ionic order by *James Salisbury*. At Lawers Crichton stretched colonnades across the outer bays and added new bow-fronted end pavilions. Heavier in detail and of Roman stolidity is Inchyra House of *c.* 1810, the centre of its polished ashlar front marked off by coupled giant Doric columns, the ends by pilasters. Much less accomplished although full of ambition was Kilgraston House (now School) designed as his own seat by the amateur architect, *Francis Grant*, in 1795, with symmetrical elevations but juxtaposing classical, Gothic and castellated elements.

The CASTELLATED STYLE IN MANSIONS AND COUNTRY HOUSES, introduced to Scotland by Roger Morris for the rebuilding of Inveraray Castle (Argyll and Bute) in 1744, was first taken up in Perth and Kinross by George Paterson in 1777, the year in which he bought Castle Huntly from the Earl of Strathmore. Paterson had acquired a fortune in the service of the East India Company and his acquisition and remodelling of Castle Huntly, built originally by an ancestor of his wife, a daughter of Lord Gray, have something of the character and actions of a *parvenu* eager to establish himself in local society. His alterations to the house were carried out in two stages, the first (in 1777–83 by *James Playfair*) the addition of battlemented wings, the second (in 1792–5 by *John Paterson*) the erection of an entrance hall and porch between the wings and a remodelling of the old tower house as a martially battlemented and turreted keep. Part of another newly acquired fortune, that of John Richardson, the dominant figure engaged in the commercial fishing and export of salmon from the River Tay, was spent on the construction of Pitfour Castle in the 1790s, its design clearly derived from R. & J. Adam's Seton Castle (Lothian), with castellated low service ranges bounding a defensive-seeming forecourt in front of the towered keep of the main block.

In the same general manner, although without the outer defences and verticality of Pitfour, is Strathallan Castle of *c.* 1800 built for General Andrew Drummond, a professional soldier who had petitioned unsuccessfully for restoration of the viscountcy of Strathallan forfeited after his grandfather's participation in the Jacobite uprising of 1745–6. Drummond's new house, named after the lost viscountcy rather than its geographical position (in Strathearn, not Strathallan) used some round-headed windows, as favoured by Robert Adam, and a few playful touches (e.g. cinquefoil panels on the battlement) to lighten its impression of military purpose. In 1797 another general, Alexander Campbell of Monzie, commissioned *John Paterson* to add a castellated mansion to the existing C17 laird's house of Monzie Castle. Rigorously symmetrical, this is a serious-minded toy fort with a heavy rectangular central tower and large round towers at the outer corners, delicacy eschewed, perhaps lest this bachelor soldier be suspected of effeminacy. More light-hearted and with something of the villa about it was another house built for General Drummond. This was Culdees Castle, designed *c.* 1810 by *James Gillespie Graham*. Again it is a towered and battlemented fort but the most striking element is an asymmetrically positioned large round tower, both its design and placing perhaps influenced by the work of John Nash in England. Almost frivolous in its mixing Gothic, including oriel windows, into a castellated symmetrical mass is the small mansion house of Kincardine Castle built in 1801-3.

By far the largest and internally most magnificent of these castellated houses is Taymouth Castle, built for the first and second Marquesses of Breadalbane between 1801 and 1842. In 1792 John Campbell of Carwhin, an unimportant Argyll laird, succeeded a distant cousin to become fourth Earl (later first Marquess) of Breadalbane and the owner of vast landholdings. Like some recent lottery winners his reaction to this good fortune seems to have been to 'spend, spend, spend'. Luckily, the Breadalbane estates, boosted by the spectacular rise in agricultural prices during the French Revolutionary and Napoleonic Wars, were able to fund his expenditure. The house which existed at Taymouth in 1792 had developed from the C16 into a sizeable but not especially imposing mansion, remarkable neither for architectural flamboyance nor venerable antiquity. By 1801 the new Earl had begun building a new house 'in the Stile of a Castle' to a design by *John Paterson*, its main block *c.* 30 m. square, with a Gothic-windowed round tower at each corner and a square central tower, all finished with battlements, the elevations all symmetrical. In 1804, before completion of the shell of the main block, Paterson was replaced by *James* and *Archibald Elliot* who raised its height from three to four storeys, the top floor pierced by pointed windows, designed a taller and elaborately Gothic central tower and wrapped a 'cloister' round the ground floor, alleviating the stodginess of the original design. They also enlarged and Gothicized a couple of the principal (first-)floor windows lighting the ends of the two most important rooms. It was, however, the interior which made Taymouth one of the most spectacular houses in Scotland.

The principal rooms of most castellated houses in Perth and Kinross were placed on the ground floor but at Taymouth they occupied the first floor and formed a circuit. This is reached by the imperial Great Stair within the central tower, the tower's soaring empty space above enclosed by Gothic stuccoed walls under a vaulted ceiling, an evocation of the immensely tall Perpendicular lantern of some great English church except that the canopied niches at the level of the stair formerly contained suits of armour in honour of the house's castle status. At the W end of

Taymouth Castle.
Elevation of south front in 1856

the stair landing was a door into the Billiard (later Print) Room which served as an ante-room both to the family bedchamber and dressing rooms in the W pavilion and to the Dining Hall along the N side of the main block. The Dining Hall evokes a medieval great hall, the Late Gothic vaulting of its plaster ceiling inspired by St George's Chapel, Windsor, the huge W window filled with stained glass portraying ancestors of the Breadalbanes around that family's heraldic achievement. A door at the Dining Hall's far end opened into the Dining Room on the block's E side, decorated, like the other principal rooms, in a late Gothic manner. S of this, an ante-room to the Great and Small Drawing Rooms, opening into each other through double doors and occupying the whole S side of the main block. The Great Drawing Room's E end formed a fan-vaulted apse. From this room a door provided an exit for the visitor back onto the landing of the Great Stair.

This first major phase in the rebuilding of Taymouth Castle was completed in 1812. Six years later the C18 E quadrant and pavilion were removed and a huge complex of bedrooms, domestic offices and stables built round a courtyard and joined to the main block's NE corner. Designed by *William Atkinson* in a Tudor manner, this appears like a sizeable Oxbridge college, with a 'chapel' (actually, stables) at the E end of the S front. In 1826–8 Atkinson replaced the C18 W quadrant and recast the adjoining pavilion in castellated style and deepened it to the N to provide new bedroom and dressing room accommodation for the Breadalbanes. Then, in 1838 the second Marquess of Breadalbane employed *James Gillespie Graham* (assisted by *A. W. N. Pugin*) to clothe the W link and pavilion in more heavily detailed castellated garb, the link's S side being almost filled by a huge first floor Gothic window. The whole upper floor of the link was given over to a Baronial Hall, its hammerbeam roof painted with heraldry showing the descent of the Breadalbanes 'through the Blood Royal of Scotland & England the Lords of the Isles & the Lords of Lorne'. Inside the pavilion was made a gallery off which opened a Gothic library formed from three C18 rooms, the library's entrance screen and bookcases elaborately carved, its magnificent Tudor Gothic roof adorned with blue and gold painted panels. At the same time, the richness of the early C19 Great and Small Drawing Rooms' decoration was given a new opulence, with new carved doorcases and window pelmets. A more boldly modelled ceiling was installed in the Great Drawing Room and both this and that of the Small Drawing Room were painted with depictions of monsters, medieval knights, heraldry and foliage. With the completion of Gillespie Graham's work in 1842 Taymouth Castle was a fit setting for the reception of the Queen and Prince Consort who duly paid a four-day visit.

Taymouth Castle's combination of a castellated main block containing the principal rooms and extensive but lower collegiate Tudor service quarters built round a courtyard and extending from one end was found also at Scone Palace after its comprehensive remodelling for the third Earl of Mansfield in 1803–12,

Rossie Priory. Perspective of south front from J. P. Neale,
Views of Seats, 2nd ser., ii, 1825

at Kinfauns Castle built for the fifteenth Lord Gray in 1821–6 and, but with the main house in ecclesiastical Gothic garb, at Rossie Priory (now largely demolished) constructed for the eighth Lord Kinnaird in 1807–15. At all these, the principal rooms were placed on the ground floor, with each opening into the next to form a processional route but also entered from a broad passage (the Inner Hall of Scone Palace, the Gallery of Kinfauns Castle and the Cloisters of Rossie Priory) covered with Gothic plasterwork in evocation of a medieval cloister. Scone Palace and Rossie Priory, both designed by *William Atkinson*, each contained a second 'cloister' at right angles to the first, Scone Palace's Long Gallery a remodelling of the house's early C17 Long Gallery, leading to the family's private rooms. At these houses both 'cloisters' led off the main entrance hall, the shape and some of the feeling of this room (the Octagon) at Scone Palace perhaps in tepid imitation of the octagon of Fonthill Abbey. The decoration of the principal rooms themselves was predominantly Gothic but with an admixture of Tudor and, at Rossie Priory and Kinfauns Castle, classical elements.

A similar use of vaulted passages or 'cloisters' was made by *Richard Crichton* and his nephews and successors, *R. & R. Dickson*, at the (demolished) Tudor Gothic houses of Abercairny, begun in 1803, and Millearne, begun in 1821. Abercairny's entrance hall, its hammerbeam roof of plaster grained to imitate wood, opened into the East Corridor which ran N–S and was covered with Gothic plasterwork of Strawberry Hill character. From the East Gallery's S end a door opened into the Gallery running E–W and also vaulted, on whose S side were the principal rooms (dining room, music room, library and double drawing room), all with elaborate Gothic decoration. At Millearne the interior provided a juggling of heights and spaces to surprise the visitor. As at Abercairny there was an E–W Gallery, here with a semi-octagonal end, on whose S side were placed the dining room and drawing room. Near its W end, the Gallery opened into a N–S claustral passage with a vaulted conservatory (the Cloister) on its W side and the library at its N end. Again, the rooms were Gothic, the dining room ceiling, pendant bosses hanging from the trusses, copied from the C15 roof of Crosby Hall, London (illustrated in A. C. Pugin's *Specimens of Gothic Architecture*), the drawing room ceiling from New Walsingham Church, Norfolk (illustrated in Pugin's *Examples of Gothic Architecture*), the Gallery, passages and stairs all covered with Gothic vaults and ceilings.

The largest of these Tudor Gothic mansions would have been Dunkeld Palace (a replacement for the late C17 Dunkeld House) designed by *Thomas Hopper* for the fourth Duke of Atholl. Work on its construction, begun in 1828, was abandoned soon after the Duke's death in 1830 and the building later demolished. Here, a 15 m.-long vestibule was to have led to one end of the Great Hall (27 m. long) at whose end a screen opened onto the Grand Staircase to the principal guest bedrooms on the first floor. Off the Great Hall's S side would have been the dining room and breakfast room, the first in an L-plan sequence of interconnected public spaces which continued with the library, conservatory and drawing room. Off the drawing room would have opened the boudoir, the first of a suite of private rooms for the Duke and Duchess at the house's NW corner. E of the entrance extended a large courtyard bounded by lower ranges containing service quarters and bedrooms.

Tudor of a more domestic variety was introduced to the region by *Robert Smirke* c. 1820 in his design for Cultoquhey House, manorial in general appearance but with a low tower. Smirke's former pupil, *William Burn*, popularized the use of TUDOR AND JACOBEAN MANORIAL STYLES with a succession of houses (e.g. Freeland House (now Strathallan School), Faskally House, Pitcairns, near Dunning, Auchterarder House, Lude House), all competent but unexciting, the main block often with an asymmetrical entrance front but a symmetrically composed arrangement of bay windows to light the principal rooms overlooking the garden, as at Lude House or the largely demolished Dunira. Dupplin Castle (demolished) had more of the character of a prodigy house and House of Urrard, near Temandry, also Jacobean, was unusually tightly composed and vertical in emphasis, with a pair of shaped gables. The interiors of most of these houses were planned according to a formula developed by Burn, with a large service range to one side and other servants' rooms confined to a basement, the principal rooms (usually, dining room, library and drawing room) in a line along one side of the main block and entered from a hall, often a stair hall, or broad passage-gallery, and the family bedroom and dressing rooms placed in one corner of the main block beside a private stair to the nursery rooms above. The Tudor or Jacobean manner extended to the interiors although these often contained Frenchy chimneypieces. Much of the internal finishing was routine, the top-lit central hall of Freeland House with rows of angels fronting the roof trusses unusually ostentatious.

Much grander than anything put up by Burn in Perth and Kinross would have been the new Murthly Castle designed by *James Gillespie Graham* in the late 1820s to fulfil Sir John Stewart Drummond of Grandtully's desire to live in a 'Palace' suitable for one who claimed, on the strength of distant kinship with the Stewart dynasty, to be 'intimately connected with Kings'. Only the shell (since demolished) of this Jacobean prodigy house was completed, the main block's symmetrical elevations with ogee-roofed corner towers, shaped gables and large bay windows and the centre surmounted by a huge tower. Some of the intended interiors, designed with assistance from *A. W. N. Pugin*, were installed in 1850 in the old Murthly Castle, the Great Hall covered by a hammerbean roof, the Music Room, most unusually for those who see Pugin only as a fanatical Gothicist, in best Louis XIV manner.

The last house designed by Burn in the region, Dunira of 1852, followed his general manorial prescription but had turrets and crowstepped gables to show that it was Scottish. National detail was used at the same time and with more panache by *A. & A. Heiton* in their design for Dunalastair. Strongly Scottish, although little concerned with archaeological accuracy, were attempts to revive the spirit of the soaring Scottish tower house, most memorably at the towered and turreted Dall House of 1854–5 (by *Mackenzie & Matthews*), Dalnaglar Castle of 1864 and Allean House, near Strathtummel, of 1865, all prominently sited, two overlooking large lochs, the third on a steep hillside in Glen Shee. Most powerfully redolent of a baronial stronghold is Blackcraig Castle, designed for himself by *Patrick Allan-Fraser* in 1856, and approached by a fortified bridge.

Soberer use of the SCOTTISH BARONIAL STYLE continued until the end of the C19 with *David Bryce*'s additions of 1866–7 to Culdees Castle, *Peddie & Kinnear*'s Kinmouth of 1876–8, *Andrew Heiton Jun.*'s work at Hallyburton and Tower of Lethendy in the 1880s, and *Thomas Leadbetter*'s 1890s addition to Grandtully Castle, its huge tower overpowering the earlier house. Most prominent and best-known of these houses is Blair Castle as remodelled in 1869 by Bryce, who gave the house's sprawling mass a determinedly Baronial outline, the design of his new entrance tower derived from the equivalent early C17 tower at Fyvie Castle, the walling all covered in brilliant white harling.

Inside, most of these houses contained rooms fitted up in the unadventurous Jacobean manner of William Burn, but the 1870s work at Hallyburton is constructed round a great hall and similar halls were added to Arthurstone (the library) *c*. 1870, to Freeland House by *Wardrop & Reid* in 1880 and to Blair Castle (the Ballroom) by *D. & J. Bryce* in 1876–7. At Arthurstone, the

Blair Castle.
Watercolour perspective of east front by David Bryce, 1869

Neo-Jacobean finishing of the library and dining room are in masculine contrast to the femininity of the Louis XV drawing room, a throwback to the contrast between the Great Hall and the Music Room in Murthly Castle designed forty years before.

Great halls were also provided in 1880s alterations to two other houses where the new work was influenced by France. *James Thomson* remodelled Belmont Castle for the Francophile politician and plutocrat, Sir Henry Campbell-Banerman, providing a huge central hall in French Renaissance manner. Off one side opened a suite of three drawing rooms, all decorated in French C18 taste, off another a Neo-Jacobean dining room, off a third, the stair hall sumptuously finished, again in a French manner. At the same time *John J. Burnet* extended Auchterarder House for the locomotive manufacturer, James Reid, the new and richly detailed Scottish Renaissance style porte cochère giving a much needed punch to Burn's staid architecture of the 1830s. Inside, Burn's rooms were grandly redecorated in a mixture of Scottish and French Renaissance. The new billiard room added to the house was again Scottish Renaissance but with intimations of Arts and Crafts. It was linked to the house by a winter garden whose tiles and marble work conspired to produce a classical setting which could have come from the imagination of Alma-Tadema.

A few Late Victorian houses broke decisively with Scottish Baronial or Scottish Renaissance. In 1876 *David Bryce* produced designs for the remodelling of Meikleour House as a chateau of the French Renaissance, although these were sadly cut down in execution. In 1899 *John Watherston & Sons* built the Neo-

Georgian Dunsinnan House, the centre and end bays of its front pedimented and Venetian-windowed and with a semicircular Roman Doric porch.

COUNTRY VILLAS in well-planted parks on small estates were built through the C19, often by new owners who had made money in the professions, commerce or industry. One of the earlier and hardly altered is Balhary designed in 1817 by the local architect, *John Carver Sen.*, its front dignified by a Doric portico under a three-light window. It was built for a Writer to the Signet (solicitor), John Smythe. Wholly a villa in concept and of only one storey is the broad-eaved Tudor Gothic Glendevon House of 1818. Endearingly bumptious is Airleywight, near Bankfoot, built for a Perth merchant *c*. 1810, with a half-domed semicircular portico squeezed between a pair of domed round towers. More self-assured although idiosyncratic is the classical villa of Ballindean House which *William Trotter*, a former Lord Provost of Edinburgh, designed for himself in 1832, the principal elevations designed to appear to advantage from the oblique views on the approach and with the circular cupola over the central stair hall standing above the roof.

Also self-confident in its villa status is the broad-eaved and informally composed Keithick, designed by *David A. Whyte* for a Perth physician, Dr James Wood, in 1818. About fifteen years after its completion in 1823 two of Keithick's principal rooms were redecorated by the London firm of *G. Morant*, the drawing room painted in Italian Neoclassical style with wall panels bordered by stylized candelabra and foliage and enclosing depictions of playful cherubs, the library fitted up with elegantly detailed birch bookcases. Another painted scheme but the pastoral scenes inspired by Watteau was introduced at the same time to the drawing room of Kinnaird House, the residence on a sporting estate beside the River Tay. That other shooting lodges might enjoy decoration other than a display of stags' heads is demonstrated by Glenalmond House whose drawing room was redecorated in 1907 in very best Adam Revival manner.

A different sophistication is shown by *C. G. Soutar*'s use of an English Arts and Crafts style in his remodelling of the interior of Kinloch House, near Kinloch, for the Dundee industrialist, John Paton, in 1909–10, the central galleried stair hall lit from a delicately patterned stained-glass ceiling. Also Arts and Crafts but inspired by C17 Scottish lairds' houses was the remodelling and extension of Glenlyon House in 1891 by the London architects, *W. Dunn & R. Watson*, for the shipping magnate, Sir Donald Currie. Harled, with crowstepped gables, small windows and a round stair-tower in the inner angle of its L-shape, Glenlyon is satisfying, the more so since the interior is finished in a supremely comfortable but quite unshowy manner. A less successful essay in the same idiom is Glenfarg House of *c*. 1910, by *J. B. Dunn* of Edinburgh. It is also harled, with crowstepped gables and the inner angle containing a tower whose ogee roof was copied from C17 work at Grandtully Castle, but the ground-floor windows are large, some of them forming canted bays, and the effect busy.

More delicately detailed was another evocation of a C17 laird's house, *Robert S. Lorimer*'s remodelling and extension of Briglands for the advocate (later, judge), J.A. Clyde, in 1897–1908. The exterior is, of course, harled and crowstepped, with a round stair-tower in an inner angle, but it also boasts an ogee-roofed corner turret and boat-shaped and gabled dormerheads. Some of the dormerheads and skewputts are enlivened with carving. Inside, Lorimer introduced plasterwork which displays his favourite motifs of vines, local plants and birds and, on the elliptical vault over the house's Long Gallery, reliefs of the Four Seasons. Lorimer's Scots manner was used dramatically in the remodelling he began in 1916 of the hitherto very ordinary late C16 tower house of Balmanno Castle for a Glasgow shipowner, William S. Miller. On the approach he provided a gatehouse and walled forecourt to create a tidy barmkin. The harled house, filling the courtyard's W side, was made theatrical by Lorimer's lowering of the eaves to steepen the roof pitch, adding decorative dormerheads over the top floor's windows and, most effective of all, heightening the inner angle's stair-turret by a full storey and giving it a tall ogee-profiled roof. The interior is an exhibition of early C20 Scottish craftsmanship in wood (panelling by *Scott Morton & Co.*, *Nathaniel Grieve* and *John Watherston & Sons*), plaster (by *Samuel Wilson* and *Thomas Beattie*), ironwork (by *Thomas Hadden*) and stained glass (by *Walter Camm*). The inspiration is generally of the C17 but ranges from Jacobean to post-Restoration and varies in character from room to room, the plasterwork plentifully enriched with vines and flowers and, in one bedroom, modelled with a medieval hunting scene. Originally, the ensemble was completed by the furniture, all by the Edinburgh firm of *Whytock & Reid* from designs produced under Lorimer's direction.

Completion of work on Balmanno Castle in 1921 marks the effective end of Lorimer's vision of a national domestic architecture drawing free inspiration from the past, especially from the C17, and enriched by superlative craftsmanship. His own firm of *Lorimer & Matthew* provided competent but unoriginal interiors for a remodelling of Jordanstone in 1928–9 and *George Bennett Mitchell* the large but unimaginative Scots-style shooting lodge of Dalmunzie House built for a Calcutta businessman in 1920. A much more self-confident but smaller country house-villa, its overt Scottish references limited to crowsteps, is Tirinie, near Blair Atholl, designed in 1923 by *Oswald Milne*, a pupil of *Edwin Lutyens* who had himself completely eschewed direct Scottishness at his Queen Anne style Straloch House a few years before. During the later C20 the Tudor Gothic Millearne and Abercairny and the shell of Gillespie Graham's Murthly Castle were all demolished, as were William Burn's Dupplin Castle and, less regrettably, his Snaigow House, while Moncreiffe House was lost to a fire. A handful of Neo-Georgian replacement houses have been built, e.g. Dupplin, by *W. Schomberg Scott*, and Abercairny by *Claud Phillimore* but, at the beginning of the C21 the region still lacks a work of Modernist daring.

PALACES, MANSIONS AND COUNTRY HOUSES

LANDSCAPE GARDENING. C17 gardens associated with mansions and lairds' houses might be laid out as PARTERRES, as at Drummond Castle and Kinross House. SUNDIALS were sometimes placed at the focal points of such layouts. Still in place at Drummond Castle is the tall sundial commissioned from *John Mylne Sen.* in 1630, its shaft bearing coats-of-arms and surmounted by a polyhedron whose faces are all carved with dials, as is the crowning finial. Another early C17 sundial made for the second Earl of Perth is at Stobhall, a Doric column encased in a square band and topped by a cubical stone, both this finial and the band carved with dials. Almost certainly the dials and heraldry of these were originally painted as were those of two (now lost) made for Taymouth Castle, in 1661 and in 1710–15, the second of these carved with 130 dials and showing, as well as the time of day at Taymouth, the times at London, Paris, Dublin and Jerusalem.

From the C18 most country houses were set in PARKLAND. The formality typified by *Sir William Bruce*'s single axial avenue leading to Kinross House (*see* p. 484) gave way before the mid C18 to a multiplication of avenues to provide walks and rides from the mansion house, often with clumps of trees ('wildernesses') placed beside or at their ends. Such a scheme was prepared for Blair Castle in 1723 by the Duke of Atholl's sister-in-law, *Margaret, Lady Nairne*, who suggested the planting of Scottish oaks on the main avenues and offered to provide Scots pines for the evergreen 'wildernesses', these clumps' centres to be filled with holly trees. From the 1730s successive Dukes of Atholl planted the castle's grounds and surrounding hillsides with larch, a process which continued well into the C19 although by then, as elsewhere, in much less regular dispositions. The great deerparks of both Blair Castle and Taymouth Castle were laid out from the C18 both with straight avenues and with winding walks through woodland, some bounding their respective watercourses, the River Tilt and Banvie Burn at Blair Castle, the River Tay at Taymouth Castle.

In these settings were placed STATUES, FOLLIES, TEMPLES AND GROTTOES. By the 1760s, at Blair Castle, just W of the lawn (a replacement of 1751 for a parterre) behind the house, a wooded knoll was surmounted by an obelisk carved with heraldry. On the lawn E of the house stood a clock tower. The Banvie Burn bounding the lawn was crossed by bridges, including one in the 'Chinese' taste. E of the burn, an avenue (the Hercules Walk) led to a giant lead statue of Hercules overlooking the S side of a walled garden. This contained a lake, partly crossed by another 'Chinese' bridge and with islands on which stood thatched houses for ornamental waterfowl. Placed in the garden were painted lead statues. At its far end the Hercules Walk opened onto a path along the bank of the River Tilt beside which stood a grotto. Another avenue led from the castle's E lawn to the 'wilderness' of Diana's Grove in which stood a statue of Diana and Actaeon overlooking a circular Temple of Fame. From one side of Diana's Grove another avenue was focused on The Whim, a castellated folly on the slope of Craig Urrard from which could be enjoyed the view over the park and down the River Garry to Killiecrankie. On a hillside to the E stood a stone urn and, E of that, on a knoll just outside the park, a ball-finialled obelisk around which had been constructed a summer house in which antlers were hung as festoons over the windows. Almost all this had been created in the 1740s and 1750s by the second Duke of Atholl.

The third Earl of Breadalbane showed similar ambition in his embellishment of the policies of Taymouth Castle from the 1760s. There, a lime avenue, planted probably in the late C17, led from the back of the house to a wooden 'Chinese' bridge over the Tay. A wooded walk along the river's N bank led E to the Star Seat, a mock fortification occupying a promontory, and W to Maxwell's Building, an open-sided summerhouse. In the deerpark surrounding the house on the S side of the Tay were knolls on which stood Temples of Venus and Apollo. On the steep hillside to the S was placed The Fort, a long castellated folly with a spectacular view over the valley of the Tay and along Loch Tay, and, behind it, another battlemented folly, The Tower. Of all these only The Fort and The Tower survive. Some of the other structures were not demolished until the C20 but others were replaced in the early C19 by the fourth Earl (later, first Marquess) of Breadalbane, the new works mostly designed by *William Atkinson*. A new cast-iron Chinese Bridge, Tudor Gothic despite the name, was constructed over the Tay behind the house. The Star Seat was replaced by the Star Battery, its appearance suggesting real military purpose, and Maxwell's Building by Maxwell's Temple, a serious-minded version of the Eleanor Cross at Northampton. In the park itself, the site of the Temple of Venus was taken over by the ornamental Dairy within whose white quartz walls counterpointed by tree-trunk verandas the Countess could take the role of a milkmaid once acted by Marie Antoinette.

Outside the deer parks of Dunkeld House and Taymouth Castle but intended to be viewed by those houses' more adventurous inmates or guests were HERMITAGES, both constructed in the later C18 overlooking waterfalls. The Hermitage, near Inver across the Tay from Dunkeld House and standing beside the River Braan, was built in 1757 and appears externally as a summerhouse. The inside was a stage set where, from 1783 to 1869, a doorway in the circular entrance hall was filled with a cloth portraying the Gaelic bard, Ossian, which parted to reveal the main room whose end opened onto the cascade of the Back Lynn Fall, its foaming water reflected in mirrors on the walls and ceiling. The Hermit's Cave W of Taymouth Castle, on a hillside above Acharn beside Loch Tay, is spookier, a sinuous artificial rock passage which leads to a room whose open side is filled with the aweful view of the tumultuous water of the 73m.-high Fall of Acharn. Originally, the passage walls were covered with moss and its stone benches with animal hides.

On the E edge of the park of Taymouth Castle stand the STABLES AND COACHHOUSES (now Newhall) designed in 1800 by *John Paterson* with a light-hearted Gothic screen front towards the former drive from the mansion house to Aberfeldy. Such offices were a necessary appendage of any country house until the C20. Often they formed part of a service court attached to the house itself, as was originally the case at Kinross House, at Lawers House and Rossie Priory and as provided in the extensions of 1818–22 to Taymouth Castle. Stables and coachhouses sited away from the house are often surprisingly plain. At Scone Palace the stable courtyard of 1810 makes no attempt to emulate the grandeur or style of the mansion itself. The 1780s stables of Kinross House originally had only a pedimented centrepiece to give the front distinction. Similar is the near-contemporary stable courtyard at Strathallan Castle, although with the addition of pyramidal-roofed end pavilions. Smarter is the D-plan court at St Martin's Abbey, probably of 1785, the curved range's entrance framed by an aedicule, the centre of the straight block crowned by a doocot tower. At Keithick, the front of the stables of *c.* 1825 has a pyramid-roofed central tower and pedimented ends. However, *c.* 1810, *James Gillespie Graham* designed a courtyard in heavy battlemented Gothic manner for Culdees Castle. Scots style appeared in 1919 at Dunira where was built a large stable courtyard, the walls harled, some of the gables crowstepped and the S front sporting a pair of conical-roofed turrets. Behind the plain stables of 1797 at Arthurstone rises a tall ogee-roofed water tower added in 1838 in prominent celebration of the new amenities enjoyed by that estate.

On the other side of the tower at Arthurstone is the walled garden of *c.* 1800, with a battlemented octagonal tower rising above its far wall. WALLED GARDENS for the production of vegetables, fruit and flowers had been formed from the C17. Probably of the late C17 is the garden beside Murthly Castle, the ogee-roofed pavilion in one corner apparently added in 1712–13, the corniced gatepiers constructed *c.* 1740. C18 walled gardens were generally placed at a little distance from the house, probably to avoid disturbance to its inhabitants but also to give them a goal for a walk. The Hercules Garden formed at Blair Castle in the 1750s, with its lake, islands and swans, was laid out as a pleasure ground, the ornamental character strongest at the W wall where niches contain statues of the Four Seasons to one side of a pyramidal-roofed summerhouse (the Apple House). At Blair Adam's almost contemporary walled garden, *John Adam* intended the N wall to be surmounted by urns and placed at its centre a Venetian-windowed gardener's house. Garden walls of the late C18 and early C19 were often faced with brick internally or entirely of brickwork (e.g. the gardens at Dupplin Castle and Rossie Priory), a material which provides greater warmth for espaliered fruit trees than does stone. Sometimes the walls were artificially heated and contained flues. Greenhouses were common, often intended for specific types of plant, such as the vineries and peach houses built at Taymouth Castle in 1807 and at Blair Castle sixty years later. From the late C19 these could be ordered from the catalogues put out by specialist firms such as

Mackenzie & Moncur who supplied greenhouses for the garden of Rossie House *c.* 1900. Shortage of labour, the financial retrenchment of many landowners and the increased availability of produce from commercial sources in the C20 caused many, though far from all, walled gardens to be abandoned or given over to grass or the production of Christmas trees. Some (e.g. the gardens of Arthurstone and Taymouth Castle) have been filled with houses. Perhaps the restoration of the Hercules Garden at Blair Castle now in progress will provoke action elsewhere.

DOOCOTS, their possession a privilege reserved for lairds, were a common appendage of mansion houses. A large domical-roofed circular beehive dovecot, probably of the C16, survives at Elcho Castle, a smaller D-plan example of lectern type (i.e. with monopitch roof), probably of the mid C17, at Ecclesiamagirdle House. They continued to be built for new or remodelled country houses until the C19. The late C17 square and pyramid-roofed doocot at Castle Huntly is dressed up with conical-roofed bartizans as a symbol of baronial status. Less demonstrative but prominently sited is the large lectern doocot, probably of the early C18, at Kinnaird Castle, the flight-holes placed in the riser of a step in the monopitch roof. Another lectern doocot, dated 1751, survives at Tulliebole Castle but the Late Georgian doocot at Rossie House is a battlemented concave-sided octagon. Other late C18 and early C19 doocots were incorporated in stable and coachhouse buildings. Unusually late is the free-standing pyramidal-roofed tower of a doocot built at Killiechassie, near Weem, in the 1860s.

GATEWAYS AND LODGES stood and still stand at the entrances to the parks of country houses. At the end of the drive to Castle Huntly is a gateway of the later C17 embellished with attached Tuscan columns and pyramid finials. Much more assuredly classical are the corniced and panelled gatepiers surmounted by carved urns erected, probably in the 1680s, at the end of the avenue leading to Drummond Castle, the cast-iron overthrow above the gates bearing the coroneted coat-of-arms of the Earls of Perth. Similar gates were erected *c.* 1730 at Dunkeld House (later moved to the entrance to Dunkeld Cathedral's graveyard), at Gleneagles House in 1749, the inner faces of these carved with fluted Ionic pilasters, the outer with rosettes, and, in more advanced Neoclassical form and with urns of cast iron, at Rossie House *c.* 1800. Perhaps the grandest and one of the earliest essays in this manner was the Great Gateway (now rebuilt in the garden wall) to Kinross House of 1684, carved with Doric pilasters and banded rustication. The present entrance gates to Kinross, in the same general style but without the swagger, were provided in 1902 by *Thomas Ross*. A more ostentatious throwback to the manner of *c.* 1700 is the gateway to Dupplin Castle designed by *James Miller*, 1928. An enjoyable contrast to the smoothly detailed ashlar stonework of these is made by the gateway from Kenmore to Taymouth Castle, built in 1828–9 but of rubble and in a C18 rustic Gothick manner. It suggests the entrance to the pleasure grounds and castle of a family of antique lineage.

Until the end of the C18 most lodges were probably no more than cottages to house watchmen. At the beginning of the C19, however, gateways and lodges were erected in combinations which conspired to proclaim the importance of the house beyond. In 1809 *Archibald Elliot* provided a battlemented archway between martial towers flanked by lodges, also battlemented, at the entrance to Dunkeld House. More frivolous are *William Stirling I*'s Tudor Gothic gateway accompanied by a battlemented lodge with a Gothic corner tower, built in 1812 at the E drive to Monzie Castle. Also of 1812 is the larger and more grandly tower-flanked Tudor Gothic NW gateway and lodge of Taymouth Castle, and Tudor Gothic of a more serious sort was used by *C. H. Tatham* in his design of 1809 for the Granite Lodge at Ochtertyre. Monzie Castle's West Lodge of *c.* 1830 is, like the E, battlemented but more martially detailed and it stands at the end of a bridge entered through 'Saxon' archways, the bridge and archways also topped by battlements. Quite without martial threat are the N gateway and lodges of 1820 at Megginch Castle, the gatepiers with obelisk finials in a C17 manner, the lodges with quatrefoil panels to remove any fear of hostility which might be implied by their battlements. Less frivolous are the Neoclassical Roman Doric-columned archway and accompanying lodges to Kilgraston House (now School). Also Neoclassical but of rustic simplicity and on a small scale are the lodges of *c.* 1825 at Keithick. These were built for a prosperous physician. The West Lodge of Blair Castle was built in 1866 for a duke, although at the expence of a railway company, and is a Baronial assertion of his status. Quite domestic were the red tile-roofed lodge designed by *Wardrop & Anderson* in 1891 at Freeland House (now Strathallan School) and *Robert S. Lorimer*'s over-determinedly Scots lodge of 1898 at Briglands.

ROADS, RAILWAYS AND HARBOURS

Established tracks and paths must have been used in Perth from prehistoric times. Well-used routes are likely to have been improved by the laying of stones to provide a hard surface in marshy spots or to improve fords across burns and rivers. The earliest true road, gravelled along its length and capable of carrying wheeled traffic, was that formed by the Roman army in the late C1 A.D. which ran from Camelon, near Falkirk, (Stirling and Central Scotland) to Braco and along the Gask Ridge to Bertha on the W bank of the Tay N of Perth. A few roads along which could pass wheeled traffic, although probably with difficulty and only in summer, are likely to have been in existence by 1296 when the army of Edward I made a triumphal landward progress through much of Scotland, on its way N from Stirling to Aberdeen and Elgin passing through Auchterarder and Perth to the castles of Kinclaven, Clunie and Inverquiech and, on the return S, along the Carse of Gowrie from Dundee to Perth and from there along the S shore of the Tay by Abernethy into Fife.

MEDIEVAL BRIDGES are known to have stood along certain routes. A bridge over the Tay at Perth existed by 1209 when it was destroyed by a spate. The bridge was quickly replaced and its successors spanned the river until 1621 when, after another destructive flood, a ferry took over until 1771. Higher up the Tay, at Dunkeld, construction of a bridge was begun in 1469. This, if completed, was replaced by a new bridge built in 1513–c. 1520 but that bridge was swept away, probably in the C17, and the crossing then served by a ferry until the early C19. Perhaps constructed in the C15 was the former Bridge of Earn which carried over the River Earn the major land routes to Perth from Stirling along the s side of Strathearn and from Fife along the s side of the Firth of Tay. Ashlar-built and of five arches, its width of 3.81 m. allowed for two carts to pass each other. One medieval bridge which still stands is Ardoch Old Bridge at Braco, built in 1430 to carry the road from Stirling to Perth over the gorge of the River Knaik. This is a very simple rubble arch, the roadway's width of only 1.83 m. but probably just enough to allow a cart to cross. Too narrow for a cart is the Old Pack Horse Bridge, perhaps originally constructed in the early C16, at Alyth, also of rubble but with two unequally sized arches and sloping steeply from one bank to the other of the Alyth Burn.

An act of the Scottish Parliament in 1617 stipulated that roads between market towns were to be at least 20 feet (c. 6m.) wide, and the inhabitants of each parish they passed through were to be responsible for their maintenance, together with that of roads leading to the parish church. Enforcement of the act was entrusted to Justices of the Peace who were appointed from local landowners. The legal provisions were strengthened in 1669 by an Act for Repairing Highways and Bridges which required tenants to labour on the roads for a few days each year and allowed for taxes for road maintenance to be levied on landowners by the shires' Commissioners of Supply, themselves almost all landowners.

Although SEVENTEENTH- AND EIGHTEENTH-CENTURY ROADS were maintained after a fashion, the legislation was not designed for their improvement and its implementation depended on the goodwill of landowners. Some bridges were repaired (e.g. the Old Pack Horse Bridge at Alyth in 1646 and 1674), widened (e.g. Ardoch Old Bridge in 1741–2), or built or rebuilt (e.g. bridges over the Tay at Kenmore in 1627, over the South Queich at Kinross in 1687 or over the Devon at Rumbling Bridge c. 1713) but, generally, until the end of the C18 landowners seem to have been unwilling to do much. As late as the 1790s roads in several parishes in Perth and Kinross were reported to be 'almost impassable' in winter or wet weather whilst, of two bridges over the River Farg, one was described as 'old and ruinous' and the other as 'too narrow for carriages, and ... some distance from the public road'.

Major improvements to the road system in parts of Perth and Kinross in the mid C18 were the work of central government and, at least initially, designed to facilitate the deployment of troops through potentially disaffected Highland areas and their passage between forts N and S of the region. Between 1725 and 1736 *General George Wade* constructed MILITARY ROADS from Dunkeld to Inverness and, leading off this, from Dalnacardoch, N of Blair Atholl, W along Strath Tummel and, then, S to Aberfeldy, Amulree and Crieff to join the road to Stirling which was itself improved in 1741–2. In the 1750s a new military road was constructed from Blairgowrie to the Grampian forts of Braemar Castle and Corgarff Castle and ended at the huge new Highland fortress of Fort George, then under construction. The military roads, generally *c.* 5 m. wide, were usually formed by removing soil to expose the underlying stone on which gravel was laid to form a fairly even hard surface but the excavation of soil and its banking at the sides meant that the roads ran in trenches liable to fill with snow in winter. The straight lines favoured by military engineers paid little attention to the steepness of gradients.

Associated MILITARY BRIDGES were mostly utilitarian such as the surviving rubble-built Bridge of Tummel or the ferociously humpbacked Glenshee Bridge at Spittal of Glenshee. Quite exceptional is the Tay Bridge at Aberfeldy whose marble inscription panel boasted of the Government's achievement in providing a safe means of communication between the Highlands and the towns to the S. The bridge itself was architectural propaganda for the Hanoverian regime. Designed by *William Adam* in 1733, it is a forceful assertion of the military and civilizing presence of the army, the arches' Gibbsian rustication combining with the parapets' pyramids and obelisks, cannon spouts and the relief of an unsheathed sword and scabbard under the royal crown to suggest it belongs to a new Roman Empire.

95, *p. 137*

A few sizeable BRIDGES OF THE LATER EIGHTEENTH CENTURY, mostly of an economical elegance and gently humpbacked, were put up in the region. One, the five-span Bridge of Couttie over the Isla, near Bendochy, was built in 1766 at Government expense as an improvement to the S approach from Perth and Coupar Angus to the military road up Glen Shee. Also paid for by the Government, through the Commissioners for Annexed Estates, was the bridge of four arches over the River Tummel at Kinloch Rannoch on the forfeited estate of the Jacobite Robertsons of Struan. Although military considerations may have played a part, this seems to have been erected primarily as a spur to agricultural improvement in this remote district. A desire to improve the productivity and profitability of his estate apparently lay behind the third Earl of Breadalbane's replacement of the early C17 bridge at Kenmore in 1771–4 and the construction from it of a road along the S side of Loch Tay. The new bridge by *John Baxter Jun.* has large circular openings piercing the spandrels, a practical provision to deal with flood water but one which imparted a certain distinction to the design. The inspiration for this may have come from the decorative oculi (filled with black stone) of *John Smeaton*'s Perth Bridge. This had been built in 1766–71, a very belated successor to the bridge over the Tay destroyed in 1621. Over half its cost of £26,500 was provided by the Government out of the revenues of the Commissioners of Annexed Estates, the rest raised by subscription, including £2,000 from the city of Perth and £500 from the Earl of Kinnoull who took a leading part in this project and, at the same time, built a bridge over the Earn near Forteviot, linking two parts of his estates. In 1777 another major bridge, over the Ericht at Blairgowrie, was constructed, serving routes from Perth, Dunkeld and Glen Shee into Strathmore and, *c.* 1793, public subscription paid for the four-span Kinkell Bridge over the Earn.

From 1790 acts of Parliament were passed to establish turnpike trusts in Perth and Kinross. These took responsibility for the construction or reconstruction and maintenance of major roads and their associated bridges, recouping their costs by the levying of tolls. Among the TURNPIKE ROADS were those from North Queensferry (Fife) via Kinross to Perth, from Kinross to Stirling, from Blairingone and Rumbling Bridge through Glendevon to Auchterarder, from Crieff to Perth, from Perth through the Carse of Gowrie to Dundee, and the roads through Strathmore to Coupar Angus and Blairgowrie. In 1803 Parliament established also a Commission 'for making Roads and building Bridges in the Highlands of Scotland' with power to pay for half the cost of such works, the other half to come from local landowners whose estates would profit from the improved communications. The new turnpike and Highland roads were constructed to a high standard and carried over rivers by substantial bridges. A comparison between one such new bridge (of 1816) and its predecessor (of *c.* 1713) at Rumbling Bridge demonstrates the advances made in engineering skill and availability of money during the course of a century. The earlier bridge, narrow and without parapets, is placed down in the gorge of the Devon just above the level of the river, the later and much broader spans the top of the chasm and is decorated with slits piercing the spandrels and string courses under the parapets. Grandest of these new bridges is *Thomas Telford*'s five-span ashlar-faced Dunkeld Bridge over the Tay, built in 1805–8 by the parliamentary Commissioners for Highland roads. The turrets surmounting its cutwaters make a gently martial approach to the town's new principal street which carried the main road to Inverness E of the parkland of Dunkeld House. Most elegant of the region's early C19 bridges is Dalcrue Bridge, near Pitcairngreen, designed by *W. H. Playfair* in 1832 and built by the connoisseur, Lord Lynedoch, to complement the same architect's contemporary farmhouse on the hill above, the two forming an Italianate incident on the road between Lynedoch's pleasure house of Lynedoch Cottage and his seat of Balgowan House. TOLL HOUSES were single-storey cottages. Most have been badly altered but one of *c.* 1835 at Lawers is picturesque with broad eaves and jerkin-head gables. More urbane is the early C19 toll house at Barnhill on the approach to Perth from the Carse of Gowrie, its front gable's window placed between Greek Doric columns.

After 1879 roads became the responsibility of County Road trustees and, from 1889, of the newly created county councils.

Coincidentally or not, during the next twenty years, a number of bowed truss or girder steel road bridges were erected in Perth and Kinross, e.g. at Comrie, Forteviot and Keltneyburn. The two largest (*c.* 128 m. and *c.* 113 m. long), over the Tay, both named Victoria Bridge and since replaced, were at Caputh (by *William Arrol & Co.*, 1887–8) and Perth (by *Blyth & Westland*, 1899–1900), each with lattice-girder spans carried on stone piers, the piers at Perth garbed in turreted Baronial dress. The present Caputh Bridge of 1993 continued the use of steel for its girders but these are carried on concrete piers. At Perth, the Queen's Bridge, which replaced the Victoria Bridge in 1960, is of prestressed concrete, the elliptical arches faintly reminiscent of Late Georgian bridges in the region. Similar but more powerful is the slightly earlier (1949) Aldour Bridge at Pitlochry designed by *Sir Alexander Gibb & Partners* with *Tarbolton & Ochterlony* as architectural consultants.

Central government took over the care of trunk roads after 1936 and major works on those in Perth and Kinross were carried out from the 1970s. The main road from Glasgow to Perth (A9), was made a dual carriageway for its whole length and by-passes formed round the few towns and villages on the route. The A85 E from Perth along the Carse of Gowrie to Dundee also became a dual carriageway and had its route adjusted to by-pass villages, although underpasses or bridges to carry minor roads across it have been constructed only slowly. Stretches of dual carriageway and by-passes have been formed along the A9's progress N of Perth towards Inverness. The most important of these late C20 roads is the M90 motorway from the Forth Road Bridge to Perth completed in 1980, by-passing Kinross, Milnathort, Glenfarg and Bridge of Earn. All these routes meet at the Perth by-pass built in the 1970s and 1980s round the S and W sides of the city. At the by-pass's S end and outclassing all other road structures in its length, height and sense of purpose is the Friarton Bridge of 1975–8 (by *Freeman, Fox & Partners*) which carries the M90 in a *c.* 0.8 km. long sweep over the Tay S of Perth.

Relief from the stress of travelling on the region's motorway or dual-carriageway roads can be found by walking over one of its few SUSPENSION BRIDGES. The earliest is that of *c.* 1835 over the Ericht at Glenericht House, near Bridge of Cally, the one with the most stomach-churning sway that of 1913 over the Tummel at Pitlochry, the most recent the glass-fibre bridge of 1992 at Aberfeldy Golf Course, the utilitarian purpose of each lightened by a touch of frivolity.

RAILWAYS made their first tentative appearance in Perth and Kinross in 1836–7 with the construction of the short Newtyle & Coupar Angus Railway, a branch line from the Newtyle (Angus) terminus of the Dundee & Newtyle Railway which had opened in 1831 as a communication from the farmland of Strathmore to Dundee. On both the lines, from Dundee to Newtyle and from Newtyle to Coupar Angus, the carriages were pulled by horses, assisted by a sail in favourable weather. Such railways offered little advantage over roads and, unsurprisingly, there was a pause before more were constructed. In the late 1840s, however, no fewer than four main lines, all meeting at Perth and designed for steam trains, were completed in the region. The Dundee & Perth Railway, running from Dundee through the Carse of Gowrie, was opened to Perth's E suburb of Barnhill in 1847 and, after completion of a viaduct over the Tay, to the centre of the city in 1849. A second route E of Perth, the Scottish Midland Junction Railway, was opened in 1848. Its line crossed the Tay on a viaduct at Cargill and then passed through Strathmore (incorporating the line of the Newtyle & Coupar Angus Railway) to Forfar (Angus) where it joined the Arbroath and Forfar Railway, itself linked to the main line between Aberdeen and Dundee. Also opened in 1848 were two lines from Perth to the S. The Scottish Central Railway passed through Bridge of Earn to run W through Strathearn to Auchterarder and then S through Stirling and Castlecary to join the line from Glasgow to London. The Edinburgh & Northern Railway opened a line from Perth to Ladybank (Fife) on its existing line between the ferries over the Forth and Tay at Burntisland and Tayport, the first section of the new line sharing the Scottish Central Railway's track N of Bridge of Earn. All these lines were constructed by individual companies, their directors and shareholders drawn largely from local landowners who hoped to profit from the greater ease and speed of getting agricultural produce to market and from the development of villages on their estates. The landowners' other interests sometimes influenced the path of the lines. The Dundee & Perth Railway, for example, was sited well S of the parkland of Rossie Priory, the seat of its chairman, Lord Kinnaird, although he enjoyed a branch line for horse-drawn carriages from the main line to Inchture village at the entrance to the park.

The enthusiasm and investment of landowners remained strong during the next development of the railway system in the 1850s and 1860s. In 1856 was opened the Perth & Dunkeld Railway's line from Perth to Birnam, its route much influenced by the wishes of Sir William Drummond Stewart of Grandtully, owner of the Murthly Castle estate. The line was extended (as the Inverness & Perth Junction Railway) N to Inverness in 1863. 1856 was also the year in which opened the Crieff Junction Railway, a branch from the Scottish Central Railway's Crieff Junction (now Gleneagles) Station, near Auchterarder, N to Muthill and Crieff, much of the route through land belonging to Lady Willoughby de Eresby, proprietor of Drummond Castle. Two years later a line (the Perth, Almond Valley & Methven Railway) was constructed from Perth W to Methven and was extended to Crieff by the Crieff & Methven Junction Railway in 1866. In the E of Kinross-shire in 1858–60, two originally separate companies, the Kinross-shire and the Fife & Kinross Railways, formed a loop line which curved NE from Cowdenbeath (Fife) on the main line of the Edinburgh, Perth & Dundee Railway and ran through Kinross and Milnathort back to the main line at Ladybank. In 1863 the Devon Valley Railway opened a line W from Kinross to Rumbling Bridge and, in 1871, extended it through Clackmannanshire to join the line from Tillicoultry to Alloa, the junction with the line from Dunfermline to Stirling.

Two important developments of the railway network affected the region in the 1890s. Associated with construction of the Forth Railway Bridge in 1883–90 was the upgrading of the main line from Edinburgh to Perth and Inverness which included the opening of a shorter route from Milnathort to Bridge of Earn through Glen Farg in 1890. A line from Tyndrum (Stirling and Central Scotland) to Fort William (Highland and Islands) which crossed the W tip of Perth and Kinross was opened in 1894, together with the solitary Rannoch Station standing in the wilderness of Rannoch Moor.

Several branch lines were formed in the later C19 and first decade of the C20. The earliest, apart from the short branch to Inchture village, were those opened from Coupar Angus to Blairgowrie in 1855 and from Alyth Junction on the Scottish Midland Junction Railway to Alyth in 1861. The promoters of these may have hoped that their N termini would become part of a line W to Birnam or of one N to Braemar and Deeside. Another branch line which perhaps aimed to be part of a greater network was the Aberfeldy Branch Railway, opened in 1865, which ran on the S side of the Tay W from Ballinluig on the Perth–Inverness main line to Grandtully and Aberfeldy. Its possible W continuation to Kenmore and, beside Loch Tay, to Killin (Stirling and Central Scotland) on the main line from Glasgow to Oban was no more than a vision, although there was a regular passenger service by horse-drawn coaches from Aberfeldy to Kenmore and thence by a steamboat on Loch Tay to Killin. A later attempt to link Perth to the railways to the W Highlands was made with construction of a line W from Crieff. The Crieff & Comrie Railway was opened in 1893 and the line extended in 1903–5, as the Comrie, St Fillans & Lochearnhead Railway, along the N shore of Loch Earn to Lochearnhead and Balquhidder (Stirling and Central Scotland) where it formed a junction with the main line to Oban and Fort William, although lack of co-operation between railway companies forced passengers to wait there for many hours to board an ongoing train. Least ambitious of the region's branch lines was the short one which ran from Luncarty on the Perth–Inverness main line to Bankfoot. Opened in 1906, it closed to passenger traffic twenty-five years later.

Between 1950 and 1971 many other railway lines in Perth and Kinross were closed. The only survivors are the lines crossing Rannoch Moor and those from Ladybank to Perth (reopened in the 1970s after the more direct line from Milnathort had been taken over by the M90), from Stirling and Auchterarder to Perth, from Dundee to Perth, and from Perth to Inverness. VIADUCTS along both closed and open lines still stand. Although generally engineers tried to lay out railway routes with as few road and river crossings as possible, some were unavoidable and the branch line from Ballinluig to Aberfeldy crossed forty-one bridges, mostly small but including three-span viaducts over the

Tummel and the Tay. A couple of the earlier viaducts were partly or largely of timber construction. The Dundee & Perth Railway's viaduct, built over the Tay at Perth in 1848–9, was wholly of wood except for one section where stone piers supported an iron swing bridge of *c.* 15m. span. The Scottish Midland Junction Railway's contemporary viaduct further upstream at Cargill had stone piers but, until replaced with steel girder beams *c.* 1890, a wooden deck. Massive and consciously architectural viaducts were designed by *Joseph Mitchell* and built in 1861–3 by the Inverness & Perth Junction Railway over the Braan at Inver and the Garry at Struan, both of hammer-dressed masonry, one with battlemented turrets, the other with bartizans, the Braan viaduct displaying the heraldic achievement of the Duke of Atholl on whose land it stood. Bull-nosed masonry, perhaps chosen to give a reassuring impression of structural strength, was used by *William R. Galbraith* for the viaducts on the line formed through Glen Farg in 1887–90 but the soffits of their round-headed arches are faced with brick. The viaduct of 1862–4 with which *Blyth & Westland* replaced the earlier viaduct over the Tay at Perth is disappointing, an unambitious edifice of wrought-iron girders carried on stone piers and with stone flood arches at the ends. More ornamental is *J. Mitchell & Co.*'s contemporary viaduct over the Tay at Logierait, all except the abutments of iron, the spans supported on decoratively detailed piers and columns.

RAILWAY STATIONS provided shelter for passengers and housing for railway company offices and employees. The earliest and largest is the polite Perth Railway Station designed by *William Tite* in 1847, a long and low Tudor building, its battlemented end tower failing to provide excitement for the traveller. The small piend-roofed former station building of 1848 at Denmarkfield, near Luncarty, is wholly domestic. More consciously picturesque is *A. & A. Heiton*'s Dunkeld and Birnam Railway Station of 1856 at Birnam. This is a sizeable Tudor cottage with mullioned and transomed windows and bargeboarded gables. The platform's decoratively treated canopy is a happy replacement of 1863. Rather in the same manner but with crowstepped gables to proclaim its nationality is the Pitlochry station of 1882. By contrast, English picturesque was the manner adopted for the stations at Rannoch Station (by *James Miller*, 1894) and St Fillans of 1901, the walls of the first of wood with half-timbering, the other also with half-timbering but applied to walls of brick and harl and its roofs covered with red tiles. A promise of comfortable sporting holidays for the well-heeled is given by Gleneagles Railway Station, near Auchterarder, designed in 1919 by *James Miller* to serve the Caledonian Railway Co.'s huge resort hotel. The wood and glass waiting rooms are dignified with some English Baroque detail, the station-master's house and booking office dressed in welcoming Scottish costume. Some late Victorian FOOTBRIDGES have survived, such as the lattice-sided examples at Birnam and Rannoch Station. At Perth, the footbridges supplied by the *Sun Foundry* in 1884–6 enjoy Gothic balustrades.

HARBOURS in the region existed only along the lower Tay. By the late C18 there were small quays and piers at Inchture and Inchyra, near St Madoes, for the shipment of agricultural produce from the Carse of Gowrie. Probably slightly later were the quay and pier at Kingoodie, near Invergowrie, constructed for the transport of stone from the adjacent quarries. Perth itself, well-sheltered at the head of the Tay estuary, is a port of long standing. Its first harbour, probably formed by the C12, was along Watergate between the E ends of High Street and South Street. Later, its position was shifted S to beside Greyfriars Cemetery just S of the old city walls. In 1752 a new harbour was constructed still further S. This was reconstructed early in the C19, when it acquired a wooden steamboat jetty, and remodelled in 1840–1 by *Robert Stevenson & Sons*. They formed a masonry-walled tidal basin although their proposals for construction of a wet dock linked to the basin by a canal were not carried out. The need for these harbours was largely lost with the development of the region's railway system from the late 1840s. What remains of them fails to evoke delight.

BURGHS AND VILLAGES

Still predominantly rural in character, Perth and Kinross contains only one major urban conurbation, that of Perth itself. None of its other burghs can claim to be more than a market town or tourist centre, although large housing developments, often as dormitories for those working outside the region, now encircle them.

Burghs and Villages Before the Later Eighteenth Century

From the C12 until the end of the C17 the right to engage in foreign trade was monopolized by merchants in royal BURGHS (under the direct overlordship of the Crown) and most domestic commerce could take place only in royal burghs or in burghs of regality or barony (under the overlordship of ecclesiastical or secular lords).* The practice of most crafts was restricted to inhabitants of burghs. Perth was a royal burgh by the early C12, as was Auchterarder by 1246 although it later lost burgh status. Dunkeld and Abernethy, both ecclesiastical centres of some antiquity, were made burghs of barony in the late Middle Ages, as were Alyth *c.* 1455, Dunning in 1511 and Kinross in 1541, followed in the C17 by Coupar Angus, Meigle, Crook of Devon, Blairgowrie, Crieff and Longforgan. Most of these, however, were never more than sizeable villages.

The medieval burgh of Perth was surrounded by a town wall and moat, the River Tay on the E serving as both defence and

---

*The distinction was one of nomenclature. In the case of a burgh of barony its feudal superior held his lands from the Crown as a barony, in the case of a burgh of regality the feudal superior held his lands as a regality.

harbour. Inside the wall, the town was laid out, probably in the C12, with two broad E–W streets (High Street and South Street). Extending backwards from these were strips of lands, each intended originally to accommodate the house, workshop and garden of one burgess family. Narrow lanes or vennels connected the main streets. Between them, in the centre of the town, was the burgh's St John's Kirk with a marketplace to its W. Burghs of barony and large villages with the right to hold fairs seem also generally to have had a central 'square' as a focus for trade. Irregularly shaped marketplaces survive at Sandport in Kinross, Tron Square in Dunning and the spaces known as The Cross at Abernethy, Coupar Angus and Errol. When Dunkeld was rebuilt after 1689 the line of the main street (High Street and Cathedral Street) was moved to the W but its central broadening to form The Cross may reproduce the medieval pattern. When Crieff, a burgh which had been 'burned to the last house' in 1716, was created anew from the 1730s, a marketplace (James Square) was formed at the centre of the High Street.

VILLAGES, distinct from small ferm touns of perhaps fifteen or twenty houses, were rare before the late C18. Those which did exist were populated by tradesmen, such as smiths, serving the surrounding area or home-workers such as handloom weavers. Generally, their buildings seem to have clustered around a parish church.

MARKET CROSSES were symbols of burgh status, although some were erected also at villages which had been granted the right to hold trade fairs on stated days each year. By far the grandest in Perth and Kinross, as befitted the only royal burgh, was the 'cross' (a replacement for an earlier one) put up at Perth in 1668–9 by *Robert Mylne*, Master Mason to the Scottish Crown. Like the early C17 market crosses of Edinburgh and Preston (Lothian), it consisted of a round building whose flat roof served as a platform from which could be read public proclamations and on which stood a shaft carved with the royal arms and those of the city.* An impediment to wheeled traffic, it was demolished in 1765 but its general appearance was reproduced in the city's King Edward VII Memorial (by *Alexander K. Beaton*) of 1913. Other market crosses in the region are variously finialled shafts standing on one or more steps. The earliest, perhaps late medieval, may be that of the former village of Old Scone in the grounds of Scone Palace, the finial of its octagonal shaft carved with a rosette. The finial at Kinross, perhaps of the earlier C16, is, unusually, a roughly shaped cross. Another crude cross finial is at Meikleour. This market cross, dated 1698, bears the same mason's mark as the similarly ungainly example erected at Kinrossie twelve years before, with four finger-like protuberances extending in a saltire arrangement from its rounded head. Hardly more sophisticated is the monolithic market cross at Alyth, its

---

*Perth has long been regarded by its inhabitants and most outsiders as a city although this title has not been recognized officially by Government bureaucrats.

octagonal head carved with a lion rampant (the royal arms) and the initials of James, Earl of Airlie, superior of the burgh, together with the date 1670. Another lion rampant but perhaps in allusion to the coat-of-arms of the Earls of Strathmore, the feudal superiors, appears as a finial on the Corinthian column erected in the late C17 at Longforgan. Corinthian columns were used also as the shafts of two crosses of the earlier C18, the Dalguise Pillar (now in the John Kinnaird Hall at Birnam) and the cross at Rossie Priory, one surmounted by a block carved with reliefs of dragons and a sphinx and bearing a heraldic unicorn as finial, the other with a ball finial supported by lions and unicorns.

TOLBOOTHS, buildings to store the tolls levied on traders and used also for meetings of burgh officials and as courthouses, must have existed in some form in all burghs. Probably, few were of much architectural significance. At Perth, however, the medieval St Mary's Chapel, notable for its tower, was converted to the city's tolbooth (demolished) after the Reformation and a sizeable new building was added beside it in 1693–6. A tolbooth tower (since demolished) was erected at Crieff in 1685 and the rather plain Tolbooth Steeple at Coupar Angus in 1762.

Tolbooths housed the burgh courts. Outside the burghs, courts with local jurisdiction were often held in the halls of lairds' houses. In the district of Atholl, however, regalian jurisdiction over all criminal cases except high treason was vested in the Earls (later, Dukes) of Atholl until 1747. This regality's court house, built at Logierait in 1707 and demolished later in the C18, contained a hall over 21 m. long with a gallery at each end. Outside the regalities and generally after 1747, Commissioners of Supply for each county were responsible for the provision of sheriff court houses and prisons. In 1771 the County House containing a courtroom and prison was put up at Kinross, distinguished from an ordinary tenement by its bowed end's giant Tuscan pilasters, niches and entablature, these embellishments paid for and and presumably designed by *Robert Adam* who sat as M.P. for Kinross-shire as well as heading the leading architectural practice of his day. Of rather similar character were the MEETING PLACES OF THE GUILD AND TRADE INCORPORATIONS of merchants and craftsmen in Perth. The hall of the Wrights' Incorporation, built in Watergate in 1725, survives, a three-storey and attic block with a broken-pedimented doorpiece at its ten-bay front. The Guildhall, the meeting place of the pre-eminent Merchants' Guild, built in High Street in 1722, was demolished in 1906.

A handful of ALMSHOUSES existed in burghs. St George's Hospital at Dunkeld was founded by Bishop George Brown in 1510 to house seven poor men and a master and *c.* 1585 James VI provided an endowment for support of the poor of Perth. The C16 St George's Hospital was destroyed with almost all of Dunkeld in 1715 but a substantial three-storey replacement (now The Ell House) was built in 1753. Very much larger was the King James VI Hospital at Perth, its erection in 1748–52 funded partly by the C16 royal endowment and partly by public subscription. This almshouse is a four-storey H, with pedimented centres at the principal elevations, an aedicular Roman Doric doorpiece and a central cupola surmounting the roof.

SCHOOLS, formally attached to religious houses or taught by parish priests or noblemens' chaplains, existed before the Reformation. From the later C16 the reformed Church and Scottish parliaments tried to establish an educational system with a school or schools in each parish. By the beginning of the C18 this had been largely achieved, payment of the schoolmaster's salary and his accommodation the legal responsibility of heritors aided by the charging of fees. School buildings were often primitive, sometimes containing a single room to serve as both the schoolroom and the schoolmaster's dwelling. At Caputh in 1724 the heritors agreed to build a new school with a thatched roof, the cost limit set at £3 4s. 0d. sterling. The school provided at Abernyte in 1737 was thatch-roofed and *c.* 12 m. long internally. It cost £2. More extravagant were the heritors of Logierait who, in 1733, spent *c.* £11 on repairs to the existing schoolroom and the erection of a new one-room schoolhouse. This was *c.* 9.8 m. by 3.7 m. but only 1.8 m. high, its dimensions very similar to those of the single-room dwelling which originally occupied the w half of the C18 longhouse at Nether Camserney, near Dull (*see* pp. 124, 327–8). Presumably, it served as kitchen, living and sleeping quarters for the master and his family.

A few parish LIBRARIES were formed in the C17 and C18 but almost all were small collections of books in the care of the minister or schoolmaster. An exceptionally large collection was held at Innerpeffray where a library was founded in the C17 by the third Lord Madderty and much augmented in the C18 by Robert Hay, Bishop of St Asaph (later, Archbishop of York), his successor as owner of the Innerpeffray estate. In 1758–62 Bishop Hay put up a two-storey U-plan building to house the library, with a school on the ground floor. Designed by *Charles Freebairn*, this is decidedly a public building but one which eschews pomposity, the reading room lit by a large Venetian window.

Hardly any DOMESTIC BUILDINGS earlier than the C18 survive in the towns and villages of Perth and Kinross. Perth's great C16 and C17 town houses built in Watergate for local magnates (the Earls of Atholl, Gowrie and Kinnoull and the Bishop of Dunkeld) were mostly removed in the C18. The largest, Gowrie House (not demolished until the beginning of the C19), was built round two sides of a courtyard and had a garden going down to the River Tay. The C16 and C17 houses of merchants and the richer craftsmen seem to have been of two or three storeys, constructed of stone but often with wooden galleries cantilevered out for *c.* 2 m. from the front walls. Some idea of the appearance of a Perth house of the early C17, although without galleries, can probably be got from the 1890s rebuilding (a rather free reconstruction) of the Fair Maid of Perth's House in North Port. A stair-tower projects towards the street at one end of the front. A similar stair projection (now at the back but entered originally from the street before its line was changed *c.* 1690) is found at The Old Rectory in Dunkeld, a much altered house dating probably from *c.* 1600. Here the entrance was at an intermediate level between the present basement (the original kitchen) and the ground floor. In Perth, too, the lowest floors of C16 and C17 buildings are reported to have been often a little below street level. By the 1760s the Perth city council insisted that, in any rebuilding of houses, galleries were to be replaced by stone fronts. In 1781 the council outlawed the use of thatch for roofing or re-roofing of houses and stipulated the use only of tiles or slates. A similar insistence on the use of slate for the roofing of new houses in Dunkeld ('not only ane advantage to the proprietors thereof, But allso a beutifying of the place') had been made by that burgh's superior, the first Duke of Atholl, in 1716. These houses in Perth and Dunkeld, as in other burghs and villages, formed terraces but of small-scale and informal design. At Dunkeld in the C18, only a pair of three-storey blocks on the W side of The Cross, the marketplace, broke the two-storey norm of High Street and Cathedral Street. The interior of The Old Rectory, however, with mid-C18 panelling in the principal rooms and a tendrilly display of plasterwork over the stair, is exceptionally well finished, perhaps by tradesmen employed on the reconstruction of Blair Castle.

The Later Eighteenth Century to the 1830s

From the later C18 Perth and other burghs expanded in fairly orderly fashion. New SUBURBS began to be laid out on the W side of Perth from *c.* 1760. After the opening of Perth Bridge over the Tay in 1771, a broad N–S thoroughfare (George Street and St John Street) was pushed through the E edge of the medieval town and 'New Towns' begun to the N and S. At about the same time Crieff expanded on a grid-iron pattern. Grid-iron 'New Towns' were also formed beside other burghs at the end of the C18, as at Alyth, where land S of the Alyth Burn was laid out for the town's expansion in 1786, or Blairgowrie, which developed on a regular street pattern S of the original settlement beside the parish church after 1790. Similar planned developments but with unified elevational designs were begun at Dunkeld and the intended spa of Bridge of Earn in the 1820s.

PLANNED VILLAGES were also founded in the later C18 and the beginning of the C19, usually intended to attract tradesmen and industrial workers. Many of these inhabitants were hand-loom weavers, generally working at home, but some were employed in textile-spinning mills. Most villages consisted of no more than a single street, exceptionally long and sinuous at Muthill, or were built round a roughly oblong green or square, e.g. Moulin (now part of Pitlochry), Kinloch Rannoch, Kenmore, Pitcairngreen or Spittalfield. Exceptionally large for a late C18 village but housing the workforce of the region's largest cotton mill was Stanley, laid out in 1785 by *James Stobie* on a grid-iron plan occupying level ground above the mills.

Late Georgian urban expansion was accompanied by the erection of some consciously grand PUBLIC BUILDINGS. At Kinross, a new sheriff court house (the County Buildings) was built in 1824–6. Robert Adam's nephew, William Adam of Blair Adam, was Preses (Convenor) of the Commissioners of Supply and instrumental in the choice of *Thomas Brown* of Uphall as architect for the work. This heavy but dignified classical edifice, standing a little aloof from the street, contained a courtroom, witnesses' room, two rooms for the Sheriff Clerk, a records room, three rooms for the detention of debtors, two prison cells and a guardroom and cost *c*. £2,000. Very much larger and costing more than ten times as much were the Perth County Buildings (now Perth Sheriff Court) erected beside the River Tay in 1816–19, a worthy but unexciting example of *Robert Smirke*'s Greek Revivalism. The entrance in the Doric temple centrepiece opens onto a two-storey hall behind which was placed the semi-circular Justiciary Courtroom in which presided a judge of the High Court when on circuit. N of the hall was a pair of sheriff courtrooms and, behind the building and joined to it by an undergound passage, was a prison with two cell blocks and a governor's house. But the Commissioners of Supply for Perthshire, prominent landowners of the county, had not contented themselves with edifying a simple palace of justice for, S of the central hall, they had placed a double-height assembly or ball room of *c*. 21 m. by 12 m., a committee room *c*. 9 m. square and, on the first floor, a tea or card room of *c*. 13.5 m. by 9 m., all elegantly decorated and hung with portraits of leading figures of the shire.

THEATRES AND MUSEUMS also served the social and intellectual needs of the well-heeled inhabitants (lairds, army and naval officers, merchants and their families and widows) of Perth's new suburbs. The Theatre Royal was opened in 1820. Unfortunately, according to David Peacock's description in 1849, 'while it is too small for its purpose when the leading dramatic *stars* visit us, it is too large for the ordinary run of business.' That the city's inhabitants could rise above frivolity is shown by the Perth Museum and Art Gallery, built in 1822–4 as a monument to the city's historian and former Lord Provost, Thomas Hay Marshall, and to house the library and collection of the Perth Literary and Antiquarian Society. The Society's Secretary, *David Morison*, prepared the design. Inspired by the Pantheon, this is a domed rotunda but with its E segment sliced across to form a straight side framed by a giant Ionic portico. Some of the building's vertical dominance was lost in 1931–5 when *Smart, Stewart & Mitchell* added a large S extension.

INNS had existed by the beginning of the C18, e.g. the Losset Inn at Alyth and the inn at Inver beside the ferry crossing over the River Tay, both unpretentious two-storey buildings. However, in 1773 construction of a new bridge over the Tay at Kenmore was accompanied by the erection of the substantial Kenmore Hotel of three storeys with a five-bay front, and the turnpike roads formed from the late C18 were bordered by new and more comfortable hostelries. Roughly contemporary with the early C19 bridge over the River Devon at Rumbling Bridge is the adjacent coaching inn. Another coaching inn associated with a bridge is the tall block of the Weem Hotel of *c.* 1800. More picturesque are some roadside inns of the earlier C19. The Loch Tummel Inn at Strathtummel is gabled and gableted, with horizontal window panes and a tree-trunk porch. The broad-eaved Meikleour Hotel, built in 1819–21, has hoodmoulded attic windows above a veranda. Also hoodmoulded is the entrance to the bay-windowed and bargeboarded Inchture Hotel.

The late C18 and early C19 'New Towns' laid out at Perth and Dunkeld after their bridges over the Tay had been opened in 1771 and 1808 included large HOTELS. At Perth in 1798, the Royal George Hotel in the newly formed George Street contained over fifty bedrooms, two coachhouses and stabling for fifty-one horses round a 70m.-long yard. Two hotels were prominent in the redevelopment of that city's medieval South Street. In 1824–5 the site of the former Grammar School (Nos. 29–37 South Street) was filled by the City Hotel, the pedimented centre of its front quietly asserting that this was something of a public building. More blatant in its self-advertisement is the Salutation Hotel of *c.* 1800, the principal portion of the façade treated as a triumphal arch, its first floor's centre filled by a huge three-light window under a segmental-arched fanlight. In Dunkeld, Bridge Street and Atholl Street, laid out along the new line of the road from Perth to Inverness, contain a pair of big Late Georgian hotels. The Atholl Arms, by *W. M. Mackenzie*, dominates the SE corner of Bridge Street overlooking the bridge. The Royal Dunkeld Hotel forms part of a terrace but its central part soars two storeys above the houses. An exuberant competitor to these rather stolid hostelries was created in the 1830s and 1840s with the development of the Birnam (now Birnam House) Hotel on the opposite side of the Tay. Built in stages, it became a massive edifice formed from the mating of an overweight *cottage orné* with a Baronial adventurer. By 1836 this hotel boasted several bathrooms and, by then or soon after, its principal public room was 'a splendid HALL, finished in the most gorgeous style'. These hotels provided the setting for dances and other social gatherings. Less formal meetings could take place in COFFEE HOUSES – the Exchange Coffee Room in George Street, Perth, was built in 1836, its polished frontage, designed by *W. M. Mackenzie*, incised with Soanean ornament.

Parish SCHOOLS and SCHOOLHOUSES became more comfortable from the end of the C18. Probably not much larger than earlier examples were those put up at Coupar Angus in 1792 and Kirkmichael in 1813, each with a schoolroom and master's house, the house at Coupar Angus containing one room and a kitchen, that at Kirkmichael two rooms.

However, two-storey buildings, the schoolroom occupying one floor, the schoolhouse the other, were put up at Blairgowrie in 1772, at Logierait in 1806–7 and at Arngask in 1811–12, the cost (*c.* £180–£190) of those at Logierait and Arngask comparable to that of a new farmhouse of the time. The fashion for two-storey parish schools was short-lived. In 1825–6 the upper floor of Arngask School was removed, the remodelled building being used hereafter only as a schoolroom, and a new schoolhouse added at one end. By then, a general type of school had been established. It consisted of a single-storey schoolroom and adjoining schoolhouse, often of two storeys, the walls all built of lime-mortared stone and the roofs covered with blue slate. Pleasant but unpretentious examples of the type, dating from the 1830s, survive at Comrie and Cleish, the Comrie schoolhouse (now Ruchearn) with a pilastered doorpiece, the Cleish school with a ball-and-spike finial on one gable. A quite different expression of educational and architectural ambition is given by the Public Seminaries put up as the centrepiece of Rose Terrace in Perth in 1803–7 to house two institutions, the Perth Grammar School, which claimed a medieval origin, and the Perth Academy, founded in 1760 and proud of its teaching of the classics. Designed by *Robert Reid*, it is a smooth exercise in Robert Adam's classical manner, with three-light windows under fanlights and, at the centre, an order of attached Roman Doric columns. The principal room of the Perth Academy's quarters was an octagon, its domed ceiling enriched with plasterwork like an open umbrella.

From the end of the C18 TENEMENTS AND HOUSES in towns and villages were almost all built with stone walls. Slate had become the common roofing material but pantiles were also used in some areas and survive on houses in a few villages, e.g. Blairingone, Keltybridge and Scotlandwell. Thatch had been generally abandoned as a covering but the roofs of some cottages, probably of the early C19, seem always to have been thatched with reeds, a much more durable material than straw or broom.

Modest TERRACED HOUSING of the late C18 and earlier C19 characterizes such villages and small burghs as Abernethy, Errol and Comrie. Hardly more ambitious, although given a more strongly urban air by their parade of ground-floor shops are the Late Georgian or Georgian survival tenement terraces in the main streets of Auchterarder, Blairgowrie and Crieff. Although of fairly standard height and appearance, these were built piecemeal, not attempting real unity of design, far less to be palace fronts.

Not surprisingly, the grandest terraced housing is found in Perth itself. On the N side of Charlotte Street is a short terrace built in 1786–9, the back windows looking over the parkland of the North Inch. Each house is individually designed, Nos. 1 and 3 with giant pilasters at the corners and columned doorpieces. On the street's S side stands a three- and four-storey tenement terrace of the early C19, the block of Nos. 2–8 with a pedimented and Venetian-windowed projection breaking forward from the E gable, Nos. 10–18 with channelled and rusticated stonework at the two lower floors and channelled pilaster strips at the ends and centre of the front. The L-plan tenement of Charlotte House (No. 20) was designed in 1830 by *W. M. Mackenzie*, the front block's bowed end with ground-floor shop windows framed by attached Greek Doric columns. At the S wing, the entrances to the upper floors' flats are also columned. Late Georgian tenements of three and four storeys line the N end of St John Street, two of the fifteen bays of the front of Nos. 25–37 marked off by anta-pilasters and containing three-light windows. The block at Nos. 26–30 is of only three bays but all its first- and second-floor windows are Venetian.

Terraced housing of unified elevational design appeared at the end of the C18 and in the early C19. The smartest is again in Perth where Atholl Crescent and Atholl Place, looking over the North Inch, were built in the 1790s: the houses of Atholl Crescent form a concave palace front articulated by giant pilasters, the centrepiece pedimented. Also beside the North Inch is the larger palace-fronted terrace built from *c*. 1800 in Rose Terrace, its houses' round-headed ground-floor window overarches and fanlit entrances set in rusticated masonry, the Adamish centrepiece provided by the Public Seminaries. On the s edge of the city centre, beside the South Inch, are the palace-fronted terraces of Marshall Place designed by *Robert Reid* in 1805, each with a three-storey centrepiece and end pavilions linked by long two-storey sections. The debt to Robert Adam is evident although the detail lacks his lightness of touch. In the following year *Robert Reid* prepared a very grand scheme for the 'New Town' of Dunkeld which included a square surrounded by three-storey terraces, their ends treated as pyramidal-roofed pavilions, the concept a much simplified version of Adam's Charlotte Square in Edinburgh. This proved over-ambitious and, from 1827, Bridge Street and Atholl Street in Dunkeld were developed with simply detailed terraced housing and two sizeable hotels, two of the terraces with moulded architraves to the first-floor windows, the elevations following or adapted from designs by *W. M. Mackenzie*. These were similar to those provided by *William Burn* in 1823 for terraces at Bridge of Earn where one was built in Main Street, quite plain but with slightly advanced and taller parapeted end blocks.

Late Georgian expansion of towns saw the advent of SUBURBAN VILLAS. At Bridgend (Perth), the tall Inchbank House of *c*. 1790 has giant Roman Doric pilasters at the ends and, at the centre, a console-corniced doorpiece, its frieze prettily enriched, and a Venetian-windowed attic gablet. Blackfriars House in Perth's North Port is a substantial late C18 house, the three-storey main block, with a pilastered doorpiece under a corniced window, flanked by lower pavilions, one with a bowed end. In nearby Barossa Place, the ground floor of the early C19 No. 7 is crossed by a Roman Doric pilastrade and the huge fanlight over its door filled with the most elaborately patterned glazing. On the edge of Muthill is Dalliotfield of *c*. 1830, its front's slightly advanced and gabled centre containing a pilastered doorpiece and, high up, an oval plaque. In the windows is horizontal-paned glazing. Tulach of 1832, in Kirk Wynd, Blairgowrie, is also piend-roofed, with a Roman Doric portico to the front and pediments at the sides.

Victorian and Edwardian Burghs and Villages

The Municipal Reform Act of 1833 provided for the election of town councils in royal and 'parliamentary' burghs. Perth, the only such burgh in the region, thus acquired responsibility for a number of public services. From 1850 'populous places', defined as having populations of over 1,200, could become 'police burghs' with councils responsible, as were those in existing royal burghs, for policing and fire services, lighting, paving, drainage and sewerage. Blairgowrie and Crieff assumed 'police' powers soon after 1850 and three new 'police' burghs were erected later in the C19: Alyth in 1875, Aberfeldy in 1887 and Auchterarder (a medieval royal burgh which had lost that status in the C17) in 1894. Their new burgh status did not mean that these towns were big. Of the three largest, Blairgowrie and Crieff had populations of about 4,000 and Perth itself no more than about 30,000 by the end of the C19.

Purpose-built COUNCIL OFFICES of this period are few. In 1850 Crieff's crowstep-gabled Town Hall was built on the site of its C17 tolbooth (demolished in 1842) and has a pyramidal-roofed tower in reminiscence. Perth's C17 tolbooth, a conversion and extension of the medieval St Mary's Chapel, was replaced in 1878–9 by *Andrew Heiton Jun.*'s Old Council Chambers, Flemish Gothic in style but with the design of the tower at the High Street front derived from that of the chapel. Alyth, however, eschewed tolbooth references in 1886 when it erected an overblown villa (by *Heiton & Grainger*) to serve as its town hall. Victorian and Edwardian PUBLIC HALLS for meetings or concerts are more prominent. A City Hall (demolished in 1877) was built at Perth to *W. M. Mackenzie*'s design in 1844. The top-lit main hall, c. 30 m. by 20 m., was much larger than Smirke's County Hall in the County Buildings. Although intended for serious meetings rather than balls, it was not without grandeur. The ceiling's richly modelled plasterwork was painted and gilded. Elaborately carved capitals surmounted the sixteen supporting columns to which were attached gas lights, making them 'look like as many magnificent candelabra'. A more economical town hall built in the centre of Kinross in 1837 was rebuilt in 1868–9. It abuts the steeple of the demolished Parish Church of 1751, the two combining to suggest a tolbooth. Also of tolbooth inspiration is the Milnathort Town Hall of 1853–5 whose C17-style steeple and dominant central position indicate that village's desire to be thought a burgh. Perhaps in anticipation of regaining burgh status, Auchterarder acquired the Aytoun Hall in 1870–2, its street front with Venetian Gothic detail and a dominant clock tower. This was designed by *Charles S. Robertson* who, in 1883, was responsible also for the free Jacobean Birnam Institute. Coupar Angus chose a French municipal manner for its Town Hall (by *David Smart*) erected to celebrate Queen Victoria's Golden Jubilee of 1887. The small Town Hall at Pitlochry (by *Alexander Ness*, 1898–1900) is Jacobean, an ogee-roofed tower covering the join of its elaborately detailed front block to the plain hall behind. Free of historicist references is the low and harled Aberfeldy Town Hall of

1889–91, by *J. M. MacLaren*, its bargeboarded front gable's loggia influenced by contemporary American work. Single-mindedly a hall, undistracted by other functions, is the huge Beaux-Arts classical Perth City Hall, designed in 1908 by *H. E. Clifford & Lunan*, a chilling authoritarian presence in the heart of the city. The same city's Guildhall of 1722 was replaced in 1906–8 by *A. G. Heiton*'s Burnetian Baroque essay embellished with sculpture emblematic of Industry and Commerce supporting the city's coat-of-arms under the Scottish crown.

Most VILLAGE HALLS date from the early C20, sometimes paid for by families that had recently established themselves as local landowners. Glenfarg, a new village developed from 1890 beside the railway, was given the Corbett Institute (now Arngask Library) in 1892. Designed by *A. N. Paterson*, this is Scots Renaissance on a domestic scale but with touches of expensive carving and a cupola. Also Scots Jacobean and with a bowed tower over the entrance is *J. Macintyre Henry*'s Village Hall at Blair Atholl of 1906–7. Such extravagance, however, is rare and village halls were often simple harled buildings, perhaps enlivened by bargeboards, as at Caputh (by *Ebenezer Simpson*, 1909) or Balbeggie (by *G. P. K. Young*, 1910–11), the Caputh Hall with an Art Nouveau ventilator, or with touches of half-timbering like *G. P. K. Young*'s Public Hall and Institute of 1908 at Bridge of Earn.

After 1854 burghs were empowered to finance public LIBRARIES from the rates but were slow to do so. It was not until 1898 that the Sandeman Public Library was opened in Perth. By *Campbell Douglas & Morrison*, it is a classically detailed but asymmetrically composed red sandstone edifice with a small corner turret. Serving a much smaller population is the dumpy Kinross Public Library, designed by *Peter L. Henderson* in 1904, with crow-stepped gables and a battlemented tower. Smaller still is the library built in 1884–5 in The Square at Kenmore. Fish-scale red tiling and tree-trunk verandas make it a picturesque presence on the approach to the W gateway into the park of Taymouth Castle. Other late Victorian and Edwardian libraries form part of town or village institutes or public halls.

PUBLIC BATHS were provided by the Victorians so that the urban poor could wash themselves and their clothes. At Perth, baths and washhouses were built in Mill Street in 1846, a very early example of such a facility, and Canal Street in 1902. Municipal SWIMMING POOLS were first provided at Perth in 1889 (since demolished), an acknowledgement that immersion in water might be enjoyable as well as hygienic. Surprisingly lacking enjoyment is the Perth theatre in High Street, built in 1898–1900. Fronted by a gruesomely plain tenement, part of the same development designed by *William Alexander*, it is quite without drama, although the interior is appropriately plush.

One Victorian public institution of national importance in the region was the PRISON at Perth. This had begun as Scotland's principal prison for French prisoners-of-war, a grouping of barracks blocks surrounded by the defences of a Georgian fort but with the guns trained in rather than out, designed by *Robert Reid* and built in 1811–12. It was taken over in 1839 by the General Board of Directors of Prisons in Scotland for erection of a General Prison for Scotland to house all convicts serving sentences of nine months or more. This General Prison, designed by *Thomas Brown Jun.*, was built in 1840–2 and replaced Reid's prisoner-of-war barracks with cell blocks (originally two, the number increased to four in 1852–9) radiating from a semicircular observation corridor which allowed warders to monitor activity in the galleried atrium of each block, a pioneering example of the prison planning which afterwards became general in Britain. The convicts were kept in solitary confinement, unable to distract each other from self-reflection and rehabilitation. Three of the cell blocks are still in use but the 'separate' system of solitary confinement was abandoned in the C20 and communal facilities provided. Rehabilitation of the inmates remains a professed aim of the Scottish Prisons Service.

County police forces were established in the 1850s and POLICE STATIONS built in some towns and villages. At Perth, *David Smart*'s Italianate Classical new County Buildings of 1864 contained the county's police headquarters as well as an office for the Procurator Fiscal. Premises solely for police occupation, designed by *A. G. Heiton*, were put up in Tay Street in 1895–6. Also of 1864, by *James C. Walker*, is Pitlochry's polite Georgian survival police station. More authoritarian is *David Smart*'s police station built at Crieff in 1898–1900.

After a Government postal service was set up in 1808 some specially designed POST OFFICES were built but the few significant examples in Perth and Kinross date from the later C19 or early C20. *Robert Matheson* of *H. M. Office of Works* at Edinburgh designed Perth's Italianate General Post Office on High Street's corner with Tay Street in 1866. Matheson's successor, *W. W. Robertson*, produced a free Renaissance replacement on another High Street site in 1897–8. Both have been demolished and the city's principal post office now appears a shop rather than a public building. The post office of 1897 at Aberfeldy, by the local architect, *William Bell*, has carved bargeboards to fit in with this decorous Victorian holiday resort. More obviously a representative of bureaucracy and designed by *H. M. Office of Works* in 1906 is the Scots Renaissance Crieff Post Office of 1906.

The Poor Law Act of 1845 regularized the system of relief and its funding. Some parishes combined to build large POORHOUSES to accommodate their paupers. Two in the region are the Perth Poorhouse (now Rosslyn House) of 1859–61 and the Atholl and Breadalbane Combination Poorhouse built at Logierait in 1861–4. Both are careful to avoid extravagance, the first being plainest Jacobean, the second adorned only with some bargeboards and a prominently hung bell.

Although medical and surgical HOSPITALS had been founded in Edinburgh, Glasgow and Dundee in the C18, it was not until 1838 that the Perth City and County (later Perth Royal) Infirmary was built. The façade, now part of the A.K. Bell Library, was designed by the City Architect, *W. M. Mackenzie* in a dignified but not ostentatious manner, a porte cochère the principal ornament. It was succeeded in 1911–14 by new buildings, the present Perth Royal Infirmary, on a suburban site. Designed by *James Miller* in his polite Neo-Georgian manner, these are now beleaguered by less soft-spoken additions of the late C20. Slightly earlier than the Infirmary was the region's first LUNATIC ASYLUM, the Murray Royal Hospital at Perth, designed by *William Burn* and built in 1822–7. A big but unexciting block, the front's centre marked by a Roman Doric portico and surmounted by an octagonal tower, it does, nevertheless, suggest treatment rather than incarceration of the insane. The Murray Royal Hospital was extended considerably in the later C19 and earlier C20, the Edwardian additions consisting of villa-like detached blocks, their Arts and Crafts manner indicative of a further advance in attitude towards the mentally ill. Also of considerable size although architecturally undistinguished was the Perthshire District Lunatic Asylum, by *Edward & Robertson*, built at Murthly in 1861–4 and demolished in the late C20. COTTAGE HOSPITALS to serve small towns were put up in the late C19 and early C20, sometimes accompanied at a discreet distance by isolation hospitals for the treatment of infectious diseases. The Blairgowrie Cottage Hospital (by *Lake Falconer*, 1899) is like a bargeboarded villa, St Margaret's Hospital at Auchterarder (by *Stewart & Paterson*, 1926), Scots Jacobean.

From the end of the C19 until the discovery of effective drugs in the 1950s, many victims of tuberculosis were treated in SANATORIA, often sited on well-drained hillsides to avoid damp and enjoy the benefit of fresh breezes. The largest of these in Perth and Kinross was the Ochil Hills Sanatorium (demolished), by *Robert Duncan*, 1900–2, a huge French Renaissance crescent, looking very like a hydropathic hotel, perched high above Milnathort with a spectacular view to Loch Leven. Also overlooking that loch but less precipitously placed was the smaller and more cottagey Glenlomond Hospital (now housing), near Kinnesswood, of 1919. The Hillside Hospital at Perth, situated unusually low beside the Tay, was designed by *J. Murray Robertson* in 1898 as a tightly composed large villa of Late Georgian inspiration.

The educational system based on parish SCHOOLS, whose construction and maintenance was the responsibility of local landowners, continued until 1872. From the 1830s greater attention was given to their architecture and to the comfort of teachers occupying the schoolhouses. In addition, some schools, usually for the education of girls in domestic science and often named industrial schools,* were established by wealthy benefactors. After 1843, the Free Church of Scotland built its own schools as rivals to the Church of Scotland-controlled parish schools. A conjunction of two types of school was built at Monzievaird in

---

*The term 'industrial school' did not, in Scotland, necessarily imply that these were for delinquents or paupers.

1859–61 where two single-storey schoolrooms (the parish school and an 'industrial school') flank a two-storey schoolhouse, making a picturesquely broad-eaved symmetrical group. Decorative detail was, however, limited. The Old School at Forteviot, by *W. M. Mackenzie*, 1839–40, has widely spaced crowsteps on the gables. The windows of the school (now Meigle Museum) built at Meigle in 1844 are hoodmoulded. At Newton of Pitcairns on the edge of Dunning, the former parochial school of 1839 is a Tudor *cottage orné* but the front gable of the rival Free Church School of 1847 boasts a Venetian window. Logierait Parish (now Primary) School at Ballinluig, of 1863–4, has a pyramid-roofed tower. This seems a surprisingly costly embellishment but the school stood beside the road between the Duke of Atholl's seat of Blair Castle and the park and pleasure grounds of his uncompleted (since demolished) Dunkeld Palace. The sixth Duke, 'being willing to erect an ornamental building', met over half the cost. The appearance of this school was, at least in part, the work of *Anne, Duchess of Atholl*. Ten years before she had employed *R. & R. Dickson* to design the girls' industrial school (now Duchess Anne Halls) which dominates the informal square at the centre of Dunkeld. As at Logierait, there is a tower for emphasis but the style is urbane Tudor and the building is of two storeys, one floor containing the schoolmistress's house.

Architectural ambition beyond that of the generality of rural parish schools is shown by some other mid-C19 educational buildings. In 1833 the heritors of Longforgan erected an idiosyncratic Jacobean L-plan schoolhouse (the contemporary school later rebuilt), designed by *John Bell*. A triangular bay window projects from the jamb's gable, a very shallow bay window from the main block, and a turret-buttressed porch stands in the inner angle. The front of Blairgowrie Parish (now St Stephen's Primary) School of 1841 is dignified with a pedimented 'portico', its arched openings round-headed. At Crieff, Taylor's Institution of 1842–3, by *Andrew Heiton Sen.*, is Jacobean, the schoolhouse with a shaped gable, the school itself with a bellcote. Another prominent bellcote surmounts the front gable of Crieff Parish (now Primary) School designed by *Thomas Pilkington & Son* in 1856 but the gable also contains a five-light Gothic window. Gothic too is *J., W. H. & J. M. Hay*'s contemporary Female Industrial School (now Community Centre) at Errol.

A few Early Victorian schools are of a quite different order of magnitude. In 1860 Sharp's Educational Institution, founded with a legacy from a local baker, was built in Perth. This is Italianate, by *David Smart*, a central tower and portico the main features of the front. Also opened in 1860 was Morrison's Academy at Crieff, the product of a bequest from a Perthshire-born Edinburgh builder. Here, *Peddie & Kinnear* provided a not very exciting long Baronial exterior but, inside, a first-floor great hall *c.* 11.3 m. square and 9 m. high filled the whole depth of the centre. The largest, in terms of area, of the region's educational establishments is Glenalmond (originally Trinity) College, founded in the 1840s as a combined Episcopalian theological college and boarding school where both ordinands and schoolboys could be kept safe from the perils of Presbyterian heresy and urban depravity. It was set in rural surroundings, 5.6km. distant from the nearest village, Methven, whose population was not notorious for debauchery. The buildings, designed by *John Henderson*, 1842, in a Collegiate Gothic manner, were placed round a quadrangle, its S side intended to be closed by a cloister. Projecting E of the quadrangle's SE corner was the chapel, its appearance derived from the C13 chapel of Merton College, Oxford. Almost three-quarters of the intended buildings were completed by 1863 but in 1875 the ordinands found the damage caused by a fire to their quarters an opportune excuse to decamp to Edinburgh. In 1891–3 a boys' boarding house was built in place of the originally intended library in the E range. Only in 1906 with the opening of the Memorial Library as a monument to former pupils killed in the South African War was scholarship given architectural recognition. Unfortunately for Henderson's design, this library usurped the place of his proposed cloister. A cloister (the Gladstone Cloister), sited further S and inconsequentially detached from the quadrangle, was at last built in 1926–7. It serves as a passage to shelter pupils waiting to enter classrooms behind rather than as a place for contemplation.

p. 384

The Education Act of 1872 transferred responsibility for the former parish and burgh schools to elected local School Boards. At the same time the newly established Scotch Education Department laid down standards for school buildings. Most of the more recently constructed parish schools met these. Nevertheless, there was a flurry of school building in the 1870s. BOARD SCHOOLS of this first generation usually consisted of a single-storey classroom block in which were separate rooms for infants and more senior pupils, and a schoolhouse, usually two-storey, containing a kitchen, parlour and three bedrooms. Local considerations, such as the aesthetic interest or ignorance of School Board members and the abilities of the usually local architects employed, affected the appearance of these new schools. *Charles S. Robertson*'s school at Bridge of Earn was embellished only with bracketed eaves and a pair of flèches over the classrooms' rooftop ventilators but at Burrelton Primary School *G. T. Ewing* provided bargeboards to the gables and a cupola to house the ventilator. Invergowrie Primary School was clothed by *Duncan D. Stewart*, architect to the Rossie Priory estate, in that estate's architectural livery so that it appears as a wrought-iron finialled *cottage orné*. More assertive is the Gothic Alyth High School, designed in 1876 by *John Carver*, with a spired and finialled bellcote surmounting the gable of one wing of its U-plan front. The broad-eaved Auchterarder School had a low Italianate tower. Also Italianate but with details taken from the work of 'Greek' Thomson is *Andrew Heiton Jun.*'s Kinnoull Primary School at Perth while English Elizabethan architecture influenced *John McDonald*'s design for the school (now Robert Douglas Memorial Institute) at New Scone.

By the 1890s secondary education was being provided by some burgh School Boards. At the same time, new schools, some of two storeys, were being planned round central halls. By 1906 the Scotch Education Department had made such halls obligatory for any new school designed to accommodate more than 500 pupils. At Perth in 1890 *Andrew Heiton Jun.* designed the Caledonian Road Primary School as a tall two-storey block, the classrooms grouped round a top-lit hall. The Flemish Renaissance exterior, faced with red Corncockle sandstone, was not of the cheapest. Between 1898 and 1908 *G. P. K.Young* added a huge wing to Perth's Southern District School and designed new Central and Northern District Schools for the city, all of two storeys with central halls, the external elevations Wrenaissance in character. These are or were (only the Northern District (now Balhousie Primary) School surviving) decidedly public buildings. So too, although on a smaller scale, is *Charles S. Robertson*'s Errol Primary School of 1897, the freely treated English Renaissance exterior expensively clad in polished ashlar.

The mid and late C19 saw a proliferation of commercial buildings in the burghs, most notably in Perth. The most expensive and dignified are BANKS. Banking companies in Scotland had been established since the foundation of the Bank of Scotland in 1695 and a total of thirty-five, most serving local areas, had been founded by 1845. These included two Perth-based companies, the Perth Bank begun in 1787 and the Central Bank of Scotland founded in 1834. Both erected new purpose-built head offices in the mid C19. These are palazzi. The three-storey Central Bank in St John Street, built in 1846–7, was designed by *David Rhind* with pilastered entrances at the end bays and Corinthian pilastered aedicules framing the first-floor windows. At the Perth Bank in George Street, by *A. & A. Heiton*, 1857, lions' heads poke out from the frieze over the ground floor and segmental pediments surmount the first-floor openings. Each of these contained a banking hall on the ground floor and a first-floor boardroom. The region's other banks were built as branch offices and each operated under the control of an agent, often a local lawyer. Except for the banking hall, the whole of a branch bank building was occupied by the agent as his own offices and house, the domestic quarters often of considerable size and even opulence.

Some branch banks were, not surprisingly, domestic in appearance. The British Linen Co. Bank (by *George Alexander*, 1810) in George Street, Perth, and the Perth Bank of 1851 in Wellmeadow, Blairgowrie, resemble well-finished tenements. Slightly more pompous in the treatment of their architraved and aproned windows are the Royal Bank of Scotland and the Clydesdale Bank, built beside each other in Allan Street, Blairgowrie, in the 1870s. Smart villas were built to accommodate their agents' houses and banking offices by the British Linen Co. Bank at Kinross in 1830 and the Commercial Bank of Scotland at Dunkeld in 1834, the first with its entrance set behind a screen of Ionic columns, the second (by *James Gillespie Graham*) with an Ionic portico.

More pompous is *David Rhind*'s Commercial Bank (now The Old Bank House) of 1837 at Blairgowrie, with a Greek Doric portico, consoled balconies and an urn-topped wall-head balustrade, but in 1852 Rhind designed a much less formal and very Scottish crowstepped villa (now Bank House) for the Commercial Bank at Pitlochry. Several branch offices were, like the head offices of the Central and Perth Banks, housed in palazzi, e.g. at Perth, *James Smith*'s restrained Bank of Scotland of 1853–6 in St John Street and the vertically proportioned Royal Bank of Scotland of 1899–1902, by *David Smart*, in Kinnoull Street or, at Dunkeld, *A. & A. Heiton*'s self-important Central Bank (now Bank of Scotland) of 1857. At Crieff three palazzi were built for rival banks (the Union, Commercial and North of Scotland) between 1868 and 1878. By contrast and perhaps in an appeal to the nationalism of potential clients, Crieff's Bank of Scotland of 1883 is crowstep-gabled and the corner entrance surmounted by a conical-roofed spire. Twenty years later the British Linen Co. joined the banking competition in Crieff, putting up an office designed by *Peddie & Washington Browne* in a free Jacobean-French Renaissance manner, the polished red ashlar front adorned with sculpted decoration. Even freer in its mixture of styles, culled from the early C17 and early C18, is *Sydney Mitchell & Wilson*'s Commercial (now Royal) Bank of Scotland of 1884–5 which fills one side of The Square at Aberfeldy.

By the mid C19 most towns in Perth and Kinross had one or more respectable new HOTELS, usually of unexciting Georgian survival character, such as the Royal Hotel of 1852 in Blairgowrie or the string of hotels along the main street of Auchterarder. The coming of railways to the region made it much more easily accessible to tourists and new hotels were built for their accommodation. Some of these were put up by the railway companies. *Andrew Heiton Jun.*'s Flemish-Gothic Station (now Quality) Hotel, beside the railway station at Perth, was built in 1887–91 for one company. Another employed *Duncan Cameron* to design the Jacobean-style Palace Hotel, also next to a railway station, at Aberfeldy in 1898. Two hotels were built at Glenfarg soon after the opening of its railway station in 1890. The Lomond Hotel is rather English in manner, with half-timbering and a veranda, the Glenfarg Hotel (by *David Smart*) defiantly Scots with crow-stepped gables and a battlemented tower. Scots style but quite peaceful in character was adopted also by *W. Dunn & R. Watson* for the Fortingall Hotel, a comfortable resting place for hill-walkers in Glen Lyon whose beauty was widely acclaimed despite it not being served by a railway. Also without railway communication until 1905 but famed in the C19 for its setting beside Loch Earn was St Fillans where the Drummond Arms Hotel was built to *Andrew Heiton Jun.*'s design *c.* 1875, the main block Georgian survival but broad-eaved and the centre rising as a tower whose top stage is detailed in the manner of 'Greek' Thomson.

Very much larger but, despite their hilltop positions, less suggestive of fun are the region's two HYDROPATHICS, hotels intended to host those recovering from illness or the strain of work. These institutions were noted for not serving spirits and sometimes no alcoholic drink and their architecture is sober. Designed in a joyless Jacobean manner by *Robert Ewan*, the Strathearn House Hydropathic (now Crieff Hydro) was built on the edge of Crieff in 1867–8 at a cost of £30,000. The dining and drawing rooms, *c.* 25.6 m. by 9.2 m. and 25.6 m. by 4.6 m. and 9.2 m. high, were too large to be cheerful but the Turkish baths perhaps gave opportunity for self-indulgence. Even more expensively constructed, at a cost of *c.* £55,000, and almost as forbidding, despite its iron-crested Frenchy roofs, was *Andrew Heiton Jun.*'s Atholl Hydropathic (now Atholl Palace Hotel) of 1875 at Pitlochry. Attempting to combine the size of the hydropathics with a promise of holiday pleasure and cocktails, the Caledonian Railway opened the 300-bedroom Gleneagles Hotel in 1924, its design of 1914 by *James Miller* altered by the company's architect, *Matthew Adam*. The site, overlooking golf courses and with views along Strath Allan, Strathearn and Glen Eagles, deserved better than this huge but timidly Neo-Georgian dumpling. The interior, however, has the luxury of an ocean liner but without the risk of shipwreck.

TEAROOMS have long served or, after five p.m., refused to serve residents and visitors to Perth and Kinross. A few were purpose-built. In Crieff, on the corner of King Street and Commissioner Street, is a former tearoom of 1906–7, by *Gordon L. Wright*, with a domed corner tower and large round-arched s-facing first-floor window fronted by an Art Nouveau balcony. Still serving meals is the The Dome Cafe in Blairgowrie, the large eating room at the back added by *W.J. Brewster, Grant & Henderson* in 1925, its domed ceiling carried on Tuscan columns.

SHOPS occupy the ground floor of many C19 and early C20 buildings in the principal streets of the region's towns and villages. Generally, their fronts are straightforward expanses of plate glass set in wood or stone frames, sometimes overlaid with plastic. A few occupy whole buildings. In Perth, the small Baroque block at Nos. 31–33 Kinnoull Street was designed in 1906 by *McLaren & Mackay* as premises for the wine and whisky merchants, Matthew Gloag & Son, the firm's trade proclaimed by a vine swag carved above the entrance. A crowstep-gabled shop building of 1899–1900 (by *William Bell*) on the corner of Dunkeld Street and Moness Terrace in Aberfeldy stands as a proud but not boastful advertisement for the Scottishness of the tweeds available inside. Also Scottish, with a comfortable round tower and gablet dormerheads, is the small block at Nos. 1–3 Dunira Street, Comrie, designed by *Honeyman, Keppie & Mackintosh* in 1904. Cosmopolitan sophistication is shown at *Smart, Stewart & Mitchell*'s Frenchy remodelling in 1931 of the mid-C19 shopfront at Nos. 58–60 St John Street, Perth.

OFFICE BUILDINGS in Perth and Kinross are relatively few, most of the region's businesses occupying former housing or shop premises. One late Victorian purpose-built office block is the long and low free Jacobean red sandstone building (now Perth Christian Centre) designed by *Andrew Heiton Jun.* in 1893 for the whisky-blending firm of John Dewar & Sons in Glasgow Road, Perth. Also of the 1890s but standing on the corner of High Street and Tay Street in the city centre is the former head office (now Council Buildings) of Perth's General Accident, Fire & Life Corporation. Designed by *G. P. K. Young*, this swaggering assertion of financial muscle is dressed in costliest *fin de siècle* Baroque, with a cupolaed corner tower and richly sculpted ornament.

Much of the Victorian and early C20 HOUSING of the region's small burghs and villages is quite without pretension. C19 village dwellings are often pleasant but plain, not infrequently with bracketed broad eaves and gabled dormers, sometimes with decorative bargeboards, as at Glencarse, Inchture and St Fillans. At Kenmore in the mid C19, latticed porches were added to many of the houses in The Square. These belonged to the Breadalbane estate. So too did the village of Acharn where tree-trunk porches give a picturesque air to a couple of short cottage-terraces. A more ambitiously composed cottage-terrace, of almost civic dignity, is at Blair Atholl where *R. & R. Dickson*'s Blair Cottages, built in 1840, form a U, the crowstep-gabled two-storey projecting wings joined by single-storey sections to the three-storey towers which flank the main range's two-storey centrepiece. Almost pompous is the three-storey Scots Renaissance Murthly Terrace of 1862–9 at Birnam with its oriel windows, shaped gables and conical-roofed round turrets. Birnam may have had ambitions to develop into a burgh. Fortingall's late C19 owner, Sir Donald Currie, was determined to maintain a village and, in 1889, employed *J. M. MacLaren* to design quintessentially cottagey housing whose thatched roofs form rounded gablets over the attic windows. Despite crowstepped gables, the effect is southern English although quite at ease in the Highland setting of Glen Lyon. Unbothered with Scottish references is the model housing designed by *James Miller* and built by the first Lord Forteviot in the 1920s at Forteviot and Pitheavlis Cottages (now in a Perth suburb). Both schemes are U-plan, the harled houses with red brick dressings and tiled roofs, their prominent gables, tile-hung at Pitheavlis Cottages, without crowsteps.

Victorian and Edwardian free-style TENEMENTS are present in quantity in Perth and, more sporadically, elsewhere. Many are plain but the grander are generally in a heavily detailed Renaissance manner, e.g. the 1890s blocks by *David Smart* and *James Smart* in Kinnoull Street and Scott Street, Perth. One of the largest and most striking is the four-storey block of 1906–7 by *G. P. K. Young* at Nos. 1–9 York Place, with strongly modelled classical detail and an octagonal cupola over the corner with New Row.

Some WORKING-CLASS HOUSING was provided at the end of the C19 by enlightened employers. In the Tulloch area of Perth, the dyeing and dry-cleaning firm of J. Pullar & Sons built the two-storey terraces of Tulloch Terrace in the 1880s and 1890s. These display a variety of bracketed broad eaves, triangular gablets, semicircular-pedimented dormerheads and oriel windows. Other housing was provided by co-operative societies.

In 1895 the Perth Co-operative Society employed *Charles S. Robertson* to design Unity Place in Victoria Street, a decent but inexpensively detailed Scots Jacobean tenement. A small amount of municipal housing was built at the beginning of the C20. At Perth, also in Victoria Street, the large L-plan St Johnstoun's Buildings, by *R. McKillop*, was put up in 1902–3, the broad-eaved blocks not extravagant but with touches of half-timbering, oriel windows and swan-neck pedimented dormers.

The variety of Victorian and Edwardian architectural styles is displayed by VILLAS at Bridgend in Perth. The mid-C19 Rose Cottage is Georgian survival, Bowerswell of 1848 and Braco House of *c.* 1860 Italianate with pyramid-roofed towers, Knowehead House of 1852 energetically crowstepped, Ardchoille of 1851 and *Dunn & Findlay*'s Balnacraig of 1892 Baronial, St Leonard's Manse, by *C. J. Menart*, 1904, Baroque, and the double house of Craigievar and Darnick (Nos. 1–3 Dundee Road) Ruskinian Gothic of *c.* 1870 by *Andrew Heiton Jun.* Also Gothic but on a small scale and weirdly idiosyncratic is Inchglas in Broich Terrace at Crieff. Designed for himself by *F. T. Pilkington* in 1859, the external treatment is consistently varied, the interior planned round a top-lit stair hall, the drawing room covered by a plaster tunnel vault. Two villas at Auchterarder, Coll Earn House of 1869–70 and Ruthven Towers of 1882, were designed by *William Leiper* in his Jacobean manner, the exteriors adorned with plentiful carving, the interiors with Glasgow-style stained glass by *Daniel Cottier*. Much starker is Glentower House at Glendevon, the main block plain except for bracketed broad eaves and jerkinhead gablets but joined to an immensely tall tower from whose top the owner could enjoy the view up the glen. More discreet are the balcony and viewing platform looking over the Firth of Tay at the red brick villa of Brantwood in Invergowrie which *James Hutton* designed for himself in 1900. Far too many of the region's Victorian and Edwardian villas are routine, making resort towns like Crieff and Pitlochry disappointingly dour. One of the largest and stylistically the most eclectic villa in Perth and Kinross has been demolished. This was St Mary's Tower at Birnam, built for Lord John Manners in 1861 when the *Perthshire Courier* published a description: 'It seems to combine all the styles of architecture from the Conquest downwards; it has windows of all shapes and sizes, and roofs of many forms and elevations. It is almost 100 feet (30m.) high, and bristles with cannon. It has numerous port holes.'

The Earlier Twentieth Century to the Present Day

Local government reorganizations in the late C19 and C20, the establishment of county as well as burgh councils in 1889, the replacement of both by a two-tier system of district and regional councils in 1975 (Perth and Kinross forming one district within the region of Tayside) and their replacement in turn by unitary authorities, with Perth and Kinross as a single local authority, have not been accompanied in this region by the erection of governmental edifices. Perth and Kinross County Council adapted the former Perth City and County Infirmary for its offices, and the present council's headquarters are in the former head office of the General Accident, Fire & Life Corporation (*see* above). This readiness to adapt existing structures as PUBLIC BUILDINGS has been extended to the former Perth Waterworks (*see* Industrial Buildings), now serving as the Fergusson Art Gallery. The 1830s façade of the Perth City and County Infirmary is now incorporated as the centrepiece of the front of the A. K. Bell Public Library (by *Perth and Kinross District Council*, 1992–4), the additions stretching out either side in heavy Postmodern fashion. Surprisingly, the interior of the new building is without tricks, a light and agreeable space in which to study or browse. Much less happy has been the erection as the Perth and Kinross Police Headquarters of a shoddy-looking six-storey tower block of 1977 beside Perth's inner city ring road.

A few INTERWAR SCHOOLS, mostly to cater for an increased number of secondary pupils, were put up in the region. The polite Neo-Georgian of *T. Aikman Swan*'s design for Perth Academy, built in 1928–32, was followed by the County Architect, *A. Watt Allison*, for the Royal High School of Dunkeld at Birnam in 1930 and the Robert Douglas Memorial School at New Scone in 1933, both built of red brick. POST-SECOND WORLD WAR SCHOOLS, either replacements for Victorian buildings or serving new housing developments, are common. Most of those put up in the 1960s and 1970s, usually designed by the Perth and Kinross County Architect, *Ian A. Moodie*, or his successor, *John Nicol*, are flat-roofed and lightweight-looking, although aggregate cladding gives a sense of dour purpose to Perth High School (by *Bett-Bison*) and Perth Grammar School. More playful are the opposed monopitch metal roofs held apart by a flat-roofed central block at *Boswell, Mitchell & Johnston*'s Inchture Primary School of 1973. Ribbed metal roofs, but of curved profile, surmount Abernethy Primary School (by *Perth and Kinross Council*, 2001–2) and The Community Central School of Auchterarder, built to *Anderson Christie*'s design in 2000–4.

MEDICAL BUILDINGS have been built widely, although often on a small scale, in the region during the late C20. The largest, although architecturally undistinguished, have been the additions to Perth Royal Infirmary put up between 1979 and 1993. Efficiency rather than cheerfulness is suggested by Crieff's replacement of 1993–7 for its Edwardian cottage hospital. Much more satisfactory is the children's hospice, Rachel House at Kinross, designed by *Alan Marshall* in 1994, admirably optimistic in appearance, the generally Postmodern manner mercifully free of laboured jokes. Even more straightforward is *Gordon & Dey*'s Upper Springland Centre for the disabled built on the NE edge of Perth overlooking the Tay in 1974–5.

SPORTS BUILDINGS contribute a touch of gaiety to the area. *Faulkner Browns*, Perth Leisure Pool promises frolicsome enjoyment. Soberer, although not without style, are the buildings of Perth's Gannochy Trust Sports Complex: the domed hall of the

Bells Sports Centre, by *D. B. Cockburn*, 1975–9, the adjoining Gannochy Sports Pavilion, by *Gordon & Dey*, 1975–9, and the link of 1989–91 between the two. Dewar's Rink at Perth of 1989–90 (for skating and curling) is stodgy, the Kinross Leisure Centre, begun in 1991, flashy.

CINEMAS in the region were never numerous and few have survived. The former Picture House at Blairgowrie, by *W.J. Brewster Grant & Henderson*, 1925, and Perth's Playhouse in Mill Street, by *Alexander Cattanach Jun.*, 1933, are Art Deco but without flair. The Moderne front of The Birks (now an amusement hall) built at Aberfeldy in 1939 is restrained as if fearful of disturbing the slumber of that early-to-bed resort. Set a little apart from its burgh is the Pitlochry Festival Theatre, by *Law & Dunbar-Nasmith*, 1981, its glazed foyer overlooking the River Tummel to give the playgoer a sense of occasion. Hidden away in back streets is the Perth Concert Hall (by the *Building Design Partnership*, 2003–5), its oval shape deprived of elegance by the addition of seemingly arbitrary angular projections and the bulbous copper roof over the auditorium.

COMMERCIAL BUILDINGS of the mid and later C20 are either over-polite or over-brash. Bank agents were replaced by salaried managers and, in the interwar years, both the managers and the banking premises were exemplars of financial prudence. The squared-up Neo-Georgian façade of the 1930s Commercial Bank in Wellmeadow, Blairgowrie, offers little hope of an overdraft. The Thatcherite era's greater willingness to fund the entrepeneur is represented by the loud-mouthed assertiveness of the *Cunningham Glass Partnership*'s Clydesdale Bank of 1990–1 in South Methven Street at Perth. Trying rather too hard to fit into a tight urban setting are the entrances to Perth's St John's Shopping Centre, by *William Nimmo & Partners*, 1985–7, the front to King Edward Street a bland ashlar-faced U-shape, that to South Street hiding under a canopy, both half-ashamed of the mall behind. More self-confident, perhaps because placed away from any streetscape worth respect, are the hypermarkets opened at Perth in the 1990s. Their commercialism is honest. Less immediately obvious but just as ruthless in its money-making purpose is the shopping complex of The House of Bruar ('The House of Country Clothing') built in 1994–5, its appearance presumably attempting to suggest an Edwardian shooting lodge.

OFFICE BUILDINGS of size are scarce. The General Accident insurance firm's offices (now Tayside Nursing Home) built in 1966 in the suburban setting of Isla Road at Perth are long, low and devoid of frills. These are by *James Parr & Partners* who in 1986 designed the firm's new headquarters (now Norwich Union) offices off Necessity Brae, a complex of courtyards whose surrounding flat-roofed blocks step with confidence down the slope of Craigie Hill.

After the passing of the Housing and Town Planning (Scotland) Act in 1919 local authority HOUSING became widespread. Often consisting of two-storey flatted blocks, with harled walls and slated pitched roofs, much is little more than utilitarian externally. In Parkside Road at Alyth, however, in 1938 *Johnston & Baxter* designed two-storey housing whose first-floor windows rise into curvaceous gablets. Perth's Hunter Crescent (Tulloch) and Muirton housing schemes of the 1930s were by the Burgh Surveyor, *Thomas McLaren*, with *John A. W. Grant* acting as consultant. Of two and three storeys, these tenements were simple but effectively treated Neo-Georgian, the harling of the walls relieved by red artificial stone dressings, the doorpieces all corniced and some pedimented. Misguided attempts from the 1990s to make them cheerful have destroyed their quiet dignity. In 1958–62 *E. V. Collins* of *George Wimpey & Co.* designed Perth's multi-storey blocks of flats at Pomarium Street and Potterhill (Bridgend), straightforward flat-roofed towers with rendered and partly glazed balconies. A much busier approach was used by the *Nicoll Russell Studios* in 1990–2 for Servite House on the corner of West High Street and Comrie Street in Crieff, the blockwork walls ending in half-octagons with the recessed entrance set between. The most recent tenement blocks, now proliferating on the edge of the Perth city centre, have adopted a half-hearted Neo-Victorian manner. Much more successful have been Perth's earlier low-rise developments at Bridgend of the 1970s, the Commercial Street terraces by *James Parr & Partners*, with steep slated roofs and reddish blockwork fronts arranged in staggered formation, and *Alex Strang & Associates*' Bridgend Court which fronts a line of houses stepping downhill to the river.

The C20 contributed few villas of originality. Two, in Bridgend (Perth), are worth mention. Manderley, by *Cecil Stewart* and *G. P. K. Young & Son*, 1938, with its pyramidal roof and vertical windows is a happy example of Modern-Traditionalism. The elegantly composed and detailed single-storey Meadowland by *Morris & Steedman*, 1964–6 (extended in the 1970s), makes the most of its site overlooking the Tay. It shows how the Modern Movement could and should have preluded humane and unmeretricious architecture, free of superfluous ornament and show-off tricks. Sadly, the same spirit is lacking in the massive housing developments of the late C20 and early C21 in the region, most notably on the W side of Perth although still contained within the *cordon sanitaire* of the dual carriageway A9 ring road.

RURAL MANSES, FARMHOUSES AND STEADINGS

Agriculture in Perth and Kinross, as elsewhere in Scotland, changed little from the Middle Ages until the late C18. The rural population was grouped in ferm touns, each usually containing between ten and twenty-five families, growing crops predominantly of barley and oats and raising some cattle or sheep. The arable land was divided between the infield which was under constant cultivation and on which was spread all available manure and the outfield where an elementary rotation was practised by which a third was left fallow each year. Hill land was used as summer pasture for the beasts, most of which were sold or slaughtered annually before the onset of winter. Those that were kept were housed under the same roofs as their owners. Buildings were often constructed with mud or drystone walls and roofed with rough timbers covered with straw, turf, ferns, broom or heather.

The MANSES of the parish ministers were, beside the houses of lairds, the most substantial rural dwellings until the agricultural revolution of the late C18 and early C19. For much of the C17 these were built or improved at the expense of the ministers themselves. On the death or demission of a minister his manse was valued and he or his family paid its worth by his successor. The valuations of manses varied considerably. In 1624 the manses at both Scone and Errol were valued respectively at *c.* £27 and *c.* £49 sterling but £22 of the worth of Errol Manse resulted from work carried out on it during the previous ten years. In the 1650s and 1660s valuations of the manses at Dupplin, Dron and Kinfauns ranged from £36 to £55.

In 1663 an act of the Scottish Parliament laid down that the construction of manses and major repairs during a ministerial vacancy were the responsibility of the heritors (landowners) who were to provide manses worth between *c.* £27 and £85, the cost varying according to the wealth of the parish. The cost covered also the provision of offices, usually a barn, stable and byre, needed by the minister to farm his glebe. Some early manses were constructed cheaply. In 1719 the roof of Kinloch Manse seems to have been covered with turf and, in the 1720s, the manses of Abernyte, Caputh and Lethendy were thatched. The manse built at Blairgowrie in 1704 had a roof of grey slate (sandstone slabs) but its offices were thatched and thatch was used also as a covering for office houses at Lethendy in 1739 when the manse itself was rebuilt with a slate roof and at Dron in 1769. However, most manses built from the early C18 were slated and some seem not to have been without comfort. In 1715 a new manse costing *c.* £145 sterling, well above the legal requirement, was built at Dull, measuring *c.* 14.6 m. by 6.1 m. externally, was of two storeys and an attic and covered with a slate roof. It contained two rooms and a pantry on the ground floor and two rooms on the first floor whilst the kitchen presumably formed part of the office houses. Very similar in cost (*c.* £124), size and accommodation was Kenmore Manse of 1729.

Slightly larger manses seem to have been erected at Forteviot in 1721 and Forgandenny *c.* 1740, each with a dining room, bedchamber, kitchen and pantry or closet on the ground floor and three bedchambers and one or two closets on the first floor. Unusually, one attic room of the Forgandenny manse was equipped with a fireplace. Manses of this general size were put up during the rest of the C18 and reluctance of heritors to spend money on decent housing for the ministers was obviated by the Court of Session which ruled in 1760 that the 1663 act's upper cost limit on the building of new manses did not apply to the rebuilding of existing ones. From the mid C18 good-quality West

Highland slate was available and, in the 1780s, Easdale slates from Argyll were used for the roofs of manses and offices at Kinross and Milnathort. In 1800 it was specified that the new offices of Abernethy Manse were to be covered with blue slate and given a lead ridge.

Agricultural prosperity, the result of improved farming techniques and of the steep rise in prices during the French Revolutionary and Napoleonic Wars between 1789 and 1815, appears to have raised the expectation of ministers as to the size and quality of their manses and to a willingness among landowners to satisfy this. In 1803 *Robert Reid* designed a new manse at Logierait which, although externally plain, contained seven rooms, a pantry and closet on the ground and first floors and two further rooms and a closet in the attic. A fair number of other new manses were built during the first decades of the C19. They followed a standard formula, usually built of harled rubble with slate roofs and containing two storeys and an attic which was often lit originally from windows in the gables. The entrances of their three-bay fronts might be given economical dignity by an architraved surround as at Dull Manse (now Appin House) of 1841–2, a consoled cornice as at Kinnaird in 1832, or a pilastered and corniced frame as at Fortevoit in 1826 or Fortingall in 1835. Tibbermore Manse of 1824 is unusually smart, with panelled pilasters at the entrance, three-light windows to the ground floor and a wall-head parapet. A few designs broke from this pleasant but unadventurous Late Georgian norm. The ground-floor windows of Kinloch Manse (now The Old Pastorie) of 1847–8 are placed in shallow rectangular bays. Aberdalgie Manse, designed in 1832 by *William Burn*, architect of the nearby Dupplin Castle, is plain Tudor in style and Methven Manse (now Lynedoch House) by *W.M. Mackenzie*, 1830, is Jacobethan. At Monzievaird *William Stirling I* produced a *cottage orné*. Some manses were extended later in the C19, generally with utilitarian back wings but the wing added to Kilspindie Manse in 1862–3 is Jacobean. Madderty Manse (later rebuilt) acquired bay windows in 1887. Bathroom additions were common between 1890 and 1910, e.g. at Moneydie in 1899 or Muthill in 1903.

AGRICULTURAL IMPROVEMENT in Perth and Kinross hardly began before the 1770s. An act of 1770 'to encourage the Improvement of Lands, Tenements and Hereditaments in that Part of Great Britain called Scotland' allowed owners of entailed estates to borrow money against the security of their estates for such purposes as fencing, hedging, tree-planting, and the erection of farmhouses and farm buildings. This, combined with a greater general prosperity in Scotland from the mid C18, the substantial income some landowners received from holding government or judicial positions and, in some cases, money gained through marriage to heiresses, brought about a major, though sometimes gradual, reorganization of farms and farming practices. Tile drainage was widely used to bring potentially fertile but waterlogged land into production. Lime came into general use as a fertilizer and a proper rotation of crops of greater variety was introduced. Ferm touns were replaced by individual holdings, each leased to a single tenant expected to be able and willing to borrow for improvement. In upland areas, sheepwalks replaced the previous mixture of subsistence farming and cattle rearing. Leases of farms were offered for a substantial number of years, usually nineteen by the early C19, giving tenants a reasonable security. Between the 1770s and the 1790s agriculture was revolutionized in the Carse of Gowrie, whose heavy clay soils were drained, and the hills bordering Glen Devon were given over to sheep walks. In the year before he took a twenty-one year lease of the lands of Stanley House in 1785 Captain George Murray, an uncle of the Duke of Atholl, had spent £1,200 on their improvement. However, as late as the 1840s, agriculture around Coupar Angus in the fertile vale of Strathmore had undergone only limited change. The financial benefits of improved agriculture were relatively shortlived. In the late C19, imports of wheat from North America and, after the introduction of refrigeration on ships, of beef, lamb and mutton from Argentina and the Antipodes depressed prices. Many sheepwalks were converted to deer forests. In lowland areas, some further amalgamation of farms to provide economies of scale to pay for mechanization and larger cattle courts took place from the end of the C19 but a significant amount of farmland was abandoned in the 1920s and 1930s. Brought back into productive use during the Second World War, it has continued to be cultivated, with agricultural incomes subsidized by the Government or the European Union.

Very few FARMHOUSES AND STEADINGS from earlier than the end of the C18 survive. A rare example, at Nether Camserney, near Dull, is a longhouse, probably built in the C18. It is long and relatively narrow, *c.* 22 m. by 5 m., the structure consisting of paired crucks standing on stone slabs and joined at the top by yokes above collar-beams. A longitudinal spar supports the ridge of the thatched roof. The walls are of rubble, with small windows to the s. Originally, the building contained one room in which the farmer's family lived, the smoke from its central hearth rising into a hanging chimney constructed of wattle and daub, and a byre for the cattle. By contrast, James Robertson reported of the houses being built in 1797 on newly laid out and improved farms in the region: 'In place of the mean hovels, in which their fathers lived, without light and without air, in the midst of soot and smoke, many farmers now live in houses, substantially built with stone and lime, having two floors, and a covering of blue slate.'*
Robertson was describing a process of building new farmhouses which was at its beginning or mid-point in different parts of the region. In some areas, such as that around Fowlis Wester, only a few farmhouses in the 1790s had slated roofs and some of these were covered with grey rather than blue slates. Most were thatched with straw. However, by the 1830s it was rare for a farmhouse not to be slated. In lowland areas, most steadings were

---

*James Robertson, *General View of Agriculture in the County of Perth* (1799) pp. 51–2

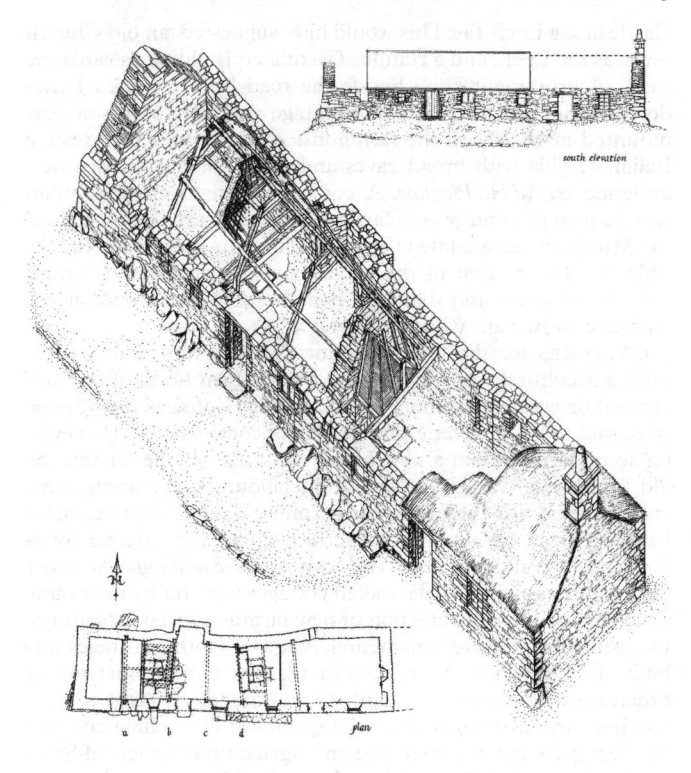

Dull, Nether Camserney, longhouse.
Axonometric view

rebuilt in the late C18 or earlier C19, often constructed as U-plan courtyards set a little back from the farmhouse. In arable areas, from the beginning of the C19, a round or octagonal horsemill for threshing grain usually projected behind the barn. The walls, like those of the farmhouses, were usually of lime-mortared stone, often harled, and the roofs slated.

Most Late Georgian farmhouses and steadings, if not too drastically altered, especially in the lowland areas, appear pleasantly prosperous but architecturally unpretentious. A few attempted more, sometimes because they could be seen from a road used for afternoon excursions by guests at the estate's mansion house. At Culdaremore, near Fortingall, near the road which encircles Drummond Hill behind Taymouth Castle, the principal range of the late C18 farmhouse and steading complex was treated as a palace front, the pend entrance placed in a pedimented centrepiece which is linked by low blocks to piend-roofed pavilions, one containing the farmhouse, the other part of the farm offices. In 1798 *John Paterson* prepared an unexecuted design for a farmhouse at Callelochan, near Acharn, on the road W from Taymouth

Castle along Loch Tay. This would have suggested 'an old Church towards the Loch, and a ruinous Castulated Building towards the road'. A prominent knoll beside the road between Lord Lynedoch's residences of Lynedoch Cottage and Balgowan was surmounted in 1832 with the farmhouse of Dalcrue, a picturesque Italianate villa with broad eaves and a pyramidal-roofed tower, designed by W. H. *Playfair*. A conical-roofed tower and broad eaves adorn the *cottage orné* farmhouse of Stewart Tower built on the Murthly Castle estate in 1848–9. The same estate was responsible for the erection of the gabled and gableted Bee Cottage, with broad eaves and diamond-pane-bordered windows, at the entrance to Birnam Wood in 1841.

COTTAGES for the lesser peasantry and farm servants were, until agricultural improvement had taken firm hold, often built of mud or wattle and daub. As late as 1843 cottages near Scone were said to be 'in several places, very uncomfortable'. However, on some farms, when a new house was built for the tenant, the old farmhouse was given over to his labourers, apparently providing them with slightly better accommodation. That seems to have occurred at Nether Camserney where the original longhouse was converted into two two-room dwellings. At other farms stone-built and slate-roofed cottages were built at the same time or soon after the erection of new farmhouses and steadings. Occasionally, they are ornamental. A row of Gothic cottages was built at Milltown of Aberdalgie in 1826–31 and a courtyard of broad-eaved cottages, also with Gothic detail, at Achloa, near Keltneyburn, in 1839. The design quality of the Achloa cottages was recognized by the Highland and Agricultural Society of Scotland which awarded its gold medal to the Marquess of Breadalbane for the work.

INDUSTRIAL BUILDINGS

Containing only a handful of burghs, medieval Perth and Kinross had limited industry. The sole royal burgh,* Perth itself, served as an entrepôt port for the export of agricultural produce, especially wool and hides, and the import of luxury goods including dyes and wines. Early C13 Perth contained craftsmen employed in cloth-making, dyeing, and leather and metal working. By the late C17 the city was exporting linen in some quantity, most of the cloth made by rural handloom weavers working in their homes, the flax supplied and the finished goods traded by Perth merchant-capitalists. The populations of some villages or burghs of barony, such as Errol or Coupar Angus, contained a substantial proportion of weavers. In the C18 linseed oil mills were established at Perth, their product sent mostly to London. These, like the city's grain mills, were powered by water carried in the great lade which had been cut in the C12 from the River Almond

---

*Auchterarder was a royal burgh by 1246 and represented in the Parliament of 1584 but thereafter lost all burgh status.

c. 5 km. to the NW and circled the city before discharging into the Tay.

By the late C18, when the lintseed oil industry was in decline, the introduction of improved machinery for scutching flax (separating the fibres from the woody parts) and spinning yarn led to the erection of TEXTILE MILLS. The first of these in the region may have been the flax-spinning Meikle Mill built at Blairgowrie in 1778. Similar machinery was used for cotton spinning and cotton mills were founded at Cromwellpark, near Pitcairngreen, beside the River Almond and Stanley beside the River Tay in the 1780s. Cotton, linen and woollen mills appeared at Kinross and Milnathort early in the C19. Not infrequently, mills founded for the manufacture of one class of textile were adapted for another, as at Milnathort where cotton manufacture was replaced by that of woollens or, much later, at Stanley where the manufacture of acrylics took over from cotton. Blairgowrie's linen mills, established in the late C18 and early C19, were converted to jute mills in the later C19. All the textile mills erected before the mid C19 were originally served by water carried from rivers (e.g. the Almond, the Ericht and the Tay) in lades, the velocity and depth controlled by sluice gates, to turn wheels which powered the machinery. The mills at Stanley had seven huge water wheels until 1921 when they were replaced by a hydro-electric power station, itself served by the mills' (reconstructed) lade from the Tay. At several of the Blairgowrie mills wheels survived until the later C20 and varied in width from just over 3 m. to a little under 6 m. and in diameter from 5.5 m. to 7.3 m. Steam power was introduced from the mid C19. At Perth in the 1860s the linen-weaving firm of John Shields & Co. built the steam-powered Wallace Works (demolished), originally housing 300 looms but expanded to contain 900 by the end of the C19.

The size of mill buildings varied widely. The piend-roofed factory (now The Muckle Hoose) built at Spittalfield in 1767 is of two storeys, the windows of the five-bay front very small. The Ericht Works, built at Blairgowrie in 1867, was eighteen bays long but of only one tall storey. Of similar length but rising to four or five storeys and with an attic or basement are the cotton mills at Stanley. The earliest of these, the Bell Mill of 1786–7, attempts a few architectural flourishes. Its two lowest storeys are of rubble, those above of red brick and with elliptical-arched windows. The W side, facing the approach, boasts a slightly advanced and pedimented (off-centre) 'centrepiece' and the N gable is surmounted by a birdcage bellcote. At Blairgowrie, the Ericht Works had round-headed windows and a cast-iron cornice, and one gable of the Keathbank Mill of 1864–5 was ball-finialled. Appearing almost like a frivolous extravagance is the early C19 Gothick-windowed manager's house at Stanley Mills.

Linen or cotton, whether produced by home-workers or in mills, required to be bleached by being first steeped in a hot alkaline solution and then, after being washed and dried, having acid, usually vitriol (sulphuric acid) applied. Commercial BLEACH WORKS were founded at Tulloch, near Perth, in 1735, Luncarty in 1736, Huntingtowerfield in 1774 and Stormontfield in 1788. Like mills, their machinery was originally water-powered, the works at Stormontfield served by a canal or lade from the River Tay, c. 5km. long and 5m. wide, and the buildings utilitarian although those at Stormontfield were said in the 1790s to be 'remarkably neat and commodious'. Of the Huntingtowerfield works there survives one block (of 1867) with a heavy clock tower.

Sizeable DYEWORKS AND PRINTWORKS for the dyeing of cloth, often in printed patterns, were erected, often in proximity to textile mills, from the late C18, e.g. at Cromwellpark, Ruthvenfield and Tullochfield in the 1780s and at Perth in 1814. The largest dyeworks in C19 Scotland was the North British Dye Works at Perth. This belonged to the firm of John Pullar & Sons which had been founded in the 1820s but expanded massively from c. 1850. Taking full advantage of Perth's position as a node of Scotland's railway system, the firm received cloth and garments for dyeing from almost the whole country. In 1870 it branched out into dry cleaning. The Perth works in Kinnoull Street were rebuilt in 1865 on a massive scale, although without bombast, a pedimented centrepiece the principal display at the twenty-nine bay front. Major additions, designed by *J. Murray Robertson* in 1899, continued the same general manner but with crowstepped gables. Unashamed of its industrial purpose is Pullars' dyeworks building of 1919–21 in St Catherine's Road designed by *Smart & Stewart*, constructed of reinforced concrete, the exposed frame filled externally with panels of brick and glass.

PAPER MILLS existed in the region by the late C18 when they used rags of bleached linen or cotton as their raw material, largely replaced in the later C19 by esparto grass and then wood pulp. Most seem to have been small, such as one at Huntingtower Haugh outside Perth which, in the 1790s, employed between twenty-five and thirty workers. Much larger was the Bullionfield Paper Mill established at Invergowrie in 1846 when the Penicuik (Lothian) paper-makers, Alexander Cowan & Sons, bought a bleach works (formerly a flax-spinning mill) there and installed machinery for the manufacture of paper. Enlarged and modernized later in the C19, it was steam-powered, with a chimneystack c. 77m. high. All that now remains is a martially parapeted late Victorian water tower.

From the Middle Ages until the end of the C18 peasant and tenant farms were compelled by law to take their corn and oats to GRAIN MILLS belonging to local lairds. After an act of 1799 allowed commutation of this servitude in return for payment of a sum of money, almost all new steadings incorporated their own threshing mills and most former mills were demolished or converted to other uses. The City Mills at Perth, first established probably in the C12, continued in use. Powered by water brought from the Almond along the Town Lade, they were rebuilt in the late C18 and early C19 and form a pleasingly informal rubble-walled complex, now used as a hotel. Some other mills, generally in or on the edge of upland areas whose farms' relatively small production of cereals made it uneconomic for them to have their own mills, were built or rebuilt in the C19. One, at Crook of Devon, has a pyramidal roof over its kiln which was used for drying grain. This was water-powered as was the corn mill of 1834 at Alyth. The Aberfeldy Water Mill was built in 1825–6, with Gothic windows decorating the N front. The kiln, added in 1841, is also pyramid-roofed. The Old Mill at Acharn on the Breadalbane estates was constructed in 1851–2, its bargeboards a picturesque embellishment perhaps designed to please visitors passing from Taymouth Castle to the Hermit's Cave on the hill above.

MALTINGS for barley to be used for distilling or brewing could be substantial. At Coupar Angus, the maltings built in the mid or later C19 form a broad triple-pile with the kilns at one end. Also impressive for their size are the maltings, originally part of a brewery, at Blackford which were designed by *Russell & Spence* in 1897, a tall engine house rising above the E end.

DISTILLERIES existed in Perth and Kinross in the C18 but reluctance to pay the punitive duties then levied on whisky meant that much distilling took place privately. Nevertheless, the Glenturret Distillery at Hosh was founded in 1775 and both the Blackhill Distillery at Logierait and the Tullibardine Distillery at Blackford in 1798. Further distilleries were established at Ballechin, near Strathtay, by a consortium of farmers in 1810, at Auchnaguie, near Ballinluig, in 1812, Balnacraig, near Pitlochry, and Grandtully in 1825. Of these early distilleries only the Glenturret Distillery and the Blair Atholl Distillery, which was founded at Pitlochry in 1826, still operate. A major reduction of excise duties in 1828 was followed immediately by invention of the Stein and Coffey stills, allowing continuous distillation which had not been possible with the previously used pot stills. Thereafter, new distilleries were founded, e.g. the Edradour Distillery in 1837 and the Isla Distillery at Perth *c.* 1850, and existing distilleries rebuilt although, as late as 1887, Alfred Barnard found the Grandtully Distillery to consist of a single building, *c.* 22 m. by 6 m., 'the most primitive work we have ever seen'.* The smaller surviving distilleries, such as Glenturret and Edradour, are simple collections of whitewashed buildings. Edradour consists only of a single-storey malt barn and store, a two-storey still house with a pagoda-roofed kiln at one end, and, standing a little apart, the manager's house. Much larger and dourer are the long rubble-walled block, also with a pagoda-roofed kiln, of the Aberfeldy Distillery of 1896–8. Designed by *C. C. Doig* of Elgin, a specialist in such work, it was built for the Perth whisky-blending and bottling firm of John Dewar & Sons who, in 1911, erected a large brick bonded warehouse beside the railway in Perth. In 1962 this was superseded by a new bottling plant (closed in 1994) at Inveralmond on the N edge of Perth, adjacent to the A9 and the dual carriageway and motorway roads linking that city to Edinburgh, Glasgow and Dundee.

*Alfred Barnard, *The Whisky Distilleries of the United Kingdom* (London, 1887), 277.

GAS WORKS were constructed in every town in the region and also at some country houses and mills from the early C19. Perth's first gas works was built in Canal Street in 1824 to a design by *Adam Anderson*, the Rector of Perth Academy. A second gas works, in Blackfriars Street on the N edge of the city centre, followed in 1844, both superseded by the new gas works opened at Friarton in 1901. The replacement of coal gas by natural gas in the later C20 has made gas works redundant. Among the few surviving remnants are a round sunk-pit gasholder of 1842–3 at Crieff, the tall brick chimney of the gas works constructed at Stanley Mills, *c*. 1830, and the battlemented tower which contained a chimney of the gas works put up in 1854–5 at Aberfeldy.

Commercial and municipal generation of ELECTRICITY became common from *c*. 1900. At Perth, a red brick steam-powered generating station was opened at Shore Road in 1901 when electric street lighting was introduced to the city. The Central Electricity Act of 1926 provided for the establishment of a national grid making it financially viable for companies to generate electricity in sparsely populated areas for use elsewhere. As a result, the Grampian Electric Supply Co., strongly supported by the eighth Duke of Atholl, owner of the largest estate in Perth and Kinross, undertook the region's first major hydro-electric scheme (the Loch Ericht–Loch Rannoch Scheme), constructing dams at Loch Ericht and the E end of Loch Rannoch in 1928–30. Further development of hydro-electric power followed the passing of the Hydro-Electric Development (Scotland) Act in 1943 and the subsequent establishment of the North of Scotland Hydro-Electric Board. In the 1940s and 1950s the Board carried out four major schemes, each designed by a different firm of engineers, the Tummel–Garry Project (by *Sir Alexander Gibb & Partners*), with new lochs (Loch Faskally and Loch Errochty) formed by the construction of dams across the Rivers Garry and Tummel and the Errochty Water, the Gaur Project (by *Babtie, Shaw & Morton*) with a dam across the River Gaur to form Loch Eigheach, the Lednock–Earn Scheme (by *Sir Murdoch MacDonald & Partners*) with dams across the Rivers Lednock and Earn near Comrie and St Fillans, and the Lyon Scheme (by *James Williamson & Partners*) damming the River Lyon W of Innerwick. All the dams are powerful concrete structures, thankfully unsoftened by concessions to ideas of good taste. The POWER STATIONS themselves are less confident, most designed in a Modern-Traditional manner with flat roofs and rubble walls, although the sides of *H. O. Tarbolton*'s Pitlochry Power Station of 1951 are formed of pre-cast slabs of reconstituted Aberdeen granite. *Robert H. Matthew* placed pitched roofs over his stations of 1954–7 at Cashlie and Lubreoch, near Innerwick. Just as powerful as the dams constructed for the hydro-electric schemes is one by *Babtie, Shaw & Morton*, 1963–8, at the Loch Turret Water works although its sloping outer face is covered with turf. It forms one end of a 3.6 km.-long reservoir.

A much earlier WATERWORKS whose machinery was placed in a grandly designed and boldly positioned public edifice was that designed by *Adam Anderson* in 1830 to supply Perth with water from the Tay. The reservoir tank was housed in a Graeco-Roman domed rotunda behind which rises the engine house's chimney contained in an urn-finialled Doric column like some great commemorative monument.

GAZETTEER

ABERARGIE

Hamlet beside the River Farg.

DESCRIPTION. On the N side of the A913, a picturesque single-storey cottage terrace of c. 1840. Bracketed broad eaves, gablets, and projecting front gables containing round-headed dummy slit windows; originally the windows had horizontal-paned glazing. Behind, in NETHERMILL PLACE, a contemporary but plain curved terrace of cottages.

RAILWAY VIADUCT, Glen Farg, 2.7 km. SSW. Disused. By *William R. Galbraith*, 1887–90. Of hammer-dressed ashlar, four 15 m. high round-headed arches built on a skew; brick soffits.

RAILWAY VIADUCT, Kilnockiebank, 1.3 km. SW. Disused. By *William R. Galbraith*, 1887–90. Of hammer-dressed ashlar, five 19 m. high round-headed arches; brick soffits.

AYTON HOUSE. *See* p. 175.

GLENFARG HOUSE. *See* p. 403.

ABERCAIRNY
2.2 km. SW of Fowlis Wester

Harled Neo-Georgian mansion house, by *Claud Phillimore*, c. 1960. – Array of C18 and early C19 STATUARY along the terrace in front. – STABLES to the NE. Tudor Collegiate, by *R. & R. Dickson*, 1841–2. Two-storey ranges round back-to-back courtyards. Large square tower at the centre of the S elevation. Octagonal towers flank the W entrance to the S courtyard. – N LODGE of c. 1865, with bargeboards and a tree-trunk veranda; shouldered-arched windows in the W front. – SE LODGE. Tudor of c. 1840. Contemporary GATEPIERS in the same manner.

ABERDALGIE

Just the church and manse on the edge of the policies of Aberdalgie House.

PARISH CHURCH. Rubble-walled T-plan kirk of 1773, the burial vault of the Earls of Kinnoull protruding as a terrace from under its E end. In each gable of the main block, a Diocletian window (the E blocked in 1928–9) under a Venetian. At the top of the E gable, a dummy oculus. On the W gable, a large birdcage bellcote, its rectangular openings framed by fluted Roman Doric pilasters, the ogee-profiled roof topped by a weathercock. The bellcote is a replacement by *Lorimer & Matthew* who recast the church in 1928–9. At the long S elevation they retained the two tall round-headed centre windows and the gallery-level oculi of the end bays but they built up the door below the E oculus and encased the corresponding W door in a plain porch. The piend-roofed N jamb retains its C18 appearance, with two tiers of windows and, on its W side, an open-pedimented and chimneyed wallhead gablet.

The interior is almost all by Lorimer & Matthew, who removed the C18 end galleries and created a 'sanctuary' at the E end. Compartmented ceiling, high panelled dado, and simple pews, all of Austrian oak. Also of 1928–9 is the frame of coupled Ionic pilasters at the opening to the laird's loft in the N jamb. Behind the loft, a retiring room. – COMMUNION TABLE of *c*. 1900. – PULPIT of 1912. – STAINED GLASS of 1930–1 (Moses; the Sower; 'Bear ye one another's burdens') in the lights of the E Venetian window, a colourful display of stylized realism.

At the E end of the S wall, a Gothic recess made in 1904 to contain a medieval incised GRAVE-SLAB which had been in the medieval parish church (sited some way to the NE of the present building) and left without adequate protection after that building's demolition in 1773. It is of Tournai stone and presumably made in northern France or Flanders. The inscription, now weathered away, was recorded in 1719 as commemorating Sir William Olifaunt, lord of Aberdalgie, †5 February 1329 (i.e. 1330 N.S.), apparently either Sir William Oliphant who was Constable of Stirling Castle in 1304 or his cousin, Sir William Oliphant of Dupplin. The slab is carved in flat relief, the effect much like that of a monumental brass, with the effigy of a knight, his feet resting on a pair of back-to-back dogs. To the r. of the knight's head, a shield bearing the Oliphant coat of arms; the outline of an answering shield on the l. was still visible in the 1890s. Above the effigy, a canopy of three cusped and crocketed arches springing from side-shafts, each panelled with three canopied niches containing small figures dressed in civilian clothes (one of the figures now weathered away and four only fragmentary). At the bottom r. corner, a winged ox (the symbol of St Luke); presumably there were emblems of the other Evangelists in the other corners. That the effigy is shown dressed in armour of mixed mail and plate (not the mail with no or very little plate reinforcement worn by an early C14 knight) suggests, despite the recorded inscription, a date of the later C14 (perhaps the 1360s) for the monument.

In the GRAVEYARD a few HEADSTONES of the mid and later C18, their tops carved with angels' heads (souls).

MANSE to the NW, plain Tudor by *William Burn*, 1832–3.

GRAVEYARD, Kirkton of Mailler, 3.1 km. E. The site of a vanished medieval chapel. Most of the HEADSTONES are C19 but a few are earlier. Roughly in the centre, the stone to Alexander Low, tenant in Tarsappie, †1775. W face topped by an angel's head (the soul) above reliefs of a plough, a salmon and the aerial view of a boat containing a pair of salmon; at the bottom, crossbones, a skull and hourglass. – SE of this, Margaret Imbrie, the top of the stone's W face bearing the date 1775 and an anchor. Another aerial view, in quite high relief, of a boat containing salmon; hourglass, crossbones and skull at the bottom. – To its NE, the headstone of 1745 to Helen Blyth, the W face with an angel's head above a weaver's loom and shuttle, and with a skull, bones and hourglass at the bottom.

ABERDALGIE HOUSE, 0.2 km. E. Smart little mansion house of c. 1800. Two storeys and a basement. S front of three bays with panelled giant pilasters at the ends. Slightly advanced and pedimented centre, its fanlit door in a Roman Doric pilastered and corniced surround.

MILLTOWN OF ABERDALGIE, 0.4 km. N. Three blocks of rubble-walled cottages with pointed doors and windows. They were built in 1826–31.

DUPPLIN CASTLE. See p. 356.

ABERFELDY

8040

Small Highland town (granted burgh status in 1887) which began as a village beside the Tay Bridge of 1739 carrying General George Wade's military road from Crieff to Dalnacardoch across the river. Some rebuilding and expansion took place in the earlier C19 and more followed after the opening of the branch railway from Ballinluig (on the main line from Edinburgh and Perth to Inverness) in 1865. Tourism of a discreet and decorous nature is the main industry.

CHURCHES

Former ABERFELDY FREE CHURCH, Taybridge Road. Now Church Hall. By *Peter Skeen*, 1843–4, the hall at the S added in 1887; both much altered in 1960–4. The rubble-walled church's diagonally buttressed W tower retains its original appearance. Hoodmoulded ogee-arched door at the bottom. In each face, a pointed belfry opening under a chamfered cornered clock stage. Copper-clad spire and weathercock.

ABERFELDY FREE CHURCH. Chapel Street. Secularized. Lumpy Dec, by *David Morris*, 1907. At the S corner of the front (W) gable a sturdy buttressed tower, its pyramidal roof slated. Inside, a floor has been inserted at gallery level.

ABERFELDY PARISH CHURCH, Crieff Road. By *John Young*, 1883–4. Early Gothic, built of squared and coursed rubble. Nave, W transepts and a low semi-octagonal W apse containing the vestry. Angle-buttressed porches, the N of two storeys, the S single-storey, flank the E gable. This gable, also angle-buttressed, has a slightly advanced centre containing a vestibule window of three cusped lights sharing a continuous hoodmoulding. Above, a large Geometric four-light gallery window with quatrefoil tracery at the head; small foliage-carved label stops at the hoodmould. Plain lancet windows at the N and S sides and the transepts. Rose window in the W gable of the

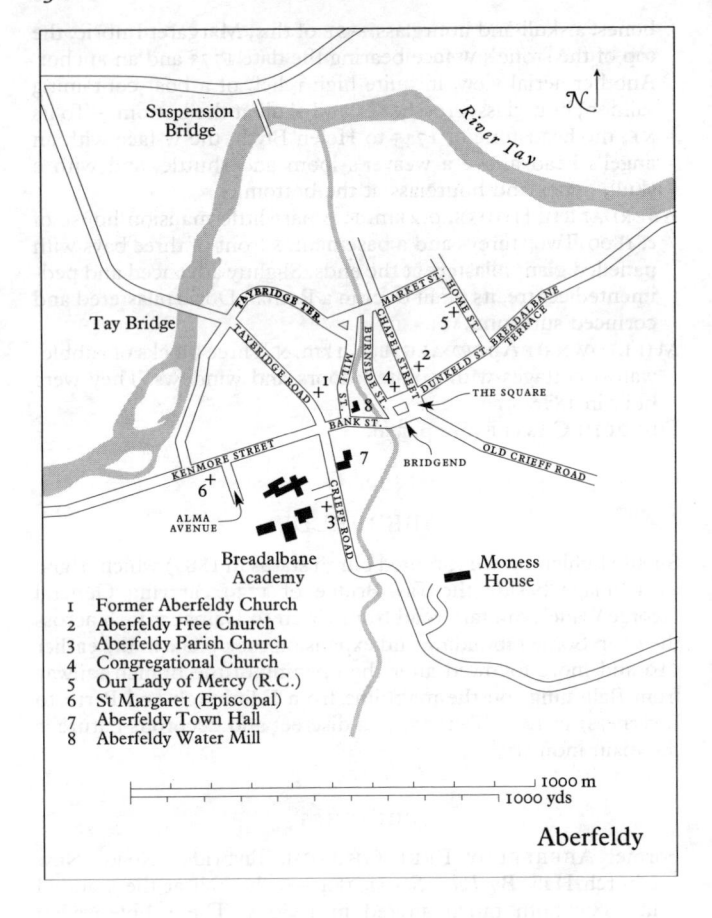

Aberfeldy

- 1 Former Aberfeldy Church
- 2 Aberfeldy Free Church
- 3 Aberfeldy Parish Church
- 4 Congregational Church
- 5 Our Lady of Mercy (R.C.)
- 6 St Margaret (Episcopal)
- 7 Aberfeldy Town Hall
- 8 Aberfeldy Water Mill

nave. Slated flèche of French derivation over the crossing. Triangular dormer-ventilators along the roof.

Spacious but plain interior with a collar-braced roof and E gallery. Scoto-Catholic arrangement of furnishings.

CONGREGATIONAL CHURCH, The Square. Secularized. By *Mackenzie & Matthews* of Aberdeen, 1877–8. Lancet-windowed broad box; at the NE corner, a steeple with a splay-footed spire. Contemporary hall against the E side. The building was converted to a community centre by *Gaia Architects*, 2000.

OUR LADY OF MERCY (R.C.), Home Street. Erected 1885, a small cruciform church of white-painted corrugated iron, the detail Gothic. Carved wooden bargeboards and iron cresting on the roof ridge. Only the base remains of the flèche which formerly surmounted the E gable.

ST MARGARET (Episcopal), Kenmore Street. Now a house (THE AULD KIRK). By *Bell & Cameron*, 1906–7. Simple and small, a harled and buttressed nave and chancel, the windows pointed. Much altered on its conversion.

PUBLIC BUILDINGS

ABERFELDY TOWN HALL, Crieff Road. Free Style with a Richardsonian North American accent, by *J. M. MacLaren*, 1889–91, red sandstone dressings contrasting with the white harled walls. SE wing with bracketed eaves at its gables and gablets. The main hall is in the NW range. Bargeboarded broad gable to the street. At its ground floor a loggia of three round-headed arches; above, a five-light stone-mullioned window lighting the gallery. Battered slate-covered ventilator flèche finished with an ogee-roofed cupola and elaborate iron weathercock. At the back, the former FREE CHURCH SCHOOL of *c.* 1845.

BREADALBANE ACADEMY, off Crieff Road. The detached S range is by *William Bell*, 1886–7. Multi-gabled and gableted, with bracketed broad eaves and a spired flèche. To the N, a two-storey block by the Perth & Kinross County Architect, *Ian A. Moodie*, 1958, its walls of contrasting harl and 'Fyfestone'; flat-roofed clock tower.

SUSPENSION BRIDGE over River Tay, Aberfeldy Golf Course, off Taybridge Terrace. By *W. J. Harvey* and students of *The University of Dundee Department of Civil Engineering*, 1992. Elegant glass-fibre span, carried on tall A-frame uprights.

TAY BRIDGE, Taybridge Road. Designed and built by *William Adam* in 1733 to carry *General George Wade*'s military road from Crieff to Dalnacardoch over the Tay. The purpose of the bridge is stated by the inscription (copied in 1932 from a tablet of 1733) on one of the obelisks as being WITH THE ROADS & OTHER MILITARY WORKS FOR SECURING A SAFE AND EASY COMMUNICATION BETWEEN THER HIGH LANDS [*sic*] AND THE TRADEING TOWNS IN THE LOW COUNTRY. It is a symbol of the civilizing power brought by the Hanoverian monarchy to Highland Scotland.

The bridge is hump-backed, the shape disguised externally by the parapets which rise in two slopes to a flat-topped centre. Rubble-built of chlorite schist with ashlar dressings. Five

Aberfeldy, Tay Bridge.
Elevation and plan by William Adam, *c.* 1733

segmental arches, their size increasing towards the central span; Gibbsian rustication at the voussoirs and the piers which flank the central arch. Pedestals bear panelled pyramids at the outer ends of the parapeted approaches which are pinched in at the beginning of the bridge proper. This has splay-sided piers, the top of each forming a pedestrian refuge, from which project triangular cutwaters. At the sides of the outer piers, cannon spouts, and, on the piers' inner faces, moulded frames intended to enclose white marble panels. On the parapet above the central piers are panelled obelisks. On the W face, over the centre arch, a white marble tablet carved with the relief of a crossed sword and scabbard under a crown.

DESCRIPTION

DUNKELD ROAD is the approach from the NE. The Aberfeldy Distillery (*see* Industrial Buildings, below) is an outpost of the town whose real start is BREADALBANE TERRACE. This, built up only on the N, begins with harled local authority housing of the 1930s, gablets providing interest. There follows a three-storey and attic six-bay flatted block of *c.* 1890. Small consoles carry the cornices over the doorways. Shouldered arches to the second-floor windows. Obtusely pointed attic windows in the second and fifth bays which are slightly advanced, with carved bargeboards at their gables. Similar but simpler two-storey and attic block of 1880–6 at Nos. 2–5. Then the PALACE HOTEL by *Duncan Cameron*, 1898–9, the dark-coloured rough ashlar of its walling enlivened by plentiful bands and dressings of red sandstone. Jacobean, with shaped gables and parapeted two-storey bay windows. Columned doorpiece, its shafts of polished granite, surmounted by a balustraded and ball-finialled balcony. This is at the splayed corner whose steep pediment contains a datestone set in a roundel which is keystoned at the cardinal points; behind the pediment, an iron-crested French pavilion roof. In HOME STREET, the Church of Our Lady of Mercy (*see* Churches, above).

DUNKELD STREET begins with buildings of the later C19 with bracketed broad eaves. At VIEWFIELD on the corner of Home Street, horizontal-paned windows, those of the second floor topped by gablets. Then, also on the N, the STATION HOTEL of 1884. Frilly bargeboards and cast-iron foliaged finials on its many gablets. A slated octagonal spire, again with a finial, over the splayed SE corner. Plain building of 1881 at Nos. 37–39 and mid-C19 blocks at Nos. 19–33. Opposite, on the corner of Moness Terrace, No. 32 by *William Bell*, 1899–1900, the walling of red Keithick sandstone with dressings of red Ballochmyle stone. Crowstepped gable and gablets. Conical slated roof over the bowed corner whose ground floor contains the shop entrance set back behind cast-iron columns. Then, on the N, the POST OFFICE of 1897, also by *Bell*, with ornamental bargeboards for decoration. At the street's fi end, on the corner of Chapel Street, THE BIRKS (originally a cinema, now an amusement hall) of 1939. Unflashy rendered moderne front hiding the shed behind.

In CHAPEL STREET, on the E, Aberfeldy Free Church (*see* Churches, above). Further down, on the W, Nos. 37–39, a Late Georgian double house. Similar double house but of the later C19 and with bargeboarded gables at the adjoining Nos. 43–45. At the N end of Chapel Street, on its NE corner with Market Street, remains of the GAS WORKS, by *A. & A. Heiton*, 1854–6, a rubble-built industrial shed, with a crudely battlemented tower-like chimney at the S end.

THE SQUARE at the W end of Dunkeld Street is Aberfeldy's not very formal centre. On the N side, the mid-C19 Nos. 1–3 with curvaceously carved bargeboards to the gablets and horizontal-paned windows, followed by the roughly contemporary but plainer Nos. 4–6. To the W, the Congregational Church (*see* Churches, above). On the W side of The Square, THE ROYAL (originally COMMERCIAL) BANK OF SCOTLAND by *Sydney Mitchell & Wilson*, 1884–5. Free mixture of Jacobean and Early Georgian, built of chlorite schist with dressings of red sandstone. Steep open pediments over the end bays, one containing a segmental-pedimented attic window, the other's attic window surmounted by a panel carved with strapwork and the date 1885 and topped by a triangular pediment. Pedimented Gibbs surround to the entrance.

On the E side of The Square, a large block (Nos. 2–6 Dunkeld Street and No. 23 The Square) of 1898, plain despite the broad eaves, bargeboards and a slated octagonal spire on the NW corner. To its S, Nos. 21–22 The Square on the corner of Old Crieff Road is of the later C19. The splayed corner is dressed up with a curvy topped gable containing a corniced and keystoned architrave to the door; first-floor window with a lugged architrave; round window at the attic. Broad oriel window at the elevation to Old Crieff Road. Adjoining, No. 1 OLD CRIEFF ROAD of *c*. 1860, its bracketed broad eaves broken by wallhead dormers. On the S side of The Square, on the W corner of Old Crieff Road, STRUAN HOUSE of 1891, large but not very competent free Baroque. An early C19 vernacular building to its W. In front of this, a cast-iron DRINKING FOUNTAIN by *Walter Macfarlane & Co.* of the *Saracen Foundry* presented by Gavin, Marquess of Breadalbane, as a memento of his and his wife's visit there in July 1886. Leafily capitalled fluted columns carry a canopy topped by a marquess's coronet. On the sides, panels bearing an inscription, the Breadalbane coat of arms (twice) and the relief of a heron. Under the canopy, a bowl surmounted by a bulbous stem of foliage on which stands the figure of a heron.

BRIDGEND exits The Square to the W. On both sides are plain buildings of the later C19 although the BREADALBANE ARMS HOTEL incorporates earlier work. Set back on the S, the burgh's WAR MEMORIAL archway, by *W. Erskine Thomson*, 1922, the round-headed opening set in a framework of red sandstone ashlar, with panelled pilasters and a parapeted cornice. Spandrels carved with claymores and targes. The archway is flanked by urn-topped pedestals. At Bridgend's W end, a plain rubble BRIDGE, probably of the later C19, over the Moness Burn.

BANK STREET'S S side begins with the BANK OF SCOTLAND of c. 1865. Asymmetrical Elizabethan manorial; plain bargeboards and horizontal-paned windows. Opposite, on the N, a long red sandstone ashlar block (Nos. 2–12) of 1910. Two tall storeys, the ground floor occupied by shopfronts, their large expanses of plate glass set between piers of polished pink granite. The upper floor is free Jacobean, divided into three sections by pinnacled fluted pilasters. Over the one-bay E section a steep gable; pedimented mullioned and transomed window of three lights. Centre section of three bays, the masonry channelled, the windows two-light, again mullioned and transomed. The W section is of two bays surmounted by a pair of steep gables topped by scrolls which form ball-finialled crown spires; pedimented three-light windows like that of the E bay. Then the CROWN HOTEL, of the later C19 with bracketed broad eaves, followed by a roughly contemporary two-storey terrace, the upper windows with gableted dormerheads. On the S, a two-storey and attic building (Nos. 13–15) of c. 1900 with oriel windows at the first floor's outer bays. The W end of Bank Street mostly contains plain housing of the mid C19. At Nos. 21–23, a stone carved with a rope-moulded oval panel bearing the date 1838. At the S side's corner with Crieff Road, the former UNION BANK (now COUNCIL OFFICES AND LIBRARY), English Baroque of two storeys and an attic, by *Bell & Cameron*, 1904–5. At the N front, a pair of first-floor bowed oriels, the l., above the pilastered entrance, bearing the bank's coat of arms; at the attic, three wallhead dormers, the outer two with triangular pediments, the centre with a segmental pediment. Two-storey bow window at the rear wing to Crieff Road.

Running N from the middle of Bank Street is MILL ROAD. On its E side, the Aberfeldy Water Mill (*see* Industrial Buildings, below). On the W, Nos. 1–5, a two-storey rubble-built tenement of the earlier C19, the first-floor windows rising into gablet dormerheads.

CRIEFF ROAD goes uphill to the S from the W end of Bank Street. At its bottom, on the W side, ROSEMOUNT and IVYBANK, a mid-C19 double house, a bargeboarded gable over the l. bay and gablets at the three r. bays; horizontal window panes and pilastered and corniced doorpieces. Further up, Aberfeldy Town Hall (*see* Public Buildings, above) on the E and Late Victorian villas. On the W, Aberfeldy Parish Church and, to its W, the Breadalbane Academy (*see* Churches and Public Buildings, above).

TAYBRIDGE ROAD continues Crieff Road N of Bank Street. On its E side, the former Aberfeldy Free Church (*see* Churches, above). Otherwise, pleasant late Victorian villas. At the road's N end, the Tay Bridge (*see* Public Buildings, above). Just W of the bridge, the BLACK WATCH MEMORIAL, a large and kitsch sculptured sandstone group by *W. Birnie Rhind*, 1887. Cliff-like rocky pedestal, its front (E) face carved with the relief of a soldier of the Black Watch (dressed in Late Victorian uniform) drawing a line under a list of the regiment's battle honours. On the w face, a panel bearing a relief bust of Queen Victoria. On top of the pedestal, giant statue of a soldier of the Black Watch (in Highland dress of 1739), his hand on his sword.

KENMORE STREET continues the line of Bank Street w. At its E end, two-storey terraced housing of the earlier C19, with bracketed broad eaves and the occasional pilastered and corniced doorpiece. This is followed by late C19 villas. Among them, the former St Margaret's Episcopal Church (*see* Churches, above).

INDUSTRIAL BUILDINGS

ABERFELDY DISTILLERY, Dunkeld Road. By *C. C. Doig*, 1896–8. Long rubble-built double-pile front block of three storeys, with an off-centre and taller pagoda-roofed kiln. Late C20 still house extension at the w. Plain bonded stores of 1896–8 behind.

ABERFELDY WATER MILL, Mill Street. Informal rubble-built mill begun in 1825–6 when it seems to have been L-plan, the main block at the sw, the jamb projecting to the NE. Agreeably crude little Gothic windows to the N; eight-spoke wood and iron water wheel on the s. The jamb's kiln, its wooden pavilion roof topped by a pagoda vent, was added by *Robert Robertson*, mason, and *James Kippen*, wright, in 1841. The jamb may have been further extended soon after, perhaps at the same time as the addition of a broad-eaved but plain two-storey store at the E end of the main block whose upper windows' bargeboarded gablets also look mid C19.

MONESS HOUSE
Moness Drive

Harled laird's house of 1758 (the date on the rear elevation). Two storeys above a fully exposed basement. s front originally of five bays but extended E by a further three in the early C19; the porch may have been added about the same time. Further additions later in the C19. It now forms part of a large leisure complex.

BOLFRACKS. *See* p. 235.

ABERNETHY

At the point where the land route along the coastal plain on the s side of the Firth of Tay squeezes past the NE end of the Ochil Hills into Strathearn, Abernethy was probably the seat of a bishopric in the early C8 and housed a community of *Céli Dé* soon after. It was made a burgh of barony in 1459. By the early C19 this was a weaving and salmon-fishing centre and, later in that century, a resort for summer visitors but neither the weaving nor tourist industries have survived.

CHURCHES AND PUBLIC BUILDINGS

ABERNETHY AND DRON PARISH CHURCH (KIRK OF ST BRIDE), School Wynd. By *James Ballingal*, 1801–2. Broad box, built of red sandstone, the s front of droved ashlar, the rest of rubble. Pointed windows. In the s front, large centre windows and, in each of the outer bays, a two-storey arrangement of smaller windows, the lower one converted from a door in the late C19. Two-storey window arrangement at the back. On the w gable, a pyramid-roofed bellcote with short Roman Doric corner pilasters and a pointed panel at each face. At the E end, a session house by *Ballingall*, 1829; enlarged in 1937. Late C19 w porch.

INTERIOR. Round three sides, a semi-octagonal panelled GALLERY supported on stumpy wooden columns. – At the centre of the s wall, a late Victorian Gothic PULPIT. – Large circular stone FONT of 1892. – Victorian PEWS. – STAINED GLASS. The large narrative windows flanking the pulpit (the Annunciation to the Shepherds and, below, St Mungo and St Columba Exchanging Pastoral Staffs; the Maries at the Tomb and, below, King Gartnaidh, the Founder of Abernethy Church, Inspecting the Building) are of 1922. – In the s wall's outer bays, under the gallery, windows (the Adoration of the Magi; Our Lord's Entry to Jerusalem) by *William Wilson*, 1964. – The N wall's central window under the gallery (St Columba, and smaller figures of St Bride and St Ninian) is of 1935, sketchy in strong colours.

The GRAVEYARD WALL was rebuilt by *Thomas Malcolm* in 1829–30, its elliptical-arched s GATEWAY dated 1830. – In the centre of the graveyard, a rectangular grouping of corniced BURIAL ENCLOSURES of the Moncrieffs of Culfargie and Bandirran, probably of the early C19. Built into the internal s wall of the w enclosure, a large stone PANEL of 1892, carved in high relief with the coats of arms of Sir Alexander Moncrieff of Culfargie and Bandirran and his wife, Harriet Mary Rimington Wilson.

ABERNETHY ROUND TOWER, in the graveyard's sw corner, is one of two surviving Early Christian detached circular towers (the other is at Brechin Cathedral, Angus) in Scotland. Built for a monastic house of *Céli Dé*, probably in the later C11, it stands *c.* 27.6 m. high, with a diameter which tapers from *c.* 4.57 m. at the base to *c.* 3.96 m. at the top. Masonry of ashlar, the bottom twelve courses of greyish stone and perhaps earlier than the work above, the rest of buff-coloured sandstone, the top and cornice restored in 1868 probably when a square clock face was erected. Except for a few roughly shaped small openings, architectural detail is confined to the entrance and top stage. The entrance, a little above the present ground level, is a round-arched doorway, with inclined jambs; any carved decoration has been lost to weathering. At the top, probably a belfry, four large round-arched openings set in round-arched recesses, the jambs again inclined. Inside, a metal spiral stair constructed in 1982. Six string courses round the walls indicate the position of missing wooden floors, the lowest (now a metal deck) placed just above ground level. – Built into the tower's s segment, JOUGS, probably of the C17. – Beside the tower, a Pictish SYMBOL STONE, probably of the C7, incised with a 'tuning fork' flanked by a hammer and anvil and surmounting a 'crescent-and-V-rod'.

ABERNETHY UNITED PRESBYTERIAN CHURCH, Kirk Wynd. Secularized. Ambitious but ungainly Gothic, by *Charles S. Robertson*, 1866–7. NE steeple, the angle-buttressed tower broached to an octagon pierced with quatrefoil lights. Rising from the stone-slabbed roof, a gableted octagonal belfry, gargoyles projecting from its corners, surmounted by a slated spire finished with a wrought-iron finial. Alterations, including the insertion of a large elliptical-arched opening in the s side, were made by *Kirkland Restoration Ltd.*, 2006.

ABERNETHY PRIMARY SCHOOL, Main Street. By *Perth & Kinross Council*, 2001–2. Single-storey classrooms flanking a taller central hall. Walling of ashlar, render and glass under curvaceous ribbed metal roofs.

SCHOOL, School Wynd. Converted to housing, 2006. Tall single-storey block by *Charles S. Robertson*, 1874, with mullioned and transomed windows in the gable. Two ventilators, one covered by a spire, the other by a pyramidal roof. Slightly earlier two-storey w block. Mid-C19 schoolhouse at the N.

WILLIAMSON HALL, Kirk Wynd. Simple Romanesque of 1881–2.

DESCRIPTION

PERTH ROAD, the entry from the W, starts as a bungaloid approach to the burgh. Its first architectural incident is provided by the mid-C19 PITVERSIE BANK on the r., Georgian survival but with bracketed eaves and a steep pediment over the door. Then, set back from the road, PITVERSIE HOUSE, a late C19 villa with a low octagonal tower at its NW corner, followed by the pleasantly plain early C19 BLAIRERNO and CHERRY BANK. Then, ANNFIELD of the earlier C19, its piended roof flanked by chimneystacks. After the junction with Main Street the line of Perth Road is continued by the curving BACK DYKES. On the r., the early C19 THE HOLLIES. Giant pilasters at the ends of its painted ashlar front whose centre, slightly advanced under a blocking course, contains a round-headed doorpiece. On the l., set below road level, the harled C19 ROSE COTTAGE, its thatch replaced by concrete tiles but ungentrified and the attic still lit only by small windows in the gables.

MAIN STREET leads to and through the centre of the burgh. At its start, on the l. and placed behind a front garden, is the mid-C19 harled BALLOBURN, its parapeted porch probably a later addition. On the r., No. 2, also of two storeys, is of *c.* 1840, its stugged masonry now painted; corniced doorpiece. The road bends s. On the bend, No. 3, a mid-C19 cottage with a fluted eaves course and skewputts carved with pointing hands and topped by sphinxes. The housing now establishes an early/mid-C19 two-storey norm, with walls of whinstone, some painted, rendered or harled, enlivened by dressings of buff-coloured sandstone. On the l., No. 1 BARMORE PLACE, a rendered cottage, probably late C18, presents a crowstepped gable to Main Street. Further along Main Street, also on the l., the early C19 CROFT COTTAGE, with rope-moulded club skewputts. The next door CROFT HOUSE is a Victorian intruder, its stugged grey ashlar and segmental-arched windows and door discordant in this context. Beside it, No. 39, a gable-ender of *c.* 1800.

Main Street broadens out to form a rough triangle at THE CROSS. Here stands the WAR MEMORIAL, by *Mills & Shepherd*, 1920. Of mercat cross type, the shaft topped by a stone carved with a coat of arms on each face and the date 1458 (for the foundation of the burgh). From the s point of the triangle SCHOOL WYND leads s past the graveyard (*see* Churches and Public Buildings, above). On the l., MORNINGTON COTTAGE of *c.* 1800, each of its skewputts carved with a stylized rosette. At the house's s end, a gateway to the back garden, its lintel inscribed with worn initials and the date 1757. S of this, a low two-storey stable range, probably Late Georgian, with a broad elliptically arched cartshed door and small horizontally proportioned first-floor windows. Below this, the piend-roofed early C19 MORNINGTON HOUSE. On the other side of the road, the School (*see* Churches and Public Buildings, above).

MAIN STREET E of The Cross continues on the r. with a short early C19 terrace (Nos. 46–50), the windows and doors of Nos. 46 and 48 with Gibbsian surrounds. At the end of the terrace, the entrance to KIRK WYND which leads uphill to the s. On its l., WILLESDENE where the upper windows are small and the lintel of a built-up door bears a heart flanked by the initials IC and MW and the date 1764, likely enough for the origin of this rubble-walled house but it seems to have been reconstructed in the earlier C19 and its thatch replaced by slates in the C20. Further up, on the r., the former Abernethy United Presbyterian Church and the Williamson Hall (*see* Churches and Public Buildings, above).

In MAIN STREET E of Kirk Wynd, the narrow windows (one enlarged) of Nos. 52–54 on the r. suggest a late C18 date. No. 56 is of the earlier C19, its painted ashlar channelled at the ground floor which is marked off by a cornice. Rusticated quoins to the upper floor, its windows set in moulded architraves. Opposite, the early C19 No. 65 has Gibbsian surrounds to the doors and windows, as at Nos. 46–48 (*see* above). Consoled cornice over the door of the mid-C19 No. 66 (ST LEONARD'S). Then the street bends in an S-shape. On the l., THE CROSS INN, Georgian survival of 1843, with a first-floor sill course and later porch. Lower and rougher office range, perhaps contemporary, attached to its W end. Main Street ends with Abernethy Primary School (*see* Churches and Public Buildings, above) at the junction with the A913 running E towards Fife.

FORT, Castle Law, 1 km. SW. Iron Age fortification, probably of the earlier first millennium B.C., enclosing the level summit of a precipitously sided knoll which rises from the steep E side of Castle Law. The massive main wall, *c.* 5.5 m.–6.6 m. thick and still standing to a height of *c.* 2.1 m. rears up from the steep slopes to the N, E and S of the summit. In the wall's outer face, a double tier of rectangular holes contained horizontal beams *c.* 2.4 m.–3.0 m. in length. The enclosure inside the wall is roughly oval (narrower at the E end), *c.* 41 m. by 15 m., and contains a rock-cut well. A second wall, *c.* 4.3 m. thick, has curved out from the enclosure to defend an annexe.

ABERNYTE

2030

Agreeably informal small village, the houses mostly C18 and C19 vernacular.

ABERNYTE FREE CHURCH, 1 km. SE. Secularized. Built in 1854 to a design by *Thomson*, inspector at Lochton. Sturdy rubble-built and lancet-windowed T.

ABERNYTE PARISH CHURCH, 0.9 km. E. Rubble-built and cruciform, the product of several stages of development. The first was in 1736 when *David Smart*, mason in Dundee, and *James Morris*, wright in Longforgan, contracted to rebuild the existing church as a straightforward oblong with a bellcote on the W gable. A large transeptal N 'aisle' or jamb was added *c.* 1800. Then in 1870 *Edward & Robertson* extended the church with a short chancel on the S side of the C18 main block and a gabled porch at the N end of the jamb. At the same time they removed the W bellcote and erected a new gabled bellcote on the jamb which now acquired the status of a nave, the E and W ends of the original church becoming transepts. Simple detail of various dates. Small rectangular Georgian side windows to the jamb, the S on the W side checked for shutters, now filled with Victorian Gothic lights. In each transept gable, a mullioned window of three rectangular lights, the centre taller than the others, probably of 1870. At the top of the W gable, a datestone of 1672 reused from the previous church on the site. Fleur-de-lys finial above, probably of 1870. In the S side of the W transept, a Georgian door.

Inside, open wooden roofs, pews and pulpit of 1870. – COMMUNION TABLE of 1939 in the chancel. – STAINED GLASS. Brightly coloured pictorial S window (Our Lord Walking on the

Water; a Female Saint; a Mother and Children) of 1877. – Similar window of 1894 (Our Lord Leading a Girl to Paradise) in the E transept.

GRAVEYARD. Several C18 HEADSTONES of note. Propped against the S side of the W transept, an aedicular stone commemorating Jean Boyd †1746 and William Paterson †1759. Ball-finialled pilasters carry the curvy pediment, its tympanum carved with cattle who support a panel depicting a butcher at work. Below, a pair of angels' heads (souls) above a shield carved with the figure of a man; an hourglass, skull and crossbones at the base. – W of this, Jean Wardraper, erected in 1758 by her husband James Benvie, wright in Abernyte, the W face displaying the tools of his trade; emblems of death in the curly pediment. – To its SW, George Geikie, †1747, the E face with an angel's head above a shield bearing a crowned cordiner's knife; emblems of death at the bottom. – S of the church, William Duncan, weaver in Burnside of Pitkindie, †1738, the W face decorated with a skull and bone above a weaver's loom and shuttle flanked by hourglasses. – To its E, the stone erected by Patrick Lowson, 'flesher [butcher] in Glen Lyon', in memory of his father, †1729, and wife, †1736, the W face a curvily pedimented aedicule. Poking inward from its Corinthianish pilasters are the heads of sheep who look at the central scene of a butcher killing a steer whose throat is gripped by a bulldog; above this scene, a heart bearing the tools of a butcher, below are emblems of death. – To the S, a stone erected in 1789 by William West, tenant in Kirkton Mill, in memory of his son, Peter. W face carved with figures of two men in C18 dress; an angel's head in the curly pediment. – Propped against the churchyard's E wall, a C17 GRAVE-SLAB bearing the initials IM and EM. A shield at the top; at the bottom, an hourglass and skull flanked by a pair of crossbones.

Two-storey harled MANSE (now GAVINTOWN HOUSE) to the E. The main part was built by *David Smart*, mason in Dundee, 1756, its S front partly rebuilt and the window openings altered by *John Cross*, wright in Coupar Angus, 1820. Off-centre addition, with a bowed S front, of 1821–2. At the house's SW corner, a reused datestone of 1666.

ABERNYTE PRIMARY SCHOOL. By *James Findlay*, 1906. Red brick and plain but with a hint of Jacobean.

ABERUCHILL CASTLE

2.4 km. SW of Comrie

Harled laird's house built from the early C17 to the late C19.

In 1594 Sir John Campbell of Lawers acquired the lands of Aberuchill as an estate for his second son, Colin, who apparently built the core of the present house in 1602 (the date on a reset dormerhead). This is a three-storey and attic L, the roofs of both the main block and the NE jamb running E–W.

Conical-roofed round turrets on the s corners of the main block and the NE of the jamb; rounded stair-tower in the inner angle (now hidden inside Victorian additions). The principal (s) front appears quite peaceful. Its ground-floor window, probably originally small, has been enlarged, perhaps in the C18. At the E end of this front, a heavy Neo-Jacobean porch of 1869; also late C19 are the attic's gabled dormers.

An E wing of two storeys and an attic was added *c.* 1800. s side of three bays (but only two windows to the ground floor), plain except for the square bartizan on the E corner. This really belongs to the broad four-bay E gable which is dressed up with playful castellated detail. At its corners, corbelled bartizans with quatrefoil dummy windows surmount slightly advanced slender 'towers' decorated with pointed dummy windows, those of the ground floor hoodmoulded. Between the towers rises a battlement which, together with the tops of its merlons, slopes on the line of the roof pitches over the outer bays. Over the two centre bays it is horizontal, with tiny conical-roofed corner turrets. Hoodmoulds over the two centre windows of the first floor.

Sprawling low service wings were added in 1869 and 1873–4 (by *Robert Ewan*). Scots manorial in style with crowstepped gables and a sparing provision of turrets with tall conical roofs.

Rubble WALLED GARDEN, probably of *c.* 1800, to the w.

ABERUTHVEN

9010

Village of plain houses, mostly C19 vernacular, the former churches standing at opposite ends of the main street.

ABERUTHVEN FREE CHURCH. Now a house. Rubble-built oblong of 1851–2. Tudor-arched windows and a gableted bellcote. Tall w porch. The low session house was added to the E end in 1863–4.

ST KATTAN'S CHURCH. Roofless remains of a medieval church which was abandoned for worship at the end of the C17; few dateable features but it might be C13. The building is a narrow rectangle, *c.* 19.8 m. by 6.6 m., the walls of rubble. On the w gable, a pyramidal-roofed birdcage bellcote built by *David Fenton* and *Robert Richard*, masons, in 1721–5. Windowless N wall. In the E gable, a low door inserted in the late C16 or C17 and a pair of lancet windows, the head of each carved from a single large stone. Only the w end of the s wall survives, now forming one side of the GRAEME MAUSOLEUM which occupies this part of the building, its Tudorish arched door apparently of the earlier C19. Abutting this is the DUFF-DUNCAN MAUSOLEUM roughly in the centre of the church but its s front set back from the line of the church's s wall. Entrance through a mid-C19 four-centred arch. Occupying the E end of the church and projecting s from it is the detached MONTROSE MAUSOLEUM designed by *William Adam* and built by the apparently unrelated *John Adam*, mason in Buchanan, 1736–8. This is square, the walls (originally of ashlar but now rendered) rising to a bold cornice; urn-topped pyramidal roof. Inserted in the s wall by *John Steven*, 1785, a Venetian doorway, the volutes of its Ionic pilasters now broken off, the keystone carved as a grotesque head. – In the GRAVEYARD some C18 HEADSTONES carved with grisly reminders of death and angels' heads (souls).

ACHARN

Small village on the s side of Loch Tay.

DESCRIPTION. At the E end, on the N side of the road and at right angles to it, a symmetrical row of rubble-built and broad-eaved two-storey mid-C19 cottages (THE MANUFACTORY), their Gothic first-floor windows rising into gableted dormer-heads and with a pair of gabled wings projecting from the E front. Then, a slightly later U-plan row fronting the road, the windows enlarged in the later C20. Set back on the road's s side, a rather altered mid-C19 double house with broad-eaved gabled porches and a Gothic dummy window in the E gable. To the s, PINE COTTAGE, also mid-C19, with carved bargeboards to the gables and dormerheads. In the centre of the village, THE OLD MILL of 1851–2. Harled and picturesquely bargeboarded. Cupola-ventilator on the roof; water wheel at the w end. It stands beside the rubble-built segmental-arched BRIDGE, probably of the early C19, over the Acharn Burn. w of the bridge and facing each other across the road, a quadruple cottage (FERNBANK, ROSE COTTAGE, LAURELBANK and TAY VIEW) and a double cottage (DRUMMOND VIEW and HAUGH COTTAGE), both mid-C19 with bracketed broad eaves, small-paned windows and tree-trunk porches. In the same manner the contemporary former school (THE OLD SCHOOL HOUSE) beside the path up to the Hermit's Cave.

HERMIT'S CAVE, 0.7 km. s. A 'hermitage' constructed on the w bank of the Acharn Burn *c*. 1800 to allow visitors a spectacular view of the Falls of Acharn. Built into the bank, two rubbly entrances at the ends of an S-shaped passage, its stone-slabbed sides pierced by small openings and punctuated by stone ledge seats set in recesses. Off the main passage, a shorter passage leads to a polygonal chamber, now roofless, its open E side giving a frontal view of the waterfall.

REMONY, 0.4 km. E. Villa of 1924, by *William Kerr* of *John Melvin & Son*. Rubble-built, the general inspiration taken from Cotswold manor houses but with a Scots inflexion and some weatherboarding.

ALDIE CASTLE see HOUSE OF ALDIE

ALMONDBANK

Two settlements (Almondbank and Bridgeton) separated by the River Almond, both built to house workers in cotton mills and now serving as dormitories for Perth.

ALMONDBANK TIBBERMORE (ST SERF'S) CHURCH, Main Street. Originally Almondbank St Serf's United Free Church. Sizeable but plain late Gothic, by *Hippolyte J. Blanc*, 1904–5, built of squared and stugged grey rubble with dressings of polished red sandstone. Nave and narrow aisles under a single bellcast-eaved roof; NW transept and SW hall. Only the bottom stage of the intended NE tower was built.

THE NEW HOPE CENTRE, Scroggiehill. Built as the Victoria Guild Hall in 1899. Buttressed red brick rectangle with a Dutch-gabled W front, its porch an addition of the 1990s. Flèche surmounted by an elaborate wrought-iron finial.

BRIDGE, Main Street. Mid-C19, a single segmental arch over the River Almond. Ashlar, the N parapet rebuilt in the late C20 with artificial stone.

DESCRIPTION. Almondbank's MAIN STREET S of the bridge (*see* above) is mostly C19 vernacular. Off its W side, overlooking the River Almond, is RIVER LODGE of *c.* 1900. Picturesque, the ground floor of painted brick, the attic of wood with decorative panels composed of saplings; broad-eaved and bargeboarded roof covered with fish-scale slating. Late C20 E addition. N of the bridge the road climbs up to Bridgeton. At its S end, a pink granite cenotaph WAR MEMORIAL of *c.* 1920 in front of a handful of plain Late Georgian houses, one dated 1799. Just beyond, on the road's W side, Almondbank Tibbermore (St Serf's) Church (*see* above).

ALYTH

A settlement which possessed a mill, smithy, brewery, meat market and inn by 1468, Alyth became a burgh of barony *c.* 1485, this status confirmed in 1624 when the superiority was acquired by James, seventh Lord Ogilvy of Airlie (later, first Earl of Airlie). The early buildings stood near the former Parish Church at the N end of the present town.

Development S of the Alyth Burn followed *William Panton*'s layout of Airlie Street and the land to its E for building in 1786, although not much took place before the early C19. In the mid C19 Market Square and Commercial Street were formed, providing a link to the earlier settlement, followed by new streets W of Airlie Street. Alyth became a police burgh in 1875 but in size has remained little more than a large village with only a main shopping street and square to justify its burghal pretensions.

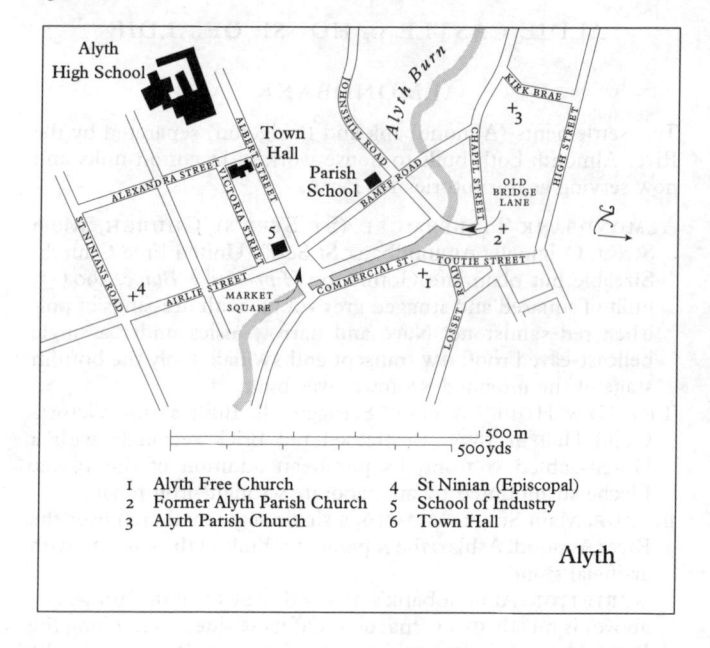

1 Alyth Free Church
2 Former Alyth Parish Church
3 Alyth Parish Church
4 St Ninian (Episcopal)
5 School of Industry
6 Town Hall

CHURCHES

ALYTH FREE CHURCH, Commercial Street. Disused. Built in 1843, a tall red sandstone ashlar box, with pointed windows and birdcage bellcote.

Former ALYTH PARISH CHURCH, off High Street. Standing in a graveyard, a sizeable fragment of the medieval church dedicated to St Moluag. This church, perhaps built in the C13, was originally a simple rectangle, *c.* 24.4 m. by 7.3 m. Probably in the C15 a chapel was constructed on the N side of the chancel and a three-bay N aisle added to the nave *c.* 1500. Of this there survive the arcade between the nave and aisle, much of the N wall of the chancel (now sloped towards the E and adorned with C19 crowsteps), and low walls on the chapel's E and N sides. The arcade consists of round-headed chamfered arches carried on octagonal piers with simply moulded bases and capitals. Jostled by the E end of the arcade is a partly blocked high-set round-headed tall window, presumably part of the fabric of the church's original N wall. E of this, a (built-up) round-headed doorway which opened from the chancel into the chapel. In the chancel's N wall, a sacrament house partly blocked by a monument. In this wall's N side (i.e. the S side of the chapel), two aumbries, the W triangular-headed, the E square.

ALYTH PARISH CHURCH, Kirk Brae. Unarchaeological Romanesque by *Thomas Hamilton*, 1836–9. Tall red sandstone cruciform, the broad N, S and E limbs equally sized but the E with aisles whose outer corners are clasped by pinnacled buttresses. Low vestry addition by *I. R. Dalgetty*, 1956, at the end of the E limb. More pinnacled clasping buttresses at the corners of the shorter and narrower W limb, a steeple at its end. In each gable of the N, S and E limbs, three windows to light the area and, above, a four-light gallery window, its head filled with a rose. The steeple's tower is of three stages, the lowest buttressed and containing the broad round-headed entrance under a Neo-Jacobean mullioned and transomed rectangular window. At each exposed face of the second stage, a window of two round-headed lights under a quatrefoil head. Above, blind arcading under the belfry openings which are surmounted by clock faces. Stone spouts project from the parapet. Within it rises the octagonal stone spire, a lucarne at each of the cardinal point faces.

The interior was renovated in 1934 and recast by *Ian Macdonald* in 1972–5 when the E limb was blocked off to form a hall, the E gallery being moved to the W side and the pulpit (its canopied top altered at the same time) moved from the W to the E. Scalloped-capitalled cast-iron columns support the galleries, the panels of whose fronts are decorated with friezes of round-headed arcading; Jacobean pendants drop from the undersides. Coomb ceiling strengthened by wooden braces which intersect over the crossing.

STAINED GLASS. Under the N gallery, the W window (Our Lord and the Samaritan Woman) is by *A. Ballantine & Son*, 1905. – To its E, a window (a dark version of Holman Hunt's *The Light of the World*) of 1906, by *Stephen Adam*. – Beside it, a strongly coloured light (Our Lord and Little Children) by *Margaret Chilton* and *Marjorie Kemp*, 1925. – The W window under the S gallery (the Sower) is also by *Marjorie Kemp*, 1948, an example of restrained expressionism. – Beside it, a window (the Man of Sorrows) of 1913, by *Alfred A. Webster*. – The E window on this side (Our Lord and St Peter) is by *William Wilson*, 1954. – Gallery window of the N limb (Scenes by *Stephen Adam*, from the Life of Our Lord) 1904, realistic but bad. – Much better the lushly coloured post-Raphaelite S gallery window (the Agony in the Garden and Our Lord Carrying the Cross, flanked by David and Isaiah), by *Henry Holiday*, 1907. – ORGAN in the W gallery, by *David W. Loosley*, 1978, reusing pipes (by *Harrison & Harrison*, 1913) from the former Blairgowrie Parish Church and a console from the former Dysart Parish Church, Kirkcaldy (Fife).

In the porch, a CROSS-SLAB, perhaps of the late C7, the front incised with a cross, its inner angles containing rope coils; on the back, part of a 'double-disc-and Z-rod' symbol.

CHURCHYARD. At the entrance a large Romanesque round-headed ARCHWAY, by *Thomas Hamilton*, 1839.

ALYTH UNITED PRESBYTERIAN CHURCH, Airlie Street. Secularized. By *John Haggart*, 1867–8. Gothic red sandstone rectangle. Pinnacled diagonal buttresses at the corners of the front gable which has a lower projecting gabled centrepiece hinting at a nave and aisles behind. On top of the front gable, a fussily detailed bellcote.

ST NINIAN (Episcopal), St Ninian's Road. Romanesque, built of squared and stugged masonry, by *David Bryce*, 1857. Nave and a lower apsidal-ended chancel. SW steeple containing the entrance; NE vestry and NW organ chamber. Wheel window in the W gable. Cushion-capitalled nook-shafts to the other windows of the nave and chancel. Under the chancel's eaves, a corbelled-out band course. Bowed stair-turret at the W face of the steeple's two-stage tower. Rising within its tall corbelled parapet, a slated pyramidal spire.

Inside, an open roof over the nave, a ribbed plaster vault above the chancel. Round-headed chancel arch. – Simple bench PEWS of 1857. – PULPIT of *c.* 1945. – ALTAR RAILS of *c.* 1940. – Stone FONT of 1863, carved angels' heads round the base of the bowl. It was formerly in the demolished St Margaret's Episcopal Church at Meigle. – In the W gallery, a CHAMBER ORGAN by *John R. Miller*, 1909.

STAINED GLASS. In the chancel three lights (St Mary Magdalene, the Good Shepherd, St Martha) by *O'Connor*, probably of *c.* 1860. – In the W gable, a wheel window (the small roundels containing portraits of prophets and Evangelists 'arranged' by Sir James Ramsay of Bamff) by *Clayton & Bell*, 1880. – Also in the gable, two lights (Angels) of *c.* 1890. – In the N wall, one light (David) by *John Blyth*, 1952, colourful but not very good.

S of the chancel arch, a marble MONUMENT to Jane Oliphant, wife of Sir James Ramsay of Bamff, with a relief of the Burial of Our Lord. It is signed by *Holme Carmichael*, 1869. – On the N wall, a pair of bronze MEMORIAL TABLETS, both with relief portraits. One (depicting an officer of the Black Watch) is to Lieutenant Nigel Neis Ramsay, †1899, the other to Charlotte Fanning, †1904, the wife of Sir James M. Ramsay of Bamff.

PUBLIC BUILDINGS

ALYTH HIGH SCHOOL, St Andrew Street. By *John Carver*, 1878. A tall single storey in picturesque School Board Gothic, built of red sandstone. U-plan S front, the gable of its W wing topped by a tall bellcote, with a wrought-iron finial on its fish-scale slated spired roof.

PARISH SCHOOL, Bamff Road. Now in other use and the walls covered with drydash, the roof with concrete tiles. By *John Carver Sen.*, 1835, and extended in 1862 when the advanced centre was given a pointed door and Gothic bellcote.

SCHOOL OF INDUSTRY, corner of Airlie Street and Albert Street. Now housing. Plain school and schoolhouse of 1855, built of red sandstone.

TOWN HALL, Albert Street. By *Heiton & Grainger*, 1886. Like a gargantuan villa. Applied half-timbering in the gables, bracketed broad eaves and quatrefoil-pierced bargeboards. At the NE tower a half-timbered jettied belfry, its openings topped by slated dormerheads protruding from the pyramidal roof. Over the main entrance a stone balcony, its parapet pierced by pointed arches.

DESCRIPTION

AIRLIE STREET is the approach from the S. At its start, a WAR MEMORIAL of 1921 designed by *James Riddel*. Tall battered pedestal of ashlar surmounted by a bronze statue by *Kellock Brown* of a crouching woman holding a scabbarded sword in one hand and, in the other, an orb topped by a figure of Victory. The street's architecture soon establishes itself as plain small-town C19 vernacular. On the W, St Ninian's (Episcopal) Church and, further on, the former Alyth United Presbyterian Church and School of Industry, with Alyth Town Hall in ALBERT STREET to the W (*see* Churches and Public Buildings, above).

MARKET SQUARE is the burgh's central space, its buildings continuing the character of Airlie Street. At the square's NW corner, a polished granite FOUNTAIN of 1913, the water issuing from a bronze lion's head. Behind the fountain and also of polished granite, the SOUTH AFRICAN WAR MEMORIAL of *c.* 1905, an obelisk with Neo-Egyptian detail.

COMMERCIAL STREET on the E side of the Alyth Burn runs N from the end of Market Square. Buildings only on the E side. Among them, the ALYTH MUSEUM (former YMCA) of 1901. Two storeys, the upper floor tall, the pedimented gable front topped by a squat Baroque chimney. Adjoining, No. 16, a two-storey house of 1827, its rough ashlar front of three bays. At the street's N end, the former Alyth Free Church (*see* Churches, above). Facing Commercial Street from the W side of the Alyth Burn is PITNACREE STREET, dominated by a plain late C19 industrial building. At the street's N end, the OLD PACK HORSE BRIDGE. It was perhaps built in the C16 but repaired in 1646 and 1674. Two segmental rubble arches of unequal size and the E at a higher level than the W; triangular cutwaters at the central pier. Above the S cutwater, a shield said* to have borne the coat of arms of the Ramsays of Bamff and the initials VR, perhaps for William Ramsay, Baron-Bailie of Alyth in 1674. Crudely corbelled parapets added *c.* 1800 and heightened about forty years later.

TOUTIE STREET continues the line of Commercial Street uphill to the N. On its corner with LOSSET ROAD, the C18 harled LOSSET INN. Quite small windows. They now have cement margins and the building was reroofed in the late C19 when it acquired mean bargeboards. In the front, a stone, probably not *in situ*, incised with the initials and date 17DO♡MM30. In PARKSIDE ROAD off Losset Road, piend-roofed and harled

---

*By James Meikle, *An Old Session Book* (Paisley, 1918), 151.

local authority HOUSING by *Johnston & Baxter*, 1938, with first-floor windows rising through the eaves into curly-topped gablets.

On Toutie Street's s corner with Bank Street, No. 16 Toutie Street. Its s front of 1823 and w gable have been drydashed and altered but in the long rubble-built N elevation are small blocked windows and the NE corner is rounded below corbelling to bring it to a right angle under the eaves, suggesting this part may be of C16 or C17 origin. In HILL STREET at the top of Toutie Street, No. 1, originally a double house of 1814. Ashlar front with rusticated quoins and a Gibbsian door surround (the opening now a window) at the l. part; the r. part's ground floor has acquired a shopfront.

HIGH STREET runs w. At the start on its s side, OAKLEY, an L-plan house, now rendered and the windows altered in the C19 and C20 but its origin probably disclosed by one first-floor opening whose lintel is incised with the initials and date IG.IM.1690. It stands on the side of a short close leading to the graveyard surrounding the former Alyth Parish Church (*see* Churches, above). On the N side of High Street, on the axis of Toutie Street, a little garden. On its retaining wall stands the ALYTH MARKET CROSS, a small monolith, the shaft (originally taller) with a panel bearing the date 1670. Octagonal finial carved with the relief of a lion rampant and the initials I^{E}A (for James, [second] Earl of Airlie, the burgh's feudal superior). In BAMFF WYND, on the corner with High Street, the rubble-built and small-windowed No. 7, the attic lit by openings in the gables; it is probably late C18. KIRK BRAE leads down to Alyth Parish Church (*see* Churches, above). Opposite the church, on the s side of BAMFF ROAD where the ground falls precipitously to the bank of the Alyth Burn, a tall piend-roofed and rubble-built T-plan former CORN MILL of 1834. In Bamff Road SE of the Alyth Burn, the former Parish School (*see* Public Buildings, above).

LANDS OF LOYAL HOTEL
off Loyal Road

Originally Loyal House. Enjoying a superb view over Strathmore, a substantial villa of 1850 designed by *A. & A. Heiton* for a naval officer, Commander William Ogilvy. Broad-eaved, bargeboarded and bay-windowed exterior with some Jacobean touches, the walls of stugged red sandstone ashlar. At the entrance (W) elevation, a Jacobean Gothic porch. Near-symmetrical S front but the bay windows of its broad gabled ends are canted at the W and rectangular at the E; hood-moulded centre window of three lights, a gablet over the window above. At the E gable, the ground-floor window enjoys a large ogee-arched hoodmould with pendant label stops and a foliaged finial, its appearance Late Georgian. Recessed wing in the same manner added for Professor George Gilbert Ramsay by *Andrew Heiton Jun.*, 1877–8.

Inside the porch, a hammerbeam roof. Entrance hall with a compartmented ceiling. It opens onto a top-lit inner hall formed *c.* 1900. Two storeys in height finished in the Lorimerian Scottish Arts and Crafts manner. The plaster ceiling is a segmental tunnel vault divided into compartments by bands enriched with oakleaves and acorns; vine frieze. Vine embellishment also on the oak panelling of the walls. At the E end, a T-plan stair, its newel posts topped by figures of lions. At first-floor level, a gallery along the hall's E and S sides and the E end of the N side. Large canopied chimneypiece of veined marble at the N. The other principal rooms are ranged along the house's S front, all with Jacobean compartmented ceilings of 1850, most elaborate in the E room whose plasterwork includes (twice) the figure of a lady holding a portcullis (the Ogilvy crest).

FORT, Barry Hill, 2.4 km. NE. On a hilltop overlooking Strathmore, an Iron Age fort, probably of the first millennium B.C. It has been constructed in two principal phases. The first entailed the building of a rampart to enclose a broad roughly oval terrace from whose centre rise the steeply sloping sides of the flat-topped knoll which forms the summit of the hill. The area enclosed by this rampart is *c.* 155 m. by 88 m. and was entered from the SE. An annexe extending *c.* 35 m. from the enclosure's W side was also surrounded by a rampart. The second stage of work saw the construction of a new earth rampart, up to 15 m. thick and backed by a ditch, along the S and E sides. Its long S stretch overlies the original rampart, its blocking of the original entrance perhaps dating from a later phase of work, but its N return at the E end is inside the original enclosure. Probably at the same time the hill's oval summit was fortified as a citadel, *c.* 80 m. by 25 m., surrounded by a massive bank of rubble masonry, probably laced with timber and over 10 m. thick, which still rises on the S from the inner side of a ditch to a height of up to 6.8 m.

SYMBOL STONE, Bruceton, 4.7 km. ENE. Boulder, 1.37 m. high, one face incised, probably in the C6 or C7, with paired horseshoe and 'Pictish beast' symbols.

BALHARY. *See* p. 177.
BAMFF. *See* p. 189.
BARDMONY HOUSE. *See* p. 192.

AMULREE

Hamlet on the military road from Crieff to Aberfeldy, its multi-gabled HOTEL rebuilt *c.* 1910.

AMULREE AND STRATHBRAAN CHURCH. Harled oblong kirk designed by *John Douglas* and built in 1743–52 but remodelled in 1881–2. Round-headed windows, perhaps mid C18, in the S side. The E gable's large pointed window and its intersecting tracery are probably of 1881–2, the date of the W end's gabled bellcote, hoodmoulded round window, lean-to porch and piend-roofed NW outshot containing the gallery stair.

Inside, the w gallery and space below were partitioned off in 1960. At the E end, a Scoto-Catholic arrangement of late Victorian FONT, oak COMMUNION TABLE of 1916 and oak PULPIT of 1904, its faces carved with shields bearing emblems of the Passion, a sounding-board above. – STAINED GLASS. Competent but uninspired E window (Faith, Hope and Charity) of *c.* 1905.

GRAVEYARD. Immediately E of the church, a HEADSTONE of 1759 to the children of Donald McLean, maltster. On the w face, an angel's head (the soul) above a shield bearing a maltster's implements; at the bottom, a skull, crossbones and hourglass. – s of this, a stone of 1780, its E face carved with an angel's head above a heraldic achievement; reminders of death at the bottom. – To its SW, a headstone of 1828 commemorating John McFarlane, the w face a swan-neck-pedimented aedicule framing a heraldic achievement.

AMULREE FREE CHURCH, Glenquaich, 3.5 km. w. Disused. Built in 1862 to a design by the clerk of works at Taymouth Castle (q.v.). Whin rubble walls, the roof with broad eaves and carved bargeboards. w front of three bays, the centre (now containing a large C20 garage door) advanced and surmounted by a ball-finialled birdcage bellcote. Round-headed lights in the rectangular windows.

STONE CIRCLE, Meikle Findowie, 6.2 km. ENE. On a hillside in Strath Braan, a double circle of standing stones erected, probably in two stages, in the third or second millennium B.C. The outer and perhaps later ring, 7.92 m. in diameter, was composed of nine stones (three now fallen), the two largest (both fallen) *c.* 1.83 m. and 2.13 m. tall and placed in the SW arc. The inner ring, not quite concentric to the outer, is *c.* 3.81 m. in diameter. Eight small stones still stand, none more than 0.25 m. above the ground.

ARDBLAIR CASTLE
1.5 km. WSW of Blairgowrie

Laird's house of the Blairs (later, Blair-Oliphants) of Ardblair which has developed from the C16 to the early C20 round a courtyard.

The site, evidently occupied from an early date, a Pictish quaich having been discovered during repairs to the NW tower, is naturally defensive. A loch (now drained) formerly surrounded it on the S, E and W, the approach from the N presumably was once defended by a ditch and rampart. The lands of Ardblair or Mureton were held in the C14 by Thomas Blair, son of Blair of Balthayock, but the earliest part of the present house is the NW tower built, probably in the early C16, at one corner of what may well have been an existing barmkin enclosure. Probably in the late C17, perhaps in 1668 when the courtyard was given a new N entrance, a self-contained range was built on the courtyard's E side; it may have been intended as a jointure or dower house. A W range was built against the S side of the tower, probably in the early C18, with an office wing extending W from its S end. For most of the C19 the buildings were used as a farmhouse and steading but after the sale of Gask House (q.v.) *c.* 1903 the complex became the principal residence of the Blair-Oliphants for whom it was repaired, altered and extended by *Sydney Mitchell & Wilson* between 1894 and 1908.

Like all the buildings in the complex, the NW TOWER is of harled rubble; base constructed of boulders. Main block of three storeys and an attic, with a three-storey jamb, its floors placed at a slightly lower level, which projects both W and S of the main block. In the W inner angle, a stair-turret projected on continuous corbelling; its conical roof is of 1894–5. In the N gable of the jamb, an oval gunloop; round shot-hole in its W side. Irregularly disposed openings to the N and W, with slit windows at the ground floor (the window in the W gable of the main block enlarged in 1895), large first-floor windows and smaller but comfortably sized windows at the second floor. The catslide dormers on the main block's N side were added in 1894–5 when most of the gables' crowsteps were replaced.

At the tower's inner faces to the courtyard, a large wallhead chimney on the S side of the main block. Same hierarchy of windows as at the outer faces, the main block's first-floor S windows and the jamb's second-floor E window with rounded margins. The second-floor window of the main block has a chamfered margin and pedimental top (renewed in the C20). The tower's entrance is placed, conventionally enough, in the E face of the jamb but its frame, probably of the early C17, is far from conventional. The inner part has a roll-moulded surround with a rope-moulded cornice, a pendant corbel at its centre, topped by a badly weathered shield. Flanking this are superimposed baluster-like attached columns with rope-moulded capitals and diagonally fluted bulbous bases and finials, their design perhaps derived from those for contemporary bedposts. Now placed above but almost certainly not *in situ* is the round-headed frame for a missing panel. It is carved in high relief with figures of a unicorn, stag, musician, angel, beasts, etc.; weathered unicorn finial. What is this and where did it come from?

The courtyard's N ENTRANCE is of 1668. Roll-and-hollow-moulded jambs supporting imposts from which spring a round-headed arch. On the wallhead, a scroll-flanked aedicule with squat panelled pilasters and a steep pediment, its tympanum carved with the date 1668 and the monogrammed initials BS (for Blair of Ardblair and Stewart of Pittendreich). Inside the aedicule, a strapwork-surrounded circular shield bearing the impaled arms of Blair and Stewart. Behind this wall, the plain single-storey flat-roofed N RANGE of 1894–5. It contains a large entrance hall providing a link between the NW tower and the E range.

The courtyard's W RANGE S of the tower, also quite plain, is of two storeys, the first-floor windows taller than those below.

Its N part and the W service wing are probably early C18 but the wing was remodelled in 1894–5. The range S of that is a tactful addition of 1907–8.

The two-storey E RANGE, perhaps late C17 in origin, was recast in 1895–6, the likely date of its gabled dormer windows. Over the door to the courtyard, a worn armorial panel. Most of the W elevation is overlaid by a two-storey corridor addition of 1907–8 which ends at a conical-roofed stair-tower in the inner angle with the contemporary S RANGE. This is of two storeys and plain Georgian in manner except for round-headed doorways to the courtyard and garden.

INTERIOR. The ground-floor room in the main block of the NW tower, probably originally a store, was vaulted until 1895 when it became an inner hall opening off the main entrance hall in the new N range. In the tower's jamb, a comfortable turnpike stair to the first floor. Tighter stair in the turret to the floors above. The C16 hall on the first floor of the main block became a parlour in the early or mid C18 when its walls were panelled and a basket-arched chimneypiece introduced. More panelling in the Long Gallery which occupies the first floor of the W range. That of the room's N part may be C18 but the panelling in the S part must date from the range's extension in 1907–8. Also of this date the Georgian Revival drawing room on the first floor of the S range.

In the courtyard, a multi-faceted SUNDIAL, perhaps of the later C17. – Also here, one of a collection of fairly crudely carved stone STATUES of Greek deities. The other four (Aesculapius, Prometheus (?), Ceres and Flora) are in the garden E of the house. They may be early C19.

ARDLER

Village laid out in the later C19, with a main E–W street and three streets running off it to the S. Much of the housing is plain; large parsonical former MANSE (by *Alexander Johnston*, 1884–5) at the E end.

ARDLER CHURCH, Church Street. Converted to a house in 1988. By *Alexander Johnston*, 1883. Busy but unexciting Dec, the walls of stugged red sandstone, the roof covered with bands of grey and green slates with iron cresting on the ridge. N transepts and an apsidal chancel, its windows rising into gablets. SW steeple, the square tower broached to an octagonal belfry finished with a stone spire.

SCHOOL, off Wallace Street. Built, *c.* 1840. Single-storey with simple Jacobean detail, the hoodmoulds of the rectangular windows with pendant label stops. It was extended at each end in the same manner by *Alexander Johnston*, 1888–9; carved bargeboards to the gables.

ARTHURSTONE. *See* p. 160.

ARDOCH see BRACO

ARDVORLICH HOUSE
6.5 km. w of St Fillans

Rubble-built laird's house overlooking Loch Earn. The two-storey and attic main block was built by the master mason, *Robert Ferguson*, in 1790. s front of three bays, the centre with an urn-finialled gablet containing a Venetian window. In 1839 the house became a U by the addition of low rear wings, the w with a chimney-topped crowstepped gable at the centre of its outer side; horizontal panes to the windows. Further work was carried out in 1890 when round turrets and crowsteps were added to the w gable of the C18 house and its s front's entrance given a Neo-Jacobean pedimented porch. Contemporary E addition, its crowstepped broad s gable projecting beyond the C18 front; French pavilion roofed tower at the NW.

ARLARY HOUSE
2 km. NE of Milnathort

Laird's house which has developed in pleasant though not very orderly fashion. The main block is early C18, of droved ashlar, with a second-floor lintel-cum-eaves course and rusticated quoins. The entrance seems originally to have been at the N elevation whose two-bay centre is advanced under a rather steep pediment. A new principal entrance was made at the centre of the s front *c.* 1800. This is contained in a suave porch of triumphal arch inspiration, its grey stone a contrast to the red masonry of the earlier walling. Framework of polished ashlar in which are set droved panels. Over the door, a semi-circular fanlight. In each panelled spandrel of the arch, a round boss. Probably contemporary is the single-storey piend-roofed pavilion at the house's E end, its front gable's two windows set in round-headed overarches. The plain NW wing butting into the centre of the N elevation is probably mid-C19.

Early C19 WALLED GARDEN to the N, its dwarf s wall topped by cast-iron railings. At the w end of the N wall, a doorway with chamfered margins and, on its lintel, the date 1700. Possibly it came from the house or, more probably, from its predecessor.

ARNGASK see GLENFARG

ARNOT TOWER
2 km. E of Scotlandwell

On a hillside above Loch Leven, a Victorian villa with a roofless C15 tower house in the garden.

The VILLA is of 1878. Walling of bullnosed masonry. Bracketed broad eaves to the jerkin-head roofs, now covered with concrete tiles. Brick-built extension to the rear by *Peddie & Washington Browne*, 1904.

The TOWER HOUSE, probably a replacement for an earlier wooden structure, stands just to the E at a higher level, its defensive site presumably formerly enclosed by a barmkin wall. The house is a simple four-storey oblong, *c.* 9.88m. by 8.05m. Except at the SE corner which has been removed, the rough ashlar walling, unbroken by string courses, mostly stands to the wallhead whose plain moulded corbels have carried a parapet. The entrance must have been at the SE. Just W of its presumed site, the S wall has a slit window just above ground-floor level and presumably to light a stair. At the first floor, N and S windows, both altered but seemingly smaller originally than the unaltered sizeable second-floor window; all have chamfered margins.

Inside, the ground floor has been occupied by a store covered by a stone tunnel vault whose springing survives. Each of the upper floors, the corbels supporting the wooden structure of the top two still in place, seems to have contained a single room with a fireplace (now missing) in the W gable. At the first-floor hall, the S window is placed in a segmental-arched embrasure which has contained a stone window seat. Better-preserved seat in the window embrasure of the second-floor upper hall. The third-floor room is windowless but has cupboards in the S and W walls.

A rubble-built two-storey range has been built, probably in the C16 or C17, against the S side of the tower and along the W side of the likely barmkin court. Its windowless W wall survives with some of the corbels which supported its upper floor.

ARTHURSTONE
1 km. N of Ardler

Pleasantly restrained country house of the late C18 and C19 enclosing an opulent Late Victorian interior. It was converted to flats in 2004.

The earliest part faces W, a three-storey piend-roofed house built for Colonel William Rattray, *c.* 1795. Walling of squared and cherry-cocked red sandstone rubble. Five-bay front, the centrepiece a full-height splay-sided projection containing the tall Roman Doric columned and pedimented entrance. Tall windows at the ground floor, a sill course under those of the first floor, small and square openings at the second floor. Wallhead blocking course topped by small stone urns at the ends and the outer corners of the centrepiece. At the rear (E) elevation, now largely covered by C19 additions, a central round-headed stair window.

At the S gable is a rectangular bay window added by the Murrays of Simprim who bought the estate in 1838. They also built the long, three-storey SE wing which resembles a Jacobethan manor house with a near-symmetrical S front of six bays, the centre four topped by gablets. Advanced and gabled ends, a two-storey rectangular bay window at the l., an oriel window at the r. A service range of one and two storeys joins the mansion to its coachhouse (*see* below). Peter Carmichael, a partner in the Dundee flax-spinning firm of John Baxter & Son, bought the estate in 1869 and soon after added the single-storey NE wing (replacing an earlier one). In its W front, aligned with that of the 1790s house, a mullioned and transomed three-light window under a panel carved with back-to-back Cs. At this wing's long N side, a couple of bay windows, one rectangular, the other canted. At the back of the C18 house, various C19 additions, the most significant a single-storey Jacobethan corridor extension of *c.* 1870 which connects the E wing and contained a new principal entrance surmounted by the Carmichael coat of arms.

INTERIOR. The E entrance hall of *c.* 1870 opens through a large Gothic arch into the contemporary ground-floor corridor. Wooden chimneypiece of Gothic character flanked by heavy wooden doorcases on the corridor's W side. At its N end, the entrance to the library or billiard room of *c.* 1870. This is a Jacobean great hall, the beams of its double-pitch ceiling carried on corbels modelled as human heads. Large wooden chimneypiece with a mirrored overmantel.

The corridor opens W into the STAIR HALL of the late C18 house. Stair with a cast-iron balustrade of pierced oval panels. Delicate Gothic arcaded cornicing at the landings and ceiling. A large Gothic arch of *c.* 1870, like that from the entrance hall to the corridor, opens into the 1790s circular ENTRANCE HALL (the Victorian garden room), its cornice repeating those of the stair hall. Over the door to the garden (the 1790s front door) the stained-glass coat of arms of the Carmichaels. To the S, the DINING ROOM. Its ceiling's cornice, enriched with a Greek key pattern, oval paterae and acanthus decoration, is Late Georgian but cut into by the beams added when the room was remodelled *c.* 1870 in an exuberant and expensive Jacobean manner. At the intersections of the beams, bosses carved with flowers, foliage and a grotesque head. The beam at the opening into the bay window is supported by carved wooden figures of satyrs. The walls' lower two-thirds are covered with panelling, the Artisan Mannerist pilasters bearing reliefs of lions' heads and supporting wooden statues of medieval men and women. Large wooden chimneypiece, the bases of its Corinthian columns carved with grotesque heads; on the frieze, a hunting scene in high relief. Overmantel with atlantes holding bunches of grapes above their heads at the ends; between them, a medieval battle scene in high relief.

N of the C18 entrance hall, a double DRAWING ROOM, its S compartment formed from a late C18 room, the N contained in the wing of *c.* 1870. Lavish decoration of *c.* 1870 in a Louis XV manner, the walls plaster-panelled, the painted wooden chimneypieces carved with cherubs and relief panels of pastoral scenes; mirrored overmantels.

On the first floor of the 1790s house, a circular BEDROOM above the original entrance hall contains a Late Georgian pine and gesso chimneypiece, its acanthus-capitalled pilaster-jambs decorated with foliage pendants and surmounted by reliefs of urns; on the frieze, a panel with gryphons facing an urn. In the rooms either side, Victorian chimneypieces: they contain Late Georgian cast-iron grates, the SE room's bearing the crest of the Prince of Wales, the NW classical urns.

The COACHHOUSE to the E, tenuously joined to the house by the early C19 service range, is of 1797 (the date together with the initials of Colonel William Rattray on a small panel on its W front). Two storeys and rubble-walled, the main roof piended and with Victorian cast-iron urn finials. A pyramidal roof, its cast-iron urn-and-spike finial also Victorian, over the advanced centrepiece which contains an elliptical-arched carriage entrance under a round-headed window. Projecting from this, a double-pitch-roofed Victorian porte cochère with bundle-shafted columns and bargeboards pierced by Gothic motifs. Several of the building's doors and windows have been altered and a single-storey C19 extension built at the rear.

A screen wall runs W from the coachhouse and links it to a tall and square ogee-roofed rubble-walled WATER TOWER designed by *George Stewart* in 1838. On its S front, a panel bearing the crest of the Murrays of Simprim. Set into the tower's W face, a late C16 semicircular dormerhead, its border carved with dogtooth ornament; inside the border, a coat of arms and initials identified by the basal inscription as those of COLIE CAMPBELL. Probably it came from an earlier house on the site built after the estate had been acquired by the Campbells in the mid C16.

WALLED GARDEN of *c.* 1800, now filled with late C20 housing, to the E. Along the outside of its N side, a single-storey piend-roofed rubble-built cottage range, also of *c.* 1800. At its centre, a tall octagonal red sandstone tower, its four stages marked off by string courses. At the third stage, circular dummy windows; oval dummies at the tall top stage. Crude battlement with tall merlons carried on moulded corbels. Inside the garden, on this side, a late C19 greenhouse, its length curtailed when it was adapted as a conservatory for the housing behind.

ARCHITECTURAL FRAGMENTS were brought here in the late C19. Some, if not all, came from demolished buildings in Coupar Angus. On the external face of the garden's S wall, an aedicular doorpiece composed of disparate elements which were probably put together in 1883. The columns' weathered shafts may be late C17 or C18 but their bases look late C19. The columns' badly worn foliaged capitals, each with a rectangular outer section, may be late medieval and from Coupar Abbey, Coupar Angus, where they perhaps belonged to responds. The lintel is probably of 1883, the modillion cornice C18. Projecting from the garden's NW corner, L-plan walling, probably built in 1883 to house the architectural fragments. SW stretch pierced with four round holes and topped by a couple of crude merlons. Built into its S face, a moulded doorpiece of 1749 with a lugged architrave and pediment on whose top has been placed part of a late medieval wall-shaft of trefoil section, probably from Coupar Abbey. Each side, a rectangular fragment, perhaps from a frieze, and also probably late medieval and from Coupar Abbey. Probably from the same source is the springer of an arch inserted in the wall's N face. Built into the wall's return to the SE, a steeply pedimented doorpiece of the late C16 or early C17, its tympanum containing a circular recess probably intended to house a panel carved with a coat of arms or inscription.

SE of the walled garden, a red sandstone rubble-built and crowstep-gabled lectern DOOCOT moved here from Coupar Angus in 1883. One rat course which rises at the gables in crowstepped fashion. At the SE front, immediately above the rat course, a row of flight-holes. The SW skewputt is carved with the date 1610, presumably that of its original construction, the SE with a weathered coat of arms. Low doors in the gables. Built into the E wall is a late medieval scalloped capital, probably brought here from Coupar Abbey and inserted in 1883.

At the drive's NW end, a late C19 crowstep-gabled LODGE, with Gothic windows and door to its porch. – Low corniced GATEPIERS with large ball finials, also Late Victorian.

ASHINTULLY CASTLE
2.3 km. NE of Kirkmichael

Pleasingly unpretentious rubble-walled laird's house, the product of two main building periods.

The earlier part is at the W, a three-storey and attic L-plan house, the jamb projecting both W and S of the main block and with its W side's base built of boulders. In the jamb's E face, a wide-mouthed gunloop beside the original entrance, the lintel of whose roll-and-hollow-moulded surround is carved with the date 1583, presumably that of the house's construction. Above the door, a heraldic panel on which the initials AS (for Andrew Spalding of Ashintully) flank a shield bearing the impaled arms of Spalding and Wemyss. This is set in a roll-and-hollow-moulded surround under the re-cut inscription THE.LORD. DEFEND.THIS.HOVS, the whole flanked by baluster-like attached shafts and a cornice which breaks into capitals over the ends and centre. C16 windows with rounded margins survive at the jamb, the second floor of the main block's S front and its W gable. Blocked slit windows and a gunloop at the jamb's S face; another gunloop at the S end of the main gable. Massive chimney on the original E gable. The crowsteps on the gables of the jamb and the main block's W end were renewed in 1831 as was a corbelled battlement on the E side of the jamb. At the jamb and the W gable of the main block, fairly small C16 windows.

The main block E of the jamb was remodelled in 1831 when a large E extension was built incorporating earlier work (e.g. a built-up elliptical pend arch now containing a door), perhaps of an office range. The extension, together with the recast C16 main block, produced a nearly regular three-storey range, its S front of six bays, the windows grouped 2 (the C16 main block, its ground and first-floor windows enlarged and the openings imperfectly aligned) and 4 (the 1831 extension). A door opening and tall ground-floor windows at the four E bays. All the first-floor windows are tall; small windows to the second floor, those of the E extension larger than the C16 windows to their l. Also of 1831 is the lean-to two-storey service range at the back, the main roof swept down to cover it but without skews. In this range's W gable, a first-floor Gothic window. Rising from the back of the main roof, a conical-roofed turret containing the stair to the attic. Some quite tactful alterations (the blocking and insertion of doors and windows and the addition of a catslide-roofed dormer) were made at the rear by *Robert Hurd & Partners* in 1966.

Inside, on the first floor of the back range, a long gallery covered by a plaster ribbed tunnel vault; it is probably of 1831.

Detached rubble-built court of offices to the E, probably of the 1830s, its two-storey principal (S) range piend-roofed. Rubble WALLED GARDEN, also probably of the 1830s, to the W.

Beside the drive, 1.4km. S of the house, a two-storey piend-roofed and rubble-walled STORE, probably of the early C19. – At the S end of the drive, a LODGE of the earlier C19. Carved bargeboards and valenced broad eaves. One corner of the porch is clasped by an octagonal buttress topped with a foliage-finialled pinnacle.

AUCHLEEKS HOUSE
6.1 km. W of Struan

Small but smart two-storey piend-roofed mansion house built for the Robertsons of Auchleeks, *c*. 1820. Ashlar-faced five-bay front, with rusticated quoins at the slightly advanced ends and narrower centre whose pediment's tympanum is carved with the Robertson coat of arms. At this centrepiece, a Roman Doric columned and corniced frame to the segmental-fanlit entrance; above, a three-light window. Late C19 pedimented dormer windows.

Early C19 corniced GATEPIERS at the end of the drive. – Below the terrace in front of the house, WALLED GARDEN, also early C19, part of the enclosure provided by cast-iron railings. – On the S edge of the parkland, the piend-roofed and rubble-built U-plan STABLES (now DOOCOT COTTAGE) of c. 1820. Elliptical-arched carriage entrances (now containing a door and windows) on the S side of the S range. Above the E range, a pyramid-roofed doocot tower.

AUCHTERARDER

9010

Small town which was a royal burgh by 1246 but seems to have the lost the status of a burgh of any sort by the end of the C17. Warren Hastings found 'a Village . . . indifferently large but composed of Hutts' on his visit in 1793 when linen weaving was the principal activity of the inhabitants. Woollen manufacture succeeded that of linen in the C19, the town's growth aided by the opening of the railway line to Perth and Stirling in 1848. Auchterarder became a police burgh in 1894 and was reinstated on the roll of the Convention of Royal Burghs in 1951.

CHURCHES

AUCHTERARDER FREE CHURCH, High Street. Secularized. By *Cousin & Gale*, 1843–5. Crowstep-gabled box with two tiers of rectangular side windows. The N bay is slightly narrower than the rest and parapeted. From it projects an angle-buttressed square tower, its unarchaeological Romanesque detail still Georgian in feeling. Shallow battlement, pinnacles at its corners. The interior has been converted to a shop.

Attached to the church's SW corner, a HALL by *Smart, Stewart & Mitchell*, 1926–7, a low tower at the centre of its crowstepped front gable.

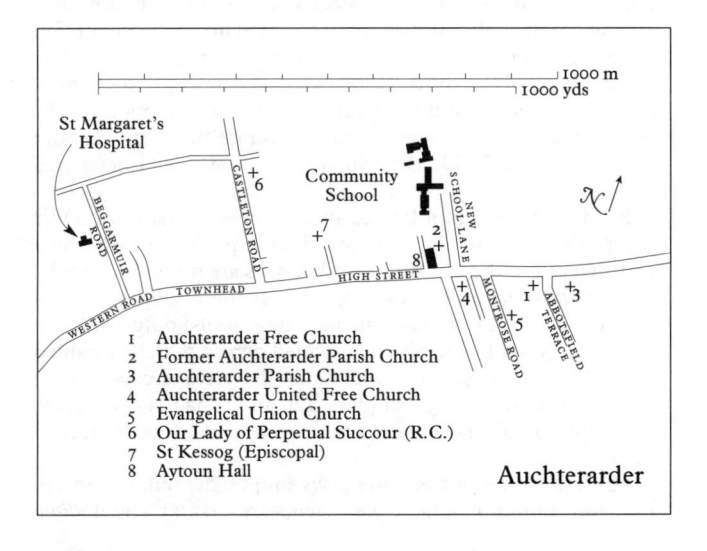

1 Auchterarder Free Church
2 Former Auchterarder Parish Church
3 Auchterarder Parish Church
4 Auchterarder United Free Church
5 Evangelical Union Church
6 Our Lady of Perpetual Succour (R.C.)
7 St Kessog (Episcopal)
8 Aytoun Hall

Auchterarder

Former AUCHTERARDER PARISH CHURCH, High Street. Some of the overgrown rubble N wall of the church rebuilt in 1784 survives. So too does the church's mid-C17 W tower. Rubble-built walls with a single intake. Pyramidal slated roof with bellcast eaves. In the outer faces rectangular door and windows (two now built-up) and, at the top, pointed belfry openings; in the E face, a round-arched door to the gallery. Inside the tower, a tunnel-vaulted ground-floor store. On the tower's E side, roof raggles at three different pitches.

GRAVEYARD. At the entrance, the SECOND WORLD WAR MEMORIAL GATEWAY by *R. M. Mitchell*, 1948. Round-headed arch containing wrought-iron gates. – On the site of the former church, the FIRST WORLD WAR MEMORIAL by *John Stewart* of *Stewart & Paterson*, 1921. Octagonal limestone shaft carved with coats of arms of regiments, the burgh and nation; Celtic cross finial.

AUCHTERARDER PARISH CHURCH, High Street. Early Gothic with hints of Art Nouveau, by *Honeyman, Keppie & Mackintosh*, 1904–5. Broad nave and chancel, W aisle and NW tower, built of squared purplish sandstone rubble. The nave is severe. Hoodmoulded stepped arrangement of three lancet windows in the N gable. The windows of the buttressed E side are each of two broad pointed lights, alternating quatrefoils and trefoils in their heads. Angle-buttressed NE porch, the label stops of the hoodmould over the entrance carved with male and female human heads. Short low chancel with a window of three stepped lights. At the W aisle, tall hoodmoulded two-light pointed windows rising into gables alternate with rectangular windows kept below the wallhead.

The squat square tower is of three stages. At the lowest, clasping buttresses. Main entrance in the N face, its hoodmould's label stops carved with men's heads. Moulded central jamb between the doors, a foliaged capital on its boldly projecting nook-shaft. Arched tympanum flanked by quatrefoil panels. Narrow cusped windows at the tower's second stage. At each face of the third (belfry) stage a pair of pointed openings, their hoodmoulds again carved with human heads. Grotesque faces and animal heads decorate the cornice under the battlement. Inside the battlement, a low slated octagonal spire.

Inside the church, a braced open roof over the nave. Over the gabled bays of the aisle are double-pitched roofs which broaden out to the W. Over the other bays are monopitch roofs, their tie-beams and braces supported at the E side on corbels over the arches of the nave arcade; these roofs' outer ends are supported on a beam which is carried across the taller gabled bays. The broad pointed arches of the nave arcade spring directly from the octagonal piers. Tall and broad chancel arch, its hoodmould's label stops yet again carved with human heads.

FURNISHINGS of 1905, the pews simple, the pulpit, lectern, font and communion table Neo-Jacobean. – ORGAN by *William*

Hill & Son and Norman & Beard, 1929. STAINED GLASS. S window (Our Lord with Moses and Isaiah) by *Douglas Strachan*, 1905. Small panes and strong colours. – In the E wall, War Memorial window (Our Lord giving the Crown of Life to a kneeling knight) of 1921. – To its N a window (the Martyrdom of St Stephen) by *Alexander Kerr*, 1960. – N of that, a window (Faith and Love) by the *Abbey Studio*, 1919. – In the W wall of the vestibule under the tower, two late C19 lights (St John and St Paul). – On the vestibule's E wall, a marble MONUMENT to the Rev. George Jacque designed by *William Leiper* and executed by *W. Birnie Rhind*, 1895, with a portrait bust in relief. – Also in the vestibule, the weathered stone bowl of a medieval FONT. It came from St Mackessog's Church (*see below*). – Again in the vestibule, two BELLS from the former Auchterarder Parish Church, both by *George Watt*, 1754.

AUCHTERARDER UNITED FREE CHURCH, High Street. Early C20. Like a hall, with a bargeboarded front gable whose basket-arched door and rectangular windows are set in extravagantly Gibbsian surrounds.

EVANGELICAL UNION CHURCH, Montrose Street. Secularized. Built in 1856 but altered *c.* 1880 and again in 1889 when it became a United Presbyterian church. Broad nave and narrow aisles fronted by a triple gablet, the thrifty Gothic detail partly lost in the building's conversion to a workshop.

OUR LADY OF PERPETUAL SUCCOUR (R.C.), Castleton Road. Built in 1879. Plain rectangle constructed of hammer-dressed squared masonry, the walls rising from a battered base. Depressed-arched windows. Small gabled ventilators on the roof. W porch added *c.* 1970.

ST KESSOG (Episcopal), St Kessog's Place. Gothic, 1896–7, by *Ross & Macbeth*, built of purplish local sandstone with dressings of pale Auchmithie stone. Nave with a full-height S (liturgical E) chancel, the join marked by a buttress on the W side, a gabled bellcote on the wallhead of the E, and a square pyramidal-roofed ventilator on the roof. Transeptal SE vestry. Buttressed NW porch; above its entrance, a niche containing a statue of St Kessog carved by *James Young*. In the church's N gable, a window of three lights, a trefoil in the head of the tall centre opening, quatrefoils in the others; above, a vesica light. Paired lancet windows in the four-bay side walls of the nave. At the chancel's E side, paired lancet lights, shorter than those of the nave, in the N bay; a triplet of lancets placed high up in the S bay. High up in the chancel gable, a broad pointed overarch containing a stepped arrangement of three lancet lights.

The interior is covered by an open wooden roof. Stone chancel arch filled by a tripartite two-tier stone screen, its arches cusped; at the centre opening of the upper tier, a sculptured Crucifixion with kneeling figures of Our Lady and St John. – Stone PULPIT of 1897 on the r. of the chancel arch. – In the chancel, a stone ALTAR and REREDOS by *Alexander Neilson* of Dundee, 1897. On the altar's front, a central panel decorated with a mosaic of the *Agnus Dei* adored by angels.

The brightly coloured panels of the reredos contain depictions of Our Lord in Glory flanked by the Annunciation and Our Lady and St John at the Empty Tomb, designed by *Ada Currey* and executed by *James Powell & Sons*. – On the l. side of the chancel, the ORGAN by *Ingram & Co.*, 1935; rebuilt by *A. F. Edmonstone*, 1995. – STAINED GLASS. S (liturgical E) window (the Crucifixion, flanked by St Kessog and St Margaret of Scotland) by *C. E. Kempe*, 1897. – N window (scenes from the life of St Agnes) of 1899 and also by Kempe.

ST MACKESSOG, Kirkton, 1.1 km. N. Ivy-covered ruin of the medieval parish church of Auchterarder, perhaps built in the C14 or C15. The E and W gables and parts of the side-walls still stand. It has been a rubble-built oblong, c. 24.7 m. by 7.5. Inside, near the E end of the S side, a polygonal-headed piscina – In the SE corner of the drystone-walled GRAVEYARD, the mid-C19 MAUSOLEUM of the Johnstons of Kincardine. Battered walls and a stone-slabbed roof. Roll-and-hollow moulded entrance; crenellated skews. – A fair number of weathered C18 GRAVE-SLABS and TABLE STONES, some carved with coats of arms, angels and emblems of death.

PUBLIC BUILDINGS

AYTOUN HALL, High Street. By *Charles S. Robertson*, 1870–2. Two-storey stugged ashlar front, a tower at its SW corner. Venetian Gothic openings to the ground floor; above, an iron balcony under a window of three round-arched lights, all stilted and exaggeratedly so at the centre. The tower is tall and square. Its base was adorned in 1905 by the addition of a drinking fountain framed in an open pedimented Ionic aedicule, the columns' shafts of polished granite. Narrow round-headed first-floor windows and large pointed openings to the belfry. Above, a 'machicolated' top hamper which rises at the centre of each face to form a boat-shaped gablet containing a clock face. Truncated slate spire finished with iron cresting.

THE COMMUNITY SCHOOL OF AUCHTERARDER, New School Lane. By *Anderson Christie*, 2000–4. Relaxed group of buildings, all with walls of brown brick and render covered by shallowly curved, ribbed metal roofs. To the NW, the broad-eaved former AUCHTERARDER SCHOOL, by *William Simpson*, 1875. At the S front, an off-centre Italianate low tower, its pyramid roof with bellcast eaves.

GLENEAGLES RAILWAY STATION, 2.8 km. SW. By *James Miller*, 1919, built to serve the Caledonian Railway Company's Gleneagles Hotel (q.v.). On the W platform, a central block of station offices. Wood and glass above an ashlar base, with touches of English Baroque detail; awnings over the platform. On the E platform, a shorter block, similar to the one on the W but with only a W awning. The platforms are joined by a lattice-sided footbridge. At its ends, pyramidal-roofed pavilions, the W oblong, the E square, both with bowed oriel windows. A second footbridge gives access from the W pavilion to the single-storey former station-master's house (now CALE-DONIAN COTTAGE). This is free Scottish domestic, harled and crowstep-gabled, with bow windows and an awning over the entrance.

ST MARGARET'S HOSPITAL, St Margaret's Drive. Built as a cottage hospital in 1926; *Stewart & Paterson* were the architects. Scots Jacobean, U-plan with crowstep-gabled wings. At the main block, shaped and triangular dormerheads carved with foliage. Ionic pilastered doorpiece, the cornice surmounted by a coat of arms.

DESCRIPTION

FEUS is the E beginning of the long main street through the town. Dour C19 vernacular housing of one and two storeys, enlivened a little by the oriel windows of *c.* 1900 at the harled No. 61 on the N and the skewputts carved with human heads at the early C19 Nos. 70–72 on the S. At the top of ABBEY ROAD, the former GOOD TEMPLAR HALL of 1894, originally plain and now rather altered. To its S, ABBEY MOUNT of the later C19, with bargeboards and bracketed eaves. ABBEYHILL is of *c.* 1840, a piend-roofed two-storey house, with a block-pedimented doorpiece and horizontal-paned windows at the three-bay front. A little further S, Ruthven Towers (*see* Villas, below). Near the bottom of Abbey Road, RUTHVENVALE TERRACE, a severe late C19 terrace of mill workers' housing stepping down the slope. At the bottom are the Glenruthven, White's and Halley's Mills beside the Ruthven Water (*see* Industrial Buildings, below). HUNTER STREET goes N from Feus. On its N corner with Collearn, the single-storey and attic EAST EARN LODGE, the former lodge to Coll Earn House (*see* Villas, below). Like the main house it is by *William Leiper*, 1869–70. L-plan, the main block crowstepped and with a bowed projection bearing a coat of arms at its S end. Battlemented porch in the inner angle. Projecting blocks on the skews of the E wing, its gable with a panel carved with the relief of a farm labourer and two farm girls. At the N end of the street, GREENBANK, an early C19 two-storey harled house with a broad chimneyed gablet over the centre bay whose first-floor window is Venetian, the central light a dummy, surmounted by a roundel displaying a heraldic achievement.

HIGH STREET, continuing the line of Feus, begins on the N with the CRAIGROSSIE (former RAILWAY) HOTEL of *c.* 1850. Georgian survival but the windows are two-light. Over-large capitals to the doorpiece's Ionic pilasters which support a block pediment, its tympanum adorned with consoles which serve as supporters to a shield bearing the relief of a railway engine. On the S side of the street, the roughly contemporary QUEEN'S HOTEL, heavily detailed Georgian survival, the two-light windows linked by sill and lintel courses; rusticated quoins at the corners. Then, on the N, CRAIGROSSIE HOUSE of *c.* 1870. Almost symmetrical three-bay front but one of the full-height and gabled bay windows is rectangular, the other canted. Gothic windows to the first floor; carved bargeboards. Opposite, Auchterarder Parish Church (*see* Churches, above) followed by the entrance to Coll Earn House (*see* Villas, below). Behind, the former Auchterarder Parish Manse (MANSEFIELD) by *Andrew Heiton Sen.*, 1847, the three-bay front's open-pedimented door flanked by niches instead of windows; bracketed eaves to the piended roof. Behind this and entered from ABBOTSFIELD TERRACE is Dunearn House (*see* Villas, below).

W of these High Street's general character is low-key Georgian and Victorian with a few commercial touches of the C20. No. 50 has been up-market Late Georgian with rusticated quoins, a cornice enriched with ball ornament and squat consoles under the architraves of the first floor's centre window. The other windows were enlarged in the C20. No. 52 is commercial architecture of *c.* 1900. Balustraded parapet and a bowed and gabled corner to Montrose Street. In MONTROSE STREET to the S, the former Evangelical Union Church (*see* Churches, above) on the E and, on the W, Drumcharry (*see* Villas, below).

In High Street W of Montrose Street, the early C19 Nos. 61–63, the unaltered first-floor windows with consoled architraves like that at No. 50. At the parapeted Nos. 65–67 of *c.* 1840 the E two-thirds of the ground floor (containing a shop and the entrance to the upper floor) are slightly advanced and corniced; to the W, a shallowly projecting corniced rectangular bay window, the architrave lugged. Shouldered architraves to the first-floor windows which are joined by a lintel course. On the E corner of Ruthven Street on the N side, Nos. 73–76 High Street, late C19 commercial with a conical-roofed bowed corner; bracketed broad eaves and a bargeboarded large dormerhead.

NEW SCHOOL LANE leads N to The Community School of Auchterarder (*see* Public Buildings, above). On the W corner with High Street, the graveyard containing the former Auchterarder Parish Church (*see* Churches, above). W of the graveyard, the late C18 MASONIC HALL (Nos. 85–89 High Street), originally with segmental-arched ground-floor doors (now partly built-up) and a Venetian window at the centre of the upper floor. The Roman Doric columned doorpiece is an early C19 embellishment. Another Roman Doric doorpiece at the early C19 GIRNAL HOUSE whose first floor has a central round-headed niche flanked by narrow rectangular lights forming a sort of Venetian window. The dormer windows are Edwardian. Then, Aytoun Hall (*see* Public Buildings, above).

On HIGH STREET'S S side W of the former Auchterarder Parish Church graveyard, Nos. 86–88 with club skewputts; the building is perhaps late C18 but now rendered and the ground floor converted to shops. Uninspired Italianate of two tall storeys at the later C19 Nos. 92–94. An oriel window of *c.* 1900 on No. 96. Early C19 Nos. 102–106 but the ground floor boasts an Edwardian shopfront, its cornice carved with thistles; Art Nouveauish apples on the entrance to the upper floors.

On the N side of High Street the squared-up free Scots Renaissance block at Nos. 109–113, by *James Marshall*, 1904–5, was built as a post office. It is followed by the STAR HOTEL of c. 1840, with an anta-pilastered doorpiece. The second-floor windows acquired triangular and segmental-pedimented dormerheads c. 1900. Opposite, Nos. 112–114, originally mid-C19 but given a harled Edwardian top hamper with bracketed broad eaves and half-timbered gablets. Also Edwardian is No. 125 on the N, its gablets crowstepped or shaped, some carved with swags and shields; delicate Queen Anne doorpiece. Further W, on the S, the two-storey GOLF INN (No. 138) built as the Relief Church Manse in 1837, a consoled pediment over the central door. It is followed by the gatepiers of the drive to Ochil Tower (*see* Villas, below). Opposite, on the N side of High Street, the early C19 two-storey and attic Nos. 149–151. Roman Doric doorpiece; first-floor windows in architraves which are lugged at all corners and surmounted by dentilated cornices. Further W, the late C19 Nos. 173–175, plain Jacobean with tall stepped gablets. Adjoining, the entrance to ST KESSOG'S PLACE leading to St Kessog's Episcopal Church (*see* Churches, above). The W end of High Street is generally plain C19 but the early C19 two-storey ashlar front of Nos. 200–206 has a continuous entablature over the ground floor, its E section supported on Roman Doric attached columns, the W on piers; at the wallhead a heavy cornice and blocking course.

TOWNHEAD'S buildings are mostly plain Victorian domestic. On the N, No. 9 of 1871. Vermiculated and rusticated surround to the elliptically arched door which is flanked by windows each of two elliptical-arched lights. The arched windows of the upper floor are set in spike-finialled stone gablets, these and the E gable adorned with rope-moulded club skewputts. No. 11 is a stolid two-storey house of c. 1840 with a heavy anta-pilastered doorpiece. Behind the mid-C19 double cottage of Nos. 51–53 the contemporary brick-built square double PRIVY, a ventilator cupola on the slated pyramidal roof. At the N end of ST MARGARET'S DRIVE, St Margaret's Hospital (*see* Public Buildings, above).

WESTERN ROAD contains prosperous but unexciting Victorian villas, some with monkey-puzzle trees in the gardens. ORCHIL ROAD leads off to the W. On its corner with Tullibardine Road, a tall domed CAIRN erected for Queen Victoria's Golden Jubilee of 1887. At the NW end of TULLIBARDINE ROAD, a STANDING STONE, a large sandstone slab, probably erected in the second millennium B.C.

VILLAS

ABBEY ROAD. RUTHVEN TOWERS. Built in 1882 for the mill-owner, J. Halley, designed by *William Leiper*. Relaxed Scots Jacobean, built of squared pinkish stone with buff-coloured dressings. Uncrowded display of a conical-roofed corner tower, a balustraded bow window and a semicircular oriel window, its stone-slabbed sloping roof surmounted by the figure of an aged harper. On the entrance (w) front's crowstepped gables, statues of a monkey and a lion. At this front, a pair of steeply pedimented scroll-sided dormer windows with rose and thistle finials; in their tympana, reliefs of a sun-surrounded head and of a girl's head and the motto HE BUILDS TOO LOW WHO BUILDS BENEATH THE SKIES. Another relief of a woman's head in a panel over a first-floor window. Shaped dormerheads at the S elevation. Extensions of the later C20 to the E and SE. Inside, high wooden dadoes and panelled wooden ceilings. At the entrance hall, STAINED GLASS by *Daniel Cottier* depicting ladies playing the lute, dancing and painting; more stained glass containing panels of female heads at the stair window. Stained glass again in the upper panes of the windows of the principal rooms.

ABBOTSFIELD TERRACE. DUNEARN HOUSE, by *Andrew Heiton Jun.*, is a broad-eaved villa of the later C19, with a pyramidal-roofed tower.

HIGH STREET. OCHIL TOWER, Jacobean of *c.* 1850. – The red sandstone COLL EARN HOUSE of 1869–70 was designed by *William Leiper* for an advocate, Alexander Mackintosh. Jacobean and relaxed but the house's relatively small size makes the emphasis vertical, this verticality reinforced by the conical-roofed NE corner tower, a band under its eaves inscribed A FAST TOWER IS OUR GOD; on top of the tower's roof, the statue of a man holding a weathervane. Plentiful detail. Buff sandstone carved reliefs (e.g. on the tower a double panel carved with the relief of a woman with children (Mercy) and a woman looking in a mirror (Truth) and the inscription LET NOT MERCY AND TRUTH FORSAKE THEE, and, on the E front, a figure of Justice). On the N front, a pair of elaborate shaped dormerheads and a coat of arms. Another coat of arms in a dormerhead on the E side, its skews surmounted by figures of wolves. At the S elevation, crowstepped gables, one with the figures of a squirrel on a skewputt and a deer on the apex, another with figures of birds. Between these two gables, a gablet dormerhead bearing a coat of arms. Single-storey and attic service range to the W, one skew of its crowstepped S gable supporting the figure of a rabbit; N gable with figures of beasts and birds. The interior is a Gothic–Jacobean mixture, with stained glass in the manner of Daniel Cottier.

HUNTER STREET. GREENBANK, a harled two-storey early C19 house. Three-bay front, the first-floor centre window Venetian, its centre light a dummy. Chimneyed wallhead gablet containing a circular armorial panel.

MONTROSE STREET. DRUMCHARRY is by *Alexander MacGregor*, *c.* 1860. Round-headed windows, bracketed broad eaves and carved bargeboards.

INDUSTRIAL BUILDINGS

GLENRUTHVEN MILL, Abbey Road. Rubble-built and plain, of 1877, a red brick chimney at the N end.

HALLEY'S MILL (Gleneagles Knitwear Co.), Abbey Road. Built in 1873–4. Single-storey, the W front of stugged ashlar with segmental-arched windows and, near the S end, a free Jacobean aediculed doorpiece.

WHITE'S MILL, Abbey Road. The surviving part is now a house, its concrete crowsteps and concrete tiled roof late C20. It was built *c.* 1874, the main windows segmental-headed; round windows in the tops of the gables.

CASTLE MAINS
0.5 km. N

Mid-C19 farmhouse, a conical-roofed tower at the back. In the steading, a square FOLLY, also mid C19, its E wall's round-headed openings and the W wall's double keyhole gunloops designed to recall the medieval Auchterarder Castle, a fragment of whose walling may survive in the thick but featureless S wall.

AUCHTERARDER HOUSE
1.8 km. NNE

Large but understated mansion house designed by *William Burn* and built for Captain James Hunter in 1832–3 but given some opulent additions and a lavish interior by *John J. Burnet* of *John Burnet, Son & Campbell* in 1886–9 after the estate had been acquired by the locomotive manufacturer, James Reid.

The 1830s house is of two storeys, built of purply-red sandstone ashlar, an asymmetrical Elizabethan manor but with crowstepped gables as a concession to its nationality. L-plan with a large but low service wing tenuously attached to the main block's NW corner. At the join of the two parts, a round tower, originally conical-roofed but heightened and finished with a corbelled and balustraded platform and ogee-roofed caphouse in the 1880s, the new work of a brighter red Dumfriesshire sandstone than the original masonry.

On the E elevation, a pair of slightly advanced gables, the S fronted by a two-storey rectangular bay window. Single-storey bay windows, one rectangular and the other canted, at the ends of the S elevation; shaped dormerheads above the first-floor windows. Similar dormerheads along the W elevation; at its S end, a two-storey canted bay window. Burnet's additions are at the main block's NE corner where he placed a huge porte cochère projecting to the N and, to its E, a winter garden and billiard room. The porte cochère is swaggering Jacobean Renaissance, the round-headed entrances with cartouche keystones and framed by Roman Doric attached columns and tall panelled bases and surmounted by consoles which form the ends of the stepped parapets. On the side parapets, boldly modelled cartouches. At the front, a pair of cartouches flank a large panel carved with another cartouche and surmounted by a ball-finialled pediment; ball finials also on the porte cochère's front corners. The interior of the porte cochère is covered by a domical vault. Behind, a porch with stone benches along the side walls and, at the S end, the house's principal entrance under a segmental pediment broken by an heraldic shield. Set back and at right angles to the porch is the tall single-storey winter garden, its N and S sides almost filled by large windows, the wallhead surmounted by a strapwork parapet. Across the E end is the crowstep-gabled billiard room, its side walls with strapwork parapets and ball finials on the corners. In the centre of the N gable, a sloping-roofed splay-sided projection under a pedimented window. In the E side and S gable, three-light windows framed by columns standing on consoled bases.

INTERIOR. The entrance hall is of the 1880s, its decoration of free early C18 inspiration. Marble-clad walls and floor, a beamed ceiling supported on corbels. Set into the walls are scrolled metal radiator grilles. Off the entrance hall's E side, the winter garden, filled with light from the side windows and glazed collar-braced roof. Terrazzo floor. The end walls are marble-clad to three-quarters of their height. At the E, a pair of glass-panelled doors flank a broad window framed by marble columns, their bulbous capitals carved with interlacing in the manner of H. H. Richardson; originally, a marble basin sat in front. The winter garden opens into the W side of the billiard room. This is a great hall covered by a collar-braced queenpost truss roof; pendants below the braces. The room's N end is filled by a splay-sided inglenook entered through a shouldered arch, its lintel carved with foliage and bearing the monogrammed initials of James Reid and his wife, Charlotte Geddes, together with the inscription CHEAT FAIRE.MIND H^{E}ARTS AR^E.AYE TR^{V}MPS BVT LVCK'S A. Half-timbering on the wall above which is pierced by an oval window. Inside the inglenook, a wood-panelled ceiling and walls, the lower panels each side of the fireplace with swan-neck tops.

Off the entrance hall's W side, the inner hall, its decoration of the 1880s with wood carving, as elsewhere in the house, by *William Sherriff*. Elaborate panelling in an early C18 manner. Enriched plaster ceiling of later C18 style but with Neo-Jacobean touches. White marble chimneypiece carved with reclining ladies learning against a shield carved with a human head. Off the hall's N side, a washroom and lavatory, both with wooden panelled ceiling and large windows filled with obscured glass in Jacobean patterned panes. The hall's W end opens onto a broad corridor running down the centre of the main block, its position and size, like those of the principal rooms, as designed by Burn, the decoration by Burnet. Opulent free Jacobean Renaissance with swan-neck-pedimented door cases and pendants hanging from the ceiling. Off the corridor's W side, the dining room, the framework of its Jacobean ceiling of the 1830s but the compartments enriched with plaster roses in the 1880s. Also of the 1880s the Jacobean Renaissance doors set in pedimented surrounds and the carved wooden chimneypiece with snarling lions' heads on the consoled jambs. s of the dining room, the stair hall, its panelled wooden ceiling of the 1880s as are the stair's wrought-iron balustrade adorned with James Reid's monogrammed initials and its wooden handrails whose ends are carved as dogs' heads.

At the s end of the ground floor corridor are the interconnecting drawing room and library. In both rooms, Jacobean ceilings of the 1830s. The drawing room's Frenchy chimneypiece is of the same date but has been moved here, probably from elsewhere in the house, in the later C20. The 1880s oval-mirrored wooden overmantel with reliefs of cherubs in the spandrels has lost its crowning swan-neck pediment on whose sides reclined figures of youth and at whose centre stood a cherub. The library chimneypiece, also Frenchy and of veined marble, is of the 1830s but altered in the 1880s when bronze heads of Plato and Homer were placed on the jambs. Burnet's bookcases survive, as does his plaster frieze modelled with fleurs-de-lys and fruiting foliage. The upper sashes of the windows of both rooms contain Glasgow style stained glass borders depicting stylized foliage and flowers.

LODGE to the NW, by *John Burnet, Son & Campbell*, c. 1887. Single-storey English picturesque, with broad eaves, bargeboards and half-timbering above a carved bottom rail. Balustrading at the rear. – HOME FARM on the W side of the B8062. Late C19 bargeboard-gabled farmhouse and steading (now housing). At the centre of the steading's front, a three-storey tower with three-light windows to the two lower floors and a round window to the second, all contained in a giant overarch.

CLOAN. *See* p. 270.
GLENEAGLES HOTEL. *See* p. 396.
KINCARDINE CASTLE. *See* p. 454.

AYTON HOUSE
0.4 km. SE of Aberargie

Laird's house, its unsatisfactorily disjointed Georgian and Georgian survival character the product of several building periods. The first, in the mid C18, produced a piend-roofed main block of three storeys, harled and with rusticated quoins; five-bay E front, the windows grouped 1:3:1. The band course under the first floor and its tall windows' cornices and aprons were all probably provided in 1830 by *William Burn* who added the r. bay's pilastered squat porch. The porch's coat of arms dates from alterations made to the house in 1878 by *D. & J. Bryce* and was moved to its present position probably in 1907–9 when

Robert S. Lorimer added a two-storey balustraded canted bay window overlaying the l. two of the front's three centre bays.

The late C18 house is bullied by a large ashlar-faced N addition of 1830, also by Burn and of three storeys but taller than the C18 house. Projecting from the addition's pedimented E gable, a parapeted two-storey broad canted bay window. The addition's N elevation is of three bays. At the two E bays, corniced first-floor windows similar to those of the C18 house but without aprons and fronted by a balustraded stone balcony supported on consoles. Slightly advanced and pedimented W bay with a bay window just like that at this addition's E gable. W of this, a harled two-storey wing by Lorimer, 1907–9.

BALBEGGIE

Roadside village of generally undistinguished C19 and C20 housing.

BALBEGGIE CHURCH (United Free). Built as an Antiburgher church in 1832. Plain box with pointed windows. The N gable's stone bellcote has been removed and the slates replaced with concrete tiles.

ST MARTINS PUBLIC HALL. By *G. P. K. Young*, 1910–11. Harled, with sturdy buttresses at the side wall. Bargeboarded front gable whose flat-roofed porch projects from below a semicircular window.

BALEDGARNO

Hamlet on the W edge of the parkland of Rossie Priory (q.v.), laid out as a planned village by George, seventh Lord Kinnaird, *c.* 1790.

DESCRIPTION. On the E side of a green, rubble-built cottage-terraces, probably of *c.* 1790 in origin but reconstructed in the mid or later C19 and with windows enlarged in the mid C20. Bowed N end to the S terrace. Bargeboarded gablets over the doors of the other terraces. On the W side of the green, two-storey mid-C19 housing, the upper windows gableted, and a plain STEADING, probably of the earlier C19 in origin but altered and extended by *Duncan D. Stewart*, 1879. FARMHOUSE to the NW, built in the earlier C19 but enlarged in 1879 by Stewart who added a two-storey canted bay window, its rectangular openings containing Gothic lights. S of the hamlet, a former SCHOOL of *c.* 1840, like a *cottage orné*, with bracketed broad eaves.

CASTLEHILL, 0.3 km. NW. Rubble-built courtyard steading of 1838–40. The N range consists of a terrace of two-storey houses with hoodmoulds over the ground floor openings and gableted angular Gothic windows to the first floor. The ground floor windows were widened in the mid C20 and all have lost their latticed glazing. Built in above the door and adjoining window of the E house are a lintel incised with the date 1698 and a stone carved, perhaps in the C18, with the relief of a bull. On the steading's s side, the broad-eaved harled farmhouse, its first floor windows gableted. At its E end, a single-storey Gothic dairy pavilion. Inside the courtyard, the broad-eaved but plain single-storey estate office of 1907.

ROSSIE PRIORY. *See* p. 680.

BALEDMUND
1.6 km. N of Pitlochry

Prominently sited and tall, harled shooting lodge. The earliest part is the present E wing, an unpretentious three-storey three-bay Late Georgian house, the veranda across the ground floor probably a late C19 embellishment. In 1895 was added the present U-plan main block, also of three storeys but much more vertical. At its centre, a crowstepped gable with a red sandstone second-floor oriel window to the front and a conical-roofed round turret at the SW corner. Diagonally placed battlemented SE tower. At the SW and also diagonally placed, a full-height wing, its bowed end surmounted by a corbelled-out rectangular top floor. Short single-storey W wing.
In a field s of the house, a STANDING STONE erected probably in the third or second millenium B.C.

BALENDOCH
3.1 km. N of Meigle

Rubble-walled laird's house of *c.* 1800. Two storeys and a basement, the attic lit originally by windows in the gables but now with two large C20 dormer windows. Three-bay s front, the Venetian door contained in an overarch and reached by a flyover stair. Piend-roofed pavilions at the ends, the W of a single storey above a basement, the upper floor perhaps an early addition, the E of a single (basement) storey.

BALHARY
2.6 km. SE of Alyth

Laird's house of 1817–21, designed by *John Carver Sen.* for a lawyer, John Smythe. Main block of two storeys, faced with stugged ashlar. Entrance (NE) front of three bays, the broad centre slightly advanced, the door set behind a screen of Doric columns *in antis* and surmounted by a three-light window. Five-bay SE elevation, the centre projecting as a shallow canted bay. A single-storey NE wing joins the main block to a pavilion, its segmental-arched front window of the three lights. This sits at one corner of a service court whose NW screen wall is curved. – Behind, rubble-built quadrangular STABLES of

1839–41. Front (SE) range of two storeys with an advanced and pedimented centrepiece fronted by a wooden porte cochère. – W of the house, a FOOTBRIDGE over the burn, the ashlar piers on the approach dated 1830. The 27.4m. long wrought-iron lenticular truss bridge itself is of 1873, its wooden deck a mid-C20 replacement. W of the bridge, a rubble WALLED GARDEN of the earlier C19, with various datestones from 1810 to 1840. Over the corniced SE entrance, a stone brought here from the demolished Crandart Castle in Glen Isla (Angus). It is inscribed I.SHALL.OVERCOM.INVY.VIT/.GODS.HELP.TO.GOD. BE.AL./PRAIS.HONOVR.AND.GLORIE/1660.

BALLATHIE HOUSE
1.8 km. S of Kinclaven

Standing beside the Tay, a rambling two-storey fishing lodge of the 1890s, picturesquely bargeboarded and with a couple of conical-roofed low turrets and a Jacobean porch. – Harled and half-timbered LODGE, presumably contemporary.

BALLINDEAN HOUSE
1.6 km. NW of Inchture

Idiosyncratic classical villa of 1832 designed for himself by *William Trotter*, a former Lord Provost of Edinburgh and supplier of luxury woods for furniture. Harled walls with polished ashlar dressings; mutuled eaves cornice. Long piend-roofed S front of two storeys, with tall ground-floor windows. Nine bays, the centre three slightly advanced and pedimented. The centrepiece's ground-floor is covered by an ashlar porch whose heavy corner piers and balustraded cornice frame a screen of

Ballindean House.
Perspective sketch, by David Walker, *c.* 1965

more delicate piers containing the entrance door and flanking lights, all with horizontal-paned glazing; horizontal panes also in the side windows of the porch.

The house's side elevations are intended to be seen obliquely from the approach. The E is also of two storeys. Six bays, the third to fifth slightly advanced under a pediment and fronted by a broad single-storey canted bay window, its parapet decorated with small round-headed blind arches. The W side is of five bays. The advanced and pedimented centre and the two bays to its N are of three storeys but with low and small-windowed ground and second floors so their overall height is only slightly above that of the rest of the house. Rising from the centre of the roof, a glazed circular cupola. A long, low and narrow block extending across the back, is a remnant of the previous laird's house (begun 1711 and enlarged 1789), which was remodelled by Trotter as a service wing but demolished *c.* 1962.

INTERIOR. Large ENTRANCE HALL, its walls wood-panelled for two-thirds of their height. Consoled cornice over the broad glazed door to the stair hall (*see* below). Frenchy marble chimneypiece on the N side. Panelled plaster ceiling, the centre panel with a foliaged rose. Similar ceiling and centre rose in the DINING ROOM which occupies the house's SW corner; black marble chimneypiece. In the SE corner of the house, the DRAWING ROOM, the principal panels of its plaster ceiling with delicate roses. Empire garlands on the white marble chimneypiece. Console-corniced doorpieces, the N doorway very broad and filled with glazed folding double doors. This opens into the EAST DRAWING ROOM. Panelled plaster ceiling; consoled cornices to the doorpieces. On the N side, a brute classical black marble chimneypiece. At the E end, a Corinthian columned screen to the bay window whose lights rise from the floor.

In the centre of the house, with console-corniced doors to the entrance hall, East Drawing Room and a W service passage, is the large and square top-lit STAIR HALL. On its W side, another black marble chimneypiece with panelled pilaster jambs supporting foliaged 'capitals' and an egg-and-dart cornice. Flying stair round three sides, its cast-iron balustrade restrained and light. At the upper level, on each side, pilasters framing a trio of arches, the outer two round-headed, the centre segmental-arched, their heads springing from console-corbels. The arches on the E and W sides are open and contain cast-iron balustrades fronting passages, those on the N and S being dummies, the S fronted by a gallery. Over the stair hall, a panelled dome on rosetted pendentives, its cut-out top surmounted by a glass-sided domed cupola, also with a ceiling rose.

SOUTH LODGE. Also by *Trotter*, *c.* 1832, and harled, with red sandstone dressings. Single-storey, with broad eaves to the piended roof. U-plan S front, the l. with a three-light window, the r. with a canted bay window. Pedimented porch at the E end. Rectangular windows but with round-headed glazing to their upper sashes.

Estate HAMLET to the W, with broad-eaved and lattice-glazed COTTAGES of the earlier C19 and a contemporary two-storey piend-roofed FARMHOUSE at the E end, all built of red sandstone.

BALLINLUIG

Small village of C19 and C20 housing cut off from the River Tummel by the A9.

LOGIERAIT PRIMARY SCHOOL. School and schoolhouse of 1863–4 designed by *Anne, Duchess of Atholl*, plain except for a pyramid-roofed tower and a canted bay window. It was extended to the N by *Bell & Cameron*, 1911. E addition of the late C20.

HALL. By *Erskine Thomson & Glass*, 1931. Harled walls, the roof with a jerkin-head gable to the front and a prominent spired ventilator.

TULLIEMET HOUSE. See p. 740.

BALLINTUIM

Hamlet in Strathardle.

ST MICHAEL AND ALL ANGELS' CHURCH (Episcopal). By the *Rev. Edward Sugden*, 1899. Very simple but picturesque, built of sneck-harled granite and whinstone. Gabled hood over the entrance; cusped lights in the rectangular window openings. Carved bargeboards and a metal-clad flèche.

BALMYLE HOUSE, 1 km. N. Piend-roofed and harled two-storey house of *c.* 1830, with tall windows at the ground floor of the three-bay front whose porch is an addition. Also an addition, probably of the mid or later C19, is the bay window at the centre of the W side.

CAIRNS, STANDING STONES AND HUT CIRCLES, Stylemouth, Balnabroich, 1.7 km. N. On rough pasture and moorland in Strathardle, a remarkable scattering of funerary, ritual and domestic structures of the third to first millennia B.C. interspersed with more recent heaps of stones cleared from fields and the remains of a couple of C18 farmsteads. Set in a gap between two small forestry plantations is the largest of the surviving prehistoric monuments, the circular GREY CAIRN. Perhaps of the third millennium B.C., this is a mound of stones *c.* 29 m. in diameter and formerly over 7 m. high. Excavation in the C19 discovered a passage leading towards the centre where was found an area of burning under a layer of boulders. It stands at the E end of a rough oval (*c.* 0.45 km. by 0.31 km.) of CAIRNS, all probably of the third or second millennium B.C.

One of these, 0.09 km. NE, is a roughly circular ring-cairn, *c.* 6.5 m. in diameter and 0.3 m. high, with an outer kerb of small stones still in place round the S segment and four larger stones standing at the inner face of the bank. To its ENE, 0.18 km. NE of the Grey Cairn and immediately beside a hut circle (*see* below) on the crest of a knoll, is a burial cairn, now also 6.5 m. in diameter but perhaps originally smaller and 0.4 m. high. Another round burial cairn, 0.4 km. E of the Grey Cairn, is *c.* 12 m. in diameter, its rough kerb of boulders fairly intact at the E and SE segments. It seems to have stood only 0.3 m. high. Exposed in its centre is a large stone-slabbed cist, *c.* 0.8 m. by 1.15 m. A second ring-cairn, 0.3 km. SE of the Grey Cairn, is roughly oval, 7.5 m. by 6.8 m. in diameter, with boulders of its outer kerb still standing at the N, E and S segments. These seem to have been graded in height with the largest (0.4 m. high) at the S. The open centre is roughly square, with its kerb's prostrate stones, their upper faces flush with the top of the bank, still in place along the E and S sides and one remaining on the W. – The last of these cairns, 0.05 km. S of the Grey Cairn, is a round burial cairn, now *c.* 10.5 m. in diameter and 0.5 km. high. – Standing within this oval of cairns and placed 0.14 km. ESE of the Grey Cairn is a STONE CIRCLE, *c.* 7 m. in diameter and formed probably in the third or second millennium B.C. Of its nine formerly upright boulders, all now fallen or semi-prostrate, the largest, at the WSW, is 1.2 m. long and 1 m. broad. A STANDING STONE 10 m. NNW may have served as an outlier. – A little way W, N and E of the Grey Cairn are remains of HUT CIRCLES, probably of the late second or first millennium B.C., now appearing as roughly circular hollow banks. Adjoining the burial cairn 0.18 km NE of the Grey Cairn is a pair, both with S entrances, the W circle (*c.* 8 m. in internal diameter) with a curved outer bank on its N side which may have formed part of an eccentric outer enclosure which extended to the E but was largely removed when the adjacent circle (*c.* 10 m. in internal diameter) was constructed. Remains of two hut circles with concentric double walls survive *c.* 0.21 km NE and *c.* 0.65 km N of the Grey Cairn.

STANDING STONES, Balnabroich, 2.2 km. NW. Beside the A924, a pair of boulders, 3 m. apart, erected probably in the third or second millennium B.C. The N, still almost upright, is 1.35 m. high, the S now leans badly.

BLACKCRAIG CASTLE. *See* p. 200.

BALMANNO CASTLE
0.4 km. SE of Dron

1010

Originally a severe, almost utilitarian, laird's house built for George Auchinleck shortly before he received a charter of part of the lands of Balmanno from Alexander Balmanno of that Ilk in 1580. In 1916–21 it was remodelled for a Glasgow shipowner,

William S. Miller, as the epitome of a Scottish tower house. The architect was *Robert S. Lorimer* and the work was carried out by his favourite craftsmen.

The site is a low eminence formerly encircled by a moat which had been partly infilled by the late C19 and completely so in the early C20. The approach from the E leads to a crowstep-gabled GATEHOUSE of 1916–21. Rubble-built, of two storeys, the upper floor jettied at the wide V of the E front whose windows rise into tall gablet dormerheads. At the centre of this front, a gable, also crowstepped, containing the large round-headed moulded entrance to the pend, its oak double doors with vertical panels crossed by a swan-neck rail; in place of two of the panels, a wicket door. Above the arch, a stone panel in a moulded frame. At the gatehouse's U-plan inner face, a trio of crowstepped gables. W of the gatehouse, a paved FORECOURT, its N and S sides bounded by creeper-clad rubble walls, also of 1916–21. Lorimer marked off the forecourt's W end with a balustrade. At its centre, on the axis of the entrance through the gatehouse, a pair of panelled gatepiers with ribbed half-globe finials and scrolly wrought-iron gates (by *Thomas Hadden*). This inner court's W and N sides are bounded by the white harled house itself.

The HOUSE as built in the C16 was a sizeable, tall, four-storey L, with a main block (c. 15.5 m. by 7.9 m.), and jamb (c. 11 m. by 7.6 m.) projecting N from its W end. In the NE inner angle, a taller rectangular tower (c. 4.3 m. by 5.2 m.); corbelled out from the second floor in its SE inner angle with the main block is a round stair-turret, which rose to a caphouse above the tower. Crowstepped gables to the main block and jamb, ashlar parapets at the flat-roofed tower and turret, the tower's with a corbelled round at the NE corner and cannon spouts at the N face. Continuous corbelling under the turret and angle round. Entrance at the S end of the jamb's E side and, high above it and to the r., a square frame for a heraldic panel. Almost all the windows were altered and probably enlarged in the C18 and early C19 when the first-floor windows of the W elevation were given segmental-arched heads and the central S window of the main block was converted to a door reached by a forestair.

Most of the existing fabric was retained by Lorimer but he rebuilt the S forestair in more assertive form, blocked one of the two Georgian segmental-headed first-floor windows in the main block's W gable and gave the other a rectangular head, and built up the tiny attic windows which had pierced both gables of this block. More important were his alterations to the top floor, which changed the character of the house from a sturdy residence of a C16 laird to a much more decorative and light-hearted exemplar of the early C20 vision of Scottishness. The eaves level of the roofs was lowered by over 0.9 m. and the remodelled third-floor windows provided with dormerheads, a segmental-pedimented one at the jamb's E front, scroll-sided gablets over the tall S windows and simpler stone gablets over the W windows of the jamb. On the new roof ridges, stone carvings of grotesque crouching beasts executed from models by *Louis Deuchars*. Lorimer's most theatrical touch was the heightening of the stair-turret by an extra storey surmounted by a tall slated ogee roof topped by a large weathercock.

At the same time as he remodelled the C16 house Lorimer added an extensive single-storey and attic L-plan SERVICE WING to its NE. Harled, with stone dressings and slated roofs of the same pitch as those of the main house, crowstepped gables and window pediments giving a strongly Scots Jacobean flavour but with a two-bay round-arched loggia at the N range's W elevation. In 1958 *Ian G. Lindsay & Partners* extended the upper floor of the E jamb to the E above a flat-roofed single-storey store of 1916–21.

INTERIOR. The entrance opens onto a passage running through the tower. On its S side, two C16 doorways converted to windows by Lorimer to give borrowed light from the adjacent HALL. This, entered from a third doorway at the passage's W end, was formed by Lorimer from a pair of C16 stores, their individual vaults replaced by a single plaster tunnel vault. In the W wall, a door, its ogee-arched moulded stone surround with a fleur-de-lys finial, was inserted in 1916–21 to give access to the C16 wine cellar (formerly entered from the N), which Lorimer converted to a cloakroom, with the N end partitioned off for its original purpose. The tunnel-vaulted ground-floor room in the house's jamb was the C16 kitchen, its N wall occupied by an elliptical-arched fireplace flanked by arches to an oven and cupboard. In Lorimer's remodelling this became the DINING ROOM, the arches flanking the fireplace were converted to entrances to the loggia and service wing's corridor. Oak radiator cases, also of 1916–21, pierced with Gothic traceried panels.

Access to the first and second floors of the C16 house is by a comfortable turnpike stair in the tower, its windows containing stained-glass panels emblematic of 'The Months' by *Walter Camm*, 1921. Also of 1921, the second-floor landing's wrought-iron balustrade by *Thomas Hadden*, the outer panels containing curvaceous stylized thistles, the centre panel the monogrammed initials of William Miller and his wife; topping the newel post, the depiction of a cockatoo. Over the stair, a plaster ceiling also designed by Lorimer in an early C17 manner, its compartments containing floral motifs modelled by either *Samuel Wilson* or *Thomas Beattie* who were responsible for all the early C20 plasterwork in the house.

In the C16 the first and second floors probably contained identically planned suites of rooms, each with a hall occupying the jamb and an inner or drawing room and bedchamber in the main block. In the C18 or early C19 a staircase between the two floors was inserted between the two rooms of the main block. This stair was removed by Lorimer, who reinstated these rooms to their probable original dimensions. The decoration of these two floors and also of the third floor is all his. The C16 first-floor hall in the jamb he made into a BILLIARD ROOM.

Trabeated plaster ceiling, the beams enriched with fruiting vines; flowers in the corners of the panels. The walls are panelled in oak and walnut (by *Scott Morton & Co.*), the style that of the late C17 work at the Palace of Holyroodhouse (Edinburgh). The DRAWING ROOM occupies the W two-thirds of the main block. Its ceiling is by Wilson, the heavily moulded central roundel surrounded by vine branches, all contained in a foliaged oblong border. At each end of the room, three panels, their centres and borders enriched with floral motifs. Oak panelling by *Nathaniel Grieve*. The fireplace at the W end is flanked by elliptical-arched recesses, the N containing a window. E door into the PARLOUR. Here, a coved ceiling executed by Beattie. On each side of the coving's lower part, the relief of a large basket of flowers. Above this, a heavy plain border and, in the corners at the top of the coving, fleurs-de-lys. On the flat, a floral circle. Mahogany panelling by *John Watherston & Sons*, the fireplace framed by Ionic pilasters flanked by segmental-arched recesses with lugged and keystoned architraves.

The second and third floors are linked by the C16 narrow turnpike stair in the turret and also by a scale-and-platt stair of simple late C17 character, inserted by Lorimer at the S end of the jamb. The bedrooms are all finished in the same manner as the principal first-floor rooms with plaster ceilings in the style of the early C17 and panelling (simpler than on the first floor). In one (the Hunter's Bedroom) the ceiling has a freely modelled frieze depicting a medieval hunting scene. In the bedroom at the top of the tower, a plaster tunnel vault enriched with floral motifs contained in roundels and curvaceous ribbed compartments radiating from a small central roundel.

The GARDEN to the N was formed by Lorimer. WALLS of crazy-paved rubble enclose the oblong space bisected by a central E–W path. At the NW corner, a two-storey square PAVILION in a late C17 manner, the first-floor door and window openings rising through the eaves of the ogee roof to stone dormerheads.

BALNAKEILLY
1.9 km. N of Pitlochry

Piend-roofed laird's house built in 1821, the design a cheaper version of that used at Auchleeks House (q.v.). Like Auchleeks it is two-storey, with a front of five bays, the end and narrower pedimented centre slightly advanced and with rusticated quoins at the corners, but the walling is of rubble instead of ashlar. Also as at Auchleeks, the fanlit entrance is framed by a Roman Doric columned and corniced doorpiece but the window above is of one not three lights and the ground-floor windows of the end bays are hoodmoulded.

BALTHAYOCK CASTLE AND HOUSE
1 km. NE of Kinfauns

Not especially happy juxtaposition of a medieval tower house and a Victorian villa standing on the edge of a steep slope above the Carse of Gowrie.

BALTHAYOCK CASTLE was built for the Blairs of Balthayock c. 1400 and restored in 1864. It is oblong, c. 16m. by 12m. externally with walls over 3m. thick. These are constructed of rubble; at the N end of the E face their masonry is partly supported on a relieving arch although without any evidence of there having been an opening here. Slit windows to the ground floor. At the upper floors, irregularly disposed openings, several enlarged, perhaps in the C16, and with chamfered margins. A C19 stone forestair rises to the E side's first-floor entrance. This, a round-headed door with a chamfered surround, seems original. Towards the E end of the S front, a second-floor splay-sided garderobe projection supported on moulded corbels. Heavy C19 battlement with a caphouse at the SE corner. Lower down at this corner, tusking provides evidence of a medieval barmkin wall. On the line of this wall, a C19 gateway surmounted by a panel carved with the date 1578 and the initials and impaled arms of Alexander Blair of Balthayock and Egidia Mercer, his wife. The panel formerly adorned a house which stood immediately NE of the tower and was demolished c. 1865.

INTERIOR. The first-floor entrance opens onto a passage through the E gable wall. At the passage's W end, before its entrance to the hall, a door on its l. side into another passage which is contained in the thickness of the S wall and leads to a straight stair down to the ground floor's tunnel-vaulted store.

The first floor is occupied by a high tunnel-vaulted HALL. At its W end, a fireplace, probably of 1864 but in the position of a medieval fireplace and flanked by high-set windows. A couple more windows are placed lower at the W end of the N and S walls. In the E ingo of the S of these is the entrance to a tunnel-vaulted garderobe in the wall thickness. At the hall's W end, the opening from the entrance passage is balanced by a window; between them but at a higher level, another window, possibly intended to light a gallery above a screens passage.

Off the S side of the S wall passage to the stair to the ground floor is the well of a turnpike stair (now missing) to the second floor and wall-walk; off this turnpike, a short flight gave access to the S garderobe projection. At the second floor is another high room, but unvaulted, with a fireplace in the N side.

E of the tower and fronted by a formal terrace is BALTHAYOCK HOUSE, designed c. 1865 by *James Maclaren* for the businessman, William Lowson, who had just bought the estate. It is a prominently gabled and bay-windowed large Jacobean villa, the polished granite of its porte cochère's Ionic pilasters a nouveau riche contrast to the stugged ashlar of its main walling.

LODGE at the W end of the drive, built in the mid C19. Harled, with a reed-thatched pyramidal roof topped by a central chimney. – Harled circular GATEPIERS of *c.* 1865 surmounted by stone urns with console handles and obelisk finials.

BALVAIRD CASTLE

3.8 km. ESE of Glenfarg

Hilltop group of buildings and enclosures developed after the marriage in *c.* 1495 of Sir Andrew Murray to Margaret Barclay, heiress of the baronies of Arngask and Kippo which included the lands of Balvaird. The castle had become the family's principal seat by 1572.

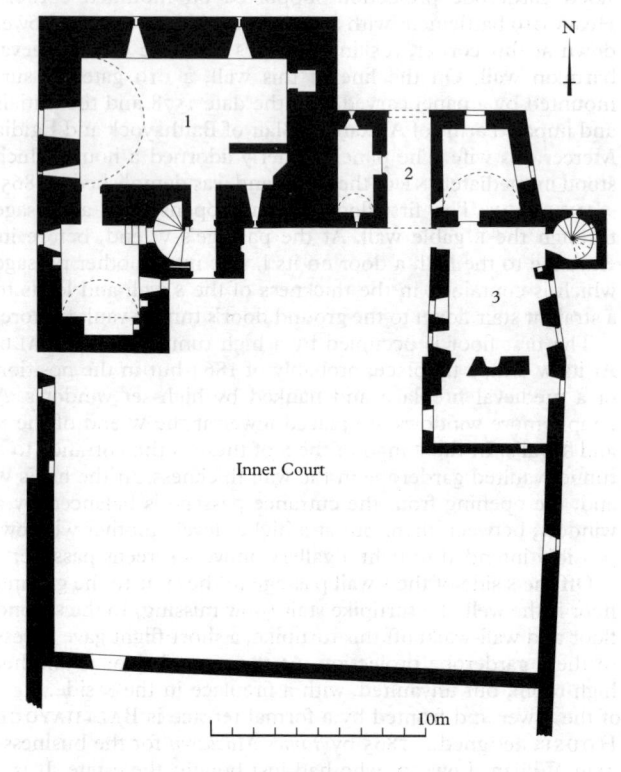

1. Tower House
2. Gatehouse
3. East Range

Balvaird Castle.
Ground-floor plan

The group comprises an outer courtyard at the N end, an inner court, with a tower house occupying its NW corner and lower ranges round the other sides, a walled garden S of the inner court, and pleasure grounds to the E. The OUTER COURT is now marked out only by some fragmentary walling; further walling survives round the extensive PLEASURE GROUNDS.

The TOWER HOUSE is of *c.* 1500. L-plan but with a stair-tower 56 in the inner angle of the main block and its SW jamb. Masonry of a mixture of whinstone and red sandstone rubble, the walling of the stair-tower's E face intaken above the ground floor, the dressings all of sandstone. All of three-storey and attic height (the jamb containing an extra floor) similarly detailed. At the wallhead, moulded corbels and a cavetto cornice under the battlement which has shallow crenelles and is pierced by drainage holes. At the corners and in the centre of the house's N and W sides the battlement breaks into rounds, their individual moulded corbels projected on courses of continuous corbelling. Within the battlement rise crowstepped gables, their large chimneys' copes carved with reliefs of moulded corbels, and, at the stair-tower, a tall battlemented caphouse which gives this tower the appearance of a castellated telescope. At the ground floor of the main block, a purposeful display of inverted keyhole gunloops (several now blocked) to the N and W and with one to the S to cover the entrance to the tower. A small horizontally proportioned gunloop (also blocked), is placed at a higher level at the S end of the W wall of the jamb. Chamfered margins to the windows. These are tall at the first and second floors of the main block and, at the W side of the main block and jamb, aligned above each other but less formally arranged at the other elevations. At the E end of the N wall and set below the level of its first-floor window, an ogee-arched frame composed of two stones; it resembles an image niche but was probably intended for a heraldic panel. The door in the W side is an insertion, perhaps of the C18.

The house's round-arched entrance in the S face of the stair-tower is surmounted by a three-tier arrangement of panels of diminishing size, their heraldic carving badly mutilated but the impaled coats of arms on the lowest supposed to be those of Sir Andrew Murray and Margaret Barclay.

Inside, the entrance opens into a small vestibule at the foot of the stair-tower. Ahead and down a few steps is a high tunnel-vaulted room, formerly divided by an entresol floor. A stub of wall shows that a small chamber has been partitioned off at the SE corner's lower level; in its S wall, the (blocked) gunloop commanding the approach to the house's entrance, so perhaps this was a guardroom. The main room's lower level is lit only from the gunloops in the N and W walls; a locker in the E wall. The entresol level has small E and W windows with elliptically arched embrasures, the E window blocked by the addition of the gatehouse (*see* below). S of the E window, a door to a wall chamber which has had its own small window (also blocked by the gatehouse) and, in the floor, a hatch to a pit-prison. In the room's SW corner, the entrance, possibly an insertion, into the jamb's tunnel-vaulted ground-floor room which is also entered from the foot of the stair. This was the KITCHEN. Large elliptically arched S fireplace, a small recess, probably a salt-box, in its E side. Small (built-up) windows in the E and W walls. To the r. of the E window, a plain wall cupboard. Large locker under the W window and, to its l., a slop drain.

At the upper floors, reached by the turnpike stair, there is no direct communication between the rooms in the main block and those in the jamb. However, they have adjoining garderobes (in the wall thickness of the main block's SW and the jamb's NW corners) whose flues descend into a single chute. At the main block's first-floor HALL, windows to N, W and S, all with stone seats in their segmental arched embrasures. At the hall's E (high table) end is a long chimneypiece, its corniced deep lintel carried on bundle-shafted columns. To the r. of the fireplace, a door (perhaps formed from a window) into the gatehouse; a wall chamber to the l. of the fireplace. In the N wall, to the r. of the window and serving the high table end of the hall, an elaborate ogee-arched and crocketed aumbry, its top of yellow rather than red stone; it has been much patched with cement and cusping has been lost. To the l. of the window, a large rectangular wall cupboard. Small and utilitarian cupboard in the S wall beside the garderobe entrance. On the second floor, an upper hall of similar but simpler character. N fireplace, the lintel projected on rounded corbels and supporting the chimney breast above.

Each upper storey of the jamb contains one room. Above the first floor they have had wooden floors (now missing), their joists supported on corbels. Each has been well appointed, with aumbries or lockers, stone seats in the window embrasures (the first floor's now missing), and a fireplace. The first-floor E fireplace's moulded jambs survive. At the third floor, the lintel and chimney-breast project on corbels from the W wall.

The present INNER COURT was formed in 1567 when a gatehouse was built against the tower house's E side and W, S and E ranges erected to the S. These additions, now fragmentary on the S and E sides of the courtyard, are again constructed of a mixture of whinstone and sandstone rubble but with dressings of buff-coloured as well as red sandstone. The GATEHOUSE (NE) block is set back from the N elevation of the tower house but its S wall is aligned with the tower's S side. In the N front, the roll-moulded and round-arched entrance flanked by an oval gunloop on the r. and a (built-up) roll-moulded rectangular door under a small square entresol window on the l. The upper floor is jettied out above a cornice carried on moulded corbels. At this level, above the entrance to the pend is a moulded stone frame for a heraldic panel of which a fragment bore the date 1567. To the l. of this, a narrow roll-moulded window. The jettying of the upper floor on individual corbels continues for a little way along the splayed E side before they are replaced by continuous corbelling and then both corbelling and jettying abandoned just N of the projecting rectangular stair-tower. Jettying on continuous corbelling resumes S of the stair-tower. At this elevation, a mixture of chamfered and roll-moulded window margins.

The transe through the gatehouse is tunnel-vaulted. On its W side, a tunnel-vaulted narrow guardroom. Joist holes show that it contained an entresol floor. The lower level is lit from a gunloop to the N and a slit window into the courtyard behind. S window at the entresol level. On the transe's E side, a broader room, also tunnel-vaulted and with joist holes for an entresol floor. Originally it was entered only from the N but this door has been built up and the present S entrance formed, perhaps in the C18. At the lower level, a slit window into the transe and a fair-sized window to the E. Small N and E windows at entresol level. S of this, remains of two ground-floor rooms, the N entered from the courtyard. Each has contained a narrow fireplace. Off the E side of the N room is the turnpike stair to the upper floor.

The court's S and W ranges have been robbed of much of their masonry. In the S ground-floor room of the W range, the roll-moulded jambs of a fireplace.

S of the inner court, the lower courses of walls which enclosed a GARDEN.

BAMFF
3.8 km. NW of Alyth

Not very gainly harled mansion on the lands of Bamff, which have been held by the Ramsays since the C13.

The earliest part, at the house's SW corner, is the surviving main block of a late C16 house which probably originally occupied the S two-thirds of the W side of a rectangular barmkin enclosure. It is of four storeys, with an attic lit only by a window in the S gable. At the ground floor of the two-bay W elevation, a pair of oval gunloops. Chamfered margins to the windows of the upper storeys, those of the first floor taller than the others. The third-floor windows rise through the eaves to gablet dormerheads, the l. with a crescent finial, the r. with a cross.

Probably in several stages but all of the C18, the sides of the likely former barmkin were all lined with buildings. A two-storey N addition to the C16 house completed the W side while office ranges, also two-storey, were constructed along the N and E sides. On the S, perhaps replacing a shorter jamb of the C16 house, was built a range of the same four-storey height and length as that house's main block but with its S front dressed up with a battlement and bartizans of light-hearted Late Georgian character. In 1828 this S range was extended E by three further bays, the addition of the same height as the earlier work but containing only three floors.

Considerable further alterations were made in 1844–7 to designs by *William Burn* but modified by the executant architect, *James Ballingall*, with crowsteps added or restored to gables to produce a more Scottish appearance. A full-height gabled addition was built covering the front of the C18 W part of the S range (deprived of its battlement and bartizans), with a conical-roofed round turret in the E inner angle and a simple Neo-Jacobean entrance. At the first floor, a window of three equal-sized lights, the two windows at the second floor aligned with its outer openings and flanking a heraldic achievement; two-light third-floor window under a blank panel. The 1828 E part of the S range was given steeply pedimented and rosette-finialled dormerheads standing on the eaves above the second-floor windows. Over the first-floor windows were erected three panels carved by *John Blackadder* with crests and a monogram. At the W range, the C18 N extension was heightened by a storey and given a parapeted two-storey rectangular bay, its first-floor window of three lights. Inside the courtyard, the back of the S range was remodelled, with tripartite windows to light a new principal stair, while an existing circular stair-tower in the court's SE corner was heightened with a conical roof. At the same time a pair of crowstep-gabled service ranges were built N of the main quadrangle.

Further work was carried out in 1926 when the E range was heightened to three storeys, the second-floor windows of its three S bays surmounted by pedimented dormerheads like those added to the S front in the 1840s and the broad N bay given a crowstepped gable. In 1988 *Simpson & Brown* removed the quadrangle's N range, making the house a U.

INTERIOR. The ground floor of the C16 part at the SW corner contained two tunnel-vaulted stores but the tops of their vaults have been removed. Chamfered door in the partition wall. Otherwise, the interior is mostly of the 1840s. Neo-Jacobean ENTRANCE HALL in the centre of the S range. At its N end, a trio of arches, the outer two segmental, the broader central opening elliptical, open onto the stair hall. The principal stair rising to the second floor continues the Neo-Jacobean character, with pendants at the bottom of the newel posts. Over the stair, a plaster ceiling (by *James Annan & Son*) with floral enrichment in the corners.

The main rooms form an interconnecting L along the first floor of the S and W ranges. At the S range's E end, the drawing room of 1828 (now DINING ROOM) remodelled in the 1840s with a compartmented Neo-Jacobean plaster ceiling enriched with simple gilded motifs and pendants. It is grained, as is the wallpaper. Painted wooden chimneypiece in an early C19 manner, with acanthus-capitalled pilaster jambs carved with pendants of drapery. On the frieze, rosettes, swags and a central panel with the relief of a classical scene. It does not look like 1840s work but is it of 1828 or 1926? W of this, above the entrance hall, a T-plan second drawing room (now MORNING ROOM), the ceiling of similar design but painted cream. Brown marble Frenchy chimneypiece of the 1840s. The S room of the W range, the 1840s LIBRARY but presumably the hall of the C16 house, is plain, its roll-and-hollow moulded stone chimneypiece probably of the 1840s. N of this, the 1840s dining room (now KITCHEN), also with a Neo-Jacobean ceiling but its black marble chimneypiece removed.

At the s end of the drive, SOUTH LODGE by *James Ballingall*, 1839. Single-storey and broad-eaved, with a semi-octagonal projection on the E side.

BANKFOOT

Village laid out in the early C19 on the estate of Airleywight.

AUCHTERGAVEN PARISH CHURCH, Cairneyhill Road. Designed and built by *John Stewart*, 1811–13, but left a roofless shell after a fire in 2004. It was a tall and broad box with urn-finialled corners, the sides and rear harled, the W end and the tower projecting from it of sneck-harled rubble. The tower, rather low in relation to the body of the early C19 church, is of three stages, the upper two intaken. Hoodmoulds over the door, windows and belfry openings; clock faces of 1868 at the belfry. Gabled piers at the corners of the battlement. Flanking the tower are battlemented low vestries added by *Lyle & Constable* in 1898–9. A scheme has been prepared (2006) by *Raymond Angus* of *Building Design Centre* for restoration of the tower, replacement of the early C19 church by a considerably smaller building, and for the erection of a new church on a different site.

GRAVEYARD. Plain Tudor GATEPIERS of 1838–9. – Good collection of C18 and early C19 HEADSTONES, almost all with an angel's head (the soul) carved at the top and emblems of death (an hourglass, crossbones and skull) at the bottom. Some way s of the church, in line with its w gable, the stone erected in 1778 by James Duff, tenant in Sutterhill, to his wife Ann Thomas, the W face carved with the relief of a mounted knight. – ESE of this, a broken stone of 1836 commemorating Andrew Muir bears a weaver's shuttle and loom. – To its N, a swan-neck-pedimented stone with a heraldic achievement. It was erected by John Scott, tenant in Newmiln of Nairn, and Helen Scobie, his wife, to their daughter in 1779 and 'restored' (i.e. probably re-cut) in 1932. – Just s of the church's E end, a couple of small C18 stones, one to Ann Campbell carved with the tools of a millwright. SE of this, a stone of 1747 commemorates Isoble [*sic*] Young, the W face bearing crossed keys above pincers and a hand holding a hammer over an anvil which is flanked by a vice and a ploughshare and coulter. – A little to the SE, a stone of 1701 to Janet Robertson, the E face elegantly decorated with an angel's head above a shield carved with a weaver's shuttle. – Built into a short stretch of wall to the NE, a round-headed MONUMENT to the Rev. Alexander Anderson, minister of Auchtergaven, †1665. At the top, a shield, its l. half bearing a coat of arms, its r. blank (presumably Anderson's wife was not armigerous), and flanked by the initials A^M^A and GB for Mr Alexander Anderson and his wife, Grisell Ballendene. Open Bible in the middle of the inscription. An hourglass, skull and crossbones at the bottom of the stone.

AUCHTERGAVEN UNITED PRESBYTERIAN CHURCH, Church Lane. Now a hall. By *William McLaren*, 1883. Broad-eaved and bargeboarded but unadventurous, with plain round-headed windows; heavy-handed Romanesque carving at the porch door.

DESCRIPTION. Near the village's s end, the V-junction of CAIRNEYHILL ROAD and Main Street watched over by the rustic cairn WAR MEMORIAL of 1921. Further up Cairneyhill Road, aloof from the village, is Auchtergaven Parish Church (*see* above). In MAIN STREET the housing is predominantly early and mid C19, of one or two storeys. Near the s end, the early C19 BANKFOOT INN, its three-bay s part with a central chimneyed gablet; broad Roman Doric portico of 1822 erected here, *c.* 1911; it came from Tullybelton House (q.v.). Five-bay s part with a wallhead chimney and elliptical pend arch whose painted date of 1826 is not implausibly that of the inn's construction.

AIRLEYWIGHT, 0.7 km. w. Villa-like laird's house of *c.* 1810 built for an entrepreneurial Perth merchant, James Wylie. Two-storey main block and single-storey lateral wings, all constructed of a mixture of stugged and droved ashlar, with pilasters at the corners. Pedimented gables to the main block whose N front is of five bays. At its centre, a half-domed semicircular Roman Doric portico squeezed between the domed round towers of the adjacent bays.

TULLYBELTON HOUSE. *See* p. 740.

BARDMONY HOUSE
3.3 km. s of Alyth

Small Neoclassical mansion house of 1830. Two-storey main block, its three-bay front of polished reddish-coloured ashlar, the corners gripped by anta-piers, their bold cornices continuing along the wallhead. Advanced and pedimented centre with a Roman Doric portico fronting the sidelit entrance, which is surmounted by a segmental fanlight. Remains of an earlier house at the rear; single-storey w wing, perhaps a midC19 addition.

BATTLEBY
0.7 km. N of Redgorton

Informally composed villa-like mansion house designed by *David Smart* and built for the Maxtone Grahams of Cultoquhey in 1861–3, its stables redeveloped as a conference and exhibition centre in the 1970s.

The Victorian house is mostly of two storeys, built of squared and stugged ashlar, with broad-eaved roofs. Piend-roofed single-storey porch near the s end of the w front. To its N, placed between two first-floor windows, is a large and elaborately mantled shield carved with the impaled coats of Carnegie (for John Graeme of Balgowan and Elizabeth Carnegie, his wife). It came from the pediment of the early C18 Balgowan House (demolished in 1861).

Inside the porch, Greek Revival plaster reliefs on the walls. Ionic columned doorpiece into the stair hall where there are more classical reliefs and also one depicting the Covenanters' assassination of Archbishop Sharp on Magus Muir in 1679. Simple Jacobean stair; another aedicular doorpiece at the E end. On the stair hall's s side, the drawing room with a panelled dining room to its E. E of that, the library (perhaps originally morning room) containing an Adam Revival chimneypiece.

A flat-roofed rendered link of *c.* 1977 joins the E end of the house to the BATTLEBY CENTRE which is by *Morris & Steedman*, 1974. It takes the form of a courtyard surrounded by rubble-walled ranges of a tall single storey with glazed elliptical-headed 'cartshed' openings to the S and E. The courtyard itself is filled with an octagonal auditorium flanked by foyers.

BELMONT CASTLE
0.7 km. s of Meigle

Sumptuous late C19 interior in an architecturally unexciting container. The house (originally Kirkhill) was begun in the early C16. A large addition was built in 1752 and the whole was clothed in castellated dress in the early C19. In 1884 it was gutted by fire and bought the next year by the future Prime Minister, Sir Henry Campbell-Bannerman, who employed *James Thomson* of *John Baird & James Thomson* to repair and remodel the shell and add a sizeable N extension. Further work was carried out by *Allan & Friskin* in 1931 when the house was converted to an eventide home.

The much altered C16 house is incorporated at the NE corner of the harled and piend-roofed main (s) block. This block retains much of its general external appearance from before the 1884 fire but with its Georgian battlement replaced by Thomson in 1885 with one of unequivocally Victorian character. It is of two storeys, with hoodmoulded windows. At the N end, a square early C19 clock tower. At the S elevation, a three-storey centrepiece flanked by round towers, the centre's gabled attic and the towers' conical-roofed crowning turrets additions of 1885. Also of 1885 are this block's bay windows and Neo-Jacobean E porch, its hammer-dressed masonry aggressive.

Extensive castellated N additions of 1885, the principal one with bay windows at the ends of its harled W front, the first-floor windows of the intermediate bays linked by continuous hoodmoulding. To the E and N the additions are faced with hammer-dressed masonry. Low E additions of 1931.

INTERIOR of 1885. The main door in the E porch opens onto the ENTRANCE HALL. Groin-vaulted stone ceiling. In the side walls, stained-glass windows, their central panels emblematic of the arts; at the top of each, shields bearing the royal arms of Scotland and a saltire, at the bottom a thistle. Black marble chimneypiece. The porch opens into a huge top-lit LIVING HALL. Ceiling with heavy plasterwork of French Renaissance character forming a border for stained glass composed of abstract motifs, stylized flowers and panels containing lions rampant and thistles. At the centre of the S wall, a massive red marble Frenchy chimneypiece, the high-relief head of a bearded man in the centre of the frieze. Mirrored overmantel with the head of a woman at the top of its gilded frame. Doors on all sides, their panels enriched in an C18 French manner. At the W, N and E walls they are placed in doorcases decorated with foliage and surmounted by curvy sided and corniced panels. At the S wall, two doorcases (the third door is a later insertion) with consoled swan-neck pediments broken by foliage and bow-tied branches on the tympana.

The principal rooms open off the hall. On the S, three interconnecting DRAWING ROOMS, the N and S with bay-windowed ends. All are decorated in French C18 style, their curvaceous liver-coloured marble chimneypieces with mirrored overmantels. Coved cornices, that of the E room bearing classical scenes, those of the other rooms with floral arabesques and corner panels bearing depictions of dogs. In the W drawing room, tall cupboards flank the chimneypiece and the E door.

W of the central hall, the DINING ROOM, its compartmented plaster ceiling Jacobean in general design but with Neoclassical detail. More wholeheartedly Jacobean are the oak dado and the Artisan Mannerist fireplace surround, its overmantel containing an C18 landscape painting. Off the hall's E side, the LIBRARY. Simple pine dado and fireplace surround. Trabeated ceiling with circles of inlay on the beams.

The central door on the hall's N side opens into the sumptuous STAIR HALL. Imperial stair, its partly gilded cast-iron balusters rising from the outstretched hands of small figures of fishtailed boys. The stair's soffit and the walls are decorated with arabesques of gilt thistles; on the walls, a *trompe l'œil* panelled dado and stylized foliage borders. Coved ceiling, its painted panels containing back-to-back mythical creatures; in the centre of each the CB monogram for Campbell-Bannerman. Cupola filled with stained glass, a head of Apollo in the centre.

STABLES to the NW, also of 1885 and by *James Thomson*. Two-storey ranges round a courtyard, the external elevations of hammer-dressed masonry. At the battlemented S range, a Tudor gateway with ogee-topped turret-buttresses; a conical-roofed low round tower at the SE corner. Parapets at the E and W ranges, crowstepped gables at the N. To the N, a single-storey crowstep-gabled detached block with a low corner tower topped by an ogee-roofed cupola.

GATEWAY AND LODGES of the earlier C19 to the SW. Ashlar-battlemented harled gateway pierced by a hoodmoulded elliptical arch. Single-storey lodges, also harled, with ashlar battlements and hoodmoulded windows. – Beside the S lodge, 'MACBETH'S STONE', an exceptionally large upright boulder, *c.* 3.6 m. high, which tapers roughly to a point. Both the principal faces are carved with cup-marks, twenty-four visible on the W and about forty on the E. The stone was probably upended and carved in the second millennium B.C.

BENDOCHY

Church and former manse sitting above the River Isla.

BENDOCHY PARISH CHURCH. Built *c.* 1600 but transformed in 1884–5 by *Alexander Johnston*. Originally the church seems to have been a long low rectangle to which a piend-roofed N 'aisle' was added, probably in the C18. Johnston added diagonal buttresses to the W gable, a small porch at the W end of the S side, a transept near that side's E end, a session house on the N, and provided a gableted new bellcote and Gothic windows.

The INTERIOR was rearranged in 1884–5 with plain PEWS and curvaceous GAS LAMP BRACKETS along the side walls. At the E end, an early C17 wooden PULPIT, the panels of its bowed front carved with stylized foliage. The MINISTER'S CHAIR and a couple of ELDERS' CHAIRS are also C17 or incorporate woodwork of that date; one has a panel with the initials W.R/I.G (for William Roger and Janet Gellatly) which was probably added on their marriage in 1796. – STAINED GLASS. Pictorial W window (the Good Shepherd) of 1901.

Now inserted in the S end of the E gable is a badly worn early C16 SACRAMENT HOUSE which was discovered under the floor of the church. The rectangular aumbry opening is set in a vine-decorated overarch. In the arch's head, the relief of a chalice or monstrance; below the opening, the initials (VT) of William Turnbull, Abbot of Coupar Angus from 1510 to 1526. – On the W end of the S wall, the well-preserved GRAVESLAB of John Cumming of Couttie †1606 carved in high relief with the effigy of a knight clad in armour, his hands raised, his feet on a dog. His head is flanked by shields displaying the coats of arms of Cumming and Crichton, his legs by shields with the arms of Ogstoun and Moncur. – On the W gable, S of the window, a WALL MONUMENT to Leonard Leslie, Commendator of Coupar Angus Abbey, †1605. Above the inscription panel scrolls (inscribed EX.MORTE VITA) flank a smaller fleur-de-lys-finialled panel bearing the impaled coats of arms of Leslie and Ramsay between the initials LL and BR (for Leonard Leslie and B. Ramsay, his wife). Each side of the inscription panel, a smaller panel bearing a pair of shields, those on the l. with the arms of

Leslie and Cadell, those on the r. with the arms of Ramsay and Crichton. – N of the W window, a small late medieval STONE with an inscription commemorating Matilda, a nun, under the weathered relief of an angel. – On the wall beside it, a GRAVESLAB, also weathered, to Nicolaus Campbell of Keithick †1587. Long Latin inscription bordering a pair of heraldic shields. – On the W end of the N wall, the worn GRAVESLAB of David Campbell of Denhead †1584. It is divided into three panels, the top one carved with a skull and crossbones, the central with two shields.

The GRAVEYARD is entered through a WAR MEMORIAL GATEWAY, by *Reginald Fairlie*, 1921, the round-headed opening surmounted by a panel carved with the Pelican in Piety. – S of the church, a good number of late C17 and early C18 GRAVESLABS and TABLE STONES, most weathered but some still displaying shields, angels' heads (souls) and emblems of death.

MANSE (now BENDOCHY HOUSE) to the N, built in 1815, the E front's porch probably a slightly later addition. The building was re-roofed by *John Carver* in 1861. – In the garden to the S, the birdcage BELLCOTE of *c.* 1600 removed from the church in 1884–5. Two-tier rectangular openings with rounded mouldings; a ball-finialled obelisk on the flattened ogee roof. – W of the manse, two ranges of single-storey piend-roofed OFFICES, by *John Carver Sen.*, 1826.

BRIDGE OF COUTTIE, over the River Isla, 1 km. SW. Elegant gently humped bridge of five segmental arches built in 1766 but widened in the later C19 when lower arches with small pointed cutwaters were added on each side.

BIRNAM

Village at the S end of the crossing of the River Tay to Dunkeld. A layout plan and elevations for a village 'on rather a splendid scale' composed of 'splendid villas, cottages ornées [*sic*], with gardens, terraces, &c.' was prepared by *James Gillespie Graham c.* 1840* but the house plots offered for sale found no takers. Development of Birnam as a small resort began a little later, aided by the opening of the railway from Perth in 1856.

CHURCHES

LITTLE DUNKELD KIRK, School Lane. Harled rectangle, designed and built by *John Stewart*, wright in Dunkeld, 1797–8. On the W end, a birdcage bellcote, its two-tier baluster supports looking old-fashioned especially by comparison with the swagged urns on top of the E gable and at the corners of the S front; the pedestals of the S urns bear the date 1798. At the S front, tall round-headed windows with projecting imposts and keystones, their glazing altered, probably as part of *Alexander Duncan*'s work in 1896–7. They are grouped 1:2:1

---

* *Perthshire Courier*, 13 August 1840.

and the outer bays also contain lowish blocked doors, also round-headed. At each gable, a round-headed gallery window above a circular window flanked by a plain door and rectangular window, these lower openings perhaps dating from C19 alterations. Vestry addition on the N side.

Inside, a gallery along the N sides and ends, the panelled fronts embellished with husk pendants. At the centre of the S side, the PULPIT. Its back, also with husk pendants, and bell-cast octagonal canopy surmounted by a gilded dove finial are of the 1790s; the body and flanking sections with Neo-Jacobean round-headed panels date from 1896–7; curvaceous brass gaslight fittings also of the 1890s. – Simple PEWS of 1896–7. – ORGAN in the N gallery, by *Abbot & Smith*, 1935.

ST COLUMBA (R.C.), St Mary's Road. By *Reginald Fairlie*, 1932. White-harled and simple, with small round-headed windows. E apse; porch across the W end.

ST MARY (Episcopal), Perth Road. Surprisingly unified product of several building phases, the general effect that of an English country church. The nave and chancel are by *William Slater*, 1856–8. The W tower,* intended from the start, is of 1870. A vestry on the N side of the chancel was added *c.* 1880 and the squat N aisle and baptistery by *Norman & Beddoe*, 1883. It is all built of whin with buff-coloured stone dressings. Geometric detail. At the tower's belfry stage, round clock faces (by *James Ramsay*, 1882) set between the pointed openings; above, a corbelled battlement.

Inside, simple open wooden roofs. Broad stone chancel arch springing from corbels carved with the heads of a man and woman. N arcade with broad pointed arches on pillars of quatrefoil section. The aisle's W bay beside the tower contains the baptistery. At the entrance to the chancel, a stone SEPTUM, its frieze carved with foliage, surmounted by a brass Gothic railing. Is this of 1858 or an addition of 1883? In the sanctuary's S wall, a single-seat SEDILIUM and a PISCINA. – ORGAN with stencilled pipes on the N side of the choir, by *Forster & Andrews*, 1874; rebuilt by *John R. Miller*, 1908.

In the baptistery, a circular stone FONT, probably of the late C19, the bowl carved with Scenes from the Life of Our Lord. Steepled and foliage-finialled oak cover of 1908. – Victorian PEWS in the nave, probably of 1858. – Elaborately carved oak PULPIT of 1897. Octagonal base, its panels depicting the Holy Family, Our Lord with the Doctors in the Temple, and the Nativity of Our Lord. The body is circular but divided into panels by pilasters which form the backdrop for figures of angels. On the panels, scenes of the Agony in the Garden, the Crucifixion and the Ascension. – Brass eagle LECTERN of 1895. – Late C19 oak CHOIR STALLS with fruiting foliage carved on the ends. They were designed by the *Rev. Edward Sugden.* – Stone REREDOS, probably of 1858. It is divided into three panels by arches carried on marble-shafted columns. A marble

---

*Really SW. Liturgical directions are used here for convenience.

cross on the centre panel, marble bosses on the outer panels. On the spandrels, emblems of the four Evangelists.

STAINED GLASS. Three-light E window (the Crucifixion) by *C. E. Kempe*, 1895. Clearly drawn and well coloured, blues predominant. – In the chancel's S wall, a brightly coloured but horribly pictorial window (Moses; St John the Baptist) by *James Ballantine & Son*, 1864. – In the S wall of the nave, a window (the Agony in the Garden; the Ascension), again brightly coloured but more accomplished, by *Alexander Gibbs*, 1883. Similar are this wall's other two windows (the Baptism of Our Lord and Our Lord with Little Children; the Annunciation and the Nativity of Our Lord) of *c.* 1890 and *c.* 1895. – In the N aisle, a lush window (King David and St John) by *Morris & Co.*, 1890, from designs of 1866 and 1869 by *Edward Burne-Jones*. – Also by *Morris & Co.*, the figures pale against a rich background of vegetation, is this aisle's other window (Miriam and Ruth) of 1904, the designs, again by *Burne-Jones*, dating from 1886.

PUBLIC BUILDINGS

BEATRIX POTTER GARDEN, Perth Road. Laid out in 1991–2 by *Perth & Kinross District Council*. – Bronze SCULPTURES by *David Annand* of characters (rabbits, Mr Tod, etc.) from the works of Beatrix Potter, who visited the area frequently in her youth.

BIRNAM INSTITUTE AND JOHN KINNAIRD HALL, Station Road. The Institute at the N end of the complex is by *Charles S. Robertson*, 1883. Plain, with free Jacobean touches and an octagonal cupola. Glazed link to the John Kinnaird Hall added by *Maclachlan Monaghan*, 2000–1. The hall itself is tall, with bowed ends, the walls wood-boarded except for full-height glazing at the centre of the long W side. Wrapped round the S end, a stone-clad bow containing a stair. Projecting from this end, a low glazed triangle containing exhibition space. Behind, a narrow two-storey block. Heart-raisingly light interior, a top-lit atrium serving the various parts. In the exhibition space is the DALGUISE PILLAR, perhaps designed as a market cross, a fluted column whose Corinthian capital is surmounted by a square block carved with dragons and a sphinx. Above this, an entablature stone topped by a unicorn bearing a scroll carved with a thistle. It came from Dalguise House (q.v.) and is probably early C18.

DUNKELD AND BIRNAM RAILWAY STATION, S of the A9. By *A. & A. Heiton*, 1856. Cottage Tudor, with mullioned and transomed windows and carved bargeboards. The platform awning supported on cast-iron brackets with cherry decoration is a replacement of 1863. – Lattice-sided FOOTBRIDGE of standard Highland Railway type and probably erected later in the C19.

ROYAL SCHOOL OF DUNKELD, School Lane. By *A. Watt Allison*, 1930. Harled, with dressings of red brick. Perfunctorily classical, a small pediment over the centre of the front.

DESCRIPTION

PERTH ROAD enters from the SE. The village is heralded by a mid-C19 short terrace of three cottages on the r. side, the first of *c*. 1830, the centre house mid C19 and boasting a trio of bracketed broad-eaved gablets, the third late C19 and bargeboarded. Then, late C20 housing but a line of trees on the r. offers compensation. The next incident, again on the r., is TORWOOD PLACE, two parallel short terraces of mid-C19 two-storey houses. The front row is of six bays, the second and fifth slightly advanced and gabled, the others with steep gablets, all topped by stone finials carved as fleur-de-lys, thistle, star and crescent. The back row is lower and plainer, the first floor windows gableted but without finials. On the corner of ST MARY'S ROAD, a single-storey mid-C19 *cottage orné* which presents an extravagant display of carved bargeboards. A path leads uphill from St Mary's Road to St Columba's R. C. Church (*see* Churches, above). In St Mary's Road, several large Victorian villas, the white harled BIRCHWOOD HOUSE of 1858 the most light-hearted, with broad eaves, bargeboards and small towers.

NW of St Mary's Road, Perth Road becomes suburban with semi-detached villas of *c*. 1900, half-timbering in their gables. Mid-C19 housing, the first-floor windows gableted, in GLADSTONE TERRACE and BIRNAM TERRACE to the SW. Further along Perth Road, the single-storey early C20 GENERAL STORE TEA ROOM, its walls of split logs, followed by St Mary's Episcopal Church (*see* Churches, above). On the l., a mid-C19 harled cottage with broad eaves and a tree-trunk porch. Beyond, on the E corner of STATION ROAD, a large block (TOWER BUILDINGS) of 1859, a steeply pyramid-roofed tower projecting at the canted corner. On the W side of Station Road, the Birnam Institute (*see* Public Buildings, above).

MURTHLY TERRACE, on Perth Road's NE side, is a long three-storey Scots Renaissance block of 1862–9. Oriel windows under shaped gables, gableted dormerheads and conical-roofed round turrets. At the terrace's W end, a DRINKING FOUNTAIN by *Beveridge* of Perth, *c*. 1915. Ball-finialled fat sandstone column on a pedestal, its sides panelled with polished grey granite. Then the bulk of the BIRNAM HOUSE HOTEL, a mid-C19 eclectic mixture of Baronial display and the *cottage orné*. Tower with bracketed broad eaves under an extravagantly bellcast pyramidal roof. The huge mullioned and transomed window to the l. is an insertion of 1913 when the building was reconstructed after a fire. Some gables are crow-stepped but others bargeboarded. To the W, stone piers, the outer pair with acorn finials, the inner topped by balls, between which are cast-iron screens and gates of *c*. 1870 at the end of the former drive to Murthly Castle (*see* Murthly). Above the gates, a cast-iron overthrow surmounted by morose lions. The screen and gates link the hotel to CARTERS LODGE (also of *c*. 1870), a tall two-storey Baronial building with a jettied upper floor, crowstepped gables and gablets and a pyramidal-spired entrance tower. Opposite the hotel, the Beatrix Potter Garden (*see* Public Buildings, above). To the W, C20 bungaloid development. Set back on the r., in SCHOOL LANE, the Royal School of Dunkeld and Little Dunkeld Kirk (*see* Churches and Public Buildings, above). At the end of Perth Road, NURSERY COTTAGE of the earlier C19. Broad-eaved piended roof; lattice glazing in the pointed windows.

BEE COTTAGE, 3.3 km. SE. Picturesquely gabled and gableted rubble-walled cottage of *c.* 1830. Broad eaves and a small canted bay window. Diamond-paned borders to the windows.

ROHALLION LODGE. *See* p. 678.

BLACKCRAIG CASTLE
1.3 km. S of Ballintuim

Over-the-top towered and crowstep-gabled Baronial dream house of the artist and amateur architect, *Patrick Allan-Fraser*, built in 1856 round an unpretentious earlier core.

It is an irregular Z-plan constructed of whinstone rubble with dressings of red sandstone. Huge rectangular NW corner tower, the top stage jettied on a single course of continuous corbelling, its wallhead finished with huge moulded corbels which carry a balustrade between parapeted corners on three sides; on the E the wallhead rises into a square caphouse. Inside the balustrade, an attic storey. The house's three-storey main block extends S from the E side of the tower. At the gabled N bay, a canted oriel window, its mullions formed as columns whose bases and capitals are carved with human heads. At this block's S end, a large squinch arch. The house's SE jamb is formed by an L-plan tower house, its inner angle filled by a large conical-roofed round tower containing the principal entrance whose stone canopy is surmounted by the half-length figure of an angel. Rounded corners to this tower house's main block and jamb but on these are placed corbels to carry the rectangular top floor. Conical-roofed corner turrets, one on the jamb bearing a clock face. A pair of service courts behind; on the S of these, a screen wall with a round turret.

BRIDGE over the River Ardle on the driveway from the E, of *c.* 1870 and also designed by *Allan-Fraser*. Its relatively utilitarian river crossing, of one broad segmental span flanked by narrower round-headed arches, is made a symbol of baronial status by the massive upper work, a two-storey gatehouse constructed of bull-nosed ashlar masonry. Conical-roofed towers at the S corners and, above the tall transe, an L-plan lodging, its NE jamb forming a rectangular corner tower from which a parapeted wall-walk on the N side leads to a formidable battlemented round bartizan. In the sides of the transe, balustraded openings giving views over the river. From the lodging's SW corner, a high-level bridge to the conical-roofed round tower of a lodge beside the drive.

LODGE of *c.* 1856 at the E end of the drive. Crowstep-gabled and with a canted bay window whose column-mullions are like those of the castle's oriel window but without the carved human heads; gabled S porch. Diagonally set square GATEPIERS surmounted by carved piles of leaves topped by dogs' heads.

BLACKFORD

Village, formerly a small industrial centre having breweries, tanneries and a sawmill, the buildings mostly Victorian.

CHURCHES

BLACKFORD FREE CHURCH, Moray Street. Secularized. Gothic Georgian survival by *William Henderson*, 1865, built of purplish ashlar, the dressings of stugged buff-coloured stone. It is a big buttressed box with a stone-spired S steeple. Pinnacles on top of the angle buttresses of the church and steeple; below the steeple's belfry are lozenge-framed clock faces.

Former BLACKFORD PARISH CHURCH, off Moray Street. A long narrow rubble-walled rectangle (*c.* 23.5 m. by 7.6 m.), now roofless, it was rebuilt, probably on medieval foundations, in 1738–9. On the W gable, a birdcage bellcote, its pyramidal roof with a ball finial; moulded skewputts. Long S front originally of seven bays, the end doors (the W now blocked) under elliptical-arched fanlights. Over the centre door, a segmental-arched fanlight, its imposts bearing the initials AM (for Archibald Moncrieff, minister of Blackford from 1697 to 1739); the door's lintel is inscribed W 1739 M, the initials those of William Moncrieff who was appointed assistant and successor to his father in 1738. At the intermediate bays, tall rectangular windows, their margins checked for shutters; they were enlarged as part of *James Gillespie Graham*'s alterations of 1821.* Placed high up each side of the central door, a rectangular window inserted in 1821. W of the door a very short stretch of wall joins to a ruinous octagonal session house, probably added in the later C18.

In each gable a rectangular gallery window of 1738–9. The E gable's round-arched door was inserted by *James Ritchie* in 1877. At the N side low windows under the original E and W galleries. The tall rectangular windows between were probably blocked in 1821 when a N gallery was erected, entered from a central door approached by a forestair.

At the entrance to the GRAVEYARD, a stone GATEWAY, probably of *c.* 1740, with chamfered segmental-arched openings, the side walls of the interior containing recesses. Lying inside this gateway, a broken C18 HEADSTONE decorated with an Ionic

---

* *William Stirling I* was executant architect.

pilastered panel bearing a relief of three women; weathered angel's head (the soul) at the top. – W of the church, a badly worn HEADSTONE of 1731 carved with the initials FH and MC and reliefs of a man and woman under an angel's head. – Adjoining HEADSTONE to MA dated 1684 and bearing a very crude skull and crossbones.

BLACKFORD PARISH CHURCH, Moray Street. Gothic, by *David MacGibbon*, 1858–9. Originally T-plan, each broad gable containing a stepped arrangement of three lancet lights. Below them, a porch at the E and depressed arched windows at the N and S. The W limb, its gable again with a three-light window (perhaps reused) and with a round window at the top, was added in 1892. Tall and thin square steeple at the SE corner, the tower's four stages marked off by string courses. Pointed belfry openings. Stone spire with gableted clock faces and small lucarnes. The small porch in the SE inner angle was added in 1866–7 by *Henry Robertson*.

Inside, scissor-truss roofs. Galleries with plain Gothic fronts in the E, N and S limbs. The W chancel was refurnished in the mid C20. – ORGAN by *Ingram & Co.*, 1898. – STAINED GLASS. Three-light W window (the Risen Lord with St Peter and St John) by *A. Ballantine & Gardiner*, 1900. – In the S side of the W limb, one light (the Sower) of 1890. – In the N side of this limb, a light (the Good Shepherd), also of *c.* 1890. – Two figurative lights (the Good Shepherd, and Dorcas) of 1957–8 and 1962. – In the N wall under the W gallery, a window (an execrable version of Holman Hunt's 'The Light of the World') by *John C. Hall & Co.*, 1917.

PUBLIC BUILDINGS

BLACKFORD PRIMARY SCHOOL, Moray Street. Utilitarian, by *John Donaldson*, 1869; ragbag additions.

BLACKFORD VILLAGE HALL, Moray Street. Dated 1887. Tall single-storey block, the windows rising into pedimented dormerheads. Entrance framed by tall panels topped by stumpy Ionic pilasters, the frieze's intended carving unexecuted; above the cornice, a coat of arms in a pedimented surround.

DESCRIPTION

Two parallel streets. The broad MORAY STREET contains most of the churches and public buildings, (*see* above) and the MALTINGS by *Russell & Spence*, 1897, of four-storeys and eleven-bay with the engine house rising above the E end. In front of the maltings, the BLACKFORD HOTEL of the later C19, the walls painted white with black trimmings. Bargeboarded dormerheads to the windows of the upper floor. Octagonal corner turrets with witches' hat roofs; over the centre, an iron-crested French pavilion roof. Otherwise, Moray Street's buildings are dour C19 small-town architecture. STIRLING STREET running parallel to the SE contains C19 vernacular houses, the atmosphere jollier and more villagey. Set back at the NE end of the village, the small broad-eaved RAILWAY STATION by *A. & A. Heiton*, 1854, and, on the SE side of the road, an early C20 SIGNAL BOX, very like a bowling green clubhouse. Prominent on a hill to the N, the former Blackford Parish Church (*see* Churches, above).

SYMBOL STONE, Peterhead, 2.6 km. ENE. Undressed boulder, 1.38 m. high, one face incised, probably in the C6 or C7, with paired goose and 'rectangle' symbols.

GLENEAGLES HOUSE. *See* p. 397.

BLAIR ADAM
1 km. WNW of Keltybridge

1090

Sprawling makeshift of a laird's house and offices constructed round a courtyard in the C18 and C19. That this was the seat of the Adam family, Scotland's dominant architectural dynasty in the C18, is hardly evident.

The architect and builder, *William Adam*, bought the estate of Blair Crambeth (from *c.* 1769, Blair Adam) in 1731 and a year or two later built a house to accommodate his resident factor and himself on his visits to the property, with an L-plan set of offices behind. This house forms the centrepiece of the present E range. It is a straightforward harled block of two storeys (a built-up window in the N gable formerly lit the roof-space). Five-bay front, the shallowly projecting portico erected by *Simpson & Brown c.* 1990 to replace a porch added by William Adam's eldest son, the architect *John Adam*, in 1775. The portico's stone pediment and end piers are reused from the porch, the wooden Roman Doric columns new. The projection of the house's eaves gutter on shallow wooden blocks is a late C19 alteration.

By 1736 William Adam had enlarged the house by the addition of harled single-storey lateral wings, each originally of three bays. Both were extended by John Adam in 1775, the S wing being heightened and given a bowed end. The three N windows of its E front seem to be in their original position but with ashlar work above, perhaps to support the additional masonry of the heightening. The additional S window is set close to its 1730s neighbour. The N wing was made an L by the construction of a piend-roofed block across its end and stretching back to the W. This addition's E front is of two bays, its N elevation of three, the windows grouped 1:2, the E window of three lights.

At its W end the addition joined the house to the existing N range of OFFICES, which is rubble-built and of two storeys. Apparently quite plain when built in the 1730s, the E half of this range's N front was remodelled in 1815–16 when one upper window was built up and the other two given heavy roll-and-hollow mouldings of early C17 type and heightened to rise through the eaves to pedimented dormerheads. One dormerhead is carved with the Adam coat of arms, the other with the arms of the wife, mother and grandmother of William Adam, Lord Chief Commissioner of the Jury Court of Scotland, who had succeeded his father, John Adam, as owner of the estate in 1792. Probably at the same time a weathered panel bearing the royal arms of Scotland was inserted in the wall. It looks late C16 and may have been brought here from the Palace block or (demolished) Queen's House at Dunfermline Abbey (Fife). The W half of this range is less altered but roofless. Against its N side, a rubble-walled tower which was added in 1815–16. It is of two stages, with narrow rectangular windows. Unmoulded corbels under the parapet which is pierced by quatrefoils; pyramid roof.

The house's principal entrance was moved to the S in the C19. It is now contained in a single-storey piend-roofed block abutting the C18 house's S wing. Masonry of roughly squared and coursed blocks; side-lit door. Rising behind it is the gable of an addition (replacing a late C18 addition) built at the back of the original house to *David Bryce*'s design in 1859. W of the entrance, a second but taller and broader piend-roofed building, also of 1859. Its three-light S window has been converted from a side-lit door, perhaps reused from an entrance of 1807 in this position. W of this, a plain two-storey block of 1847, its E end all harled. The ground floor of its W two-thirds is timber-framed and infilled with rubble. The frame is the surviving structure of a veranda which fronted a three-storey block built in this position in 1805. The upper floor, supported by the timber frame, is of stretcher bond brickwork and harled. At the W end, a two-storey but lower harled short block of 1805 which contains a tunnel-vaulted cellar.

A late C19 screen wall, of stugged ashlar with Roman Doric pilasters and entablature of polished ashlar, hides the W SERVICE RANGE from the drive. This is rubble-built of two-storeys, its S end ruinous; mainly C18. Segmental-arched entrance to the stables. The N gable's crowsteps and large but plain cross finial are late C19, contemporary with a single-storey N addition, also crowstepped and cross-finialled.

Inside the courtyard, an informal jumble of rear elevations. Along the side of the S range, a late C19 lean-to addition. Projecting from the W range, a square rubble-built clock tower of 1815–16, its stages marked off by unmoulded string courses; small openings at the top.

INTERIOR. The S range's late C19 entrance hall is top-lit. At its N end, a short passage, also top-lit and with a heavy egg-and-dart cornice, gives access to the DINING ROOM on the W which was formed by *David Bryce* in 1859. It is lit by an elliptical-arched opening in the N wall and a three-light window (the centre light originally a door) in the S. Huge Neoclassical cast-iron chimneypiece, presumably supplied by the *Carron Ironworks* of which the Adams were major shareholders. Arabesques of foliage round the fireplace opening; urns and foliaged pendants on the jambs. At the ends of the fluted frieze, reliefs of Europa and the Bull; at the centre, a panel of a lady patting a lion. Egg-and-dart cornice.

N of the passage behind the entrance hall is THE CORRIDOR formed by Bryce in 1859. This is the house's principal room and occupies a space between the C18 house and a service passage (constructed in 1847 as a link between the N and S ranges). It is lit by a pair of large lunettes placed high in the W wall. At the same level in the N wall, a broad segmental-arched recess containing a bust; under this, a plain chimneypiece of veined white marble, the Adam crest at the centre of the frieze. Plaster ceiling of three compartments with foliaged borders, a rose in the centre compartment. In the centre of the E side, a door into the C18 STAIR HALL, the stair's cast-iron balustrade a replacement, probably of 1847. Fluted pilasters mark the division between the stair hall and the original ENTRANCE HALL, the pilasters and the entrance hall's palmette and anthemion frieze and acanthus cornice looking like late C18 embellishments. This entrance hall is flanked by two rooms, the S the owner's PARLOUR (now a bedroom) with an early C18 basket-arched and keystoned grey marble chimneypiece, its wooden surround added in the later C19, the N the FACTOR'S ROOM (now also a bedroom), its keystoned grey marble chimneypiece also early C18 and with an added wooden surround but plainer. Similar early C18 chimneypieces, their quality differentiating the owner's bedroom to the S and the factor's to the N, in the two rooms above.

N of The Corridor is the top-lit ANTE-LIBRARY, also of 1859. Off its E side, the LIBRARY in the 1730s N wing; it was used as the drawing room by the late C18. Tunnel-vaulted plaster ceiling. Huge mid-C19 white marble chimneypiece imported from the boardroom of the Carron Ironworks in the later C20. It is still Late Georgian in feeling, the jambs' console-capped pilasters carved with husk swags and floral pendants. At the centre of the frieze, a deeply undercut floral swag. N of this, entered off a short passage N of the Ante-Library, the cove-ceilinged SCHOOLROOM added by John Adam in 1775 as the dining room and well lit from two windows in the E wall and a three-light window in the N. Pine chimneypiece of late C18 type decorated with husk swags and pendants; on the central panel of the frieze, swags of vines framing an urn surmounted by back-to-back lions. N of this and also of 1775, the kitchen (the late C18 principal bedroom) with a coomb ceiling and, at the S wall, a recess intended to be occupied by a bed.

Propped against the S side of the house is a steeply pedimented stone DORMERHEAD of *c.* 1600, the tympanum carved with fleurs-de-lys above a pair of circles which contain the initials IL and EC for James Lindsay of Dowhill and Elizabeth Colville, his wife. It probably came from Dowhill Castle (q.v.).

COACHHOUSE, 0.2 km. WSW of the mansion house. Mid C18. Rubble-built S front of five bays, its slightly advanced and pedimented ends of two-storey height, each with a tall round-headed window with projecting imposts, the E window with a dummy head and flanked by two first-floor openings, probably C19 insertions. At the three centre bays, segmental-arched carriage doors and late C19 round-headed dormer windows.

The WALLED GARDEN, 0.4 km. NE of the house, was formed by *John Adam* in 1755–61. It is entered from the W through corniced and channelled ashlar gatepiers of the earlier C19, the iron gates with rosettes at the intersections of their latticework. In the NW corner of the garden's W part, a corniced pedestal MONUMENT by *Thomas Brown* of Uphall, 1833. Panelled sides, the W bearing an inscription commemorating William Adam's layout of the landscape of Blair Adam (THEN A WILD UNSHELTERED MOOR) in 1733 and John Adam's continuation of the work and creation of the walled garden, WHICH HAS BEEN PRESERVED WITHOUT CHANGE OF DESIGN OR ALTERATION OF EFFECT EXCEPT WHAT GROWTH HAS PRODUCED. At the garden's main part, a tall N wall (intended to be surmounted by urns) with crude guttae under the cope. At the wall's centre, a pyramidal-roofed two-storey GARDENER'S HOUSE of the 1750s. In its S front, an overarched dummy Venetian window under a small and square first-floor opening. Short return walls at the E and W ends of the garden's N side, their copes carried on simple moulded corbels. In the W wall, a rusticated and pedimented Gibbsian door. The corresponding E door (now built up) is a Doric aedicule with banded pilasters; it was intended to open into a semicircular temple or summer house.

NORTH BLAIR, 0.2 km. NW of the walled garden, built in 1760–3, was designed by *John Adam* as the SE pavilion of an otherwise unexecuted quadrangle of offices. Rubble-walled and piend-roofed, with a Venetian window (the sidelights dummies) in each of the E and S faces. The E front's upper windows have been given C19 dormerheads. N addition, probably of 1814 when the pavilion was converted to a house.

BLAIR ATHOLL

Strung-out but fairly small village in Glen Garry and just outside the park of Blair Castle (q.v.), developed from the 1830s as housing for estate workers, hotels serving tourists from the 1860s after the arrival of the railway.

CHURCHES

BLAIR ATHOLL PARISH CHURCH. By *Archibald Elliot*, 1824–5. Sneck-harled rubble-built cruciform, with short low transepts (the S a vestry, the N a vestibule fronted by a battlemented porch); narrow chancel-like outshot at the E gable. Round-headed windows, some dummies. Battlemented W tower of three intaken stages. At the lowest, round-headed windows in the W and S faces, the latter a dummy; rectangular N door, perhaps an insertion. At each exposed face of the second stage, a pair of small and narrow round-headed lights. Round-headed belfry openings at the top stage.

The interior was recast in 1950–1. – ORGAN by *John. R. Miller*, 1910.

ST ADAMNAN-KILMAVEONAIG (Episcopal). On the site of the medieval church of Kilmaveonaig which was rebuilt or reconstructed in 1591 (the date on a stone now in the S wall which bears the initials of Alexander Robertson of Lude and his wife, Agnes Gordon).

The present church was built in 1794 (the date on a badly worn stone in the W gable), one of the first Episcopalian churches erected after the repeal of the penal laws in 1792 and indistinguishable from a Presbyterian country kirk of the same date. *Charles Robertson* was the mason and *John Stewart* the wright and architect. It is a rubble-built box (originally harled), a ball-finialled birdcage bellcote on the W gable. Round-headed windows in the S wall. In each gable, a door under a gallery window, both again round-headed. At the N side was a vestry and two forestairs for access to the galleries inside. Alterations were made in the 1890s to designs by the *Rev. Edward Sugden* of Coupar Angus. In 1893 he inserted three pointed and cusped lights under a foiled circlet in the central S window, provided a new vestry and removed the N forestair (a wooden replacement of *c.* 1870 for the stairs of 1794). Five years later he placed similar lights but without the traceried head in the other two S windows and the window of the W gable. At the same time Sugden formed a chancel at the E end, raising the sill of the E window of the S wall, building up the E door and inserting a rectangular window at the E end of the N side. In 1899 he added a battlemented Gothic porch at the W end. Further alterations took place in 1906 when the vestry was enlarged and an addition containing a new stair to the W gallery and a bedroom for a visiting priest built beside it.

INTERIOR. The porch doubles as a sacristy, its centre occupied by a Purbeck marble square FONT of 1900, a scaled-down copy of the C12 font in Galway Parish Church, decorated with low relief patterns.

The church itself originally contained galleries along the N side and the E and W ends, the E gallery deeper than the W and the space below occupied by a room and the burial vault of the Robertsons of Lude; the pulpit stood at the centre of the S wall with a small communion table in front. Sugden's alterations removed the N gallery in 1893 and the E gallery in 1898 when the present chancel was formed.

The W GALLERY is of 1794, its front of fielded panelling with a dentilled cornice; on the centre panel, a high-relief heraldic achievement of the Robertsons of Lude, originally at the E gallery and moved here in 1898. – The PEWS are mostly Victorian. – On the N side of the entrance to the chancel, a very simple semi-octagonal PULPIT enclosure, formed with communion rails of the 1860s. – Elaborate but charmless wooden

LECTERN, Gothic of 1899, on the S side. – Oak ALTAR of 1900; its panels, carved by *Bridgeman* of Lichfield with reliefs of the *Agnus Dei* flanked by angels, were added in 1908. – Fumed oak REREDOS by *Robert S. Lorimer*, 1912, with late Gothic enrichment. On its back a central crucifix carved at Oberammergau flanked by figures of angels holding chalices; angel trumpeters on top of the slender columns either side of the central panel. – CHAMBER ORGAN of *c.* 1780, placed in the church in 2000.

On the chancel's N wall, a large but crudely lettered early C17 GRAVE-SLAB commemorating Agnes Gordon †1634 and her son, Alexander Robertson of Lude, †1639. – Above it, a stone dated 1665 bearing two coats of arms identified by the accompanying initials as those of Alexander Robertson of Lude and Katharine Campbell, his wife. – Two HATCHMENTS. The larger is on the N wall and commemorates James Robertson of Lude †1803. Around the heraldic achievement at the centre are painted coats of arms, those on the l. representing the wives of his ancestors; skulls at the top and bottom. The hatchment on the S wall is to Margaret Nairn †1802, wife of James Robertson of Lude, the achievement surrounded by painted foliage; an angel's head (the soul) at the top, a skull at the bottom.

STAINED GLASS. Strongly coloured E window (Christ the King) of 1898. – The chancel's two-light N window (St Euan or Adamnan and St Bride) is by *Margaret Chilton*, 1925, clearly drawn and coloured. – Rich but lightly handled three-light S window (St Columba, St Ninian and St Margaret of Scotland) by *Clayton & Bell*, 1900.

At the entrance to the small rubble-walled graveyard, a simple wooden LYCHGATE of 1901, the centre of each gable supported by a Celtic cross.

ST BRIDE'S KIRK, Old Blair, 1.2 km. NW. Disused since 1825. Probably built in the later C16, it is T-plan with an off-centre S 'aisle'. The roofless body, apparently standing on medieval foundations, was partly rebuilt in 1742, the walls constructed of thin stone slabs. At the W gable, low remains of a tower. The gable's entrance is a round-headed door almost entirely robbed of its dressings. In the N wall, E of its centre, a minister's door (blocked in 1864) under a horizontally proportioned window, its lintel now missing. At the E end of this wall and set even higher, an elliptically arched gallery window with rounded jambs. In the E gable, a pair of fairly small rectangular windows with rounded jambs. Near the top of this gable, two blocked gallery windows. In the S side, E of the 'aisle', a rectangular door with chamfered jambs, and above but not aligned, a rectangular gallery window. At the 'aisle', rectangular gallery windows and a W door, all with chamfered surrounds. On the W wall, a pair of heraldic MONUMENTS in ogee-arched frames, the l. of 1575 and commemorating 'IS', the r. to John Stewart, fourth Earl of Atholl, †1579 and his second wife, Margaret Fleming. In the main block's S side W of the 'aisle', remains of three gallery windows, one still with chamfered jambs, and, near the w end, a built-up door and a small ground-floor window.

Inside, the groin-vaulted 'aisle' is entered through a moulded segmental arch provided by *David Bryce* in 1865. – MONU-MENTS. On the N wall of the church, a small weathered tablet of 1579 with two coats of arms and the initials GL and IG, probably for George Leslie, Captain of Blair, and J. Gordon, his wife. – On the s wall of the 'aisle', a large marble monument to George, sixth Duke of Atholl, erected in 1869, was carved by *John Steell* with the relief of a mourning Atholl Highlander beside a lopped tree, the duke's mantle hanging on one branch; above, a ducal coronet. – Against the 'aisle's' E wall, two medieval SLABS, one incised with a cross, the other with foliage.

PUBLIC BUILDINGS

BALVENIE PILLAR, Tom na Croiche, 1.1 km. N. On the edge of a wood but intended to be clearly visible from the parkland of Blair Castle, a crude rubble obelisk originally surmounted by a gilded ball finial. It was erected in 1755 by James, second Duke of Atholl, in commemoration of the place where executions formerly took place and of his own regalian jurisdiction (lost in 1747) over all criminal cases in Atholl except high treason.

BLAIR CASTLE CARAVAN PARK. The park was opened in 1971. RECEPTION CENTRE by *Michael Gray Architects*, 2002. Two-storey pavilion, the exposed V-shaped struts supporting a curved roof of ribbed metal. Under this, walling of glass, metal, painted plywood and varnished pine. Inside, a full-height reception area. On one wall, a large *Coade* stone PANEL of 1809 bearing the heraldic achievement of the Dukes of Atholl. It belonged to a gateway (now demolished) at Dunkeld House.

BRIDGE OF TILT. By *John Mitchell*, 1823. Three segmental arches; triangular cutwaters. A cantilevered footpath was added on the s side, *c*. 1960.

RAILWAY STATION. By *Peter Wilson* of the Highland Railway Co., 1869. On the N platform, the plain broad-eaved and rubble-walled main building of one and two storeys. On the s platform, a wooden waiting room. – Lattice-girder FOOTBRIDGE of standard Highland Railway type.

RAILWAY VIADUCT over the River Tilt. By *Joseph Mitchell*, 1861–2. A single lattice-truss span. At each end, a large and heavily detailed castellated stone archway.

SCHOOL. Now a museum. L-plan school and schoolhouse built by *James Robertson* and *John Fergusson*, 1833. The school was lengthened in 1849 and further altered and extended in 1865. The gablet dormerheads of the single-storey and attic schoolhouse seem to be of 1833 but the sturdy gabled porch was added in 1861.

VILLAGE HALL. Rubble-built domestic Scots Jacobean, by *J. Macintyre Henry*, 1906–7. Crowstepped gables at the ends and the slightly advanced broad centre from whose W inner angle a slate-roofed bowed tower pushes out. At the centre, a canopied round-arched door under a mullioned and transomed three-light window, its centre light's segmental pediment carved with a thistle. Three-bay ranges either side of the centre, the l. with swept dormerheads over the first-floor windows, the r. with tall gableted dormerheads.

DESCRIPTION

The B8079 runs through the village. On the N side, the park wall of Blair Castle (q.v.). On the S, set back at the W end, the Railway Station (*see* Public Buildings, above). It is followed by the large ATHOLL ARMS HOTEL, symmetrical squared-up Scots Jacobean by *R. & R. Dickson*, 1856. Opposite, the WAR MEMORIAL of 1924, a huge boulder from Craig a Barns, near Dunkeld, its top roughly worked to suggest a lopped tree. It was executed from sketch designs by *John, eighth Duke of Atholl*. E of the hotel, FORD ROAD leads S across the railway line to THE MILL, a plain rubble-built water mill of *c.* 1833; single-spoke mid-breast shrouded paddle wheel. In the main street E of Ford Road, BLAIR COTTAGES, a carefully composed rubble-built terrace, symmetrical but diversified, by *R. & R. Dickson*, 1840. Projecting at each end, a crowstep-gabled and prominently chimneyed two-storey wing. Single-storey links, the broad centre of each boldly advanced under a crowstepped gable, join to square three-storey pyramid-roofed towers. These flank the terrace's advanced two-storey centrepiece, its corners splayed at the ground floor and corbelled out to the square above; straight skews to the gable. Part of the E link has been overlaid by a later shopfront. Then, the Village Hall (*see* Public Buildings, above) followed by the small tea-caddy-roofed BANK OF SCOTLAND by *George Arthur & Son*, 1925, its ground floor's rounded corners corbelled out to the square at the jettied upper floor. After Blair Atholl Parish Church and the former School, Bridge of Tilt (*see* Churches and Public Buildings, above). E of the bridge, the BRIDGE OF TILT HOTEL of *c.* 1840. At the centre, a corniced and pilastered doorpiece under a three-light first-floor window. The roof has been heightened and altered, probably early in the C20. Late C20 sun lounges fail to enliven the architecture. Opposite, a path leads through fields to St Adamnan's-Kilmaveonaig Episcopal Church (*see* Churches, above).

OLD BLAIR, 1.3 km. NW. Harled former inn, its external appearance of the C18 with C19 embellishments. Main block of two storeys and an attic with an early C19 trellis-sided porch and mid-C19 Neo-Jacobean dormer windows standing on the wallhead. Long single-storey and attic E wing, its upper windows rising into gablet dormerheads. Shorter piend-roofed W wing. To the W, a detached L of cottages.

TIRINIE, 2.5 km. NE. On a hillside in Glen Fender, a harled two-storey villa designed in 1923 by *Oswald Milne* for a solicitor,

David Tod, and his wife, Lady Helen Murray, sister of the eighth Duke of Atholl. Anglo-Scottish Arts and Crafts. Symmetrical s front with advanced gables at the ends; the first-floor windows of the three centre bays rise into triangular-gableted dormerheads. Prominent tall chimneys on the high slated roof.

CAIRN, Monzie, 3.9 km. NE. In moorland beside the Fender Burn, a large round cairn, *c.* 24 m. in diameter, constructed of waterworn boulders. It probably dates from the third millennium B.C.

CAIRN, Strathgroy, 2 km. E. Round cairn, probably of the late third or early second millennium B.C., standing high on a hillside above the River Garry. It is 38 m. in diameter and rises to a height of *c.* 5.5 m. There has been a stone kerb round the base. Sticking out of the top, slabs of a cist burial, presumably an insertion.

LUDE HOUSE. *See* p. 512.

BLAIR CASTLE
1 km. NW of Blair Atholl

8060

One of Scotland's best-known sights, the huge and stark-white ancestral seat of the Dukes of Atholl standing in the wooded valley of the River Garry just s of the desert bleakness of the moorland of the Grampians. Hugely popular with tourists, it has been often but quite undeservedly spurned by supposed connoisseurs of architecture.

HISTORY

The Pictish kingdom of Atholl had become an earldom before 1136 when granted to Malcolm III's nephew, Mathad, whose descendants held it until the Wars of Independence. Construction of a castle at Blair, at the N end of the fertile lands of the earldom, did not take place until 1269. Then, according to Walter Bower's *Scotichronicon*, one was built there by Sir John Comyn, lord of Badenoch, provoking a quarrel between him and David, Earl of Atholl, which was settled by the King in favour of the Earl. Presumably this was a castle of enclosure, its buildings probably of timber except for a small stone keep later known as Cumming's (or Comyn's) Tower.

After the Wars of Independence the earldom became an appanage of the Crown until 1439 when the lands were granted to Sir James Stewart, the Black Knight of Lorn, on his marriage to James I's widow Joan Beaufort. About 1530 their great-grandson, John Stewart, Earl of Atholl, added to Cumming's Tower a substantial three-storey block, its upper floors containing a hall and upper hall.

In 1629 the earldom of Atholl, having reverted to the Crown as a result of the failure of the male line of the Stewart earls, was revived in favour of John Murray, a grandson of the fifth Earl. Soon after, he extended the house further s, the addition's first

Blair Castle.
Elevation of east front, c. 1750

floor containing a drawing room, bedchamber and closet leading from the existing hall, a similar suite of rooms probably intended for the floor above. This was, however, uncompleted when the mid-C17 civil wars brought work to a stop.

About 1676, John, second Earl (of the new creation) and first Marquess of Atholl, built Dunkeld House which seems to have served as the principal residence of the family (Dukes of Atholl from 1703). It was not until 1736 that James, second Duke of Atholl, commissioned *John Douglas* to prepare plans for the completion and reconstruction of Blair Castle as a great Palladian mansion and then, in 1743, an alternative and more castle-like design from *James Winter*. Both schemes would have provided a grandly planned interior with a state stair giving access to a ducal apartment or suite of rooms on the first floor and a state apartment on the second. Neither was executed and, instead, the Duke began a great new house on the lower ground to the S of the castle, its general form perhaps derived from Hopetoun House (Lothian) which was then being remodelled and extended by William Adam, to provide a main block from which extended two wings, one housing a state apartment, the other the owner's suite of rooms. What was built at Blair in 1743-4 was a two-storey 51 m.-long detached range, apparently intended as the new house's ducal (N) wing.

After the Jacobite rising of 1745-6 when Blair Castle had been garrisoned by government troops, the Duke of Atholl minuted that he 'Took the Resolution to take down the Castle of Blair', stating that, were the castle to undergo a straightforward repair, 'there might be a danger of making it a garrison again.' This implies a decision to continue with the building of a new house to the S. If so, he quickly changed his mind and, instead, between 1747 and 1758, he joined the 1740s range to the house whose exterior was drastically remodelled in a surprisingly cheap manner. All its parts were raised or lowered to a relatively uniform three- and four-storey height and the window openings altered but without any attempt at symmetry, let alone magnificence. The principal architect seems to have been *John Douglas* with *James Winter* as executant architect. On completion of the work, Blair Castle was renamed Atholl House.

John, seventh Duke of Atholl, succeeded his father in 1864 and five years later employed *David Bryce* to baronialize the

Blair Castle.
Perspective of east front, *c.* 1840

exterior of what again became Blair Castle, its outline doggedly diversified and equipped with a panoply of crowstepped gables, battlements and turrets. Further Baronial alterations and additions were provided later in the C19 and at the beginning of the C20 but the Baronial manner, even in ironic Postmodern form, has been rightly and successfully eschewed for the latest work, carried out in the 1990s by *Jamie Troughton & Hugh Broughton*.

EXTERIOR

Brilliant white harling unifies the disparate elements and covers up evidence of the long and complex development of the castle. At the N end of the E-facing main block is CUMMING'S TOWER, the C13 keep which had been raised from two or three to five storeys in the C16 and reduced to three in the C18 before being again heightened, with an attic storey, in 1869–72. The three lower floors retain their Georgian appearance with a staidly regular two-bay disposition of windows at the E front. But the attic, its windows' margins exposed to contrast with the harling (as elsewhere in Bryce's alterations), is Baronial with crowstepped gables, the N and W set behind battlements, a corbelled and conical-roofed NE turret and NW angle round with a bold cannon spout. The Tower's SW jamb, perhaps an addition of *c.* 1300 and originally of two or three storeys, had attained a dizzying six-storey height before it was cut down to three storeys in 1748. Bryce restored the missing top three floors, their NW corner jettied out, the oversailing SW corner supported by a corbelled turret carried on a squinch arch; cannon spouts under the unarchaeologically bold battlement which breaks into a NW angle round. At the ground floor of the W face the harling has been stripped to expose what seems to be a crudely constructed built-up pointed doorway, a puzzling feature as it would have opened onto the rock round which the ground-floor walls of the jamb were built. Perhaps it was a relieving arch.

s of Cumming's Tower is the C16 three-storey MAIN BLOCK. Its W elevation was left untouched by Bryce except for a door which he remodelled with a hoodmoulded round-headed arch. On the E front this block's N end is covered by an early C17 stair-tower whose corner turrets had been removed and the roof replaced in the mid C18. Bryce remodelled the top, giving it a battlement studded with cannon spouts. The central feature of Bryce's remodelling of this front is his boldly advanced three-storey and attic entrance tower (replacing a single-storey C18 porch), its design derived from the early C17 entrance tower of Fyvie Castle (Aberdeenshire). The centre bay of its two lower floors is recessed between bowed ends, the upper two floors making a crowstep-gabled rectangular top hamper jettied out on corbelling which forms an elliptical arch at the centre; conical-roofed fat turrets at the corners of the second floor. Round-headed and stop-chamfered principal entrance surmounted by a knot-ended rope moulding. The space between the door and the first-floor window is filled by a panel carved with the heraldic achievement of the Dukes of Atholl.

In the SE inner angle of the entrance tower and the main block is a round C16 STAIR-TOWER whose original two-storey rectangular top hamper and slender NE turret were removed in the mid C18. Bryce replaced the low C18 roof with a taller conical one. At the S end of this E front, a shallow two-bay projection. The two lower floors of its N half were built as part of the uncompleted early C17 S addition, the second floor and the S bay (containing the Picture Staircase) added in the mid C18. Bryce added an attic, its crowstepped gable flanked by a battlemented bartizan and a conical-roofed corner turret. At the early C17 S extension's W elevation, completed in plain Georgian dress in the mid C18, Bryce placed a crowstepped gablet above its join to the C16 hall block and a battlement over the bay to the S. The SW jamb was given an attic, with conical-roofed turrets at the corners of its crowstepped gable.

The S side of the forecourt is bounded by the low LINK of c. 1750 between the main house and the 1740s wing of the intended new mansion house to the S. It is of two storeys but sited on much lower ground so that the first floor is below the main block's ground-floor level. Originally quite plain, the link's battlemented W end is an addition of 1905 by *J. Macintyre Henry*, its E end's pair of crowstepped gables of the mid C19. Its C18 first floor N porch to the forecourt was rebuilt in 1814–15 as a clock tower which was remodelled in the late C19 when it acquired gableted belfry openings and a pyramidal spire roof, its spear-shaped finial (pierced by shrapnel) taken from the Mahdi's tomb in Omdurman and erected here in 1899; Neo-Jacobean porch added by *Henry & Maclennan*, 1908. The 1740s SOUTH WING extending from the link's E end

BLAIR CASTLE 215

is of the same height. On its E side, a ground-floor porch and two-storey stair-tower. The N part of this side's ground floor is hidden by banking and overlaid by the single-storey flat-roofed and top-lit extension of 1998. The S end of the wing was heightened by *D. & J. Bryce* in 1876–7 to form a crowstep-gabled small tower with a conical-roofed round turret. A similar heightening of the centre was carried out by *James C. Walker* in 1885–6.

N of the main block is the mid-C18 well-house court (the courtyard itself roofed over by *J. Macintyre Henry* in 1904–5). On its E side, a passage whose external face is pierced by round windows. On the court's W side, a screen wall, given a battlement in 1904–5 and with an addition built against it in 1998–9. On the court's N side, the crowstep-gabled BALLROOM added in 1876–7 by *D. & J. Bryce*. Single-storey and attic, with bargeboarded gabled dormers and wallhead chimneys along the N side; bartizans, one round and one square, at the E gable. The ballroom forms the SE wing of a U-plan SERVICE COURT whose mid-C18 W range and NE wing are of two storeys, the wing extended E in 1998–9, the crowstepped gable which it had acquired in the later C19 replicated in the late C20 work. Also of 1998–9 is the glass-fronted E addition to the front of the main range. At the S end of the W elevation, the former CHARTER ROOM added by *J. Macintyre Henry* in 1904–5. Right at the N end of the straggling complex is the L-plan former ARMOURY of the Atholl Highlanders (the private army of the Dukes of Atholl), by *Henry & Maclennan*, 1908, domestic in scale and crowstep-gabled.

INTERIOR

Many of the C18 family rooms are in the SOUTH WING (not open to the public). This wing is entered on the E side through *Jamie Troughton & Hugh Broughton*'s addition of 1998, its S side fully glazed. The ground floor's centre room, overlooking the garden to the W, was the PARLOUR. Like the other rooms in this wing it was finished in 1747–8, with panelling by *Archibald Chessels* and plasterwork by *Thomas Clayton*. Pendants of fasces and flowers flank the chimneypiece which is enriched with flowers and shells and surmounted by an overmantel whose shell-topped lugged frame encloses a swag of flowers.

To the E, the delicately detailed stair, with turned wooden balusters. A tunnel-vaulted corridor on the E side runs the whole length of the FIRST FLOOR. The rooms, most still with 1740s decoration and coved ceilings, open off this but each also opens into the next through a door at the W end of its N wall. The S bedroom was Victorianized in 1876–7. To its N, a bedroom whose chimneypiece, with a pulvinated frieze and a panel carved with a floral swag, is surmounted by stucco trophies. Then, a room with a simple enrichment of shells and flowers on the chimneypiece's frieze; shell-topped overmantel with a guilloche border. Two dressing rooms to the N, the

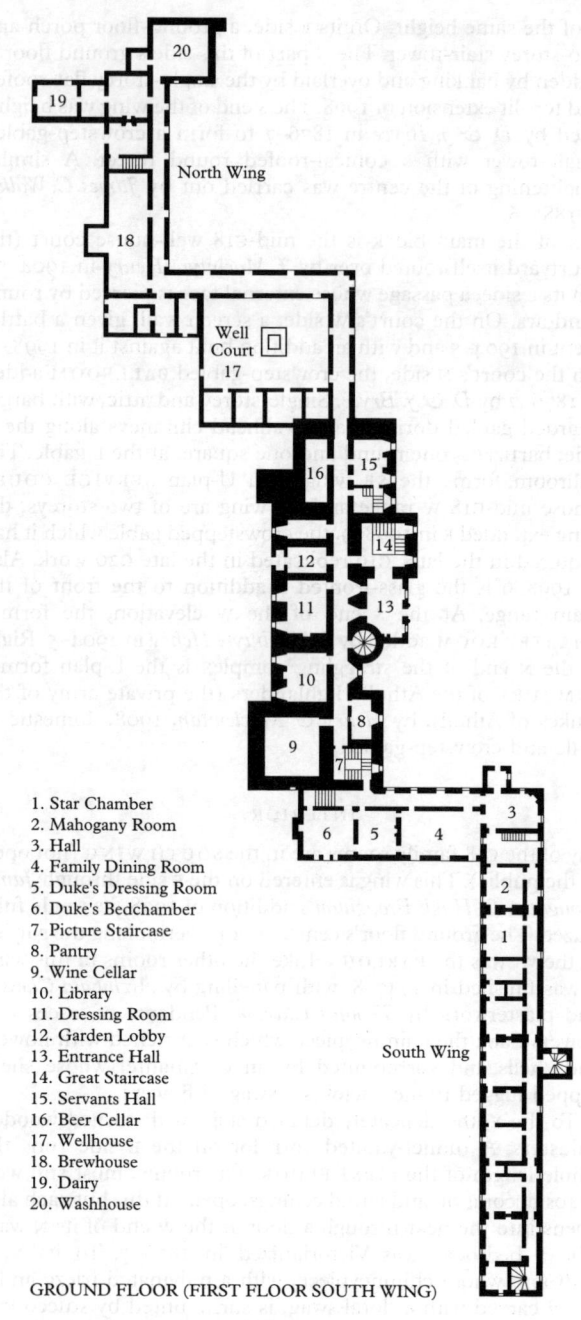

1. Star Chamber
2. Mahogany Room
3. Hall
4. Family Dining Room
5. Duke's Dressing Room
6. Duke's Bedchamber
7. Picture Staircase
8. Pantry
9. Wine Cellar
10. Library
11. Dressing Room
12. Garden Lobby
13. Entrance Hall
14. Great Staircase
15. Servants Hall
16. Beer Cellar
17. Wellhouse
18. Brewhouse
19. Dairy
20. Washhouse

GROUND FLOOR (FIRST FLOOR SOUTH WING)

Blair Castle.
Reconstruction of plans in c. 1760

FIRST FLOOR   SECOND FLOOR

|―――――――――――| 30m

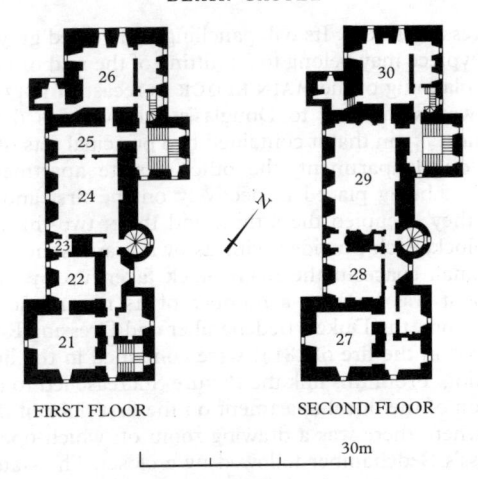

21. Small Drawing Room
22. Duchess' Bedchamber
23. Closet
24. Great Dining Room
25. Anteroom
26. Nursery
27. Derby Bedroom
28. Red Bedroom
29. Great Drawing Room
30. State Bedchamber

Blair Castle.
Main block, first and second floor

chimneypiece of the N with a grotesque head at the centre of its pulvinated frieze. On the S wall of the next room (now a sitting room), a panel with a double-lugged architrave intended to frame a landscape painting. Off-centre N chimneypiece, its frieze decorated with latticework and flowers, its shell-topped overmantel (also intended for a landscape) with a lugged architrave. The N of the 1740s rooms in this range was originally known as the STAR CHAMBER. On the S wall, a panel (presumably for a landscape) with a double-lugged architrave, shells at its corners and a shell and foliage on top. Off-centre N chimneypiece with a lugged surround and Doric frieze and cornice. Lugged overmantel, its upper corners again decorated with shells and topped by shells and swags of flowers. Ceiling enriched with uncluttered Rococo ornament. Foliage motifs at the corners. In the centre, a circle of ribbons and bows enclosing the star of the Order of the Thistle.

The interior of the link between the S wing and the main block was destroyed by fire in 1814 and remodelled in 1815. Its E rooms, C20 in their present form, now make up an office. The principal room at the W end is the cove-ceilinged LIBRARY formed in 1815 from the C18 Duke's Bedchamber and Dressing Room. Its oak panelling and veined grey marble chimneypiece may belong to a refitting of the mid or later C19.

The planning of the MAIN BLOCK as recast in 1747–58 may have owed something to Douglas's and Winter's designs of 1736 and 1743 in that it contained two principal sets of rooms, one a ducal apartment, the other a state apartment, but, instead of being placed respectively on the first and second floors, they occupied the S third and the N two-thirds of the main block, each provided with its own grand stair. The relatively small space in the main block taken up by the ducal apartment was because a number of its rooms including a dining room, the Duke's Bedchamber and Dressing Room (all destroyed in the fire of 1814) were contained in the link from the S wing. From this link the Picture Staircase led to the continuation of the ducal apartment on the first floor of the main block where there was a drawing room off which opened the Duchess's Bedchamber followed by a closet. The state apartment began at the main block's entrance hall off which was the Great Stair leading to the first-floor Anteroom and Great Dining Room. This stair continued up to the second floor's Great Drawing Room off which, in Cumming's Tower, were the State Bedchamber, Closet and Dressing Room.

A door from the passage on the N side of the library opens onto the foot of the PICTURE STAIRCASE in the SE corner of the main block. Constructed in 1748–50, this rises from the first-floor level of the link from the S wing (i.e. a little below the ground-floor level of the main block) to the main block's first floor. The woodwork is by *Archibald Chessels*, the plasterwork by *Thomas Clayton*. Turned balusters to the stair. Walls of grained plaster divided into panels, their surrounds modelled with egg-and-dart and enriched with shells, foliage and flowers. At the first-floor landing the wall decoration becomes lavish, with trophies suspended from ducal coronets. Rosettes between the modillions of the cornice. Ceiling divided into two panels and with a shallow dome at the centre. In each panel, foliage at the corners and a high basket of flowers in the centre. The dome is placed in a foliaged surround and enriched with panels bearing shallow reliefs of foliage; leafy central pendant.

Running S–N through the GROUND FLOOR of the main block from the Picture Staircase is an elliptically tunnel-vaulted PASSAGE, constructed as part of the C16 and early C17 additions and extended N through Cumming's Tower to join to the E passage of the well-house court in the mid C18. Its egg-and-dart cornice is of the later C19. On the passage's W side, in the C16 and C17 work, are tunnel-vaulted rooms, the S originally a kitchen but which became a wine cellar in the mid C18, the others stores. In EARL JOHN'S ROOM (fitted up in the C18 as a library and in the C19 as the duke's sitting room), plain panelling of the mid C18 and a Victorian chimneypiece. THE STEWART ROOM (used as a dressing room in the C18 and as a smoking room in the later C19) has painted panelling, also mid-C18, and a Victorian Frenchy marble chimneypiece carved with the relief of a head. N of this, THE TERRACE ROOM, its door to the garden formed in the mid C18. At both this door and the room's entrance from the passage are doorpieces of 1755–6, with pulvinated friezes squashed under segmental pediments. The ground floor of Cumming's Tower, probably originally a single room and perhaps vaulted, was divided from the mid C18 by the passage into two unvaulted rooms and with a service stair in the SE corner.

The Ducal Apartments

Off the first-floor head of the Picture Staircase opens the SMALL DRAWING ROOM, the drawing room of the C18 ducal apartment, its mid-C18 decoration intact. Walls covered with painted panelling, with delicate bead enrichment at the stiles except in the deep window embrasures where they are carved with a diaper pattern and rosettes. Foliaged plaster frieze under an egg-and-dart cornice. Pedimented doorpieces, their pulvinated friezes carved with flowers. Ionic columned and pilastered E chimneypiece of white and buff marble made by *Thomas Carter*, c. 1750. Mirrored wooden overmantel carved by *Charles Ross* in 1755 from a design by *Abraham Swan*, the mirror flanked by foliage-decorated upside-down consoles which face both forward and to the sides; pediment broken by an obelisk-finialled pediment.

N of this, the TEAROOM (the mid-C18 Duchess's Bedchamber), its painted panelling like that of the Small Drawing Room. Flower-enriched frieze and another egg-and-dart cornice. Doorpieces with lugged architraves, their acanthus-leaf friezes squashed under heavy cornices. N chimneypiece, probably also by *Carter*, heavily enriched with flowers and foliage. More foliage carving at the wooden overmantel (by *Ross*, 1755), its pediment broken by the bust of a woman. N of this, a tiny panelled closet, with a low coved ceiling. This was the final room of the ducal apartment but provided access, perhaps for the ceremonial entry of the Duke and Duchess to a banquet, into the Great Dining Room (*see* below).

The C16 turnpike stair on the E side of the main block's S end was remodelled in 1756. It gives access to the S end of the main block's second floor which is occupied by three mid-C18 bedrooms and a dressing room. In the SW corner is the DERBY BEDROOM (named from the bed hangings said to have been embroidered in the C17 by *Charlotte de la Trémouille, Countess of Derby*, mother-in-law of the first Marquess of Atholl). Wall panelling, some of the panels' corners cut out to allow for rosettes; egg-and-dart enrichment on the stiles of the shutters. Pedimented doorpieces, their friezes carved with rosetted circles. Elaborate white marble chimneypiece of c. 1750 by *Thomas Carter*. At the sides, fruit-swagged upside-down consoles from which grow the heads of boys. Another swag of fruit on the central panel of the frieze. Mirrored wooden overmantel of 1755 by *Charles Ross* from Swan's design, also with carved fruit at the sides and on the frieze; pediment broken by the bust of a woman.

Off this room to the E, the DERBY DRESSING ROOM. Similar panelling and doorpieces. Chimneypiece enriched with carved flowers; broken-pedimented overmantel, its mirror in a lugged architrave. N of the Derby Dressing Room, another C18 bedroom (now the BOOK ROOM). Pretty panelling, with egg-and-dart enrichment on the stiles of the shutters and at the cornice of the doorpiece. Chimneypiece carved with flowers and foliage. Pedimented overmantel, its mirror in a double-lugged architrave. N of the Derby Bedroom is the RED BEDROOM. Also panelled, the corniced doorpieces with lugged surrounds and pulvinated friezes carved with acanthus leaves. Rococo wooden chimneypiece (by Ross, 1755), its mirrored overmantel under a broken segmental pediment, all enriched with carved foliage and flowers.

The State Rooms

The processional route to the state rooms begins at Bryce's ENTRANCE HALL of 1869–72, a Neo-Jacobean setting for a display of weaponry. Two-storey height with a balcony across the W side and a compartmented plaster ceiling, the panels enriched with egg-and-dart. At the S wall, a massive canopied fireplace on which stands the heraldic achievement of the Dukes of Atholl. On the N side, the C18 broad segmental-arched opening to the Great Staircase, the keystone of the arch carved with a head of Diana.

The GREAT STAIRCASE, replacing a C17 stone stair in the same position, was erected in 1753–8 to a design by *Abraham Swan*, with plasterwork by *Thomas Clayton*. It rises from the ground to the second floor. The stair itself is of mahogany, the newel posts and turned balusters carved with foliage, the stringers with rinceau decoration, all by *John Caitcheon*. The walls of the stair hall are crossed by friezes enriched with foliage and fruit. These mark off three-storey elevations with the first floor significantly higher than the other two. At each level, stucco wall panels, their stiles enriched with stylized foliage. The ground floor's W door has a frieze squashed under its cornice. More elaborate decoration at the first floor, the plasterwork with boldly modelled flowers, fruit and foliage in high relief. Pedimented doorpieces with lugged architraves. At the second floor, the walls uninterrupted by the rise of the stair, each elevation seems to aspire to symmetry. This is achieved only at the W where a lugged centre panel, heavily enriched with foliage, is flanked by doors whose lugged surrounds are surmounted by swan-neck pediments encrusted with foliage. The N and S elevations are mirror images, each with a door at its W end of the same design as those at the W wall, a lugged horizontal centre panel and, at the E end, a square panel with roses in its cut-out corners. At the E wall, a central panel repeating that of the W wall. Flanking it, on the s, a panel like the E panels of the N and S walls, and, on the N, a panel of the same type but truncated to allow room for a lug-architraved window below. Compartmented plaster ceiling with guilloche enrichment on the flat of the stiles and egg-and-dart at their sides. A rosette of swirling foliage in each compartment, the central rosette forming a large pendant.

The W door from the first floor stair landing opens into the ANTE-ROOM. Simple mid-C18 decoration, the panelled walls originally intended to be hung with antlers and studded with cloak pins, presumably for the use of visitors; chair rail carved with a relief of intersecting lozenges. Acanthus-leaf cornice. The flat of the ceiling is enriched with a circlet of flowers round a leafy pendant from which a chandelier was intended to hang.

S of the ante-room is the GREAT DINING ROOM, its stucco decoration (by *Thomas Clayton*, 1751–3) almost too rich for the height. The general scheme is of panelled walls, aedicular door-pieces, a lavish chimneypiece and a Rococo ceiling. The narrow subsidiary panels and the panels of the deep window embrasures have stiles delicately enriched with stylized flowers and foliage; chair rail with a pattern of intersecting lozenges like that of the ante-room. The five large panels have lugged surrounds surmounted by shells and foliage. In these are placed paintings of local scenes (four landscapes, three showing waterfalls, and a view of the W front of Dunkeld Cathedral) by *Charles Steuart*, 1766–78. The centrally placed panel of the S wall is flanked by a pair of doors, each with a leafily enriched frieze and segmental pediment broken by an urn; above the doors, swags of flowers. Very grand entrance at the centre of the N end. The door, surmounted by plaster swagged drapery, is set in a Doric aedicule, the columns circled by spiralling oak leaves, the metopes of the frieze carved with swords and shields, boats, anchors and, in the centre, a grotesque face. In the pediment's tympanum, a helmet placed against foliage. Reclining on the sloping sides of the pediments are statues of two ladies. The chimneypiece of veined white marble (by *Thomas Carter*) has consoled jambs and a frieze carved with rosettes at the ends and a head of Apollo in the centre. The cornice supports the overmantel's marble base. On this, between upside-down consoles, a long panel carved with quivers and fruiting branches; at the centre, a harp placed against crossed trumpets. Above, a huge and boldly modelled stucco trophy, the banners displaying devices from the coat of arms of the Dukes of Atholl. The top of the trophy rises almost into the dining room's frieze whose deeply undercut enrichment bears foliage, shells and human heads. Rococo plasterwork on the ceiling enriched with foliage, baskets of fruit, human heads and eagles; a large leafy pendant, intended for a chandelier, in the centre. In the corners, roundels containing paintings by *Thomas Bardwell* of putti emblematic of the Four Seasons. The N half of the ceiling collapsed in 1985 and was subsequently re-erected by *L. Grandison & Son* from casts taken from the S.

On the first floor of Cumming's Tower N of the anteroom is a set of rooms (not part of the state apartment and approached by a staircase behind the Great Stair) fitted up in 1755–6. The rooms consist of the BLUE BEDROOM (used as a nursery in the C18), with a closet in the medieval jamb to its W and a dressing room to its E. In both the Blue Bedroom and the BLUE DRESSING ROOM are panelled walls, the stiles of the panels of the deep window embrasures and the shutters delicately carved with flowering branches, the corniced doorpieces with leafy pulvinated friezes. More foliaged enrichment at the chimneypieces and the broken-pedimented mirrored overmantels. Bedroom ceiling with a mutuled cornice above a foliaged frieze like that in the Small Drawing Room (*see* above). Modillion cornice to the dressing room ceiling.

At the head of the Great Stair, a balcony-landing with two W doors. The l. is a dummy. The r. opens into the GREAT DRAWING ROOM of the state apartment. Formed in 1755–8 and occupying the whole space above the first-floor anteroom and Great Dining Room, it is almost a double cube, c. 15.9 m. by 8.2 m. and 8.2 m. high, its coved ceiling giving it the height which the Great Dining Room lacks and the sumptuous decoration appearing less crowded. Four regularly spaced windows along the W side. At the E side, doors (the s a dummy) opposite the end windows and a chimneypiece at the centre. At each end wall, two doors flanking a tall alcove. All the doorpieces have foliaged friezes under consoled cornices. The white marble chimneypiece (by *Thomas Carter*) has consoles to the front and sides; frieze carved in high relief with bunches of grapes. The wooden overmantel (by *Charles Ross* from a design by *Abraham Swan*) is a Corinthian-columned broad aedicule, the swan-neck pediment broken by a vase filled with fruit. The end walls' alcoves, also by Ross, are narrower versions of the overmantel. Each contains a round-headed opening, its keystone carved with the relief of a grotesque head, its spandrels with foliage. *Thomas Clayton*'s stucco ceiling enrichment is Baroque. Deeply undercut foliage on the coving. The flat is enclosed by a guilloche border and divided into three panels, the end panels octagonal and filled with stylized foliage; at their centres, foliaged roses intended for chandeliers. The much larger circular centre panel is enriched with a circle of foliage enclosing a sunburst, a head of Apollo at its centre.

The state apartment continues in Cumming's Tower to the N with a bedchamber, closet and dressing room. The state bedchamber (now the TAPESTRY ROOM) was fitted up in the 1750s around an existing state bed of 1700 and Mortlake tapestries (illustrating the history of Diana and Callisto) of 1696. Corniced doorpieces with lugged architraves and squashed pulvinated friezes carved with leafy enrichment; simple lugged architraves to the window surrounds. The frieze under the ceiling is also pulvinated and enriched with oakleaves. Tall chimney surround. Simple lugged architrave to the fireplace opening but no mantelshelf so the chimneypiece and overmantel combine to form a single aedicule, its panelled ends suggestive of pilasters and bearing foliage pendants. More foliaged enrichment on the frieze under the consoled cornice which carries a pediment broken by an overflowing flower vase. All this is a frame for an oval mirror set between palm fronds and foliage. More mid-C18 decoration in the W closet (now TULLIBARDINE ROOM), the chimneypiece enriched with carved foliage and flowers, and the TAPESTRY DRESSING ROOM to the E, its doorpieces and broken-pedimented mirrored overmantel enriched with foliage, its modillion cornice with rosettes.

The BALLROOM, added by *D. & J. Bryce* in 1876–7, feels institutional. Hammerbeam roof. At the centre of the S side, a balcony looking like a laird's loft, its front bearing the heraldic achievement of the Dukes of Atholl. The wall panelling was introduced in 1899.

GARDEN AND PARKLAND

In the GARDEN immediately W of the house, lead STATUES of Apollo, Ceres and Flora by *John Cheere*, 1740, and a SUNDIAL held by a kneeling figure of Father Time of 1743 and also by Cheere. – In a wood, W of the garden, an ashlar OBELISK of 1742, its pedestal carved with reliefs of the star of the Order of the Thistle, the crest of the Dukes of Atholl, a ducal coronet and the heraldic device of the Isle of Man whose superiority was held by the Dukes from 1736 to 1765.

The PARKLAND was laid out from the early C18, *Margaret, Lady Nairne*, providing sketch designs in 1723. This layout was one of avenues radiating from the house, several of them leading to or through 'wildernesses' of trees. The main approach avenue (Castle Drive) from the SE survives. At its start at the edge of the village of Blair Atholl, the castle's principal GATEWAY, by *David Bryce*, 1869. End piers with cushion-banded rustication and topped by swagged urns are linked by screen walls to a pair of similar tall piers with scrolled crown-spire finials. Cast-iron gates decorated with the crest of the Dukes of Atholl; a ducal coronet on the overthrow. Crowstep-gabled LODGE of 1871, also by Bryce. – A secondary drive just to the W starts with another crowstep-gabled late C19 LODGE. – Just off this drive, the ESTATE OFFICE (originally STABLES), by *James Winter*, 1743–4, but much altered in 1877. – A third drive begins 2.4 km. to the W at the WEST LODGE designed by *Joseph Mitchell* in 1866 and built at the expense of the Highland Railway Co. whose line encroached on the edge of the castle's park. Gateway with a round-headed arch under a corbelled parapet, its central panel bearing a coroneted 'A'; conical-roofed round turrets at the ends. Two-storey and attic L-plan LODGE to the N, with crowstepped gables, a turret and a bartizan; conical-roofed round tower in the inner angle.

An avenue (the HERCULES WALK) laid out in 1743, aligned on the castle's entrance, runs E to a colossal lead STATUE of

Hercules resting on his club which is draped with the pelt of the Nemean lion. It is by *John Cheere*, a copy of the C3 statue in the Palazzo Farnese in Rome, and was erected here in 1743. – N of the Walk is the HERCULES GARDEN, its rubble walls built in 1751–4; the N wall was rebuilt in 1868. At the end of its S wall whose centre is lowered to allow a view of the statue from the garden, are GATES with coroneted JKA monograms (for John and Katharine, [eighth Duke and Duchess of] Atholl). They were designed by *J. Wilson Paterson* and erected in 1924 to commemorate their Silver Wedding. In the centre of the garden, the CANAL POND (formed in 1751) which is crossed by the CHINESE BRIDGE, a 1990s copy of the bridge designed by *Abraham Swan* which was erected over the Banvie Burn in 1754. In the S stretch of the garden's W wall, pointed niches containing marble statues of the Four Seasons (by *John Cheere*, 1742). At the centre of this wall, the pyramid-roofed C18 APPLE HOUSE. At the N end of this wall, a piend-roofed two-storey GARDENER'S HOUSE of 1873. At the centre of the garden's E side, an ogee-roofed pavilion with a veranda (MACGREGOR'S FOLLY) designed by *Amelia Murray MacGregor* and built in 1888. In front of it, lead STATUES. Four are of pudgy boys and were made by *John Cheere* in 1740. The other two (a Shepherd and Shepherdess) were cast *c.* 2000 from mid-C18 statues by Cheere and erected here as a memorial to the tenth Duke of Atholl. – On the bank of the River Tilt, 0.3 km. E of the Hercules Garden, is a GROTTO of 1758. Semicircular-arched rubble entrance to a half-domed chamber.

Just N of Blair Castle is the densely planted DIANA'S GROVE, a 'wilderness' formed in the 1730s when it was planted with European larch, these trees supplemented in the C19 with American firs and Japanese larch but many replaced after a storm in 1893. In the centre of the Grove, a STATUE of Diana and Actaeon. It is a replacement of 1893 for a statue of 1871, itself a replacement for a statue of 1740 which had been removed in the late C18 or early C19. At the N end of Diana's Grove, a rubble-built semicircular-arched BRIDGE, perhaps of the later C18. Similar BRIDGE to its E.

On the wooded side of Craig Urrard, 1 km. NW of Blair Castle, is THE WHIM, a folly of 1762. Rubble-built and formerly harled screen wall of three arches, the outer two round-headed, each surmounted by a deep crenelle. The tall centre arch is pointed. Above it the battlement rises to suggest a turret pierced by a small pointed opening. In front of this, a retaining wall whose parapet links the screen to a pair of square pavilions covered with steep pyramidal roofs and with round-headed arches in their N and S sides.

BLAIRGOWRIE

Standing on the River Ericht, at the N edge of the plain of Strathmore, with hills rising steeply behind, Blairgowrie was erected a

BLAIRGOWRIE 225

burgh of barony under the superiority of the Drummonds of Blair or Newton in 1634. However, the burgh comprised only a group of thatched cottages near the parish church in 1790 when Colonel Macpherson of Blairgowrie laid out new streets for development. There followed the growth of a flourishing linen industry, the mills originally powered by water from the Ericht. Rattray on the river's E side, and originally a separate village, also developed as a weaving centre in the early C19 when it spread W from its parish church towards the bridge linking it to Blairgowrie. Industry has now largely departed but the town serves as a commercial and tourist centre for the surrounding rural hinterland.

CHURCHES

BLAIRGOWRIE BURGHER CHURCH. *See* Public Buildings: Royal British Legion Hall.

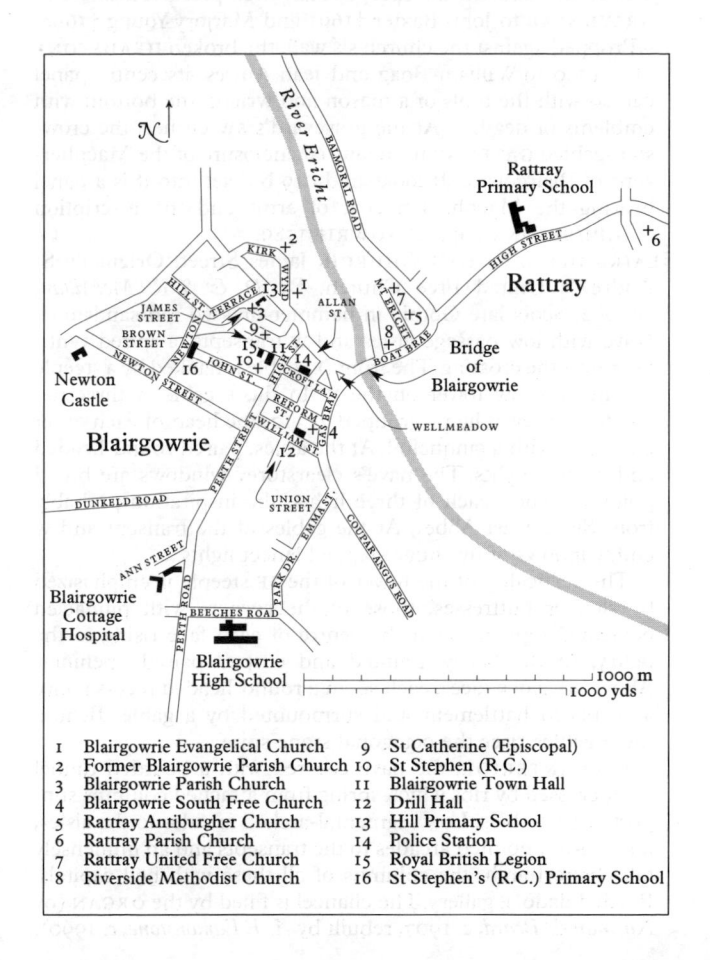

1 Blairgowrie Evangelical Church
2 Former Blairgowrie Parish Church
3 Blairgowrie Parish Church
4 Blairgowrie South Free Church
5 Rattray Antiburgher Church
6 Rattray Parish Church
7 Rattray United Free Church
8 Riverside Methodist Church
9 St Catherine (Episcopal)
10 St Stephen (R.C.)
11 Blairgowrie Town Hall
12 Drill Hall
13 Hill Primary School
14 Police Station
15 Royal British Legion
16 St Stephen's (R.C.) Primary School

BLAIRGOWRIE EVANGELICAL CHURCH, KirkWynd. Originally the hall of the former Blairgowrie Parish Church, it is by *Robert Reid*, 1901. Gothic, built of hammer-dressed squared and coursed red sandstone.

Former BLAIRGOWRIE PARISH CHURCH, KirkWynd. Disused. Built in 1824, full advantage of its hilltop site taken by the S tower. This is square, of four intaken stages, the three lower all with pointed windows which diminish in size upwards. At the bottom stage the windows are set in overarches, the corbels at their rectangular heads supporting the cornice over this stage. Chamfered corners to the top (belfry) stage. The top stage is pagoda-like, pierced by pointed and cusped openings and finished with bold stone brackets. These support the broad eaves of the roof which is scooped up to a ball-finialled cupola surmounted by a weathercock. The body of the church is a piend-roofed red sandstone ashlar box with large pointed windows. Battlemented porches at the ends added in 1882.

E of the church, an exceptionally well-preserved late C17 GRAVE-SLAB to John Baxter †1691 and Marjory Young †1698. – Propped against the church's S wall, the broken HEADSTONE of *c.* 1700 to William Boag and Jean Amres, its centre panel carved with the tools of a mason and wright, the bottom with emblems of death. – At the graveyard's SW corner, the crow-step-gabled GATEWAY to the burial enclosure of the Macphersons of Blairgowrie. It looks mid C19 but set into it is a panel bearing the Macpherson coat of arms and the inscription MACPHERSON/OF/BLAIRGOWRIE/1789.

BLAIRGOWRIE PARISH CHURCH, James Street. Originally St Andrew's United Free Church. By *D. & J. R. McMillan*, 1900–2. Scots late Gothic in hammer-dressed red sandstone. Nave with low passage aisles and W transepts, a spired ventilator over the crossing. The front (E) gable is flanked by a steeple on the S, a low tower on the N. In the E gable, a three-tier window of seven lights grouped 2:3:2, the head of each outer pair filled with a cinquefoil. At the aisles, paired round-headed and cusped lights. The nave's clearstorey windows are broad pointed arches, each of three lights, the inspiration probably from Sweetheart Abbey. At the gables of the transept and W end, windows of five huge stepped lancet lights.

The verticality of the tower of the SE steeple is emphasized by slender buttresses, those of the corners with pinnacled octagonal tops, those at the centre of each face rising to the belfry. At the belfry, pointed and cusped paired openings. Above are clock faces, each set in a round-headed recess above a corbelled battlement and surmounted by a gable. Behind these gables rises the octagonal stone spire.

Lofty INTERIOR, the nave covered with a boarded tunnel vault crossed by ribs which spring from attached columns supported by corbels. Low segmental-arched arcades to the aisles, tall two-bay pointed arcades to the transepts and an immensely tall chancel arch, the columns of all these with bell capitals. Reeded dado. E gallery. The chancel is filled by the ORGAN (by *Norman & Beard, c.* 1907; rebuilt by *A. F. Edmonstone, c.* 1990).

In front, a routine Gothic oak PULPIT of c. 1925. – STAINED GLASS. Brightly coloured chancel window (scenes from the Life of Moses) of 1902.

HALL (originally BLAIRGOWRIE FREE CHURCH SCHOOL) to the W, begun c. 1845 and extended s in 1849, the s gable pierced by pointed windows.

BLAIRGOWRIE SOUTH FREE CHURCH, Reform Street. Disused. Simple Gothic of 1858. Big buttressed box, built of red sandstone rubble with buff-coloured dressings. The N gable front just manages to suggest a nave and aisles. NW steeple. At each face of the angle-buttressed tower is corbelled out a two-light belfry opening under a gablet containing a clock face. Rather small corbels under the boldly projecting cornice which supports the octagonal broach spire, its roof enlivened by bands of fish-scale slating and a tier of gableted lucarnes.

RATTRAY ANTIBURGHER CHURCH, Mount Ericht Lane. Now housing and rather altered. Built in 1835. *James Readdie* was inspector of work, *John Fleming* and *William Wilson* the masons, *John Readdie* the wright. Oblong, now drydashed. Front of four bays. At the two centre bays, tall round-arched windows; at each outer bay, a rectangular lower window under a round-arched gallery window.

RATTRAY PARISH CHURCH, High Street Rattray. By *William Stirling I*, 1820. Preaching box built of sneck-harled whinstone rubble with dressings of red sandstone. Tall round-arched and Y-traceried windows. At the W end, a slender square tower, its five stages marked off by string courses; paired round-arched openings to the top (belfry) stage. Hat-like pyramid roof with bellcast broad eaves.

Inside, a panel-fronted semi-octagonal GALLERY carried on slender Doric capitalled columns along the N side and ends. At the centre of the S wall, an octagonal oak PULPIT, its ogee-roofed canopy's urn finial surmounted by a carved dove. – Jacobean Renaissance COMMUNION TABLE of c. 1900. – Plain boxy PEWS of 1820. – STAINED GLASS. Two large and lush s windows (Our Lord and the Samaritan Woman; the Prodigal Son) of c. 1900.

S of the church, the roofless MAUSOLEUM of the Whitsons of Parkhill. Broad pointed arch at the W gable; at the E gable, a stone carved with the sun, its centre an opening to give light to the interior. – E of this, the BURIAL ENCLOSURE of the Clark Rattrays of Rattray, built in 1876. On the E wall, round-headed arches containing the inscriptions; above, a coat of arms.

RATTRAY UNITED FREE CHURCH, Balmoral Road. Now Rattray Parish Church Hall. By *Lake Falconer*, 1912. Sturdy Late Gothic, the walls of hammer-dressed red sandstone. SE steeple, the tower angle-buttressed and battlemented, the spire slated.

RIVERSIDE METHODIST CHURCH, corner of Boat Brae and Riverside Road. Scots Late Gothic, by *David Smart*, 1887. Cruciform, a steeple in the S inner angle of the nave and W transept; low vestry at the N end. Cusped loop tracery in the large windows at the nave's front (s) gable and the transepts.

The steeple's tower is diagonally buttressed; octagonal stair-turret at its NW corner. At each face of the top stage, a Y-traceried two-light window. Broached octagonal stone spire, its large lucarnes containing the belfry openings.

Inside, hammerbeam roofs. In pride of place at the N end, the huge ORGAN by *Albert Keates*, later altered by *H. Hilsdon Ltd.* – STAINED GLASS. Four-light S window (St George, St Paul, Job and General Charles Gordon symbolizing Courage, Endurance, Fortitude and Self-Sacrifice) designed by *R. Anning Bell* and executed by *J. & W. Guthrie & Andrew Wells Ltd.*, 1922. – In the W transept, a window (Faith) of 1900.

ST CATHERINE (Episcopal), George Street. Small lancet-windowed Gothic box, a lower and narrower chancel at the N end. It was built in 1842–3 to a design by the incumbent's fifteen-year old stepson, *J. B. Henderson*.

Inside, the nave is covered by a depressed arch ceiling, its pine boarding added in the early C20. Pointed chancel arch, its soffit decorated with Tudorish plaster panels. – PULPIT of *c.* 1895, the stone base supporting an oak body carved with linenfold panelling and floral decoration. – Brass eagle LECTERN by *Hardman, Powell & Co.*, 1897. – On the W wall, PANELLING of the C16 or C17, probably Italian, depicting the Ascension. It was placed here in 1894. – STAINED GLASS N (liturgical E) window (the Ascension), probably of the 1840s.

To the N, a plain Gothic SCHOOL added *c.* 1850.

ST STEPHEN (R.C.), John Street. By *E. W. Pugin*, 1856. Plain Gothic rectangle, now roughcast except for the front (S) gable which has been cement-rendered. This gable contains a tall window of three cusped lights. Originally the building's S end contained a school, the side windows each of two obtusely pointed lights, the N end the church, its windows again two-light but pointed and cusped. Three tall hoodmoulded windows in the N gable. Short outshot at the NW.

Inside, the nave's three S (liturgical W) bays are unaisled; gallery over the first two. The three N bays have aisles, the arcades' pointed arches springing directly from the pillars. One-bay chancel, with smaller arches to the aisles. Scissor-truss roof.

STAINED GLASS. Two-light N window of the chapel at the end of the W aisle (Our Lady and St Joseph) of the late C19. – Late C19 glass again in this aisle's S window (St Stephen). – More late C19 glass in the E aisle's S window (Our Lady and St Anne). – Colourful late C20 glass (the Good Shepherd) in the chancel's three-light N window.

PUBLIC BUILDINGS

BLAIRGOWRIE COTTAGE HOSPITAL, Beeches Road. Thriftily bargeboarded and villa-like, by *Lake Falconer*, 1899. Large and low SW extension of 1979–82.

BLAIRGOWRIE HIGH SCHOOL, Beeches Road. By the Perth & Kinross County Architect, *Ian A. Moodie*, 1956–8.

BLAIRGOWRIE TOWN HALL, Brown Street. Neo-Georgian front block by *W. J. Brewster Grant & Henderson*, 1939. Behind, a rubble-built hall of 1860, by *John Carver*.

BRIDGE OF BLAIRGOWRIE over the River Ericht. Constructed in 1777. Rubble-built with arch rings of dressed stone. Four segmental arches, the E over a mill lade; triangular cutwaters. Cantilevered concrete footpaths added by *James Leslie* in 1871–2.

DRILL HALL, Union Street. Plain, by *Robert Reid*, 1897–8.

THE HILL PRIMARY SCHOOL, Upper Allan Street. Main (W) block by *John Carver*, 1879. School Board Gothic in red sandstone. The centre range was heightened to two storeys by *D. & J. R. McMillan*, 1908–9. To the E, a single-storey harled and piend-roofed block and a two-storey piend-roofed block, the walls of brick and harl, by *Johnston & Baxter*, 1939–41.

POLICE STATION, Ericht Lane. Cheerless Baronial, by *Smart & Stewart*, 1913.

RATTRAY PARISH CHURCH HALL. *See* Rattray United Free Church.

RATTRAY PRIMARY SCHOOL, High Street Rattray. Main block by *L. & J. Falconer*, 1886. Plain except for bracketed broad eaves.

ROYAL BRITISH LEGION HALL, corner of George Street and Brown Street. Built as Blairgowrie Burgher Church, 1830. Two-storey piend-roofed rectangle; six-bay front of rough ashlar. Rather altered for its present use.

ST STEPHEN'S PRIMARY SCHOOL, John Street. Built as Blairgowrie Parish School in 1841. Tall single-storey piend-roofed rectangle. At the centre of the front, a pedimented and round-arched 'portico' but with no entrance behind. Later additions.

DESCRIPTION

PERTH ROAD is the principal approach from the S. On the E, the long garden wall of FALCON HOUSE, a bargeboarded and bay-windowed villa, late C19 in appearance but with hoppers dated 1901; Ionic columned entrance to the porch. Opposite, on the N corner of Essendy Road, the late C19 DUNCRAGGAN. Single-storey and attic, built of hammer-dressed red sandstone with chimneys of dark red brick; under the wallhead cornice, a red tile frieze with anthemion and palmette decoration. Bowed SE corner rising into an ogee-roofed squat tower. Segmental-pedimented dormers. A little to the N, on the W side of Perth Road, an early C20 double house (LOCHLANDS and WESTDENE), the white harled walls enjoying black painted trimmings. At each end of the front, a rectangular bay window under a broad jettied gable. Opposite, a procession of six double cottages, each with a bargeboarded advanced end bay and a canted bay window; hoodmoulds over the other windows and doors. In WESTPARK ROAD, a two-storey double house (WESTERTON and DALMORE) of *c.* 1900, the ground floor of red sandstone, the jettied upper floor harled and half-timbered;

red tiled roofs. A pair of gables at the front; jerkin-head gables at the ends of the main roof. On the s side of BEECHES ROAD, Blairgowrie High School (*see* Public Buildings, above). On the N side, harled local authority housing of the 1930s, its exaggeratedly steep front gables colliding with each other; demure piended dormerheads. The original slating of the roofs has mostly been replaced with concrete tiles and the astragalled Neo-Georgian windows with a mixture of late C20 designs.

PERTH STREET continuing the line of Perth Road N of Beeches Road begins with solid-looking but quite small late C19 villas among which Blairgowrie Cottage Hospital (*see* Public Buildings, above) fits in quite happily. s of the hospital, on the street's W side, a couple of gabled and bargeboarded cottages (THE SHAMROCK and ISLA COTTAGE) of the 1860s (Isla Cottage dated 1867) and, N of Shaw Street, a similar double cottage (Nos. 119–121 Perth Street) of 1868, each of their gabled porches bearing a quatrefoil panel. The street's general character now develops into late C19 cottage vernacular followed by dour Late Victorian two-storey housing, its scale but not its mood broken by the three-storey and attic No. 16 on the E.

REFORM STREET goes off to the E and introduces the town's commercial centre. On the s, the single-storey and attic late Victorian No. 5. Gable front with bracketed eaves and roundheaded windows. Adjoining two-storey block of 1873, the windows of its triple-gabled upper floor pointed; former hall behind. On Reform Street's N side, the rendered Art Deco front of the former PICTURE HOUSE by *W. J. Brewster Grant & Henderson*, 1925. For the Drill Hall in UNION STREET running s from Reform Street, *see* Public Buildings, above. Near Reform Street's E end, the former Blairgowrie South Free Church (*see* Churches, above).

JOHN STREET leads W from the top of Perth Street. On its N side, St Stephen's (R.C.) Church and, closing the vista at the end, St Stephen's Primary School (*see* Churches and Public Buildings, above).

HIGH STREET continues the line of Perth Street N of John Street. The buildings are mostly C19 and of two storeys, containing shops under housing, but there are some C20 intruders. On the W, the former MECHANICS' INSTITUTE (Nos. 33–37) by *Alexander Johnston*, 1869–70. Three storeys, with simplified Ruskinian Gothic detail. Also three-storey but much lower, the early C19 block at Nos. 23–27 High Street with a bowed quadrant corner to BROWN STREET. Another early C19 block (Nos. 2–3 Brown Street) on the opposite corner, again with a bowed quadrant corner across which the cornice is carried on corbels. On the s side of Brown Street, Blairgowrie Town Hall (*see* Public Buildings, above). Further along Brown Street, on the N side, the early C19 ST CATHARINE'S HOUSE of two storeys and three bays, a traceried rectangular fanlight over the door. It adjoins St Catherine's Episcopal Church (*see* Churches, above) on Brown Street's NW corner with GEORGE STREET.

On the opposite corner, the Royal British Legion Hall (*see* Public Buildings, above). Across Brown Street's w end is THE OLD BANK HOUSE (originally the Commercial Bank of Scotland), by *David Rhind*, 1837. Three-storey Georgian survival with a hint of Italianate and not without pomposity. Ashlar front of three bays, moulded sill courses under the windows of the upper floors. On the ground floor, a Greek Doric portico, its balustraded top serving as a balcony to the central first-floor window; under the other first-floor windows, stone balconies supported on huge consoles. Urn-topped balustrade over the wallhead cornice. The view N up George Street is closed by No. 15 JAMES STREET, a two-storey house of 1832, the front now covered with render in imitation of bullnosed ashlar, but the frieze of the pilastered and battlemented doorpiece is carved with rosettes. No. 13 James Street behind is probably also early C19, a single-storey cottage, its pilastered doorpiece a forgivable attempt to raise its status. To the w, Blairgowrie Parish Church (*see* Churches, above).

In High Street's last N stretch, on the w, the late C18 three-storey and attic No. 21 (the former QUEEN'S HOTEL), its rubble front (now harled) of three bays, the centre slightly advanced under a pediment, its ends surmounted by urns, the apex by a bust of Queen Victoria. At Nos. 11–13 High Street, a small late C19 block, its corner's rounded oriel window rising into a conical-roofed turret. Facing down High Street from the foot of ALLAN STREET is the three-storey ROYAL HOTEL, built in 1852 but still Georgian in feeling. Front of painted ashlar, the first- and second-floor windows linked by sill courses. Heavy cornices over the entrance and the window above, that of the door with large three-quarter-round rosettes. Over the centre of the wallhead cornice a blocking course flanked by scrolls. To the NW, in UPPER ALLAN STREET, The Hill Primary School (*see* Public Buildings, above) looking over to Blairgowrie Parish Church (*see* Churches, above).

KIRK WYND leads upwards off Upper Allan Street to the N. On its E side, the Blairgowrie Evangelical Church (*see* Churches, above). To its N, THE BRAES, an early C20 single-storey and attic house, the walls harled, the large roof covered with red tiles. Boat-shaped door and low horizontal lead-paned windows; curvaceous Art Nouveauish chimney pots. The ascent up Kirk Wynd is overlooked by TULACH (formerly Hillbank) of 1832, a piend-roofed two-storey villa, a Roman Doric portico at the front; central pediments at the side elevations. For Blairgowrie Parish Church, *see* Churches above.

On the downhill-sloping ALLAN STREET'S N side, E of the Royal Hotel, the asymmetrical frontage of Nos. 49–51 of 1871, its character Gothic although some of the first-floor windows are round-headed. On the s, Nos. 18–32, a plain Georgian survival block of 1890. Below this, THE ROYAL BANK OF SCOTLAND by *Peddie & Kinnear*, 1871–2. Two-storey polished ashlar front of five bays, the aproned ground-floor windows with moulded architraves, their sills consoled; anthemion-decorated cast-iron rainwater head. Contemporary CLYDESDALE BANK next door. Lugged architraves to the first-floor windows, again with aprons and consoles under the sills, here decorated with guilloche ornament. UPPER MILL STREET leads downhill to the N to the former Ericht Works (*see* Industrial Buildings, below). Allan Street's S side ends at the E with the early C19 Nos. 2–6, a quadrant corner to Leslie Street; anthemion-decorated rainwater heads like the one at The Royal Bank of Scotland and presumably replacements of *c.* 1870.

LESLIE STREET runs S from Allan Street's E end. On the E side, THE DOME CAFÉ, a straightforward early C19 building but at the rear is a restaurant added in 1925 by *W. J. Brewster Grant & Henderson*, its domed ceiling carried on Tuscan columns. In ERICHT LANE to the W, the Police Station (*see* Public Buildings, above). Near the S end of Leslie Street, on the W, No. 46, a two-storey mid-C19 house. Full-height rectangular bay windows with bracketed sills to the first-floor openings, the central bay's upper part supported on a Roman Doric portico. Panelled wallhead parapet, a pediment at the centre.

WELLMEADOW at the E end of Allan Street is a triangular space, its centre occupied by a WAR MEMORIAL of 1920 designed by *Reginald Fairlie*. This is of market cross type, a stepped ashlar base and a tall square pedestal supporting a cushion-capitalled octagonal shaft surmounted by a figure of the pelican in piety. At the front, the bronze statue of a soldier with arms reversed, by *Alexander Carrick*. On the W side of Wellmeadow, the three-storey former PERTH BANK (Nos. 29–30) of 1851. Georgian survival, the ground floor with V-jointed rustication and cavetto splays to the doors and windows. Bottom-lugged architraves at the windows of the upper floors. On the N side of Wellmeadow, the former COMMERCIAL BANK OF SCOTLAND (No. 14) of the 1930s is squared-up Neo-Georgian. To its E, on the E corner of Mill Street, a two-storey harled and half-timbered block (No. 13) of *c.* 1900, the bowed corner finished with an ogee dome enlivened by a band of fish-scale slating. Wellmeadow's SE corner is the entrance to a car park but, at its E end on the corner of Tannage Street, the BRIG O' BLAIR HOTEL, late C19 Georgian survival.

The Bridge of Blairgowrie (*see* Public Buildings, above) crosses the River Ericht to the formerly separate village of Rattray. At the foot of BOAT BRAE, the Riverside Methodist Church (*see* Churches, above). Behind, in RIVERSIDE ROAD, ERICHT BANK, an early C19 single-storey and attic house with a chimneyed central gablet and a pilastered and corniced doorpiece. In MOUNT ERICHT ROAD, the former Rattray Antiburgher Church (*see* Churches, above). Further up Boat Brae on the N side but entered from Balmoral Road, MOUNT ERICHT, a rendered two-storey villa of *c.* 1840. Full-height canted bay windows flank a screen of Roman Doric columns *in antis* in front of the entrance. In BALMORAL ROAD, the former Rattray United Free Church (*see* Churches, above). Further N, the harled Late Georgian ROSEBANK HOUSE with a pilastered doorpiece. Then, HOPE PARK, a villa of the later C19. Harled, with buff sandstone dressings. Display of bargeboards, canted bay windows and gableted dormerheads; a Frenchy tower over the entrance. At the N end of Balmoral Road, the Keathbank Mill, Brocklebank Works and Westfield Mill and, in OAKBANK ROAD on the W bank of the River Ericht, the Oakbank Mill (*see* Industrial Buildings, below).

HIGH STREET RATTRAY is Rattray's architecturally dour Victorian main street running E from the top of Boat Brae. On its N side, Rattray Primary School (*see* Public Buildings, above) and, at its E end, Rattray Parish Church (*see* Churches, above).

INDUSTRIAL BUILDINGS

BRAMBLEBANK WORKS, Balmoral Road. Linen mill begun in the mid C19, the main block of two storeys and an attic, originally of nine bays but later extended to fourteen.

ERICHT WORKS, Mill Street. Former linen mill built in 1867. Main block of one tall storey, its coursed and squared rubble main (E) elevation to the River Ericht of eighteen bays, the higher three at each end slightly advanced and with round-headed windows; cast-iron cornice (partly missing). Behind, piend-roofed weaving sheds. At the SE corner of the complex, a piend-roofed office block.

ERICHTSIDE WORKS, Haugh Road. Begun *c*. 1836 but enlarged later in the C19 and C20. Utilitarian. Tall round chimney of red and white brick, probably of the late C19.

KEATHBANK MILL, Balmoral Road. Built in 1864–5. Rubble-walled main block of three storeys and an attic, the front of eight bays; ball finial on the S gable. N additions, partly heightened in brick in the C20. Tapering octagonal chimney, probably of the late C19.

OAKBANK MILL, Oakbank Road. Rebuilt after a fire in 1872. Rubble-walled three-storey and attic five-bay block. Roofless remains of a wheel house from which a vertical drive shaft climbs up the building.

WESTFIELD MILL, Balmoral Road. Substantial remains of a mid-C19 spinning mill of one and two storeys. Tall octagonal brick chimney, perhaps added in *Lake Falconer*'s reconstruction of 1902.

NEWTON CASTLE
off Newton Street

Covetable harled and crowstep-gabled laird's house, probably built soon after 1565 when George Drummond received a Crown charter confirming the grant to him by the Commendator of Scone Abbey of the lands of Newton.

The S-facing late C16 building is of three storeys and an attic. Z-plan, with a square stair tower at the SE, a small bowed turret corbelled out at second-floor level in the N inner angle. At the house's NW corner, a round tower surmounted by a rectangular attic top hamper projected on heavy corbelling. The first and second floors of the main block and NW tower are lit by reasonably sized windows, those of the tower with chamfered surrounds, the surrounds of the main block's windows variously chamfered or with roll-and-hollow mouldings. The ground-floor openings of the main block and NW tower are insertions, probably of c. 1700 (the r. opening of the main block's S front originally a door converted to a window, c. 1920). Early C19 gableted dormer windows, crowstepped at the main block but with straight skews at the NW tower. In the E gable of the main block, tiny windows lighting a private stair from the first floor to the attic. Small stair windows at the SE tower. In this tower's W face, the C16 entrance with a roll-and-hollow-moulded surround. The approach to it is covered by a large oval gunloop at the E end of the main block. A second gunloop S of the door has been harled over. Another entrance, its steep pediment giving a Scots Renaissance flavour, was provided at the main block's E gable in 1920, at the same time as a short garden wall was built running S from the SE tower and pierced by a gateway surmounted by the coat of arms of the Macphersons, who had acquired the estate in 1788.

Short three-storey NE addition of 1883, its second-floor windows rising into crowstepped dormerheads. It is tactful, as is the low two-storey extension of 1920 to its N. N of the house, rubble-built L-plan stable offices, the E range with a piended roof. They may be of c. 1800.

The C16 entrance opens onto the foot of a broad turnpike stair rising the full height of the house. Behind this, at the E end of the main block, the entrance hall of 1920 and, to its W, the contemporary dining room (presumably on the site of the C16 kitchen), the plaster ceilings of both with modelled wild cats (the Macpherson crest) in their corners. In the SW tower, a domical-vaulted round store. The first floor of the main block contains one room (the C16 hall and C18 parlour). Its walls are covered with panelling of c. 1700. Lugged architraves to the doors which are surmounted by horizontal panels, as is a china cupboard in the N wall. Another horizontal panel forms the overmantel of the fireplace, whose surround has a lugged architrave and pulvinated frieze; flanking the fireplace are fluted Ionic pilasters. More panelling of c. 1700 in the first- and second-floor rooms of the NW tower. In the NE wing of 1883, a first-floor library, its fireplace surround a heavy-handed version of early C18 work.

STANDING STONES, Courthill, 2.9 km. NE. One massive sloping-sided and flat-topped boulder rises from a base, measuring c. 2.6 m. by 1.7 m., to a height of 2.5 m. It was probably erected in the second millennium B.C. Four more stones, 0.4 km. S, all now fallen and one broken, have marked the corners of an approximately 4 m.-square space. Also probably erected in the second millennium, none would have stood more than c. 1 m. above the ground.

DRUIDSMERE, 2.4 km. s. Tall four-storey villa of 1885, by *Andrew Heiton Jun.* in his Rhineland-Baronial manner, built of bullnosed red sandstone masonry. Conical-roofed round towers with massively battered bases and jettied top floors at the s corners; stretched between them are cast-iron balconies (by *McDowell, Steven & Co.*). Bargeboarded dormerheads over the third-floor windows. Rectangular NE tower containing the entrance. Low NW service wing.

CRAIGHALL-RATTRAY. See p. 287.

BLAIRINGONE

9090

Little more than a hamlet, a few of its C19 cottages still roofed with clay pantiles but most with concrete replacements.

CHURCH. Disused. Built as a chapel of ease in 1836–8. Tallish T-plan, of sneck-harled rubble. In each gable, a segmental-arched window, its stone mullion and cusping provided in the late C19 or early C20. In the inner angles, small piend-roofed porches. The s jamb's bellcote has been removed.

Inside, a gallery in the jamb. – STAINED GLASS. W window (Our Lord and Little Children) of *c.* 1890. – E window (Angels symbolizing Peace and Hope) of 1919.

ARNDEAN, 1.6 km. NE. Two-storey Jacobethan laird's house of *c.* 1820, the rubble walling originally all harled. Ladder-like horizontal-patterned glazing in the windows. The entrance (W) front is of three bays, the l. advanced and gabled, with a hoodmoulded four-light window to the ground floor and a window of two lights, also hoodmoulded, above. In the two bays to the r., hoodmoulds over the door and the four-light window to its s; above, two-light windows rising into gablet dormerheads. Five-bay garden (s) elevation, the advanced and gabled W end with hoodmoulded windows. At the four E bays, the outer windows of both floors are taller than the others (one now a door), the upper openings again with gablet dormerheads. Inside, the drawing room in the SW corner has a reeded white marble chimneypiece with floral panels on the frieze.

DEVONSHAW, 2.1 km. NE. Mechanically detailed ashlar-faced laird's house of the earlier C19. Asymmetrical Jacobethan, with hoodmoulded mullioned windows; steep gablets over the first-floor openings. – Contemporary LODGE to the N, with broad eaves to its piended roof.

SOLSGIRTH HOUSE. See p. 698.

BOLFRACKS

8040

3.5 km. WSW of Aberfeldy

Dotty castellated harled villa of the early C19 perched on a hillside above the River Tay. The principal (N) front is composed of three sections tied together by a first-floor sill course. At the l., a two-storey and attic battlemented gable, its crowning merlon with a quatrefoil panel; bartizans with crosslet dummy arrowslits at the corners. Hoodmoulds over the first-floor and attic windows. Next, a two-storey link, also battlemented, with a three-light window to the ground floor and a hoodmoulded window of two lights above. The w element is a three-storey tower, its corners clasped by turret buttresses, their faces pierced by dummy crosslet arrowslits and slit windows. Narrow windows flank the entrance. Above, hoodmoulded three-light windows and a corbelled battlement, its large central merlon with a quatrefoil panel.

LODGE of the mid C19, its bargeboards carved in the usual Breadalbane estate style.

BONHARD HOUSE
1.1 km. E of New Scone

Jacobean mansion house of 1847–9, built of stugged ashlar. Almost square two-storey main block from whose w face projects an ogee-roofed three-storey tower now fronted by a late C20 porch. Gently asymmetrical treatment of the principal elevations, the s end bays of the w and E fronts and the w bay of the s with crowstepped gables flanked by ogee-roofed turrets, the last also with a bay window. Low ogee-roofed tower at the SE corner. Lower service wings at the N, with strapworked dormerheads to the upper windows.

A large rendered lectern DOOCOT (now derelict) to the N. One ratcourse which jumps up at the gables of which the w still has its crowsteps. The skewputts bore the date 1709, presumably for the doocot's construction.

BONSKEID HOUSE
1 km. E of Glenfincastle

Dizzyingly vertical Baronial mansion house of greyish rubble with buff-coloured dressings. It was designed by *Andrew Heiton Jun.* in 1881 for G. F. Barbour who had married the heiress to the estate, on which already stood a small house of *c.* 1805. This now forms a two-storey wing, plain except for Late Victorian string courses. To its E bay Heiton added a boldly projecting, crowstep-gabled two-storey and attic porch, its ground floor with rounded corners, the rectangular upper floors carried on continuous corbelling. Polygonal-headed entrance, two-light first-floor window in an elliptical overarch, a slit window to the attic. On the porch's E side, a conical-roofed round tower.

Heiton's mansion is tall and tower-like, of three storeys and a high attic. Crowstepped gables, a corbelled battlement along the E and W sides, the E with a massive wallhead chimney, the w with a Jacobean dormer window. Conical-roofed round turrets are corbelled out from three corners. At the NW corner, a round tower surmounted by a large square caphouse finished with a tall pyramidal spire roof. The principal (S) gable is a powerful display of bourgeois Baronialism. Two-storey canted bay window, the splay of the sides reduced by corbelling at the upper level and brought to the rectangular under a battlement. Huge oriel window to the attic. Quieter but determinedly Baronial block of two storeys and an attic to the N, with crow-stepped gables, a full-height canted bay window, its sides also corbelled out to a rectangle; conical-roofed NW angle turret. Early C19 service ranges (remodelled in the late C19), the battlemented S front overlaid by a flat-roofed dining hall added c. 1960 when the house was used as a youth hostel.

BRACO

Village which grew up beside Ardoch Parish Church from the early C19. Most of the housing is now Victorian or C20.

ARDOCH PARISH CHURCH, Feddal Road. Simple rectangular kirk of 1780–1, now drydashed. Rope-moulded scrolled skewputts. Ball-finialled birdcage bellcote of 1836 on the W gable. Set rather high in the long S wall are round-headed windows with projecting imposts and keystones; simpler N windows, also round-headed. In 1890 *William Simpson* added the low lancet-windowed chancel at the E end and the buttressed porch, its W end pierced by a round window, the horseshoe-arched door set in a gabled shallow projection on the S side.

GRAVEYARD. Immediately S of the church's W end, a pair of almost identical TABLE STONES of the 1790s (to James Read †1797 and Lily Sharp †1792), each with an oval panel containing the relief of a sock and coulter. – SW of these, a HEADSTONE of 1795 to M. B. and H. H., decorated with an oval panel containing the relief of a plough.

BRACO FREE CHURCH, in a graveyard on the corner of Church Street and Feddal Road. Only the battlemented tower survives of the church built in 1844–5. This is rubble-built, of three stages. At the bottom a hoodmoulded and nook-shafted round-headed door. The second stage is the belfry, its openings each of two tall and narrow round-headed lights. Above, circular clock faces.

BRIDGES over the River Knaik. The A822 is carried on a single-span rubble bridge of c. 1900. Immediately to its N and at a lower level, ARDOCH OLD BRIDGE, its general appearance that of the bridge erected here in 1430. One rubble-built elliptical arch, only c. 1.83m. wide and without parapets. It was widened to the N in 1741–2 but the C18 work collapsed in 1896 leaving the bridge in its earlier form. Renovated, 1989.

LITTLE ARDOCH, Front Street. Two-storey piend-roofed early C19 house. Three-bay front of stugged ashlar; pilastered doorpiece and horizontal-paned windows.

KAIMES COTTAGE, 3.4 km. NE. Harled single-storey house of the earlier C19. S front of five bays, the ends slightly advanced under piended roofs and with hoodmoulded rectangular windows. The centre is also advanced but gabled and with a hoodmoulded Gothic window. The windows of the intermediate bays have been widened to two lights.

NETHER BRACO, 0.9 km. NW. On the approach to Braco Castle (*see* below), a harled farmhouse and rubble-built steading of *c.* 1810. The house is of one storey and an attic, its piended roof with broad eaves. Smart front of three bays. The advanced centre, diagonally buttressed and gabled, contains a Gothic door flanked by pointed windows and, at the attic, a two-light hoodmoulded window. In the outer bays, hoodmoulded ground floor windows, each of two arched lights. The canted dormers are probably additions of the mid or later C19. Contemporary courtyard steading behind (now partly derelict). In the S gables, Gothic arched recesses.

6 ROMAN FORT, Ardoch, 0.3 km. E. Rising from a field, the oblong platform on which stood the fort buildings, surrounded by massively defensive ditches and ramparts. These defences are the product of three stages of work in the C1 and C2. The fort was first constructed *c.* 85 A.D. as one of the line of 'Agricolan' forts and fortlets between Camelon (Falkirk) and Bertha, near Perth. It then consisted of an oblong *c.* 230 m. by 152 m. enclosed by an earth rampart and two outer ditches across which causeways led to the two gateways placed a little S of the centre of the long E and W sides. Abandoned within a few years, the fort was reoccupied *c.* 140 as a forward defence to the Antonine Wall. At this time, the enclosure was made shorter and slightly narrower (201 m. by 145 m.), curtailed significantly at the S end, and surrounded by a new earth rampart, its front revetted with turf. The entrances in the E and W sides occupied the same positions as those of the C1 fort but there were also entrances at the ends, the S roughly central, the N some way E of centre. The space between the new rampart and the existing outer ditches was filled with additional closely spaced ditches so that the rampart was surrounded by six ditches on the E side and S end, five on the W and three on the N. About twenty years later the fort was again reconstructed, its enclosure's N end shortened by 40 m. The rampart was given a stone outer face and, presumably to provide a sound foundation for this, the fort's innermost ditch infilled. In the space between the new rampart of the curtailed N end and the earlier N rampart, retained as an outer defence, were dug two ditches, the line of the N angled so that the ground between them formed a 'ravelin' through whose apex passed the path to the fort's N entrance, now placed centrally. The defences, all grass-covered and threatened by burrowing rabbits, survive intact at the N end and most of the E side. At the S end, only parts of the four outer ditches are visible and the rampart has been mostly destroyed. On the W side, the rampart is fragmentary and only the N two-thirds of the inner ditch survive, the outer

ditches obliterated by construction of the military road immediately to the W in the C18.

Much less distinct to the N and NW are remains of the ditches and ramparts which surrounded an ANNEXE and two MARCHING CAMPS. The annexe, just N of the fort, has been a 270 m.-long oblong. Its N side is overlaid by the SE corner of a 55 ha. camp whose own W side is overlaid by a 25 ha. camp. The annexe was presumably in use at the same time as the fort, in the late C1 or mid C2. The camps probably date from the Roman campaigns against the Caledonians at the beginning of the C3. On the E side of the 55 ha. camp is the double-ditch enclosure for a watch tower which was erected, probably in the late C1, beside the Roman road from Ardoch to the fortlet at Kaims Castle (*see* below).

ROMAN FORTLET, Kaims Castle, 3.2 km. NE. Surprisingly well-preserved defences of a late C1 Roman fortlet which covered an overall area of *c*. 61 m. by 55 m. They consist of a counterscarp, two curvilinear ditches and a rectangular earth rampart still standing to a height of 1 m. which surround an enclosure *c*. 22.5 m. by 21 m. The entrance was on the long S side, probably surmounted by a wooden tower.

ORCHIL HOUSE. *See* p. 564.

BRACO CASTLE
2 km. NW

Sizeable but inexpensively detailed rubble-built mansion, the product of several stages of development.

The house was probably begun soon after 1585 when John, third Earl of Montrose, granted the lands of Braco to his second son, Sir William Graham, who seems to have put up a tall four-storey L-plan house, the only surviving detail of that date a small third-floor window with chamfered margins at the W end of the N side. This house was remodelled at the beginning of the C18 after the property had been acquired by the Graemes. In 1801 the estate was sold to James Masterton of Gogar who further enlarged and remodelled the building in a gently castellated manner. More work was carried out later in the C19 and in the early C20.

Nearly symmetrical S front, its present appearance mostly early C19. It is U-plan, the W wing and main block representing the house of *c*. 1590, the E wing dating from the beginning of the C19 as does the lower block which fills and projects slightly from the central hollow. This centrepiece, architecturally the most satisfactory part, is of two storeys and battlemented, with a broad central bow pierced by hoodmoulded windows, tall at the first floor to denote the *piano nobile*; in front, a battlemented porch. Rising behind, the three-bay front of the earlier house's main block, dressed up with an early C19 battlement, the third-floor windows enlarged to two lights in the later C19, the second-floor windows hidden from view by the addition's battlement. The front gables of the wings, the W remodelled when the E was built, appear as siblings rather than twins. Each is crowstepped, has a conical-roofed round turret at the inner corner, a circular attic window and hoodmoulds over the openings below. But the E gable is broader and its three bays of windows, tall at the first floor, are regularly disposed across its three storeys. The gable of the W wing is now also of three bays but some of the windows are wholly or partly dummies and the central first-floor window is placed at a lower level than its flanking neighbours in a not very satisfactory attempt to pretend that the four-storey block behind is of only three storeys. Over the ground-floor window, a heraldic panel bearing the coat of arms of Masterton of Gogar.

Plain W elevation, the windows Georgian, the polygonal-headed door an insertion of the earlier C20. The E wing's side is of four bays, the r. two united at the ground and first floors by the mid-C19 addition of a parapeted bay window with hoodmoulded openings.

Service ranges, also of the mid or later C19. Two-storey and attic NE wing, its E side battlemented and with oriel windows to the W and E, its N gable topped by a chimney whose arched open centre contains a bell. Lower wings to the N of the NE wing and, with a battlemented front, E of the main block.

LODGE of the later C19 at the entrance to the drive beside the River Knaik from Braco village. Broad-eaved, with a gabled wooden rustic porch. Some latticed glazing survives in the windows. Pyramid-topped low ashlar GATEPIERS, probably contemporary.

BRIDGE OF CALLY

Scattered hamlet at the confluence of the Rivers Ardle and Ericht, the Bridge of Cally Hotel at its S end, Netherton Church at the NE.

NETHERTON CHURCH. Built as Netherton Free Church in 1891. Small but tall Gothic-windowed oblong, a gableted bellcote on the S end, an octagonal ventilator-flèche on the roof. SE porch; NW vestry. – STAINED GLASS N window (Our Lord) by *James Powell & Sons*, 1892.

PERSIE CHURCH, 3.1 km. N. Now an agricultural store. Built as a chapel of ease, *c.* 1785. Rectangular-windowed box, the rubble walls partly harled. Ball-finialled birdcage bellcote on the W gable.

BRIDGE OF CALLY, over the River Ardle. Mid C19. Rubble-built, of one segmental arch.

BRIDGE OF CALLY HOTEL. Begun in the mid C19 as a broad-eaved block, with hoodmoulds over the first-floor windows of its three-bay S front, it has been extended to the E and N in the same manner.

ASHMORE HOUSE, 1.6km. N. By *Lake Falconer*, 1882. Large gabled villa, a square tower at its S end.

GLENERICHT HOUSE, 3.2km. SE. Large harled shooting lodge of later C19 character. – WEST LODGE beside the A93. Gothic of *c.* 1840, with pinnacled corners and a piended roof. At the S front, a gabled projection with tabernacled corner niches and a hoodmoulded door. – SUSPENSION BRIDGE carrying the W drive over the River Ericht, by *John Justice*, *c.* 1835. Network of rods running diagonally from wrought-iron arches to support the wooden deck. – Beside the bridge, a single-storey Gothic LODGE, probably of the early C19.

CAIRNS AND HUT CIRCLES, Middleton Muir, 4km. SW. Several sizeable round and oval prehistoric CAIRNS, probably of the third or second millennium B.C., stand on the hillside. One of the larger is circular, 12.5m. in diameter but now only 0.4m. high. Still in place are some of the kerb's boulders, the largest (0.3m. tall) at the SW segment of the edge. A second, 35m. to the E, is oval, 10.5m. by 9.6m., also with a kerb of boulders but these are up to 0.6m. tall, the largest also at the SW. On a low knoll, 500m. N, another round cairn, 9.8m. in diameter, edged by a kerb of boulders up to 0.3m. tall. Exposed at the centre, a 0.75m.-long slab which may be part of a cist. – Surrounding and interspersed with the cairns are the remains of about thirty HUT CIRCLES, some very indistinct, the internal diameter of their enclosures varying in size from 6.2m. to *c.* 16m. Several are double-walled. The houses were probably constructed at various times in the second and first millennia B.C.

STONE CIRCLE, Parkneuk, 5.7km. E. Four standing stones (one now fallen), probably erected in the second millennium B.C. to mark out an oblong space, *c.* 4.8m. by 3.9m. The two largest (1.2m. and 1.38m. tall) stand at the SE and NW corners. The NE stone is 0.9m. high.

BRIDGE OF EARN

Sizeable village sitting below Moncreiffe Hill, at the E end of the broad valley of Strathearn. It developed in the late C18 and early C19, partly to house visitors taking the waters at Pitkeathly Wells 1.8km. to the SW. Large late C20 housing developments to the S serve as dormitories for Perth.

CHURCHES

DUNBARNEY FREE CHURCH, Back Street. Now housing (IMRIE COURT). Built in 1843. Innocent Gothick three-bay front, the gabled centre marked off by tall attached columns, much like those at St Paul's Church, Perth (q.v.), carrying panelled pedestals surmounted by obelisk finials. On the gable, a

Tudorish birdcage bellcote with obelisk finials at the ends and apex.

DUNBARNEY PARISH CHURCH, Manse Road. Red rubble T-plan kirk built in 1787 (the date on the keystones of S windows). The front is of five bays. In the outer bays, tall round-arched windows, the inner two with projecting keystones; at the centre bay, a round window above a blocked door. Originally, each end bay had two tiers of windows, the upper round-arched, the lower rectangular, but the intervening masonry was removed c. 1880 in a recasting which also introduced thinly detailed Neo-Romanesque lights into the window openings, built up the S door, added a ventilator to the roof, and replaced the W gable's C18 bellcote with one which is pedimented and ball-finialled. The ringed cross on the E gable may belong to a later stage of alterations, probably early C20, in which a bowed porch was added at the W end. On the gable of the N jamb, a ball finial, probably of 1787. Piend-roofed vestry at the E end of the N side, perhaps a mid-C19 addition.

The interior, originally with galleries at the E and W ends and in the jamb, was refurnished c. 1880 when the pulpit was moved from the centre of the S wall to the E end whose gallery was removed; the other galleries were rebuilt with Neo-Jacobean fronts. – Lorimerian SANCTUARY FURNISHINGS (communion table, pulpit, font and organ case) of 1923. – Also of 1923 the brightly coloured STAINED GLASS E window (Scenes of Hope and Youth). – ORGAN by *John R. Miller*.

At the entrance to the graveyard, a piend-roofed single-storey SESSION HOUSE, its door lintel dated 1818.

CEMETERY

DUNBARNEY CHURCHYARD, 1.9 km. W. Walled graveyard, the site of the medieval Dunbarney Parish Church before it was supplanted by a new building at Bridge of Earn (since replaced by the present church there) in 1689. At the W end of the S wall, early C19 corniced GATEPIERS. – In the SE corner, a BURIAL ENCLOSURE of the earlier C19, a hoodmould over the entrance. – Good collection of C18 and early C19 HEADSTONES, the carved reliefs well preserved, the inscriptions more weathered. At the SW corner, Robert Wright, surgeon, the swan-neck pediment containing the head of a dozy angel (the soul); below, a panel bearing surgical instruments. On the back, a skull and crossbones above the inscription. – Immediately behind, a large stone dated 1768, commemorating William Stoddart. Angel's head above a shield bearing initials and farming implements; reminders of death at the bottom. – Due N of the entrance, a stone of 1771 to David Millar, plasterer, again with an angel's head at the top. Under a helm and mantling, a shield bearing the tools of Millar's trade. – N of this, Emilia Don †1772, with an angel's head and a shield carved with tools. – To its E, a stone dated 1809. Under an angel's head, a large relief of setsquare, dividers, saw and axe, so presumably this was for a wright. – Immediately behind, a late c18 stone with an angel's head, an oval panel carved with tools, and high-relief emblems of death at the bottom. – Some way to the N, a very similar stone of 1790 to Jannett Peddie. – E of this, a stone with fluted Roman Doric pilasters and a heraldic achievement erected by William and James Robertson to their mother, Elispet Erich, †1780. – Behind, another c18 stone, badly weathered except for the reminders of mortality at the bottom. – To the S, a stone dated 1767, with an angel's head above a stag. – Beside it, a worn swan-neck-pedimented c18 stone, a shield on the front. – A little further S, the small curly-topped headstone of Elizabeth Mirr †1718, wife of William Deuar, wright in Kilgraston, an angel's head above the inscription; on the other face, a setsquare, dividers and an axe under a skull and crossbones. – To the E, a stone dated 1790 to Anne Rattery, wife of James Low, smith. Aedicular front with Roman Doric pilasters and an open swan-neck pediment enclosing an angel's head; below, a shield bearing a crowned hammer. – To the W, a small curly-topped stone of 1719 to Margaret Warer, carved with an angel's head above reminders of death. – Further W, an c18 stone to George Martine, maltman, with a jolly angel's head above a shield displaying a maltster's tools; the usual emblems of mortality at the bottom.

PUBLIC BUILDINGS

BRIDGE OF EARN. By *James Jardine*, 1821–2, but widened in concrete by *W. L. Gibson*, the Perthshire County Engineer, 1933. The appearance from a little way away is still Georgian. Three segmental arches with rusticated voussoirs; rounded cutwaters at the piers which rise a little above the parapet whose ends curve outwards.

PUBLIC HALL AND INSTITUTE, Station Road. English Arts and Crafts, by *G. P. K. Young*, 1908. Harled walls, buttressed on the S side and at the W corners. Red sandstone dressings at the broad elliptically arched entrance which is set in a slightly advanced gable, its top half-timbered. – Beside the Hall, a red sandstone Celtic cross WAR MEMORIAL of *c.* 1920.

SCHOOL, Main Street. By *Charles S. Robertson*, 1874–5. Single-storey and picturesque, with bracketed broad eaves and two ventilator flèches. Large S addition by *Tayside Regional Council*, 1993–5, a heavy-handed reworking of the style of the original.

DESCRIPTION

The approach from the N over the Bridge of Earn (*see* Public Buildings, above) leads to MAIN STREET which begins scrappily, the buildings mostly small suburban villas of the later c19. More such villas in MANSE ROAD which goes off to the W leading to Dunbarney Parish Church (*see* Churches, above).

On the S corner of Manse Road and Main Street, the school (*see* Public Buildings, above). S of the school, the corner of STATION ROAD on whose N side stands MARYFIELD, a pompous two-storey villa of the later C19, its polished sandstone ashlar front garishly yellow as a result of cleaning; rusticated pilaster strips at the ends. Three-bay front, with two-light windows in the outer bays; at the centre, an Ionic portico, the corners of its curvy parapet topped by ball finials. At the wallhead, a parapet which sweeps curvaceously up over the outer bays. Further W, the Public Hall and Institute (*see* Public Buildings, above).

S of Station Road, Main Street's W side is occupied by a bowling green and, to its S, a solid-looking late C19 broadeaved block containing housing above shops. On the E side of Main Street, a two-storey and attic terrace of the 1830s, a fragment of an intended 'New Town' scheme for the development of Bridge of Earn which *William Burn* had produced for Sir David Moncreiffe of that Ilk in 1823. Plain but the end buildings (THE LAST CAST HOTEL and THE BRIDGE HOTEL) are slightly advanced, taller than the others and corniced and parapeted. S of Side Street, the first three houses of a similar and contemporary terrace but its first house (THE SURGERY), although again taller than the rest and with a cornice and parapet, is not advanced. Side Street leads E to BACK STREET. In Back Street's stretch to the S of Side Street, the former Dunbarney Free Church (*see* Churches, above). To the N of Side Street, Back Street has some housing of the late C20 but the character is predominantly Late Georgian. On the E side, the ashlar-fronted BURNBRAE, dated 1800 at its central chimneyed gablet. Another chimneyed gablet on the front of the late C18 CYPRUS INN which faces a path down to the Earn.

BALLENDRICK HOUSE, 1.5km. W. Unexciting piend-roofed laird's house of *c.* 1825, built of red sandstone rubble. Main block of two storeys, with a Roman Doric columned and corniced doorpiece in the centre of the S front. Single-storey rectangular bay window of the mid or later C19 at the W gable. At the E end, a plain two-storey wing, probably late C19, and a Victorian conservatory.

STABLES E of the house. Rubble-built piend-roofed U, mostly of two storeys with very small first-floor windows and segmental-arched carriage openings. Over one door of the S range, a datestone of 1827 and, in this range's W gable, another of 1829, the dates very likely those of the buildings' construction.

OLD HILTON HOUSE, 2.5km. NW. Harled small laird's house of 1732. Two storeys and an attic which is lit from windows in the gables. N front of four bays, the openings grouped 3:1 and the ground-floor window in the second bay from the E very small. In the next bay, the basket-arched and bolectionmoulded main entrance. Over the entrance, a corniced panel incised with the initials and date GW/JM/1732 and framed by panelled pilasters without capitals. Stepped skews and moulded skewputts at the gables, the W side door converted from a window in the late C20. Rear elevation of five bays, the windows grouped 2:3 and with an additional tiny ground-floor window r. of the door opening in the centre bay. Also in the centre, a small window under the eaves which lights the top of the stair. Inside, a stone staircase with silhouette balusters (some of the top flight's late C20 replacements). The W first-floor room is partly panelled and with a lugged surround to its fireplace.

PITKEATHLY WELLS, 1.8 km. W. Built *c.* 1760 as a three-storey and attic house with a round-headed door in the centre of the S front but remodelled in the 1920s to its present appearance as a two-storey piend-roofed and harled box. – To the SE, WELLHOUSE COTTAGES. A group serving the mineral well here, which attracted visitors from the C18. At their centre, a rubble-built round tower pierced by large crosslet 'arrowslits'. It was put up in 1834 to cover the well. The tower is ringed by a circular single-storey building with bracketed eaves which was added in the late C19 to house cubicles for visitors. Mid-C19 N wing, originally a detached house.

DRUMMONIE HOUSE. *See* p. 325.
DUNBARNEY HOUSE. *See* p. 329.
KILGRASTON SCHOOL. *See* p. 450.
MONCREIFFE HOUSE. *See* p. 535.

BRIDGE OF GAUR 5050

Place name provided by the bridge, with Braes of Rannoch Church standing on a hillside to the E.

BRAES OF RANNOCH CHURCH. By *P. Macgregor Chalmers*, 1907. Nave, semicircular apse, and NW porch. On the W gable of the nave, a ball-finialled bellcote, probably of *c.* 1775 and reused from the church's two predecessors. Otherwise, very simple Early Christian detail, with unmoulded round-arched openings. Inside, walls of hammer-dressed granite. Round-headed chancel arch. Simple FURNISHINGS of 1907. – ORGAN by *F. Rothwell*. – On the W wall, a stone WAR MEMORIAL of *c.* 1920, an image niche containing the figure of a soldier with arms reversed.

BRIDGE OF GAUR. Slightly humpbacked bridge of 1838. Three segmental arches and triangular cutwaters.

GAUR POWER STATION, 3.6 km. W. Hydro-electric station constructed for the North of Scotland Hydro-Electric Board in 1951–3 with a dam across the outfall of Loch Eigheach into the River Gaur. Austere concrete DAM by *Babtie, Shaw & Morton*, *c.* 107 m. long and with a maximum height of *c.* 13.7 m. To its E, a concrete BRIDGE over the River Gaur, the abutments of crazy-paved local granite rubble. This gives access to the modern-traditional GENERATING STATION itself designed by *J. W. Manson* of *James Miller, Son & Manson*, a parapeted two-storey oblong, the walls also of granite rubble, the ground-floor windows tall.

RANNOCH POWER STATION, 3.2 km. NE. Built in 1930 for the Grampian Electricity Supply Co.'s Tummel Valley hydro-electricity scheme. Of hammer-dressed stone with polished ashlar dressings, all now painted. Two storeys, the immensely tall ground floor with keystoned segmental-arched windows. Smaller contemporary version of the station at the valve house uphill to the N.

TOWER, Eilean nam Faoileag, 3.1 km. NE. On an island, probably a crannog, in Loch Rannoch, a battlemented square tower of the early C19.

BRIGLANDS
1 km. ESE of Rumbling Bridge

The rural retreat created for the Edinburgh advocate (and later judge), J. Avon Clyde, in 1897–1908 by *Robert S. Lorimer*. He recast and extended an unassuming Georgian house in a free interpretation of C17 Scottish architecture unified by harling and stone dressings.

The house which existed when Lorimer began work was a long two-storey building. Its earliest (E) part, perhaps of 1743 (the date on a stone now on the S front), seems to have been of two storeys and five bays. This had been roughly doubled in size, possibly in 1759 (the date on a stone moved from the former W gable to the N elevation in 1908), and remodelled *c.* 1830.

Lorimer's work was carried out in two stages. The first, of 1897–8, saw a remodelling of the existing house's E part which was heightened, with a steeper-pitched roof, and extended by the addition of a S wing covering the two W bays of its original front. At the same time, a kitchen wing was added on the N side of the house's W part. In the second stage, of 1907–8, Lorimer added a full-height bow at the back of the original E part, an L-plan wing across the house's W end and a circular stair-tower in the W inner angle of the Georgian house and his 1890s kitchen wing.

The principal approach is from the E to which the C18 house presents a gable, whose height, pitch and crowsteps, their skewputts carved with animal heads, are all of 1897–8. Extending S from this gable, a screen wall pierced by an archway, its segmental head with Gibbsian rustication, containing a simple wrought-iron gate. The screen wall forms the E side of a small courtyard whose other sides are bounded by the S front of the original house, the S wing of 1897–8 and, on the S, a retaining wall to the garden. The r. ground-floor window and three first-floor windows of the original house are still visible, the l. first-floor window peering through a notch in the NE corner of the S wing, all with broad surrounds of polished ashlar. Lorimer built up the ground-floor window of the C18 second bay and inserted a new window between it and the

Briglands.
Perspective and ground-floor plan (by V. D. Horsburgh), c. 1907

position of the C18 door (also built up and partly overlaid by the wing). At the second floor which he added to the C18 house, a pair of windows rise into boat-shaped dormerheads, the r. carved with a rose (probably emblematic of Mrs Clyde's interest in gardening), the l. with panels containing a bird, a fish and foliage (emblematic of J. Avon Clyde's pursuits of shooting, fishing and arboriculture).

The 1890s S wing had, at the N end of its E side, in the position usual in a C16 or C17 laird's house, the main entrance with a roll-and-hollow-moulded surround and surmounted by a large panel carved with a coat of arms, the frame decorated with roses and, at the sides, curved stems of foliage. No windows to the first floor of this elevation. One second-floor window towards the S end; it rises into a gableted dormerhead whose sides are covered with scrolled foliage and whose front bears the initials JAC (for James Avon Clyde). Projecting from the wing's SE corner, a diagonally set stone sundial, its narrow SE side carved with foliage and the motto VIVITE FVGIO. It is surmounted by the figure of a lion holding a shield; on the wall behind, the date AN^O DOM/1898. In the wing's crowstepped gable, its skewputts again carved with animals' heads, windows with rounded margins. The two at the ground floor are placed close together in the centre; at each of the upper floors, a single opening near the l. corner.

The later C18 two-storey W extension's front is of six bays, the windows originally aligned above each other but the spaces between them not quite regular and the two r. windows of the ground floor smaller than the others. In his remodelling of 1907–8 Lorimer replaced the lower windows of the third and fourth bays from the r. and the first-floor windows of the third, fourth and fifth bays with new ones, the position of the l. of the upper windows shifted a little to the r. of its predecessor. Also of 1907–8 the high mansard roof fronted by shaped stone dormer windows.

Lorimer's W addition of 1907–8 provided a solid stop to the house. This is a three-storey L with a massive chimneystack in the NW inner angle and an ogee-roofed round turret at the main block's SW corner. Tall second-floor windows light the billiard room inside, those of the gables surmounted by ashlar panels in the form of shaped gablets of Cape Dutch inspiration; boat-shaped dormerheads to the W windows of the main block.

The rear (N) elevation of the C18 house is mostly overlaid by Lorimer's additions. Projecting from its W part, a twin-gabled block of 1897–8 with a round tower of 1907–8 in the W inner angle. At the earlier E part of the house, a boat-shaped dormerhead of 1897–8 to a second-floor window and, at the E bay, a fat full-height bow of 1907–8, the top floor jettied and ogee-roofed.

The INTERIOR is almost all by Lorimer. The principal entrance opens onto a small vestibule. In the STUDY (originally, smoking room) to its S, a stone chimneypiece carved with roses and surmounted by a panelled overmantel. N of the vestibule, a SITTING HALL, its chimneypiece's deep lintel carried on rounded corbels. E of this, the panelled DINING ROOM, with a bow window at the N. C18 stair to the first floor. Its E room is the DRAWING ROOM, also with a bow window. Panelled overmantel above the fireplace in the E wall, this wall decorated with a foliaged plaster frieze modelled, like the rest of the 1890s plasterwork, by *Samuel Wilson*, its centre displaying the initials JAC and AMC (for James Avon Clyde and Anna Margaret Clyde) and the date 1898. The room W of the staircase (now a bathroom) was the BOUDOIR in the 1890s when it was given its panelling and a plain green marble chimneypiece; in the top of the fireplace opening, a copper plate decorated with a relief of flowers and birds in a tree. At the second floor of the house's original part and the 1890s S wing, three BEDROOMS with coved plaster ceilings of the 1890s. The E bedroom's coving is enriched with birds among vines; a small vine in each corner of the flat. In the room W of this, the relief of a fruit or vegetable on each coved side. Vine and flower enrichment on the coving of the bedroom in the S wing.

From the first floor of the original part of the house, the entrance to a narrow stair at the E end of the LONG GALLERY which fills the mansard-roofed attic of 1907–8 above the house's C18 W extension. The walls of the long gallery are covered with simple oak panelling. At the W end, a doorway in an Ionic pilastered aedicule, the pediment carved with reliefs of birds among foliage and broken by a cartouche. The gallery is covered by a plaster elliptical tunnel vault divided into compartments in Lorimer's Neo-Jacobean manner. The central compartments are filled with floral enrichment. In the side compartments, more flowers but also emblematic figures of the Four Seasons on the S side and the Four Quarters of the World on the N. W of the gallery and filling the top floor of the 1907–8 wing, a BILLIARD ROOM covered by a plaster tunnel vault.

GARDEN to the S and W of the house laid out in the 1890s with topiary a major feature. W of the house, a square pavilion with a steep ogee roof. Another square pavilion at the SE corner, of two storeys, with a steep pyramid roof. SW WALLED GARDEN. On its N side, a BOTHY, perhaps of the early C19 but altered c. 1900 by Lorimer who provided a boarded gable and jerkinhead roof. The walled garden's W side is bounded by a STEADING range of the early C19. It was remodelled by Lorimer in the 1890s when an ogee-roofed round tower with a heart-shaped dormer window was added to the E side and a triple-gabled addition to the W. W of this, an L-plan range, also probably early C19 but given jerkin-head and gambrel roofs c. 1900, the N range's with small gablet ventilators.

OUTBUILDINGS N of the house. L-plan S range and NW jamb, perhaps early C19 but remodelled c. 1900, again with a jerkin-head roof. Flat-roofed garage extension on the N side, by *Lorimer & Matthew*, 1936.

Harled Scots Renaissance LODGE at the NE end of the main drive. By *Robert S. Lorimer*, 1898, incorporating the structure but not the detail of a Late Georgian single-storey one-room oblong house. Lorimer inserted a NW corner window overlooking the drive, added a jettied upper floor under a tall piended roof with bellcast eaves and, at the N front, a bowed stair tower, its upper part also jettied; single-storey store under a catslide roof in the NE inner angle. Segmental-pedimented dormerheads to the N and S first-floor windows.

BRUAR

Late C20 commercial development sited in rural seclusion beside the A9 on the N edge of Perth and Kinross where the wooded ribbon of Glen Garry gives way to the desert of the Grampian Mountains.

THE HOUSE OF BRUAR. By *Mason Gillibrand*, 1994–5. Sizeable shopping complex, the architecture intended to evoke the spirit of a Late Victorian shooting lodge. Walls mostly harled, the roofs with bracketed broad eaves and gableted dormers. A huge conical-roofed round tower is the dominant feature.

WOODHOUSELEE. Harled 1990s version of a C17 laird's house, with crowstepped gables and a conical-roofed round tower, but looking like a suburban villa. The Edwardians did this better.

BURLEIGH CASTLE

0.8 km. E of Milnathort

Remains of a C16 courtyard house built as the principal residence of the Balfours of Burleigh. The buildings comprised a NW tower of *c.* 1500 and W and S ranges, with SW and SE towers, all built in 1582; the courtyard's E and N sides were probably enclosed by a barmkin wall. The S range and SE tower were demolished in the C19. The surviving parts are all of reddish rubble.

The now roofless NW TOWER is a rubble-built oblong (*c.* 9.75 m. by 8.2 m.) of three storeys and an attic. The missing parapet was supported on moulded corbels placed above a string course which forms the top course of the continuous corbelling under the angle rounds at the NW, SW and SE corners; caphouse at the NE corner. In the tower's E face towards the courtyard, an off-centre ground-floor door, its jambs and pointed head renewed. At the N end of this wall, slit

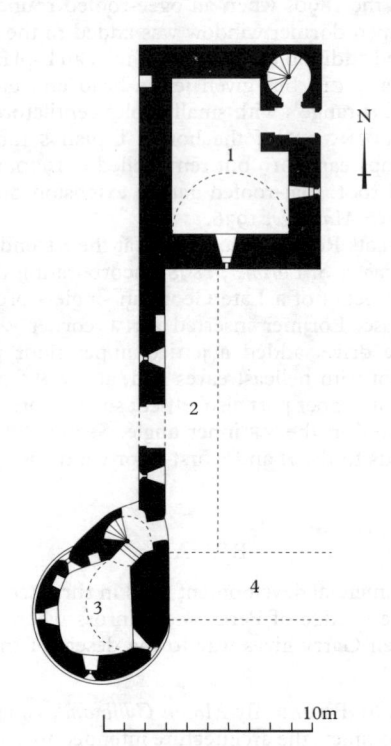

1. North-West Tower
2. West Range (site of)
3. South-West Tower
4. South Range (site of)

Burleigh Castle.
Ground-floor plan

stair windows. Larger ground-floor slit windows in the E and S faces; at the W side, a chute with, above it, slit windows lighting the garderobes which it served. A first-floor window in each face, the W robbed of dressings, the N with rounded jambs, the E with a moulded surround, the S with chamfered jambs. Second-floor E and W windows, both with chamfered margins. A roof raggle at the N gable shows that a two-storey addition, perhaps of the C17, formerly covered its W two-thirds.

INTERIOR. The E entrance opens into a vaulted vestibule whose S wall, and the W wall of the stair well, take a notch out of the NE corner of the tunnel-vaulted storeroom occupying the ground floor of the tower. Off the N side of the vestibule is the turnpike stair which formerly rose the full height of the building but has been removed above first-floor level. Unvaulted first-floor hall, again with a notch taken out of its NE corner. There was probably a screens passage across the N end. Fireplace in the E wall, an aumbry in the S. Dog-leg garderobe in the wall thickness of the NE corner. Well-appointed second-floor room, its E and W windows both provided with window seats; S fireplace. Garderobe, also dog-legged, in the NE corner. The attic room, its walls now fragmentary, has had a fireplace in the N wall and an aumbry in the S.

The W RANGE, whose surviving front wall continues the line of the NW tower's W side, has been of two storeys and an attic, its former height and *c.* 3 m. width shown by a roof raggle at the NW tower's S gable. Very tall ground floor, its W wall pierced only by the roll-moulded, round-headed and hoodmoulded off-centre entrance and its flanking oval gunloops, the N set at a higher level than the S. The range's upper floor is jettied out on a rounded string course of buff-coloured ashlar, the floor level of the windowless part N of the entrance higher than that of the shorter part to the S which contains a window with rounded margins. Above the entrance itself, the string course rises to form a rectangular overarch containing the moulded frame for a heraldic panel. Unvaulted entrance transe, its inner face surmounted by a rectangular hoodmould. Inside, at the ground floor, immediately N of the transe, a windowless wall chamber, its entrance checked for a door. High up in the N wall, above and N of the entrance, the moulded corbels which originally carried a wooden upper floor. S of the entrance, the large segmental-arched embrasure of the S part's first-floor window.

The line of the W range's front wall forms the E side of the three-storey SW TOWER. This is L-plan, with a bowed stair jamb in the inner angle of its main block and the W range. The two lower floors of the main block form a three-quarter circle projecting from the straight E side. The top floor is an oversailing rectangle except for a slightly bowed S face, its SE, SW and NE corners carried on continuous corbelling which starts at a lower level at the S corners than at the NW. At the W gable, wedge-shaped skewputts, the N carved with the date 1582, the coat of arms of Balfour of Burleigh (on a chevron, an otter's head, in base, a rose, the difference of Burleigh) and the initials

I^{S}B and MB (for Sir James Balfour of Pittendreich and his wife, Margaret Balfour, heiress of Burleigh),* the S with a rose. Chimney at the E gable, whose S skew is crowstepped. The string course under the W range's first floor is carried across the stair jamb, steps down to support the jettied first floor of the main block, and then rises again at the join with the missing S range. At the main block's low ground floor, four oval gunloops; a small square window above the gunloop in the W segment. At the first floor, large W and S windows in moulded surrounds, their upper halves grooved for glazing; large gunloop in the SE segment. In the N segment of the main block, a very small garderobe window and an adjacent round shot-hole, both with moulded surrounds. At the top floor of the main block, good-sized W and S windows, both with glazing grooves in the upper part of their surrounds and with shot-holes below. At the top of the stair jamb, a tiny window in a moulded surround and, to its E, a larger window whose lintel and l. jamb have been renewed but whose r. jamb has a full-height groove showing that it was intended to be fully glazed. At each of the two upper floors of the tower's E side, a built-up door into the courtyard's missing S range. Just to their N, the built-up C16 ground-floor entrance to the stair jamb. The present entrance to the tower, probably formed in the C18, is in the NW segment of the stair jamb.

Inside, the tower has a tunnel-vaulted ground-floor room, its only light provided by gunloops, their embrasures fitted for wooden gun mountings of which the remnants of two survive at the NW and SE. Small fireplace, perhaps an C18 insertion, in the SW corner. Turnpike stair in the NE jamb, its steps (renewed except for the bottom two) now rising only to the first floor. This is occupied by an irregularly shaped pentagonal room. In its E wall, a small plain fireplace, apparently an C18 replacement, flanked by a pair of cupboards, the r. with a shot-hole in its back. Another but smaller cupboard in the W wall. The S and W windows, their breasts pierced by shot-holes, are placed in segmental-arched embrasures. In the NW wall, the entrance to a garderobe, its NW side with a small window and shot-hole, its SW side with a lamp recess. The floor of the room above is missing but joist holes show that it was of wood. Its N and W windows both have shot-holes in their breasts but the embrasure of the W is elliptically arched, that of the S straight-lintelled. Small cupboard beside the W window. NW garderobe, a small window in its NW side, a lamp recess in the NE.

BURLEIGH CASTLE STEADING, on the S side of the road, was built in 1840. Rubble-built regularly disposed ranges. The E and W are two-storey, with basket-arched cartshed openings and slated roofs. Between them, a single-storey H-plan building, its roofs pantiled, that of the cross-bar piended. The

---

*Although Sir James Balfour had been declared a traitor and his lands forfeited in 1579, his wife was granted a life rent of the lands in 1580 and she and her son acquired full rights over them in 1584.

complex was converted to housing in 1996 by the *Watson Burnett Design Partnership* who added a tactful garage range at the s. s of that, BURLEIGH HOUSE, a substantial farmhouse, probably c18 in origin but thickened in 1840 when it was given a bay-windowed s front.

BURRELTON AND WOODSIDE

Originally two villages which now run into each other. The s is Burrelton, named after the Hon. Peter Drummond Burrell (later, second Lord Gwydir and twenty-second Lord Willoughby de Eresby), husband of Clementina Drummond, heiress of the Drummond Castle and Stobhall estates, and laid out in 1812 with three main streets (North Street, High Street and South Street) and a not very formal green at the N end. A few early c19 cottages survive but most of the houses are of the mid or later c19 and a good number of the c20. Woodside, on the Balgersho estate, was founded in 1832. Looser-knit layout, the houses predominantly of the later c19 and c20.

CARGILL-BURRELTON PARISH CHURCH, corner of Church Road and Manse Road. Built as Burrelton Free Church in 1854–5. Gothic-windowed oblong, constructed of hammer-dressed red sandstone. Projecting from the centre of the s side, a porch topped by a stone-spired octagonal belfry. Ball-and-spike finials on the spire and gables. Late c20 porch at the w end. Inside, FURNISHINGS of 1923–4. – STAINED GLASS. Two colourful lights (the Good Shepherd; Our Lord) in the w gable, by *William Meikle & Sons*, 1924. – Outside, immediately s of the church, an octagonal stone FONT BOWL, perhaps late medieval.

   MANSE in Manse Road. Mid-c19 Georgian survival, with a heavily corniced pilastered doorpiece.

BURRELTON PRIMARY SCHOOL, School Road. By *G. T. Ewing*, 1877–8. One tall storey, with bargeboards and a cupola-ventilator. It was extended s and a double porch with a veranda added to the centre of the E front by *L. & J. Falconer*, 1898.

HALL, High Street. By *James Smart*, 1896. Walls of red brick with white brick trimmings; jerkin-head roofs.

WOODSIDE, Station Road. Bargeboarded and multi-gabled overgrown villa of the later c19. The entrance is contained in a thriftily Jacobean tower with French cresting on the roof.

KEITHICK. *See* p. 438.

CAMBUSMICHAEL

Ruin of a medieval church in a graveyard beside the River Tay.

CAMBUSMICHAEL PARISH CHURCH. Substantial remains of the church whose parish was united with St Martins in the late c17. Its present form seems late medieval. It is a straightforward oblong, 15.5m. by 6.4m., the rubble walls incorporating a good number of ashlar blocks, perhaps from a C12 predecessor. Remains of a projecting splayed eaves course whose line is continued round each gable as a chamfered offset, the recessed walling above giving a pedimental effect. On the W gable, a pyramidal-roofed bellcote, its sides pierced by rectangular openings (small to the N and S). Is this late medieval or a post-Reformation addition? The E gable has been surmounted by a cross standing on a gableted base. Round-headed slit window high up in the E gable. At the W end of the S wall, a round-headed door with a chamfered surround. At the centre of this side, another slit window, also round-headed. There was probably a similar window between it and the door. To its E, the sill of a larger window lighting the chancel. Inside, a small aumbry immediately E of the entrance, probably intended to contain a stoup. Another rectangular aumbry, perhaps a sacrament house, at the E end of the N side.

GRAVEYARD. C18 and C19 HEADSTONES, mostly weathered. The W face of one stone, S of the church's entrance, is a Corinthian pilastered aedicule, the tympanum of the curly pediment carved with an angel's head (the soul); relief of a weaver's loom and shuttle.

CAPUTH

Small village with a handful of C19 and early C20 cottages beside Caputh Church and Hall; a plain late C19 harled terrace at the bottom of the hill.

CAPUTH CHURCH. Outwardly ungainly product of successive alterations and additions. The church was begun in 1798, the date on a rope-moulded oval panel in the W gable, and opened in 1800. In this first incarnation it was a tall rubble-walled oblong with a W birdcage bellcote. Blocked rectangular gallery windows survive on the N side. This building was recast in 1839 when the present tall pointed windows were introduced to the W gable and N side, the W window later extended downwards, the N windows with pendant label stops to their hoodmoulds, their cusped lights and quatrefoil heads inserted by *W. Erskine Thomson*, 1918. A transeptal S 'aisle' was added in 1865–7, its stonework, like that of subsequent additions, of stugged grey masonry. In its gable, a large four-light plate-traceried window, its hoodmould also with pendant label stops. Also of 1865 is the tower in the W inner angle of the 'aisle' and church, its lower part of hammer-dressed masonry, its belfry stage with a large rectangular opening in each face; a slated pyramidal spire roof rises within the chunkily corbelled battlement. A plain vestry was added to the centre of the N side in 1891.

The last major change took place in 1912–13 when *A. G. Heiton* removed the W bellcote and gave heavy buttresses to the corners of the original E gable to which he added a buttressed semi-octagonal chancel designed in a restrained Late Gothic manner. Either side of the chancel are contemporary outshots, the N an organ chamber, the S a porch. The porch's pointed door, with the hoodmould's label stops carved as men's heads, is reused from a porch of 1839. At the same time Heiton added a buttressed S aisle, the label stops of its Gothic windows foliaged, on the E side of the 'aisle' of 1865 and filled the W inner angle of that 'aisle' and the tower with a porch, its entrance also reused work of 1839. On the porch's SW corner, a brass sundial of 1627 from the church's predecessor.

The INTERIOR, thoroughly remodelled by Heiton, 1912–13, in a Lorimerian Late Gothic manner, is surprisingly unified. It consists of a broad nave (the 1798 church), chancel and S aisle (the transeptal 'aisle' of 1865 and the early C20 aisle to its E) which is separated from the nave by two broad pointed stone arches, now filled with a discreet wrought-iron screen of the later C20. The S aisle's two compartments are divided by another pointed stone arch. Over the nave, a boarded tunnel vault with surface ribs and rosetted bosses. At the nave's E wall, a high stone dado, its outer top corners carved in high relief with angels at prayer, the inner corners with IHS and AΩ set among foliage. Stone chancel arch surmounted by a small pointed window. The chancel walls are ashlar-clad. In their corners, columns from which spring the braces of the elaborately carpentered roof structure under a plaster ceiling.

Expensive but unshowy furnishings of 1912–13. At the nave's W end, a deep GALLERY, its front with linenfold panelling and supported on octagonal pillars, their capitals enriched with carved foliage and fruit. The space under the gallery has been tactfully screened off to form a kitchen and session room. – Oak PEWS. – On the N of the chancel arch, the PULPIT. Stone base carved in mannered shallow relief with an inscription. Body of oak linenfold panelling under a vine-carved frieze. – Late Gothic oak LECTERN, also with a vine frieze, to the S of the chancel arch. – More linenfold panelling and vine friezes at the chancel's oak CHOIR STALLS. – The COMMUNION TABLE, also of oak and with a frieze carved with corn and vines, is in keeping with the early C20 work but not introduced until 1956. – Flanking the table, a pair of tall and ornate Gothic wrought-iron STANDARDS for oil lamps; they are of the mid or later C19. – On the N side of the chancel, an early C19 ORGAN in a late Georgian Gothick case. Formerly at Delvine House, it was gifted to Caputh Church in 1909 and rebuilt by *John R. Miller.* – In the nave's SE corner, an elaborately carved small stone FONT of 1866. – The blocked centre window of the N wall contains a carved wooden MONUMENT to Caroline Graham Murray †1912, by *Robert S. Lorimer.* The frame, carved with vines and crowns, encloses a cusped arch. Within the arch, the inscription and, below it, a relief of two angels holding an inscribed scroll; above the main inscription, the relief of a dead lady upon whom descends a pair of angels, one holding a laurel wreath, the other a crown.

STAINED GLASS. In the N wall of the nave, a window (St Margaret, Dorcas, St Cecilia and Joan of Arc) by *R. Anning Bell*, 1919, the figures well drawn and strongly coloured. – The chancel's colourful glass was all executed by *John Jennings*. The central three-light window (Our Lord Worshipped by Saints), designed by *T. Millie Dow* is of 1913–14, the flanking single lights (Angels) of 1922. – In the aisle, a two-light S window (the Risen Lord Commanding His Disciples to Preach the Gospel) of 1964 by *Gordon Webster* with characteristic small-scale drawing and strong colours. – The aisle's two-light E window (St Francis and St Columba) by *The Abbey Studio*, 1962, is competent but a touch disappointing in this company.

At the NE entrance to the churchyard, a wooden LYCHGATE of 1928, its roof covered with stone slabs.

CEMETERY, 0.6 km. W. On top of a well-wooded low hill. At the W end, the early C20 BURIAL ENCLOSURE of the Lyles of Glendelvine, its off-centre gatepiers and corner piers ball-finialled and of early C18 character. Inside, the MONUMENT to Elizabeth Moir, wife of Alexander Park Lyle, †1918, a bronze statue by *E. Cole* of Mrs Lyle accompanied by a naked boy and girl. – Near the cemetery's E end, the MAUSOLEUM of the Mackenzies of Delvine, formed from the chancel of the former Caputh Parish Church which had been built *c*. 1500 and whose body was demolished in 1798. The pyramidal roof is of *c*. 1800, the Neo-Romanesque entrance (W) front of red sandstone ashlar constructed in 1879. Inside, at the centre of the E wall, a white marble MONUMENT to John Mackenzie †1778. On the consoled sides of the inscription's frame, carved floral pendants. Pediment, its ends surmounted by flaming sauceboat urns, its top by a larger vase-like urn. – Beside it, the MONUMENT, also of white marble, erected in 1714 to commemorate John Mackenzie and Margaret Hay and designed by *James Smith*. Segmental pediment bearing their coat of impaled arms and topped by the hand-held quill crest of the Mackenzies of Delvine. At the bottom, an angel's head above a swag of drapery and flowers.

Good number of C17 and C18 GRAVE-SLABS, HEADSTONES and TABLE STONES. Immediately SW of the mausoleum, a late C17 grave-slab to David Ambros †1670 and his wife, Isobel Anguis, †1688, crudely incised with a share and coulter, a powder horn and gun above a skull and hourglass. Behind the mausoleum, several C18 table stones and headstones carved with angels, reminders of death and trade emblems, the best-preserved the headstone erected by Charles Duncan to his first wife, Christian Straithearn, †1763. Above the E face's inscription, an angel's head (the soul). The W face is carved with another angel's head above a helmet-crested and mantled shield which bears a weaver's loom, shuttle and stretcher. Built into the cemetery's S wall in line with the mausoleum, a couple of C17 slabs, one incised with reminders of death.

CAPUTH BRIDGE, 0.5 km. S. By *T. J. Donechy* of *Tayside Regional Council*, 1993. Three-span bridge over the River Tay. Concrete piers with rounded ends support welded steel plate girders which form very shallow elliptical arches. On this structure, a gently curved deck of reinforced concrete.

CAPUTH HALL. By *Ebenezer Simpson*, 1909. Single-storey, picturesque with harled walls and red-tiled roof. Battered buttresses, lunette windows, broad eaves and bargeboards. On the roof, a squat Art Nouveau ventilator-cupola with a galley weathervane.

STANDING STONES, East Cult, 2.6km. NW. On the ridge of a low hill, a 25m.-long line of three stones, erected probably in the second millennium B.C., the W stone standing 1.8m. high and the central stone *c.* 2.1m. high. The E stone has fallen but its exposed upper face is carved with at least one hundred and thirty cup-marks, some formed as 'dumb bells'.

CARDNEY HOUSE
3.4 km. NE of Dunkeld

0040

Pleasant but unpretentious harled two-storey laird's house of *c.* 1800, extended in Neo-Georgian manner by *Peddie & Forbes Smith* in 1913. The S front was originally a five-bay U. At the advanced E bay, a three-light ground-floor window, the corresponding window at the W bay of two lights, both perhaps enlarged in the mid C19. The broken-pedimented centre door is of 1913, as is the stone panel (replacing a window) above. Also of 1913 the bow-ended wings projecting at the W and E, each with a three-light window to the ground floor, and the balustrades which extend from them across the front terrace. – Harled and piend-roofed LODGE of 1913 to the SW.

CARGILL

1030

Church and a handful of houses beside the River Tay.

CARGILL FREE CHURCH. *See* Wolfhill.
CARGILL PARISH CHURCH. Now a house. By *W. M. Mackenzie*, 1831–2. T-plan, with a short E jamb, built of sneck-harled rubble. Pedimented gables, the jamb's with a circular window in the tympanum. Tall round-headed windows in the side walls and (overarched) in the gable of the jamb. The main block's gables contain rectangular windows to light the area under round-headed gallery windows. Gallery windows of the same type in the sides of the jamb with block-pedimented doors below. The jamb's bellcote was removed in 1975.
CARGILL-BURRELTON PARISH CHURCH. *See* Burrelton and Woodside.
GRAVEYARD. On the W side of the village and entered through an elliptical-arched GATEWAY of 1810 (the date and its surmounting sundial now hidden by ivy). – Near the graveyard's W end, the WRIGHT BURIAL ENCLOSURE of *c.* 1835, built on the site of part of the former Cargill Parish Church. Quite elaborate ironwork in the door. Inside, at the S wall, a large GRAVESLAB commemorating George Wright of Lawton †1692. Reliefs of a skull and crossbones and of a gravedigger's tools above

and below the inscription. Propped against the outside of the enclosure's back wall is a broken long SLAB carved with round-headed arcading, the three panels bearing reliefs which appear to depict Abraham and Isaac, the ram, and Adam and Eve. It is perhaps of *c.* 1600. – On the N side of the graveyard, a large sandstone MONUMENT of 1765 to Patrick Thomson †1762 and members of the McGregor family. It is aedicular, the Ionic pilasters with flattened volutes, the pediment broken by an armorial panel; at the base, the relief of a corpse lying between two skulls. – Just N of the Wright Burial Enclosure, the egg-and-dart-bordered slab of a TABLE STONE, probably early C18, carved with a shield at the top and emblems of death at the bottom. – More reminders of mortality on the adjoining GRAVE-SLAB of 1715; at its top, an oval panel containing the relief of a grinning head, probably intended as an angel (the soul). – Several C18 HEADSTONES, most of them fairly weathered. A little N of the burial enclosure is the stone to David Pirrie, farmer in Redstone, †1749 and his son, Robert Pirrie, millwright, †1769, the S face bearing a heraldic achievement, the supporters in C18 dress and carrying axes, the shield carved with the relief of a millwright's tools. Crossbones, skull and hourglass at the base. – Some way further N, the headstone erected in 1770 by John and James Corse to their parent, with the relief of a figure, also in C18 dress, being greeted by an angel; an angel's head at the top, reminders of death at the bottom.

RAILWAY VIADUCT over the River Tay, 0.3 km. N. Five-span, the hammer-dressed stone piers built in 1848 for the Scottish Midland Junction Railway. They carried a wooden deck, which was replaced *c.* 1890 by parallel steel trusses.

BALHOLMIE, 0.5 km. S. Long Scots Manorial villa built in 1901 for the barrister Ernest (later, Sir Ernest) Moon. Harled walls, with sandstone dressings, crowstepped gables and pedimented dormerheads. Conical-roofed round towers at the entrance and the SW corner; turrets at the NW corner and projecting from the S end.

CUP-AND-RING-MARKED STONE, Newbigging, 1.8 km. SSE. Large boulder, one face carved in the second millennium B.C. with about thirty cup-marks, most of which are placed in a line and several surrounded by one or more complete or partial rings. From some extend tail-like grooves, with three of these forming a border.

RINGWORK, Mains of Cargill, 0.9 km. NE. Probably constructed at the end of the C12 for Richard de Montfiquet who was granted the lands of Cargill for one knight's service, *c.* 1190. A castle, its tower presumably of wood, was in existence here by 1199. The D-shaped flat top of a steeply scarped natural mound beside the River Tay has been defended on the landward sides by a broad earth rampart, still standing up to 2 m. high. Evidence of the surrounding ditch at the base of the mound has been mostly obliterated by ploughing.

STOBHALL. *See* p. 704.

CARNBANE CASTLE
6.4 km. W of Fortingall

Roofless ruin of a house built by Duncan Campbell of Glenlyon in 1564. The site is a promontory with steep drops to the N, S and E. The house itself, a rubble-walled oblong (c. 15.24 m. by 10.05 m.), has been of at least two storeys. In the surviving stretches of the S, W and N walls, gunloops in rectangular surrounds. In the centre of the E wall, a segmental-arched doorway, probably inserted in the C18. There seems to have been a stair at the NW corner.

CASTLE CLUGGY
2.1 km. ENE of Monzievaird

On a steep-sided mound, perhaps partly artificial, at the neck of a promontory (the 'Dry Isle') poking into Loch Monzievaird, substantial remains of a rectangular building which has been of at least three storeys. It is said* to have been described as '*antiquum fortalicium*' ('the old fortalice') in a charter of 1467 and possibly dates from the C14. Now c. 7 m. square, the house has been curtailed in size, perhaps in the C17, the present E external wall having originally been an internal cross wall. Masonry constructed of thin slabs. Externally quite plain, with a few narrow rectangular windows (one to the ground floor in the S wall, two first-floor openings – one to a wall chamber – in the W wall and one in the S) and, in the E wall, a small first-floor window, now robbed of dressings, and a slightly larger second-floor opening with a chamfered surround. Large holes in this side's masonry at the ground and first floors may indicate the position of former doorways.

Inside, joist holes show that the building was unvaulted. Now, a single room on each floor. The ground-floor room was presumably a store. The first-floor room's S and W windows' round-headed embrasures have risen above the level of the joist holes of the floor above. In the W window's embrasure, stone seats. There has been a fireplace at the E end of the N wall. At this wall's W end, a wall chamber with its own window to the outside.

CASTLE HUNTLY
1.1 km. SW of Longforgan

Rising from the formerly marshy coastal plain beside the River Tay, a volcanic mound of dolerite on which stands a large and starkly vertical C15 tower house. This was remodelled in the C17 and again in the late C18 when it was clad in Georgian castellated dress and much extended. It is now an open prison.

---

*By Thomas Hunter, *Woods, Forests, and Estates of Perthshire* (Perth, 1883), 456.

In 1452, the same year that he was appointed Master of the Household to James II, Andrew, first Lord Gray, was granted a royal licence to build a castle on such part of his lands as he thought proper, and Castle Huntly must have been erected soon after. In 1613 Andrew, sixth Lord Gray, sold the estate of Castle Huntly to Patrick, first Earl of Kinghorne, whose son, John, second Earl of Kinghorne, remodelled the house (renamed Castle Lyon) in the 1630s as his summer seat. Following the second earl's death in 1646 Castle Huntly was occupied by his widow until her own death thirteen years later, after which it was abandoned as a residence and stripped of furniture. On attaining his majority at the age of eighteen in 1660 Patrick, third Earl of Kinghorne (from 1677, Earl of Strathmore and Kinghorne), found both his principal houses of Glamis Castle and Castle Huntly in disrepair and himself encumbered with debts of c. £400,000 Scots (£33,333 sterling). For the next ten years he took up residence at Castle Huntly where he remodelled the interior of the house and laid out the gardens and parkland. During the first half of the C18 the castle was again occupied as the jointure (dower) house of the widows of successive Earls of Strathmore and Kinghorne but abandoned on the remarriage of the fourth Earl's widow in 1745. Thirteen years later Sir William Burrell found the house 'large & well contrived, to receive a numerous Family, but is now entirely uninhabited, the last Dowager having carried away all the Furniture'.

In 1777 the Castle Huntly estate was sold to George Paterson who had made a large fortune in the service of the East India Company. He married Anne, daughter of John, twelfth Lord Gray, and a descendant of the house's first owner. The house was extensively enlarged and remodelled by Paterson in two stages. The first, in 1777–83 and apparently with *James Playfair* as architect,[*] entailed the construction of a pair of wings on the E side of the C15 main block, the second, in 1792–5 and designed by *John Paterson*, the erection of a single-storey block to fill the space between the wings. At the same time the medieval house was remodelled, *The Statistical Account of Scotland* reporting c. 1795 that: 'The castle itself, although completely modernised within, has assumed even a more castellated appearance outwardly than formerly. The wings, embattled walls, round tower, and corner turrets, have been given it by the present proprietor . . .'[†]

Some remodelling of the 1790s entrance block was carried out in 1937–8 for Colonel A. G. Paterson, while institutional use since 1947 (as borstal, Young Offenders Institution and open prison) has littered the parkland with low-rise buildings. The castle's site forms an almost sheer cliff on its S and W sides. The C15 house was built against the W face of the rock, its two lowest floors (a basement and sub-basement) below the level

---

[*] An account for painter work in 1778 is endorsed 'Examin'd Ja⁵ Playfair'.
[†] *The Statistical Account of Scotland*, xix (1797), 478.

of the summit on which stand the late C18 additions. Walling of local rubble, the consistency of material combining with the Georgian battlements to give a superficial unity. The entrance front faces E.* From the corners of the three-storey side of the C15 house project the two-storey and attic wings of 1777–83, the space between them filled by the single-storey 1790s addition. The tops of the wings' gables, projected on corbelling, are crowstepped and pierced by large crosslet 'arrowslits'. Unashamedly large Georgian windows to the ground and first floors. Projecting from the wings' outer corners, bows at the ends of their battlemented side elevations. These extend back across the ends of the C15 tower. The front block between the wings was remodelled in 1937–8. As built in the 1790s it projected beyond the wings and had battlemented round towers at its E corners. In the remodelling the towers were removed and the parapeted front rebuilt (to the 1790s design) slightly behind the gables of the wings. At the minimally advanced ashlar-clad centrepiece, the sidelit entrance with acanthus-capitalled pilasters and an overall elliptical fanlight.

The C15 tower rises above and behind the late C18 additions, its E windows irregularly disposed, some with late C17 moulded margins, others with late C18 surrounds. Curiously, its age is disguised rather than enhanced by the archaizing Late Georgian remodelling which provided its wallhead's corbelled tall battlement and conical-roofed round corner turrets. An L, with the jamb projecting W from the S end of the main block, the tower is exceptionally large, the main block *c.* 18.9 m. by 11.6 m., the jamb *c* 7.0 m. by 9.1 m. At the main block, a not very regular array of Georgian windows, one at the principal floor on the E side inserted in a blocked larger opening, perhaps of the late C17. The most dramatic view is from the W where the jamb, raised in the late C18 to the same height as the main block, rises from the low carse ground on this side to a dizzying 35 m., the lowest part of the walling (against the rock face) with three intakes below the sub-basement above which are a basement and four storeys. The masonry is undisturbed by string courses below the corbelling on which is projected the crowstepped top of the gable flanked by conical-roofed corner turrets; battlements finish the side elevations. In the jamb's W face, a slit window to the sub-basement and small windows to the two floors above. At the three upper floors, larger paired openings (dummies at the top floor) all of the late C18. The N inner angle of the main block and jamb is filled by a late C17 single-storey and basement block of stores, its windows blocked in the mid C20 when its battlement, probably a late C18 embellishment, was replaced by an unadorned parapet.

The E entrance opens into a mean lobby of the 1930s. Behind, a top-lit oval saloon of 1793–5. Plaster frieze enriched with anthemion and urns. At the S end, a high-quality chimneypiece

---

*Really NE but E for ease of description.

of painted pine and gesso. Slender coupled columns at the jambs, the ends of the frieze with reliefs of ladies playing lyres. On the frieze's intermediate panels, swags and birds. At the centre, the relief of a cherub gazing on frolicking maidens. The basement of the C15 house was originally its ground floor, entered through a round-headed door in the N side of the jamb. Tunnel-vaulted stores in the jamb (hidden by a suspended ceiling) and main block. In the floor of the jamb, the opening for a trap door to a pit-prison in the sub-basement. The main block's first-floor room (the GOWRIE ROOM) was the C15 hall. Long fireplace at the N end, its stone surround of the 1930s, the remainder of the decoration Late Georgian.

ICE HOUSE, *c.* 0.1 km. N. Semicircular forecourt cut into the hillside, bounded by a retaining wall and reached by a flight of steps. On the court's straight SE side, a doorway into the ice house itself where a short passage covered with a brick tunnel vault leads to the egg-shaped brick chamber.

GATEWAY, 0.6 km. NE, at the entrance to the drive. Erected in the later C17 by Patrick, third Earl of Kinghorne, at the end of the former 'Grand Avenue' from Longforgan to Castle Huntly. Rebuilt here in 1783. It is of ashlar. Large piers with pulvinated friezes and cornices surmounted by diagonally set steep pyramid finials. Attached to the N and S faces of each, Tuscan half-columns standing on pedestals and with their entablatures just below those of the piers. Extending from these piers, curvaceously topped screen walls, each pierced by a round-headed footgate; on the ends of the screen walls, tall front-facing pyramid finials.

DOOCOT, 0.3 km. N of the mansion house, beside the back drive, also of the later C17. Rubble-built square; corbelled out at the corners, circular bartizans, now missing the top part of their walling and their conical roofs. The doocot's lantern-topped pyramidal roof has been removed. Pointed doorway in the S side. Stone nesting boxes survive inside.

CASTLE MENZIES
0.7 km. W of Weem

Large but unshowy mansion house built for James Menzies of that Ilk in 1571–7. Since the building's acquisition by the Clan Menzies Society in 1957 later additions at the back have been removed but an Early Victorian wing still projects from the W side.

The late C16 house is rubble-built with in-and-out quoins at the corners. Z-plan, the four-storey main block *c.* 23 m. by 9 m., and the NE and SW jambs each *c.* 7.5 m. square and of the same height as the main block but containing more floors. Identical squat conical-roofed round turrets on continuous corbelling at the main block's SE corner, the NE corner of the NE jamb and the SW corner of the SW jamb. Originally the main entrance was in the SW jamb which has its own small NW jamb containing part of the house's principal stair.

The entrance was moved to the centre of the main block's s front in the mid C18. It is now covered by a Neo-Jacobean porch added by *William Burn* in 1839–40, its segmental pediment broken by the heraldic achievement of the Menzies of that Ilk. Flanking the porch are horizontally proportioned small windows with chamfered surrounds and randomly placed oval gunloops; at the E end of this front, a larger kitchen window, its surround also chamfered, and a rectangular water inlet. At the first floor, four large windows with roll-and-hollow mouldings, their relieving arches pierced by holes of uncertain purpose; the windows' 3:1 grouping discloses the hall and chamber inside. At the second floor, four reasonably-sized but smaller windows, also with roll-and-hollow mouldings. Again they are grouped 3:1 but only the E window is directly above a first-floor opening. Between the two centre windows, a moulded frame encloses a panel carved with the Royal Arms of Scotland (indicating that Sir James Menzies, the builder of the house, held his barony directly from the Crown). The third floor's regularly spaced windows rise through the wallhead as dormers. These are aedicular, the pediments alternately triangles supported on superimposed pilasters and semicircles carried on superimposed attached columns, the order of both the pilasters and the columns Doric of a sort. Finials at the ends and apices of the pediments whose tympana are variously decorated, the W with herringbone enrichment, the next with a semicircular version of this, the third elaborately carved and displaying the initials IM and BS (for James Menzies and Barbara Stewart, his wife) and the date 1577, the fourth with a sunburst. The windows of the block's SE turrets are placed in punchily moulded surrounds. Towards the S end of the gable, a tier of roll-moulded windows light the upper floors. At the gable's N end, an oval gunloop at the ground floor and, above, a stack of small garderobe windows, some with chamfered, others with roll-moulded surrounds. The S slope of the gable is crowstepped, the N half carried up as an undemonstrative caphouse, its roof ridge at right angles to that of the main roof.

The NE jamb contains five floors instead of the main block's four. The plain ground-floor window in the S face is probably an C18 insertion. The E face's ground-floor window is of reasonable size but with an oval gunloop below to deter an attacker. At the first floor, roll mouldings to the S window and to the l. window of the E face but this face's r. window has chamfered margins. Roll-moulded margins to the S and E windows of the second and third floors and to the fourth floor's gable window. At the jamb's E face, the fourth-floor window breaks through the eaves as a repeat of the W third-floor window of the main range's S front. The N face of this jamb is broken only by an oval gunloop at the ground floor and a (blocked) opening at the first floor. At the W face, blocked openings, one with a roll moulding. The jamb's S gable is crowstepped. Its N gable is topped by a huge chimney, quite disproportionate to the single flue which it contains.

At the N elevation of the main block, large built-up windows and a big wallhead chimney.

The SW jamb contains five storeys and six in the NE corner. At the N end of the E face, an oval gunloop under a fairly small vertically proportioned ground-floor window, and, at this face's S end, a round gunloop. These gunloops cover the off-centre roll-moulded original entrance to the house. Above the door, a panel bearing the initials and impaled arms of James Menzies of that Ilk and Barbara Stewart, the lintel carved with the date 1571. In the jamb's S face, the pair of comfortably sized ground-floor windows with stop-chamfered margins are presumably insertions of 1839–40. At the E and S faces, near the SE corner, tiers of roll-moulded windows lighting the upper floors, the top window of the E face placed in an aedicule whose detail repeats that of the E top-floor window of the main block. At the N end of the E face, tiny garderobe openings and a stack of small windows, their margins chamfered or roll-moulded. The S gable's E slope is crowstepped, the corresponding W part occupied by the corner turret. At the W face of the jamb, a tier of stair windows at the N end, their margins chamfered or roll-moulded, the top window rising through the wallhead as a simple triangular-pedimented aedicule. Otherwise, this face is broken by an irregular disposition of chamfered and roll-moulded windows and garderobe slits. Top-floor window of the main block's pilastered type but its tympanum is undecorated. Crowstepped N gable.

Projecting W from the house's NW corner is a four-storey wing added by *William Burn* in 1839–40, a very early example of his Scottish Baronial style. From the C16 house are copied the aedicular windows of the top floor, the conical-roofed turrets but here of two storeys, the crowstepped gables and roll-moulded window margins, but the careful scholarship is let down by tall first-floor windows and rectangular bay windows at the S and E.

INTERIOR. The late C16 entrance in the SW jamb contains an outer door and iron yett. Inside the jamb, a small vestibule. Like all the C16 GROUND FLOOR rooms it is tunnel-vaulted. Off its S side, a guardroom with a gunloop in its E wall. W of the guardroom but entered from the vestibule, a store with a gunloop in the W wall and, N of the store, the principal stair. On the S side of the main block's ground floor, a passage. Originally there seem to have been three stores off its N side. The W two survive, each with a gunloop in the N wall. In the W embrasure of the W room's N window, the entrance to a service stair to the hall above, so presumably this room was the wine cellar. In the thickness of the W gable, a roughly oval chamber with a tiny window to the outside (now into the passage to Burn's wing). The door between these two stores is probably an insertion. The third (E) store was opened up into the passage to form an entrance hall in the C18. E of this and occupying the full width of the main block is the KITCHEN. Most of its E gable is occupied by the segmental-arched fireplace. In the fireplace's back, at its N end, a gunloop. In the N side of the fireplace, a round-headed embrasure (much renewed in brick) containing a pointed arch constructed of two stones which opens into a half-domed oven. Large aumbry in the fireplace's S side. At the E end of the kitchen's S wall, a water inlet. Diagonally opposite, in the N wall, a sink and drain. At the centre of the W wall, a recess and, to its N, an aumbry. Another store at the ground floor of the NE jamb, with gunloops in the N and E walls. Blocked door, probably C18, in the W wall.

The PRINCIPAL STAIR behind the SW jamb begins with a straight flight of five broad steps before it continues as a turnpike. In the space under the rising turnpike, a small irregularly shaped chamber, a gunloop in its N side. At the first floor the W two-thirds of the main block is occupied by the C16 HALL, later remodelled as the dining room. The walls' plaster panelling, with bead enrichment on the stiles and a rosetted frieze below the cornice, is of *c*. 1800, the doors, dado and shutters mid C18, the large Roman Doric columned chimneypiece of yellow-veined black marble an insertion of 1840. Beyond the dining room, occupying the E third of the main block, is the CHAMBER or withdrawing room. Walls covered with Victorian pine panelling with spaces left for tapestries, a not unconvincing imitation of late C17 work were it not for the doors. Basket-arched stone chimneypiece, probably of 1840.

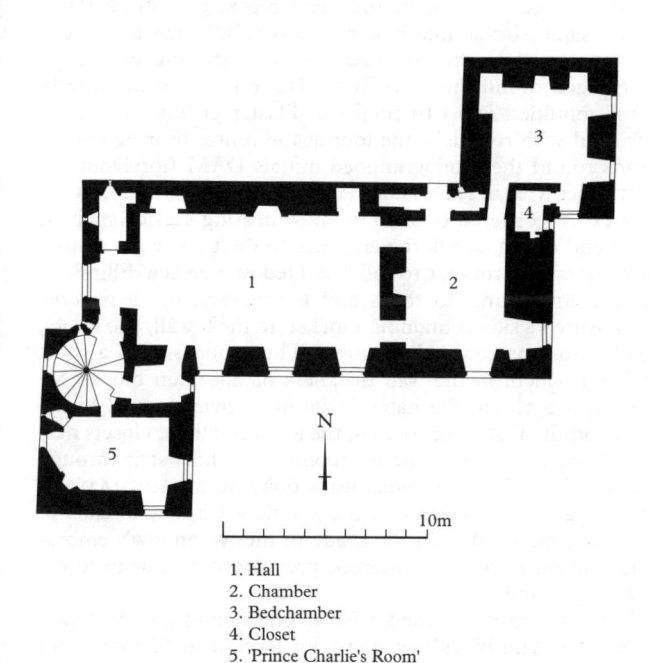

1. Hall
2. Chamber
3. Bedchamber
4. Closet
5. 'Prince Charlie's Room'

Castle Menzies.
First-floor plan

Compartmented plaster ceiling of *c.* 1660. In each outer compartment one of the national emblems of the countries claimed by the monarchs of Great Britain (the rose of England, the thistle of Scotland, the fleur-de-lys of France, and the harp of Ireland). The dividing ribs and central compartment's border are decorated with rinceau, amorini and human half-figures. In the centre, a concave-sided pediment enriched with rose-filled flower pots. In the room's N wall, a pair of doors. The W opens into a vestibule in the wall thickness. A door on the vestibule's W side formerly gave access to a service stair (removed in the C18); E door into a garderobe. The other N door from the withdrawing room opens into a BEDCHAMBER in the NE jamb. Mid-C18 panelling on the walls. In the W side of the S window embrasure, a door into a closet contained in the wall thickness of the main block's E gable. A window grooved for glazing in the closet's E wall; in its S, a cupboard.

Off the main stair, at an intermediate level between the first and second floors, is a small room in the SW jamb's NE corner. Three steps further up the stair, the entrance to PRINCE CHARLIE'S ROOM which was refitted *c.* 1730, with a basket-arched chimneypiece and panelling; at the W wall, pilasters flank a basket-arched broad panel intended as a backdrop for a bedhead. In the wall thickness of the NW corner, an ovoid garderobe provided with a lamp recess and a small window.

On the second floor of the main block, an UPPER HALL of the same size as that below. It was subdivided in the C18 but reinstated in the late C20 with its panelling of *c.* 1730 rearranged round the walls. Towards the E end of the N wall, a roll-moulded late C16 fireplace. Plaster ceiling of *c.* 1660 enriched with roundels, the four at the centre bearing angels' heads round the monogrammed initials DAM (for Dominus Alexander Menzies and Dame Agnes Menzies, his wife). At the room's NE corner, a door to the now missing service stair. At the S end of the E wall, the entrance to the UPPER CHAMBER or withdrawing room. C16 roll-moulded W fireplace. Elliptical-arched embrasures to the S and E windows, the E window embrasure's S side containing a locker. In the N wall, two doors, the l. into a narrow wall chamber. The r. opens onto a short stair off which, in the wall thickness of the main block's NE corner, is a closet, the hatch in its floor giving access to the closet off the first-floor room in the NE jamb; these closets may have been designed as charter rooms. The short stair through the N wall of the main block leads down to a BEDCHAMBER in the NE jamb. Fireplace in the N wall, a window in each of the other three sides. In the S side of the W window's embrasure, the entrance to a garderobe provided with a lamp recess and small window.

In the NE corner of the SW jamb, one step of the main stair above the main block's second-floor level, a small room with an E window and an ovoid garderobe off the SE corner. Above Prince Charlie's Room, a room of the same size but now quite plain; again a garderobe off the NW corner. At the room's SW corner, a door into a closet occupying the turret. At the top of the main stair are silhouette banisters of the mid C17.

In the Early Victorian w wing, a first-floor drawing room (the DEWAR ROOM) with bay windows to the s and w. Routine Neo-Jacobean compartmented ceiling and a grey-veined white marble chimneypiece, both typical of Burn.

Immediately N of the house, a partly demolished service court, its remaining buildings of 1839–40. On the courtyard's N side, a GATEWAY, perhaps of the C19 but restored in 1984. Above its round-headed arch has been placed a wedge-shaped stone of the later C17 bearing the crowned initials C RII.

Sloping rubble-built WALLED GARDEN, probably of the late C18, to the NE of the house. – At the entrance to the E drive, early or mid-C18 corniced GATEPIERS of V-jointed ashlar, their urn finials carved with acanthus leaf ornament.

CHAPELHILL

0030

Little more than a C19 vernacular inn on the B8063 and the Logiealmond Parish Churchyard to the s.

LOGIEALMOND PARISH CHURCHYARD, 0.3 km. s. Low rubble walls mark out the shape of the former PARISH CHURCH which was built in 1834, incorporating a chapel of 1643. – Just inside the entrance to the churchyard, a sturdy rubble-built MAUSOLEUM, possibly C17, a stepped buttress at each side wall, the entrance in the E gable. Tunnel-vaulted interior. – Among the HEADSTONES s of the church are some of the C18. Towards the churchyard's w end, a tall and narrow stone of 1764 to James Nockel, an angel's head (the soul) in the shaped top. Below this, figures of Adam and Eve above a display of reminders of death. – Some way to the SE, a small stone, also narrow and carved with an angel's head and emblems of mortality.

CHESTHILL

6040

4.4 km. w of Fortingall

Two-storey shooting lodge of the earlier C19. Symmetrical s front of five bays, with three-light windows in the broad and gabled ends. Gableted dormerheads over the upper windows of the three centre bays; a gabled porch. Horizontal glazing in the windows.

CLEISH

0090

Tiny village round the Parish Church.

PARISH CHURCH. By *D. McIntosh*, 1832–3. Tall ashlar-walled box of three bays by two, the E corners chamfered. Hoodmoulded windows, each of two round-arched transomed lights except in the W bay of the N side where there are two tiers of windows with rectangular lights. Between the two E bays of the N side, a buttress-like chimney, perhaps a late C19 addition. Corbelled out from the W gable, an octagonal birdcage bellcote with chamfered and panelled corners. The SW tower was added by *Hardy & Wight* in 1897 to commemorate Queen Victoria's Diamond Jubilee. In the E face of the tower, a hoodmoulded door, perhaps moved from the E bay of the church's S wall. At the tower's belfry, broad pointed openings. Also of 1897 is the Gothic chancel at the E end. In its SW inner angle with the body of the church, a flat-roofed vestry added in 1966. In the S wall of the church, a small SUNDIAL of 1732 reused from the previous church on the site; at its top, the relief of a rosette.

Inside, a Perp ceiling rose of 1832–3. The rest of the interior is of 1897 when the 1830s galleries were removed, a new W gallery erected and new furnishings arranged on 'ecclesiological' lines with the chancel, entered through a Tudor arch, as the focus of worship. – ORGAN by *Evans & Barr Ltd.*, 1927, originally in the Lockhart Memorial Church, Edinburgh, and rebuilt here by *Ron Smith* in 1992. – STAINED GLASS. Three-light E window (Our Lord's Agony in the Garden of Gethsemane) of *c.* 1905. – In the S wall, a two-light window (the Resurrection) of *c.* 1930.

GRAVEYARD. At the S entrance, the damaged round bowl of a FONT, quite plain but presumably medieval. – Built into the W wall, the aedicular HEADSTONE which commemorates Janet Steedman †1780, whose initials appear on the tympanum of the swan-neck pediment. The ends of the pediment are carved with skulls. Below the weathered inscription, reliefs of an hourglass flanked by crossed spades and bones. – At the E end of the churchyard, a fragmentary C13 or C14 CROSS-SLAB decorated on both front and back with a circle enclosing a Maltese cross. It was discovered at Cleish in 1980 and erected here in 1994.

HALL. Built in 1928. Drydashed, with a corrugated-iron roof.

SCHOOL. Single-storey T-plan, built in 1834–5. The gable of the N jamb is finished with a spike-and-ball finial; in the gable, a clock. To the W, the SCHOOLHOUSE built by *Thomas Davison*, mason, and *Edward McKillop*, wright, in 1795. It is of two storeys with a three-bay front. On the street side of the garden wall, a PUMP under a cast-iron lion's head; it is probably of the earlier C19.

DESCRIPTION. On the S side of the B9097, just a handful of cottages and, at their W end, the school (*see* above). On the N side of the road, at the E end of the village, the MANSE. It is double-pile, the narrow back block dating from 1744–5, the front block an addition of 1836. The stone skews are returned across the ends of the gables to suggest open pediments. The front block's pilastered doorpiece is of 1836, the adjoining bay window a later addition, perhaps part of the alterations made by *Robertson* of Dollar in 1893. Immediately W of the Manse, the Parish

Church (*see* above). In front of its graveyard entrance, the single-storey BEADLE'S HOUSE, its present appearance mid-C19 with crowstepped gables and panelled chimneystacks. The front windows have been enlarged. In the w gable, a tiny window formerly used by an elder to take collections for relief of the poor of the parish.

CLEISH CASTLE
1.2 km. w

Substantial but much altered tall and gaunt tower house, probably of the late C15 and apparently in existence by 1505 when the estate of Cleish was acquired by Robert Colville, Director of Chancery.

The house is a four-storey and attic L, the SE jamb slightly taller than the main block, all built of roughly squared rubble. Unusually, the walling of the jamb's s gable is intaken above the ground floor and again above the second floor, perhaps to lessen the weight over the kitchen fireplace inside. At the E side, marking the join of the main block and jamb, is a rounded stair-turret projected on continuous corbelling from the second-floor level. In the sw inner angle of the main block and jamb is the entrance, its rectangular doorway with a roll-and-hollow moulding. This looks like a replacement, perhaps of 1600, the date that is carved with the initials R.C. and B.H. (for Robert Colville, third of Cleish, and his wife, Beatrix Haldane) on a steeply pedimented dormerhead now built into the E stair-turret. This dormerhead was probably resited as part of *John Lessels'* reconstruction of the house in 1846–7 when the wallheads and gables' crowsteps were restored, the house re-roofed, the turret given a bellcast-eaved conical roof, most of the windows enlarged and provided with chamfered margins, the attic windows surmounted by new steeply pedimented dormerheads of Jacobean character, and a first-floor entrance reached by a balustraded forestair formed above the original entrance. Probably at the same time a single-storey crowstep-gabled addition was built at the w end of the main block. This addition's N gable incorporates a round-arched doorway (now the overarch to a window) whose roll-and-hollow moulding suggests a date of *c.* 1600. On the gable's E skewputt, a stone sundial of 1723.

The main block (much altered internally by Lessels) underwent a further reconstruction in 1972 when *Michael Spens* restored the entrance to the ground floor. Inside, he altered the ground and first floors of the main block to form a galleried two-storey slit of a room, its ceiling panelled with sculptured reliefs by *Eduardo Paolozzi* (now in the Scottish National Gallery of Modern Art). Further major work, removing almost all evidence of the 1970s alterations, was carried out by *Marcus Dean* in 1993–4. In 2001 an undistinguished extension w of the main mid-C19 addition was replaced by a new block, also single-storey but taller, designed by the owner, *Simon Miller*, in association with *Frederick Gibson*.

INTERIOR. The entrance in the inner angle opens onto the foot of the circular stair well. The stair itself, which rises to the second floor, is a C19 replacement, its balusters imported in the 1990s. Above the second floor, an original tight turnpike stair in the turret. The ground floor of the jamb is occupied by the tunnel-vaulted C15 kitchen (now a lavatory). Huge elliptical-arched fireplace filling its s end. The ground-floor vault of the main block was removed in the 1840s. The rooms (a kitchen and dining room) now there were formed in 1993–4. At the first floor, the original door from the stair into the main block's hall was a little to the E of the present door and at a slightly higher level. The hall itself is now divided as a study and drawing room. The drawing room's Late Georgian appearance dates from the 1990s when it was given a coffered ceiling and an imported white marble chimneypiece. The jamb's first floor room (now a library) has a beamed ceiling painted in the 1990s by *Jenny Merredew* with motifs relevant to the history of the house and the Miller family.

Crowstep-gabled LODGE of *c.* 1850 to the NE.

DOOCOT STEADINGS, 1.5 km. W. Formerly Cleish Mains. Early C19 irregular U-plan steading (now housing), the E range dated 1808, the N 1820. At the E range, a pair of basket-arched cartshed openings. Flight-holes in the s gable of the w range, so this contained a doocot. Late C20 conical-roofed round tower in the NE inner angle.

HARDISTON HOUSE, 2.1 km. W. Two-storey harled house of *c.* 1800, the first-floor windows linked by a lintel course under the eaves. The flat-roofed porch is an addition. Back wing, with shaped gablet dormerheads added to the upper windows *c.* 1900. Single-storey pantiled offices at the rear, probably contemporary with the house.

DOWHILL. *See* p. 313.
DOWHILL CASTLE. *See* p. 314.

CLOAN
2.3 km. SE of Auchterarder

Placed high on a hillside overlooking the broad valley of Strathearn, an unpretentious laird's house transformed into a Franco-Scottish château, the walls covered in peach-tinted harling.

The earliest part, at the centre, built in 1820, perhaps incorporating earlier work, comprised a two-storey and attic main block with lower lateral wings. The estate was bought by a lawyer, Robert Haldane, *c.* 1852 and in 1855 he employed *A. & A. Heiton* to replace the w wing with a massive three-storey and attic tower, its French pavilion roof finished with iron cresting, a two-storey canted bay window projecting from its

N front and a spire-roofed square bartizan at the sw corner. Conical-roofed tall round tower, its top floor jettied on continuous corbelling, in the tower's NE inner angle with the original main block to whose W bay was added a two-storey gabled porch. In 1905 *Harry Ramsay Taylor* raised both the 1820 main block and its 1850s porch to three storeys, the porch's new gable finished with heavy crowsteps, the new second floor windows to the E with gableted dormerheads which rise through the corbelled eaves. At the same time Taylor replaced the E wing with a second tower. Like the 1850s tower, it is of three storeys and an attic with an iron-crested French pavilion roof but is lower and with conical-roofed round corner turrets and gableted attic windows. Behind, plain rubble-built farm offices of the early or mid C19, the E range's S end containing a doocot, its E side's flight-holes forming a ladder-like diagonal, those in the S gable more conventionally arranged.

CLOCHFOLDICH
2.1 km. w of Strathtay

8050

Neoclassical small mansion house of 1828. Two storeys, the ashlar-faced N front of five bays with giant anta-pilasters at the ends and a wallhead blocking course. Greek Doric portico at the slightly advanced centre. Sill courses under the windows, the ground-floor openings corniced. Circular windows in the E side.

CLUNIE

1040

Just the church, manse and a motte beside the lake.

CLUNIE CHURCH. Sited on a rise in the graveyard. Tudor Gothic, by *W. M. Mackenzie*, 1839–40. Tall and broad crowstep-gabled box, built of stugged and squared red sandstone rubble. In the N and S sides, mullioned and transomed two-light windows. In the W gable, two shorter windows with a circular light above; a low semi-octagonal vestry projects from this gable. At the E gable, pointed windows above a pair of Tudor doors. These flank the tower. Chamfered corners at its bottom two stages which contain a broader hoodmoulded door under a taller two-light window. Then, a string course and, at the corners, corbels carved as human heads which support attached columns rising to the battlement. At each face of the belfry stage, a pair of pointed openings. At the corners and the centre of each face of the battlement are octagonal-shafted pinnacles finished with large crocketed finials.

34

The tower door opens into a small vestibule. At each side, a four-centred arch into a passage leading to a gallery stair; off the passage's W side, two arched doorways into the church. One side of each arch springs from a plaster corbel modelled as a human head.

In the church proper, a large Tudor ceiling rose. – U-plan GALLERY supported on sturdy Tudorish octagonal wooden pillars with concave faces. The pine front is decorated with square panels above a frieze stencilled with stylized flowers. – Boxy pine PEWS. – At the W end, the PULPIT, also Tudorish, its back with attached octagonal pillars supporting an entablature and a pointed-arched top. The enclosure in front of the pulpit was intended for a long communion table, now replaced by a smaller one of the later C20. – STAINED GLASS in the W windows by the *City Glass Co.*, 1947, with inscription scrolls and small panels bearing sacred motifs set against a pale background.

S of the church, a medieval fragment, perhaps a SACRISTY, of the church's predecessor. It is small, the walls of harled rubble, the roof double-pitched. In the S gable, two small round-arched windows, the blocked upper window in a moulded surround of square section as if designed for a shutter. But there is no evidence of the opening inside and has the surround been reused as decoration? In the N gable, an elliptically arched doorway, its soffit enriched with dogtooth ornament. More dogtooth ornament on the outer order of the roll-and-hollow moulding of the door's hoodmould, which has been carried on nook-shafts whose capitals survive. The building may be C14.

GRAVEYARD. Built into the outer face of the churchyard wall beside the entrance to the E of the church, a STONE dated 1672 and inscribed 'Keep thy foot When thou goest to the house of God'. – Inside the entrance, just S of the gateway, the coped GRAVE-SLAB of Jean Young †1704, the flat top carved with reliefs of a horse and emblems of death. – Most of the monuments are routine, of the C19 and C20, but among them a number of C18 HEADSTONES and TABLE STONES bearing various combinations of angels' heads (souls), mantled shields and reminders of mortality. – SE of the church, two very similar HEADSTONES, one dated 1819 and commemorating James Robertson, the other with a quotation from Job 19:26 ('And though after my skin worms destroy this body...'). The front of each is carved with ball-finialled pilasters and a panel bearing the relief of a tree set in a border of leaves.

MANSE, S of the churchyard. Built in 1799–1800. Harled, of two storeys and an attic. The three-bay front's flat-roofed porch is a C20 addition. Single-storey rubble-built and piend-roofed offices built by *William Keillar* and *James Fife* in 1811.

CLUNIE CASTLE, 0.1km. E. A roughly oblong natural hillock, its summit *c.* 90m. (N–S) by 30m. (E–W), which may have been fortified by the C9 but was developed from 1141 as the site of a hunting lodge serving the royal forest of Clunie to the N. The sides of the hillock have been terraced and a path led from its SW corner across the hillock's S end up to the summit. At the summit's SW corner, very scanty remains of a small stone-built tower and a curtain wall extending N from it. The castle seems to have been abandoned *c.* 1500 and its buildings quarried for the construction of Loch of Clunie Castle (q.v.).

CAIRN, Muir of Gormack, 3.2 km. NE. On the edge of a plantation, a small ring-cairn, probably of the late third or early second millennium B.C. only 4 m. in diameter. The outer face of the bank is edged with a boulder kerb, the stones graded in height with the tallest (0.25 m. high) at the SW. Similar grading of stones at the kerb round the roughly rectangular internal court.

FORNETH HOUSE. *See* p. 371.
KINCAIRNEY HOUSE. *See* p. 454.
LOCH OF CLUNIE CASTLE. *See* p. 505.

COLLACE

2030

Rural hamlet.

COLLACE FREE CHURCH. *See* Kinrossie.
COLLACE PARISH CHURCH, Kirktown of Collace, 0.9 km. ESE. Built in 1812–13. Crowstep-gabled broad box, with a tower at the N end; the detail is Georgian Perp. The buttressed W side (facing the road) and gables are of ashlar, the E side of rubble. Angle buttresses surmounted by pinnacles at the battlemented tower.

The interior was recast in 1908 when plaster was stripped from the walls and the plaster ceiling removed to expose the kingpost-truss roof structure. N gallery of 1813, supported on bundle-shafted cast-iron columns and with a panelled front. At the S end, the COMMUNION TABLE of *c.* 1925 and, to its l., the PULPIT of 1908 in a heavy simplified Jacobean manner. – Brightly coloured figurative STAINED GLASS S window of *c.* 1920 (Scenes from the Life of Our Lord).

GRAVEYARD. Just E of the church, the NAIRNE MAUSOLEUM, a battlemented oblong burial enclosure of 1813. The E entrance is a reused archway of *c.* 1200, its chevron-decorated hoodmould a restoration if not an invention of the C19. Three orders, the outer two springing from waterleaf-capitalled nookshafts, the inmost from pendants. Stop-chamfered outer order. Middle order with a roll-and-hollow moulding. Plain inmost order. Is this the chancel arch of the medieval parish church which stood on the site but was described in the 1790s only as 'an old and indifferent fabric' with no mention of carved work? Or has it been imported, perhaps from Coupar Abbey at Coupar Angus? In the enclosure's W wall, a pair of square dummy windows. – At the churchyard's NE corner, a large rubble-built early C19 MORT-HOUSE. Small pointed side windows. Pinnacled S gable pierced by two small circular openings above the entrance. (Vaulted interior.)

14

Just E of the Nairne Mausoleum, a TABLE STONE to John Beaton †1750, its top end carved with a coat of arms flanked by angels' heads (souls) and surmounted by a crown and floating angels; at the bottom end, a skull, crossbones and an hourglass. – A little to its E, a HEADSTONE of 1763 to John Wills, 'REVISED' (i.e. re-cut) in 1865, the S front with an angel's head and Ionic pilasters which frame a relief of the tools of a mason above a shield bearing a ploughshare. Coffin, skull and hourglass at the base. – N of the Beaton table stone, C18 TABLE STONES and HEADSTONES, one headstone carved with the relief of a ship, another with a heraldic achievement, its shield displaying a pair of ploughshares.

COLLACE PRIMARY SCHOOL, Kirktown of Collace, 0.9 km ESE. By *Stevens*, 1876–7, recasting and extending the parish school of 1825. School and schoolhouse, the school's bargeboards failing to provide jollity. At the back, a roughcast square tower, probably of the earlier C20, its top stage louvred; pyramid roof with a weathervane.

FORT, Dunsinane Hill, 1.7 km. E. Spectacularly sited on a ridge of the Sidlaw Hills, an Iron Age fort, probably of the first millennium B.C. It occupies a knoll, the slopes of its N and E sides fairly gentle, those of the S and W much steeper. An area of 2.16 ha. on and just below the summit has been surrounded by a stone rampart, best preserved on the S where it is 2.5 m. thick. The entrance to this large enclosure seems to have been from the N. Within the enclosure the ground rises to the summit of the knoll which has been fortified as a citadel. These defences, possibly replacing earlier ones, are clearly later than the outer rampart since they cut across the original entrance through it. They consist of two ramparts and a massive inner wall of *c*. 9 m. in thickness. Vitrified stones (i.e. hardened by fire) within the fort but not *in situ* suggests that some of the defences have been constructed of timber-laced masonry.

COLQUHALZIE
1.3 km. SE of Innerpeffray

Harled Early Georgian laird's house of the Hepburns of Colquhalzie, tactfully extended in 1826 and 1928. The main block was built in 1729. Two storeys over a basement which is now hidden on the S (entrance) side by the early C19 ramping of the ground but fully exposed to the N. Tall ground-floor windows. High piended roof. Symmetrical entrance front, originally of five bays, the centre three slightly advanced under a pediment. Doorpiece with a lugged architrave and segmental pediment. In 1826 the house was extended W by one bay and an almost identical E wing added by *Stewart & Paterson* in 1928. The additions' wallheads are of the same height as the main block's, the ridges of their piended roofs slightly lower. Both project N of the main block, their three-bay side elevations with prominent wallhead chimneys. At the garden (N) elevation the three centre bays of the original house form a full-height canted bay, its centre pierced at the top floor by a circular dummy opening flanked by rectangular windows.

INTERIOR. The entrance opens onto the stair hall, the geometric stair with twisted oak balusters, its curved wall painted by *William Fielding* in 1967 with a view of Colquhalzie seen

COLQUHALZIE 275

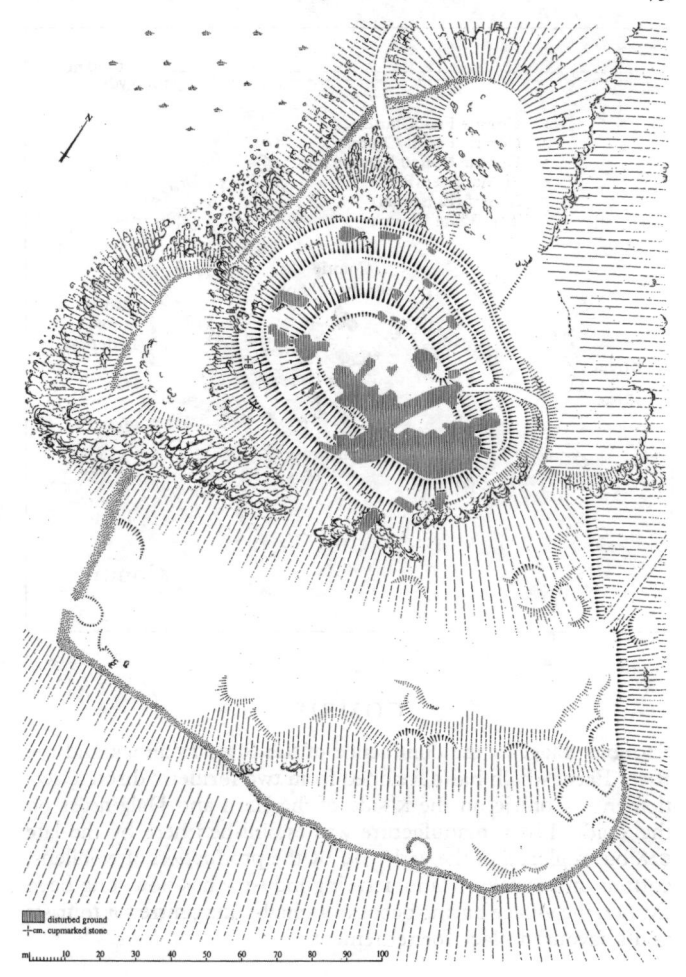

Collace, Dunsinane Hill, fort.
Site plan

from the ruin of Innerpeffray Castle. Behind, at the centre of the N side, an octagonal dining room (the C18 parlour), its original decoration intact. Coved ceiling with stucco heads at the corners. On the E side, a pedimented chimneypiece with reliefs of sheet music and musical instruments. On the W, a shell-headed alcove framed by an aedicule whose coupled pilasters support a broken pediment, its ends surmounted by flower baskets.

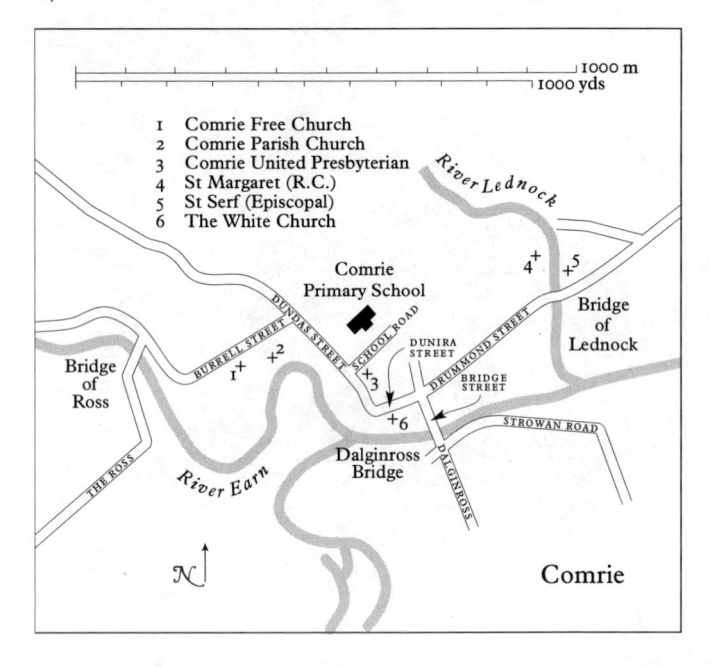

COMRIE

Sizeable village at the confluence of the River Lednock and the River Earn, which has developed from two formerly discrete settlements, Comrie on the N side of the Earn and Dalginross on the s side. Linen manufacture was established here by the late C18 but replaced in the early C19 by the production of woollens, cottons and whisky. Manufacturing industry has now long been extinct, the village having become a small-scale centre for tourists and a favoured place for retirement.

CHURCHES

COMRIE FREE CHURCH (now COMRIE HALL), Burrell Street. Rubble-walled box of 1843. Pointed windows. At the front (N) gable, now deprived of its bellcote, a plaque carved with a quatrefoil enclosing the date of the church's construction. It was converted to a hall in 1885 after the opening of a new church (now Comrie Parish Church).

Former COMRIE PARISH CHURCH. *See* The White Church, below.

COMRIE PARISH CHURCH, Burrell Street. Originally Comrie Free Church. French Gothic, by *G. T. Ewing*, 1879–81. Huge broad rectangle, built of squared and coursed hammer-dressed masonry banded with buff-coloured polished ashlar; very tall steeple at the NE corner. At the centre of the angle-buttressed front (N) gable, a crocket-finialled porch, the entrance a depressed arch, stiff-leaf capitals on its fat nook-shafts. Each side of the porch, a two-light window, its column-mullion with a stiff-leaf capital, the lintel decorated with cusped blind arcading. Above the porch, a polished ashlar band, its arcaded panels (half of them containing windows) with rosetted heads. The centre of the band is broken by the bottom of a six-light window, its head filled with circled tracery. Another band of blind arcading under the gable's crocket-finialled apex. In the buttressed sides, two-light windows, each with a circle in the head.

Angle-buttressed steeple with tall two-light belfry openings. At the pinnacled top stage of each front, a gablet containing a clock face. Octagonal ashlar spire, its principal faces lucarned.

The interior is one huge space, the wagon roof supported by collar-braces topped by arcading. – Gothic-fronted N GALLERY and PEWS of 1881. – The S end was arranged in Scoto-Catholic fashion in 1959, the communion table the focus. In this 'chancel', oak FURNISHINGS designed by *Smart, Stewart & Mitchell*, 1931. In the SW corner, the ORGAN by *Thomas C. Lewis*, formerly at Kilmacolm (Renfrewshire) and introduced here in 1959, its case Victorian.

Detached HALL to the SE, also by *Ewing*, 1879–81. Sparing Gothic touches; slate-spired ventilator on the roof.

COMRIE UNITED PRESBYTERIAN CHURCH, Dundas Street. Secularized. By *John Melvin*, 1866–7. Small but broad buttressed Gothic box. At the bellcoted W gable a four-light window, its head filled with quatrefoiled plate tracery, the hoodmould's label stops carved as human heads. On the S side of the gable, a low tower, its fish-scale slated French pavilion roof now bereft of cresting. Rose window in the E gable.

Inside, a W gallery. Gothic enrichment on the plaster ceiling.

ST MARGARET (R.C.), Drummond Street. Broad-eaved rubble-built rectangle of 1914. Just like a small hall except for the cross on the S gable and the high-relief sculpture of the Virgin and Child above the door.

ST SERF (Episcopal), Drummond Street. Deceptively simple small harled church, a flèche on the bargeboarded slated roof. The chancel, E end of the nave and the vestry N of the chancel were built in 1884, the sketch design of *R. T. N. Speir* of Culdees adapted by *G. T. Ewing*. The walls were of white-painted wood and the roof covered with red tiles. Four years later the nave was lengthened and the vestry enlarged. In 1897 *Ewing* again lengthened the nave and enlarged the vestry; at the same time he added the transepts and the S porch. In 1957–8 *Peter Beaton* yet again lengthened the nave, enlarged the vestry and porch, cased the building's wooden walls in harled brickwork and slated the roof. A hall (St Fillan's Room) was added to the N side of the nave in 1991.

Inside, a collar-braced kingpost roof over the nave. Pointed chancel arch. – STAINED GLASS. Five-light E window (figures of Justice, Fortitude, Charity, Courage and Generosity) by *Morris & Co.*, 1908, using designs of 1880–95 by *Edward Burne-*

Jones. – Contemporary two-light window (the Archangels Gabriel and Raphael) in the N transept. It is also by *Morris & Co.*, the *Burne-Jones* designs dating from 1893. – In the S transept, a two-light window (St Ninian and St Columba) by *William Wilson*, 1962, colourful stylized realism. – The two-light W window of the nave (the Risen Lord appearing to the Maries at the Tomb) of 1878 was formerly in the demolished St Columba's Episcopal Church at Crieff.

THE WHITE CHURCH, Dunira Street. Originally Comrie Parish Church and now a community centre. Designed and built by the carpenter–architect *John Stewart*, 1803–5. Tall white-harled* oblong, a steeple at the W end. Simple Gothic detail, with Y-traceried pointed windows in the long N and S sides; in the S side are also two doors, intersecting tracery in their pointed fanlights. Above the door in the E gable, a three-light window with intersecting tracery; quatrefoil dummy window at the gable's apex. The steeple tower is of five intaken stages, the windows dummies. At the third stage, louvred belfry openings. The top stage is a battlemented octagon, its principal fronts bearing clock faces. Rising within the battlement, an ashlar spire topped by a weathercock.

The interior was subdivided *c*. 1965 and further altered by the *James Denholm Partnership*, 2000.

GRAVEYARD. Directly E of the church, a HEADSTONE to Donald Macewen †1789, each face of its swan-necked pediment containing the relief of an angel's head (the soul); at the bottom of the W side, carved reminders of death. – SE of the church, several other late C18 HEADSTONES displaying trade symbols and emblems of mortality.

PUBLIC BUILDINGS

BRIDGE OF LEDNOCK over the River Lednock, Drummond Street. Early C20 steel bowed-truss bridge, the abutments of hammer-dressed masonry.

BRIDGE OF ROSS over the River Earn, Burrell Street. Built in 1791. Rubble-built humpbacked bridge, the main span a segmental arch; small flood relief arch on the S side.

COMRIE PRIMARY SCHOOL, School Road. By *G.T. Ewing*, 1908–9. Tall single-storey. S front of nine bays, the centre three advanced under a broad gable on which hangs a bell sheltered by a broken segmental pediment. At each of the three-bay outer sections a central shaped gablet. Columned and domed cupola on the roof. Porches are set well back at the ends.

DALGINROSS BRIDGE over the River Earn, Bridge Street. Designed and built by *Sir William Arrol & Co.*, 1904–5. Three-span steel-girder bridge, with two double cantilevers carried on oval piers of hammer-dressed ashlar. At the sides, railings with round-headed arcading under a circle-studded top.

---

* Harling was first applied in 1814.

DESCRIPTION

Drummond Street is the entry from the NE. On its N, St Serf's Episcopal Church followed by the Bridge of Lednock. Immediately across the bridge and set well back on the N is St Margaret's (R.C.) Church (for all these, *see* Churches and Public Buildings, above). Then come Glenbuckie, a late C19 bargeboarded villa in a large garden on the S and, on the N, the late C19 bay-windowed Comrie Hotel. On the W side of Nurse's Lane beside the hotel, an early C20 Hall. Tall single-storey, a ventilator on the broad-eaved and piended roof. Further down, on the E side, Millside of *c.* 1800, a plain rubble-built two-storey house, its attic lit by windows in the gables; three-bay front. At the N end of the lane, the beginning of the drive to Comrie House (*see* below).

Drummond Street's character is quickly established. One- and two-storey vernacular terraced housing of the early and mid C19 interspersed with a handful of larger late C19 buildings. On the S, on the W corner of Manse Lane, St Kessac's Masonic Lodge, its tall single storey the same height as the adjoining two-storey houses. Front of whinstone with dressings of polished red sandstone ashlar. Elliptical arched lights to the windows. Small gabled and louvred dormers on the roof. On the W side of Ancaster Lane the three-storey Ancaster Arms Hotel, with canted bay windows and a trio of bargeboarded gables. On the N side of the street, at the E corner of Melville Square, the single-storey early C20 Clydesdale Bank, ashlar-faced, its splayed centre pedimented. Opposite, on the corner of Bridge Street, The Royal Bank of Scotland of *c.* 1900 with a slated ogee-roofed corner turret.

Bridge Street is a diversion to Dalginross Bridge (*see* Public Buildings, above). S of the bridge, on the W side of Dalginross, Combruith was designed by *Robert Ewan* and built as the Bridgend Temperance Hotel in 1895. Bargeboarded gables and bracketed eaves; slate-spired octagonal corner turret. Then terraced housing and villas of the C19. On the N corner of Barrack Road, the white-harled single-storey No. 1 Mid Square, a late C20 replica of its predecessor of *c.* 1800 and the three-bay S front incorporating its Roman Doric pilastered doorpiece, the metopes carved with saltires and roses. On the S corner of Mid Square and Camp Road, The Bothy, another single-storey cottage of the early C19, again with a pilastered doorpiece.

Dunira Street continues the line of Drummond Street. At its start, on the corner of Melville Square, Nos. 1–2 Dunira Street, a harled two-storey block by *Honeyman, Keppie & Mackintosh*, 1904. Fat corner turret; at the building's lower W section, wallhead gablets skied above the first-floor windows. A little to its W, the late C19 free Scots Renaissance Nos. 7–8, a tall and narrow three-storey and attic façade of stugged buff masonry. Cornice over the ground-floor shop surmounted by a two-storey bay window under a crowstep-gabled top hamper which is corbelled to the square under the eaves. On the S side of the street, The White Church (*see* Churches, above).

DUNDAS STREET leads N. At its start, on the W, the former PARISH SCHOOL designed by *Peter Comrie*, wright in Comrie, 1833. Two-storey piend-roofed schoolhouse (now RUCHEARN), a heavy pilastered and corniced doorpiece at its rough ashlar front. The school itself (now THE OLD SCHOOL) forms a NW wing. It is of a single tall storey and now rather altered. On Dundas Street's E side, on the S corner of School Road, the former Comrie United Presbyterian Church (*see* Churches, above) and, in SCHOOL ROAD, Comrie Primary School (*see* Public Buildings, above). The rest of Dundas Street contains pleasant and little-altered C19 vernacular housing. More C19 vernacular in BURRELL STREET. On its S side, Comrie Parish Church followed by the former Comrie Free Church (*see* Churches, above). At the W end of Burrell Street, the Bridge of Ross (*see* Public Buildings, above).

COMRIE HOUSE, off Nurse's Lane. Harled and piend-roofed two-storey Georgian laird's house. It seems to have begun, probably in the mid C18, as a straightforward oblong, the W front of four bays. Probably as part of *William Stirling I*'s work here in 1803, a pair of shallow bows were added to the end bays, the N bow with a deep ground-floor window. Probably also of 1803 is the N wing which ends with a semi-octagon. On this wing's W front, a STONE carved with the heraldic achievement of the Dundases of Beechwood, brought here in the later C20 from Dunira (q.v.) and presumably of the 1850s. In the inner angle of the main block and N wing, a broad-eaved splay-fronted porch of the later C19. A SE wing was added *c.* 1920.

DRUMEARN, The Ross. Villa, by *Andrew Heiton Jun.*, built in two stages. The first, of 1856, was unassuming. Three-bay S front, the first-floor windows of the two E bays with gablets. Bargeboarded gable to the advanced W bay from which projects a two-storey canted bay window. In 1870 Heiton added a further bay to the W, also with a bargeboarded gable, the openings of its three-light first-floor S window with Gothic dummy heads. At the E end of the front, a tall entrance tower, its pyramidal roof with fish-scale slating. Conical-roofed round tower at the house's NW corner. – In a field to the E, the EARTHQUAKE HOUSE, a pyramid-roofed square gazebo built in 1875 to shelter equipment for measuring tremors along the seismic fault on which the village stands.

HOUSE OF ROSS, The Ross. Harled and rambling two-storey U-plan mansion house designed by *G. T. Ewing* in 1908 but rebuilt with alterations by *C. T. Ewing* after a fire in 1914. Main block at the W end, its S front of five bays with a bowed Roman Doric portico projecting from the advanced and pedimented centre.

MELVILLE MONUMENT, Dunmore Hill, 1.6km. N. Erected in 1812 to commemorate Henry Dundas, first Viscount Melville, the manager of Scottish politics in the late C18 and beginning of the C19 and owner of the Dunira estate. In a square railed enclosure, a corniced pedestal surmounted by an obelisk rising from a bulbous base, all constructed of granite ashlar.

ABERUCHILL CASTLE. *See* p. 146.
DUNIRA. *See* p. 331.
LAWERS HOUSE. *See* p. 497.

COMRIE CASTLE
2.1 km. wsw of Dull

7040

Small roofless tower house in a cottage garden close to the River Lyon. It was probably built for Duncan Menzies of Enoch who was granted the lands of Comrie, formerly the property of Alexander Menzies of that Ilk, in 1603.

The house is a rubble-built L, the oblong main block of three storeys, the taller square jamb (containing the stair to the first floor) tenuously attached to the sw corner. In the SE inner angle, a rounded turret projected on continuous corbelling contained a stair from the first floor to the top of the building. Across the NW inner angle, a splayed projection corbelled out from halfway up the main block's second storey and surmounted by a second projection higher up. Cavetto-moulded skewputt on the jamb's NW corner. Round-headed and roll-moulded door in the E face of the jamb. Immediately to its l. one of several ground-floor gunloops, that at the W end of the main block's S elevation below a horizontally proportioned rectangular window. Generously sized first-floor windows to the main block. In its N wall, a large gap under a relieving arch, presumably marking the former position of the hall fireplace.

BRIDGE OF COMRIE over the River Lyon immediately to the N. By *William Bell*, 1896. Steel truss bridge; piers of hammer-dressed red sandstone with boat-shaped cutwaters.

COUPAR ANGUS

2040

Small town at the SW end of Strathmore. There was probably a settlement here by the 1160s when the Cistercian abbey of Coupar was founded. After the dissolution of the monastery in 1560 its remaining possessions were made into a temporal barony granted to James Elphinstone, Lord Coupar, in 1607, and at the same time a burgh of barony was founded under his superiority, its inhabitants enabled to work as craftsmen and to hold four fairs a year. By the late C18 the burgh housed hand-loom linen weavers, and by the end of the C19 linen works, a jute mill, maltings and a tannery had been established. Much of the industry closed down in the 1930s and the town's ambitions to be a tourist and local shopping centre have been thwarted by the neighbouring Blairgowrie and the much larger conurbations of Perth and Dundee.

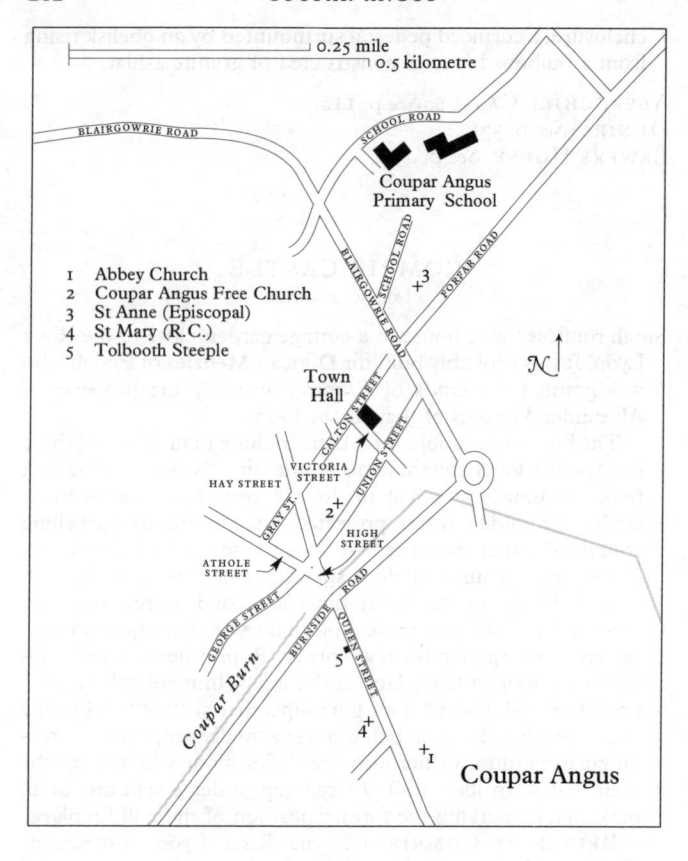

1 Abbey Church
2 Coupar Angus Free Church
3 St Anne (Episcopal)
4 St Mary (R.C.)
5 Tolbooth Steeple

CHURCHES

ABBEY CHURCH, Queen Street. Standing in a large graveyard, probably roughly coterminous with the medieval abbey precinct. By *John Carver*, 1859–60. Large but economical Gothic, built of coursed and stugged red sandstone, with dressings of buff-coloured stone, the roof covered with bands of grey and green slate. Sturdily buttressed broad nave, falsely suggesting aisles inside. Rather small pyramidal-roofed NW tower; tall SW porch, a statue of a man in C18 dress in a niche over the door. Session house at the E end added by *P. R. Donaldson* in 1969–71. Inside, a hammerbeam roof, the spandrels of the arched and cusped scissor-braces pierced by quatrefoils. W gallery, its panelled front displaying small coats of arms erected in 1964. Simple Victorian PEWS. At the E end, the PULPIT (designed by *Heiton & Grainger*) backed by the false pipes of the ORGAN, both pulpit and organ introduced in 1891–2. – Oak COMMUNION TABLE of *c*. 1920 in a routine Lorimerian manner. – Behind, the minister's and two elders' CHAIRS of *c.* 1955. – FONT in the NE corner, constructed from stones of a bundle-shafted column, probably of the C13, from the demolished church of Coupar Abbey; waterholding base and moulded capital.

STAINED GLASS. In the N wall, the E window (Our Lord with a Knight and a Girl) is of *c.* 1920. – On the S side, the W window (Our Lord Healing the Sick) of 1939. – Adjoining similar window (the Adoration of the Shepherds and the Magi) of 1938. – Next, a war memorial window (a Knight receiving the Crown of Life) by *James Ballantine II*, 1920. – Then a window (Faith, Hope and Charity) of 1911.

In the nave's SE corner, the weathered EFFIGY of a knight, probably of the C15; it was moved here from the churchyard in 1964. – Built into the W wall of the SW vestibule is a small heraldic PANEL bearing the lozenge-framed coat of arms of the Haliburtons of Pitcur, the initials HH and ML and the date _ _71 (probably 1571). – Built into the N wall of this vestibule are two SLABS, probably from the base of a tomb of *c.* 1400. Each is divided by buttresses into three crocketed arched panels. The panels of the l. slab contain reliefs of three knights, those of the r. slab what seem to be a pair of remorseful malefactors and a nonchalant executioner holding an axe. – In the NW vestibule are two GRAVE-SLABS. One, commemorating Isobell Blair †1692, is carved with a skull flanked by bones and, below, the tools of a butcher (?). The other, to John Schanwel, Abbot of Coupar, †1506, bears the relief of a coped and mitred abbot. – Also in this vestibule, the worn SCULPTURE of the head of a man, probably late medieval and from Coupar Abbey.

GRAVEYARD. Immediately beside the church are medieval STONE FRAGMENTS from Coupar Abbey. Between the two W buttresses of the S side of the nave is the waterholding base of a respond, probably of the C14. At the W end of the N side, part of a plain column and also a stone bearing the relief of a cross, possibly a ceiling boss. Halfway along this side, a badly weathered small effigy.

At the SW corner of the churchyard, the remains of a GATEHOUSE, presumably into the precinct of Coupar Abbey and the only part of the abbey buildings still visible on site. It perhaps dates from the C15. Built of squared blocks of red sandstone, the building seems to have been of three storeys. Stepped diagonal buttress at the SE corner. Ground floor pierced by a round-headed tunnel-vaulted pend. Cavetto-moulded E jamb of an off-centre first-floor window and, above, what seems to be another window jamb. – Immediately E of the gatehouse, a couple of medieval stone COFFINS.

N of the abbey gatehouse, the MAUSOLEUM of the Murrays of Simprim, built in the earlier C19, a hoodmoulded door in the N gable. – Some way to its NE, an octagonal red sandstone WATCH HOUSE of 1829. One course below the eaves is a frieze formed of simple medieval mouldings reused from Coupar Abbey. S door with one chamfered jamb, the other with a roll-and-hollow moulding. They may be of the late C16 or early C17 when part of the Abbey buildings, probably the cloister, was fitted up as a house. – Propped against the walls of the watch house are GRAVESTONES. At the SW side, a large slab commemorating George Wighton, a merchant, †1703, carved in shallow relief with a skeleton, scales and an angel's head (the soul). – On the W side, a headstone erected by Charles May, writer, to his wife, Ann, †1760, bearing the crisp relief of a monogrammed shield supported by men carrying swingle-trees; crossbones at the base, an angel's head at the top. – At the SE side, a headstone, probably of the early C18, with crude reliefs of angel's head above a catalogue display of emblems of mortality (an hourglass, skull, bone, coffin, gravedigger's tools and bell). – At the watch house's W side, a broken headstone, dated 1731, with a badly weathered relief of angels trumpeting news of the Resurrection to a skeleton.

COUPAR ANGUS FREE CHURCH, Union Street. Now church hall. Built in 1843. Simple Gothic on a small scale, the front gable flanked by low towers with piended platform roofs.

ST ANNE (Episcopal), Forfar Road. By *William Hay*, 1847–8. Very simple lancet Gothic, with a nave and chancel, porch and vestry.

Inside, a scissor-truss roof over the nave, a braced-collar roof over the chancel. Pointed chancel arch. The sanctuary floor is covered with floral-patterned ENCAUSTIC TILES by *G. H. Potts*, 1871. – Altar REREDOS with a C17 German wooden relief of the Last Supper. – Routine Gothic wooden PULPIT of 1897. – Brass LECTERN by *Cox & Sons*, 1883. – ORGAN on the E (liturgical N) side of the chancel, by *Harrison & Harrison*, 1887. – PEWS of 1871.

Complete scheme of STAINED GLASS. Colourful mid-C19 S (liturgical E) window (Scenes from the Life of Our Lord). – In the chancel's W side, two lights (St Anne; St Margaret of Scotland), rather pale stylized realism, by *Alexander L. Russell*, 1954–5. – The nave's side windows (the Beatitudes) are all of 1890 by *Clayton & Bell*, accomplished and well-coloured. – Jewel-like glass (Job) in the N windows, by *Gordon Webster*, 1962.

ST MARY (R.C.), Queen Street. Originally Coupar Angus United Presbyterian Church. By *John Haggart*, 1864–5. Box, with round-headed windows in the rubble-built sides. Gable front of stugged ashlar, its diagonal buttresses sloped into the corners which are surmounted by panelled bartizans. Projecting from the centre of the gable, a buttressed tower, its spire replaced by a mid-C20 curved roof. Across this front, a mid-C20 porch.

PUBLIC BUILDINGS

COUPAR ANGUS PRIMARY SCHOOL, School Road. By *Ireland & Maclaren*, 1875–7. Single-storey, built of grey sandstone rubble, the style hinting at Gothic. Broad eaves to the gables where some flowery wrought-iron finials survive. Curtain-walled two-storey E extension of 1960.

TOLBOOTH STEEPLE, Queen Street. Built in 1762, its lower floors originally used as a prison. Square tower, the red sandstone rubble walling divided by intakes into three stages, each of two storeys. Rectangular windows except at the top where they are round-headed. Between the top-floor windows of the N and S sides, C19 circular clock faces. Slated Victorian broach spire.

TOWN HALL, Union Street. By *David Smart*, 1886–7, built to commemorate Queen Victoria's Golden Jubilee. Front (S) block in a small-scale French municipal manner, with iron-crested pavilion roofs over the outer bays whose doors' heavily moulded consoled cornices support balustraded stone balconies. At the centre, a full-height semi-octagonal bay window surmounted by a slated spire. The hall behind links to a two-storey back block, with a central chimneyed gable and heavy console-cornieed doorpiece.

DESCRIPTION

QUEEN STREET carries the A923 in from the SE. On its r. side, the Abbey Church and churchyard (*see* Churches, above). On the l., No. 23, probably of the early C19 but built into its front wall is a weathered late medieval carved stone on which the Royal Arms of Scotland used to be discernible. Then, St Mary's (R.C.) Church (*see* Churches, above) after which a norm of Georgian and Victorian vernacular just about establishes itself. On the W, the Tolbooth Steeple (*see* Public Buildings, above) followed by Nos. 1–5, built as Coupar Angus Parish Manse in 1781, its plain three-bay front facing W. Opposite, the harled late C18 STRATHMORE HOTEL. Symmetrical five-bay front, the ground-floor windows small, those of the first floor denoting the principal floor; Victorian gabled dormers and tree-trunk portico. Then the by-pass of Burnside Road cuts through the N–S street line. On its N side, a BRIDGE over the Coupar Burn. Single rubble-built segmental arch built in 1795 but widened to the E in the C20.

HIGH STREET, N of the bridge, forms a triangle with THE CROSS (a short section of the town's historic main E–W street) on its N side. On High Street's E and W sides, an unpretentious medley of the C18, C19 and C20. At its NW corner with George Street, the ashlar-fronted ROYAL HOTEL of 1809. Piered doorpiece with a Neo-Jacobean parapet added *c.* 1840. Late C19 attic with an octagonal corner turret. The rear wing along GEORGE STREET is also of 1809, its stonework now painted. Two storeys, the very tall first-floor windows disclosing the former presence of an assembly room; almost flat pend arch at the W end.

ATHOLE STREET continues High Street to the NW. On its corner with George Street, the former POST OFFICE by *David Smart*, 1902, its canted corner topped by an octagonal turret. Athole

Street's line is carried on by CAUSEWAYEND, a long but undistinguished stretch of C19 vernacular housing. At the street's NW end, a development for the Burgh Council (STUART CRESCENT and Nos. 1–10 STRATHMORE AVENUE) by *R.W. Lowe*, 1935. Stuart Crescent forms a gentle curve of semi-detached rubble-walled houses, the end blocks piend-roofed, the others with M-shaped centre gablets. Piend-roofed blocks in Strathmore Avenue.

GRAY STREET runs NE from the NW end of Athole Street. Its l. side starts with No. 7 of *c.* 1800. Three-light windows and a pilastered and corniced doorpiece at the rendered ground floor. The upper floor's outer bays are of rubble; pedimented ashlar centrepiece containing an overarched and aproned Venetian window. No. 3, dated 1796 on the lintel of the first floor's centre window, has been altered but retains its corniced doorpiece, a heavy keystone breaking its pulvinated frieze. Opposite, the MASONIC HALL which was built as a school and schoolhouse in 1792. At the main (school) block, a corniced entrance and round-headed first-floor windows. Contemporary block (No. 20 COMMERCIAL STREET) to its NE, a Venetian window at the splayed corner. HAY STREET runs uphill to the N. On its W side, the late C18 two-storey rubble-built No. 2, with a lugged architrave and pulvinated frieze to the door.

CALTON STREET is a NE continuation of Gray Street. Its SE side starts with the sizeable three-storey CUMBERLAND BARRACKS (No. 1) built of harled rubble in 1766 but altered later and 'restored' on its conversion to flats in 1974. Front block of five bays with a centre gablet. SE rear wing, a gabled projection in the inner angle. At each of the gables' skews, a projecting stone to give the impression of stepping. Calton Street's NW side is late C18 and C19 Georgian and Georgian survival vernacular, most of the houses altered and now rendered. No. 11, with small original windows and large late C20 roof-lights, is dated 1774 on the door lintel. On the W corner of Hill Street, the grander AVIEMORE of *c.* 1800, with pedestal skewputts surmounted by urns. Near the street's end, on the NW side, the harled two-storey UNION BANK BUILDING, its late C18 three-bay main block (rather altered) with a Venetian first-floor centre window under a chimneyed gablet. Early C19 E addition with three-light windows in its shallowly bowed front. Opposite, the back of the Town Hall (*see* Public Buildings, above). In FORFAR ROAD, across Blairgowrie Road, St Anne's Episcopal Church (*see* Churches, above).

UNION STREET leads from Blairgowrie Road back to the town centre. On its NW side, the Town Hall (*see* Public Buildings, above) followed by THE ROYAL BANK OF SCOTLAND, a stolid mid-Victorian Georgian survival villa. Set well back behind a garden is DALBLAIR, the former Coupar Angus Free Church Manse of 1845, a corniced doorpiece its only adornment. Then, the former Free Church (*see* Churches, above). Opposite, the early C19 KLYDON HOUSE, a lugged architrave at its doorpiece; canted SW corner scooped up to form a right angle at the upper floor.

MALTINGS, St Catherine's Lane. Built in the mid or later C19, the masonry suggesting two stages of construction. Rubble-built three-storey triple pile with pyramid-roofed kiln vents at the S end.

BALGERSHO, 1.5km. S. Unpretentious red sandstone Georgian and Neo-Georgian country house. The two-storey main block is late C18, its front of three bays with a three-light window at the centre of the first floor. This was overlaid *c.* 1830 by a single-storey extension, and piend-roofed pavilions, also of one storey, were added at the ends. About 1900 the outer bays of the front extension were heightened to two storeys, with piended roofs and three-light first-floor windows, and a splay-sided porch added to the centre. Long rear wing, its S end probably C18, the N part and pyramid-roofed tower at the join built in 1958.

CRAIGHALL-RATTRAY

1040

2.8 km. N of Blairgowrie

Unpretentious but architecturally complicated small mansion house of the Rattrays (later, Clerk-Rattrays) of Rattray.

The site, a high peninsula above a ford in the River Ericht, with sheer drops on three sides, is of great natural strength and the approach from the S was formerly defended by a ditch and two round towers. It was probably occupied from an early period but the present house seems to have originated in the mid C17 as a U-plan building, probably with a screen wall closing the S side of its courtyard.

Extensive alterations to the house were made in the early C19 for James Clerk-Rattray, a Baron of the Court of Exchequer, who had succeeded to the estate in 1799. The first of these, probably soon after he inherited, entailed the reconstruction or rebuilding of the N range as a plain two-storey and basement harled block with a bowed N end pierced by tall ground-floor windows opening onto a balcony supported by crude piers. On the block's E side, a whin-walled stair-tower.

In a second stage, of *c.* 1830, a whin-built rectangular attic storey was dumped on top of the N range, its N end set back from the front of the bow and with its N corners supported on corbelling. At the same time the E and W ranges were remodelled in Elizabethan manorial style and refaced in a mixture of red sandstone and whin and new roofs constructed which covered both them and the intervening courtyard. A tower was built on the W side. This is of three storeys above a basement. Bartizans at the corners of the pinnacled W gable, its top floor projected on moulded corbels; round-headed first-floor window under a rectangular hoodmould. A rectangular two-light dummy oriel window on the tower's S side. The E range is domestic, with a canted bay window to the E and a rectangular bay window to the S. Also at the S front, over the first-floor windows, ogee-arched dormerheads flanked by ogee finials.

Much more assertive additions were designed *c.* 1890 by *Andrew Heiton Jun.* who added a heavy battlemented tower to the SW corner. At the same time he built a boldly advanced and gabled two-storey and attic block in front of the centre of the S elevation, its canted ground floor forming a porch, the central opening surmounted by the heraldic achievement of the Clerk-Rattrays, the corners of the upper floor corbelled out to right angles; under the attic window, crests of the Clerk and Rattray families, perhaps reused from the earlier C19 work. In the inner angle of this addition and the S front of the E range, a spire-roofed octagonal stair tower.

Built into the 1830s external walling are ARCHITECTURAL FRAGMENTS brought here by James Clerk-Rattray from demolished buildings in Edinburgh. In a screen wall to the W is a deep lintel carved in low relief with a banded pilaster, thistle, fleurs-de-lys and rosettes which flank an inscription SOLI DEO/HONOR ET GLORIA/NAMQUE ERIT ILLE MIHI/ SEMPER DEUS and the initials and monogram of NM and IF and the date 1614. A showier sculpture, built into the E gable at the E range's S end, was provided by *John Mylne Jun.* in 1656 on the house built by him for the Professor of Divinity at the College of Edinburgh with money left for the purpose by Batholomew Somervell. It is a scroll-flanked and curvaceously pedimented aedicule containing an angel's head above a shell-headed niche in which stands a half-length relief portrait of Somervell. Below, an inscription panel flanked by strapwork which encloses ovals carved with fruit.

INTERIOR. A broad corridor, on the site of the earlier courtyard, runs from the entrance to the bow-ended early C19 drawing room at the N end. In the drawing room, tall windows rising from floor level and a plain white marble chimneypiece; guilloche border to the ceiling. Simple Jacobean compartmented ceiling of *c.* 1830 in the dining room (now kitchen) at the house's SE corner. On the ground floor of the SW tower, the smoking room of *c.* 1890, its Neo-Jacobean chimneypiece with Arts and Crafts hints.

STABLE AND COACHOUSE immediately to the SW. L-plan, the NE jamb containing the stable probably of *c.* 1890, with round-headed windows in the E gable. The longer coachhouse range is of *c.* 1830, its N part's E front convex and containing segmental-arched carriage doors under gableted loft openings. At the S end, an E gable surmounted by a birdcage bellcote, its weathervane pierced with the crest and coat of arms of the Rattrays.

CRAY

Just the church beside the entrance to the former drive to Dalnaglar Castle.

Cray Free Church. Disused. Plain Gothic box of sneck-harled rubble, built in 1844. The E tower was added in 1864, its walling of pinned rubble. Tall Gothic E door. Intaken belfry stage with pointed openings, paired at the E face, single-light at the others. Rising within the corbelled parapet, a fish-scale slated pyramidal spire. – MANSE (now BLAIR HOUSE) of 1845 to the SW.

DRUMFORK 4km. S. Harled two-storey villa, by *Andrew Heiton Jun.*, 1878. U-plan S front, the centre set behind a parapeted loggia whose W bay forms a gabled porch. At the bargeboard-gabled E end, a full-height canted bay window, its first floor openings surmounted by a large sundial. The broader W end is carried up as a square tower fronted by a two-storey canted bay window; four-light mullioned and transomed window to the second floor. French pavilion roof but with bargeboarded dormer windows and topped by a square cupola, its sides glazed, the piended roof surmounted by cresting. In this tower's inner angle with the NW range, a conical-roofed round tower.

FINEGAND FARM, 2.7km. N. U-plan group of house and steading of *c.* 1800, all built of whitewashed rubble. The central range is occupied by the two-storey farmhouse, its S front of three bays. The steading ranges project on either side. On the W side of the l. range, a circular horsemill.

GLENKILRIE HOUSE, 3.3km. S. Whitewashed and crowstep-gabled mid-C19 small laird's house, with a conical-roofed round tower. Courtyard of offices at the rear.

CAIRN, Lair, 0.8km. W. On a low knoll, a large circular ring-cairn, probably of the late third or early second millennium B.C. It is 15m. in diameter and stands 0.3m. high. Fairly intact boulder kerb at the outer face of the bank. Only two boulders remain of the inner kerb round the circular court which is *c.* 4m. in diameter and placed E of centre.

STANDING STONES, Broughdearg, 3.5km. NNW. Pair of flat-topped stones, *c.* 1.6m. and 1.5m. high, erected probably in the second millennium B.C. They stand *c.* 3m. apart.

DALNAGLAR CASTLE. *See* p. 311.

CRIEFF

8020

Occupying a steeply sloping site, Crieff is a medium-sized town and the capital of Strathearn. It began as a burgh of barony founded in 1672 under the feudal superiority of the Earls (later, in the Jacobite peerage, Dukes) of Perth. Whatever existed of that settlement was 'burned to the last house' by the Jacobite army in 1716 and the present town developed from the 1730s when James Drummond, titular third Duke of Perth, laid out James Square and granted feus for houses to be built along most of High Street and West High Street. After the 1745 Jacobite rising the Drummonds' estates were forfeited and *c.* 1774 the Commissioners of

Annexed Estates laid out and granted feus in Commissioner Street, the N part of King Street, Galvelmore Street and Tainshe's Lane to the S of High Street and, to the N of High Street, in Hill Street and the backlands of High Street as far W as Comrie Street. Soon after being granted the forfeited estates of the Drummonds of Perth in 1785 Captain James Drummond of Lundin (later first Lord Perth of Stobhall) extended King Street further S and laid out Mitchell Street, Miller Street, Comrie Street and Milnab Street to the N and NW of High Street and West High Street. Perth Road at the E end of the town was formed *c.* 1790 and Comrie Road at the W end in 1804. By the 1790s Crieff, although its population was still under 600, was a summer resort for 'people of taste and science' attracted by its setting and 'the serene air, and the dry healthy situation'.[*]

The population had risen to over 3,000 by the 1820s and to over 3,500 by 1850. A further fillip to expansion and prosperity was given by the opening of the railway to Auchterarder and thence to Perth and Stirling in 1856. In 1882 the *Ordnance Gazetteer of Scotland* asserted that, 'where scarcely thirty years ago villas and cottages ornées [sic] were almost totally wanting, they now may be counted by dozens, and only within the last decade £200,000 has been expended on new building.'[†] Industrial undertakings (tanneries, woollen and linen mills, a brewery, a vitriol works) had been established, not always successfully, at Crieff since the late C18 and continued through the C19 and much of the C20 but the town's dominant character is that of a commercial centre for the rural hinterland and the tourists who descend upon it.

CHURCHES

CRIEFF BAPTIST CHURCH, corner of King Street and Addison Terrace. Built in 1925–6. Small harled rectangle, the door and windows roundheaded.

CRIEFF FREE CHURCH, Comrie Street and Coldwells Road. Secularized. By *J.J. Stevenson* and *Robert Ewan*, 1881–2, and dominating its corner site. Austere Gothic, much of the detail culled from Dunblane Cathedral, executed in hammer-dressed Alloa red sandstone, the roofs covered with green slates. Nave with W and E aisles and small S transepts marked off by stepped buttresses whose tops slope into the walling; NE steeple. Advantage is taken of the steep slope of the site to provide a basement at the S end, its entrance a moulded doorway in the front gable. Above this entrance, three plain and narrow rectangular windows light the church's vestibule. At gallery level, a trio of tall and narrow windows (cf. Dunblane Cathedral), each of two lancet lights with blind arcaded panels at the bottom and a quatrefoil in the head.

---

[*] So reported *The Statistical Account of Scotland*, ix (1793), 590.
[†] *Ordnance Gazetteer of Scotland*, ed. Francis H. Groome, ii (1882), 307.

Crieff

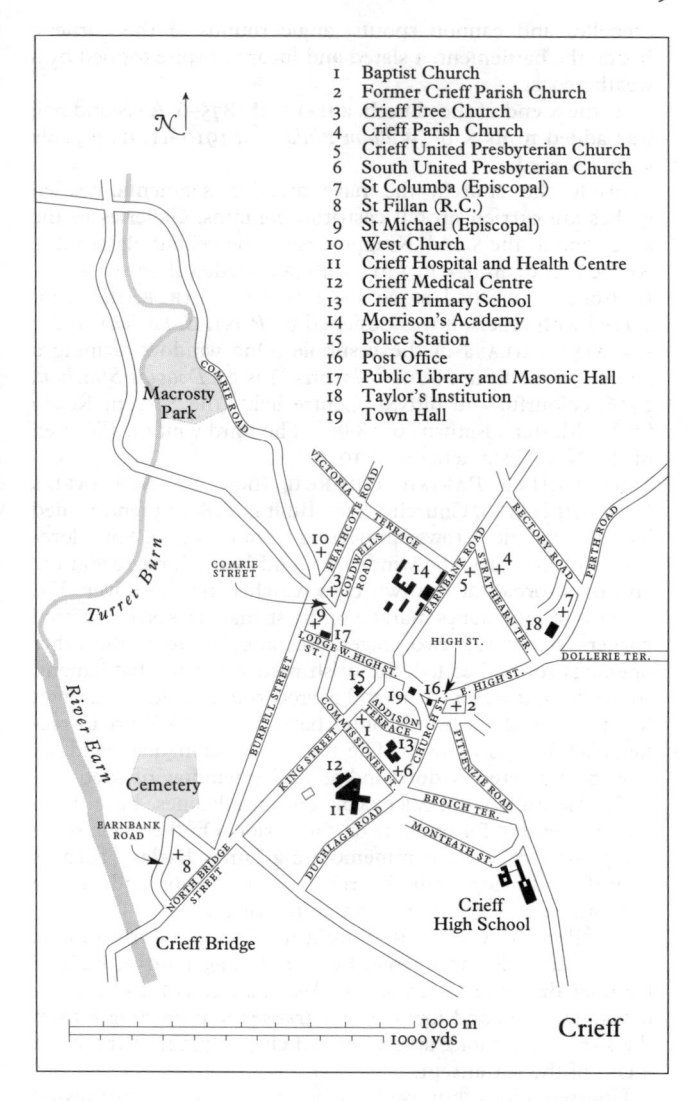

1 Baptist Church
2 Former Crieff Parish Church
3 Crieff Free Church
4 Crieff Parish Church
5 Crieff United Presbyterian Church
6 South United Presbyterian Church
7 St Columba (Episcopal)
8 St Fillan (R.C.)
9 St Michael (Episcopal)
10 West Church
11 Crieff Hospital and Health Centre
12 Crieff Medical Centre
13 Crieff Primary School
14 Morrison's Academy
15 Police Station
16 Post Office
17 Public Library and Masonic Hall
18 Taylor's Institution
19 Town Hall

In the gable of each entrance, a traceried circular window. At the E transept, the hoodmoulded and nook-shafted entrance to the church; blind arcading in the pointed head. In the sides of the nave, Y-traceried clearstorey windows. The main windows to the aisles are each of four narrow lancet lights contained in a broad pointed arch (cf. Dunblane Cathedral). The tops of the aisle walls are marked off by string courses to suggest parapets which are pierced by quatrefoil lights.

The design of the steeple is also derived from Dunblane Cathedral. Two-light belfry openings. Battlement with broad crenelles and cannon spouts; angle rounds at the corners. Inside the battlement, a slated and lucarned spire topped by a weathercock.

At the N end of the church, a HALL of 1875–6. A second hall was added to its N by *William Finlayson*, 1910–11, its E gable jerkin-headed.

Inside the church, the nave arcades' segmental-headed arches are carried on tall cast-iron columns. Galleries in the aisles and at the S end. Kingpost roof, the ceiling plastered. – At the N end, an oak PULPIT with late medieval decoration. – In front, a polished stone COMMUNION TABLE, the front carved with reliefs; it was designed by *Robert S. Lorimer*, 1929. – STAINED GLASS in the vestibule. One window (arming a knight (scene from *Pilgrim's Progress*)) is by *Douglas Strachan*, 1926, colourful and bitty. – Centre light (the Servant Ready for his Master's Return) of 1888. – The third window (Women of the New Testament) is of 1929.

Former CRIEFF PARISH CHURCH (now ST MICHAEL'S CHURCH HALL), Church Street. Built in 1786, a piend-roofed harled rectangle, a tower projecting from its S side. This elevation is of five bays, the windows round-headed, narrow at the end bays, broad at the two bays which flank the tower. The tower is of four stages marked off by string courses; chamfered corners at the top two stages. Rectangular door, the other openings round-headed. Tudorish merlons at the battlement. In the W gable a pair of tall and narrow round-headed windows like those of the S front's outer bays. This gable's broad rectangular door is of 1890. The E gable's rectangular windows have been altered. N door and adjoining window of 1890.

Rubble-walled GRAVEYARD. The headstones have been removed except for one line on the W side. On the S side some GRAVE-SLABS. One, commemorating James Barlas †1810, is carved at the top with the relief of an anchor and, at the bottom, with skulls, bones and an hourglass.

CRIEFF PARISH CHURCH, Strathearn Terrace. Early Gothic with a very tall NW steeple, by *G. T. Ewing*, 1880–2, built of hammer-dressed red sandstone. Aisled nave, its E end a semi-octagonal apse, and low two-bay transepts; projecting E from the S transept, a long apsidal-ended chapel; plain vestry at the E end of the N transept.

Unostentatious but well-heeled detail. At the buttressed aisles windows of three stepped cusped lights. Rose windows at the nave's clearstorey. The transept and apse windows are each of two pointed lights with a quatrefoil in the head. Cusped lights to the SE chapel. The W corners of the nave are clasped by pinnacled octagonal turrets from which project set-back buttresses. At the nave's W gable immensely tall windows, each of three lancet lights; circular window in the apex of the gable. Broad but simple pointed entrance flanked by small windows whose hoodmoulding is carried as a string course across the corner turrets and the ends of the aisles. In the W end of each aisle, a pair of pointed lights.

The steeple dominates by height rather than elaboration. At its belfry very tall pointed openings, and blind arcading under the wallhead cornice. At each face, a gable pierced by a rose window, its outer lights dummies. A small lead spire rises within the gables.

Inside, pointed arches to the nave arcades, the columns' capitals left in block. The label stops of the hoodmoulding over the E arches are carved with the heads of John Knox on the N and the Rev. John Cunningham, Minister of Crieff when this church was built, on the S. Boarded wooden roof over the nave. Arcaded panels on top of the braces of the aisle roofs. W gallery with a plain Gothic front.

On the N side of the entrance to the chancel, the PULPIT made by *D. Beveridge* in 1890. Columns of veined marble support its white marble octagonal body, one face carved by *W. G. Stevenson* with a relief of Our Lord. – In the centre of the chancel, a Lorimerian oak COMMUNION TABLE of 1921. – FONT very similar to the pulpit and perhaps also by Beveridge. – ORGAN behind the communion table, by *H. Hilsdon Ltd.*, probably also of 1921.

STAINED GLASS. The three windows of the apse (the Crucifixion) are of *c.* 1910. – In the S transept, a narrative window (Our Lord with the Doctors in the Temple) by *Camm & Co.*, 1895. – This transept's other window (Faith; the Sower) is of *c.* 1900. – In the S aisle, a three-light window (St Paul) by *W. & J.J. Kier*, 1882, bright and cheerful. – Modernistic window of *c.* 1945 to members of the Morton family. – Also modernistic but better, a window (Scenes from the Life of Our Lord, and St John the Baptist) by *Marjorie Kemp*, 1950. – In the N transept, two late C19 windows (Martha and Mary; Ruth and Naomi; Simeon and Our Lord; Jacob and Pharaoh). – At the E end of the N aisle, a lushly coloured narrative window (Abraham and Angels) by *Heaton, Butler & Bayne*, 1889. – To its W, a characteristically colourful window (the Good Shepherd) by *William Wilson*, 1947. – Then another window by Wilson (Our Lord calling the Apostles) of *c.* 1950. – In the W window, three lights. The centre light (St Michael) is by the *Abbey Studio*, 1958. The side lights (David; a Woman and Children) were added *c.* 1960.

In the vestibule, a wall MONUMENT to James Drummond of Milnab †1882, with a portrait bust in relief. – Also in the vestibule, a BELL of 1605 from the medieval Crieff Parish Church demolished in the 1780s.

Flanking the path to the entrance of the church, a pair of tall cast-iron LAMP STANDARDS of 1882 designed by *George Gilbert Scott Jun.*

CRIEFF SOUTH UNITED PRESBYTERIAN CHURCH, corner of Commissioner Street and Duchlage Road. Secularized. By *John Glendinning*, 1856–7. Broad and low Gothic box. Pinnacled diagonal buttresses at the corners of the front gable.

CRIEFF UNITED PRESBYTERIAN CHURCH (now ST ANDREW'S HALLS), corner of Ferntower Road and Strathearn Terrace.

By *T. L. Watson*, 1883–4, the general composition taken from J.J. Stevenson's former Kelvinside Free Church (Glasgow) of 1862. First Pointed, built of hammer-dressed red sandstone. Nave, its N (liturgical W) end apsed, and tall aisles stopped one bay short of the S end; NW transept and NE steeple. Paired lancet windows at the aisles. The transept's lancets have hood-moulds with foliaged label stops. At the nave's N apse, tall nook-shafted cusped lights, their hoodmoulds' label stops again foliaged. On the roof of the nave, a slated octagonal flèche.

The steeple is tall but austere. At the corners of the lower four stages, set-back buttresses. Above, at the ashlar-faced belfry, these are surmounted by spired octagonal buttresses. In each of the belfry's main faces a tall nook-shafted opening, its hoodmould's label stops again foliaged. Small lucarnes at the octagonal spire.

Inside, tall stilted pointed arches at the E and W arcades. Curvaceous front to the N gallery. – At the S end, a hugely roomy PULPIT backed by the case of the ORGAN of 1905 (by *Norman & Beard*). – STAINED GLASS. In the E wall, a two-light medievalizing window (Dorcas and Lydia) of 1936. – In the W wall, under the gallery, a strongly coloured three-light window (Martha, St Francis and St Ronan) by *Gordon Webster*, 1971. – In the vestibule, two lights (St Andrew and St James) of 1969 and also by Webster.

ST COLUMBA (Episcopal), Perth Road. By *McLaren, Murdoch & Hamilton*, 1987. Broad and low rectangle, the side walls dry-dashed, the roof covered with concrete tiles. Broken-pedimented front gable of buff-coloured blockwork. Hall accommodation is placed at the E end, the church itself, marked out by larger windows, at the W.

Inside, a couple of mementoes of the previous church on the site. Brass eagle LECTERN gifted in 1881. – STAINED GLASS window on the N side (Adoration of the Magi) by *Wailes & Strang*, 1888.

ST FILLAN (R.C.), Chapel Road. By *Andrew Heiton Jun.*, 1871. Buttressed Gothic box, its N (liturgical E) end apsidal, built of bullnosed masonry. Large rose window and 'bellcote' at the S gable whose harled and half-timbered porch looks an addition of *c.* 1900.

Inside, a hammerbeam roof. – STAINED GLASS. At the N end, two brightly coloured Late Victorian lights (St Fillan and St John the Baptist). – In the E wall, two windows. One (St Theresa of Lisieux) is painterly but not accomplished of the earlier C20. – The other (Our Lord bearing a chalice) of 1990 is signed by *A. McK/Glass/George Young*. – In the W wall a narrative light (the Miraculous Draught of Fishes) of 1999.

ST MICHAEL (Episcopal), Lodge Street. Secularized. Simple Gothic of 1846–7. Nave with a gabled S porch; lower and narrower chancel at the E end.

West Church (now St Ninian's Centre), corner of Comrie Road and Heathcote Road. Secularized. Built as a chapel of ease to serve this end of the town, 1837–8. Large and prominently sited but architecturally disappointing Georgian Gothic box, the front faced with coursed squared masonry, the dressings of broached ashlar. At the outer corners of the front (s) gable, octagonal clasping buttresses, the tops of their pinnacles now missing. At the centre, a tower. Three of its sides are contained within the church, so the exposed s front, marked off by stepped buttresses, appears as the ashlar-clad centrepiece of the gable. In this face of the tower, a narrow pointed and hoodmoulded window. Topping the tower is the belfry, each of its faces containing a pair of pointed openings and finished with a gable, only the corbelled base of its central pinnacle surviving; at the corners, octagonal clasping buttresses, the tops of their pinnacles also lost. The impact of the front, diminished by the loss of original detail, has been further weakened by the addition in 1982 of a flat-roofed and 'Fyfestone' walled porch and small octagonal chapel to the sw. Tall pointed windows of the 1830s in the rubble-built sides of the church. The interior has been reconstructed for its present use as a lay training centre.

CEMETERY AND PARK

Crieff Cemetery, Ford Road. Laid out c. 1855 and later extended. The main entrance is of the 1850s. Corniced gatepiers flanking the carriage entrance and round-arched gateways for pedestrians. – Immediately s of the entrance, a naturalistically painted cast-iron fountain by *George Smith & Co.* of the *Sun Foundry*, Glasgow, 1887. Figures of herons surround and perch on a lotus.

Macrosty Park, Comrie Road. Well-wooded park between Comrie Road and the Turret Burn, laid out by *Donald McOmish*, 1902. – Octagonal cast-iron bandstand by the *Albion Foundry*, 1906. Corinthian capitalled slender columns support the roof; balustrade with swagged panels round the stage.

PUBLIC BUILDINGS

Crieff Bridge over the River Earn, North Bridge Street and Bridgend. Built in 1866–8; *Alexander Hair* was superintendent of work. Four segmental arches of hammer-dressed masonry; boat-shaped cutwaters.

Crieff High School, off Monteath Street. By *Perth & Kinross County Council*, 1966–70. Five-storey curtain-walled main block, the stair-towers protruding. Single-storey buildings cluster round the base.

Crieff Hospital and Crieff Health Centre, King Street. Single-storey buildings, their walls mostly covered with drydash. The HOSPITAL by the *Common Services Agency* (completed, after the Agency's privatization, by *W. S. Atkins Health Care Ltd.*), 1993–7, has a large expanse of concrete-tiled roof and a Postmodern porch. – Flat-roofed and boxy former HEALTH CENTRE of 1970 immediately to the W.

CRIEFF MEDICAL CENTRE, King Street. By *Panton Sargent*, 2001. Butterfly plan with a two-storey central block and single-storey wings. Drydashed, with brick trimmings; shallow-pitched ribbed metal roofs.

CRIEFF PRIMARY SCHOOL, Commissioner Street. The earliest part of the two-storey front block, at the W end, is by *Thomas Pilkington & Son*, 1856–7. First-floor window of five Gothic lights in the bellcoted front gable. Plain E extensions of 1874 and 1938 (by the Perth County Architect, *A. Watt Allison*). At the back, a two-storey NE wing of 1938 and a single-storey NW wing by *Robert Ewan*, 1898.

MORRISON'S ACADEMY, Ferntower Road. Founded with a bequest from Thomas Morrison, a native of Muthill and builder in Edinburgh. The main school building designed by *Peddie & Kinnear* in 1859 was constructed in two stages, the first, of 1859–60, providing the centrepiece and part to its E, the second, of 1878, the W part. Unaggressive Scottish Baronial, built of stugged and squared masonry. Long S front, its centrepiece of two tall storeys with crowstepped E and W gables and bargeboarded small attic windows. Projecting from this, a three-storey and attic tower, its front gable finished with a gableted bellcote. At the tower's base, the elliptical-arched entrance in a rectangular surround whose hoodmould rises above a panel carved with the academy's coat of arms. Three-light mullioned and transomed first floor window; canted oriel window to the jettied second floor and a small light to the attic. In the inner angles, large conical-roofed round turrets. On each side of the centrepiece, slightly recessed two-storey four-bay sections, their upper windows rising through the eaves to steeply gabled dormerheads with crescent moon, thistle, star and rose finials. Advanced and crowstep-gabled ends, each with a two-storey canted bay window, the E covered by a sloping roof, the W finished with a parapet.

Inside, the first floor of the centrepiece is occupied by the galleried Memorial Hall, its panelling installed by *Scott Morton & Co.* in 1920. The S window is filled with brightly coloured STAINED GLASS by *Douglas Strachan*, 1924. In the central lower light, a depiction of a hand holding a torch. In the upper lights, emblematic figures of Christian Virtues and the scene of a dying soldier given water by a comrade. Set into the panelling of the E wall, a bronze relief bust of Henry Drummond †1897. Opposite, a similar bronze of Daniel John Cunningham by *Oliver Sheppard*, 1911.

Two-storey and attic JOHN SMITH BUILDING to the SE. Of 1956 but in the manner of fifty years earlier. Built of bullnosed ashlar from the demolished Duncrub Castle but quite plain except for crowstepped gables and a canted bay containing the entrance. – Broad-eaved and bargeboarded LODGE at the SE entrance, by *Peddie & Kinnear*, 1859–60.

POLICE STATION, King Street. Plain Scots Jacobean, by *David Smart*, 1898–1900. At the recessed S bay, a stone bearing the initials IW, a crowned thistle, the tongs, horseshoe and hammer of a blacksmith, and the date 1736.

POST OFFICE, High Street. By *H.M. Office of Works* (superintending architect: *George Hislop*), 1906. Scots Renaissance in polished ashlar. Bowed oriel window over the canopied round-arched entrance.

PUBLIC LIBRARY AND MASONIC HALL, corner of Comrie Street and Lodge Street. Built in 1816 by *James Marshall*, mason, and *John Keay*, wright, for St Michael's Lodge of Freemasons. Partly rebuilt in 1888. The ashlar-faced two-storey front to Comrie Street was originally a symmetrical five-bay U, the sides of the recessed centrepiece splayed, its middle topped by a parapet displaying a panel inscribed in flowery lettering with 'St Michael's Lodge/1816'. Central entrance, the necks of its columns decorated with upright acanthus leaves. Above the entrance, a three-light window, the outer openings dummies. At the outer bays, almost square first-floor windows. Giant pilasters at the outer corners. A late C19 shopfront now occupies the ground floor of the two S bays. The N two bays forming the r. limb of the U were rebuilt in 1888 and project further towards the street and are higher than originally, the first-floor windows taller than the Georgian windows of the rest. A basement at the long S elevation to the steeply falling Lodge Street. Very tall ground-floor windows. At first-floor level, moulded oblong panels, one inscribed MASONS HALL.

TAYLOR'S INSTITUTION, Perth Road. Now a house and Royal British Legion Club. Built as a charity school under the will of the tallow chandler, William Taylor, it is by *Andrew Heiton Sen.*, 1842–3. Jacobean front block (OLD SCHOOLHOUSE), its porch with pinnacled pilasters and a curvilinear gable. Gablets over the first-floor windows. Behind and at right angles, the single-storey school proper, a Jacobean bellcote crowning an advanced gable. Addition by *Andrew McNeil*, mason in Crieff, adapting a design by *Robert Wright*, 1860.

TOWN HALL, High Street. Built in 1850. L-plan, the jamb largely hidden, and with low outshots S of the main block; a tower for civic importance. The main block is crowstep-gabled, built of squared and coursed hammer-dressed masonry. In its W side, shouldered-arched ground-floor windows under obtusely pointed relieving arches. At the first floor, tall pointed windows rising into crowstepped dormerheads; glazing pattern of round panes set in a grid. Tall pointed window in each gable. Projecting from near the N end of the W side is the plain tower containing the pointed entrance under an empty panel frame. The main block's wallhead cornice is carried across the tower as a sill course under a pointed window. High up in each side, a clock face in a Georgian Gothic surround. The tower's wallhead cornice is broken by small pointed and gableted belfry openings. Extravagantly bellcast eaves to the slated pyramidal spire.

DESCRIPTION

COMRIE ROAD, cut into the steep slope of hillside down to the Turret Burn, is the entry from the NW. On its E side, set back above the road to enjoy the view are villas of the later C19, mostly bay-windowed and bargeboarded, with bracketed eaves. At DUNFILLAN, an Italianate low tower. On the W side of the road, the Macrosty Park (*see* Cemetery and Park, above). At Comrie Road's SE end, on the W corner of Heathcote Road and looking down Burrell Street, is the former West Church (*see* Churches, above).

COMRIE STREET continues the line of Comrie Road to the SE. At its start, on the SW side, the town's Lorimerian WAR MEMORIAL of *c.* 1920, constructed of diagonally broached ashlar. Battered octagonal base supporting an octagonal stepped and battered pedestal surmounted by a cross-finialled shaft, also octagonal, its cornice carved with thistles and coats of arms. The buildings are mostly mid- and late C19 commercial architecture. Free Jacobean Nos. 42–50 of 1894 on the SW side, the front of bullnosed red sandstone. An oriel window, its parapet pierced, projects from an off-centre gablet. A tall vertical accent on the W corner of Coldwells Road is provided by the former Crieff Free Church (*see* Churches, above). At the street's SE end, on the corner of Lodge Street, the Public Library and Masonic Hall (*see* Public Buildings, above).

BURRELL STREET running downhill to the S from Comrie Street's NW end starts off with vernacular housing of the early and mid C19. More of the same at BURRELL SQUARE, its earlier name of The Octagon a more accurate description of its shape. Standing in its NE corner, an early C19 LAMP STANDARD. Corniced ashlar pier with panelled sides and a rosetted frieze. On it, a large urn to which are fixed the remains of a lampholder. In Burrell Street S of Burrell Square, mid-C19 vernacular housing, mostly of two storeys, predominates. Fixed to the S gable of No. 19, on the W side, a carved early Victorian heraldic achievement of the royal coat of arms, its base bearing the painted inscription 6/7 BN THE BLACK WATCH R.H.R. No. 45 (SAUCHIE COTTAGE) of the later C19 displays folk art. The ground-floor windows and door are set in Doric pilastered surrounds, the windows' pilasters with leafy enrichment under the capitals, the pilasters and frieze of the door carved with leafy branches and rosettes. In BROICH ROAD to the E, the former gasworks (*see* below). NORTH BRIDGE STREET continues Burrell Street SW. On its SE side, No. 2, an early C19 house of two storeys and an attic. Front of broached ashlar with rusticated quoins and a mutuled cornice. Fluted frieze at the console-cornered doorpiece. In CHAPEL ROAD to the NW, St Fillan's R.C. Church (*see* Churches, above). At the SW end of

North Bridge Street, Crieff Bridge crosses the River Earn (*see* Public Buildings, above).

LODGE STREET, running E from Burrell Square, is the introduction to Crieff's commercial centre. On its N side, the former St Michael's Episcopal Church and the long side elevation of the Public Library and Masonic Hall (*see* Churches and Public Buildings, above). On the S, at the corner of Galvelmore Street, the crowstep-gabled BANK OF SCOTLAND of 1883, a tall conical-roofed slated spire over the bowed corner.

WEST HIGH STREET continues the line of Lodge Street. On its E corner with Comrie Street, SERVITE HOUSE (No. 29 Comrie Street) by *Nicoll Russell Studios*, 1990–2, a four-storey and attic block of flats over shops. W and S elevations of blockwork with tiled pitched roofs. Corner entrance recessed between the semi-octagonal ends of the street elevations, the High Street end projected above the ground floor as a corbelled-out tower supported on slender columns. The result appears contrived although not without presence. Opposite, on the S side of West High Street, the CLYDESDALE BANK (originally the Union Bank), a palazzo of 1868, the first-floor window surrounds pilastered and corniced. Then solid Victorian small-town commercial architecture. On the N, the late C19 two-storey and attic No. 11. Gablets over the end bays. First-floor windows in nook-shafted architraves; below them, a band of polished ashlar decorated with a pair of panels carved with quatrefoils under each opening.

JAMES SQUARE'S N side continues the building line and roadway of West High Street. First, the GLENBURN HOTEL of 1887. It is of three storeys and an attic. Three-bay façade. At the steeply gabled outer bays, balustraded two-storey oriel windows sitting on the cornice over the ground-floor shopfronts. Corniced first- and second-floor windows at the centre whose wallhead supports a tall chimney. Next door, the WAVERLEY HOTEL, also late C19 and of three storeys and an attic but the front of only two bays, again with balustraded oriels supported by the shopfront's cornice; a pair of Jacobean stepped gablets at the attic. Then the four-storey ANCASTER HOTEL, plain Late Georgian but the front covered in render masquerading as bullnosed masonry.

Beyond this, THE ROYAL BANK OF SCOTLAND and DRUMMOND HOTEL, both designed by *David Rhind* and built as a single development by the Commercial Bank of Scotland in 1872–4. The three-storey and attic front is all of hammer-dressed masonry, the floors and wallhead line through, and at each outer corner is a channelled pilaster strip topped by an urn but it is divided into two unequal parts by a tower (belonging to the hotel). The W part (the bank) is a Baroque three-bay palazzo. Lugged architraves and bracketed sills at the ground-floor windows. At the outer bays of the first floor, round-headed and keystoned windows framed by pilasters and surmounted by triangular pediments. Centre window of three round-headed and keystoned lights, again framed by pilasters which support a single cornice breaking forward on consoles to carry a segmental pediment over the middle light. Under this window, a balustraded balcony carried on heavy foliaged consoles. Small second-floor windows with double-lugged architraves. Mutuled wallhead cornice on which stand three heavy dormer windows, all with consoled broken pediments, the outer two triangular, the centre segmental. The off-centre unadvanced tower is a storey higher and marked off by channelled pilaster strips. Two-storey canted oriel on heavy corbelling. At the top, ball finials on the corners. Iron-crowned French pavilion roof, a heavy segmental-pedimented stone dormer at its front. The two-bay hotel frontage E of the tower is plain except for the pilastered and keystoned round-arched entrance under a balustraded stone balcony borne on heavy consoles.

s of the main road James Square slopes steeply downhill but at its centre the level of the road is maintained by a D-shaped platform formed in 1882. At each end of the platform's semicircular railing, a cast-iron dolphin-entwined LAMP STANDARD made by *George Smith & Co.* of the *Sun Foundry*, Glasgow, and erected in 1889 as a belated commemoration of Queen Victoria's Golden Jubilee. On the centre of the platform is the MURRAY FOUNTAIN by *William Mossman*, 1893–4, ERECTED BY THE INHABITANTS OF THE BURGH OF CRIEFF A RECOGNITION OF MANY BENEFITS RECEIVED FROM THE MURRAYS OF OCHTERTYRE. Large polished grey granite square structure. At each face, a round-headed arch framed by Corinthian pilasters, their shafts of polished pink granite. Beneath each arch, a lion's-head spout to pour water into a pink granite basin. On top, a dome almost hidden by four cavorting dolphins whose upright tails support a ball finial of pink granite; the grinning heads of the N and S dolphins bear shields displaying coats of arms.

On the E and W sides of James Square, undistinguished architecture, Victorian on the W, of 1969 on the E. On the S side of the square, on the W corner of King Street, the former NORTH OF SCOTLAND BANK of 1878, a pompous little palazzo. Granite shafted columns at the portico whose parapet is carved with a shield bearing a saltire. Over the splayed NE corner, an iron-crested and fish-scale-slated small dome of French inspiration. On the E corner with King Street, a plain early C19 block (No. 29 James Square).

KING STREET's buildings are mostly vernacular of the mid and later C19. Set back on the W side, the Police Station (*see* Public Buildings, above). On the S corner of Addison Terrace, Crieff Baptist Church (*see* Churches, above). Opposite, Nos. 37–41 King Street, originally the UNIONIST CLUB, by *G. T. Ewing*, 1901. Two tall storeys. The ground floor is occupied by shops. Above them, a corbelled cornice supporting the fronts of two oriel windows, one tower-like and of ashlar, the other gabled and mostly of wood. On the NW corner of King

Street and Commissioner Street, an Edwardian Free Style block (Nos. 49–55 King Street and Nos. 55–59 Commissioner Street) by *Gordon L. Wright*, 1906–7. Walls of purplish hammer-dressed masonry with dressings of buff-coloured polished ashlar; bracketed broad eaves. At the fat domed corner turret, a first-floor window in a Baroque aedicule. At the front to Commissioner Street, a large round-arched first-floor window (originally lighting a tearoom) fronted by an Art Nouveau iron balcony. Far drabber is the red sandstone block (Nos. 58–64 King Street and Nos. 51–53 Commissioner Street) of *c.* 1890 on the opposite corner, its conical-roofed corner tower routine. C19 vernacular to the s.

In COMMISSIONER STREET E of King Street, Crieff Primary School and the former Crieff South United Presbyterian Church (*see* Churches and Public Buildings, above).

HIGH STREET leading E from James Square is of mixed character but commercial architecture of the later C19 dominates. Among this, on the s side, Nos. 13–17, a two-storey and attic building of the earlier C19. Pilastered centre door under a three-light window (the centre light a dummy) and a chimneyed gablet. On the N side, the former BRITISH LINEN CO. BANK (Nos. 30–32) of *c.* 1905 by *Peddie & Washington Browne* and in the inventively detailed Jacobean-French Renaissance manner used by them for that company's premises. Three storeys, of polished red sandstone ashlar. Conical-roofed round tower containing the principal entrance. This is an elaborate pedimented aedicule, the stumpy pilaster shafts decorated with lozenges. Capitals of Corinthian inspiration but the volutes are formed by dolphins and surmounted by cherubs' heads; a carved shell in the pediment. The main ground-floor window lighting the banking hall is a broad segmental arch springing from attached piers, their shafts panelled with lozenges, their capitals carved with foliaged volutes and cherubs' heads. First-floor windows, all mullioned and transomed, set between pilasters, their shafts decorated with round and semicircular panels, their capitals carved variously with dolphins, upside-down volutes, fruit and dragons. Above the first-floor windows, a band carved with shells. At the top floor of the tower, corniced windows set between panelled pilasters. At the main elevation, a pair of pilastered second-floor windows rising into shaped dormerheads. Neo-Jacobean panelling survives in the former banking hall. For the Town Hall and Post Office on the s side of High Street, *see* Public Buildings, above.

EAST HIGH STREET is predominantly Victorian, the commercial character still strong. On the N side, at the start, a late C19 cast-iron BAILIE'S LAMP by *Walter Macfarlane & Co.* of the *Saracen Foundry*, Glasgow. On the s side, on the E corner of Ramsay Street, the late C19 two-storey CROWN INN HOTEL, its splayed corner topped by a squat ogee-roofed dome. Opposite, on the N of East High Street, Nos. 28–30, built for the Co-operative Society in 1912. Three-storey front of polished ashlar divided into two broad bays by pilasters at the ends and centre. The first-floor windows are tripartite, with consoled cornices and pediments over the centre lights. Plain three-light windows to the second floor. Further E, on the S side, THE CRIEFF HOTEL. Its main block is of 1901. Sitting on the cornice over the ground floor are canted oriel windows finished with crenellated parapets. At the attic, a semicircular-pedimented dormer window flanked by gablets. Further out on the S side at Nos. 77–83, two-storey terraced houses of the later C19, the detail mostly Georgian survival with heavy anta-pilastered doorpieces but corbels under the wallhead cornice. Beyond is the TOWER HOTEL. Set-back main block of the mid C19, the first-floor windows hoodmoulded. The NE jamb may be late C18 in origin but its tower, covered with a steep pyramidal slated roof, is of the mid or later C19. In the E gable of the adjoining Nos. 89–91 of the earlier C19, a large Gothic dummy window.

STRATHEARN TERRACE leading off East High Street to the NE contains Victorian villas. Among them, No. 10 is of the 1860s, the detail Gothic. Two storeys of stugged purplish ashlar with buff-coloured polished dressings. Asymmetrical U-plan front, the l. of the gabled wings broader and higher than the r. and with a two-storey sloping-roofed bay window which narrows at the upper floor. At the r. wing, splayed corners corbelled to the square under the eaves. Central porch, the stonework energetically corbelled under the eaves of the sloping roof to form pointed arches containing the entrance and sidelights. All windows pointed, the two first-floor ones of the centrepiece with gableted dormerheads. On the S side, a two-storey bay window narrowed at the upper floor. For the competing ecclesiastical edifices of Crieff Parish Church and, on the corner of Ferntower Road, the former Crieff United Presbyterian Church (St Andrew's Halls) *see* Churches, above. Also in FERNTOWER ROAD, Morrison's Academy (*see* Public Buildings, above).

PERTH ROAD at the end of East High Street leads out of town. Near its start, on the l., the former Taylor's Institution and St Columba's Episcopal Church (*see* Churches and Public Buildings, above). Immediately N of the church, THE OLD RECTORY which was built as the parsonage of St Columba's Episcopal Church in 1870. Large two-storey villa, gabled and gableted, the stonework of hammer-dressed masonry. Pointed windows to affirm its ecclesiastical status. Further out, a broad-eaved LODGE of 1817 to the demolished Ferntower. Gabled splay-sided front projection with Gothic windows and the heraldic achievement of Mary Anne Menzies, *suo jure* Baroness Abercromby, then owner of Ferntower.

CRIEFF HYDRO, Ewanfield. Large and bleak Scots Jacobean, by *Robert Ewan*, 1867–8, built of purplish masonry (hammer-dressed at the ground floor, stugged above) with buff dressings. Conical-roofed round corner towers; round and square turrets with conical or pyramidal roofs. N entrance under a glazed awning supported on cast-iron brackets. Above it, a huge tower, its parapet in the form of a shaped gable, with ogee-roofed square corner turrets. The main block's S wings were extended in 1878. Between them, a two-storey Winter Garden of 1903–4, its elaborate cast-iron and wooden structure vaguely Italianate; it was extended in 1991 by *James Denholm Associates*. E wing of 1888 and W wing of 1894, both in the same manner as the 1860s work. Extensive late C20 additions.

INCHGLAS, Broich Terrace. Idiosyncratic Gothic villa designed in 1859 by *F.T. Pilkington* as his own home and office. Walling of purplish squared rubble crossed by bands of buff-coloured stone. Two storeys over a sunk basement, the first-floor windows rising into dormerheads with carved bargeboards. The general shape is an L, with a NE jamb. Splayed across the SE inner angle, a porch under a triangular oriel window. At the W end of the main block's S front, a full-height bow abutting the end gable which is finished with a ringed cross. Oriel window near the W elevation's N end. Varied treatment of the windows, some segmental-headed, others round-arched or with sawtoothed shouldered arches.

INTERIOR. A door on the E side of the porch opens into what was Pilkington's study (now dining room). Behind, the former drawing office (now kitchen) with a beamed ceiling. The family rooms are grouped round a stair hall entered from the porch's N side. This stair hall is top-lit, the cupola shaped like a miniature house. Stair balustrade in a stripped Gothic manner and pierced by quatrefoils. Round-headed doors to the ground-floor rooms, each divided into panels by a saltire. On the S, the morning room, its chimneypiece with a sawtoothed shouldered arch. At the SW, the C19 dining room (now drawing room). Gothic chimneypiece and a beamed ceiling. At the N wall, a trio of stilted segmental-headed arches springing from bell-capitalled columns. The outer two contain doors, the centre a sideboard recess.

On the first floor the room doors are four-panel with sawtooth decoration. Above the original dining room, the C19 drawing room (now a bedroom). Tunnel-vaulted plaster ceiling divided into compartments, with delicate plaster enrichment to the stiles and cornice. Gothic chimneypiece. The other bedrooms are also tunnel-vaulted but plainer.

GAS WORKS, Broich Road. Built in 1842–3. There survives a sunk-pit circular gasholder with lattice-girder guides.

CAIRN, Rottenreoch, 2.5 km. SW. On a gently sloping hillside above the River Earn, a grass-covered long cairn, probably formed in the third millennium B.C. and now standing $c.$ 1 m. high. It is $c.$ 49 m. long with rounded ends, the NE $c.$ 13.7 m. broad, the SW $c.$ 10.7 m. but, roughly in the centre, the cairn bulges out to a breadth of $c.$ 15.2 m. The mound covers at least two earlier and originally free-standing chambered tombs which were probably constructed in the fourth millennium B.C. Some of the slab walls of one of these protrude at the NE end and show that it was at least 3.7 m. long and $c.$ 1 m. broad. The second tomb is placed *c.* 10m. to the sw, the barely visible tops of three slabs suggesting it was only *c.* 1.5m. long. Four other upright slabs are visible at the sw end where there may have been another tomb.

CROOK OF DEVON

Village at the crossing of the Devon on the road between Kinross and Stirling. It was made a burgh of barony in 1615.

FOSSOWAY, ST SERF'S AND DEVONSIDE CHURCH, Church Road. Simple harled kirk of 1805–6 designed by Mr *Black*, architect at Harviestoun, perhaps *James Black*. It is a straightforward rectangle with a ball finial on the E gable. On the W gable, a bellcote, its stone pyramid roof supported by two tiers of balusters on the N and S sides and with the E and W sides open; it is very similar to the bellcote of 1729 at Orwell Parish Church in Milnathort (q.v.) and presumably reused from the previous church on this site, also built in 1729. s front of four bays, the outer two containing pointed doors; big Y-traceried windows (originally flanking the pulpit) in the centre bays. Quite small pointed windows in the N side and, in the centre of this wall, a datestone of 1729 from the previous church. A tall and narrow round-arched window in the E gable. A similar window in the W gable was blocked in 1966 when the session house of 1847 was enlarged and heightened to two storeys. Piend-roofed hall extension of 1988 to the W.

The interior was remodelled and refurnished in 1924–5 when a chancel was formed at the E end and a gallery erected at the w. – STAINED GLASS. In the two s windows, brightly coloured glass of 1877, abstract except for panels of foliage and coats of arms. – In the N wall, two lights ('Suffer the little children to come unto me'; Our Lord with Martha and Mary) by *William Wilson*, 1962. – E window (the Good Shepherd) of 1946 by *Alexander Strachan*, a disappointing example of his work.

GRAVEYARD. At its NE corner, a rubble-built HEARSE HOUSE, dated 1836. Pointed window in the W gable, a broad pointed door in the E.

s of the church, a number of mid- and late C18 HEADSTONES and TABLE STONES. Among them, immediately E of the church, a stone carved with reminders of death and dated 1736 which commemorates the children of William Belfrage. – Immediately s of the church, a stone of 1742 with the initials DK/MB above an engagingly inept angel's head (the soul). – Just to its SE and much smarter, the stone of 1768 to JD and GL. Aedicular with fluted pilasters and a swan-necked pediment, its tympanum carved with a relief of two heads. – To its s, a similar aedicular stone, dated 1776, bearing the initials AC, IB, the pilasters framing an angel's head. – Another aedicule but cruder and steeply pedimented to its E, commemorating James Thomson †1761, an angel's head in the pediment. – Beside this, the slab from a table stone to Andrew Patton and

Isabella Jamie. It is dated 1754. An angel's head at the top, a coat of arms in the middle, and an hourglass at the bottom. – Beside it, the curly pedimented HEADSTONE of 1766 to JK and MM, the front carved in relief with the figure of a woman. – Further W, a large headstone, also of 1766, to James Graham, decorated with emblems of death. – More grisly symbols of mortality, together with a book and an angel's head, on John Toshoch's headstone of 1752 to the NW. – Almost in the SW corner, under a holly tree, the big table stone of 1746 to Andrew Campbell Jun. of Pitfar. Sturdy balusters support the slab which is carved at the top with an angel's head between two trumpeters; at the bottom, a skull, crossbones and hourglass. – To its W, beside the churchyard wall, a headstone to Henry Watson, dated 1741, the carving still crisp, with an angel's head at the top and with a setsquare and dividers to identify Watson as a mason. – Several early C19 headstones N of the church state how many 'Layers' (lairs or burial plots) belong to each.

INSTITUTE, Main Street. Early C20. Harled building, plain except for a faintly Art Nouveau cupola-ventilator.

DESCRIPTION. MAIN STREET is *c.* 0.7 km. long but the character given by its predominance of plain Victorian cottages and small houses, backed and sometimes invaded by C20 housing, is architecturally disappointing. CHURCH ROAD leads off to the S to Fossoway, St Serf's and Devonside Parish Church (*see above*). NAEMOOR ROAD, the N continuation of the line of Church Road, crosses a rubble-built humpbacked single-span BRIDGE constructed over the Devon in 1767. N of the bridge, the harled BRIDGE HOUSE, formerly Fossoway Free Church Manse, of *c.* 1840 with a Tudorish bay window and horizontal glazing. In Main Street, a little to the E, the centre of the village is marked by THE INN, crisply dressed in white harl with black-painted window and door surrounds. It is C18 vernacular but some windows were enlarged and dormerheads were added in the C19 and the roof covered with concrete pantiles in the C20. Further E on the N side, a pair of semi-detached cottages, BARNHILL (now pebbledashed) dated 1838 on a skewputt, and GROVE COTTAGE, its rubble walling still exposed, with a skewputt bearing the date 1833. At the E end of the village, on the S side of the road, the INSTITUTE (*see above*). In front stands the WAR MEMORIAL of *c.* 1920, a craggy stone with a foliage-carved panel. Opposite, a MILL of the earlier C19, rubble-built with a ventilator on the pyramidal roof and a wheel at the N end. The building was extended and prettified on its conversion to a shop in the later C20. On the E side of the lane which goes past the mill, the early C19 TULLIBOLE MILL HOUSE, its pilastered doorpiece eroded by cleaning. Contemporary courtyard steading behind.

HOUSE OF ALDIE. *See* p. 413.
TULLIEBOLE CASTLE. *See* p. 737.

CROSSMOUNT HOUSE
4.5 km. ESE of Kinloch Rannoch

Harled laird's house of *c.* 1800. Main block of two storeys above a half-sunk basement; piended platform roof. Three-bay S front, the centre advanced and battlemented. At the ends, single-storey and basement pavilions with tall ground-floor windows. – Broad-eaved LODGE of 1858. – Early C19 corniced GATEPIERS.

CULDEES CASTLE
2.1 km. ESE of Muthill

Red sandstone ashlar mansion, its mixed castellated and Scottish Baronial character the product of two main stages of development, the first, designed by *James Gillespie Graham* for General Andrew John Drummond *c.* 1810, the second by *David Bryce* and built for R.T.N. Speir in 1866–7.

Gillespie Graham's house was a Georgian battlemented toy fort. Two storeys over a basement. Nearly but not quite symmetrical entrance (S) front of five bays between square corner turrets, the two E bays wider than the W two. Advanced and taller centrepiece, its ground floor fronted by a porch in the form of a miniature castle; above, a hoodmoulded Gothic window of three lights. At the outer bays, two-light hoodmoulded windows, the two at the ground floor E of the porch Gothic, the others with Gothic lights in rectangular surrounds. The general composition of the N elevation mirrored that of the S. Again, an advanced and taller centrepiece placed slightly W of the true centre, its corners here gripped by octagonal turrets pierced by slit windows; at each floor, a rectangular two-light window containing Gothic lights, hoodmoulded at the two main floors. E of this, two bays of bipartite rectangular windows, also with Gothic lights at the main floors. At the NE corner, a slender round tower. W of the centrepiece, a single broad bay, its rectangular and hoodmoulded ground- and first-floor windows each of four Gothic lights. NW corner turret like those at the S elevation but it fronts a large round three-storey and basement tower with tall hoodmoulded rectangular windows to the ground floor and Gothic windows at the basement and two top floors; boldly moulded corbels under the battlement.

In Bryce's remodelling of 1866–7 the entrance was shifted to the N where Gillespie Graham's centrepiece was given a battlemented porch, the door contained in an overarch, and the windows above altered to simple mullioned and transomed openings without hoodmoulds. A similar treatment was accorded to the windows to the l. but those of the principal floor retained their hoodmoulds. The NE tower's battlement was replaced by a corbelled parapet under a fish-scale-slated conical roof. W of the centrepiece the windows of the two main

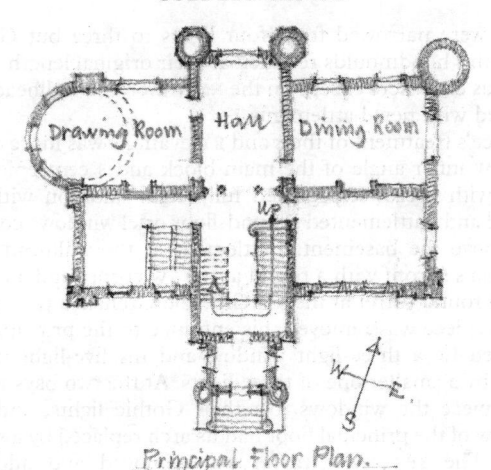

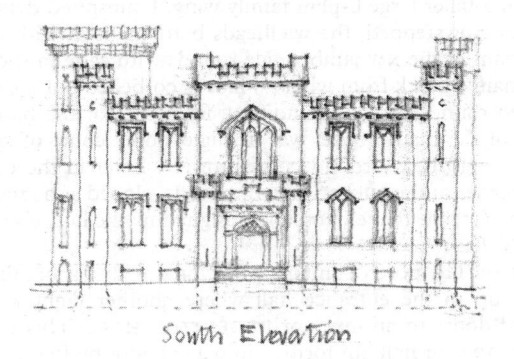

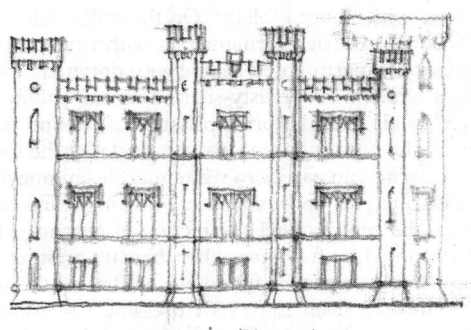

Culdees Castle.
Sketch reconstruction of elevations and principal floor plan in c. 1810

floors were narrowed from four lights to three but Gillespie Graham's hoodmoulds retained at their original length. At this front, as elsewhere except on the NW tower, the wallheads were finished with new battlements.

Bryce's treatment of the S and E elevations was more drastic. The SW inner angle of the main block and S centrepiece was filled with a crowstep-gabled full-height addition with large canted and battlemented ground-floor oriel windows corbelled out above the basement. Battlement at the wallhead of the addition's S front with a round at the SW corner and a conical-roofed round turret at the SE. Gillespie Graham's porch at the S centrepiece was removed, his entrance to the principal floor replaced by a three-light window and his five-light window above by a smaller one of three lights. At the two bays E of the centrepiece the windows lost their Gothic lights, and the E window of the principal floor had its arch replaced by a straight lintel. The SE corner turret was removed and additional windows inserted in its place. To the house's E end, set well back from the N front but projecting boldly to the S, Bryce added a taller large L-plan family wing. Uninspired detail, the gables crowstepped, the wallheads battlemented, with square bartizans at the NW jamb; angle rounds with cannon spouts at the main S block from whose S face is corbelled out a conical-roofed round turret. Extending E from this, at the basement level of the main house, was a single-storey court of kitchen offices with heavy round corner towers. Later in the C19 the NW corner of the kitchen court was redeveloped as a crowstep-gabled Gothic chapel, possibly designed by the house's owner, *R.T.N. Speir*.

INTERIOR. The porch contains a vestibule with a short flight of steps up to the entrance hall where another flight leads to glazed doors to an inner or RECEPTION HALL. This was the early C19 stair hall but formed into a corridor by Bryce, which was remodelled in 1923 by *Robert S. Lorimer* in a free Jacobean manner. Very broad stone chimneypiece on the W side, its surround carved with stylized foliage. On the walls, oak panelling below a deep plaster frieze ornamented with vine enrichment. Curvaceously compartmented ceiling with floriated bosses. On the E side, a screen with a twisty-shafted central column opens onto Bryce's stair hall, the principal stair of routine Jacobean character. In the bow-ended DRAWING ROOM at the Georgian house's NW corner, an early C19 white marble chimneypiece in the Adam manner, the ends of its frieze bearing reliefs of standing cherubs, the centre panel a depiction of peacocks drawing a chariot occupied by two more cherubs with another following behind. The CHAPEL at the E end of Bryce's family wing has a nave formed from the 1860s dressing room and bathroom. The late C19 chancel to the E is entered through a screen of two pointed arches, the principal arch carried on squat round columns of Romanesque character. Also Romanesque the chevron carving over the pointed lights of the E window. Encaustic tiles on the floor; stencil decoration on the walls.

The C19 mansion house has been abandoned. A new house (CULDEES MANSION HOUSE) was built just to its W in 1966–7.

STABLES, 0.3km. E, by *Gillespie Graham*, c. 1810. Castle-style, with battlemented towers and Gothic openings. Small-scale but heavy-handed. – Broad-eaved LODGES of the later C19.

CULTOQUHEY HOUSE
0.7km. SE of Gilmerton

Competent but unexciting Tudor manor house designed by *Robert Smirke* and built for Anthony Maxtone, c. 1820. Generally of two storeys, with a basement to the S, built of polished red sandstone ashlar, all tied round with a first-floor string course.

At the entrance (N) front, advanced and gabled end bays with round-headed slit windows at their top, the E with hood-moulded three-light windows to the main floors, the W with a parapeted porch containing a hoodmoulded four-centred arched door; single-light first-floor window, also hood-moulded. From these ends extend linking sections, the E of two bays with single-light windows, hoodmoulded at the ground floor, the taller W link of one broad bay with hoodmoulded three-light windows and a pedimented dormer window at the attic. The links join the ends to a three-storey tower, its corners with flat clasping buttresses, its plain parapet projected on blocky corbels; hoodmoulded windows, the second floor's of two narrow Gothic lights and placed above a sill course at the level of the W link's wallhead cornice.

W side of four bays, the N with hoodmoulded windows and a narrow additional ground-floor opening inserted in the C20. The advanced S three bays are treated as a unit, their outer bays with narrow first-floor windows, the slightly advanced and gabled centre with a plainly parapeted mullioned and transomed canted bay window containing Gothic lights to the ground floor, a hoodmoulded two-light window to the first floor and a round-headed slit to the attic.

The S elevation to the garden is a variant of the N. Advanced and gabled end bays, also with round-headed slit attic windows. At the E end, three-light windows to the other floors; at the W, a three-light first-floor window. The lower E link has a three-light window to each floor. The one-bay W link and centrepiece are on the same plane, with simply treated windows; over the centrepiece a gable containing another round-headed slit attic window.

Low service courtyard to the E, its E range with a tall hood-moulded S window of three Gothic lights.

Inside, Jacobean compartmented ceilings and Frenchy chimneypieces in the dining and drawing rooms, an Adamish Neoclassical chimneypiece in the library.

DALGUISE HOUSE

4.5 km. s of Logierait

Unpretentious mansion house of the Stewarts of Dalguise, altered and extended in the C19 and C20.

The earliest part is at the s, a harled three-storey block, the windows of its five-bay front quite small. The lintel of the ground floor's centre window (originally the entrance) provides a date of 1753. W of this, a harled two-storey W addition, probably of the 1830s, with tall ground-floor windows at its two-bay S front. E of the original house, another harled extension. It is by *James Gillespie Graham*, 1827. Two tall storeys, with tall windows. S front of two bays, with a Roman Doric pilastered porch, probably a late C19 addition, at the l. bay; at the r., a full-height bow. The house was further extended in 1885 by *Andrew Heiton Jun.* who provided a single-storey bowed and balustraded link from the 1827 extension to a battlemented L-plan tall tower constructed of sneck-harled masonry. Square bartizans at the corners. Tall windows to the ground floor; above these and the first-floor openings are prominent segmental-headed relieving arches. On the tower's E front, a reused coat of arms carved in 1827.

The INTERIOR was altered in 1885 and again in the later C20. The Late Victorian work survives best at the tower's ground-floor room, probably the billiard room, its walls and ceiling pine-panelled in a Baronial manner, with some Gothic detail at the overmantel of the fireplace. Spindly Jacobean stair in the tower's S jamb.

S of the house, a rubble-built STABLES courtyard of the later C18. On its W side, a piend-roofed two-storey house. The E range's outer front has pyramid-roofed end pavilions and, at the centre, a gable containing a round-headed pend arch. – At the S end of the drive, a U of Late Georgian COTTAGES (now, the STANLEY NAIRNE CENTRE) built of white-painted rubble. The N range is divided in two. Each pair consists of a two-storey end house and a pair of single-storey cottages. The short piend-roofed single-storey E and W ranges formerly contained stores but were converted to housing in the later C20.

DALL HOUSE

7 km. WSW of Kinloch Rannoch

Prominently sited harled shooting lodge looking over Loch Rannoch, built in 1854–5 for Thomas Vernon-Wentworth of Wentworth Castle (Yorkshire) to a design by *Mackenzie & Matthews*. Scottish Baronial but lighthearted in its display of crowstepped gables, round towers and turrets with witches'-hat roofs, and steeply pedimented dormerheads. Tall main block, a rectangular turret corbelled out at the NW corner, a tower at the NE. On its W side, the entrance contained in a bowed tower topped by a rectangular caphouse; in the tower's inner angle, a tall round turret. Extensive lower service wing to the s. Behind, undistinguished late C20 structures put up when the house served as the main building of Rannoch School.

DALMUNZIE HOUSE
2 km. NW of Spittal of Glenshee

Large informally composed villa by *George Bennett Mitchell*, built in 1920 for Sir Archibald Birkmyre, a Calcutta industrialist and merchant. It incorporates a small L-plan house of 1874 which peeps through at the centre of the w side and the NE corner.

Scots style, the walls mostly harled, with stone dressings, the gables crowstepped, the dormers gableted. At the stepped s front, a rubble-built small tower containing the entrance under a panel bearing Birkmyre's coat of arms. At the w gable of this front block, conical-roofed corner turrets. The N block's w end is treated as a tower house with gables at the exposed faces. Conical-roofed round tower at its s corner and, at the N, a tower whose bowed sides are surmounted by a rectangular top. Between these towers, the gabled shelter for a bell. Rambling office buildings to the N. The interior, reconstructed after a fire in the 1990s, attempts to evoke the spirit of the 1920s.

LODGE of *c.* 1920 at the s end of the drive. Single-storey, with a conical-roofed round tower.

DALNAGLAR CASTLE
1.1. km. N of Cray

White harled Baronial extravaganza set among trees on a hillside in Glen Shee, it was built in 1864 for one Robertson, a London banker who had been born at Blairgowrie. Two-storey main block, its s front with gablets over the upper windows and an inconsequential conical-roofed round turret. At this front's w end, a full-height bow, the walling corbelled out to a shaped-gabled rectangle at the front of the upper floor. At the E end of the front, a tall French-roofed tower with conical-roofed corner turrets and a battlemented two-storey bay window on its E side. The entrance on the house's w side is contained in a battlemented tower with round turrets at three corners and a fatter and taller round stair-turret at the NW. N of this, the battlemented screen wall of a service court, another conical-roofed round tower on its NW corner. Low rubble-walled N elevation, a tower at its E end.

In front of the entrance, a stone STATUE of Field-Marshal Lord Clyde dressed in kilt and cloak, by *J.H. Foley*, *c.* 1860.

At the end of the present drive from the E, cast-iron octagonal GATEPIERS, probably of the 1860s. – At the end of the former s drive from Cray, corniced ashlar GATEPIERS, also probably of the 1860s.

DERCULICH

2.3 km. SW of Strathtay

Standing on a hillside above the River Tay, a harled Baronial-manorial mansion house which grew from an unpretentious Georgian origin.

The house began as a double-pile late C18 tacksman's residence of two storeys above a basement that is fully exposed in the fall of the ground to the E. Three-bay W front, the centre slightly advanced; at the centre of the rear, a canted bay. In the mid C19 the house was baronialized by the addition of conical-roofed round towers to the corners, each with a Neo-Jacobean pedimented dormer window rising through the eaves. At the same time an attic was added to the C18 house, also with pedimented attic windows, a crowstep-gabled top hamper was corbelled out at the centre of the front which acquired a battlemented porch, and the canted bay at the back was heightened as a tower finished with a corbelled battlement. The house's walling was decorated with symmetrically disposed circular 'shot-holes'.

The house was further enlarged and remodelled in 1929 by *James Gillespie & Scott* who lengthened it to the S by two bays, rebuilding the mid-C19 S corner towers at the new end. The extension's roof-line continues that of the earlier building but the wallhead is higher, a difference masked on the W front by the first bay of the extension rising into a crowstepped gable. At the end bay, the walling above the level of the earlier house's eaves is faced with ashlar instead of harling; at this bay's ground floor, a three-light window under a round-headed fanlight. At the N elevation, the Georgian valley gutter is hidden by a tall ashlar parapet. Similar parapet at the new S end where the principal floor enjoys an oriel window carried on continuous corbelling. At the E elevation, a parapeted three-storey canted bay window; between it and the earlier 'tower', a balustraded Tuscan-columned loggia. Plain low N wing of the later C20.

DOWALLY

Hamlet of C19 cottages, now rather altered, beside the church.

ST ANNE'S CHURCH. Built in 1818, a rubble T, the N jamb lower than the body. On the W gable, a birdcage bellcote with two-stage baluster piers and a ball-finialled ogee roof. In each gable of the main block, two small and narrow pointed windows flanking the tall central light (the outer windows of the E gable and half of its central opening dummies). Pointed windows also in the S side but its end doors, the E now built up, the W covered by a porch of 1985 (replacing one of 1946), are rectangular. In the N side of the main block, one rectangular gallery window. Double tier of rectangular windows in the jamb's W side. – On the S wall, just W of the blocked E door, the weathered RELIEF of an angel holding a shield, probably of c. 1500. E of the door, iron JOUGS, probably C18.

The interior was recast in 1907 when the N gallery was removed and a sanctuary formed at the E end, its Perpendicular panelling (by *Archibald Elliot*, 1814–20) formerly part of the pew of the Dukes of Atholl in Dunkeld Cathedral. Also from Dunkeld Cathedral, the ORGAN (by the *Positive Organ Co. Ltd.*, 1900) on the sanctuary's S side. – PULPIT of 1907 on the N side. – STAINED GLASS. E window of c. 1910, a realistic depiction of the Supper on the Road to Emmaus. – Two early C20 windows in the S wall, one depicting Angels, the other (by *James Ballantine II*, c. 1920) St Anne and St Columba.

In the SE corner of the GRAVEYARD, a handful of late C18 HEADSTONES, each with an angel's head (the soul) above a shield, one carved with a plough, and with emblems of death at the bottom.

DOWHILL
2.4 km. E of Cleish

1090

Agreeable laird's house, formerly named Barns, built in the early C18 and remodelled and enlarged in the early C19.

The original house is of two storeys, its three-bay S front built of droved rough ashlar; at the back, a central projection containing the stair. In 1821 the Barns estate was inherited by Captain (later, Admiral Sir) Charles Adam who soon after recast the C18 house, wrapped rubble-walled gently Jacobean additions round its N, E and W sides and moved the main entrance to the N. At the new N front, the W two-thirds of the original house is masked by a single-storey wing, its W gable containing a crosslet 'gunloop' and surmounted by a large cross-finial, its N elevation with a broad shaped gablet bearing the Adam coat of arms. This wing is halted at the E against a two-storey wing projecting from the E bay of the original house and fronted by a brute classical piered portico which fills the inner angle of the wing and a longer broad addition against the E side of the C18 house. This addition's N gable is crowstepped. At the E side, tall hoodmoulded ground-floor windows, the N of three lights; the first-floor windows rise through the wallhead into steeply pedimented dormerheads. Shallow canted bay window at the S gable's ground floor, a two-light window at the first. The C18 house's S front was dressed up with a piered and pedimented portico, hoodmoulds over the first-floor windows and gableted stone dormers rising from the wallhead. To its W, a single-storey C19 wing, plain except for hoodmoulds to the windows which were deepened c. 1985.

Inside, the early C19 entrance hall and dining and drawing rooms in the E addition are tall but economically finished.

DOWHILL CASTLE
2.4 km. ESE of Cleish

On a hilltop which rises above what used to be marshy land, the remains of the late medieval residence of the Lindsays of Dowhill built along the S and some, at least, of the W sides of a barmkin enclosure.

The earliest part which forms the E end of the S range was built *c.* 1500 and comprised a rectangular tower house, *c.* 10.7 m by 7.9 m. and of three or four storeys. Probably *c.* 1600* this was extended W by *c.* 12.8 m., the addition having a round tower at its SW corner; the S end of the largely missing W range was built at the same time.

The surviving S range still stands to the height of two storeys but only the ground floor of the W range's S end survives. Walling of ashlar, grey coloured at the S front, red-stained at the N where some pock marks in the stone are probably the product of vandalism rather than a mason's tooling. In the N (courtyard) side of the original house, a slit window to the ground floor and a fairly small first-floor window. Towards the N end of its E gable, a garderobe chute. Roughly in the centre of the bottom part of this gable, a joint which suggests that a much narrower building may have been intended at first and

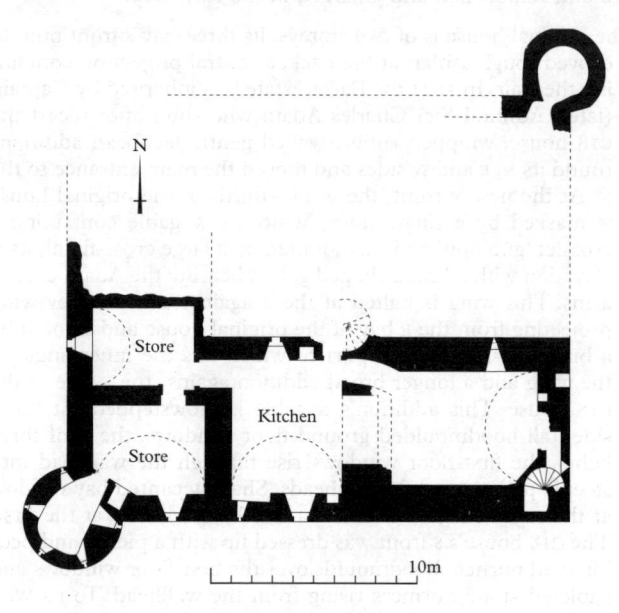

Dowhill Castle.
Ground-floor plan

*A dormerhead, now at Blair Adam (q.v.), probably came from Dowhill Castle. It bears the initials of James Lindsay of Dowhill and his wife, Elizabeth Colville. They married in 1592.

the size of the tower house increased at an early stage of construction. At the level of an entresol floor, a roughly central fairly small window with a chamfered surround. At the centre of the first floor, a window whose chamfered margins are grooved for glazing. The opening to its S is not a window but the result of stone having been quarried from the house. Slit stair window towards the S end of the gable.

At the S front of the tower house of *c.* 1500, towards the E end of its ground floor, a rectangular door under a round-headed relieving arch. This door, now partly reopened, was blocked *c.* 1600 when a new entrance was made on the courtyard side. To its E, another slit window to the stair. At the first floor, an E window, its roll-and-hollow-moulded surround perhaps a replacement of *c.* 1600. To its l., a smaller window with a chamfered surround. This opening has been contracted, the new opening within it also with a chamfered surround. W of this, a third window, robbed of dressings, which was probably formed *c.* 1600 since a disturbance in the masonry below it indicates that this W end of the original house was rebuilt when the W extension was added. W of this is the extension. Two ground-floor windows with roll-and-hollow surrounds; under each, a shot-hole robbed of its outer facing. Between the windows, a quatrefoil shot-hole. At the W end of the first floor, the jambs of a window, also with a roll-and-hollow moulding. The SW tower gives a martial display of quatrefoil shot-holes (one robbed of its outer facing). One first-floor window with a roll-and-hollow surround and a round shot-hole in the breast. Only the ground floor of the S range's W gable survives. A fairly small window (robbed of dressings) at the join with the fragmentary W range. Above it, continuous corbelling which has carried a rounded turret.

Of the courtyard (N) elevation of the S range's W extension only the ground floor remains. In it, a window, again with a roll-and-hollow surround. At the join with the original house, fragmentary remains of a rectangular stair tower which contained the new entrance provided *c.* 1600.

INTERIOR. The original entrance at the E end of the S side opens into a small tunnel-vaulted lobby contained in the wall thickness. On the lobby's E side, the entrance into a small chamber at the foot of a ruined turnpike stair in the wall thickness of the house's SE corner. The N side of the lobby opens into the ground-floor room of *c.* 1500, its floor level now above the original. This and the entresol floor above (its wooden floor now missing) were covered by a tunnel vault. The ground floor is lit only by a slit window in the N side; aumbry in the E gable. E window to the entresol. The W wall, perhaps originally containing a kitchen fireplace at the ground floor, was rebuilt *c.* 1600 when the extension was added and a tunnel-vaulted KITCHEN provided in its E ground-floor room. This wall has since been removed but the elliptical arch of its huge kitchen fireplace remains. In this kitchen's S wall, an aumbry, in the N a cupboard; a sink in the sill of the S window. Off the kitchen's

NW corner, a short passage to a tunnel-vaulted storeroom. S of this, another tunnel-vaulted store which opens into the SW tower's ground-floor room, also tunnel-vaulted but lit only by shot-holes. In the wall thickness of the tower's E segment, a narrow service stair to the first floor.

The original principal access to the first floor by the SE stair was replaced *c.* 1600 by a stair in the tower on the S range's courtyard side. On the first floor, the E room of the S range was the HALL of the tower house of *c.* 1500. It was comfortable, each of the windows' elliptical-arched embrasures provided with stone seats and a cupboard. In the wall thickness of the NE corner, a garderobe; at its entrance, the hatch to a pit-prison. The fireplace must have been in the missing W wall. No detail now survives in the first-floor room of the W extension but it may have served as a new hall, the original hall being used as an inner chamber after *c.* 1600.

At the NE corner of the former courtyard, a round tower, probably of *c.* 1600, its rubble walling rising from a projecting base. At the first floor, a circular shot-hole in the W segment. Small N window with a chamfered surround and with another circular shot-hole in its breast. The tower has been converted to a doocot, perhaps in the C18; some of the stone nesting boxes survive.

DRON

Hamlet at the foot of the N slope of the Ochil Hills.

DRON PARISH CHURCH. Disused. Georgian Gothic rubble-walled box with a battlemented W tower, by *William Stirling I*, 1824. Hoodmoulded windows containing cusped lights. Above the two windows of the E gable, an oculus. Foliage-topped pinnacles on the corners of the tower's battlement. Inside, a W gallery on Roman Doric columns.

GRAVEYARD. SW of the church, a GRAVE-SLAB commemorating Laurence Johnston †1713, the moulded border incised with stylized foliage. At one end of the slab, a coat of arms under angels' heads (souls). – Beside it, another early C18 slab (to John Johnstoun †1703), again with two angels' heads at one end; at the other, a skull, crossbones and an hourglass. – Near the S edge of the churchyard, a TABLE STONE, the baluster legs probably C19. The slab is early C18 and very like the grave-slabs near the church, carved with a pair of angels' heads at one end and, at the other, a skull, bones and an hourglass. – Immediately to its E, a C18 HEADSTONE, the curvy top enclosing a pair of angels' heads surmounting a shield; at the bottom, crossbones, a skull and an hourglass.

MANSE of *c.* 1810 to the W. Plain harled front of two storeys and three bays. Rear addition by *W. M. Mackenzie*, 1836–7.

SCHOOL. By *W. M. Mackenzie*, 1839, but recast and extended in 1907, broad eaves the principal architectural feature.

BALMANNO CASTLE. *See* p. 181.

Dron Parish Church.
Sections by William Stirling I, 1824

DRUMKILBO

1.6 km. E of Meigle

Large and bland harled Neo-Georgian house with a Georgian core.

The earliest part is the centre, a laird's house, probably of the mid C18. Two storeys over a basement, the windows of the six-bay S front grouped 3:3 and with the entrance placed between the third and fourth bays. Originally the roof was tall and piended, with bellcast eaves. In 1811 the entrance was given a pedimented doorpiece and a long low single-storey and basement wing added at the E end. In the mid C19 broad, single-storey and basement canted bay windows were built to cover the two outer bays at each end of the main block's front. The building was further extended in 1920 by *Robert S. Lorimer*, who added a SW wing of the same height as the original house, whose roof was extended W to join to that of the wing. Tall ground-floor windows announce the presence of a grand drawing room inside the wing. Finally, in 1963, *Robert Hurd & Partners* remodelled and heightened the E wing, giving its principal floor tall windows like those of Lorimer's addition and with small windows to the new top floor whose wallhead rises above that of the original house.

Inside, the principal rooms are C20. In the SW wing, the drawing room of 1920 with a carved chimneypiece designed in an early C18 manner. Free Restoration revival trabeated plaster ceiling with bay leaf roundels in the compartments. Dining room in the E wing treated in mid-C18 style, with a corniced doorpiece.

DRUMMOND CASTLE

2.6 km. NW of Muthill

The site of a late medieval castle standing sentinel over the approaches from the W and N to the broad and fertile valley of Strathearn, now occupied by a mansion house overlooking a spectacular formal terraced garden.

In 1474 James III granted the heritable offices of Steward, Coroner and Forester of the earldom of Strathearn (forfeited to the Crown in 1437) to John Drummond of Cargill who, fourteen years later, was created Lord Drummond and in 1493 received a Crown charter of extensive lands within the earldom. Two years before this charter he had received a royal warrant to build a castle at his house of Drummond. This castle was apparently habitable although unfinished in May 1496, when James IV spent a night there and paid two shillings 'to the masounis of Drummyne, of drinksiluer'. Work had probably been completed some years before 1509 when Drummond received a new royal charter of lands in Strathearn including those of '*Drummane, cum castro, fortalicio, manerio, pomeriis et ortis earundem*' ('Drummond, with the castle, fortalice, manor, gardens and orchards of the same'). This castle occupied the ridge of a hill with naturally defensive steep drops on all sides. The plateau seems to have been enclosed by walls, the space within divided into two courtyards, both probably largely surrounded by buildings, with Drummond's own private quarters contained in a tower (the keep) at the NW corner.

James, fourth Lord Drummond, was created Earl of Perth in 1605. In 1629-30 his brother, John, the second Earl, employed *John Mylne Sen.* to carry out work at Drummond including the erection of a new gatehouse adjoining the keep. At about the same time the steep slope on the S side of the castle seems to have been terraced and laid out as a garden.

James, fourth Earl of Perth (from 1701, Duke of Perth in the Jacobite peerage) was Lord Chancellor of Scotland from 1684 until the Revolution of 1688. The next year, while he was imprisoned in Stirling Castle, Drummond Castle was garrisoned by government troops and its defences strengthened. In 1693 his eldest son, James, Lord Drummond (later titular second Duke of Perth), returned from exile and soon after demolished the defences and most of the buildings of Drummond Castle except the keep and gatehouse range. At the same time he built a detached and quite pacific mansion house of no especial pretension, perhaps incorporating earlier work, roughly in the centre of the castle's plateau site. After 1734 his son, James, titular third Duke of Perth, carried out estate improvements, possibly including work on the mansion house. The Drummond estates, forfeited to the Crown after the third Duke's participation in the Jacobite rising of 1745, were granted to his non-Jacobite heir male, Captain James Drummond of Lundin (later, Lord Perth of Stobhall) in 1785. Immediately after, he employed *John Steven* to remodel the mansion house. Lord Perth's daughter and heiress, Clementina, married the Hon. Peter Burrell (later, second Lord Gwydir and twenty-second Lord Willoughby de Eresby), himself heir to substantial estates in Lincolnshire, Kent and Wales. The wealth of this couple doubtless encouraged them to commission in 1828 a grandiose scheme from *Charles Barry* for the creation of a huge new Drummond Castle in the romantic castellated style. Their possession of three other country houses may, however, have deprived them of any urgent need to carry this out and Barry's scheme for the house remained unexecuted, but between 1828 and 1838 the gardens to the S were laid out by him. This was done as a huge parterre lavishly adorned with Italian statuary, in conjunction with *Lewis Kennedy*, a landscape architect who had become factor for the Drummond estate in 1818.

A three-day visit to Drummond Castle by Queen Victoria and the Prince Consort in 1842 preluded a reconstruction of the keep and additions to the mansion house to designs produced in the same year by Lewis Kennedy's son, *George P. Kennedy*, an assistant in Barry's office. Work was not completed until 1853. Clementina Drummond and her husband both died in 1865 and in 1878 their daughter, Clementina, Lady Willoughby de Eresby, commissioned *G. T. Ewing*, the Crieff architect and factor for the Drummond estate, to remodel the mansion house to something of the appearance of a C17 laird's house. Following a fire, further remodelling of the mansion was carried out in 1899 for Gilbert, twenty-fifth Lord Willoughby de Eresby and first Earl of Ancaster.

EXTERIOR. The main approach is off the A822 to the E. On the E side of the road, a mid-C19 semicircular sweep of low walls between ball-finialled piers, the central pair of piers flanking the entrance to a track. On the S side of the track, the contemporary single-storey ashlar-clad EAST LODGE. At its NW corner, a square low tower, the eaves cornice under its pyramidal roof supported on huge brackets. Short S wing with a conical-roofed bow at the end. – On the W side of the road, at the entrance to the castle's drive, tall panelled, cornised and urn-finialled GATEPIERS of *c.* 1685. Wrought-iron gates, with flowerhead bosses at the intersections of their lattice work. Delicately foliaged elaborate iron overthrow displaying the coroneted coat of arms of the Earls of Perth. The gate piers

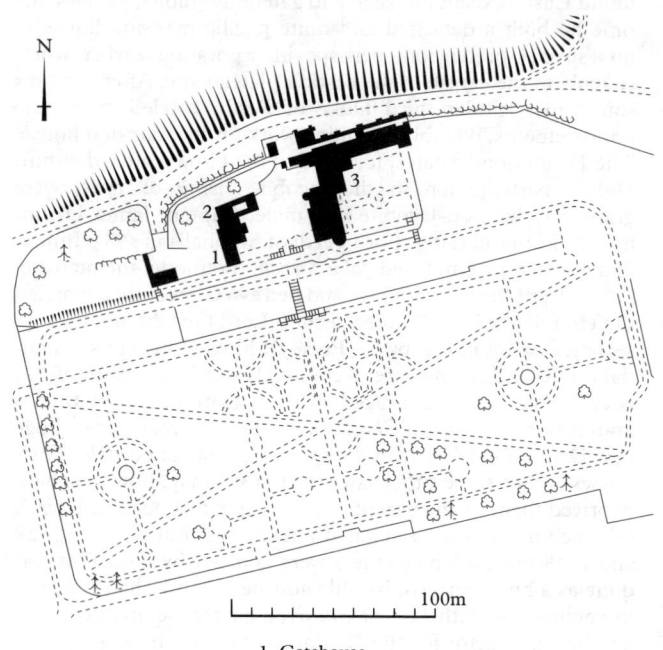

1. Gatehouse
2. Keep
3. Mansion House

Drummond Castle.
Site plan

DRUMMOND CASTLE

are joined by concave screen walls to mid-C19 ball-finalled outer piers. Inside the gates, a 1.6 km.-long beech avenue to the ridge on which the castle stands. The ridge's sloping N side has been cut through to provide a terrace carrying a road past the castle. On the S side of the road, a retaining wall, heavily buttressed and with low towers, this work apparently executed in the 1840s. The entrance to the castle is at the ridge's SW corner, where an outer courtyard, also formed in the 1840s, is entered from the N through a round-headed archway. Low W wall equipped with stone seats; a round-headed doorway in the S wall which blocks the view of the gardens.

On the outer courtyard's E side is the castle's crowstep-gabled GATEHOUSE, built for the second Earl of Perth by *John Mylne Sen.* in 1630, its front partly overlaying the late C15 keep. Like all the castle buildings, it is rubble-walled. Three storeys, the ground floor very tall and pierced by a tunnel-vaulted pend, its round-arched roll-and-hollow-moulded entrance containing an iron yett. This entrance is placed just N of the centre of the gatehouse's front, and the upper floors' openings are similarly disposed giving an effect of near symmetry. Above the gateway, a moulded frame enclosing a panel carved with the heraldic achievement of the Earls of Perth. To the r. of the gateway, at the ground floor, a moulded circular gunhole. At the first floor, N of the gateway, a pair of smallish rectangular windows (the r. built up), both with roll-and-hollow-moulded surrounds and equipped with grilles. Second-floor windows, also with roll-and-hollow mouldings, grouped 2:2 either side of the pend. They rise through the wallhead into pedimented dormerheads whose tympana are carved with a weathered shield, a coronet above the date and initial 16 E [presumably for Earl] 30, the coroneted Drummond coat of arms flanked by the initials EP (for Earl of Perth), and a coroneted shield flanked by the date 1630. The same date appears on each skew-putt of the front. Inside the pend, on the S side, the roll-and-hollow-moulded entrance to a tunnel-vaulted guardroom.

The pend opening and a blocked first-floor window are at the N end of the gatehouse's shorter E elevation, butted against the S gable of the keep. S of the pend, a small ground-floor window, probably an insertion. At the second floor, a pair of centrally placed windows like those of the W front, the tympanum of the l. bearing a coronet and the initials I^{C}P (for Jean, Countess of Perth), that of the r. carved with a coroneted shield displaying the impaled arms of Drummond and Ker (for John, second Earl of Perth, and his wife, Jean Ker). On this elevation's S skewputt, the coroneted coat of arms of Drummond and the initials IP (presumably for John [Earl of] Perth).

On the N side of the gatehouse and projecting to its E is the oblong KEEP (*c.* 13.1 m. by 11.3 m.), its N end built against a rock outcrop, a rectangular stair-tower projecting from the E side. The three lower floors are of the 1490s, the two tall upper floors and attic added by *George P. Kennedy* in the mid C19, making the building appear as an early Victorian illustration of some tale of medieval chivalry. The walls rise sheer, except for plinths on the E and S sides, to the corbelled battlement, its S corners with small angle rounds. Kennedy raised the stair-tower high above the main block to finish with a platform providing a stunning view over the gardens. Surrounding the platform, a corbelled but uncrenellated parapet, its NE corner topped by a square caphouse surmounted by a tall bellcote whose fluted piers were renewed c. 2000. Also by Kennedy is the keep's buttressed and crowstepped N gable rising high above the main battlement. In its N side, a huge round-headed blind arch. It is joined at the E to a rubble-walled water tank, also of c. 1850.

The mid-C19 remodelling of the keep, far-reaching though it was in its dramatic heightening of the building, left its earlier detail almost untouched. In the W face, the outline of a blocked ground-floor door, perhaps an C18 insertion, is marked out in the mortar of the sneck harling. The windows of the three lower floors are mostly of the 1490s. S of the blocked door, a slit window with an angular pointed head. Reasonably sized first- and second-floor windows aligned above each other in the centre of this elevation. Below the second-floor windows are moulded round shot-holes like those of the gatehouse and probably insertions of 1630. Above these windows, mid-C19 shields bearing the arms of Lord Willoughby de Eresby. The same armorial bearings appear above the S gable's pair of second-floor windows whose roll-and-hollow mouldings may be replacements of c. 1630; beneath the E window, another round shot-hole. At the S side, to the l. of the stair-tower, a narrow window with an angular pointed head lights a stair in the wall thickness. Above, a small first-floor window and a second-floor opening shaped as an inverted keyhole. More inverted keyhole openings in the stair-tower's S side; slit windows in its E face. N of the stair-tower, a first-floor door with chamfered jambs. Its stone forestair is probably of c. 1850. The mid-C19 openings to the top floors emphasize the keep's verticality. Very tall third-floor windows with roll-and-hollow-moulded surrounds and surmounted by the coroneted coats of arms of the Lords Drummond. Tall keyhole-shaped slits at the fourth floor. A Gothic panel decorates the S gable's chimney.

From inside the keep's first-floor entrance lobby a straight stair in the thickness of the E wall leads down to the ground floor which is occupied by a room covered by a tunnel vault pierced by a (blocked) hatch. The N half of the E wall is thicker than the S, possibly the result of a repair to the building. The floor's cobbles may have been laid in the C18 when this room was perhaps used as a stable. At the W end of the S wall, the deep embrasure of a tiny window which has been blocked by the construction of the gatehouse. E of this, a rough recess, its W jamb's top shaped as a rounded corbel as if to carry a lintel. In the E wall, a crude aumbry and, to its N, what may have been a water inlet, now blocked by the forestair. Tunnel-vaulted first-floor hall. Victorian chimneypiece at the S end. In the SE corner, a Georgian cupboard formed from a late C15 garderobe. The stair-tower contains a turnpike to the floors above. The upper hall on the second floor is now Early Victorian in character with a large canopied stone chimneypiece at the s end. To the N, a tunnel-vaulted charter room. The third and fourth floors are occupied by a single two-storey-height room with a large stone fireplace of neo-medieval character. The attic's floor has been removed.

E of the gatehouse and keep is a courtyard paved with granite setts laid in concentric circles. On the courtyard's N side, a rock outcrop; on the s a balustrade. The courtyard's E side is filled by the w range of the MANSION HOUSE begun by James, Lord Drummond, in the 1690s. By the mid C18 that house had developed as an L-plan, the two-storey N and double-pile w ranges meeting at a three-storey NW tower. In *John Steven*'s alterations of the late 1780s the NW tower was given a pediment over its E face and probably another over the w, and the w range's E part was extended s with a full-height bow embellished with a balcony under the deep ground-floor windows. *G. T. Ewing* in 1878 removed the 1870s pediment or pediments from the NW tower to which he gave a Frenchy attic storey, heightened the w range's w part to three storeys and added to its N end a round tower containing the new principal entrance, moved here from the E side. Finally, in 1899, the s two-thirds of the w range's w part was rebuilt and thickened to the w.

The NW tower is plain except for pedimented dormer windows. Immediately to its s, at the N end of the w range's w façade, the conical-roofed round entrance tower of 1878. Above the round-headed doorway, a panel carved with the heraldic achievement of the Drummond family. The adjoining bay of this front also represents Ewing's work of 1878, the top floor marked off by a corbelled sill course and with a window rising through the eaves to a Neo-Jacobean pedimented dormerhead carved with heraldry. Similar detail, replicated or reused from the 1878 work, appears at the slightly advanced four bays rebuilt in 1899 to the s. Boredom is fought off by the presence of an off-centre broad and chimney-topped crow-stepped gablet and, at the SW corner, a tall conical-roofed turret with a rope-moulded eaves course and armorial-decorated segmental pediments over its windows. The first-floor windows of the N bay and the s gable mix Palladian and Jacobean inspiration not very happily, each centre light topped by a pair of small openings under a pediment. Carved heraldry again, including a panel displaying the achievement of the Earls of Ancaster, on the crowstepped gable.

The two-storey E side of the w range is less Victorianised. The bowed s end's late C19 recasting gave the first-floor windows pediments carved with heraldic motifs. Otherwise the E elevation is plain. Roll-and-hollow surrounds to the windows, those of the fairly regular seven-bay first floor probably of the 1790s, those of the ground floor Victorian except for the N window whose chamfered margins may be C18. Above one pair of ground-floor windows, smaller than the others, are reused early C17 steep pediments, the l. displaying the impaled arms of Drummond and Ker and the initials I^{E}P and I^{C}P (for John, second Earl of Perth, and Jean [Ker], Countess of Perth, his wife), the r. more weathered but its shield apparently flanked originally by the same initials. Round-arched off-centre door of 1878, apparently in the position occupied by the house's main entrance in the late C18. In the inner angle of this front and the NW tower, a two-storey projection, perhaps of the late C18 but given a flat roof surrounded by a battlement in 1899. Also of 1899 is the single-storey battlemented corridor which is wrapped round this projection, the NW tower and the W end of the N range.

The crowstep-gabled but plain N range was heightened in the late C19. Its present windows seem all to be Victorian; in the walling, evidence of blocked earlier openings. More Drummond and Willoughby de Eresby family heraldry on the pedimented dormerheads over the second-floor windows. Along the back of this range, an addition of one and two storeys built *c.* 1850. At the E end, a square tower with a conical-spired caphouse rising from one corner. At the W end, a battlemented tower, a blind oriel window projecting from its W face.

In the courtyard garden enclosed by the mansion house's two ranges, a mid-C19 FOUNTAIN. Rising from the centre of the octagonal bowl, a leafily capitalled shaft, its finial the coronet and sleuth hound crest of the titular Dukes of Perth.

INTERIOR. Inside the mansion house, the principal rooms are in the W range. At its N end, the panelled entrance hall and plain Neo-Jacobean staircase, both of 1878. The rooms to the S are of 1899. On the ground floor, a large SW DINING ROOM. Plain except for a chimneypiece in late C18 manner with high reliefs of women and children at the ends of its frieze; central relief of a boy in pursuit of a wolf which has stolen a lamb. At the SE, a BILLIARD ROOM with a wooden Artisan Mannerist chimneypiece. On the first floor, a LIBRARY at the SW, with a Frenchy white marble chimneypiece. At the SE corner, the DRAWING ROOM, its elliptically tunnel-vaulted plaster ceiling crossed by rope-moulded ribs and forming a half-dome at the bowed S end. Late C18 revival white marble chimneypiece with consoles under the mantelshelf. To the N, a coomb-ceilinged ANTE-ROOM. The N wall's columned white marble chimneypiece is flanked by niches, the r.'s dummy bookcase a door which opens into a closet. N of the closet, the principal BEDROOM. Its decoration is again late C18 revival, with a coved ceiling and a round-arched dressing table recess at the N end. Neo-Adam white marble chimneypiece with face-to-face sphinxes at the centre of the frieze.

The GARDENS S of the castle were formed in two principal phases. The first, in the early or mid C17, terraced the slope. The second, *c.* 1830, restored the terracing, added balustrades and parapets and introduced statuary and ornamental architecture to the terraces and the great parterre on the flat ground below. Stretching between the castle's gatehouse and mansion house, a balustrade of round-headed arcading surmounts the topmost retaining wall. The terrace below is bounded on the S by a parapet topped by marble busts. In the centre, flanking the opening to the stair to the terrace below, a pair of pedestals which support flat brass SUNDIALS, each bearing the coroneted initials of James, fourth Earl of Perth, and with an inscription stating that it was made by *John Marke* of London in 1679. From this level, a double stair to the terrace below where the space between the flights is filled by a segmental-arched grotto recess of rusticated stonework, the keystone carved with the head of a bearded man. At the ends of the terrace, round-arched gateways. Their carved floral swags and human head keystones are perhaps late C17 and said to have been imported from a demolished church in London. Below this terrace the ground slopes steeply down to a retaining wall on which stand panelled pedestals surmounted by tall urns.

The great PARTERRE on the flat ground below the terracing is still in the form laid out by *Charles Barry* and *Lewis Kennedy* c. 1828 and one of the most ambitious such schemes of the earlier C19, although the present planting scheme dates from the 1950s. Its dominant feature is a box-edged saltire but crossed by N–S paths and with topiary and C17 or C18 Italian urns and statues providing emphases; fountains near the E and W ends. In the centre, a tall SUNDIAL made by *John Mylne Sen.* in 1630. Corniced square shaft, its N face bearing impaled coats of arms identified for those ignorant of heraldry as being those of IOHN.E.PERTH and IEAN.C.PERTH; Latin verses refer to the sundial's function in marking the passage of time. The shaft's other faces are carved with hollowed-out motifs, several in the shape of hearts. On the shaft is poised a polyhedron, its faces all bearing dials, surmounted by a tall obelisk whose faces are divided into dial panels; ball-and-spike finial.

At the S end of the central path is the GRIMSTHORPE FAÇADE erected in 1930, incorporating C18 stonework from Grimsthorpe Castle, the Lincolnshire seat of the Earl of Ancaster. Fronted by a basin, the façade consists of a round-headed archway flanked by niches which contain figures of Pan and Actæon and are fronted by Roman Doric porticoes. E and W of this are archways of the same type as those at the ends of the central terrace but surmounted by busts. They give access to the walled kitchen garden behind.

At the E end of the formal garden, a battlemented rubble-built BRIDGE of c. 1790. Four-span, the outer two arches round-headed, the wider central ones segmental. Circular panels recessed in the ends of the walling.

DRUMMONIE HOUSE
1.8 km. SW of Bridge of Earn

Small late C17 harled mansion house built for the Oliphants of Pitkeathly. It is one of a group of houses put up from the 1660s which consist of a three-storey U wrapped round a flat-roofed and balustraded two-storey centre. The s-facing main front is very like that of Prestonfield House (Edinburgh) but with crowstepped instead of shaped gables gripping the one-bay centrepiece. The centrepiece's door is early C19, with sidelights and an overall segmental fanlight, all in a Roman Doric columned and corniced surround. On the centre of the wallhead's balustrade, a cubical stone sundial. The flanking front gables are each of two bays with small and square second-floor windows (those of the E gable now dummies), all with chamfered margins. The side elevations were probably identical originally, each of three bays with evenly spaced windows, the s two of the second floor rising just above the eaves to catslideroofed dormerheads, the N bay formed by the crowstepped gables of the N range (cf. Methven Castle). The W side has retained its C17 appearance but the E side's second-floor windows were blocked and its first-floor windows enlarged when a tall room inside was formed in the early C19. N elevation of five bays, the openings symmetrically disposed but expressing the different floor levels inside.

Plain two-storey harled E wing, perhaps mid C18, its S door's reused lintel bearing the initials LO (for Laurence Oliphant) and the date 1697. Lower and longer rubble-built office wing to its E which was converted to housing in 2003 when the three dormer windows at the E end of its S front were added.

DULL

Small village of late C19 and C20 housing.

DULL PARISH CHURCH. Disused. Long rubble-built rectangle, possibly C16 in origin and certainly in existence by 1614 when it was repaired. Further recorded repairs and alterations were carried out in 1717, 1819 (by *James Cattle*), 1840 (by *John Scrimgeour*) and 1879 (by *Robert Yuille*, the clerk of works at Taymouth Castle). The bellcote on the W gable has bulgy baluster piers topped by stumpy obelisks at the corners of its concave-sided pyramidal roof; it was rebuilt in 1819, probably reusing the stonework of the bellcote erected in 1717. In the W gable, a rectangular gallery window with chamfered margins, perhaps of the C17. In the E gable, a built-up door, perhaps also C17. The blocked window above it was inserted in 1717. The other detail is of 1879. Round-headed doors and windows; little triangular dormer-ventilators on the roof. Flanking the S side's E door are fragments of two medieval SLABS incised with crosses.

GRAVEYARD consisting of two tenuously linked enclosures, the lower surrounding the church, the other uphill to the NE. S of the church, a GRAVE-SLAB, probably early C18, its top end carved with emblems of death under an angel's head (the soul). – In the NE portion of the graveyard, an aedicular swan-neck-pedimented HEADSTONE of 1834 to Robert Dewar, the W face carved in quite high relief with a coat of arms displaying a ship under sail. – To the E, a similar stone to Tavish Campbell †1809, the coat of arms displaying a boar's head; angel's head at the top. – E of this, another GRAVE-SLAB probably of the early C18, the top end carved with reminders of death under an angel's head.

DULL AND WEEM PARISH CHURCH. *See* Weem.

SCHOOL, W of Dull Parish Church. Now in other use. School and schoolhouse by *John Douglas*, 1851. Picturesque, with bracketed broad eaves.

CROSS, E of Dull Parish Church. Large roughly hewn stone, one arm missing. Perhaps C8, it was one of four which marked the sanctuary limits of the Celtic monastery of Dull (for two others, *see* Weem: Former Weem Parish Church (Menzies Mausoleum)).

APPIN HOUSE, 0.4 km. W. Originally Dull Parish Manse, built in 1841–2 to a design by *James Laing*, clerk of works at Castle Menzies. Rubble-walled and piend-roofed, with broad eaves. Main block of three bays by two, the front's centre door architraved. Rear wing, its eaves bracketed and with gablets over the first-floor windows. Behind, a piend-roofed rubble-built office range of 1842.

NETHER CAMSERNEY, 1 km. E. Immediately NW of the Victorian farmhouse, a single-storey C18 LONGHOUSE, *c.* 22.1 m. by 5.2 m., with gently undulating rubble walls, the E gable rebuilt in the building's restoration in 1992–7. The roof is covered with rye straw laid on divots, the ridge at the E end with heather divots. At the W end a round chimney formed of wood faced with divots, roughly in the centre a gabled chimney, a conventional chimney on the E gable. Towards the W end of the N wall, a small roughly rectangular projection, apparently an addition. In the S side, small windows and a couple of doors, the l. *c.* 1.5 m. W of a blocked earlier door. Immediately E of the r. door is a drain suggesting that this part of the building was originally a byre. The roof is carried on crucks, renewed at the E half of the building in the 1990s, the feet of each pair standing on stone slabs and rising to a yoke. Below the yoke, a collar-beam; above, a spar supporting the roof ridge.

The interior is now divided into two almost equally sized rooms by a stone wall. This may have replaced an earlier partition when the building's E end, probably originally a byre, was converted to a house, perhaps *c.* 1800. In this conversion two rooms were formed separated by a lobby and the stair to a loft. The stair and loft floor were removed in the 1990s. Inserted in the E end, a conventional stone fireplace which served this house's E room. At the W end, built beside the partition wall, a hanging chimney of lath and plaster, its construction strengthened in the 1990s by the addition of horizontal laths. In the wall N of the fireplace, a wooden saltbox with a circular opening. The W room which had also been subdivided has been restored as a single space, presumably its original form. Roughly in the centre, a hanging chimney constructed of wattle and daub, its E and N sides rebuilt in 1997.

COMRIE CASTLE. *See* p. 281.

DUNALASTAIR
4.8 km. E of Kinloch Rannoch

Roofless and overgrown ruin of a fairy-tale Baronial mansion house designed by *A. & A. Heiton* for General Sir John Macdonald in 1852. Two storeys, built of stugged ashlar, with a restless string course under the upper floor. Projecting from the centre of the seven-bay W front, a tall round tower finished with a steep conical roof. The tower's entrance has a rope-moulded and keystoned elliptical-arched door surround framed by a Jacobean Renaissance pilastered aedicule, its cornice surmounted by obelisks flanking a deeply cut heraldic achievement. Over the tower's first floor windows, carved stars framed by shaped 'gablets' formed by the jettied walling of the tower's top stage. This is embellished with oval panels under the attic windows whose steeply pedimented dormerheads rise through the eaves. Similar pediments above the eaves level surmount the upper windows of the front's linking sections which join the tower to the advanced ends. Projecting from each of these, a canted bay window at the ground floor above which the walling is corbelled out in two stages to a rectangular crow-step-gabled attic. Strapwork embellishment above the cornices of the first floor windows; small round-headed lights to the attic. Corbelled-out from these end bays' inner corners are heavy chimneys; on the outer corners, conical-roofed tourelles. Answering tourelles at the W end of the N and S elevations where they are placed in the inner angles of the advanced and crowstep-gabled end bays. Steep pediments, like those on the entrance front, over the upper windows of these sides' outer bays. At the centre of the N side, a full-height crowstep-gabled bay window with chimneys rising above the splayed sides and a stone balcony fronting the segmental-pedimented first floor openings. Oriel window to its W. The S side's centre bay is advanced and crowstepped. Another crowstep-gabled bay to its E.

STABLES, also of the 1850s, to the SW. Front with a crowstep-gabled central tower and more crowsteps on the dormerheads of the first floor windows.

Broad-eaved NORTH LODGE of 1857, with a tree-trunk porch and horizontal-paned glazing in the windows. Its hammer-dressed and ball-finialled gatepiers are probably of the 1890s as is certainly the ironwork of the gates which bears the coat of arms of James C. Bunten, a railway magnate who acquired the estate in the late C19. – Ironwork of the same design at the EAST LODGE AND GATEWAY designed by *Thomas Leadbetter* in 1893. This appears a purposeful defence, the main gateway and flanking pedestrian gates all round-headed and set in a screen wall finished with a corbelled parapet, its W end with a battlemented angle round, its taller centre with corbelled and parapeted angle rounds and a box bartizan. At the wall's E end, a conical-roofed fat three-storey tower, the top windows with steeply pedimented dormerheads. The tower is attached to a crowstep-gabled lodge, its flat-roofed porch surmounted by a balustrade.

DUNBARNEY HOUSE
1.9 km. W of Bridge of Earn

Comfortable and quite classy laird's house built in two main stages, the walling all of red sandstone. The earlier part is the rubble-built W block put up by the Craigies of Dunbarney c. 1700. Three storeys, the windows with chamfered margins, the skews stepped. Six-bay front, the first-floor openings linked by a sill course, the second-floor openings very small. The two centre bays are occupied at the ground floor by a sidelit door behind an early C19 Roman Doric portico with, at the back, half-columns instead of pilasters. The ground-floor windows to its l. were altered c. 1900.

The parallel E block was added c. 1800. It is of the same height but contains only two floors. Five-bay E (garden) front built of ashlar, with very tall round-headed windows to the first floor. Two dummy windows of the same design in the S gable.

Inside, a ground-floor living hall formed c. 1900, with a Roman Doric columned screen along its E side. Flying stair of c. 1800 in the house's NE corner. First-floor drawing room, its Adamish decoration more likely to be of c. 1900 than c. 1800.

N of the house, STABLE OFFICES of 1772, with a birdcage bellcote, probably of 1787 and reused from Dunbarney Parish Church at Bridge of Earn. – Rubble-walled GARDEN, probably also late C18.

DOOCOT S of the house, dated 1697. Rubble-built and pantile-roofed, it is of lectern type. A single ratcourse rises at the crowstepped gables. S entrance under a triangle of circular openings.

WINDMILL, 0.3 km. SW of the house, perhaps of the early C18. Rubble-built tapering round tower with a basement containing a segmental-arched cart entrance which was approached by a sunken driveway from the S. The superstructure and machinery have been removed.

DUNCRUB PARK
1 km. NW of Dunning

The huge but stark Elizabethan mansion house, designed by *William G. Habershon* and built for the tenth Lord Rollo in 1861–3, was demolished in 1950. It was joined by a corridor link to a CHAPEL of 1858, also by Habershon. This survives (converted to holiday housing). Early English, the walls of bullnosed ashlar masonry, the roofs covered with patterned slating. Buttressed nave ending in an E apse containing the sanctuary; short aisles at the W end of the N side and along the S where its E end abuts the corridor. Pointed windows and W door, their hoodmoulds with headstops; above the W gable's trio of windows, a cusped vesica. Overpowering NW steeple with massive angle buttresses, its two lowest stages quite plain except for the pointed N entrance. At the third stage, marked off by a string course, cusped blind arcading springing from polished granite shafts. Another string course under the belfry where each face is pierced by a quartet of tall pointed openings, the hoodmoulds also with headstops. A tall needle spire rises within the high parapet.

STABLES to the W. Of 1833–4, a rubble-built U, the main range two-storey with gablet dormerheads over the upper windows, the single-storey E wings' gables finished with pediments containing oculi. – 0.4 km E, in the garden of St Andrew's Cottage, a rubble-built square DOOCOT of 1725, its slated ogee roof surmounted by a weathercock.

DUNFALLANDY

1.1 km. S of Pitlochry

Austere rubble-built mansion house of 1818. Main block of three storeys, a Victorian porch at the centre of its three-bay front. Each side, a long lateral wing of one tall storey.

BURIAL ENCLOSURE, ESE of the house. Later C19, the cross-finialled cast-iron railings decorated with foliage. The enclosure contains a MONUMENT to Archibald Fergusson †1854. It is a sarcophagus, the front carved with quatrefoils enclosing blank shields, placed within an angle-buttressed stone shelter. In the S front, a large pointed arch, its hoodmould's label stops carved as angels. More carved angels on the back wall above the sarcophagus.

The DUNFALLANDY STONE, a cross-slab of the C8 or C9, stands immediately S of the enclosure. The S face is carved with the relief of a cross, its limbs decorated with interlaced work and bosses. At each side of this face, a tier of figures of animals and angels. The N face is carved with a frame formed by two serpents, their tongues meeting at the top, their tails curled in the bottom corners. Within this frame, at the top, two seated figures (St Paul the Hermit and St Antony of Egypt, exemplars of the eremitical and monastic life) flanking a cross above which are Pictish symbols ('linked discs', a 'moon and axe-head', a 'Pictish elephant'). Below the figures, the relief of a horseman above a hammer, tongs and anvil.

Dunfallandy Stone

DUNIRA
3.9 km. NW of Comrie

Of the Scottish Baronial mansion house designed by *William Burn* and built in 1852 for Sir David Dundas of Beechwood only a fragment survives. That comprises the house's single-storey service court and the roofless E bay of the mansion's two-storey and basement E wing. This part of the wing has a crowstepped S gable from which projects the canted bay window of the business room. At the S front of the service court, three broad gables (for the kitchen, scullery and laundry), the E crowstepped. At the E range, a splay-sided triple-gabled projection (the dairy) with round-headed windows. Battlemented W range.

W of the mansion, late C20 HOUSING. Among it, a harled Scotstyle STABLES courtyard of 1919, with some of its gables crowstepped, conical-roofed round turrets at the s corners and a round-headed pend entrance in the E side. – Behind, a rubble WALLED GARDEN, probably of the early C19, now containing housing. – WEST LODGE to the SW, of the earlier C19, its broached ashlar painted white. Single-storey, the broad-eaved roof with a jerkin head at the SE gable whose pedimented window contains three round-headed lights under a simply traceried rectangular head. Hoodmoulds and mullions to the other windows; a consoled block pediment over the door.

DUNKELD

Small town beside the River Tay and at the NW tip of Strathmore, which began in the later Middle Ages as a burgh of barony under the superiority of the Bishops of Dunkeld whose cathedral church and palace stood immediately to the w. From 1704 the superiority was assumed by the Dukes of Atholl whose seat of Dunkeld House and accompanying parkland bounded the N side of the burgh. Almost all the town's houses were burned in an attack by Jacobite forces in 1689 and the subsequent rebuilding provided one street (Cathedral Street, High Street and Brae Street) running E from the cathedral churchyard, the houses being described in 1758 as 'very good being mostly new built & Slated ...' In 1806 when construction of Dunkeld Bridge, replacing a ferry over the Tay, was begun, a cross-street (Bridge Street and Atholl Street) was laid out to carry the new line of the road from Perth to Inverness through the burgh. Although now bypassed, the town has remained an agreeable staging post on that road, not developing beyond its early C19 size. Restoration work begun in the 1950s was among the earliest of The National Trust for Scotland's 'Little Houses' schemes.

Dunkeld.
View of town from J. Slezer, *Theatrum Scotiae*, 1693

DUNKELD CATHEDRAL
Cathedral Street

Partly roofless but potent symbol of the medieval Church's wealth, power and civilizing mission.

A monastery at Dunkeld is traditionally claimed to have been founded by Constantine, son of Fergus, overlord of Dál Riata and Picts, c. 815, and it was to Dunkeld that Kenneth mac Alpin, King of Scots, brought relics of St Columba from Iona in 849. By 845 the Abbot of Dunkeld was also the chief bishop of the Pictish kingdom of Fortriu, although the abbotship had become hereditary by the C10 and the bishopric appears to have been abandoned. In the early C12 the bishopric was revived, perhaps with a community of *Céli Dé* forming the bishop's *familia*. Bishop Gilbert established a college of canons at the cathedral c. 1230, its constitution modelled on that of Salisbury Cathedral. By 1238 the chapter consisted of a dean, precentor, archdeacon, treasurer, sub-dean, succentor and a number of canons, presumably including a chancellor. This provision of a new and resident chapter of canons preluded a remodelling of the cathedral church. Work started with the construction of a new and presumably much larger choir which may have been largely complete by 1249 when Bishop Geoffrey was buried in the cathedral.* Remodelling of the choir took place during the episcopate of William Sinclair (1312–37) who, from 1318, employed *Robertus Cementarius* (*Robert* the Mason) as master mason for the work. This was apparently complete when Bishop Sinclair was buried in front of the high altar in 1337.†

Rebuilding of the nave was begun by Bishop Robert de Cardeny in 1406 and had reached the height of the triforium stage by the time of his death thirty years later. Work seems then to have been discontinued under his immediate successors but quarrying of stone was undertaken by Bishop John Raulston (1447–50) and construction was resumed by Bishop Thomas Lauder (1450–81) who dedicated the completed church in 1464 when work on the chapter house, begun by Lauder in 1457, was probably also complete. In 1470 Lauder began work on the great bell-tower at the NW corner, probably designed some years before, which seems to have been completed by Bishop George Brown (1484–1514) who hung two bells and apparently commissioned a third.

After the Reformation of 1560 the cathedral church was purged of images, the nave abandoned for worship and unroofed, and the choir fitted up as a parish church. Repairs and re-roofing of the choir were carried out early in the C17, in 1691 and 1762. The parish minister described it in c. 1795 as 'a decent and not incommodious place of worship; though from the height of the walls

p. 32

---

*Bishop Geoffrey's six predecessors had been buried at Inchcolm Priory (later, Abbey) or Newbattle Abbey.
†But the early C16 history of Alexander Myln, *Vitae Dunkeldensis Ecclesiae Episcoporum*, ed. T. Thomson (Bannatyne Club, 1831), 13, credits Bishop Sinclair with building the choir '*a fundamentis*' ('from the foundations').

and the want of ceiling, it is not only bare and meagre to the eyes, but is . . . cold during the winter.' Some of these problems were overcome in 1814–20 by *Archibald Elliot* who constructed a new roof at a lower level than its predecessor but with a neo-medieval plaster vault, opened up windows which had been partially blocked and inserted new tracery in them, walled off the E end as a vestibule and erected a gallery at each end. In 1908 Sir Donald Currie, the shipping magnate and owner of the Glenlyon and Garth estates, commissioned *W. Dunn & R. Watson* to carry out an extensive restoration of the choir. They removed the early C19 roof and provided a new one at the height and pitch of the medieval roof, rebuilt the W wall dividing the choir from the remains of the nave, replaced Elliot's vestibule partition with a lower wooden screen, and provided new furnishings. Consolidation of the roofless nave and NW tower was undertaken by *H.M. Office of Works* in 1922–6.

Exterior

The church consists of a fully aisled seven-bay nave, the bell-tower projecting from the W end of its N aisle and a porch sheltering the people's entrance on the S side, and an unaisled choir of four bays with a two-storey chapter house on its N. All, except the rubble-walled chapter house, is built of greyish ashlar, some at least of the stone of the nave taken from the nearby Burnbane Quarry.

The WEST FRONT as completed together with the NW tower *c.* 1500 forms a composition carelessly indifferent to symmetry or balance but executed with a panache which arouses the indulgence of the more susceptible onlooker. As first designed at the beginning of the C15 for Bishop Robert de Cardeny, it seems to have been staid enough. At the end of each aisle, a narrow pointed window and, above and placed nearer the join of the aisle to the nave, a small rectangular light. The join of each aisle to the slightly advanced gable of the nave was marked by a turret-like buttress finished with crocket-finialled clustered pinnacles. In the centre of the nave gable was the processional W door, almost certainly intended to have a large window directly above, probably surmounted by a roundel light in the apex of the gable. The symmetry was disturbed by the projection of a tall octagonal stair-turret just S of the door and set in from the corner of the gable which was roughly balanced by a semi-octagonal buttress at the N corner of the gable (now subsumed in the bell-tower's stair turret).

The design of the front was radically revised after 1470 with the addition of the tower at the W end of the N aisle and the enlargement of the W window to occupy the full available width between the stair-turret and the tower. The end of the S aisle, probably already completed, was left as originally intended. The stair-turret, however, was perhaps carried higher than first envisaged and finished with a high quatrefoil-pierced

DUNKELD CATHEDRAL 335

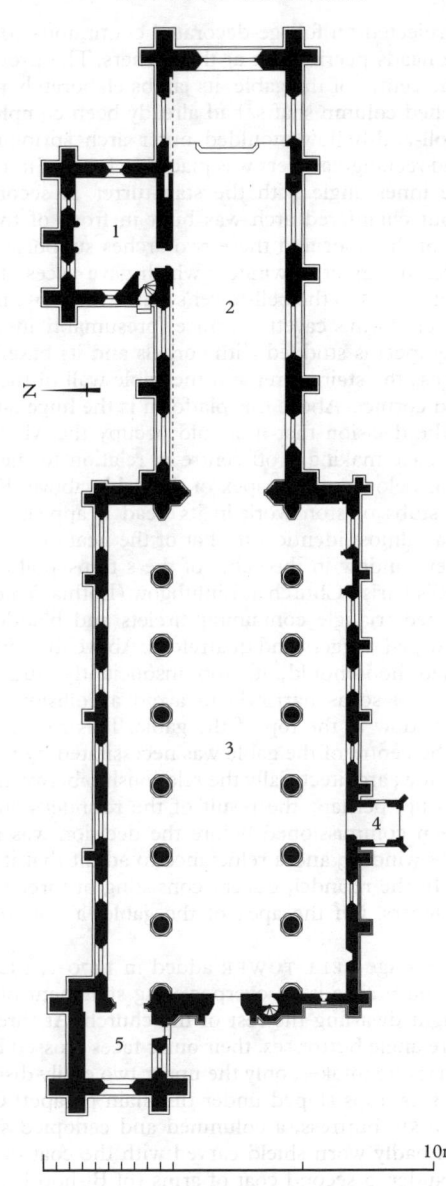

N

1. Chapter House
2. Choir
3. Nave
4. Porch
5. Bell Tower

Dunkeld Cathedral.
Plan

parapet projected on foliage-decorated continuous corbelling, grotesque heads peering out at the corners. The processional door at the centre of the gable, its jambs elaborately moulded with attached column shafts, had already been completed but a plain roll-and-hollow-moulded outer arch springing from unadorned rectangular piers was placed in front of it, the S pier filling the inner angle with the stair-turret. A second plain pointed but chamfered arch was built in front of the nave's walling N of the door and these two arches supported a platform under the great W window which gave access from the stair-turret to its S to the bell-tower's stair which rose from this level. The platform's cavetto cornice (presumably intended to carry a parapet) is studded with corbels and its baseline continues across the stair-turret and the gable wall of the nave as a moulded cornice. Above this platform is the huge late C15 W window, the decision that it should occupy the whole of the available space making it off-centre in relation to the processional door below and the apex of the gable above. From the surviving stubs of stonework in its head it appears that the tracery was almost identical to that of the near-contemporary but shorter window in the gable of the S transeptal chapel of St Michael's Parish Church at Linlithgow (Lothian), i.e. a huge curving-sided triangle containing circlets and bladder forms filled by cusped daggers and quatrefoils. Above the window, an ogee-arched hoodmould, its top insouciantly nudged over towards the N so as narrowly to avoid a collision with the roundel window at the top of the gable. This roundel's position S of the centre of the gable was necessitated by the size of the W window; architecturally the relationship between the two is a botch-up, perhaps the result of the roundel's stonework having been commissioned before the decision was made to enlarge the window, and a reluctance to admit that it was not required. In the roundel, tracery consisting of three spiralling cusped daggers. On the apex of the gable, a floriated stone cross.

The four-stage BELL-TOWER added in 1470–*c.* 1500 at the W end of the N aisle is an overpowering statement of ecclesiastical might dwarfing the rest of the church. At three of the corners are angle buttresses, their outer faces crossed by string courses marking intakes, only the upper two easily discernible, the buttresses' tops sloped under the main parapet. On the S face of the SW buttress, a columned and canopied surround encloses a badly worn shield carved with the coat of arms of Bishop Lauder; a second coat of arms (of Bishop Livingston, i.e. of between 1476 and 1483) in a similar surround is placed near the top of the buttress. At the SE corner of the tower, an octagonal stair-turret rises, unbroken by string courses, to a parapeted caphouse. At the S face of the tower's bottom stage, an off-centre round-arched low door and a two-light window, also off-centre, its head containing cusped loop tracery apparently renewed. At the second stage, a round-arched cusped light, its sill sloped down to a string course; pendant label stops to the hoodmould. At the W face of the tower's bottom stage, a three-light hoodmoulded window, its sill again sloped down to a string course. In the window's head, tracery, also apparently renewed, of daggers under a quatrefoil. At the second stage of this face, a window like that of the S face but the hoodmould's label stops are carved as human heads. The third stage of the W and S faces is blind. At each of the N and E faces, a narrow depressed-arched window, the hoodmould of the N with pendant label stops, the label stops of the E hoodmould carved as human heads. At each face of the fourth stage, a belfry opening of two pointed lights, the sill sloped to a string course, the hoodmould's label stops carved as human heads; in the openings are lozenge-shaped clock faces erected in 1814 when the clock (by *Handley & Moore*) was installed.

The nave's seven-bay AISLES were buttressed. Only bases survive of the N aisle's buttresses but the S aisle's are intact. Carried round all the buttresses is the splay-topped base of the aisle's walling. Above, the S buttresses rise unbroken by intakes but with a moulded string course on the outer faces to sloping tops under the aisle's cavetto-moulded cornice from which project stone spouts. The similar cornice of the N aisle is now missing. The tops of the buttresses flanking the S porch are set lower than the others to allow for surmounting image niches, their presumably canopied tops now missing. Angle buttress at the nave's SW corner, its sloping top surmounted by an octagonal turret, a stone sundial on its S face. On top of the SE angle buttress, a slenderer octagonal turret. At the buttress to its W the sloping top is masked by the front face being carried up as a gablet.

At each aisle the splayed sills of the windows are linked by a string course which is interrupted by the buttresses. The hoodmoulds of the S aisle's windows have had label stops, probably all carved as headstops like those surviving at the E bay and the second bay from the W. The N aisle's hoodmoulds end in simple lateral returns across the wall.

The window in the W bay of the N aisle may originally have been similar to the corresponding window of the S aisle (*see below*) but was replaced *c.* 1500 by Bishop George Brown who erected his coat of arms above it. It is rectangular, the sill and lintel with straight splays, the jambs cavetto-splayed, the three lights each containing diagonally set cusps at the top corners. In the next bay of this aisle and in its fourth and fifth bays, two-light windows, the head of each filled with a simple quatrefoil. In the aisle's third bay from the W, a pointed and hoodmoulded door. Ambitious tracery in the three-light window of the next bay whose head is filled by a large squashed sexfoil flanked by flowing trefoil lights. In the E bay, the three-light window has reticulated tracery of three quatrefoils.

In the W bay of the S aisle, a humble single-light window, its head cusped. In the next bay, a two-light window, its head filled with a Geometric arrangement of three trefoils circling a fourth. In this aisle's third bay from the W, a round-headed overarch springs from the buttresses to frame the original entrance, which was covered *c.* 1470 by the porch (now roofless) added by Bishop Thomas Lauder. At the porch's S corners, diagonal buttresses, the E still with a weathered pinnacle. The moulded S entrance survives up to the springing of its arch; plain rectangular windows in the E and W faces. Raggles on the aisle's wall show that the porch roof was double-pitched, its ridge running into the worn armorial panel over the earlier C15 door. In the two windows E of the porch, two-light windows, the head of each filled with a simple quatrefoil, very like the corresponding windows of the N aisle. Three-light window at the next bay, its head filled by a large trefoil flanked by smaller trefoil lights. In the E bay of the S aisle, another three-light window but its tracery consists of sinuously curved and cusped dagger shapes set between quatrefoils.

On both sides of the nave, simple two-light clearstorey windows, each with a quatrefoil in the head; pendant label stops to the hoodmoulds survive on the N side A corbel-studded cavetto cornice remains on the S.

The general appearance of the unaisled CHOIR is C13, most of the detail Elliot's of the early C19. It is long and narrow, *c.* 31.4 m. by 8.8 m., of four bays, the W shorter than the others. The sloped base of the walls is carried across the side buttresses. The offset tops of the S buttresses support early C19 gableted and crocketed pinnacles. At the E corners' angle buttresses the foliage-finialled pinnacles are also early C19 but octagonal and carried on continuous corbelling across the inner angles. On the E face of the SE buttress, the weathered base and canopy of an image niche. Sill courses along the sides and, at a higher level, across the E gable which is crossed also by a string course extending from the bottom of the window's hoodmould; another string course above the window. Great E window of five lights, its rectilinear tracery of 1817–20. Near the apex of the gable, a wheel window, the tracery again of 1817–20. Four-light side windows except at the W bay of the S side where the window is of only two lights, all with early C19 tracery consisting of circlets and quatrefoils. Tudor-arched doors, again of 1817–20, at the S side's end bays. Carried all round the choir's wallhead, a corbel-studded cavetto cornice and early C19 battlement.

The same cornice and battlement surmount the two-storey CHAPTER HOUSE of 1457–*c.* 1460 which projects from the choir's N side. It is an austerely detailed rectangle, *c.* 7.01 m. by 10.36 m., of the same height as the choir. Angle buttresses at the outer corners and another buttress at the centre of the long N face, all with intakes and offsets. On the E face of the NE buttress, the ogee-arched and cusped surround for a heraldic panel. The ground-floor windows are tall and narrow pointed lights. The upper floor has been lit by small rectangular windows in the E and W walls, the E windows probably later enlarged so that they break down through the original sill course, the w window now blocked. At the s end of the w wall, a low door under a tier of narrow rectangular stair windows, the top breaking through the upper floor's sill course. In the w bay of the N side, a Perp door inserted in the early C19.

Interior

The NAVE is relentlessly focused on the E end, the three storeys of arcades, triforium and clearstorey marked off by the lines of the capitals of the arcade piers and the sill courses which give an unremitting horizontality to each level reinforced by the corbel-studded cavetto cornice at the wallhead. The arcades' sturdy circular piers are strongly reminiscent of Romanesque work, their deeply moulded round bases standing on octagonal sub-bases, but their multiple-moulded octagonal capitals carry pointed arches. The arches of the N arcade have chamfer and convex mouldings, those of the S roll-and-hollow, perhaps indicating a pause in the building work although both arcades apparently belong to Bishop Robert de Cardeny's operations in the early C15. The triforium arches are all semicircular, each containing three lights, the outer two pointed, the centre trefoiled, the mouldings on each side repeating those of the arcades below. At the clearstorey there is further evidence of staggered construction but here it is of *c.* 1450–64 when Bishop Thomas Lauder completed the nave. Each pointed opening contains two cusped lights under a quatrefoil head but the windows of the N side and in the three E bays of the S have simple internal splays and are placed at the outer face of the wall while those of the four W bays of the S side have chamfered mouldings and are set well back from the wall face. The missing roof seems to have been of wood, perhaps a tunnel vault.

Broad pointed arch to the choir (now blocked) at the nave's E end. The w view looking down the nave makes the off-centre position of the w window even more startling than it is from outside.

Sill courses along the side walls of the nave's aisles. In the N aisle, stone corbels, the W two carved with foliage, apparently to support a wooden vault. At the S aisle, corbels and tas-de-charge, the corbels of the E bay carved with human heads and one at the w bay with a weathered beast, the others with foliage. It looks as if a stone vault was intended but the metal pins on the upper side of the tas-de-charge may have been fixings for a wooden roof; if so, it was presumably an afterthought. Above the responds of the nave's E bay, slots, presumably the seating for a wooden rood loft. At the S aisle's two E bays are slots in the arcade piers and cut through the wall's sill course to support wooden screens erected in the early C15 by Bishop de Cardeny who formed a chapel here. In this chapel's E wall, a piscina and, above, horizontal grooves, perhaps fixings for an altarpiece. At the w end of the N aisle, a pointed arch into the NW tower.

Propped against the N wall of the nave, a couple of late C18 HEADSTONES, both decorated with skulls, crossbones and hourglasses. One, dated 1797, displays a heraldic shield, the other an angel's head (the soul). – At the E end of this wall, a badly weathered red sandstone GRAVE-SLAB, perhaps C17, carved with the reliefs of small human figures and a skeleton at the bottom. – Against the E wall, three early C18 GRAVE-SLABS (one commemorating Robert Stewart †171–, another Katren Paton †1723, the wife of David Hill, merchant in Dunkeld), each carved with a skull and crossbones. – Built into the E end of the S wall is the TOMB of Bishop de Robert Cardeny †1437. Sarcophagus base, its front carved with angels holding shields and, between them, small human figures. Above the sarcophagus, a segmental-arched recess, its ogee-arched hoodmould crocketed and foliage-finialled. Lying on top of the sarcophagus, the effigy of a bishop. – Just W of the S door, a GRAVE-SLAB, possibly late C16 incised with what looks like a spade. – W of this, a HEADSTONE to H [?] B †1757 [?] carved with an angel's head (the soul) at the top, reminders of death at the bottom.

Inside the NW TOWER, the tall ground-floor room is covered with a stellar vault. Two of the bosses are carved with shields bearing the gryphon rampant coat of arms of Bishop Thomas Lauder. In place of another two bosses are holes for bell ropes. In the centre, a large circular opening to enable bells to be hoisted. On the vault, remains of painting. More painted decoration on the walls, the scenes, appropriate to the room's original use as a court, including the Judgement of Solomon on the N and the Woman taken in Adultery on the W. On the E side, a large pointed arch into the N aisle. It springs from bundled shafts, their capitals carved with a continuous band of foliage; roll-and-hollow moulding at the head. At the N end of the E wall, a rectangular door, placed a little above floor level, into a small chamber. – On the floor of the tower, a recumbent HOGBACK GRAVESTONE, perhaps of the C11, one side incised with scalloping, the other with a now mutilated cross standing on a stepped base. – Fixed to the wall above is a GRAVE-SLAB of *c.* 1550 commemorating Alexander Douglas, Rector of Moneydie, incised with the figure of a priest dressed in a chasuble but with a tasselled cloth on his head.

The CHOIR (now the parish church of Dunkeld) has ashlar walls with string courses along the sides. At the W half of the N wall, two sections of C13 blind arcading, the cusped and moulded arches (restored in 1908) springing from columns with stiff-leaf capitals (many now mutilated). Between the two sections has been placed a heraldic stone, perhaps reused from a dormerhead, bearing the arms of Stewart quartered with those of Muir (?) and the initials I^{M}S and MM above and below. Round-arched door to the chapter house above which is placed a late C17 heraldic achievement of the Marquesses of Atholl. Further E in the N wall, a squint from the chapter house and E of the squint, another six bays of wall arcading; two of the arches now forming a canopy over a headless alabaster EFFIGY (not *in situ*), perhaps of Bishop William Sinclair †1337; above the effigy, a damaged stone carved with a shield bearing a bird. At the N end of the E wall, one blind arch continues the arcading. Near the S wall's E end, a triple SEDILIA, perhaps an early C14 insertion, the cusped arches surmounted by continuous hoodmoulding.

The choir's roof, furnishings and much of its present character date from *W. Dunn & R. Watson*'s restoration of 1908. The roof is of oak, its curved ribs suggesting a pointed tunnel vault, the cornice carved with fruiting vines. At the W end of the choir, an oak ORGAN GALLERY of Late Gothic character. – ORGAN, by *Bevington & Sons*, 1906; rebuilt by *A. F. Edmonstone* in 1988. – In front of the organ screen, a stone FONT carved with Neo-Celtic enrichment; presumably of *c.* 1908. – The E bay of the choir is partitioned off by an oak SCREEN, again in a Late Gothic manner. Protruding from its N corner, the PULPIT, again carved with fruiting vines. – Simple but dignified oak PEWS. – STAINED GLASS E window (the Annunciation to the Shepherds, with small figures emblematic of Christian virtues above and a depiction of St Columba preaching below) by *Burlison & Grylls*, 1908.

MONUMENTS. Free-standing Glen Tilt marble TOMB (not *in situ*) of Alexander Stewart, Earl of Buchan (the 'Wolf of Badenoch') †*c.* 1405. Sarcophagus, its sides divided into canopied niches, each containing the figure of a knight. On this rests the more than life-size recumbent EFFIGY of a knight in full armour (the l. shoulder and elbow reused from another and smaller effigy), his hands folded, his feet resting on a lion. The style of armour suggests that the effigy was executed *c.* 1420. – High up on the E end of the N wall, a white marble MONUMENT by *J. G. Lough*, 1847, to Major-General Sir Robert Henry Dick, carved with a relief depicting Dick's death at the Battle of Sobraon.* – On the E wall, the huge BLACK WATCH MONUMENT, again of white marble, by *John Steell*, 1872, sculpted with the high relief of an officer of the Black Watch searching for a missing comrade among tumbled corpses. The subject was inspired by lines in the *Ingoldsby Legends* ('But a sombre sight is a battlefield,/To the sad survivor's sorrowing eyes'). – On the S wall, two weathered ARMORIAL STONES. One, immediately W of the screen, bears the coat of arms of a bishop, the other is near the W end.

The interior of the CHAPTER HOUSE is of two bays, covered with flattish groin vaulting, the ceiling ribs and E and W wall ribs elliptically arched, the N and S wall ribs pointed; bosses carved with foliage decoration. The vaulting is cut into at the SW corner by a splayed projection containing a turnpike stair to the room above (probably the cathedral's charter room). – MONUMENTS. John, fourth Duke of Atholl, is commemorated

---

*Erected in Logierait Parish Church in 1848 and moved to Dunkeld Cathedral in 1854.

by a free-standing white marble STATUE by *John Ternouth*, 1835, a more than life-size depiction of the duke dressed in the robes of the Order of the Thistle. – On the N wall, the uncompleted MONUMENT to John Stewart, Earl of Atholl, †1603. The general conception, a tomb-chest set in a recess large enough to contain an effigy, is medieval, the detail classicising. At the ends of the chest and recess, superimposed fluted pilasters, the lower order Doric, the upper Ionic of a sort, the capitals topped by angels' heads. Above the recess, an entablature, the frieze carved with square and faceted blocks. Above, scrolls flank a corniced panel, the inscription unexecuted, which supports a pediment bearing the arms and initials of John Stewart, Earl of Atholl. The recess now contains an alabaster BUST of Sir Donald Currie †1909. – On the E wall, a MONUMENT to Lord Charles Murray †1821. It is again by *Ternouth*, the inscription panel surmounted by a high-relief urn carved with a sheep and with a broken bow resting against it. – On the S wall, the MONUMENT to John, first Marquess of Atholl, and his wife, Lady Amelia Stanley, designed by *Alexander Edward* and executed by *Patrick Murray* in 1704–5. Huge open-pedimented Corinthian aedicule, the fluted columns bearing relief busts of the Marquess and his wife. Flaming urns on the ends of the pediment, its tympanum carved with two heraldic achievements. Inside the aedicule, the inscription panel flanked by a display of carved and painted coats of arms of those related to the Earl on the l. and to his wife on the r. Above the panel, a trophy; more arms below, flanked by skulls and bones. – Free-standing slab (the 'APOSTLES' STONE') carved rather crudely, probably in the C9. On one side, two tiers of cloaked forward-facing figures (twelve in all) and, above, a shield and an array of heads depicted in profile. On the other side, a depiction of Daniel in the Lions' Den; above, a display of corpses, one dismembered, under a group of warriors shown in profile. On one edge, a horseman, also in profile, above cloaked and hooded men, shown frontally and with one much larger than the others. – Plain CROSS-SLAB of the C8 or C9, rather weathered. – Large BELL by *John Meikle*, 1688.

At the E end of the CHURCHYARD, at its entrance from Cathedral Street, wrought iron GATES of *c.* 1730, originally at the entrance to Dunkeld House and re-erected here in 1832. Delicate, with urn-topped piers. At the overthrow, foliage encloses a coroneted roundel bearing the initial A (for Atholl).

CHURCHES

CONGREGATIONAL CHURCH, Atholl Street. Secularized. Harled rectangle of *c.* 1800.

DUNKELD FREE CHURCH, Tay Terrace. Secularized. Geometric, by *David Smart*, 1874–5. Four-light window in the gable front which is flanked by a steeple, its Frenchy pyramid roof covered with bands of grey and green fish-scale slates, and a battlemented tower. Over the steeple and tower entrances,

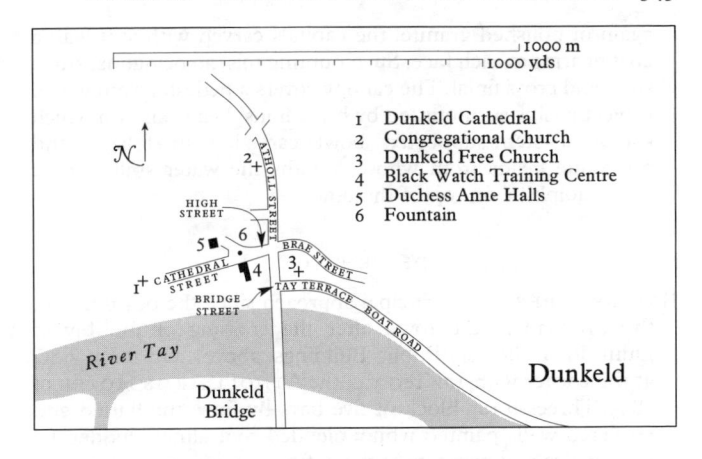

```
                    1000 m
                    1000 yds

1  Dunkeld Cathedral
2  Congregational Church
3  Dunkeld Free Church
4  Black Watch Training Centre
5  Duchess Anne Halls
6  Fountain
```

hoodmoulds whose label stops are carved (by *John Dick*) as human heads.

The interior has been partly floored over at gallery level. Ceiling painted blue with stencilled gold stars. – STAINED GLASS N window, with emblems of the Free Church of Scotland and of the eleventh Earl of Dalhousie to whom it is a memorial, by *James Ballantine & Son*, 1875.

PUBLIC BUILDINGS

THE BLACK WATCH TRAINING CENTRE, High Street. Built in 1950. Harled Neo-Georgian, desperately anxious to fit in with its surroundings.

DUCHESS ANNE HALLS, High Street. Originally the Duchess of Atholl's Industrial School. By *R. & R. Dickson*, 1853–4. Two-storey asymmetrical Tudor, a small steeple giving an off-centre accent to the ashlar façade.

DUNKELD BRIDGE over the River Tay. By *Thomas Telford*, 1805–8, the successor to medieval bridges, the last of which had fallen by the C18 and been inadequately replaced by a ferry. Almost 210 m. long, gently humpbacked and elegant, built of ashlar, the voussoirs' stonework channelled. Five broad segmental arches over the river, the pointed cutwaters surmounted by semicircular turrets with dummy crosslet arrowslits. Semicircular floodwater arch at each end. Mutuled cornice under the parapet.

FOUNTAIN, High Street. Erected to commemorate the sixth Duke of Atholl, 1866; *Charles S. Robertson* was the architect, *John Rhind* the sculptor. French Gothic of Eleanor Cross type. The canopy is supported by four columns of polished Peterhead granite, their capitals lavishly carved with birds and foliage. At each face, an elaborately cusped gabled arch. Above, an octagonal superstructure, its small columns' shafts again of polished granite, the capitals carved with stiff-leaf; a coat of arms at each face. Surmounting this, an octagonal stone spire and cross finial. The canopy covers a pedestal from which project basins surmounted by brass lions' heads and on which stands a stem-supported bowl carved with foliage and grotesque heads from whose mouths the water spills down; metal dolphins on top of the bowl.

DESCRIPTION

BRIDGE STREET, the principal approach since the beginning of the C19, enters the town after the crossing of the Tay at Dunkeld Bridge (*see* Public Buildings, above). On the E side, at the corner with Tay Terrace, the ATHOLL ARMS HOTEL of 1833. Three-storey block of five bays by four, the harled and rendered walls painted white; piended roof almost hidden by the cornice and parapet. At the W front, an off-centre entrance (now a window) with unfluted Greek Doric columns *in antis*. At the N bay, a segmental-arched pend (now blocked). In TAY TERRACE to the E, the former Dunkeld Free Church (*see* Churches, above) followed by the large and prosperous former COMMERCIAL BANK OF SCOTLAND, by *James Gillespie Graham*, 1834. Three storeys, basement and attic, the windows of the three-bay polished ashlar front architraved and linked by sill courses. Broad Ionic portico at the slightly advanced centre. Blocking course over the wallhead cornice. To its E, the TAYBANK HOTEL, a white-painted Jacobethan villa of the earlier C19. Thistle, rose and cross finials on the gablets and the slightly advanced and oriel-windowed end bay. The label stops of the round-arched entrance are carved with the heads of hirsute gentlemen. In the SE corner of the garden, a pyramidal-roofed early C19 gazebo (THE MAGAZINE), its door and windows pointed.

Bridge Street's E side N of the Atholl Arms Hotel consists of a two-storey and attic terrace, to a design of 1827 by *W.M. Mackenzie*. Ashlar front (partly painted and the upper floor of No. 6 now harled), the first-floor windows set in moulded architraves and linked by a sill course, the wallhead cornice supporting a blocking course. Quadrant corner at the N. The W side of Bridge Street begins with Nos. 1–5, by *W.M. Mackenzie*, 1827. Again of two storeys and an attic (and a basement and sub-basement at the back), moulded architraves to the first-floor windows and a blocking course above the wallhead cornice. Projecting bow at the S end. The rest of this side of Bridge Street is also early C19, a plainer version of the E side's terrace but with pilastered doorpieces. The consoled cornices at the ground-floor windows of the two N houses are mid-C19 embellishments. The terrace's canted corner to High Street is scooped up to the square under the eaves course.

BRAE STREET leads steeply uphill to the E from Bridge Street's N end. On the S side, SUNDIAL HOUSE of 1757, its name and date provided by the sundial at the SW corner which also bears the names of John Ballantine and Jannet Stewart. Three-storey and attic main block, built of painted rubble, the N wall now demolished (2006). Single-storey NE wing and two-storey E wing. Further up, on the N side, HILLHEAD OF DUNKELD, a sizeable Tudor villa of *c.* 1840, a bellcote on its single-storey office wing. Contemporary but plain stables to the N. Then, on the s, a crowstep-gabled mid-C19 villa (TAYHILL).

HIGH STREET, leading w off the top of Bridge Street into the town laid out after 1690, is an irregular triangle, broadest at the w. In the centre, the fountain commemorating the sixth Duke of Atholl (*see* Public Buildings, above). On the s side, after the Bridge Street corner, a three-storey rubble-built block (Nos. 1–5), perhaps of *c.* 1810. Then the palazzo-like BANK OF SCOTLAND (originally Central Bank of Scotland), by *A. & A. Heiton*, 1857, also of three storeys but taller and its front of polished ashlar, channelled at the ground floor. Round-headed ground-floor openings, the end doors set behind Roman Doric pillared porticoes; segmental pediments over the first-floor windows. Then the two-storey C18 Nos.17–19, its harl and painted margins dating from 1955 when the Perth & Kinross County Architect, *Ian A. Moodie*, adopted the formula used at the same time by The National Trust for Scotland's Little Houses Scheme for the repair and internal modernisation of nearby buildings. A basket-arched pend at the w end opens onto a lane leading down to the River Tay. The adjoining two-storey but much taller house (now THE SCOTTISH HORSE REGIMENTAL MUSEUM), now also harled and with painted margins to fit in, is mid-C19. Mullioned and transomed windows, those of the ground floor hoodmoulded; heavy doorpiece with block consoles under the cornice. Next door, The Black Watch Training Centre (*see* Public Buildings, above).

On High Street's N side, after the corner block (*see* Atholl Street, below), the PERTH ARMS HOTEL. It is composed of two harled blocks. The E, probably early C19, is a tall three-storey building with an anta-pilastered doorpiece. The w, also of three storeys but lower, is probably C18 but much altered. Next, a plain two-storey C18 house (No. 15), one of a group restored for The National Trust for Scotland by *Ian G. Lindsay & Partners* in 1955–6. It is dressed in the Little Houses Scheme's uniform of harl and painted margins. Then another two-storey C18 building (No. 14) but it is of six bays, the windows grouped 4:2. At the centre of the wallhead, a chimneyed gablet containing a round-headed attic window; sundial on top of the w skewputt. There follows a simple C18 harled house (No. 12) after which the building line is set back and has a more pronounced splay to the NW. Interrupting the restored C18 group, a harled block built by the *Scottish Special Housing Association* in 1953. Would-be C18 manner but the chimneys are too few and too mean; elliptical-arched entrances to a pend and a shop. The last building on this side (No. 11), again C18 and harled but for once without painted margins, is enlivened by a forestair. Then a wall containing the round-arched entrance to Stanley Hill and, at High Street's NW corner, a harled and pyramidal-roofed PUBLIC TOILET of c. 1970.

STANLEY HILL, now Dunkeld's well-wooded public park, was terraced by the second Duke of Atholl in 1730 as part of his improvements to the parkland of Dunkeld House (*see* below). Excavated in the hill's W side, an earth-covered C18 ICE HOUSE. Round-headed entrance into the stone-lined domical chamber.

At the W end of High Street, the Duchess Anne Halls (*see* Public Buildings, above). To the S, the C18 harled three-storey CASTLE CLEIRACH or CONACHER'S BUILDING which presents a gable (now minus its chimney) to the street and a four-bay elevation to a close. It was restored in 1964. On the N corner of Cathedral Street, THE ELL HOUSE, again harled, built as an almshouse (St George's Hospital) in 1753. Three storeys, the second-floor windows' gabled dormerheads added in the C19. At the first floor, two frames for armorial panels, now containing the painted coats of arms of Bishop George Brown who founded the institution in 1510 and The National Trust for Scotland who restored the present building in 1954.

CATHEDRAL STREET, laid out c. 1690, runs W from the SW corner of High Street to the gates into the Cathedral churchyard (*see* Dunkeld Cathedral, above). On both sides two-storey terraced housing of the earlier C18 (No. 6 of 1725, No. 19 with a roll-and-hollow-moulded doorpiece, perhaps reused). Most of the houses were restored (No. 7 rebuilt in replica, and Nos. 12–14 and No. 17 built to fill gap sites) in 1954–6, those on the S side for Perth & Kinross County Council by the County Architect, *Ian A. Moodie*, those on the N for The National Trust for Scotland by *Ian G. Lindsay & Partners*. All display The National Trust for Scotland's Little Houses Scheme's trademark harling and painted margins. The S terrace is broken by the entrance to the garden of the MANSE, its gatepiers of the early C19. The house itself is C18, of two storeys with a pair of piended gables to the rear. Single-storey offices, probably also C18, fronting Cathedral Street.

Set back at the W end of the N side is THE OLD RECTORY (No. 25), its two-storey, basement and attic five-bay front mid C18 except for C20 flat-roofed dormers and a wooden porch of c. 1945, but the house incorporates earlier work. Inside, at the basement's W wall, a huge kitchen fireplace, with a chamfered elliptical-arched opening. It seems to be of c. 1600, perhaps dating from a rebuilding of the former manse of the prebendary of Craigie by William Banerman who obtained a Crown charter to the property in 1599. At the half landing of the stair from the basement, a chamfered door, the house's entrance before the formation of Cathedral Street. Above this level, the interior is mostly mid C18. The E room of the ground floor is panelled but with an Edwardian chimneypiece imported in the 1960s. In the W room, a fragmentary C18 cornice. At the end of the entrance hall, a pair of elliptical arches with stucco shells at their ends open onto the stairs to the basement and the first floor, the latter with silhouette balusters. Over the stair to the first floor, a coved ceiling, its corners ornamented in stucco with bows and shells from which hang fruiting branches. On the flat, a tendrilly star. More panelling in the two first-floor rooms.

ATHOLL STREET continues the line of Bridge Street to the N. On both sides early C19 two-storey and attic rubble-built terraces, the first-floor windows linked by sill courses (partly missing on the W), the S corners canted, that of the E terrace corbelled to the square under the wallhead cornice. At the beginning of the W terrace, at No. 1, a Scots Renaissance shopfront of the late C19 and contemporary architraves to the first-floor windows. The taller mansard-roofed block at Nos. 20–24 is an insertion of *c.* 1900. At the end of the W terrace, the ROYAL DUNKELD HOTEL, its central portion rising to a dizzying four storeys and with unfluted Greek Doric attached columns at its ground floor. Inside, an elaborate cast-iron balustrade to the staircase. On the first floor an assembly room, the enrichment and rose of its coved ceiling looking like C20 embellishments. To its N, the former Congregational Church (*see* Churches, above) followed by some C20 housing and a car park. The gateway and lodges at the entrance to Dunkeld House (*see* below) mark the N end of the burgh.

DUNKELD HOUSE
off Atholl Street

Overgrown harled two-storey villa designed by *J. Macintyre Henry* and built for the seventh Duke of Atholl in 1898–1900. It has bay windows fronted by balconied verandas; over the entrance, a square tower, its pyramidal roof with bellcast eaves. Large late C20 extension, also with a tower, for the house's present use as a hotel. – GATEWAY AND LODGES fronting the road. Castellated, by *Archibald Elliot*, 1809. Built to serve the late C17 mansion of Dunkeld House (demolished, 1828). The gateway itself, placed between battlemented towers decorated with dummy crosslet 'arrowslits' and blind shields, is a pointed arch surmounted by a battlement carried on arcaded corbelling; on each face of the battlement's central merlon, the heraldic achievement of the Dukes of Atholl. On either side of the gateway, parapeted screen walls pierced by pointed footgates link to lodges. Each is a battlemented single-storey rectangle with hoodmoulds over the door and windows; corner turrets, their walls with dummy crosslets, their parapets pierced by quatrefoils and diamonds.

CARDNEY HOUSE. *See* p. 257.

DUNNING

A burgh of barony founded in 1511 under the superiority of the Rollos of Duncrub. The houses, grouped not very formally beside the medieval parish church (St Serf), were rebuilt after their destruction during the Jacobite rising of 1715–16 and, again, from the end of the C18 when a 'new town' on the E side of the Dunning Burn was begun and the hamlet of Newton of Pitcairns laid out for weavers' cottages. Weaving was the principal occupation of the inhabitants until the mid C19, after which Dunning's character changed from that of a small industrial centre to a drowsy village.

CHURCHES

BURGHER CHURCH, Townhead. Secularized. Rubble box, dated 1806. Front of four bays, with a door at each end; at its centre, a pair of large round-headed windows with projecting imposts and keystones.

DUNNING CHURCH, Perth Road. Originally Dunning United Free Church. Geometric Gothic, by *W. Carruthers Laidlaw*, 1908–9. Buttressed broad rectangle, built of bullnosed squared rubble; SW porch. Metal flèche on the roof. Hall and vestry at the N end.

Inside, the walls are of squared and stugged stone, the short chancel lined with Gothic panelling. Pointed chancel arch. Wagon roofs, the nave's with collars which spring from stone corbels carved with angels and are surmounted by arcading, the chancel's compartmented. Routine Gothic COMMUNION TABLE and PULPIT, both designed by Laidlaw and executed by *Brown Bros*.

STAINED GLASS. S window (the Four Evangelists) of 1909, by *A. Ballantine & Son*. – Also of 1909 the brightly coloured narrative S window of the E wall (St Paul). – To its N, a Modernistic window (Baptism; Eucharist) by *Martin Farrelly*, 2002. – Next, another window (the Maries at the Tomb) by *A. Ballantine & Son*, 1909. – This wall's strongly coloured N window (the Adoration of the Magi) was designed by *Fiona Forsyth* and executed by *Martin Farrelly* in 2000. – In the W wall, the two S windows (Easter and Pentecost; Genesis and the Burning Bush) are also by Farrelly, 2002. – Then, a window (Our Lord Blessing Children) of 1909 by *A. Ballantine & Son*. – More colourful this wall's N window (an Angel Blessing a Knight) of 1917. – N window of chancel (Our Lord Carrying the Cross) by *A. Ballantine & Son*, 1909.

ST SERF, Kirkstyle Square. Sizeable parish church built *c.* 1200 but altered, enlarged and partly rebuilt in the centuries after the Reformation.

The medieval church consisted of a nave (12.8 m. by 8.3 m.), a lower chancel (7.9 m. by 6.5 m.) and a very tall W tower (5.15 m. by 5.45 m.). The tower has been little altered. Gently battered walls built of coursed and squared masonry rise through six unequal stages. The first three are unbroken by string courses. In the S face, a ground floor door which appears to occupy the position of an original entrance although its present plain appearance probably dates from alterations of 1808–11. To its l., a tier of small rectangular openings lighting the internal stair. At the third stage and aligned with the door, a rectangular window. In each of the two lowest stages of the W face, a narrow round-headed window. These are off-centre but aligned with each other; flanking the upper window is a pair of putlog holes. At the S face's second stage, a pair of putlog holes but no window. Another pair of holes at the third stage where they flank a centrally placed window. The tower's fourth and fifth stages are marked off by string courses. At each face of the low fourth stage, putlog holes flanking a rectangular window, now largely hidden behind a clock face (by *H. & R. Millar*) placed here by *William Jones* in 1890. Similar arrangement of putlog holes and belfry openings at the tall fifth stage but the belfry openings consist of round-headed recesses, each containing two lights, also round-headed, divided by a cushion-capitalled column (renewed in 1890). No string course between the belfry and the low top stage which is pierced by rectangular windows flanked by putlog holes. The tower is finished with a saddleback roof, its crowstepped gables, perhaps rebuilt in the late C16 or C17, with cavetto-moulded skewputts carved with reliefs of human heads; a weathercock on the ridge.

The chancel seems to have been raised to the same height as the nave in the late C17 when the gallery of the Rollos of Duncrub was erected there, and both chancel and nave were extensively remodelled by *Alexander Bowie* and *John Frazer* in 1808–11. In these early C19 alterations the S wall of the nave was rebuilt and the chancel widened S to the same line, both chancel and nave were covered with a single roof, its pitch flatter than that of the medieval nave as evidenced by a raggle on the tower's E face, and a large transeptal 'aisle' was built out from the N side of the E part of the nave. Bowie and Frazer's six-bay S front is built at least partly of medieval masonry including carved fragments, e.g. the mutilated remains of a cushion capital in the base of the wall, a fragment of arcaded ornament and, at the E end, a fragment of chevron, all perhaps from a doorway. In each end bay, a two-storey arrangement of plain rectangular windows. In the intermediate bays, rectangular doors (the W a dummy). At the centre bays, tall pointed windows, their wooden mullions inserted *c.* 1900. The E gable incorporates medieval stonework. Built against it is a late C17 forestair to the door to the E gallery. The door, probably replacing a medieval E window, has a lintel carved with the impaled arms and initials of Andrew, third Lord Rollo, and Margaret, Lady Rollo, together with the date 1687. The windowless original N wall of the chancel survives, with a row of weathered corbels which formerly supported a parapet (removed when the chancel was heightened). Projecting from the E end of the nave is the N 'aisle' of 1808–11, quite plain, with rectangular windows and doors. In the 'aisle's' W inner angle with the nave, a forestair, now partly removed to reveal the medieval door at the W end of the nave. This is of two orders, the inner with a roll-and-hollow moulding. The hoodmoulded outer order has been carried on nook-shafts of which survive the base of the W and the cushion capital of the E. At the W end of the nave's S wall, a few weathered corbels which formerly supported a parapet which was stopped against a broad skew sloping down from the tower.

INTERIOR. Medieval work survives at the W end where there is a steeply pointed arch into the ground floor of the tower. It is carried on semicircular responds with scalloped capitals, the N capital smaller than the S, so its abacus is placed at a slightly lower level. Both abaci are simply moulded with an incised fillet and are continued as a string course across the W wall of the church. The tower arch is of three orders, the inner plain and the outer with a simple moulding. The middle order is decorated with scallops and darts, the darts pointing down to knops; at the top, a leaf ornament. In the tower's ground-floor room, the stair walls muscling into its SW corner, a W window with deeply splayed ingoes.

Services in the church were discontinued in 1974 but the furnishings remain. GALLERIES of 1808–11 at the E and W ends and in the N 'aisle', their panelled and pilastered fronts with dentil cornices. – Plain PEWS of 1868. – At the centre of the S side, an oak PULPIT of 1914 imported from the demolished Auchterarder West (originally South United Presbyterian) Church, c. 1955. – Simple Gothic COMMUNION TABLE by *J. & E. Wilson*, 1895. – STAINED GLASS. In the S wall, the E and W windows under the gallery (the Sower; the Good Shepherd) are by *A. Ballantine & Gardiner*, 1899. – In the two large windows flanking the pulpit, figures emblematic of Justice, Humility and Fidelity, by *A. Ballantine & Son*, 1910. – E and W gallery windows (the Angel Reaper; Our Lord) of 1907 and also by *A. Ballantine & Son*. – MONUMENTS. At the E end, white marble tablets bearing coats of arms, by *Thomas Gaffin*. They commemorate John, eighth Lord Rollo, †1846, and William, ninth Lord Rollo, †1852. – On the S wall, a stone bearing the Drummond coat of arms and motto GA VARLY (Go Warily), the initials VD and IK for William Drummond of Pitcairn and Jean Ker, his wife, and the date 1615. – To its W and placed high up, a round marble monument, also with a coat of arms, to James Graeme of Garvock †1812. – On the E wall of the 'aisle', a monument of 1612 to Ninian Graeme of Garvock, its weathered shield surmounted by a skull. – Under the tower, against the N wall, a weathered and broken Early Christian SLAB. It has been carved in relief with two ringed crosses (one partly broken off) with short shafts and round hollows at the bosses. The sides are decorated with interlace ornament.

The DUPPLIN CROSS was erected under the W tower in 2002. Nearly 3m. high, this is a magnificently carved high cross of local sandstone. Formerly on a hillside SW of Dupplin Castle, it was one of two crosses, the other being at Invermay to the S, which overlooked the former Pictish royal palace at Forteviot. A very badly weathered panel on the W face bears an

Dunning, St Serf's Church, Dupplin Cross

inscription, largely indecipherable, which begins *CU[...] NTIN/FILIUS FIRCUS* and presumably refers to Constantine, son of Fergus. Constantine, very likely the son of a Scottish father and Pictish mother, was ruler of the Pictish kingdom of Fortriu c. 789–820 and also of the Scottish kingdom of Dál Riata c. 811–20. There is a strong possibility that the Dupplin Cross was erected in the early C9 either by Constantine himself or to commemorate him, and its design seems to be derived from a mixture of Scottish, Irish, Pictish and Northumbrian sources. The general shape, an uncircled high cross with curvilinear arms and rounded armpits, was probably influenced by work on Iona (Argyll and Bute), its tegulated top from Irish high crosses, the differentiation in the treatment of the head and the shaft from Northumbrian crosses, while most of the carved detail and its iconography is Pictish.

Roughly shaped top carved as a tiled roof. The central intersection of the four arms of the head is marked on the broad E and W faces by prominent bosses, both decorated with a sunburst outer ring, the centre of the W with a Greek cross.

Surrounding the E boss and filling most of the arms is a depiction of two snakes, their tails dividing and intertwining; above, a panel of diagonal key pattern. Around the W boss, interlaced work ending in the heads of beasts and, at the ends of the arms, curvilinear patterns. On the narrow N face, the top arm has a panel of interlaced work above another which contains key pattern decoration. Diagonal key pattern on the end of the N arm. Another panel of interlaced work on the bottom arm. At the top of the S face, a pair of panels, the upper with interlaced work, the lower with a diagonal key pattern. On the end of the S arm, a panel bearing two crosses. At the bottom of the lower arm, a panel with diagonal key pattern and a central spiral.

The shaft is divided into panels, several bearing scenes expressive of Constantine's kingship. On the E face, the top panel is carved with a heavily moustachioed king on horseback, probably a depiction of Constantine as over-king. Tall panel below showing four clean-shaven warriors dressed in long tunics and armed with spears and shields. On the bottom panel, a pair of hounds hunting, a favourite motif of Pictish sculpture. The top panel of the weathered W face bore the inscription. Centre panel with a circle filled with interlaced work surrounded by birds. On the bottom panel, a relief of King David, the Biblical exemplar of kingship, shown twice, in the upper part killing the lion and, below, killing the bear which had stolen a lamb from his father's flock (a reference to David's boast to Saul of his fitness to challenge Goliath). The shaft's N side is also divided into three panels. In the top, a mythical beast. Centre panel showing King David playing the harp, its top carved with an eagle's head, the back of his chair with a duck's head. Interlaced work in the bottom panel. On the shaft's S side the top panel contains a pair of embracing pigs, each sticking a foreleg into the other's mouth. On the central panel, two warriors dressed and armed like those on the S face but moustachioed and perhaps representing under-kings. At the bottom, a triangular panel (the shape dictated by that of the stone) containing interlaced work.

GRAVEYARD. At the S entrance, a SESSION HOUSE of 1837, a ball finial on the S gable and a diagonally set chimney on the N. – Just E of the session house, a couple of early C17 small HEADSTONES, one of 1623 to Thomas Rutherford carved with a skull, the other of 1624 to James Dougal. – Between the session house and the church, the SLAB top of a table stone commemorating William Stewart †1742, decorated with reliefs of a skull, crossbones, hourglass and tools. – N of this, another C18 HEADSTONE displaying the same motifs but more crudely executed. – Beside it, a badly weathered HEADSTONE to MH, an angel's head (the soul) carved at the top. – E of this, several more C18 HEADSTONES and GRAVE-SLABS bearing varied combinations of emblems of death and angels' heads, one also with the crowned hammer of a smith, another of 1754 ('repaired', i.e. probably re-cut, in 1798) with the crowned last and shoe of a cobbler, a third with a tailor's scissors and iron.

PUBLIC BUILDINGS

DUNNING COMMUNITY ASSOCIATION HALLS, Newton of Pitcairns. Originally Dunning Free Church School. Dated 1847. In the front gable, a large Venetian window under a small round-headed niche.

DUNNING HALL, Auchterarder Road. Dated 1909. Small Edwardian Free Style, with some Neo-Jacobean touches.

DUNNING PRIMARY SCHOOL, Station Road. By *William Jones*, 1866. Broad-eaved and prominently gabled and gableted school and schoolhouse. Sparing Gothic detail; a big ventilator flèche, its steep pyramidal roof with bellcast eaves and a weathervane.

SCHOOL, Newton of Pitcairns. Dated 1839. Broad-eaved Tudor *cottage orné*.

DESCRIPTION

PERTH ROAD leads in from the NE past Dunning Parish Church (*see* Churches, above). From here LOWER GRANCO STREET goes downhill to the NW. At the top, on the l., a house (ROUND GABLE and WEAVERS BEAM), perhaps of the late C18, its corner gable gently bowed. Further down, set back on the r. and at right angles to the street, the OLD BANK HOUSE, also probably C18 in origin. Otherwise, pleasant but plain mid-C19 houses of one and two storeys. At the end, across a ford over the Dunning Burn, a short two-storey mid-C19 terrace (THE GRANCO).

UPPER GRANCO STREET, running SE from the Perth Road junction, begins with WILLOWBANK HOUSE (the former Union Bank), a prosperous but unadventurous villa of 1883, followed by a two-storey three-bay house of *c.* 1800 and one- and two-storey terraced housing of the early and mid C19. At the SE end of the street, the early C19 THE KNOWES stands guardian on the corner with Bridge of Earn Road. Here, on the axis of Upper Granco Street, a PUMP of the earlier C19, the water issuing from a brass lion's head; plaque bearing the name of *J. McEwan*, plumber, Auchterarder, who presumably erected it.

In Perth Road, SW of the junction with Lower and Upper Granco Streets, a grassed triangle with a Celtic cross WAR MEMORIAL of *c.* 1920 at its W end, overlooked by two-storey terraced houses, mostly of the mid C19. Then a T-junction with Bridge of Earn Road, the Perth Road vista closed by an early C19 double house (CORSHELLACH), its wallhead cornice supported on small blocks. Corniced doorpiece at the N house, the doorpiece of the S a replacement of *c.* 1900.

In BRIDGE OF EARN ROAD's E stretch, mid-C19 vernacular terraces. The street is continued SE by NEWTON OF PITCAIRNS. On the r., the former Newton of Pitcairns School and its Free Church rival (now, Dunning Community Association Halls), for which *see* Public Buildings, above. Beyond these, the hamlet of Newton of Pitcairns, a street of one- and two-storey C19 housing, mostly terraced but with a few plain villas and the occasional C20 interloper. At the end the street bends twice. On the second corner, the mid-C19 GLENROSSIE HOUSE, Tudor manorial on a modest scale.

At the NW end of Bridge of Earn Road, a BRIDGE over the Dunning Burn, built in 1777 but widened in the C20. This leads to KIRKSTYLE SQUARE, a roughly triangular small space, St Serf's Church (*see* Churches, above) on the N side; on the S, the early C19 KIRKSTYLE INN, with a pilastered and corniced doorpiece. The road continues NW into TRON SQUARE, the scale and character of its early and mid-C19 two-storey housing broken by the tall three-storey commercial block of 1874 on the corner of Muckhart Road. On the N side of Tron Square, a FOUNTAIN gifted to the burgh in 1874 by Alexander Martin. Buttressed Gothic octagon topped by a metal lotus flower. From beside the fountain KIRK WYND leads downhill past St Serf's Churchyard. On its l. side, a two-storey rubble-built house STRAW HOUSE, perhaps of the early C18. Ground floor of three bays with chamfered jambs to the door, first floor of four; moulded skewputts.

MUCKHART ROAD leads S from Tron Square. Set well back on the r., the former MANSE (now, THE GLEBE) by *William G. Habershon & Pite*, 1863, an overgrown villa with jerkin-head roofs. S of this, an early C19 house (THORNTREE VILLA), its broached ashlar front now painted; pilastered and corniced doorpiece. On the r. side of the road, the Burgher Church (*see* Churches, above).

AUCHTERARDER ROAD exits W from Tron Square. Plain C19 housing and the Dunning Hall (*see* Public Buildings, above). At the end of the road, another PUMP of the earlier C19, its design the same as that in Bridge of Earn Road (*see* above) but the lion's head replaced by a gryphon's.

In STATION ROAD opening out of Tron Square's NW corner, more plain mid-C19 housing but THE DUNNING HOTEL has raided the dressing-up box to deck itself in white-painted render, with margins picked out in black and 'shutters' painted beside the windows. Further out, on the r., Dunning Primary School (*see* Public Buildings, above).

INVERDUNNING HOUSE, 1.4 km. NE. Miniature mansion house of the early C19, happily mixing architectural styles. Rubble-built two-storey main block of three bays, the outer two shallowly bowed, an architraved and corniced doorpiece like that at Leadketty (*see* below) in the centre. Hoodmoulded windows, the centre first-floor opening Gothic and tripartite with narrow sidelights. Moulded cornice under the broad eaves. Set back at each side, a single-storey and attic one-bay wing, with a pointed attic window in its shaped gable.

LEADKETTY, 1 km. N. Rubble-built but superior farmhouse of *c.* 1800. S front of three bays, the outer two bowed and with Venetian windows at the ground floor. Architraved and corniced doorpiece like that at Inverdunning House (*see* above).

The roof has been altered so that its eaves now project in a straight line in front of the bows. – Extensive rubble-built STEADING behind, mostly of the mid C19.
PITCAIRNS, 0.9 km. SE. Asymmetrical gabled and gableted Elizabethan manor house designed by *William Burn* for John Pitcairn in 1827, a low service range and courtyard at the E. – Contemporary broad-eaved LODGE to the N.

DUNCRUB PARK. *See* p. 329.
GARVOCK HOUSE. *See* p. 380.
KELTIE CASTLE. *See* p. 440.
KIPPEN HOUSE. *See* p. 494.

DUNSINNAN HOUSE
1.3 km. SE of Wolfhill

Neo-Georgian mansion house designed in 1899 by *John Watherston & Sons* for J. Mackay Bernard, Chairman of the Edinburgh brewing firm of Thomas & James Bernard Ltd. A Georgian house forms one rear wing.

The front block is a long two-storey ashlar-clad range, the first-floor windows linked by a sill course. The principal front is to the S, with pediments over the broad centre and end bays, all with first-floor Venetian windows. At the ends, three-light ground-floor windows; at the centre, a semicircular porch with Roman Doric attached columns. In the links, single-light ground-floor windows and, at the upper floor, two-light windows in the outer bays. Three-bay side elevations. Single-storey piend-roofed NE wing, also of 1899 and ashlar-faced. The much less regular and rubble-walled NW wing is made up of parts of the house which existed before the 1890s. At its S end, an C18 block of three storeys but lower than the 1890s S range. W front of three bays with small second-floor windows. Slightly advanced at its N end, the piend-roofed gable of an early C19 addition, probably of 1821 but perhaps of 1828–30 when the S range's Neoclassical predecessor was built; its windows have been altered to two-light, perhaps in the 1890s. N of this, a piend-roofed two-storey block, the ground floor probably of the earlier C19, the upper floor an addition, probably of the 1890s.

STEADING NE of the house, by *Andrew Heiton Sen.*, 1835–6. At the centre of the S range, a two-storey farmhouse, the advanced and pedimented centre of its three-bay front with a pilastered doorpiece. Lateral single-storey wings, their end bays slightly advanced and pedimented and now containing two-light windows, probably enlarged in the 1890s. Two-storey E range and single-storey W range, both rubble-built and piend-roofed. In the courtyard, a circular well-house of 1878, its tall conical roof with a fleur-de-lys finial. – Ashlar-walled STABLES just to the E, of *c.* 1900 and presumably by *John Watherston & Sons*. U-plan, the open S side with a wall topped by railings;

ball-finialled gatepiers at its centre. The buildings are of a tall single storey and attic. Diocletian windows in the front gables of the E and W ranges. – LODGE at the S end of the drive. Early C19 but the roof was covered with red Rosemary tiles *c.* 1900. Single-storey, with three-light windows in the end bows. Corniced and ball-finialled squat GATEPIERS of *c.* 1900.

DUPPLIN CASTLE
2.5 km. WSW of Aberdalgie

The present Neo-Georgian mansion house is by *W. Schomberg Scott*, *c.* 1970. – To the N, STABLES by *William Stirling I*, 1814–18. Piend-roofed ranges faced with droved ashlar, of two storeys, the first floor windows low and horizontally proportioned. U-plan S front, the main block with a slightly advanced and taller two-bay centrepiece finished with a cornice and blocking course, the upper windows taller than the others of this floor and segmental-headed. The wings end in pyramidal-roofed pavilions, with elliptical-arched carriage doors in their inner sides; at the S front of each, a three-light window under a Diocletian opening. Large but plain courtyard behind. Across its SW corner, a bowed porch with a primitivist Doric column between the two doorways. – Contemporary piend-roofed HOUSING to the NW. Two-storey two-bay centre block, the first floor windows also small and horizontal, the ground floor windows with consoled block-pediments. Slightly recessed single-storey two-bay lateral wings. Single-storey piend-roofed NW wing (ESTATE OFFICE) by *William Burn*, 1831, its W front U-plan, a cast-iron columned veranda fronting the recessed three-bay centre block; elliptical-arched windows. – WALLED GARDEN, probably early C19, on the steeply sloping hillside to the W, the external faces of rubble, the internal of brick.

EAST GATEWAY at the end of the drive, by *James Miller*, 1928, in the manner of *c.* 1700. Outer court entered between urn-finialled piers of channelled ashlar with panelled faces and bounded by balustraded screen walls, the N higher than the S. At the court's W end, piers of the same design as those to the E flank taller piers, their faces Ionic-pilastered, surmounted by much taller urns. Elegantly detailed wrought-iron gates, the central overthrow with the coat of arms of Lord Forteviot of Dupplin surmounted by a baron's coronet. Inside the gateway, on the N side of the drive, a contemporary two-storey Jacobean LODGE. L-plan, with a strapwork parapet over the inner angle's porch. – SOUTH LODGE of 1832–3. Single-storey, with broad eaves forming open pediments at the gables. Hoodmoulded Gothic window to the S; to the W, a canted bay window under its own bellcast piended roof. – WEST GATEWAY beside the A9, the gatepiers of channelled ashlar with panelled faces, by *James Miller*, 1928. Contemporary lodge with mullioned windows on the S side of the drive. On the N side, an early C19 lodge, with bracketed broad eaves and round-headed door and windows.

ECCLESIAMAGIRDLE HOUSE
2.8 km. SE of Forgandenny

On the S shore of a small loch, a rubble-walled and crowstep-gabled mid-C17 laird's house built for either David Carmichael of Balmedie who acquired the estate in 1628 or his son, Sir David Carmichael, who inherited it eighteen years later.

Three storeys, part of the ground floor at the W end of the S front overlaid by a later terrace, and T-plan, the tail provided by a stair-tower projecting from just E of the centre of the S front. In the E inner angle, a bowed turret carried on continuous corbelling. At the S face of the stair-tower and also placed E of centre, the C17 moulded entrance under a Doric-columned aedicular frame for a missing heraldic panel. Small windows, some blocked, to the stair-tower. Comfortably sized windows at the upper floors of the main block. The original first-floor window W of the stair-tower has been converted to a door, probably in the C19 when the W second-floor window of the front was deepened and its crowstepped dormerhead, together with the others, renewed. Single-storey W wing, perhaps of the early C19.

Of the barmkin wall which enclosed a courtyard on the S side of the house there survives the W GATEWAY, a moulded segmental arch under a heraldic panel bearing the initials D^{S}C and AC (for Sir David Carmichael and his first wife, Anne Carmichael) and the date 1648, perhaps that of the erection of the house. To its E, perhaps at the former barmkin's SE corner, a narrow D-plan lectern DOOCOT, probably also of the mid C17.

CHAPEL immediately to the SW, probably built c. 1500 when Ecclesiamagirdle was the site of a hospice belonging to Lindores Abbey. It is a roofless rubble-walled oblong, c. 7.8 m. by 4.9 m. Chamfered margins to the openings. Entrance at the W end of the S wall and, at this wall's E end, a round-headed window. Tall round-headed window (built-up) in the E gable. In the W gable, a sizeable rectangular window, perhaps C17, now built-up and containing a round-headed opening, also blocked, perhaps a C19 insertion. Inside, near the N side's E end, an aumbry checked for a door.

The surrounding yew-shaded GRAVEYARD's rubble wall was erected by Sir David Carmichael in 1651. Small but notable collection of monuments. S of the chapel and roughly aligned with its door, the HEADSTONE of Margaret Chrystie †1732, the W face carved with the relief of a weaver's shuttle above incised emblems of death. – To the E, a large HEADSTONE to Dugal Wright †1699, the W face bearing emblems of death. On the E face, Ionic pilasters with upside-down volutes frame a crudely lettered verse inscription round a wreath. At the top, an angel's head (the soul); at the bottom, the setsquare and hatchet of a wright. – N of this, the small HEADSTONE of 1718 commemorating William Wadderspoon, the E face with a shield displaying a ploughshare above a skull, crossbones and hourglass. – Further N, the TABLE STONE of 1674 to Margaret Williamson, the marginal inscription framing depictions of a crossed hatchet and setsquare, a cross and a skull and crossbones. – Small HEADSTONE to Elizabeth Donaldson †1703 to the SE, the W face with the relief of a skull and crossbones. – NE of this, a GRAVE-SLAB, probably of the early C17, commemorating Laurns Drone is incised with a marginal inscription and reminders of mortality. – To its S a curly-topped HEADSTONE to MO †1716, the E face bearing the high relief stack of a crossbones, skull and hourglass. – Immediately S of this, the TABLE STONE of Thomas Smal WHO.DIED.FOR RELIGION.COVENANT.KING.AND.COVNT RIE.ᵬE.I.OF SEPTEMBER.1645, a skull and crossbones incised below the inscription. It is probably of the early C18 rather than the mid C17.

EDRADOUR

9050

Little more than a single-storey row of cottages overlooking the distillery beside the Edradour Burn.

BRIDGE. Rubble-built segmental arch over the Edradour Burn, probably mid-C19, widened to the N in the later C20.

EDRADOUR DISTILLERY. Tiny whitewashed complex built in 1837. At the S end, a single-storey rubble-walled MALT BARN (now Reception Centre) with piended transverse roofs. To its NW, a small STORE, also of one storey. N of the malt barn, the two-storey DISTILLERY, its original rubble walling largely replaced by brickwork. Quite plain, with small windows to the upper floor. Uphill to the NW, the MALTINGS. Two-storey, with low horizontally proportioned first-floor windows at the main block which is covered by a piended platform roof; forestair to the first-floor doorway. Pagoda-roofed kiln at the S end. The interior has been converted to an exhibition space. On the W side of the Edradour Burn the former MANAGER'S HOUSE (now shop), a broad-eaved cottage much extended to the N in the late C20.

123

ELCHO CASTLE
0.9 km. NE of Rhynd

1020

63, p. 70 Large mid-C16 mansion of the Wemysses of Wemyss, displaying the full baronial panoply of towers, turrets, caphouses, gunloops and crowsteps. Abandoned in the C18 it was reroofed early in the C19 and has since been preserved as a monument.

Constructed of large blocks of sandstone rubble with in-and-out dressings at the corners, the house consists of a four-storey oblong main block, *c.* 18m. by 8.8m., its E gable splayed, a conical-roofed round turret projected on continuous corbelling at the SE corner, a round tower at the NE, a semicircular tower near the N side's E end; at the W corners, square towers with splay-sided stair-turrets corbelled out in their W inner angles with the gable of the main block, the S stair turret partly supported on a bowed projection; large chimney-breast in the NW tower's E inner angle.

The composition of the towers' upper works is remorselessly varied. Corbelled out on the top of the round NE tower is a crowstep-gabled rectangular caphouse placed at a diagonal to the main block. On the off-centre round N tower, another crowstep-gabled caphouse, also on continuous corbelling but at right angles to the main block and with a rounded turret in the SE inner angle. Crowstepped gable to the NW tower which is placed slightly askew to the corner of the main block. The large SW tower is finished with a parapet from which project stone rainwater spouts; at the tower's corners, angle rounds, their continuous corbelling placed above the base of the parapet. Inside this tower's parapet, a crowstep-gabled attic, a large chimney in its S gable.

The detail is also varied. Round the ground floor of the house, a purposeful array of gunloops and, at the main block's S front, three irregularly spaced square windows with splayed jambs; two more ground-floor windows in the W gable and one at the E end of the N side. Generously sized roll-moulded windows to the first and second floors; roll mouldings also at the third-floor windows of the SW tower and the E gable of the main block. Many of these openings are covered by metal gratings. At the SE turret, windows with moulded sills, the centre and ends of the dummy SW window's sill projecting as if to provide bases for columns; under this window, a round shothole. At the top floor of the main block's S front the two end windows rise through the eaves to moulded lintels under catslide dormers. The centre window of this front has protoclassical attached columns and a flat-topped pediment, its tympanum carved with a roundel. Stone dormerhead to the NW tower's W window and a catslide dormer in the SE side of the NE tower's caphouse.

At the main block's S front the openings are irregularly spaced but all the windows of the r. bay are aligned above each other, as are the second- and third-floor windows of the centre bay and the ground- and first-floor windows of the l. bay. At the S face of the SW tower, a centrally placed tier of windows and, above the first-floor opening, the large moulded frame for a missing heraldic panel. At the W faces of this tower and of the NW tower, off-centre tiers of windows aligned above each other.

INTERIOR. The roll-and-hollow-moulded entrance in the SW tower's E face opens into a lobby, tunnel-vaulted like all the ground-floor rooms. The main stair (*see* below) opens off its S side. On the W side, a guardroom which has a window as well

SECOND FLOOR

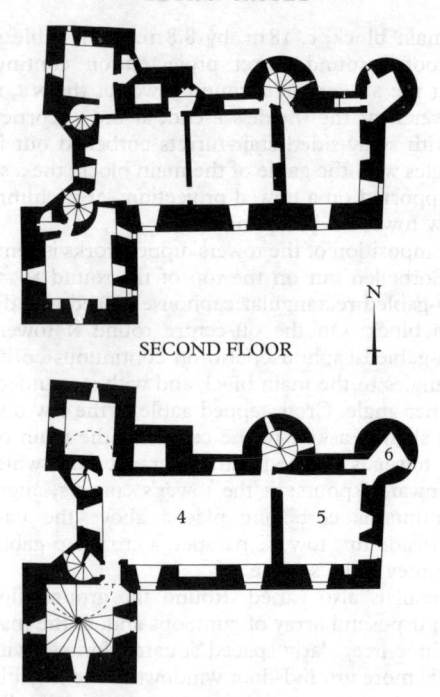

FIRST FLOOR

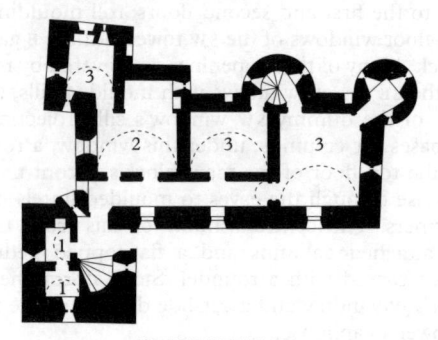

GROUND FLOOR

|_____|_____|
0   30m

1. Guardroom
2. Kitchen
3. Store
4. Hall
5. Chamber
6. Closet

Elcho Castle.
Plans

as a door into the lobby; gunloop in the W wall. S of the guardroom, another small room with gunloops in its S side. Along the S side of the main block, a corridor, well lit from a W window and two S windows, these placed above gunloops under which are stone ledges on which to mount the weapons. The W room N of the corridor, and with a window looking into it, is the KITCHEN; lighting it from outside is a window in the W gable. Segmental-arched N fireplace, an oven in its SE corner. At the kitchen's NW corner is the entrance to the ground-floor room of the NW tower. A high-set slit window in its N wall suggests that this store may have contained an entresol floor. E of the kitchen and entered from the corridor, a windowless store, perhaps the wine cellar, with a door to the service stair in the N tower. The main block's full-width E room is lit from a fair-sized N window. In the E wall, a gunloop, again with a mounting ledge below. At the N wall's W end, a door into a lobby to the service stair. At the NE corner, the entrance to a roughly wedge-shaped room at the base of the NE tower. In its walls, three gunloops, also with ledges.

The SW tower's stair to the first floor is a broad turnpike under a tunnel vault. The W two-thirds of the first floor is occupied by the HALL, its N and S windows set in segmental-arched embrasures. Fragmentary remains of a plaster frieze enriched with a zigzag motif and roses and fleurs-de-lys at the E, W and S walls. In the S wall, a broad fireplace with a simple roll-moulded surround. The slight projection of the wall's W end at the entrance from the stair may indicate the position of a screens passage. At the N end of this putative passage, the entrance to a tunnel-vaulted room in the NW tower. At the E end of the hall's N wall is a door from the N tower's service stair.

E of the hall is the CHAMBER. In its SW corner remains of a plaster cornice and frieze, again enriched with zigzag ornament and with roses, thistles and fleurs-de-lys. The use of the emblems of England, Scotland and France suggests that the plasterwork was executed soon after the Union of the Crowns in 1603. In the E wall, a plain fireplace. Locker in the S wall. In the adjoining NE tower, a closet with a garderobe in the wall thickness.

The floors above hall level are reached from the N service stair (serving the main block) and from stairs in the turrets adjoining the W towers, the N of these stairs giving access to the upper floors of the NW tower but by-passing the second floor of the main block. At each of the three top floors of the NW tower, a small room containing a simple moulded chimneypiece and with a garderobe which is contained in the wall thickness of the splay-sided turret in the inner angle with the chimney-breast of the main block's kitchen. Each of the second- and third-floor rooms of the SW tower is very comfortably appointed with good-sized windows, a fireplace, aumbries and a garderobe, the lower with a lamp recess. Attic room with a fireplace in the SE corner.

At the second floor of the main block, the space above the hall originally contained two rooms, each with an end fireplace; aumbry to the S of the E room's fireplace. Garderobes off the N side of each room. In the room above the chamber, an E fireplace and a S aumbry. At the top storey (its floor now missing) there has been a similar arrangement of three rooms. In the NE tower, a closet at each level, each with a garderobe.

At the top of the stair in the N tower, the caphouse room has a S fireplace. From this room a W door opens onto a very short stretch of parapeted wall-walk leading to an attic garderobe. E door from the caphouse onto a slightly longer wall-walk to the caphouse above the NE tower, which contains a room with a fireplace at its NE end.

The house originally formed the N range of a courtyard or BARMKIN. The base of the rubble walls and most of the featureless S gable of a two-storey building on the courtyard's W side survive. More substantial remains of the barmkin's D-plan SE tower, with a caphouse carried on continuous corbelling and oval gunloops. Built against this corner tower's N side is a mid-C19 small VILLA of two storeys, the upper windows rising through the broad eaves into gabled dormerheads; tree-trunk porch.

On the edge of the farm steading of Easter Elcho, a rubble-built beehive DOOCOT, probably of the C16. Two ratcourses, the walling slightly intaken above each. The pigeons' entrance has been from a hole in the domical roof. Interior lined with stone nesting boxes.

ERROL

Substantial village, formerly a weaving centre.

CHURCHES

ANTIBURGHER CHURCH, Hall Wynd. Converted to a hall and with a harled foyer added to the front gable in the mid C20. Rubble-walled oblong, built in 1809. A pair of pointed windows in the centre of the E side; at the end bays, a double tier of rectangular windows disclosing the former presence of galleries inside.

ERROL FREE CHURCH, Church Lane. Secularized. Tudor Gothic of 1843. Rubble-built nave and aisles, the roofs, piended at the aisles, now covered with corrugated iron. Lean-to vestibule across the front at whose centre rises a pyramidal-roofed squat tower.

ERROL PARISH CHURCH, North Back Dykes. Georgian Romanesque of 1830–3, by *James Gillespie Graham*. Built of Knockhill sandstone ashlar, droved at the main walling, polished at the buttresses. The church is a tall Greek cross but with full-height projections in the inner angles and a N tower. Clasping buttresses topped by crocket-finialled pinnacles at the main S, E and W gables, gableted diagonal buttresses, each with a deep intake, at the other corners. Round-headed windows and doors with cushion-capitalled skinny nook-shafts and hoodmoulds whose label stops are carved as grotesque human heads. In the four-light S window, late Gothic tracery, with mouchettes and a wheel head. Boldly projecting tower, its hoodmoulded entrance under an inverted V-shaped string course suggestive of a gablet. Three-light belfry openings, the centre of each obscured by a clock face (by *George Rattray*, 1901). Crocket-finialled pinnacles on the corners of the battlement.

INTERIOR. In the vestibule in the N tower, a curved double stair to the gallery. In the church proper, a huge ceiling rose with radiating round-headed panels, the effect more Late Georgian Perpendicular than Romanesque. Cast-iron columns with trumpet capitals support the U-plan gallery, the panels of its front decorated with interlaced blind arcading. The areas under the gallery in the church's E and W transepts were partitioned off to provide vestry accommodation, etc., by *P. Macgregor Chalmers* in 1915–16. In the partition walls, four-light Gothic windows. In 1996 *Murdoch Architects* partitioned off the space under the gallery's N end to form further rooms. The focus is on the S end of the church where the sides of the short rectangular chancel are covered by divided Gothic ORGAN CASES (by *John R. Miller*, 1905). At the front of the chancel, the PULPIT in a routine Late Gothic manner, by Chalmers, 1915–16. – COMMUNION TABLE of 1905. Early Christian with some Neo-Celtic motifs. – Plain boxy PEWS of 1915–16, also by Chalmers. – STAINED GLASS. In the great S window, brightly coloured patterns and, at the top, small-scale Scenes from the Proverbs and the Life of Our Lord, designed by *J. Murray Drummond* of Megginch and executed by *James Ballantine & Son*, 1867. – In the E transept's partition wall under the gallery, a Second World War memorial window (David Pouring Out as an Offering to God the Water Brought him by his Soldiers from Bethlehem; the Pelican in Piety; the Phoenix) of 1947, a well-executed and strongly coloured example of stylized realism.

GRAVEYARD
School Wynd and Church Lane

The site of the medieval parish church and its successor (also demolished) of 1765. At the W end, the HEADSTONE to Mary Duff erected and presumably executed by her husband, *David Sprunt*, mason in Errol, in 1763. On the W face, an angel's head (the soul) above a shield bearing the tools of a mason; emblems of death at the bottom. – In the middle of the graveyard, a pair of C17 sarcophagus MONUMENTS. The sloping sides of the top of the W, commemorating the Rev. Alexander Omay †1639, are carved with human figures, Father Time, trumpeting angels and symbols of mortality. On the more weathered E monument, to the Rev. William Bell †1665, emblems of death. – To the SE, the HEADSTONE of 1754 erected by Robert Hill, tenant in Inchmichael, to his daughter Margaret. The curvy top is carved with two pudgy naked children. On the W face, angels' heads and a crown above a helmet-crested and mantled shield bearing the initials RH and KM (for Hill and his wife, Kathanne Mitchell) flanked by torches; an hourglass and crossbones at the bottom. On the E (inscription) face, a cartouche containing the relief of a plough. – Just to its SE, the HEADSTONE of Andrew Adam †1746. Skulls and crossbones at the top. On the W face, two shields, one bearing a weaver's shuttle; on the E, an angel's head above the inscription. – To its S, a curvy topped stone of 1767 to Robert Pirie, wright in Thornlebush. On the W face, angels' heads, torches and a shield with the tools of a wright.

PUBLIC BUILDINGS

ERROL COMMUNITY CENTRE, North Back Dykes. Originally Female Industrial School. By *J., W.H. & J.M. Hay*, 1855–6. Single-storey school and two-storey schoolhouse, both with shouldered arched windows, the prettily detailed house also with windows of a more strongly Gothic character and an oriel.

ERROL PARISH SCHOOL, School Wynd. Early C19 rubble-walled school and schoolhouse. The plain two-storey schoolhouse is little altered but the school (now housing) was recast and extended by *William Watson*, 1863–4, a bargeboarded gable the main feature.

ERROL PRIMARY SCHOOL, Station Road. By *Charles S. Robertson*, 1897. Ashlar-faced, of one tall storey, in a symmetrical Free English Renaissance manner, with Venetian windows in the Dutch gables at the ends of the front and on the E side; a central cupola on the roof.

VICTORIA HALL, High Street. By *Alexander Johnston*, 1897. Built of red brick with white trimmings. In the front gable, round-headed windows and door, with a circular window above.

DESCRIPTION

HIGH STREET's W end is overlooked by the East Lodge of Errol Park (q.v.). On the N side, the ashlar-fronted Nos. 1–2 KIERSLAND of *c.* 1800, with small second-floor windows, followed by C19 vernacular. On the S, ARDYNE, a bargeboarded cottage of 1886. One front window is mullioned and transomed, the other a triangular bay. Then, the early C19 two-storey DALGLEISH HOUSE. Stugged ashlar front of four bays, the windows grouped 3:1. At the centre of the three-bay E part, a round-headed door in an anta-pilastered and corniced surround. The ground-floor W window is contained in a round-headed over-arch. At the rear, piend-roofed offices with an elliptical-arched cartshed opening. Then the Victoria Hall (*see* Public Buildings, above) and the contemporary ALBERT HOUSE, also of red and white brick. The street widens out to the s to form THE CROSS, an informal small square. In this, a FOUNTAIN erected by Sir William and Lady Ogilvy Dalgleish of Errol Park, 1899, in belated celebration of Queen Victoria's Diamond Jubilee. It was designed by *Johnston & Baxter* and executed by *Alexander Neilson*. Trefoil-shaped bowl of polished pink granite from which rises a circular pedestal with an egg-and-dart cornice. On this stands a thistle-capitalled column of red sandstone (now painted) topped by a unicorn who holds a shield bearing the Royal Arms of Scotland. The resemblance to a market cross presumably alludes to the apparently mistaken story that William the Lion had erected a burgh of barony at Errol in the late C12.

HIGH STREET E of The Cross continues with C19 vernacular, mostly harled or rendered but some of the fronts and most of the chimneys are of red and white brick. Down a lane to the N is the late C19 NORTHFIELD with an octagonal tower. N of that, THE BIRKS, the former Errol United Associate Manse of 1826, its rubble-built E front of three bays.

SCHOOL WYND leads s from High Street. On its E side, the former Errol Parish School (*see* Public Buildings, above) and an entrance to the graveyard (*see* above). On High Street's E corner with School Wynd, the COMMERCIAL HOTEL, its door lintel inscribed 17 JK♡JC 93. Set back in HALL WYND is the former Antiburgher Church (*see* Churches, above). The next street leading s from High Street is CHURCH LANE. On its W side, the former Errol Free Church (*see* Churches, above) followed by rather altered Late Georgian vernacular housing including KIMBERLEY HOUSE with a pediment over the door. More C18 and C19 vernacular houses in SOUTHBANK at the end of Church Lane.

CHURCH AVENUE leads N from High Street to Errol Parish Church (*see* Churches, above). On the E side, Nos. 1–3, squared-up Jacobean of 1904. E of this High Street turns to the NE and becomes STATION ROAD. On its corner with NORTH BACK DYKES, Errol Community Centre (*see* Public Buildings, above). Then late C19 and late C20 villas and cottages in Station Road. Among them, Errol Primary School (*see* Public Buildings, above).

MOTTE, Law Knowe, Mains of Murie, 2.3 km. E. Probably formed in the late C12 by the Hays who were granted the lands of Errol for two knights' service *c.* 1180. It is an 8 m.-high artificial earth mound of inverted pudding basin type, *c.* 30 m. in diameter at the base and with a flat oval summit of 12 m. by 11 m. Presumably it was surmounted by a wooden tower.

ERROL PARK
0.4 km. W

Large ashlar-faced mansion house, by *Alexander Johnston*, 1875–7. Pompous updating of the Georgian classical manner, the s end containing the principal rooms marked out by consoled triangular and segmental pediments over the ground floor openings and ball-and-spike finials on the wallhead parapet. Disconcertingly asymmetrical E (entrance) front, the ends advanced, the S with a chimney-topped pediment and a balustraded rectangular bay window. The entrance itself is off-centre placed in a balustraded large porch fronted by an Ionic-columned portico; wallhead pediment to mark the importance of this bay. The S elevation overlooking the garden is regular, of six bays, the centre two very slightly advanced under a pediment. Full-height canted bay windows at the more boldly advanced ends.

STABLES to the N, of 1811. Two-storey ashlar circular building round a courtyard. At the cardinal points, straight three-bay sections, each with an advanced and pedimented centrepiece. Over the N centrepiece, a tower, its lowest stage a high square plinth. Above, the corners are scooped out to form a tall octagon, its corniced windows surmounted by clock faces. The tower was heightened by *Johnston & Baxter* in 1899 to house a cistern which supplied water to the village, this top stage with round-headed openings. SOUTH-WEST LODGE, probably of the 1870s. Pompous Neoclassical. – Harled early C19 SOUTH LODGE, with Gothic windows and a bowed S end. Now rather altered. Late C19 corniced ashlar GATEPIERS. – EAST LODGE of the 1870s and Italianate.

MEGGINCH CASTLE. *See* p. 515.

EVELICK CASTLE
1.5 km. W of Kilspindie

Roofless but substantial ruin of a four-storey tower house built for the Lindsays of Evelick in the late C16 and sited high up on a steep hillside looking over the Carse of Gowrie to Fife.

Originally standing at the NW corner of a barmkin (tusking for its N wall surviving at the house's NE corner), the tower is a rubble-walled L-plan. The SW jamb projects W as well as S of the main block; a bowed stair-tower in the inner angle. Chamfered surrounds to all the windows. On the ground floor of the main block's S front and W gable these are of reasonable size but there are only a slit opening and a garderobe chute in the exposed N side. On the first floor, tall windows and a tiny one at the W end of the N wall. Smaller openings to the top floors. Plentiful supply of oval gunloops on all sides of the main block, those of the E gable placed in the third floor's window breasts. They make a show-off display around and above the door in the stair tower's E segment; l. of the gunloop and window above this entrance, the moulded frame for a heraldic panel.

The interior is now choked with debris but the ground floor seems to have contained vaulted stores in the main block and a kitchen in the jamb, a hall on the main block's first floor and a chamber in the jamb, and two rooms at the second floor of the main block and another in the jamb.

Carse of Gowrie from Kinnoull Hill, Perth; Kinnoull Tower, by W.M. Mackenzie, 1829 (p. 651)
Glen Tilt from near Blair Atholl (p. 1)

3. Alyth, Barry Hill, fort, iron age (p. 155)
4. Kenmore, Croftmoraig, stone circle, third or second millennium B.C. (p. 446)
5. St Fillans, Dundurn, fort, C7 and C8 (p. 685)
6. Braco, Ardoch, Roman fort, C1 and C2 (p. 238)

3	5
4	6

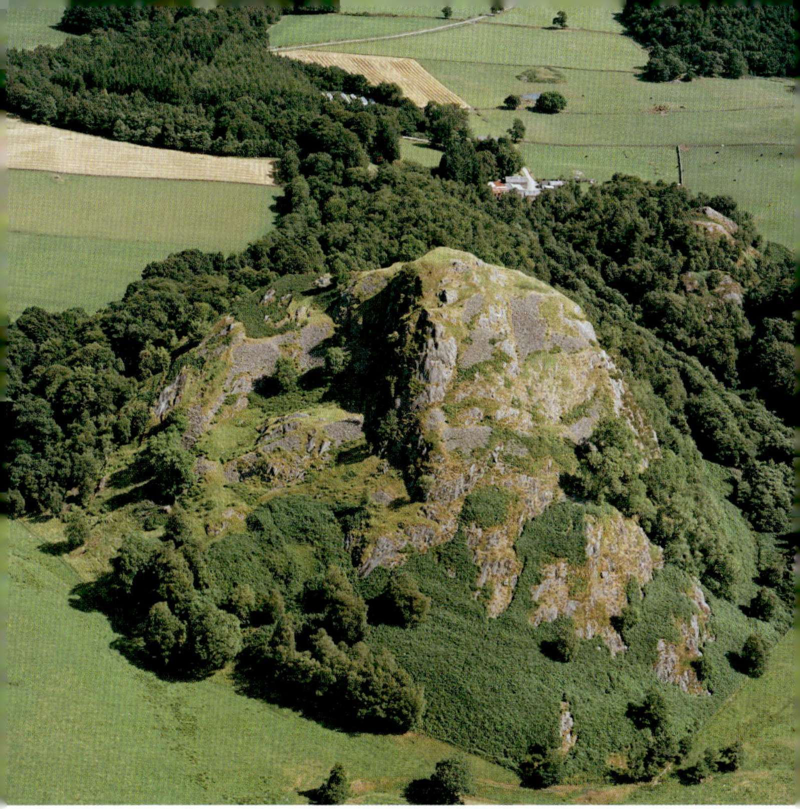

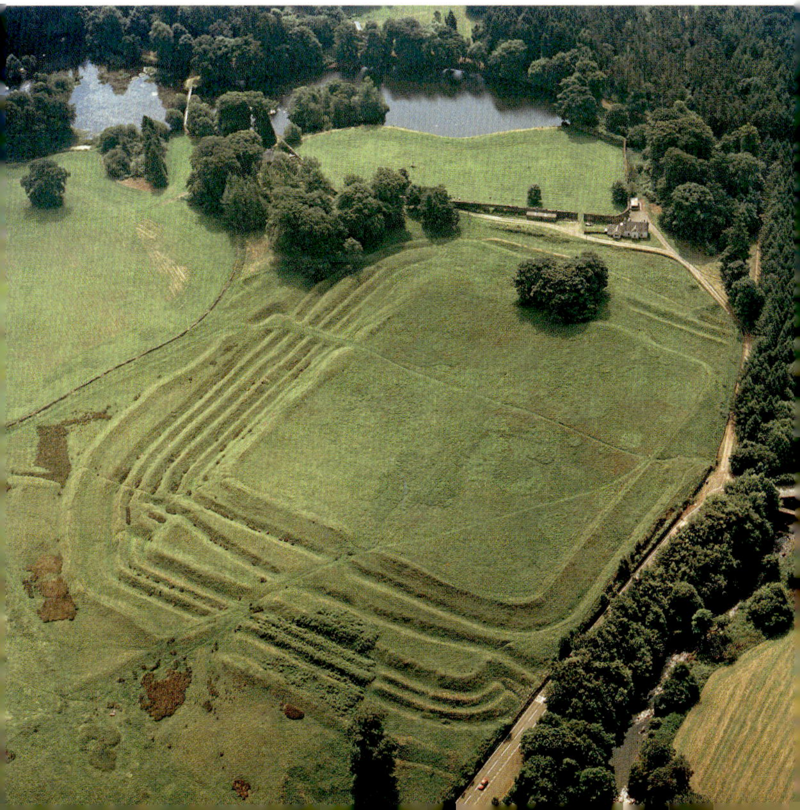

7. Meigle Museum, end of tombstone (Meigle 26), perhaps C10 (p. 521)
8. Meigle Museum, top of tombstone (Meigle 26), perhaps C10 (p. 521)
9. Meigle Museum, cross-slab (Meigle 2), C9 (p. 519)
10. Dunkeld Cathedral, 'Apostles' Stone', probably C9 (p. 342)
11. Meigle Museum, cross-slab (Meigle 2), C9 (p. 518)
12. Dunfallandy, Dunfallandy Stone, C8 or C9 (p. 330)

7	9	10
8	11	12

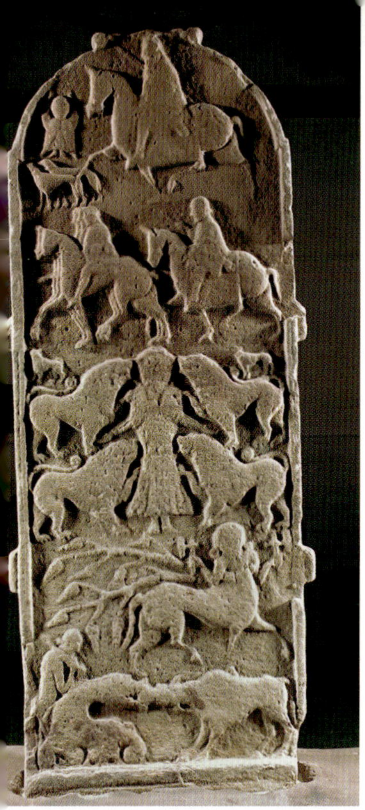
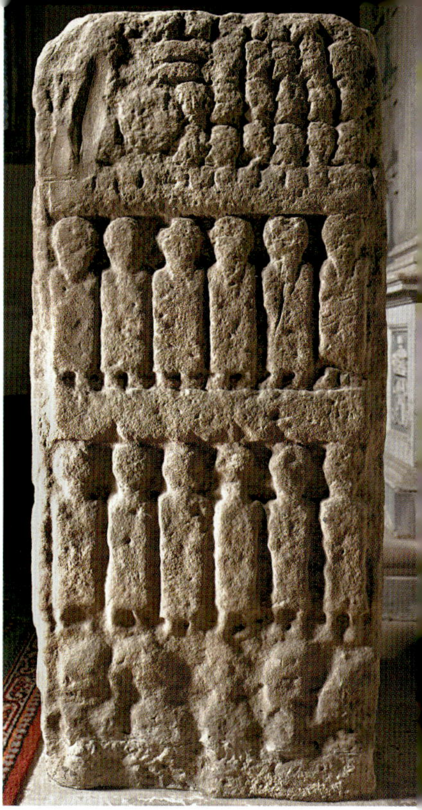
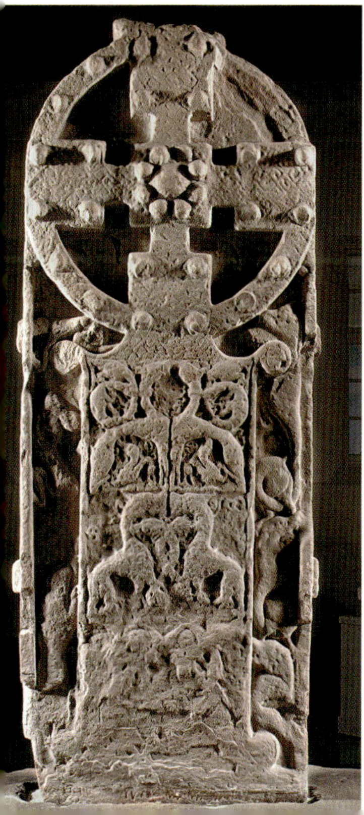
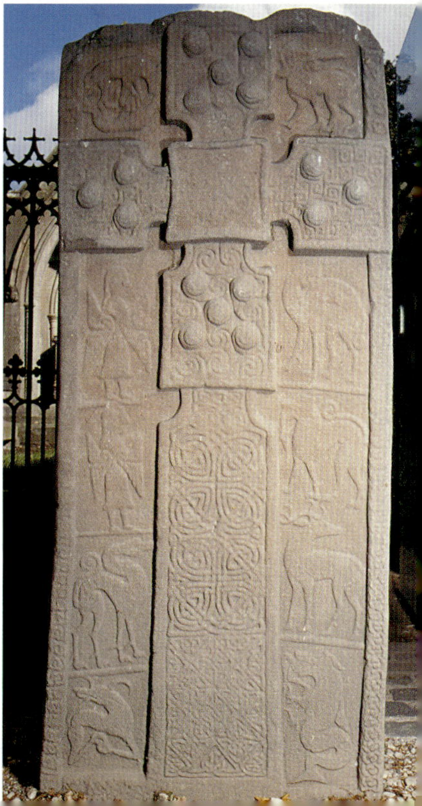

13. Muthill Old Church, tower, C12, and nave, *c.* 1425 (p. 553)
14. Collace Parish Church, Nairne Mausoleum, archway, *c.* 1200 (p. 273)
15. Perth, St John's Kirk of Perth, C15, remodelled by Robert S. Lorimer, 1923–6 (p. 570)
16. Methven, Methven Aisle, probably *c.* 1510–16 (p. 526)

13	15
14	16

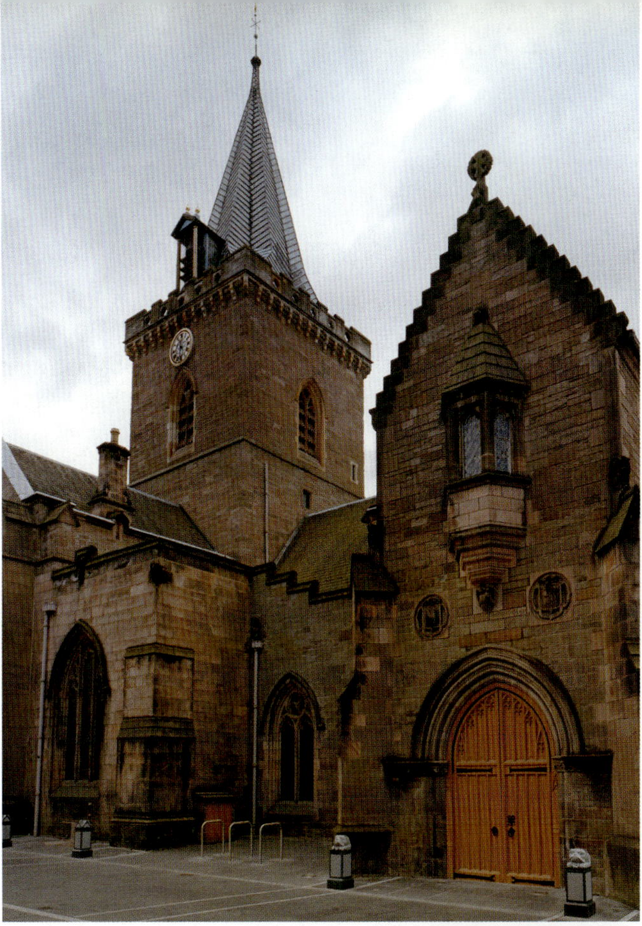

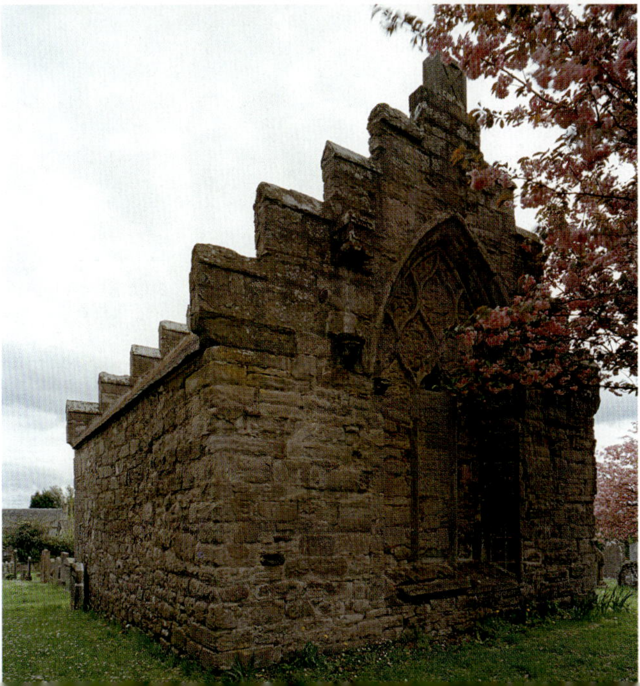

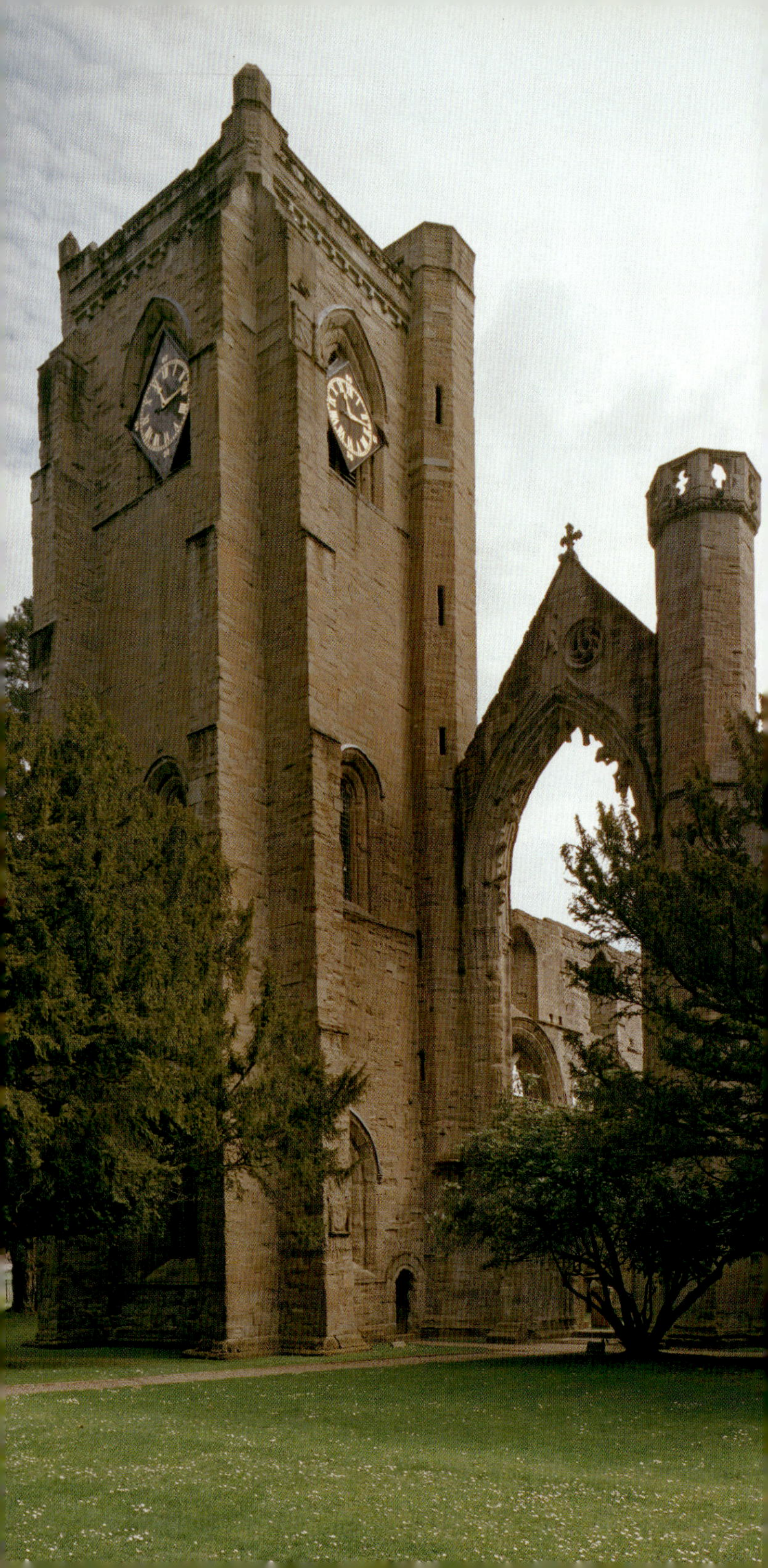

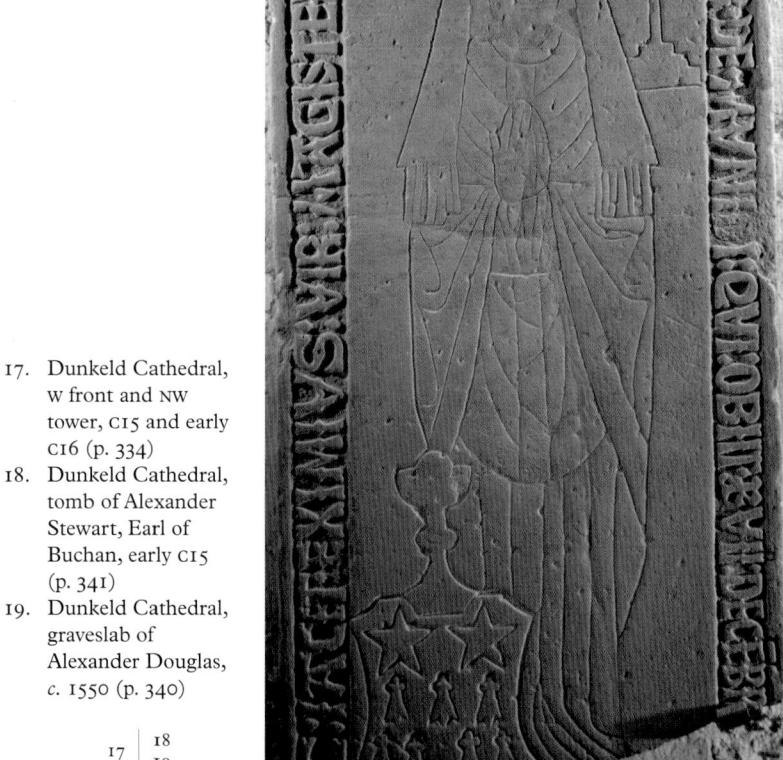

17. Dunkeld Cathedral, w front and NW tower, C15 and early C16 (p. 334)
18. Dunkeld Cathedral, tomb of Alexander Stewart, Earl of Buchan, early C15 (p. 341)
19. Dunkeld Cathedral, graveslab of Alexander Douglas, c. 1550 (p. 340)

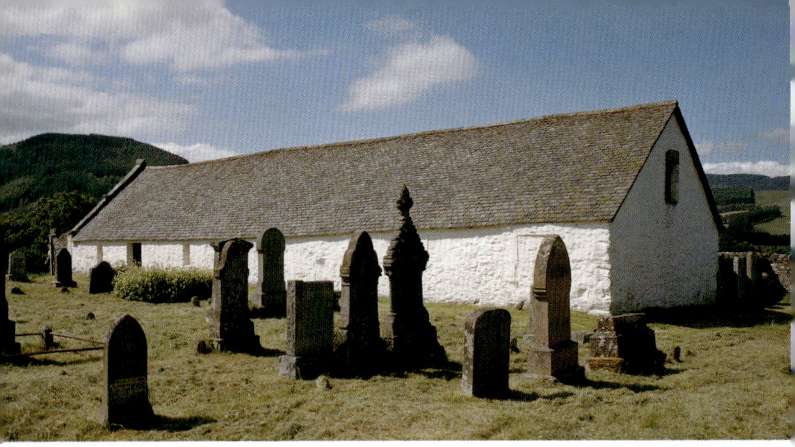

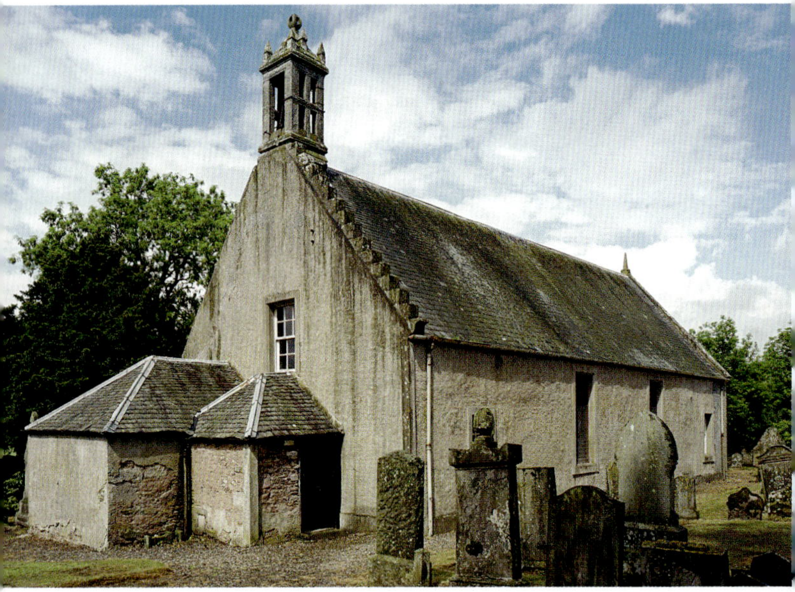

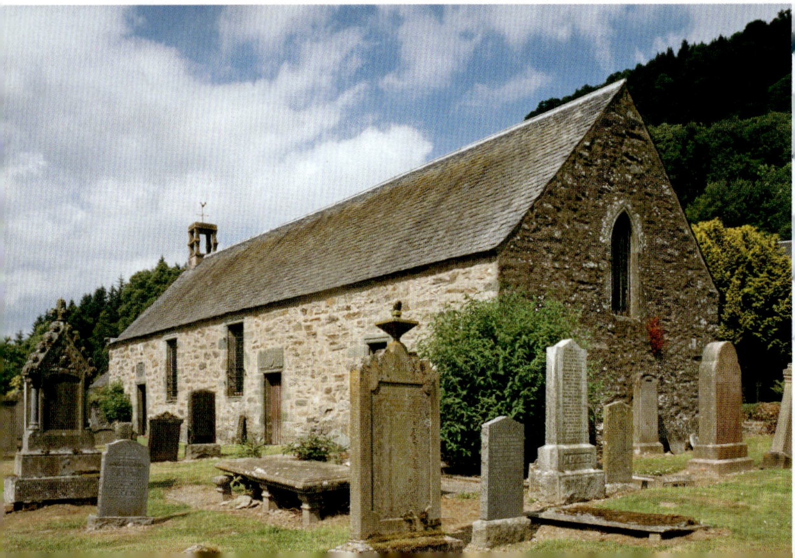

20. Grandtully, St Mary's Church, early C16, extended in early C17 (p. 405)
21. Tibbermore Parish Church, c. 1500, remodelled, 1632, 1789 and 1808 (p. 732)
22. Weem, former Parish Church, 1609–14, altered, 1753 (p. 742)
23. Grandtully, St Mary's Church, painted ceiling, early C17 (p. 405)
24. New Scone, Scone Old Parish Church, Stormont Pew, 1616 (p. 558)

20	23
21	
22	24

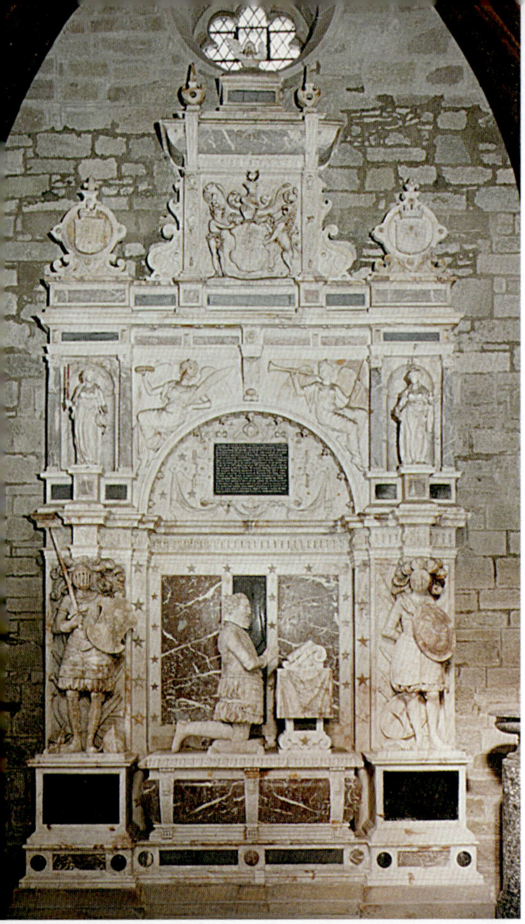

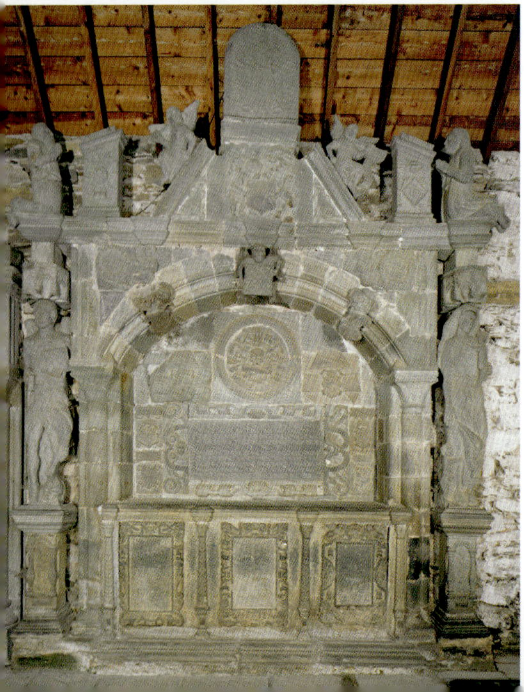

25. Scone Palace, Mausoleum, monument to David, first Lord Scone and Viscount Stormont, by Maximilian Colt, 1618–19 (p. 695)
26. Weem, former Parish Church, Menzies monument, 1616 (p. 742)
28. Perth, former Kinnoull Church, monument to George, first Earl of Kinnoull, *c.* 1635 (p. 649)
28. Dunkeld Cathedral, monument to John, first Marquess of Atholl, by Alexander Edward, 1704–5, and statue of John, fourth Duke of Atholl, by John Ternouth, 1835 (p. 342)

25	27
26	28

29. Comrie, The White Church, by John Stewart, 1803–5 (p. 278)
30. Scotlandwell, Portmoak Parish Church, by Andrew Cumming, 1831–2 (p. 697)
31. Methven, Lynedoch Mausoleum, by James Playfair, 1793 (p. 527)
32. Grandtully, St Mary's Church, headstone of James Thomson †1780 (p. 406)

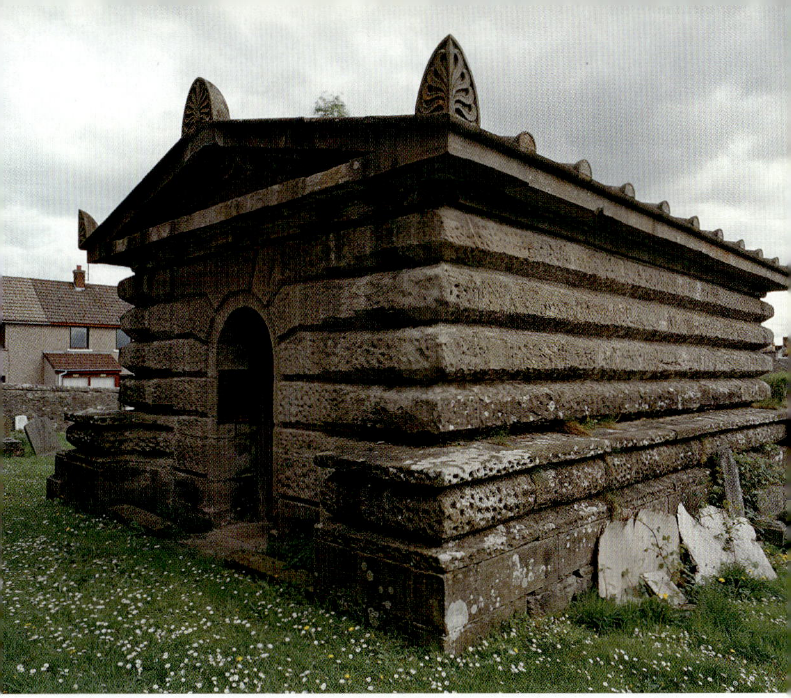

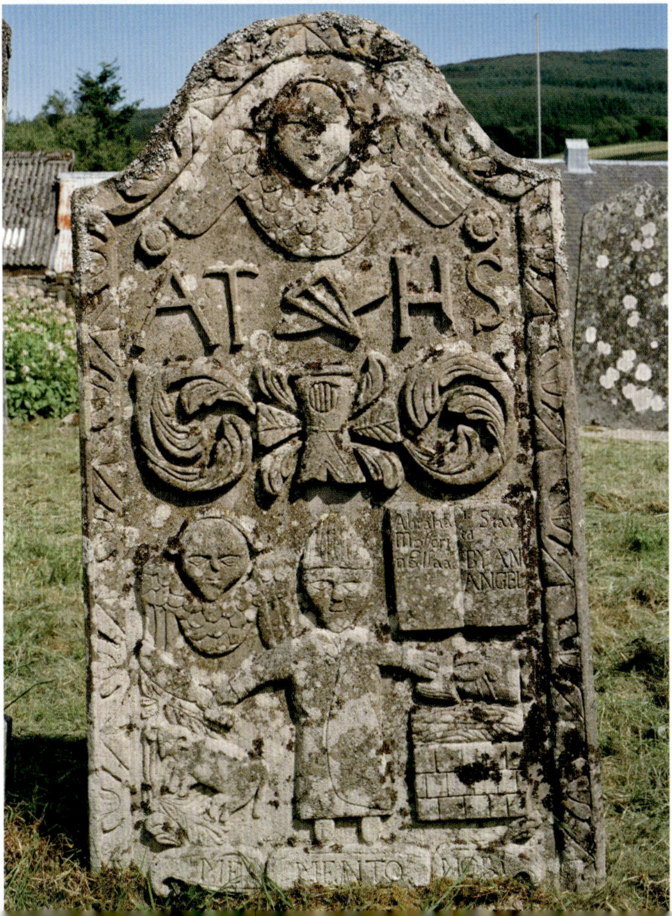
AT HS
BY AN
ANGEL

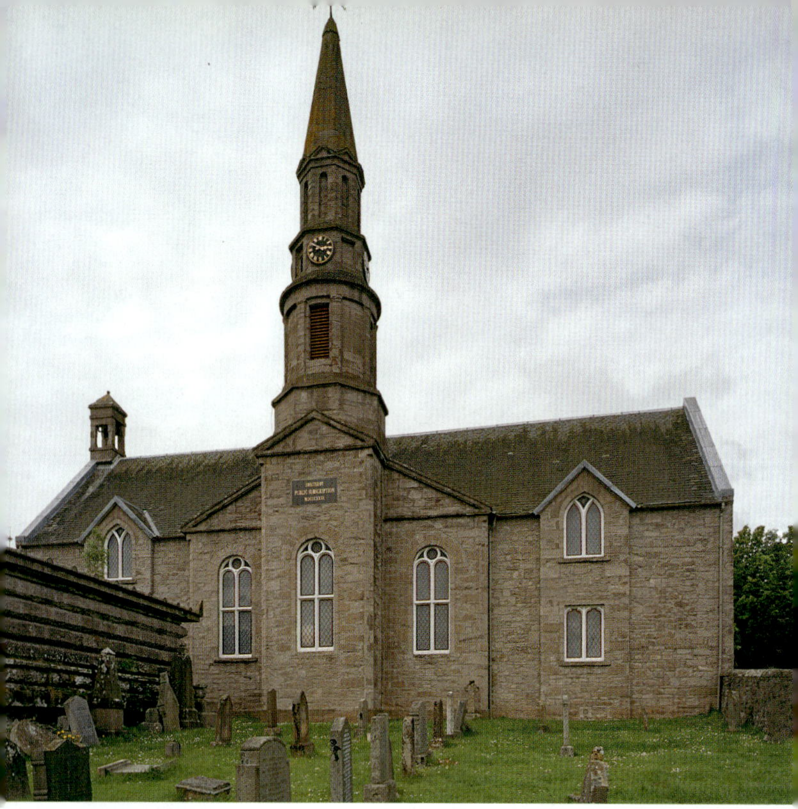

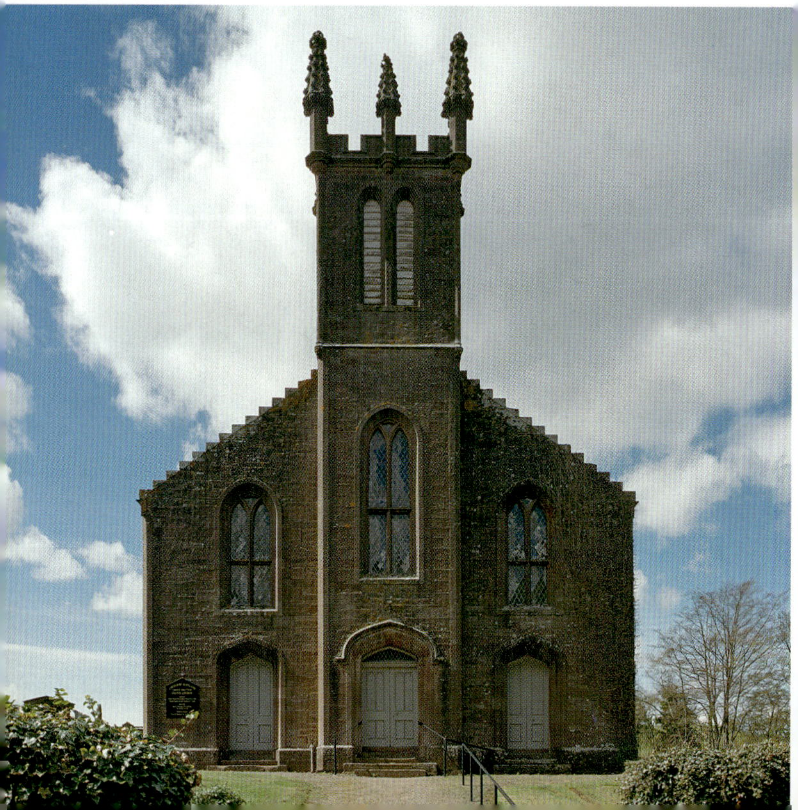

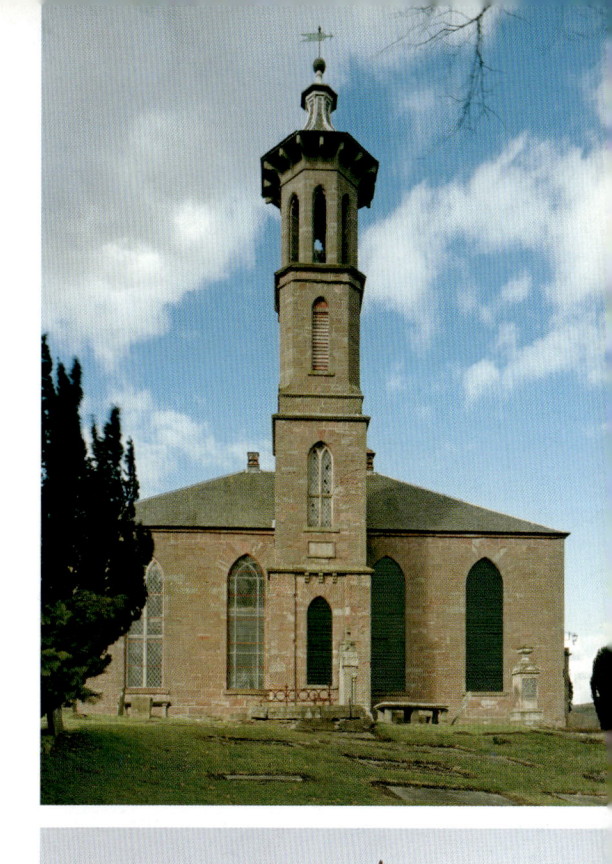

3. Methven, Methven and Logiealmond Parish Church, 1782–3, enlarged and remodelled by W. M. Mackenzie, 1825–6 (p. 526)
4. Clunie Church, by W. M. Mackenzie, 1839–40 (p. 271)
5. Blairgowrie, former Blairgowrie Parish Church, 1824 (p. 226)
6. Errol Parish Church, by James Gillespie Graham, 1830–3 (p. 362)

| 33 | 35 |
| 34 | 36 |

37. Perth, St Paul's Church, by John Paterson, 1806–7 (p. 592)
38. Alyth Parish Church, by Thomas Hamilton, 1836–9 (p. 150)

KIRK BRAE

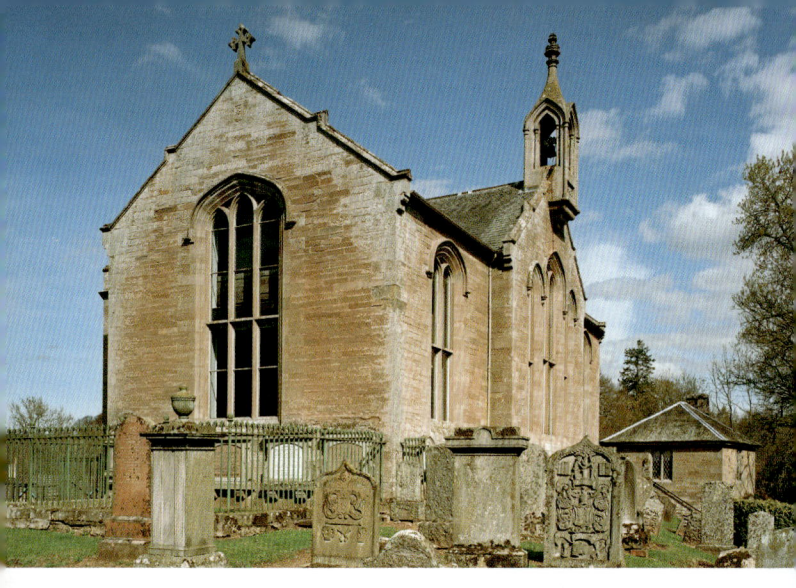

39. St Martins Parish Church, by Andrew Heiton Sen., 1842 (p. 687)
40. St Martins Parish Church, pulpit, 1842 (p. 687)
41. Murthly Castle, Chapel of St Anthony the Eremite, by James Gillespie Graham, 1845–6, and chapel (r.), c. 1600, remodelled as mausoleum, 1845–6 (p. 550)
42. Murthly Castle, Chapel of St Anthony the Eremite, interior, 1845–8, with painting over arch by Thomas Faed; Stewart monument at E end, late C17 (p. 551)

39	41
40	42

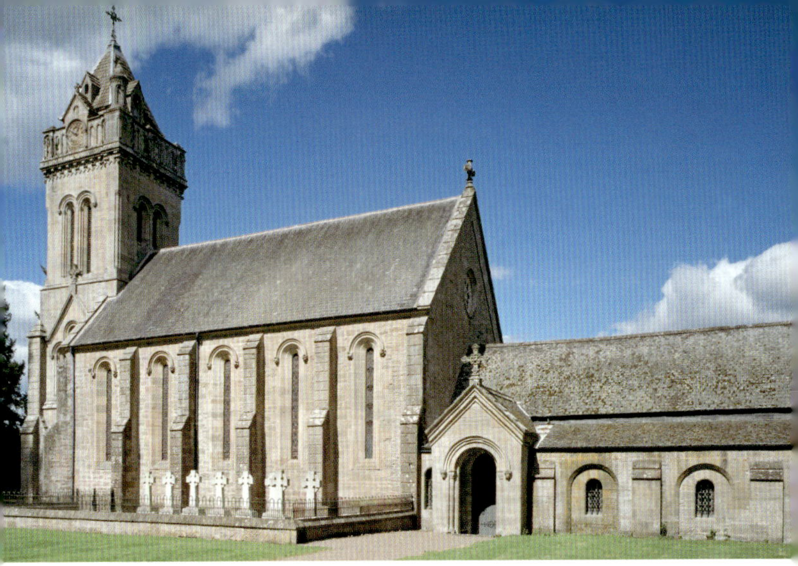
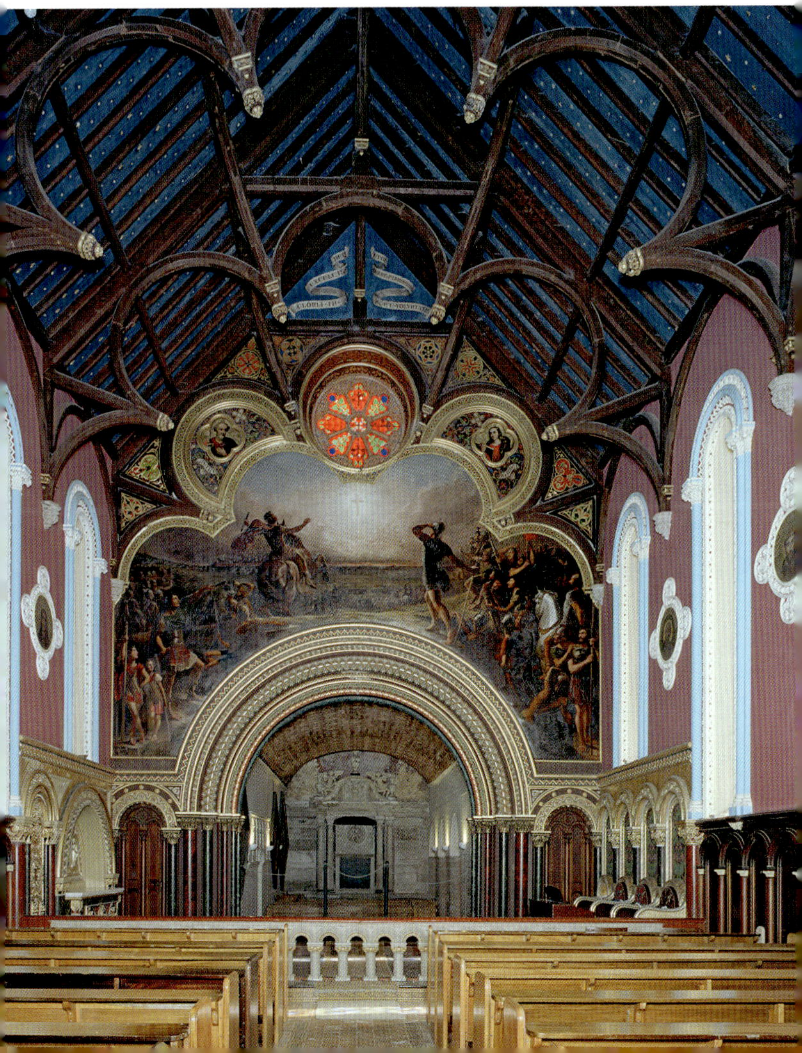

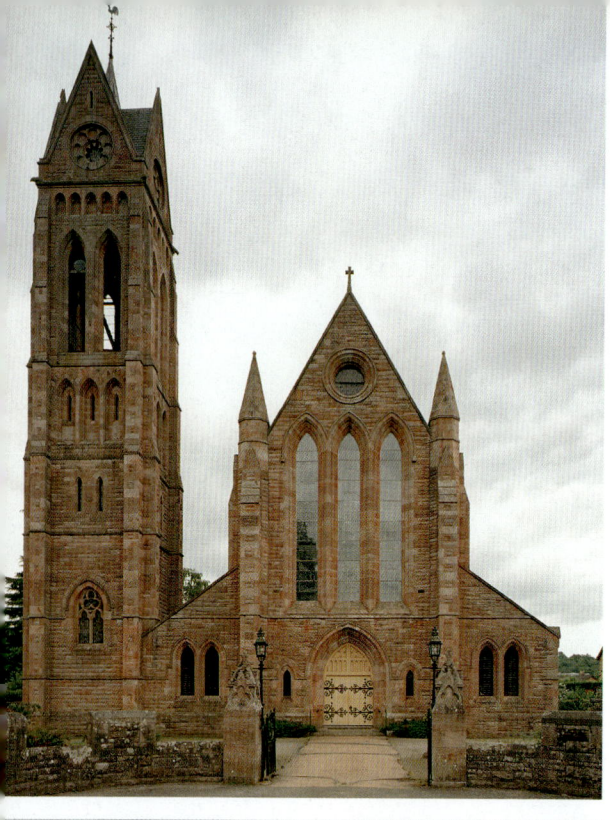

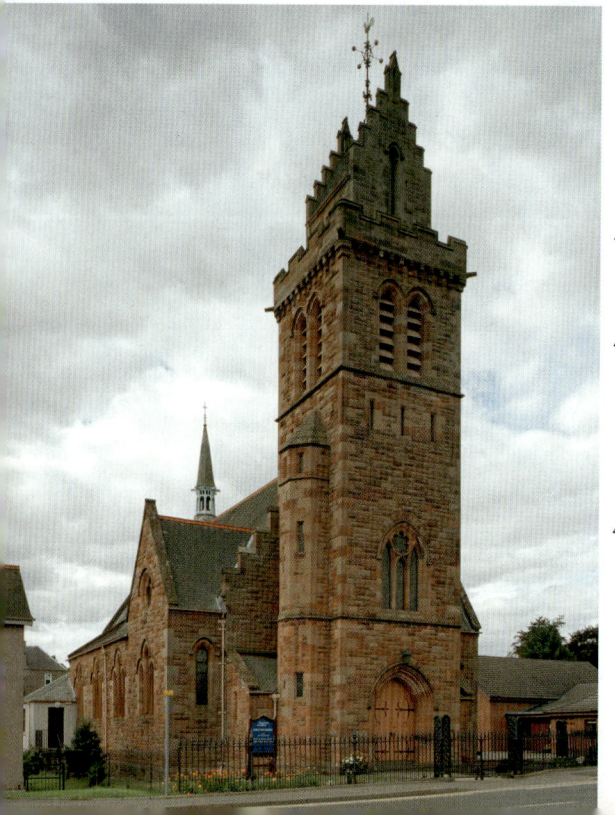

43. Crieff Parish Church, by G.T. Ewing, 1880–2 (p. 292)
44. New Scone, Scone New Church, by Sydney Mitchell & Wilson, 1886–7 (p. 557)
45. Crieff United Presbyterian Church (St Andrew's Halls), by T.L. Watson, 1883–4 (p. 293)

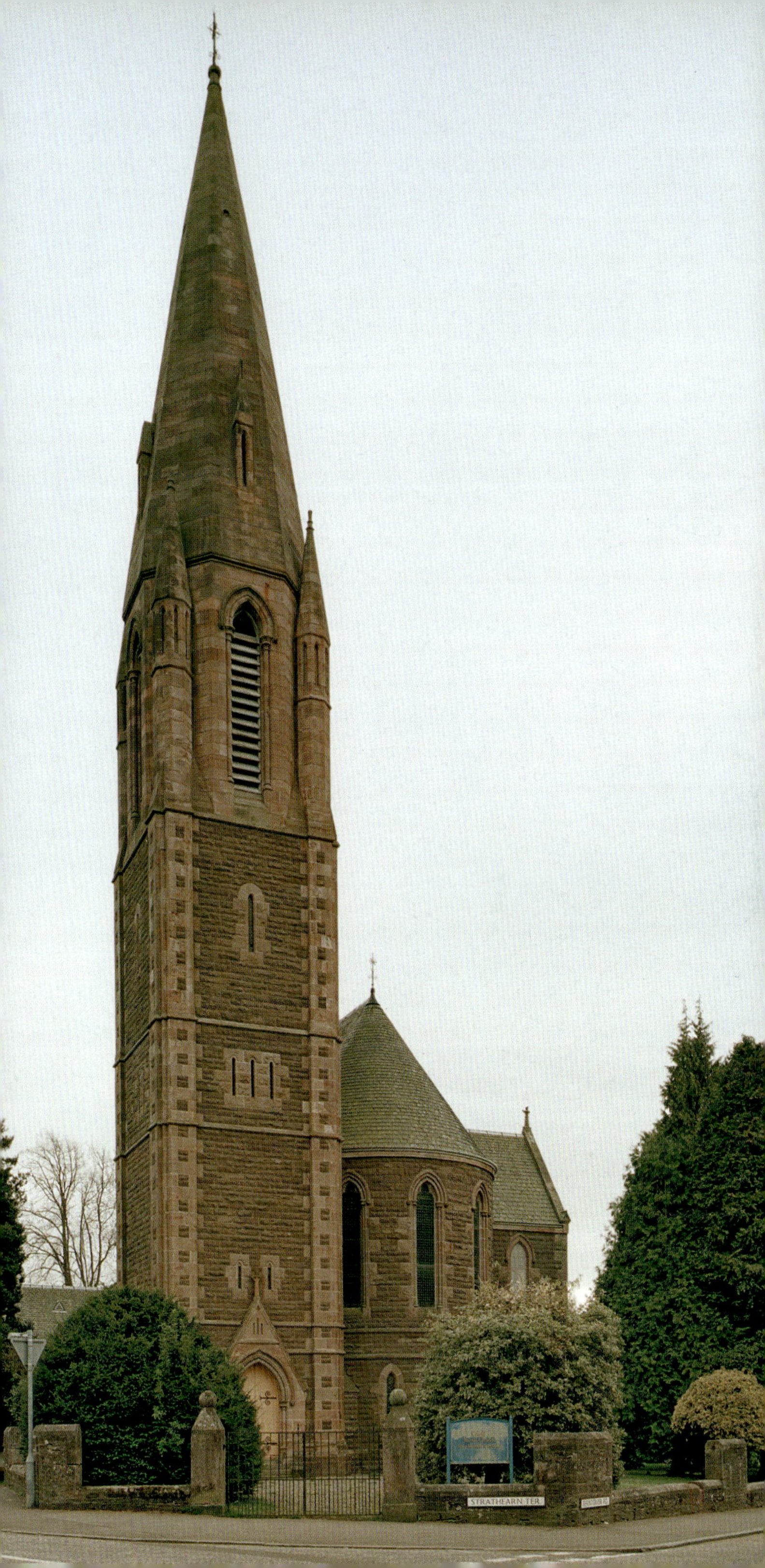
STRATHEARN TER.

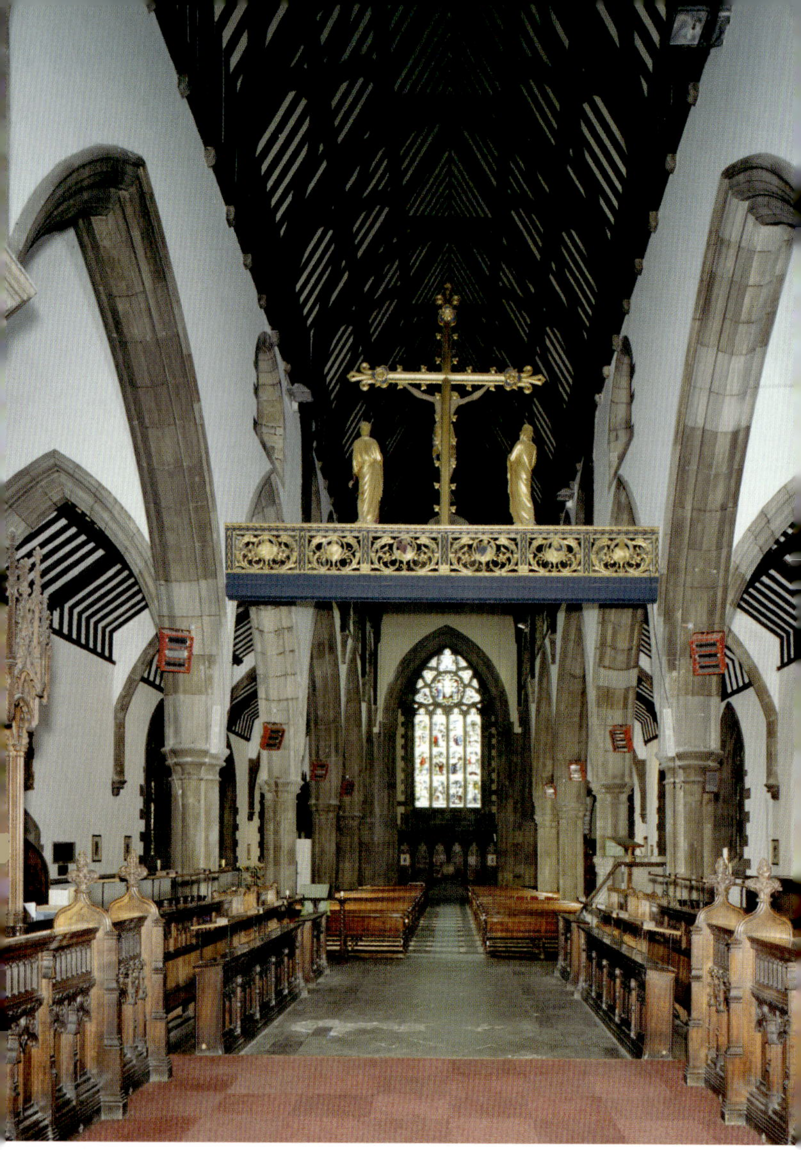

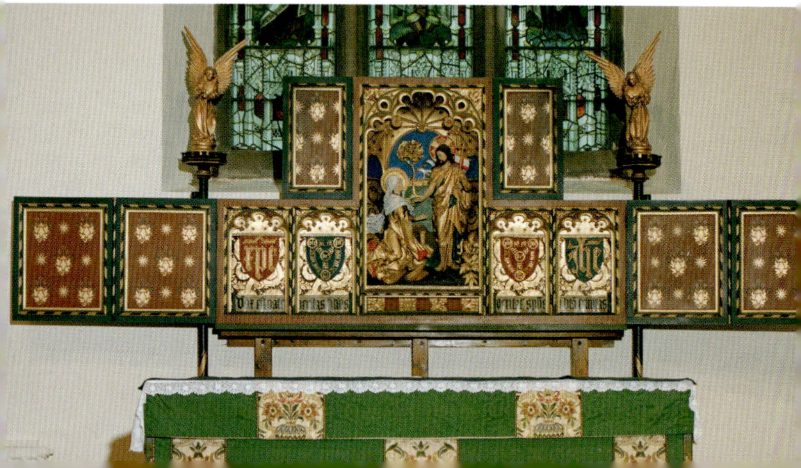

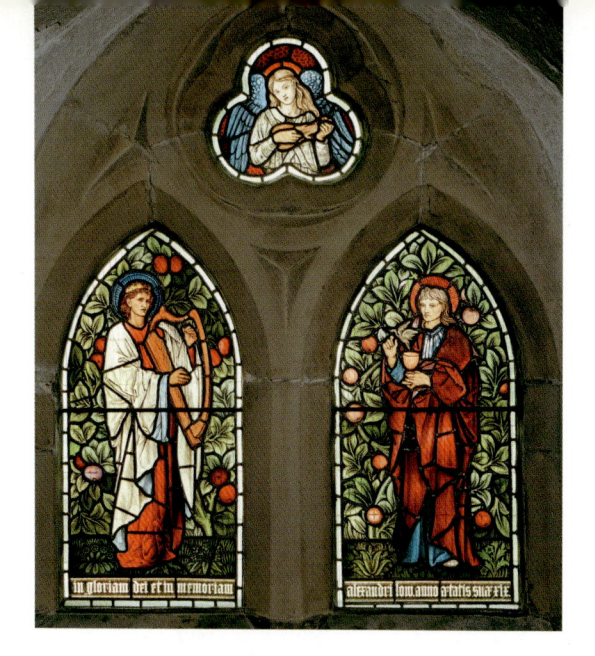

46. Perth, St Ninian's Episcopal Cathedral, interior looking w, by William Butterfield, 1848–90, with alterations and furnishings by F.L. Pearson, 1899–1901, and rood beam by J. Ninian Comper, 1924 (p. 590)
47. Pitlochry, Holy Trinity Episcopal Church, reredos, by J. Ninian Comper, 1893 (p. 669)
48. Birnam, St Mary's Episcopal Church, stained glass, by Morris & Co., 1890 (p. 198)
49. Perth, St Ninian's Episcopal Cathedral, baldacchino, by F.L. Pearson, 1908–11, and stained glass, by Alexander Gibbs, 1877 (p. 591)

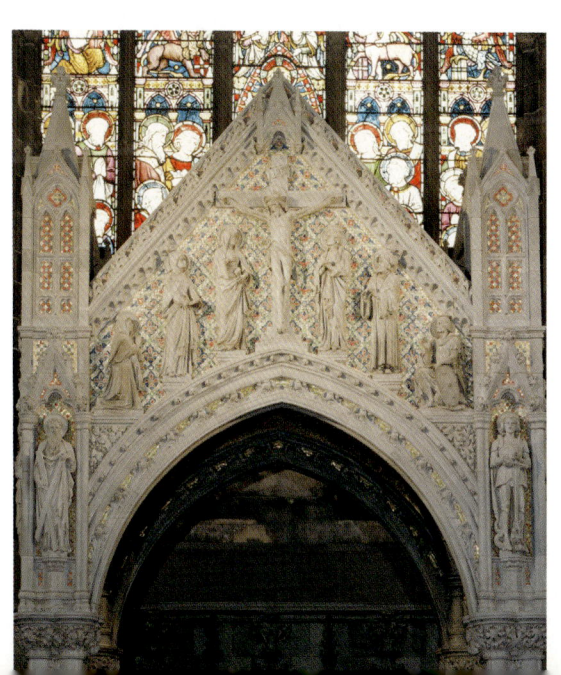

| 46 | 48 |
| 47 | 49 |

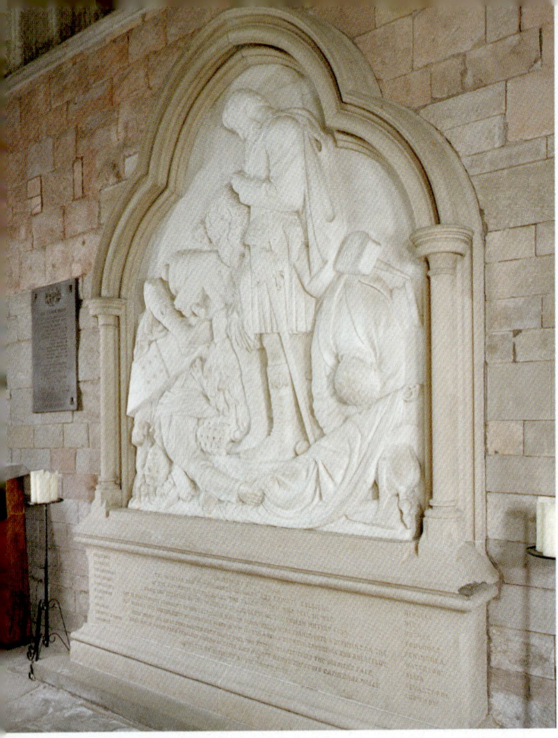

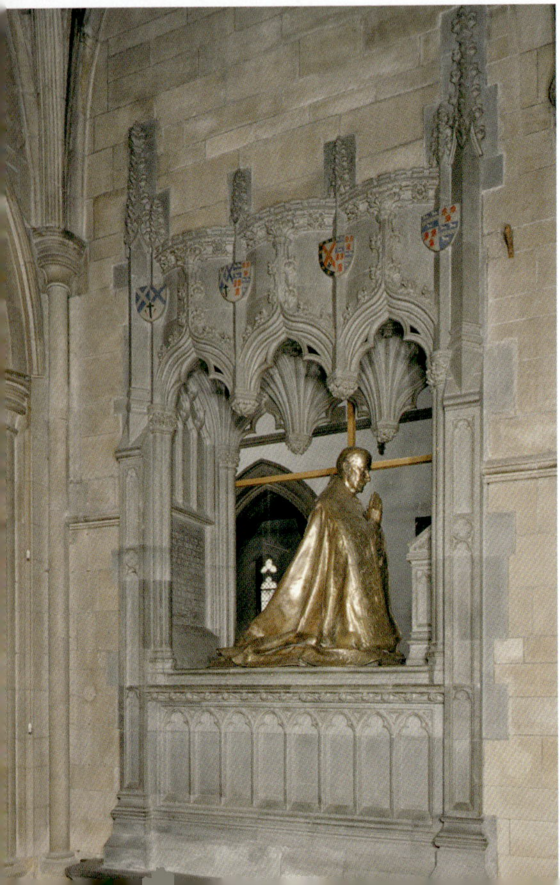

50. Dunkeld Cathedral, Black Watch Monument, by John Steell, 1872 (p. 341)
51. Perth, St Ninian's Episcopal Cathedral, Wilkinson monument, by F.L. Pearson and George Frampton, 1910–11 (p. 592)
52. Auchterarder Parish Church, by Honeyman, Keppie & Mackintosh, 1904–5 (p. 166)
53. Glencarse, All Saints' Episcopal Church, by Duncan D. Stewart, 1878 (p. 390)

50	52
51	53

54. Lochleven Castle, tower house, C14, and curtain wall, C14 and C15 (p. 501)
55. Burleigh Castle, NW tower (left), *c.* 1500, W range and SW tower, 1582 (p. 250)
56. Balvaird Castle, tower house, *c.* 1500 (p. 187)
57. Huntingtower Castle, E tower (right), *c.* 1400, remodelled, *c.* 1500, W tower, early C16, and link between towers, C17 (p. 415)

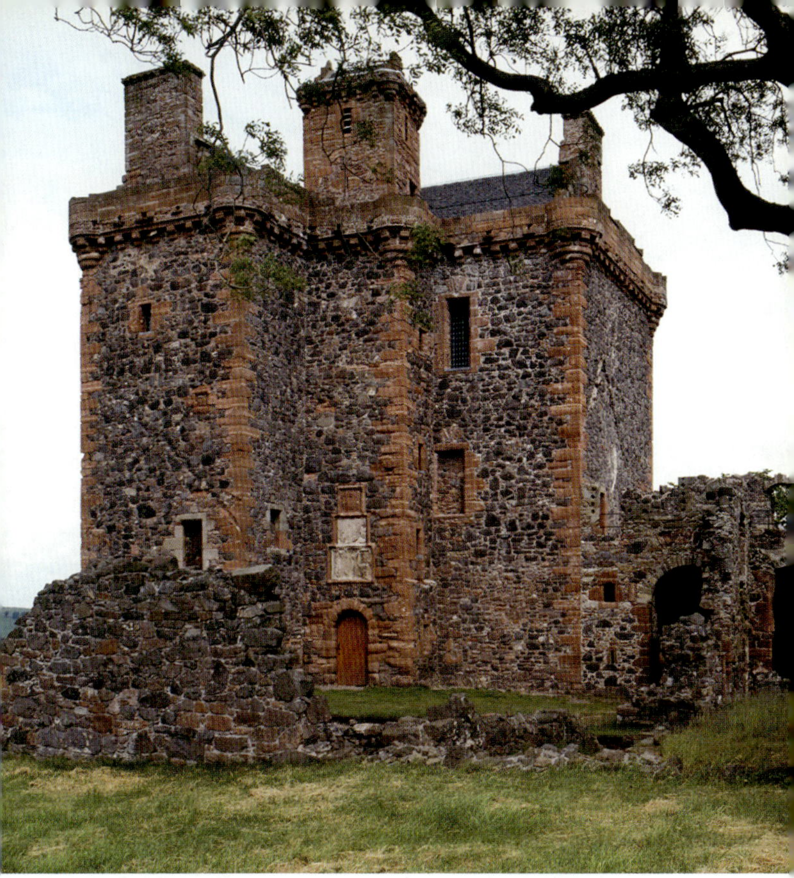
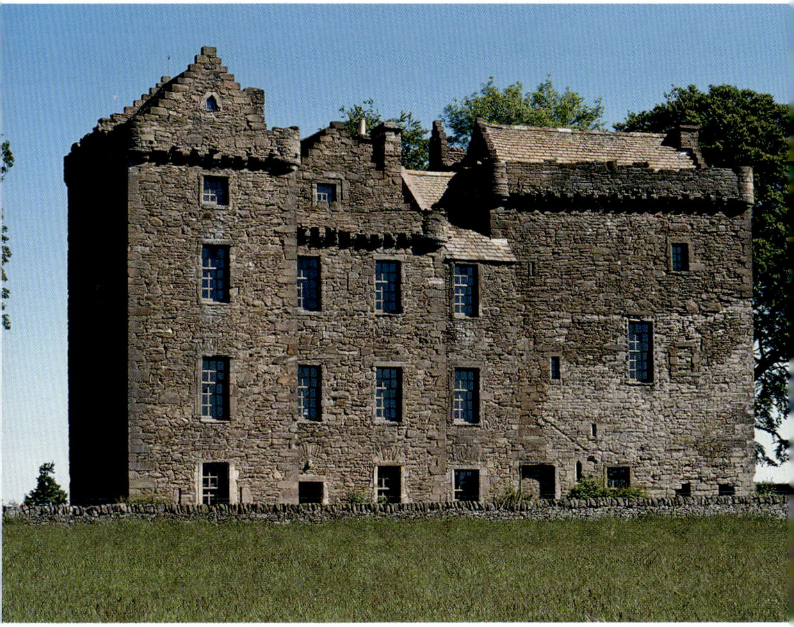

58. Drummond Castle, keep, late C15, remodelled and heightened by George P. Kennedy, 1842–53, and gatehouse, by John Mylne Sen., 1630 (p. 321)
59. Kinnaird Castle, c. 1500, restored, 1854–5 (p. 471)

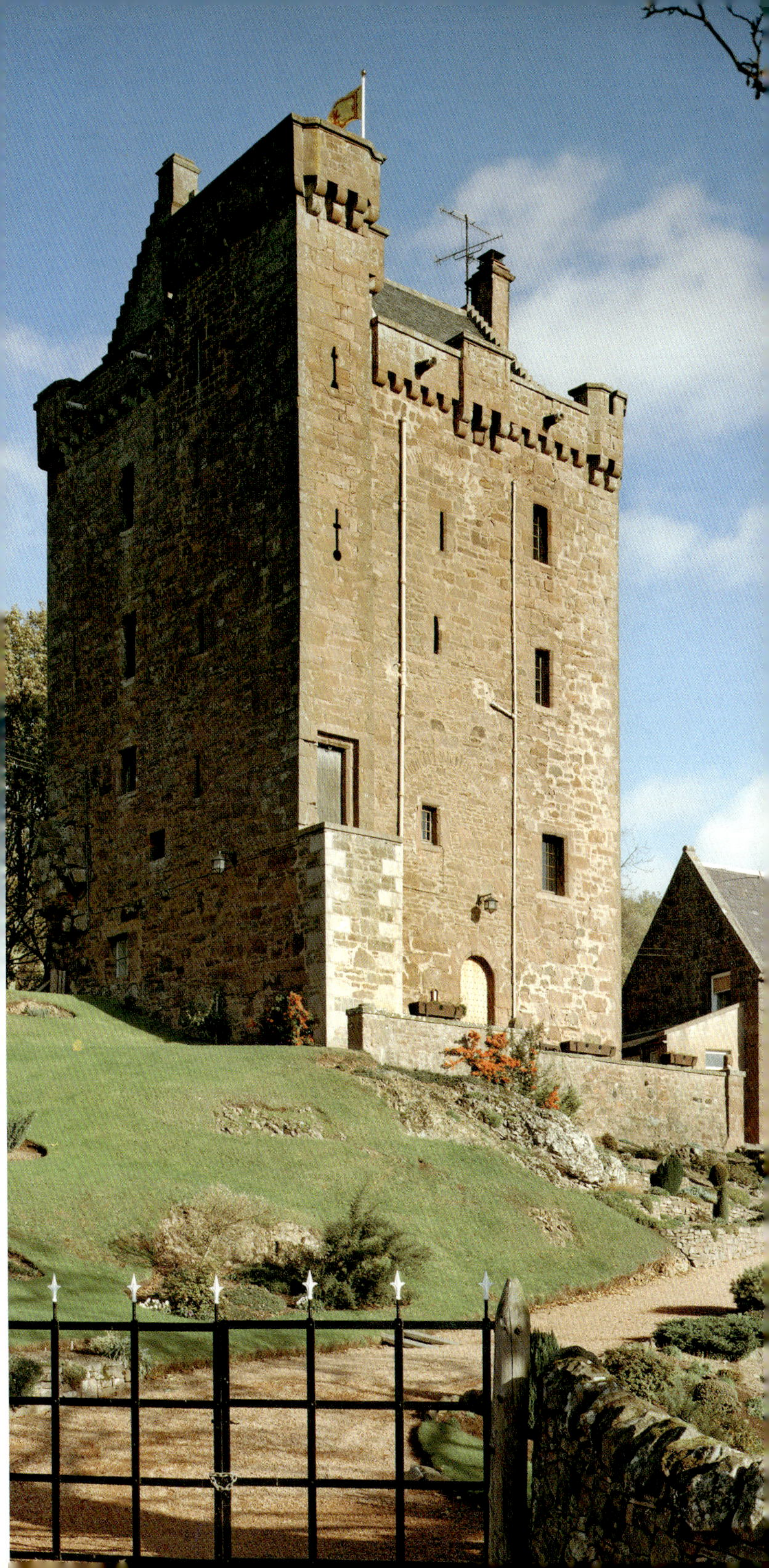

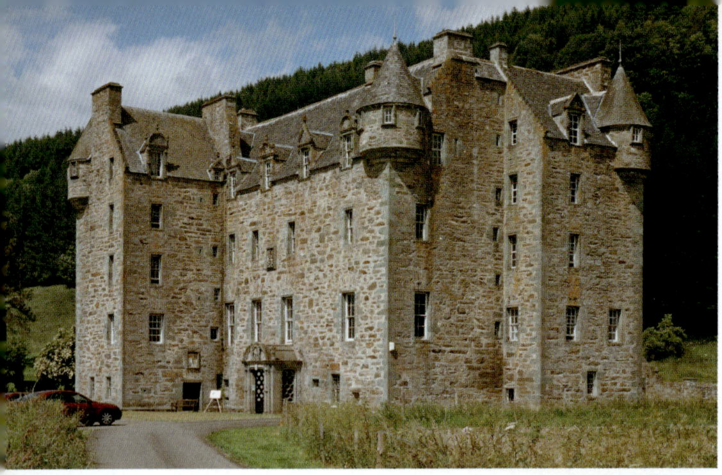
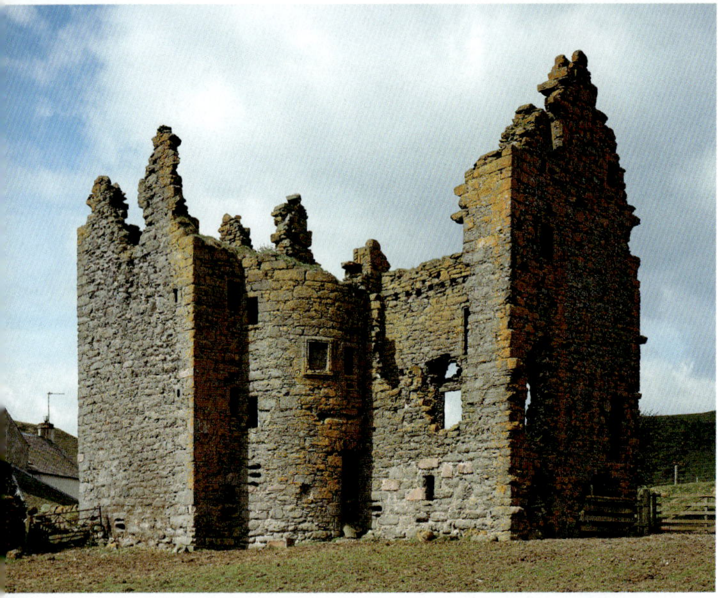
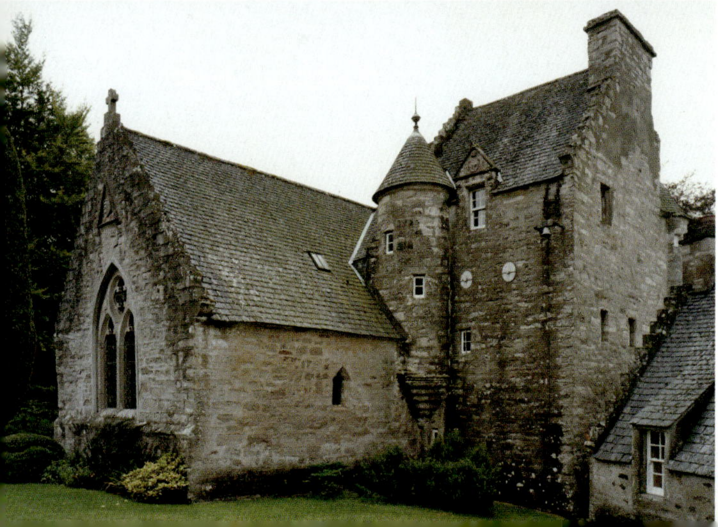

60. Castle Menzies, 1571–5, with porch by William Burn, 1839–40 (p. 262)
61. Evelick Castle, late C16 (p. 366)
62. Stobhall, 'Chapel', 1578 (p. 706)
63. Elcho Castle, mid C16 (p. 358)
64. Stobhall, 'Chapel', painted ceiling, early C17 (p. 707)

60	63
61	64
62	

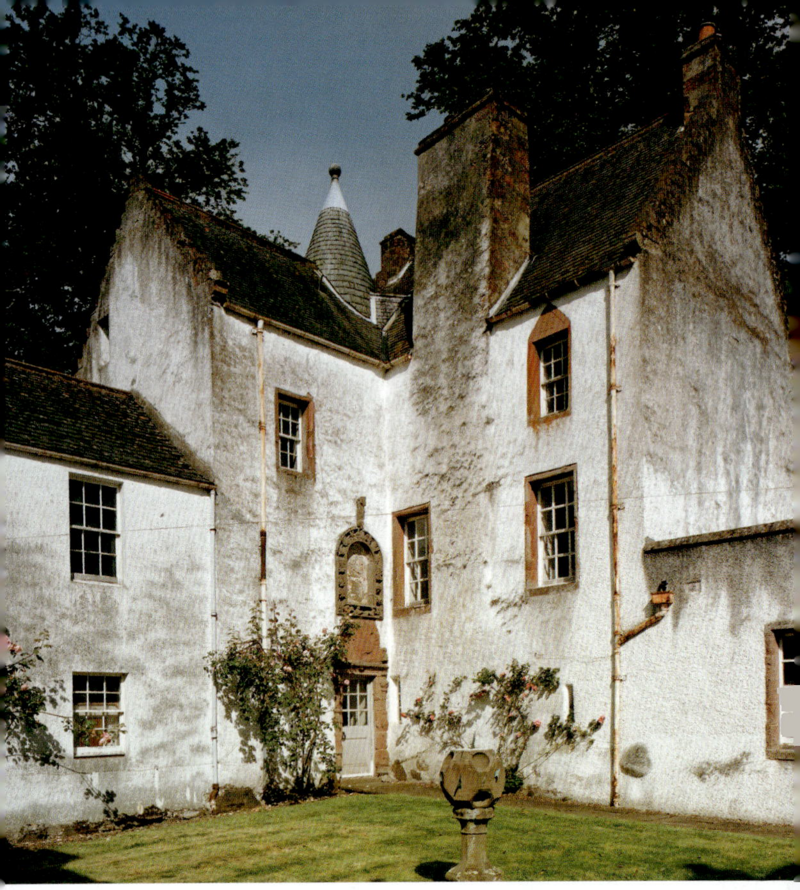
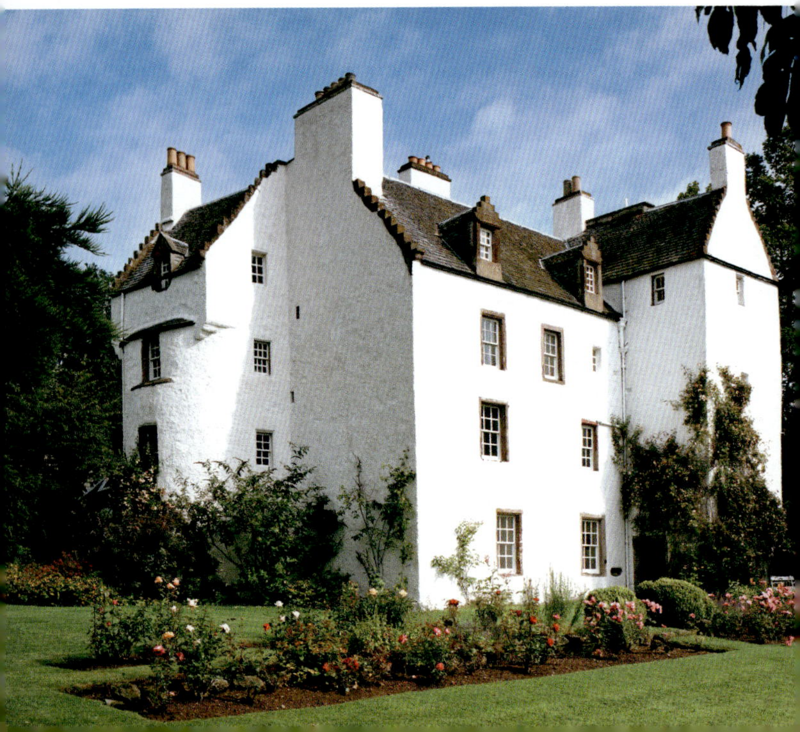

5. Ardblair Castle, NW tower, probably early C16, with doorpiece probably of early C17 (p. 157)
6. Blairgowrie, Newton Castle, late C16 (p. 233)
7. Drummonie House, late C17, with early C19 doorpiece (p. 325)
8. Methven Castle, 1678–81, altered, *c.* 1800 (p. 528)

65	67
66	68

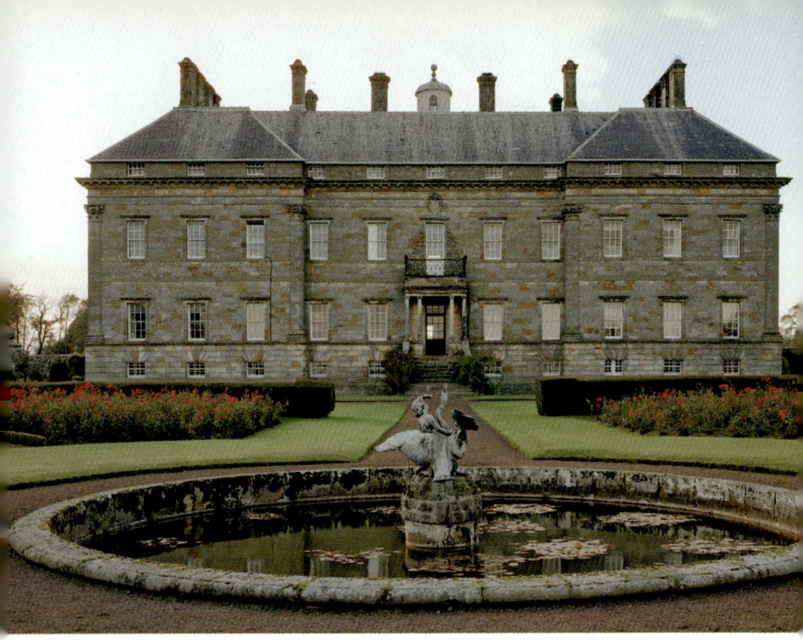

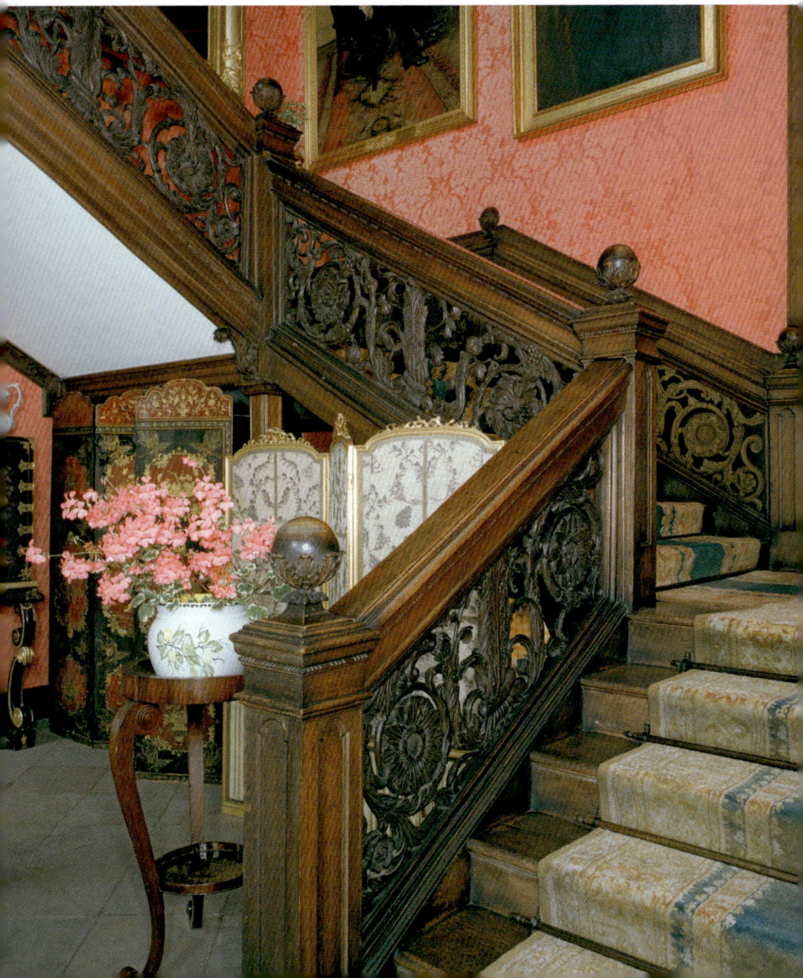

69. Kinross House, E front, by Sir William Bruce, 1685–93 (p. 488)
70. Kinross House, Great Stair, 1693 (p. 493)
71. Kinross House, Fish Gate, c. 1690 (p. 489)
72. Kinross House, Oak Drawing Room, chimneypiece, c. 1690 (p. 492)

69	71
70	72

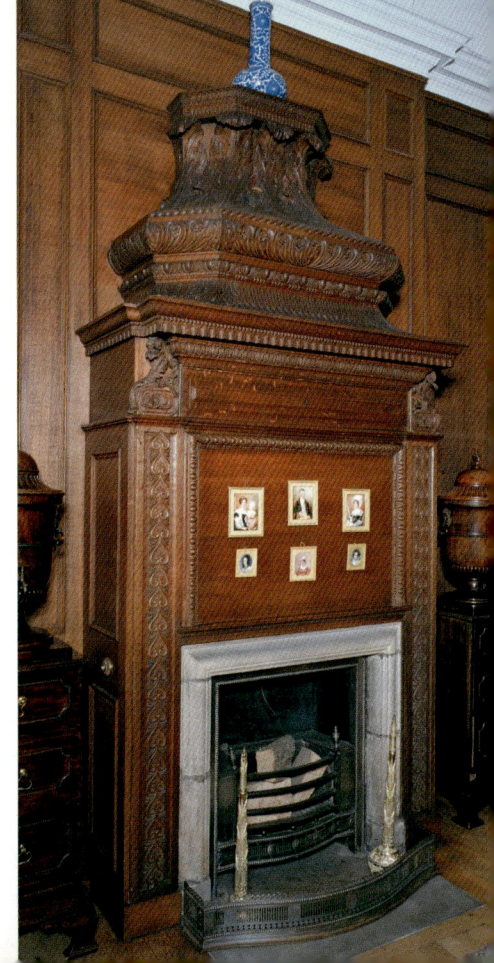

73. Murthly Castle, entrance block, by John Douglas, 1735–8; behind, Prince Charlie's Tower, probably c16 (p. 546)
74. Blair Castle, parlour, plasterwork by Thomas Clayton, 1747–8 (p. 215)
75. Blair Castle, Picture Staircase, woodwork by Archibald Chessels and plasterwork by Thomas Clayton, 1748–50 (p. 218)

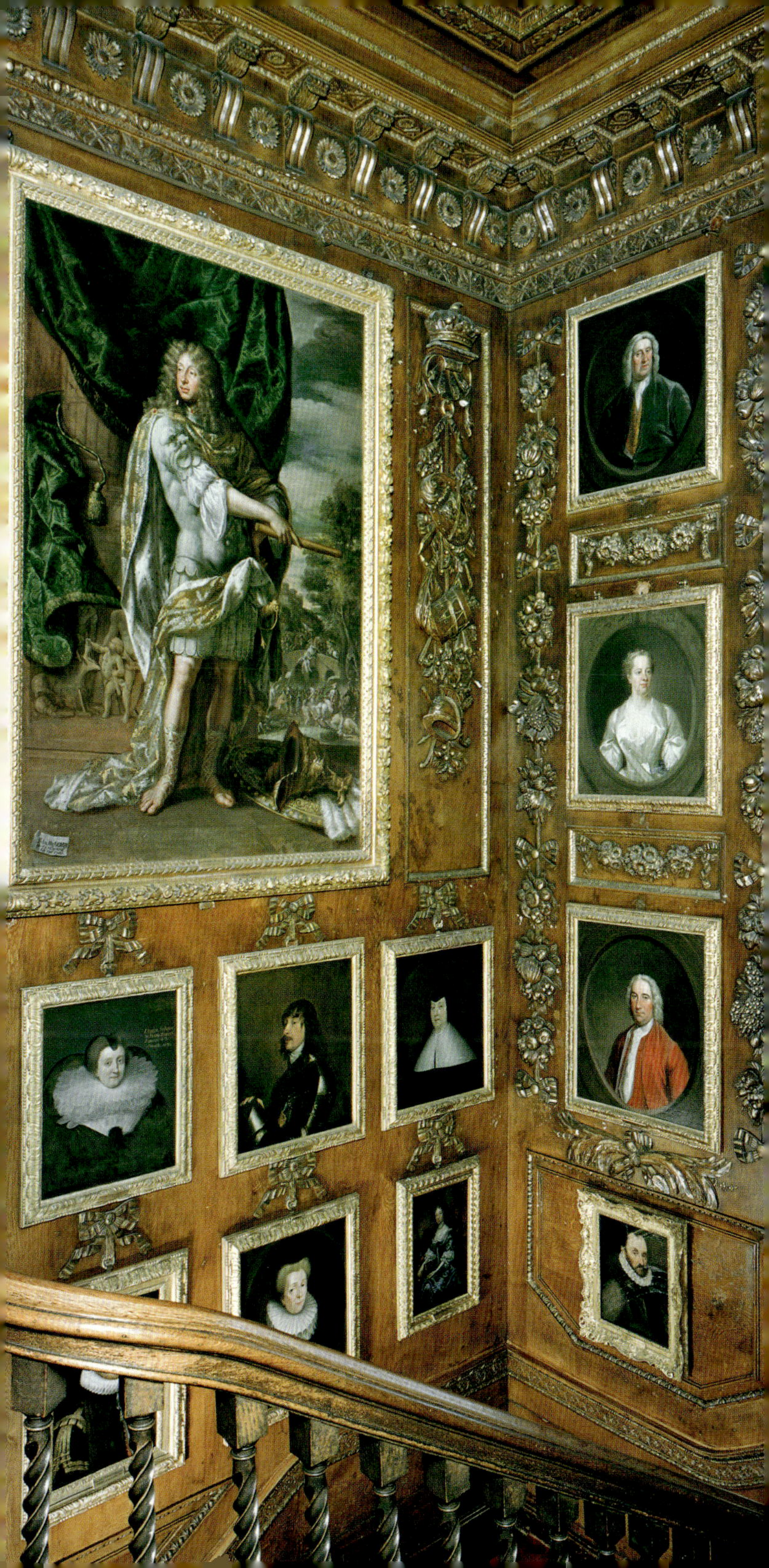

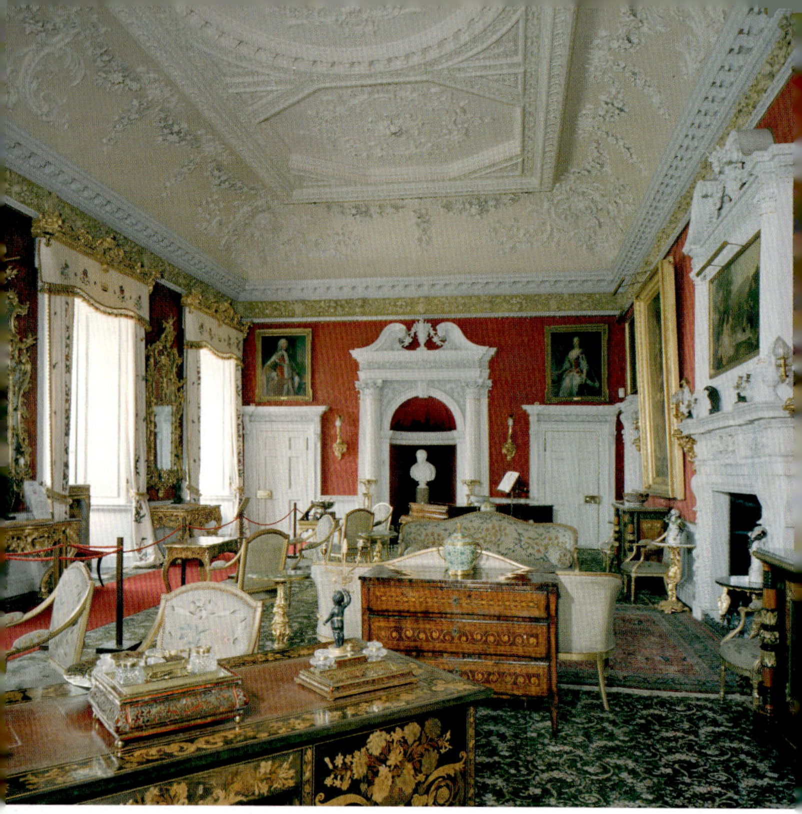

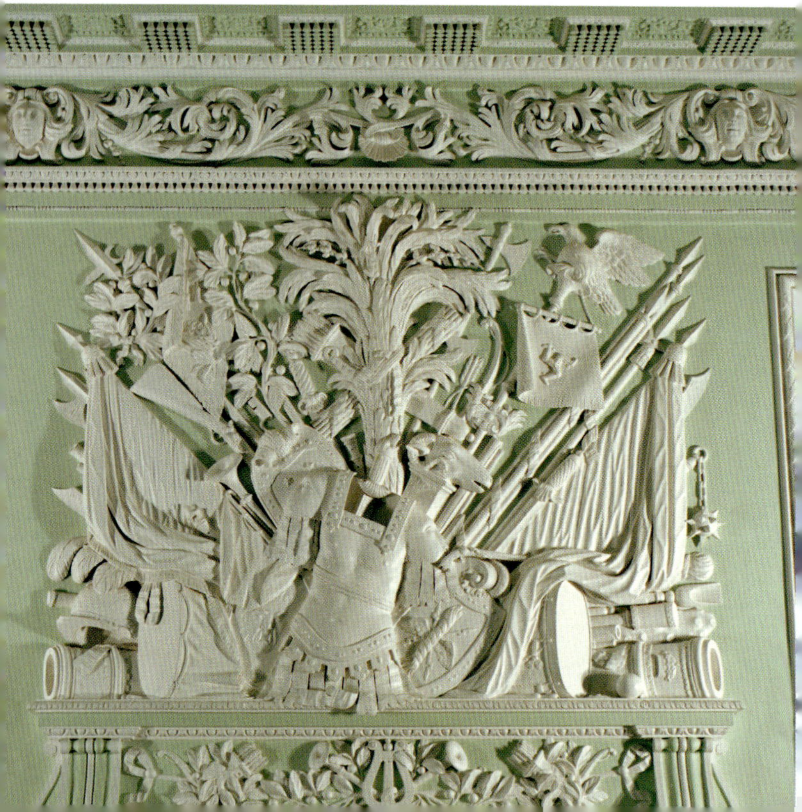

76. Blair Castle, Great Drawing Room, chimneypiece by Thomas Carter, woodwork by Charles Ross and plasterwork by Thomas Clayton, 1755–8 (p. 222)
77. Blair Castle, Great Dining Room, stucco overmantel by Thomas Clayton, 1751–3 (p. 221)
78. Blair Castle, Tapestry Room, 1750s (p. 222)

79. Scone Palace, Drawing Room, by William Atkinson, 1803–12 (p. 693)
80. Scone Palace, Octagon, by William Atkinson, 1803–12 (p. 691)
81. Inchyra House, *c.* 1810 (p. 422)
82. Keithick, by David A. Whyte, 1818–23 (p. 438)
83. Keithick, drawing room, decoration by G. Morant, probably 1839 (p. 439)

79	81
80	82
	83

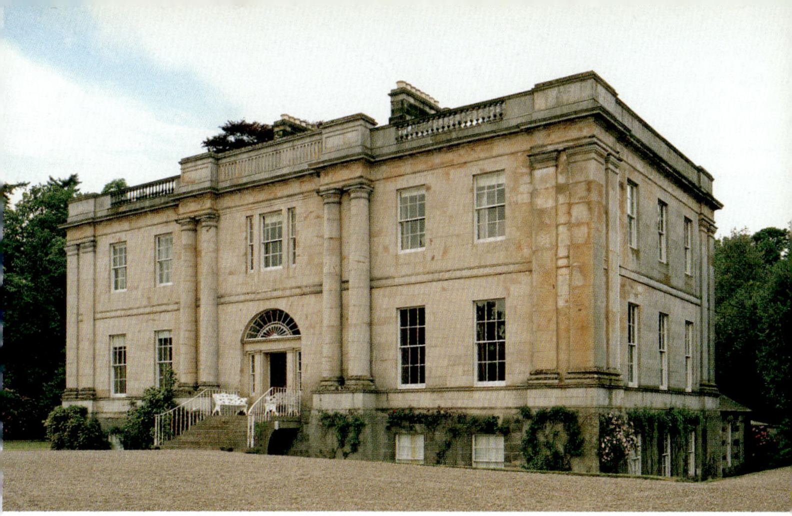

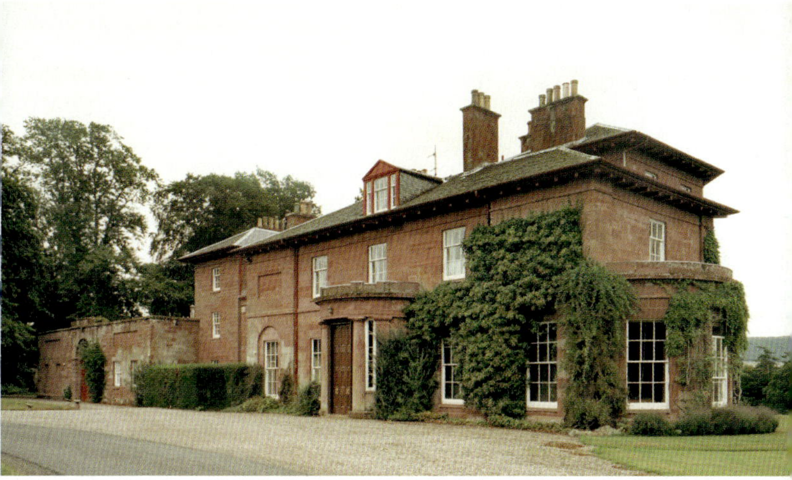

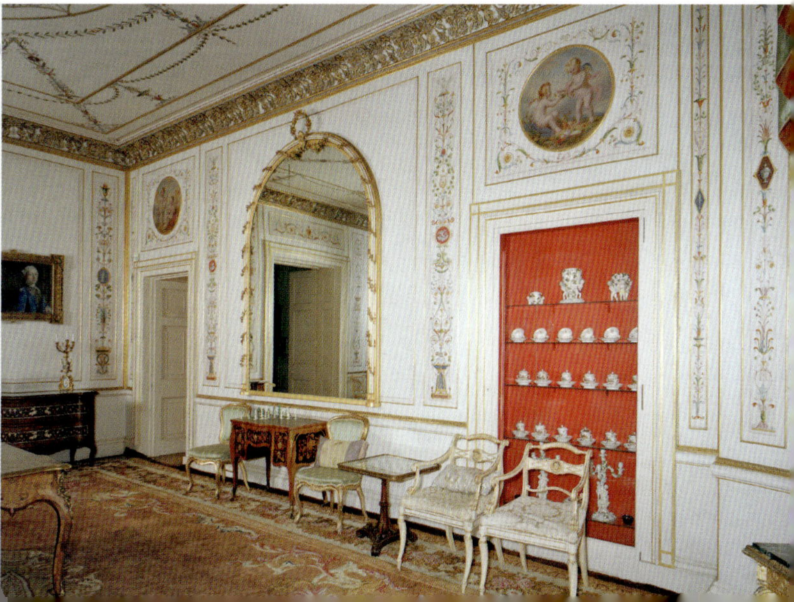

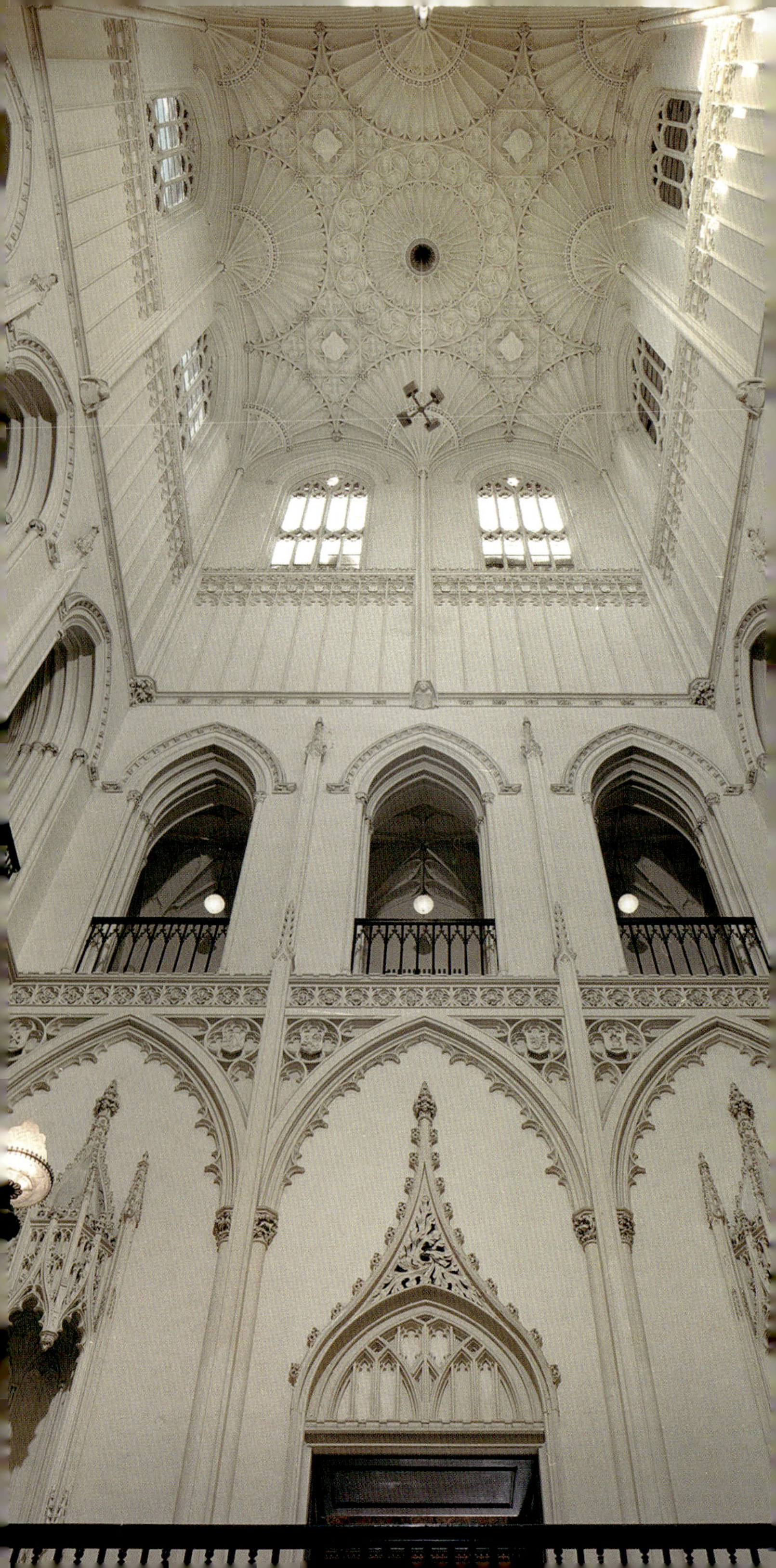

84. Taymouth Castle, stair hall, plasterwork by Francis Bernasconi, 1809–11 (p. 721)
85. Taymouth Castle, main block by John Paterson, 1801–4, heightened and altered by James and Archibald Elliot, 1805–12; East Wing (right) by William Atkinson, 1818–22; West Wing by James Gillespie Graham, 1838–42 (p. 717)
86. Taymouth Castle, Library, by James Gillespie Graham and A.W.N. Pugin, 1839–42 (p. 726)

84	85
	86

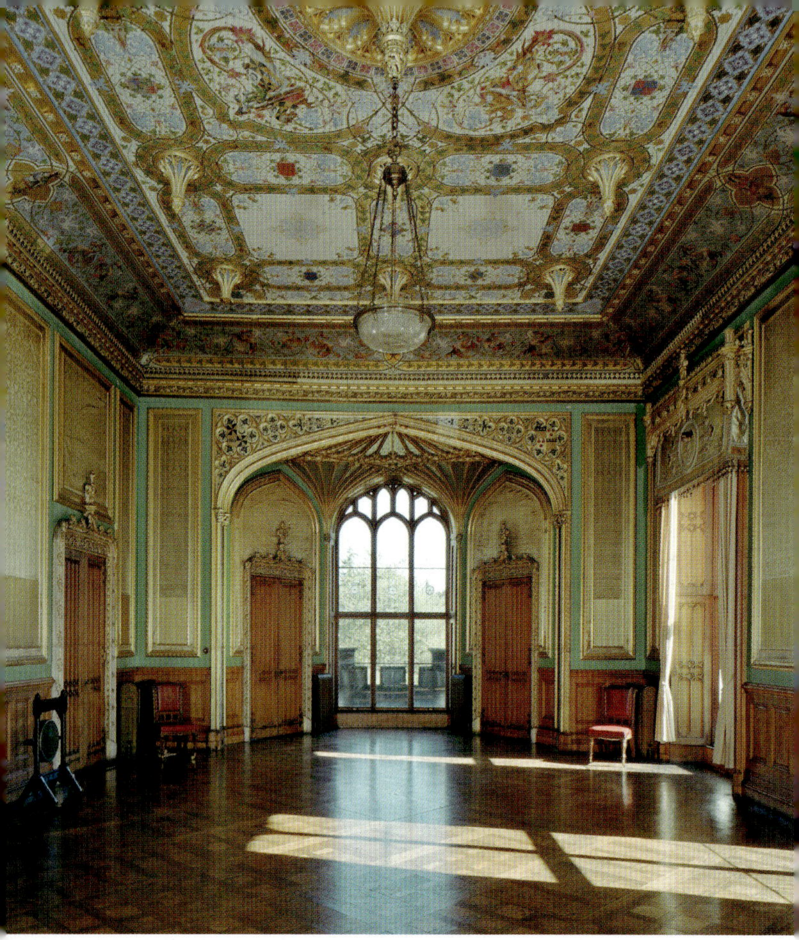

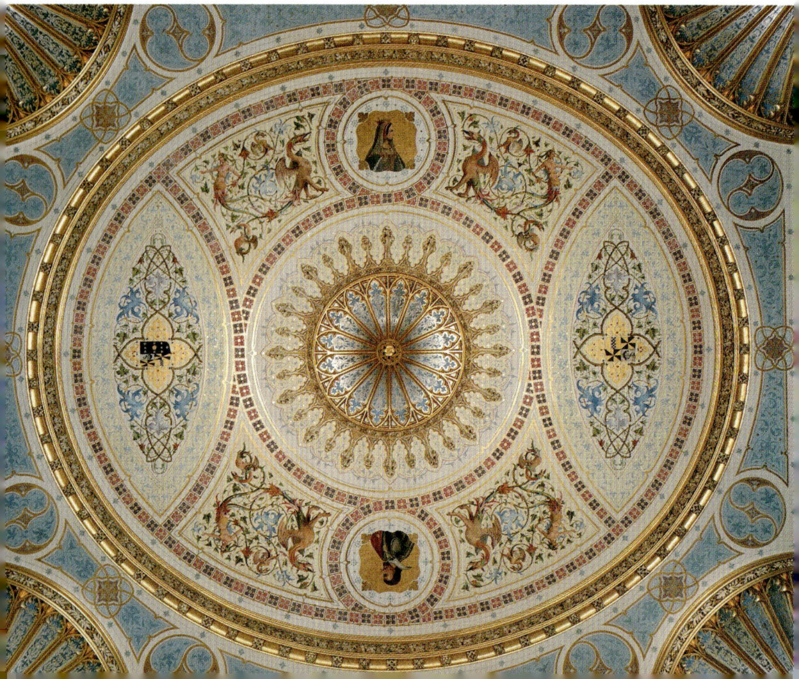

87. Taymouth Castle, Great Drawing Room, by James and Archibald Elliot, 1809–12, altered by James Gillespie Graham and A.W.N. Pugin and painted decoration by Frederick Crace & Son, 1842 (p. 722)
88. Taymouth Castle, Small Drawing Room, ceiling, plasterwork by Francis Bernasconi, 1809–11, painted decoration by Frederick Crace & Son, 1842 (p. 723)
89. Blair Castle, E front, by David Bryce, 1869–72 (p. 213)
90. Dall House, by Mackenzie & Matthews, 1854–5 (p. 310)

87	89
88	90

91. Drummond Castle, sundial, by John Mylne Sen., 1630 (p. 325)
92. Kinnaird Castle, doocot, probably early C18 (p. 472)
93. Megginch Castle, North Gateway, 1820 (p. 516)
94. Kilgraston House, Gateway, *c.* 1820 (p. 453)

	92
91	93
	94

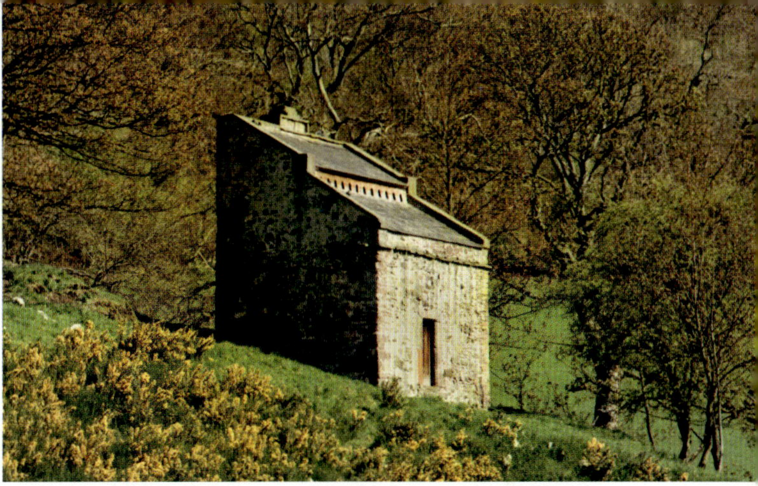

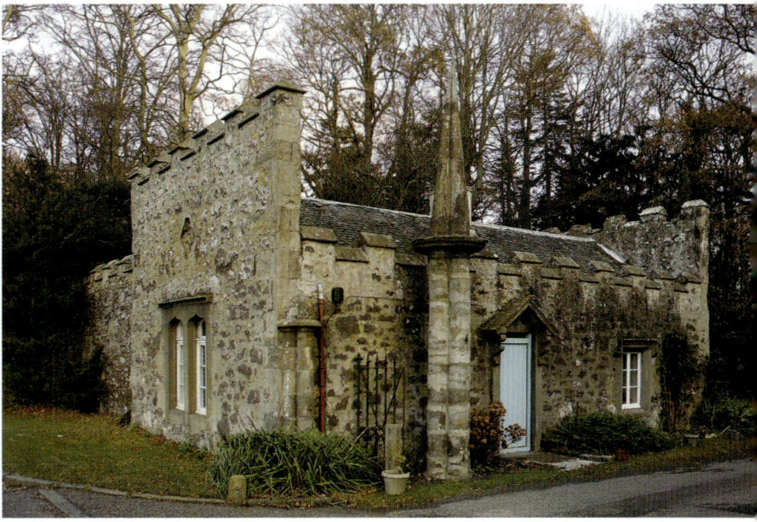

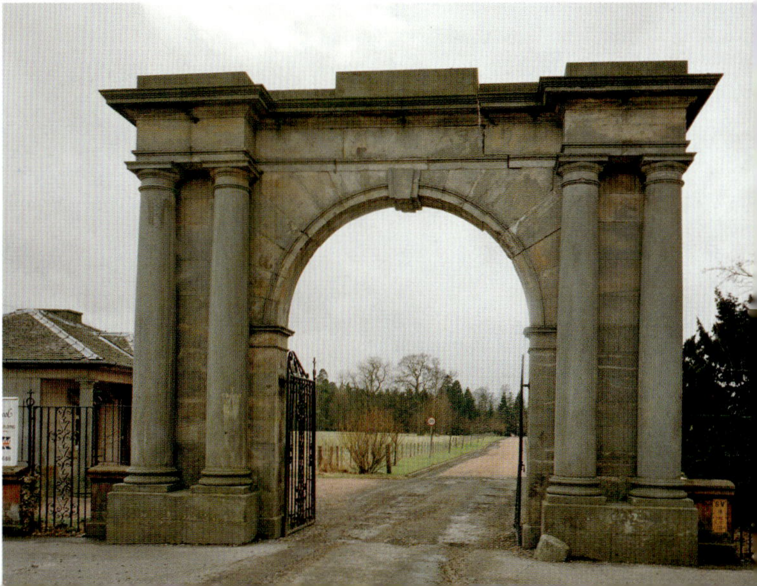

95. Aberfeldy, Tay Bridge, by William Adam, 1733 (p. 137)
96. Struan, road bridge and railway viaduct, by Joseph Mitchell, 1862–3 (p. 716)
97. Glenericht House, Bridge of Cally, bridge, by John Justice, *c.* 1835 (p. 241)
98. Aberfeldy, suspension bridge, by W.J. Harvey and students of The University of Dundee Department of Civil Engineering, 1992 (p. 137)

| 95 | 97 |
| 96 | 98 |

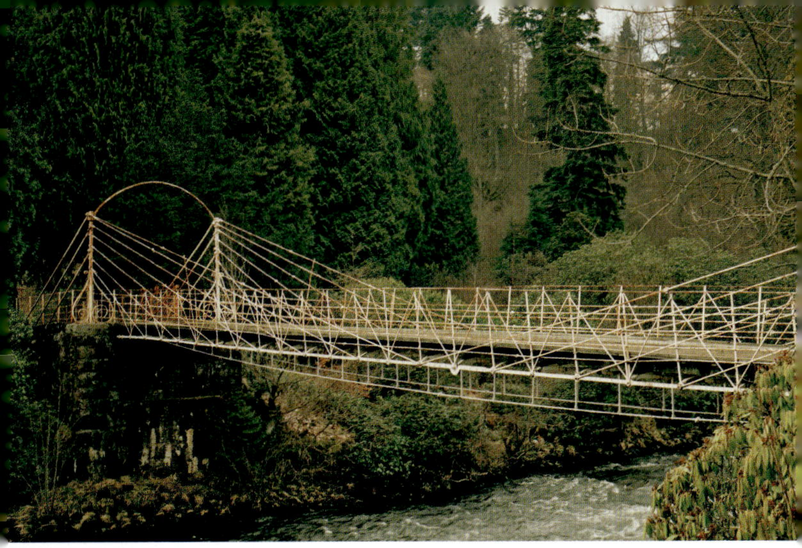

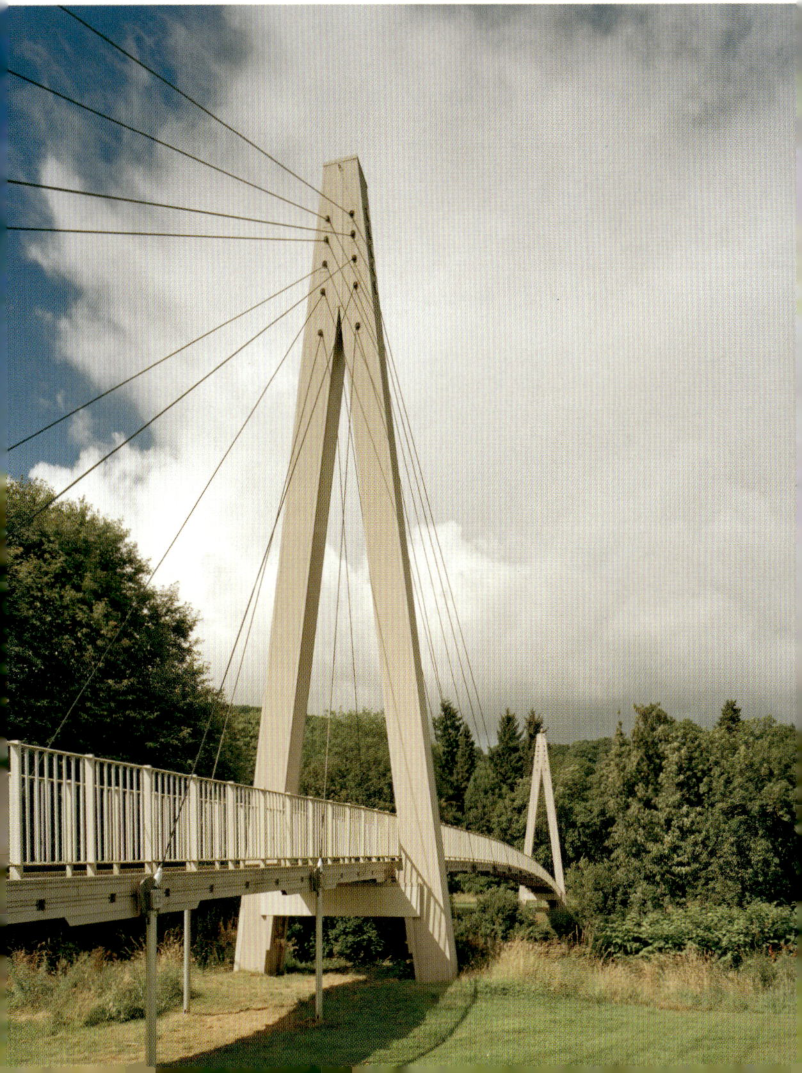

99. Abernethy, The Cross, War Memorial, by Mills & Shepherd, 1920, and Abernethy Round Tower, probably late C11 (pp. 144, 142)
100. Dunkeld, High Street, Fountain, by Charles S. Robertson and John Rhind, 1866; behind, The Ell House (left), 1753, and Duchess Anne Halls, by R. & R. Dickson, 1853–4 (pp. 343, 346)

101. Rait, cottages, probably early C19 (p. 676)
102. Meikleour, Mercat Cross, 1698 (p. 522)
103. Kinrossie, Mercat Cross, 1686 (p. 494)

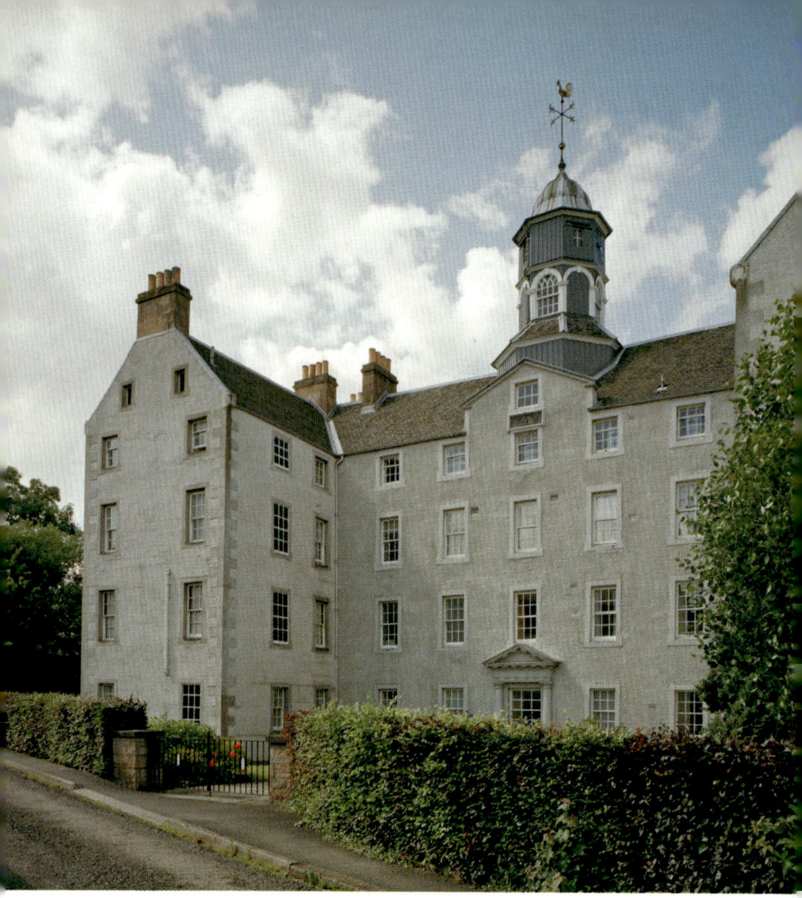

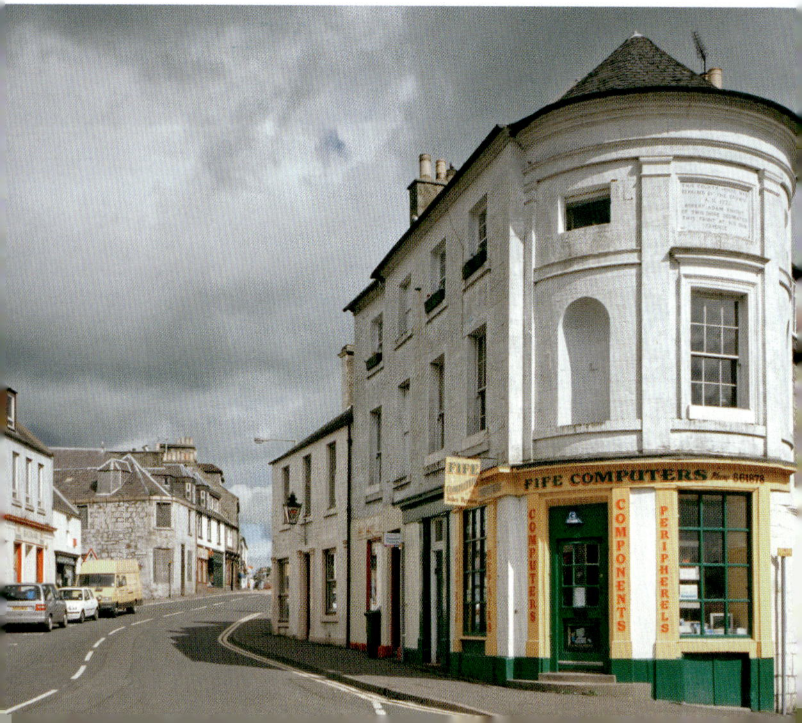
FIFE COMPUTERS
COMPUTERS
COMPONENTS
PERIPHERELS

04. Perth, King James VI Hospital, 1748–52 (p. 603)
05. Kinross, County House, by Robert Adam, 1771 (p. 477)
06. Innerpeffray Library, by Charles Freebairn, 1758–62 (p. 425)
07. Perth, Atholl Crescent, 1790s (p. 612)

104	106
105	107

108. Perth, Public Seminaries, by Robert Reid, 1803–7, with clock and sculpture added, 1886 (p. 610)
109. Perth, Salutation Hotel, *c.* 1800 (p. 635)

110. Perth Sheriff Court, by Robert Smirke, 1816–19 (p. 609)
111. Perth Museum and Art Gallery, by David Morison, 1822–4 (p. 605)

| 108 | 110 |
| 109 | 111 |

112. Perth, St John Street, Nos. 48–50 (former Central Bank of Scotland), by David Rhind, 1846–7 (p. 631)
113. Crieff, High Street, Nos. 30–32 (former British Linen Co. Bank), by Peddie & Washington Browne, c. 1905 (p. 301)
114. Perth, Old Council Chambers, by Andrew Heiton Jun., 1878–9 (p. 603)
115. Perth, Council Buildings, by G.P.K. Young, 1898–1901, W extensions of 1920 and 1932 (p. 599)

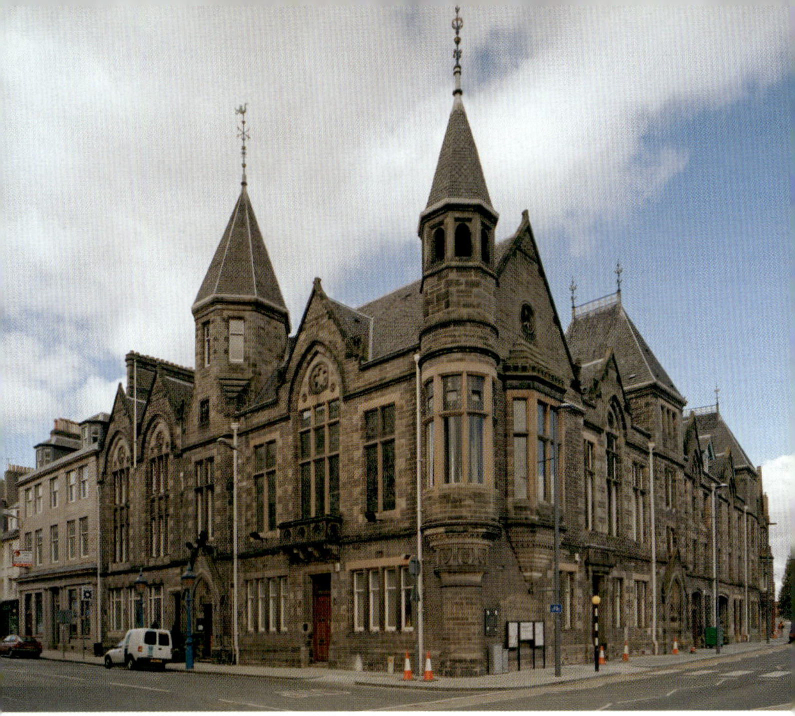

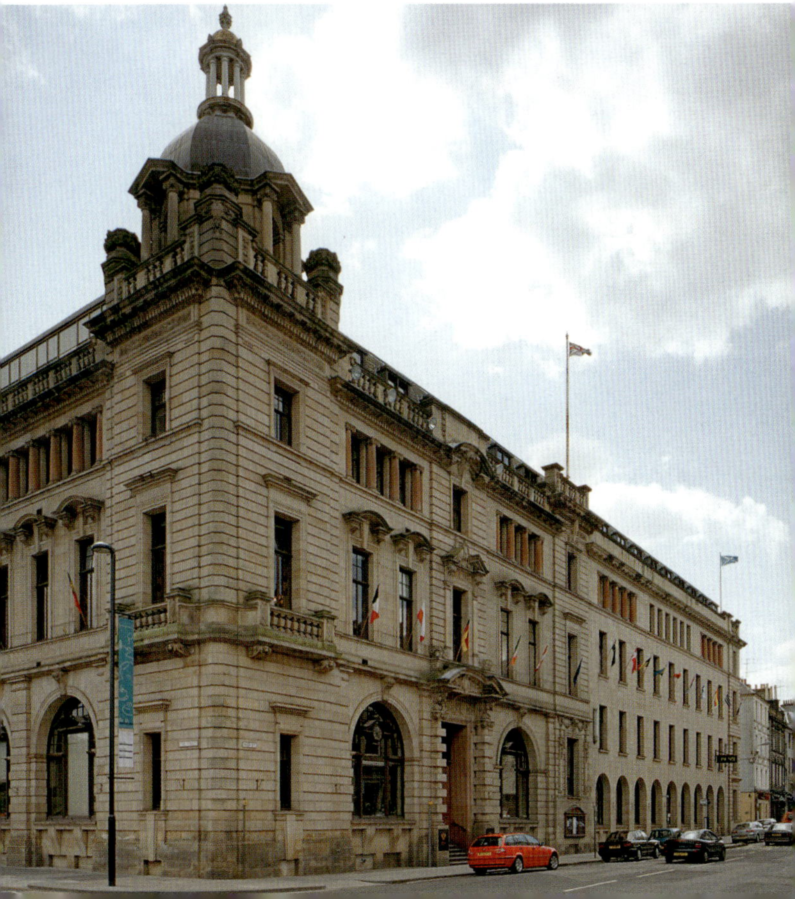

116. Fortingall, Kirkton Cottages, by J.M. MacLaren, 1889 (p. 374)
117. Glenfarg, Arngask Library, by A.N. Paterson, 1892 (p. 402)

118. Forteviot, Village Hall, by James Miller, 1927 (p. 372)
119. Pitlochry Festival Theatre, by Law & Dunbar-Nasmith, 1979–81 (p. 671)

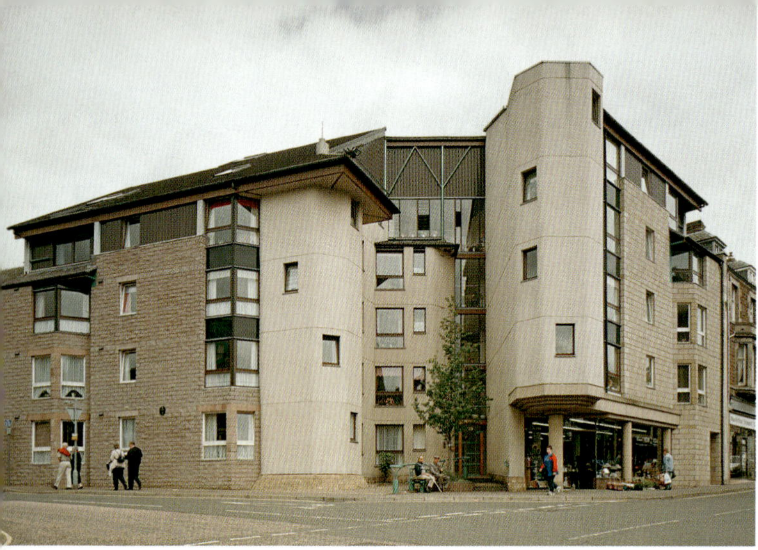

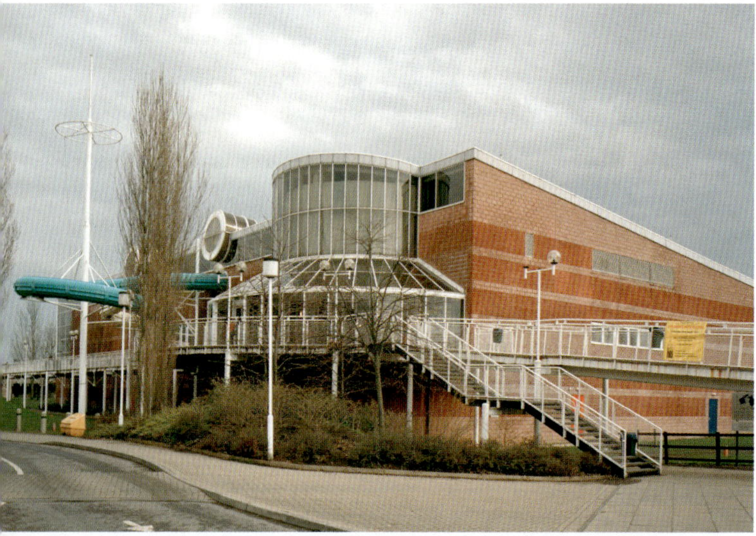

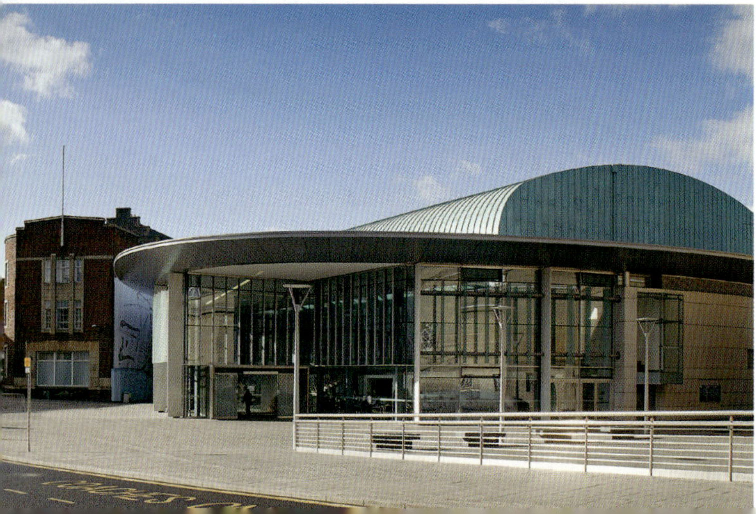

120. Crieff, Comrie Street, No. 29 (Servite House), by Nicoll Russell Studios, 1990–2 (p. 299)
121. Perth Leisure Pool, by Faulkner Browns, 1985–8 (p. 663)
122. Perth Concert Hall, by Building Design Partnership, 2003–5 (p. 605)
123. Edradour Distillery, maltings, 1837 (p. 358)
124. Aberfeldy Distillery, by C.C. Doig, 1896–8 (p. 141)

120	123
121	124
122	

125. Stanley Mills, Bell Mill, by Richard Arkwright, 1786–7 (p. 702)
126. Pitlochry Dam, by Sir Alexander Gibb & Partners, and Power Station (l.) by H.O. Tarbolton, 1947–51 (p. 671)

0.4km. WSW, an Iron Age FORT, probably of the first millennium B.C., occupies 0.55ha. of a natural terrace on the side of Pole Hill. The precipitous slopes to the E and S may have required no additional defence except perhaps an earth mound. On the more easily accessible N and W sides have been placed a formidable array of banks and ditches, the outer two presumably a second-stage reinforcement since they block the fort's original W entrance. The only entrance now is from the N. Inside the enclosure, sites of ring-ditch houses. – On the summit of Pole Hill, 0.5km. NW of the fort, a round CAIRN, probably dating from the second millennium B.C. It is 19.5m. in diameter and 2.2m. in height, the stepped profile suggesting three stages of construction. Extending from its SE segment, a small rectangular platform edged by boulders.

FASKALLY HOUSE
3.1 km. NW of Pitlochry

9060

On the N shore of Loch Faskally, a low-key mansion house built in 1829 and extended in 1837. *William Burn* was architect of both phases. An English Elizabethan bay-windowed manor is the general inspiration but with crowstepped gables and conical-roofed turrets to acknowledge that it is in Scotland.

FINDO GASK

0020

Isolated church of a rural parish.

FINDO GASK PARISH CHURCH. By *Richard Crichton*, 1800–1. Harled rectangle, a ball-finialled birdcage bellcote on the W gable. In the S side, a pair of round-headed windows with projecting keystones and imposts, their mullions and circular top lights inserted in the late C19; between them, a panel carved with a swag and the date 1800. Round-headed gallery window in the W gable. The projecting session house below was added in 1863. Pair of rectangular windows in the N side. Between them, a small piend-roofed boiler house of 1905. In the E gable, rectangular windows lighting the area and round-headed windows to the gallery; between them, a chancel-like bowed projection housing a stair.

Inside, the original E gallery, with a simple panelled front, survives but the W gallery has been removed. At the centre of the W end, the COMMUNION TABLE of 1949, flanked by the mid-C20 FONT and PULPIT of 1801 to its N. – PEWS of 1895 brought here in 1953 from Craigie Church, Perth. – STAINED GLASS. Pictorial W window (St John the Evangelist) of 1907.

SCHOOL, 0.4km. S. Broad-eaved school and schoolhouse, probably early C19 in origin but enlarged by *A. & A. Heiton* in 1857 and *William McLaren* in 1875, and further remodelled in 1902.

ROMAN WATCH TOWERS, Ardunie, 1.6 km. NW, Kirkhill, 0.3 km. E. and Muir o'Fauld, 2.1 km. ENE. Constructed in the late C1 beside the Roman road which ran from Camelon (Stirling and Central Scotland) to the forts at Ardoch near Braco and Strageath near Innerpeffray and then along the Gask Ridge to Bertha near Perth. Each is an enclosure on which stood a wooden tower and consisted of a roughly circular mound defended by a ditch crossed by a rampart from the N and an outer rampart.

GASK HOUSE. *See* p. 381.

FINDYNATE HOUSE
0.9 km. W of Strathtay

Tall villa-mansion house of 1873–6 designed by *Walter F. K. Lyon* in a strongly Scottish manner but, despite its hammer-dressed masonry, without the aggression of much Baronial architecture of the period. Round towers and a bay window on the garden (S) elevation, the E tower's exaggeratedly high ogee roof a replacement of 1909–10 by *F. W. Deas* for Lyon's more conventional conical covering. Entrance (E) front with the door under a rope moulding placed in a gabled shallow projection from the S end. To the N, a high block, asymmetrical like the rest. Mullioned windows. (Interior partly of the 1870s but remodelled in Arts and Crafts style by Deas in 1909–10.)

Single-storey and attic LODGE of the late C19. Heavily detailed, with crowstepped gables and one corner notched under corbelling to support the eaves; bow window facing the drive.

FORDEL HOUSE
2 km. N of Glenfarg

Classical villa of 1784 aggrandized by *Andrew Heiton Jun.* in 1875, the walls rendered and with rusticated quoins. Main block of two storeys. S front of five bays, the centre three surmounted by a pediment; urns on the pediment and the outer corners. To this front Heiton added broad canted bay windows, a pedimented porch and a terracotta wallhead balustrade. Extending from the main block are one-bay links, each originally single-storey and with a three-light S window. The links were heightened to two storeys in 1875. Also heightened in 1875 were the Venetian-windowed single-storey end pavilions, their 1780s pediments reused above Heiton's upper floors.

FORGANDENNY

Small village on the edge of the policies of Strathallan School (q.v.).

FORGANDENNY FREE CHURCH. Now Village Hall. By *J. J. Stevenson*, 1883–5. Small but sturdy box of stugged red sandstone with buff-coloured dressings. Diagonally buttressed gable front, its centre slightly advanced and rising into a large 'bellcote' gablet; projecting from the centre, a gabled porch. Flattened ogee-arched tops to the windows.

FORGANDENNY PARISH CHURCH. Medieval kirk, partly Georgianized and later 'restored' with unconvincing Neo-Romanesque detail by *T. S. Robertson*, 1902–3.

The main body of the church is a straightforward rectangle, *c.* 23.6 m. by 8.2 m., the W porch and the vestry and boiler house on the N side added in 1902–3. Projecting from the S side is the Ruthven Aisle, the mausoleum-cum-laird's loft of the Ruthvens of Freeland, an addition probably of *c.* 1600.

The stonework of the church's E gable up to a height just below the eaves level is of large squared blocks and consistent with a C12 date, as is the splay-topped base course along this gable. The other walls are of rubble and probably date from a late medieval rebuilding but they were heightened in 1770, a likely date also for the intaken top of the E gable now with a fleur-de-lys finial of 1902–3. Perhaps also of 1770 but perhaps of 1749 (the date on the bell*) and reused is the pyramid-roofed and ball-finialled birdcage bellcote on the W end. Built into the S wall but not *in situ* is the chevron-decorated head of a round-arched Romanesque door or window; it may have belonged originally to the church but its provenance is unknown. The windows are all of 1902–3, those of the side walls rectangular and each containing two round-arched cusped lights. In the E gable, a round-arched four-light window. In the W gable, above the porch, a quatrefoil light. In Robertson's porch, a rectangular door in the S wall; pointed W window.

The RUTHVEN AISLE is two-storeyed, the upper floor reached by a forestair. A date of *c.* 1600 seems likely but it was remodelled in the later C18 (probably 1774) when the S gable was given stone acorn finials at its ends and a swagged urn on top. Also late C18 is the Venetian door to the upper floor but in 1903 the round-arched top of the centre opening was built up and the flanking openings given windows of the same type as those of the church. Above the door, a C18 stone plaque carved with the heraldic achievement of the Lords Ruthven of Freeland. Over each sidelight, a square panel, the l. probably of *c.* 1600 but reported[†] to have borne the improbable date of 1369, the r. dated 1774. Both have the same inscription (with minor differences of spelling): ALL MEN THINK ON YOUR DYING DAY: TIS JOY TO DIE TO LIVE FOR AY. At the Aisle's lower floor, a low door and narrow slit windows, their round-arched tops restored in 1903.

---

*The bell seems to have been recast, perhaps *c.* 1900.
[†] By A. Jervise, 'Notices and Examples of Inscriptions', *Proceedings of the Society of Antiquaries of Scotland*, iv (1860–2), 581.

The church's interior was recast in 1902–3 when Robertson provided the arch-braced kingpost roof. Simple boxy PEWS. – COMMUNION TABLE and PULPIT of 1964 at the E end. – The late C19 hanging lamps were installed here in 1962. – In the porch, a Covenanter's TOMBSTONE, probably of the early C18, inscribed: HERE LYES/ANDREU BRODIE WRIG/HT IN FORGUNDENNY WHO/AT ƷE BREAK OF A MEETING/OCBR 1678 WAS SHOT BY A/PARTY OF HIGHLAND MEN/ COMMANDED BY BALLECH/EN AT A CAVES MOUƷH FLY/ING ƷIƷHER FOR HIS LIFE &/ƷHAT FOR HIS ADHERENCE/TO ƷE WORD OF GOD & SCO/TLANDS COVENANTED/WORK OF REFORMATION/REV 12C VII [i.e. 'And there was war in the heaven: Michael and his angels fought against the dragon; and the dragon fought and his angels'].

The entrance to the GRAVEYARD is from the S by a red sandstone gabled GATEWAY of c. 1920. S of the church, a collection of HEADSTONES of the mid and late C18, some pedimented or with curvaceous tops, carved in relief with reminders of death and most with angels' heads (souls). Among them, due N of the entrance, the stone of 1774 to William Hume, displaying a crown and emblems of death, the carving crude but well preserved. – S of the centre of the church, Charles Millar, dated 1753, bearing the tools of a tailor. – E of this, two stones carved with ploughs. One, dated 1783, commemorates Alexander Robertson, tenant in Over Bunzion, the other, dated 1788, William Graham, tenant in Wester Colteuchar. – Behind the stone to Alexander Robertson is one of 1741 to Alexander Boig, weaver, displaying a shuttle. – Due S of this, near the churchyard wall, James Glass, dated 1789, with a particularly well-toothed skull. – E of this, James Thomson, smith, dated 1772, with a crowned anvil and a tiny hammer to one side. – At the E end of the churchyard, Colin Brown, merchant, with a shield bearing a merchant's mark (like the numeral 4). – To its N, Janet Richardson, daughter of William Richardson, shoemaker, dated 1782, a crowned last on its shield. – NW of this, John Condie, dated 1740, and Thomas Condie, dated 1745, both carved in exceptionally high relief.

SCHOOL. Mid-C19; L-plan arrangement of a single-storey school and two-storey schoolhouse. Picturesque, the broad eaves broken by the gableted dormerheads over the upper windows of the schoolhouse. The school was extended N by *Cairns & Barlass*, 1875–6, and the windows of the original part widened in 1890 when the schoolhouse was enlarged.

DESCRIPTION. Two parallel streets separated by a field and woodland. The S street, containing the Free Church (*see* above) is a ragbag of C19 and C20 housing. In the N street, off which a path beside the school leads to the Parish Church (for these, *see* above), several picturesque broad-eaved mid-C19 cottages with gableted canopies over their entrances.

FORT, Culteuchar Hill, 3km. S. Badly ruined stone defences of an Iron Age fort, probably of the first millennium B.C., standing on the summit of a steep-sided site. The two principal walls, the outer *c.* 4.6m. thick, the inner *c.* 5.5m. and with slits for wooden beams in its outer face, are roughly concentric and enclose outer and inner oval areas, the outer *c.* 100m. by 49 m., the inner *c.* 55m. by 21m. In the centre of the outer wall's E end, a gateway which has been equipped with bar-holes. From the gateway's S side a wall extends W across the outer enclosure and is continued for a short distance into the inner enclosure. Outside the main fortification the ground to the N slopes gently for *c.* 40m. before falling abruptly. At the outer edge of the slope a substantial wall has enclosed an annexe to the fort. Below the S side of the fort are remains of ditches enclosing a terrace.

ECCLESIAMAGIRDLE HOUSE. See p. 357.
GLENEARN HOUSE. See p. 401.
ROSSIE HOUSE. See p. 679.
STRATHALLAN SCHOOL. See p. 713.

FORNETH HOUSE
0.6km. N of Clunie

Harled two-storey and basement laird's house overlooking the Loch of Clunie, built *c.* 1780 for Thomas Elder, Lord Provost of Edinburgh and Postmaster-General of Scotland. N front of three bays, the centre slightly advanced and pedimented. Its cast-iron portico was added early in the C19 when the S windows of the principal floor were deepened, given cornices and linked by a sill course. The house was remodelled in 1904 by *Lake Falconer* who added a sizeable and slightly taller W extension, with a pyramidal-roofed tower at its junction with the C18 building. On the W side, a two-storey bay window fronted by an iron balcony with steps down to the garden. S elevation with corniced windows like those of the earlier house at the principal floor. The S windows of the fully exposed basement are recessed in round-headed overarches, this treatment also extended by Falconer to the basement windows of the original house. Also of 1904, the STABLES court E of the house, with a square cupola-ventilator on the roof, but the pedimented rubble-built E gable with a giant round-headed dummy arch looks late C18. On the S side, a veranda at the level of the main house's principal floor and with steps down to the garden. – Broad-eaved EAST LODGE at the end of the drive, also of 1904.

FORTEVIOT

Early C20 model village built to serve the Dupplin estate which had been acquired by the whisky-blending millionaire, Liberal M.P. and philanthropist, Sir John Dewar (later first Lord Forteviot of Dupplin) in 1910.

FORTEVIOT PARISH CHURCH. Rubble-walled box built in 1778, the solidly classical birdcage bellcote on the W gable looking rather later, perhaps a replacement of 1830 when *William Stirling I* and *Andrew Heiton Sen.* carried out repairs. In the S wall, two round-arched and keystoned windows of 1778 and two more of the same type in the W gable. The other windows are in a thin Romanesque manner and date from *David Smart*'s alterations of 1867. So too do the gabled N porch, the lean-to vestry on the N, and the gableted skewputts of the main block.

Inside, plain PEWS of 1867. – At the E end, PULPIT and COMMUNION TABLE of *c.* 1920. – One-manual ORGAN by *D. & T. Hamilton*, *c.* 1870, renovated by *A. F. Edmonstone* and installed here in 1997. – Medieval octagonal stone FONT BOWL from the former Muckersie Parish Church. On one face, a coat of arms. – In the porch, early medieval carved stone FRAGMENTS, two bearing interlaced work, one also displaying the relief of a bull, a third showing a man on horseback.

GRAVEYARD. At the entrance, a small plain SESSION HOUSE built by *Charles McCulloch*, mason, and *Alexander Comb*, wright, in 1845. – A few HEADSTONES worth notice. Just E of the church, John Mitchell, dated 1730, carved with a skull, crossbones and an hourglass in quite high relief. On the back, an angel's head (the soul). – To its SE, William Houtan, dated 1729, with worn reliefs of an angel's head above two dancing figures. – Beside it, the polite battlemented Georgian Gothic headstone of Grizel Guthrie †1816. – Close to the S side of the church, a headstone of 1790 to Ann Williamson, wife of Nicol Deas, tenant in Cree of Innermay. Pedimented front, an angel's head in the tympanum; shield bearing a plough above a skull and crossbones.

BRIDGE over the River Earn, 1.1 km. NW. Rubble-built bridge of *c.* 1766. Four elliptical arches and a segmental flood arch. The triangular cutwaters form small pedestrian refuges at the parapet.

BRIDGE over the Water of May, 0.2 km. W. Constructed by *Arrol's Bridge & Roof Co. Ltd.*, 1899. Lattice-sided iron bridge supported on stone abutments.

FORTEVIOT PRIMARY SCHOOL. By *A. Watt Allison*, 1925–7. Buttressed walls which are harled above a brick base.

VILLAGE HALL. By *James Miller* of Glasgow, 1927, built as part of Lord Forteviot's new model village (*see* below) and in the same English Garden City manner. White-harled walls with brick dressings. At the buttressed sides, tall windows rising through the eaves into piended dormerheads. Jutting out from the front gable is a narrow gabled projection on which is a clock face.

DESCRIPTION. On the approach from the E, first the school (*see* above) set back on the N. It is followed by the OLD SCHOOL, a school and schoolhouse of 1839–40 designed by *W. M. Mackenzie*, with widely spaced crowsteps at the gables. S wing added in 1887, small-scale but aggressive Baronial. These prelude the model village built by Lord Forteviot in 1925–7;

the architect was *James Miller* of Glasgow. On the s side of the road, the SMITHY, a couple of single-storey harled and tile-roofed buildings, picturesque, with small-paned windows. Between them, a lane leads back to the former MANSE, by *William Stirling I*, 1825–6. Three-bay front with a pilastered doorpiece and a cornice incorporating a gutter. After the Smithy, the 1920s model village continues with the Village Hall (*see* above). It faces across the road to terraced HOUSING of 1925–6. This forms a single-storey and attic U-plan, the walls white-harled with brick dressings, the roofs covered with red tiles, the windows containing small panes. The manner is that of Raymond Unwin at Hampstead Garden Suburb and his First World War munitions-workers' townships. Symmetrical but picturesque, dominated by tall triangular gables. To the w, the Parish Church (*see* above) on the N side of the road; on the s, an early C19 *cottage orné*.

INVERMAY. *See* p. 433.

FORTINGALL

Small village, the church and much of the housing built for the shipping magnate, Sir Donald Currie, who bought the Glenlyon estate in 1884 and employed as his architects, first *J.M. MacLaren* (†1890) and, then, his former assistants, *W. Dunn & R. Watson*, who continued the firm under their own name after MacLaren's death.

FORTINGALL FREE CHURCH, 0.9 km. E. Now an agricultural store. Built in 1864, a sizeable Gothic-windowed harled box under a broad-eaved roof. Gothic birdcage bellcote on the w gable, a ball finial on the E in which a large doorway has been inserted.

FORTINGALL PARISH CHURCH. By *W. Dunn & R. Watson*, 1901–2. Studiedly simple Scots late Gothic, built on the foundations of the nave and chancel of its pre-Reformation predecessor, the walls harled, the roofs slated. Crowstepped end gables, the rounded corners of the w corbelled to the square below the eaves. Over the join of the nave and narrower chancel, a birdcage bellcote replicating the C18 bellcote of the previous church, with two-tier baluster uprights and a corbelled cornice; obelisk finials at the corners of its stone-slabbed and ball-finialled pyramidal roof. Low side windows to the nave; taller lights in the sides of the chancel whose E gable is windowless. W window of six lights, the head filled with cusped loop tracery. Straight skews at the gabled sw porch, the moulding of its entrance's pointed arch dying into the splayed jambs; stone sundial above the door. Set into the E end of the church's s wall, an ARMORIAL STONE, the incised inscription now illegible, the shield bearing a chevron.

The tone of simplicity without penny-pinching continues inside. Boarded pitched roof but below it the framework of a semicircular tunnel vault of Hungarian oak decorated with carved bosses. Walling of hammer-dressed Polmaise stone above a Hungarian oak dado. Round-headed stone chancel arch, the moulding, like that of the porch entrance, dying into the semi-octagonal responds. – Oak bench PEWS in the nave. – At the E end, a Scoto-Catholic arrangement, the linenfold panelled oak PULPIT on the N side of the chancel arch, the round stone FONT on the S. – Behind the focal communion table, an oak REREDOS with an intricately carved late Gothic tabernacled top; like the rest it was designed by *W. Dunn & R. Watson* but is of 1913. – Above and either side of the reredos are contemporary stone TABLETS carved with the Lord's Prayer and the Ten Commandments. – Sitting on the sills of the chancel's S windows are fragments of STONES carved with interlaced work, perhaps of the C9; they were uncovered on the site during the building of the church. – In a recess in the chancel's N wall, a HANDBELL, probably of the C7. – On the sill of the window beside the pulpit, a BELL cast by *Johannes Sprecht* of Rotterdam in 1765.

GRAVEYARD. Beside the E side of the church porch, a large hollowed boulder FONT, possibly of the C8. – At the church's W end, the rubble-walled mid-C19 BURIAL ENCLOSURE of the Stewarts of Garth, upright slabs set into the top as a rough cope. In this has been placed the C18 birdcage BELLCOTE of the church's predecessor, overshadowed by a yew tree thought to be *c.* 3,000 years old; the tradition that the tree was planted by Pontius Pilate's father is appealing but unlikely.

VILLAGE HALL. 1936 by *W. Curtis Green* of London, a former partner of W. Dunn & R. Watson. Harled and crowstep-gabled U, the roofs of the wings lower than that of the main block. Tall narrow windows in the gables; shallowly projecting buttresses at the centre.

DESCRIPTION. At the village's E end, almost hidden in a well-planted garden, the piend-roofed rubble-built former MANSE, by *John Marshall*, 1835–7. Pilastered and corniced doorpiece; horizontal-paned glazing in the windows. It is followed by Fortingall Parish Church (*see* above). Behind the church and manse, mid-C19 vernacular cottages and outbuildings. E of the church but set back from the road, the harled FORTINGALL HOTEL, by *W. Dunn & R. Watson*, *c.* 1890. C17 Scots revival, with crowstepped gables, corbelling at some corners and a couple of thistle-finialled gabled stone dormerheads. E of the hotel and coming forward to the road, KIRKTON COTTAGES, by *James M. MacLaren*, 1889. Z-plan group, the NE arm provided by a detached cottage, the rest by an L of terraced housing. Thatched roofs, the thatch rising over the wallheads' attic windows as rounded dormerheads. At the SE corner of the L, crowstepped gables and a battered chimney; jettied upper floor on the SW wing. The small-paned windows have survived. A more conventional mid-C19 cottage, its walls harled, the roof slated, intervenes between this group and MacLaren's MENZIES COTTAGE and CAIRN COTTAGE, a harled double house of 1889, the thatched roof again rising into rounded gablets over the attic windows; jerkin-head gable at the E end. MacLaren's manner was continued in 1914 by *W. Dunn & R. Watson* at THE NEW COTTAGES to the W, a symmetrical short terrace, the ends advanced with jerkin-head gables, the familiar rounded gablets at the centre, but the thatch was replaced by slates in *Kenneth Darling*'s reconstruction of 1980 after a fire. These are followed by a double house of the later C19, its bargeboards carved; contemporary range of cottages and outbuildings behind. To the W, FENDOCH, also of the later C19, a cottage with gableted wallhead dormers. Then, THE DIAL HOUSE, by *Roger Wilson*, 2000, a self-conscious evocation of the spirit of MacLaren and Dunn & Watson, with harled walls and bracketed eaves, but the huge clearstoreyed pitched and slated roof does not disguise the verticality of this three-storey house. To its W, the Village Hall (*see above*). Set well back at the village's W end, BALNALD. A small house of the later C19 in front of an extensive group of farm buildings and housing, by *J. M. MacLaren*, 1886. Picturesque, with tile-hanging and touches of half-timbering.

CULDAREMORE, 1.3 km. W. Surprisingly smart late C18 rubble-built farmhouse and steading courtyard group. The main range faces E. At its centre, a two-storey and attic one-bay block, the top of its gable pierced by the flight-holes of a doocot and crossed by a ledge giving a pedimental effect. At the ground floor, the segmental arch of a pend entry (converted to a window in the C20). Flanking this, single-storey links, each with a segmental-arched opening (now a window), to two-storey three-bay piend-roofed blocks, the N the farmhouse, the S originally with dummy windows and part of the steading. Piend-roofed steading ranges of one and two storeys behind.

CAIRN, 1.1 km. WSW. In a field beside the River Lyon, a grass-covered long cairn, probably formed in the third millennium B.C. over several earlier individual burial chambers. Composed of a mixture of earth and stones, it is of fairly uniform 1.5 m. height, *c.* 32 m. long and narrows slightly in breadth from *c.* 11.6 m. at the W end to 9.1 m. at the E. – 0.2 km. S, a 2 m.-high STANDING STONE, erected probably in the second millennium B.C.

HOMESTEAD MOAT, 0.9 km. WSW. Defensive enclosure near the River Lyon, constructed perhaps in the C13. It consists of a roughly rectangular space, *c.* 42 m. by 30 m., enclosed by a *c.* 15 m.-wide ditch which has been crossed by a causeway at the E side's N end. Remains of an inner rampart survive along the N and W sides of the enclosure. Presumably this was the site of wooden buildings.

STANDING STONES, 0.3 km. E. In a field between the road and the River Lyon, the remains of three settings of quite low but large boulders, all probably erected here in the third or second millennium B.C. Each of the two principal settings, the E now of four stones, the W of three, was discovered by excavation in 1970 to have consisted originally of eight stones arranged to enclose a roughly oblong space with the largest stones at the corners. The intermediate stones in the sides were, perhaps, erected in a second stage. Between these settings, a massive recumbent boulder flanked by smaller stones.

CARNBANE CASTLE. *See* p. 259.
CHESTHILL. *See* p. 267.
GARTH HOUSE. *See* p. 379.
GLENLYON HOUSE. *See* p. 404.

FOSS

Isolated church with just a cottage for company.

FOSS KIRK. Built in 1824. Sneck-harled rubble box, a ball-finialled birdcage bellcote on the W gable. Rectangular windows; E and W porches. Set into the S side is a large hollowed boulder FONT, probably early medieval.
    Inside, a bow-fronted PULPIT at the centre of the S wall. – PEWS of 1904.
    In the graveyard, a crudely battlemented BURIAL ENCLOSURE, its date provided by the inscription on a panel over the entrance PROGENITER OF THE OLD STEWARTS/ OF KINNOLLAN AND KINNEARD/MDCCCXIII. Above the inscription, reliefs of two angels trumpeting a fanfare to a monogram. Flanking the inscription are two roundels, one carved with a skull, the other with a hand holding a coronet.

FOWLIS WESTER

Pleasantly informal village of unremarkable C19 and C20 cottages and houses. At the centre, a small square on which stand a replica of a Pictish cross-slab (one of several now inside the parish church) and a Victorian cast-iron PUMP with a lion's-head spout.

FOWLIS WESTER PARISH CHURCH. Late medieval, with a C17 transeptal N 'aisle', but remodelled in the C18 and C19 and then recast in medieval dress by *J. Jeffrey Waddell*, 1927. The church is a rubble-built T, the gables' crowsteps added by Waddell. On the W gable, a birdcage bellcote, probably of the C18. The gable's pointed window is of 1927. So too is the door, also pointed, one of its hoodmould's label stops carved with interlaced work, the other with its date. Waddell added a couple of buttresses to the main block's S side, the E buttress marking off the chancel. At each end of this side, a small rectangular window, perhaps inserted in the C17 to light the area under end galleries. A little to the r. of the W of these and at a higher level, a built-up taller window; beside it, the fragment of a heraldic stone bearing the arms of the Moray family. This block's other windows are all of 1927. Pointed two-light Y-traceried windows in the nave's S side. Rectangular window, also of two lights, in the S wall of the chancel whose E window is pointed and of three lights. Similar windows in the N side but the presence of an organ chamber restricts the nave's E window to a single light. Another pointed one-light window in the w bay.

In each side of the C17 N 'aisle', a rectangular window with chamfered margins (the w largely renewed in 1927), and, to its s, a pointed window, the w built up when a door was inserted, probably in the C19. At the chimney-topped N gable, a hood-moulded Tudor door of *c.* 1840 under a panel, also hood-moulded, which bears the coat of arms of Colonel William Moray-Stirling of Abercairny, the panel placed in the blocking of a round-headed gallery window. Above this, a stone inscribed W^{S}M, the initials probably those of Sir William Moray of Abercairny †1640. In the 'aisle's' w wall, a stone, not apparently *in situ*, carved with the date 1641.

Waddell stripped the interior's walls of plaster. On the s side, evidence of built-up round-headed Georgian windows. Near the N end of the chancel's gable, a small medieval aumbry, probably a sacrament house, the lintel carved with 'ihs + mā'. Collar-braced queenpost-truss roof of 1927. Also of 1927 the segmental-headed stone chancel arch. The segmental arch into the N 'aisle' is (restored) C17 work. The end of this 'aisle' was partitioned off to form a vestry in 1927.

Oak FURNISHINGS of 1927, with discreet Neo-Celtic interlaced work at the pulpit, lectern and choir stalls. Gothic-arcaded front to the communion table which stands in the centre of the chancel. Behind it, a MINISTER'S CHAIR by *Donald McGarva*, 1980, in a late C20 update of Waddell's manner. – Two Gothic ELDERS' CHAIRS of the earlier C19 bearing the coat of arms of Drummond of Blair Drummond and Abercairny. – The small stone FONT is of 1911. – ORGAN of 1927 by *The Positive Organ Co. (1922) Ltd.* on the N side of the chancel.

STAINED GLASS. Carefully realistic E window (Our Lord as the Light of the World flanked by St Andrew and St John the Evangelist) of 1945. – In the s wall of the nave, a two-light window (Our Lord Teaching, with the Sower behind) of *c.* 1930. – In the nave's N wall, a single light (the Presentation of Our Lord in the Temple), cool and accomplished, by *Mary I. Wood*, 1944–5. – Garish w window (Our Lord in Glory) of 1971.

On the w wall, a broken PEDIMENT with a fleur-de-lys finial, the tympanum inscribed with a verse from *Ecclesiastes*, 5:1

T[A]K
HEE[D].THY
FOOT WHEN THOV
ENT[RE]ST.INTO.THE
[HOWS O]F.GOD.164[4]

Formerly it was above the churchyard gate. – At the w end of the N wall, a triangular-headed HERALDIC STONE, the helmet-crested and mantled shield bearing a Moray coat of arms; below, the initials and date W.M.1678.PM.

In the N 'aisle', two CROSS-SLABS of c. 800. The larger, the tallest Pictish symbol stone in Scotland (3.14 m. high), formerly stood in the village square. It had been brought there from the (demolished) St Bean's Chapel, at Buchanty 4.1 km. N of Fowlis Wester, and was placed here in 1991. It is a red sandstone monolith, the front carved with the weathered relief of a cross decorated with interlacing, the arms notched at their join to the centre. On the back, at the top, a 'double-disc-and-Z-rod' symbol, the rod's upper arm missing, under an almost obliterated smaller symbol, possibly a 'double-disc'. Below, a hunting scene with a (now headless) hound and three horsemen, one with a hawk on his arm. Under this, the relief of a man leading a cow who wears a bell round her neck and is followed by six more men carrying small shields. At the bottom, two more symbols, a 'crescent-and-V-rod' and the outline of an eagle. – The smaller (c. 1.57 m. high) and better-preserved sandstone slab had been built into a wall of the church where it was found in 1927. Only its front is carved. This has a ringed cross decorated with interlaced work. At the top, on the l., a sea monster, sword and round shield; on the r., a monster swallowing a man, probably Jonah. The cross-shaft is flanked by richly dressed seated figures, perhaps a depiction of the meeting of St Paul the Hermit and St Antony of Egypt in the desert. Below, on the l., two more smaller figures, probably ecclesiastics, walking towards the cross. The corresponding figures on the r. are missing, this part of the slab having been broken, probably before the carving was completed. – On the partition wall of the 'aisle' are placed fragments of two more early Christian CROSS-SLABS, both crosses decorated with interlaced work.

GRAVEYARD. S GATEWAY, possibly C17, with a plain round-headed arch. Above, a pediment of 1927, a reconstruction of the broken pediment in the church, the fleur-de-lys finial inscribed with the Hebrew letters IHWH (Iahweh or God), the English inscription complete. – Immediately S of the church, a large Tudor Gothic sarcophagus MONUMENT to the Rev. Alexander Maxtone †1851. It was designed by *A. & A. Heiton* and executed by *James Buchan.*

SCHOOL. Now in other use. Mid C19 and plain except for mean bargeboards.

VILLAGE HALL. By *Finlayson & Campbell*, 2000. Harled, in a Victorian estate village revival manner, with bracketed broad eaves.

WEST TULCHAN, 4.7 km. NE. Whitewashed farmhouse of the earlier C19, the two-storey main block with a broad-eaved piended roof; full-height semi-octagonal projection at the centre of the N front. Single-storey lateral wings. Short E and W ranges of farm offices, also of the earlier C19, at the back.

STANDING STONES, Thorn, 0.7 km. W. Pair of stones, erected probably in the second millennium B.C. Both are c. 1.9 m. high and stand c. 3.5 m. apart.

STONE CIRCLES, 1 km. NW. Two circles of standing stones, erected probably in the third or second millennium B.C. The apparently earlier W circle, its stones all fallen, was 7.3 m. in diameter, with the stones graded in size, the largest in the SW arc. A large outlying stone stood c. 5 m. due E. A further 12 m. E is the second circle, blocking the first circle's axial alignment on the equinoctial sunrise. It has been double, the outer ring, only four of its eleven stones in place, c. 7.6 m. in diameter. The almost intact inner ring is a kerb of contiguous stones which seem to have formed the edge of a burial cairn. Below the ground surface of the kerb's SSW segment was a cup-marked stone aligned with the edge of a 1.8 m.-tall outlying stone which stood 9.5 m. away.

ABERCAIRNY. *See* p. 133.
GLENALMOND HOUSE. *See* p. 390.
KEILLOUR CASTLE. *See* p. 438.

FREELAND HOUSE *see* STRATHALLAN SCHOOL

GARTH CASTLE
1.7 km. NNE of Keltneyburn

7050

On a formidably strong promontory site bounded by the gorges of two burns, a starkly simple rubble-walled tower, perhaps built soon after 1379 when Alexander, Earl of Buchan, son of Robert II, was granted lands in Perthshire including those of Garth. It is an unadorned four-storey oblong, c. 8.8 m. by 5.2 m., with rectangular door and window openings. The present ground floor door on the E side may be an insertion, the original entrance having been on the W at first floor level and reached by a wooden stair. The plain wallhead and flat roof date from repairs carried out in 1890 (by *Andrew Heiton Jun.*) and 1963.

Inside, a vaulted ground floor, originally containing two stores. Stair to the upper floor in the thickness of the E and S walls. The rooms on the upper floors are now late C20 in character but the first and second floors, apparently a hall and upper hall, were formerly covered by vaults which had been removed by the C19.

GARTH HOUSE
1.7 km. NE of Fortingall

7040

Architecturally unambitious mansion house of c. 1830 designed by *Andrew Heiton Sen.* for Lieutenant-General Sir Archibald Campbell who had acquired the estate after the death of his brother-in-law, John Stewart of Garth. The house was extended and embellished by *Andrew Heiton Jun.* c. 1882 for Sir Donald Currie, founder of the Castle Steamship Co.

The early C19 house was a large Elizabethan villa of two storeys and a basement, the walls faced with cement render lined in imitation of ashlar, channelled at the basement. S front of five bays, the ends and centre slightly advanced and gabled. The corners of the centrepiece are clasped by turret buttresses which are square at the basement and ground floor but octagonal at the first floor and finished with foliaged finials. First-floor Gothic window under an ogee-arched hoodmould which rises into a foliage-finialled octagonal pinnacle. Projecting in front of the Gothic entrance, a heavy porte cochère, its corners clasped by battlemented octagonal turret buttresses, its parapet with a broad merlon at each side. The porte cochère's vaulted wooden ceiling is probably of *c.* 1882. At each end bay, a two-storey and basement canted bay window under a small attic opening. Corbelled out from the outer corners of the front are turrets added in the 1880s, their lower parts octagonal, their upper parts circular and surmounted by fish-scale slated witches' hat roofs. Straightforward side elevations, the W with a canted bay window. NE addition of the 1880s with an octagonal tower, its parapet supported on Romanesque arcaded corbelling, its spire roof removed in the C20.

Inside, the entrance opens onto a full-height square hall, its vaulted plaster ceiling pierced by a cupola. Stair hall to the NW. The stair's late C19 balustrade is of cast and wrought iron lavishly ornamented with foliage. Window of heraldic stained glass, also late C19. The principal rooms, ranged along the E and W sides are large but unexciting.

GARVOCK HOUSE
1.8 km. E of Dunning

Ungainly small mansion house of 1826, the design perhaps the result of changes of mind during construction.

The principal block is a two-storey rubble-built oblong, its first-floor windows linked by a sill course. E front of six bays, the S two slightly advanced, as is the fourth bay which is finished with a pediment, its formality contradicted by the off-centre windows. At the third bay, a heavy Roman Doric portico. At the N end of this front, a pyramid-roofed square tower, its E face with three-light windows to the ground and first-floors and, on the second, a window of two round-headed lights; two-light windows in the N face.

At the back, a short full-height NW wing in a plain Jacobean manner. Projecting to its W, a lower two-storey wing with slit windows to provide a martial touch. From its W end, a single-storey stable block returns to the S, with pointed windows in its E and W sides, the W window now blocked. A C17 laird's house, which provided a second W wing behind the main block, was removed *c.* 1980.

GASK HOUSE
1.5 km. SW of Findo Gask

Smart classical mansion house designed by *Richard Crichton* and built for Laurence Oliphant of Gask in 1801–5 but remodelled, not altogether happily, in 1964–6 by *Claud Phillimore & Jenkins*.

Crichton designed a three-storey piend-roofed main block of five bays by four, joined by deeply recessed single-storey links to low pavilions. Ashlar-faced S front, the upper floors marked off by sill courses. Overarched tall ground-floor windows at the outer bays. Slightly advanced and broad pedimented centrepiece, its Ionic portico with widely spaced columns and a roundel-decorated frieze. This fronts the side-lit entrance which is surmounted by an overall segmental fanlight and flanked by round-headed niches. Above, window-like rectangular first-floor niches flank an Adamesque three-light window with Roman Doric column-mullions, its segmental fanlight rising into the floor above where it is flanked by a pair of roundels. In the 1960s alterations the top floor was removed except at the centrepiece which now looks over-assertive.

The single-storey links are each of five bays with attached Roman Doric columns along their fronts. The end pavilions provide monumentality. Each is of two storeys and three bays wide. Low horizontal-proportioned first-floor windows at the outer bays. Slightly advanced and broad centre bay, the ground-floor window and dummy oculus above contained in a giant overarch.

At the rear of the house, a fully exposed basement. The main block's three centre bays are advanced, with a broad Roman Doric portico at the centre of the basement and three-light windows above. N wings extend back from the pavilions.

OLD HOUSE OF GASK, 0.1 km. SE. Remains of a courtyard with domestic ranges occupying two sides. The house was built as the seat of the Oliphants of Gask in the earlier C17, largely demolished after the building of Gask House but partly restored in the 1930s. The entrance to the former courtyard is from the N through a round-headed and keystoned arch piercing the stub of a rubble wall. On top of the wall, probably rebuilt here in the 1930s, a bellcote with solid E and W sides. Segmental dormerhead dated 1632 at the N face, a steep swan-neck-pedimented dormerhead on the S, both perhaps reused from elsewhere in the complex. In the wall's S face, W of the arch, a recess whose lintel is supported by balusters, also probably reused.

The courtyard's W side is occupied by a T-plan three-storey rubble-walled and pantile-roofed house, its general shape and much of the ground-floor masonry C17, the rest of the 1930s with crowstepped gables (narrow at the W jamb) and catslide-roofed dormers. Probably original are the roll-and-hollow-moulded jambs of the broad E door but its lintel, with the centre tweaked up as a cusped arch, may be of the 1930s. The S range's S wall survives. Also rubble-built, of two storeys, with scroll-sided dormerheads over the first-floor windows, one dated 1641. At its E end, a round doocot, its thatched conical roof an invention of the 1930s.

CHAPEL to the S, by *James Gillespie Graham*, 1845–6. Buttressed Romanesque box. Gabled S porch containing the hood-moulded entrance. Low W tower, a splay-footed slated spire rising within its corbelled parapet.

NORTH LODGE of the late C19. Single-storey, with a shaped gable, the pedimented doorpiece with heavily banded pilasters. Contemporary GATEPIERS, also heavily banded and corniced; urn finials.

GILMERTON

Hamlet developed from the early C19.

MONZIE FREE CHURCH. Now a house. Unambitious Dec of 1869, built of purplish rubble enlivened by bands and dressings of buff ashlar. Simple oblong with a flèche on the roof. SW steeple, a porch clamped between its W buttresses; two-light belfry openings. Rising within the battlement, a splay-foot stone spire topped by a weathercock.

DESCRIPTION. Most of the houses are Georgian survival of the earlier C19. SOUTHWICK HOUSE, a double house of 1888, stands out. Crowstepped gables and gablet dormerheads, the centre dormerhead of each house with a thistle finial.

CULTOQUHEY HOUSE. *See* p. 309.

GLASCLUNE CASTLE
2.3 km. N of Kinloch

Disjointed hillside ruin of the C16 mansion house of the Herings of Glasclune. The site is formidably defensive, the E end of a ridge bounded on the N and E by a bend in the Glasclune Burn and, on the S, by the very steep slope to the Lornty Burn.

A fortalice was built here by 1510 and perhaps formed part of the missing main block of the Z-plan house whose surviving parts are of the later C16. These consist of a S range which projected W of the main block, together with a fragment of the barmkin wall running W from its SW corner, and a round tower which stood at the NE corner of the main block. Walling of grey boulder rubble with red sandstone dressings.

The S range's crowstepped gables, S side and the W end of its N side survive fairly intact. It has been of two storeys, the lower windows quite large but set well above the ground level, the first-floor windows rising through the eaves. All the windows have had chamfered margins and round shot-holes in the breasts, and the first-floor S windows have had grilles. Continuous corbelling at the SE corner for a round turret, its upper part and conical roof now missing. At the centre of this range's N side, there survives the lower part of a round stair tower with

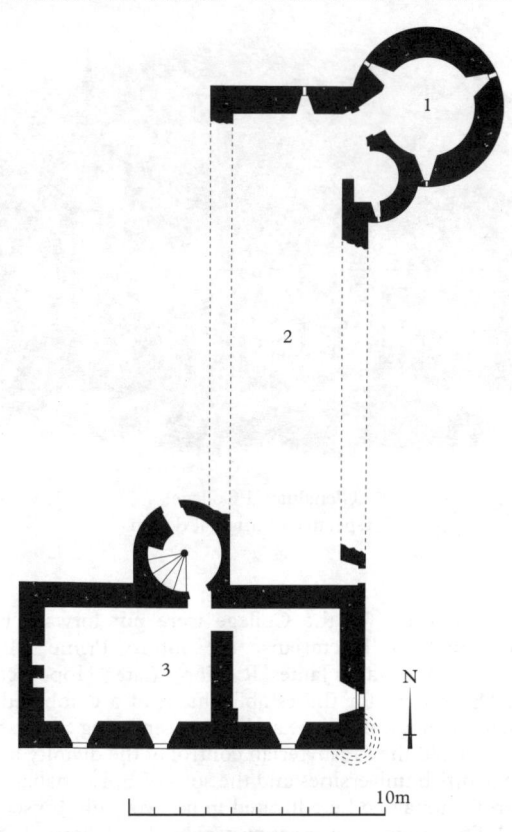

1. North-East Tower
2. Main block (site of)
3. South Wing

Glasclune Castle.
Ground-floor plan

an oval gunloop in its NW segment and one jamb of its N door. This has occupied the W inner angle of the S range and the demolished main block which was *c.* 19.2 m. by 6.1 m. The N segment of the round tower at the main block's NE corner stands to a fair height and has been of at least three storeys with windows like those of the S range. There was a round stair tower in its E inner angle with the main block.

GLENALMOND COLLEGE
5.6 km. NW of Methven

One of the first Victorian public (i.e. private) schools founded in Britain, its architecture inspired by the colleges of Oxford and Cambridge but its setting quite rural.

Glenalmond College.
Perspective of original design

The first proposals for the College were put forward by two leading Scottish Tractarians, the future Prime Minister, W. E. Gladstone, and James R. Hope (later Hope-Scott) in 1840. These were for the establishment of a combined Episcopalian theological college and school, enabling Scottish ordinands to avoid the Presbyterian control of the divinity faculties of the Scottish universities and the sons of Episcopalian gentry and professionals to be educated in an avowedly Episcopalian school. The proposals were approved by the College of Bishops of the Scottish Episcopal Church and subscription lists opened in 1841. The site, deliberately chosen to be far from the sinful influences of any large town (Perth, the nearest, 15 km. away), was acquired and designs for the buildings prepared by *John Henderson* the next year. These designs were for a quadrangle, the W range containing a gatehouse flanked by blocks containing accommodation for theological students and tutors and with the Warden's and Sub-Warden's Houses at the ends. The N range was to contain schoolrooms and dormitories and the E range the Hall and Library, with the Chapel projecting E from this range's S end. The S side of the quadrangle was to be closed by a cloister linking the W range to the Chapel.

Construction began in 1843. The N and W ranges were completed in 1849 and the Chapel dedicated two years later. The Hall, also to Henderson's design, was built in 1861–3. After a fire in 1875 had gutted their quarters (soon repaired) the theological students moved to Edinburgh and stayed there. In 1891–3 the E side of the quadrangle was completed by the addition of the New Wing (now Skrine's) between the Hall and Chapel but as accommodation for pupils instead of the originally proposed Library and to a design by *George Henderson*. A more significant departure from the 1840s designs took place in 1904–6 when *A. G. Heiton* provided the Memorial Library (commemorating Old Boys killed in the South African War) as the centrepiece of the intended but unexecuted s cloister. When a s cloister (the Gladstone Cloister) finally came in 1926–7 it was s of the original position and detached from the other buildings of the quadrangle. The cloister's architect was *Godfrey D. B. Shepherd* who two years earlier had provided an E extension of the N range (the Matheson Building).

Ancillary buildings (a lodge, sanatorium, housing for college servants and staff, and games pavilions) were scattered round the surrounding parkland in the C19 and earlier C20 but it is only from the late C20 that classrooms and boarding houses have escaped the confines of the quadrangle which still forms the heart of the complex.

At the s end of Front Avenue, the principal drive from the public road, a GATE LODGE of 1862–4 and probably by *J.L. Pearson*. Two-storey gatehouse, the tall lower floor pierced by a Gothic pend. Octagonal-spired round stair tower in the inner angle of the gatehouse and a single-storey W wing. – Just to its N, the former SANATORIUM (now REID'S), by *J. L. Pearson*, 1861–2. Two-storey, with Gothic touches, but the stonework has been harled and a large three-storey flat-roofed s extension added by *Basil Spence & Partners* in 1963. Immediately to the N, a picturesque detached INFECTIOUS DISEASES WING of 1894, by *Sydney Mitchell & Wilson*. N of this, Front Avenue curves gently on its approach to the main quadrangle.

QUADRANGLE. The W RANGE of 1843–9 sets the collegiate Gothic tone. Built, like the other quadrangle ranges, of squared reddish local sandstone, it comprises a four-storey gatehouse joined by two-storey and attic links to the former Warden's and Sub-Warden's Houses (now GOODACRE'S and PATCHELL'S) which are boldly advanced, with battlemented towers in the inner angles. The links are similar, their W front articulated by projecting chimneys which rise from the ground with intakes at the first-floor and eaves. Carried across the chimneys are string courses which form continuous hoodmoulding over the ground-floor windows of the links. Individual hoodmoulds over the first-floor windows. The ground- and first-floor window openings are all rectangular containing pointed lights. Pairs of gabled wooden dormers at the attic. The impression is of symmetry but the N link is slightly longer than the s which, in turn, has larger windows to its ground-floor (originally occupied by the theological students). The diagonally buttressed towers in the inner angles of the links and end houses are identical, their floors marked off by string courses, their windows hoodmoulded. Human-head corbels under the battlements whose tall merlons are panelled with Gothic dummy arches. At each end house, a prominent diagonally buttressed front gable with a battlemented bay window but the bay window of the former Sub-Warden's House is of one storey, that of the former Warden's House of two. The former Warden's House was extended s in similar style by *Godfrey D. B. Shepherd* of *Mills & Shepherd*, 1935-6.

The central GATEHOUSE is of two parts. Its w half is a tower which dominates the w front. Like the towers in the inner angles with the end houses it is of four storeys but much larger and higher. Angle buttresses at the w corners. In the w face, a broad Gothic entrance to the pend, the pointed arch carried on bell-capitalled shafts and with cusped arcading in the spandrels. Above, a two-storey battlemented oriel window. Dog-tooth ornament on the panels under the cusped first-floor openings and blind arcading under those of the second floor. At the tower's very tall top floor, a w window of three cusped lights set between slender crocketed pinnacled piers standing on human-head corbels. More human-head corbels under the battlement. Octagonal caphouse turret at the SE corner. The pend under the tower is covered with vaulting, the ribs springing from pendant corbels and meeting at foliaged bosses. The pend is divided into two bays by a central arch whose functional purpose is to support the E side of the tower above. The gatehouse's second (E) part, facing the quadrangle, is lower, of three storeys and an attic, its buttressed and oriel-windowed gable advancing into the quadrangle. On this side the links of the w range, buttressed at the ground-floor, present a regular array of pointed and hoodmoulded ground-floor windows and smaller first-floor windows arranged in hoodmoulded pairs; in the attic, dormer windows like those of the w front. Spire-roofed semi-octagonal tower at the s link's join to the former Warden's House. In this house's gable to the courtyard, a window of four pointed lights contained in a broad squat arch.

The N RANGE is also of two storeys and an attic. Symmetrical s front to the quadrangle with a three-storey central tower, its corners with lateral buttresses rising from the main wall-head. Inside the tower's battlement, a pyramid-roofed cupola. Projecting from the tower is a gabled and buttressed Gothic porch, the entrance to the lean-to buttressed cloister carried across the front of this range's ground-floor. The cloister's windows, each of four cusped lights, now contain square-paned glazing which replaced the original diamond panes in 1938. At the range's first-floor, pointed windows, alternately of one and two lights, under rectangular hoodmoulds; tiny windows splayed across the inner angles with the quadrangle's E and w ranges. Attic windows like those of the w range. *Godfrey D. B. Shepherd* of *Mills & Shepherd* extended the N range E of the main quadrangle to form the N side of Back Quad in 1924-5. Simplified collegiate Gothic, the walling of artificial stone. At the E end, a further extension but flat-roofed, by *Basil Spence & Partners*, 1957. At the back, a bridge to the SCIENCE BUILDING, by *McEachern, MacDuff*, 2001. Pitch-roofed; the part of the s elevation fronting the stair fully glazed.

The N half of the E RANGE is occupied by the HALL of 1861-3, its two tall storeys rising above the adjacent N range and originally with a flèche (now lost except for its octagonal base). The W front to the quadrangle is articulated by buttresses with steeply gabled tops. At the ground-floor, simple hoodmoulded, Gothic windows except at the N bay which contains a large pointed archway. Under the first-floor windows, a frieze of circles containing foliage. The first-floor windows are paired and hoodmoulded Gothic lights with circled quatrefoils in their heads. At the slightly advanced S bay, a large oriel window projected on continuous corbelling and covered with a copper-roofed octagonal spire. Under the windows, a panelled frieze bearing coats of arms of benefactors of the College. In each face, a pointed window of two cusped lights with a circled quatrefoil in the head. Another oriel window but plainer and finished with a battlement at the S bay of the heavily buttressed E elevation. Here the N bay is advanced; a large octagonal spired turret at its SE corner. The pend under the Hall block's N end begins at the W with brick vaulting, the stone ribs meeting at foliaged bosses. E of this, a tunnel vault, also of brick. Off the N side of the pend, a stair hall. Gothic panelled stone dado rising in line with the stone stair and forming a pierced parapet at the first-floor landing. Here a fat central column with a foliaged capital supports the vaulted roof of painted brickwork, the stone ribs again meeting at foliaged bosses. In the stair hall's E wall, a pair of three-light windows, the N filled with STAINED GLASS (the Story of Gareth, from Tennyson's *The Idylls of the King*) of *c*. 1895. Off the landing is the Hall itself. Elaborate open roof with hammerbeams supported on foliaged corbels. Oak dado of linenfold panelling. N gallery with an upward-curved front. At the N wall, Gothic fireplaces, their friezes and spandrels carved with foliage.

The NEW WING (now SKRINE'S) S of the Hall built in 1891–3 occupies the position originally intended for the Library. This would have been of one very tall storey and an attic. What was built (containing classroom and dormitory accommodation) was of the same height but contains two storeys and an attic, with plain rectangular windows, some mullioned and transomed, instead of the Gothic openings shown in the 1840s design. Piended dormers to the attic.

The CHAPEL overlays the S gable of the E range, projecting slightly to its W and some way to the E. In the inner angle with the range, the base of an uncompleted steeple, the pointed door in its W face intended to open onto the end of the unexecuted S cloister shown in John Henderson's design. The Chapel itself is a buttressed seven-bay rectangle, its design and detail closely derived from the choir of the late C13 chapel of Merton College, Oxford. Like the prototype it is Dec. Gabled buttresses along the sides, the tops of those of the S, like those at Merton, with arcaded panelling under trefoils. Elaborate tracery copied from Merton College in the side and E windows. There was no direct precedent at Merton College for the seven-light W window but it also contains accomplished Dec tracery; its hoodmould's label stops are carved with the heads of kings. Above, a triangular window with curved sides containing cusped ovals, its hoodmould's label stops carved as female heads. Gabled porch in the last bay but one.

INTERIOR. The porch in the tower is covered by vaulting, a circular bell-hole in the centre. Over the chapel itself, an open hammerbeam roof. Originally, the space was divided by a screen into a three-bay ante-chapel and four-bay chapel. The ante-chapel was reduced to one bay in 1962 when *Basil Spence & Partners* provided a new W GALLERY and SCREEN of fumed oak in a flashy post-Comper modern Gothic manner, its E front bearing a central roundel displaying the seal of the College (a figure of St Andrew) flanked by shields painted with coats of arms, alternately those of the older British universities and of benefactors of the College. – In the ante-chapel, PEWS of 1962. – GALLERY PEWS of the 1990s. – In the chapel proper, Victorian Gothic pine pews arranged in collegiate fashion to face each other across the aisle. – Gothic pine DADO along the walls of the five W bays; it is of 1851 but extended W in 1956. At the E bay (the sanctuary), a more elaborately Gothic oak dado designed as a First World War memorial by *J. Ninian Comper*, 1922. At the E wall this forms a REREDOS of elaborately cusped and crocketed arcading, the canopied niche behind the altar filled with small statues of Scottish saints representing each part of the kingdom. These are flanked by two laurel-wreathed roundels, one bearing a relief of St George (emblematic of the type of Christian chivalry), the other a relief of St Andrew and St Denys (emblematic of the comradeship in war of the Scots and the French). – ALTAR of rose-coloured alabaster, designed by *F. L. Pearson* and executed by *James Powell & Sons*, 1901. Central front panel with a mosaic depiction of Our Lord as the Good Shepherd; in flanking panels, mosaics of angels holding scrolls. – ORGAN by *Harrison & Harrison*, 2007.

In the centre of the ante-chapel's W wall's plain Gothic panelling (of 1934), the SOUTH AFRICAN WAR MEMORIAL, designed by *A. G. Heiton* and executed by *James Powell & Sons*, 1905. Mosaic of three arches, the outer two enclosing the names of the fallen and the interlocked triangles emblematic of the College's dedication to the Holy Trinity; at the centre, a figure of St Andrew. – On the ante-chapel's N wall's panelling (of 1938), a carved wood MEMORIAL of 1939 to Edward William Neish, by *J. Ninian Comper* in his highly coloured late manner. Coat of arms flanked by figures of St Edward the Confessor and St William, Duke of Aquitaine and Provence; below, an inscription panel held by a pair of cherubs. – Also in the ante-chapel, a marble BUST of Bishop Charles Wordsworth †1892, first Warden of the College.

STAINED GLASS. In most of the side windows, abstract-patterned glass by *James Powell & Sons*, 1851. – E window (small-scale Scenes from the Life of Our Lord) also of 1851. – The sanctuary's N window (Apostles) is late C19. – S window of the sanctuary (St Martin, flanked by King David and St David of Scotland) by *J. Ninian Comper*, 1923. – Brightly coloured W window (small-scale Scenes from the Lives of Old Testament Heroes, of Our Lord and of the Apostles) by *Henry Hughes*, 1859.

A. G. Heiton's MEMORIAL LIBRARY of 1904–6 stands in the centre of where the quadrangle's originally intended S cloister would have been. It is simple collegiate Gothic in manner. Two storeys, the upper floor tall. Diagonally buttressed S gable and buttressed sides; towards the S end of the E side, a battlemented chimney. Rectangular windows, each of two or three pointed lights. Near the N end of each side, a pointed archway (now glazed) intended to open into the cloister. Display is reserved for the angle-buttressed N gable. Hoodmoulded pointed entrance with foliage-capitalled stumpy attached columns. These make up the bottom part of a frame whose ashlar stonework contrasts with the squared and stugged masonry of the rest. The frame's sides rise to form the outer corners of an oriel window, its stonework decorated with a foliage-carved frieze under inscription panels flanking a central panel carved with blind arcading and a shield bearing the College emblem. The upper lights above the oriel's transom are cusped. At the Library's NW corner, a battlemented octagonal stair tower, its frieze carved with foliaged panels.

Inside the Library, a stone stair to the upper floor. At its bottom flight, a wooden balustrade, the newels topped by lions who hold shields bearing the College emblem. On the first-floor landing, a moulded stone seat. The ashlar-walled Library itself is covered with an oak wagon ceiling, one panel pierced with the familiar interlocked triangles. Oak bookcases. Near the N end, a screen of late Gothic character.

Lying S of the Victorian quadrangle and detached from it is the GLADSTONE CLOISTER with the present WARDEN'S HOUSE at its W end. These are by *Godfrey D. B. Shepherd* of *Mills & Shepherd*, 1926–7. The cloister is single-storey, its N (cloister) side buttressed and with gabled porches at the E end and centre. Classrooms on the S side of the cloister. The Warden's House at the W end is collegiate Gothic in the manner of its Victorian predecessor, with a two-storey bay window to the W and an oriel window to the E.

On the S side of Back Quad, E of the main quadrangle, a THEATRE (ROBIN THOMSON BUILDING) by *Bob McEachern* of *Honeyman, Jack & Robertson*, 1972–3. Prestressed concrete frame filled with aggregate panels. Immediately below the oversailing fascia, windows with elliptically arched lintels and sills. Elliptical-arched canopy over the entrance. – S of this, on Back Avenue, the MUSIC SCHOOL, by *Peter S. Ferguson* of *Basil Spence & Partners*, 1963. Careful arrangement of flat-roofed brick boxes, the E side fully glazed. – Further S, the harled and flat-roofed SWIMMING POOL (by *Honeyman, Jack & Robertson*, 1965) and the GANNOCHY HALL (by *Blockley, Goodwin & Warner*, 1971), its walls of corrugated metal. – CRICKET PAVILION, Big Cricket, by *Godfrey D. B. Shepherd* of *Mills & Shepherd*, 1911. Harled, with a piended roof swept down over the veranda; central gablet containing a clock.

GLENALMOND HOUSE
4.8 km. N of Fowlis Wester

Sizeable but undemonstrative mansion house of a sporting estate.

In 1805–8 the Glenalmond estate was acquired from the Duke of Atholl by Thomas Hay Marshall, Lord Provost of Perth, and inherited from him in 1808 by James Patton of The Cairnies, Sheriff-Clerk of Perthshire, who purchased a further tranche of land. The present house was begun either by Patton or, soon after his death in 1831, by his eldest son, James Murray Patton. In 1907, following a fire, the building was repaired and remodelled by its then owner, the railway magnate Sir Alexander Henderson (later, first Lord Faringdon). Further work was carried out by *Bell Ingram Design*, 2003.

The main part is a piend-roofed two-storey L-plan. Ashlar-faced S front of seven bays, the two at each end slightly advanced, their ground-floor overlaid by flat-roofed octagonal bay windows added in 1907 and extended outwards *c*. 2000. Harled NE wing, its two N bays slightly advanced. Projecting from its S end, a pedimented full-height addition of 1907. In its S inner angle, the house's principal entrance under a bracketed gabled canopy. Rubble-built W and N service ranges. On the W side, a large bay window addition of 2003, a conservatory in its S inner angle, and a large gabled porch of the same date. Similar porch on the internal courtyard's S side where the back of the front block was tactfully thickened at the same time.

Inside, at the back of the S block, a long double corridor, its S part of 1907, the N of *c*. 2000. Drawing room of 1907 at the SW corner, lavishly decorated with an enriched plaster ceiling (remodelled at the bay window in 2003) and marble chimneypiece in best Adam Revival style.

GLENCARSE

Village of picturesque mid-C19 houses of one and two storeys, mostly sneck-harled, including a terrace (NEWTON COTTAGES) with bargeboarded dormer windows. All Saints' Church provides a centrepiece.

ALL SAINTS' CHURCH (Episcopal). English village Picturesque, by *Duncan D. Stewart*, 1878. Nave, transepts (the N a vestry, the S originally an organ chamber), SW porch and semi-octagonal chancel. Walls of white-painted concrete, the S front (visible from the street) enlivened by black-painted applied half-timbering; red tiled roof with a spired bellcote at the W end. Rectangular window openings containing cusped lights, those in the sides of the nave with quatrefoil-traceried heads.

Inside, a kingpost roof, the collar supported by braces which are pierced by small quatrefoils in the chancel whose floor is laid with encaustic tiles. The chancel's canted walls are stone-lined; a credence on the S side, a sacrament house on the N. Pointed chancel arch springing from responds. In the arch, a wooden Gothic SCREEN designed by the *Rev. Edward Sugden*, 1897, with carved dragons climbing down between the arched openings. – Red sandstone REREDOS of 1887, also designed by Sugden. Above the tabernacle, a Caen stone statue of Christ the King, executed by *Cox & Buckley*. – Octagonal oak PULPIT of 1910, carved by *Agnes Watson* and *Caroline Greig* with small emblems of the Evangelists at the top and, below, panels bearing reliefs of a floral cross, flowers and the crowned IHS monogram. – FONT of 1878 by *Cramb & Beveridge*. Polished granite columns support the quatrefoil-shaped Caen stone bowl carved with flowers, a cross and a dove. – STAINED GLASS. The four windows of the chancel (St John the Baptist, St Stephen, St Joseph, the Blessed Virgin Mary, St John the Evangelist, St Peter, St Columba and St Augustine) are by *John Hardman & Co.*, 1881–2. – In the nave's S wall, a colourful narrative window (the Sermon on the Mount) by *Mayer & Co.*, 1894. – Then, a good-quality gently archaising window (Our Lord in the House at Bethany; the Risen Lord Appearing to Mary Magdalene) by *John Hardman & Co.*, 1886. – Contemporary window to the W (the Good Shepherd) also by *Mayer & Co.*

N of the church is the RECTORY, built in 1880, also with white-painted walls and a red tiled roof.

HALL, W end of the village. Built *c.* 1900. Of red brick, with white brick trimmings; jerkin-head roof.

NEWTON HOUSE, E end of the village. Large villa of *c.* 1860. Harled, with ashlar dressings; gentle Jacobean detail.

GLENCARSE HOUSE
1.1 km. N

Originally a smart though unostentatious villa designed by *R. & J. Adam* for Thomas Hunter, 1790, but enlarged and altered in the late C19 and early C20 when the original work was rendered and given quoins and parapets, the result a pompous mess.

The Adam design provided a piend-roofed main block of two storeys with a fully exposed basement to the rear (S) and single-storey wings projecting to the N. The main block's entrance (N) front is of five bays, the centre slightly advanced and with a first-floor three-light window. The central entrance was originally recessed behind a screen of Roman Doric columns *in antis*. At the end bays were flat-roofed single-storey projections. In 1923 these were remodelled and linked by a pilastered addition across the ground-floor of the three centre bays, all the new windows elliptically arched; at the centre of this, a Roman Doric portico. The pedimented front gables of the wings survive, each with a Roman Doric pilastered three-light window, but the E wing was heightened (reusing the pediment) in 1889 and the W wing enlarged to the W in 1923.

The 1790s S front had a full-height central bow flanked by pilastered and corniced windows to the principal floor. In the alterations of 1889 the top floor's outer windows were enlarged to three-light, and a balustrade as well as a parapet added to the bow which was given a conical-roofed round cupola. Also of 1889 is the full-height two-bay E addition, the l. bay slightly recessed, the r. pedimented, both with three-light windows to the principal floor, the l. set in a single-storey and basement rectangular projection. A slightly recessed one-bay W addition, replicating the l. bay of the 1889 extension, was built in 1923. Low additions, the E with a pedimented section, the W with a conservatory, of about the same date further extend the house.

GLENDOICK HOUSE. See p. 395.
INCHYRA HOUSE. See p. 422.

GLENDELVINE HOUSE
1.1 km NW of Spittalfield

Sizeable but unpretentious Elizabethan manor house, plentifully provided with gables and gablets, by *George Angus*, 1839–40. It was remodelled c. 1900 for the shipowner, Sir Alexander Lyle, who harled the rubble masonry, added a heavy battlemented tower on the W, removed a bay window from this side's S bay, added another on the E, and placed small panes in the upper sashes of the windows. – In the garden to the S, a round CAIRN, possibly of the fourth millennium B.C. but probably of at least two periods of construction and use. About 17 m. in diameter, it now stands to a height of 1.5 m. On its E side, a 1.8 m.-high STANDING STONE, probably erected in the second millennium B.C. – N of the house, a harled and half-timbered block of GARAGES AND COTTAGES of c. 1900. – Contemporary S LODGE in the same manner.

GLENDEVON

Hamlet in the eponymous glen, Glentower House at its E end. The hamlet's centre is marked by the white-painted mid-C19 TORMAUKIN HOTEL, the ends of its four-bay front projected as semi-octagons.

GLENDEVON PARISH CHURCH, 1.3 km. NW. Harled rectangle, probably of post-Reformation origin, its present appearance partly the result of a remodelling and E extension of 1803 but the projection of the slated roof over the gables is a slightly later alteration. On the W gable, a very simple pyramid-roofed birdcage bellcote, perhaps of the C17 or early C18. The five-bay s front with regularly spaced rectangular windows retains the appearance it acquired in 1803. In the E gable, a pointed window, probably an insertion or remodelling of the earlier C19. The w window, an elliptical arch containing three cusped lights, was inserted in 1913. On the N side, a late C19 porch and a session house-cum-vestry extended in 1960.

Inside, a late C19 kingpost roof decorated with Gothic arcading. – PEWS provided by *Thomas Frame & Son* in 1886 when the position of the pulpit was shifted to the w end. – Early C20 PULPIT and COMMUNION TABLE, probably of 1929. – STAINED GLASS. w window (the Good Shepherd) of 1913. – E window ('By Works was Faith Made Perfect') by the *Abbey Studio*, 1951. – On the E wall, MONUMENT to Walter Nicol Russell, with a bronze relief depicting an angel and a portrait bust of Russell, by *G. H. Paulin*, 1917.

GRAVEYARD. Against the w gable of the church, a swan-neck-pedimented HEADSTONE bearing the initials AF, IF and the date 1716. Its front is divided into two panels, the l. carved with scales above a merchant's mark (looking like the numeral 4), the r. with a skull, crossbones and an hourglass.

White-painted former MANSE to the E. The main block, built *c.* 1830, was originally of two storeys but given a third by *James Mitchell* in 1896, its windows rising into piended dormerheads. Plain porch added by *William Kerr* of *John Melvin & Son*, 1913. Two-storey rear wing built in 1840 by *Robert Hardman*, mason, and *David Millar*, wright, to Millar's design. Single-storey offices built by *Andrew Goold*, mason, 1793.

GLENTOWER HOUSE, E end of the hamlet. Picturesque villa of 1880, perched on the steeply sloping bank of the Devon. Its most striking feature is the very tall but stark battlemented tower. The main block is of a single storey with an attic and a basement which becomes a full ground-floor in the slope of the ground to the sw. Bracketed broad eaves and jerkin-head gables with decoratively carved bargeboards. At both the NE and sw fronts, an off-centre 'centrepiece', its roof running tranversely across the main roof and its gables' bargeboards carved with arcading. The single-storey SE wing may date from the earlier C19 and have belonged to the house's predecessor.

Inside, the pitched-ceilinged attic rooms of the 'centrepiece' are surprisingly sumptuous. In the NE, on one wall, a plaster plaque with a relief of dolphins ridden by putti; ceiling painted with fruit in a Louis XV manner. The ceiling of the sw room is divided into panels by ornate plaster stiles.

The house is set in a large garden entered at the sw through a battlemented Gothic GATEWAY of the early or mid C19. At its ends, fluted and banded pilaster strips topped by quatrefoil-decorated panels flanked by pinnacle-topped narrow pedestals whose fronts display double-keyhole dummy gunloops. Foliaged label stops to the hoodmould of the carriage entrance; plain footgate. – At the NW corner of the garden, an octagonal TOWER with huge crosslets, contemporary with the gateway.

WESTER GLENSHERUP, 2.4km WNW. Nondescript harled farmhouse of the later C19. Beside it, its predecessor of 1693 (now gutted and used as a store), a rubble-built oblong of two storeys, with an attic lit from windows in the crowstepped gables; roof now covered with corrugated iron. In the front, small windows and a first-floor door, presumably once reached by a forestair; a garage door has been inserted at the ground-floor. – On the approach, a hump-backed rubble BRIDGE of one segmental arch over the River Devon. It is probably late C18.

GLENDEVON CASTLE
1.8km. NW

Mutilated tower house, its hillside position still making it a notable presence in Glen Devon.

The house was built shortly before 1605 when it was sold, together with a small estate, by John, Lord Lindsay of the Byres, to Patrick Monypenny of Pilrig. It was a harled Z, with SW and NE jambs. The SW jamb's W side is aligned with the W gable of the main block, the NE jamb projects E of the main E gable; bowed W tower at the join of the main block and SW jamb. The four-storey SW jamb has survived to its full height. Rounded margins to the windows. Entrance on the E side, now covered by a porch. The main block and NE jamb were remodelled, perhaps in 1766, when both were reduced in height and given monopitch roofs which rise to wallheads finished with very widely spaced crude merlons. The main block's W end was demolished in the later C20. (Inside, a vaulted ground-floor room in the main block.)

GLENDEVON HOUSE
1.2km. NW

Enjoyable Tudor Gothic villa built for the Rutherfords of Glendevon in 1818. Only one storey and rubble-built but smartly detailed, with a broad-eaved piended roof. Entrance (W) front of six bays. The three l. bays are treated as a unit, its slightly advanced centre containing the pointed door, the outer bays tall pointed windows, all the openings hoodmoulded. The two bays to the r. are slightly set back, their hoodmoulded rectangular windows containing Gothic lights. The front's deeply recessed S bay is treated in the same manner.

N elevation with splayed corners corbelled to the square under the roof. At the centre, a canted bay window with Gothic lights; narrow four-centred arched windows at the outer bays. (Inside, Gothic doorcases and an octagonal library.)

The approach from the SE begins with a rubble-built humpbacked BRIDGE over the River Devon, built or reconstructed in 1757 and widened to the W in 1775. Two segmental arches, a long curved cutwater on the E side, triangular cutwater on the W. – At the beginning of the drive, a round-headed

GATEWAY arch in a corniced rectangular rubble frame. It is early C19 but the arch's keystone, presumably reused, is carved with the date 1766 and the Rutherfords' initial and mermaid crest. – Just inside the gateway, an early C19 single-storey LODGE, its front originally of three bays with hoodmoulded rectangular door and windows. It was extended at both ends in the C20.

GLENDOICK HOUSE

2020

2.2 km. NE of Glencarse

Laird's house built *c.* 1750 for the Lord Advocate, Robert Craigie (later a judge with the judicial title of Lord Glendoick), the exterior of marked but modest pretension, the interior a display of the stuccoist's art.

The house is an oblong, of two storeys above an exposed basement marked off by a string course; high piended roof with two tall panelled chimneystacks, the neat front dormers probably later additions. Harled walls with sandstone dressings and rusticated quoins. S front of five bays, the centre slightly advanced under a pediment, a small oculus in its tympanum. Here, a broad flying stair to the entrance, a 'Tuscan Venetian' door, the keystoned head of the opening breaking the pediment, the design derived from Batty Langley. At the outer bays, tall pedimented windows at the ground-floor denote the *piano nobile*. Side elevations, each of three bays (the centre window omitted at the top floor), with a Venetian ground-floor window at the centre of the E elevation, the door below probably converted from a window in the C19. Behind the house, a low office courtyard, the piended S gables of its E and W ranges appearing as recessed pavilions to the main house, the W with a round-headed ground-floor window, the E with a Venetian window at the ground-floor and a segmental-pedimented window to the first-floor which was added by *A. G. Heiton* in 1911.

Inside, the principal rooms are on the ground-floor, with the entrance hall and main stair occupying the centre, the dining room along the whole of the E side, the drawing room occupying the S two-thirds of the W side with what was probably the principal bedroom behind. All are panelled in painted pine. The only division between the ENTRANCE HALL and stair is a basket arch springing from capitalled consoles, the plaster soffit of the arch enriched with interlaced ornament and floral motifs. On the arch's keystone, high-relief male and female heads look forwards to the entrance and backwards to the stair. At the N end of the entrance hall's E side, a fireplace. Simple basket-arched chimneypiece barely large enough to support the Baroque overmantel whose stucco work is almost certainly the work of *Thomas Clayton*. Its base is a horizontal panel enriched with crossed branches; at the ends, heavy fluted consoles to the front accompanied by shadow-like later consoles either side. Above, a tall broken pedimented aedicule, its pilasters flanked by lateral consoles and pendants of foliage; foliaged pendants also on the panelled fronts of the pilasters. Huge shell-like leaf in the pediment and a small shell on the frieze. All this is the surround for an overmantel painting under a stucco swag of flowers.

Behind the entrance hall, the flying STAIR which rises round three sides of the oblong well, its Rannoch pine barley-sugar balusters and handrail continued round the first-floor landing on the well's S and E sides; another balustrade of the same design in front of the N wall's first-floor stair window. Over the stairwell a Rococo stuccoed ceiling. Central acanthus leaf rose, the fronds curling over, with flower-bud spikes projecting at the cardinal points. More budding spikes at the curvaceous floral enrichment in the ceiling's corners.

In the DINING ROOM, E of the entrance hall, the wall panelling is finished with a mutule cornice. Tall chimneypiece at the N end. At the W wall opposite the E side's Venetian window, a slightly advanced centrepiece designed as a Baroque version of a triumphal arch. Tripartite, with fluted Ionic pilasters at the ends and framing the centre where they support a swan-neck pediment. Inside this frame, a round-headed alcove, its arch's keystone carved with foliage. On the alcove's half-dome, a stucco flower basket. The DRAWING ROOM, W of the entrance hall is smaller but much richer. Double-lugged architraves to the walls' panels, those over the doors intended to contain landscapes. Broken pediment over the horizontal panel (containing a landscape) above the veined marble chimneypiece. Rococo ceiling, with large displays of tendrilly foliage in the corners of the cove. On the flat an acanthus-leaf rose in a curvaceous border with flower-bud spikes projecting from acanthus leaves at the cardinal points and, at the corners, candelabra-like fronds issuing from shells and ending in more flower-bud spikes. The room behind had its ceiling lowered when an additional bedroom was inserted above it *c.* 1900.

GLENEAGLES CASTLE see GLENEAGLES HOUSE

GLENEAGLES HOTEL
2.9 km. WSW of Auchterarder

Huge resort hotel built by the Caledonian Railway and now surrounded by golf courses and equestrian and shooting centres. The King's and Queen's Golf Courses, intended as prime attractions for visitors here, were laid out by *James Braid* in 1910 and 1919. Construction of the hotel itself began in 1914 to *James Miller*'s design but was halted by the First World War. Work resumed in 1922 but now with *Matthew Adam* of the *Caledonian*

Railway Divisional Engineer's Office as architect, and was completed two years later.

The architecture is disappointing. English Baroque of a sort, the harling of the walls relieved by stone dressings. At the S front, some balustraded canted bay windows. Projecting from the segmental-pedimented centrepiece, a large shallowly bowed and large-windowed single-storey block. At the W elevation, a balustraded tower fronted by an angle-pilastered porch. Large late C20 additions to the W.

Expensively finished INTERIOR, the circulation spaces in an early C18 manner, the principal rooms mostly Adam Revival. In the Bar beside the entrance hall, a square central serving space placed in screens of Ionic piers; Ionic pier screens also at the W and S bay windows. Columned screens and Adam Revival chimneypieces at the ends of the Terrace Room. Huge Art Deco lights in the ocean liner-style Glendevon Room at the centre of the S side. The Strathearn Restaurant is divided into a nave and aisles by Ionic columns; Ionic pilasters along the walls and another Adam revival chimneypiece. At the entrance to the Ballroom on the main block's N side, an apse containing a stair designed to show the descent of gowns to maximum effect. Ceiling in the early C18 manner, modelled with large circles enriched with naturalistic fruit and flowers, two pierced by cupolas. Ionic pilastered walls; in each bay, a mirror under a Diocletian 'window'. Proscenium arch and stage at the N end.

Single-storey GARDEN PAVILIONS, also of the 1920s, at the outer corners of the S lawn which commands a view down Glen Eagles. – To the S, the DORMY CLUBHOUSE, the hotel's original golf clubhouse. Neo-Georgian with a Roman Doric columned and piend-roofed portico. Ogee-roofed cupola on the W wing. The building has been tactfully extended. – NE LODGE, again of the 1920s. Harled Neo-Georgian.

GLENEAGLES HOUSE
3.1 km. E of Blackford

Strung-out harled laird's house of the Haldanes of Gleneagles, the product of several stages of development over successive centuries.

The house, consisting of two unequally sized blocks linked by a screen wall fronted by a veranda, began, probably in the early C17, as a two-storey and attic block. In the earlier C18 it was decided to construct a new house just to its W consisting of a main block, probably of three storeys, flanked by two-storey pavilions. The pavilions, the E adjoining the W end of the C17 house, were built but the intended centre block was not and the C17 house, instead of being removed, was enlarged to the E. Further work in the C19, late C20 and the beginning of the C21 has failed to impose architectural unity.

Gleneagles House.
Drawing of north front, by David Walker, *c.* 1967

The early C18 W pavilion retains much of its original appearance. It is a two-storey oblong, the piended roof with bellcast eaves; rusticated quoins and a moulded eaves cornice. The long N and S elevations are each of four bays with small, almost square, windows to the ground floor and tall first-floor windows; originally, there was a door in the N front's W bay but this was converted to a window and a door was formed at the E bay in 1985. The linking veranda with a gableted centre is probably mid C19 in its present form.

The larger E block comprises both the E pavilion of the intended C18 mansion and the enlarged and remodelled C17 house. Its pavilion section (at the W end) was originally identical to the W pavilion, except that its N door is at the E end and there is an additional ground-floor window at the S elevation. The late C19 remodelling raised this part to three storeys, the second-floor windows rising into gableted dormerheads. In this remodelling the C18 eaves cornice was reused at the S elevation and copied elsewhere, as was the general appearance of the C18 roof. At its E end, the slightly recessed N front of the C17 house. Alterations in the C18 and late C19 and the addition of an extra floor have made its original appearance barely recognizable. At its E end, a large panel bearing three badly weathered heraldic shields and, higher up, a small stone with the date 1759 (perhaps that of the E extension). At the S elevation of this part of the house, a lean-to outshot, probably C19, across the ground floor, but the regular four-bay design of the first floor may represent the original design although the windows seem to have been remodelled in the C18. The original height of the C18 one-bay E extension is revealed by scrolled skewputts carved with floral decoration. Victorian windows to its N front. At the gable, a broad segmental-arched coachhouse opening (now a window). A pavilion-roofed conservatory was added to the S wing by *The Hurd, Rolland Partnership* in 2001.

INTERIOR. The internal plan of the W pavilion was originally tripartite with, at ground and first floor, a large room occupying the centre two bays, a small room at the W end and the stair at the E. Above the stair hall's entrance to the main ground-floor room has been placed a steep wooden pediment broken by the pedestal top of a heraldic achievement displaying the impaled arms of (Sir) John Haldane of Gleneagles and his first wife, Katharine Wemyss, under their initials and flanked by the date 1624, possibly that of the earliest part of the present mansion house. The main ground-floor room (its w wall removed) was the kitchen, its large fireplace and ovens surviving at the E end. On the first floor, the main room has a simple moulded stone chimneypiece at the W wall whose fielded panelling is partly original and partly replicated in *The Hurd, Rolland Partnership*'s restoration of the pavilion in 1985.

The plan of the early C18 E pavilion (i.e. the W end of the main block) seems originally to have been identical but reversed. Here, the principal ground floor room was the C18 PARLOUR, its decoration intact. Fielded panelling; over each door, a band of stucco enrichment with a central shell. Basket-arched fireplace, its stone surround panelled and keystoned; stucco overmantel of a richly modelled trophy. The room above has been subdivided.

In the C17 block immediately to the E, the W ground-floor room contains an original stone chimneypiece, the lintel projected on corbels which are set slightly on the diagonal so as to point outwards. Above, a re-set late C17 stone bearing the heraldic achievement of the impaled arms of John Haldane, fourteenth of Gleneagles, and his wife, Mary Drummond. Stone stair to the E. On the first floor, the W room is finished with early C18 panelling.

In the C18 E extension, the ground-floor room (now dining room) seems originally to have been a coachhouse. In the room above (now drawing room), a late C19 cornice and ceiling rose but an C18 basket-arched stone chimneypiece.

STABLES immediately W of the house. Probably mid C18, a two-storey piend-roofed block of six bays by two, the upper windows small and square. Rubble-built, the N front harled and with a large garage opening inserted at the W end. A two-storey house, added probably in the mid C19, forms a SE wing.

CHAPEL, 0.2 km. N. Early C16 rubble-built and crowstepped rectangle, the E gable with an intake. Its gableted finial (now surmounted by a stone cross), perhaps originally the top to a buttress, looks C14 and has presumably been reused from elsewhere. On this gable's S skewputt, a weathered shield which displayed the Erskine coat of arms, presumably for Margaret Erskine who married Sir James Haldane, sixth of Gleneagles, in 1518. The hoodmoulded and pointed E window of two lights under a quatrefoil dates from *Reginald Fairlie*'s restoration of the chapel in 1925. Roughly in the centre of the N side, a rectangular door (unblocked in 1925) and a window, also rectangular, to its E. In the S side, two rectangular windows, the E larger than the W. Elliptical-arched door in the W gable.

Inside, the roof structure was renewed by *The Hurd, Rolland Partnership* in 1996 but its earlier form respected. The use of wall-posts makes it similar to the roofs in Tullibardine Church (q.v.) but here there is a single tier of collars. Stone floor laid in 1925. – Wooden ALTAR by *Alan Shaftoe*, 1995. – STAINED GLASS E window (St Andrew and St Mungo, his face modelled on that of Bishop Alexander Chinnery-Haldane), clearly drawn, by *Arthur L. & Charles E. Moore*, c. 1925. – Erected against the W wall is the weathered GRAVE-SLAB of Malcolm Fleming †1657, carved with a coat of arms.

In the chapel's drystone-walled small GRAVEYARD, the MONUMENT to Bethia Dundas, wife of George Haldane, eighteenth of Gleneagles, †1770, a rusticated ashlar obelisk on a corniced pedestal.

GLENEAGLES CASTLE, 0.3 km. N of the chapel, was the residence of the Haldanes before the building of Gleneagles House. It stands on a steep-sided natural mound, its N and E sides circled by a burn, the S and W formerly bordered by a loch (now drained). The building itself is of the late C15, a simple rectangle, c. 17.1 m. by c. 11.9 m., the rubble walls standing to a height of two storeys except at the E end where only their base survives. At the W end of the S side, the base of a porch, probably an addition of the later C16. Behind, the chamfered W jamb of the house's C15 entrance survives. W of this, a pair of narrow ground-floor windows, the E robbed of dressed stonework, the W still with most of its chamfered W jamb. In the centre of the gable, an inverted keyhole gunloop at the ground floor and, above, a reasonably sized first-floor window robbed of dressings. At the ground floor of the N side, remains of two more inverted keyhole gunloops. Between them, at the bottom of the wall, a garderobe chute which has discharged into a stone drain. E of this, remains of a ground-floor window. At the upper floor, jambs of a narrow window roughly in the centre of the wall.

INTERIOR. The entrance is above the internal floor level to which a short flight of steps descended. On the l. of the entrance, remains of the well of a turnpike stair. On the r., a dog-leg wall chamber, its N part interfered with by the insertion, perhaps in the C16, of a service stair. In the wall thickness of the NE corner, a pit-prison which must have been entered from a first-floor hatch. The main ground-floor room (later subdivided) was the kitchen with a large fireplace at the E end. In the N side, between the E window and the E of the two gunloops, a slop drain which has also served as the outlet for two drains contained in the wall thickness and which served an upper floor. Except for the N side's window all the openings are placed in elliptical-arched embrasures; a locker in the E side of the embrasure of the N side's E gunloop. At the W end of the N wall, an aumbry and another tiny one above. Another aumbry but dog-legged at the N end of the W gable. In the wall thickness of the SW corner, a windowless round cell, its roof rising as a domical vault but finished with a flat lid. The surviving upper floor has been an entresol, it and the ground floor covered by a single tunnel vault whose haunches survive. In the thickness of the entresol's N wall, a garderobe and, to its W, a stair to the now missing floor above. Flue of a narrow fireplace at the N end of the W gable. At this gable's S end, a dog-legged cupboard. Outside the house, fragments of a BARMKIN WALL.

GATEPIERS at the E end of the main drive to Gleneagles House bear the initials of Mungo Haldane (fifteenth of Gleneagles) and the date 1749. They are of ashlar, with panelled faces and egg-and-dart cornices. On the E face of each, a rosette and, on the W, a fluted Ionic pilaster. Urn finials carved with floral ornament.

GLENEARN HOUSE
2.8 km. SE of Forgandenny

Stuccoed two-storey villa of c. 1830, with a broad-eaved piended roof. E front of three bays. Segmental-headed door in a slightly lower central projection, its roof also piended. This is flanked by bows, their ground floor covered with trellised cast-iron verandas. – Contemporary single-storey LODGE beside the drive. Walls of red sandstone ashlar, the piended roof with a carved valance and slight projection at the centre; Neo-Jacobean glazing in the windows. – At the entrance to the drive, late C18 GATEPIERS, also of red sandstone ashlar and with urn finials.

GLENFARG

Rather dour village which developed after the opening of the railway from Edinburgh to Perth via the Forth Railway Bridge in 1890.

Former ARNGASK PARISH CHURCH, 0.9 km. E. Roofless rubble-built rectangle designed by *Adam Horsbrough*, wright in Milnathort, 1806. At the S side, a rectangular door flanked by two round-headed windows. Two rectangular windows in the N side. At each gable, a door to the area, the E off-centre, the W now blocked. Also at the E gable, a forestair, presumably an addition of 1821 when galleries were erected to the design of *Joseph Low*, builder in Perth. The SE Session House looks a later addition. At the W end, a gableted bellcote by *George Washington Browne*, 1907. It is flanked by diagonally set corniced piers, the W a chimney.

The church stands in the NW corner of the GRAVEYARD. At the graveyard's centre, a spire-topped birdcage BELLCOTE of 1806 which was removed from the church and re-erected here in 1907. – Beside it, a roofless rubble-walled WATCH HOUSE built, together with the churchyard wall, by *John Stewart*, mason in Collessie, in 1820. – Beside the watch house, a weathered effigy said to be that of Margaret Barclay, heiress of the baronies of Arngask and Kippo and wife of Sir Andrew Murray; if so, it is early C16. – E of the watch house, the HEADSTONE of Elizabeth Peat †1792. Aedicular front with squat Ionic attached columns and a curly pediment; high reliefs of a skull and hourglass. – To its SE, a scrolly-topped HEADSTONE to John Gib †1719, the front carved with reminders of death under an angel's head (the soul). – Lying on the ground beside it, the C18 HEADSTONE of a smith bearing his trade emblems. – Beside that, a large late C17 or early C18 TABLE STONE to WB and IW, the slab bearing an hourglass and sexton's tools above a mantled shield.

ARNGASK PARISH CHURCH, Church Brae. Originally Arngask United Free Church. Simple Dec, by *Sydney Mitchell & Wilson*, 1906–7, built of squared rubble. Nave, with a double-pitch roofed and narrow E aisle. Slightly tapering SE tower, the late Gothic detail at its belfry hinting at Art Nouveau; inside the parapet, a slated pyramid roof topped by a weathercock.

Inside, boarded roofs. Wooden chancel arch, its spandrels traceried. The basket arches of the three-bay nave arcade are carried on wooden piers. – STAINED GLASS (the Good Shepherd) of 1944 in the aisle's N window.

ARNGASK LIBRARY, Greenbank Road. Originally the Corbett Institute. By *A. N. Paterson*, 1892, in a Scots domestic manner. Single-storey, the walls harled and with red sandstone dressings, the roof covered with green slates and surmounted by a clock-faced cupola-topped ventilator. Ornately carved semicircular dormerhead. One canted bay window and one bow window. The bow is covered by a flattish conical roof over a corbelled eaves course; mullions with corbelled attached columns, their capitals carved with thistles. Touches of Scots Renaissance detail at the adjoining cottages built as part of the same scheme.

ARNGASK PRIMARY SCHOOL, Main Street. By *John M. Robertson* of Perth, 1904–5. Single-storey, built of squared rubble, the roof with bracketed broad eaves and a spired octagonal ventilator. Symmetrical triple-gabled front.

VILLAGE HALL, Greenbank Road. Built as Arngask Parish School in 1863, it was designed by *James C. Walker*. Single-storey school, with bracketed broad eaves and a slate-spired ventilator. Pointed windows to the school; rectangular windows to the two-storey schoolhouse.

GLENFARG HOTEL, Main Street. By *David Smart*, 1899–1900. Like a tall villa, with crowstepped gables and a battlemented tower, the walls of hammer-dressed grey ashlar, with dressings of polished red sandstone.

LOMOND HOTEL, Main Street. Built, *c.* 1900. Harled, with some applied half-timbering. Roman Doric columned short veranda. Brick tops to the Art Nouveauish chimneys.

ARNGASK HOUSE, 0.8km. NE. Dour Late Georgian house of *c.* 1830. The main block is a two-storey oblong box of three bays by two, the walls of coursed whinstone with sandstone dressings at the rusticated quoins, doors and window openings and the wallhead's blocking course which rises to a small parapet over the centre of the W front. Diagonally set chimneys on the piended platform roof. The large W porch is probably an addition of the later C19, its corners' Roman Doric columns reused from a portico. Also of the later C19 the full-height SE wing which extended the S elevation from two bays to six, the centre two slightly recessed. Single-storey N wing of the late C19 or early C20.

BALVAIRD CASTLE. *See* p. 186.
FORDEL HOUSE. *See* p. 386.
ROSSIE OCHIL. *See* p. 679.

GLENFARG HOUSE
0.5 km. N of Aberargie

Sprawling white harled two-storey Scotstyle villa by *J. B. Dunn*, c. 1915, but built in two stages. The original house was a quite tautly composed H-plan. Projecting from the end of one wing on the entrance front and of both wings at the garden elevation are flat-roofed single-storey bay windows. Curvaceous M-roofed dormerheads over the first floor windows of the entrance front; to the garden, a central semicircular-topped dormerhead flanked by triangular dormerheads. The second stage of work doubled the size of the house with an L-plan extension, in the same manner but with catslide-roofed dormerheads over the upper windows. In the SE inner angle of the SW wing and the original house, an octagonal tower, its ogee roof copied from the C17 stair tower of Grandtully Castle (q.v.).

Contemporary GARAGE, STABLES AND LAUNDRY to the E, also by Dunn. Built round a courtyard, one side closed by a screen wall. Single-storey ranges with crowstepped gables and a loft opening placed in a tall dormer with a shaped head. – White harled and jerkin-head gabled LODGE of the earlier C20.

GLENFINCASTLE

Chapel standing at the mouth of the glen.

GLENFINCASTLE CHAPEL. Built as a Free church in 1843–4. Rubble-built box with a S porch. On the N gable, a bellcote, its open wooden superstructure finished with a fish-scale slated pyramidal spire. Minimally pointed windows; bracketed broad eaves.

To the S, a small octagonal SUNDAY SCHOOL of 1930. Wooden walls above a stone base; bellcast eaves to the slated roof.

BALAVOULIN, 1 km. NW. Originally a two-storey three-bay farmhouse, probably of the early C19. It was recast in 1905 by *Ramsay Traquair* who added an attic, its gabled dormers rising from just below the eaves, and a full-height piend-roofed central projection. This contains the entrance, its roll-and-hollow-moulded stone surround under a coat of arms contrasting agreeably with the harled walling. Club skewputts.

BONSKEID HOUSE. *See* p. 236.
OLD FINCASTLE. *See* p. 563.

GLENLYON CHURCH see INNERWICK

GLENLYON FREE CHURCH see INNERWICK

7040
GLENLYON HOUSE
0.8 km. w of Fortingall

Arts and Crafts epitome of a harled laird's house formed by the 1890s remodelling of the late C17 and early C18 residence of the Campbells of Glenlyon.

The house was begun by Captain Robert Campbell at about the same time as he sold Meggernie Castle in 1684. He built a straightforward two-storey oblong, now the SW wing. In 1729 his son, John, doubled the building's size and made it L-plan with the construction of the NE range. In 1891, a few years after his purchase of the Glenlyon estate, the shipping magnate, Sir Donald Currie, employed *W. Dunn & R. Watson* to carry out major alterations.

The exterior is a tactful reworking of the unassuming C17 and C18 work. The two main ranges are both crowstep-gabled and with small ground floor windows. Large wallhead chimney on the s front of the 1729 two-storey NE wing which was left largely unaltered. The SW wing was heightened to three storeys, its second floor windows rising through the eaves to triangular and shaped dormerheads; oriel window at the s gable. In its SW inner angle was placed a conical-roofed round tower, its upper floor jettied on continuous corbelling. Also of the 1890s is the short two-storey and attic NW wing, its top floor jettied, its crowstepped gable's lack of a chimney disclosing its date. In its inner angle with the SW wing, a tower-like piend-roofed projection, its ground floor serving as a garden porch.

Interior of the 1890s. Entrance hall panelled in late C17 manner but with a beamed ceiling. Billiard room at the s end of the SW wing, dining room in the NW wing, both well finished but unshowy. The whole first floor of the SW wing is occupied by the drawing room, its plaster ceiling Jacobean in style, its end chimneypiece in the manner of the later C17.

LAUNDRY AND GARAGES to the NW, of 1913 and also by *W. Dunn & R. Watson*. Harled and crowstep-gabled Scotstyle U, of a single storey and attic loft. – Adjoining STEADING immediately N of the house, by *J. M. MacLaren*, 1889. Single-storey harled ranges round a courtyard, with elliptical-arched cartshed openings. Bracketed broad eaves to the roofs from which rise red sandstone shaped dormers. At the SW corner, an octagonal spire-roofed tower, its upper stages of red sandstone, the top containing the flight-holes of a doocot. – s of the steading, FARMHOUSE, also of 1889 and by MacLaren. It is Scots but without self-conscious historicist references, a squared-up harled composition preluding the Modern Movement but with Art Nouveau chimneys. Two-storey and attic L-plan, the broad

NW wing slightly lower than the main block and with a jettied first floor and an attic set back behind a parapet forming a low battlement to the W. On the N side of the house the main roof is swept down over a long and low lean-to whose W front forms a segmental-arched porch for the back door.

GLENSHEE PARISH CHURCH see SPITTAL OF GLENSHEE

GRANDTULLY

Strung-out small village, the buildings of the later C19 and C20.

ST MARY'S CHURCH, Nether Pitcairn, 3.2 km. SW. On the edge of a hilltop farm steading, an externally quite unassuming long and low chapel. It seems to have been built in or shortly before 1533 when Alexander Stewart of Grandtully endowed a curacy and chaplainry there, specifying that prayers were to be offered for the soul of the reigning king, James V, and those of Stewart and his family. It was a rectangle, c. 14.3 m. by 7 m. In the S wall were four rectangular windows, the E, lighting the sanctuary, much larger than the others, and, towards the W end, a door (all these now built up). The present N door, probably an C18 insertion, may be in the position of a C16 priest's door. High up in the E gable, a window, also rectangular, its rounded jambs grooved for glazing. The lintel is carved with the initials of Sir William Stewart of Grandtully (1567–1646) and his wife, Dame Agnes Moncrieff, and the window was probably replaced or inserted in the early C17, perhaps in 1636 (the date on a stone now in the chapel but formerly over the churchyard entrance). Also in the early C17 the building was extended W by c. 9.14 m., possibly to provide living accommodation for a chaplain. In the S wall of this part is a door flanked by two narrow windows. The W gable has a projecting stone on each skew to suggest stepping and a now shapeless stone finial.

Inside, at the S end of the E wall, an aumbry. Another aumbry in the N wall, its hinges probably C16, its doors C20 replacements for ones which existed into the late C19.* The W extension is separated from the chapel itself by a stone partition.

Over the extension and the chapel's W end the roof structure is exposed but the chapel's E half containing the burial vault of the Stewarts of Grandtully is covered by a wooden tunnel vault. Its boards display a remarkable scheme of early C17 PAINTED DECORATION (much restored and its former delicacy sacrificed from c. 1950), the scheme simulating a panelled and coffered ceiling, the *trompe l'œil* coffer cartouches in

---

*They are mentioned in David MacGibbon and Thomas Ross, *The Ecclesiastical Architecture of Scotland*, iii (1897), 572.

strapworked frames joined by bands. The panels between the coffers are decorated with brightly coloured depictions of fruits, birds and angels trumpeting news of the Resurrection. The centrepiece is a Corinthian columned and pedimented aedicule* containing a scene showing Death holding an arrow with which he is about to 'sting' a man lying on a bed, which stands on a chequered floor (possibly a reference to the chequered band of the Stewart coat of arms). On the r. of the bed, figures of the dead rise from their graves in response to the pair of angels sounding the last trump at the top of the scene.

Each of the two coffers immediately E and W of this centrepiece contains the monogrammed initials of Sir William Stewart and Dame Agnes Moncrieff, the E monogram designed to be seen from the W, the W from the E. The E coffer of the central row is painted with the sun in glory, the W with the moon encircled by stars and clouds. Each side of this row, an intermediate line of coffers on the curve of the vault. The four W contain depictions of the Evangelists, each holding or writing his gospel and accompanied by his attendant symbol. E of these are coats of arms. The first two are those of THE.LAIRD.OF./GRAINTVILIE on the N and DAM.AGNES./MONCRIEF on the S. Next, those of the two great nobles of the line of Stewart, the DVIK OF LENNOX (the arms barely visible) on the N and, on the S, the EARLE.OF.ATHOIL. The two E coats of arms on each side are royal – on the N the arms (badly worn) and initials of Anne of Denmark and of James VI; on the S the arms of Henrietta Maria and the arms and initials of Charles I. As well as proclaiming the loyalty of a subject to the Crown these probably celebrate both Sir William Stewart's presumed kinship with the Stewart kings and also his personal relationship to James VI whom he had served successively as a page of honour and a Gentleman of the Privy Chamber and by whom he had been knighted in 1606. The bottom row of coffers on each side contain emblematic human figures, some at least symbolic of Christian virtues.

Displayed on the W wall of the chapel's interior is a large broken slab inscribed .W·S·S. .A.·D·M 1636. It was formerly over the entrance to the graveyard.

GRAVEYARD on the S side of the church. Its HEADSTONES are almost all Victorian but at the W end is the curvaceously topped stone to James Thomson, late tenant in Donvorist †1780, its piecrust-bordered W front carved with a smiling angel's head (the soul) above the initials of Thomson and his wife Hellen Stuart which flank a crowned scot and coulter. Below is mantling above a depiction of Abraham and Isaac accompanied by the inscription 'Abraha Stay/Mosscri/ng Isaac BY AN ANGEL'; at the bottom, the inscription ME MENTO MORI.

---

*Formerly sited so as to be seen from the E. It was turned round c. 1960 so as to be seen from the W.

GRANDTULLY CASTLE
2.8 km. SW

Tall C16 laird's house of the Stewarts of Grandtully which became a secondary residence after their acquisition of Murthly Castle (q.v.) in 1615 but received a massive Baronial addition in the 1890s when it served as the dower house of the widow of the last Stewart in the direct male line.

In its present form, the building is L-plan but with towers projecting from the main ranges. The C16 house, occupying the E part of the S range, was probably built in two stages. The first, of *c.* 1500, was a rubble-walled oblong (*c.* 10.36 m. by 9.45 m.) of three storeys and an attic, its main entrance perhaps at the W end of the N side. In the second stage of *c.* 1560 the main block was reconstructed and extended to a Z-shape by the addition of identically sized four-storey and attic rubble-built square jambs at the NW and SE corners, with a round stair-tower in the SW inner angle of the SE jamb. In this late C16 form the house was comfortable but not ostentatious. Crow-stepped gables to the main block and jambs. At the main block's NE and SW corners, conical-roofed round turrets on continuous corbelling. Box-machicolation serving a garderobe at the top of the SE jamb's gable. Inverted keyhole gunloops to the ground floor, decently sized windows above. The buttress in the W inner angle of the main block and SW jamb is probably an addition. A touch of swagger was provided in 1626 when the round stair-tower was heightened and given an ogee-profile roof, the windows of its new top floor rising into ball-finialled gablets, one bearing the date of 1626, and the coat of arms and initials of (Sir) William Stewart of Grandtully.

The extension built for Lady Stewart in 1892–6 is by *Thomas Leadbetter*. This is mostly of three storeys and an attic forming an irregular L-shape with one range extending W from the C16 house and the other returning to the N. Rubble-built and crowstepped in a fairly pacific interpretation of Scots Baronial but with a battlemented and bartizaned five-storey SW tower from whose outer corner is corbelled out a tall round turret under a saddleback-roofed rectangular caphouse. Catslide roofs to the main ranges' dormer windows. On the N range's gable are conical-roofed corner turrets like those of the earlier house, on its E side, a conical-roofed round tower.

INTERIOR. At the C16 entrance in the SE jamb, an iron yett. Tunnel-vaulted lobby with a pair of doors in its S side. The l. opens into a vaulted guardroom whose floor contains the hatch to a pit-prison, the r. onto a stone turnpike stair. On the ground floor of the main block, a passage with a pair of vaulted cellars to its W, the N now the inner hall giving access to the stair hall formed by Leadbetter in the C16 NW jamb. On the first floor of the C16 main block, the HALL, an immensely broad fireplace at its W end, the walls lined with 1890s oak panelling. Contained in the thickness of the N wall, a passage room which led from the hall's NE corner to the NW jamb.

The other principal rooms are all contained in Leadbetter's extension. In the S range, W of the hall, the LIBRARY, also oak-lined but the panels conceal bookshelves; chimneypiece in a late C18 manner. Double doors open to the DRAWING ROOM occupying the house's SW corner in which are a similar chimneypiece and panelling. DINING ROOM with a thinly ribbed ceiling at the S end of the N range. At this range's other end, the BOUDOIR, its end wall filled by an inglenook, the opening framed by foliage-capitalled pilasters supporting the long lintel whose lower half is fronted by a bracketed shelf intended for the display of china, the upper carved with festoons of foliage hanging from bow-tied ribbons. Shell-headed niches in the splayed sides; a pair of windows flanking the chimneypiece which is in the manner of *c.* 1700 with a lugged architrave and pulvinated frieze.

HALLYBURTON HOUSE
1.1 km. ESE of Kettins

Large Elizabethan Revival manor house of 1880–4 designed by *Andrew Heiton Jun.* for Robert Stewart Menzies, a member of an Edinburgh brewing family, and remodelled and enlarged in 1903 for W. G. Graham Menzies by *Robert S. Lorimer*, the interior much more interesting than the exterior.

Like the previous house on the site which had belonged to the Hallyburtons of Pitcur, it is triple pile. Two storeys and an attic above a fully exposed basement, built of pinkish stugged ashlar. Mullioned openings, with rectangular or canted bay windows to the principal rooms. The W (entrance) front is dominated by a battlemented four-storey entrance tower with a taller octagonal SW corner turret. At the front's N end, a lower tower and, beyond this, a low battlemented wing, its upper floor added in 1903 but with the 1880s battlement reused, projects W to join a battlemented archway, the entrance to the N service court.

The S elevation's centrepiece, recessed between the gables of the W and E piles, contains a huge five-light Gothic window, its upper lights cusped; above, a large bargeboarded wooden dormer window, its corner columns with elongated bell capitals, the tympanum of its gablet decorated with the relief of a shell. In the inner angle with the E pile, a splay-cornered projection built in 1903 when Lorimer extended this pile ·S, his windowless gable with a large chimney corbelled out from the wall face very like Heiton's earlier gable.

The E front to the garden is composed of several parts. Tall S section of three bays, the S an addition by Lorimer together with the present canted bay at the centre (a replacement for Heiton's lower rectangular bay window), its parapet rising to enclose the central relief of a rosette, and the wallhead's tall stone dormer windows whose gabled heads rise between scrolls. N of this and slightly set back, a lower three-bay section of the 1880s, its battlement broken by a central gablet. Central partly glazed and pointed broad door from the drawing room, the sidelights and fanlights with cusped arcading and quatrefoils. It opens onto a stone stair; the simple iron balcony in front of the flanking windows was added in the C20. N of this, the surviving single bay of a N wing added to the previous house in the 1860s. Its triangular bay window under a gableted parapet is of that date but the tall first-floor window is of the 1880s when a gabled attic storey was added.

The rest of the 1860s wing was rebuilt in 1903, with a canted bay window and wallhead dormers which are smaller versions of those Lorimer added to this front's S end. To the N was a lower five-bay addition, also of 1903. This was demolished in 1988 except for the lower part of its front which forms a screen wall pierced by door and window openings. At the wall's S end, a stair to a balcony in front of a built-up window, the balustrade of curvaceous ironwork and with a wrought-iron rose in front of the window.

INTERIOR. Double-height ENTRANCE HALL of the 1880s, its walls ashlar-clad above a high oak-panelled dado. Jacobean Renaissance wooden chimneypiece. Trabeated wooden ceiling, its beams carried on stone corbels carved with shields. At the N end, a stair up to a gallery fronted by a glazed screen. From this gallery is entered the two-storey SALOON, also of the 1880s, which occupies the S half of the house's central block. This is a Neo-Jacobean great hall (*c.* 18.3m. by 6.1m. and 8.2m. high), covered with a wooden vaulted ceiling, the ribs of its sexpartite compartments springing from moulded stone corbels and meeting at foliaged bosses. Walls covered with panelling for half their height; above, they are plastered and half-timbered, with oriel-like balconies giving borrowed light to the first-floor corridors behind. At the S end, the huge Gothic window. On the E side, a large Jacobean Renaissance chimneypiece, its bulbous columns of white-veined black marble supporting a wooden entablature with a foliage-carved frieze; above, the coat of arms of the Menzies of Hallyburton. At the N end, a Gothic screen of three depressed arches carries a minstrels' gallery. The space under the gallery, also covered by a vaulted wooden ceiling, is more domestic, with a bay window to the W and an inglenook to the N, both entered through depressed arches, the inglenook's stone fireplace of Late Gothic character with columned jambs and a quatrefoiled frieze. N of this, a rather small Jacobean STAIR HALL.

Off the W side of the saloon, in the house's SW corner, the LIBRARY/BILLIARD ROOM, its 1880s character intact. Heavy beamed ceiling. Bay windows in the W and S sides, both marked off by depressed arches springing from bell-capitalled columns. Columns of the same type support the entablature of the bookcases whose arched openings are shouldered. Elaborate Artisan Mannerist wooden chimneypiece with paired figures of crouching satyrs under the mantelshelf. The overmantel consists of decoratively panelled cupboards, the tall centre one designed to hold billiard cues.

The other principal rooms face the garden to the E. Off the saloon is the DRAWING ROOM, also of the 1880s but much lighter in character. Compartmented plaster ceiling bearing motifs of the rose, thistle, fleur-de-lys, etc. At the ends, identical wooden chimneypieces of early Georgian inspiration, each with Ionic columned jambs and a foliaged frieze with, at its centre, the head of a man wearing a winged helmet. Wooden Gothick window surrounds at the E wall mask the contrast between the arched and glazed garden door in the centre and the rectangular windows which flank it. Large Gothick doorpiece on the W side.

The rooms to the N are entered off a CORRIDOR running from the stair hall. This was remodelled by Lorimer who provided fumed oak panelling (by *John Watherston & Sons*) sparingly ornamented with carved fruits. The S part is a top-lit square, the cupolaed plaster ceiling enriched by the *Bromsgrove Guild* with four large roses on the flat and small fruits on the coving. Off this, the BOUDOIR, its triangular bay window of the 1860s, its decoration of 1903. The walls are covered with C18 tapestries set into painted wooden panelling, its design of French inspiration but given a characteristic Lorimerian twist with reliefs of birds pecking at the fruited swags which are carved on the tops of the narrow panels. Plaster ceiling, its cove enriched with vine garlands.

The corridor's narrower N continuation, also panelled, is covered by an elliptically arched plaster tunnel vault crossed by rosetted bands. On its E side, Lorimer's DINING ROOM. Square, except for a bay window, and high. On the walls, fumed oak panelling, the lower part a linenfold dado, the upper framing five large French tapestries of c. 1500. Ceiling, also of oak, with heavy beams encrusted with carved and painted stylized fruiting branches; circular bosses carved with rosettes. Each compartment is divided into four by delicate ribs intersecting at floriated square bosses. At the bay window, a lighter version of the main ceiling. Simple and low stone chimneypiece, its keystone carved with the relief of a shell.

GATEWAY to an arboretum immediately NE of the house, by *Lorimer*, 1903, in the manner of c. 1700. Tall polished ashlar piers with ogee tops and simplified urn finials. Climbing up from low walls on either side are large wrought-iron scrolls of foliage and flowers. More foliage and flowers at the overthrow above the gates. – Garden GATEWAY of 1908, 0.2 km. SW of the house; presumably by Lorimer. Widely spaced channelled ashlar piers surmounted by figures of boys holding shields. Between the piers, wrought-iron screens and gates in the manner of c. 1700. – STABLES 0.1 km. NE of the house, by *John Ramsay*, 1857–8. Two storeys, the S window of the upper floor rising into gablets. – LODGE at the end of the S drive, by *Andrew Heiton Jun.*, c. 1882. Jacobethan, of two storeys, with a Gothic porch and spired octagonal tower. The accompanying

GATEWAY is buttressed and battlemented, with a depressed arch.

THE HERMITAGE
1.7 km. wsw of Inver

Land belonging to the Dukes of Atholl on the W side of the River Tay at its confluence with the River Braan, with the wooded slopes of Craigvinean rising behind, was laid out in the C18 as public pleasure grounds and found popularity with visitors to Dunkeld. A path beside the turbulent Braan enabled a stroller to enjoy the 'picturesque' surroundings, although their effect was vitiated for some by patches of shrubbery and flower beds (long since removed). The path survives, as do buildings designed to exploit the 'sublimity' of the surroundings.

At the E end of the path, HERMITAGE BRIDGE of *c.* 1785, constructed of rustically set rough masonry, the segmental arch over the river founded on rock and with slab voussoirs. A semicircular foot arch at the E end allows access from the S to a fissure in the rocky bank allowing a view of the river below. At the bridge's W end, the pathway passes through a crude arch.

THE HERMITAGE itself was built for John Murray of Strowan, nephew and heir of the second Duke of Atholl, by *John Neaper* in 1757, rebuilt after being being blown up by vandals in 1869, and altered by *Basil Spence* in 1951. Externally, it retains much of its mid-C18 appearance, as a single-storey

The Hermitage.
Engraving after a pastel by George Walker, from James Cririe, *Scottish Scenery*, 1807

summerhouse with bowed ends, the walling of the s bow of corduroy-textured droved ashlar crossed by a band course which forms imposts for the semicircular fanlight over the door; heavy blocks under the eaves cornice. The other walls are of rubble. The curve of the N bow, originally a wall pierced by a three-light window, is now marked only by metal pillars provided in 1951 to support the roof.

The interior is mid C20 but retains the C18 two-room layout. Circular entrance hall, now with pointed arches to the doors and wall niches. From 1783 until 1869 the doorway opposite the entrance was filled by a painting of Ossian (commissioned by the fourth Duke of Atholl and executed by *George Steuart*, adapting van Dyck's portrait of Belisarius) which, at the working of a secret pulley, divided into two parts which slid into openings in the wall thickness to reveal the principal room beyond (from 1783 known as Ossian's Hall). This is oblong with bowed ends, the N bow now an open viewing platform. Panelled walls and plasterwork in a polite late C18 manner. All this is mid C20. In the late C18 the walls and ceiling were mostly covered with mirrors reflecting the churning waters of the Black Lynn Fall of the river.

OSSIAN'S CAVE, 0.4 km. SW, also on the bank of the Braan is a largely artificial grotto of the later C18 formed of huge boulders.

HOSH

Hardly more than a place name to mark the site of the Glenturret Distillery.

GLENTURRET DISTILLERY. Founded in 1775 but the general appearance unpretentious C19. The principal block is a piend-roofed range, probably of the early C19, built of whitewashed rubble, with a slightly taller pavilion-roofed mash house at the s end. S of this, a detached mid-C19 house with canted dormers; glass-fronted single-storey addition of 2002 at the back whose upswept roof provides a terrace for seating. S again, the conference centre formed in 1998, its piend-roofed main block of *c.* 1890 but the pagoda-roofed 'kilns' at the ends are of the 1990s. To the NE of the complex, the large bronze-plated STATUE of a grouse (in honour of *The Famous Grouse* blend of whisky) erected in 2002.

LOCH TURRET WATER WORKS, 4.6 km. NW. 334 m.-long dam across the SE end of Loch Turret, by *Babtie, Shaw & Morton*, 1963–8. Both faces are sloped, the SE covered with grass, the NW of exposed concrete. Parapet of crazy-paved rubble. At the foot, a contemporary CONTROL HOUSE, the walls of hammer-dressed grey granite ashlar enlivened by touches of pink granite; double-pitch roof. – At the N end of the dam, a late C20 BOATHOUSE. Harled low walls under high slated roofs inspired by the Sydney Opera House. Wedge-shaped W end where the roof projects as a low triangular canopy. The E end is bowed.

HOUSE OF ALDIE
2.7 km. SE of Crook of Devon

Formerly the property of the Mercers of Meikleour who had acquired the lands of Aldie in the C14, the present house grew in several stages from the early C16 to the late C17. Abandoned in the early C20, the building was acquired in 1947 by Archibald Hope Dickson and restored for him by *Ian G. Lindsay*, *c.* 1950. It is now covered in pink-washed harling.

The earliest part is at the N, an oblong tower house of *c.* 1520. Tusking at its SW corner shows that it was intended to have a three-storey jamb to the S. The jamb was either not built or removed in the late C16 when the lower SW kitchen wing was built. Further remodelling and extension took place in the earlier C17 when a S range, possibly a jointure or dower house, was built on the E side of the jamb making the house a U, its small courtyard open to the E. At the same time the original tower was remodelled and its top storey added or replaced. In the late C17 the courtyard's E side was closed by the construction of an entrance block.

The crowstep-gabled N tower is of four storeys. At three corners of the early C17 top floor, conical-roofed tall round turrets carried on continuous corbelling and pierced by windows above gunloops set in rectangular surrounds; a crowstep-gabled caphouse over the turnpike stair at the SW corner. Most of the tower's window openings are of the early C17, their margins chamfered, but a large inverted keyhole gunloop at the second floor of the N side may be original. At the N end of its E gable, a ground-floor door inserted perhaps in the C18; above, a small cement heraldic panel of the late C20. A tier of slit windows at the S end of the W gable discloses the position of a stair. The third-floor windows rise through the eaves to crowstep-gabled dormerheads. Large off-centre wallhead chimney at the N side.

The late C16 SW wing is of two storeys and crowstep-gabled, its windows with chamfered margins, some with holes for iron grilles. The three-storey S wing has second-floor windows which rise into crowstep-gabled dormerheads. The first-floor windows here also have chamfered margins, again with holes for grilles. At the S side's ground-floor, a couple of slit windows and, at a lower level, the outlet for a wall chute, presumably a drain. At the E gable, windows with chamfered margins and grille holes. At the E end of the N side, commanding the approach to the entrance, a pair of ground-floor gunloops, one an oval, the other a stumpy inverted keyhole.

The short late C17 E block across the outer side of the courtyard is of two storeys, the upper floor minimally jettied and containing a much restored window with chamfered margins.

Off-centre ground-floor door, its surround with a roll-and-hollow moulding. Above, a moulded frame containing a stone panel carved with the heraldic achievement of the Mercers of Meikleour.

INTERIOR. The late C17 E entrance in the E block opens into a tunnel-vaulted entrance hall. Off its S side, a chamfered-margined door into the S wing. The W side of the entrance hall originally opened onto the small internal courtyard created by construction of the E block and which was roofed over *c.* 1950. On the N of this former COURTYARD, a door, with chamfered jambs, inserted in the early C17 to give access to the ground floor of the tower. At the former courtyard's SW corner, the bottom steps of a late C17 stair (*see* below). In the former courtyard's W wall, two doorways into the late C16 SW jamb. The N is checked for an outward-opening outer door with an inward-opening door behind and opens onto a lobby. On the lobby's N side, an entrance formed in the late C16 to give access to the bottom of the turnpike stair in the wall thickness of the tower's SW corner. The S doorway, its margins chamfered, opens into the KITCHEN which occupies most of the SW wing's ground floor. It is covered by an elliptical tunnel vault. At the S end, a huge elliptically arched fireplace.

The tower's ground floor is occupied by a single room (now DINING ROOM but originally a store) covered with a semicircular tunnel vault. Just above the springing of the vault on each side, a row of holes from which have been removed corbels which supported the floor joists of an entresol room which was entered from a hatch at the SE corner of the first-floor hall. At the room's W end, a sizeable window, enlarged probably in the early C17, with a couple of stone steps in its embrasure. At the S end of this wall, a locker. It is now jostled by the projection of the wall enclosing the bottom of the tower's turnpike stair which was extended down to this level in the late C16. It has partly blocked the original S entrance to the room whose lintel and E jamb are still visible showing that the level of the floor (paved in the mid C20 with stone slabs from Perth Prison) has been raised.

Two approaches to the first floor, one by the turnpike stair, the other by the late C17 stair entered at the former courtyard's SW corner. This rises in a narrow block built against the N side of the S wing, its W first floor window still exposed, to a landing where there is a chamfered-margined entrance to the wing. From this landing, another flight of steps in the late C17 E block leads to the doorway to the first floor of the tower. This was the early C16 external entrance, originally reached by a forestair. It opens onto a tunnel-vaulted lobby in the wall thickness. On the lobby's W side, a door, also with chamfered margins, into a long passage or gallery in the thickness of the tower's S wall.

At the W end of the gallery, a small opening, presumably a 'laird's lug', into the HALL. The hall itself is covered by a beamed ceiling which was painted in 1988 by *Michael Pinfold* with colourful patterns and depictions of the fauna and flora of Kinross-shire. Elliptical-arched window embrasures. At the hall's W end, a large rectangular fireplace, its roll-and-hollow-moulded surround perhaps a late C16 or early C17 replacement. At the E end of the N wall, a door to the surviving base of a stair which rose in the wall thickness to the floor above. The wall enclosing the tower's principal turnpike stair nudges into the SW corner of the hall.

The first floor of the late C16 SW wing is occupied by a single room (now the YELLOW ROOM), probably originally a withdrawing room, its wooden tunnel vault provided by Ian G. Lindsay, *c.* 1950.

The second floor of the tower was formerly one room. In its N wall, a fireplace with a chamfered surround and an aumbry to its E. Simply moulded stone cornices along the N and S walls. Garderobe in the thickness of the W wall. The room was subdivided *c.* 1950 when the resultant E bedroom was given a modelled plaster ceiling of early C17 inspiration, its roundels containing reliefs of pomegranates, angels' heads and coats of arms; outside the roundels, roses, thistles and naked ladies issuing from leaves.

SUNDIAL, E of the house. By *Archibald Handyside*, 1732. Multi-faceted head on a classical pier. It was formerly at Cramond House (Edinburgh) and erected here in 1960.

N of the house, facing each other across the drive, a crow-step-gabled C19 COTTAGE, extended in the late C20, and a late C20 GARAGE BLOCK, also crowstep-gabled.

HUNTINGTOWER CASTLE
0.6 km. SE of Ruthvenfield

Tall and informally composed mansion house, its present form created in the C17 by the linking and remodelling of a pair of late medieval tower houses. Formerly named Ruthven Castle, the site was the chief stronghold of the Ruthvens of that Ilk (Lords Ruthven from 1488 and Earls of Gowrie from 1581) from the late C12 until their forfeiture after the Gowrie Conspiracy, a purported attempt to assassinate James VI, in 1600.

A castle of enclosure was probably constructed here soon after the lands came into the Ruthvens' possession and the earliest part of the present mansion was built, perhaps *c.* 1400, as a gatehouse on the S side of the likely enclosure. About a century later the enclosure's entrance was moved to the W side and the gatehouse remodelled and heightened as a tower house. Soon after, a second tower house, detached but only 3 m. away, was built to the W, the earlier tower house perhaps becoming a jointure (dower) house. In the C17, when Ruthven Castle was a possession of the second Earl of Tullibardine and then of the Earls of Atholl and rechristened Huntingtower Castle, a short linking block was built to join the two tower houses.

The rubble-walled E TOWER HOUSE is oblong, *c.* 11m. by 7 m., and, when first built as a gatehouse, seems to have been of two storeys. Evidence of the original round-headed archways to the transe is given by the remains of chamfered jambs at the S side and, at the N, by the surviving E half of the entrance. Also perhaps of *c.* 1400 is the pointed slit window towards the W end of the S side's ground floor. In the remodelling of *c.* 1500 the building was heightened to three storeys and an attic, the reddish stone of the new work contrasting with the grey-coloured original masonry, the original transe was blocked and a tall round-arched new doorway inserted at the W end of the N side. At the wallhead of the new work, a parapet projected on moulded corbels, with continuously corbelled rounds at the corners; a crowstep-gabled caphouse set back from the NW round. Inside the parapet, the crowstep-gabled attic, its walls set back to allow a wall-walk all round. Thrifty provision of not very large windows in the N, S and W walls, the W openings now inside the linking block, the S side's first-floor window built up, probably in the C17, when a larger window was inserted to its W and a large window inserted at the ground floor of this side, together with a tall basket-arched S entrance (now blocked). In the W gable (now inside the linking block), at the level of an entresol floor, an inverted keyhole gunloop of *c.* 1500 which must have lost its purpose after the building of the W tower. A roof raggle at the E gable shows that there has been a single-storey building against this end, perhaps put up in the C17.

The larger W TOWER HOUSE, set slightly forward of the S side of its E neighbour, is also rubble-walled but L-plan, the main block again of three storeys and an attic, the SW jamb a floor higher. The wallheads are mostly treated like those of the E tower, the parapets projected on moulded corbels except at the jamb's N gable where the parapet is formed by an upward extension of the main walling; continuously corbelled angle rounds. Crowstep-gabled attics; a pointed opening in the S gable of the attic of the jamb. At the NW corner of the main block, a rounded projection (containing the stair) finished with a caphouse. At the N gable of the jamb, a lean-to covers steps which rise behind the parapet to give access from the wall-walk of the main block to that of the jamb. In the exposed faces of the jamb and the main block's W side, inverted keyhole gunloops to the ground floor. Chamfered margins to the windows of the upper floors, those to the S apparently enlarged in the C17. Garderobe outlets at the base of the jamb's N side and the main block's W. The ground floor S door of the main block is an insertion, probably of the C19. Visible inside the C17 infill block are two blocked earlier doors, both perhaps original, to the E side of the ground floor. The original principal entrance, now approached by a rubbly forestair, is at first-floor level at the W end of the main block's N gable. A roof raggle shows that a two-storey block containing a great hall (probably removed in the early C19) was built against the N side of the tower's main block, probably in the mid C16.

HUNTINGTOWER CASTLE

Uniting the two tower houses is the narrow one-bay C17 section aligned with both the N and S gables of the W tower house. Chamfered margins to the windows. Tusking at the E corners suggests that an unexecuted scheme for rebuilding the E tower, perhaps to form a symmetrical U-plan S front, was intended.

INTERIOR. The ground floor of the E tower house contains a tunnel-vaulted room. The masonry of the E wall shows that the former transe at this end was covered by a tunnel vault, removed when this building was remodelled *c.* 1500. In the N

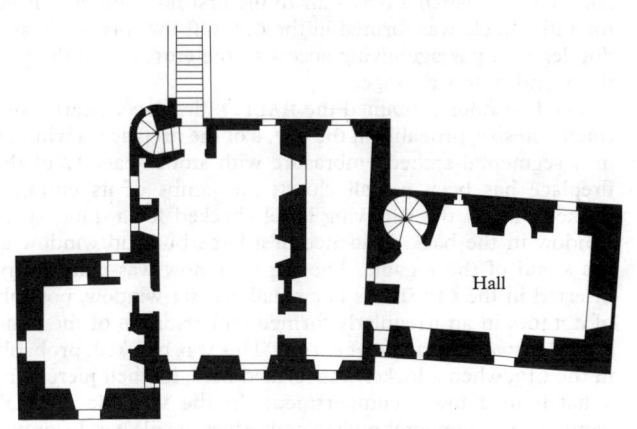

FIRST FLOOR

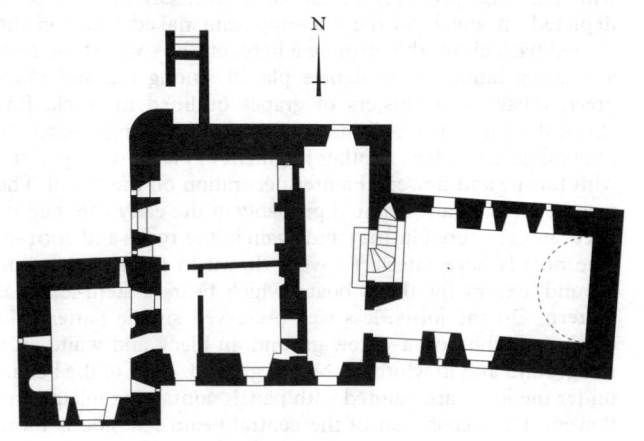

GROUND FLOOR

Huntingtower Castle.
Plans

wall, a fireplace with a simple moulded surround, flanked by a pair of windows, their sills stepped, all these of *c.* 1500. Under the sill of this wall's W window and on its W side, the remains of a stone frame. Stepped sill to the slit window in the S wall. A door and window in the W gable, a high-set S window and joist holes in the N wall show the room was formerly divided by an entresol floor which seems to have stepped up at the E end and, at the W, cut across the arched top of the tower house's entrance. The ingoes of the S window suggest that this floor was removed when the present vault was introduced, probably in the early C16. In the room's NW corner, remains of the lowest part of the tower's turnpike stair, the steps of this part removed when a new stair to the first floor, entered from the infill block, was formed in the C17. Off the turnpike was a dog-leg wall passage giving access to the entresol; gunloop at the N end of this passage.

The first floor contained the HALL. N fireplace, clearly contracted in size, probably in the C17. E of the fireplace, a window in a segmental-arched embrasure with stone seats. W of the fireplace has been a wall closet, the jambs of its entrance hacked off but the surviving lintel checked for a door; small window in the back. Evidence of a large built-up window at the S end of the E gable. The big S window was enlarged or inserted in the C17. To its E, a small low-set window, possibly of *c.* 1400, in an irregularly formed embrasure. E of the main S window was a window of *c.* 1500. This was blocked, probably in the C17, when a locker was formed here, its shelf pierced by a hatch to a lower compartment. In the W gable, a small window in a segmental-arched embrasure, its plaster decorated with painting, probably of the early C16. On the N ingo is depicted an angel, on the S a supplicant naked man, on the arched back above the opening a hare, on the soffit of the arch a running hind, all the figures placed among red and blue-green foliage and clusters of grapes outlined in black. Just above the window, a red lion *passant guardant*. Immediately W of the large S window, another fragment of plasterwork painted with foliage and flowers. Fainter decoration on the E wall. The wooden ceiling, also painted probably in the early C16, had its decoration restored in 1913 and again in the 1930s and 2001–2. The boards have interlaced work drawn in black on a white ground, except for the N board which bears a stem-and-leaf pattern. On the joists, less well-preserved simple patterns in black and white on a yellow ground, in black and white on a red ground and in white on a black ground. Four of the beams under the joists are painted with panels containing foliage and flowers. The decoration of the central beam's W side is more ambitious, the panels containing, from the N end, a foliaged design, foliaged strapwork ending in dragons' heads, another dragon's head rising out of foliage, and a hound. A garderobe in the wall thickness of the room's SW corner has been cut through, probably in the C18 or C19, to provide the hall with a direct communication to the C17 infill block.

At the second floor, an UPPER HALL. Large E fireplace of
c. 1500 with shafted jambs and a high corniced lintel. To its N,
a small cupboard. At the E end of the N and S walls, windows
in elliptical-arched embrasures containing stone seats. At the
N wall's W end, a large cupboard. Small aumbry in the S wall.
In the SW corner, a garderobe. The attic, its floor now missing,
has been entered at its W end by a door from the wall-walk.

The C17 infill block between the two tower houses contained
a narrow ground floor hall with a large scale-and-platt stair at
its N end. This gave access to an ante-room at each of the first
and second floors from which was entered the early C16 W
tower house. The C17 stair and floors have been removed and
a stepped wooden bridge now connects the main first-floor
rooms of the two tower houses. The simple moulded stone
chimneypiece of the first-floor ante-room survives.

In the W tower house, an unvaulted ground floor, now a caretaker's house. From the first floor, a turnpike stair in the NW
corner rises to the wall-walk off which is entered the jamb's
top room. At each upper floor (the floors above the first floor
removed), a large room in the main block and a smaller room
in the jamb. Simple moulded early C16 chimneypieces at the
second floor of the main block and the first and second floors
of the jamb. The present first-floor door into the C17 block has
a chamfered inner surround and may have originally opened
into a wall chamber. First- and second-floor garderobes in the
NW corner of the main block. Another first-floor garderobe in
the jamb's NE corner. Beside the original first-floor external
entrance into the main block are remains of black-and-white
painted decoration, an axonometric representation of building
blocks. On the N ingo of the W window in the jamb's first-floor
room, a fragment of plaster painted with a lozenge-framed coat
of arms, presumably C16. The attic of the jamb has contained
a doocot, its walls lined with stone nesting boxes.

HUNTINGTOWERFIELD

Small housing development of c. 2000 around the former bleach
works.

BLEACH WORKS. Now housing. The surviving block of the works
founded by Richardson & Co. in 1774 is of 1866. It is of two
storeys and piend-roofed, the sides and rear elevation harled.
Ashlar-faced S front with a slightly advanced and parapeted
centre. From this centre projects a tower, its bottom stage with
channelled stonework. Round-headed slit windows at the
second stage. The third stage is a belfry with a keystoned
round-headed opening in each face. At the top stage are clock
faces. Broad-eaved low pyramidal roof surmounted by an iron
cage containing a bell and finished with a weathervane finial.

HUNTINGTOWER HOTEL. Large harled and half-timbered
villa, by *A. G. Heiton*, 1892. Late C20 additions for its present
use.

INCHAFFRAY ABBEY
1 km. NE of Madderty

Fragmentary remains of the Augustinian abbey founded by Gilbert, Earl of Strathearn, in 1200. The buildings seem to have been of standard monastic plan with the abbey church on the N side of the cloister. The only substantial surviving part is the N gable of the W range which presumably originally contained the guesthouse and was c. 29.6 m. by 7.9 m. externally. The gable is of four storeys, with chamfered margins to the narrow windows; chimney with an outwardly splayed cope. This may be of the late C16, perhaps dating from a reconstruction of the guesthouse as a mansion for James Drummond (later, Lord Maderty) who acquired the abbey lands in 1560.

INCHBERVIS CASTLE see STANLEY: STANLEY HOUSE

INCHMARTINE HOUSE
1.8 km. SW of Inchture

Small harled three-storey mansion of early C18 origin but remodelled c. 1800. Six-bay W front with tall first-floor windows. At the centre of the ground floor, a tetrastyle Roman Doric portico fronting a pilastered door and sidelights. Strip quoins; wallhead cornice and a blocking course which rises to form a low parapet at the centre. On the N side of the house, an oriel window of c. 1830; on the S side, three-light windows to the ground floor (one now a door) and first floor (one a dummy). Low rubble-built office wings, probably of the early C19, at the rear.

The drive crosses an elliptical-arched Late Georgian CULVERT, its SW keystone bearing the initials of Sir Patrick Ogilvy of Inchmartine, the NW the date 1643; both seem originally to have been skewputts. – Single-storey LODGE of c. 1830, its walls of polished ashlar. Broad-eaved jerkin-head roofs. One canted bay window, the other windows with stone canopies; decorative Neo-Jacobean glazing. Low octagonal GATEPIERS.

E of the mansion house, STABLES AND COACHHOUSE (now housing) of c. 1800. A rubble-built, mostly harled U. Piend-roofed main W range with a taller pedimented centrepiece containing the round-headed pend and surmounted by an ogee-roofed octagonal ashlar cupola, with round-headed dummy windows in its sides. – Immediately E of this a former Roman Catholic CHAPEL of the mid C19. Stripped Romanesque, built of squared masonry, with moulded corbels under the eaves. It is disused and rather altered.

INCHTURE

Small village, home to a brewery in the C19, the architectural character controlled by the owners of the Rossie Priory estate.

INCHTURE PARISH CHURCH. By *David Mackenzie*, 1834–5. Georgian Gothic, the s side (out of public view) harled, the rest of red sandstone ashlar, stugged at the main walling, polished at the dressings and buttresses. T-plan, with a N jamb and full-height porches in the inner angles. At the jamb, clasping buttresses, angle buttresses at the other corners, all pinnacled. On the jamb's gable an octagonal bellcote with a stone spire rising inside its battlement. Ornate cross of 1875 on the E gable. The doors have ogee-arched and foliage-finialled hoodmoulds, their label stops carved with grotesque heads at the main entrances and with shields at the narrow doors in the sides of the jamb.

The interior was completely remodelled by *Duncan D. Stewart*, 1891, after a fire. Braced and boarded wagon roof. Gothic arcade dividing the body from the N 'aisle' (now partitioned off behind the arcade). – PEWS and PULPIT of 1891. – On the s wall, a MONUMENT of 1899 to the Rev. John Adamson Honey. Tudor Gothic frame enclosing a panel carved with a portrait bust in relief. – STAINED GLASS. Modernistic E window (a cross and with four angels representing the Four Seasons) by *Sep Waugh*, 2000.

GRAVEYARD. Propped against the church's w gable, a HEADSTONE of 1745 with the initials AJ and MG. It is aedicular, the pilasters bearing torches and topped by heads of men wearing full-bottomed wigs; a trumpeting angel floats in the curvy pediment. – Immediately s of the church's w end, a Neoclassical pedestal MONUMENT decorated with a shield above a husk garland. It was erected by Alexander Rae, tenant farmer in Millhill, to his wife, Elizabeth Matthew †1796. – Beside it, a medieval coped GRAVESTONE, the top shaped as a disc-headed cross, the N side incised with a sword. – Immediately to its w, the semicircular pedimented HEADSTONE erected by Thomas Ranken to his daughter Janet †1730. In the E face's pediment, an angel's head (the soul). The w face is aedicular, the attached columns surmounted by roundels carved with stars and flanking a helm-crested and mantled shield displaying crossed scythes and Ranken's initials; a pair of angels' heads and stars in the pediment. – To its SE, a HEADSTONE of 1748 commemorating the children of William Kininmont. Segmental pediment, the top carved with a pair of skulls; ball finials at the ends. Badly weathered aedicular w face, the leafily capitalled pilasters bearing high-relief torches. At the E face, an angel's head in the pediment. The inscription is flanked by emaciated figures, probably corpses, one standing on an hourglass, the other on a skull.

INCHTURE PRIMARY SCHOOL. By *Boswell, Mitchell & Johnston*, 1973–4. A pair of single-storey ranges with ribbed metal monopitch roofs facing each other across a flat-roofed centre block.

INCHTURE VILLAGE HALL. Originally Inchture Parish School. By *William Scott*, 1851. Broad-eaved red brick school and schoolhouse, the school with hoodmoulded windows.

DESCRIPTION. Short main street lined with mature trees. At its SW end the two-storey INCHTURE HOTEL of the earlier C19, Picturesque with carved bargeboards, a hoodmoulded entrance and two-storey canted bay window. These motifs recur variously in the mid- and late C19 cottages which follow. Set back are the Inchture Village Hall and, near the NE end, the Parish Church aloof in its graveyard (for these, *see* above). Beyond the Primary School (*see* above) is a mid-C19 former LODGE to Rossie Priory (q.v.), the drive now cut through by the A85. Gothic Picturesque, with carved bargeboards and canted bay windows still containing Jacobean paned glazing.

BALLINDEAN HOUSE. See p. 178.
INCHMARTINE HOUSE. See p. 420.
MONCUR CASTLE. See p. 536.

INCHYRA HOUSE
0.5 km. W of Glencarse

Urbane classical villa–country house built *c.* 1810 for an Edinburgh lawyer, John Anderson, whose father had completed the acquisition of the small estate of Inchyra in 1786.

Simple but imposing oblong of two storeys over a half-sunk basement, the front and sides of polished sandstone ashlar, the utilitarian rear of cherry-cock-pointed whinstone rubble. S front of five widely spaced bays. Coupled giant pilasters at the ends; paired Roman Doric three-quarter giant columns marking off the centre whose entrance door has sidelights and an overall segmental-arched fanlight; above, a three-light window. The line of the plinths under the columns and pilasters is continued as a band course under the tall ground-floor windows. Narrower first-floor band course the full width of the front and threaded through the columns and pilasters. The band courses are continued across the house's three-bay sides which also has coupled giant pilasters at the corners. Wallhead cornice surmounted by plinths above the columns and pilasters; balustrades over the intermediate bays of the front, a fluted parapet over the centre and plain parapets at the sides.

The expensively finished INTERIOR is partly of *c.* 1810 and partly of 1956 when *Martyn Beckett* carried out alterations for the diplomat, Sir Frederick Hoyer Millar (later, Lord Inchyra), who had acquired the property the year before. Large ENTRANCE HALL, the ceiling's delicate plaster enrichment of *c.* 1810 with an outer circle set in a square; inner circle enclosing a foliaged rose. Also of *c.* 1810 the simple chimneypiece. The doorcases' pediments are of 1956. At the house's SE corner, the DINING ROOM, its plaster wall panels of 1956, its reeded and rosetted cornice of *c.* 1810. Exceptional late C18 pine and gesso chimneypiece imported in 1956. Pilastered jambs; on the centre of the frieze, shells among which stands the emblematic figure of Hope resting her elbows on an anchor while she contemplates a snarling crocodile. DRAWING ROOM occupying the SW corner of the house, also with plaster wall panels of 1956 and a rosetted cornice of *c.* 1810. The E wall's broken-pedimented doorpiece is of 1956. At the N wall, a white marble chimneypiece, the fluted pilaster jambs topped by reliefs of urns; in the centre panel of the frieze, the relief of a mythological scene. It is probably late C18 and imported in 1956.

Behind the entrance hall is the STAIR HALL, its Late Georgian finishings intact. Simple flying stair. The first-floor level is marked on the walls by a plaster band enriched with reeding and rosettes. Ceiling on pendentives, the flat decorated with two oval bands, the outer rosetted, the inner with Vitruvian scroll enrichment; foliaged rose surrounded by husk swags. Each side of the stair hall, at the ground floor, a round-headed arch into a short passage. The E leads to a D-plan MORNING ROOM, its present character of 1956. Round-headed niches in the curved E corners. Late C18 pine and gesso chimneypiece. At the end of the W passage is the LIBRARY, formed from two rooms in 1956, its E end marked off by a screen of Roman Doric columns *in antis*, the pilasters and columns standing on tall panelled plinths. In the N wall of the main part, a chimneypiece probably of the later C18, with pilastered jambs and urns and swags carved on the frieze.

Behind the house, a piend-roofed rubble-built STABLES courtyard, probably of *c.* 1810. Segmental-arched coachhouse openings. The SE corner has been heightened in the late C19 to form a two-storey house. – N of this, a STEADING, also piend-roofed, built in 1877 for James Watson, then the owner of the estate. At the centre of the S front, a gable containing a tall round-arched doorway. Behind, a broad-eaved FARMHOUSE, probably also of 1877, with bargeboards to the porch and the dormerheads of the upper windows; horizontal-paned glazing.

W of the house, the early C19 WALLED GARDEN, the walls constructed of whin rubble, the E side now buttressed, and lined internally with brick.

LODGE to the SW, contemporary with the house. Single-storey, of polished ashlar, the bowed and pilastered S end displaying a coat of arms. – Pyramid-topped GATEPIERS of polished ashlar and also of *c.* 1810.

INNERPEFFRAY

Church, Library and School forming a small group, Innerpeffray Castle by itself a little to the SSE.

CHURCH OF THE BLESSED VIRGIN MARY. A collegiate church completed in or just before 1507 when John, first Lord

Drummond, provided the endowment for four chaplains. It is a long rectangle, *c.* 24.7m. by 8.2m., rubble-built with a splayed base course and a cavetto wallhead cornice along the N and S sides. Intaken tops at the gables, the W with a chimney. The windows are all rectangular. At the W end of the N wall a small high-set slit stair window. A little to its E, a built-up rectangular door with chamfered jambs. Further E a blocked window. A fair way E of this, another window. Then a roughly arched door to the demolished sacristy and, to its E, a small window (now blocked internally) with a splay to the exterior; it probably served as a squint. High up on the windowless E gable, an ogee-arched image niche. At the E end of the S wall, a rectangular door with cavetto splayed jambs, the soffit of the lintel carved with a shield bearing the Drummond coat of arms. W of this, two large windows, their jambs double-chamfered. A third window is similar but much lower. Next, a rectangular door, its surround with a roll-and-hollow moulding, its lintel again carved with a shield bearing the Drummond coat of arms. Above the door a narrower pointed dummy window or fanlight. W of this door, a pair of low windows very like that to the E of the door but narrower. In the centre of the W gable a door with a roll-and-hollow surround. Immediately above, a large window, its jambs moulded with a double chamfer and a rounded inner order. Small window, its surround chamfered, high up in the gable.

The INTERIOR was originally divided into three unequal-sized compartments. The W bay was a vestibule marked off from the church proper by a round-headed arch, probably filled originally with a wooden screen. In the stub wall S of the arch, a squint into the church. The vestibule's NW corner is occupied by a splayed projection containing the turnpike stair to a small upper room, its W window giving light from outside, its E looking into the church. Simply moulded W fireplace, possibly a replacement of the mid C17 when this part of the building was converted to a library and the room's floor lowered so that it cut across the top of the vestibule's arch. The underside of the floor (i.e. the ceiling of the vestibule) is boarded and painted in tempera with a badly damaged depiction of the sun among clouds; angels were formerly also visible.

The church's two bays E of the vestibule comprised a short square nave. Corbelled out beside the S door is a moulded stoup. Over the S window to the E of the door are a pair of corbels with a third to their E; at the N wall one corbel (in line with the S wall's W corbel) survives. These corbels clearly supported the rood loft over the screen which cut off the nave from the canons' long choir. The choir is well lit from its large S windows which, together with the door to their E, have segmental-headed rear arches, that of the door moulded. Aumbry at the E end of the S wall. – C16 stone ALTAR at the E end of the choir. – Painted CONSECRATION CROSSES, two on the S wall, one on the N and one on the W wall of the vestibule, survive.

At the W end of the church, a MONUMENT to Joanna Murray †1707, wife of James Faichney ('Faichni'), which formerly stood outside in the graveyard. Ambitious but endearingly inept advertisement of the skills of its mason-sculptor. It is a large aedicule but the 'pilasters' are composed of the superimposed figures of Murray's ten children, their names and dates of birth provided by an incised inscription. Above, a heavy moulded cornice which breaks forward at the ends to support statues of a cloaked man and woman, their heads surmounted by large globes decorated with foliage and grapes. On the centre of the cornice, a large shaped panel carved with a wreath containing high-relief figures of a man and woman identified by initials as portraits of James Faichney and Joanna Murray; in the panel's bottom corners, a battlemented tower and a rosette. On top of the panel, the large bust of a woman, her hair combed with rigorous exactitude and falling to a waved fringe. The main panel inside the aedicule contains a coat of impaled arms flanked by JFJM monograms. Above the shield, a pair of trumpeting angels; below, reliefs of a woman's head, a hand holding a book, an hourglass and a skull.

On the N wall of the church, a mid-C17 MONUMENT to Sir James Drummond of Machany †1650 and his wife, Dame Katharine Hamilton, †1638, their coats of arms and the inscription placed in an acanthus-bordered frame whose cornice is surmounted by a skull, its base supported on an angel's head (the soul); lions' heads protrude from the sides. – On the N and S walls, two identical white marble TABLETS, one commemorating the Hon. James Drummond †1799, the other his father, James, Lord Perth, †1800. Each is elegantly lettered and bears an oval panel carved with the Perth crest. – On the N wall, two early C19 HATCHMENTS, one erected on the death of Clementina, Lady Perth, in 1822.

GRAVEYARD. At the S wall, aligned with the church's W end, a couple of C18 HEADSTONES, each carved with an angel's head; the angel on the E stone of 1773 (to William Drummond) blows a trumpet. – Also at the S wall but in line with the E end of the church, the HEADSTONE erected by Andrew Morison, labourer in Cultoquhey, to his children †1793–1817, the top bearing reliefs of a chisel, mallet and setsquare. – Beside it a HEADSTONE, probably C18, carved with a crowned hammer, the emblem of the smiths.

INNERPEFFRAY LIBRARY. Designed by *Charles Freebairn* and built by *John Faichney*, master mason, 1758–62, to house the public library and school endowed in the C17 by David Drummond, third Lord Maderty, the library augmented in the C18 by Robert Hay, Bishop of St Asaph (and later Bishop of Salisbury and Archbishop of York), who had inherited the Innerpeffray estate. Two-storey U-plan, the main block's upper floor much taller than the lower, the lower wings projecting N, all with piended roofs, the walls' harling enlivened by ashlar dressings. Windowless N front, the only openings the doors in the inner faces of the wings. At the main block's S elevation to the churchyard three ground-floor windows linked by a lintel course; large Venetian window to the first floor. The Library occupies the first floor of the main block. Bookcases round the walls; chimneypiece with panelled jambs and a corniced mantel.

SCHOOL. Mid-C19 single-storey school and two-storey schoolhouse. Set into the front wall of the house a scroll-topped early C17 dormerhead bearing the Drummond coat of arms flanked by the initials LM (for Lord Maderty who endowed a school at Innerpeffray in the C17). Curly-topped bellcote over the diagonally set porch of the school.

DOLLERIE HOUSE, 2.3km N. Complex but not especially prepossessing rubble-built small laird's house. Probably begun in the early C18 as a two-storey and attic block, it was extended N in the late C18 with an addition of three storeys but the same height and width. In 1840 an ogee-roofed tower was built at the original house's E front. Then, in 1867, both the original house's part N of the tower of 1840 and the late C18 addition were widened to the E and the original house to the W. Battlement along this new part of the E front whose entrance is placed in a parapeted porch; N of this, a three-light window. Perhaps also of the mid or later C19 is the single-storey and attic wing extending S from the S side of the tower. The second-floor windows of the late C18 N addition were built up in 1928.

INNERPEFFRAY CASTLE
0.5 km. SSE

Roofless but largely intact remains of an austere house of the mid C16. It is a crowstep-gabled L, the jamb projecting to the SW; square stair-tower in the inner angle. Rubble walls with in-and-out quoins. Exceptionally large chimneys on the jamb's gable and the wallhead of the main block; at the walls beneath these chimneys relieving arches mark the positions of the fireplaces at the ground-floor kitchen in the jamb and the first-floor hall in the main block. Slop drains in the N side of the jamb and at the S end of the E side. Small ground-floor windows. Door at the stair-tower, its lintel roll-moulded. Very tall windows to the first-floor hall in the main block, the N window partly built up.

At the main block's NW corner there survives a jamb of the archway which gave access to a courtyard enclosed by a barmkin wall on the house's W side.

INNERWICK

Little more than a place name in Glen Lyon, with just the church and a handful of Victorian cottages and the shooting lodge of Innerwick House nearby.

GLENLYON CHURCH. Originally Innerwick-in-Glenlyon Church. Harled 'Parliamentary' church* (i.e. to *William Thomson*'s design) of 1828. Tudor windows and a spikily pinnacled birdcage bellcote. A porch has been added at the W end of the S front and a door at the front's E end built up, probably in 1898; small vestry at the NE corner, also an addition. Inside, an oak SCREEN of *c*. 1965 across the W end. – PEWS and PULPIT of 1898. – Neo-Romanesque COMMUNION TABLE of 1914, originally in Rosehall United Free (now Priestfield) Church, Edinburgh. – STAINED GLASS E window (St Andrew standing in Glen Lyon and holding a brace of salmon) of *c*. 1960, brightly coloured and realistic. – In a niche in the porch, ST ADAMNAN'S BELL, a square-plan bronze handbell with tapered sides, of *c*. 800.

GLENLYON FREE CHURCH, Camusvrachan, 3.1 km. E. Much altered on its conversion to a house (Cille Fionn) in the later C20. Built in 1847–8, a simple rubble-walled oblong with a Gothic birdcage bellcote on the W gable.

CASHLIE POWER STATION, 9.3 km. SW. Concrete DAM over the River Lyon, designed for the North of Scotland Hydro-Electric Board by *James Williamson & Partners*, 1954–9. To the N, a GENERATING STATION of 1958–9, by *Robert H. Matthew*, the walls of crazy-paved rubble; double-pitch roof.

LUBREOCH POWER STATION, 15.2 km. SW. Across the E end of Loch Lyon, a huge concrete DAM, designed for the North of Scotland Hydro-Electric Board by *James Williamson & Partners*, 1954–7, its sloping E face buttressed; two square towers. It dwarfs the GENERATING STATION of 1956–8, looking very like Cashlie Power Station (*see* above) and also designed by *Robert H. Matthew*.

GALLIN, 5 km. SW. Late C19 steading of rubble-built broad ranges covered with shallow pitched roofs; touches of half-timbering and a cupola.

MEGGERNIE CASTLE. *See* p. 514.

INVER

Hamlet at the confluence of the River Tay and River Braan.

BRIDGE over River Braan. Of rubble, built by *Thomas Clark*, mason in Dunkeld, *c*. 1740. Two segmental arches, with broached triangular cutwaters at the central pier.

INN (now housing). C18 harled U-plan, the main (N) range of five bays, its heavy pilastered doorpiece an addition of the mid C19. Rubble-built NW office range. – To the S, a pair of rubble-walled COTTAGES of the earlier C19.

---

*Built with government finance under An Act for Building Additional Places of Worship in the Highlands and Islands of Scotland (1823). In 1825 the Commissioners for Highland Churches appointed under that act adopted a design for a 'Standard Church'.

RAILWAY VIADUCT over River Braan, 0.3km. w. By *Joseph Mitchell*, 1861–3. Built of ashlar, hammer-dressed at the main walling, stugged at the arch rings and parapets. Segmental arch over the river flanked by battlemented turrets; a small semicircular flood arch at each end. The parapets rise over the centre where they bear the heraldic achievement of the Dukes of Atholl. – Beside the viaduct, a contemporary LODGE, its walls also of hammer-dressed masonry. Baronial, with conical-roofed towers, some jettying of the upper floor and one gable whose canted corners to the ground floor are corbelled out to the square above. Bargeboarded and iron-crested roof. Porch with wooden columns.

THE HERMITAGE. *See* p. 411.

INVERGOWRIE

Sizeable village which developed from the early C19 to house workers at the Bullionfield mill (successively a flax-spinning mill, a bleach works and, from 1846 until its closure in 1965, a paper mill). From the late C19 housing has spilled downhill towards the railway station and the Firth of Tay. It is now a dormitory of Dundee.

CHURCHES

ALL SOULS (Episcopal), Main Street. An Early English miniature cathedral designed by *Hippolyte J. Blanc* and built in 1890–6 by Frances, Lady Kinnaird, as a memorial to her High Church husband whose Episcopalian chapel at Rossie Priory (q.v.) had been closed when his Evangelical brother succeeded him in 1878. Cruciform, with a five-bay nave and low aisles, transepts and crossing tower, semi-octagonal-ended chancel, angle-buttressed SW* porch and a flèche-topped NE hall, all built of red Corsehill sandstone squared rubble, the roof covered with Westmorland slates. Angle buttresses at the corners of the nave and transepts. The chancel, sited away from the road and not easily seen, is severe and cliff-like. Simple detail, with hoodmoulds over the windows, only the label stops of the S aisle carved with the intended foliage. At the W gable, a three-light window with bell-capitalled nook-shafts, its head filled with a cinquefoil flanked by trefoils; vesica in the apex. At the aisles, lancet windows; two-light clearstorey windows with curved triangular heads. A window of the same design and placed at the same level in the each side of the chancel's W bay. The transepts' gable windows are of two lights with traceried heads.

---

*The orientations given here are liturgical. The church's chancel (liturgically E) is really at its S end.

The crossing tower dominates. Angle buttresses with crocketed pinnacles; bestial gargoyles at the parapet. In each face, a large two-light belfry opening flanked by dummy arches, all with bell-capitalled nook-shafts. Rising within the parapet and tied to its corners by flying buttresses is an octagonal stone spire with tall and narrow lucarnes.

INTERIOR clad with red sandstone ashlar, all the label stops and corbels carved with foliage; large panels along the sides of the aisles bear reliefs (executed c. 1900) of STATIONS OF THE CROSS. Parquet floor in the nave. Its arcades' pointed moulded arches are carried on bell-capitalled pillars of quatrefoil section, perhaps in conscious reminiscence of the chapel formed at Rossie Priory by Lady Kinnaird's husband thirty years before. Corbels support the stone vaulting shafts which carry the hammerbeam roof, its collars surmounted by kingposts. Simple monopitch roofs over the aisles whose windows are placed in broad depressed rear-arches; narrow and low pointed arches at the aisles' E end opening into the transepts, the N containing an organ chamber, the S a side chapel. The transepts are covered by open wooden roofs, their braces carried on stone vaulting shafts which rise from corbels, the central shaft of the S transept's E wall stumpy and set immediately above the tabernacle canopy over a stone statue (by *Farmer & Brindley*, 1896) of Our Lord standing on a corbel and holding a sacramental host. In the S wall of this transept, a large cusped-arched piscina, its base formed by a corbel carved with vines and a lamb lying on a cross (a motif taken from the chapel at Rossie Priory).

At the crossing, a square one-bay choir, its tiled floor raised two steps above that of the nave. In each side, a tall pointed arch springing from bundled shafts, the innermost order rising from foliaged corbels. Wooden vaulting with a large centre roundel as if to cover a bell-hole.

The chancel's tile-floored W bay is raised another two steps above the choir, its stone-paved E end by a further three, wooden vaulting carried on stone shafts. One shaft on the S side is carried on a corbel placed above the cusped-arched triple sedilia. At the E end are stumpy shafts rising from corbels which surmount tabernacle canopies over alabaster statues (also by *Farmer & Brindley*, 1896) of the Virgin and St John standing on corbels. In the N splay of the apse, a simple aumbry for the reserved sacrament; in the S splay, a cusped-arched piscina.

Stone FONT at the W end of the N aisle, by *Carnegie & Son*, 1896, a shaft of quatrefoil section with a cushion capital for the bowl. – On the N side of the crossing arch and entered through the wall from the transept, the Gothic PULPIT, also executed by *Carnegie & Son*, from a design by *James Hutton*. – On the S side of the crossing arch, a brass LECTERN. North Italian Baroque, perhaps of c. 1700. – Under the crossing arch, a stone SEPTUM pierced by Gothic arcading. It replaced a screen, c. 1920. – In the choir, oak STALLS, SIDE SCREENS and ORGAN

CASE designed by *Freeman & Ogilvy*, 1912. Lorimerian, embellished with reliefs of flowers and foliage. – Contemporary ORGAN (now largely dismantled) by *John R. Miller*. – Wooden COMMUNION RAIL in the same manner as the septum but of *c.* 1960. – HIGH ALTAR and REREDOS by *Farmer & Brindley*, 1896. The altar is of black marble inlaid with alabaster floral designs and a central cross, the reredos a tall cusped and crocketed arch containing a giant alabaster crucifix placed against a painted cloth background. – The side chapel's ALTAR was made by *Allardice & Napier* in 1865–6 for the chapel at Rossie Priory. Stone front, the central slab of polished Kemnay granite flanked by soapy looking side panels carved with vines in high relief. Mosaic-clad retable, its surmounting marble and mosaic cross a C20 addition.

Former INVERGOWRIE PARISH CHURCH, Station Road. Roofless but substantial remains of a church of *c.* 1500 whose parish was united to Liff and Benvie (Angus) in 1613 but which continued to be used for worship into the C18 and was then taken over as a burial place. Long rubble-walled rectangle (16.2 m. by 6.2 m.), the masonry of both gables intaken at main wallhead level. Remains of a cavetto cornice on the S side's E end. In the W gable (its top now missing), a four-centred arched doorway of the earlier C19, its hoodmould now lost. Towards the W end of the S side, a late medieval round-headed doorway with a chamfered surround. Inside the church, immediately to its E, was a holy water stoup. Towards the E end of this side, a rectangular door, also with a chamfered surround but an insertion, probably of the C17. Immediately W of this door, a badly weathered built-up window, its surround also chamfered; vestiges of cusping show that it had a trefoil head. E of the door and also built up, a rectangular window, probably enlarged in the C17 when it was given a mullion. Near the W end of the N side, a rectangular door (built up) with a chamfered surround, again probably a C17 insertion. Of about the same date the large round-headed doorway (built up) roughly in the centre of this side. This opened into the church from a transeptal N 'aisle' added after the Reformation but remodelled and extended W in the earlier C19 as a mausoleum, its now missing parapet carried on corbels. Tall pointed entrance at the W gable; at the E, a hoodmoulded and pointed dummy window, its blocking decorated in cement with a Gothic glazing pattern. Built into the mausoleum's N wall, a cannon spout.

Immediately S of the church's W end, the large HEADSTONE erected in 1762 by James Witton, wright in Ninewells, to his wife, Elizabeth Nichol, and their children. In the E face's curly top, a relief of the tools of a wright. On the W face, a laudatory inscription placed between an angel's head (the soul) and emblems of death.

INVERGOWRIE PARISH CHURCH, corner of Main Street and Errol Road. Dec with a Scots accent, by *John Robertson* of Inverness, 1906–9, built of hammer-dressed greyish buff stone.

Four-bay nave, with a N aisle and NW tower, a slightly lower chancel at the E end. The battlemented tower dominates. It is of three stages with rounded corners and, at the NE, a taller turret which rises as an octagon above a circular base. At the tower's bottom stage, a pointed W door with fat roll-and-fillet mouldings. Quite small windows at the second stage; very tall belfry openings above. In the W gable of the nave is the principal entrance, a larger version of the tower door, under a four-light window with cinquefoil tracery in its head. Pinnacled buttresses at the nave's outer corners; sloping-topped buttresses mark off the intermediate bays. In the bays of the aisle, trios of pointed lights with, like all the openings, moulded surrounds; large clearstorey windows of cinquefoil shape above. The nave's S side is pierced by tall two-light windows with cinquefoiled heads. In the sides of the chancel, paired pointed windows. E window of three lights under a cinquefoil flanked by loop tracery.

Spacious INTERIOR, a W gallery over the vestibule, the nave covered by an open wooden roof, its collar braces pierced by Gothic arcading, the trusses above also with arcading but their openings are cusped. Depressed arches at the N arcade into the aisle and a tall arch to the chancel which contains the communion table. On the chancel's side walls, the divided ORGAN by *Joseph Brooks & Co.*, *c.* 1900, originally in the former Carnoustie United Presbyterian Church (Angus) and erected here in 1934. – Gothic PULPIT S of the chancel arch, its ogee-arched panels carved with floral decoration. – STAINED GLASS in the aisle's E door. A window of 1906 (the Rev. R. S. Walker Conducting an Open Air Communion Service after the Disruption) originally in the former Longforgan Free Church and moved here in 1945.

HALL at the NE of 1909–11 and also by *Robertson*. Determinedly ecclesiastical, with tall Gothic windows, pinnacled buttresses and an array of apses.

LONGFORGAN FREE CHURCH, Main Street. Now Bullionfield Recreation Hall. Built in 1843–4, a box of stugged masonry with round-headed windows. E aisle, probably an early addition, in the same manner. Projecting from the S gable, a tower added in 1906 by *Thoms & Wilkie*. Plain Romanesque for the most part but with a more expensively detailed belfry-cupola surmounting the truncated pyramid roof.

PUBLIC BUILDINGS

BULLIONFIELD RECREATION HALL. *See* Longforgan Free Church, Churches, above.

INVERGOWRIE PRIMARY SCHOOL, corner of Main Street and Errol Road. By *Duncan D. Stewart*, 1874–5. School and schoolhouse in a tall *cottage orné* manner, with wrought-iron finials on the gables. S addition of *c.* 1910, a forceful parade of steep gables at the S front.

DESCRIPTION

MAIN STREET is aptly if unimaginatively named. At its E end and slightly below road level, No. 1, a late C18 bow-ended toll house. Then, plain late C19 and early C20 housing of one and two storeys, with local authority housing of the early and mid C20 in the streets to the S. Further W, on Main Street's N side, the former Longforgan Free Church (*see* Churches, above) and, at No. 54, its manse of 1849, a consoled pediment over the door. Invergowrie Parish Church and All Souls' Episcopal Church, kept apart by Invergowrie Primary School (*see* Churches and Public Buildings, above), give the village an ecclesiastical centre. W of All Souls' Church and set back from the street, is its former Rectory (No. 63 Main Street) of *c.* 1890, a sizeable broad-eaved villa, its Gothic entrance in a wing whose upper floor is projected on corbelling and finished with carved bargeboards. Contemporary coachhouse to the NW in the same manner. At the W end of Main Street, the single-storey Tudor OLIVEBANK, a former toll house by *David Mackenzie*, 1834. Irregular T-plan with a ball-finialled porch in the SE inner angle, a rectangular bay window at the S gable and a canted bay window at the E; late C20 N addition. A monkey-puzzle tree marks the exit from the village. Off Mill Road to the N, among the housing development of 2003–4 in ALASTAIR SOUTAR CRESCENT, a late C19 square WATER TOWER (now converted to flats) survives from the Bullionfield Paper Mill. It is finished with a top-heavy machicolated parapet with angle rounds.

ERROL ROAD, its housing mostly early C20, leads S from Invergowrie Parish Church and Primary School to Station Road. In STATION ROAD, Nos. 12–14, a harled double house by *William Gauldie*, 1927–8, the N gables of its M-roof supported on paired bay windows. Similar blocks (also by Gauldie, 1924–5) at No. 16 Station Road and Nos. 2–6 STATION CRESCENT but with the outer corners of the gables carried on columns. On the N side of Station Road, BRANTWOOD (No. 13), designed by *James Hutton* for himself in 1900, a red brick two-storey villa which possesses a viewing platform and balcony to enjoy the vista over the Firth of Tay to Fife. Stretching back from it and also by Hutton, *c.* 1895, a single-storey and attic cottage terrace (Nos. 1–5 STATION TERRACE), with canted bay windows, their upper sashes with diamond panes, broad eaves supported on cast-iron brackets, and segmental pediments bracketed out over the dormer windows. At Nos. 11–13 Station Terrace, a late C19 single-storey and attic double villa, canted bay windows supporting the twin-gabled harled and half-timbered upper floor, its windows covered by canopies. Low ogee-roofed tower at the SE corner. Further NE in Station Road, the former Invergowrie Parish Church (*see* Churches, above).

INVERMAY

1.7 km. s of Forteviot

Harled mansion house, built, probably *c.* 1750, for John Belsches, Deputy Sheriff Clerk of Edinburgh. His father, Alexander, Sheriff Clerk of Edinburgh, had bought the estate in 1717. Piend-roofed main block of three storeys above a basement, with a two-storey and basement bowed projection at the back. w front of five bays, the second-floor windows small, the centre slightly advanced and pedimented. Its three-light first-floor window may have been enlarged in 1806 when *Robert Burn* added single-storey and basement bows with tall ground-floor windows to the outer bays of the front and a bowed Roman Doric portico to its centre. Behind the portico, the entrance flanked by sidelights, its general appearance probably of 1806, but the sidelights' pilastered and corniced surrounds seem to be embellishments of *c.* 1900. At the N end of the house, a single-storey and basement addition, also of *c.* 1900, its gable front with a steep pediment containing an oculus. This is set back behind a terrace built over the basement area which was formerly surmounted by a conservatory.

Inside, a mid-C18 stair with turned wooden balusters. In the principal rooms, early C19 decoration spiced up with late C18 revival work of *c.* 1900.

0.2 km. N on the s neck of a promontory formed by a sharp bend in the Water of Invermay is the rubble-built OLD HOUSE OF INVERMAY. This is probably the survivor of a group of buildings which formerly occupied the easily defensible site. Oblong main block, perhaps begun in the late C16 as a two-storey building, the lines of the original wallhead and gables evident in the masonry; windows with chamfered jambs. The house was later raised to three storeys, probably in the earlier C17. At the centre of the s side, a tapering bowed tower, now with a sloping roof; a couple of slit windows on the first floor. Above the entrance has been placed a dormerhead bearing the Drummond coat of arms and the initials of David Drummond of Invermay and his wife, Elizabeth Abercrombie, and the date 1633. NW stair-tower of the late C16 or early C17, with a crow-step-gabled top hamper projected on continuous corbelling. In its E face, a door in a chamfered surround and two dummy gunloops of inverted keyhole type. E of this, a two-storey addition, perhaps C17. At its ground floor, a slit window and a C19 door. Three windows to the upper floor, the centre now blocked, the other two heightened, probably in the early C19, to rise through the eaves. Large E chimney. At this building's w end, a crowstep-gabled coachhouse wing, perhaps of the C18, with a large segmental-arched opening in the gable. Inside, a vaulted ground floor. On the first floor, a fireplace at each end. Above the w fireplace, a fragment of a moulded stone, possibly from a dormerhead.

On the lawn between the old and new houses, a mid-C17 SUNDIAL. It stands on a corniced pillar very like the one supporting the sundial of 1630 at Drummond Castle (q.v.) and, like that example, its faces' raised panels are carved with geometric shapes and hearts. Standing on this pillar, four small balls which support the sundial proper. It is square, each side consisting of two dial faces, the lower sloped outwards, the upper inwards. Above, also supported on small balls, an obelisk, its faces' raised panels showing no evidence of having had gnomons.

0.2 km. S of the mansion house, the early C19 STABLE COURTYARD (HILL OF INVERMAY), now converted to a house. Only the N and W ranges of the intended U were built. Two storeys, the walls of rough ashlar. The W range's W front is of five bays, the broader ends and centre slightly advanced and pedimented. Two-light windows at the end bays; at the centrepiece, three-light windows contained in a segmental-headed overarch. The linking bays' upper windows have been heightened to rise through the moulded eaves cornice and their ground-floor windows converted to doors. Pedimented gables. At this range's E elevation to the courtyard, a slightly advanced and pedimented two-bay centrepiece (off-centre because of the absence of the intended S range) with a pair of elliptically arched coachhouse entrances (built up) under a three-light window. At the E gable, a pilastered and basket-arched overarch with rosetted spandrels.

MAUSOLEUM, 1.3 km. ESE of the mansion house. On the site of the medieval Muckersie Church whose parish was united with Forteviot in 1618. It is a rubble-walled rectangle, now roofless, rebuilt in the mid C19 as a mausoleum. Hoodmoulded and pointed W door. In the E gable, a pair of pointed windows, their external dressings of the C19 but their round-headed rear-arches are possibly medieval as may be much of the gable's stonework. On the inside of this gable, four regularly disposed square recesses looking like putlog holes but not penetrating the wall.

LODGE AND GATES of *c.* 1900, 0.9 km. W of the mansion house. The lodge is harled, with touches of half-timbering and a veranda porch. Rosemary tiled roof. Heavy Neo-Jacobean gatepiers, now with cast-iron horses'-head finials of 1803 moved here from the former entrance to the drive some way to the S.

INVERQUIECH CASTLE
3.3 km. E of Alyth

Fragments of a C13 castle of enclosure, apparently dismantled in the mid C14 and only partly brought back into use later.

The site is a steeply banked promontory bounded by the River Isla on the E, the Burn of Quiech on the SW and a deep natural gully on the N; the W side may have been defended by a ditch. Walling of squared and roughly coursed masonry survives at the castle's obtusely angled NW corner, the N stretch now pierced by a wide-mouthed horizontal gunloop, probably inserted in the early C16 when the Earls of Crawford owned a fortalice or tower here. Two more substantial survivals at the N end of the promontory's E side show that the wall was of at least two storeys in height. In the N of these, remains of a garderobe and its chute. The S has contained a postern gate.

ISLE OF LOCH TAY
0.6 km. W of Kenmore

7040

A well-wooded CRANNOG in Loch Tay on which stands the ruin of a sizeable manor house of *c.* 1500 built for the Campbells of Glenorchy.

The artificial island was formed, perhaps in the early medieval period, by depositing boulders on a natural gravel bank. Joining it to the N shore of Loch Tay is a 100 m.-long causeway *c.* 1.2 m. below the surface of the loch. Reputedly the burial place of Alexander I's queen, Sibilla, it was held by Scone Abbey from the C12 until 1492 when granted by James IV to Sir Duncan Campbell of Glenorchy who, according to the C17 *Black Book of Taymouth*, 'biggit the great hall, chapel, and chalmeris in the Isle of Lochhtay' before his death in 1513.

The island is oval, *c.* 0.7 km. by 0.5 km., with steep rocky banks except at the E end where a sloping beach sheltered from the prevailing wind provides a harbour from which an easy path gives access to a flat-topped NW plateau. This has been enclosed by a barmkin wall, also the work of Sir Duncan Campbell, of which only foundations remain. On the N side and W end of the enclosure, below the level of the plateau, a rubble plinth or retaining wall rises from the shore. Set just back from the plinth's outer N face is the ivy-covered ruin of the HOUSE of *c.* 1500. It is a single long range, the W part *c.* 24.7 m. by 9.5 m., the E part, slightly angled to the S in conformity with the shape of the island, *c.* 18.6 m. by 7.3 m. Rubble-built, of three storeys, the S wall now mostly missing. In the E gable and the adjoining end of the N wall, some small and crudely formed rectangular openings without dressings, probably windows rather than gunloops. At the two upper floors of this end, fairly small windows, also rectangular, with chamfered margins. The presence in the N wall of gunloops which had been blocked internally was noted in the 1930s* but these are now hidden by ivy. Immediately S of the house's W gable the plinth is cut through by a path from the rocky shore and the remains of a small square building project from the line of the barmkin wall beside the path; probably there was a postern gate here.

Internally, the house seems to have been divided into distinct sections, each apparently entered from the courtyard to

---

*By William A. Gillies, *In Famed Breadalbane* (1938), 407.

the s. At the E end, a section apparently containing one room on each floor, the ground floor probably a store with a door and a hatch in its w wall. These opened into the ground floor of what was probably the section containing the hall, probably placed above stores. In the N wall's E end, the sill of a ground-floor window survives. No evidence of a fireplace or flue which presumably was contained in the missing s wall. In the section w of this, the foundation of a cross wall shows that it contained two ground-floor rooms, probably stores, and probably one or two rooms on each of the upper floors. No evidence now of fireplaces. In the house's w section, remains of a large w fireplace in the ground floor room which seems to have been the kitchen.

SE of the house, an irregular polygonal-sided rubble-walled PIT, perhaps a (blocked) well or for storage.

JORDANSTONE
2.9 km. SE of Alyth

C18 laird's house overwhelmed by Neo-Georgian additions of the 1890s and 1920s, the interior a display of wealthy good taste.

The house is all of two storeys, basement and attic, the walls harled, with red sandstone dressings and rusticated quoins. In the middle is the late C18 house, whose s front is of three bays, the centre slightly advanced under a pediment, its tympanum containing a dummy oculus, its ends and apex surmounted by urns. The entrance, originally flanked by sidelights, was altered to a glazed screen in 1928–9 by *Lorimer & Matthew* who added the glass-roofed veranda across the ground floor. Pedimented dormer windows, probably also of the 1920s. The rear elevation is utilitarian except for a round-headed and keystoned stair window.

The first addition, at the E end, was designed by *J. Murray Robertson* and built in 1895 for James Archibald Duncan who had acquired the estate after making a fortune as a merchant in Dundee and New York. L-plan, the broad sw limb projecting slightly in front of the original house's s elevation, its façade with a ball-finialled overall pediment pierced by an oval window. At each of the ground and first floors, a large three-light window above a sill course, the upper window flanked by square panels carved with coats of arms. The NE jamb's E gable is also finished with a ball-finialled pediment. Projecting from it, a two-storey and basement canted bay window. In the inner angle, an ogee-roofed round tower.

The second principal addition, at the house's w end, was designed by *Lorimer & Matthew* and built for James (later, Sir James) A. L. Duncan in 1928–9. Again it is L-plan but with its small NE jamb tucked away at the back of the house. The main block's s front is almost a twin of that of Robertson's addition but slightly and disconcertingly narrower and with an oculus instead of an oval opening in the pediment. Plain elevations to the w; splayed across the inner angle with the jamb, a Doric portico in front of the house's new main entrance. Also of 1928–9 is the addition at the rear of Robertson's NE jamb.

INTERIOR. Lorimer & Matthew's entrance opens into a vestibule, also of the 1920s and covered with a groin-vaulted plaster ceiling. In the E wall, a blocky stone door surround carved with the initials of James A. L. Duncan and Adrienne G. St Quintin, his wife. Entering from this door, the outer hall* formed by Lorimer & Matthew in the NW corner of the C18 house. N of the outer hall, the BOUDOIR in the NE jamb of the 1920s addition. Walls covered with oak woodwork except for a walnut panel above the green marble chimneypiece and three panels formerly filled by landscape paintings (removed in 2004). Built-in bookcases decorated with small reliefs of fruit and birds carved by *Scott Morton & Co*. Also opening off the outer hall and filling the main block of the 1920s extension is the DRAWING ROOM. Elaborate plaster ceiling, the beams and cornice enriched with floral ornament, the compartments of the flat with exaggeratedly large simplified roses placed between reliefs of flowers and birds. Large but simple marble chimneypiece in a late C17 manner.

s of the outer hall and entered through a wide rectangular archway, the HALL formed in the 1920s by throwing together the C18 entrance hall and the room to its w (a library in the 1890s). At its w side, a large stone chimneypiece, its hood carved with the coat of arms of the Duncans of Jordanstone. Off the E end of its N side, the C18 principal staircase, quite unpretentious and rather small for the house after its remodelling in the 1890s and 1920s. E of the hall, a corridor formed in the 1890s. Off its s side, the BUSINESS ROOM occupying the SW corner of the Georgian house, its late C18 pine and gesso chimneypiece decorated with classical motifs probably imported in the late C19 or early C20. E of this, the 1890s DINING ROOM, with a simple compartmented ceiling and high painted wooden dado. Expensive white marble chimneypiece with Ionic pilasters. At the ends of its fluted frieze, panels carved with putti, one holding a spear, the other a bow. Swagged central panel, also with a relief of putti but here they are cavorting. Is this of the 1890s or the 1920s? N of the corridor's bowed E end, in the 1890s NE jamb, Robertson's BILLIARD ROOM, its ceiling and dado (here of unpainted pine) like those of the dining room. In the N wall, a broad opening to the 1920s LOUNGE which occupies the ground floor of Lorimer & Matthew's NE addition. This is lower than the billiard room and dominated by a stone chimneypiece bearing the date 1929 and, in the spandrels of the segmental-arched fireplace opening, reliefs of pheasants. On the first floor, rather small bedrooms and a few bathrooms of the 1890s and 1920s.

---

*The room names used in this description are those shown on Lorimer & Matthew's plans.

In the SW bedroom, a stone chimneypiece of 1895, its frieze carved with oak branches.

KEILLOUR CASTLE
5 km. ENE of Fowlis Wester

Tall villa of Rhineland inspiration, by *Andrew Heiton Jun.*, 1877, built of bullnosed red sandstone masonry. S-facing main block, its W half of three storeys, with bracketed broad eaves through which the top-floor windows rise into piended dormerheads. It is fronted to the S by a sloping-roofed two-storey bow window on a boldly battered base; jerkin-head gable on this block's W side. The block's E half is carried up for a further storey under a pavilion roof. At the NE corner, a conical-roofed round tower containing the shouldered-arched entrance. Lower wings, also with bracketed broad eaves and jerkin-head gables, project to the N.

KEITHICK
1.1 km. N of Burrelton and Woodside

Villa-country house designed by *David A. Whyte* and built for a Perth physician, Dr James Wood, in 1818–23. Its walling of droved red sandstone ashlar, the house is an irregular composition of piend-roofed blocks, most with bracketed broad eaves and those containing the main rooms tied round with string courses. Each contains a discrete set of rooms, the ground floor's principal apartments distinguished by tall windows. Two-storey NW block containing the entrance hall, principal stair and drawing room. N front of five bays, the ends slightly advanced, with segmental-headed overarches to the ground-floor windows (the W a dummy) and horizontal panels on the first floor. Dummy ground-floor windows flank the central semicircular porch which has rather the appearance of a bowed screen, with closely set paired Greek Doric columns at the front and pilasters at the back corners. The door was moved from the back of the porch to the front and the spaces between the columns filled with windows in *David Bryce*'s alterations of 1839. Also of 1839 the pedimented dormer windows. Projecting from this block's W side, a flat-roofed and parapeted large single-storey bow pierced by three windows; a single light above.

The house's second element is a big three-storey tower containing the library. It projects from near the W end of the NW block's S front. Two-bay W elevation. Splayed S front of three bays, the centre with a French window at the ground floor and a horizontal stone panel in place of a window at the second floor. E of this tower and built against most of the E three-fifths of the NW block's S side is a third block which contains the dining room. Two storeys, the front of three bays. Another pedimented dormer window was added here in 1839.

E of the principal parts of the house and set back from both their N and S elevations, a short and low narrow-eaved two-storey block originally containing pantries at the ground floor and a nursery and bathroom above. Another dormer window of 1839 at its S front. Built across its E end and projecting minimally to the N and more forcefully to the S, a tower-like three-storey block which contained the housekeeper's room and servants' hall with the night nursery and bedrooms above. Bracketed broad eaves but no string course.

At the E end of the house, a service court, its S and E ranges with bracketed broad eaves to their piended roofs. The principal (N) front is of five bays, the walling carried up as a screen to suggest an upper floor. Round-headed archway at the slightly advanced broad centre. One long horizontal panel above each pair of flanking windows (the E dummies).

INTERIOR. The N porch was remodelled in 1839 when Bryce provided its door and cupboards. Spacious oblong ENTRANCE HALL to its S, the plaster frieze enriched with gryphons and garlands. On its E side, segmental arches, the N replacing a columned screen, the small S arch marking the former site of a short passage whose N wall was removed by *Maclaren, Soutar & Salmond* in 1926. This wall had abutted the bottom flight of the flying stair whose cast-iron balustrade is decorated with ovals containing acorns.

W of the entrance hall, the bow-ended DRAWING ROOM whose painted decoration by *G. Morant*, probably of 1839, makes it a delight. This is executed in an Italianate C18 manner, the colours of a pastel palette. On the walls, large panels intended to contain mirrors or pictures. Between them, narrow vertical panels painted with tall candle-like stalks of delicate stylized flowering foliage issuing from Neoclassical vases or pedestals, some held aloft by feminine angels. Over the S doors, oblong panels, their floriated borders framing roundels containing depictions of cherubs at play. Cavetto cornice enriched with gilded naturalistic flowering foliage. On the flat of the ceiling, over the oblong main part of the room, a leafy plaster rose surrounded by a painted open umbrella whose spokes extend to a broad oblong border embellished with stylized foliage and husk swags. Over the room's W bow, a painted fan with foliaged long thin spokes. The white marble chimneypiece, probably a replacement of 1839, is carved in high relief with bunches of flowers and a flower basket on the ends and centre of its fluted frieze.

To the S, entered through a walnut-veneered door, the LIBRARY, its S end a canted bay. Acanthus-leaf cornice. Rather small Late Georgian classical chimneypiece of white and liver-coloured marble, its frieze's centre panel carved with the relief of an urn, its ends with rosettes. Birch bookcases finished with concave cornices. Large DINING ROOM to the E. Two-tier cornice (egg-and-dart under acanthus leaf) under the cove of the ceiling. Simple Tudorish chimneypiece of grey marble veined with gold. Broad elliptical arch to the sideboard recess at the E end.

On the s lawn in front of the house, an early C19 stone SUNDIAL copied from a C17 example at Stobhall (q.v.). The shaft, banded by an angular stone bearing dial faces and the coat of arms of the Collins-Woods of Keithick, supports a cubical finial, its faces hollowed for dials; ball finial.

WALLED GARDEN, 100m. NW, of *c.* 1825, the masonry of rough ashlar. Cast-iron s gate with quatrefoil panels. – Immediately W, STABLES, also of *c.* 1825. Two-storey s front of cherry-cock-pinned rough ashlar. Seven bays, the ends slightly advanced and pedimented, the first-floor windows E of the centre heightened in the mid or later C19. The broad centrepiece is a pyramidal-roofed tower. At the lower stage, a pair of coachhouse doors in an elliptical overarch. Above, a doocot with a trio of round-headed entries for the birds. On the outer face of the stables' w range, a round horsemill.

LODGES at the N and s ends of the drive, both of *c.* 1825. Single-storey, built of droved ashlar and with broad eaves. At each side, fronting the drive, a piended gable in which the entrance is recessed behind octagonal pillars of primitive Doric type. At the s lodge and contemporary with it, squat corniced ashlar GATEPIERS.

KELTIE CASTLE
1.6 km. SW of Dunning

Pleasingly unpretentious three-storey and attic rubble-built laird's house built, *c.* 1500, for the Bonars of Keltie but extended and altered in later centuries.

The original building seems to have been a simple oblong, the entrance perhaps at the first floor on the W side. At the SE corner, a second floor rectangular turret projected on continuous corbelling. From this first period of construction survive also one inverted keyhole gunloop at the ground floor of the E side and another in the S gable.

The first major alteration, perhaps in 1686 (the date on a door lintel inside), was the addition of a NW wing with a stair tower in the inner angle. Further work was carried out in 1712, the date carved on the lintel of an enlarged or inserted ground floor E window together with the initials of John Drummond of Keltie, whose uncle had acquired the estate twenty years earlier, and those of his wife. This work probably included the thickening of the main block W to the line of the C17 stair tower whose presence is disclosed externally by tiny W windows. The first floor W window of the extension has rounded jambs like those in the wing's S side; perhaps they are reused. Possibly at the same time, the original upper windows of the main block's E side were built up and new openings inserted to produce a regular three-bay elevation but the present large first floor windows here are of *c.* 1820.

Also of *c.* 1820 may be the small pinnacled finials on the steps of the s gable and on the skewputts of the wing's w gable. A pair of dormer windows were added to the E side *c.* 1920.

Of the same date is the pointed door (replacing a rectangular entrance) to the wing. Above it, the (renewed) frame for an armorial panel. It now contains a pedimented dormer head, the top enriched with scrollwork and with rosette-finialled stalks at the ends.

Interior mostly of *c*. 1920 but, in the thickness of the E wall, remains of a stair, presumably of *c*. 1500, which rose from the ground to the first floor.

KELTNEYBURN

Mill, smithy and monument beside the bridge over the eponymous burn.

BRIDGE over the Keltney Burn. Lattice-girder bridge constructed in 1896.

MONUMENT. Stone statue of Major-General David Stewart of Drumachary and Garth in the uniform of a Highland regiment; by *H. S. Gamley*, 1924.

MILL AND SMITHY. Picturesquely informal group of mill, smithy and housing, probably early C19 but extended in 1859, perhaps the date of the mill's wavily bargeboarded kiln ventilator and jerkin-headed gables.

ACHLOA, 1 km. SW. Two-storey rubble-built steading of the earlier C19, with Gothic windows to the upper floor. At the roofless central range, a gabled centrepiece containing the Gothic entrance.

COMRIE COTTAGE, 0.9 km SE. Set below the road, a two-storey cottage of *c*. 1830, its Gothic first floor windows with gablet dormerheads. Latticed glazing.

COMRIE FARM, 0.7 km. SSE. Mid-C19 rubble-built group. At the W, a detached farmhouse with broad eaves and gablet dormerheads. L-plan steading (now housing) of two tall storeys. At its NW corner, a tower with carved bargeboards.

RUSTIC LODGE, 2.1 km. S. Built in 1840–1 at the end of a path from Newhall Bridge (*see* Taymouth Castle, q.v.) to Drummond Hill. Single-storey and picturesque. Rubble-walled main block extending back into the hillside. Across its S end, a large tree-trunk portico, the uprights supporting the wavy eaves of the piended roof.

FORT, Dun MacTual, 1.4 km. S. On a rocky knoll rising from the slope of the forested Drummond Hill, remains of an Iron Age fort, probably of the first millennium B.C. The site's roughly oblong summit, *c*. 91 m. by 64 m., is enclosed by a wall, *c*. 2.74 m. thick at the base but with a marked batter on the inner face. It may have risen to a height of *c*. 4 m. A curved wall extending NE from the main fortification encloses a relatively narrow annexe, *c*. 50 m. long, the steep fall of the ground to its E apparently obviating the need for a wall on this side. Outside the W side of the main enclosure, a pair of curved walls provide further defence across the easiest route to the summit.

GARTH CASTLE. *See* p. 379.

KELTYBRIDGE

Small village extending N from the Kelty Burn.

DESCRIPTION. At the s end is the small rubble BRIDGE over the Kelty Burn, built by *John Bachop* in 1696. A single round-headed arch over which are elliptically curved parapets. Immediately E, a few late C20 bungalows along the side of the burn. The main street runs almost due N. On its w side and set below the road level, the mid-C19 BRIDGE HOUSE with gableted dormers. On the E, at right angles to the street, the early C19 BURNSIDE, its walling constructed of cherry-cocked rough ashlar, the roofs now covered with concrete pantiles. Behind and parallel to Burnside is a pair of crowstep-gabled houses. The W, built of rough ashlar, is mid C19. At the rubble-walled E house, the door lintel is inscribed with the initials PR and EB and the date 1751, a likely date for the house's construction. To the N, a U-plan group of pantile-roofed C18 and C19 cottages (Nos. 17–27). No. 17 in the s range is dated 1777, No. 19 facing the road bears the date 1808 but both have mid-C19 window surrounds. Further out, on the w side of the road, a pair of early C19 houses (No. 14 and Nos. 18–20), both of two storeys with pantiled roofs. At No. 14, widely spaced crowsteps at the W gable and small gableted dormerheads (perhaps additions) over the upper windows. Moulded skewputts at the E gable of Nos. 18–20.

Standing by itself to the N of the village is the late C18 MIDDLETON HOUSE. Two storeys and an attic which is lit only from tiny windows in the gables. Rubble-built with rusticated quoins and a band course under the eaves. The gabled stone porch is a mid-C19 addition. Single-storey rear wing with a pantiled roof.

BLAIR ADAM. *See* p. 203.

KENMORE

Picturesque estate village at the E end of Loch Tay, sitting just outside the parkland of Taymouth Castle.

CHURCH AND PUBLIC BUILDINGS

KENMORE PARISH CHURCH, The Square. Built in 1760, perhaps to a design by *William Baker* of Cheshire who a year earlier had received 6 guineas from the Earl of Breadalbane, the sole heritor of the parish, 'for plans of a Kirk', but the design was modified by *Paterson*, builder (probably *George Paterson*). It is cruciform, with an E tower. Gabled Victorian porch, perhaps of 1870, in the SE inner angle. Harled walls, with ashlar strip quoins at the corners. Simple round-headed windows, their wooden mullions and tracery inserted in 1870; in the S transept's window, much more delicate tracery of

1923–4 by *J. Jeffrey Waddell & Young* executing a scheme prepared in 1916 by *P. Macgregor Chalmers*. High up in the gable of each transept, a vesica light. At the W end of the nave's S side, a round-arched C18 door under a large circular window, perhaps inserted or altered in 1870. C18 pointed minister's door in the S transept's W side. The skews and cross finials on the gables and the roof cresting all date from 1870; originally the roofs were piended.

The tower is of three stages marked off by unmoulded string courses. At the bottom stage, a round-arched E window; in the N face, a round-arched door but its roll-and-hollow moulding looks like work of 1923–4. Low second stage, a round window in each exposed face. Tall belfry, heightened in 1870, with round-headed openings, the E containing a clock made by *John Peatt* in 1781–2. The battlement's pinnacles were removed in 1950.

Inside, coombed plaster ceilings, strengthened by hammer-beam supports of 1870 which intersect over the crossing. At the E end of the nave, a Victorian Gothic gallery, probably of 1870, supported on cast-iron columns with stiff-leaf capitals. The W bay of the nave is divided off by a pointed arch, again probably of 1870, its hoodmould's label stops carved with foliage. This bay formerly contained the Breadalbane Gallery but it was removed in 1923–4 by J. Jeffrey Waddell & Young who filled the bay's lower part with simple oak panelling sparingly ornamented with Gothic detail and placed the organ above. – Victorian PEWS. – 'Chancel' FURNISHINGS (PULPIT, LECTERN, READING DESK, MINISTER'S AND ELDERS' SEATS and COMMUNION TABLE) all of 1923–5, in a simple Arts and Crafts manner with sparing use of Gothic and Celtic detail. – Small Early Christian FONT, also of the 1920s. – ETCHED GLASS in the chancel's N and S windows (Scenes of Local Life and Christian Symbols) by *Anita Pate* of *Glass from Vitrics*, 1990–1 and 1999. – STAINED GLASS. The N transept's strongly coloured N window (St Columba and a Knight) is by the *Abbey Studio*, 1947. – Much more effective the S transept's S window (David and St John the Baptist) by *William Wilson*, 1970. – Paler but also of quality a window in the N side of the nave (St John the Divine, the Good Shepherd) by *Herbert Hendrie*, 1947.

GRAVEYARD. At the E entrance, a LYCHGATE, its sides of stone and wood, the roof of red tiles, erected *c.* 1905 as a memorial to Queen Victoria. – HEADSTONES. Most are Victorian or C20 and routine but a fair number survive from the C18 and early C19. A little W of the church, a round-headed stone to Christa Tindle †1784, daughter of Charles Tindle, overseer at Taymouth. On the W face, an angel's head (the soul) above fluted pilasters which frame a relief of dividers under a pot of foliage; emblems of death at the bottom. – To its N, an early C19 segmental-pedimented stone to Alexander MacDougall, the W face displaying a large coat of arms. – Some way N of that, a couple of early C19 stones, both pilastered aedicules framing coats of arms and with angels' heads in their swan-neck pediments. One (to David McGrigor) is of 1814 and fairly crude, the other, much larger and more accomplished, is of 1820 and commemorates John MacGregor. – Similar but exceptionally well-preserved stone of 1813 to Archibald Marquis, the carving in quite high relief, some way to the E. – Near the W end of the graveyard, a small headstone to John Crerar, fowler to the Earl of Breadalbane, †1781, the W face carved with a gun, powder flask, etc. – Almost at the W wall, the headstone of James Campbell, Minister of Kenmore, and his wife, both †1780. Double-arched top. On the W face, a pair of angels' heads above an open Bible; symbols of death at the bottom. – Quite a number of Georgian headstones S of this. – Lying on the ground at the graveyard's SW corner, a small stone, probably of the earlier C18, its face carved in exceptionally high relief with folk art depictions of an angel's head above a skull, hourglass, coffin, crossbones and the inscription MEMENTO MORI; below, a sock and coulter, so presumably this commemorates a farmer.

BRIDGE over the River Tay. By *John Baxter Jun.*, 1771–4. Humpbacked, built of rubble (formerly harled), with ashlar dressings. The three main arches are elliptical, the spandrels pierced by large circular openings to allow flood water to pass through; low triangular cutwaters. At each splayed-out end a smaller round-headed arch; three utilitarian flood-water arches to the N.

LIBRARY, The Square. Now in other use. Built in 1884–5; according to *The Architect* it was designed by *Alma, Countess of Breadalbane*.* Symmetrical but picturesque. Bargeboard-gabled centrepiece, a round window above a canted bay window whose roof's red fish-scale tiles are repeated at the tree-trunk verandas wrapped round the building's front and ends. Red tile ridge to the main roof, a small ventilator-flèche over the centre.

VILLAGE HALL, The Brae. Now a shop. Built in 1902. A tall single-storey building with prominent gables, one with a central buttress. Mullioned and transomed windows, pointed doors; a flèche on the roof.

DESCRIPTION

ABERFELDY ROAD enters from the S. On its E side, two blocks of traditionally detailed harled housing of 1955–6. At the foot of THE BRAE, on the W, the former Village Hall (*see* Church and Public Buildings, above). On The Brae's E side, a harled cottage terrace, probably C18 in origin but heightened and given wallhead dormers in the mid C19. At the top of the street, on the W, an unaltered C18 survivor with small windows and moulded skewputts.

---

* *The Architect*, xxxi, 270.

THE SQUARE epitomizes the planned village of C18 and C19 Scotland. At the E end, the gates opening to the approach to Taymouth Castle (q.v.); at the W end, Kenmore Parish Church (*see* Church and Public Buildings, above). In the centre of the N side, the harled KENMORE HOTEL, begun in 1773 as a three-storey five-bay block but given an attic with two large front gablets and carved bargeboards in 1857 when the slightly lower W wing was added or remodelled. Behind, C18 stables and a piend-roofed coachhouse, its doorways elliptically arched. W of the hotel, a single-storey harled cottage, the small windows suggesting an C18 origin but the lattice-sided porch and bracketed broad eaves are mid-C19 embellishments. The house to its W and those occupying the W two-thirds of The Square's S side are probably also of C18 origin but all heightened and given gabled wallhead dormers and latticed porches in the mid C19. E of the hotel, the former library (*see* above). Opposite, at the E end of the S side, AM FASGADH and THE GATEHOUSE, a two-storey block of 1875. Carved bargeboards to the gables and the gablets of the first-floor windows; a battlemented canted bay at the E end. The main road exits from the NW corner of The Square, jinking round the churchyard's side before running N towards the bridge over the Tay (*see* Church and Public Buildings, above). Just before the bridge, set back on the W, is THE ORPHANAGE, a harled late C18 building of one storey and an attic.

MAINS OF TAYMOUTH, 0.4km. N. Late C19 courtyard STEADING (now in other use), the rubble-built ranges dressed up with gables and bargeboards. Principal entrance from the W through a round-headed pend arch above which a tower rises to a gabled wooden bell house. To the N, a contemporary tall WATER TOWER, the battered rubble sides surmounted by a corbelled parapet topped by iron cresting. A second tower to the S, originally of the same design but now without its cresting. – To the W, between the A827 and Loch Tay, a rubble WALLED GARDEN formed in 1835 to serve Taymouth Castle (q.v.) but now choked with housing. In the S side, an agreeably crude Gothic gateway, much like the Kenmore Gate to Taymouth Castle.

PORTBANE, 0.9km. SW. Rubble-built cottage of the earlier C19 with small-paned windows, broad eaves and elaborately carved bargeboards to the gables and dormerheads.

RUSTIC LODGE, 1.2km. W. Built *c.* 1840 at an entrance to a walk along the S side of Drummond Hill, it is set into a niche carved out of the hillside and backed by battlemented boulder-built retaining walls. Battlemented Gothic folly with a round tower at the W end, all faced with craggily projecting boulders. In front, a retaining wall and round piers in the same manner.

CRANNOG, Scottish Crannog Centre, 0.5km. SW. Reconstruction of 1994–7 by the Scottish Trust for Underwater Archaeology of the likely appearance of the crannog of the earlier first millennium B.C. excavated at Oakbank, Fearnan, near

Fortingall, on the N side of Loch Tay. It consists of oak uprights which rise from the floor of the loch to support a circular platform on which stands a roundhouse, its walls of wattle, the conical roof thatched with reeds. Joining the platform to the shore is a wattle-sided bridge carried on oak uprights.

STONE CIRCLE, Croftmoraig, 3.1 km. NE. Double circle of standing stones erected in the third or second millennium B.C. on the site of an earlier setting of wooden posts whose former existence was discovered by excavation. The inner 'circle', really a rough oval, c. 6.09 m. by 7.62 m., consists of eight boulders (one fallen) all standing 1.4 m.–1.6 m. high and graded in height with an alternation of slightly higher and slightly lower stones. The NW face of a stone in the oval's NE segment is carved with a small group of cup-marks. The surrounding second circle, c. 12.2 m. in diameter and apparently erected later, is composed of nine massive stones, 2.15 m.–2.75 m. high. Just outside this outer circle are remains of a roughly circular stone bank edged with an outer kerb which survives at the SE segment. The bank may be contemporary with the first circle of standing stones. In the SW segment of the bank lies a long stone whose upper face is carved with twenty-three cup-marks. Outside the bank's ESE segment, a pair of massive stones standing 2.18 m. and 2.28 m. high, probably erected at the same time as the outer circle.

ISLE OF LOCH TAY. *See* p. 435.
TAYMOUTH CASTLE. *See* p. 717.

KETTINS

Small village on the edge of the Hallyburton House estate.

KETTINS PARISH CHURCH, Newtyle Road. Georgian kirk with Victorian additions.

The body of the church is a red sandstone rubble-walled oblong designed by *William Mitchell*, mason in Coupar Angus, built in 1767–8. It was repaired and probably altered by *Peter Brown* in 1790–1.* The principal (S) elevation is of six bays. In the end bays, a double tier of segmental-headed windows. In the next bays, large round-headed windows with projecting keystones and imposts, their Y-tracery probably introduced in the 1870s. In each of the two centre bays, a smaller round-headed window under a dummy oculus. High up at the centre, a shield bearing the date 1768. Cast-iron rhone decorated with arcading and with hoppers in the form of griffons; they probably date from 1878 when *John Carver* repaired the roof. Above the gutter, an C18 cavetto cornice which is returned across the gables as the base of their pediments. In each pediment, a seg-

---

*A report of 1789 by *James McLeran* had recommended rebuilding the front wall and heightening the building by c. 0.6 m.

mental gallery window. Below, a Venetian window lighting the area under the gallery.

The N side of the church is mostly Victorian. In each end bay, a round-headed upper window and a lower of two elliptically arched lights, probably of 1870–1 when *John Carver* added the N jamb. In the jamb's gable, a pair of close-set elliptically arched ground-floor windows and three round-headed windows above. On the gable, a polished granite MONUMENT to the Rev. James Fleming, by *Robert S. Lorimer*, 1914. Inscription tablet decorated with a few flowers. Double-lugged frame carved with rosettes and surmounted by a steep pediment, its tympanum with the Burning Bush emblem of the Church of Scotland in high relief. In the E inner angle of the jamb, a porch, also of 1870–1. The steeple in the W inner angle was built to *Alexander Johnston*'s design in 1893. Tower of three stages, its walling of coursed squared masonry from Leys Quarry, the openings round-headed and hoodmoulded, the belfry marked off by a string course and with large paired lights. Parapet carried on simple moulded corbels. Inside it there rises an octagonal stone spire studded with small lucarnes and finished with a wrought-iron weathervane.

Inside, a plaster elliptical tunnel vault with applied ribs which spring from a cornice decorated with foliaged panels and with a couple of fleur-de-lys ventilator openings, all this looking of the earlier C19. Semi-octagonal pine GALLERY of 1870–1, the front panelled with round-headed blind arcading. At its centre, a clock made by *James Ivory* in 1769. PULPIT, also of 1870–1 and with round-headed blind arcading, the brackets under the lectern carried on Gothic attached columns; round-headed back covered in buttoned velvet. In front, a Gothic COMMUNION TABLE of 1923.

STAINED GLASS. The four windows at the centre of the S wall (Hope and Faith, flanked by scenes of the Annunciation to the Shepherds, the Baptism of Our Lord, the Resurrection and Ascension) are all Glasgow style of 1878, perhaps by *Stephen Adam* who improved them in 1908 'by putting in better glass and touching up the figures and borders'. – At this wall's W end under the gallery, a window (the Presentation of Our Lord in the Temple) by *A. Ballantine & Gardiner*, 1892–3. Like the rest of the glass in the church it is in a colourful narrative manner. – Gallery window (Dorcas) of 1900. – At the E end of the S wall under the gallery, a window (Our Lord Blessing Little Children) by *James Ballantine & Son*, 1891. – Contemporary gallery window (Our Lord Bearing the Cross), also by Ballantine & Son. – In the W gable under the gallery, another window (the Good Samaritan, flanked by figures of the Sower and the Reaper) by Ballantine & Son, 1891. – Contemporary gallery window (Our Lord as Judge) by the same artists. – The E gable's window under the gallery (the Last Supper) is by Ballantine & Gardiner, 1892, its gallery window (the Agony in the Garden) by Ballantine & Son, 1891. – In the N wall, two windows (the Parable of the Talents; the Maries at the Tomb) of 1892–3 by Ballantine & Gardiner. – In the vestry in the N jamb, two lights (the Calling of St Peter and St Andrew; the Holy Family with Simeon in the Temple) of 1913.

GRAVEYARD. At the E entrance, a LYCHGATE of 1902 by G. H. *Fowler Jones* of York, that city's demolished buildings the source of the oak of its superstructure; roof covered with Staffordshire tiles. Immediately E of the church, a badly weathered late medieval red sandstone octagonal FONT BOWL standing on the shaft, also octagonal, of the former MARKET CROSS of Kettins which may be C17. Immediately W of the church, its former BELLCOTE which was removed in 1893. Of birdcage type with coupled piers and a weathervane in the form of a flag pierced by the date 1768. It contains a BELL decorated with a band of fleur-de-lys enrichment and a Flemish inscription recording that it was given to MARIA TROON (i.e. the convent of Maria Troon at Grobendonck near Antwerp) in 1519 by *Hans Popen Ruider*, a gun founder of Mechlin (Malines), who presumably cast it.

Good number of HEADSTONES and GRAVE-SLABS of the C17, C18 and early C19. A little W of the church, the stone of 1737 to David Howleson, gardener at Hallyburton, with a mantled helm over a shield carved with a gardener's tools. – To its E and immediately NW of the bellcote, the stone erected by John McDougall, cooper, to his daughter †1797. On the W face, an angel's head (the soul) above the relief of dividers and a cooper's hammer; skulls and crossbones at the bottom. – SW of the church, another C18 stone with an angel's head at the top and emblems of death at the bottom. In the middle, a mantled helm and shield flanked by torches. – By the graveyard's S wall, a little W of the church, two slabs. One, erected by James Fyfe to his wife, Elspeth Jack †1684, bears a crudely executed low relief of crossbones, a skull and hourglass. On the other, to Anton Ramsay †1700 and his wife, Janet Small, the relief of a skull and a bones and the inscription:

THIS.HONEST.MAN.IS.FROM.VS.GONE.
WHOSE.BODY.LYES.WITHIN.THIS.TOMB.
HIS.HONEST.REPVTATION.SHALL.
REMAIN.TO.GENERATIONS.ALL.
HIS.BLESSED.SOVL.FOR.EVERMORE.
DOTH.MAGNIFY.THE.KING.OF.GLORE.

To its NE, a headstone of 1778 erected by Patrick Forbes to his wife, Elizabeth Och. Swan-neck pediment with an angel's head above a frame of drapery containing a mantled helm and a shield carved with the initials of Forbes and his wife; crossbones, skull and hourglass at the bottom. – A little to its E, the stone of 1781 commemorating Thomas Souttar and his wife, Agnes Petrie. Aedicular W face with ball-finialled attached columns under an open pediment. Within this frame, a relief of two pudgy trumpet-wielding angels above a skull and bone; at the base, a panel with hourglasses and a gravedigger's tools in high relief. – Some way to the E, the stone erected by James Balardie, miller, to his father, John, a tailor, †1735 and mother, Helen Stubbles, the W face bearing a shield incised with shovels, the E with another shield incised with a tailor's goose, shears, etc. under the very shallow relief of an angel's head. – S of the church, in the graveyard's E section, a large stone erected in 1812 to Alexander Heron, brewer in Inchture and Forgan, its W face with an angel's head above a shield which displays barley sheaves flanking a brewer's shovels and fire-hook. – Just N of this, the headstone of 1763 erected by Alexander Soot to his father, William, the E face carved with a crowned shoemaker's knife above a skull and coffin. – To its NE, a stone of 1778 to John Angus, very like the contemporary stone to Patrick Fyfe (*see* above), the shield bearing a crossed shovel and broom. – Behind it, a stone erected in 1761 by David Robertson and his wife, Margaret Herauld, to their children. Segmental-pedimented E face containing an angel's head. Below, torches flank a mantled helm and shield bearing the crowned knife of a shoemaker; emblems of death at the base. – To its E, the stone to Catherine Baillie †1748, with an angel's head above a shield carved with ploughshares and flanked by an hourglass, bone and spade.

KETTINS SCHOOL, School Park. Built in 1874. Plain except for bargeboarded gables with wrought-iron finials and a chimney-like bellcote. – To its NW, the single-storey former PARISH SCHOOL (now housing) and two-storey SCHOOLHOUSE of the mid C19.

DESCRIPTION. At the village's E end, some housing of the late C20 and early C21. SCHOOL PARK containing the school and its predecessor (*see* above) forms a crescent round the S side of the village. The main road crosses the Kettins Burn by a single-span ashlar BRIDGE of 1838 and becomes NEWTYLE ROAD. On its S side, a triangular green in front of Kettins Parish Church (*see* above). Behind the church, the harled former MANSE designed by *James Ballingal* and built in 1791–2. T-plan, of two storeys with an attic lit from round-headed windows in the gables. Extension by *John Ramsay*, 1852, filling the W inner angle. Single-storey rubble-walled office range of 1802 projecting to the W. On the N side of Newtyle Road, a mid-C19 cottage with carved bargeboards at the gables and porch. Stone canopies over the front windows, in the gables, hoodmoulded windows under large panels containing crosslets. The housing to the W is mostly C20 but SMITHY COTTAGE is mid-C19. U-plan front with crosslets in the bargeboarded gables and hoodmoulds to the windows. Simple mid-C19 cottages to its W.

SOUTERRAIN, Pitcur, 2.2 km. SE, in a field. Excavated in 1878. Probably formed in the later first millennium B.C., it consists of three inter-connected chambers, their boulder-faced walls standing up to 2 m. high. The gently curved E chamber, *c.* 2 m. broad, is now *c.* 10.2 m. long but originally continued further, its side walls corbelled inwards to carry roof-slabs, still in place.

Near the E end of the N side and the W end of the S, wall cupboards. In the N wall, opposite the W cupboard, a stone incised with graffiti of uncertain date, including the depiction of a fish and what looks rather like a champagne glass. W entrance, its jambs rebated for a door. It opens into a narrower passage, only *c.* 1.1m. long, leading from the central compartment. In the passage's N wall, a reused cup-marked stone, its carvings probably of the fourth or third millennium B.C. Also *c.* 2m. broad, the central compartment extends in a sinuous line for *c.* 23m. W before curling round to the SE in a hook-shape. Its walls are still substantial but have been partly removed, as have all the roof-slabs. At the W end, a short S passage, still roofed, slopes steeply down from the ground outside. Lying on the W of this passage, a boulder carved with cup-marks, some surrounded by rings. On the S side of this compartment's W hook, another passage, constructed in two angled sections. In its E side, a reused stone carved with cup-marks from which extend tail-like grooves. The passage communicates with the third compartment which forms a concentric ellipse round the W end of the central compartment. This compartment is wider than the other two, broadening from *c.* 2m. at its SE end to *c.* 3m. at the N. In the S side of the S segment, a wall cupboard and two entrances, presumably to passages originally leading to a building or buildings above.

SYMBOL STONE, High Keillor, 3.6km. E. 1.98m.-high undressed pillar, one face incised, probably in the C6 or C7, with the crude depiction of a wolf and 'double-disc-and-Z-rod' and 'comb' symbols.

HALLYBURTON HOUSE. *See* p. 408.
PITCUR CASTLE. *See* p. 666.

KILGRASTON SCHOOL
1.1 km. SW of Bridge of Earn

Complex developed round a late C18 mansion house, which was converted to a girls' school in 1930.

KILGRASTON HOUSE, the main edifice, was built and largely designed by *Francis Grant* soon after he inherited the Kilgraston estate from his brother in 1793. Rather in the manner of Robert Adam but without his flair, the architecture mixes classical, Gothic and castle details but the result is barracks-like, accentuated now by the loss of astragals from all except the ground-floor windows.

The house is H-plan, the ends of the long N and S ranges treated as towers. Three storeys (with an extra floor squeezed in at the S end of the cross-bar and with flat-roofed dormer windows added in the C20), the ground floor low and basement-like, the height of the first floor an over-emphatic proclamation of a *piano nobile*. Walling of red sandstone, predominantly of rubble but at the entrance (S) front and W side the ground floor is faced with channelled ashlar, its top course linking the sills of the first-floor windows.

Classical S front of nine bays, with a three-bay centrepiece joined by two-bay sections to the slightly advanced and taller ends. The centrepiece's ground-floor walling is minimally advanced to serve as a plinth for the pilasters above. In its outer bays, segmental-headed windows. At the centre bay, a plain entrance flanked by rectangular sidelights, all fronted by a low hexastyle Doric portico, its outer columns coupled. This ground-floor doorway and portico look like the result of a half-baked afterthought, replacing an originally intended grand stair to an entrance on the floor above. On the two upper floors of the centrepiece, giant pilasters with Prince of Wales-feathered necks under Ionic capitals. They support a broad pediment, its tympanum pierced by an oculus, the ends surmounted by figures of seated lions, the apex by a large swagged urn, this statuary all of artificial stone. Inside this aedicular frame, the first-floor window of the broad centre bay has a consoled pediment, each of the outer two windows of this floor a cornice above a plain frieze.

The linking sections are quite plain except for segmental-arched ground-floor windows and wallhead balustrades. At each end bay, a Diocletian window at the ground floor, an over-arched Venetian window with dummy sidelights at the first floor and a three-light window above a sill course at the second. At eaves level, a panel with guttae at its centre; above, a pediment topped by an artificial stone swagged urn. Each of the side elevations has battlemented end towers and a recessed centre, its wallhead parapet pierced by round-headed arcading. Otherwise, detail differs.

The W side (now partly overlaid by C20 extensions) with its channelled ashlar ground floor has been the smarter. At each of its towers, a triplet of ground-floor windows, the elliptical arches of their heads springing from imposts, a first-floor Venetian window but with round-headed sidelights and a rectangular Jacobean hoodmould, and a three-light second-floor window above a continuation of the second-floor sill course which is here decorated with faceted blocks and breaks forward on a pendant corbel under the window's centre light. At the elevation's recessed centre, the second-floor windows have latticed stone aprons above a string course.

The masonry of the E elevation is all of rubble. Plain rectangular ground-floor windows. At the first floor of the towers, conventional Venetian windows (the S a dummy); at the second floor, pairs of pointed windows above a sill course. The recessed centre is quite plain.

Plain rear elevation, now much overlaid by additions. The corner towers project boldly and have long fronts. Pointed windows at the second floor. Battlement across the centre as well as the towers.

The INTERIOR was gutted by fire in 1872. In the subsequent reconstruction, probably designed by *David Smart* who produced survey plans, the late C18 layout was retained but the style, although in late C18 manner, is unmistakably Victorian. The front door opens into a two-storey height ENTRANCE HALL largely filled by the double stair to the *piano nobile*. Fluted Doric pilasters round the walls whose frieze is studded with alternating heads of lions and of women. Elliptical-arched ceiling crossed by transverse ribs. At the head of the stair, the round-headed entrance to the saloon (now CENTRAL HALL) in the middle of the house. Bowed ends. Attached Corinthian columns round the walls. Aediculed doorpieces, the detail too heavy to be mistaken for genuine C18 work. In the centre of the N wall, a chimneypiece of veined white marble, its Corinthian columns more Neo-Jacobean than Neoclassical. Compartmented plaster ceiling with a large centre oval opening into the UPPER SALOON above and receiving borrowed light from its cupola. In this upper saloon, which provided circulation space serving the bedrooms, the centre containing the oval well is marked off by Corinthian columned screens supporting a pendentived dome, its plasterwork's coffers decorated with rosettes, the dividing stiles with guilloche and more rosettes.

The principal rooms of the *piano nobile* were rather awkwardly arranged. Along the S side, E of the entrance, was a suite of dressing room, family bedroom and boudoir. At the NE corner, the dining room. W of the entrance hall were the drawing room, a sitting room or ante-room at the house's SW corner, the library in the centre of the W side and a billiard or smoking room in the NW tower. In most of the rooms, smart doorpieces, some with consoled cornices, rounded reeded ceiling cornices crossed diagonally by narrow bands, and marble chimneypieces. The drawing room (now LIBRARY) is the grandest, with a slightly French flavour. Cornice enriched with swags and musical instruments, relief panels of classical deities at the overdoors, and a chimneypiece of honey-coloured and white marble. At the E end, a pilastered segmental-arched recess, its head filled with a plaster fan.

At the back of the house, a low courtyard of SCHOOL BUILDINGS added by *Gillespie, Kidd & Coia* in 1961. The N side is filled by the CHAPEL, a simple flat-roofed and brick-walled oblong with bands of clearstorey glazing, deeper at the S wall, along its sides. Boarded ceiling; W gallery. Behind the altar at the E end, a stone CRUCIFIX, by *Hew Lorimer*, 1961.

Attached to the W end of the main house, a harled DORMITORY addition of the 1930s. Behind, the former CHAPEL of 1930 [?] looking like a cheap hall. On rising ground behind the main house, a long two-storey range of the later C20, its E part flat-roofed and of 1960–1, the W part (BARAT WING) of 1987, brick-built and with a pitched roof.

W of the main complex, a rubble-built and turf-covered ICE HOUSE, probably of *c.* 1800. Broad rounded E end containing the chamber. The entrance is at the W in a round-headed gable. – Immediately W of this, the early C19 STABLES (now THE

GRANGE). Piend-roofed two-storey ranges round a courtyard, the E, N and S ranges faced with droved red sandstone ashlar, the S of rubble. E front of seven bays, the first-floor windows small and of horizontal proportion. At the ground floor's end bays, large elliptically arched coachhouse doors. At the advanced centre, a basket-arched pend entrance; wallhead pediment of polished ashlar. The N elevation is a repeat of the E but without the pedimented centrepiece. In the W elevation, rectangular slit windows and a pair of segmental-arched doors. The S elevation is utilitarian. The internal courtyard was covered with a glass roof and the rooms converted to classrooms by *Fred Multon*, 1992. NW of the stables, a SPORTS HALL by *Brown Construction*, 1991. 'Fyfestone' walls and a piended metal roof.

At the end of the E drive, a GATEWAY of c. 1820, built of polished grey ashlar. Keystoned round-headed arch framed by paired giant Roman Doric columns supporting a parapeted entablature. Red sandstone dwarf walls join this to low square 'pavilions', their corners with Roman Doric pilasters. Niches in their front and inner faces. These are probably of the later C19. Just inside the gateway, a broad-eaved LODGE, also of c. 1820 and built of grey sandstone. On its W side, a Roman Doric columned veranda which forms a portico at the centre; stone canopies over the windows. Tactful rear addition of the C20.

KILSPINDIE

Church and manse on a hillside above the Carse of Gowrie.

KILSPINDIE AND RAIT PARISH CHURCH. Rubble-built rectangle of 1795. The S wall incorporates several C16 or C17 stones with roll-and-hollow mouldings including, at its W end, the head of a window. These may have come from the demolished Kilspindie Castle. Near the E end of this wall, an incised sundial, its gnomon missing, which bears the date 1666. Otherwise, straightforward Late Georgian detail, with pointed doors and windows (now with late C19 glazing) in the S wall and a rectangular gallery window in each gable. On the W gable, a birdcage bellcote, its finial missing. Mid-C19 vestry at the NE corner.

The interior was recast in 1938–9 by *D. A. Stewart* of *Smart, Stewart & Mitchell* who removed the N and E galleries and rearranged the seating to face E. The surviving W GALLERY is probably of 1795, its panelled front displaying the painted coat of arms of the Murray Thrieplands of Fingask, the principal heritors (landowners) of the parish. – Plain rather boxy Late Georgian PEWS. – At the E end, the COMMUNION TABLE flanked by a large PULPIT and small LECTERN, all of 1938–9, the pulpit with some Neo-Celtic enrichment. – Early C20 ORGAN by *John R. Miller*, originally in Errol Free Church.

The GRAVEYARD is entered through a bargeboarded and half-timbered First World War memorial LYCHGATE of c. 1920.

Immediately E of the church, the corniced and parapeted MAUSOLEUM erected in 1822 to the memory of Lieutenant-General Robert Stuart of Rait. Above a vermiculated base, walls of polished ashlar, with round-arched M-shapel panels. In the centre of the S side, an oval inscription panel of marble. At the W end, the M-arched entrance under a round plaque bearing an Arabic inscription; above, a rectangular panel bearing the Stuart crest. – Some C18 HEADSTONES carved with the usual repertoire of emblems of death and several with an angel's head (the soul). At the churchyard's SW corner, a stone of 1786 also displays a cordiner's knife. – To its E, a contemporary stone commemorating Robert Sharp, the W face bearing a loom and shuttle. – Propped against the S wall of the churchyard, a stone of 1781 for Charles Spence, also with a loom. – Just E of the church, a large stone of 1796 to Andrew Duncan, with a shield bearing a coulter.

MANSE to the S. Plain rubble-walled L, built by *William Lindsay*, wright in Perth, 1765. Simple Jacobean W wing added by *James Ritchie*, 1862–3.

KINCAIRNEY HOUSE
2.3 km. W of Clunie

Laird's house, the piend-roofed two-storey front block built c. 1835. Principal elevation of five bays, with an Ionic portico at the centre. Two-bay side elevations, each with a chimneyed pediment. Horizontal-paned glazing in the windows. Harled rear block probably of the C18 but reduced and remodelled c. 1920. – Broad-eaved LODGE, also of c. 1835 and with horizontal-paned glazing, its W elevation facing the drive with a gablet over the r. window and a canted bay window at the l.

KINCARDINE CASTLE
1.5 km. S of Auchterarder

Castellated small mansion house of 1801–3, built of coursed and squared red sandstone rubble. Two storeys over a basement which is partly exposed at the back. The house is a symmetrical piend-roofed oblong of five bays by two, with battlemented octagonal clasping turret-buttresses at the outer corners and marking off the three-bay centrepieces of the NW and SE elevations, all tied together by a first-floor sill course. The entrance front faces NW. At its outer bays, Gothic canted oriel windows to the ground floor, their parapets' corners with spike finials, and hoodmoulded first-floor windows, each of two Gothic lights. Cast-iron battlement, the gableted merlons pierced by arched openings, the crenelles' bases by quatrefoils. Over the centrepiece, a taller stone battlement with broad crenelles and a stepped central merlon. The entrance, sadly bereft of its splay-sided Gothic portico, is flanked by hoodmoulded rectangular windows. First-floor windows of the same design flank a hoodmoulded Gothic window of two lights with a quatrefoil in the head.

At the end elevations, hoodmoulded windows and continuations of the front's cast-iron battlements but with broad stepped merlons in the centre.

At the rear, hoodmoulded windows to the ground and first floors, the three centre bays forming a bow surmounted by a stone battlement, again with a stepped central merlon but also decorated with panels containing diamonds enclosing quatrefoils; cast-iron battlements over the outer bays.

w of the house, STABLES AND COACHHOUSE, also of 1801–3. Two rubble-built ranges, the N with segmental-arched coachhouse doors. Gothic dummy windows in the N gables. The first-floor windows have been heightened in the mid or later C19 and given dormerheads.

At the N end of the drive from Auchterarder, an ashlar-faced LODGE of c. 1805. Twin-gabled E front with diagonally set gabled buttresses at the corners; hoodmoulded Gothic windows. At the N end, a large octagonal projection surmounted by a round chimney. – s of the lodge, the drive passes under the KINCARDINE GLEN VIADUCT carrying the railway over the Ruthven Water. By *Locke & Errington*, c. 1846–8, built of bullnosed masonry. Six segmental arches and a smaller round-headed W arch over the drive.

sw of Kincardine Castle, RAUN GATE, a harled single-storey cottage of the earlier C19. Thatched jerkin-head roof with broad eaves.

KINCLAVEN

Just the church and a handful of buildings.

KINCLAVEN CHURCH. Built in 1848. Long rectangle, the stugged and squared masonry of the walls articulated by hammer-dressed stonework at the barely projecting buttresses which clasp the corners and mark off the gabled centres of the N and S sides. Round-headed windows at the centre of the sides and, in a stepped arrangement, at each gable, rectangular windows in the sides' outer bays, all hoodmoulded. w porch; a blocked door at the E gable which is surmounted by a carpenter's Gothic bellcote, with pinnacled corner piers and a tall finial.

The INTERIOR was thoroughly remodelled in 1893. The roof is a showpiece of carpentry, with scissor trusses, hammerbeams and kingposts dropping down to pendants. Raked floor, the PEWS of standard Late Victorian type. Corniced wooden DADO. At the E end, on either side, the canopies for LAIRDS' PEWS, the N deeper than the s. Oak COMMUNION TABLE of 1935 in a tepid Lorimerian manner. The PULPIT of 1893 now stands to one side of the 'chancel'. On the other side, a lumpy Gothic stone FONT of 1883.

STAINED GLASS. Late C19 E window. Patterned background against which are set panels containing lushly coloured depictions of fruit and flowers; in the two centre lights, figures of St John the Evangelist and St Paul. – In the E bays of the side walls, two similar windows, both probably of *c.* 1895, with identical backgrounds of flower-patterned grisaille roundels. Against these, at the top of each, two small panels framed by wings and containing portraits in youth and age of those commemorated (General Richardson Robertson of Ballathie at the N and Jessica Mary Stewart Richardson at the S). At the centre of each window, a pair of scenes (the N showing the Angel of the Lord Smiting the Army of the Assyrians and Gideon's Army Attacking the Host of Midian, the S the Nativity of Our Lord and Our Lord Setting a Child among His Disciples). – The central N window is by *Stephen Adam & Co.*, 1896, a pictorial depiction of the Parable of the Good Samaritan. – The W window of this side is similar to its E window and also of *c.* 1895 but, instead of portraits at the top, there are angels holding scrolls. At the centre, two scenes depicting the Virtuous Woman and her Family. – The centre window of the S side with realistic figures of two Evangelists is of 1903. – This side's W window of *c.* 1920 (the Presentation of Our Lord in the Temple; Our Lord and Little Children) is almost certainly by *Douglas Strachan*, a restrained example of sketchy stylized realism. – Great W window of *c.* 1900. Clearly drawn and well-coloured Scenes from the Life of Our Lord. – In the vestibule, two lights. The N (Our Lord with a Cripple and a Boy) is by *John Blyth*, *c.* 1990. – The S window (Our Lord as the Good Shepherd), its realism less stylized, is of *c.* 1960

GRAVEYARD. At the entrance, an ashlar-walled war memorial LYCHGATE, by *Reginald Fairlie*, 1919. Round-headed moulded arches surmounted by panels, the S carved with a relief of the Pelican in Piety, the N with the Burning Bush. Bellcast eaves to the roof. – S of the church's W end, a sarcophagus MONUMENT to John Windram, merchant, its top slab carved with an angel's head (the soul) above a panel bearing initials, the date 1740 and a merchant's mark (like the figure 4); at the foot of the slab, an hourglass, skull and crossbones. – To its E, the HEADSTONE of James Miller †1716, its top a rounded M-shape, the W face carved with a loom and a tailor's goose and scissors; skull at the bottom. – SE of this, a pedimented C18 HEADSTONE, rather weathered, the W face with a weaver's loom and shuttle. – Much crisper carving on the HEADSTONE of 1768 commemorating James Rattray, the W face with an angel's head above a shield displaying a tailor's goose and scissors; emblems of death at the bottom. – To the E, a couple of C18 GRAVE-SLABS. One, to William Watson, cordiner in Cairko (Kerkoch), has a marginal inscription round weathered panels, one bearing reliefs of a cordiner's knife, an awl and knives, the other, of 1739, to Thomas Galatly, tenant in Drum of Muckery, an angel's head at the top and the usual crossbones, skull and hourglass at the bottom. – E of the church, a HEADSTONE, its E face with an inscription of 1842 to James Cathrow, the W face with the date 1755 and reliefs of a weaver's loom, shuttle and stretchers above emblems of death.

BRIDGE OF ISLA, 1.3 km. E. Built in 1794–6 to a design by *Patrick Brown Jun.* who, with his father, *Patrick Brown Sen.*, was also the contractor. Slightly hump-backed five-span bridge, rubble-built with dressed stone arch rings to the segmental arches; triangular cutwaters.

KINCLAVEN CASTLE, 1 km. SE Now hidden in a wood, the remains of a royal castle which was in existence by the early C13 but whose defences were dismantled in 1337.

The site is a low hill beside the River Tay which provided an outer defence on the E side, this apparently supplemented by an encircling ditch. The castle is a rubble-walled enclosure, *c.* 40 m. square, which had a tower at each corner, these perhaps demolished in 1337. The principal entrance was near the SW end of the NW side. NE of the entrance the walling seems to have thickened internally, perhaps indicating the former presence here of a stair to the wall-walk. Roughly in the centre of the SW side, remains of a buttress or possibly one side of a tower at the external entrance to a postern gate which opens into a wall passage. The passage has a small window into the courtyard into which its NW end opens. The walls stand to a fair height but robbed of their outer facing and dressed work.

BALLATHIE HOUSE. *See* p. 178.

KINFAUNS

Standing on a steep hillside overlooking the River Tay, a short string of late C20 houses between the Parish Church and its former manse (now, Kinfauns House).

KINFAUNS PARISH CHURCH. Disused. By *Andrew Heiton Jun.*, 1869–70. Plain Gothic, built of squared and coursed bullnosed masonry of a purplish colour. Nave, W transepts and a low chancel-like E vestry. Plate-traceried circular windows in the nave gables. In the inner angle of the nave and S transept, a tower finished with a slated steep pyramid roof.

The church stands in a W extension of the GRAVEYARD. In its earlier E part, the ivy-clad and roofless FORMER PARISH CHURCH, perhaps C15 but much altered after the Reformation. It is oblong, the rubble walls formerly harled; an intake in the E gable. In the N wall, rectangular windows, probably all of post-Reformation date, but a little W of the centre of this side is a minimally pointed entrance with a simple roll moulding which appears to be medieval. The entrance in the E gable must be post-Reformation. The S wall's E window is rectangular with a chamfered surround but its internal splay suggests it may be original. The other openings in this wall are post-Reformation, the broad entrance W of the Charteris Aisle made in 1838 when a s 'aisle' (since demolished) was built here.

The CHARTERIS AISLE projecting from the S side, and still roofed was built in 1598 both to house the pew of the Charterises of Kinfauns and to serve as their burial place. It is a small ashlar-walled rectangle; at each skew a single crowstep. S entrance flanked by two high-set windows and surmounted by a double tier of frames for heraldic panels. Chamfered surrounds to the openings and the empty lower frame. The upper frame has a cavetto-moulded surround and a cornice. In it, the crest (a helmet) for a coat of arms which has weathered away; part of the Charteris motto (TREV TO THE KING) survives below.

Inside the church, immediately E of the C19 S entrance, a rather crude ogee-arched medieval stoup. Near the E end of the N wall is a late medieval tomb-recess which probably doubled as an Easter sepulchre. Elliptical arch with simple roll mouldings which die into the jambs, the hoodmould now fragmentary and with its crockets chipped off. The outer corners of the arch have been carried on squat nook-shafts with simple capitals and bases, now buried. – Propped against the W end of the S wall, a medieval STONE carved with a cross.

The Charteris Aisle originally opened into the church through a segmental arch. This has been built up and a doorway formed in the blocking. The Aisle's interior is covered with a groin vault, the moulded ribs springing from pendant corbels and meeting at a pendant boss. On the ribs, four small shields, the NE and SW carved with the arms of Charteris, the NW and SE with the Chisholm arms. On the E and W walls identical classicizing monuments, presumably erected in 1598. Each is of three compartments separated by leafily capitalled fluted pilasters. In the two l. compartments of the E monument are heraldic achievements, one displaying the impaled arms of Charteris and Chisholm (for John Charteris of Kinfauns and Janet Chisholm, his wife) above the inscription JOHN.CHARTRVS/JIAN|NAT.CHISOLM/IN/OR.TYM.BVIDIT.THIS, the other the arms of Charteris above the inscription GEORGE.CHARTVS.SON/AN.HAR.TO.THE.S&.IOHN./AND. DEPPARTIT.BOT.SUCCE|SSWN. In the centre compartment of the W monument, a heraldic achievement of the impaled arms of Lindsay and Chisholm (for Henry Lindsay or Charteris, later thirteenth Earl of Crawford, the adopted son of John Charteris of Kinfauns and Janet Chisholm, and for his wife, Helen Chisholm) above the initials HC. Below the E monument, a single strapworked panel and three more such panels are below the W monument, their inscriptions worn away.

Beside the graveyard's E entrance, a plain WATCH HOUSE, probably of the earlier C19, with a small window overlooking the graves; inside is a fireplace but the chimney has been removed. – At the NE corner of the churchyard, an ivy-clad rubble-built BURIAL ENCLOSURE of the C18 or early C19. –

Built into the former Parish Church's N wall, near its E end, a MONUMENT to John Blair and Margaret Johnston †1829 with a Roman Doric columned and corniced surround. – To the S and SE of the Former Parish Church are several C18 GRAVE-SLABS and HEADSTONES carved variously with angels' heads (souls), shields and emblems of death. Some of the headstones merit individual mention. Just S of the Charteris Aisle, the stone erected in 1782 by James Morrison, gardener in Perth, to his parents, the W face carved with a relief of Eve offering Adam the apple from the Tree of Knowledge. – To its S, the stone of John Buist †1761, the shield on its W face bearing a salmon, knife and rowing boat in which lies another salmon. – W of this, the headstone of Andrew Imrie, smith at Glendoick, †1776, the W face with his trade emblem of a crowned hammer. – Immediately to its S, the headstone of 1723 to William Sharp, the shield of its W face bearing a weaver's shuttle. – Quite a bit further E, the headstone erected in 1780 to Alexander Rogers, wright in Glendoick, the shield on its W face carved with dividers and a setsquare.

SCHOOL. Two buildings, both now converted to housing. The W is the broad-eaved Parish School of 1830, by *W. M. Mackenzie*. The E, also broad-eaved but with its windows brutally enlarged in the late C20, is the Board School, by *H. J. Bell*, 1902.

KINFAUNS HOUSE. Originally Kinfauns Parish Manse. Two-storey and basement main block, designed and built by *Patrick Brown*, mason at Dryburgh (near Dundee), 1798–1800. E wing, at right angles, added by *W. M. Mackenzie*, 1840. The building was harled and the N porch added, *c.* 1960.

KINFAUNS HOME FARM, 1.5km. W. Plain rubble-built farmhouse of 1814, the main block of two storeys and three bays; piend-roofed single-storey lateral wings. – To the SE, the DAIRY by *Lorimer & Matthew*, 1928, a single-storey octagon, the large ogee roof swept down over a surrounding veranda. Small N wing with a keel-shaped gable. – Piend-roofed L-plan whinstone-rubble STEADING of 1813 to the W but with flat-roofed dormer windows added to the main block, an octagonal brick chimney, probably late C19, on the W side and a NE wing, perhaps of 1928, with bellcast eaves to the piended roof.

TOWER, Binn Hill, 1km. W. Built *c.* 1815 by Francis, fourteenth Lord Gray, the owner of Kinfauns Castle, as an observatory and castellated romantic feature perched on a crag high above the Carse of Gowrie but now hidden in woodland. Tall rubble-walled rectangular tower finished with a battlement (partly missing) carried on small rounded corbels. In the W face, a four-stage tier of Gothic windows. In each of the other faces only the ground and top floors are pierced by openings, also Gothic. At the tower's NW corner, a taller octagonal stair-tower with broad slit windows. Intake at second-floor level; under the top stage, a continuation of the string course of the main tower's battlement. Only corbels survive of the battlement.

KINFAUNS CASTLE
1.6km. W

Poised on a hillside above the Tay, the large asymmetrically composed castellated mansion designed by *Robert Smirke* and built for the fifteenth Lord Gray in 1821–6.

The building comprises an L-plan main house and a courtyard of offices to the N. Walling all of pink-coloured ashlar, polished at the principal elevations. At the centre of the E (entrance) front, a boldly projecting battlemented porte cochère; at its outer corners, tall towers with small round-headed dummy windows. In its front, a pointed footgate under a narrow dummy window, again pointed. Tall pointed carriage arches in the sides. Heraldic shields under the porte cochère's battlement whose S face bears the heraldic achievement of the Lords Gray. Inside, the porte cochère is covered with a vaulted ceiling, the ribs springing from pendant corbels and meeting at a foliaged boss. In the W side, the tall round-headed entrance into the house's battlemented porch. This porch is of one tall storey with a trio of round-arched windows in each side. It joins onto a sturdy three-storey battlemented tower, its E face pierced by a window of three round-headed lights.

Flanking the E front's central tower are two-storey four-bay ranges. The N of these is the E range of the service court, its battlement formed by a simple crenellation of the wallhead, unprojected on corbelling. Continuous hoodmoulding over the bipartite front windows, those of the ground floor with rectangular lights and stone mullions, the first-floor windows' lights round-headed; an extra first-floor window has been inserted at the S bay. At the range's N end, a rather small square clock tower, also battlemented.

The S range is generally similar but its extra height and continuously corbelled battlement denote the importance of the rooms inside. Continuous hoodmoulding again over the rectangular ground-floor windows but they are taller than those of the N range and contain pointed lights and wooden mullions; rectangular lights in the first-floor windows which are linked by a sill course. At the house's SE corner, a massive square tower, of three storeys but lower than the E front's centre tower. Severely plain clasping buttresses at the corners. The battlement is carried on one course of continuous corbelling over the buttresses but projected to the same plane on heavy rounded individual corbels at the main wall faces between. Identical E and S elevations, each pierced by a ground-floor window of three round-headed lights, its hoodmould with pendant label stops. Hoodmoulds with pendant label stops also at the first floor's three smaller windows but these are pointed and linked by a continuation of the E range's sill course which is carried across the corner buttresses and extends along the house's S elevation. At the second floor, three round-headed lights, smaller again and without hoodmoulds but placed above a string course which continues the line (interrupted by the corner buttresses) of the continuous corbelling under the battlements of the E and S ranges.

The S range's ground floor, containing drawing rooms which enjoy the view over the Tay to Fife, is placed between the SE tower and a taller but slimmer battlemented circular tower which projects boldly from the SW corner. The S range itself, battlemented like the principal E range, is symmetrical. Two-storey three-bay sections, their rectangular windows joined by continuous hoodmoulding, flank the broad three-storey gabled centre which is marked off by clasping buttresses and finished with a pierced parapet. A hoodmoulded three-light window at each of the upper floors, that of the second floor quite small and with pointed openings. Projecting from the ground floor, a tall canted bay window with slender buttresses at its corners. In each face, a mullioned and transomed window with four-centred arched lights. Under the bay window's battlement, a frieze studded with heraldic shields. A hoodmoulded first-floor Venetian window in the W gable of the S range.

On the W side, the main house and the service courtyard's N range form a U-plan courtyard, its elevations faced with vertically broached ashlar. On the courtyard's S side, at the back of the main house's S range, a four-storey tower, its recessed top floor, visible from afar, faced with polished ashlar and crowned with a battlement and round corner turrets. In the tower, round-headed openings, the large lowest window (lighting the principal stair of the house) a sort of Venetian. Across the ground floor of the courtyard's plain E side (the back of the main house's E range), a single-storey Gothic windowed projection (containing the Gallery). Buttressed N range (the S range of the service court) in a collegiate manner, the wallhead crenellated but not projected on corbelling. At this range's W end, a squat tower (originally containing the kitchen) of one very tall storey, a window of three round-headed lights in each exposed face. Plain service courtyard to the N.

INTERIOR. The main entrance from the porte cochère opens into a porch or OUTER HALL containing a flight of steps up to the ground floor. Plaster vaulted ceiling, its ribs enriched with dog-tooth ornament and meeting at a foliaged boss. At the head of the stair, a round-arched opening filled with a partly glazed Gothic door gives access to an INNER HALL. Over this, a trabeated ceiling, the main hammerbeams with foliage-carved pendants and carried on foliaged stone corbels. At the N wall, a Gothic chimneypiece of veined green-grey marble, with stepped and gabled buttresses at the ends. Like the other principal chimneypieces of the 1820s it was designed by *Smirke*. Originally in the principal stair hall, it was made by *Shillinglaw & Scott* in 1824–5 and moved here in 1904. At the end of the inner hall, a door into the GALLERY which runs along the W side of the E range. The Gallery is divided into three spaces by broad depressed arches, their sides and soffits with delicately detailed Gothic panelling. Over each space, an identical ceiling (as elsewhere in the house, the plasterwork by *Annan & Imrie*

Kinfauns Castle, Gallery.
Engraving after a painting by Robert Gibb, *c.* 1827, from J. P. Neale,
Views of the Seats, 2nd ser., iv, 1828

with composition ornaments by *William Bryson*) divided into small square compartments containing quatrefoils. The central space's W side forms a broad and shallow canted bay window. Opposite, a stone chimneypiece (probably one of the many less important chimneypieces supplied by *David Ness*), its depressed-arched fireplace opening under a crocketed hoodmould. Below the battlemented top, a frieze studded with heraldic shields. On the Gallery's E side is the DINING ROOM. Tudorish black marble chimneypiece of the 1820s. The rest of the decoration probably dates from alterations made in 1904 by *F. W. Deas* for Morton Gray Stuart Gray (later, seventeenth Earl of Moray) who had inherited the Kinfauns estate three years before. Simply compartmented depressed-arched ceiling; foliaged and rosetted bosses along the frieze. Panelled oak dado and doors.

At the Gallery's S end is a fourth space intended by Smirke to serve primarily as an ANTE-ROOM to the Large Drawing Room to its S. It is taller than the Gallery and covered by a vaulted ceiling whose diagonal ribs spring from foliage-encrusted corbels surmounted by angels bearing shields. Circular central compartment enriched with Gothic arcading placed in panels round a pendant. The space was originally marked off by an arch of the same design as those which divide the Gallery itself but Deas replaced this by a simple Tudor arch in 1904 and also substituted an arch for the wall which had divided this space from a BILLIARD ROOM to its W, so making the former billiard room part of a processional route from the Gallery to the stair hall at the centre of the S range's N side.

Deas remodelled the former billiard room in Lorimerian manner, the main feature a chimneypiece (sited N of the position of the 1820s fireplace) of veined green and pink marble in an Artisan Mannerist wooden surround, the leafily enriched overmantel intended to frame a painting. In each of Smirke's three pointed N windows was placed a panel of C17 German stained glass (one dated 1657, another 1659) depicting people, a skeleton and coats of arms.

A round-headed door of 1904 opens into the STAIR HALL to the W. This was entirely remodelled by Deas, the woodwork executed by *Scott Morton & Co*. Walls panelled in oak up to the level of the first floor. Against the S wall, a Corinthian columned oak screen containing a pair of doors, one a dummy, the other the entrance to Lady Gray's Room. Imperial STAIR (the treads of teak) in best Jacobean manner, the balusters' bulbous bases carved with foliage, the newel posts surmounted by statues of birds, beasts, an angel, a cherub and a knight, all holding shields carved with the coats of arms of past owners of the Kinfauns estate. Under the banisters, a pierced frieze of vines in which are set naturalistic carvings of beasts and birds. At the upper floor, screens to the S and E, their columns with idiosyncratic voluted capitals. Plaster cornice enriched with foliage. Coved plaster ceiling enriched with vines among which are birds at play. Heraldic achievements in the centre of three sides of the coving.

Smirke's principal rooms on the ground floor of the S range's retain their decoration almost intact. The SE room is the LIBRARY. Almost all the E and S walls are occupied by windows, their Gothic pelmets still in place. On the other walls, Gothic bookcases articulated by slender buttresses and foliaged friezes; carved musical instruments on the W bookcases. In the centre of the W side, a battlemented white marble chimneypiece, its recessed overmantel with a mirrored back and fan-vaulted canopy. Compartmented ceiling of grained plaster enriched with Gothic panels and pendants. On the flat are circles enclosing quatrefoils which contain shields displaying the impaled coats of arms of successive Lords Gray and their wives.

W of the library is the LARGE DRAWING ROOM. Gothic panelled dado and a buttressed white marble chimneypiece. The walls are finished with a frieze of grapes under a cornice on which stand flowers in front of broad elliptical arches under the simply compartmented Tudor ceiling, its ribs meeting at foliaged bosses. Doors with reeded panels except at the W end where a battlemented doorpiece frames Gothic panelled double doors into LADY GRAY'S ROOM or SMALL DRAWING ROOM in the centre of the S range. Most of this room's S side is occupied by a bay window, the walls at its entry covered with Gothic panelling. Simple compartmented ceiling, with foliaged bosses at the intersections of the ribs. Lavish white marble chimneypiece at the W wall. At its ends, standing female figures, their hands on top of their heads to support the rosetted ends of the entablature. The main part of the frieze is carved with a cornucopia of flowers flanking the central panel which bears a relief of Ceres sitting in a chariot drawn by snakes and accompanied by putti, two holding torches, the third a wreath above the goddess's head.

In the garden N of the house, a pair of crudely carved early C19 sandstone STATUES of Bruce and Wallace.

BALTHAYOCK CASTLE AND HOUSE. *See* p. 185.

KINGS OF KINLOCH
1.9 km. W of Meigle

Laird's house built in 1798 for the radical politician, *George Kinloch* of Kinloch, who produced the design. It was remodelled by *John Carver* in 1865. The C18 house was a rubble-walled and piend-roofed oblong of two storeys above a basement which was half-hidden at the front by ramped ground, the tall ground-floor windows identifying the *piano nobile*. S front of five bays, the centre three slightly advanced and originally surmounted by a pediment. Two-bay side elevations, the W with Venetian windows at the ground floor and three-light windows above, the S a dummy. Rear elevation of five bays. A piend-roofed single-storey and basement E wing does not appear on the surviving designs of 1798 but may be an afterthought or, more probably, an addition of the early C19.

In the remodelling of 1865 the pediment was removed from the front, to whose centre was added a three-stage balustraded tower built of lightly stugged ashlar with polished dressings. At the tall bottom stage rising from the external ground level to the house's principal floor, a round-headed door in a Roman Doric pilastered and pedimented surround. In the front of each upper stage, a two-light window, the second stage's pedimented. Also of 1865 is the large but plain NW wing of three storeys and a basement, again faced with stugged ashlar. A two-storey and basement bay window projecting from its N end; the coat of arms (of Rose-Cleland) on the W front is an embellishment of 2003.

INTERIOR. The doorway in the S tower opens into an ENTRANCE HALL of 1865 whose straight flight of stairs, the cast-iron balustrade decorated with birds and foliage, rises to the house's original doorway. This has sidelights and an overall segmental fanlight, its tracery probably replaced in 1865, but has lost its C18 Ionic pilastered surround. Under the sidelights, panels carved with the coat of arms of Kinloch of Kinloch. At the INNER HALL (the 1790s entrance hall), each of the pilastered side walls has a segmental blind arch flanked by narrower round-headed arches, the N on the E side now opening into a short corridor formed in the early C20, the other three framing console-corniced doorpieces which look like early C20 work. At the hall's N end, a panelled segmental arch to the flying stair, its cast-iron balustrade with anthemion-filled ovals.

E of the inner hall was the C18 drawing room (now DINING ROOM). In the early C20 this was subdivided, a business room being formed in its SW corner with a short corridor behind which leads to the room's E end. This was opened up through an elliptical arch into the front room of the E wing, the walls of both parts covered with oak panelling; small Edwardian fireplace in the W part. On the W of the entrance hall, the LIBRARY (the C18 dining room), its ceiling's swagged and triglyphed frieze late C19 Adam revival, the veined grey marble chimneypiece a replacement of the early or mid C19. To its N, occupying the NW corner of the Georgian house, the SMALL DRAWING ROOM formed, probably in the early C19, from the 1790s family bedroom and closets, its decoration probably of the late C19 but in a late C18 manner. Console-corniced doorpieces. Window surrounds with acanthus-capitalled pilasters; garlands above the sidelights of the Venetian W window. Plain Victorian white marble chimneypiece. In 1865 the E of this room's N windows was converted to a door to give access to the LARGE DRAWING ROOM filling the principal floor of the 1860s NW wing. Here is a compartmented plaster ceiling with Rococo central rose. White marble chimneypiece, the jambs carved in high relief with pendants of flowering foliage and baskets of flowers, the centre of the frieze with a basket of fruit flanked by birds.

Rubble-built STABLES of *c.* 1800, 0.1 km. W. Now a ruin but the tower at the centre of the S range survives. This was originally of two storeys with a round-headed arch to a tunnel-vaulted pend under the first floor S opening, also round-headed, which served as the birds' entry to a doocot containing stone nesting boxes, the human entry being by a N door; below the door, a couple of corbels, probably of the later C19, set at different heights but supporting a stone ledge. Also of the later C19 the tower's gabled clock-stage.

At the end of the drive from the SE, Victorian Tudor GATEPIERS surmounted by stone eagles which may be Georgian.

KINKELL

9010

Place name commemorating a medieval parish which was united to Trinity Gask in the mid or late C17.

ANTIBURGHER CHURCH. Now a house. Simple harled box of *c.* 1790. In the four-bay S front, two tall round-arched windows (formerly flanking the pulpit). The other windows of this front and in the rear elevation are rectangular and placed below the level of the interior's former gallery. Two tiers of windows in the gables.

ST BEAN'S CHURCH. The former Kinkell Parish Church, now roofless and ivy-covered. It is probably of *c.* 1600, perhaps built on medieval foundations. Long narrow rectangle (*c.* 19.8 m. by

7.0m.), traces of harling still adhering to the rubble walls. There has been a w bellcote. In the s wall, three irregularly disposed windows and a door near the w end; a window placed high in each gable. All the openings are rectangular, with chamfered margins. The interior has been partitioned into burial places.

KINKELL BRIDGE over the Earn, 0.8 km. NW. Constructed *c.* 1793. Rubble-built, slightly humpbacked and on a gentle curve. Four segmental arches; triangular cutwaters rising to pedestrian refuges at the parapet. At the s end, a buttress on each face. – At the N end, the contemporary OLD TOLL HOUSE. Harled single-storey cottage, a pointed window in the s side of the w porch.

EARNBANK HOUSE, 0.8 km. NW. Two-storey house of the earlier C19, built of white-painted rubble. Bracketed broad eaves and horizontal-paned windows. Consoled cornice over the door. Contemporary low outbuildings to the E.

MILLEARNE. See p. 529.
STRATHALLAN CASTLE. See p. 710.

KINLOCH

Hamlet on a hillside above Loch Marlee.

KINLOCH PARISH CHURCH. Disused. Harled box of *c.* 1792, the gables' skews removed in 1862, the small piend-roofed end porches added in 1867 and 1872, and the ball-finialled birdcage bellcote renewed in 1964 when the roof was given concrete tiles. In the s side, a pair of round-headed windows with projecting keystones and imposts. Rectangular gallery windows in the gables. The N side's rectangular windows under the gallery were inserted by *David Smart* in 1877.

Inside, a semi-octagonal gallery round the ends and N side, its panelled front of *c.* 1792, the cast-iron columns of 1877. PULPIT of *c.* 1792 at the centre of the s side.

GRAVEYARD. Some GRAVESTONES worth noting. s of the church's E end, a grave-slab to Androw [*sic*] Mitchell †1699 and his wife, Jean Baxter †1693. In one of its triangular ends, reliefs of a shoemaker's knife, pincers and a pick. – Beside it, the curvy-topped headstone of John Cathro †1768. On the w face, an angel's head (the soul) above flaming torches which flank a shield carved with two picks, a rhind and a coulter. – Immediately to the s, the similarly shaped headstone of 1776 erected by David Weddal, smith, and his wife, Janet Robertson, to their son, David, the w face carved with Ionic pilasters. These frame the relief of a pair of angels above a shield which bears the tools of a smith; emblems of death at the base. – Further E, the headstone erected in 1782 by John Anderson, tenant in Burnside of Marlee, to his parents and children. On the w face, an Ionic pilastered aedicule, an angel's head in the pediment. The aedicule encloses a heraldic achievement, the supporters in C18 dress, one holding a pick, the other a sickle. The shield displays a plough and has a horse for crest. Reminders of death below.

SCHOOL. Now a house (THE OLD SCHOOL). By *Robert Keiller*, wright in Blairgowrie, 1857–8. Single-storey, built of red sandstone squared rubble; hoodmoulds over the windows.

MANSE (now THE OLD PASTORIE). By *W. M. Mackenzie*, 1847–8. Two storeys, of red sandstone rubble. Piend-roofed main block, its S front's three-light ground floor windows set in shallowly projecting rectangular bays.

MARLEE HOUSE, 0.2 km. S. Harled early C18 laird's house. Two-storey main block, its S front of five bays, the openings grouped 2:1:2. Neo-Georgian doorpiece added by *A. J. Meacher*, 1890. This block is joined by lower concave links to two-storey piend-roofed SE and SW pavilions, also of the early C18. Larger pavilions, probably early C19, at the N corners.

CAIRN, 0.7 km. W. Standing between the A923 and the Loch of Drumellie, a large round cairn, over 30 m. in diameter and 2.5 m. high. It was probably formed in the third millennium B.C.

STONE CIRCLE, Leys of Marlee, 1.3 km. SE. On low ground between Rae Loch on the N, Fingask Loch on the S and Loch of Drumellie to the W, a setting now composed of six large boulders (two re-erected), bisected by the B947. They form a rough oval, *c.* 16 m. by 11.5 m., but the three W stones stand in an almost straight line. They were probably erected in the third or second millennium B.C.

KINLOCH HOUSE
1.5 km. W

Unpretentious but self-assured laird's house of *c.* 1840 with a satisfying Edwardian interior. Two storeys, built of cherry-cocked whin rubble. S front of five bays, the centre three forming a splay-sided projection. The long L-plan NE back wing is original. Later in the C19 a second wing was added forming a courtyard which was roofed over as a stair hall as part of *C. G. Soutar*'s alterations of 1909–10 for John Paton, a partner in the Dundee and Montrose flax-spinning firm of J. & G. Paton Ltd. Also of 1909–10 the recessed two-storey E addition containing the entrance, its doorcase of Wrenaissance character. At the W end, a flat-roofed single-storey extension and conservatory of the later C20. The over-large diagonally set SE wing with a conical-roofed corner tower was added in 1988–9 for the house's present use as an hotel.

Inside, the principal rooms were remodelled in 1909–10. Small entrance hall with Jacobean patterned glazing in the N window which contains three stained-glass heraldic crests. W of this, a beamed LIVING HALL, its oak-panelled dado rising as an elliptical-arched overmantel above the large Arts and Crafts stone fireplace whose cornice bears shields displaying a rose and thistle and, at the centre, an eagle; fireplace surround of Delft tiles. This room is open to the STAIR HALL formed from the former courtyard. Arts and Crafts again, divided by panelled oak piers into a nave and aisles, the stair itself in the centre of the nave, the aisles and nave ends occupied by balconies. Over the stair well, a glazed ceiling, its accomplished stained glass in the manner of Oscar Paterson. Pale grey quarries, stylized designs in purple and blue with discreet touches of yellow; bay-leaf oval garland at the centre. The house's mid-C19 main rooms are placed along the S side of the ground floor. Plain DINING ROOM at the E, now missing its chimneypiece. In the centre, the drawing room with an Adam Revival pine chimneypiece. The W room was probably the LIBRARY, its ceiling decorated with little squares of flowers and foliage (roses, thistles, oak leaves, etc.) in the Lorimer manner. Panelling imported in the late C20.

COACHHOUSE AND STABLES (now a house) to the W. Also of *c.* 1840. The main (S) front is of two storeys with slightly advanced end bays. The pyramidal-roofed centre, projecting a little more boldly, contains an elliptical-arched pend under an oculus. – N of the house and probably contemporary with it, the steeply sloping WALLED GARDEN. W entrance with a heavily consoled cornice; frieze carved with branches between rosettes. Urns on the corners of the rubble walls. – LODGE at the entrance to the drive, also of *c.* 1840. Single-storey, the ashlar walls finished with parapets; a canted bay window to the S. Panelled GATEPIERS with low pyramidal tops.

GLASCLUNE CASTLE. *See* p. 382.

KINLOCH RANNOCH

Village at the E end of Loch Rannoch.

ALL SAINTS (Episcopal), The Square. Plain Gothic, by *Andrew Heiton Jun.*, 1864. Nave and a lower chancel, a low outshot at its E end. At the join of the nave and chancel, a S tower, its slated spire truncated and topped by a belfry-cupola finished with a Frenchy spire. Large round window in the W gable. SW porch.

Inside, a pointed chancel arch. Open roof over the nave. The chancel ceiling is stencilled with gold stars on a blue ground; at the top of the chancel walls, stencils of sacred symbols above a band of vine decoration. – Victorian FURNISHINGS. – STAINED GLASS. Three-light E window (the Ascension) of *c.* 1870 in the brightly coloured manner of illustrations to a children's Bible. – S window of the chancel (the Good Shepherd) of *c.* 1905. – One S window of the nave (the Maries at the Tomb) is of 1936. – One light in the nave's N wall (Angels) of *c.* 1895. – Late C19 glass (the Good Shepherd) in the round W window.

THE OLD KIRK OF RANNOCH, Schiehallion Road. Oblong 'Parliamentary' church* (i.e. to *William Thomson*'s design) built in 1829. Tudor windows in the sides and N gable. On the S gable, a birdcage bellcote with spiky obelisk finials at the corners and a spired roof. This gable's large round window (now blocked) is an insertion, probably of 1893 when the wood and glass porch and NE vestry were added.

Inside, FURNISHINGS of 1893 but the 'chancel' arrangement at the N end is of *c.* 1930. – STAINED GLASS window (the Good Samaritan) in the E wall, by the *Glass Co*. of Glasgow, 1904, a woefully bad example of narrative art. – Display of C19 collecting LADLES on the S wall.

GRAVEYARD, Lassintullich, 3.5km. ESE. Rubble-walled burial ground, the site of a medieval chapel dedicated to St Blane. On the N side, the rubble-built oblong MAUSOLEUM or burial enclosure of the Stewarts of Inverhadden, *c.* 8.3m. by 4.3m. and 1.6m. high. No evidence that it was covered by a roof. Rectangular door in the centre of the S side and, opposite, a round-headed N window; slit windows in the end walls. It is perhaps C17.

BRIDGE over the River Tummel. Rubble bridge of 1764. Four segmental arches; the triangular cutwaters have stepped tops.

DESCRIPTION. Most of the buildings around THE SQUARE are of the mid or later C19, with gablets, bargeboards and bracketed eaves but failing to be picturesque. On The Square's W side, the DUNALASTAIR HOTEL, perhaps mid C19 in origin but much enlarged in 1881 and given a conical-roofed round tower. On the N side of The Square, All Saints' Episcopal Church; on the S side of the River Tummel, The Old Kirk of Rannoch (for these and the bridge, *see* above).

CRAIGANOUR LODGE, 4.6km. W. Sprawling two-storey rubble-built shooting lodge. The taller W part, with broad eaves and horizontal-paned glazing, is of *c.* 1840. Long late C19 extension to the E.

CROSSMOUNT HOUSE. *See* p. 306.
DALL HOUSE. *See* p. 310.

KINMOUTH HOUSE
1 km. SSE of Rhynd

By *Peddie & Kinnear*, 1876–8, a starkly vertical ashlar-walled Baronial mansion house overlooking the S end of Strathearn. Asymmetrical but tautly composed main block of two storeys above a tall basement, plentifully equipped with crowstepped gables and mullioned windows. NW corner tower containing the entrance and rising a storey above the rest, its top floor

---

*Built with government finance under An Act for Building Additional Places of Worship in the Highlands and Islands of Scotland (1823). In 1825 the Commissioners for Highland Churches appointed under that act adopted a design for a 'Standard Church'.

jettied on continuous corbelling. Semicircular pediment over the attic window in its rosette-finialled N gable and a tall aedicular steeply pedimented dormerhead over the W attic window. At the tower's SW corner, a round tower, its conical roof covered with fish-scale slating. Between the chimneys which surmount the gable of the N front's E bay, a short but boldly corbelled battlement. S (garden) front of three bays, the l. with a gable between corbelled-out and spire-roofed square bartizans, the centre bay's top floor jettied on corbelling and with a steeply pedimented dormerhead over the top window; at the E end, a full-height canted bay window whose splayed sides are surmounted by corbelling to form a rectangular attic storey. In the bay window's W inner angle, a conical roofed circular turret. Rectangular bay window to the W elevation and, to its N, a bowed window under a corbelled-out diagonally set tophamper. Low service range projecting to the NE.

KINNAIRD

Beside a motte, now topped by a late C20 house (BARTON HILL), an informally laid out small village, the cottage gardens of more note than the architecture.

INCHMARTIN CHURCH, Westown, 1.4 km. S. Substantial though roofless and ivy-clad remains of a late medieval church abandoned after the union of its parish with Errol in 1628. It originally consisted of a nave and chancel. The chancel's E end has been demolished and only the W stubs of its side walls survive. The nave walls are largely intact. They are built of ashlar and pierced by putlog holes which penetrate the whole thickness of the masonry, perhaps intended as decoration as well as to provide supports for scaffolding during the building's construction. In the S wall's E end, a pair of rectangular windows, their roll-and-hollow-moulded surrounds containing glazing grooves. Near this side's W end, a segmental-arched door. The W gable is crowned by a sturdy gabled bellcote, its E and W faces with tall rectangular openings, the sides with oval openings. It may be an addition of the late C16. High up in this gable, a rectangular window. In the church's N side, a little W of centre, a rectangular door with a chamfered surround, almost certainly a late C16 or early C17 insertion. At the E end of this side, directly opposite the E window of the nave's S wall, a pointed window with a cusped head, its moulded surround again grooved for glazing. The chancel has been marked off from the nave by a cross wall pierced by a broad pointed arch flanked by a pair of putlog holes. The arch (now blocked) is of two orders with chamfered mouldings and springs from respond capitals, the inner apparently surmounting a pendant corbel rather than a shaft. Inside, splayed ingoes to the windows. Just E of the S door, remains of a recess, probably for a stoup.

s of the church, the GRAVE-SLAB of Alexander Hood, probably of the C17, its W end rounded. Incised marginal inscription and, in the centre, an array of tools.

KINNAIRD PARISH CHURCH. Built in 1815. Simple rubble-walled rectangle, a birdcage bellcote on the W gable. Pointed windows, now with wooden mullions and circled heads of 1893, in the gables and S side whose end bays are occupied by pointed doors under quatrefoil dummy openings. On the S wall, a well-lettered MONUMENT of c. 1930 to the Threiplands of Fingask.

GRAVEYARD. Beside the entrance, a rubble-built and piend-roofed windowless SESSION HOUSE of the early C19. – A few GRAVE-SLABS are propped against the walls. At the N end of the W wall, a slab, perhaps C17, carved with angels' heads (souls) and emblems of death. At the S end of this wall, a mid-C17 slab incised with crossbones. At the S wall, a couple of C18 slabs, both bearing shields and emblems of death. One is of 1741. The other, of the 1780s and commemorating Thomas Ogilvie, a farmer, has ploughs on the shield which is adjoined by a beaker and jug.

DELFORD HOUSE. Built as Kinnaird Parish Manse. By *W. M. Mackenzie*, 1831–2. Piend-roofed two-storey house, a blocking course at the slightly advanced centre of the three-bay front. Console-corniced doorpiece; wooden mullions to the three-light ground-floor windows.

KINNAIRD CASTLE
0.2 km. N

Tall tower house built for the Kinnairds of Kinnaird c. 1500. 59 Roofless and partly demolished by the late C18, it was restored in 1854–5 by Sir Patrick Murray Threipland whose family had acquired the property in 1674 as an adjunct to their estate of Fingask.

The site, on the top of a knoll cut off from the higher ground to the N by the steep banks of a burn, is naturally defensive but was strengthened by a barmkin wall with the tower standing at its NW corner. The tower is a rubble-built L. Main block (c. 11.7 m. by 8.3 m.) of four storeys with a crowstep-gabled attic, apparently in the place of a similar original feature, built in the 1850s; NW jamb, only c. 1.8 m. square but rising a storey higher, its join to the tower with a splay across the SE inner angle. Enough of the rounded corbels of the battlements survived by the 1850s for a reconstruction of their general appearance, with bartizans at the corners of the main block and a box machicolation over the entrance in its W side, but the uncrenellated parapet and cannon spouts are conjectural. Most of the walling below the battlements is C15. In the W side of the main block, two broad relieving arches, one at the first, the other at the second floor, are formed by the exposed outer ends of vaults over wall chambers inside. At the ground floor of this side, the round-headed principal entrance. A second (rectangular) doorway at the first floor of the jamb's W end gave access from the tower to the wall-walk of the barmkin which is now represented by a platform built in 1966 but incorporating a stub of medieval masonry. This entrance's moulded surround shows that it contained an inner and outer door, the outer folding down in drawbridge fashion. At the ground floor of the main block, slit windows in the gables and (lighting the lower flight of a stair) W side. More slits (lighting wall chambers) at the upper floors of the W side's N end and the NE corner where they serve mural garderobes. Decent-sized windows to the upper floors. In the jamb's faces are decorative slits of keyhole type, the rounds at their base intended as shot-holes, some with cross-bars.

The principal entrance, containing a round-headed iron yett, opens onto a lobby in the thickness of the W wall. E of this, a single room, its N and S ends forming tunnel-vaulted recesses, the room's centre covered with a flat ceiling, the wall-plates supported on corbels. At the NE corner, a round shaft, *c.* 5.5 m. deep, cut through the rock; it was probably a well. A doorway at the room's N end opens onto a wall passage leading into the jamb. In the floor of the passage, a trap door to a pit-prison. Off the N side of the entrance lobby, a straight flight of stairs contained in the thickness of the W wall leads to a turnpike stair in the wall thickness of the house's NW corner which rises to the attic and battlement's wall-walk. Each upper floor of the tower contained a single main room with a fireplace in one wall, windows equipped with stone seats and, at the NE corner, a garderobe, the garderobes at the second and third floors entered from window embrasures. At each level and entered from the stair, a narrow room in the thickness of the W wall.

Immediately S of the tower and at a lower level, a rubble-built plain COTTAGE. Its first-floor W window has a chamfered surround and is surmounted by a steeply pedimented dormerhead carved with the date 1610 and the initials PT, II and MO, the date not improbably that of the building but none of the initials relating to owners of Kinnaird Castle at that time. Perhaps it has been re-set here, possibly by the Threiplands in the late C17. Inside, the whole of the ground floor was originally occupied by a kitchen, presumably serving the tower, with a huge arched fireplace occupying its S end.

DOOCOT, *c.* 100 m. SE, probably of the early C18. Rubble-built, of lectern type, the roof rising as two identically pitched slopes interrupted by a central step which contains the flight-holes.

KINNAIRD HOUSE
2.2 km. SE of Logierait

Sprawling mansion house, begun *c.* 1805 for Charles Izzet, an Edinburgh hatter, who built a piend-roofed rubble-walled villa of two storeys above a basement (the S part of its front area later covered over). Three-bay w front, the centre slightly advanced under a pediment; ground-floor Venetian windows in the outer bays.

The estate was sold to the fourth Duke of Atholl in 1824 and sixteen years later the house was enlarged as a residence for Emily, Lady Glenlyon, widow of a brother of the fifth duke. The 1840 full-height but plain addition is on the back (E) of the original house and projects to its N. At its S gable and the S bay of its E elevation are single-storey and basement parapeted bay windows. Above the E bay window, a three-light window to the first floor. A porch was placed in the NW inner angle with the original house.

In the third stage, of 1913, *P. Macgregor Chalmers** extended the 1840 wing N by a further three bays and overlaid its W side with an addition, the porch being removed. To the E this work appears as a tactful continuation of the earlier extension, including a bay window of the same design but with two-light windows at the N bay. To the w it is free Elizabethan with hints of Neo-Georgian; round-arched entrance.

The house's final stage of growth took place in 1928–9 when Sir John Ward commissioned *Forsyth & Maule* to add a wing across the N end and extending W, making the building an irregular U shape. At this wing's E elevation, another bay window of the 1840 pattern. Two more bay windows but a storey higher at the long N side and, between them, a prominent chimneystack rising from the basement. On the S front towards the entrance court, a ground-floor Venetian window.

The interior is, unsurprisingly, a mixture but redolent of early C20 house parties. Large living hall of 1913 S of the entrance. At the SW corner, the drawing room (now dining room) of 1840 with a Frenchy chimneypiece and Watteauesque painted decoration of pastoral scenes on the walls. Also of 1840 the dining room to its N (now, Small Dining Room). N of this, along the E side, rooms of *c.* 1900 (formerly, a sitting room, dressing room and bedroom) with gentle Arts and Crafts plasterwork. In the N wing of 1928–9, two large rooms, the w (originally, smoking room) lined with cedar, the E (billiard room) also wood-lined.

In a hollow, just NW of the house, a rubble WALLED GARDEN, probably of *c.* 1810. – N of this, early C19 STABLE OFFICES. Two ranges, the S formed by a rubble-built double house, the N by piend-roofed cottages and stables (rather altered). Two-storey gabled centrepiece with segmental-arched coachhouse doors and, at the apex of the gable, the shaped base of a missing finial.

KINNESSWOOD

Village, known for its manufacture of parchment from the C16 until the C19, sited on the E edge of the low ground between Loch

---

* Tom Davidson Kelly has confirmed that Chalmers was responsible for work in 1913.

Leven and the Lomond Hills. It has been considerably enlarged in the late C20 but its size is still modest.

GLENLOMOND HOSPITAL, 2 km. NW. Built as a tuberculosis sanatorium in 1919. Simple blocks with white-harled walls, the roofs covered with red Rosemary tiles.

LOMOND HOUSE, the principal building, has wallhead gablets and a doorpiece with a semicircular open pediment. Closed in 1961, the hospital has been converted to housing and a nursing home, with additional residences built in the grounds.

DESCRIPTION. MAIN STREET is built along the A911. Near its S end, on the r., is RANNOCH, a Georgian cottage which was given a mansard roof and chunky oriel windows *c.* 1900. On the l., THE LOMOND COUNTRY HOTEL, its present appearance also of *c.* 1900, with a veranda between full-height canted bay windows. The majority of the village's buildings are simple vernacular, mostly of the earlier C19, some with pantiled roofs. But LOCH LEVEN VIEW on the l. side of the street has small splay-margined windows and a moulded and corniced doorpiece; it is probably early C18. Opposite, on the N corner of The Cobbles, the early C19 DOUGLAS HOUSE, its piended roof now covered with concrete tiles. Three-bay gable front of squared masonry with a heavy pilastered doorpiece, a band course above the ground floor and a first-floor sill course. In THE COBBLES, an uncobbled street which rises uphill to the E, informal C19 vernacular, some buildings rather altered. On the l., the early C18 rubble-built and pantiled MICHAEL BRUCE COTTAGE, birthplace of the poet Michael Bruce (1746–67). Two low storeys; small windows. The skews of the W gable have steps. At this gable, the S skewputt is moulded and topped by a stone ball.

ST SERF'S PRIORY. *See* p. 688.

KINROSS

Small town beside the main land route from Edinburgh to Perth and the capital of the former county of Kinross-shire. A burgh of barony under the superiority of the Douglases of Lochleven was created here in 1541 and the earliest houses probably stood near the W shore of Loch Leven in what is now the park of Kinross House to the E of the present town. This developed in the C18 as a centre for the manufacture of cutlery and linens, with cotton and woollen mills arriving in the early C19. A woollen industry continues but Kinross serves also as a golfing centre and a dormitory for Edinburgh and Perth.

CHURCHES

ANTIBURGHER CHURCH, Mill Street. Secularized. Rubble-built box of 1796–7. At the gables, plain club skews and ball

Map Legend

1. Antiburgher Church
2. Kinross Parish Church
3. St James (R.C.)
4. St Paul (Episcopal)
5. West United Presbyterian
6. Old Parish Churchyard
7. County Buildings
8. County House
9. Library
10. Rachel House
11. Town Hall

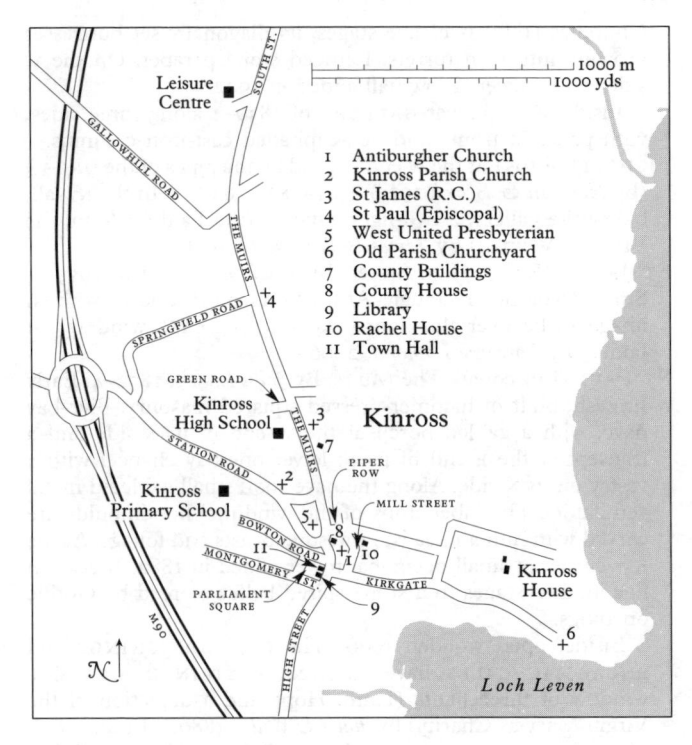

finials, the s gable's finial now missing. Metal ventilators on the roof, probably dating from alterations made in 1850. In each gable, a pair of rectangular windows and a round opening near the top. At the sides, rectangular windows in the end bays, taller round-headed windows in the centre. Early C20 porch at the centre of the E side. Projecting from the centre of the W side, a short link to a low hall added in 1890–2. Like the church, the hall is built of rubble with a ball finial on its front gable which is pierced by a pointed window under a small pointed dummy window. At the entrance from Mill Street to the courtyard formed by the church, link and hall, heavy gatepiers of 1892 supporting an iron overthrow.

KINROSS PARISH CHURCH, Station Road. 1831–2, by *George Angus*, and very similar to his contemporary Kettle Parish Church at Kingskettle and Tulliallan Parish Church at Kincardine-on-Forth, both in Fife. Like them it is Perpendicular, ashlar-built and large. M-roofed main block with diagonal corner buttresses. Porch at the E end. At the W end, short transepts and a tower. In the sides and E gable of the main block, hoodmoulded and tall two-light transomed windows, those of the gable topped by roundels containing stone S-tracery. Three-light windows at the transepts. The tower, exactly the same as those of Kettle and Tulliallan Parish

Churches (Fife) is of five stages, its diagonally set buttresses growing into slim turrets. Latticed stone parapet. On the w side of the tower, a low hall added in 1902.

Inside, a rectilinear GALLERY of 1830–2 along three sides, with panelled fronts and bell-capitalled cast-iron columns. – PULPIT of 1951 at the W end backed by the pipes of the ORGAN (by *Norman & Beard*, 1911). – STAINED GLASS. In the N wall, below the gallery, a two-light window (the Faithful Man; the Virtuous Woman) by *James Ballantine II*, 1926.

ST JAMES (R.C.), High Street. By *William W. Friskin*, 1955–6. Small drydashed rectangle. At the S end, a brick porch with an image niche over the door. – STAINED GLASS window (St James) by *Lorraine Lamond*, 2006.

ST PAUL (Episcopal), The Muirs. By *John Lessels*, 1872–4. Early English, built of hammer-dressed squared masonry. Five-bay nave, with a gabled porch at the W end of its S side and a transept at the E end of its N; lower one-bay chancel with a vestry on its N side. Along the nave roof, small gabled metal ventilators. The label stops of the windows' hoodmoulds are carved with human heads, grotesque beasts and foliage. At the NW corner, a small octagonal tower added in 1882. It rises in five intaken stages to a stone-spired belfry pierced by Gothic openings.

Inside, open wooden roofs. The C19 FURNISHINGS and ENCAUSTIC TILES have survived. – STAINED GLASS. E window of three lights (Faith, Hope and a depiction of the Virgin Mary as Charity) by *Jones & Willis*, 1880. – In the S wall of the nave, an expressionist window (St Peter) by *David Smith*, 1939. – A strongly coloured but less wilful mid-C20 window (St Margaret) is signed by *Douglas Hamilton*. – One light (St Paul) of *c*. 1910 and another (the Ascension) of 1882. – In the N wall, one light (the Risen Lord) by *Clayton & Bell*, 1898. – Another window (Our Lord Blessing Little Children) is of 1882. – Busily expressionist W window of three lights (Our Lord with the Doctors in the Temple; the Presentation of Our Lord in the Temple; the Maries at the Tomb) of *c*. 1935.

WEST UNITED PRESBYTERIAN CHURCH, High Street. Now a hall (Kinross Church Centre). Uninspired and uninspiring Gothic, by *Robert Baldie*, 1883–4. Nave and aisles, their join marked by pinnacled buttresses at the front gable. Over the gabled entrance, a five-light window with intersecting tracery. Lancet windows in the buttressed sides.

CEMETERY

OLD PARISH CHURCHYARD, Kirkgate. The medieval Kinross Parish Church, standing in isolation beside the shore of Loch Leven, was abandoned in 1743 when a new church was built in High Street.* Of it there survives only the BRUCE MAU-

---

* Itself demolished after the opening of the present Parish Church in Station Road in 1832.

SOLEUM built as a laird's aisle and mausoleum by *Sir William Bruce* after his purchase of the Kinross estate in 1675 but reconstructed in 1860. Its appearance is entirely Victorian. In the s gable, a hoodmoulded round-arched door. At each of the E and W sides, a large recessed panel topped by corbels supporting the masonry under the eaves; in these panels, round-headed dummy slit windows of 'Saxon' character.

On the s side of the graveyard, a battlemented square WATCH TOWER rebuilt in 1851–3. – In the graveyard, a number of C17 and C18 TABLE STONES, some of the C17 ones decorated only by inscriptions. Others have slabs carved with reminders of death. The earliest of these seems to be the stone dated 1690 to AM and IB. On it, a cartouche topped by a pediment whose sides are formed by carved bones; the tympanum displays a skull, spade and pick. – More emblems of mortality on a few C18 HEADSTONES. – In the graveyard's SW corner, a MONUMENT to Robert Burns-Begg by *Stewart McGlashan & Son*, 1902. It is a rough granite pillar carved with Celtic motifs. Set into the sides, bronze inscription tablets; at the front, a high-relief portrait bust of Burns-Begg by *D. W. Stevenson*.

PUBLIC BUILDINGS

COUNTY BUILDINGS, High Street. Now the Kinross Neighbourhood Office of Perth and Kinross Council. Classical, by *Thomas Brown* of Uphall, 1824–6. Main block of two tall storeys, faced with broached ashlar eroded by cleaning. Symmetrical front of five bays, the first-floor windows linked by a sill course and taller than those of the ground floor. The broad end bays are advanced and pedimented. In each pediment, a moulded roundel, the N containing a clock face. At each of these end bays, a door with a delicately consoled pediment and a consoled cornice over the window above. In the centre bay, a round-arched door in a pedimented aedicular frame with unfluted Greek Doric columns, the heaviness of this feature a contrast to the delicacy of the consoles at the end bays. Flanking the centrepiece, round-headed ground-floor windows in rectangular overarches. At each end and slightly set back, a single-storey pavilion, its front wall carried up as a screen above the level of the main block's first-floor sill course.

In front, a stone WAR MEMORIAL of *c.* 1920, its top a simplified Celtic cross.

COUNTY HOUSE, Nos. 109–113 High Street, on the corner of Burns-Begg Street. Now in commercial use, a three-storey block faced with droved ashlar (now painted). On it, an inscription recording that THIS COUNTY HOUSE WAS REPAIRED BY THE CROWN A.D. 1771 ROBERT ADAM KNIGHT OF THIS SHIRE DECORATED THE FRONT AT HIS OWN EXPENSES. Whatever earlier fabric is incorporated, nothing of the building's appearance now looks earlier than 1771. The decorative work which was paid for and presumably designed by *Robert Adam* who sat as M.P. for Kinross-shire between 1768 and 1774, is at the bowed S end where giant Tuscan pilasters mark off the upper floors' three bays and are surmounted by an entablature with a deep frieze and bold cornice. In the outer bays, round-headed niches at the first-floor and horizontal windows at the second; in the centre bay, a corniced first-floor window, with the inscription panel above. The ground floor's pilastered shopfronts are probably of the earlier C19.

KINROSS HIGH SCHOOL, High Street. Tall single-storey U-plan main block, by *Andrew Muirhead*, 1906–7. At the advanced ends, shaped gables containing round-arched and keystoned windows. To the NW, a harl and brick extension by *A. Watt Allison*, 1930. NW of that, a further extension by the Perth & Kinross County Architect, *Ian A Moodie*, 1961. In the playground, the round-arched bellcote from the demolished Parish School which was designed by the mason-architect *John Simpson* in 1823.

KINROSS PRIMARY SCHOOL, Station Road. By the Perth & Kinross County Architect, *John Nicol*, 1967–9. Functional-looking boxes of one and two storeys.

LEISURE CENTRE, The Muirs. Flashy Postmodern shed, by *Perth & Kinross District Council Architectural Services Department*, 1991.

LIBRARY, High Street. By *Peter L. Henderson*, 1904–5. Dumpy Baronial, with big crowsteps and a battlemented squat tower.

RACHEL HOUSE, off Avenue Road. A children's hospice. Accomplished Postmodern, by *Alan Marshall* of *Gray, Marshall & Associates*, 1994–6. Low, colourful and friendly, with prominent swept-up green slate roofs. At the pedestrian entrance, a blue-painted iron gate by *Ironhorse Studios*, the uprights in the form of stylized plants.

ST SERF'S HALL, The Muirs. Dated 1926. Utilitarian except at the front gable where a steep gable is marked out by cement dressings and the entrance has simplified Doric columns.

TOWN HALL, High Street. A ragbag development on the site of the former Kinross Parish Church of 1742–3, which was demolished after the completion of the present parish church in 1832. There survives the steeple which was added in 1751. Its slightly battered tower is of reddish sandstone with buff-coloured strip quoins and dressings. The E, W and S faces are all of rubble. The principal front to the N is faced with rough ashlar and divided by unmoulded string courses into four stages. At the bottom stage, a round-arched door, its surround hinting at Gibbsian influence. At the second stage, a moulded frame containing a panel carved with the profile of a lion rampant holding a shield which bears a saltire. In each corner of the panel, a fleur-de-lys. Above the panel, a round-arched window, the surround again Gibbsian. Blind third stage. At the top stage, a clock face in a simple moulded stone surround under a plain round-arched belfry opening. The same combination of a clock face and a belfry opening appears at the other sides of the tower but at the E front the clock is off-centre. The tower is finished with a rather crude balustrade projected on simple moulded corbels. Within the balustrade, a broached slated spire topped by a weathercock.

Built across the S side of the steeple but not quite at right angles to it is a two-storey piend-roofed office dated 1841, its grey ashlar front a contrast to the steeple's red rubble. Three-bay E front, the pilastered doorpiece flanked by canted bay windows. Rubble-built NW wing, its NW corner splayed. Projecting between this wing and the steeple, a crowstep-gabled two-storey block (formerly a Post Office), probably also of 1841 but built of red sandstone. S of the office block and set well back from the street is the Town Hall itself, a replacement by *Andrew Cumming*, 1868–9, for a hall put up in 1837 but which had been found too small. The present hall is a very tall single-storey block, the roof piended to the S, faced with stugged grey ashlar. Advanced and open-pedimented centre containing a lugged-architraved and corniced door. In the side elevations of this centrepiece, tall and narrow hoodmoulded windows. In each of the two outer bays, a two-light mullioned and transomed window.

DESCRIPTION

The B996 is the approach from the S. On the r. of the road the start of the town is announced by the large LOCHLEVEN MILLS, mostly a utilitarian late C20 brick complex but its N end incorporates a long late C19 range of weaving sheds, built of coursed masonry and covered by a series of double-pitch roofs whose gables front the road. The mills stand on the S side of the South Queich which is crossed by a single-span BRIDGE built in 1812 by *Pearson* with advice from *John Paterson* who may have designed it. The elliptical arch and outer faces are of ashlar, the inner sides of the parapet of rubble.

HIGH STREET starts with the white-painted BRIDGEND HOTEL of the mid or later C19 on the E. Its plainness sets the character of this stretch of the street, most of whose terraced houses are unambitious examples of one- and two-storey C19 vernacular. A few are earlier. At Nos. 233–237 on the r., a two-storey block with a mutuled cornice; it looks late C18 but the ground-floor windows have been enlarged. Set back from the street on the l. is No. 194, rubble-walled and pantile-roofed, its door lintel dated 1736.

SANDPORT is formed by three groups of buildings round a green which is open (except for discreet public lavatories) to High Street on the W. In the centre of the green, the old MARKET CROSS,* a roughly shaped stone cross to which is attached the rusty chain of a jougs. The cross may date from *c*. 1541 when Kinross first became a burgh but its base was

---

*It stood outside the County House until 1824 when it was removed to a disused quarry. Re-erected on approximately its old position in 1886, it was moved to a site beside the Town Hall in 1893 and to Sandport, *c*. 1955.

renewed in 1886. On the E side of the green, the gable and garden wall of the rubble-walled No. 8 Sandport built as Kinross Parish Manse in 1768 by *James Flockart*, mason in Annafreich. The pilastered doorpiece looks an addition of the early C19, a likely date for the enlargement of the ground-floor windows and perhaps also for the broad bowed dormers. The concrete roof tiles are C20. To its N, the early C19 BLINKHOOLIE (No. 10), the gable of its back wing extending to Sandport. The piend-roofed main block's W front is of two storeys and four bays.

SOUTH STREET leads W off High Street opposite Sandport. In it, C19 vernacular cottages, mostly now concrete-tiled but the roof of No. 4 is still covered with clay pantiles, although its dominant feature is a gabled dormer window of *c*. 1900. Closing the view down South Street is a single-storey T-plan former WASHHOUSE in MYRE TERRACE, built in the earlier C19 to serve the adjacent bleaching green (now playing field); hoodmoulds over the door and windows.

MONTGOMERY STREET is the next W branch off High Street. At the beginning of its S side, MYRE WELL HOUSE, the L-plan two-storey main part probably early C19, with a S-facing front, its C20 box dormers mercifully hidden from the street. Projecting N from the rear jamb is a single-storey drydashed cottage, its door lintel inscribed 17 DM MC 84. Also on the S side of Montgomery Street but further out, Nos. 15–23, a single-storey and attic terrace of the later C19, the roofs now with concrete pantiles but each house still boasting a large bargeboarded wallhead dormer.

The first stretch of High Street ends with the library and Town Hall (*see* Public Buildings, above) which provide a civic centre for the burgh. Immediately N of the Town Hall, an octagonal Gothic FOUNTAIN of 1886. At each face of the pedestal, a pointed blind arch springing from attached columns; over the arches, continuous hoodmoulding with foliaged label stops. At alternate faces the arches frame badly worn carved lions' heads designed to spit out water into stone bowls (one now missing). The pedestal supports an octofoiled basin, its soffit carved with foliage, from whose centre rises a finial composed of four back-to-back gryphons. Just to the N, Nos. 98–102 High Street, probably the tenement which was described as 'new' in an advertisement in the *Edinburgh Evening Courant* in 1801. This is of two storeys and an attic, its ashlar front slightly bowed and with a broad pedimental chimneyed gablet at the centre of the wallhead. Opposite is the former County House (*see* Public Buildings, above) on the corner of Burns-Begg Street from whose E end KIRKGATE leads between the park wall of Kinross House (*see* below) and Loch Leven to the Old Parish Churchyard (*see* Cemetery, above). In High Street immediately N of the County House, a plain and rather altered house of *c*. 1840, the pilastered doorpiece now bereft of its cornice. It is followed by a set-back development by *James Shearer & Annand*, 1970–4, whose commercial blocks form a gateway to housing in MILL STREET at whose E end, overlooking Burns-Begg Street, stands the former Antiburgher Church (*see* Churches, above).

SWANSACRE continues the line of Mill Street W of High Street. On its S side and continuing SW into SCHOOL WYND, heavily reconstructed C18 and C19 vernacular housing covered in drydash and render, the houses in School Wynd roofed with pantiles. The N side of Swansacre begins more suavely with the early C19 Nos. 2–4. At their W end, presenting a gable to the street is the LOCHLEVEN INN, its walling now rendered and lined as ashlar. Three storeys, the unaltered small windows of the W front's upper floors disclosing its early C18 date. Just to its W, a late C19 pair of cottages (Nos. 8–10 Swansacre); built into their front wall is a lintel inscribed WS.EW.1716.

AVENUE ROAD, the next street exiting E from High Street, leads to the gates and lodges at the entrance to the park of Kinross House which is visible at the end of a long avenue (for these, *see* Kinross House, below). Off the end of Avenue Road, a short drive to Rachel House (*see* Public Buildings, above). In High Street opposite the entrance to Avenue Road, a mid-C19 block (Nos. 72–74), its ground floor's shop windows surmounted by a cornice supported on consoles rising out of carved shells. On the N corner of High Street and Avenue Road, the harled three-storey SALUTATION HOTEL, still with shaped skewputts but the fenestration altered. At the W gable, an early C19 doorpiece framing what is now a window opening whose lintel is inscribed WW ED.1721, a likely enough date for the building. A little further along High Street, on the corner of Piper Row, the former West United Presbyterian Church (*see* Churches, above).

STATION ROAD's S corner with High Street has been opened up as a car park for a shop. The road's first part forms the N side of a triangle whose SE side is provided by Swansacre. At the junction of Station Road and Swansacre, the MONUMENT erected in 1914 to James Mungle. Kemnay granite pedestal with a projecting basin. On the pedestal, a bronze bust by *John S. Rhind*. Just W of the monument and set back from the road is Kinross Parish Church (*see* Churches, above). Opposite the church is the substantial but plain piend-roofed EAST HOUSE of *c.* 1830. Immediately to its W, the former KINROSS PARISH MANSE (now Nos. 3–4 LOMOND MEWS) built and perhaps designed by *Thomas Falconer* in 1784–5, the front (S) windows enlarged by *Smart & Stewart* in 1910. The rear wing visible from the street is probably an addition of 1812. The mutuled cornices of its sides return across the N gable to form a pediment. Further out, on the N side of Station Road, No. 28, dated 1889, a sort of *cottage orné* but over-large and over-serious for the genre although the wacky battlemented tower over the entrance is enjoyable. On the S side, after Kinross Primary School (*see* Public Buildings, above), VIEWFIELD (No. 41) with Italianate windows and elaborate bargeboards; it is dated 1879.

High Street starts to alter character N of the junction with Station Road. The change is announced by THE ROYAL BANK OF SCOTLAND (No. 53) on the E side, by *David Smart*, 1900. Villa-like but stolid with heavy consoles under the projecting ends of the corner over the door. A little further on, No. 45, a genuine villa of *c.* 1830, with an architraved and corniced doorpiece, small rectangular overarches to the ground floor windows, and a blocking course over the centre of the main cornice. Another villa (No. 41) is of *c.* 1815 but altered *c.* 1900 when it was given a porch, two-storey bay windows and big piended dormers, the porch and bay windows surmounted by pacific battlements with circular central merlons. The original walling is of broached ashlar with rusticated quoins; the additions are built of polished ashlar. Next door, the piend-roofed CLYDESDALE BANK (No. 39) is also of *c.* 1815 and faced with broached ashlar (now painted). Quite ambitious, with giant pilasters at the ends of the front, round-headed overarches to the ground floor windows, and a Roman Doric columned doorpiece. At the house's S end, a single-storey addition of *c.* 1900, a heavy consoled pediment over the entrance. Opposite, Nos. 18 and 20 (KIRKLANDS HOTEL) were originally a pair of detached early C19 houses, both built of broached ashlar and having identical pilastered doorpieces with rosetted friezes and chimneystacks topped with triangular merlons, but the roof of No. 18 is piended, that of No. 20 has straight skews. The houses are now linked by a slightly recessed extension added to No. 20 in the mid C19. There follow the County Buildings and St James (R.C.) Church on the E and Kinross High School on the W (*see* Churches and Public Buildings, above).

High Street ends with detached villas. On the E, No. 3, dated 1865, has carved bargeboards and Tudorish first floor windows. No. 1, also bargeboarded, was built in 1867 but acquired a round conical-roofed SW corner tower in 1896. Opposite, the BANK OF SCOTLAND (No. 2) was built as the British Linen Co.'s Bank in 1830, a most superior piend-roofed villa of two storeys and three bays. In front of the entrance, a screen of Ionic columns *in antis*; aprons under the windows of the outer bays. The S ground floor window is of three equal-sized lights, perhaps the result of a later enlargement. Octagonal chimney stacks at the gables.

THE MUIRS, the N continuation of High Street, begins on the W with THE GREEN HOTEL, its main block built in 1829 but altered later in the C19; in the C20 it was extended to the N and W in a Neo-Georgian manner. Harling and black-painted margins give a superficial unity. Further out, the piend-roofed MOSS GROVE (No. 18) of the earlier C19. Two storeys and three bays, the N bay projecting as a full-height bow; anta-pilastered doorpiece. On the E, St Serf's Hall and St Paul's (Episcopal) Church (*see* Public Buildings and Churches, above). Far out on the W, Nos. 74–78, a pair of tall late C19 villas, their gables' half-timbering including depictions of thistles. At the N end of The Muirs and of the town, the Leisure Centre (*see* Public Buildings, above).

SECESSION MONUMENT, Gairneybridge, 3.7 km. S. By *A. Macdonald & Co.*, 1883. Large polished granite obelisk erected to commemorate the 150th anniversary of the formation of the first presbytery of the Secession Church.

KINROSS HOUSE
off Avenue Road

Architecturally the most ambitious work of late C17 Scotland, placed in a setting of formal gardens and historical landscape which combine with the house to make a huge processional apartment focused on the distant Lochleven Castle.

History

The Kinross estate was bought in 1675 by *Sir William Bruce* of Balcaskie, the leading architect and arbiter of taste of his time. No less importantly for contemporaries, Bruce was also a political protégé of the Duke of Lauderdale and, at that time, Clerk of the Bills, Surveyor-General and Overseer of the King's Buildings in Scotland, Receiver of Fines, Commissioner of Excise in Fife and farmer of the customs of Scotland. On his purchase of Kinross he became also hereditary Sheriff of Kinross-shire and his erection of Kinross House was doubtless intended to be accompanied by his (unrealized) elevation to the peerage as Viscount of Kinross.

When Bruce bought the estate there already existed a substantial mansion, known as Newhouse, standing some way NE of the present house, which had been built in the late C16 to provide a more comfortable residence than the island fortress of Lochleven Castle (q.v.). Although Bruce repaired and occupied Newhouse, it was literally marginal to his new garden and landscape layout which assumed the construction of a new mansion as its centrepiece. Work on levelling of the site and construction of garden walls began in 1679 and the next year stone was quarried at Nivingston for a great gateway at the entrance from the town of Kinross to an avenue on the approach to the new house. In 1682 Bruce's son, John, sent his father horse chestnuts, shrubs, seeds and flower roots from Paris, and the main elements of the park and garden layout were probably in place by 1684 when *Tobias Bachop* contracted to build 'the Great Gate in the outmost Sweip', four years after stone had begun to be quarried for its construction. At the same time work was in progress on building coachhouse and stable blocks.

Bruce was appointed a member of the Privy Council in May 1685, and contracts for construction of the mansion house itself were signed in the same year. Tobias Bachop seems to have been the principal mason. The basement was built in 1686 and decorative carved stonework produced at the same time by *Peter Paul Boys* and *Cornelius van Nerven*. Despite Bruce's dismissal from the Privy Council and other government offices by James VII in 1686 and his imprisonment as a Jacobite sympathiser at times during the reign of William III work continued. Kinross House was roofed in 1691 and, the next year, hangings and pictures were provided for the interior, whose Great Stair seems to have been completed in 1693. Financial, if not physical constraints seem to have precluded the fitting out of the house's first floor, which had been intended as a *piano nobile* housing the state apartment, in anything more than rudimentary fashion. Daniel Defoe related in 1722, however, that 'the great salon is crowded with pictures . . .'

Sir William Bruce's heirs failed to carry the work to completion and in 1758 Sir William Burrell noted that 'a very small proportion of that Part of the House is finished, being only bare, the Garden produces Hay & Barley instead of Fruit & Flowers . . . the Back of the House is planted wth Fruit & other Trees, but the Winds have demolished some of them entirely, & makes continual attacks on the rest.' In 1777 the Kinross estate was sold to George Graham, a Calcutta merchant. Soon after, he carried out repairs and more work was done *c.* 1810 by his brother and heir, Thomas. On Thomas Graham's death in 1819 the estate passed to his daughter, Helen, wife of Sir James Montgomery of Stanhope who had built himself the large country house of Stobo Castle (Borders) and for whom Kinross House was apparently superfluous. Although it was reroofed in 1869 Kinross was unoccupied by its owners for the rest of the C19. However, when Sir Basil Graham-Montgomery inherited in 1902 he decided to live at Kinross and carried out substantial work to the house and gardens, including laying out a parterre where one had been intended by Bruce. *Thomas Ross* acted as architect for this work.

Plan

Bruce's layout of the house, gardens and landscape was rigorously unified, the most complete and uncompromising expression of the processional planning which he had introduced to Scottish architecture. Underlying this was the French conception of a royal palace as a sequence of rooms (guard hall, presence chamber or throne room, privy chamber, bedchamber and closet) of increasing grandeur or intimacy, a visitor's rank or place in royal favour determining how far he could progress before being refused admission to the room beyond. At Kinross Bruce included the approach to the house and, beyond it, the garden, Loch Leven and its castle in a processional sequence of exceptional length and inexorable linearity. From the great gateway at the W edge of the park a 0.3 km.-long avenue led to a second gateway flanked by stable and coachhouse blocks occupying the W range of a gravelled outer court, its other sides enclosed by screen walls. A third gateway, at the centre of this court's E side, opened into the smaller inner court, laid out as

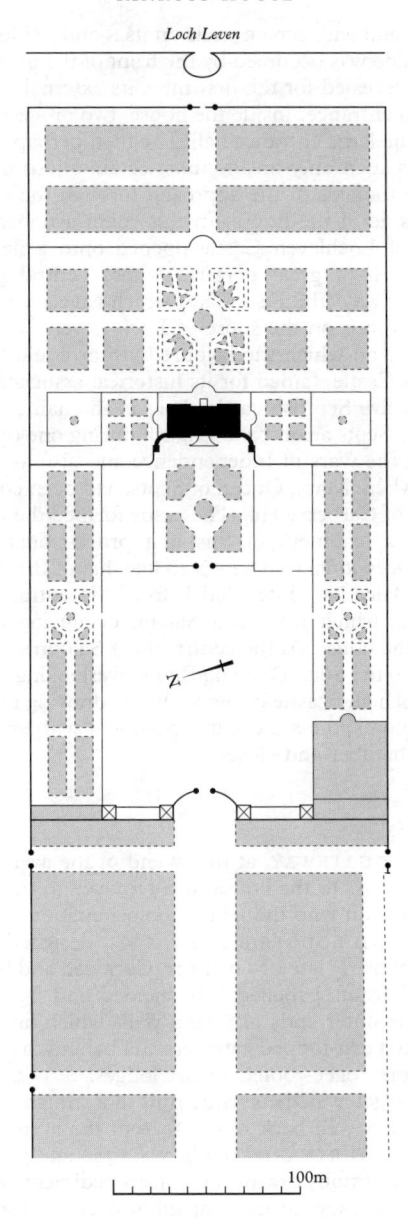

Kinross House.
Reconstruction of site plan of c. 1685

a parterre and with screen walls on its N and S sides. The inner court's E side was occupied by the front of the mansion house, here fully revealed for the first time, its external stair rising to the central entrance. Inside the house, two processional routes led from the large entrance hall. The first, perhaps intended to be used as such only on the most ceremonious of occasions, continued the axis of the approach through the Garden Hall on the E side of the house. In this room a doorway framing the view of Lochleven Castle opened onto a flight of steps descending to a great parterre whose central path led to another gateway (the Fish Gate) which gave access to a small circular harbour on the shore of Loch Leven. In the harbour was a barge on which the favoured visitor could be rowed to Lochleven Castle, famed for its historical associations both as one of the five Scottish castles held in the name of the rightful King of Scots against the English during one of the darkest periods of the Wars of Independence and also as the place of captivity where Mary, Queen of Scots, had been confined after the Battle of Carberry Hill. The castle formed the final 'room', effectively a 'cabinet', of this first processional route. The second processional route, its plan like that of Bruce's previous house at Balcaskie (Fife), led l. from the entrance hall to a Great Stair which rose to a Saloon occupying the five-bay centre of the house. At the centre of the Saloon's E side a door opened into the State Drawing Room overlooking the parterre, with the loch and castle beyond. Off the drawing room ran two suites of rooms, the S the state apartment with an ante-room, state bedchamber and closet.

Description

Bruce's GREAT GATEWAY, at the W end of the avenue from the town of Kinross to the house, was removed in the late C18 by George Graham who thought it too ostentatious. The present GATEWAY AND LODGES are of *c.* 1905, designed by *Thomas Ross* in a scholarly late C17 manner. Corniced and ball-finialled piers, their fronts panelled with banded and fluted pilasters, stand at the outer ends of screen walls which link to banded and corniced urn-topped gatepiers. Set behind the screen walls are two-storey ogee-roofed square lodges.

From the gateway the avenue runs in a straight line towards the house. Set well back to the N from the avenue's E end is the STABLE COURTYARD built here *c.* 1780 and probably originally unpretentious except for a steep pediment with a circular dummy window in its tympanum over the round-headed entrance. This front range was dressed up in late C17 style by Ross at the beginning of the C20 with round-headed windows in rusticated surrounds and two-storey ogee-roofed end pavilions, their ground-floor openings overarched. Inside the courtyard, a round tower, a cupola on its truncated conical roof. From the E side of the stables extends a wall which marks the N boundary of Bruce's formal landscape and gardens. At

KINROSS HOUSE

this wall's W end, beside the stables, a pair of tall urn-topped GATEPIERS, probably of the late C17. They stand at the entrance to a woodland ride.

The OUTER COURT's buildings and walls have been demolished except the N and S ends of its E wall which were extended in the C19 across the former orchards to the boundary walls, the extensions pierced by round openings. Each of the late C17 stretches of these walls runs between piers, the outer with an urn finial, the inner surmounted by a sundial, its underside decorated with foliage. The sundials were carved by *John Hamilton*, servant to the architect and master mason, *James Smith*; their copper gnomons were supplied by the smith, *John Callander*, in 1686. In the centre of each of these walls, a round-headed gateway surmounted by ball finials flanking a stone pineapple; iron gate, the overthrow with acorn and tulip finials.

From the inner ends of these screen walls extend the curvaceous walls which formed the N and S sides of the INNER COURT. These are convex, articulated by pilaster strips surmounted by finials in the shape of acorns and flaming urns (the latter probably carved by *James Anderson* in 1686). Between the pilasters are set tethering rings held in the mouths of friendly-looking carved stone lions' heads. At their E end these convex walls are joined by short stretches of straight walling to the house's square PAVILIONS, the ogee roof of each finished with a foliaged iron finial. The pavilions are of a single storey, basement and attic, their rubble walling probably intended to be harled, and with rusticated quoins. In the W face of each, a round-arched and keystoned ground-floor window; small horizontally proportioned openings to the basement and attic. At each inner face to the court, a door under a pulvinated frieze and cornice which supports a pedestal surmounted by a roundel on which are displayed the monogrammed initials WMB (for [Sir] William Bruce and Mary Bruce, his wife) and set in a carved surround of fruiting foliage. In each pavilion's E front facing the garden, a round-headed niche. The outward-looking faces of the pavilions abutted piend-roofed low wings, the N housing the kitchen, the S the 'woman house' (female servants' quarters), which were demolished in 1853. At the N pavilion, a round-headed basement door, probably late C17. The S pavilion's ground-floor door, also round-headed, may be an insertion; above it, a small stone carved, perhaps in the C16, with a weathered coat of arms and the letters Rd M. Balustraded concave basement links join the pavilions' inner W corners to the W corners of the main block of the mansion house.

The main block of the MANSION HOUSE is of two storeys and an attic above a basement, all built of warm yellow polished ashlar. This masonry is channelled at the upper part of the basement whose lower part was intended to be hidden by a terrace (now removed from the sides and E elevation). W front of eleven bays, the three at each end slightly advanced and with a single giant Corinthian pilaster at each corner, their wide spacing probably derived from Bernini's first project of 1664 for the Louvre illustrated in *Le Grand Marot* (*c.* 1670). Other details all of a similarly refined austerity. Horizontally proportioned basement windows with voussoir lintels; between the outer windows of the centrepiece are small circular openings. The basement is finished with a sill course under the ground-floor windows and forming the lowest course of the pilasters' bases. Another sill course at the first floor. The ground- and first-floor windows, all apparently sashed from the start, have lugged architraves and cornices. In the centre bay, the house's entrance fronted by a broad elliptical sweep of steps whose bottom flights extend beyond the centrepiece; their present appearance is the result of an afterthought or perhaps an early C18 replacement, a narrower stair of rectangular plan having been intended originally.

The entrance itself is set behind an Edwardian portico, its coupled Ionic columns replicas of those designed by Bruce. Bruce originally intended the portico to be surmounted by a wrought-iron balustrade and the ironwork for this was supplied by the smith, *James Horne*, in 1689–90, but the balustrade was replaced by a pediment either as a change of mind in the 1690s or as an early C18 alteration. The Edwardian rebuilding of the portico also provided a pediment but it looks steeper than the one shown in the early C18 engraving of the house published in *Vitruvius Scoticus*. The window above the portico is framed by triangular enrichments carved into the wall surface, probably as an afterthought, in fairly shallow relief with downward-spilling trophies, the shields bearing grotesque heads. Above the window, a cartouche surmounted by Bruce's crest of a sunburst and bearing the impaled coats of arms of Sir William Bruce and his first wife, Mary Halket. This stands proud of the house's entablature and modillion cornice. Above the entablature, a low 'parapet' under the eaves of the piended roofs. It is pierced by the small horizontally proportioned attic windows (originally casements), a detail probably taken from Palladio's design for a villa for the Mocenigo family illustrated in *I Quattri Libri*. On the centre of the high roof, an ogee-roofed and ball-finialled octagonal cupola. Regularly disposed panelled and corniced chimneys.

The house's five-bay end elevations are almost identical. The detail repeats that of the front but the ground-floor windows (the W curtailed to allow for the roofs of the quadrant links to the pavilions) are less tall, giving space for the horizontal openings (originally containing casements) of a mezzanine floor above, the centre mezzanine window of each end having a keystoned basket arch.

The house's E front is a repeat of the W except at the centre bay. Here, instead of the W elevation's curved flight of steps, is a straight stair, its squashed stone balusters giving way at the bottom to curlicued wrought-iron railings. The late C17 portico survives, again with coupled Ionic columns but surmounted not by a pediment but by a wrought-iron balustrade (by *James*

Horne, 1689–90) round the flat roof which serves as a balcony onto which opens a window-door framed, like the corresponding window of the W front, by triangles of shallow relief carving, here of fruit. In the cartouche above, the impaled coats of arms of Sir William Bruce's son, John, and his wife, Christian Leslie, perhaps not executed until after 1700 when they took over the house from Sir William.

For the interior of the house, *see* below.

Sir William Bruce designed a great parterre E of the house. Whatever of this was executed was swept away, except for a large basin on the central axis, in the late C18. The present PARTERRE was created by Sir Basil Graham-Montgomery at the beginning of the C20. At the N end of the garden's W wall, a pair of corniced GATEPIERS, with channelled stonework. They may be late C18. A little to the NE and SE of the house, pedestals surmounted by large stone STATUES of recumbent lions, perhaps of the late C17. Directly in front of the house, the parterre, its centre occupied by the basin which seems to have been placed there *c.* 1690 and in which stands a rather small lead STATUE of a boy with a swan. At the ends of the SW compartment of the garden, Ionic columned shelters of *c.* 1910. In the centre of the path between them, a lead STATUE of Atlas, probably C18. E of this, at the garden's S boundary, a widely spaced pair of PIERS, probably of the late C17, surmounted by carved stone baskets of fruit. Panelled faces with, at the N, bowed projections under foliaged pendants; at the inner faces, scroll-topped rectangular projections. At the corresponding point of the garden's N side, much larger PIERS, the centre of each face carved with a broad Doric pilaster, the whole crossed by banded rustication. These are clearly the reused gatepiers of the Great Gate which *Tobias Bachop* contracted to execute in 1684. Large and elaborately swagged urn finials, apparently provided as afterthoughts, perhaps in the early C18, in place of the originally intended globes. Further E, facing each across the garden, two Doric columned SHELTERS, perhaps of the late C17. The N shelter's back wall bears a MONUMENT of 1929 to Sir Basil Graham-Montgomery with a bronze relief bust by *Thomas Good*. E of these, rubble garden walls with moulded copes, the N wall pierced by a round-arched gateway, probably of the C17, which provided access to the path to the former mansion of Newhouse (demolished in 1723).

The E GARDEN WALL is articulated by panelled and corniced piers, the outer ones with fir cone finials, the inner surmounted by lions holding shields. In the centre of this wall, directly aligned on Lochleven Castle (q.v.), is the late C17 FISH GATE. At its ends, corniced piers crossed by bands of frosted rustication and topped by fish-tailed cherubs. The tops of the piers are flanked by scrolls from which the walling is scooped down each side, the broad scoop between the piers crowned with long cornucopias. In the centre of this part, a round-headed arch, its keystone supporting the carving of a plaited basket filled with fish. Until the lowering of the water level of Loch Leven in 1836 the Fish Gate opened onto a landing place beside the small harbour which housed a barge to carry visitors to Lochleven Castle.

INTERIOR OF MANSION HOUSE. In the basement, tunnel-vaulted rooms (cellars, larders, kitchens and stores). The stairs down have late C17 wrought-iron balustrades of simple curlicue design but surprisingly smart for this position.

The late C17 PLAN of the ground and first floors survives largely intact although, not surprisingly, rooms have changed their functions. Inside the front door is a large entrance hall and ahead, the Garden Hall (now Drawing Room), with a garden door on the axis of the approach from the W and of Lochleven Castle to the E. S of the Garden Hall was the principal suite of family rooms consisting of a drawing room, bedchamber, closet and dressing room. N of the Garden Hall, another bedchamber and closet. A third bedchamber, with closet and dressing room, occupied the SW corner of the house. Most of the house's NW corner was filled by the Great Stair entered from the N side of the entrance hall; behind it were a charter room and Sir William Bruce's closet. The Great Stair gave access to the first-floor Saloon (now Ballroom) occupying the central five bays of the house's W side. Opening off it to the E was a State Drawing Room with a door onto the flat roof of the portico (i.e. on the axis of Lochleven Castle). The state apartment continued to the S with an enfilade of antechamber, bedchamber and closet. Two more bedchambers, each with a closet, were provided in the house's SW and NE corners. In the middle of the house and opening each side off the E end of the entrance hall were secondary stairs and, beyond them, tunnel-vaulted passages. Near the ends of these passages and contained in wall thicknesses were very tight turnpike stairs to small servants' bedrooms which occupied the centre of the N and S ends of the house on the mezzanine and first floor. More bedrooms were placed in the attic.

The ENTRANCE HALL is T-plan, the short tail projecting E. The arms of the T are marked off by screens, each with a close-set pair of Ionic columns standing on a tall pedestal and well separated from the end pilasters. The screens seem to have been an afterthought since the design of *c.* 1685 shows walls in their place and the building accounts for 1691 mention mason work (presumably paving) as having been carried out in the 'Ante Cham[ber] next Stair Case' (i.e. the present N arm of the T). Stone flagged floor. Panelled walls. The entrance from the W is placed in a lugged architrave which encloses a long horizontal panel above the door opening, the architrave framed by an Ionic columned aedicule. Opposite, another Ionic aedicule framing the segmental-arched E door into the former Garden Hall. This is flanked by a pair of dummy doors, their lugged architraves with bead-and-reel enrichment, set in segmental-headed overarches. Similar doors and overarches at the sides of the tail. This central space is finished with a modillion

KINROSS HOUSE

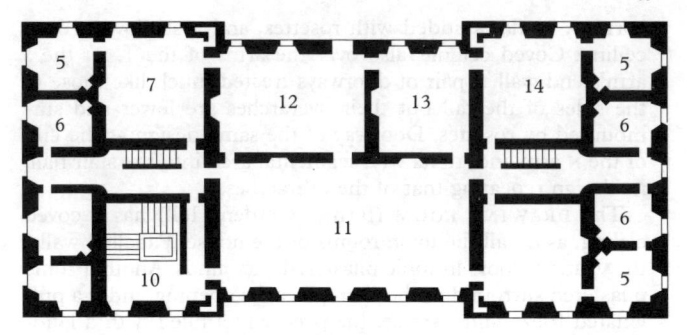

FIRST FLOOR

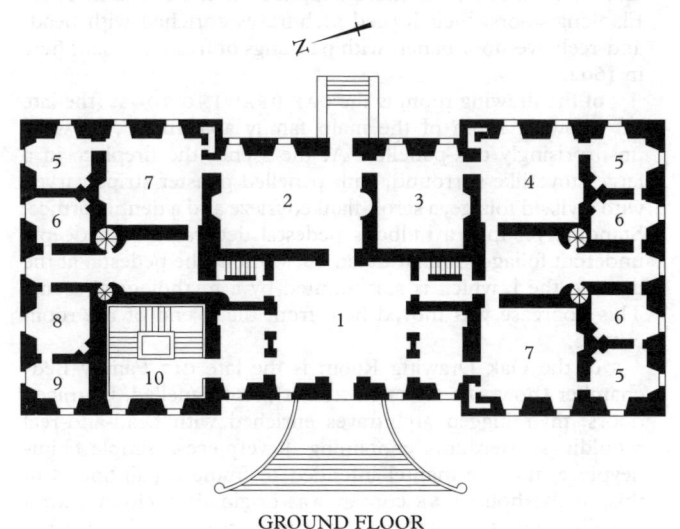

GROUND FLOOR

|—————————————————| 30m

1. Entrance Hall
2. Garden Hall
3. Oak Drawing Room
4. Family Bedchamber
5. Closet
6. Dressing Room
7. Bedchamber
8. Sir William Bruce's Closet
9. Charter Room
10. Stair Hall
11. Saloon
12. State Drawing Room
13. Ante-Chamber
14. State Bedchamber

Kinross House.
Plans of house in *c.* 1700

cornice, its flat studded with rosettes, and a shallowly coved ceiling. Coved ceilings also over the arms of the T. At the S arm's end wall, a pair of doorways treated much like those of the sides of the tail but their overarches are lower and surmounted by rosettes. Doorway of the same design at the end of the N arm and, to its W, a segmental arch into the stair hall, its design repeating that of the overarches.

The DRAWING ROOM (former Garden Hall) has a coved ceiling, as do all the main rooms of the house. Panelled walls, the W and S doors in Ionic pilastered surrounds. Another Ionic pilastered surround to the N fireplace, its opening under a pulvinated frieze and cornice, the overmantel filled with a landscape painting, one of those supplied for the house in 1692. Flanking doors, their lugged architraves enriched with bead-and-reel; overdoor panels with paintings of fruit, also sent here in 1692.

S of the drawing room is the OAK DRAWING ROOM (the late C17 drawing room of the main family apartment), its walls unsurprisingly oak-panelled. At the S end, the fireplace in a large stove-like surround, with panelled pilaster strips carved with stylized foliage, a scroll-flanked frieze and a dentil cornice. Standing on this, a bulbous pedestal decorated with deeply undercut foliage. Similar detail but without the pedestal at the door to the l. which is surmounted by a mythological scene. This doorcase was moved here from the N end of the room c. 1902.

S of the Oak Drawing Room is the late C17 Family Bedchamber (now BIG SITTING ROOM), also panelled. Corniced doors, their lugged architraves enriched with bead-and-reel mouldings; overdoors containing flowerpieces. Simple chimneypiece, the overmantel intended to frame a painting. S of this, at the house's SE corner, was originally a closet with a dressing room to its W, both with corner fireplaces. In the early C20 they were thrown together to form the LITTLE SITTING ROOM, the walls covered with reused or replicated panelling; chimneypiece in a simple late C17 manner.

N of the Drawing Room is the DINING ROOM formed c. 1902 from a late C17 bedchamber, closet and dressing room. One doorcase, placed across the SW corner, is corniced and surmounted by an ogee roof with a fir-cone finial. Does this incorporate work from a late C17 corner chimneypiece removed from a former closet or dressing room? Smart Adam Revival marble chimneypiece.

Opening off the SW corner of the entrance hall is another late C17 bedchamber (now LIBRARY). Corniced doorpieces with pulvinated friezes. Adam revival chimneypiece of the early C20. To the S, a panelled closet known as the TOBACCO ROOM since 1692, so perhaps used as a smoking room in the C17. The door and corner fireplace have very similar detail to those at the S end of the Oak Drawing Room but the fireplace's surmounting pedestal is larger and of flatter profile. E of this but now entered from a passage on its E side is a dressing room converted, *c.* 1902, to the MARBLE BATH-ROOM but still with a late C17 corner fireplace.

Off the NW corner of the entrance hall is the square STAIR HALL containing the late C17 Great Stair to the intended state apartment on the first floor. At the lower part of the stair hall the walls are articulated by skinny pilaster strips. The arch from the entrance hall is set in a bead-and-reel-moulded wooden frame with a wooden panel above. In the N wall opposite, two doors, both with lugged architraves. The r., under the stair's half landing, also enriched with bead-and-reel, originally gave access to Sir William Bruce's Closet (now laundry). The l., opening onto a vaulted charter room (now lavatory), is surmounted by the wooden high-relief achievement of Sir William Bruce flanked by foliaged scrolls and topped by carved fruit and flowers; this is probably identifiable as the carved coat of arms executed for Bruce by *Jan van Santvoort* in 1679 and perhaps erected initially in Newhouse. The scale-and-platt stair itself is of oak, the edges of its underside carved with foliage and flowers. More carved flowers and leaves in the pierced scrollwork of the wooden balustrade whose panelled and corniced newel posts support leaves cradling ball finials. The design of the balustrade is repeated on the walls as a painted dado (by *James Alexander*, 1693). Here the newel posts are mirrored by wooden pilasters with half-round finials. At the top landing, doors with lugged architraves to the E and S. Over the E door, a pulvinated frieze and modillion cornice with rosettes on the flat support a segmental pediment broken by a foliaged pendant. The door to the S, opening into the Saloon, is grander, its entablature and pediment carried on Ionic pilasters. Over the stair hall, a lavishly enriched coved ceiling, the plasterwork deeply undercut. Large leaves at the corners. Foliaged border to the square panel of the central flat whose boldly modelled flowering and fruiting foliage encloses a roundel, probably intended for a painting, the roundel's outer border modelled with egg-and-dart enrichment, its inner with beading.

The S door of the Great Stair's landing opens into the Saloon (now BALLROOM). Bruce intended this as a magnificent space, *c.* 17.4 m. by 7.6 m. and 9.14 m. high, the lighting from its W windows supplemented by top lighting from the cupola on the roof of the house. At the centre of the E wall, above the door to the State Drawing Room, was to have been a musicians' gallery. However, the room seems to have been finished in the late C17 in only perfunctory fashion and the present appearance is *Thomas Ross*'s work of *c.* 1902. This is in a scholarly approximation of Bruce's manner but without the richness of decoration which must have been intended originally. Large leaves at the corners of the coved plaster ceiling. On its flat, four square compartments, each containing foliage surrounding a circular centre panel. Simply corniced doorpieces with pulvinated friezes. At the E wall, two fireplaces flank the central door. This opens into the intended STATE DRAWING ROOM and, as at the drawing room below, is aligned on the view of Lochleven Castle seen through a half-glazed door above the garden front's portico. The room itself is of *c.* 1902, its chimneypiece of Late Georgian derivation in white and honey-coloured marble.

LOCHLEVEN CASTLE. *See* p. 501.

KINROSSIE

Broad street of late C18, C19 and C20 cottages now fronted by lawns. One house (THE WHIGMALEERIE) boasts a reed-thatched roof.

COLLACE FREE CHURCH. Converted to Village Hall in 1962. Rubble-built buttressed box of 1843, the side windows rectangular. At the front (s) gable, round-headed dummy windows and a door which is placed in the front of the minimally projecting pyramid-roofed squat tower. In the tower, round-headed belfry openings, the W covered by a clock made by *Victor & Sons*.

MERCAT CROSS. Dated 1686 and bearing the same mason's mark as the cross of 1698 at Meikleour (q.v.). Roughly circular weathered red sandstone monolithic shaft and rounded head from which extend four finger-like projections in a saltire pattern; ball finial.

KIPPEN HOUSE

1.7 km. S of Dunning

Bloated cottage-villa with Baronial pretensions, by *Andrew Heiton Jun.*, *c.* 1875, tacked onto a pleasantly unpretentious laird's house. The original house is at the SW corner, a small Tudor manor house of *c.* 1840, the first floor windows rising into gablet dormerheads. Rectangular bay window at the S front's advanced and gabled centrepiece. Crowstepped gables and a conical-roofed SW corner turret (the balancing SE turret removed in the 1870s) to show that it belongs to Scotland.

Heiton's additions are overpowering and not especially welcome, their bargeboarded gables and bracketed broad eaves failing to be picturesque. Two-storey link from the earlier house's E end to a conical-roofed round tower of quite peaceful character. E of that, a much taller two-storey main part, with a full-height canted bay window at the gabled E end of the S elevation. At the N corner of the E (entrance) front, a tall and massive square tower, its high battlement carried on heavily moulded deep corbels; conical-roofed turrets at three corners and, at the NW, a caphouse whose truncated conical roof is topped by a spired cupola. Projecting from this tower, an incongruously cottagey gabled portico.

KIRKMICHAEL

Village in Strathardle, the house plots laid out by *Robert Reid* in 1811. The buildings along the A924 are very simple of the early or mid C19 with some Victorian embellishments but the tall late C19 KIRKMICHAEL HOTEL has gabled end bays, the l. with a large oriel window. On the s side of Kirkmichael Bridge, mid-C19 broad-eaved cottages.

DUFF MEMORIAL FREE CHURCH. Disused and altered for storage. By *L. & J. Falconer*, 1890. Sturdy buttressed and lancet-windowed Gothic box. sw steeple, its square tower broached to an octagonal belfry under the lucarned and slated spire roof.

KIRKMICHAEL PARISH CHURCH. Set well below the level of the main road, a harled kirk of 1791–2, the long s side with round-headed windows at the centre and small rectangular windows at the end bays. In each gable, a short Venetian window above a rectangular door. Plain birdcage bellcote on the N gable. The roof's bracketed broad eaves probably date from *James C. Walker*'s repairs of 1874 or perhaps from the alterations made by *John Sim* in 1892–3. Certainly of that date is the addition of the N jamb, with a corniced gallery door at road level and a round window above. Probably contemporary are the gallery windows of this side which are carried up through the eaves into gableted dormerheads.

Inside, gallery of 1792 round three sides. In the centre of the s wall, a roomy PULPIT with a pedimented back, the manner Late Georgian but it probably dates from the alterations of 1892–3, as do the simple PEWS. – STAINED GLASS W window by *Heaton, Butler & Bayne*, c. 1895.

GRAVEYARD. On the N side, immediately w of the church, is the two-storey former PARISH SCHOOL designed and built by *Daniel McDonald*, wright in Balnakeilly, 1813, extended one bay to the E in 1819 and first harled in 1837. A window was converted to a door into the churchyard in 1896 when the ground floor became the church vestry. – Several C18 HEADSTONES. One, to the w of the church, has an angel's head (the soul) carved in the swan-neck pediment; below, a shield and mantled crest. – E of this, a stone to WS and AM with a sorrowful angel's head above the tools of a mason; at the base, an open Bible, crossbones and an hourglass. – Further E, a stone to FB incised with a very crude angel's head. – Near the graveyard's E end, the well-preserved headstone of John Yeaman †1772, its W face carved in relief with a shield bearing a dyer's rail, fulling bottle, press and round dish, with male supporters in C18 dress and a mantled helm for crest; an angel's head at the top, emblems of death at the base.

KIRKMICHAEL PRIMARY SCHOOL. Villa-like, begun in 1850 but much enlarged by *James C. Walker*, 1877, and *Lake Falconer* in 1912.

CAIRN, Balchrochan, 1.4 km. s. Rounded mound, 15.5 m. in diameter and c. 3 m. high, formed of small boulders and slabs, now covered with grass and a few trees. It may date from the late third or early second millennium B.C.

ASHINTULLY CASTLE. *See* p. 163.
WHITEFIELD CASTLE. *See* p. 745.

KIRKTOWN OF COLLACE *see* COLLACE

KNAPP

Hamlet on the N edge of the policies of Rossie Priory (q.v.).

CHAPEL, Dron, 1.3 km. NE. Fragments of a late medieval chapel, probably built to serve the N part of Longforgan parish. What remains are parts of the chancel which measured *c.* 10.4 m. by 7.6 m. The E gable, built of slab rubble and now featureless, appears not to have contained a window. The pointed and chamfered chancel arch is intact, its semi-octagonal responds with simple moulded bases. Walling each side of the arch shows that the missing nave was broader.

DESCRIPTION. Mostly estate housing of the C19. On the S side of the road through the hamlet and set below it, the rubble-built MILL COTTAGE of the earlier C19. On the N side of the road, the two-storey NYE COTTAGE (originally a double house), also of the earlier C19 but consciously picturesque. Hoodmoulded ground-floor openings and gablets over the first floor windows whose latticed glazing survives; bracketed broad eaves. DOVECOT COTTAGE is a huge rubble-built and crow-step-gabled early C18 lectern doocot which was converted to a house *c.* 1900. Ratcourse across the gables and back wall which rises to form a trio of crowstepped and ball-finialled gablets.

LAWERS

Hamlet N of Loch Tay.

Former LAWERS CHURCH, 0.7 km. E. On the edge of the steep bank of Loch Tay, the ruin of a rubble-walled T-plan kirk built in 1669 and repaired in 1754. The corniced base of a bellcote survives on the SW gable. The windows have been rectangular, their margins chamfered except at the gable of the SE jamb where they are rounded. The interior has contained galleries.

LAWERS CHURCH. Disused. By *John Murray*, 1833–4. Partially harled rubble-built rectangle, with elliptically arched windows in the E and W sides. On the S gable, a pinnacled birdcage bellcote with round-headed openings. The interior was recast in the late C19 to leave a gallery at the S end facing the pulpit at the N.

DESCRIPTION. On the approach from the S, Lawers Church (*see* above) and its former MANSE (now, THE OLD CHURCH HOUSE) and BEN LAWERS HOTEL, both mid C19 and broad-eaved, the hotel with horizontal-paned glazing and some Gothic windows with gableted dormerheads. N of this group, the path down to the former Lawers Church (*see* above) and the ruin of LAWERS HOUSE, a long and skinny rubble-built two-storey oblong, probably of the C17. On the main road, at the NE end of the settlement, the OLD TOLL HOUSE of *c.* 1835, a whitewashed cottage with jerkin-head-gabled broad-eaved roofs to the main block and its porch.

STONE CIRCLE, Machuim, 0.8 km. NE. Beside the road along the N side of Loch Tay is an oval mound, *c.* 13.7 m. by 11 m., perhaps artificial. On top and slightly W of the centre, a roughly oval circle, *c.* 6.7 m. by 5.8 m., of standing stones erected probably in the third or second millennium B.C.. It has comprised six massive boulders, two now fallen, which stood 1.13 m.– 1.47 m. high, graded in height with the lowest at the NE and the tallest at the SW. Small stones, only *c.* 0.25 m. high, have been placed between some of them.

LAWERS HOUSE
2.7 km. E of Comrie

Pink sandstone mansion house designed by *William Adam* and built for Colonel (later, Lieutenant-General Sir James) Campbell of Lawers in two stages in 1724–6 and 1737–44 but remodelled for the London banker, Henry Drummond, by *James Salisbury* in 1783. It was further altered and extended for the judge, David Williamson, Lord Balgray, by *Richard Crichton c.* 1815.

The house built in 1724–44 consisted of a double-pile two-storey main block, with lower two-storey piend-roofed wings extending laterally from the sides of the S range, all built of rubble. Adam's principal front faced S. The main block's seven-bay façade was dignified by a three-bay centrepiece, taller than the rest and slightly advanced under an urn-finialled pediment. The centrepiece's ground floor contained segmental-arched windows flanking the segmental-pedimented entrance and its first-floor tall keystoned round-headed windows, their arched tops blind. In Salisbury's remodelling of 1783 the centrepiece was refaced in ashlar, the ground-floor openings altered to form three tall windows in elliptical-headed overarches and an order of attached Ionic columns added at the upper floor to support the reused early C18 pediment.

Crichton's alterations of *c.* 1815 were more far-reaching, and this elevation became the garden front. Its outer bays were refaced with ashlar and the front walls of the wings brought forward to the line of the main block. The l. wing was raised to the same height as the main block, had an additional window inserted at each floor and its first-floor windows enlarged to match those of the main block. The r. wing was both heightened and extended E as a three-bay continuation of Adam's main block. A Doric colonnade was carried across the ground floor each side of the centrepiece. The wallhead over the outer bays may have been finished with a parapet or perhaps, though it looks a little later, the present balustrade with urns surmounting the corner plinths. To each end Crichton added a boldly projecting single-storey pavilion. Each pavilion's bowed front has five large windows separated only by pilasters, and with paired chimneys joined by a round-headed arch, quoting the treatment of the early C18 chimneys on the outer bays of the N elevation.

The present rubble-walled N (entrance) elevation was the back of the early C18 house. Main block of nine bays, the outer three at each end with an attic and finished with a shaped gable surmounted by the Vanbrughian device of paired chimneys joined by a round-headed arch; urns on the outer corners of the gables. The centre three bays are slightly advanced and were, perhaps, originally finished with a parapet or balustrade but a piend-roofed attic has been added, probably c. 1815. The portico of four evenly spaced Roman Doric columns fronting the ground floor of the centrepiece is of 1815. Undistinguished mid-C19 wings of one (W) and two (E) storeys now extend from the sides of this block.

The stable courtyard at the house's W end is also an addition of c. 1815 by Crichton. Two-storey E and W ranges, the windows of their pedimented gables contained in giant round-headed overarches. On the courtyard's S side, a screen wall to the garden. On the N, low ranges, now with C20 windows, flanking a central tower whose bottom stage is pierced by an overarched pend. This stage's flat roof supports a panelled square plinth from whose corners rise columns enclosing the boldly corniced clock stage; at the top, a cupola. The NW wing, also with a pedimented gable, is an addition, perhaps of c. 1920.

The INTERIOR is a mixture of Georgian and Georgian revival, the later work carried out for Captain Norman Rockey and his wife whose parents gave them the estate on their marriage in 1918. The ENTRANCE HALL at the centre of the N front was formed in the early C19 by enlarging Adam's ground-floor N room (probably the parlour) S to the line of a columnar screen at the back of the early C18 entrance hall but retaining the position of the W fireplace, now badly off-centre. Decoration of c. 1920 by *William Black* in deliberate evocation of the manner of William Adam. The fireplace is framed by Ionic pilasters and an overmantel topped by a semicircle of foliage in a swan-neck pediment. More foliage and a vase in the broken pediment over the broad W doorpiece, its frieze carved with swags. Swagged friezes and pediments, one swan-neck, the other broken and enclosing foliage, at the S and E doors. Rococo plasterwork on the ceiling, its central sunburst surrounded by foliage, some rising out of baskets. In the centre of each side, the monogrammed initials RS for the surnames of Rockey and his wife (a Stewart); more foliage in the corners.

At the entrance hall's SE corner, a broad opening, its beam supported on pairs of swagged consoles, to the top-lit STAIR

HALL. Its general character appears mid C19, the Ionic pilasters at the first floor landing perhaps embellishments of *c.* 1920. Probably also mid C19 is the form of the well stair itself, its newels with foliaged finials and pendants, but the turned balusters and closed outer string carved with leafy Vitruvian scroll ornament may be reused mid-C18 work. Off the entrance hall's W side, a second stair which is of the 1740s. It is scale-and-platt with turned balusters. At the half-landing, a keystoned basket arch springing from panelled pilasters. S of the entrance hall, the MORNING ROOM which occupies the S three-quarters of the original entrance hall. Its N wall has been formed by building behind Adam's screen whose fluted Roman Doric columns and basket arches survive. The room's other decoration is of late C18 type but may well be of *c.* 1920. The walls bear large plaster panels with rosettes in their cut-out corners. Black marble chimneypiece on the E side, a niche on the W, both in projecting breasts enriched with plaster reliefs of urns and pendants. Framing the S wall's central window (in the position of Adam's principal entrance to the house) is a pair of fluted Doric columns. Delicate parasol centrepiece to the ceiling.

The principal first-floor room is Adam's SALOON which fills the S two-thirds of the house's centre. This is a noble space covered with a coved ceiling, its heavy cornice of the earlier C18 but the delicate enrichment on the flat (a foliaged oval inside a swagged oval and corner roundels) of the 1780s. William Adam's design provided symmetrical elevational treatments of the four sides. On the S, three windows, the narrow panels between them now missing. Adam's published designs for the E and W walls were transposed in execution. In the centre of the E wall, a white marble chimneypiece, the jambs carved with pendants dropping from consoles; on the frieze, shells and a central swagged urn. Overmantel, probably designed for a landscape or mirror, framed by pilasters which narrow towards the base, their fronts carved with husk pendants. They support a pediment broken by a shell; crossed branches on the frieze. Each side of the chimneypiece was a panel and a door. The S door has been built up and extra panels put in its place. The N door, with a lugged architrave, pulvinated frieze and cornice, survives; the open-pedimented overdoor containing a landscape painting which was added to it in the 1780s was removed in the mid C20. The design of the W wall was identical but with a large central panel with a lugged architrave and swan-neck pediment instead of the chimneypiece. This survives, as do the doors. At the N wall were panels flanking a triangular-pedimented doorpiece. The doorpiece seems to have been replaced in the 1780s by one with a swan-neck pediment which was set in an Ionic-columned and broken-pedimented aedicule.

The room N of the saloon (probably originally the DRAWING ROOM) seems also to have been redecorated in the 1780s. Ceiling enriched with an oval of ribbon-tied husks enclosing a concave-sided lozenge and central rosette; rinceau ornament at the ends. E chimneypiece with a lugged architrave and carved frieze. Overmantel, probably intended for a painting, with a double-lugged architrave surmounted by swags.

Some BEDROOMS have 1740s work. In one, E of the saloon, wall panels and corniced doorpieces. E chimneypiece, its broad jambs and frieze carved with foliage; overmantel with a swan-neck pediment broken by an acorn. In another bedroom Ionic pilasters flank the fireplace whose high frieze contains a mirror; overmantel with a cartouche breaking the pediment.

In parkland S of the house, the rubble-built E gable of a CHAPEL, probably of 1519. On the gable's exterior, the moulded frame for a pair of panels, probably heraldic. At the SE end of the drive, a broad-eaved single-storey LODGE of the later C19.

LENDRICK MUIR
1.1 km. NE of Rumbling Bridge

Lumpish Georgian-survival classical mansion house of c. 1875, the ashlar walling channelled at the ground floor. Three storeys, the top floor's small windows denoting the unimportance of the bedrooms within. Advanced and pedimented narrow centrepiece on the S front, its ground and first floor windows of three lights. Pedimented porch at the S end of the E side and a balustraded bow window in the same position on the W. Large lower wings extend to the rear.

LETHENDY

Just the Parish Church at Kirktown of Lethendy, the Free Church, manse and school some way to the E.

LETHENDY AND KINLOCH FREE CHURCH, Chapel of Lethendy, 1.5 km. E. Now a house. By *David Steven*, 1843–4. Rubble-walled Gothic box, a Georgian survival birdcage bellcote on the E gable. This gable contains the entrance under a circular window topped by a small quatrefoil light. Another quatrefoil light above the broad pointed window of the W gable.

Immediately to the E, the mid-C19 former FREE CHURCH SCHOOL, single-storey with broad eaves. – To its E, the two-storey former FREE CHURCH MANSE of 1850–1 by *Wilson*, with a meanly corniced doorpiece.

LETHENDY PARISH CHURCH, Kirktown of Lethendy. Now roofless. Oblong, of red sandstone rubble, built in 1758. Windowless except at the S front which was rebuilt in 1847–8 to a design by *John Ramsay*, with shouldered-arched openings. Also of 1847–8 the birdcage bellcote on the W gable.

GRAVEYARD. A number of C18 GRAVE-SLABS and HEADSTONES. Among them, in the SW corner, the headstone erected in 1765 to John Irons, the top of its W face carved with the relief of a weaver at his loom; below, stylized foliage and, at the base, emblems of death. – Adjoining headstone of 1722 (with the initials W/W), the E face displaying a heraldic achievement, the supporters in C18 dress. – Immediately S of the centre of the church's S wall, the stone of 1773 to John Waddell, smith. Ineptly detailed Ionic pilasters and foliage frame a shield bearing the tools of a smith; below, a jolly skull, coffin and a gravedigger's shovel and spade.

GOURDIE HOUSE, 1km. NW. C18 laird's house said to have been dated 1705 or, more probably, 1765. Two storeys over a basement, harled with rusticated quoins. Five-bay S front, the Gibbsian central doorpiece linked by a stone panel to the window above. Small corbels under the eaves cornice. Built into the NW back wing, a steeply pedimented dormerhead carved with a coat of arms, the date 1661 and the initials GN and MK; immediately below, a lintel incised with the initials DK flanked by the date 1674.

TOWER OF LETHENDY. *See* p. 733.

LOCHLANE
1.7 km. SE of Monzievaird

Smartly detailed harled laird's house of 1710. Two storeys and an attic, the roof steep and piended. At the S front, four regularly disposed windows at the first floor. These are placed above the ground-floor windows (the E now a door) but at that level the house's entrance (now a window), its pediment carved with a coat of arms, is squeezed in at the centre. At the attic, a central steep triangular gablet, its window flanked by carved scrolls and surmounted by a coat of arms and the date 1710. In front of the house, a small forecourt with rubble-built dwarf walls and panelled and corniced ashlar gatepiers, their ball finials topped by metal spikes.

LOCHLEVEN CASTLE
1.9 km. E of Kinross

Island fortress famous as Mary, Queen of Scots' place of imprisonment in 1567–8. The castle's position near the strategically important main overland route from Edinburgh to Perth was of some importance during the Wars of Independence. Its existence is not mentioned in accounts of Edward I's invasion in 1296 but, according to a C17 source (Sir James Balfour of Denmilne), a siege of the castle was relieved by Sir John Comyn in 1301 and it may have been first fortified just before. Certainly it was in existence by 1313 when Robert I stayed there and, according to Barbour, he imprisoned John of Lorn in Lochleven Castle three years later. In 1329 the castle was significant enough to serve as a deposit for part of the royal exchequer. Three years later, the castle's keeper, Alan Vipont, was paid 7s. 6d. for cords *'pro machinis ad Lacum de Leuyn'* ('for the machines at Loch Leven') and, after the Battle of Halidon in 1333, Lochleven Castle was said to have been one of only five castles or fortresses still held in the name of David II. In 1335 a siege by Sir John Stirling, the English Governor of Edinburgh Castle, was unsuccessful. Five years later there is evidence of building activity, possibly to do with construction of the keep, £900 being paid to Reginald, Chamberlain of Scotland, *'pro expensis quas fecit in mora sua infra castrum Laci de Leuin, tam pro edificiis infra dictum castrum constructis, quam pro diuersis victualibus que in dicto castro dimisit'* ('for the expenses which he made during his stay at Lochleven Castle, as well for buildings erected in the said castle as for various victuals which he sent to the said castle') and in 1359 £20 was paid *'pro reparacione murorum et edificiorum, et supportacione aliorum onerum dicti castri'* ('for the repair of the walls and buildings and the support of other burdens of the said castle'). Lochleven remained a royal castle until 1390 when it was granted to Sir Henry Douglas, husband of the King's niece. The castle was held by the Douglas family until the C17 when it seems to have been

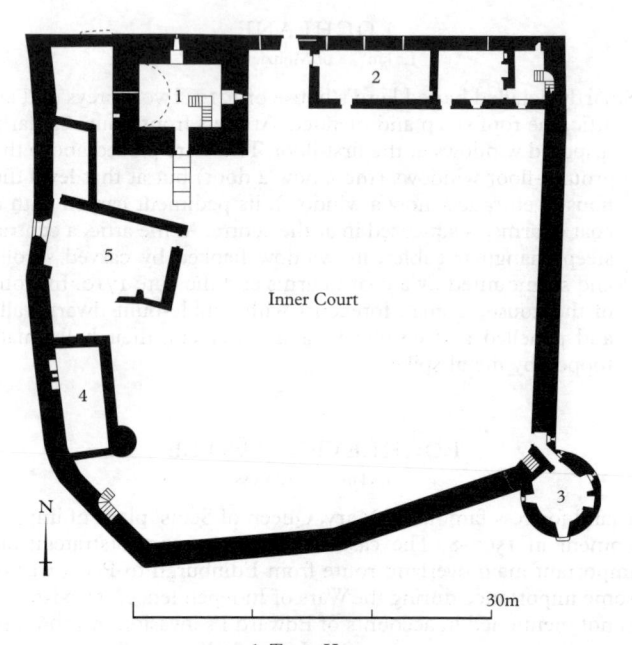

1. Tower House
2. North Range
3. Glassin Tower
4. Kitchen
5. Hall

Lochleven Castle.
Ground-floor plan

abandoned as a residence, but the ruins maintained as an eye-catcher from Kinross House (q.v.).

The island site now rises from a wooded lochside fringe to a plateau on which stand the castle buildings. Until the lowering of the loch's water level in 1836 and a consequent increase in the island's size from 0.7 ha. to c. 3.2 ha. only the plateau stood above the water, seemingly surrounded by a curtain wall and divided into an outer (N) and inner (S) court. Of the outer court's defences, possibly originally provided by a palisade which was replaced by walling in the C15, only scanty fragments of masonry survive. At its SE corner, low remains of a BAKEHOUSE, perhaps of the C16, with the base of a large semi-circular oven projecting S from its E end.

The CURTAIN WALL of the inner court encloses a roughly oblong area, c. 44 m. (E–W) by 38 m. (N–S), but with irregular S and W sides adjusted to the contours of the site. This area was probably enclosed c. 1300 and at the S side the lower part of the curtain's rubble masonry is constructed of roughly cubical blocks characteristic of work of that date. Cubical blocks have been reused elsewhere in the wall but most of this probably dates from a C15 reconstruction. At the S end of the E side, a C16 gunloop formed when the Glassin Tower was built, at the W side the gable of a hall and, at the N, the tower house (for all these, *see* below). Just W of the tower house, a jettied projection, perhaps of the first-floor room of a demolished building inside the courtyard, above a built-up doorway of uncertain date but unlikely to be earlier than the late C16. The N curtain wall E of the tower house is pierced by the narrow ground-floor windows of the courtyard's N range. Between the tower house and this range, the round-headed entrance into the courtyard. On its W side, just below the springing of the arch, a small shield, probably intended to bear a coat of arms but with no evidence of carving. Inside the courtyard, at the curtain's SW corner, steps up to the wall-walk.

The castle's dominant building, its N side interrupting the masonry of the curtain, is the C14 TOWER HOUSE. This is of four storeys and an attic. Rubble masonry, many of the stones roughly squared, intaken above the first floor. Parapet carried on rounded individual corbels; continuous corbelling under the rounds at the NE, NW and SW corners. At the SE corner the parapet was carried up to form the outer sides of a caphouse at the top of the internal stair. Narrow N and E windows to the ground floor; at the base of the E side, a garderobe outlet. Above this level, on all sides, reasonably sized windows, also rectangular, light the main rooms; narrow openings to garderobes in the W wall and the stair in the SE corner. Unusually, the attic windows pierce the parapet. In the S side and well below the present courtyard level is an unadorned ground-floor entrance formed in the place of a window in the C19. Principal entrance at the second floor on the E side, reached by an external wooden stair (a late C20 restoration).

The apex of its round-headed arch is carved with a shield; remains of a hoodmould.

INTERIOR. The ground floor contains a tunnel-vaulted room, its windows with stepped sills. A hatch near the W end of the vault was originally the only communication with the kitchen above but a dog-leg stone stair was cut through the vault's SE corner in the C19. Access to the first-floor KITCHEN was originally from a tight turnpike stair descending from the second floor in the wall thickness of the tower's SE corner. The kitchen is covered by a tunnel vault, its E end pierced by a hatch to the second-floor hall. E fireplace, now opened up as high as the relieving arch but with stubs of the elliptically arched former lintel surviving; salt-box in the back of the fireplace. Stone seats at the N windows and at the S wall's E window which is equipped also with a slop drain below the sill. In the wall thickness of the SW corner, a garderobe with a small window and a lamp recess. Low down at the E end of the N wall, a pair of aumbries, their openings without door checks.

Immediately inside its E entrance from the external stair to the second-floor HALL, the hatch to the kitchen whose length indicates the width of the screens passage, its position confirmed by the survival of holes for the ends of the missing wooden screen. At the screens passage's S end, a depressed-arched door to the house's SE stair. At the W end of the hall, a plain fireplace, narrowed in the C17. N and S windows with stone seats in their round-headed embrasures; small W window to the N of the fireplace.

The third floor contained an UPPER HALL or solar, its now missing wooden floor supported on simple moulded corbels. Towards the E end of the N side, an elliptical-arched roll-and-hollow-moulded fireplace. Windows at the E end of the N wall and just off-centre in the S, the floors of their segmental-arched embrasures a step above the general floor level of the room. Stone seats at the N window. At the S window's embrasure, a stone seat on the E side but, on the W, a basket-arched narrow door to a wall chamber. At the S end of the W wall and again with a step up from the main floor, the basket-arched entrance to a garderobe.

The ATTIC, also apparently containing a single room, had a wooden floor, its simply moulded corbels extant at the N wall. Towards the E end of this side, a fireplace flanked by smallish windows. Towards the W end of the S wall and the N end of the W wall are larger windows, with seats in their embrasures. Narrow rectangular door to the garderobe in the SW corner.

The round mid-C16 GLASSIN TOWER, projecting from the courtyard's SE corner, is also largely intact though roofless and missing the top of its walls. Rubble-built, of three storeys above a basement. At the basement, wide-mouthed gunloops in the SE and NW segments, a water inlet in the E and an outlet at the SW. Above the outlet, remains of a ground-floor oriel window with minimally canted sides. Small rectangular W window, its surround chamfered. Also at this level, two gunloops in the N and NE segments and one first-floor gunloop in the N segment, all of the same design as the one in the curtain immediately to the N. At the first floor, a couple of circular shot-holes, a gunloop of the same type as at the ground floor and curtain wall, and a window in a chamfered surround.

From the courtyard a pair of entrance doors, both with chamfered surrounds. The r. door, placed slightly below the l., opens onto a steep flight of steps down to the tunnel-vaulted basement. The l. door is the entrance to a small lobby at the foot of the stair to the upper floors. In the E side of the lobby, the gunloop piercing the curtain wall. In the tower's well-lit ground-floor room, a narrow fireplace, its back pierced by a hole, perhaps the remains of a shot-hole. N of the fireplace, a recess pierced by a gunloop. The first-floor room was probably a bedchamber. Rectangular wall recesses in the W and NE segments. Fireplace with a chamfered surround. To its l., a small wall chamber, perhaps a close garderobe, its entrance checked for a door, a gunhole in its back wall. W fireplace in the second-floor room.

Scantier remains of the other medieval buildings round the courtyard include a WEST RANGE of which little more than low walls survive.

At the range's S end has been a kitchen, with a S fireplace and a round oven projecting from the SE corner. N of this was a C16 hall, a fireplace in the S wall. The hall's W gable forms part of the curtain wall. In it, a good-sized rectangular window with a simple roll-and-hollow moulding, the upper part grooved for glass. It has been covered by an iron grille. Fragmentary remains of buildings to the E and N of the hall.

A NORTH RANGE E of the entrance to the courtyard contained three ground floor rooms, the centre room with an E fireplace, the E room with a narrow chamber in the N wall and, at the E end, steps up to the curtain wall's wall-walk. In each of these two rooms survive the lower parts of the surround of a S window, grooved for glazing, and of doorways with chamfered jambs. The long W room seems to have been lit only by narrow slits in the N side. Perhaps it was a stable.

LOCH OF CLUNIE CASTLE
0.4 km. E of Clunie

Roofless but largely intact late medieval retreat of the Bishops of Dunkeld, its tree-fringed island site probably of artificial origin.

The house, begun in the later C15 but mostly built *c.* 1506–10, is rubble-walled, constructed partly of stone taken from Clunie Castle (q.v.) on the shore of the loch. L-plan, the main block of three storeys, the slightly taller NE jamb of five. Unusually, the jamb's roof was parallel rather than at right angles to the main block. In the inner angle but reading visually as the S end of the jamb is an irregularly rounded projection containing the principal stair, this projection and the main body of the jamb both crossed by a second-floor string course. In the s front of the projection, the house's entrance, with a machicolation above. Slit windows, several built up, once lit the ground floor and stair. The first-floor windows were enlarged in the C18 or C19. The top windows of the W side were heightened and given pedimented dormerheads in the later C16.

Inside, the ground floor of the main block contained a tunnel-vaulted kitchen, its N end partitioned off in the C18 or C19. At the same time its broad segmental-arched fireplace was contracted. In the kitchen's original N wall, a straight service stair to the first-floor hall. The main staircase is a turnpike.

LOGIEALMOND see CHAPELHILL

LOGIERAIT

Scrappy hamlet beside the River Tay.

LOGIERAIT PARISH CHURCH. Harled rectangle, designed and built by *John Stewart*, 1804–6. Round-arched windows, narrow at the N side. On the W gable, a late C20 version of a birdcage bellcote, not an entirely happy substitute for its Georgian predecessor. Swagged urns on the ends of both gables and at the apex of the E. Round-headed E door, its flanking rectangular windows perhaps inserted as part of the alterations made by *A. C. Duthie* in 1878.

The interior was recast by *J. Jeffrey Waddell* in 1928 when the E end was partitioned off to form a Neo-Georgian vestibule with a room each side. In the church itself, FURNISHINGS of 1928, the pulpit, lectern, communion table, high-backed minister's chair and font sparingly decorated with Early Christian motifs. Good-quality dark panelling in a Georgian manner on the W wall. – STAINED GLASS narrative window of 1900 (the Maries at the Tomb) in the N room off the vestibule.

GRAVEYARD. S of the church, a low enclosure containing three iron MORT SAFES, two of them adult-sized, the third for a child. – HEADSTONES. Immediately E of the church, a curly-headed stone of 1781 to Peter McFarland and his two wives. At the top of the W face, a carved angel's head (the soul). Below, a piecrust bordered panel containing a shield bearing the initials of McFarland and his second wife, Ann Stewart, and a relief of a sock and coulter; below the shield, a relief of Adam and Eve, the serpent twining round the Tree of Knowledge, and the inscription THE.SERPENT.BEGUILED EVE. On the stone's E front, emblems of death below the main inscription. – SE of this, a smaller stone of 1784 to William Husband, again carved with an angel's head and a relief of Adam and Eve accompanied by the same inscription. – To its E, a large stone of 1794 to Duncan McPherson, the W face displaying an angel's head above a coat of arms bearing the tools of a shoemaker; hourglass, crossbones and a skull at the bottom. – SE of this, the headstone of 1790 commemorating William Berry, its W face carved with the usual angel's head at the top and reminders of death at the bottom; in the centre, initials in an oval frame formed by the carved representation of a tasselled cord flanked by foliage. – Immediately SE of the church, a headstone of 1784 to Margaret Connachar, the N face again carved with a relief of Adam and Eve; angel's head above, emblems of death below. – W of this, a curly-headed stone of 1782 to Patrick McFarland with a shield bearing what looks like an upside-down iron. – Between these last two headstones, a broken CROSS-SLAB, perhaps of the C8. On the E face, a cross with bossed hollows at the inner angles and a circled centre. On the W face, the relief of a horse above a spear entwined by a serpent.

LOGIERAIT PRIMARY SCHOOL. *See* Ballinluig.

POORHOUSE. Now housing. By *James C. Walker*, 1861–4. Understandably thrifty rubble-built three-storey block. Advanced ends with bargeboarded gables. A bell hangs at the two-bay gabled centre. Late C20 E addition.

RAILWAY VIADUCT over the River Tay. Disused. By *J. Mitchell & Co.*, 1863. Bullnosed ashlar abutments, their inner ends topped by cast-iron piers, support the outer ends of short straight cast-iron floodwater spans, their inner ends resting on oval piers, also of cast iron, surmounted by bundle-shafted cast-iron columns rising from bulbous bases. Two lattice-girder spans over the river itself.

LOGIERAIT HOUSE. Originally Logierait Parish Manse, it was designed by *Robert Reid* and built by *John Stewart* in 1803–4. Harled, of two storeys and an attic. Front of three bays, the gabled porch added in 1838, the dormer windows in 1874.

DALGUISE HOUSE. *See* p. 310.
KINNAIRD HOUSE. *See* p. 472.

LONGFORGAN

Long roadside village founded as a burgh of barony under the superiority of the Earls of Strathmore, owners of Castle Huntly (q.v.), in 1672. By the 1790s it had a population of over 600, with agriculture and weaving the principal occupations, and the cottages were being rebuilt with lime-mortared stone walls and roofs of thatch, tiles or slate. The decline in handloom weaving in the C19 was accompanied by a fall in the population of Longforgan which, by 1900, was half what it had been a century earlier. However, from the beginning of the C20 it began to grow as a commuter outpost of Dundee. By-passed since 1971, the A85 forms a barrier to expansion to the N but plentiful housing, discreetly tucked away, has been developed to the S in the late C20 and early C21.

CHURCHES

LONGFORGAN FREE CHURCH. *See* Invergowrie.
LONGFORGAN PARISH CHURCH, Main Street. Tall rubble-built oblong, by *John Paterson*, 1794–5, incorporating some earlier work, perhaps of *c.* 1600, at the W gable from which projects a tower of 1690. A short chancel was added to the E end by *Alexander Hutcheson* in 1899–1900.

The tower (largely rebuilt in replica after being struck by lightning in 1981), which hides the segmental arch of an earlier W window, rises to a balustraded wallhead. In each face, circular windows and, at the top stage, a rectangular belfry opening under a pair of dummy oculi. The entrance at the base of the W side is of 1899–1900, and the round inscription panel above which records the tower's erection in 1690 by Patrick, Earl of Strathmore, is a replacement for a panel now housed inside. Within the balustrade, a square ashlar plinth surmounted by a lucarned splay-foot spire, presumably a replacement of the later C19, from whose W side projects a clock face (a 1980s replacement of one erected in 1878). In the tower's S inner angle with the church, a Gothic-windowed projection of 1899–1900 containing a stair to the W gallery; in the N inner angle, a bowed heating chamber, probably of the mid C19. In the church's W gable, N of the tower, a blocked rectangular gallery window, perhaps of the early C18. This is placed at a level below that of the 1790s gallery windows in the N wall. These, like the area windows below, are rectangular and quite plain, their round-headed glazing pattern of 1899–1900.

The S side of the church was the 1790s show front. It is of five bays, the outer bays with large two-light Y-traceried pointed openings, the centre with the head of a similar but dummy window which surmounted a door (built up in 1899–1900) which gave the minister access from the outside to the pulpit. On the church's SW corner, a stone sundial. High up on the C18 E gable, a panel, perhaps C17, carved with a human head and a shield. The chancel of 1899–1900 is plain and low. In its E gable, a window of three lancet lights. Flanking the chancel, a vestry on the S and organ chamber on the N.

The INTERIOR is mostly of 1899–1900 when the N and E galleries were removed, a new W gallery provided (the space below divided off in 1994 by a screen, its lower part of late Victorian woodwork, its upper part of glass with an etched cross by *Anita Pate*), and the position of the pulpit shifted from the centre of the S side to S of the new broad and round-headed chancel arch. It is flanked by two large oak PANELS designed by *Robert S. Lorimer* and erected in 1900 to commemorate the Patersons of Castle Huntly, their cresting carved with foliage and fruit. On the r. panel, more roses and thistles and a shield bearing the impaled arms of Paterson and Gray in honour of George Paterson who bought Castle Huntly in 1776 and his wife, Anne Gray, a descendant of the first Lord Gray who had built the house in the 1450s.

The tall PULPIT is probably of the late C19 but its bowl makes a setting for woodwork, perhaps of early C18 South German workmanship. This comprises alternating narrow panels, each carved with the high relief of a cherub's head set among vines, and broader panels whose reliefs depict the Holy Family, the Good Shepherd, the Risen Lord, and Our Lord Blessing. – In the chancel, a COMMUNION TABLE of c. 1900. – N of the chancel arch, a crude but agreeable oak eagle LECTERN of c. 1900. – On the chancel's N side, the ORGAN, by *John Compton Ltd.*, 1924. – Nave PEWS of 1899–1900. – Under the W gallery, a BELL, its inscription stating that it was made by *John Meikle* and given to Longforgan Church by Patrick, Earl of Strathmore, in 1690.

STAINED GLASS. E window (the Ascension), strongly coloured and realistic, by *Clayton & Bell*, 1900. – In the N wall of the nave, the E window (Abraham and an Angel) is best Glasgow style, by *Stephen Adam*, 1895. – The two windows to the W (Our Lady and Children; David and Jonathan) are early C20. – In the S wall, E window (St Modwenna, reputed founder of the first church at Longforgan, cradling the model of a church, and St Peter) by *Margaret Chilton*, 1956, the realism stylized. – In the W bay in front of the gallery, a window (the Nativity of Our Lord) by *Emma Butler-Cole Aiken*, 2003, an undisciplined swirl of strong colours.

Exceptional array of MONUMENTS. At the E end of the nave's N wall, the early C14 GRAVE-SLAB identified by its marginal inscription as belonging to John de Galychtly, lord of Ebroks, and his wife, Mariota, incised with full-length nearly life-size portraits of an armoured knight and his lady, their hands joined in prayer, their heads turned to gaze on each other, each accompanied by a heraldic shield. He stands on a hound which looks up at him; at her feet, the diminutive full-frontal figure of a knight, possibly representing their son. Between their heads, a small figure of St Andrew. Elaborate tabernacle work at the top. – W of this, the grey and white marble classical MONUMENT to the Rev. George Lyon of Ogil and his wife, Margaret Rodger, both †1793. In the segmental pediment, a relief of books, manuscripts and a broken column. At the base, a shield bearing their impaled coats of arms. – W of this, the elegantly lettered veined marble SLAB commemorating the Rev. David Forrester †1697. Its stone surround, the base carved with crossed bones, the top surmounted by skulls flanking a pediment, looks a C19 replacement. – On the nave's W wall, N of the door from the tower, the GRAVE-SLAB of James Fyf †1588. Latin marginal inscription enclosing three panels, the top one carved with the relief of a skull and bone, the foliage-bordered centre panel with a shield bearing a cross and flanked by Fyf's initials. On the bottom panel, four coats of arms, each identified by a name (VEMYS, MONORGVNS, HERIN and ANDERSON). – On the same wall, S of the entrance from the tower, the GRAVE-SLAB of Jean Fledger, wife of John Millar, †1660, with a piecrust outer border and marginal inscription. Within this frame, emblems of death and the initials IM and IF above and below the verse inscription:

> BIRTH.IS.A.BRAGGE.
> GLORY.A.BLAZE.
> HONOVRS.EARTHS.
> POMPE.RICHES.A.GAZE.
> FAME.IS.BVT.WINDE
> BEAVTY.A.FLOVER.
> PLEASVRE.A.DANCE
> THE.WORLD.A.BOVER.
> IN.HEAVEN.WITH.THEE
> LORD.LET.ME.BE.
> ON.EARTH.MY.HEAVEN.
> WAS.STILL.IN.THEE.

At the S end of this wall, the MONUMENT to Apollonia Kichlais, wife of David Lyon, †1695. Ionic aedicule, the curvaceous steep pediment carved with the monogrammed initials of DAL and the date 1698. At the base of the inscription, crossbones, a skull and hourglass in high relief. – On the N wall of the porch under the tower, a pair of large medieval GRAVE-SLABS, each with a ringed cross rising from a stepped base, the cross's arms ending in fleur-de-lys finials. The r. slab's carving is in relief and its cross-arms extend beyond the ring. Above the cross, the initials BS and, above its arms, the initials AF. The shaft is flanked by arched panels, the l. inscribed 'ihs' (for Jesus), the r. 'ma' (for Maria). The l. slab is much cruder, with incised carving. – On the S wall of the porch, the GRAVE-SLAB of ANE.TREV.COVENANTER.NAMED.ANDROV.SMYTH †1643, a delightfully incompetent display of the rural mason's craft. Within a marginal inscription, three panels. On the top, its border inscribed MY.SAVL.TO.PRAIS.THE.LORD AS.EF, an incised skull above a triangular object. The centre panel is carved with a circular object, possibly a shield, inscribed MEMENTO MORI. On the bottom panel, a sexton's tools displayed saltire-wise and the date 1644. – On the floor of the porch, fragments of a FONT, perhaps of the C15. Four of these come from the bowl and bear panels carved in relief with Scenes from the Life of Our Lord, apparently representing the Agony in the Garden, the Scourging, the Entombment and the Harrowing of Hell. – Also in the porch, the late C17 ROUNDEL moved here from the exterior of the tower which records its erection in 1690 by Patrick, Earl of Strathmore.

The GRAVEYARD's rubble wall was built in 1839. Of that date also the plain ashlar GATEPIERS to Main Street and the castiron GATES, their centre rail pierced by quatrefoils, their uprights with foliaged spearheads and, at the ends, urn finials. – W of the church, the HEADSTONE erected by William Fender, weaver, to his son, James. Aedicular E face with Roman Doric pilasters and a segmental pediment. Within this frame, an angel's head (the soul) from whose wings hangs a lion's head, its mouth holding a ring through which passes a drape over a shield which bears the date 1800. A bone, skull and coffin at the base. – Just S of the church's W end, a HEADSTONE, the E face with an inscription of 1837 to the Thornton family but the top incised with the date 1763, that of the carving on the W face, an angel's head above a shield with a mantled helm which displays a weaver's loom and shuttle; emblems of death below. – Immediately to its E, the GRAVE-SLAB of James Fyf †1659. Piecrust-bordered marginal inscription enclosing a cartouche and, at the bottom, a skull, crossbones and hourglass. – Similar GRAVE-SLAB to Janet Fyf †1652 just to its SE. – Further S, a curly-headed C18 HEADSTONE, the E face now with a C20 inscription to Peter Miller Smith and Elizabeth Campbell. At the top of the W face, a sorrowing angel. The main panel is carved in high relief with a pair of angel trumpeters above emblems of death flanking the sock and coulter of a farmer. – Immediately E of the church, the HEADSTONE of Eupham Elder †1731, with a curvaceous segmental pediment. At the top of the main panel, a pair of angels' heads; reminders of death at the bottom. – To its E, the vine-bordered GRAVE-SLAB of a woman †1698, also with a skull and crossbones.

LYCHGATE by *Thoms & Wilkie*, c. 1920, at the entrance to the graveyard's S extension. On the extension's S wall, a Lorimerian MONUMENT of the earlier C20 to the Patersons of Castle Huntly, with a rosetted border and the same coat of arms as on their memorial panels in the church. – In the W extension of this part, the HEADSTONE of the artist, Alberto Morrocco, erected in 2001. It is carved by *Vincent Butler* with the relief of a stylized depiction of the Annunciation, the archangel floating towards the striding figure of the Blessed Virgin Mary.

PUBLIC BUILDINGS

LONGFORGAN PRIMARY SCHOOL, Main Street. Jacobean single-storey and attic schoolhouse fronting the street, by *John Bell*, 1833–5. L-plan front, a triangular bay window at the gable of the NW jamb, a very shallow canted bay window at the main block. In the inner angle, a parapeted porch with an octagonal buttress-turret clasping its outer corner. The main block of the school behind is by *James Findlay*, 1908–9. One tall storey of hammer-dressed masonry. S front with gabled end bays and a large mullioned and transomed centre window breaking up through the bracketed broad eaves.

MARKET CROSS, Main Street. Erected c. 1675 but moved to the parkland of Castle Huntly in the late C18 and re-erected on the present site in 1989. Octagonal step supporting a corniced pedestal on which stands a Corinthian column, its capital eroded, surmounted by a badly weathered lion rampant, the heraldic emblem of the Lyons, Earls of Strathmore, the feudal superiors of the burgh.

WAR MEMORIAL, Main Street. Erected c. 1920. Tall red sandstone pillar with a blocky Greek cross-head. On one face, the relief of a Celtic cross.

CASTLE HUNTLY. See p. 259.

LUDE HOUSE
1.2 km. E of Blair Atholl

By *William Burn*, 1837–9, a two-storey ashlar-faced Jacobethan manor house, crowstepped gables the only overtly Scottish touch. The main block's symmetrical principal front faces S. Slightly taller (two-storey and attic) broad centrepiece with a parapeted two-storey canted bay window under a three-light attic window. At the flanking bays, single-storey bay windows, also canted and parapeted; tall first-floor windows which rise through the eaves to steeply pedimented dormerheads. The N elevation's W end is advanced and fronted by the console-pedimented main entrance surmounted by an oriel window. Extensive service ranges, in the same manner and also of two storeys, project to the NE, the recessed S front's E bay with a large oriel window under a basket-arched porch.

STABLES to the NW, the front (S) range castellated Tudor Gothic of 1824. – To the W, beside the Bridge of Tilt (*see* Blair Atholl), a battlemented Tudor GATEWAY of 1839 flanked by a contemporary lodge and thin tower.

LUNCARTY

Nondescript village, formerly the home of a large bleachfield, the housing mostly of the C20 and C21 sprinkled with a few earlier examples.

GRAVEYARD, off Main Road. At the SE corner of the rubble-walled enclosure, a MORT-HOUSE, also of rubble and dated 1832 on the lintel of the S door. Elliptically arched concrete roof (a C20 replacement) expressing the profile of the tunnel vault inside. Oculus above the door; slit windows in the other walls.

HEADSTONES. Roughly in the centre of the graveyard, the stone to Alexander Rutherford †1744, its E face's curvaceous pediment enclosing an angel's head (the soul). The W face is carved with a hand holding a crowned hammer (the emblem of a smith) above an anvil which is flanked by a boat and the figure of a man holding a gun. – To its W, a stone of 1787 to David Gellatly, late tenant in Barley Mill of Huntingtower, the W face displaying an angel's head above a low relief of two trees and the tools of a millwright; at the bottom, emblems of death. – Beside the mort-house, a stone, also of 1787, commemorating James Dougall, the W face carved with the relief of an angler and more emblems of death.

HALL, Main Road. English Picturesque, by *J. C. McKellar*, 1902. Harled, with touches of half-timbering and a Rosemary tiled roof. Rather altered and with a flat-roofed extension on the W side. – In front, WAR MEMORIAL of *c.* 1920, a blocky red sandstone cross, its stepped base incorporating red granite inscription tablets.

RAILWAY STATION, Denmarkfield, 1.7 km. S. Only the station building (now Belvedere House) remains. It is of 1848, a two-storey and basement piend-roofed house. Built into its back wall, three C17 stones, the l. a badly weathered dormerhead, the centre stone with a coat of arms, the initials IG and ID and the date 1627, the r. with the inscription PRAISIT/BE/GOD above the date 1601 and flanked by the initials IB and BS.

THE ARNS, Main Road. Two-storey *cottage orné* of the earlier C19, built of white-painted rubble, with a broad-eaved roof. Gothic glazing in the rectangular windows.

MADDERTY 9020

Isolated church and churchyard.

MADDERTY PARISH CHURCH. Drydashed oblong kirk built in 1668, the date on the E gable; on the S side, a stone inscribed I^{M}G for Mr James Graham, minister of Madderty, 1659–82. The W gable's ogee-roofed birdcage bellcote is a replacement of 1801. The gables' crowsteps, the windows (pointed except for the circular window in the W gable) and the N porch all date from *G. T. Ewing*'s reconstruction of 1897.

Very simple interior, mostly of 1897 when Ewing braced the roof with quatrefoil-pierced collars and provided a new PULPIT. – STAINED GLASS. Jewel-like E window (a Knight and Angel) by *Oscar Paterson*, 1919. – In the S wall, a lush three-light window (the Crucifixion) by *A. Ballantine & Gardiner*, 1897. – By the same artists the contemporary window in the W wall, the coat of arms of Anthony Murray of Dollerie its central motif, and the W rose window (Christian symbols).

GRAVEYARD. At its E entrance, a SESSION HOUSE by *Peter Skeen*, 1856, extended S in 2003. – A few C18 HEADSTONES carved with emblems of death and angels' heads (souls) but weathered.

WILLIAMSTON, 2.4 km. E. Unpretentious rubble-built mid-C17 laird's house of two storeys, with an attic lit by small square windows in the gables. The S front is dominated by a massive off-centre stepped chimney rising from the wallhead. Remains of a roll-and-hollow moulding on the l. jamb of the door. Irregularly disposed windows, mostly inserted or altered perhaps in 1802–3 when the E wing was added. Relieving arch, lintel and part of one jamb of a blocked C17 ground-floor window at the l. of the front. At the r., another blocked ground-floor window but of tiny size.

Another C17 stepped chimney on the W gable but the E gable's chimney has been rebuilt, probably in 1802–3. At the back, a bowed stair-tower under a rectangular attic projected on continuous corbelling. In the stair-tower's W inner angle, a bowed turret, also carried on continuous corbelling and finished with a sloping roof; tiny window in the turret's W face. W of the stair-tower, a first-floor window, Late Georgian in its present form, and, to its W, a blocked horizontal opening which must have lit the W ground-floor room from near its ceiling. A C20 addition covers the rear E of the stair-tower. L-plan wing of 1802–3 at the house's E end, its S front's dormer windows added in the later C19, its NE jamb's E extension of 2003.

Inside the C17 main block, a curving stone stair to the first floor and, in the turret, its continuation, but curving the other way, to the attic.

INCHAFFRAY ABBEY. See p. 420.

MEGGERNIE CASTLE
3.7 km. WSW of Innerwick

On a plain beside the River Lyon, a sprawling harled laird's house which has grown from the late C16 to the C20 in determinedly Scots style.

The earliest part, at the W end, is a four-storey and attic crowstep-gabled tower plausibly said* to have been built *c.* 1585 for Colin Campbell of Glenlyon and certainly in existence by 1603 when mentioned in a charter. It is oblong, with a pyramid-roofed rectangular turret carried on continuous corbelling at each corner. Entrance in the S front with a moulded surround. The other ground-floor openings are few and tiny. At the upper floors, a mixture of small- and medium-sized windows. The attic's pedimented wallhead dormers date from alterations of 1673. Perhaps also of that date but more probably C18 is the three-bay wing built at the E end of the tower, its tall first-floor windows denoting the principal storey. This wing was remodelled in 1848–9 by *John Henderson* who gave it a Neo-Jacobean porch and new second-floor windows which rise through the eaves into crowstepped gablets. At the same time he extended the wing E by two bays. The first of these, slightly advanced and broad, is a storey higher and with crowstepped E and W gables, its second floor projected on corbels and with a third-floor window on continuous corbelling which rises through the wallhead to a crowstepped gablet. The addition's E bay repeats the detailing of the W bays of the wing but with small versions of the C16 tower's turrets, at its crowstepped gable. Also of 1848–9 are the simple crowstep-gabled additions at the back of the house. A low service court at the house's E end was built in 1815–20 and remodelled in 1959 when its S wall acquired a battlement.

---

*By Alexander Stewart, *A Highland Parish* (Glasgow, 1928), 89.

To the NE, a harled and prominently gabled COACHHOUSE block of the later C19. – Rubble WALLED GARDEN to the W.

EAST LODGE straddling the entrance to the S drive, a two-storey and attic tower-like gatehouse of 1922 designed by *R. C. James* and *Vincent Steadman*. Very Scots, with red sandstone dressings enlivening the harling of the walls. Buttressed corners surmounted by turrets like those of the mansion house. Piercing the tall ground floor, a pend entered through round-headed arches. Crowstepped gables and dormer windows.

MEGGINCH CASTLE
2 km. N of Errol

2020

Substantial tower house of the Hays of Megginch swamped in Late Georgian additions.

The house started, perhaps at the end of the C15, with an oblong block which was extended and remodelled in 1575, this work recorded on a stone placed above one window and inscribed PETRVS.HAY.AEDIFICIVM.EXSTRVXIT.AN.1575 ('Peter Hay built this edifice in the year 1575'). Probably in the C17 the house was made L-plan by the addition of a SW stair jamb. Remodelling and the construction of large extensions was begun in the 1780s with the building of a block across the jamb's S end. In 1818–20 *W. M. Mackenzie* extended this new block futher E, probably to its originally intended length, and wrapped an L-plan addition along much of the tower house's N front and across its E end. Rubble masonry and Late Georgian battlements give some unity to the complex.

The three-storey tower house, much Georgianized, is still half-visible behind the additions. At the N corners, conical-roofed and ashlar-clad fat round turrets on continuous corbelling. Projecting from near the E end of the N side, a rounded tower with a bowed projection in its E inner angle, the main tower finished with a crowstep-gabled and ashlar-faced rectangular top storey also carried on continuous corbelling. Screen wall in front of the house W of the tower. The tower's lower part and the E end of the main block are largely hidden by the battlemented two-storey extension of 1818–20. Projecting from this extension's N front, a battlemented single-storey semicircular porch, its entrance round-headed. Canted S end to the extension's E wing. The addition across the S end of the tower house's jamb is of three storeys, the bow-ended three W bays of the 1780s, the similarly detailed three bays to the E of 1818–20. Tall windows to the first floor *piano nobile*, its importance marked by a band course; small second floor windows under the wallhead battlement. An off-centre early C19 Roman Doric portico was removed as part of alterations made by *Mills & Shepherd* in 1928.

Inside, a cupola-lit early C19 stair hall, the stair's balustrade composed of cast-iron scrolls. Inter-connecting drawing room and library on the first floor of the S block, the bow-ended drawing room's Adamish plaster ceiling, perhaps of the 1780s, with an open parasol enrichment in the centre and circles in the corners. Expensive late C18 white marble chimneypiece with Ionic columns supporting the entablature whose frieze is carved with urns at the ends and an allegorical panel in the centre. In the early C19 library, a shallowly compartmented ceiling with some floral enrichment on the stiles and a small central rose. Veined marble chimneypiece.

STABLES courtyard to the NW, entered at the SE corner through early C19 gatepiers with tall obelisk finials of C17 type. Two-storey N and E ranges, the E built of brick, of the early C19. Endearingly crude Gothic, with tall pointed openings to the ground floor and small cinquefoil windows above. Cross-finialled gabled centrepiece to the N range. In the courtyard, a free-standing two-storey octagonal DOOCOT, also early C19 and Gothic, the ground floor open, the upper storey with lozenges and arched panels containing the flight-holes; bellcast-spired roof.

CHAPEL to the N. Small crowstep-gabled and rubble-walled oblong built in 1781 on the site of a chapel of 1679. Gothic windows in the S wall, a rectangular door in the N.

NORTH GATEWAY AND LODGES at the beginning of the drive from the A85. Built in 1820. Tall obelisk-topped quatrefoil-plan gatepiers of C17 type. Each side of the drive's entrance, a single-storey battlemented lodge, its end walls carried up above the roof as battlemented screens and pierced by hoodmoulded windows of paired ogee-arched lights under quatrefoil panels.

MEIGLE

Now no more than a village but the remarkable collection of Pictish carved stones now in Meigle Museum (*see* Public Buildings, below) shows that it was an early historic centre of importance, probably the site of a monastery. In 1608 Meigle was erected a burgh of barony under the superiority of the Fullartons of Ardoch but failed to attract industry or a sizeable population.

CHURCHES

MEIGLE FREE CHURCH, Dundee Road. Now a store. Built in 1853. Nave and piend-roofed aisles, with Tudor Gothic windows. Sturdy diagonal buttresses and a hoodmoulded window at the front gable, its bellcote now missing.

Beside the church, its contemporary MANSE, a few of the windows hoodmoulded.

MEIGLE PARISH CHURCH, Forfar Road and Strathmore Place. By *John Carver*, 1869–70, a plain Victorian Gothic reworking of the Late Georgian formula of a tall T-plan kirk but with the tower placed not at one end but in the NW inner angle of the main block and jamb. Masonry of stugged purplish ashlar. At the N jamb and the N side of the main block, a double tier of windows, the lower lighting the area, the upper the galleries. Only gallery windows in the main block's gables from which project a semi-octagonal porch at the E and a vestry at the W. In the S side, tall windows to light the pulpit, flanked by a double tier of smaller windows at the end bays. The tower is finished with a pierced parapet; at its corners, spikily finialled panelled piers. Inside, a compartmented plaster ceiling, the bosses with pâtisserie decoration bearing sacred symbols; frieze enriched with human heads set among foliage. Galleries at the ends and in the N jamb. Herringbone-patterned boarding at the doors, front pews and gallery fronts. Varnished pine PEWS of 1870. Also of 1870 the Gothic PULPIT at the centre of the S side. In front of the pulpit, a routine Gothic COMMUNION TABLE of 1907.

In the porch at the base of the tower, an octagonal FONT BOWL of c. 1500 discovered on this site in the late C18. Six of the corners have bundle-shafted and pinnacled attached column-buttresses from which spring ogee arches to frame panels at seven of the faces. The eighth face has no arch and its column-buttresses are sturdier than the others and decorated with carved foliage. On this face, a relief of the Crucifixion. Six of the other faces are carved with shields bearing emblems of the Passion of Our Lord (the seamless robe, scourge and dice; the nails and hammer; the cross and crown of thorns; the pierced hands, feet and heart; the scourge and whipping post surmounted by a cock; a saltire arrangement of a ladder and sponge-topped reed and a spear). The last face contains a depiction of the Resurrection.

Well-stocked GRAVEYARD. On the E side of the church's N jamb, a WALL MONUMENT of 1661. Moulded frame for a pair of inscription panels. On top of the frame, rosetted swan-neck pediments enclosing two coats of impaled arms, the l. framed by the initials M/GS/MF (for Mr George Symmer, minister of Meigle, c. 1622–55, and his wife, Margaret Fullerton †1658), the r. with the initials M/IS/MC (for Mr John Symmer, assistant and then successor to his father as minister of Meigle, 1634–60, and his wife, Margaret Campbell). – Towards the E end of the N wall of the main block, a WALL MONUMENT erected in 1827 to members of the Scott family, the inscription panel with an egg-and-dart border and surmounted by a coat of arms.

Immediately W of the church and to its S, several C17 and C18 TABLE STONES, their top slabs carved with reminders of death, some also with coats of arms. The SW stone of the W group, N of the path, is carved with an angel's head (the soul) above a pair of angels who trumpet news of the Resurrection to a skeleton. – S of the church, C18 HEADSTONES, mostly carved with angels' heads and emblems of death. SW of the church is a stone of 1742 to James Lesley and Janet Edward, its W face with an angel's head above a skeleton which holds an hourglass and bone and is flanked by trumpeting angels. – SE of this, the stone to William Watson †1761.

On the W face, a pair of angels' heads above a crested and mantled shield which bears the shuttle and loom of a weaver. On the E face, a pair of angels blowing downward-pointing trumpets at a prone skeleton. – E of this, the stone erected in 1743 to the parents of William Anderson and Marjory Yeoman, the W face with a shuttle and loom.

KINLOCH MAUSOLEUM
1.5 km. SW

Built in 1861 for the Kinlochs of Kinloch. In appearance it is a two-bay Romanesque chapel with a W tower. In the N side, a broad door and nook-shafted narrow E window. In the E gable, a round light in a large overarch flanked by narrow windows, all with trumpet-capitalled nook-shafts. Nook-shafted small windows in the S side. Below the eaves, a 'parapet' projected on moulded corbels. Tower of six low stages marked off by string courses which form hoodmoulds over the openings. Corbelled parapet with pyramid-roofed corner turret-piers, their faces panelled with round-headed arches springing from attached columns. Coat of arms at the N face.

PUBLIC BUILDINGS

KINLOCH MEMORIAL HALL, Dundee Road. Dated 1913. Harled, single-storey, with bracketed broad eaves to the piended roofs which were formerly topped by cupolas.

MEIGLE MUSEUM, Dundee Road. Originally the Parish School, it was built in 1844. Single-storey, with hoodmoulded windows and a front porch.

The museum's sole collection is a remarkable group of PICTISH STONES, all but one found in Meigle, a few in the village but most in the churchyard or built into the former parish church, and placed here in the 1880s. All are of sandstone. They are numbered, the numbers those assigned them in J. R. Allen and J. Anderson, *The Early Christian Monuments of Scotland* (1903) and described here in that order (the missing numbers those of stones which are now lost).

MEIGLE 1 is a slab, its principal carved decoration probably of the late C8 but at the bottom of the back of the stone are incised cup and cup-and-ring marks of the third or second millennium B.C. when this was presumably first erected as a standing stone. On the front, a cross, its armpits notched, as are those of the other carved crosses in the museum, and filled with circles; interlaced work on the shaft and arms, circles on the centre of the head. The cross is flanked by sea horses and mythical beasts. On the back, a jumble of Pictish symbols (a salmon, dog's head, 'Pictish beast', 'serpent-and-Z-rod', 'mirror and comb'), animals, horsemen, a kneeling camel and an angel, the last two perhaps copied from an ivory casket imported from the Mediterranean. – MEIGLE 2 is a huge (*c.* 2.5 m. high) and elaborate slab of the C9. The front is carved with a cross, the broad shaft's upper corners scrolled. On the shaft, three pairs of front-to-front animals, their tongues and tails wrapped round them, and smaller beasts snapping at them. More beasts flank the shaft. The shaft supports a ringed head studded with jewel-like bosses. Reliefs on the back of the slab. The lowest depicts a man holding a club and watching a dog grab an ox in its jaws. The next shows a unicorn holding a cross and an axe, with branches in the background. Large relief halfway up the stone, of Daniel in the Lions' Den. Above, horsemen, the three in front riding abreast, the fourth with a large saddlecloth, probably a mark of status. At the top, a huntsman with a pair of hounds surmounted by a floating angel. – MEIGLE 3, the upper part of a slab, probably of the C9, is much smaller (originally *c.* 0.6 m. high) and probably marked an individual grave. On one face, the relief of a cross decorated with interlaced work. Below the l. arm, part of a 'double-disc' symbol. On the other face, the relief of a warrior mounted on a pony. – MEIGLE 4, perhaps of the early C9, is made up of two large fragments of a cross-slab, the missing central part replaced by an uncarved stone. The limbs and centre of the cross itself are carved with interlaced work, with a raffia-like pattern at the centre. In the spaces between the outer frame and the cross's limbs are animals, one attacking a man. At the bottom the shaft is flanked by interlacing. On the back, a medley of mounted warriors (at different scales), animals, snakes, 'Pictish beast' and 'crescent-and-V-rod' symbols and interlacing. – MEIGLE 5 is a substantial fragment. On one face, a cross, its shaft shorter than the arms, poised on the rounded top of a pedestal whose sides scroll out into animals' heads. Interlaced work on both pedestal and cross, the cross's armpits filled with circles. A bird with a snake in its beak and beasts fill the spaces between the arms of the cross. On the back, the relief of a mounted warrior, his head now missing. One of the narrow sides of the slab is incised with 'mirror-case' and 'Pictish beast' symbols. The use of incised instead of relief carving suggests that these may represent a deliberate evocation of an older tradition juxtaposed with the Christian symbolism of the cross on the main face. – MEIGLE 6 is another fragment, one face carved with the upper part of a cross-shaft decorated with a diagonal key pattern. On the back, figures of a mounted warrior, his head missing, 'double-disc' and 'crescent' symbols, and a hound, placed one above the other. – MEIGLE 7, also a fragment and worn, is the rounded top of a slab, its front bearing a cross carved with a diagonal key pattern, the head flanked by a seated naked man and a beast. On the back, 'double-disc-and-Z-rod' and 'comb' symbols. – MEIGLE 8 is a narrow slab (0.22 m. wide). Badly weathered cross on the front. On the back, a tool (?) above the heads of two animals, the r. a horse, which poke legs into each other's mouths. – MEIGLE 9 is a weathered recumbent gravestone, its top apparently cut off but with a shallow slot at one end to support an upright feature. The long sides are divided

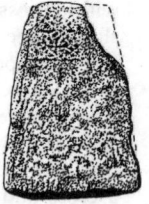

Meigle Museum, Pictish stone
(Meigle 11)

into unequally sized panels bearing reliefs of animals, a human figure and interlacing.

MEIGLE 11 is the largest of the recumbent gravestones in the museum. Sloping top with a broad slot at the higher end and a recessed panel, perhaps erasing some symbol, at the lower. On each side, a broad border with faint traces of carved decoration. On one side the border frames a scene of three horsemen and a small hound followed by a humanoid figure with a beast's head who holds a pair of entwined snakes. On the other side, an array of motifs – animals, a panel of snake-encircled bosses, a circle of bosses framed by beasts munching on a man's head and feet. – MEIGLE 12, another recumbent gravestone, is probably of the C10. Top carved with lozenges in a border of interlaced work. On one side, the relief of a fish monster. On the other, a hound biting the hind leg of a deer, and a pair of bulls about to fight. – MEIGLE 14. Only a fragment which was found in the walling of the former parish church. One side has been carved with a cross bearing interlaced work. On the other, a pair of clerics, the l. shown in profile. Only part of the full-face r. figure now survives but the whole figure, together with a third (a mirror-image of the first) was recorded in the C19. – MEIGLE 15, also a fragment, is the bottom of a small cross-slab, the cross-shaft decorated with interlacing and flanked by animals. – MEIGLE 20. Small fragment, one side carved with interlaced work, presumably of a cross-shaft, the other with legs of a horse and rider. – MEIGLE 21 is the substantial fragment of a relatively tall and narrow cross-slab, the cross-shaft carved with interlaced work, the head with loosely composed diagonal key pattern; rope circles in the notched armpits. – MEIGLE 22, a narrow panel carved only on one face, may have been part of a frieze on a Pictish church at Meigle. Relief of a seated siren, half-woman and half-fish, flanked by long-clawed beasts. – MEIGLE 23, an intact but badly weathered slab, was found in a malt kiln at Templehall, *c.* 70 m. N of Meigle Parish Church, in 1858. On one face, a ringed cross flanked by a pair of seated figures. On the other, two pairs of grappling beasts. – MEIGLE 25 is a late C10 sloping hogbacked tombstone, the sides and lower end carved with curved roof tiles. On the top, a figure with a dog's head and fish's tail. – The well-preserved MEIGLE 26 is another sloping tombstone. Slot at one end of the top which is carved with a border of interlaced work. Inside the border, at the top, a circle of three snakes. In the centre, a square panel filled with snake-entwined bosses. At the bottom, a pair of dancing sea horses. On one side, a latticed panel with, on its l., two mythical beasts, one a griffon, and, on its r., a hunting scene. The other side bears reliefs of juxtaposed scenes – two beasts eating a human corpse, a knot of four naked humans, and two animals. On the end, the figure of a man pursued by a manticore. – The remaining stones are small fragments. One side of MEIGLE 27 is carved with the shaft of a cross ornamented with double spirals and flanked by interlaced work, the other with the figure of a small man sitting on the ground behind the chair of his much larger master. – MEIGLE 28 is the bottom of a cross-slab, the shaft placed above a panel carved with double spirals and flanked by panels of key-pattern work. – One face of MEIGLE 29 is rough, so perhaps it was intended to be placed against a wall. The narrow side is carved with interlacing, the front with a relief of two clerics. – MEIGLE 30 bears the relief of a sleeping animal, perhaps a cat. – On MEIGLE 31, the head of a small cross-slab. – On MEIGLE 32, one arm of a cross carved with spirals; below the arm, part of a panel of double-spiral decoration. – MEIGLE 34 is carved with a scroll. – MEIGLE 35 is something of an intruder, the fragment of a MEDIEVAL CARVED STONE, decorated with a circle entwined with a looped pattern.

MEIGLE PRIMARY SCHOOL, Dundee Road. Red sandstone Board School, by *John Carver*, 1876–7, with a touch of asymmetry at its U-plan front and sparing Gothic detail. Carved bargeboards and a central flèche to the roof.

DESCRIPTION

ALYTH ROAD is the W entry. On its S side, remains of the early C19 STEADING of Meigle House. At its NW corner, a two-storey block, the W gable flanked by pinnacled buttresses, one fleur-de-lys finial surviving. At the upper floor, a small coat of arms of the Murrays of Simprim placed between hoodmoulded windows, the S a dummy. Extending S is an irregular cruciform building, its roof slates placed directly on the extradoi of its internal stone tunnel vaults. At the curved gable of the W limb, pinnacled corner buttresses with fleur-de-lys finials. Arched stone dormer windows.

Alyth Road ends at THE SQUARE, a formal name for a bend in the main E–W road through the burgh from which Ardler Road and Dundee Road lead out to the SW and SE. On the S side, the KINLOCH ARMS HOTEL, the lower two floors of *c.* 1770 but much altered, the top floor, dressed up with half-timbering, an addition of *c.* 1900. On The Square's SW corner, the OLD BANK HOUSE of 1771, its pedimented chimney gablet containing a Venetian window, the centre light a dummy; an urn finial survives at one end of the front.

FORFAR ROAD carries the A94 out to the E. Set back in its graveyard to the S, Meigle Parish Church (*see* Churches, above). The road's N side starts with an early C19 two-storey house, with a heavy anta-pilastered doorpiece. Built into its W gable, a C17 segmental pediment brought here from South West Fullarton (1.2km. SE). Round its top, the inscription YIS.HOVS.IS. BVLDSB[Y] ELESOBETH.BETOVN; at the bottom 'L.FVLLERTOVN'. In the centre, the monogrammed initials EB and WF. On the house's N front, two C17 stones, also from South West Fullarton, one bearing the coat of arms of Fullarton of that Ilk flanked by the initials WF, the other the arms of Beaton or Bethune of Balfour flanked by the initials EB. E of this house, the severe mid-C19 Jacobean ROYAL BANK OF SCOTLAND.

ARDLER ROAD leads to VICTORY PARK, a cricket field entered through a round-headed WAR MEMORIAL arch of hammer-dressed stone under a gambrel roof, designed by *John Bruce & Sons* in 1921.

Near DUNDEE ROAD's start, on its E side, the Meigle Museum (*see* Public Buildings, above). Then, on the W in a leafy garden, the former MEIGLE PARISH MANSE, built in 1809–10 but extended by *John Carver*, 1877, a plain agglomeration unified by harling. Further out, on the E, Meigle Primary School and the Kinloch Memorial Hall followed by the former Meigle Free Church (*see* Churches and Public Buildings, above).

BALENDOCH. *See* p. 177.
BELMONT CASTLE. *See* p. 193.
DRUMKILBO. *See* p. 318.
KINLOCH HOUSE. *See* p. 467.

MEIKLEOUR

Small estate village.

INSTITUTE. By *D. A. Stewart* of *Smart, Stewart & Mitchell*, 1930. Drydashed, with stone dressings. Single-storey piend-roofed block and a taller hall with a low clock tower at its front gable, bargeboards and hoodmoulded windows.

JOUGS. Tall pock-marked slab with a roughly triangular top and pierced by a round hole. Attached to the S face, iron jougs. It may have been erected in the C16 or C17.

MERCAT CROSS. Erected in 1698 and bearing the same mason's mark as the cross of 1686 at Kinrossie (q.v.). Monolith on a circular stepped base. The cross's pedestal is roughly square, each face bearing the relief of a saltire. Oblong shaft with diagonal projections at the corners. Each of the two main faces is hollowed out to form a tall round-headed arch containing a star-finialled attached column. On top of the shaft, a crudely modelled cross.

DESCRIPTION. At the village's S end, THE BRICK HOUSE, a harled two-storey three-bay building of *c*. 1790. Its pedimented portico is an addition, probably of the later C19. On the W side of the road, just within the parkland of Meikleour House, the jougs (*see above*). After the Institute (*see above*), the early C19 PARK VIEW COTTAGE, with bracketed eaves and hoodmoulded door and windows. C19 cottages follow, together with some late C20 housing which does its best to fit in. The mercat cross (*see above*) provides a central feature. Further N, the single-storey and attic MEIKLEOUR HOTEL built by *James Dewar*, *John Thomson* and *James Pirnie* in 1819–21. Picturesque, with a bay window, bracketed broad eaves, hoodmoulds over the attic windows and diagonally placed chimneys. Veranda at the E front. Long rear wing.

CLEAVEN DYKE, North Wood, 1.1 km. NE. Monumental Neolithic earthwork of *c.* 4000 B.C., the minor differences in alignment along its generally straight SE–NW line probably evidence of a protracted period of construction. It is a 2.3 km.-long bank, formed of sand and gravel revetted with turf, and stands up to 1.8 m. high. Mostly 8 m.–10 m. broad, it widens at the NW end to *c.* 16 m. The central gap through which passes the SW–NE path through North Wood seems to be original. Each side of the bank, a 20 m.-wide berm on platform bounded by a 4 m.-broad ditch.

MEIKLEOUR HOUSE
0.9 km. SSW

Sited in parkland above the E bank of the River Tay, an Early Georgian laird's house largely remodelled as a French Renaissance château by *David Bryce* in 1869–70.

The original house, built in 1734 for Robert Mercer (formerly Murray) who had married Jean Mercer, heiress of the estates of Aldie and Meikleour fourteen years before, faced E. It consisted of a piend-roofed main block of two storeys above a basement. Seven-bay front, the centre three slightly advanced under a segmental pediment; another segmental pediment over the central door. This block was joined by single-storey and basement wings to Venetian-windowed pavilions, also of a single storey and basement. In his remodelling for Robert Mercer's great-granddaughter, Emily Jane de Flahault de la Billerdrie, Dowager Marchioness of Lansdowne and *suo jure* Baroness Nairne, Bryce made the E front the garden façade and refaced it and all the other C18 work with squared and stugged purplish masonry to correspond with that of his additions. He also lowered the ground level to expose fully the basement, above which he stretched a full-length E balcony carried on stone corbels, its iron balustrade decorated with face-to-face Ls (for Lansdowne), anthemion and rosettes under a Vitruvian scroll border enriched with flowers. At the centre of the balcony he placed a horseshoe stair (replacing the C18 single flight of steps) down to the garden. At the same time he added an extra floor to the links and pavilions. The pavilions were given iron-crested tall French pavilion roofs and their C18 Venetian windows replaced by shallowly projecting three-light rectangular bay windows with pierced parapets; above, three-light openings with lugged architraves as have all the second-floor windows; pedimented stone windows to the attic. On the new roof over the links and main block, more iron cresting and panelled chimneystacks; four dormer windows like those of the pavilions placed between the windows below. The windows of the principal floor of the links and main block were lowered to floor level and given cornices, these being removed except at the centrepiece in the 1950s when the eight outer bays' windows acquired lugged architraves. Bryce also replaced the centrepiece's segmental pediment with a triangular pediment, its tympanum carved with the coat of arms of the Mercers, and converted the pedimented central door to a corniced French window.

At the house's short N elevation, a porch added in 2000 and fronted by a Roman Doric columned and segmental-pedimented doorpiece, its design derived from the one formerly at the house's original E entrance (*see* stables, below). At the S elevation, a two-storey canted bay window under a pierced parapet; it is of 1869–70.

Bryce's W (entrance) front is disappointing, a cheaper version of what he had originally proposed. Across the C18 main block he added a two-storey balustraded addition (the lower floor at the level of the C18 basement), its slightly advanced centre containing the side-lit main entrance, its pediment carried on leafy consoles, under a three-light window. At the end bays of this addition, a flat-roofed third storey rises behind the balustrade. In front of the C18 links and projecting slightly from his central addition he placed one-bay three-storey W wings, their windows of three lights, their intended tall French pavilion roofs replaced in the execution by low piended roofs with floriated iron finials. At these wings and the main block, pedimented stone dormers like those of the S front. At the W front's outer corners, fish-scale slated conical-roofed round towers, also with pedimented dormers; on the N tower, the coat of arms of Baroness Nairne, on the S the arms of the Marquess of Lansdowne. Attached to the NW tower, a single-storey and attic service wing added by *Andrew Heiton Jun.*, *c.* 1880. Balustraded W and S fronts of squared and stugged masonry; harled N elevation.

INTERIOR. From the W entrance a plain corridor leads N to the stair hall of 1869–70. Oak stair with turned balusters rising through three storeys. Plaster ceiling, its cornice with rosettes between modillions. At the landing to the principal floor, a doorcase with foliaged consoles and a modillion cornice. This is the entry to the LONG GALLERY, a plain but useful circulation space occupying Bryce's central W addition. At its S end, a SITTING ROOM, its late C18 pine and gesso chimneypiece imported in the later C20. It is decorated with foliage pendants and husk swags. At the top of the jambs, reliefs of jugs; at the centre of the frieze, a basket of flowers.

The main rooms, facing E, have modillioned and rosetted cornices like that of the stair hall. At the S end, the DRAWING ROOM. High-quality mid-C18 marble chimneypiece, presumably an import, perhaps from Bowood (Wiltshire) or Lansdowne House (London). Diagonally set caryatid terms at the jambs. On the frieze, swags of fruit flanking the central panel which is carved with the head of Apollo in a sunburst. Then, a study followed by a small SITTING ROOM, its Neoclassical chimneypiece of white and veined brown marble, with fluted pilasters and a rosetted frieze. This is of *c.* 1800 and probably also brought from elsewhere. The DINING ROOM occupies the three centre bays of the E front and was probably formed by Bryce from two rooms, the E the entrance hall, the W perhaps a stair hall. Another high-quality mid-C18 chimneypiece and also apparently imported. Massive foliage-enriched and urn-topped consoles projecting diagonally from the outer corners. On the frieze, the high relief head of a bearded man set in swagged drapery. Grey marble chimneypiece in Bryce's characteristic Frenchy manner in the small dining room to the N.

MOTTE to the W of the house's S end, beside the River Tay. It was probably formed in the late C12 when the lands of Meikleour were held by the Earls of Strathearn. Roughly circular 5m.-high artificial mound of inverted pudding basin type, *c.* 35m. in diameter at the base and 22m. at the flat summit. Presumably it was surmounted by a wooden tower.

STABLES, 0.2km. N of the house. Rubble-walled piend-roofed ranges enclosing a sizeable courtyard, built *c.* 1800. E range of two storeys, some of the small first-floor windows heightened in the late C19 to rise through the eaves to dormerheads. Pedimented and elliptical-arched pend entrance, its present appearance probably dating from 1870. On the courtyard's S side, a two-storey range with, at its centre, a taller two-storey house with a round-headed central door. The W range is of one and two storeys. Built into the back of its N part, the C18 former front door of the mansion house. It is a Roman Doric aedicule, the tympanum of its segmental pediment carved with the date 1734 and the monogrammed initials of Robert Mercer of Aldie and Meikleour. Inside this framework, a heavily keystoned and imposted segmental arch carried on pilasters whose fronts' outer halves are convex, their inner concave.

On the E edge of the house's parkland, beside the A93, a beech HEDGE planted in 1745. It is *c.* 0.53km. long but made quite remarkable by its height of *c.* 24m.–35m.

METHVEN

Village which developed in the late C18, handloom weaving the principal occupation of the inhabitants.

CHURCHES

MANSION NOOK CHAPEL, off Main Street. Now a hall. Rubble-walled and piend-roofed box built in 1844 for a congregation which had split from the Methven Original Secession Church. The centre of the three-bay w front is slightly advanced; rectangular windows.

METHVEN AND LOGIEALMOND PARISH CHURCH, Church Road. Large rubble-walled kirk begun in 1782–3 by *James Watt* and *John Taylor*, masons, and *James Anderson*, wright, who built a straightforward rectangular church, with a simple pyramid-roofed birdcage bellcote on the w gable. The long s wall had tall windows flanking the pulpit and, at the ends, small rectangular openings. In each gable, a round-headed door and, near the top, a small square window. In the N wall, rectangular windows and a door at each end.

In 1825–6 the church was enlarged and remodelled by *W. M. Mackenzie* who added a N 'aisle' or jamb and gave the s front a new civic dignity, recasting it as a nine-bay elevation. The fourth and sixth bays are advanced, each containing a tall round-arched window and surmounted by the outer third of a triangular pediment. The centre of this pediment is broken by the bolder projection of the central bay under its own pediment and with another round-arched window in its front. Rising above is a steeple whose octagonal base supports a pilastered drum (the belfry). On top of the drum, a low octagonal clock stage surmounted by a taller octagon with a narrow round-arched dummy window in each gabled face. The steeple is finished with an octagonal stone spire. The third and seventh bays are blind. At the second and eighth bays, full-height gabled projections, each containing a rectangular area window under a pointed gallery window. The end bays are again blind, the c18 openings built up. At the 'aisle', round-arched windows lighting the area and Tudor Gothic gallery windows with consoled sills and intersecting astragals, their tops rising into gabled dormerheads. A piend-roofed vestry in the NE inner angle was added in 1861. Further alterations were made in 1871 by *David Smart* who divided each window of the front into two lights under a circled head, a token attempt to medievalise Mackenzie's work.

Inside, a panel-fronted U-plan gallery of 1825, its cast-iron columns with foliaged capitals. In the centre of the s wall, a late c19 ORGAN, formerly in Dupplin Castle and installed here by *John R. Miller*, 1914, the date also of the PULPIT which fronts it.

GRAVEYARD. Immediately w of the church is the METHVEN AISLE, the surviving N transept of the medieval parish church, the rest of which was demolished in 1783. The church had become collegiate in 1433 when Walter Stewart, Earl of Atholl, endowed an establishment consisting of a provost, five chaplains and four choirboys. The church may well have been enlarged at that time to house additional altars but the surviving Aisle is probably an extension of *c*. 1510–16 when the college was expanded by the endowment of nine extra prebends, one by James IV. It is small (*c.* 6.7m. by 6.4m.), with extravagantly heavy gableted crowsteps (those of the S gable added in 1835). In the N gable, a three-light window (the openings now blocked) with reticulated tracery and double-splay moulded jambs. At the springing of the window arch, a moulded impost above which the section of the moulding of the sides changes. The window is flanked by a canopied image niche on the l. and, on the r., by a panel bearing a badly weathered carving of the Royal Arms of Scotland. Windowless E and W walls. At the S gable, a big pointed entrance arch, probably also of *c.* 1510–16 but with a transom introduced in 1835.

Just S of the W end of the Parish Church is the LYNEDOCH MAUSOLEUM, by *James Playfair*, 1793. It is a powerful Neoclassical rectangle of French inspiration. Walls of channelled rock-faced masonry, the lower courses projected as a pedestal. Anthemion-finialled pediments at the N and S ends. Shallow-pitched and ribbed lead roof. The round-arched N door is the only opening.

On the W end of the S wall of the Parish Church, a MONUMENT of 1840 to the Rev. John Jameson, with carvings in exceptionally high relief of two mourning ladies and an urn. – Near the S edge of the churchyard, aligned with the Methven Aisle, an C18 HEADSTONE, its top carved with an angel's head (the soul); below are torches flanking a shield. – Some way to its W and a little to the N, another C18 HEADSTONE, with an angel's head above an array of tools, the carving in quite high relief. – N of this, a HEADSTONE, now with a C19 inscription to James and John Scott and Janet Morrison but apparently C18, its front carved with an angel's head above a torch-framed shield; reminders of death at the bottom. – N of this, a foliage-bordered C18 GRAVE-SLAB. At the top end, angels' heads flanking a ship above a heraldic achievement; below the inscription, a skull, crossbones and an hourglass.

METHVEN UNITED PRESBYTERIAN CHURCH, Main Street. Now Community Centre. Dec, by *John Honeyman*, 1867–8. Buttressed box, built of stugged masonry. Wheel window in the N gable. At the front (S) gable, a three-light window with foliage-capitalled nook-shafts; the label stops of the hoodmould are carved with the heads of a man and woman. SW porch, the hoodmoulds over its entrance and S window with foliaged label stops. – HALL at the NE added by *P. Keay* and *Robert Jack* in 1908.

PUBLIC BUILDINGS

CHURCH HALL, Retinue Road. Built and perhaps designed by *J. Keay*, 1909. Harled, with red sandstone dressings; broad eaves and a big ventilator-flèche.

METHVEN SCHOOL, Main Street. By *G. P. K. Young*, 1910. Long building, the walls harled and with red sandstone dressings. Sparing Free Jacobean detail.

DESCRIPTION

MAIN STREET carries the A85 through the village. At its E end, on the N side, Nos. 8–10, a double house of the mid or later C19, No. 8 with broad eaves, gabled dormerheads over the first-floor windows, and a rustic porch. Some way further on and set back on the s, Methven School (*see* Public Buildings, above). The centre of the village is announced by the former Methven United Presbyterian Church on the N; beside it but hidden behind No. 34 Main Street is the old Mansion Nook Chapel (*see* Churches, above). Opposite but back from the road, THE OLD SCHOOLHOUSE by *Andrew Heiton Sen.*, 1839, with bracketed broad eaves. Then, CHURCH ROAD goes off to the N, with plain early C19 houses at its S end. Closing the view to the N, Methven and Logiealmond Parish Church (*see* Churches, above). Behind the church, in LYNEDOCH ROAD, is LYNEDOCH HOUSE (the former Parish Manse), Jacobethan by *W. M. Mackenzie*, 1830–1, enjoying a large sloping garden. In RETINUE ROW, the W continuation of Lynedoch Road, the Church Hall (*see* Public Buildings, above).

W of Church Road, Main Street settles down into unambitious early and mid-C19 Late Georgian and Georgian survival. Off it, on the N, THE SQUARE, a less formal space than the name suggests, its N side occupied by Nos. 6A–7B, an early C19 ashlar-fronted two-storey and attic double house. The W end of Main Street is architecturally bitty but, on the N, a row of early C19 weavers' cottages (Nos. 94–100) followed, on both sides, by other cottages of the mid and later C19.

METHVEN CASTLE
1.6 km. E

Prominently sited status symbol built in 1678–81 for Patrick Smythe, a merchant, who had acquired the estate in 1664. The general conception of a U-plan house, whose open centre is filled by a flat-roofed and balustraded block containing the entrance, had become normal for Scottish mansion houses from the 1660s but at Methven the verticality, prominent corner towers and shot-holes assert the building's right to the name of castle.

Covered in cream-coloured harl, the house is tall, of four storeys and an attic, with crowstepped gables and large ogee-roofed round towers at the four corners. Originally the ground floor was lit by small square windows, the two principal floors above by windows of decent size and the third floor by small windows under the eaves; tiny attic windows in the gables. Several of these openings were enlarged *c.* 1800. The towers were lit by tiers of small windows above round-headed ground-floor slits.

At the N-facing entrance front the gables of the E and W wings grip the balustraded centre; under one end of the balustrade, a stone spout to drain the centrepiece's flat roof, the corresponding spout at the other end replaced by a downpipe. Narrow round-headed late C17 door. In the gable of the E wing, a much larger door (now a window), with sidelights and an overall fanlight, was inserted *c.* 1800, its height requiring the curtailment of the window above. The centre's third-floor window is low and horizontal.

At the E and W side, regular four-bay elevations, the E side's S bay with windows only at the ground floor, but the symmetry of composition disturbed by the walling being carried up into the gables of the S range. Tiny slit window at the centre of the W side's first floor but at a lower level than the flanking openings. In the centre of the E side, a tier of round shot-holes, their surrounds carved with rosettes. At the four-bay S (garden) front, the (enlarged) first-floor windows have projecting sills added in the early C20 to support window boxes.

The interior, much altered in the C18 and C19, has been virtually gutted in the reconstruction begun by *Kenneth Murdoch* in 1985. Of the late C17 work there survives the stone scale-and-platt stair which rises from inside the front door at the centre of the house's N side. Also late C17 is the large roll-and-hollow-moulded segmental-arched fireplace in the NE ground-floor room, probably originally the kitchen. Of the late C20 work the most notable feature has been the opening up of the second, third and attic floors of the S range as a simple galleried space open to the roof timbers, the gallery's Oregon pine silhouette balusters gently reminiscent of the work of Charles Rennie Mackintosh.

W of the house, a rubble-built mid-C19 service building with an ogee-roofed cupola at one end. It formed part of an otherwise demolished W wing which had been added to the castle.

GLENALMOND COLLEGE. *See* p. 383.

MILLEARNE

9010

1.2 km. NW of Kinkell

The Tudor Gothic MANSION HOUSE by *R. & R. Dickson*, built for John George Home Drummond in 1821–38, was demolished in 1969 and a smaller modern-traditional house erected.

The STABLES courtyard, also Tudor, survives to the W. Gatehouse range at the E of 1824, its centrepiece a two-stage battlemented tower pierced by a Tudor pend arch under a shallow rectangular oriel window; on the S side of the tower, a taller tower, also battlemented but of four stages, with a Gothic doorway at the bottom. Plain single-storey links, the N battlemented, to the projecting gable ends of the courtyard's N and S ranges, the N a tall single storey with a four-light mullioned and transomed window, the S of two low storeys. Inside the courtyard, the N and S ranges are workaday but, rising from the N is a square tower with a crowstepped gable at each face and hoodmoulded windows to the upper stage. The S range's ivy-covered outer front is Tudor, its gabled W bay added in 1852. Screen wall on the courtyard's W side.

W of the stables, a garden TERRACE of the earlier C19, its S retaining wall with battlemented Tudor 'turrets' and fronted by a balustraded flight of steps. High N wall broken by a Gothic doorway and recesses. – Brick WALLED GARDEN of 1840 to the W. In its S side, a Tudor stone gateway carved with a pair of shields bearing the coats of arms of John George Home Drummond of Millearne and Mary Bothwell Drummond, his wife. – On the S axis of the gate, an octagonal stone 'FONT', also of the earlier C19 and Tudor, its bowl's flat top probably intended for a sundial, the sides carved alternately with the Home Drummond coat of arms and stylized foliage. – A little SW of the walled garden, a Gothic ashlar MONUMENT erected in 1840 to commemorate John George Home Drummond's mother, Janet Jardine. Angle-buttressed square pedestal supporting an octagonal pier, its base boldly moulded, its capital carved with flowering foliage. The finial is a large cross, its ends also foliaged. – Tudor Gothic GATEWAY of the earlier C19 at the S end of the main drive to the house.

MILNATHORT

A large village, now separated from the N end of Kinross only by the River North Queich, which developed around mills powered by the Fochy Burn. By the late 1790s these comprised two waulk mills and five grain mills, as well as a distillery. In the early C19 handloom production of cotton goods was the principal industry, superseded from the 1830s by the manufacture of woollens and linens. Industry declined in the C20 and the village now serves partly as a dormitory for towns accessible by the nearby motorway.

CHURCHES

ANTIBURGHER CHURCH, Church Street. Secularized, the ground-floor openings and the interior altered. Tall piend-roofed rubble-walled rectangle of five bays by four which has developed from the church built by *James* and *Robert Morison*, masons, in 1764. In 1790 *David Nicol*, mason, and *Alexander Readie*, wright, heightened the walls by *c.* 1 m. and widened the building to the N by *c.* 2.1 m. The church was further enlarged by *John Beveridge* in 1816 when the front (S) wall was rebuilt *c.* 0.6 m. further out. In the long walls, two tiers of rectangular windows. In the W gable, a pair of round-arched ground-floor windows inserted in 1816.

BURGHER CHURCH, Perth Road. Secularized. By *James Milne*, 1821–2, the roughness of its ashlar masonry just depriving it of urbanity. It is a two-storeyed broad box with pedimented gables, the NE gable's pediment with a blind oculus containing a cinquefoil. At this gable and the side walls, the upper windows are round-headed, the lower rectangular. At the SW gable, two tall round-headed windows (formerly lighting the pulpit), their stone mullions inserted in 1881, flanked by two smaller round-headed windows which lit the area under the gallery. A large door has been inserted in the NE gable and the interior gutted for the building's present use as a store.

MILNATHORT UNITED PRESBYTERIAN CHURCH, South Street and Church Street. Now HILLCREST. Tall and bare Geometric, by *William Ingram*, 1867–9. The church is a big buttressed stugged ashlar box, the breadth of its gable front partly masked by the steeple whose broached spire is relieved by lucarnes. It was converted to housing in 1994.

ORWELL PARISH CHURCH, off Manse Road. T-plan kirk built of coursed rubble, originally harled. It was begun in 1729 (the date on the sundial on the S wall) and of the original building there survive the shape and the birdcage bellcote on the W gable of the main block. This bellcote, open-sided to the E and W and with two tiers of stumpy balusters on the N and S sides, must originally have been almost identical to the contemporary bellcote of Fossoway St Serf's and Devonside Parish Church at Crook of Devon (q.v.) but was given a stone-slabbed pyramidal roof and iron cross finial in *John Lessels'* alterations of 1874. The main block of the church was heightened in 1797, the date of the moulded stone cornices on the long sides, the ball finial on the E gable, and the round-headed windows and doors of the S front and gables, the S windows now with stone tracery of 1874. In the N wall of the main block, rectangular windows. Rectangular windows also in the N jamb which was heightened in 1808 when it acquired cornices like those of the main block.

The interior was re-furnished by Lessels in 1874. At the ends of the main block and in the jamb, GALLERIES with Gothic-panelled fronts, the centre of the N gallery front with a CLOCK of *c*. 1840 by *J. & A. McNab*. Most of the N gallery was partitioned off as a room in 1996. – The windows flanking the pulpit in the centre of the S wall are filled with STAINED GLASS of *c*. 1875, garishly coloured and with depictions of stylized foliage.

The GRAVEYARD was enclosed with a wall in 1736 and enlarged in 1782 and 1808. At its S entrance, a simple SESSION HOUSE, designed and built by *Alexander Forfar*, 1828; it was converted to a hall and given a roughcast extension in 1930–1. – Against the graveyard's E wall, three aedicular HEADSTONES. One, commemorating members of the Robertson family, is dated 1760. Fluted Ionic columns support a swan-necked pediment broken by a lozenge carved with a smiling sun. Another, to John Robertson, dated 1754, is plainer, with panelled Ionic pilasters and a steep shaped pediment. The third, dated 1763, commemorates David Coventry. Orderless rudimentary columns and a curvy pediment. – Against the churchyard's W wall, the similar but more accomplished HEADSTONE of Helen Thomson †1785, with fluted Doric columns and a concave-sided pediment. – Built into the S wall of the churchyard, a

MONUMENT to Colonel John Thomson †1839, carved with the relief of a mourning lady. – Beside it, the free-standing MONUMENT to his wife, Bathurst Thomson †1845, with the statue of another female mourner. – A few free-standing HEADSTONES are worth notice. A little NW of the church is the rectangular stone, dated 1761, to David Lennox, mason, the front decorated with an Ionic-columned aedicule, its pediment topped with an acroterion. The spandrels between the pediment and the main border are carved with dividers and set-squares, open on the l., closed on the r. – SW of the church, the TABLE STONE of 1758 to James Brown, with trumpeting angels at the bottom. – To its S, the HEADSTONE of George Condie, dated 1756, its front and back both pilastered, the curvy pediment broken by a sort of pineapple. On the W face, an angel's head (the soul); on the E, a smiling sun. – S of the church's E end, a similar but simpler HEADSTONE, dated 1758, commemorating Robert Henderson and Catherine Wilson.

PUBLIC BUILDINGS

MILNATHORT PRIMARY SCHOOL, Stirling Road. By *Perth & Kinross County Council*, 1962. Buff brick and curtain walling.

TOWN HALL, New Road. By *Watt* of Kinross, 1853–5. Two-storey ashlar rectangle, a big gablet in the centre of the long W side. Pedimented S gable with narrow pointed windows. This is almost covered by a steeple, *c.* 29 m. high, its appearance Neo-C17 with pointed doors and windows to the tower within whose overall balustrade rises a ribbed metal spire. The hall was extended E in 1897.

DESCRIPTION

The shape of the village is that of a tree. SOUTH STREET forms the trunk. At its S end, a plain ashlar-built BRIDGE over the North Queich, by *Watt* of Kinross, 1841. Just N of the bridge and set well back from the street's E side, an ashlar-faced ENGINE HOUSE, the principal surviving building of the ORWELL WOOLLEN MILL built in 1861. Italianate, with round-arched windows and a tall ventilator shaft on the piended roof.

South Street proper begins on the E with the mid-C19 No. 125. Single-storey and attic with a block-pedimented door-piece, the necks of its pilasters carved with badly weathered acanthus leaves. The main floor of No. 121 is also mid C19 and built of red sandstone rough ashlar but it rests on a basement of pale buff-coloured stone, probably originally the ground floor of an C18 predecessor. Some way further up the street, on the W side, the two-storey No. 60, again of the mid C19. Over its door, a hoodmould supported on heavy moulded square corbels. No. 58, also two-storey but lower, looks C18. On the E side of the street, the mid-C19 No. 67, with moulded architraves to the windows and door and a cornice-like string course over the ground floor. To its N and sitting in a garden, DUNELLEN (No. 63), a villa of *c.* 1900, with half-timbering, bracketed broad eaves, and an ogee-roofed octagonal turret at the NW corner. The effect is Arts and Crafts but unrelaxed. On the W side, at the S corner of Church Street, the former Milnathort United Presbyterian Church (*see* Churches, above). Opposite, set back from the E side of South Street, the MILNATHORT GOLF CLUB occupying the much altered N range of a steading. The steading's S range, now roofed with corrugated iron but probably originally thatched, is dated 1839. Small horizontal-shaped openings at the upper floor which is reached by a forestair against the W gable. At South Street's N end on the E side, Nos. 7–9 of *c.* 1860, the ground floor with V-jointed rustication and an elliptical-arched shop entrance. On the W side, Nos. 2–6, probably early C19 but most of the first-floor windows now have chamfered jambs. Roman Doric pilastrade along much of the ground floor.

CHURCH STREET to the W is the first branch off South Street. In it, C19 vernacular cottages. On the N side, the former Antiburgher Church (*see* Churches, above). STIRLING ROAD is the second W branch. At its corner with South Street, a pseudo-traditional drydashed block of flats, by *Baxter, Clark & Paul*, 1998–2000. On the street's N side, at the corner with Wester Loan, the two-storey MILL HOUSE (No. 2), dated 1792 but now drydashed and with cement margins to the windows. Otherwise, Stirling Road's buildings are mostly C19 cottages, the S side largely formed by the backs of buildings in Church Street. At the E end of Stirling Road, after its junction with Church Street, Milnathort Primary School (*see* Public Buildings, above).

NEW ROAD is a branch to the E off the top of South Street. Its N side begins with the Town Hall (*see* Public Buildings, above) which gives the village a burghal character. To its E, the rendered two-storey and attic JOLLY BEGGARS HOTEL, perhaps late C18, with rope-moulded club skewputts. A little further E, Nos. 21–23 of *c.* 1800, with a moulded main cornice and scrolled skewputts, again with rope-moulded decoration. At the end, PERTH ROAD begins with THORNTON HOUSE (No. 1), a substantial early C19 house with rusticated quoins and a Roman Doric columned doorpiece. Perth Road's exit to the NE is overlooked by prosperous Jacobethan villas of which No. 3 (ORWELL AND PORTMOAK MANSE) on the N was built as Orwell Free Church Manse in 1850–1. On the S, WHITETHORN is of about the same date and MORVERN, formerly the United Presbyterian Manse, is by *John Melvin*, 1851. The junction of New Road and Perth Road is also the starting point for BURLEIGH ROAD which runs out to the SE towards Burleigh Castle (q.v.) and for Victoria Avenue which leads uphill to the NW. From Victoria Avenue's SE end, OLD PERTH ROAD goes off to the E. On its r., a simple two-storey block of *c.* 1800, built of coursed rubble, its gable gently bowed. On the l. side of the road, the former Burgher Church (*see* Churches, above).

BACK LOAN runs W from the bottom of Victoria Avenue. At its W end, on the N side, No. 9, a single-storey pantile-roofed cottage, probably C19 but with reused window lintels, one inscribed IM.IB.1700, the other M.IB.1699. At the two-storey Nos. 5–7 Back Loan of 1899, a couple more reused lintels at the paired doors, one of buff stone and inscribed B 1698, the other of reddish stone and inscribed RM 1730 EL. The harled No. 3 (HOLLYHOCK COTTAGE), snug behind a front garden, has a door lintel inscribed 17 IY BA 50, the date fitting the appearance of the house. This is of two storeys and three broad bays, the first-floor windows taller than those below. Moulded skewputts; at the chimneys, checks for thatch but the roof is now slated.

Hollyhock Cottage looks over to the back of the Town Hall (*see* Public Buildings, above) past whose W side WESTER LOAN rises to the N. On Wester Loan's l. side, the L-plan No. 13, probably C18, built of buff-coloured rubble. Moulded skewputts at the gables; the gable of the back wing has steps breaking the straight line of the skews. On the r., No. 26, its door lintel dated 1733. Two storeys and three broad bays, of red-coloured rubble, the skewputts moulded. At the top of Wester Loan, on the l., No. 45 of the earlier C19, with hoodmoulds over the ground-floor openings.

The N vista up Wester Loan is almost closed by No. 2 MANSE ROAD, again early C19 and with a pilastered doorpiece but its windows have been altered and the roof covered with concrete tiles. Manse Road then curves uphill towards Orwell Parish Church (*see* Churches, above). On its l. side, the two-storey No. 13 was built as the parish schoolhouse in 1810; *Robert Burn* was the architect. The gabled porch is a later addition. Further up, the harled ORWELL HOUSE (No. 21), formerly Orwell Parish Manse, was built by *David Nicol*, mason, and *Thomas Beveridge*, *John Bell* and *Robert Forfar*, wrights, in 1788. The dormer windows may date from *Peddie & Kinnear*'s alterations of 1891–2.

HILTON, 1.1 km. W. Prominently sited overlooking the M90, a laird's house of *c.* 1830. Two storeys, built of grey rubble, well-clad with Virginia creeper; piended platform roof. Tuscan-columned doorpiece to the three-bay front. At the E end, a spire-roofed octagonal dairy of the mid or late C19.

LETHANGIE HOUSE, 0.9 km. S. Late Georgian house much altered and extended by *John Melvin & Son* in the earlier C20 (1911, 1923 and 1935) to form a comfortable villa. Originally quite simple, of two storeys, the three-bay front of ashlar droved to a corduroy texture. The heavy block-pedimented porch was added and the two-light window to its r. inserted in 1860. In the early C20 the first floor windows were given shutters and flat-roofed dormers constructed at the attic. Also of the earlier C20 is the bow-fronted W addition. Extensive harled extensions at the rear. – In the partly walled garden W of the house, a red sandstone square GAZEBO of the earlier C19, with hoodmoulded windows and a steep pyramidal roof. Built into its S wall, an heraldic stone bearing the impaled arms of Sir William Bruce of Kinross and his wife, Mary Halkett, together with the date 1669. – WALLED GARDEN to the E and, some way beyond, a harled square DOOCOT, perhaps Late Georgian, with flight holes placed in a gablet; wrought-iron finial of the later C19 on the pyramidal roof. Inside, stone nesting boxes. – At LETHANGIE FARM behind, an aggressively crowstep-gabled steading range of the mid C19.

STANDING STONES, Orwell, 2.9 km, E. Pair of huge stones, c. 13.6 m. apart, probably erected in the second millennium B.C. The W (re-erected in the 1970s) is a whinstone boulder, c. 2.3 m. high above the ground; the E, smooth-sided and with a roughly rounded top, stands c. 3.1 m. high. Excavation in 1972 found that both had been associated with cremation deposits, with two placed in one side of the W side's socket-hole.

ARLARY HOUSE. See p. 159.
BURLEIGH CASTLE. See p. 250.

MILTON OF EDRADOUR see EDRADOUR

MONCREIFFE HOUSE
1.3 km. NE of Bridge of Earn

Harled mansion house, by *William H. Kininmonth*, c. 1960, designed to evoke but not replicate its predecessor of 1679 which was destroyed by fire in 1957; a conical-roofed round tower at the back. Reused from the earlier house is its doorpiece, a channelled ashlar basket arch with a small central pendant. This forms the background for a Doric aedicule, the pilasters fluted, the cornice projected beyond the sloping sides in a manner suggestive of Robert Mylne, the apex broken by a swagged urn. In the pediment's tympanum, a shield bearing the impaled arms of Thomas Moncreiffe of that Ilk and his wife, Bethia Hamilton; the metopes of the frieze are carved with a star and rosette and the date 1679.

On the lawn in front, the 'BORE STONE', a Pictish cross-slab, probably of the C8 or C9, which stood in a field behind Gask House (q.v.) until moved here c. 1900. The top has been broken off. On each face, a ringed cross decorated with interlace work. Pierced oval holes fill the spaces between the rings and the cross arms. On the better-preserved S face of the slab, l. of the cross-shaft, reliefs of centaurs, horses and a deer; r. of the cross-shaft, bears or dogs, one eating a salmon, and, below, two horsemen, the upper accompanied by a 'flower' symbol and surmounted by a 'serpent-and-Z-rod'. The N face is badly weathered. At the top, on either side of the cross-shaft, are beasts. Below, Biblical and hagiographical scenes – on the l., Jacob Wrestling with God and, perhaps, the Presentation of Our Lord in the Temple; on the r., St Antony and the Centaur, perhaps the Burial of St Antony by Lions, and King David (identified by a harp) Killing a Lion. – Beside the drive to the W, a STONE CIRCLE erected probably in the third or second millennium B.C. on a site 0.3 km. W and now covered by the M90. It was moved here *c.* 1980. Eight boulders stand in a circle, *c.* 8 m. in diameter, the tallest stones (1.47 m.–2.00 m. high) in the S arc. They may have surrounded a ring-cairn. A cup-marked stone was placed in the centre of the circle in the late C19.

STABLES to the NW, probably built soon after 1821 when *William Stirling I* produced a design for additions. Rubble-walled and piend-roofed main range of two storeys, the upper windows of the nine-bay front originally small but raised through the eaves to gabled dormerheads in the C20. Slightly advanced broad end bays containing segmental-arched carriage entrances. Also advanced and with a carriage entrance but narrower is the centre bay which is finished with a ball-finialled pediment into which rises the arched top of the first floor window. – W of the stables, a large crowstep-gabled lectern DOOCOT of 1729, now roofless. Ratcourse stepping up at the gables; ball finials on the back wall. – CHAPEL, SE of the mansion house, also roofless and with the W gable fallen. The main part is late medieval, a simple rubble-built oblong, *c.* 12.2 m. by 7.0 m. The plain birdcage bellcote on the E gable and the S side's rectangular windows and door are perhaps of the early C18 but the door is in the position of the medieval entrance since inside, immediately to its W, is a pointed-arched stoup. Aumbry at the E end of the N wall. A small transeptal 'aisle', placed slightly W of the centre of the N side, is an addition, probably of the C17 or early C18. At the chapel's E end, buttressed and lancet-windowed transepts and apse of 1887, built largely of stones taken from the medieval Bridge of Earn. Incorporated are heraldic stones of the C16 or C17 from an earlier Moncreiffe House.

Rubble WALLED GARDEN E of the mansion house, constructed in 1726 by *William McGaw*, mason in Newburgh. At the back, a pair of ICE HOUSES. – Mid-C19 WEST LODGE. Tudor, with latticed glazing and a jerkin-head gable.

MONCUR CASTLE
0.7 km. NE of Inchture

Standing on a low eminence, perhaps formerly surrounded by a moat, the roofless but substantial remains of a smart laird's house built for the Moncurs of that Ilk, *c.* 1600. It is a rubble-walled three-storey Z, with a long main block (*c.* 17.4 m. by 7.9 m.), a rectangular NE jamb (*c.* 6.4 m. by 5.5 m.), its E and S walls mostly fallen, and a round SW tower (*c.* 5.2 m. in diameter) with a much smaller round stair-tower (*c.* 2.7 m. in diameter) in its N inner angle with the main block. At the ground floor, oval gunloops and, set rather high, horizontally proportioned windows which, like the house's other windows, have chamfered margins. Fairly small windows at the upper floors of the SW tower. Slit windows in the adjacent stair-tower. At the main block, quite large first-floor windows in the S gable and E and W sides; towards the S end of its W side, a slit window (lighting a garderobe) under a horizontal opening like those of the ground floor. The second floor has been lit by smaller openings. Massive wallhead chimney on the E side of the main block. Only the roll-and-hollow-moulded W jamb survives of the entrance in the S side of the NE jamb.

INTERIOR. The jamb contained a (now missing) stair to the first floor in the NW corner and an adjacent vaulted guard-room. The main block's N two-thirds contained a kitchen, the springing of its tunnel vault visible. In the W side, at a point where the walling has fallen, a slop drain. The S third of this block contained a cellar, vaulted at right angles to the kitchen. Off its SW corner open doors to the stair-tower and the SW tower's vaulted ground-floor room. Of the gunloops through this room's walling, the N pierces the walling of both the tower and the stair-tower.

The first floor of the main block contained a hall above the kitchen and a chamber above the S cellar. In the hall's E side, a large elliptically arched fireplace, the surviving S jamb with a roll-and-hollow moulding. Smaller rectangular fireplace, also with a roll-and-hollow moulding, at the S end of the chamber. In this room's W side, the entrance to a slit-windowed mural garderobe. In the SW tower, a tunnel-vaulted oblong room.

MONEYDIE

0020

Rural hamlet.

MONEYDIE PARISH CHURCH. Disused. Built in 1813–14, probably to a design by the amateur architect and local landowner, *Lieutenant-General Sir Thomas Graham* of Balgowan. Buttressed box, the walls of red sandstone rubble, the acutely pointed windows filled with latticed glazing. W tower of three stages, the diagonally buttressed lowest stage containing a Tudor arched door. Pointed W window at the second stage. In the exposed faces of the third stage, paired Tudor Gothic belfry openings. Corbelled battlement. At the church's E end, a battlemented round porch containing a gallery stair.

(Inside, GALLERY supported on cavetto-capitalled columns. – Double stairs to the PULPIT whose sounding board has gableted corners.)

GRAVEYARD. S of the church, several C18 HEADSTONES, each with an angel's head (the soul) at the top of the W face on which are carved trade symbols. The W of these, to John Gow, tenant in Drukenhead, is of 1786 and bears a hand-held hammer and a ploughshare and coulter. – Then, an illegibly inscribed stone, with a shield bearing a curved knife and axe.

– To the SE, a stone to John Straton, carved with a weaver's loom, shuttle and stretchers. – Lying on the ground near the churchyard's SE corner, a long flat-topped pedimental C18 stone commemorating Thomas Alison. It bears a panel flanked by putti, one holding an hourglass, the other a scythe.

Former MANSE to the E. Built *c*. 1800 but the piend-roofed front block probably dates from *W. H. Playfair*'s enlargement of 1833. Its outer ground-floor windows are broad and elliptically arched; low windows to the first floor.

SCHOOL. Now housing. Late C19 single-storey school and two-storey schoolhouse, the house picturesquely gabled and bargeboarded.

COTTAGES, across the Shochie Burn to the N. Mid-C19 double cottage. Bargeboarded gablets over the doors. Advanced centre with a bargeboarded gable and a round-headed dummy slit above the window. Horizontal-paned glazing survives at the W cottage.

BLACKPARK LODGE, 1.9km. W. Villa of *c*. 1850, an irregular grouping of one- and two-storey elements. Roughly in the centre of the S front, a three-storey pyramid-roofed square tower from which projects a two-storey canted bay window with round-headed lights to the upper floor.

MONZIE

Little more than the church and manse beside the Shaggie Burn.

MONZIE FREE CHURCH. *See* Gilmerton.

MONZIE PARISH CHURCH. By *William Stirling I*, 1830–1. Rendered rectangle, not without modest pretension. Corbelled out from the S gable is an octagonal bellcote, its round-headed openings narrow, its stone spire topped by a heavy foliaged finial. The piend-roofed S porch with ogee-arched doors and windows looks like an addition, perhaps part of *H. B. W. Steele & Balfour*'s alterations of 1894. Flanking the porch, two round-headed windows; depressed-arched two-light window above. In the long E and W sides, pointed windows, each of two mullioned and transomed lights. At the N gable, a pointed four-light window, its head filled with very simple rectilinear tracery.

INTERIOR. The side galleries were removed in 1894 by Steele & Balfour who reconstructed the S gallery of 1831 reusing its cast-iron columns and panelled front. PEWS of 1831 in the gallery; those in the main body of 1894. At the N end, a 'chancel' formed in 1894, the back wall lined with routine Gothic panelling from which project the minister's and elders' seats. On the 'chancel's' E side, a large Gothic PULPIT, also of 1894. On the W side, the ORGAN, by *Norman & Beard Ltd.*, 1913. Near the S end of the W wall, a simple Gothic AUMBRY made in 1918. – Also on this wall, a bronze TABLET commemorating Charles Julian Maitland-Makgill-Crichton †1915, incised with the depiction of an angel standing over the corpse of a soldier.

STAINED GLASS. Four-light N window (the Four Evangelists above Scenes from the Life of Our Lord) by *Morris & Co.*, 1917, using designs of 1872–4 by *Edward Burne-Jones*. – In the E wall, another window by *Morris & Co.* (figures of Fortitude and Devotion in the upper lights, St Francis and St Christopher below). It is of 1937, the designs by *Edward Burne-Jones* and *Henry Dearle* dating from 1868 to 1923. – To its N, a late C19 heraldic window. – In the W wall, two windows (the Presentation of Our Lord in the Temple and Our Lord with the Samaritan Woman; the Resurrection and Ascension) of the 1890s by *James Steel & Co.*, like illustrations in a Victorian Children's Bible. – In the S vestibule, one light (the Good Shepherd) of *c.* 1960.

GRAVEYARD. At the SW entrance, C18 corniced GATEPIERS built of V-jointed ashlar, the ball finials standing on stepped pedestals. – Against the S end of the church's E side, the BURIAL ENCLOSURE of the Campbells of Monzie. Built into its S wall, a GRAVE-SLAB to Archibald Campbell of Laginrech †1640, the top carved with a row of emblems above a coat of arms. – Beside it, a late C17 slab to the Campbells of Monzie, its top displaying trumpeting angels who hold a laurel wreath above a crested and mantled coat of arms; below, drapery bearing the inscription. – On the enclosure's E wall, an elegantly lettered bronze TABLET commemorating Patrick Campbell of Monzie †1751.

Former MANSE on the W side of the road. Built *c.* 1790 but reconstructed by *William McLaren* in 1893–4 when it acquired bracketed broad eaves; the front's central gablet may be C18 in origin.

BRIDGES over the Shaggie Burn. Segmental-arched rubble-built ROAD BRIDGE, probably of the early C19. – To its E, a humpbacked PACK BRIDGE, perhaps early C18. Tall segmental arch; no parapets.

CONNACHAN LODGE. 3.1 km. NE. Shooting lodge of the earlier C19 designed in exuberant *cottage orné* style. Single-storey and attic, the walls constructed of boulders, with a tree-trunk and sapling veranda along the W front and wooden outshots; external shutters to the ground-floor windows. Polygonal-headed wooden dormers at the broad-eaved piended roof.

ROMAN WATCH TOWER, Fendoch, 4.6 km. NE. On a hillside at the S entry to the Sma'Glen, a fortified enclosure of the late C1 in which stood a wooden tower. The ditch and earth rampart, pierced by a SE gateway, survive. Almost nothing of the associated fort, 1.1 km. SE, is now visible.

MONZIE CASTLE
0.7 km. SW

Back-to-back conjunction of an early C17 laird's house and a much larger Late Georgian castellated mansion, both with Edwardian interiors.

In 1613 three-quarters of the lands of Monzie were granted by Margaret Scott, heiress of Monzie, to her son, James Graeme, who built a smartly detailed house here. This is a rubble-walled and crowstep-gabled L of three storeys, the second-floor windows rising through the eaves to pedimented dormerheads, Roll-and-hollow mouldings to the windows. Symmetrical s elevation with two comfortably sized ground-floor windows, five tall windows at the first floor and three windows at the second. At the NE wing's W front, the entrance in the inner angle is contained in a rusticated and pedimented surround; on the lintel, three weathered heraldic shields, the initials I^{M}S for Mr James Graeme and MG for his wife, Marjory Graeme, and the date 1634, presumably that of the house's construction. Badly eroded carving on the pediments of the second-floor windows. One bears a coat of arms, the initial M (probably surviving from I^{M}G), the date 1634 and the Latin inscription [Q]VEM COLO QVÆR[E] ('Seek the one whom I worship'). A second depicts the figure of a man in C17 dress who holds a Bible and a cornsheaf and bears the initials [I]^{M}G, the date 1634 and a Greek inscription ('I am led by Scripture'). On the third, another coat of arms, the initial G and a Hebrew inscription ('I have found his prosperity').

The estate was sold to Colin Campbell of Lagvinshoch and the Ibert in 1666 and in 1797–1800 his descendant, General Alexander Campbell, added the mansion house to the E. Designed by *John Paterson*, this is a rubble-built toy fort of three parallel parts, the N and S of three storeys with corbelled parapets and battlemented round corner towers which rise from battered bases. The battlemented centre part rises a storey higher. At the E front it projects slightly, with slit-windowed narrow end bays between which is a broad bow, its ground floor pierced by round-headed and overarched windows and the principal entrance; above the door, a rather small panel carved with the heraldic achievement of the Campbells of Monzie. String courses carried round the building delineate the floor levels inside; a sill course under the hood-moulded first-floor windows. At the outer bays of the E front were three-light windows but those of the upper floors were narrowed to single lights as part of *Robert S. Lorimer*'s alterations of 1908–12. On the N side, a low two-storey crowstep-gabled service wing of the later C19, its E end heightened in 1908–12, the first-floor windows with gablet dormerheads.

The INTERIOR of the 1790s block was gutted by fire in 1908 and reconstructed during the next four years by Lorimer who made no attempt to restore its Late Georgian appearance. Large entrance hall divided into three by sturdy Roman Doric columns. The plastered walls are treated in a free early C18 manner with double-lugged panels; moulded stone chimney-piece. Off the S side, a wood-lined LIBRARY, also in an early Georgian manner. The entrance hall's W end is open to the generously sized well stair (replacing Paterson's imperial stair), its arabesqued wrought-iron balustrade made by *Thomas*

Hadden. At the half landing below the first floor, a small balcony whose curvy front bears the monogrammed initials MC for Charles Maitland Makgill Crichton who had inherited the estate in 1900. The STAIR HALL's walls are again plasterpanelled; frieze at the second-floor level ornamented with roses and the lion crest of the Royal Arms of Scotland. The top panels are surmounted by shells. Ceiling enriched with large acanthus leaves in a late C17 manner in the corners and a basket of fruit in a slightly later style at the centre of each side; flowers and fruit round the central cupola.

At the first floor, the stair's E landing gives access to the principal rooms. Jutting into its centre, the splay-sided end of the DRAWING ROOM, its entrance in an Ionic pilastered aedicule, the steep cornice broken by a coat of arms. The drawing room (replacing Paterson's saloon) has bowed ends and plasterpanelled walls enriched with reliefs of musical instruments, bows and quivers, etc.; fruit round the fireplace's overmantel. The white marble chimneypiece, a survivor of the fire, is early C18. Terminal figures at the jambs. Frieze carved with swags of oak leaves and acorns; on the centre panel, a head of Apollo. The ceiling's Baroque plasterwork is by *Thomas Beattie*. Large centrepiece repeating the shape of the room and surrounded by floral enrichment. At the four cardinal points, oval panels bordered by foliage and flowers and enclosing figures of floating angels modelled by *Hubert Paton*.

In the DINING ROOM to the N, heavier decoration in the manner of *c*. 1700. Plaster-panelled walls, the large panel at the W end and the fireplace's overmantel double-lugged and with swagged swan-neck pediments. They are placed between Ionic pilasters with swags at the capitals. Inside the pilasters, either side of the overmantel, pendants of flowers hanging from heraldic cartouches. The white marble chimneypiece is another early C18 survivor of the fire. Consoled jambs carved with foliage and fruit. On the frieze, more fruit and a couple of small female heads. Compartmented ceiling, also by Beattie, the beams enriched with guilloche. In the corner compartments, circles of bay leaves. Large and heavily modelled oval of flowers and fruit at the centre.

S of the present drawing room, occupying the site of Paterson's drawing room, are a BILLIARD ROOM, its stone fireplace in a lugged surround, and, to its E, a MORNING ROOM, its simple marble chimneypiece of late C18 type but with a double-lugged overmantel topped by a swagged swan-neck pediment. In the NW corner of the E block, a geometric stone stair, apparently of the 1790s, rises the full height of the house.

Lorimer fitted up the interior of the C17 house as a family wing, its first floor given over to day and night nurseries and a schoolroom, the second floor to the parents' rooms, the decoration in an agreeable mixture of freely treated C17 and early C18 styles. Scale-and-platt stone stair with moulded risers, the lower flight C17, the upper of 1908–12; wrought-iron balustrade by Hadden. In the panelled first-floor SE room

(Lorimer's day nursery, now a sitting room) an immensely broad fireplace, its opening (now largely filled with Delft tiles) of C17 size, the stone chimneypiece by Lorimer apparently based on some evidence of earlier work. Pilastered jambs. Corniced deep lintel carved in relief with a swag of drapery; in the centre, a heraldic panel and the date 1634. At the ends of this frieze, initials of C17 owners of Monzie. At the second floor the SW room (a dressing room) has a tunnel-vaulted ceiling of 1908–12.

GARDEN W of the house, its rubble wall along the N and W sides built perhaps in the late C18. – NE of the house, Scots Jacobean STABLES of 1878, the courtyard's buttressed and segmental-arched entrance in a battlemented screen wall with bartizans at the corners.

On the drive to the house from the E, an early C19 segmental-arched BRIDGE over the Shaggie Burn, its sides with cast-iron railings between broached ashlar piers topped by pinnacles of polished ashlar. – At this drive's end, the EAST LODGE AND GATEWAY, by *William Stirling I*, 1812. Screen wall, its parapet carried on arcaded corbelling containing the Tudor Gothic gate flanked by pointed footgates; on the walling and the parapet, the coats of arms and initials of ancestors of General Alexander Campbell of Monzie. Built at a diagonal to the gateway, a battlemented two-storey lodge, its main block's hoodmoulded windows containing diamond-paned glazing. At its S corner, a battlemented and Gothic-windowed round tower.

WEST LODGE of *c.* 1830 0.6km. NW of the mansion house. Single-storey, the walls of rough ashlar. Broad-eaved roof, gabled at the semi-octagonal front and with jerkin-head gables at the sides. Ashlar GATEPIERS with flattened pyramidal tops. – Straddling the drive to its E, the early C19 MID LODGE AND GATEWAY. The gateway is a segmental-arched bridge over the Keltie Burn, its tall sides formed by battlemented screen walls pierced by pointed openings and with crosslet dummy 'arrowslits'. At each end of the bridge, a battlemented round-headed 'Saxon' archway with bundle-shafted columns. At the W corners, two-storey round towers with pointed doors and dummy windows; battlements carried on arcaded corbelling. Above the E archway, a box machicolation bearing heraldic shields. At this archway's SE corner, a battlemented round tower of four stages with pointed windows (dummies above the ground floor) at the lower and round-headed slits at the top. Projecting diagonally from the gateway's N corner, a square lodge with round bartizans at the corners of its battlement; hoodmoulded windows to the E.

MONZIEVAIRD

Strung along the N side of the A85, a fragment of the former Monzievaird and Strowan Parish Church and, to its W, the former schools and manse.

MONZIEVAIRD AND STROWAN PARISH CHURCH. Built in 1803–4 and demolished in 1964 except for a fragment of the S wall which serves as the backing for an angle-buttressed mid-C19 monument. – At the S side of the graveyard, the WAR MEMORIAL designed by *Reginald Fairlie* and executed by *Alexander Carrick* in 1920. Square base of Cullaloe sandstone ashlar with inscription tablets of Kemnay granite. On the front of the stepped top, a relief of the Pelican in Piety; bronze ringed cross finial.

STROWAN CHURCH, 1.6 km. S. Roofless remains of a kirk of *c.* 1600 which was abandoned after the opening of Monzievaird and Strowan Parish Church in 1804 and its W third subsequently demolished. It has been an oblong, the walls built of rubble and formerly harled. High up in the centre of the crow-stepped E gable, a rectangular window with a chamfered margin. Immediately below the window, a stone carved in relief with a quatrefoil enclosing the coat of arms of the Grahams of Strowan. Slightly below this and to its r., a PANEL of 1684 whose ill-lettered inscription commemorates Margaret Stirling, its date flanked by a crude depiction of gravediggers' tools. In the S wall, rectangular openings, the E window with a roll-and-hollow moulding on the jambs, a door with a chamfered margin and, to its W, a window checked for shutters. Inside, below the E window, a narrow cupboard. – Built into the W end of the N wall, the GRAVE-SLAB of John Murray of Strowan †1541. Unusually small (only *c.* 99 cm. by 61 cm.) but richly decorated in relief. Within a border enriched with flowers, a marginal Latin inscription encloses three panels. In the end panels, the coats of arms of John Murray of Strowan and his wife, Margaret Hepburn, each surmounting a pair of birds. In the centre panel, a helmet with two long drooping plumes issuing from its crest; below, lying on its side, a shield bearing the arms of Murray of Strowan.

GRAVEYARD. Some C18 HEADSTONES. One, to the SW of the church, erected *c.* 1780 by James McIlvride to the memory of his parents, uncle and sisters, has an angel's head (the soul) on the E face and a merchant's mark (like a numeral 4) on the W. – Just to its NW, a stone with skulls at the ends of the pedimented top.

BAIRD MONUMENT, Tom a' Chaisteil, 0.9 km. S. On the summit of a wooded hill, the site of an iron age fort, the 25 m.-high granite ashlar monument designed by *William Stirling I* and erected in 1832 to commemorate General Sir David Baird. Enclosure of cast-iron spearhead railings with ball-finialled uprights at the corners. Inside, a square pedestal on a stepped base surmounted by an obelisk (some of the stones now displaced). On the faces of the pedestal, tablets inscribed with a eulogy to Baird and the names of his battles and campaigns.

MONZIEVAIRD AND STROWAN INDUSTRIAL SCHOOL AND PARISH SCHOOL, 0.3 km. W. Near-symmetrical rubble-walled and picturesque group of two schools (now housing) and a schoolhouse built in 1859–61. The schools are each L-shaped, their plans reversed, with broad eaves and horizontal-paned glazing to their two-light stone-mullioned windows. Between them, the two-storey schoolhouse, also broad-eaved and with horizontal-paned windows. s front with paired gables and a central porch.

CLATHICK, 1.2 km. w. Broad-eaved rubble-built two-storey laird's house of 1827. Asymmetrical s front of five bays, the centre with a semi-octagonal projection, the bay to the l. recessed, the w bay with a canted bay window. – Behind, a contemporary courtyard of OFFICES. At the advanced and jerkin-head gabled s end of the w range, an elliptical-arched pend entrance with flight-holes for a doocot above.

MONZIEVAIRD HOUSE, 0.4 km. w. Originally, Monzievaird and Strowan Parish Manse. By *William Stirling I*, 1836–7. Rubble-walled two-storey *cottage orné*. U-plan s front, the outer bays broad and gabled, the centre with a gabled porch containing the elliptical-arched entrance; horizontal-paned glazing in the windows.

CASTLE CLUGGY. See p. 259.
LOCHLANE. See p. 501.
OCHTERTYRE. See p. 561.

MORENISH

Just the church and shooting lodge standing on the N side of Loch Tay.

MORENISH CHURCH. Built in 1901–2 by Joseph (later, Sir Joseph) and Aline White Todd as a memorial to their daughter. Small but sturdy broad-eaved rectangle, built of hammer-dressed granite with dressings of buff sandstone. Buttresses at the s corners and door. On the gables, large crowsteps, the top ones segmental-headed, the E carved with the relief of a floral cross. Keystoned lunette in the w gable. The round-headed and keystoned entrance has hinges in a Celtic Art Nouveau manner bearing the Todds' initials and the date 1902. E of the door, a pair of low stone-mullioned three-light windows. Round-headed and keystoned E window of five lights.

The entrance opens onto an ashlar-clad vestibule from which a round-headed door gives access to the church itself. Here the walls are plastered and the ceiling a plaster ribbed tunnel vault. In the N side, a fireplace, its splayed ingoes covered with tiles which, at the lower halves, are plain green set in floral-patterned borders and, above, are decorated with stylized floral motifs. Oak overmantel. – STAINED GLASS E window by the *Tiffany Studios*, 1902, the lower lights inscribed with the Ten Commandments in colourful surrounds, the upper containing roundels depicting realistic Biblical Scenes, Children and Angels set in jewel-like borders.

E of the church, a pair of bronze SARCOPHAGI decorated with floral reliefs. They commemorate Sir Joseph White Todd

†1926 and his wife †1924. – Art Nouveauish GATEPIERS at the entrance to the churchyard.

MORENISH LODGE, 1 km. SE. Two-storey shooting lodge built in 1841–2 and enlarged in 1862. Probably of the 1840s are the W wing and gabled W bay of the present five-bay main block whose windows have horizontal-paned glazing. The remainder of the main block seems to be of 1862. Carved bargeboards at the gables and the dormerheads over the first-floor windows.

MURRAYSHALL
1.7 km. E of New Scone

Jacobean Renaissance country house of *c.* 1930. Mullioned and transomed windows; conical-roofed corner turret. Built into the W face, a badly weathered steep triangular dormerhead, probably from the house built here in 1664 and, below it, a stone carved with three worn panels, the l. inscribed H^{ON} S^{IR} A. M. (for Sir Andrew Murray), the centre panel J.R.M.G. and the date of ··86 [?], the r. now effaced. Large late C20 N additions for the house's present use as a hotel. – Late C19 LODGE, with bracketed broad eaves.

MURTHLY

Strung-out village of C19 and C20 houses, a few with bargeboards.

MURTHLY CHURCH. Now a house (CHURCH HOUSE). Gothic mission church by *Alexander Duncan*, clerk of works to the Murthly Castle estate, 1913, a spired ventilator on the roof.

MURTHLY PRIMARY SCHOOL, 1 km. S. School and schoolhouse of the mid or later C19. Quite picturesque display of bargeboarded gables and gablets, and with a few Romanesque touches and a veranda.

ARDOCH, 0.6 km. S. Broad-eaved and rubble-walled two-storey *cottage orné* of *c.* 1850, the first-floor windows with gablet dormerheads. Three bays, the centre slightly advanced. Round-headed windows to the outer bays, a pointed first-floor window at the centre whose door is hidden by a later porch.

STEWART TOWER, 2.2 km. SW. Originally North Airntully. Broad-eaved *cottage orné* FARMHOUSE of 1848–9. Rubble-built two-storey U with a single-storey W range closing the courtyard. The principal elevations are each of three bays with round-headed windows, those of the first floor rising into gablet dormerheads; gabled porch at the E front. Conical-roofed round tower rising over the centre. On the S side of the adjacent road, the STEADING built in 1846–7. Broad eaves again and elliptical-arched openings; circular horsemill at the E end.

MURTHLY CASTLE
3.2 km. WNW

Large and rambling mansion house, the product of many stages of development from the C16 to the late C19, given some unity by its sneck-harled rubble walling. The shell of a much grander Neo-Jacobean replacement designed by *James Gillespie Graham* was built S of the garden in 1832–3 but never finished internally and demolished *c.* 1950.

The site is a broad promontory bounded by the River Tay and with steep slopes to the S and W. There must have been some residence here, probably defensible, during the Middle Ages when the barony of Murthly was held by the Abercrombies of that Ilk but the earliest part of the present F-plan house is probably C16. PRINCE CHARLIE'S TOWER at the SW corner is a crowstep-gabled five-storey oblong with a minimally projecting stair-tower at its SE corner. At its SW and NE corners, pepperpot turrets projected on continuous corbelling and with quatrefoil gunloops under the sill courses below their windows. Corbelled out at its NW corner, a pinnacled little turret, its

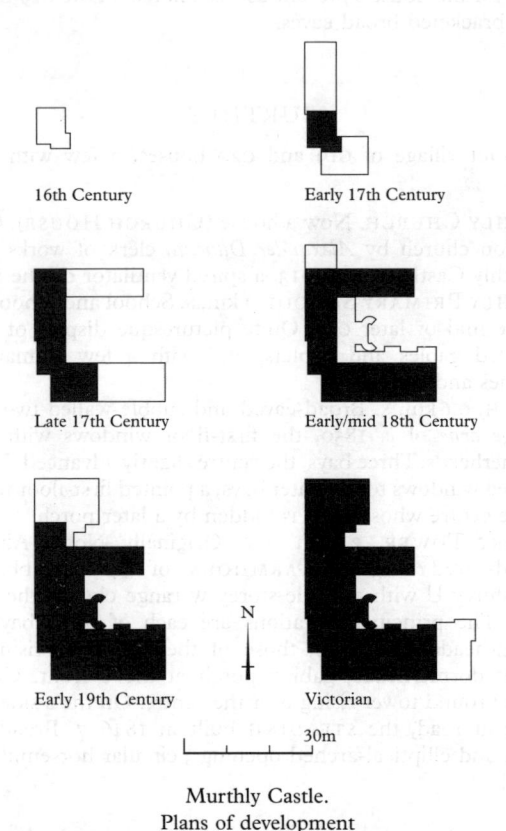

16th Century

Early 17th Century

Late 17th Century

Early/mid 18th Century

Early 19th Century

Victorian

N

30m

Murthly Castle.
Plans of development

function purely decorative. Is it original or a C17 addition? Not very regular disposition of windows, some with chamfered surrounds, the W side's top window rising through the eaves to a catslide dormerhead. Large wallhead chimney on the E side whose r. top-floor window has been filled with a C17 heraldic panel. This displays the arms of the Stewarts of Grandtully who acquired the Murthy estate in 1615 and the initials DAM for Dame Agnes Moncrieffe, wife of Sir William Stewart †1646.

The second stage in the house's development, probably in the early C17, consisted of the erection of a crowstep-gabled hall block at right angles to Prince Charlie's Tower and forming the W end of the present S RANGE. This is of two storeys and an attic. At the S front, a small blocked first-floor window with a concave moulding and, to its r., three tall windows, their chamfered surrounds much renewed in the C19. The N elevation is largely covered by an C18 addition but one small ground-floor window and a large (blocked) window at the first floor seem to be C17. In the W gable, another large first-floor window and a smaller attic window, both with chamfered jambs.

In the later C17, apparently *c.* 1666–77 (the dates provided by dormerheads now built into the late C19 addition at the E end of the S range), major extensions were built to both the S range and N of Prince Charlie's Tower. *John Pirnie* was the mason responsible for some if not all of this work. The S range was more than doubled in length by the addition of the five-storey crowstep-gabled BACHELOR'S TOWER at the E end of the existing hall block and, E of this, a block of the same height and size as the hall block, producing an approximately symmetrical composition with a tall centrepiece and a lower wing each side. Some C17 windows with chamfered margins survive but were altered in the C19 when the second-floor windows of the part E of the Bachelor's Tower were blocked. On this E part's N elevation, a stepped wallhead chimney, its present appearance probably early C19.

The W RANGE, N of Prince Charlie's Tower, is also of three storeys. At its W elevation, irregularly disposed windows, comfortably sized at the ground floor and tall at the first, all with chamfered margins. The second-floor windows rising through the eaves were finished originally with pedimented dormerheads but these were replaced with catslide tops in the later C19 when three of these windows were enlarged. Perhaps of the same date was a range which stood on the site of the present MIDDLE WING, extending E from the new W range's N end, making the house a U-shape, the courtyard's E side closed by a screen wall and gateway (now gone) which were built by *James Robertson* and *John* and *James Pirnie* in 1675. The Middle Wing was rebuilt in 1893 to a design by *Alexander Duncan*. Tactful Georgian vernacular manner with crowstepped gables and catslide dormers.

The removal of the courtyard's screen wall may have occurred in 1735–8 when a show-off new ENTRANCE BLOCK was added covering the E front of the C17 W range. The contractors for this block were the Edinburgh mason-architect *John Douglas*, who probably designed it, and *Thomas Halliburton*, wright in Dundee. It is of two storeys and five bays, the tall first-floor windows denoting the *piano nobile*. At each of the rubble-walled end bays, a dummy oculus above the first-floor window. Ashlar-fronted and pedimented three-bay centrepiece with rusticated quoins. It is fronted by a horseshoe forestair, its landing carried on a basket-arched loggia. At the first floor, the round-headed door and flanking windows combine in Palladian fashion. Lugged architraves to the windows which are again surmounted by dummy oculi. In the pediment, the impaled coats of arms of Sir George Stewart of Grandtully and his wife, Anne Cockburn. At about the same time the W range was extended N by two bays, the top-floor windows with catslide dormerheads.

The house was further extended in 1818–19 when a three-storey addition was built across the N end of the W range and projecting to its E. It was presumably designed by *James Gillespie Graham* who was responsible for internal alterations at the same time; *John Stewart* supervised the work. It is piend-roofed and with strip quoins; tall windows to the ground and first floors. Late C19 additions on its E side.

The house was enlarged again *c.* 1850 when the S range was extended E. This addition is of two storeys, its S front of rubble, the E gable's ground-floor masonry hammer-dressed. Segmental-headed windows at the ground floor, windows of late C17 type above. This block was thickened in the late C19 and given a pyramidal-roofed low tower at the NE corner. Built into the walls and the prominent N chimney are late C17 dormerheads bearing the initials of Sir Thomas Stewart and his wife, Dame Grizel Menzies, and the dates 1666, 1673 and 1677. One, at the E gable, is carved with beasts at the bottom of its steeply sloping sides, and another bears coats of arms.

INTERIOR. GROUND FLOOR. A short passage from the lower entrance hall in the 1737 addition leads to the original C16 entrance to Prince Charlie's Tower, its outer jambs rounded. It has provision for two doors (or a door and yett). The tower's ground-floor room is tunnel-vaulted. In the tower's SE jamb, a turnpike stair which becomes tighter above the first floor. In the top room of the tower, a C17 plaster panel bearing the royal coat of arms and the initials CR (for *Carolus Rex*), perhaps more likely for Charles I than Charles II.

In the S range, a tunnel-vaulted passage along the N side of the ground floor leads to a turnpike stair in the Bachelor's Tower. Off the passage are tunnel-vaulted store rooms.

In the late C17 W range, the ground-floor room adjoining Prince Charlie's Tower contains a simple moulded stone chimneypiece inserted in the original outer face of the tower. Beside it, a large double-keyhole gunloop. Is this C16 or a piece of Victorian antiquarianism? The tunnel-vaulted room to the N has been a KITCHEN. In its N wall, a large segmental-arched fireplace flanked by round-headed arched recesses, one formerly an oven, the other now a doorway. All this is work of the 1730s.

The principal stair to the FIRST FLOOR rises from the N end of the lower entrance hall and is also of 1737, with turned balusters. Its continuation up to the second floor was provided in the late C20. At the first floor, the three centre bays of the 1737 entrance block contain the UPPER ENTRANCE HALL. The round-headed end arches (to the stair and an ante-room) and the ceiling's cove are probably C18 but otherwise the room was remodelled in 1848. Pine-panelled walls. Frieze of eighty-eight small painted panels depicting knights of Catholic orders of chivalry from designs by *Alexander Christie*. Heavy Neo-Jacobean plaster panel on the flat of the ceiling. W of the upper entrance hall is the DRAWING ROOM. In the late C17 and C18 this consisted of two rooms, a three-bay dining room at the S and a two-bay drawing room to its N. In 1821 *James Gillespie Graham* converted the dining room to a drawing room. The oak panelling on the walls may be largely late C17 but the corniced doorpieces with lugged architraves and foliaged pulvinated friezes were carved by *John Steell* in 1821. So too were the Ionic pilasters with swagged volutes which flank the S fireplace and support another foliaged frieze. Massive white marble chimneypiece supplied by *David Ness* in 1821. The jambs' consoles and the frieze are carved with boldly undercut foliage and flowers. The partition wall between this room and the earlier drawing room to its N was removed *c*. 1900. In the two bays of the earlier drawing room, early C18 panelling. White marble chimneypiece of the later C19, its rather routine ornament hovering between classical and Neo-Jacobean. The character of the room to the N, apparently the C17 and C18 state bedchamber (now DINING ROOM), is mid C19 with pine panelling and a white marble chimneypiece.

The route to the S range from the upper entrance hall begins with an ANTE-ROOM. On its S wall, a stone panel carved with the Royal Arms of Scotland, the initials IR (for *Jacobus Rex*, i.e. James VI) and the date 1616. The principal rooms of the S range are mid C19 (after a fire in 1845) or of *c*. 1900. The LIBRARY at the W end has gently Neo-Jacobean panelling and a chimneypiece of *c*. 1900. Probably of the same date but more strongly Neo-Jacobean are the panelling and wooden ceiling in the STUDY (made out of two rooms, *c*. 2000) next door. E of this, the Great Hall (now BALLROOM) of 1846 occupying the site of the dining room which had been formed in 1819 and destroyed in 1845. It rises through two storeys and is covered with a dark-stained and gilded hammerbeam roof which had been made in the 1830s from *James Gillespie Graham*'s and *A. W. N. Pugin*'s design for the new Murthly Castle. The roof's sloping plaster sides between the rafters and flat ceiling are painted with golden bees (the crest of the Stewarts of Grandtully) on a blue background. More bees, together with the Stewart motto PROVYD are carved on the curvaceous overdoors at the room's N side and W end. At the E end, taller doors (the N a dummy) with lugged architraves. Large Neo-Jacobean wooden chimneypiece, the overmantel carved with the Stewart coat of arms, crest and motto. E of the Great Hall is the MUSIC ROOM, its decoration mostly executed in the 1830s for the new Murthly Castle and installed here *c.* 1850. Designed by Gillespie Graham and Pugin, it is, most unusually for Pugin, in the Louis XIV manner with elaborate *boiseries*. Frieze modelled with small plaster heads of Apollo and classical scenes; on the N side, a pair of roundels containing Dutch paintings. On the flat of the coved ceiling, a large classical scene set in a border decorated with stucco enrichment and gilded rosettes. Large and heavy grey marble chimneypiece, its classicism verging on the brutal but with some naturalistic touches; presumably it is of *c.* 1850.

In the late C19 tower at the NE corner of the S range, a square first-floor BEDROOM, with the painting of an angel on the flat of its coved ceiling. W of this, i.e. behind the music room, a BATHROOM still with a late Victorian marble bath and an overhead shower. W of this, a late Victorian stair. The ground floor of the S range's E end, under the music room and tower bedroom, is occupied by a BILLIARD ROOM, late C19 in its present form. Panelled walls and ceiling. Stone chimneypiece with foliaged capitals to its columns.

On the S side of the house, a WALLED GARDEN probably laid out in the late C17. A path on the axis of the Bachelor's Tower leads down from the terrace to a round pond with a lead FOUNTAIN, perhaps of *c.* 1700, the water issuing from the mouth of a dolphin ridden by a putto. In the garden's SE corner, an ogee-roofed two-storey GARDEN PAVILION, its rubble walling formerly harled. The first-floor SW door, reached by a forestair, and the NW window rise through the cavetto-moulded eaves cornice to triangular dormerheads which bear the initials of Sir Thomas Stewart of Grandtully and the date 1669. These are probably from the mansion house and erected here in the C19. Likely dates for the building are provided at the window's lintel which is incised with the year 1712 and the weathervane pierced with 1713. On the garden's E side, corniced GATEPIERS, probably of 1740, surmounted by stone beasts.

CHAPEL OF ST ANTHONY THE EREMITE
0.2 km. N of the house.

A two-stage building, the earlier part a chapel of *c.* 1600. This was remodelled as a mausoleum appended to the much taller chapel added to its W end in 1845–6 by *James Gillespie Graham*, possibly with some assistance from *A.W.N. Pugin*, for Sir William George Drummond Stewart of Grandtully, a Roman Catholic convert.

The earlier chapel is a rubble-walled T, the main windows presumably originally in the S side, the N jamb containing a laird's loft reached by a stair in the lean-to on its E side. The elaborate stone cross on the E gable, the low buttressed S aisle and S porch are all sturdy Romanesque additions by Graham. At the porch, the entrance's hoodmould has male and female headstops; stone cross finial.

The chapel of 1845–6 is a tall buttressed five-bay Romanesque box. Narrow side windows, their hoodmoulds' label stops carved with foliage. Wheel window in the E gable. Angle-buttressed W tower of three stages, with a bowed stair-turret on the N side. Entrance in the tower's S side, its hoodmould enriched with chevron ornament, the door hinges in the manner of Pugin. At the tower's second stage, a gableted three-light S window, the central opening tall and stilted. A single light, also gableted, to the W. The top stage is the belfry, with tall paired openings. Parapet with blind arcading, its S side surmounted by a gabled clock face (the clock itself erected in 1850, its bell originally ringing the *Angelus* three times a day). On the parapet's SE corner, a conical-roofed small turret. Rising inside the parapet, a low pyramidal spire, a large gabled stone lucarne on each face.

INTERIOR. The chapel of *c.* 1600 is covered with a wooden segmental tunnel vault painted with a floral arabesque design. Stone slab floor. Very simple S arcade of 1845–6, the round-headed arches carried on long bow-ended piers. The N jamb is separated from the body of the chapel by a wall erected in 1845–6. This is covered with painted boarding incorporating what seems to be the remains of a gallery front of *c.* 1600 with segmental-headed arcading carried on ineptly detailed Ionic pilasters. The E wall's ashlar facing is contemporary with the late C17 MONUMENT to Sir Thomas Stewart of Grandtully †1688 which stands against it. This is a huge sandstone Corinthian aedicule, its paired columns, the inner pair placed slightly forward of the outer, standing on pedestals carved with emblems of death; at the centre of the base, a panel carved with the head of a beast, its mouth stuffed with drapery. Entablature surmounted by flaming urns and a swan-neck pediment, its sides supporting figures of trumpeting angels, its finial another flaming urn; on the tympanum, a coat of arms. The aedicule frames an inscription panel, its border decorated with carved foliage. Above the panel, a roundel containing a high-relief portrait bust of Sir Thomas Stewart surrounded by coats of arms. – HATCHMENTS. On the S aisle's E wall, one bearing the coat of arms of Stewart of Grandtully. It was erected for Sir George Stewart in 1827. – On the N wall, at its E end, a hatchment with the impaled arms of Sir John Archibald Drummond Stewart †1838, its likely date, and those of his wife, Lady Jean Stewart. – To its W, two hatchments, both bearing the arms of Sir William Drummond Stewart †1871.

The N jamb was remodelled in 1845–6 to form one tall room covered with a timber-lined tunnel vault, the windows, originally lighting the laird's loft, placed very high up. In the lean-to on the E, a S passage with a late medieval STOUP. In the small room to the N, probably the site of the former gallery stair, the stone sarcophagus TOMB of the Rev. Thomas Drummond Stewart †1846.

The 1840s chapel was not intended to house a congregation of any size and the nave, entirely floored with encaustic tiles, was originally clear of fixed seating except for a low bench along the side walls and w end. A gallery for members of the Stewart family was provided in the tower giving them an unimpeded view of the sanctuary. The tower's ground floor serves as a porch and is covered with a heavily ribbed vault. In the w side, an arched recess intended to contain a font. The recess's design and detail, like that of almost everything in the chapel, is rich Romanesque. Off the N side, a very tight spiral stair to the vaulted family gallery, whose E wall is pierced by a triple-arched opening to the chapel, the central arch tall and stilted.

The chapel itself, dedicated on All Saints' Day, 1846, but the decoration not completed until 1848, has an elaborate hammerbeam roof, the woodwork dark-stained and with touches of gilding, the beams springing from foliaged stone corbels. The plaster ceiling between the rafters was decorated with gilt plaster stars (most now fallen) against a blue background. On the walls, a dado of blind arcading. The windows are framed by elaborately decorated round-headed arches, as is the W door from the tower which is flanked, at window level, by pairs of arched frames which formerly contained full-length portraits of SS Andrew, George, Catherine of Siena and Margaret of Scotland (the figures of St Andrew and St Margaret originally in the sanctuary but moved here in 1848). The figures, like the surviving portraits in the chapel, were painted by *Thomas Faed* following designs by *Alexander Christie*.

In the side windows, brightly coloured small-paned STAINED GLASS by *Ballantine & Allan* depicting sacred motifs and angels. Between the windows, elaborately bordered roundels containing portraits of saints either directly associated with Britain (e.g. St Columba and St Edward the Confessor) or who had founded religious orders which had had houses there (e.g. St Dominic, St Benedict). The sanctuary's E wall is pierced by narrow doors to the vestry and the old chapel's S aisle and a large arch (originally containing an organ screen), its carved and painted wooden surround of most elaborate Romanesque character. Above the arch, a PAINTING (also designed by Christie) depicting the Conversion of Constantine under a stained-glass roundel (again by Ballantine) which is flanked by portraits of St Peter and St John.

The sanctuary is raised one step above the nave and marked off by a Romanesque wooden ALTAR RAIL, its fat columns carved with spiralling foliage. It is a C20 replacement for the 1840s varicoloured and partly gilt marble rail. On the sanctuary's N and S sides, a marbled dado. On the S side, carved and painted blind arches, their backs decorated with stylized foliage, are fronted by SEDILIA and a PISCINA. On the sanctuary's N side, immediately inside the altar rail, a doorway, its very elaborate door's centrepiece carved with a wooden cross above a panel which slides to disclose a grille. When the door was opened against the altar rail this served as a CONFESSIONAL, the penitent kneeling in front of the rail and door, the priest behind. E of the doorway, a segmental-arched recess, its carved enrichment all of wood. On the back, a pair of high-relief angels worshipping a cross which stands in front of a triangle (the symbol of the Holy Trinity) and a sunburst. The recess contains a marbled and gilded SARCOPHAGUS, its front adorned with foliage-tipped crosses and the IHS monogram in high relief. – PEWS of *c.* 1955, formerly in St Benedict's Abbey Church, Fort Augustus (Highland and Islands), placed here, *c.* 2000.

MUTHILL

Sizeable village, its character predominantly late C18 and early C19.

CHURCHES AND PUBLIC BUILDINGS

MUTHILL OLD CHURCH, The Wynd. Remains of a medieval parish church, its tower C12, the rest built or remodelled by Michael Ochiltree, Dean (later Bishop) of Dunblane, *c.* 1425. The tower is built of rough ashlar. Four stages, a projecting string course (fragmentary on the W) above the bottom stage, the third and fourth stages intaken. At the bottom stage a built-up segmental-arched W door, perhaps inserted or altered in the C15. In each of the N and S faces, a small rectangular window; in the E face a narrow segmental-arched door, again perhaps of the C15. At the second stage a small rectangular window in the W face, and a similar opening in the N face of the third stage. The top stage has been a belfry. In each of its N and W faces, a round-arched recess; at the back of each recess, an opening of two round-arched lights with a central cushion-capitalled octagonal pier and half-round responds which taper downwards. In the S side, a plain opening of two rectangular lights, its mullion flush with the external wall. At the E elevation, an opening with downward-tapering jambs. The tower is finished with a saddleback roof, the gables' crow-steps perhaps C15.

The rubble-built early C15 church which encloses the N, S and E sides of the tower consisted of a nave, perhaps of the same size as the C12 nave, with N and S aisles and a narrower unaisled chancel which probably had a sacristy on its N side. The outer walls of the nave's S aisle are largely intact, the other walls much more fragmentary. At the S aisle's ends and side wall the principal windows each consisted of a broad and low pointed arch containing three lights, the heads of the sidelights following the curve of the outer arch until halted against the mullions of the pointed centre light, the design very close to that of the N clearstorey windows of the choir of Dunblane

Cathedral. Above the aisle's main W window but not centred on it, a narrow pointed light; quite large square window, again off-centre, above the main E window. At the centre of the S side of the aisle, a plain rectangular door, probably a post-Reformation insertion. In the W gable of the N aisle, one window jamb survives; its moulding suggests that it was of the same design as the corresponding window of the S aisle. In the N aisle's E gable, the jambs of a narrow door, apparently rectangular, which gave access to the putative sacristy on this side of the chancel. At the W end of what remains of the chancel's S side, the jamb of a door and, to its E, the jamb of another, both apparently post-Reformation. The base of the chancel's E gable, built on falling ground, is intaken at two splay-topped courses.

Inside, nave arcades of simply moulded pointed arches which spring directly from octagonal piers. The S arcade is of three bays, the N of only two, the W end of the aisle having been walled off from the rest of the church, perhaps as a chapel. Tall and broad chancel arch, again simply moulded. Inside the tower has been placed a late medieval double EFFIGY cut from a single stone, the badly worn figures of a knight and a woman identified, not necessarily correctly, in the C19 as Ada, daughter of Henry, Seneschal of Stathearn, and her husband, Sir Muriel Drummond of Concraig †1362.

GRAVEYARD. In the SW corner, the HEADSTONE erected by John Bayne, merchant in Oban, to his father, Edward Bayne, feuar in Bridgend of Crieff, the swan-neck pediment carved with the date 1791 and a merchant's mark (like a numeral 4), the base with a crude skull, hourglass and crossbones. – Even cruder the HEADSTONE of 1795 to John White which stands S of the S door of the church's nave. An angel's head (the soul) in the semicircular top, a skull, crossbones and hourglass at the base. – S of the W end of the chancel, a broken TABLE STONE, probably of the C18, one upright carved with the worn relief of a skeleton holding an hourglass. – To its E, a swan-neck-pedimented HEADSTONE (now fallen) of *c.* 1800 bearing reliefs of a setsquare, dividers, hammer and axe above bones, a skull and an hourglass; presumably it commemorates a wright. – Just E of this, the HEADSTONE of Patrick McClaren †1754, an angel's head above the inscription; on the other face a shield bearing the emblems of a farmer and the usual reminders of death at the base. – To its E, a fallen stone of *c.* 1800 which displays the implements of a maltster above the standard skull, crossbones and hourglass. – More genteel are the four early C19 stones to the S, three of them swan-neck-pedimented and pilastered aedicules, the fourth (to George Taylor †1820) with narrow side panels and a foliaged and rosetted frieze under the carving of a sunburst. – A little to the E, a tall HEADSTONE, its faces worked at different dates. The E, dated 1815, commemorating Margaret Oswald, wife of William Sharp, farmer in Forr, has console-topped pilasters which support an open pediment containing a heraldic achievement, the shield bearing the implements of a farmer, the human supporters clad in loincloths, the crest a wheatsheaf. On the back (to William Sharp †1848), a Composite columned aedicule enclosing the incompetently executed relief of an urn flanked by a muscular angel, naked except for a carefully positioned wristband, and a fully clothed and half-veiled female mourner.

MUTHILL PARISH CHURCH, off Station Road. Late Georgian Perpendicular, by *James Gillespie Graham*, 1825–8. Large buttressed box and W tower, all built of red sandstone ashlar. In the church's battlemented five-bay sides, tall mullioned and transomed three-light windows; like all the openings they are hoodmoulded. At the crowstepped E gable, topped by a weathercock, a five-light window, its head filled with wheel tracery; dummy wheel window above. The battlemented W gable has angle buttresses, the tops of their pinnacles foliaged. Two-light windows flank the boldly projecting tower. This is of three stages, the upper two intaken and marked off by heavy moulded string courses. Large Tudor door at the bottom. At each exposed face of the second stage, a two-light window. In the faces of the third stage, three-light belfry openings above lozenge-shaped clock faces. The tower's battlement is carried on moulded corbels; foliage-topped pinnacles at the corners.

The INTERIOR is a large and broad space, the W end bowed. U-plan gallery on bundle-shafted wooden columns round three sides, its front decorated with Perpendicular arcading. Spaces under the gallery at the W and E ends of the N and S sides have been partitioned off, the two at the E in 1906–7. Huge ceiling rose formed of radiating cusped arches. At the E end, the PULPIT, its elaborate Gothic (still almost Gothick) octagonal sounding-board topped by crocketed flying buttresses which form a foliage-finialled crown spire. – Plain PEWS of 1906–7.

At the W approach to the church, spired Gothic GATEPIERS, presumably of 1828.

ST JAMES (Episcopal), corner of Station Road and The Laigh Toll. Gothic, by *R. & R. Dickson*, 1835–6. Rubble-built tall cruciform, the N and S limbs just too short for it to be a Greek cross. Tall pointed windows, hoodmoulded at the more exposed W and N sides. In the W gable a very tall and narrow pointed and hoodmoulded door; above, a round window filled with cinquefoil tracery. Corbelled out at the top of this gable is a square bellcote, a pointed opening in each face, the stone-slabbed pyramid roof topped by a stone-spired octagonal turret, its faces panelled with dummy arches. The apse at the E end and porch at the W were added in 1904. The NE vestry also looks an addition but of the later C19.

The INTERIOR must have looked less bare before the removal of the W gallery in 1904 and the renewal of the roof in 1962 when coats of arms of local Episcopalian families were taken down from it and scattered round the building. The choir is marked off from the crossing by a septum surmounted by a wrought-iron railing of 1904. Bell-capitalled attached shafts carry the pointed stone arch into the ashlar-clad sanctuary.

Encaustic tiles of 1904 in the nave passage and the chancel. – Routine Gothic FONT of 1907 at the W end. – Simple boxy PEWS of 1874. – Brass eagle LECTERN of 1907. – Brass ALTAR RAILS also of 1907, designed by *R.T.N. Speir* and executed by *Duncan Campbell*. – ORGAN by *Wadsworth & Bros.*, 1888. – STAINED GLASS. Four early C20 lights (the Nativity, Crucifixion, Resurrection and Acension) in the sanctuary, one painted by *Speir* who was probably responsible for them all.

MUTHILL PRIMARY SCHOOL, Station Road. Front block by the Perth County Architect, *A. Watt Allison*, 1934. Harled with red sandstone dressings, the mullioned and transomed windows providing Jacobean hints. Broad-eaved rear block of the later C19.

DESCRIPTION

One long winding main street carrying the A822 snakes through the village. Its houses are mostly terraced dwellings of the late C18 and earlier C19, generally of two storeys but a few of one, many sneck-harled. At the village's SE end, a triangular green (the HIGHLANDMAN'S PARK) bounded by Pitkellony Street on the S, Thornhill Street on the W and Willoughby Street on the E, each with buildings only on the side away from the green. At the SE corner of the green, an early C19 stone WELL, the water issuing from a dog's head at the ogee-arched and ball-finialled front wall. In PITKELLONY STREET, No. 1 of *c.* 1800 has a central gablet. No. 14, set behind a small front garden, is dated 1814. Two-storey three-bay villa, the Ionic columned and corniced doorpiece with rosettes and a foliaged panel on the frieze; cornices over the ground-floor windows. At Pitkellony Street's W end, on the corner with Thornhill Street, another two-storey three-bay house of the earlier C19, its pedimented centre gablet pierced by a quatrefoil opening. On the W side of THORNHILL STREET, early C19 ball-finialled round GATEPIERS at the beginning of the drive to Pitkellony. In WILLOUGHBY STREET on the E side of the green, the white-painted No. 73, a single-storey and attic battlemented toy fort of the earlier C19. Round corner turrets. At the door, bundle-shafted columns carrying a parapet; hoodmoulds over the ground-floor windows. The rubble-built two-storey No. 57 is dated 1813. At the N end of the green Willoughby Road curves to run almost due N, the change of direction marked by a monkey-puzzle tree in the garden of LILYFIELD (No. 51). The street now becomes two-sided. On the E, at one corner of a small courtyard, No. 29 with a projecting corner bow; the house is probably early C19 in origin but the windows of the bow of *c.* 1850. From here a diversion up THE LAIGH TOLL leads past St James' Episcopal Church to STATION ROAD with Muthill Parish Church to the NE and Muthill Primary School to its W (*see* Churches and Public Buildings, above). On the W side of THE WARD, which runs N past the school's W side, is the early C19 No. 3, its porch's flattened gable suggestive of a pediment. In WARDSIDE to the E, on the N, the early C19 ASH-FIELD, with tiny attic windows in the gables. At the E end of the village, set back behind a garden, DALLIOTFIELD, its piend-roofed and harled front block of *c.* 1830. Three-bay front, the centre slightly advanced and gabled, with a pilastered doorpiece and an oval plaque at the top. Horizontal panes in the windows.

At the N end of Willoughby Street, the DRUMMOND ARMS HOTEL, bargeboarded but not light-hearted architecture of the later C19, its tall two-storey height something of a bully in the context. The road then turns W and becomes DRUMMOND STREET. Terraced housing of the late C18 and early C19. Projecting from the wall of No. 48, a plain SUNDIAL of 1748, apparently reused.

BENNYBEG SMITHY, 1.8 km. N. Picturesque, of the earlier C19. Two-storey rubble-built and broad-eaved house, its ground floor's tree-trunk portico flanked by hoodmoulded two-light windows; angular Gothic openings above. On the S side, a broad canted bay window under a gabled Gothic light. Diagonally set tall chimney. Behind, a single-storey L-plan office wing, with a segmental-arched cartshed opening.

CULDEES. *See* p. 306.
DRUMMOND CASTLE. *See* p. 318.

NEW SCONE

Village developed from the beginning of the C19 as a replacement for Old Scone *c.* 2 km. to the NW whose buildings were cleared to improve the policies of Scone Palace (q.v.).

CHURCHES

SCONE NEW CHURCH, corner of Angus Road and Balformo Road. Originally Scone Free Church. By *Sydney Mitchell & Wilson*, 1886–7. Simple Gothic with a strong Scots accent, built of hammer-dressed red Corsehill (Dumfriesshire) sandstone. Nave and aisles covered by a single roof. At the E end, transepts flush with the aisles and, projecting from the crowstepped gable, a tower. This is of three tall stages marked off by cornice-like string courses. At the S face, a turret, its top sloped in below the parapet. At the top (belfry) stage of the tower, paired hoodmoulded openings. Sturdy battlement supported on moulded corbels; stone spouts protrude from the corners. Within the battlement, a saddleback-roofed and crowstep-gabled caphouse surmounted by an elaborate wrought-iron weathercock. On the nave roof, a flèche with a witch's hat slate spire.

High and spacious INTERIOR. Wagon roof over the nave which is divided from the aisles by tall wooden pillars carrying broad and angular pointed arches, their wooden spandrels pierced by circles and mouchettes. E organ gallery (the organ now removed). At the w end, a shallow rectangular chancel containing the communion table. Octagonal stone PULPIT on the s side of the chancel entrance. – Simple pine PEWS.

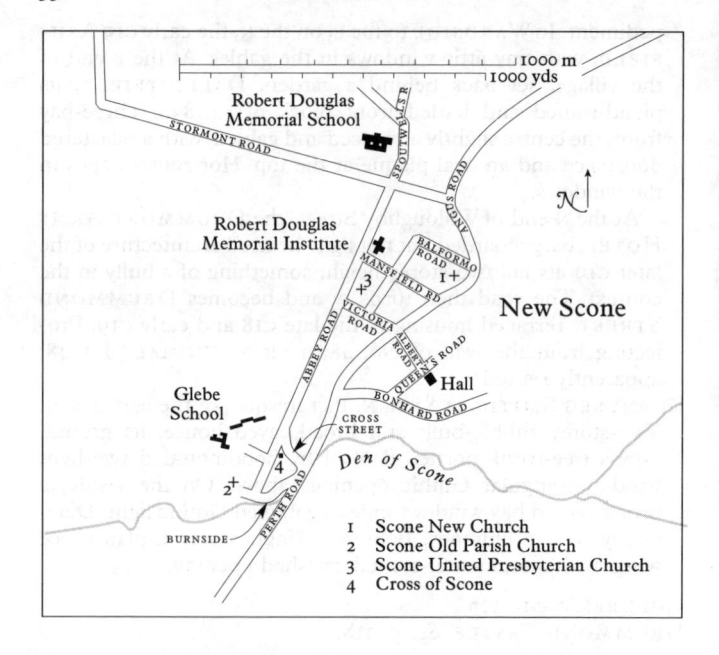

SCONE OLD PARISH CHURCH, Burnside. T-plan kirk, the main block built in 1804, the N jamb added by *John Bell Jun.*, 1833–4, all constructed of stugged rough ashlar. On the w gable of the main block, a birdcage bellcote, its ogee-profiled stone roof carried on Roman Doric columns. At each gable of this block, a rectangular entrance under a window which would be Venetian except that its centre light is pointed. In the s wall, two tall windows. In the N wall of the main block, low rectangular windows. A tall pointed window in each side of the jamb. In the jamb's N gable, an off-centre rectangular door and, lighting the gallery, a pointed window which is truncated below its arched head. The chamfered surrounds of all these openings are original but the mullions of the large s windows and of the centre lights of the E and W gable windows and the cinquefoil tracery in the jamb's N window are late C19, probably introduced as part of the alterations made by *John McDonald* in 1873.

The INTERIOR was refurnished in 1965–6 when *John S. Dow & Mills* provided a new pulpit, pews and E and W galleries. – At the N end of the jamb, the STORMONT PEW constructed in 1616 to seat the family of the parish's chief landowner, David, first Lord Scone (later, first Viscount Stormont). Made of oak, it is an exuberant demonstration of Jacobean classicism.

Panelled front and back on which stand reeded columns with large foliaged capitals supporting arches under a canopy. The larger front columns carry three M-shaped arches, their central pendants repeating the design of the columns' capitals. At the back, seven elliptical arches with fretted soffits. Entablature with guilloche-bordered niches containing entwined cones above the front columns and pendants. On the panels of the frieze are lions' heads set among foliage; egg-and-dart cornice. On top of the ends of the entablature, pediments with open spire finials. Between these, two aedicules flanked by scrolls ending in birds' heads. Each aedicule consists of coupled attached columns, again with foliaged capitals, and a steep pediment broken by a palmette-finialled rosetted pedestal, a lion's head at its base. In the pediments the heraldic achievements of DAVID.LORD.SKONE (David, first Lord Scone) and ELIZABETH.LADY.SKONE (Elizabeth Betoun, his wife). Between the aedicules, a rosetted pedestal topped by a double-spiral ornament on which stands an oval panel bearing the monogrammed initials of David, Lord Scone, and Elizabeth Betoun. The panel is flanked by the heads of bearded men and surmounted by a palmette-finialled pedestal, again with a lion's head carved at the base. On the canopy's underside are panels whose cut-out corners are filled with rosettes.

STAINED GLASS. The two S windows behind the pulpit (Faith, Hope and Charity; Christian Virtues) are of 1916. – At the W end of the main block's N wall, colourful bitty window (the Conversion of St Paul; the Risen Lord at the Sea of Tiberias) by *Alexander Gilfillan*, 1954. – At this walls's E end, a window ('To the Hills Shall I Lift Mine Eyes') depicting scenes associated with the Rev. Ronald Robertson who is commemorated here, by *Shona McInnes*, 1996.

GRAVEYARD. Beside the E entrance, a single-storey L-plan SESSION HOUSE by *John McDonald*, 1877. Georgian survival except that the inner angle is filled by a Tudorish diagonal porch. – NE of the church, a large Baroque MONUMENT to David Douglas, the botanist and plant collector who introduced the Douglas fir to Scotland. It is of 1840–1 but the inscription is dated 1847. Pilastered pedestal topped by cone-filled vases and large floriated scrolls supporting an urn.

SCONE UNITED PRESBYTERIAN CHURCH, Abbey Road. Now housing. By *W. G. Rowan*, 1885. Sturdy plain Romanesque, with massive sloping topped angle buttresses at the S gable. The buttresses along the sides were added by Rowan in 1895.

PUBLIC BUILDINGS

CROSS OF SCONE, corner of Abbey Road and Cross Street. Erected in 1820, a replica of the medieval Cross of Old Scone (*see* Scone Palace). Octagonal shaft with a floriated cross finial.

GLEBE SCHOOL, off Abbey Road. By the Perth & Kinross County Architect, *Ian A. Moodie*, 1962–5. Barrack-like, with a red-tiled roof.

HALL, Queens Road. Built in 1879–80. Thrifty Romanesque detailing at the gable front.

ROBERT DOUGLAS MEMORIAL INSTITUTE, corner of Abbey Road and Mansfield Road. Originally New Scone School. By *John McDonald*, 1876. Picturesque in a sort of English Elizabethan manner, with bracketed eaves. Large octagonal flèche with fish-scale slating. Two-storey schoolhouse at the S end in the same manner.

ROBERT DOUGLAS MEMORIAL SCHOOL, Stormont Road. By *A. Watt Allison*, 1933–5. Stolid Neo-Georgian, built of red brick with buff-coloured stone dressings. Pediment over the centre bay of the front; Roman Doric columned cupola on the roof.

DESCRIPTION

PERTH ROAD and its NE continuation, ANGUS ROAD, form the main thoroughfare, their architecture for the most part a not very appealing mixture of badly altered early C19 vernacular and late C19 and C20 housing. No. 58 Perth Road, its front facing a close, looks early C19 in its present form but the doorpiece, with Gibbsian rustication and massive keystones breaking through the heavy cornice, could be early C18. On the corner of Angus Road and Balformo Road, Scone New Church (*see* Churches, above) is a tall punctuation mark but the other churches and public buildings are scattered through the village.

BURNSIDE ROAD, going off to the SW at Perth Road's entry into the village, contains Scone Old Parish Church (*see* Churches, above). The Cross of Scone (*see* Public Buildings, above) stands on the corner of CROSS STREET and ABBEY ROAD which runs N from Burnside roughly parallel to Perth Road, on the corner of Cross Street. Further up Abbey Road, the former Scone United Presbyterian Church and the Robert Douglas Memorial Institute (*see* Churches and Public Buildings, above).

BONHARD ROAD runs E off Perth Road. In it, No. 2, a large broad-eaved villa of the later C19, its French pavilion-roofed tower still with cresting; big monkey-puzzle tree in the garden. In MURRAYSHALL ROAD running NW from Bonhard Road to Angus Road, No. 20 was built as the Scone Free Church Manse in 1848. Georgian survival but with sturdy brackets under the eaves and below the balustraded balcony which surmounts the entrance; horizontal-paned glazing in the windows. STORMONT ROAD is the W exit from Angus Road leading out of the village past the Robert Douglas Memorial School (*see* Public Buildings, above). Off it, in LYNEDOCH ROAD, No. 19, an early C19 two-storey house, its three-bay front of (painted) droved ashlar with rusticated quoins; carved foliage and rosettes on the frieze of its pilastered and corniced doorpiece.

CAIRN, Shien Hill, 3.6 km. E. High on a hillside overlooking the broad valley of the Tay, a huge round cairn, probably of the third millennium B.C., over 30 m. in diameter and 4 m. high.

The much sandier lower part and relatively stony upper portion suggest that it may have been formed in two stages.

STONE CIRCLE, Sandy Road. In a housing development, a small circle, c. 6.5m. in diameter, of standing stones erected probably in the second millennium B.C. It has contained seven boulders but four have fallen and one is missing. An urn containing a cremation and datable to c. 1200 B.C. has been excavated from the centre but may not have been contemporary with the circle.

BONHARD HOUSE. See p. 236.
MURRAYSHALL. See p. 545.
SCONE PALACE. See p. 689.

NEWTON CASTLE see BLAIRGOWRIE

OCHTERTYRE
2 km. NE of Monzievaird

8020

Prominently sited on a hillside above Loch Monzievaird, a mansion house designed by *James McLeran* and built for Sir William Murray of Ochtertyre in 1785–9.

Main block of two storeys and an attic above a basement (fully exposed on the S side), the walling of whinstone ashlar, rough and with cherry-cock pointing at the sides and the outer bays of the N front. Piended platform roof with a mutuled cornice. The N (entrance) front is of seven bays, the centre three of polished ashlar and advanced under a pediment. Pedimented porch with Roman Doric attached columns, an addition perhaps of 1838–9 when alterations were made for Sir William Keith Murray. The S front is generally similar but the stonework is all of polished ashlar and the centrepiece, of the same width as the N front's, has a single Venetian window at the first floor. Also, the centrepiece's lower floors are covered by a broad bowed flat-roofed projection, its top surmounted by a simple railing. Is this of the 1790s or an addition of the 1830s? The windows of this front's principal floor and of the two W bays of the basement have been lowered, presumably in the 1830s, and a cast-iron balconied veranda erected at the same time. Extending on each side, set well back from the S elevation and screened from the N by the basement area, are single-storey wings, each consisting of a three-bay range, the W with a round-headed door flanked by lunettes, the E with round-headed windows, and a taller piend-roofed end pavilion whose S front's slightly advanced and pedimented centrepiece contains a Venetian window (the W now a door).

Inside, a central STAIR HALL, with anthemion decoration to the cast-iron balusters of the flying stair. At the corners of the ceiling, reliefs of seated classical figures, two backed by urns and two by trophies, all framed in boughs of foliage. The ceiling's centre is a cupolaed dome, the lower part decorated with alternating fans and fan-shaped panels enriched with urns and rinceau ornament. Above this, husk swags dropping from ribboned knots and with pendant circular plaques bearing classical reliefs. DINING ROOM at the house's SE corner, with corniced doorpieces and a white marble chimneypiece of the 1790s. In the centre of the s front, the DRAWING ROOM, with pilasters at the opening to its bow. To its W, the MORNING ROOM, its chimneypiece also of white marble, with a mythological classical scene carved on its frieze; at the ends, reliefs of a woman with a corpse and a woman and child.

STABLES to the NW, built in 1838–9. U-plan, the walls of whinstone rubble. At the ends and centre, two-storey piend-roofed pavilions, the outer two with round-headed coachhouse arches in their inner sides whose blind heads have contained fan tracery; segmental arched entry to the centre pavilion.

MAUSOLEUM of the Murrays of Ochtertyre on the W side of the main drive, designed by *C.H. Tatham* and built in 1809 on the site of the former Monzievaird Parish Church. The roof is now stripped of slates and the wallhead detail lost. Serious-minded Perpendicular, the walls faced with ashlar. The N and s elevations are each of three bays marked off by buttresses, their lowest steps gabled, their tops removed. Above a sloped offset about halfway up the sides, cusped and splay-sided windows. At each gable, a Tudor door, the W a dummy. Above the E door a simple two-light window, above the W a window of three triangular-headed lights under simple tracery. – In the surrounding GRAVEYARD, some C18 HEADSTONES carved with trade emblems and reminders of death. – Immediately N, a second GRAVEYARD containing late C19 and C20 MONUMENTS.

GRANITE LODGE at the SE end of the main drive, also by *Tatham*, 1809, is a severe ashlar-faced Tudor ensemble. Octagonal gatepiers. On their W, a small square building finished with a cornice and tall parapet; hoodmoulded rectangular s window; four-centred E door. Another four-centred door in the W porch of the main lodge E of the gatepiers, this porch, the two-storey main block and the single-storey E and N wings all finished with cornices and tall parapets. In the porch's s face, a slit window. The main block is an octagon, its long s side with a hoodmoulded rectangular ground-floor window containing Gothic glazing; a tiny pointed dummy light above. In this block's SE, SW and NW sides, small pointed ground-floor windows and, at the first floor, hoodmoulded panels carved with the coats of arms of Murray of Ochtertyre, of Hope (for Lady Mary Hope, wife of Sir Patrick Murray of Ochtertyre, the builder of the lodge), and the Royal Arms of Scotland superimposed on a saltire. In the long sides of the E and N wings, hoodmoulded rectangular windows, the s still with Gothic glazing; a Gothic dummy window in the N wing's gable.

Halfway up the back drive from the SW, an early C19 LODGE,

its walls of cherry-cocked whinstone, the windows containing small-paned glazing; bracketed broad eaves. A sloping canopy over the S porch's entrance.

OLD FINCASTLE
2 km. NW of Glenfincastle

8060

Rubble-walled laird's house of the Stewarts of Fincastle who owned the estate from the later Middle Ages until the C19.

The present building consists of two parts, a main block of 1702 and an L-plan wing, perhaps originally a jointure house, of the 1750s. The main block is of two storeys with an attic lit only by a tiny window in the E gable and a piended dormer, probably C19, at the back; rounded skewputts. Symmetrically treated S front of seven bays on the ground floor, the central door flanked by small windows, and five at the first floor whose openings are grouped 1:3:1. The lintel of the entrance is incised with the initials G.S. and I.C. (for Gilbert Stewart of Fincastle and Isobel Campbell, his wife) and the date 1702. The lintel of the window immediately to the W, presumably reused from the house's predecessor, is a large stone bearing the incised inscription arranged to fit its irregularly shaped top: 1640.AG 7/BLISSIT.AR.ÞE.MERCIFVL./FOR.ÞEY.SCHAL. OBTAIN.MERCE./ÞE.FEIR.OF.ÞE.LORD.ABHOREÞ./ WICKEDNES./IS.CM, the initials those of James Stewart of Fincastle and his wife, Cecilia Mercer.

The SW wing is of two storeys but lower. Three-bay E front, the central first-floor window now a dummy, the outer windows heightened and given piended dormerheads in the C19. The lintels of the ground-floor windows flanking the central door are both incised, the l. with 17 HS 51 (the initials those of Henry Stewart of Fincastle), the r. with 17 HS CM 54 (the initials those of Henry Stewart and his wife, Charlotte Mercer), the dates probably those of the wing's construction. Panel above the door bearing the initials of Robert Stewart of Fincastle and Louise Graeme, his wife, and the date 1807. S facing jamb, its upper windows also heightened with piended dormerheads in the C19.

Inside the main block, the E room (now kitchen) was the DINING ROOM in the mid C18 when it was given a basket-arched sideboard recess, a frieze enriched with a sort of Vitruvian scroll and a foliaged cornice. Geometric stair, its anthemion-decorated cast-iron balusters perhaps of 1807. First-floor DRAWING ROOM also finished in the mid C18 with panelled walls and a wooden chimneypiece, its pulvinated frieze carved with foliage. Surprisingly grand stucco ceiling. At its centre, a head of Apollo in a sunburst. Round this, a circle of drapery bow-tied at the four cardinal points and with boldly modelled flowers and fruits at the intermediate points.

OLD HOUSE OF GASK see GASK HOUSE

ORCHIL HOUSE
3.4 km. NE of Braco

Characteristically unlovable Baronial, by *Alexander Heiton Jun.*, 1868. Large mansion displaying the full panoply of crow stepped gables, turrets, towers, battlements and bay windows, all faced in bullnosed masonry but without excitement. It was restored by *Henry & Maclennan*, 1925, after a fire but later abandoned. – NORTH LODGE on the A822, of the earlier C19 and presumably by *James Gillespie Graham* whose wife inherited the Orchil estate in 1825. Single-storey Tudor Gothic in red sandstone, with hoodmoulded and a splay-sided portico. Large late C20 addition at the back. – SOUTH LODGE of *c.* 1870, built of hammer-dressed masonry.

PERTH

Introduction	564
City Centre	570
St John's Kirk of Perth	570
Churches	582
Greyfriars Burial Ground	593
Public Buildings	599
Streets	612
Industrial Buildings	642
Suburbs	644
Balhousie and Muirton	644
Barnhill, Bridgend and Gannochy	645
Burghmuir, Dovecotland, Hillyland, Letham and Oakbank	657
Craigie and Moncreiffe	663
Tulloch	664

INTRODUCTION

By far the largest town and regarded by its inhabitants and most outsiders but not all bureaucrats as a city, Perth is the undisputed administrative, industrial and commercial capital of Perth and Kinross. Its site, in the centre of the district and of eastern Scotland, lies at the meeting point of land routes from the W along Strathalmond and Strathearn, from the E along Strathmore and the Carse of Gowrie, from the N along the Tay valley, and from the S along the narrow declivity of Glenfarg, its nodal importance strengthened, at least in its earlier history, by its position at what is both the lowest fordable point and the highest tidal point of the River Tay.

By the 1120s a motte castle, serving from *c.* 1150 as the seat of a sheriff, had been erected here and a royal burgh with the right to levy customs on foreign trade was in existence. The burgh,

Perth.
View of city from J. Slezer, *Theatrum Scotiae*, 1693

probably originating from a settlement beside an inlet of the Tay at the E end of the present High Street, was laid out on a roughly rectangular area of flat ground S of the castle and was probably surrounded by a palisade on three sides, along the lines of the present Mill Street on the N, South Methven Street on the W and Canal Crescent and Canal Street on the S, the Tay providing a natural defence on the E. Within these boundaries the town's plan consisted of two principal E–W streets (High Street and South Street) from which ran back the tofts or burgage plots of the inhabitants, each originally intended for a dwelling and workplace accompanied by ample garden ground. At the W end of each street was a gate giving access to the town. In the centre of the town, between the two streets and their tofts, were placed the burgh church (St John's Kirk of Perth) and churchyard with a marketplace to their W. N–S communication was provided by vennels or alleys (Kirkgate, Skinnergate, Meal Vennel and the probably broader Watergate). To the N and S of town were the North and South Inches, open extents of common land liable to flooding from the Tay.

The importance of Perth as a burgh was marked *c.* 1150 by the construction of a lade bringing water from the River Almond at Huntingtower Haugh, 5 km. NW, to the town's mills. At its SE end the lade was joined by ditches filled with water from the River Tay to form a moat round the town.

In 1209 a flood of the Tay destroyed the castle motte and the bridge over the river. The bridge was rebuilt within ten years but the castle abandoned, the sheriff moving his seat to Kinclaven Castle (q.v.). Perhaps partly as a result of the loss of the castle, the town's defences seem to have been strengthened with the construction of a stone wall instead of a palisade inside the line of the encircling moat. Possibly also connected with the loss of the castle was the foundation, *c.* 1235 and perhaps by Alexander II, of a Dominican friary, its site commemorated by Blackfriars Street and Blackfriars Wynd, just N of the town. Its buildings provided accommodation for the royal court on the King's visits to Perth and round them the medieval suburb of North Port was to develop. A second (Carmelite) friary, now commemorated by Whitefriars Street, was founded in 1262 and stood at Tullylumb a little W of the town and its already existing suburb of New Row. Two further religious houses, of Carthusians and Franciscans, were founded in the C15.

During the Wars of Independence of the late C13 and early C14 Perth changed hands several times, its town wall alternately levelled and rebuilt, the last time during Edward III's invasion of 1336. Despite the turmoil of these wars the town was sufficiently prosperous to rebuild the bridge over the Tay *c.* 1326. After the ending of the wars Perth served as a regular residence of the court and a meeting place of the Scottish Parliament and also housed a population of merchants and craftsmen, some employed in the manufacture of metal, wooden and leather goods. From the C14 to the later C16 it was generally ranked fourth among the Scottish burghs in terms of burgh taxation and fifth in terms of customs receipts, these levied largely on exports of raw wool from sheep reared in the town's extensive hinterland. Architectural evidence of the town's late medieval economic vitality can be found in the hugely expensive rebuilding of St John's Kirk undertaken from *c.* 1440.

In the mid C16 a French visitor, Jean de Beaugué, found Perth 'a very pretty place, pleasant and well fitted to be the site of a good town'. Although the religious houses were destroyed after the Reformation of 1560 and Parliament had ceased to meet at Perth after 1437 the town continued to be visited by the Court. Town houses of local nobles and lairds were built beside the Tay along Watergate and Speygate; the grandest of these was Gowrie House, the residence of the Earls of Gowrie until their forfeiture after the Gowrie Conspiracy, a purported assassination attempt made here on James VI in 1600. This was built along sides of a courtyard and enjoyed a riverside garden at the back. The houses of merchants and craftsmen seem also to have been of stone but frequently fronted by wooden galleries.

The union of the Crowns in 1603 deprived Scotland and Perth of the presence of the King and his court and fifteen years later Taylor the Water Poet reported of Perth that 'a fine town it is, but it is much decayed by reason of the want of his Majesties yeerely comming to lodge there . . .' Moreover, silting of the River Tay meant that Perth ceased to be one of the principal ports of E Scotland. When a new bridge over the Tay, built in 1617, collapsed four years later, it was replaced only by a ferry and by 1639 Perth had fallen to eighth place among Scottish burghs as measured by the value of their rents. However, its strategic position at the meeting of land routes across Scotland was recognized in 1654 when the South Inch just outside the burgh was chosen as the site for one of the four Cromwellian citadels built in Scotland (all demolished after the Restoration).

By the late C17 and well into the C18 Perth was primarily an entrepôt for the export of linen, grain and cured salmon, all products of the surrounding county, although the burgh also housed its own craftsmen among whom glovers were unusually prominent. In the 1720s Daniel Defoe reported of the town that 'here are abundance of new Houses, and more of old Houses new fitted and repair'd, which look like new'.

Expansion of the town outside its medieval boundaries began in the 1760s with the development of New Row, Leonard Street and the handloom weavers' settlement of Pomarium to the w and sw, and in 1766 the Town Council decided to remove the medieval gateways to the town and such of the town walls as was necessary to improve access for 'large Carriages'. At the same time the Council ordered that, in the rebuilding of houses, wooden galleries were to be omitted and, in 1781, forbade the use of thatch as a roofing material. These moves towards enlargement and upgrading of the town were accompanied by the construction of Perth Bridge in 1766–71, its opening a century and a half after the collapse of its predecessor the occasion for further expansion and remodelling of the town. A new suburb (Bridgend) was begun on the E side of the Tay. Inside the town itself, George Street was punched through the medieval layout to provide access for wheeled traffic from the bridge to High Street. Soon afterwards, land between the medieval burgh and the North Inch and along the w side of the Inch, bordering the thoroughfare from Perth Bridge to the Crieff and Dunkeld turnpike roads, was laid out as a small 'New Town' comprising Charlotte Street, Atholl Crescent and Place and Rose Terrace, and with villa plots to the NW between Rose Terrace and Melville Street. By the 1790s both the North and South Inch had been laid out as public parkland and from 1798 a second 'New Town' was laid out by *Henry Buist* between Canal Street, formed by infilling the medieval ditch on the s side of the medieval burgh, and the South Inch. Within the medieval burgh St John Street was formed in 1801 to extend the line of George Street s from the High Street to South Street from which Princes Street provided the main vehicular route through the s 'New Town' to the turnpike road from Perth to North Queensferry (Fife).

These developments, largely promoted by the entrepeneur, local historian and future Lord Provost of Perth, Thomas Hay Marshall, experienced uneven success, the new streets through the medieval burgh and the N 'New Town' built fairly quickly, the s 'New Town' not completed until half a century later. Also uneven was the development of Perth's industries. Textiles continued to be of importance for the town and surrounding area, the manufacture of linen largely replaced by that of cotton cloth by *c.* 1800, but declined with the ending of the Napoleonic Wars before seeing a revival in the 1830s and 1840s and the establishment of new steam-powered linen works in the 1860s. Iron and brass foundries were set up in the earlier C19, as were breweries, glass works, rope walks, tanneries, brick and tile works, coach-building works and a boat-building yard, many of these surviving into the C20 but mostly of small importance.

In 1847 the Dundee & Perth Railway was opened and, the next year, three further lines, the Scottish Central Railway to Stirling, the Edinburgh & Northern Railway to North Queensferry and, running NE of Perth, the Scottish Midland Junction Railway to Coupar Angus, Forfar and Dundee. The railways to Stirling and Dundee were extended to Glasgow and Aberdeen in 1850 and a line to Dunkeld opened in 1856 which was extended to Aviemore and Forres in 1863 and to Inverness in 1898. These placed Perth at the nodal point of the Scottish railway system and by the late C19 the railway companies provided the town's largest single source of employment. Closely linked to the railways was development of dyeing and of whisky blending and bottling. In 1848 the dyeing firm of John Pullar & Sons, founded about twenty years before, opened the huge North British Dye Works in Kinnoull Street to which cloth was sent from all over Scotland, the works' success helped by the introduction of a cheap parcel postal rate in 1851. About 1870 Pullars expanded into dry-cleaning, the garments also brought to and from Perth by the railway-borne postal service. By 1900 the firm employed about 2,000 workers. Perth's whisky-blending firms of Matthew Gloag & Son, J. & T. Currie, John Dewar & Sons and Arthur Bell & Sons, the first three founded by 1850, the last in 1865, used the railways to transport whisky from the distilleries to Perth and, after blending and bottling, from that town to their customers. Significant but small-scale employers until the 1890s, these whisky firms then expanded massively. Other offshoots of Perth's geographically central position were the growth of its livestock auctions, the mart sited beside the railway station opened in 1875, and a major insurance company, the General Accident Fire and Life Insurance Corporation, founded in 1885 and employing 2,000 by 1929. Two major government institutions, both housing sizeable numbers, stood on the edge of the town, the (now demolished) Perth Barracks at the NW, built in 1793–4 and finally closed in 1962, and Perth Prison at the S end of the South Inch, built in 1811–12 to accommodate French prisoners-of-war, remodelled in 1840–2 as the General Prison for Scotland, and still in use.

The growth in industrial and commercial activity in Perth in the mid and late C19 was accompanied by the building of villas, tenements and workers' housing to the N and W and, at Bridgend, a string of prosperous villas overlooking the Tay. At the same time much of the town centre was redeveloped, the scale and architectural ambition of the new buildings evidence of Perth's civic pride as a commercial and administrative centre with a panoply of government and municipal buildings, museums, an art gallery and theatre. The start of the C20 was marked by the formation of King Edward Street as another N–S thoroughfare linking the medieval burgh's High Street and South Street, and the erection there of a mercat cross (the King Edward VII

Perth.
Map of city, c. 1850

Memorial) facing across the street to the front of the Beaux-Arts bulk of the new Perth City Hall. In the 1920s and 1930s Perth expanded with new housing estates. The Gannochy lands NE of Bridgend were covered with model workers' housing built by Arthur Bell & Sons. The Town Council erected a generously laid-out scheme of Neo-Georgian housing on Muirton, between the N end of the North Inch and Dunkeld Road. Extensive housing, both public and private, accompanied by schools, sprawled W over the estates of Letham, Viewlands and Burghmuir to the W and Friarton to the S. Further housing development, especially on the W side of the town but contained within the boundary of the W by-pass opened in the 1980s, continued through the later C20 and into the C21. Also of the late C20 and early C21 has been the redevelopment for flatted housing of many sites fringing the town centre.

In the later C20 linen manufacture and Pullar's dye works and dry-cleaning services were closed and the railways ceased to be a major source of employment but whisky bottling has continued, together with a number of small industrial concerns. However, financial and service industries are now the chief source of employment. New commercial developments in the town centre and supermarkets along the main roads leading to it have continued Perth's historic role as the principal shopping centre for a wide surrounding area. Perhaps the opening of a new concert hall in 2005 will bring excitement to the town although it must be hoped without damage to its national and well-merited reputation for courtesy.

CITY CENTRE

The area W of the River Tay comprising the medieval burgh, the inner suburbs, both medieval and later, which lie between the W line of the former burgh wall and the railway, and the Georgian 'New Towns' bordering the North and South Inches. Almost all of this is laid out on a gridiron plan, pleasurably relaxed at the crescents overlooking the North Inch. The commercial streets display a variety of Georgian, Victorian, Edwardian and C20 architecture, frequently intermingled in unsatisfactorily bitty fashion. Along the High Street, Tay Street and on the Inches, carefully positioned sculpture of the late C20 and early C21 forms a public display of enlightened patronage unrivalled by any other town or city in Scotland.

ST JOHN'S KIRK OF PERTH
Kirkside, St John's Place and St John Street

The C15 burgh church of Perth, the scene of an inflammatory sermon by John Knox at the launch of the Scottish Reformation. After the Reformation the building was altered and subdivided internally but reconstructed as a single edifice in the 1920s.

History

A church existed on the site by c. 1126 when David I confirmed the grant of its advowson and tiends to Dunfermline Abbey. Of the size and appearance of that building nothing is known but they are likely to have been commensurate with the importance of the royal burgh (also known as St Johnstone) in which it occupied the central position (and it was of sufficient importance to be chosen in 1286 as the burial place for the heart of Alexander III). It was probably in response to the late medieval expansion of the burgh and the desire of individuals and guilds to endow chapels or altars for the saying of votive masses that it was decided in the C15 to rebuild the church, presumably on a substantially larger scale. In 1440 Dunfermline Abbey granted a proportion of the tiends of Perth, together with the fees levied on burials in the choir, for a period of six years as a contribution towards rebuilding the choir of St John's Kirk. Work seems to have been largely completed by December 1448, when the altar of St John the Evangelist to the N of the high altar was endowed. Construction of transepts, a crossing tower, and nave with N and S porches followed. A view of 1806 shows the upper storey of the N porch (Halkerston's Tower) pierced by a huge and ornately traceried window and the two buttressed bays of the N aisle to its E containing vast windows, suggesting that these were intended as part of a very grand scheme, probably for a hall-church nave. Presumably the scheme proved too expensive and the W end of the N aisle and the whole S aisle were completed as low unbuttressed lean-to structures, together with a not very elaborate two-storey S

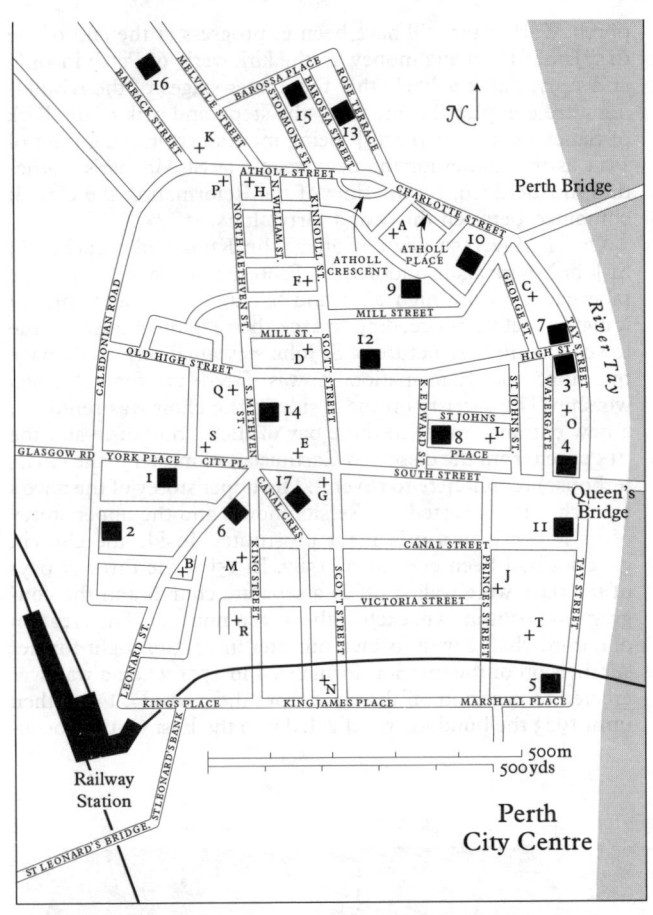

1 A.K.Bell Public Library
2 Caledonian Road Primary School
3 Council Buildings
4 County Buildings
5 Fergusson Gallery
6 King James VI Hospital
7 Old Council Chambers
8 Perth City Hall
9 Perth Concert Hall
10 Perth Museum and Art Gallery
11 Perth Sheriff Court
12 Perth Theatre
13 Public Seminaries
14 Sharp's Educational Institution
15 St John's Primary School
16 St Ninian's Primary School
17 Telephone Exchange

A Former Middle Free Church
B Free Presbyterian Church
C Middle Free Church
D North Church
E Old Light Antiburgher Chapel
F Perth Congregational Church
G Perth Methodist Church
H St Andrew
J St John the Baptist (Episcopal)
K St John the Baptist (R.C.)
L St John's Kirk of Perth
M St Leonard
N St Leonard's-in-the-Fields and Trinity
O St Matthew
P St Ninian's Cathedral (Episcopal)
Q St Paul
R Tayside Christian Fellowship
S Trinity Church of the Nazarene
T Greyfriars Burial Ground

porch. Work must still have been in progress at the end of the C15, James IV giving money 'to the kirk werk' of Perth in 1489 and 1497, but it is likely that these later stages of the rebuilding were completed soon after, 'the stepil and prik of the Kirk of Sanct Johnstoun [Perth]' being mentioned in a contract of 1511 as the model for the new steeple at St Machar's Cathedral in Aberdeen. By the time of the Reformation the church contained between thirty and forty altars.

On 11 May 1559, the day after John Knox had preached in St John's Kirk against idolatry, a Protestant mob destroyed the tabernacle on the high altar and 'all utheris monumentis of idolatrie' before proceeding to sack the religious houses in the town. The main structure of St John's escaped serious damage but after the Reformation it was fitted up for reformed worship. The sacristy on the N side of the choir was removed, a new entrance made in the E bay of the S choir aisle and the C15 porch from the dissolved Carthusian monastery (the Charterhouse) rebuilt here to cover it. The upper storey of the nave's S porch was converted to a session house and the upper storey of its N porch to a prison for prostitutes. Inside the church, galleries had been erected by 1587. In 1598, the three W bays of the nave were walled off as a separate church and the congregation split in two, each with its own minister. The creation of a third charge with its own minister in 1715 brought further subdivision of the interior, formalized in 1771 when a wall was erected to partition off the choir from the crossing. From then until 1923 the building was divided into the East Church occu-

Perth, St John's Kirk of Perth.
Engraved perspective of south elevation in 1775 after an etching by
Archibald Rutherford

pying the choir, the Middle Church in the crossing, transepts and two E bays of the nave, and the West Church in the nave's three W bays.

Some tidying up of the fabric, including demolition of the nave's S porch, took place *c.* 1800 and further destruction of medieval work followed. Soon after 1817 the upper storey of the C15 N nave porch was removed and, in 1825, *James Gillespie Graham* shortened the N transept to permit the widening of St John's Place for traffic. This opening up of the view of the church may have underlain the decision in 1828 to employ Gillespie Graham to cut back decayed stonework, carry out cement repairs to tracery and enhance the building's architectural impact by the addition of arcaded balustrades to the wallheads of the choir and aisles. Much more ambitious was his intended rebuilding of the nave (with the addition of a clearstorey), and its aisles on a much taller scale and in a Late Georgian Gothic manner. In the event this was carried out only at the E two bays of the N side of the nave where all physical evidence of the projected but uncompleted grandiose C15 design was removed.

Designs of 1889–91 by *Andrew Heiton Jun.* for a restoration of the exterior to something like its late medieval appearance and of the interior as a single church were abandoned because of the Presbytery's insistence on the building of new churches to rehouse two of the existing congregations. Instead, in 1892–6 *Heiton & Grainger* carried out refurbishment of the three-church interior and removed Gillespie Graham's nave clearstorey.

In 1918 a public meeting decided that, as a memorial to the men of the city and county of Perth who had been killed in the First World War, St John's Kirk should be restored to its medieval appearance and the interior reconstructed as a single church. *Robert S. Lorimer* was appointed architect and the work, partly a scholarly restoration and partly a celebration of the quality of early C20 craftsmanship, was begun in 1923 and completed in 1926.

Description

EXTERIOR. The general appearance is C15, much of the detail of the 1820s and 1920s. The ashlar-walled church is cruciform, *c.* 58.2 m. long, 27.7 m. broad at the transepts, and with the aisled nave and choir each *c.* 17.7 m. wide internally (i.e. of comparable size to other major late medieval burgh churches such as St Giles, Edinburgh, St Michael, Linlithgow, or St Mary, Haddington), but the copper-roofed choir is of five bays, the slate-roofed nave of six and fractionally longer (by *c.* 0.35 m.) and lower; porches project from both. Crossing tower, its broach spire covered with herringbone-patterned leadwork.

Lorimer's work on the choir and transepts was a conservative attempt to restore their medieval appearance, although Gillespie Graham's cement tracery, much of it attempting to

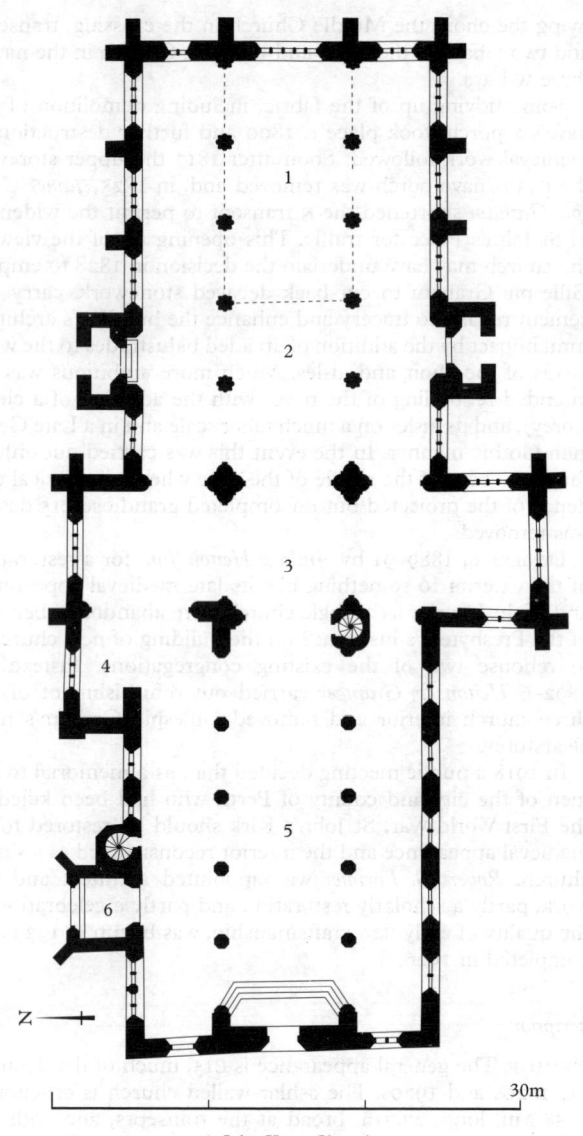

1. John Knox Chapel
2. Choir
3. Crossing
4. Shrine Chapel
5. Nave
6. Halkerston's Tower

Perth, St John's Kirk of Perth.
Plan

reproduce medieval work, was retained. At the CHOIR's E front the main gable is marked off from the ends of the aisles by sturdy sloping-topped buttresses. Gabled angle buttresses at the outer corners of the aisles. The top of the gable, its apex surmounted by a floriated cross of 1923–6, is crossed by a string course, placed just too low to form a pediment. In the tympanum, a sexfoiled roundel. The hoodmoulded main E window is tall, of five cusped lights, the tracery of cusped loops and circles containing trefoils. The window's sloping sill is continued across the walling and as a string course under the hoodmoulded windows of the aisles. The N of these is of two lights, the head filled with a cusped dagger. The S aisle's window is larger, of three tall cusped lights, again with dagger tracery in the head. Under the ends of the aisle parapets, stone figures of sleeping animals (a dog and dragon) carved by *Donaldson & Burns* in 1923–6.

In the N wall of the choir's central vessel, hoodmoulded clearstorey windows, all pointed and two-light, with soggy cusped loops in their heads. The N choir aisle, like the S, has each bay marked off by gableted buttresses and is now finished with a tall parapet of 1923–6, a narrow crenelle at the centre of each bay; stone gargoyles carved (by *Donaldson & Burns*, some from models by *Phyllis Bone*) as animals' heads. The aisle's side windows, renewed with cement in 1828 but apparently reproducing C15 work, are large and pointed. The E three are each of four lights. In the head of the first, trefoils under a circlet of swirling mouchettes. The reticulated tracery of the second window contains trefoils and quatrefoils; below this window, a straight joint of the round-headed C15 door which opened from the church into the (demolished) sacristy. The third window is similar to the first but with much larger swirling mouchettes in the head above smallish quatrefoils. The aisle's fourth bay contains an early C19 gabled porch (blocking the C15 window), its entrance arch of five orders, the attached shafts' capitals simply moulded, the hoodmould with weathered headstops. In the W bay, a three-light window with quatrefoils in the head.

The choir's S side is similar to the N. The hoodmoulded clearstorey windows, their sills lowered in a post-Reformation alteration, are round-headed single lights and smaller than those on the N. Four-light aisle windows, their hoodmoulds, except at the E bay, with pendant label stops. In the window of the E bay, tracery like that of the third window in the S side; below it, breaks in the stonework made by the erection here in the later C16 of a porch (removed, *c.* 1800) brought here from the Perth Charterhouse. The next window's tracery repeats that of the E window on the S. Reticulated tracery in the third window. At the fourth bay, an early C19 gabled porch, blocking the medieval window. The window of the W bay is generally similar to that of the E bay.

The S TRANSEPT retains its general C15 form, with a hoodmoulded window in each face, the E and S windows four-light with quatrefoil tracery in the heads. Much restoration and renewal of stonework detail was carried out in the 1820s and again in 1983.

The N TRANSEPT was shortened in 1825 but its angle-buttressed N gable seems to have reproduced its C15 predecessor, with a main window of four cusped lights, the head filled with cusped loops, trefoils, quatrefoils and a sexfoil. Above, a round window containing a whirligig of three cusped loops.

In the transept's inner angle with the N nave aisle is Lorimer's parapeted SHRINE CHAPEL of 1923–6, occupying the site of a late medieval chapel which had been removed a hundred years before. Lightly broached ashlar walling, smoother than that of the rest of the church. Shallowly projecting clasping buttress at the NW corner. Near the top of that corner, a large stone crouched lioness, again carved by *Donaldson & Burns*. In the chapel's N side, an off-centre three-light window (derived from the E window of Melrose Abbey) with tightly detailed tracery of Scots late medieval type in the heads of the outer lights. Above the window, the straight line of the parapet is broken by a merlon containing a niche.

At the NAVE, where evidence of the building's original appearance was largely uncertain, Lorimer produced a dignified version of a late medieval Scottish burgh church. The side walls of the aisles were wholly (at the S) or partly (at the N) rebuilt, heightened by *c.* 2.74 m. and given plain parapets pierced by slits to discharge water from the roof into downpipes. In both aisles, new and larger windows, those of the S aisle two-light with tracery of late medieval inspiration. The N aisle's windows are more varied. The E, next the Shrine Chapel, has a whirligig of cusped loop tracery, the next is a narrow single light. In the W bay of the aisle, a pair of rectangular windows, each of two lights containing flattened pointed and cusped openings; their design evokes the C15 three-light window shown in this position in C18 engravings.

Projecting from the N aisle's second bay from the W is HALKERSTON'S TOWER. The lower storey is that of the C15 N porch, the upper was erected in 1923–6. Its rough ashlar tries to blend with the medieval stonework but Lorimer's design was derived not from the medieval upper storey (demolished *c.* 1818) shown in a view of 1806 but from the C15 S porch of St Michael's Parish Church, Linlithgow. Intaken diagonal buttresses at the corners, each topped by a stone gryphon of 1923–6. Crowstepped N gable surmounted by a foliaged Celtic cross. In the gable, a broad pointed C15 door, its simply moulded arch springing from capitals whose carved decoration is continued to E and W as a rod-like string course crossed by weathered foliage. In the 1920s work above the door, a pair of roundels containing Tudor Rose panels carved with shields, the l. bearing the arms of the City of Perth, the r. those of the County of Perthshire. Between these, a large corbel carved with an angel violinist over which is continuous corbelling to support the upper floor's canted oriel window covered with a stone-slabbed roof. In the SE inner angle, a stair-turret, its upper part rebuilt in 1923–6.

The W FRONT is largely medieval but Lorimer added the parapets to the aisles, placed figures of a recumbent lion and horse (above the dates 1126 and 1924) on top of the buttress-like projections at the corners of the main gable, and gave that gable a floriated cross. The W window of each aisle is of two lights and plain. The nave's hoodmoulded and pointed W door is low and again plain except for a chamfered surround. Above, the walling of the gable's broad centre is recessed, probably because a huge window was originally intended. What was actually constructed was a four-light window of no great size, cusped loop tracery in the head.

Finally, the CROSSING TOWER (*c.* 9.45 m. square) which rises to a height of *c.* 47 m. above the ground. Single intake in the walling immediately above the ridge of the choir roof. Just above this, simple two-light pointed belfry openings. Clock dials (by *E. Dent & Co.*, 1879) on the N and S faces. At the SW corner, a buttress-like square stair-turret, its top sloped into the walling but originally intended to be carried higher, perhaps to a caphouse.* The tower is finished with a battlement supported on moulded corbels and pierced by quatrefoils. This dates from a restoration of 1862 which seems largely to have reproduced C15 work but also heightened the parapet by *c.* 0.35 m. and added extra corbels. Rising inside the parapet, a lead-covered splay-foot spire. From its N front projects an aedicular lucarne-bellcote, probably of the late C18, the ball-finialled pediment carried on etiolated Roman Doric columns.

INTERIOR. The lower storey of HALKERSTON'S TOWER is covered by a sturdily detailed stone vault, with tierceron ribs as well as those on the diagonal and transverse axes. At the intersections of the ribs, foliaged bosses and, in the centre, a plain shield. At the centre of each of the S, E and W walls, a corbel, presumably intended to carry an image. Round-headed and hoodmoulded S door into the church, with three orders of shafts, their capitals simply moulded. In the E wall, three doors of the 1920s, the S (now into a cupboard) in the position of the later C16 door which opened onto the stair to the floor above. The C15 entrance from the N nave aisle was reopened by Lorimer (*see* below). The first-floor room is of 1923–6, covered by a wooden tunnel vault with a square foliaged boss at the centre.

Lorimer reconstructed the interior as a single church, its surviving medieval fabric largely respected. The plan of the NAVE is C15, with five-bay arcades opening from the central vessel into the aisles. At each end bay, long abutments, those of the W formed by internal walls buttressing the corners of the main W gable. At the E bay the S abutment is provided by the large SW crossing pier containing a stair and the N abutment by an

---

*The stair inside was clearly intended to continue higher.

answering wall. The arcades are of C15 form but the piers were rebuilt, using much of the old stonework, in 1923–6. The pointed arches, simply detailed with pairs of chamfers, are carried on octagonal piers, their capitals moulded with simple filleted rolls and hollows. At the E pier of the third bay from the W on the N side, a niche, its angular pointed arch cusped internally. The niche is set low down so unlikely to have contained an image but is too shallow for a credence. Above the arcades, high blank expanses of walling crying out to be pierced by clearstorey windows.

The fumed oak roofs were provided by Lorimer. Over the central vessel, a barely pointed tunnel vault crossed by thin ribs. In some compartments, square rosetted panels. Along the ridge, panels carved by *W. & A. Clow* and painted by *Moxon & Carfrae* from designs by *Morris Meredith Williams* with depictions of Scenes from the Life of Our Lord (the Nativity at the W, Baptism, Our Lord and Little Children, Trial Before Pilate, Crucifixion and, at the E, the Ascension). Along the wall-plates are crowned shields bearing sacred symbols (the *Agnus Dei*, *Chi-Rho*, etc.). Flat compartmented ceilings over the aisles, the intersections of the ribs marked by carved and painted panels.

In the N aisle, a hole in the wall beside the entrance from the lower floor of Halkerston's Tower marks the former position of a medieval holy water stoup. To its E, in the position of its medieval predecessor, a rectangular door of 1923–6 with chamfered jambs gives access to the stair-turret in the SE inner angle of Halkerston's Tower and the nave. The E bay of this N aisle is occupied by the S end of the Shrine Chapel, entered from the W by a pair of pointed arches sharing a quatrefoil-plan pier; these were constructed in 1923–6. Above these arches, a dummy window with whirligig tracery, again of the 1920s.

The CROSSING arches are carried on massive quatrefoil NW, NE and SE piers. Even more massive and octagonal the SW pier which contains a stair. On the front of each lobe of the piers, a very broad fillet; spurs between the lobes. Simply moulded capitals. The piers carry pointed arches, moulded with hollow splays. The W arch contained the medieval rood loft, its height above the floor marked by the turret's upper door and by a simply moulded corbel. Two more of the loft's corbels, both carved with human heads, survive behind, placed partly on the E fillet of the responds and partly on the attached columns of the arches into the transepts. On the other sides of the crossing, pointed arches of the same height as that from the nave. Over the crossing is a ribbed stone vault, its centre pierced by a large hole to enable the hoisting of bells. This is now filled by a large wooden boss bearing a depiction of the *Agnus Dei* carved by *W. & A. Clow* and painted by *Moxon & Carfrae* in 1923–6. Four of the vault's ribs are pierced by small round holes for bell ropes, their placing apparently dictated by the hanging of the bells rather than any desire for symmetry.

The TRANSEPTS are covered by wooden ribbed tunnel vaults of 1923–6, decorated with bosses and panels carved with foliage. Pointed arches from the transepts into the choir aisles. In the S transept's W side, a broad pointed medieval recess, its mouldings hacked off. Its position precludes it having been a credence but it seems too small to have contained an effigy. At the N end of this transept's E wall and above the cornice of Lorimer's ceiling, corbels which supported the original wall-plate. In this wall, traces of an arched opening wider than the present arch into the choir aisle suggesting that the aisle was originally intended to be broader. The rough stonework of the N transept's N end, contrasting with the ashlar of the rest, provides clear evidence of that wall's rebuilding when the transept was curtailed in 1823. On this transept's W side, a broad late medieval arch (reopened and restored in 1923–6) which opened originally into the N nave aisle and a chapel added on its N side, probably in the early C16, but now gives access to Lorimer's SHRINE CHAPEL. This is rectangular but the short protrusion into it of the aisle's wall forms a shrine recess at the N end of its W side.

At the W end of the CHOIR, a narrow rectangular window in the crossing tower looking down the central vessel. The arcades are carried on octofoil piers with heavy filleted shafts on their four main axes and smaller keeled shafts between. The W pier on the E bay of the S arcade is carved with a band bearing the inscription *iohañes:fullar:et:vxor:eivs:mariota foullar*, the inscription crossed by and crossing two shields, each displaying a key and a spur. The arcades' tall pointed arches rise two-thirds of the height of the choir. Those of the three W bays are moulded with three orders of segmental hollows. At the two E bays, presumably the position of the medieval presbytery, the arches are more richly moulded, with bold quirked rolls and deep hollows. Plain rear-arches to the clearstorey windows (the sills of those on the S side lowered). Over the main vessel, an open wooden roof, its oak traditionally said to have been taken from Kinnoull Hill; it was uncovered and restored, perhaps with some conjecture, by Lorimer. The construction combines corbelled and arch-braced wall-posts with tie-beams, collar-beams, kingposts and scissor-braces. Over the choir aisles, roofs of 1923–6. In the choir's E wall, an ogee-arched piscina. In the S choir aisle, to the r. of the door, a (restored) stoup. In the N choir aisle's second bay from the E (now fitted up as a vestry), the lower parts of the moulded jambs of the medieval door to the (demolished) sacristy.

Lorimer's FURNISHINGS are rich but decorous. The three E bays of the choir (approximately the position of the C15 presbytery) are screened off as the JOHN KNOX CHAPEL. The W front and one-bay return of its oak SCREEN are of 1923–6, designed by *Lorimer* and executed by *W. & A. Clow*. Simple linenfold panels at the base from which rise slender uprights carrying a foliage-carved parapet, its centre displaying angels supporting a crowned shield. As first erected the screen stood one bay to the E. It was moved forward in 1970 by *W. Schomberg Scott* who designed the E two bays of the returns in a flashy late C20 Gothic manner. – In the centre of this chapel, an oak COMMUNION TABLE of 1923–6, also designed by *Lorimer* and the front carved by *W. & A. Clow* with a relief of the Last Supper.

In the choir's two W bays, CHOIR STALLS of 1923–6 (again designed by *Lorimer* and executed by *W. & A. Clow*), quite restrained with only a few of Lorimer's favourite beasts carved on them. – More beasts and some foliage enrichment on the contemporary STALLS in the transepts. – On the N side of the choir, filling the W bay of the aisle, the ORGAN, originally built by *Conacher & Co.* in 1874 at the E end of the East Church and rebuilt in its present position by *Frederick Rothwell*, 1926–8. It was renovated in 1961 by *Rushworth & Dreaper* and again rebuilt in 1985–7 by *A.F. Edmonstone*. – Oak ORGAN CASE of 1928 (by *W. & A. Clow* from *Lorimer*'s design), quite elaborately carved in a Late Gothic manner, the pierced parapet decorated with acorns and thistles; over the centre, a pair of roundels containing reliefs of angels. – Against the NE crossing pier is the oak PULPIT of 1926 (also by *W. & A. Clow* from *Lorimer*'s design). Again it is in a Late Gothic manner, the general conception derived from 'John Knox's Pulpit' in the National Museum of Scotland. The centre panel of the octagonal body is carved with the Pelican in Piety; small shields bearing sacred symbols on the other panels. Large soundingboard carved with oakleaves and acorns.

Under the S transept's S window is the GALLERY FRONT from the loft of the Wrights' Incorporation of Perth which was erected *c.* 1800 in the East Church. The front was re-erected here in 1968. It is smartly panelled in the Late Adam manner, decorated with fluting, rosettes, urns and husk pendants; on the centre panel, the large heraldic achievement of the Wrights. – On the E wall of this transept, a PANEL from the N gallery front of the East Church which marked the seat of the Procurators. Again of *c.* 1800, it is painted with a figure of Justice. – On the N wall of the N transept, a HATCHMENT of *c.* 1800 commemorating the Mercers of Aldie.

Crimean War MONUMENT to men of the 90th Light Infantry Perthshire Volunteers on the E wall of the S choir aisle, by *Samuel Manning Jun.*, 1857–8. Of marble, with high reliefs of a mourning private soldier and officer flanking the inscription panel. – In the NW recess of the Shrine Chapel, WAR MEMORIAL designed by *Lorimer* and executed by *Donaldson & Burns*, 1923–6. Painted stone inscription panel set in a moulded frame, its sides crossed by bands bearing the names of the theatres of war, the top carved with two angels who hold a shield bearing the Saltire; above, the royal arms. In each inner corner of the recess is a corbel on which stands the painted figure of an angel sculpted by *Fanindra Bose*, the l. holding a shield which bears the arms of the City of Perth, the r. a shield with the arms of the County of Perthshire. – At the SW pier of the chapel, a large bronze STATUE of St John the Baptist, by *Bose*, 1926. – The chapel's twelve-light brass CHANDELIER hung formerly above the Shoemakers' Gallery of the Middle Church. It is probably mid-C15 Flemish work. – On the E wall of the N choir aisle, a large but weathered medieval GRAVE-SLAB of Tournai marble, with the matrix for brasses of two figures, presumably a husband and wife, perhaps of the family of the Earls of Gowrie whose burial place was in this aisle.

STAINED GLASS. Choir: five-light E window (the Crucifixion) by *Douglas Strachan*, 1920, and rather bitty. – N choir aisle: well-coloured two-light E window (a Blind Boy being Led to Our Lord) by *Margaret Chilton* and *Marjorie Kemp*, 1930. – In this aisle's N wall, a badly realistic four-light window (the Resurrection) by *James Ballantine II*, 1928. – In the W bay of this aisle, now hidden by the organ, a three-light window (St John the Baptist, with Zechariah and St Elizabeth) by *Stephen Adam & Son*, 1898.

S choir aisle: three-light E window (St Andrew, St John the Baptist and St Peter) by *A. Ballantine & Gardiner*, 1894, soberly coloured realism. – In this aisle's S wall, two four-light windows. One (*Veritas, Sacrificium, Immortalitas* and *Libertas*) is of 1921 by *William Meikle & Sons*. – The other (the Feeding of the Five Thousand) is by *Margaret Chilton* and *Marjorie Kemp*, 1929.

N transept: N window (Deborah, Huldah, Miriam and Anna) by *Herbert Hendrie*, 1930, displays clearly drawn and strongly coloured figures against a pale background. – In the Shrine Chapel, N window by *Morris Meredith Williams*, 1925, depicting St Michael and pallid angels defeating Satan.

S transept: a very bright E window (Moses Striking the Rock) by *J. & W. Guthrie & Andrew Wells Ltd.*, 1932. – S window (Isaiah, Jeremiah, Ezekiel and Daniel) of 1929 by *Herbert Hendrie*, a counterpart to his N window in the N transept. – W window (Adoration of the Magi) by *Douglas Strachan*, c. 1947, uncharacteristically disciplined and realistic but disappointing.

N nave aisle: E bay (Two Soldiers of the Black Watch, with St Michael and St Andrew) by *William Wilson*, 1955, brightly coloured and realistic. – Next, a window (St Elizabeth Teaching St John the Baptist) by *Herbert Hendrie*, 1926, with strongly coloured figures against a pale background. – W of the door to Halkerston's Tower, a characteristic two-light window (St Nicholas and St Christopher) by *William Wilson*, 1956. – Then a semi-abstract window, strong blues dominating the colour scheme, by *Harvey Salvin*, 1975. – The W window's floral patterned glass looks early C20.

S nave aisle: in the two E bays (St Andrew and St Columba; St John the Baptist and St John the Divine) glass by *Herbert Hendrie*, 1936–7, examples of stylized realism. – Then a well-coloured but sentimental window (Scenes from the Life of King David) by *Louis Davis*, c. 1930. – To its W, another window (Moses and Aaron) of c. 1930, by *Herbert Hendrie*, a freer version of his window to the E. – Beside this, a crowded window (Noah, Moses, Abraham, Joshua, Samuel and David, and Elijah) by *Isobel Goudie*, 1935. – w window (the Nativity of Our Lord), strongly coloured, by *Marjorie Kemp*, 1933. – In the great w window of the nave, pale glass (Scenes from the Life of Our Lord, the Nativity the principal subject) by *Herbert Hendrie*, 1926.

BELLS. In the tower is a carillon of bells hung here in 1934 when they were provided with paper rolls punched with nineteen tunes including 'A man's a man for a' that', 'Charlie is my darling' and 'Greensleeves'. Thirty-four of the bells are of 1934, cast by *Gillett & Johnson Ltd*. The bourdon bell was cast by *Peter Waghevens* of Mechlin (Malines) in 1506. Round the top, borders of low-relief stylized foliage frame a band inscribed *iohannes baptista vocor ego vox clamantis in deserto mechline petrus wagheuens me fo'mavit sit benedictus qui cuncta creavit M ccccc vi* ('John the Baptist am I called, the voice of one crying in the wilderness. Peter Waghevens of Mechlin cast me. Blessed be He who created all things. 1506.'). On the waist, panels of stylized decoration, the founder's mark and a small relief figure of St John the Baptist.

In the lucarne-bellcote on the N side of the spire, a peal of thirteen bells. Eight were cast by *George Mears & Co.*, of the *Whitechapel Bell Foundry*, 1861–5, and four by *John C. Wilson & Co.*, 1901. The thirteenth, of the early or mid C14 and the largest of its date in Scotland, bears the inscription in Lombardic lettering: AVE MARIA GRACIA PLENA DOMINUS TECUM ('Hail Mary, full of grace, the Lord is with thee'). – Now hung on a metal frame standing on the floor at the E end of the S choir aisle are fifteen more bells. Nine are of the C18 and C19. Five are chime bells, presumably the survivors of a chime of seven noted in a visitation of the church in 1653. The three smaller are inscribed X IC BEN GHEGOTEN INT IAER MCCC-CCXXVI ('I was made in the year 1526') and the two largest X IC BEN GHEGOTEN INT IAER ONS HEEREN MCCCCCXXVI ('I was made in the year of Our Lord 1526'). The cross is identical and the lettering very similar to that on a bell now hung at the N end of the W cloister walk of Iona Abbey (Argyll and Bute) which was cast at Mechlin in 1540 by *Peter van den Ghein* who is likely to have been the founder of these. The fifteenth bell is also early C16, inscribed †*exce Agnus dei* ('Behold the Lamb of God') and bearing small reliefs of the *Agnus Dei*, a cock, flower and crown.

CHURCHES

Former BAPTIST CHAPEL. *See* SOUTH STREET.
FREE PRESBYTERIAN CHURCH, Pomarium Street. Originally Forteviot Hall. Part of a small Scotstyle group designed by *Erskine, Thomson & Glass* and built in what was then a run-down working-class area for the philanthropic Forteviot Trust in 1938–9; all harled with artificial stone dressings. Crowstep-gabled E front, the tall side windows rising through the eaves

into steeply pedimented dormerheads. On the S side, a single-storey house with a bow window at the advanced and pedimented l. bay of its E elevation. To the N, a flatted double house (Nos. 2–5 Pomarium Street) built as part of the same development and in the same manner, with crowstepped gables and gableted dormerheads.

Former MIDDLE FREE CHURCH, Blackfriars Street. Secularized. Built in 1843. Three-bay front, the low centre door flanked by Tudor Gothic windows, the l. now converted to a door.

MIDDLE FREE CHURCH, Tay Street. Now housing. Early Gothic with a French accent, by *Hippolyte J. Blanc*, 1885–7, built of red Corsehill sandstone. Cruciform, with an aisled nave. The side buttresses soar above the roofs of the aisles as fliers. Flanking the N gable, a NE porch and bowed NW stair-tower; in the gable, a large wheel window. Transept gables of two bays, each containing a tall four-light window with a quatrefoiled vesica in the head. In the inner angle of the E transept and choir is a contemporary two-storey Gothic hall.

NORTH CHURCH, Mill Street. Originally North United Presbyterian Church. Italian Romanesque, with an imposing basilica front in polished grey ashlar, by *T. L. Watson*, 1878–80. Nave and aisles, the aisles stopped short of the nave's N bay and the inner angles filled by lower semi-octagonal-ended transeptal projections. In the front (N) gable of the nave, a window of three stepped round-arched lights, the centre light stilted, the arches carried on slender attached columns with foliaged capitals; diapered hoodmoulds. More diaper ornamentation on the gable above the window; indented corbelling under the parapet. At the corners of the nave, turreted clasping buttresses. Projecting from this gable, a flat-roofed square porch. Set diagonally across its corners are pilasters whose capitals' foliaged carving is carried across the walls ending in the foliaged capitals of the granite nook-shafts of the round-arched and gabled front and side entrances. Below the level of the springing of the arches the porch walls are panelled; above they have diaper ornament. At the end of each of the transeptal projections, a heavy console-pedimented doorpiece, its tympanum carved with stylized foliage. The windows of these projections are round-arched with foliage-capitalled nook-shafts. So too are the gallery windows in the side walls of the aisles; below them, rectangular lights with very simple capitals.

The INTERIOR is divided into a nave and aisles by round-headed arcades carried on slender foliage-capitalled cast-iron columns. Tunnel-vaulted plaster ceiling over the nave; domes on pendentives over the aisles. U-plan gallery filling the aisles and across the N end. At the S, a tall round-headed arch to an apse which is filled by the ORGAN (by *John R. Miller*, 1893), its case and integral pulpit provided in 1880. – Oak COMMUNION TABLE in a Lorimerian Late Gothic manner, by *Scott Morton & Tynecastle Co.*, 1920–1. – Abstract patterned STAINED GLASS by *Adam & Small*, 1880.

OLD LIGHT ANTIBURGHER CHAPEL, off South Street. Secularized. Rubble-built rectangle of 1821, the piended roof now covered with concrete tiles. Pointed windows. The Gothic porch is a Victorian addition.

PERTH CONGREGATIONAL CHURCH, Kinnoull Street and Murray Place. Scots Late Gothic in red sandstone, by *H. B. W. Steele & Balfour*, 1897–9. Buttressed nave and aisles. Crow-stepped front gable with pinnacled corner buttresses. Spired ventilator-flèche on the roof.

PERTH METHODIST CHURCH, Scott Street. By *Alexander Petrie*, 1879. Small-scale Gothic, with acutely pointed windows. The gable front is bisected by a steeple, the tower's belfry stage (empty of bells) broached to an octagonal stone spire decorated with patterned bands.

Inside, the pulpit stood originally at the E end under a round window but has been moved to one side. – STAINED GLASS. In the round W window, a late C19 double portrait of John and Charles Wesley. – In the N and S walls, two abstract windows by *Vanessa Ohyma*, 1982, blue the dominant colour.

ST ANDREW, Atholl Street. Disused. Thrifty Dec, by *Andrew Heiton Jun.*, 1884–5. Three-gabled front, the side gables fronting the aisles. At the broad centre gable, a barely projecting porch, its gable containing a vesica with a relief of St Andrew; pointed door, its nook-shafts with foliaged finials.

ST JOHN THE BAPTIST (R.C.), Melville Street. Big bare Geometric barn, by *A. & A. Heiton*, 1854–6, incorporating at its W end the side and end walls of a church of 1832–3. E gable to the street. Over the SE porch, a slated pavilion roof topped by a wooden bellcote.

The interior is covered by an elaborate open roof with a scissor truss, its W part of 1854–6, its E part an extension by *Andrew Heiton Jun.*, 1892–3 when he remodelled the 1830s part of the building. Broad pointed arch into the W (liturgical E) apse, both arch and apse of 1892–3, flanked by narrow arches into small rectangular side chapels added in 1925. C20 E gallery. – STAINED GLASS. In the apse, three lights (Saints) of 1893, colourful but bad. – In each of the N and S walls, a two-light window (the Resurrection; the Ascension) of 1925, of similar quality. – ORGAN in the gallery, by *Norman & Beard*, 1906; rebuilt in 1968 by *Rushworth & Dreaper*.

ST JOHN THE BAPTIST (Episcopal), Princes Street. Like an English country church deprived of its graveyard and placed in unhappy urban exile. It is by *J., W. H. & J. M. Hay* of Liverpool, 1850–1. Dec cruciform, built of stugged squared masonry, a NW steeple in the inner angle of the nave and N transept, an octagonal turret at the S transept's SW corner. The W door to the nave is hoodmoulded, the stops carved as high-relief angels holding saltired shields. Dumpy steeple, its angle buttresses with steep offsets. Blind arcading under the belfry stage; below the dogtoothed cornice, a frieze of cusped arch-heads. Broached and lucarned stone spire. The battlemented low porch built against the steeple's W face was added in the

C20. Plain NE addition by *A.G. Heiton*, 1914. The day-to-day entrance is through the NW porch. In its N side, the 1850s pointed door to the tower, its hoodmould's stops carved with large representations of the Pelican in Piety and the Eagle symbol of St John the Evangelist. Less demonstrative early C20 door into the church itself.

The INTERIOR has plenty of correct C14 Gothic detail, but unusually for an Episcopalian church of its date, the plan makes only cursory acknowledgement of Ecclesiological principles: the nave is exceptionally broad in relation to its length, the roomy transepts containing galleries, the spaces below the galleries were screened off in the mid C20 to form a (N) meeting room and a (S) Lady Chapel and the chancel is shallow (its E wall has been unhappily stripped of plaster). Collar-braced roof, with hammerbeams springing from corbels carved with foliage, angels' heads and emblems of the Four Evangelists. Pointed chancel arch, its shafts with foliaged capitals, the hoodmould's stops carved as male and female human heads. It contains a simple Lorimerian SCREEN of *c.* 1925, the frieze carved with vines. – In the chancel, a wooden ALTAR of 1929 and late C19 CHOIR STALLS. – Caen stone PULPIT of 1851 with elaborate but mechanical Gothic decoration. Its marble reliefs (Scenes from the Life of St John the Baptist) by *Mary Grant* were added in 1871–2. – Well-developed wooden eagle LECTERN of the late C19, formerly in the chapel of Cortachy Castle (Angus). – ORGAN at the W end, originally in the chapel of Selwyn College, Cambridge, and rebuilt here in 1971.

STAINED GLASS. Three-light E window (Our Lord flanked by St John the Baptist and St John the Evangelist) of *c.* 1855, archaic, with primary colours dominant. – S window of the Lady Chapel. Its wishy-washy two E lights (a Chalice; the Good Shepherd) are by *Artios C.S.*, 1991. The five lights to the W (St Andrew, St Elizabeth, St John the Baptist, the Blessed Virgin Mary and St Mary Magdalene) by *Gordon Webster*, 1970, are much more strongly drawn and coloured. – The W window of the nave's S wall (the Nativity) is of *c.* 1965. – In the W porch under the organ, two lights (St Patrick and St Columba) by *Jane Gray*, *c.* 1970. They were formerly in the S wall of the nave but moved here when a S door was made in place of a window. – In the NW porch, one small early C20 light by *J. Wippell & Co. Ltd.*

ST LEONARD, King Street. Secularized. Built as a chapel of ease in 1834–6; the architect was *W.M. Mackenzie*. Neoclassical but a mixture of Italian Renaissance and Greek. At the polished ashlar E front, three tall and relatively narrow doors under semicircular fanlights. They are set in round-headed overarches whose outer mouldings spring from broad channelled pilasters. Above each opening, a long horizontal panel as if to denote an attic. Plain parapet topped by a pedestal which carries a version of the Choragic Monument of Lysicrates (i.e. an open rotunda of Corinthian columns surmounted by a finial). In the rubble-walled sides, two tiers of windows, the lower rectangular except in the E bay where they are round-headed like those of the upper tier. W apse added by *James Smart*, 1891.

Inside, a floor has been inserted at the level of the D-plan gallery whose slender cast-iron columns and panelled front survive. – STAINED GLASS. Most of the windows contain abstract patterned glass, probably of the 1830s. – More strongly coloured and with sacred motifs are the W windows, presumably of 1891. – Probably also of 1891 are the lights at the E end of each side (the Good Shepherd; the Light of the World) by *Jones & Willis*.

ST LEONARD'S-IN-THE-FIELDS AND TRINITY, Marshall Place. Originally St Leonard's Free Church. Large and sturdy Scots Late Gothic, by *J. J. Stevenson*, 1882–5, the steeple's crown spire a landmark on the approach to Perth from the S.

The masonry is of hammer-dressed and squared buff-coloured rubble. Buttressed nave and aisles; broad crenelles and low merlons at their battlements, those of the aisles pierced by quatrefoils. The aisle windows are three-light with cusped loop tracery in their heads. At the clearstorey, a procession of windows, each of two ogee-arched lights under an uncusped loop. Projecting from the crowstepped W gable of the nave, a tall semi-octagonal apse derived from the C15 apse of the Church of the Holy Rude at Stirling, its windows containing loop tracery.

The E tower is square, with corner buttresses, diagonally set at the SE and NE. At the two lower stages, detail continuing that of the nave although the windows in the first stage are of two lights rather than three. Within the continuation of the nave parapet there rises an unadorned third stage. Above this, the belfry, a pair of large pointed two-light openings in each face. From the corners of the tower's overall parapet are corbelled out the bases of the four flying buttresses of the crown spire. This is closely derived from the C15 spire of St Giles' Cathedral, Edinburgh, although here with only four fliers instead of eight. As at St Giles' there are sturdy buttresses topped by stumpy pinnacles and the fliers have curved soffits and straight tops covered with stone cresting. From the meeting point of the fliers rises a tall main pinnacle, its general appearance and height relative to the fliers close to that of St Giles' but the detail all Gothic without the admixture of classical elements which was introduced to the pinnacles at St Giles' in the early C17. On top, a tall weathercock.

Attached to the NW corner of the church, a session house and hall, both with crowstepped gables. Mullioned rectangular windows at the session house. At the hall, a Late Gothic window in the W gable, a slated octagonal flèche on the roof.

INTERIOR. In the tower vestibule, a Neo-Jacobean stone chimneypiece. The church itself impresses by size and height. Collar-braced kingpost truss roof over the nave which is separated from the aisles by arcades, their stone depressed arches carried on tall cast-iron bundle-shafted columns. At the W (liturgical E) bay, the W end of each arch springs from a foliaged stone corbel. More carved corbels support the pointed stone arch into the shallow W apse which is covered with stone groin vaulting. Galleries with simply panelled oak fronts in the aisles and across the E end. Panelled wood dado along the aisle walls. At the W end, a large oak PULPIT of 1885, its body late Gothic, the sounding board Neo-Jacobean. In front, the COMMUNION TABLE, routine Gothic of 1930. – Simple PEWS of 1885. – Original windows, their plain quarries enlivened by STAINED GLASS abstract motifs. – ORGAN in the E gallery, by *Bryceson, Son & Ellis*, 1881, and originally in the former Morningside United Presbyterian Church, Edinburgh. It was rebuilt here by *David W. Loosley* and given a modern-traditional case, its ash woodwork too pale in this context, designed by *Stewart Tod*, 1985.

ST MATTHEW, Tay Street. Originally West Free Church. Early Gothic, by *John Honeyman*, 1869–71, built of purplish stugged rough ashlar, the dressings of buff-coloured stone. Nave and double-pitch roofed aisles, transepts and a tall steeple at the E end.

The nave and aisles are of five bays. At the buttressed aisles, two tiers of windows, the lower two-light, the upper large cusped roundels. In the E front of each diagonally buttressed transept, a two-light window, its head filled with a quatrefoiled roundel, its nook-shafts' capitals and hoodmoulds' label stops, like all the label stops, carved with foliage. At the buttressed two-bay sides of the transepts, two tiers of two-light windows, the upper with nook-shafts and hoodmoulds; above, a vesica. In the E bay of each transept, a nook-shafted and hoodmoulded door. Under the transepts' eaves, corbels carved with stylized medieval motifs.

The 64.6m.-high steeple dominates. At the E front of its angle-buttressed tower, a door of three orders, the capitals of the inner and outer shafts foliaged. At the second stage, a pair of hoodmoulded pointed lights. At each of the third stage's exposed faces, blind arcading carried on ringed shafts. The tower's top stage is the belfry, its opening linked by a sill course which is carried as a moulded string course across the buttresses. In each face, a tall two-light opening, its central column with a shaft-ring, the head filled with a cusped roundel, contained in a nook-shafted overarch. Battlement projected on carved corbels, octagonal pinnacles at the corners. At the base of four faces of the octagonal stone spire are lucarnes with trefoil openings, their gablets pierced by quatrefoils. Upper tier of small lucarnes in all the faces.

INTERIOR. Vestibule in the tower, its floor of grey and white marble. Double door into the church, the pointed arches sharing back-to-back central columns, their shafts of polished granite, their capitals foliaged; above, a quatrefoiled roundel carved with a relief of foliage. In the church itself, galleries in the aisles and across the E end, their fronts with plain Gothic blind arcading; clock at the E gallery. These are supported by foliage-capitalled cast-iron columns which rise to the hammer-beams of the nave roof, its collar-braces pierced by quatrefoils. The focus is on the roomy Gothic PULPIT of 1871, originally housed in a recess but pulled forward in 1896 to make room for the ORGAN by *J. W. Walker*, rebuilt by *R. C. Goldsmith Ltd.* in 1973 and 1991. – STAINED GLASS. Brightly coloured patterned glass, probably of 1871, in the W window and the upper windows of the aisles. – In the S aisle, under the gallery, a Second World War memorial window (Our Lord Blessing Soldiers) by *Alexander Gilfillan*, 1953, formerly in the demolished Wilson United Presbyterian Church. – Under the N gallery, a window (the Heavenly Jerusalem) of 1887, from the former Middle Free Church. – Also from the former Middle Free Church and probably of 1887, the glass (flowers and sacred symbols) in the upper windows of the transepts.

Behind, a HALL by *Honeyman & Keppie*, 1895. Simple Late Scots Gothic detail.

ST NINIAN'S CATHEDRAL (Episcopal), corner of Atholl Street and North Methven Street. Consecrated in 1850, as the first cathedral begun in Britain since the Reformation. Its erection owed much to the enthusiasm of two Tractarian-inspired laymen, Walter, eighteenth Lord Forbes, and the Hon. George Boyle (later sixth Earl of Glasgow),[*] eager to provide a visible assertion of the Scottish Episcopal Church's claim to be the true Catholic Church of the land. The building is the product of a protracted period of construction, the result unified but disappointing, the lack of impact at least partly due to the choice of a site which was both too small and too weak geologically.

William Butterfield was appointed architect for the cathedral in 1848 and, by the following year, produced designs in the Tractarians' approved Dec style for a church which comprised an aisled nave of four bays, with two W towers, transepts, their gables flush with the sides of the aisles, and a chancel of two long bays containing a choir and sanctuary. The first phase of work began at once and the chancel, with a N aisle containing vestries and an organ chamber, crossing and the E bay of the nave were completed in 1850. A second phase, again to Butterfield's design, was carried out in 1888–90. This entailed construction of the three W bays of the nave and, at the end of its central vessel, the lower part of a single W tower flanked by transepts, their ends also flush with the sides of the aisles, Butterfield having decided that:

'In the absence of a central tower at the intersection of the Choir and Nave with the transepts . . . a single tower is more suitable than two would be. Two towers in that position demand a third, which in this case does not exist. Neither of

---

[*] Who had already commissioned William Butterfield to design the College of the Holy Trinity (now Cathedral of the Isles) on Great Cumbrae.

the two towers in the first design would have been imposing features, and in only one of them would have been bells to justify its existence. The single tower, with its spire, as now proposed, is of imposing proportions: it will be a commanding feature in any distant view of the Fair City, and will serve for a full peal of bells.'

Further work was undertaken in 1899–1901 when *F. L. Pearson*, using designs prepared by his father, *J. L. Pearson* (†1897), rebuilt the chancel's N aisle (moving the organ to the S transept), added a corresponding S aisle intended to end in a chapel and, S of the S transept, a single-storey range containing a cloister with, on its E side, vestries and a chapter house. In 1908–11 the Lady Chapel at the E end of the S choir aisle was built to *F. L. Pearson*'s design. At the same time he remodelled the W tower (its completion impossible because of foundation problems) as a W gable for the nave and modified the E end of the chancel. In 1936 further work was carried out by *Tarbolton & Ochterlony*. The S end of the cloister range of 1899–1901 was extended further S and a school built behind it to enclose a roughly triangular space, its N and E sides bounded by the cathedral and cloister.

EXTERIOR. The external walling is all of squared and stugged masonry. The roofs of the nave, transepts, chancel and Lady Chapel are slated, those of the aisles covered with lead. The building's 21.3 m. height is impressive and would be more so were it possible to see it from a greater distance than is allowed by its position on the corner of two not very broad streets. Roofs of the same height over the nave, transepts and chancel, the crossing marked by an open bellcote finished with an octagonal flèche. The centrepiece of the W FRONT is Butterfield's unfinished tower as completed by F. L. Pearson who removed its low second stage and made it a gabled ending to the nave, adding blind-arcaded gablets and crocketed spired octagonal turrets to the existing angle buttresses. In the gable, the large but over-delicate window of four lights under a circlet placed amidst radiating arched tracery is Butterfield's. The low hoodmoulded window above, its head containing a cinquefoil, is Pearson's. The angle-buttressed transepts flanking the tower are by Butterfield. In each, a three-light window. The N of these transepts contains what was intended as the cathedral's main entrance and is more richly treated than the S, the head of the gable being decorated with quatrefoiled panels, the doorway with bell-capitalled nook-shafts and a tympanum carved with the Tree of Life.

The side elevations of the NAVE are Butterfield's. Sturdy buttresses with offsets at the aisles; gableted pilaster buttresses at the clearstorey. Three-light aisle windows. Butterfield's design of 1849 showed a single stumpy pointed light containing a foiled circle in each bay of the clearstorey. This was carried out at the E bay built in 1849–50 but at the three W bays of 1889–90 there are paired lights.

The CROSSING TRANSEPTS are also angle-buttressed. The gable of each has a low central buttress dividing its lower part into two bays. In the W bay of the N gable, a discreet porch. In the upper part of each gable, a large rose window in a pointed overarch. In the E face of each transept, a curvy-sided triangular light containing a quatrefoil.

The CHANCEL is a Butterfield–Pearson hybrid. The parapeted aisles are by Pearson, the clearstorey walling by Butterfield, the N side's two bays divided by the surviving lower part of a chimney which served the vestries which occupied the site of the present N aisle until 1899. In the chancel's W bay, on each side a large but short four-light window with a richly traceried head. Butterfield placed angle buttresses at the E corners of the chancel. The E projection of each survives but the W projections were replaced in 1908–11 by octagonal turrets, their open tops finished with crocketed spires. In the chancel gable, a febrile five-light window of 1849–50, its head filled with a circle of foiled lights. Small round window above, also of 1849–50.

Projecting E from the S chancel aisle is Pearson's LADY CHAPEL of 1908–11. Two-bay nave and a semi-octagonal chancel, its corners' buttresses rising into slender crocketed pinnacles. Parapet pierced by trefoil openings. In the windows, Dec tracery but sturdier than that of the cathedral's main windows.

The parapeted CLOISTER range of 1899–1901 S of the S transept is staid. Dec traceried four-light rectangular N windows to the vestries. Projecting at the original S end is the taller angle-buttressed chapter house. In its E gable, a large segmental-arched four-light window, its head filled with circled quatrefoils. On the W side of this range the windows to the cloister passage are elliptically arched, of four lights with quatrefoils in their heads. At the S end of this range and just overlaying the E gable of the chapter house is the porch added by *Tarbolton & Ochterlony* in 1936–8. Squared-up modern Gothic, the walls of crazy-paved rubble. In a gable immediately S of the entrance, a tabernacled niche containing the small statue of a bishop (St Ninian). This addition joins behind onto a harled V-plan SCHOOL (also of 1936–8 and by *Tarbolton & Ochterlony*), now in other use and rather altered.

INTERIOR of impressive height. Over the nave and crossing, a steeply pitched collar-braced roof, the plaster ceiling decorated with elaborate wooden patterning. Each bay of the nave aisles is marked off by a half-arch springing from a corbel. Wooden wagon roof over the chancel, panelled at the choir, panelled and ribbed at the sanctuary. Nave arcades with pointed arches carried on bell-capitalled quatrefoil-plan piers. At the W end, a very tall arch into the intended tower which opens into the W transepts through slightly lower arches; narrow pointed arches from the aisles into these transepts. Broad rear-arches to the clearstorey windows of the nave. The main transepts are entered from the crossing through arches which simply continue the design of those of the nave arcades. Narrower arches from the aisles, the low openings into the chancel aisles (the N aisle's E end now the Chapel of St Andrew) provided in 1899–1901. On the crossing's E side, the chancel arch carried on simply moulded large corbels.

In the side walls of the W bay of the chancel are double-arched openings into the chancel aisles. These were formed in 1899–1901, the N opening replacing a single arch to the original organ chamber. The walls of the sanctuary in the E bay of the chancel were adorned in 1908–11 by F. L. Pearson with lavishly crocketed and foliaged stone arcading in which are set sedilia. One arch opens into the Lady Chapel and houses the monument to Bishop George Howard Wilkinson (*see* below).

The LADY CHAPEL, built in 1908–11 as a memorial to Caroline Menzies, wife of Atholl MacGregor, is a calm space, with ashlar-clad walls articulated by bell-capitalled attached columns. Groin-vaulted wooden ceiling (foundation problems precluded the originally intended stone vaulting), the bosses bearing the coats of arms of the diocese of St Andrews, Dunkeld and Dunblane, of the City of Perth and of MacGregor and Menzies. Trefoil-headed CREDENCE in the S wall. In the N wall, an AUMBRY for the reserved Sacrament, its stone surround carved with ballflower ornament, the wooden door decorated with curvaceous metalwork.

FURNISHINGS. The simple early fittings have all been replaced. Over the High Altar, a BALDACCHINO designed by *F. L. Pearson* and executed by *H. H. Martyn* in 1908–11. It is of Cornish polyphant, generally Gothic in character but with brightly coloured mosaic decoration, gold much in evidence. Small stone statues, the centre one depicting the Crucifixion; at the front corners, figures of St Andrew and St George facing W and of St Patrick and St David looking out to the N and S. – Simple brass SANCTUARY RAILS designed by *William Butterfield* in 1894. – In the W bay of the chancel and under the crossing, oak CLERGY AND CHOIR STALLS in a Late Gothic manner, by *F. L. Pearson*, 1899–1901, the Bishop's Throne with small figures emblematic of the Christian Virtues round the richly carved canopy, the canons' stalls (two added in 1929) also canopied but less elaborate, the choir stalls simpler again. – At the W side of the crossing, a ROOD BEAM by *J. Ninian Comper*, 1924, bearing figures of a beardless crucified Christ flanked by Our Lady and St John. Comper's triple-arched stone screen below was removed *c.* 1985. – At the NW pier of the crossing, a round stone PULPIT, by *F. L. Pearson*, 1899–1901, with a foliaged frieze and tall foliage-capitalled columns between canopied panels which are carved with scenes of St Patrick Preaching to the Daughters of King Laoghaire, St Columba Preaching to King Brude, St Kentigern Preaching to the Workmen who Built his Churches, and St Cuthbert Preaching to the Shepherds at Melrose. – Simple Victorian PEWS in the nave. – (FONT at the W end, by *Butterfield*, 1890, of Bannockburn stone, with columns of

Peterhead granite. The tall oak FONT COVER, elaborately carved and with a figure of St George on the front, was added by *F. L. Pearson* in 1920.) – ORGAN, in a Late Gothic case (by Pearson, 1901), built by *J. Robson*, 1850, rebuilt by *Conacher & Co.*, 1872, enlarged by *Eustace Ingram* in 1890, again rebuilt by *John R. Miller*, 1901, and by *A. F. Edmonstone*, 1996.

STAINED GLASS. E window of the chancel (Our Lord in Glory), brightly coloured and archaic, by *Alexander Gibbs* from a design of *William Butterfield*, 1877. – In the transepts, the E windows (the Nativity and the Crucifixion of Our Lord) are of *c.* 1910. – In the S transept's gable, a late C19 rose window (the Holy Spirit (a Dove) surrounded by angels and foliage) – The nave windows are all by *Burlison & Grylls*. In the clearstorey, heraldic glass of the 1890s. – In the S aisle, a clearly drawn window (the Raising of the Son of the Widow of Nain; the Raising of Jairus's Daughter; the Raising of Lazarus) erected in 1894 as a memorial to the children of the twelfth Earl of Kinnoull, the figures being portraits of the Earl and members of his family. – In this aisle's W bay, another well-drawn window (the Good Shepherd; the Nativity of Our Lord; the Presentation of Our Lord in the Temple) of 1891. – Also of 1891 the very accomplished window (St Ninian Carrying a Model of the Cathedral, with SS Serf, Mungo, Drostan and Columba; a depiction of Candida Casa in the tracery) (St Ninian's church at Whithorn) in the E bay of the N aisle. – In the next bay a competent early C20 window (St Margaret of Scotland, St Elizabeth of Hungary and St Catherine of Siena). – More appealing is the window of 1904 in the aisle's W bay (Our Lord with St Ninian and St Andrew, and depictions of St Ninian's Cathedral, Perth, and the medieval St Andrews Cathedral). The W window of the nave (Old and New Testament Scenes of the Fall and Redemption of Man) is of 1890. – In the Lady Chapel, the E window (*Te Deum*) is by *James Powell & Sons* and accomplished. – Muddier window (*Nunc Dimittis*) of 1929 in the chapel's S wall.

MONUMENT to Bishop George Howard Wilkinson (†1901) under the arch between the chancel and Lady Chapel, designed by *F. L. Pearson* and executed in 1910–11. Stone sarcophagus and canopy of Aberfeldy soapstone bearing shields painted with the coats of arms of the diocese of St Andrews, Dunkeld and Dunblane and the Wilkinson family. On the sarcophagus, a bronze figure of Wilkinson, by *George Frampton*. The coped bishop kneels in prayer before a prie-dieu on which is a Bible open at a verse of Isaiah ('They that wait on the Lord . . .') and looks to a relief of the Crucifixion. It is a moving evocation of piety. – At the E end of the N aisle, the WALL MONUMENT erected to the Rev. Alexander Lendrum in 1911. Marble slab bearing brass plates depicting an elaborately decorated monstrance, the *Agnus Dei* on its front, and a chalice.

ST PAUL, corner of High Street and South Methven Street. Disused. Castellated Gothic, by *John Paterson*, 1806–7. A droved ashlar octagon, with long sides facing NE, NW, SE and

SW, and, fronting the cardinal points, shorter and slightly projecting elevations, each with a two-light window above a rectangular door. Just advanced from the N face is the front of the steeple which contains the main entrance from High Street. In each long side, a tall three-light window with intersecting tracery. At the outer corners of the short sides, slender attached shafts (their fluted bell capitals badly weathered) which support angle rounds projecting from the battlement. The N steeple's tower is of three stages marked off by string courses. In the two lower stages, a rectangular door under a two-light window of the same design as those in the other short sides. The third stage, clear of the wallhead of the church, contains a two-light window in each face. At the corner of this stage, attached shafts like those at the other short sides and, like them, supporting angle rounds at the tower battlement. Inside the battlement, an octagonal belfry of two stages, the upper marked off by a cornice-like string course. At the belfry's lower stage, clock dials on the N, E, W and S sides. At the upper stage these same faces are pierced by gableted two-light openings. Above, a rather squat octagonal spire.

Inside, the octagonal space is covered with a plaster vault rising to a central cupola. Gallery on cast-iron Tuscan column, the fronts with octagonal panels. The gallery now extends along all sides but the N section, which served as an organ loft, is of 1890–1 by *Andrew Heiton Jun.* who, at the same time, lowered and remodelled the pulpit, its stairs' sides ornamented with carved vines.

TAYSIDE CHRISTIAN FELLOWSHIP, Paradise Place. Built as a hall for St Stephen's United Free Church (now demolished) in 1899–1901, it is by *McLaren & Mackay*. Mullioned and transomed rectangular windows in the side walls. In the E gable, a Y-transomed three-light pointed window.

TRINITY CHURCH OF THE NAZARENE, York Place. Originally York Place United Presbyterian Church. By *Andrew Heiton Jun.*, 1858–9. Large but thinly detailed Romanesque. Big wheel window in the front gable which is flanked by set-back towers, their bellcast-eaved tall pyramidal roofs of Frenchy appearance. The interior has been subdivided.

GREYFRIARS BURIAL GROUND
off Canal Street and Tay Street

Opened on the site of the former Franciscan (Greyfriars) friary in 1580. From the C18, it has been filled by a major assembly of headstones and grave-slabs; the largest and best collection in the region, and one of the most important in Scotland. The E entrance from Tay Street was formed in 1999–2001. Corniced and ball-finialled GATEPIERS. Metal GATES with a large sunburst enclosing the initials PK (for Perth and Kinross), the sunburst's top bearing angels' heads; at the bottom, a band with reliefs of crossbones, skulls and hourglasses, recurrent motifs on the graveyard's monuments. They were made by

Ballantine Bo'ness Iron Co. from designs by *Perth & Kinross Council* and the *Scottish Urban Archaeological Trust*.

The original (N) entrance has early C19 corniced ashlar GATEPIERS and a footgate under a re-cut Latin inscription relating the universality of death. Inside, on the wall above the footgate, a SUNDIAL topped by a skull flanked by hourglasses. It is probably C17. – Immediately E of the entrance and projecting from the N wall is the FARQUHAR MAUSOLEUM of *c.* 1830, built of polished ashlar. At its front, a broad centrepiece with Roman Doric pilasters supporting a parapeted and ball-finialled entablature; Empire wreaths on the frieze. In each of the exposed faces, a console-corniced door (the S and E dummies). – To its E, an Ionic pilastered MONUMENT to John Cleland, by *William Burn*, 1836, in a C17 Scots Baroque manner. Cherub heads on the entablature; swan-neck pediment broken by a cartouche topped by a shell-filled segmental pediment. At the bottom, a sarcophagus with the relief of a human head at its centre. Bits of strapwork embellishment.

The burial ground is divided by a central path into two halves and the E further divided by paths into three sections.

Eastern Burial Ground

Near the NW corner of the N compartment, the HEADSTONE of Emmy Marshall, dated 1782, with an open swan-neck pediment. Mantled shield on one side, an angel's head (the soul) on the other. – To its S, a large weathered HEADSTONE of 1756 to IH carved with the relief of a tailor's shears and goose set among foliage. – E of the Marshall stone, the HEADSTONE erected by David Marquharson and Hellen Butchart to their children †1820, the W face with an angel's head from whose wingtips fall tassels which frame a merchant's mark (like the numeral 4). – To its E, the GRAVE-SLAB of Jean Anderson †1749, wife of David Drummond, a wright. It is carved with low relief shields, one bearing a coat of arms, the other a wright's tools. – On the E wall, MONUMENT to the Rev. Samuel George Kennedy, by *James Ritchie*, 1837. Roman Doric pilastered aedicule, the segmental pediment broken by a cartouche. In front of the aedicule, the statue of a lady mourning over a sarcophagus. – Beside it, a large MONUMENT to the Rev. William Wilson †1741 and Lord Provost Colin Brown †1741. It looks to be of the earlier C19. Aedicule with attached Corinthian columns and a swan-neck pediment. – Immediately to the W, the HEADSTONE of 1782 commemorating Elizabeth Blair, wife of David Grant, glover, the W face with an angel's head above a shield bearing gloves and the tools of a glover; emblems of death at the base. – On the W side of the path, an early C18 piecrust-bordered GRAVE-SLAB to J^{M}F (i.e. Mr John Fleming, minister of the West Church, †1719), its top end carved with an open Bible and angels' heads, the bottom with crossbones, a skull and hourglass. – Just to its W, the HEADSTONE of 1784 to TW and MP, the W face with an angel's head in the swan-neck pediment and a shield bearing a weaver's shuttle. – Beside the path on the S of this section, the GRAVE-SLAB erected by David Gibson, shipbuilder, and Kathrine Painter to their children †1783. It bears the relief of a ship with a pair of angels' heads floating above and reminders of death below. – Set back just to the N, a line of Georgian HEAD-STONES, the W face of each with an angel's head at the top, emblems of death at the base and a shield in the middle, the shield of the E stone (to Simon McKenzie, burgess weaver, †1774) bearing the stag's head of the McKenzie coat of arms, the next (now with an inscription to John Craigie) the shovel, broom and peat hook of a maltster, the W (erected by James Cowan, baker, to his parents and daughter †1810) with a corn sheaf and crossed baker's peels, each with a pair of loaves. – On the W side of this section, beside the central path, the HEADSTONE of 1821 to Patrick Just, baker, with a shield carved in fairly high relief with a hand holding scales above a corn sheaf. – To the N, a HEADSTONE of 1792 (now with an inscription to George Speed). Aedicular W face, with an angel's head in the tympanum, a shield bearing the implements of a maltster, and emblems of death at the base.

In the central section of the cemetery's E half, on the E wall, an early C19 MONUMENT to George Pentland †1806, the tablet set in a Gothick recess framed by columns of bundled shafts; flaming urns above the entablature. – To the W, several C18 HEADSTONES with curvy or pedimented tops. They include Archibald Martin, gardener burgess, †1701, with a shield bearing garden tools. Above, an angel's head; a skull, hourglass and crossbones below. – David Rough, glover, †1780, aedicular W face with a round cartouche bearing trade emblems. – Swan-neck-pedimented aedicular late C18 stone to John and William Corrie, with an angel's head. – David Keay, dated 1763, with a helm and mantled shield under an angel's head; reminders of mortality at the bottom. – Elspeth Barland, wife of Charles Bell, shoemaker, dated 1758, with a crowned cordiner's knife under an angel's head. – Beside the N–S central path, on the W, the stone erected to Helen Grigor †1780 by Thomas and Charles Grigor, shoemakers, also with a crowned cordiner's knife. Angel's head above; below, reminders of death. – Beside the path on the S side, near the E end, another stone erected (in 1781) by a shoemaker, William McKinnon, to his children, again with a cordiner's knife, here accompanied by a foot measure. – To its W, the large headstone of 1789 commemorating the children of Stewart Imrie, flesher. On the W face, an angel's head above a helm-crested and mantled shield which bears a sharpener, cleaver and knife; a skull, crossbones and hourglass below.

Some more HEADSTONES worth note in the S compartment of the graveyard's E half. On the N, beside the path, an ogee-arched stone, probably late C18, to Andrew Allan, merchant burgess, and his son Henry. On the E face, crisp carving of their initials, a merchant's mark and emblems of death; angel's head on the w face. – To the s, a glover's headstone of 1782, the w face with an angel's head above a foliage-bordered relief of gloves, stretchers, shears and a buckle. – To its w, the large stone of James Young †1714 and nine of his grandchildren, probably erected by his son John, a merchant, †1753. On the w face, a shield bearing a merchant's mark, with an angel's head above and crossbones, a skull and hourglass below.

At the centre of the graveyard's s end, a SHELTER erected in 1999–2001 to house monuments moved here for protection from the elements. On its back wall (the s wall of the graveyard), a badly weathered stone of 1580 to IB. Set into the ground, HEADSTONES and GRAVE-SLABS, mostly arranged in pairs. At the E end, two headstones. One, dated 1701, commemorates the children of William Austine. Flanking the inscription are terminal-figured Ionic pilasters. Above, a crown over two trumpeting cherubs. – Beside it, a stone of 1745 to John Young, merchant. On the w face, the high relief of a purse set in a shallow relief of foliage and, below, a shield bearing a merchant's mark; emblems of death at the base.

Headstone of Alexander Bisset, barber and wigmaker, †1777, with a shield bearing razors, a comb and a wig stand. Again, an angel's head and reminders of death. – Grave-slab of John Shioch †1651, the front bearing a crowded relief of startlingly inept quality under the words FAITH CHARITY & HOPE. The same three nouns appear individually further down implying that the carved figures on the l. are emblematic of Faith, those in the middle of Charity and those on the r. of Hope. At the top, two angels' heads, a dove in the centre, and the bust of a figure holding a crown (of life) on the r. Below the dove, what may be intended as a representation of the Virgin and Child above a figure apparently standing in a pulpit, the tips of the fingers of his upraised hand supporting a chalice topped by a bird. Beside this figure, two birds pecking at an inverted heart. Below the round-headed arches of the pulpit's substructure, crossed bones. On the l., the figure of a man accompanying a boy, each having one hand raised, a chalice balanced on the fingertips of the man's. On the r., a couple of anchors (conventional symbols of Hope) but also a cockerel (perhaps suggesting the dawn of a new day), its humanoid face possibly the result of ineptitude rather than intention. On shields at the bottom corners of the stone, an iron and a pair of shears showing that it commemorates a tailor.

Headstone of Andrew Kippen, former Deacon of the Glovers Incorporation, dated 1761. On the E face, the inscription in a frame of flowering foliage under an angel's head. In the aedicular w face's swan-neck pediment, more angels' heads around a heraldic shield. Below, a carved display of leather breeches and gloves, stretchers, shears and a buckle. – Headstone of 1759 to Ishbel Laing, wife of David Scott, mason. On the w face, the familiar angel's head and reminders of death. Between them, a shield bearing three castles (the heraldic emblem of the masons) and a chevron formed by compasses superimposed on a setsquare. – E of this, the headstone of the Peters family, carriers, dated 1777, the reliefs including one of a horse pulling a cart and held by a diminutive man. – Headstone erected in 1782 by Daniel Cameron, gardener, to his father, John. On the W face, an angel's head above a depiction of Adam and Eve holding the Tree of Knowledge which stands on a boss carved with a gardener's tools; bones, a skull and hourglass at the bottom. – Grave-slab erected by David Scott, sailor and merchant in Bombay, †1758 in memory of his mother †1755. In the top corners, reliefs of angels' heads and, between them, a ship; below, a heraldic achievement, the supporters in C18 dress. Under the inscription, a skull, crossbones and hourglass. – Grave-slab of 1636 to Thomas Anderson, flesher. Cartouche flanked by a skull and crossbones at the top. Below, figures of Father Time and a kneeling naked man flank a skull. At the bottom, an angel's head surmounts a shield on which is depicted a butcher slaughtering an ox whose head is gripped by a dog. – Headstone to Cirsten Biset †1777, wife of Robert Browhouse, sailor. The top of the swan-neck pediment is carved with trumpeting angels and a skull. On the W face, foliage-finialled Ionic pilasters, their shafts decorated with flaming torches, frame a ship above a heraldic achievement. On the E face, an angel's head in the tympanum. Initials and skeletons on the ends of the inscription scroll; emblems of death at the base. – Headstone of 1788 to William Clement, dyer, its W face bearing the usual angel's head and emblems of death. In the middle, a shield carved with a hand, dyer's press and tongs.

Western Burial Ground

Near the S end of the W wall, a Celtic CROSS commemorating the architect Andrew Heiton Sen. †1853, presumably designed by his son and partner, *Andrew Heiton Jun.* – Set into the grass, a good number of C18 and early C19 HEADSTONES, many with the familiar angels' heads and emblems of death. Near the S end, beside the burial ground's central path, a stone of 1781 to the daughter of David Imrie, baker, with a wheatsheaf-crested shield displaying a saltire of baker's peels and loaves. – To the N, the headstone erected in 1788 by Alexander Paul, tailor, to his children, its shield with a tailor's goose, scissors and sharpener. – Some way further N, the headstone of 1787 to Christian Anderson erected by her husband, John Rodgie, maltster, with a shield bearing the tools of his trade. – To the W, a curvaceously pedimented aedicule of 1783 to the children of Charles Eldge, mason, its shield with a mason's coat of arms of three castles and a chevron of dividers superimposed on a setsquare. – Immediately to the N, Jean Culbert †1747, the daughter of James Culbert, merchant, with a merchant's mark. – E of this, near the central path, a swan-neck-pedimented stone of 1769 (now with an inscription to James Chalmers), the W face with a helm-crested and mantled lozenge carved with a mason's level above a mell, wedge, plumb line and pair of chisels. – Beside the path, the headstone of Thomas Robertson, glover, dated 1759. On the E face, a pair of small angels' heads above the inscription. On the W, the head of a third angel above a display of gloves and a glover's tools. Beside it, to the N, the swan-neck-pedimented stone erected in 1784 to the children of William Morison, maltster, with a helm-crested and mantled shield. – Immediately W, the headstone erected in 1782 by James Kermook, smith, to David Proudfoot, the W face with an angel's head in its swan-neck pediment and the crowned hammer of a smith below. – W of this, the contemporary swan-neck-pedimented stone of William McOmie, its W face with the relief of an urn above a merchant's mark. – A little to the NE, the headstone of David Cameron, erected by his father Daniel, merchant in Perth, in 1784. The aedicular W face's open pediment contains an angel's head above a swag from whose ends drop tassels to frame a shield with a merchant's mark. – Another crisply carved merchant's mark on the headstone of 1782 to Thomas Swan to the NE. – E of this, another aedicular stone erected in 1791 by Alexander Ferrier, Deacon of the Weaver Incorporation, to his children, the W face's shield bearing a macabre display of three human heads, their mouths stuffed with shuttles. – To the NE, a headstone of 1761 to the children of Thomas Bisset, flesher, the half-eroded shield carved with a cleaver and knife. – W of this, the headstone of 1774 to Ann Christy, its W face's shield surmounted by an ineptly sculpted pair of angel trumpeters. – To the NW, the stone erected in 1769 to commemorate John Stewart, merchant, the E face with an angel's head, the W with Stewart's coat of arms above a merchant's mark and emblems of death. – E of the Stewart stone, a curly-topped headstone of 1764 to the children of another merchant, Patrick Duff, its W face carved with a mounted knight (the crest of the Duffs, Earls of Fife). – NW of John Stewart's headstone, one of 1763 (now with an inscription to Archibald Menzies), its W face's shield with the mash-oar, broom and shovel of a brewer or maltster. – To the N, a stone of 1779 to Hugh Livingston, smith, its W face a pilastered and swan-neck-pedimented aedicule with an angel's head above a helm-crested and mantled shield bearing the crowned hammer of the smiths. – Just to the NE, the stone erected in 1763 by Robert McDonald and his wife, Grant Stewart, to their children. A merchant's mark on the E face; on the W, an angel's head above the Stewart coat of arms, with a skull, crossbones and hourglass below. – In the graveyard's NW corner, the headstone of 1784 erected by James Gib, hammerman (smith), to his daughter Grizel, the W face's shield with a crowned hammer. – Near the NE corner of this half of the burial ground, the headstone of Thomas Oliphant †1746, its shield with a merchant's mark. – To the SE, beside the central path, the GRAVE-SLAB (now up-ended) of William Moncrieff, shoemaker, dated 1712, its shield displaying a lion rampant and shoemaker's tools.

PUBLIC BUILDINGS

A. K. BELL PUBLIC LIBRARY, York Place. Jarring juxtaposition of two ideas of classicism. The front block, designed by *W. M. Mackenzie*, was built as the Perth City and County Infirmary in 1836–8. Two storeys of polished ashlar, the ground floor channelled except at the centrepiece. Eleven-bay E-plan N front, the end bays slightly advanced and with consoled tall parapets. Boldly advanced and taller three-bay centrepiece, its consoled parapet topped by scrolls supporting a shell finial; projecting from this centrepiece, a porte cochère with round-arched and console-keystoned openings. The entrance and flanking windows behind the porte cochère are round-arched. So too are the centrepiece's first-floor windows and central niche, all contained in overarches which spring from broad pilasters. Above the ground-floor windows of the links, a band course decorated with Empire garlands; panelled aprons under the first-floor windows. In the end bays, overarched and round-headed windows at the ground floor. The first-floor windows' architraves have an entasis and are surmounted by pediments with anthemion finials.

The former Infirmary now forms an appendage to the much larger back block added by *Perth & Kinross District Council Architectural Services Department* in 1992–4, its totalitarian Postmodern classicism strikingly unsympathetic to the gentle good manners of the 1830s work.

To the NE, a single-storey LODGE of the 1830s, built of polished ashlar. In the three-bay front, the aproned centre and the l. window's architraves have marked entasis. The r. bay of the front contains a side entrance under a panelled 'apron' to a porch whose main entrance is from the W through a screen of Greek Doric columns. The building was remodelled and repositioned by *David Smart* in 1867.

CALEDONIAN ROAD PRIMARY SCHOOL, Caledonian Road. By *Andrew Heiton Jun.*, 1890. Tall two storeys and attic, built of red Corncockle stugged ashlar with polished dressings. Flemish Renaissance, with Dutch gables and gablets. Roman Doric aedicular doorpiece with strapwork and relief busts carved at the base of the columns; foliage and a cartouche in the pediment. – To the NE and facing Kinnoull Causeway, a detached block by *A. G. Heiton*, built as the Advanced Department in 1900. Again of stugged red sandstone with polished dressings and of two storeys and an attic but lower. Squat Ionic columns across the first floor of the front.

COUNCIL BUILDINGS, corner of High Street and Tay Street. Built as the head office of the General Accident, Fire & Life Assurance Corporation, an institution of such importance in the life of Perth that the building could be regarded as 'public' even before its conversion to Perth and Kinross District Council's headquarters in 1984.

The main block is by *G. P. K. Young* but built in two stages. The first, of 1898–1901, produced the elevation to Tay Street, the corner tower and the three bays W of that facing High Street. The second, in 1920, extended the High Street frontage W by two further bays, the original end (entrance) bay becoming a centrepiece and having its top remodelled, the original crowning carved stonework and balustrade being reused at the new W bay. The style is opulent English Baroque of the Belcher/Pite school, perhaps mediated through Charles Rennie Mackintosh's unexecuted competition design of 1894 for the Royal Insurance building in Glasgow.

Three storeys and an attic, faced with yellow Woodburn (Cumbrian) sandstone, the masonry channelled the full height of the centre bay of the High Street (N) front and at the slightly advanced and taller end bays. These form the building's compositional frame, together with the mutuled and balustraded wallhead cornice over the intermediate bays which continues the line of a moulded and guttaed band across the end bays and rises, at the centre of each front, into an open segmental pediment supported on leafy consoles. At the NE corner, a tower whose consoled cornice, enriched with egg-and-dart ornament, carries a balustrade, the corners crowned by massive swagged vases (like all the carved stonework, executed by *William Shirreffs* of Glasgow). Within the balustrade of this corner tower, a domed octagonal cupola; projecting from each of its N, W, S and E faces, an open-pedimented Ionic portico fronts a round-arched keystoned opening. On top of the cupola's main dome, a small second cupola in the form of a Doric columned rotunda, its gold-coloured roof surmounted by a Baroque finial. At the three main floors of the corner tower, corniced windows; projecting in front of the tall first-floor openings are balconies, the soffits of their supporting stone brackets carved with acanthus, their fronts with lions' heads.

At the S bay of the E (Tay Street) elevation, a tall lugged-architraved door; above, a panel carved with swagged foliage and flanked by grotesque heads which serve as consoles under a cornice which is carried round the building above the ground floor. At this bay, minimally lugged architraves to the first- and second-floor windows, those of the second floor corniced. At the top, a cornice and balustrade like those on the NE tower. Very similar treatment at the W bay of the N (High Street) front but, instead of a door, a ground-floor window flanked by pilaster-like corniced panels and with swags extending from its keystone.

In the centre bay of the N front, the tall main entrance framed by banded Ionic attached columns surmounted by sculptures of kneeling gentlemen who support the ends of the segmental pediment, its tympanum bearing a cartouche; below the pediment, a frieze carved with foliage. At the first floor, a lugged-architraved window set in a quasi-Doric aedicule, its pilasters' capitals surmounted by leafy consoles under the pediment which is broken by a cartouche supported by two *putti*. At the second floor, a lugged-architraved and corniced window like those of the end bays but with its keystone expanded upwards to form a huge foliaged console under the wallhead's open segmental pediment.

The other bays of both the N and E elevations are marked off by banded quasi-Doric pilasters rising to the cornice above the ground floor which is given further support by the leafily consoled keystones of the big round-arched ground-floor windows; large plain consoles under their sills. A sill course joins the tall windows of the first floor, their architraves minimally lugged and topped at the ends by fat consoles which combine with the tall keystones to support open segmental pediments. At the second floor, small windows recessed behind screens of squat Ionic columns, their shafts of red sandstone.

Large W extension of the same height but containing an extra floor by *G. P. K. Young & Son*, 1932. It is a drastically simplified version of the original building and quotes its second-floor detail of windows recessed behind Ionic colonnades.

The entrance at the E end of the High Street frontage opens into the former general office. Occupying most of the ground floor of the original building, this is a tall space divided into three aisles by marble Doric columns. From their capitals extend large stucco leaves along the undersides of the beams of the panelled plaster ceiling. At the S end of the E aisle, a rather narrow elliptical-headed archway, its pilastered marble jambs surmounted by bronze figures of crouching allegorical ladies. Behind the arch is the stair to the upper floors, its top landing covered by a coved and panelled ceiling. Oak balustrades carved (by *John Crawford*) in a richly detailed free Scots Renaissance manner. The windows of the half-landing are filled with STAINED GLASS by *A. Ballantine & Gardiner*, incorporating emblems of the kingdoms of Scotland, England and Ireland and the coats of arms of the city of Perth and of directors of the General Accident, Fire & Life Assurance Corporation.

COUNTY BUILDINGS, corner of South Street and Tay Street. Designed as an adjunct to Perth Sheriff Court but now in other use. By *David Smart*, 1864–6. Classical with an Italian inflexion, built of polished ashlar. The polite two-storey eleven-bay front to South Street reads as two five-bay palazzi, with rusticated angle quoins, joined by a slightly recessed single-bay link. At each 'palazzo', ground-floor windows with lugged architraves and consoled sills, aproned and corniced first-floor windows, those of the outer bays with consoled triangular pediments, the centre window with a consoled segmental pediment and with scrolled bases to the sides of its architrave, and Roman Doric aedicular doorpieces. But the E 'palazzo' is more expensively detailed than the W, with three-light windows in the end bays, panelled aprons, and a columned doorpiece.

More forceful because the detail is less thinly spread is the three-bay end elevation to Tay Street. Windows like those of the E 'palazzo' of the main front. On the wallhead, a pair of scroll-sided chimneystacks linked by an attic window of two round-headed lights with pilastered mullions and jambs. w extension by *Woodside-Parker*, 2003.

FERGUSSON GALLERY, Marshall Place and Tay Street. A Graeco-Roman temple, prominently sited at the NE corner of the South Inch as if to announce to the traveller from the s the public virtue of the city of Perth. This was built to house the reservoir tank and engine house of the Perth Waterworks in 1830–2, the design provided by *Adam Anderson*, Rector of the Perth Academy.

Water taken from the River Tay passed through a filter bed on Moncreiffe Island and was piped under the river to the waterworks where it was pumped by a steam-engine into the tank. From here it was distributed through pipes to the streets of the city.

The TANK is contained in a two-stage domed rotunda. Lower stage, *c.* 12.2 m. high, of polished sandstone ashlar with Roman Doric pilasters and a balustraded entablature. Each bay is panelled. Above the s door, large but not very elegant cast-iron letters, added *c.* 1846, spell out the motto AQUAM/ IGNE ET AQUA/HAURIO ('I raise water by fire and water') which was devised by Anderson. The upper stage (the tank itself), set back behind the balustrade, was originally constructed of curved cast-iron plates (painted stone colour) made by the *Dundee Foundry Co.*, the bays divided by fluted Ionic pilasters. In each bay, a tall blind window, architraved and console-corniced. On the frieze, horizontal panels containing swags and, above the pilasters, square anthemion-decorated panels. The dome above is ribbed and surmounted by a low cupola, its drum decorated with more anthemion.

Adjoining on the N is the flat-roofed ENGINE HOUSE, of the same height as the rotunda's lower stage and with Roman Doric corner pilasters, each topped by a triglyph; panelled parapet. This block serves as a pedestal for the tall CHIMNEY disguised as a Doric-capitalled column topped by an urn (a fibreglass replacement of 1973 for the original which was struck by lightning in 1871).

The building's original use was lost when a new waterworks at Gowans Terrace was opened in 1965. It was converted to a Tourist Information Centre by *Morris & Steedman* in 1972–4 when a s addition of 1900 was removed. The interior was reconstructed in 1991–2 as a gallery displaying works by J. D. Fergusson (1874–1961) and others, by *Perth & Kinross District Council Architectural Services Department* with *McLaren, Murdoch & Hamilton*. The dome was re-roofed by *Bell Ingram Design*, 2003–4.

In front, a stylized headless bronze STATUE ('*Torse de Femme*') modelled by *J. D. Fergusson*, 1918, and cast in 1994.

FORTEVIOT HALL. *See* Churches: Free Presbyterian Church, above.

HARBOUR, Harbour Road. Small tidal basin constructed in 1840, the design by *Robert Stevenson & Sons* a modified version of one prepared by the same firm in 1834. The walls are now faced with concrete.

KING JAMES VI HOSPITAL, Albert Place, Hospital Street and King Street. Now housing. Built as an almshouse and school in 1748–52 (dated 1750 on the S front). Harled, the cement dressings provided in *J. Morrison*'s restoration of 1973. H-plan of four storeys and an attic, the third-floor windows small, the attic lit only by windows in the gables. Open pediments over the centre bays of the main block and wings. On top of the main block, an octagonal cupola with a lead-covered ogee-domed roof and copper weathercock. In each face of the cupola, a round-headed opening (dummies on alternate faces); clock dials above. The original main entrance (now a window) was in the S front, a Roman Doric columned and pedimented doorpiece with triglyphs on the frieze. The simpler pilastered and pedimented N doorpiece looks an early C19 addition, as do the single-storey piend-roofed outshots at the N ends of the wings. Above the first-floor window of the N front, a cartouche carved with a human head.

OLD COUNCIL CHAMBERS, corner of High Street and Tay Street. Flemish-flavoured secular Gothic in stugged grey ashlar, by *Andrew Heiton Jun.*, 1878–9. The building's civic importance is expressed by the S range, fronting High Street, in which is the Council Chamber itself. The range is divided into two unequal parts by a minimally advanced tower, a version of the medieval tower of St Mary's Chapel which had stood on the site. Its top stage is broached to an octagon and covered by a slated spire. At the SE corner of the range, a fat column, its top carved with shields displaying the individual quarters of the royal arms and a thistle, serves as a stem to support a slender round turret surmounted by an octagonal upper stage pierced by depressed arches and finished with a slated spire; this turret was intended as a reminder of a turret

Perth, Old Council Chambers.
Perspective

on the former Tolbooth which stood here. The presence of the Council Chamber in the E part of this range is disclosed by large mullioned and transomed S windows and, at the E gable, a canted oriel, the lowest of its supporting corbels carved with the City arms. Over this E part, a central gablet decorated with diaper work and a cinquefoil panel. At the slightly shorter E part of the S range, a couple more gablets. The tall mullioned and transomed upper windows try to suggest the presence of a second tall chamber behind but the presence of another floor is disclosed by stone panels halfway up their height.

N of the gable of the S range the Tay Street elevation is almost domestic but with giant pointed overarches and a couple of French pavilion-roofed towers. In the gablet over the entrance to the District Court, a small shield bearing a relief of Justice. S of this, a parapeted Tudorish doorpiece with a panel stating that THIS.HOUSE.LOVES.PEACE:HATES.KNAVES.CRIMES. PUNISHETH/PRESERVES.THE.LAWS.AND.GOOD.MEN. HONOURETH.

Inside, the High Street entrance, a Gothic stone staircase. At the half-landing, a STAINED GLASS window by *James Ballantine & Son*, 1880, depicting a youthful Queen Victoria and Prince Albert. The Old Council Chamber itself (restored to the 1878 design by *A. G. Heiton*, 1895–6, after a fire) is a great hall, the hammerbeam roof with stencil decoration and springing from stone corbels carved with emblems of the guildry incorporations of Perth. Canopied stone fireplace containing a C17 cast-iron FIREBACK which bears the royal coat of arms. Strongly coloured pictorial STAINED GLASS of 1880 by *James Ballantine & Son*. In the S windows portraits of historical and quasi-historical characters in Sir Walter Scott's *The Fair Maid of Perth*, in the E a scene of Robert the Bruce Recapturing Perth from the English.

PERTH BRIDGE, from Charlotte Street to Main Street. The first bridge constructed over the Tay at Perth since the collapse of its predecessor in 1617. By *John Smeaton*, 1766–71, built of pinky-coloured sandstone ashlar. Seven segmental main arches and a smaller flood arch at each end. Low triangular cutwaters. In the spandrels, large round panels of black stone. The top was widened in 1869 by *Allan D. Stewart* who added the bracketed footpaths on each side; on their metal parapets, slender cast-iron lamp standards by *Laidlaw* of Glasgow, also of 1869.

PERTH CITY HALL, King Edward Street. Beaux-Arts classical, by *H. E. Clifford & Lunan*, 1908–11, the carved detail almost mechanical in its precision. It is a large ruthlessly symmetrical corniced and parapeted box of polished ashlar with channelled strips at the corners. At the principal (W) front, a screen of paired giant Ionic columns between the advanced ends on which sit large statues of cherubs holding the ends of swags. Behind the screen, three round-headed entrances, the outer two surmounted by reliefs of crowns, the centre door by a shield bearing the coat of arms of the City of Perth. At each end of the front, a main window whose keystone rises as a flattened console into a broken pediment; at the base of the window, a pedestal breaks through the architrave. Below these windows are swags and, beneath these, small segmental-arched openings lighting a basement.

At each of the long side elevations, slightly advanced end bays, their window-surmounted entrances recessed between paired Ionic columns. The windows of the other bays are taller but less ornate versions of the front windows. At the E end, five tall round-arched windows at the centre; at each end, a double tier of rectangular lights. Dry Baroque INTERIOR. In the Main Hall, a basket-arched ceiling, gallery round three sides and huge organ at the E end. Proposals for conversion to a shopping mall were prepared in 2006.

PERTH CONCERT HALL, Mill Street. By *Building Design Partnership* (project architect: *Bruce Kennedy*), 2003–5. A large public building hidden away in back streets. The general shape is oval, the curtain walls clad in white pre-cast concrete, white render and glass and topped by a boldly oversailing canopy. Rising above the centre, a ribbed green copper curved roof over the auditorium. Arbitrary-seeming angular projections at the sides. At the S front, a rectangular notch in the oval shape contains the entrance. Inside, a glass-walled large foyer of two-storey height, its slate floor and resonant acoustic suggestive of an airport concourse. Over the foyer's N balcony, the curved underbelly of the auditorium's gallery. The auditorium itself, designed to seat 1,200, is oblong with a sloped ceiling and galleries on three sides. In the area, raked seating which can be stowed away if the floor is raised to provide a level surface. Wooden boarding on the walls of the stage at the N end.

PERTH MUSEUM AND ART GALLERY, George Street. Disjointed product of two stages of development. The N part was built in 1822–4 as a memorial ('Marshall's Monument') to Thomas Hay Marshall of Glenalmond, a former Lord Provost of the city. It housed the Perth Library and the museum of the Perth Literary and Antiquarian Society whose Secretary, *David Morison*, produced the design. Loosely derived from the Pantheon in Rome, this is a whitepainted copper-domed Ionic pilastered rotunda but with its E segment sliced off and fronted by an Ionic tetrastyle portico, the frieze under the pediment bearing the words T. H. MARSHALL, CIVES GRATI. In each curved bay of the rotunda, a tall rectangular niche with a panel below. Behind the portico, three tall dummy doors, with a single horizontal panel above their rectangular fanlights. In 1931–5 *Smart, Stewart & Mitchell* added the large S extension. This is authoritarian civic architecture built of honey-coloured ashlar. In the original portico, a bronze STATUE of Marshall erected in the mid or later C19.

PERTH PRISON, Edinburgh Road. Massive complex dominating the S approach to the city, the buildings half-hidden by the sur-

Perth Prison.
Bird's-eye view, by J. D. Collinson, *c.* 1810

rounding wall. It was begun in 1811–12 as The Depôt, Scotland's principal place of internment for French prisoners-of-war, abandoned two years after completion and largely rebuilt in 1840–59 as the General Prison for Scotland. Much piecemeal redevelopment in the later C20 and early C21.

The Depôt was designed by *Robert Reid* as a military fort but with its defences intended to withstand attack from the interior. U-shaped, with its mouth to the W, surrounded by a moat and an outer wall, the parapet reached by external stairs. Placed along the perimeter were the principal buildings, with accommodation for *c.* 7,000 men. These consisted of a two-storey block housing petty officers (the officers themselves free on parole) at the SW corner, a hospital, also of two storeys, at the NW and five three-storey barrack blocks, each for 1,140 men, along the curved E side fronted by walled exercise yards radiating from a tall observation tower flanked by kitchens. Immediately W of the moat, at the centre of the U, stood lodges flanking the drawbridge entrance. W of these, in a courtyard outside the main wall and filling the open mouth of the U, two single-storey blocks to accommodate guards and a pair of houses for the Agent or Governor and Surgeon and, across the W side of this courtyard, a pair of guardrooms flanking the outer entrance.

In 1839 the newly appointed General Board of Directors of Prisons in Scotland chose The Depôt as the site for a General Prison for Scotland to house all Scottish convicts sentenced to terms of imprisonment of nine months or more. Under the scheme prepared for the Directors by *Thomas Brown Jun.* the moat was infilled and the perimeter wall heightened and its external stairs removed. The buildings which had stood in the courtyard W of the moat and main wall were retained, the guardrooms being used as stores, the Agent's and Surgeon's houses accommodating the Governor and Chaplain and the guards' barracks prison warders. The lodges flanking the former drawbridge were replaced by a gatehouse. Inside the main wall the former petty officers' quarters housed insane convicts and the hospital continued its original use, as did one kitchen block, the other becoming a laundry. The observation tower was converted to a huge chimney serving the heating system of the new cell blocks and the two-storey block round its base rebuilt as the Governor's office and a reception centre for new inmates. The five blocks of prisoner-of-war barracks round the E curve of the U were demolished, their position and design making them unsuitable for a prison planned on the 'separate' system of rigorous solitary confinement of inmates which it had been decided should be adopted for the new General Prison for Scotland.

The planning of prisons on the 'separate' system had been standardised by the late 1830s when both the Model Prison at Pentonville, London, and the General Prison for Scotland at Perth were designed (respectively by *Joshua Jebb* and *Thomas Brown Jun.*), their layout combining the isolation of prisoners with effective but economical supervision. From a central observation block manned by warders radiated cell blocks, the sound-proof individual cells strung out either side of galleried full-height central corridors. Between the cell blocks were circular exercise yards divided by radiating high walls into compartments, each intended for the solitary and silent exercise of one prisoner at a time. In his design for the prison at Perth Brown planned four four-storey cell blocks radiating from a full-height semicircular observation corridor built behind the original observation tower of The Depôt. The central segment of the corridor and the NE and SE cell blocks were built in 1840–2. In 1852–9 the corridor was extended at each end to its originally intended length and the N and S cell blocks constructed, their design by *Robert Matheson* much more 'architectural' than Brown's blocks of ten years before. Further detached blocks to house juvenile and insane prisoners were built to the S of the main complex later in the C19. During the C20, the 'separate' system having been abandoned, communal workshops were constructed. Extensive remodelling and redevelopment, begun in the 1980s, is still in progress (2007).

A short stretch of the early C19 rubble-built PERIMETER WALL survives at the NW corner. The rest was replaced in the C20 with pre-cast aggregate panels. Near the N end of the W side, two former GUARDROOM BLOCKS of 1811–12. Each is single-storey, built of rough ashlar and with bracketed broad eaves to the piended roofs. W fronts of nine bays, the ends slightly advanced, the windows set in segmental-headed overarches. Behind the N guardroom, the contemporary former SURGEON'S HOUSE, also of rough ashlar and piend-roofed with broad eaves. Two-storey, a pilastered doorpiece bereft of its cornice at the three-bay W front. The barrack blocks behind have been replaced by utilitarian mid-C20 housing. The space behind the S guardroom, formerly the site of the Agent's house and barracks, is now occupied by the VISITOR CENTRE of 1983–6, the prison's present principal entrance. Ashlar-clad and piend-roofed but uncertain whether to respect or contrast with the C19 architecture, it is neither imposing nor friendly. To its W and SW, a large car park.

The 1840s GATEHOUSE is on the axis of the roadway between the two former guardrooms. Piend-roofed, of two storeys, the W corners splayed. W front with a battlemented centrepiece containing the segmental-arched pend entrance under a trio of round-headed windows, the central merlon bearing a clock face. Round-headed windows to the ground floor, those of the upper floor enlarged in utilitarian fashion in the C20. At the E elevation, battlements over the centre and ends, all the windows round-headed. Pyramid-roofed cupola rising behind the centre battlement. The observation tower of The Depôt which stood behind was demolished in the late C20. Behind, the semicircular curve of the 1840s and 1850s CORRIDOR BLOCK from which radiated the cell blocks. It is of four storeys, rubble-built and battlemented except at the slightly advanced centre which is finished with a plain parapet and pierced by large three-light windows. Stretching out to the S and N from its W ends are the cell blocks (A HALL and D HALL) of the 1850s, both ashlar-faced and of four storeys, with small cell windows and battlements with exceptionally long merlons along their sides. The W corners of their inner ends are clasped by towers whose battlements are carried on moulded corbels. Round-headed openings at the lower floors of these towers and elliptical-arched windows above. At the main inner gables of these blocks, three-light windows, the top floor's Venetian but with round-headed sidelights, light the cell blocks' central corridors; battlements of crowstepped form. Less emphatic towers clasp the W corners of the outer ends. The outer gables are very like the inner but the windows combined as single very tall openings, the gallery levels inside marked only by transoms. A jamb projects E of the N wing flush with its N gable. Similar jamb at the S wing but semi-octagonal-sided and with three-light windows. Over the centre of each of these cell blocks, a large battlemented octagonal ventilator tower.

Of Brown's two radial cell blocks of 1840–2 the SE (C HALL) survives, also of four storeys but rubble-walled and quite plain. Late C20 ribbed metal addition at the piended outer end.

At the prison's NW corner, the HOSPITAL of 1811–12. Two storeys, plain and rather altered, its piended roof with bracketed broad eaves. At the SW corner, some Late Victorian blocks, also plain.

PERTH SHERIFF COURT, Tay Street. Greek Revival, by *Robert Smirke*,* 1816-19. E-plan, designed to house Justiciary and Sheriff Courts and, in the s wing, the County Hall or assembly room. Tall single-storey façade of thirteen bays, built of buff-coloured polished ashlar, the wallhead finished with a triglyph frieze under a parapet. The walling of the seven-bay centrepiece is recessed but projecting from it is a Greek Doric colonnade which breaks forward at the five centre bays as an octostyle pedimented portico. Behind the portico the three centre bays are minimally advanced between pilasters and contain a trio of round-arched entrances. Over the flanking windows either side, small 'attic' openings.

At the three-bay end sections, corniced windows. The centre window of the s section is a dummy filled in 1867 with a bronze RELIEF by *John Steell* depicting Gowrie House which stood on the site until 1807; below the main relief, another bearing the Royal Arms of Scotland and the arms of the Earls of Gowrie.

In each of the N and s elevations, a trio of three-light windows with tall pilaster mullions, the N windows under Diocletian overlights, the s with semicircular fanlights. The rear is dominated by the central wing, a replacement of 1866-7 by *David Smart*. Two-storey, with round-headed windows at the upper level. Piended roof masked by a w parapet surmounted by massive corniced chimney-like ventilator shafts.

The layout of the INTERIOR is mostly as designed by Smirke, its architectural detail largely the product of *David Smart*'s remodelling of 1866-7. At the centre, a two-storey entrance hall, its plain coffered ceiling of the 1860s, broken by a central roof-light. On the w side, a T-plan stair with severe stone parapets, the shouldered arches under the side landings formed by Smart. These contain the ground-floor entrances to Court No. 1 (originally Justiciary Court), Smart's square replacement for Smirke's semicircular courtroom. Two-storey height, the coffered ceiling with rosetted stiles and a large central ventilator. High-set round-headed windows framed by pilastered arcading along three sides. Gallery on cast-iron leaf-capitalled columns at the E end. At the w, the judge's bench in a broad basket-arched recess under a bracketed canopy which extends the full length of this wall. On the ground floor of the N wing, a pair of back-to-back sheriff courts, both with compartmented ceilings. The whole of the s wing is filled by Smirke's County Hall (now general office). Panelled ceiling with rinceau enrichment on the stiles. The walls' arcading is presumably of the 1860s.

PERTH THEATRE, High Street. By *William Alexander*, 1898-1900. The front is a red sandstone ashlar tenement of plainest Georgian survival character, the theatre's presence announced by a projecting canopy added in 1967. From the entrance a

---

*Smirke was appointed after a limited competition in which designs were also submitted by *William Atkinson* and *Wyatt* (either *Benjamin Dean Wyatt* or *Jeffrey Wyatt*, later *Wyattville*).

long corridor leads to the auditorium. This is a tall and rather narrow oblong, restored after a fire in 1924, the fronts of the dress circle and upper circle breaking into shallow bows decorated with rococo enrichment.

PERTH WATERWORKS. *See* Fergusson Gallery, above.

POLICE HEADQUARTERS, Barrack Street. Built in 1977. Inelegantly proportioned six-storey tower, with alternating layers of glass and aggregate cladding. – In front, the red sandstone SCULPTURE of an eagle. It came from the former Police Station of 1895–6 in Tay Street.

PUBLIC SEMINARIES, Rose Terrace. Now offices. Built in 1803–7 as the Public Seminaries to house Perth Grammar School and Perth Academy; the architect was *Robert Reid*. Two storeys in the height of the adjoining houses' three. The manner is Adamish. Five-bay front of polished ashlar, the square-jointed rustication of the ground floor crossed by a band course at the height of the springing of the fanlights over the windows and doors. In each of the advanced end bays, a door under a semicircular fanlight. In the three centre bays, three-light windows, again under fanlights. At the first floor, in each end bay, a tall three-light window with Roman Doric column-mullions and an overall fanlight; these windows are flanked by carved stone rosettes. The walling of the three-bay centrepiece is set back from the plane of the ground floor behind a screen of attached and paired Roman Doric columns *in antis*; console-corniced windows surmounted by rectangular panels. The wallhead entablature is plain except for guttae at the end bays and rosettes over the columns of the centrepiece. Above, a balustrade broken at the centre by a stepped pedestal containing a clock face (by *James Ritchie & Son*) and surmounted by a standing stone figure (by *W. Birnie Rhind*) of Britannia accompanied by a lion, the clock and sculpture both erected in 1886.* At the rubble-walled rear, a full-height semi-octagonal wing with three-light windows at both floors, those of the first under segmental fanlights.

Inside, the octagonal SW first-floor room (originally the principal room of Perth Academy) has round-headed arcading on the walls under a rosetted frieze; domed ceiling with a large plaster rose.

QUEEN'S BRIDGE, from Tay Street to Dundee Road. By *F. A. MacDonald & Partners*, 1960. Of pre-stressed concrete construction. Three elliptically arched spans (the centre very long) carried on keel-shaped piers; simple railings at the sides of the roadway. The E abutment is a survivor of the earlier Victoria Bridge (by *Frank Young*, of *Blyth & Westland*, 1899–1900).

RAILWAY STATION, Leonard Street. Built in 1847–9 to a design by *William Tite* as a co-operative venture between the Edinburgh, Perth & Dundee Railway, the Scottish Midland Junction Railway and the Scottish Central Railway. Tite's building,

---

*Reid had intended a sculptured group at this position.

now obscured by additions, stands on the present central platform of the main part of the station. It is a tall two storeys, Tudor of a decent but unadventurous variety. At the N end of the main block, a battlemented Tudor Gothic octagonal tower with a slated spire roof. Central entrance with, on the E and W sides, a single-storey canted bay window from which projects, much like an oriel, a clock by *James Ritchie & Son* of Edinburgh. Tite's roof over the platform to the W was replaced by *Donald A Matheson* in 1910–11 with a pitched-roofed glazed awning supported on arched iron brackets which spring, on the E, from corbels and, on the W, from iron columns beyond which the awning is carried down to a pelmet-like fringed fascia. At the N end of the building, a lower two-storey extension, again Tudor, by *A. & A Heiton*, 1854.

In 1884–6 the station was much enlarged by *Blyth & Westland*, their E extension much more utilitarian than Tite's work and with its awning cutting into the E front (the original street entrance) of his main building. At the same time they produced a new curved platform at the SE for the Dundee line, its piended glass roofs supported by octagonal Gothic piers. In each of the new street fronts (to the main station and the Dundee branch), a three-bay Gothic arcade (its openings now built up). The open bottom of the V-shaped entrance court was filled by the *British Railways Board's Architects Office* with a flat-roofed addition (replacing a corridor link of 1884–6) in 1968.

Over the tracks are lattice-sided FOOTBRIDGES, that at the N of the main station made by *Alexander Findlay & Co.*, of the *Parkneuk Works*, Motherwell, 1893, and erected as part of fairly minor alterations and extensions designed by *W. A. Paterson*. The S footbridge of the main station was made by *George Smith & Co.* of the *Sun Foundry*, Glasgow, in 1884–6, with a Gothic balustrade at its approach flight of steps. Footbridge of the same type and date at the Dundee platforms.

RAILWAY VIADUCT. The railway line from Dundee to Perth, opened in 1849, was carried over the Tay via Friarton Island on a wooden bridge and then W to Perth Railway Station on an embankment with viaducts over the streets at the S end of the city centre. The bridge over the Tay and Friarton Island was replaced by *B. & E. Blyth*, 1862–4. Over the water courses, eleven spans of wrought-iron girders carried on stone piers, the W span a swing bridge. Ten narrower stone arches over the island. A footpath on the N side was added later in the C19. The artificial embankment to the W behind the buildings of Marshall Place and King's Place is of 1849, partly supported on brick and stone arches. Plate girder bridges over the streets also of 1849 but the one over King Street is a replacement by *D. A. Matheson*, 1907.

ST JOHN'S PRIMARY SCHOOL, Stormont Street and Barossa Street. By *A. Watt Allison*, 1936. Red brick with concrete dressings. On each of the E and W fronts, an entrance under a steeply pitched gablet.

SANDEMAN PUBLIC LIBRARY, Kinnoull Street. Now in other use. Free Renaissance, by *Campbell Douglas & Morrison*, 1895–8, built of polished red sandstone ashlar. The elements of the design are all classical (Ionic pilasters and columns, some windows round-arched and keystoned, others corniced, a sparing use of pediments) but the composition is asymmetrical and the height varies from two to four storeys. On the NE corner, a stone ogee-roofed turret, perversely small for the position.

SHARP'S EDUCATIONAL INSTITUTION, South Methven Street. Built as a school with a bequest from John Sharp, a Perth baker, but now in other use. By *David Smart*, 1860. Dignified but unextravagant Italianate, mostly built of rubble with polished ashlar dressings. The centrepiece is a broad pyramid-roofed clock tower of four storeys. At its channelled ashlar ground floor, a Roman Doric aediculed portico. Rusticated quoins at the upper floors. The first and second floors each have a slightly recessed three-light window; between these windows an ashlar panel. Above the second floor a cornice. On the W front of the top floor a panel containing the segmental-pedimented frame for the (missing) clock face; at each of the other fronts a round-arched window. Boldly projecting eaves cornice carried on paired consoles. At the ends of the front, tall two-storey three-bay piend-roofed pavilions, the close-set windows round-arched at the ground floor, with lugged architraves and consoled sills at the first. The pavilions are joined to the centrepiece by recessed one-bay links of a lower two storeys and attic. In the front of each, an overarched ground-floor window of two round-headed lights; above, a two-light lugged architraved window and a scroll-sided segmental-pedimented dormer.

TELEPHONE EXCHANGE, Canal Crescent. Curtain-walled, by *A. C. Shallis*, 1957–60.

STREETS

ATHOLL CRESCENT. Built in the 1790s at the SW end of the North Inch, the segment of ground in front now deprived of the railings which formerly fenced it off from the line of Atholl Street. No. 1 is three-storey and harled. Corniced three-light windows at its bowed quadrant corner to Blackfriars Street. The N front is curved to start the line of the crescent. This is a palace front, composed of seven two-storey, basement and attic houses (Nos. 2–8), each of three bays with a centre door and a sill course under the ground-floor windows; giant anta pilasters divide off each house from its neighbours. The centrepiece is the slightly advanced No. 5 whose giant fluted pilasters support a pediment with an oculus in the tympanum. The doors of the other houses are simple with cavetto splays but here the entrance is framed by Roman Doric columns supporting a triglyphed entablature.

ATHOLL PLACE. A short terrace laid out in the 1790s and placed at a diagonal to the main road along the s side of the North Inch. The triangular space in front of the houses was formerly a garden but now a car park and bereft of its railings. Nos. 1–6, built *c.* 1795–1800, are terraced houses of uniform design except that the entrance to No. 3 is in its l. bay instead of the r., and that the wallhead of No. 6 is higher than that of the others (is this is a deviation from the design or has it been raised?). Two-storey, basement and attic, now with a variety of Victorian and Edwardian dormer windows. Fronts of (painted) broached ashlar, each of three bays with a pilastered and mutule-corniced doorpiece. No. 7 of *c.* 1800, on the corner of Blackfriars Street, is a taller tenement, with a former ground-floor shop at the front; side entrance to the flats above with an anta-pilastered and corniced door.

Across the road, on the s edge of the North Inch, a stone STATUE of Prince Albert dressed in the robes of the Order of the Thistle and holding the design of the Crystal Palace; it is by *William Brodie*, 1864. Weathered Tudor pedestal. – To the NE, near the bank of the Tay, 51ST HIGHLAND DIVISION MONUMENT by *Alan B. Heriot*, 1995. Bronze statue of a girl handing a rose to a piper of the Division. On the sides of the granite pedestal, bronze reliefs of battlefield scenes. – Further to the NE, the 90TH LIGHT INFANTRY (PERTHSHIRE VOLUNTEERS) MONUMENT by *David Beveridge & Son*, 1895. Polished granite obelisk on a two-stage Ægypto-Greek pedestal.

ATHOLL STREET was developed from *c.* 1800. On the s side, at the w end of Atholl Crescent (q.v.), the curved droved ashlar frontage of Nos. 1–5 of *c.* 1800, plain except for sill courses under the windows of the two upper floors. The taller and grander No. 7 on the corner of Kinnoull Street was built as the Theatre Royal in 1820. Its three-bay front to Atholl Street is of droved ashlar above a channelled ground floor. At the ground floor, segmental-arched shop windows. At the two floors above, a slightly recessed centre; three-light windows in the outer bays, the second-floor windows lower than those of the first. Mutuled cornice topped by a parapet at the centre. Plain six-bay elevation to Kinnoull Street.

On the N side, at the corner of Rose Terrace which it serves as a slightly projecting bookend, a three-storey block by *McLaren, Murdoch & Hamilton*, 1985–6, replicating its predecessor of *c.* 1800. The s and E fronts are each of four bays. Ground floor of channelled ashlar. At the upper floors, giant fluted Doric pilasters supporting the wallhead entablature and parapet. Tall first-floor windows above a continuous cast-iron balcony, its front composed of intersecting ovals. To the w, a plain late C20 tenement in the manner of its Georgian predecessor.

On the s, after the corner block with Kinnoull Street (*see* below), two mid-C19 double houses (Nos. 11–13 and 15–17), both of two storeys and an attic, built of droved ashlar (now painted), the ground-floor windows set in segment-headed overarches and the paired doors in Jacobean-classical pedimented surrounds. At the first floor of each, above the entrances, a small two-light window, its sill supported on block corbels; under the panel-topped windows of the outer bays, delicate cast-iron balconies decorated with anthemion ornament and carried on boldly projecting console-brackets. But these double houses are not identical twins. Within the jambs of the ground-floor windows of Nos. 11–13 are half-pilasters. This double house's second and fourth bays are advanced and pedimented, the panels over the first-floor windows are contained within the architraves, and the flat-roofed C20 dormers are placed behind the parapet. At Nos. 15–17, the first-floor windows of the outer bays are surmounted by console-pedimented dormerheads; at the centre of the wallhead, an open segmental-pedimented aedicule containing a round-headed arch.

Nos. 14–24 (N side) are early C19 tenements and plain except for the one at Nos. 20–24 which was altered in the mid C19 when it was given a rendered front, with swan-necked pediments over the first-floor windows and slender giant pilasters at the ends. In the W gable, a first-floor dummy window of three lights under an overall fanlight.

On the S side, between North William Street and North Methven Street, plain early C19 tenements flank St Andrew's Church (*see* Churches, above).

Opposite, between Stormont Street and Melville Street, more plain tenements of the early C19 and one (Nos. 36–38) of the late C19. The last stretch of Atholl Street facing the long side of St Ninian's Cathedral (*see* Churches, above) begins W of Melville Street with No. 56, a low two-storey early C19 building with a bowed quadrant corner. Then, a two-storey and attic terrace (Nos. 58–64) of *c.* 1840, the front of polished ashlar, channelled at the ground floor. Pilastered doorpiece at No. 58 whose first-floor windows are architraved and aproned. Original pilastered and corniced stone shopfronts survive at Nos. 62 and 64.

BAROSSA PLACE was developed for terraced housing and villas from the early C19. On the N side's E end, Nos. 1–5, a short early C19 terrace of three two-storey, basement and attic three-bay houses. Square-jointed rustication at the ground floor whose windows are set in round-headed overarches; semicircular fanlights over the doors. The terrace is continued by No. 7, also early C19 but taller. The ground floor is treated in shopfront style with a Roman Doric pilastrade supporting a cornice. Over the door, a huge rectangular fanlight filled with intricately patterned glazing. The contemporary No. 9 is a smaller and much tamer version of this, the cornice of its pilastered entrance carried across the front. Also early C19 is the piend-roofed No. 13, the ground-floor windows set in overarches; Roman Doric columned doorpiece. Pleasant but plainer villas of the early and mid C19 to the W. On the street's S side, at Nos. 16–18, a double house of the earlier C19, the front built of polished ashlar, channelled at the ground floor whose paired entrances have Roman Doric columned doorpieces. Similar double house at Nos. 22–24, also of the earlier C19 and with channelling at the ground floor whose windows are three-light.

BAROSSA STREET was laid out *c.* 1800. On the E side, a two-storey harled vernacular terrace of *c.* 1800. It faces the back of St John's Primary School (*see* Public Buildings, above).

BLACKFRIARS STREET was formed *c.* 1800, the name commemorating the C13 Dominican friary which stood nearby. On the E side, Nos. 8–10, a pair of two-storey houses of *c.* 1840, each of three bays with a heavy pilastered and corniced doorpiece. To their S, the former Middle Free Church (*see* Churches, above).

CALEDONIAN ROAD was formed in the later C19 and is now part of Perth's Inner Ring Road. The S stretch is bordered by the railway line on the W. On the E, the Caledonian Road Primary School (*see* Public Buildings, above). N of York Place, on the W side, the rear wing of No. 35 York Place (*see* below) followed by a supermarket (MORRISONS) by *D. Y. Davies Associates*, 1991. Kitsch Postmodern, decorated with tiles bearing motifs from Pictish symbol stones made by *Westman's Pottery*. On the E, the WAVERLEY HOTEL, Scots Jacobean Renaissance of 1887. Set back in MILNE STREET, three nine-storey flat-roofed and aggregate-clad point blocks, by *Bett (Bison)*, 1979.

CANAL CRESCENT was formed in 1803, following the line of the SW arc of the medieval moat and city wall. At the SE end, on the corner of Charterhouse Lane, a wedge-shaped mid-Victorian block (Nos. 2–4), its corner hosting a pilastered shopfront with a rinceau-decorated panel above; antefixae at the wallhead. On the crescent's NE side, the Telephone Exchange (*see* Public Buildings, above). On the SE side, a harled block of 1810 with a tall pointed window at the upper floor which originally housed the chapel of an Independent congregation.

CANAL STREET continues the line of the medieval moat and S wall of the city. At the E end, the N side is occupied by the side of Perth Sheriff Court (*see* Public Buildings, above), the S by Quayside Court (*see* Tay Street) followed by a car park in front of the entrance to Greyfriars Burial Ground (*see* above). W of Princes Street, the N side begins with a multi-storey CAR PARK by *William Nimmo & Partners*, 1986, followed by the harled SPEY COURT, by *Smart & Stewart*, 1919–20. Two parallel flatted ranges with a courtyard between. The manner is English Arts and Crafts; oriel windows on the block fronting the street. Then, housing (SERVITE HOUSE) by *Keppie Design*, 1997–9, in a Neo-Victorian manner. On the S side, WALKER COURT, *Architectural Services Department, Perth & Kinross District Council*, 1983, chunkily detailed housing built of pink block-work. Then, Nos. 52–54 (LOVE'S AUCTION ROOMS) of *c.* 1900. Gabled Elizabethan, with half-timbering and pargetting. Between Scott Street and James Street, Canal Street's s side is filled by Nos. 76–106, a two-storey range of the earlier C19. Ground-floor shops; sill course at the polished ashlar first floor.

CHARLOTTE STREET was laid out in 1783 as part of the N 'New Town'. Nos. 1–13 (N side) were built in 1786–9; a short terrace, enjoying views over the North Inch from the back windows. No. 1, at the E end beside Perth Bridge, is the smartest. Two storeys above a basement, the front of painted droved ashlar. Central Corinthian columned doorpiece, the fluted frieze decorated with rosettes and an urn. The giant end pilasters support a frieze and cornice at the wallhead, the frieze fluted and with rosettes at the ends; urns over the ends of the cornice. This entablature is broken by individual entablatures over the first-floor windows whose plain friezes interrupt the fluting of the main frieze and whose cornices are formed by projections of the main cornice. A small attic window in the E gable. No. 3 is a storey higher but plainer. Giant end pilasters, the l. now largely missing. Corniced windows at the ground and first floors; Ionic-columned doorpiece at the l. bay. No. 5 was dressed up in the mid C19 when the ground- and first-floor windows were given segmental pediments and the second-floor windows heightened so that they rise into triangular-pedimented wallhead dormers. Consoled triangular pediment over the centre door. No. 7, its broached ashlar badly weathered, is quite plain except for early C19 pilastered shopfronts. At the five-bay Nos. 9–13, a cavetto splay to the doorpiece. Central wallhead gablet containing a Venetian attic window with dummy sidelights.

On the street's s side, a terrace of tenements. The three-storey and attic E building (Nos. 2–8) of *c*. 1800 has a plain frontage but, at its gable to George Street, a pedimented three-storey projection with a Venetian window at the second floor. Projecting from the two lower storeys of the gable is a bow addition of the mid C19, probably built when this became the Post Office; another mid-C19 two-storey projection, flat-fronted and pedimented, to the s of the bow. The early C19 block at Nos. 10–18 Charlotte Street is of four storeys, the masonry of its ground floor channelled; square-jointed rustication at the first floor. Channelled pilaster strips at the centre and ends of the ten-bay front. Pilastered shopfront at Nos. 16–18, probably an early alteration. On the corner of North Port (this end known as Charlotte Place) is CHARLOTTE HOUSE (No. 20) by *W. M. Mackenzie*, 1830, a taller and grander four-storey block, built of polished ashlar, the first-floor windows corniced. At its three-bay front to Charlotte Street, a plain shopfront, probably of the late C19, to which has been attached an insurance company plaque dated 1710. The long w elevation is to Charlotte Place, the N end projecting as a semicircular bow, its panelled-aproned shop windows framed by fluted Greek Doric columns. More Greek Doric columns mark the original entrances (one now a window and another built up) in the straight section to the S. The columns support an entablature which carries a first-floor balcony, its cast-iron front latticed between borders containing a simplified Greek key pattern.

COUNTY PLACE continues the line of South Street beyond the W boundary of the medieval burgh. On the N side, the rear wing of the early C19 block on the corner of South Methven Street (*see* below) is carried on at the contemporary Nos. 3–7, a two-storey and attic building (its 'mansard' roof a late C20 addition). In the centre of its first floor, a niche containing a painted STATUE of Robert Burns by *William Anderson*, 1854. At the E end of County Place, Nos. 29–39 on the corner of New Row, by *G. P. K. Young*, 1898, fairly plain free Renaissance, built of polished red sandstone ashlar. Corbelled out from the canted corner, an octagonal turret with an ogee-domed lead roof.

The S side starts with the early C19 wedge-shaped Nos. 2–8 on the corner of Hospital Street. Three storeys with sill courses at the upper floors; trefoil-plan corner. Adjoining, the four-storey late C19 Nos. 10–22. The centre of each of the first-floor windows' cornices is carried up as a small semicircular 'pediment' carved with rosettes. The COUNTY HOTEL is mid-C19, with low segmental pediments over the first-floor windows and a wallhead balustrade.

FLESHER'S VENNEL. *See* South St John's Place.

GEORGE STREET opened in 1771 as a route for traffic from the new Perth Bridge to High Street. On the E side, at the corner of High Street, Nos. 1–9, a plain late C18 four-storey block. Its N end (Nos. 7–9) acquired a two-storey shopfront in the mid C19. The upper part of this survives, its end pilasters skied, its windows dressed up with wavy-topped shouldered architraves. At Nos. 11–13, also late C18, lugged architraves to the windows of the upper floors. The two-storey Nos. 15–21 became the Conservative Club in 1887 when the front was remodelled in Renaissance fashion by *Andrew Heiton Jun*. It is of three bays, with channelled pilasters providing a framework in which are set large ground-floor shop windows. The first-floor windows are quasi-Venetian but with coupled pilasters and round-arched sidelights. Wallhead balustrade. Then, three three-storey and attic tenements of the later C18 (Nos. 23–39), all rubble-built (Nos. 35–39 now rendered), two with chimneyed wallhead gablets. No. 41 is early C19 and of four storeys. Front of polished ashlar with a pilastered shopfront and sill courses at the first and second floors. Beside it, the ROYAL GEORGE HOTEL, its late C18 N part with moulded architraves to the windows and a rectangular pend entrance. The S part, built in 1790, was given a new front by *John Young*, 1871. Two-storey canted bay windows topped by iron cresting and linked by a balustraded stone balcony over the round-arched door. Rear extensions linking to a plain mid-C19 piend-roofed block facing Tay Street which was extended at both ends in 1928.

George Street's prevalent late C18 character resumes at the four-storey and attic Nos. 59–65, a gently convex front of eight bays, the windows grouped 5:3. Over the five-bay S part, a chimneyed gablet pierced by a Venetian window with dummy sidelights. Of about the same date, the plain rendered Nos. 67–71. On the corner of Tay Street, Nos. 75–77, designed by *George Alexander*, 1810, and built as the British Linen Company's Bank. Three storeys and an attic, six bays, built of broached ashlar above a polished ashlar ground floor. Moulded window architraves and rusticated quoins. At the centre, paired doors (now windows) set in an Ionic-columned frame. At the wallhead, a blocking course with a fluted centre panel.

The W side, after the corner block with High Street (*see* below), begins with plain late C18 four-storey tenements (Nos. 10–20). Much more assertive is the former Perth Bank (Nos. 22–24) by *A. & A. Heiton*, 1857, a rendered palazzo of three storeys and six bays. Over the ground floor, a cornice-like string course with carved lions' heads projecting above the door and window openings. At the first floor, aproned and segmental-pedimented windows with lugged architraves and pulvinated friezes. Sill courses and lugged architraves to the second-floor windows. Adjoining, Nos. 26–32 by *W. M. Mackenzie*, 1836, built as the Exchange Coffee Room. Large-scale three storeys and five bays, of polished ashlar above the Edwardian shopfronts (by *G. P. K. Young*, 1905–7). The end bays of the upper floors are framed by giant orderless pilasters incised with Soanean Æegypto-Greek ornament and supporting a frieze decorated with Greek key ornament under the parapet. Cornices over the tall first-floor windows. The second-floor windows are small and square, with lugged architraves. The street continues to Bridge Lane with plain late C18 tenements, a step on the S skew of Nos. 48–50, a central chimneyed gablet at Nos. 54–56. Across Bridge Lane, the civic presence of Perth Museum and Art Gallery (*see* Public Buildings, above) followed by the corner block with Charlotte Street (q.v.).

HIGH STREET, the principal street of the medieval burgh, remains the city's commercial centre. At the E end, on the corners of Tay Street, the opposing Gothic Old Council Chambers on the N and the Baroque Council Buildings on the S (*see* Public Buildings, above). Then, on the N, THE ROYAL BANK OF SCOTLAND (Nos. 9–11), originally the National Bank, mid-C19 Georgian survival, with coupled Roman Doric columns framing the recessed entrance in the polished ashlar front. The rendered late C17 building at Nos. 13–17 is of three storeys and an attic and of six bays. Moulded architraves to the small first- and second-floor windows; Victorian dormers. The console-corniced shopfronts (also Victorian) flank a pend entrance framed by a Gibbsian surround, the top of its consoled keystone carved with a crowned head; at the ends, clamshells under a pediment whose base projects beyond the sides (an idiosyncracy associated with James Smith), the tympanum carved with a rose above the initials RG/EC (for Robert

Graham and Elspeth Cunningham) and the date 1699. This is followed by the Late Georgian block on the corner of George Street (q.v.). From George Street's w corner as far as Skinnergate, the N side of High Street continues with rendered four-storey tenements (Nos. 21–43) of the late C18 (Nos. 21–29 dated 1774 at the gable), the upper floors plain except for the window architraves at Nos. 21–37 (vestigially cornided at the first floor of Nos. 23–25). Delicately detailed two-storey Edwardian shopfront with an oriel window at No. 21. Big foliaged consoles on the Victorian shopfronts of Nos. 23–29.

On the S side, W of Watergate, Nos. 28–30, a rendered four-storey block of the late C18, its roof piended towards High Street. Above the later shopfront, the three-bay façade is divided vertically by three tiers of superimposed pilasters (the order a sort of Roman Doric) and horizontally by string courses. Over the first-floor windows, segmental pediments, the centre one broken by a coat of arms. Pulvinated friezes and triangular pediments over the second-floor windows. Is this treatment original or an early C19 embellishment? Nos. 32–34 are mid Victorian. Balustraded four-bay front of polished ashlar. Shellheaded niches over the first-floor windows. At the second floor the two centre windows have segmental pediments, the outer windows flattened triangular pediments with anthemion finials. On the E corner of St John Street, Nos. 36–38, a plain four-storey block of *c.* 1800 but badly altered by *McLaren & Mackay*, 1903. The block (Nos. 44–46) on the W corner of St John Street is of the earlier C19, with plain ashlar frontages and a canted corner. More pretentious is No. 50, probably late C18 in origin but refronted in the mid C19 when the centre windows of the first and second floors were enlarged to two-light and all the second-floor windows given cornices and panelled aprons.

High Street between Skinnergate and the junction with Kinnoull Street and Scott Street was pedestrianized in 1990 and now displays specially chosen lamp standards, planting and benches. On a bench at the beginning of this part, a realistic life-size bronze STATUE of a seated girl holding a book on her lap ('Fair Maid') by *Graham Ibbeson*, 1995. The buildings W of Skinnergate begin on the N with No. 45, a late C20 harled block, its design reminiscent of its early C19 predecessor. Adjoining is the mid-C19 balustraded Nos. 55–57. Ground-floor shop with large foliaged consoles under the pedimented ends of its cornice. The three upper floors are of polished ashlar, with channelled pilaster strips at the ends. Lugged architraves to the first- and second-floor windows; blocks under the sills of the third-floor windows. Late C20 buildings aping the Georgian vernacular of their predecessors at Nos. 61–65, followed by No. 75 (MARKS & SPENCER) by *Monro & Partners*, 1977–9, which is at least honest about its date and function. Long recessed shopfront the dominant feature. The hammer-dressed stone cladding and traditionally proportioned windows above look like perfunctory gestures towards the aesthetic sensibilities of town planners. Then, more late C20 redevelopment in an unconvincing Georgian and Neo-Victorian manner as far as Guard Vennel.

On High Street's s side, at the w corner of Kirkgate, No. 52, a late C20 shop, its two-storey scale too low in this context and its 'mansard' roof the most cursory of nods towards traditional architecture. The prevailing four-storey scale is restored at Nos. 60–64. Here is a juxtaposition of different architectural manners. Two-storey High Victorian Renaissance shopfront with superimposed Corinthian pilasters, those of the upper tier framing a five-light window whose stilted elliptical arches are carried on Corinthianesque column-mullions, their shafts of polished granite. The two floors above are Georgian survival. Mid-C19 Georgian survival at Nos. 66–68. Rinceau decoration on the friezes of the first-floor window. At the two floors above, windows with lugged architraves and consoled sills, those of the second floor linked by a sill course. Another Georgian survival variant at Nos. 70–72 of c. 1840 where the first-floor windows have cornices, the second-floor windows lugged architraves and a sill course, and those of the third floor pilasters but now without cornices. The late C19 No. 76 is a taller four storeys. At the first and second floors, a giant elliptical-headed overarch, its pilaster's shafts billowing out like consoles. Within this frame, first-floor windows under a continuous wavy cornice; at the second floor, a three-light window with broad pilaster-mullions. Another tripartite pilaster-mullioned window at the third floor but its openings are round-headed; at the ends of this floor, pedimented pilasters. A third pediment fronts the centre of the parapet which is surmounted by an aedicular gablet containing an oculus. No. 84 is late C20, the classicism of its open pediment belied by the horizontal gash of the shopfront. At Nos. 86–102, the late C20 rebuild of three tenements of the later C18. The two at the E were nearly identical, each of five bays with small centre windows, those of the l. tenement round-arched at the second floor, Gothick at the third, the centre third-floor window of the r. tenement also Gothick. The adjoining w tenement was of three bays and plain. The new would-be replica [retained?] frontages (by *Bell-Ingram*, 1979) are harled with cement margins.

Next door is the GUILDHALL (Nos. 104–106) by *A. G. Heiton*, 1906–8, replacing the previous Guildhall of 1722. Two tall storeys. At the ground floor, a pair of broad elliptically arched granite shopfronts. The upper floor, faced with buff-coloured sandstone, is Burnetian baroque. Three bays divided by Ionic pilasters supporting the mutuled cornice which rises into an open segmental pediment over the centre. All windows with lugged architraves and pulvinated friezes. The outer windows are surmounted by pediments, the central window by figures of Industry and Commerce supporting the coat of arms of the city of Perth under the Scottish crown, this sculpture all by *H. H. Martyn* of Cheltenham. Big corner block (Nos.

108–112) to King Edward Street, by *Menart & Jarvie*, 1904, in a squared-up Baroque manner. Oriel windows on both faces of the corner which is surmounted by an octagonal cupola with a copper-domed roof and tall lead finial.

At the beginning of High Street's progress w of Guard Vennel, a free-standing SCULPTURE ('Nae Dae Sae Dark') by *David Annand*, 1992. Bronze figure of a slave and his master encircled by an aluminium ring. On the N side of the street, Nos. 117–119, a tall panelled slab by *F. W.Woolworth & Co. Ltd. Construction Department*, 1964, the design explicable if complete redevelopment of the street had been envisaged but not excusable. The adjoining Nos. 121–127 (by *James Smart*, 1899), Georgian survival but with two-light windows and unequivocally Late Victorian wallhead dormers, is squeezed unhappily between it and No. 129, a three-storey brown brick block (by *R. Chatterton* of *Alexandre Ltd. Architects' Department*, 1968), its ground floor filled by a shopfront. No. 135 is probably C18 but the first floor has been eliminated in order to heighten the shop below. The late C20 Nos. 137–141 would be tactful were it placed between Georgian vernacular buildings but is followed by a long bland block of the later C20 (Nos. 143–161), its shopfront a dominating horizontal. Plain early C19 tenement at No. 165, squashed by a C20 slate-hung top hamper but with a confident Victorian shopfront, the cornice carried on hefty consoles. REID'S BUILDINGS (Nos. 171–175) is by *John W. Smart*, 1907–9. Large squared-up Jacobean in polished ashlar, three-storey oriels sitting on the shopfronts' cornice. For the horribly plain tenement (Nos. 177–187) fronting Perth Theatre, see Public Buildings, above. More enjoyable Nos. 189–191 by *McLaren & Mackay*, 1902. Free North European Renaissance, a pedimented niche rising from the top of its gable front. Shopfront with banded pilasters topped by pedimented consoles at the ends of the cornice. Two-light windows above, those of the first floor with hefty consoles round which a moulded string course breaks forward to form a cornice. For Nos. 193–195, see Kinnoull Street.

On the s side, at the corner of King Edward Street, Nos. 116–128 by *William Nimmo & Partners*, 1973, ashlar-clad and with tall brown glass oriel windows and a slate 'mansard' roof. Squeezed next door is the three-storey three-bay No. 130 of *c.* 1840 bullied on the W by the flashy-looking Nos. 132–148 (by *Monro & Partners*, 1961, the windows altered in 1968). No. 150 is mid-C19, its wallhead finished with iron cresting, its canted NW corner topped by a dormer window pretending to be an octagonal turret. Beside it, an upswept canopy over the N entrance to St John's Shopping Centre (*see* King Edward Street). To the W, late C20 attempts to imitate Georgian vernacular continue to the corner with Scott Street.

Tall blocks on the W corners of Kinnoull Street and Scott Street (*see* below). Then High Street's scale drops and Georgian vernacular takes over. On the N side, at the harled No. 205, a steep-pitched gablet. Basket-arched pend entrance at

No. 209. No. 221, a shoddy-looking commercial block, is an intruder of the later C20. For this side's W corner block, *see* South Methven Street. On the S, unpretentious Georgian vernacular, mostly three-storey and attic, up to the tall four-storey block (No. 230) by *A. G. Heiton*, 1902–3, on the corner of South Methven Street. Stripped Georgian survival with a bowed corner.

On the N, after the block on the W corner of South Methven Street (*see* below), is the two-storey GRANT MILLER MEMORIAL HALL (No. 249). Built in 1839 as a Glasite meeting house, its upper floor lit by three Venetian windows. On the S corner of South Methven Street but curiously oblivious of its site is St Paul's Church (*see* Churches, above). To the W, an undistinguished C19 and C20 medley enlivened only by the leaping salmon metal shop sign of *c.* 1930 on No. 259.

JAMES STREET. Laid out in 1803. Its N stretch, between Charterhouse Lane and Victoria Street, is plain low-scale vernacular housing of the mid and later C19. For the block on the NE corner of Victoria Street, *see* Victoria Street. S of Victoria Street, on the W side, is No. 23, a mid-C19 two-storey *cottage orné*. On the E side, Nos. 28–40, a two-storey terrace of *c.* 1840, the houses enjoying pilastered doorpieces (anta-pilasters at Nos. 28–32, Ionic at No. 34; at Nos. 36–40 a trio of doors under a continuous cornice which is supported by Ionic pilasters at the ends and consoles at the centre). The terrace is continued but its height broken by No. 42 and completed by No. 44, its doorpiece with an architrave.

KING STREET, except for its earlier N end, was laid out in 1803, the feuing plan revised by *W. M. Mackenzie* in 1830 to provide sites for villas. At the N end, the E side starts with an unpretentious harled late C18 three-storey block (Nos. 1–5), with a bowed corner at the junction with Canal Crescent. Then the mid-C19 No. 7, its ground floor now occupied by a heavy Late Victorian classical entrance and shopfront. The two upper floors are divided by pilasters into four bays, the third much broader than the others and filled by a mullioned and transomed window lighting a masonic hall behind.

On the W side, at the corner of Hospital Street, a crown-finialled PILLAR erected in 1914 to mark the site of the Charterhouse, Perth's medieval Carthusian friary; it was designed by *Alexander K. Beaton* and executed by *David Beveridge & Son*. This land is now occupied by King James VI Hospital (*see* Public Buildings, above) with to its S, the former St Leonard's Church (*see* Churches, above), unostentatious but dignified C18 and C19 edifices for the bodily and spiritual well-being of the citizens of Perth.

S of Charterhouse Lane, on the E side of King Street, Nos. 1–4 GRAHAM PLACE, two pairs of semi-detached two-storey villas of the earlier C19, their polished ashlar walling channelled at the ground floor. At each pair of entrances, a double portico whose Roman Doric columns (coupled at the centre) support an entablature decorated with cartouches in the middle and at the sides. Aprons under the first-floor windows; at the second-floor windows, lugged architraves. On each house, a pilastered and segmental-pedimented dormer, perhaps added *c.* 1900. To the S, on both sides of the street, unremarkable villas of the earlier and mid C19, several with fluted Doric doorpieces or porticoes.

KING EDWARD STREET, laid out in 1901–2 between High Street and South Street, is dominated by the Perth City Hall (*see* Public Buildings, above). For the corner blocks at the N end, *see* High Street. Below them, on the E side, Nos. 10–16, by *Smart, Stewart & Mitchell*, 1931–2. Stripped Neoclassical, with giant orderless columns on the upper floors. The shopfront was replaced in the late C20 but the broken-pedimented doorpiece at the canted corner survives. Then, Perth City Hall and, to its S, on the corner of South St John's Place, the red sandstone ashlar Nos. 22–28 King Edward Street by *David Smart*, 1901–2. Plain up to the wallhead whose parapet, decorated with round-headed blind arcading, is broken by pedimented dormers. Over the canted corner, a truncated slate spire surmounted by iron cresting.

On the W side of King Edward Street, the ST JOHN'S SHOPPING CENTRE by *William Nimmo & Partners*, 1985–7, a bland ashlar-clad three-storey U-shape front whose upper floors contain offices. Small gablet above the entrance but not much to suggest excitement within. Inside, a shopping mall running W from the King Edward Street entrance and from which short limbs (entered under upswept canopies from High Street and South Street) branch off to N and S. The mall gives access both to single-storey shops (their flat roofs providing space for car parking and rear servicing) and also to the backs of earlier developments along High Street and South Street. In the small square in front, the KING EDWARD VII MEMORIAL 1913, by *Alexander K. Beaton*, a very free re-creation of the city's former mercat cross (erected in 1668–9 and demolished in 1765). Octagonal drum surmounted by a Corinthian-capitalled pillar, its finial a unicorn holding a shield bearing a saltire. At the corners of the drum, Doric columns (now much patched with cement). On the sides, round-arched panels. The back panel contains a door, the front a polished granite inscription tablet and a high-relief bronze portrait of Edward VII by *James Ness*. In the other panels, coats of arms. At the corners of the parapet, gryphon 'gargoyles'. On the face of the parapet are roundels carved by *David Beveridge & Son* with the arms of the trade incorporations of Perth and, at the back, the arms of the Weavers Incorporation. For King Edward Street's SW corner block, *see* South Street.

KING JAMES PLACE and KING'S PLACE. *See* Marshall Place.

KINNOULL STREET was laid out *c.* 1823 but its S end has been redeveloped with Late Victorian and Edwardian large-scale commercial buildings and its N end witnesses a confrontation between the industrial purpose of the former North British Dye Works and the trivia of Postmodern detail applied to housing put up in the last years of the C20 and the first of the C21. On the E corner with High Street, Nos. 1–5 Kinnoull Street and Nos. 193–195 High Street, by *David Smart*, 1895–6. Plain classical except that the canted corner is topped by a pyramidal spire covered with grey slates enlivened by bands of green fish-scale slates. The use of a wallhead balustrade and scroll-sided open-pedimented dormer window on the Kinnoull Street elevation is repeated, together with other detail, at the contemporary Nos. 7–9 (also by *David Smart*) and 11–17 Kinnoull Street to the N. These would be twins except that Nos. 11–17 are built of red rather than grey stone and have giant fluted pilasters instead of superimposed panelled pilasters. The Late Victorian Renaissance manner is continued at Nos. 19–23 (by *James Smart*, 1895), the centre door framed by pilasters (the cornice they supported now missing) and flanked by shopfronts with consoled cornices. Pedimented dormers behind the urn-topped wallhead balustrade. Adjoining, on the corner of Mill Street, Nos. 31–33, by *McLaren & Mackay*, 1906–7, built as the premises of the wine and spirits merchants, Matthew Gloag & Son. Squared-up Baroque in polished red sandstone ashlar, the front decorated with a vine swag.

The former ROYAL BANK OF SCOTLAND BUILDINGS (Nos. 2–12; W side) is by *David Smart*, 1899–1902. The S part (Nos. 2–4) is a vertically proportioned Renaissance palazzo. Giant Ionic pilasters on the polished red sandstone ashlar front. Pediments over the first-floor windows; urns on the wallhead balustrade. At the corner, a truncated slate spire finished with iron cresting. The red sandstone walling and the main elements of the design continue at the development's N part (Nos. 6–12) but the lower floor-to-ceiling heights produce a slightly disconcerting change of scale. Polished red sandstone again at the former Sandeman Public Library (*see* Public Buildings, above).

N of Mill Street and Murray Street, on the E, the large mass of the former North British Dye Works (*see* Industrial Buildings, below). To its N, the entrance to the multi-storey KINNOULL STREET CAR PARK, by *Keppie Design*, 2000, and, N of this, CARPENTER COURT by *John Turnbull of Perth & Kinross District Council Architectural Services Department*, 1984–5. Brown brick housing, with narrow full-height slate-hung bay windows and a late C20 version of a mansard roof. N of Carpenter Street, No. 75 Kinnoull Street, a plain early C19 two-storey and attic three-bay building followed by the long side elevation of the corner block with Atholl Street (q.v.).

On the W corner of Murray Street, Perth Congregational Church (*see* Churches, above). Then, large blocks of Neo-Victorian housing, No. 32 Kinnoull Street and Nos. 1–3 Foundry Lane on the S side of Foundry Lane by *Keppie Design*, 2003–4, and KNIGHTS COURT on the lane's N side, by *McCarthy & Stone*, 1997–8, followed by THE COOPERAGE, a block of housing by *Woodside & Parker*, 1997, rendered and with Postmodern touches. This occupies the site of Perth United

Free Church (by *Smart, Stewart & Mitchell*, 1934–5) whose hall survives, its diminutive cement-rendered front a break between the fussiness of the new housing and the early C19 Nos. 48–50 Kinnoull Street, plain except for a heavy corniced doorpiece. Also of the early C19 but more ambitious is No. 52 on the corner of Atholl Street, its polished ashlar masonry channelled at the ground floor. Main entrance flanked by sidelights, all under a segmental-arched fanlight; corniced first-floor windows. Heavy wallhead cornice under a blocking course.

LEONARD STREET was laid out in the late C18 but now contains a generally undistinguished ragbag of C19 and C20 buildings. The QUALITY HOTEL (former STATION HOTEL) is set back on the W, occupying the N side of the station forecourt (*see* Public Buildings, above). It is by *Andrew Heiton Jun.*, 1887–91. Flemish, with tall crowstepped gables and gablets, built of pale-coloured stugged Dunmore ashlar with dressings of polished red Dumfriesshire stone. L-plan, the entrance placed in the gable of the SW jamb; in the inner angle, a conical-roofed fat round tower. At the SE corner, a slimmer octagonal tower, its tall spired roof with bellcast eaves. Single-storey E addition built in two stages, the piend-roofed S part designed by *Alexander Cullen, Lochhead & Brown* of Hamilton in 1919, the parapeted N part by *D. McLellan* of the *Caledonian Railway Divisional Engineer's Office* at Glasgow in 1930.

MARSHALL PLACE, KING JAMES PLACE and KING'S PLACE. One-sided street overlooking the South Inch, it was laid out for development in 1802 but not completed until the later C19 by which time the railway viaduct had been built along the N edge of its back gardens. At the E end of MARSHALL PLACE, on the corner of Tay Street, the former Perth Waterworks (now Fergusson Gallery, *see* Public Buildings, above) stands as a monument of civic virtue but is followed by THE ARCHERY, a long block of flatted housing by *McLaren, Murdoch & Hamilton*, 1994–5. The indeterminate Neo-Georgian style hovers uneasily between palace-fronted urbanity and vernacular domesticity, a louvred cupola adding the suggestion of a stable block. The rough-textured concrete-block walling is an unhappy contrast to the polished ashlar or smooth render of the buildings to the E and W. In the car park across the street, discreetly landscaped in 1995, a stylized bronze SCULPTURE ('Fish with a Boy') of a boy diving into the mouth of a leaping fish, by *Doug Cocker*, 1995.

Nos. 1–14 and 15–28 across Princes Street are a pair of thirty-one-bay palace-fronted blocks designed by *Robert Reid* in his heavy-handed Adamish manner in 1805 but not completed until 1831. Each has slightly advanced and pyramid-roofed three-bay end pavilions of three storeys and a basement, joined by ten-bay, two-storey, attic and basement links to a five-bay, three-storey and basement piend-roofed centrepiece. Sober adornment at the pavilions and centrepiece whose ground-floor windows are round-headed and overarched; round-headed overarches also at the doors but the tops of these arches are filled by fanlights. Console-corniced first-floor windows at the inner pavilions (Nos. 14 and 15) and centrepiece. At the second floor, small windows and a central Diocletian window (a lunette at Nos. 21–22). Over each of the pavilions and centrepieces, a blocking course rising to a parapet at the centre. Ball-and-spike finials survive on the roofs of Nos. 15 and 28. The unity of design is now marred by the rendering and painting of much of the polished ashlar stonework, the loss of glazing bars from windows and fanlights, and a disparate array of late C19 dormer windows. Even more regrettable has been the removal of almost all the railings from the low walls of the front gardens. Surviving fragments (at Nos. 3, 9, 11 and 17) show that these were arrow-headed with urn finials at the gateways and that there were tall cast-iron gates and lampholders.

Reid intended three shorter terraces to be built to the W and elevations for the E and central of these were produced by *W. M. Mackenzie* (almost certainly adapting designs by Reid) in 1830. However, building work did not begin (at the W of these terraces) until the mid C19, and in the 1880s the site of the intended E terrace was acquired for the erection of the assertively Gothic St Leonard's-in-the-Fields and Trinity Church (*see* Churches, above). The W terrace (Nos. 1–3 KING JAMES PLACE and Nos. 1–3 KING'S PLACE) was designed to have end pavilions like those in Marshall Place but no centrepiece, and the linking houses are of three bays rather than two. The W pavilion was built in *c.* 1840 as intended but without the Diocletian second-floor window together with the two houses to its E. The third of the houses between the pavilions was not put up until *c.* 1870, continuing the design but built of a different stone. This stone is used also for the contemporary E end pavilion which pays little respect to Mackenzie's design, its windows being all rectangular, those in the outer bays of three lights and set in shallowly projecting rectangular bays. On the S side of King's Place, on the axis of King Street, a stone STATUE, by *Cochrane Bros.*, of Sir Walter Scott accompanied by his deerhound, Maida. It was first erected in 1845 at the E end of High Street and moved here in 1877.

King's Place W of King Street is occupied by mid-Victorian villas. No. 6 is piend-roofed Georgian survival but with Baroque consoled segmental pediments over the three-light windows and doors of the ground floor. Ruskinian Gothic double house at Nos. 7–8. Nos. 11–12 are Italianate, brick-built with stone dressings.

MELVILLE STREET, laid out *c.* 1800, is the W street of Perth's Georgian N 'New Town'. On the E side, after the block on the corner of Atholl Street (*see* above), the mid-C19 classical Nos. 7–11. Tall two storeys (now with a long late C20 box dormer on the roof). Lugged architraves to the windows, their sills supported on moulded corbels. In the centre, a trio of doors under a continuous entablature supported by a Roman Doric pilaster at each end. Plain rendered early C19 tenement at Nos. 15–17.

Nos. 19–21 form a piend-roofed double house of the earlier C19, set back behind a front garden, still with some spearhead railings on its dwarf wall. Contemporary piend-roofed villa (No. 23) to the N, its polished ashlar frontage channelled at the ground floor. At the slightly advanced centre, a door (now a window) with sidelights; first-floor pedimented window of three aproned lights, the lintel supported by consoles projecting from the mullions. The outer first-floor windows are corniced and aproned. On the N side, a mid-C19 porch, the entrance pilastered. At the corner of Barossa Place, the mid-C19 No. 25, its ashlar stonework again channelled at the ground floor and with an anta-pilastered doorpiece at the three-bay W front. Two-bay N elevation, its first-floor windows architraved and aproned.

On the W side, N of the corner block with Atholl Street (*see* above), plain mid-C19 tenements and villas. Among them, the gable-fronted St John the Baptist (R.C.) Church (*see* Churches, above). Beside it, the Neo-Georgian clergy house (No. 22) by *Reginald Fairlie*, 1932, the corniced doorpiece with a lugged architrave and pulvinated frieze.

MILL STREET AND MURRAY STREET. Mill Street was developed from the C18 along the N boundary of the medieval burgh. At its E end, between Skinnergate and Kinnoull Street, the huge former North British Dye Works on the N (*see* Industrial Buildings, below) looks across to the backs of buildings fronting High Street. W of Kinnoull Street the street broadens (the result of the removal *c.* 1955 of Public Baths and Washhouses of 1846 which stood between Mill Street and Murray Street), the N side acquiring the name of Murray Street. On the S side (Mill Street), the former Sandeman Public Library followed by the North Church (*see* Public Buildings and Churches, above). On the N (Murray Street), the corner with Kinnoull Street is occupied by Perth Congregational Church (*see* Churches, above). In the middle of this N side, the PLAYHOUSE CINEMA by *Alexander Cattanach Jun.* of Kingussie, 1933. Unexciting Art Deco in cement render and brick, with metal glazing bars in the curved horizontal windows. In front of the Playhouse, a painted concrete spiral SCULPTURE ('Vortex') by *Malcolm Robertson*, 1995.

MILL WYND was the medieval route from High Street to the City Mills (*see* Industrial Buildings, below). Isolated on the E and facing a car park, the early C18 three-storey HAL O' THE WYND HOUSE. Front of five bays, the centre very slightly advanced under a shaped gable. Repairs by the *Cunningham Glass Partnership*, 1980–1, have left the centre's rubble masonry exposed so that it stands out from the harled walling of the outer bays in an uncomfortably over-emphatic manner.

MILNE STREET. *See* Caledonian Road.

MURRAY STREET. *See* Mill Street and Murray Street.

NORTH METHVEN STREET was laid out in the 1790s but the buildings are later. On the E side, for the most part fairly plain mid-C19 tenements. On the W, the tenements, except for one stugged ashlar-fronted late C19 intruder (Nos. 18–24), are early C19. At No. 32, a console-corniced shopfront. The shopfronts of Nos. 34–38 have fluted pilasters and columns. The N end of this side of the street is dominated by the E end of St Ninian's Cathedral and its associated buildings (*see* Churches, above).

NORTH PORT is a curved street laid out when a medieval suburb developed in the vicinity of the Blackfriars convent just to the W but its earlist surviving buildings are Georgian. At the N end, on the W side, BLACKFRIARS HOUSE, a harled late C18 villa. Main block of three storeys and five bays, with a Roman Doric pilastered and corniced central doorpiece; a cornice over the first-floor centre window. This is flanked by two-storey pavilions, the N bow-ended. At the front of the S pavilion, a three-light window at each floor; another three-light window at the ground floor of the N pavilion. In 1950 a new entrance was made at the N end. Late C20 additions to the S and W.

On the E side, the large tenement block on the corner of Charlotte Street (*see* above) looks as though it was intended to be the start of a grandiose redevelopment but is halted against Nos. 4–6 North Port, a tenement of the later C18, a narrow gablet on its rendered front. No. 8 is another unpretentious tenement, the windows of its five-bay front grouped 3:2. Rising from the wallhead, a chimney whose bricks are apparently original, on which is a panel inscribed P.H.E.L./1774 to date the building.

At the street's SW end, on the N side, No. 15, the surviving C18 rubble-built two-storey and attic range of a large town house. At the ground floor, three large round-headed arches, their masonry rusticated. Five-bay first floor, the window surrounds renewed, probably in the C19, but the centre opening incorporating part of the moulded jambs of an earlier window. Two neat piended dormers. To the W, the FAIR MAID OF PERTH'S HOUSE of 1893–4 by *J. & G. Young* who rebuilt a house which dated probably from the early C17. It is a rectangular rubble-built block with a catslide-roofed round stair-tower at the SE corner. In the masonry, some earlier fragments. The SW skewputt is carved with a weathered head; below it, a pointed niche. Single-storey E wing, its SW skewputt carved with a worn head and torso, perhaps of an angel.

POMARIUM STREET was the site of a settlement of handloom weavers in the later C18, of working-class housing in the C19 and redeveloped in the C20. On the E side, two blocks of flats by *E. V. Collins* of *George Wimpey & Co. Ltd.*, 1958–60. One is a slab block of eight storeys, the other an eleven-storey tower block, both flat-roofed and with rendered walls. In front of the picture windows of the living rooms, partly glazed balconies. At the N end of the W side, the Free Presbyterian Church and associated housing (*see* Churches, above).

PRINCES STREET. Architecturally bitty, the N end, between South Street and Canal Street, laid out in 1770, the S in 1802. Overlooking its N end are the pedimented Nos. 29–37 South

Street and the steeple of St John's Kirk of Perth; at the S, glimpses of the South Inch.

At the N end, the corner blocks with South Street (*see* below) provide plain Victorian (Nos. 1–3, W) and palazzo (No. 2, E) introductions to the first stretch. Then, on the W side, Nos. 5–7, mid-C19 Georgian survival with corniced first-floor windows. Of about the same date Nos. 15–19, the first-floor windows with lugged architraves and corniced. On the E, the two-storey Nos. 4–8, by *David Smart*, 1881, with tall shopfronts (now altered), lugged architraves to the windows of the upper floor, and an overall balustrade.

On the SW corner of Canal Street, the two-storey and attic three-bay No. 33 of *c.* 1800, with rusticated quoins and a pilastered entrance (the outer windows enlarged). On the SE, baldly exposed since the demolition of the former corner building, is St John the Baptist Episcopal Church (*see* Churches, above). Down a lane to the W opposite the church, DUNBAR (No. 43), a two-storey *cottage orné* of *c.* 1830, the l. of its three bays advanced and gabled; at the r. bay, a semi-octagonal projection. Between these, a screen of octagonal pillars in front of the recessed entrance; above, a window of three narrow lights. The house's S view is blocked by the backside of No. 55, a former hostel for the homeless, by *James Miller*, 1925. Neo-Georgian, in purplish brick.

On the E side of the street, S of the church, the three-storey Nos. 30–36, early C19, with a pilastered ground floor. Also three-storey but much taller and with a bracketed eaves cornice is the former warehouse of *c.* 1890 at Nos. 38–48. Polished ashlar front of nine bays, the broader centrepiece marked off by giant pilasters supporting an open pediment. Three-light windows at the centrepiece's upper floors, two-light windows in the outer bays. At the ground floor, a broad elliptical centre arch flanked by round-headed openings to the outer bays, these now fronting a loggia formed on the block's conversion to housing in *c.* 1985. The adjoining two-storey three-bay No. 50 of 1866 is agreeably pretentious with pilastered and keystoned round-arched windows at the upper floor; bracketed eaves cornice surmounted by a balustrade which is broken by an open pediment. Opposite, on the NW corner of Victoria Street, the early C19 three-storey VICTORIA BAR (No. 61), the windows of the first floor corniced, those of the second linked by a sill course. On the E side, Nos. 60–62, English Baroque of *c.* 1900. Only two storeys and three bays but the first-floor windows are canted oriels decorated with carved swags; more swags at the urns on the overall balustrade. The adjoining tenement at Nos. 64–68 (by *Charles S. Robertson*, 1898) is quite plain except for the central door's pilastered and swan-neck-pedimented surround. Then the two-storey mid-C19 No. 70, the two bays of its front divided by superimposed pilasters (Corinthianesque over Roman Doric). The small lead owl (probably Victorian) on the corner of its parapet is presumably an addition. Opposite, on the NW corner of South William Street, the Late Georgian MONCRIEFFE ARMS, its roof piended to the s. Panelled aprons under the first-floor windows of its elevation to Princes Street. Over the street's s end, a span of the railway viaduct (*see* Public Buildings, above).

ROSE TERRACE. One-sided street built *c.* 1800 on the W side of the North Inch, the railings which formerly separated the street from this public space now lost. N of the corner block to Atholl Street (*see* above), Nos. 1–12 appear, at first glance, a palace front of three-storey, basement and attic housing with the former Public Seminaries (*see* Public Buildings, above) as a grand centrepiece, but the s range of housing is of fifteen bays and the N, although occupying the same length of ground, of thirteen more widely spaced bays. These ranges have fronts of ashlar, the ground floor with square-jointed rustication (the s range now rendered, the N painted). The ground-floor windows are set in round-headed overarches; door openings of the same width as the overarches with semicircular fanlights above. The s range was restored externally and converted to flats by *McLaren, Murdoch & Hamilton* in 1985–6 when the present canted dormers were added. At the N end the terrace is continued at Nos. 13–17 with houses of the same height but of a different and simpler design which omits the rustication and overarches. Console-corniced doorpieces at Nos. 13–16, a pilastered and corniced doorpiece at No. 17.

On the North Inch immediately E of the terrace, SCULPTURE ('Seasons, Time, and Place') by *Frances Pelly*, 1991, a formal octagonal arrangement of slabs, some bearing inscriptions, those on the outer faces referring to the Seasons, those on the inner to a garden (MY GARDEN SIDE BY SIDE NATIVE PLANTS FOREIGN PLANTS GROWING TOGETHER).

ST CATHERINE'S ROAD. Now filled with the car parking and retail sheds of the late C20 ST CATHERINE'S RETAIL PARK. At the NE corner of the development, a former Dye Works (now, Highland House; *see* Industrial Buildings, below).

ST JOHN STREET. Laid out in 1795–1800 as an extension of the line of George Street s to South Street. After the NW corner building with High Street (*see* above), Nos. 3–5 (originally BANK OF SCOTLAND), by *James Smith* of Edinburgh, 1853–6, a restrained palazzo of three storeys and six bays. At the ends, Ionic columned doorpieces. Panelled aprons under the windows of the ground floor. The tall first-floor windows, all with consoled triangular pediments, open onto a continuous anthemion-decorated cast-iron balcony. Second-floor windows with lugged architraves and small consoles under the sills. The plain early C19 block of Nos. 7–13 shares a C20 shopfront with No. 15, a two-storey building of *c.* 1800, its first-floor window of three lights under an overall fanlight. On the corner of St John's Place, Nos. 19–23 St John Street, a three-storey block, by *George Alexander*, 1821, built of droved ashlar. At its bowed corner, the first- and second-floor windows are each flanked by dummy lights set just too far apart for the windows to be truly tripartite. Widely spaced mutule blocks under the wallhead cornice. Broad gablet (now without its chimney) on the elevation to St John's Place. Beyond the broad Gothic E end of St John's Kirk of Perth (*see* Churches, above), Late Georgian architecture resumes at the early C19 Nos. 25-37 St John Street on the corner of South St John's Place. Three storeys of painted broached ashlar. Front of fifteen bays, the slightly advanced fourth and ninth marked off by anta-pilasters and surmounted by panelled parapets; three-light windows at the upper floors of these bays. The pilastered doorpiece at No. 31 and the shopfronts of Nos. 25 and 29 look original. Arcaded shopfront at No. 27, perhaps formed by enlarging windows to the full extent of their former overarches. Another arcaded and pilastered shopfront at No. 33. It is of 1983, a free version of the shopfront added here by *James Smart & Son* in 1898. Then the corner block with South Street (*see* below).

At the E side's N end, Nos. 2-16, an early C19 four-storey tenement. Painted ashlar front of six bays, the windows grouped 3:3, the centre window of each trio a dummy. At No. 14 the original fanlight (a rectangle containing four oval openings) survives. Adjoining, the contemporary Nos. 18-24, its broached ashlar unpainted. Four storeys and seven bays, the only decoration a panelled band course under the second floor. No. 22 has a fanlight of the same design as that at No. 14. Another early C19 four-storey block at Nos. 26-30 but of only three bays. All the first- and second-floor windows are Venetians, still with the original glazing pattern of circles and ovals in the heads of the centre lights; simple three-light windows at the third floor.

Plain three- and four-storey early C19 buildings (Nos. 32-44) lead up to the former CENTRAL BANK OF SCOTLAND (Nos. 48-50). This is by *David Rhind*, 1846-7. Three-storey five-bay palazzo, of buff-coloured polished ashlar with rusticated quoins. At the ends of the ground floor, Roman Doric pilastered doorpieces with triglyphed friezes. The bases of the inner pilasters are linked by a balustrade under the corniced ground-floor windows of the three centre bays. Aedicular first-floor windows with Corinthian pilasters and triangular pediments. Below them, a continuous stone balcony projected on foliaged console-brackets. Above the first floor, a band of guilloche. Under the corniced small second-floor windows, a moulded sill course supported on consoles; between each pair of consoles, a panelled apron. At the wallhead, a boldly projecting consoled cornice under a balustrade. The detail of the front is carried round on the S side facing Baxter's Vennel but omitting the ground-floor balustrade and first-floor balcony. The banking hall inside has an elaborate trabeated plaster ceiling, the soffits of the beams decorated with guilloche; pendants at the intersections. Inside each compartment, consoles under the central panels, each of which contains a pair of pendant-centred roses. The banking hall was extended to the rear in 1971, the extension's Neoclassical detail a misguided attempt to be in keeping with the 1840s work.

s of Baxter's Vennel, Nos 58–60, also by *Rhind*, *c.* 1847, a huge single-storey shop, the three bays of its front divided by pilasters, each topped by a pair of consoles supporting the mutuled and balustraded cornice. The openings within this framework were remodelled by *Smart, Stewart & Mitchell*, 1931, when the windows were given Greek key-patterned metal frames and the panels above decorated with swags and plaques in a sort of Louis XV manner. Next door, the three-storey and attic Nos. 62–70 of *c.* 1800. Rendered front of seven bays, the centre three surmounted by a gablet (now missing its chimney), its central window a round-arched dummy. The C20 replacement of the sash windows with small-paned casements is incongruous. On the corner of South Street, Nos. 72–76 St John Street is similar but of *c.* 1821. Three storeys and attic, with a big chimneyed gablet containing a round-arched dummy window. Baroque shopfront dated 1906.

ST JOHN'S PLACE. The N side of the former medieval square surrounding the burgh church, the street extended w at the beginning of the C20. The s side is filled by St John's Kirk of Perth and Perth City Hall (*see* Churches and Public Buildings, above). On the N, after the corner block with St John Street (*see* above), Nos. 4 and 5–8 on the corners of Kirkgate, both early C19 three-storey blocks, built of polished ashlar and with bowed quadrant corners but the stonework of Nos. 5–8 is rougher and now much patched with cement. Plain block of *c.* 1800 at No. 10. Change of scale and style at Nos. 12–16, by *Smart, Stewart & Mitchell*, 1926, but without a hint of modernity. Front of three tall storeys and eleven bays, the centre carried up as a tower with strapwork over the mullioned and transomed window which rises through the two top floors. Lugged architraves at the first-floor windows of the outer bays. Adjoining, THE FILLING STATION (No. 1) of 1925 and also by *Smart, Stewart & Mitchell*, its tall red sandstone front treated in a free castellated manner (*see* also South St John's Place, below).

ST LEONARD'S BANK is a row of villas built along the ridge bordering the w side of the South Inch, the plots laid out for development by *W. M. Mackenzie* in 1828.

All the houses (except for the s one) are of three storeys, with three-bay fronts facing E over the South Inch from which they are set back behind large sloping gardens. They start at the s with the rendered No. 1, quite plain, of *c.* 1830. It is now linked to the ashlar-fronted No. 2 of *c.* 1870, piend-roofed Georgian survival but with bay windows and a Victorian console-corniced doorpiece. No. 3, also ashlar-fronted and piend-roofed, is of the earlier C19 with an openwork iron porch and bracketed eaves. At the back, a two-storey late C19 addition, its NE corner clasped by a conical-roofed low tower. At the w front of the addition, a first-floor round-headed window flanked by two lower rectangular lights just too widely spaced to form a Venetian window. No. 4 is early C19, piend-roofed and with a pilastered doorpiece. No. 5 is mid C19. At the ground floor of the polished ashlar front, shallow curved-sided bay windows flanking the entrance which is set behind a screen of Ionic columns *in antis*. Pedimented side elevations. At the back, a large late C19 wing with a chimneyed pedimented gablet. At No. 6 of *c.* 1830, three-light ground-floor windows. No. 7 looks a little later. At the ground floor of its polished ashlar façade, very shallow rectangular bay windows with pilastered ends and surmounted by parapets; between them an Ionic columned and baluster-topped screen in front of the entrance. Wallhead balustrade. No. 8 of the earlier C19 is plain except for a cornice over the original centre door (now a window). C19 and C20 additions at the back. Contemporary house at No. 9, with fluted Greek columns at the entrance; late C20 single-storey rear addition.

No. 10, of *c.* 1830, is grander than the other villas. Polished ashlar elevations to the E and S. Four-bay E elevation, the two centre bays of three storeys, the outer bays of two, their wallhead cornice carried across the centre bays to denote its top floor's attic status. The ground-floor windows at the outer bays are pedimented, those of the centre bays corniced, all with panelled aprons. The entrance is in the S elevation whose centre is marked off by pilaster strips; parapet over the centre, balustrades over the ends. In the outer bays, round-headed niches under corniced panels at the ground floor and dummy windows to the first floor. Balustraded Roman Doric portico at the centre. Utilitarian C20 W and N additions for the house's present use as a club. To the S, CSSC SPORTS AND LEISURE of 1979, a long low building with a shallow-pitched roof.

SCOTT STREET was laid out in 1803 but almost all redeveloped in the late C19 and C20; the N end for commerce, the S for housing. Nos. 1–7, on the NW corner with High Street, by *James Smart*, 1895, built of khaki-coloured stone. The style is mixed Georgian survival and Victorian Renaissance. Canted corner rising into an octagonal tower, its truncated spire topped by iron cresting. The W side continues with the late C19 thrifty Renaissance Nos. 9–13, followed by shops (Nos. 15–21) of 1967 by *Arthur Swift & Partners*. The scale mounts again with two large buildings designed by *James Smart* in 1897. At Nos. 23–27 the windows of the upper floors are enclosed in giant elliptical-headed overarches; skinny fluted pilasters at the ends. Free classicism at Nos. 29–35 whose shallow oriel windows are recessed within pilastered frames; Ægypto-Greek touches at the pedimented dormer windows. The scale is maintained but in red rather than buff sandstone at the corner block with South Street (*see* below).

On the E side, the late C20 corner block with High Street (*see* above) is followed by late C19 four-storey buildings, all faced in polished ashlar and of generally Renaissance character. At Nos. 8–14, by *James Smart*, 1896, skinny end pilasters and a wallhead chimney. Strapwork parapet on Nos. 16–24, by *McLaren & Mackay*, 1897. The first-floor windows of Nos. 26–28 (by *David Smart*, 1896) have triangular and segmental pediments, its wallhead a balustrade. At JEDBURGH BUILDINGS (Nos. 30–42), by *James Smart*, 1898–9, wavy-topped architraves round the first-floor windows. Then the corner building with South Street (*see* below).

Between South Street and Canal Street, plain late C19 tenements along both sides. On the W also, Perth Methodist Church (*see* Churches, above) and, on the E, the long side of Servite House (*see* Canal Street). S of Canal Street, Nos. 65–73 on the W side continue the early C19 vernacular of Nos. 80–106 Canal Street (*see* above). On the W, a large corner block by *McLaren & Mackay*, 1904–6, built for the City of Perth Co-operative Society. Stripped Jacobean-classical, with giant antapilasters and mullioned windows. It is followed by Nos. 92–94 on the corner of Victoria Street, a tenement of 1925, harled, with dressings. For the tenement on the W corner, *see* Victoria Street. S of Victoria Street, two-storey and attic vernacular housing of the early or mid C19 and, on the E, the long side of Nos. 96–98 Scott Street and No. 58 Victoria Street (*see* Victoria Street). Over the S end of Scott Street, a plate-girder span of the railway viaduct (*see* Public Buildings, above).

SHORE ROAD formed the C19 access along the W bank of the Tay to the Harbour (*see* Public Buildings, above). S of the South Inch, the T-plan SOUTH INCH BUSINESS CENTRE by *McLaren, Murdoch & Hamilton*, 1988, its frame, clad in bands of yellow and red brick, enclosing large sheets of blue-tinted glass. Gambrel roof of blue-coloured ribbed metal. Then the former MILNE'S COLD STORAGE AND ICE FACTORY of 1926, by *Alexander K. Beaton*, built of glazed red brick. Big single storey and attic, the front composed of two broad crow-stepped gables with obelisk finials; big oculi at the attic. Immediately to the S, a harled block of three-storey working-class housing by *R. McKillop*, 1901. Picturesque, with bracketed broad eaves and oriel windows under half-timbered gablets. Basket-arched shopfronts at the ground floor.

SKINNERGATE is a narrow medieval street running N from High Street, the buildings now of the C19–C21. On the E side, at the S end, the Late Victorian single-storey and attic OLD SHIP INN, with a red sandstone crowstepped gable fronting the street. On the W, SKINNERGATE HOUSE, originally a model lodging house, by *Erskine Thomson & Glass*, 1927. Red brick Neo-Georgian, the narrowness of the street precluding appreciation of its symmetry. At the E side's N end, a development displaying huge windows and prominent pitched roofs, by *Pask & Pask*, 2003–4.

SOUTH STREET was the S street of medieval Perth inside the city walls. At the E end, classical C19 officialdom, the long frontage of the former County Buildings facing the flank of Perth Sheriff Court (*see* Public Buildings, above). Then on the N side, W of Watergate a harled early C18 block (No. 7) with its gable to South Street, followed by straightforward late C18 vernacular at Nos. 11–21 and the corner block with St John Street (*see* above).

On the S side, w of Speygate, the mid-C18 three-storey and attic rendered front of Nos. 8–12. Six bays, the windows grouped 3:3. Low steps at the E and w gables, crowsteps on the gable of the back wing along Speygate. After a gap site, Nos. 20–24, also of three storeys and an attic. It is probably C18 but was remodelled in the mid C19 when it was given lugged window architraves and end pilasters whose consolecaps support the wallhead cornice. Then, the mid-C18 Nos. 26–32, again three-storey and attic. Six bays, the windows grouped 3:3; two-bay chimneyed gablet over the centre.

The tall SALUTATION HOTEL, all built of painted ashlar, is [109] one of Perth's swankiest Late Georgian buildings. The l. part of *c.* 1800 is a triumphal arch of two storeys and three bays. At the centre of the low ground floor, a three-light window. Above, a huge window, also of three lights, its mullions and jambs dressed up as a screen of Ionic columns *in antis*, surmounted by an overall segmental-arched fanlight which is flanked by round panels. Rectangular-headed niches l. and r. of the window now contain painted statues of a pipe-major and officer of the Black Watch; above the niches, rectangular panels. The lower part of the tall wallhead parapet is panelled and decorated with guttae. The surmounting balustrade continues across the hotel's r. part. This is C18 in origin but was remodelled in the mid C19, with blocky consoles under the sills of the lugged-architraved windows. Squeezed in at the l. of the ground floor is the hotel's pilastered and corniced entrance.

No. 38, on the corner of Princes Street, was built in 1856–8 as the Commercial Bank of Scotland to a design by *David Rhind*. Tall three-storey palazzo faced with lightly stugged ashlar. Windows decreasing in size at each floor. At the ground floor, the openings are round-arched with pilastered jambs and V-jointed heads, their keystones carved with bearded faces. Round-headed and corniced first-floor windows; shouldered architraves at the second floor. The chimneystacks are linked by round-headed arches.

The block on the w corner of St John Street (No. 23 South Street and No. 41 St John Street), is by *Smart & Stewart*, 1923, faced in polished red sandstone ashlar, with a squat octagonal ogee-roofed corner turret. The black granite of its shopfront, a replacement, is repeated at the shopfront of No. 27, a narrow block by *James Marshall*, 1903, with thin pilasters at the ends, and mullioned and transomed windows to the upper floors. Its Dutch gable has been replaced by a 'mansard' roof which squashes down on the mutuled wallhead cornice. The block at Nos. 29–37 was built as the City Hotel but occupies the site of the former Grammar School and has something of the presence of a public building. It is old-fashioned for its date of 1824–5. Three storeys and an attic, built of broached ashlar. Front of seven bays, the centre three slightly advanced under an open pediment containing a small Venetian window. Sill course under the second-floor windows. The shopfront with paired pilasters standing on tall bases looks late C19. The adjoining two-storey and attic No. 41, by *James Parr & Partners*, c. 1985, is a polite but self-confident newcomer to the street, built of pinkish-coloured concrete blockwork with a slated roof. Only two bays, the upper windows and metal-clad flat-roofed dormers of traditional proportions. At the ground floor, the l. bay is occupied by a recessed shopfront, the r. by a broad pend under the building's oversailing back wing. Then, Nos. 43–51 of the earlier C19, a three-storey block of polished ashlar (the three E bays now rendered). Off-centre 'centrepiece' formed by a slightly advanced rectangular bay containing three-light windows at the upper floors. Blocking course above the wallhead cornice. Victorian shopfront at No. 51, leafy consoles under its dentil cornice.

W of Flesher's Vennel, a three-storey six-bay block of c. 1840 at Nos. 55–57 South Street, the windows of the upper floors with moulded architraves, lugged at the first floor. Scrawny pilasters at the ends and centre. Then nondescript C20 development until the SALVATION ARMY HALL, by *Burns Architects*, 2000–1, of one tall storey, in a Neo-Edwardian manner. The former hall, together with housing and shops, was in the adjoining Nos. 75–81 on the corner of King Edward Street, a sizeable block by *John Hamilton*, 1904. Squared-up English Baroque, with a narrow canted corner.

On the W corner of Princes Street, Nos. 40–44, mid-Victorian commercial-Italianate, its masonry's khaki colour unappealing. Red sandstone at Nos. 46–50, by *William McLaren*, 1889. Thrifty Scots Jacobean, a panel above the central first-floor window carved with emblems of the Fleshers Incorporation of Perth. It is followed by a late C20 four-storey tenement (No. 66), the walls of concrete blockwork. Its traditionally proportioned windows try to fit in but the dormerheads give a restlessness to the top and the lack of shopfronts a torpidity to the bottom which are uncharacteristic of the rest of the street. Then, plain mid-C19 vernacular Georgian survival (Nos. 84–94), the windows now with cement margins, followed by late C20 infill, here enlivened by shops. More mid-C19 Georgian survival vernacular (Nos. 116–120) before No. 122. This is by *Inskip & Wilozynski*, 1971. A long white-harled block with a pitched and slated roof, it keeps the three-storey height of its neighbours but with the ground floor occupied by one continuous shopfront and a blind 'first floor', its lack of openings made more noticeable by the windows and chunky oriel-ventilators above. Then, a humble three-storey and attic building (No. 144), the small windows of the upper floors suggesting an C18 date. Nos. 146–150 may be Late Georgian in origin but the present appearance is mostly of c. 1900 when new shopfronts and oriel windows were added. The following narrow block (Nos. 152–156) is by *Smart, Stewart & Mitchell*, 1934, its shallow buttresses and quasi-pointed windows making it faintly ecclesiastical. Plainest Victorian commercial buildings carry on up to the corner with Scott Street, the corner block itself dated 1880.

On the N side's W corner with King Edward Street, a large red sandstone block (Nos. 83–89) by *James Marshall*, 1905. Stripped Jacobean with mullioned and transomed windows. The tall C18 tenement at Nos. 91–95 was rebuilt but the front retained in the late C20. Six bays with a chimneyed gablet over the centre. It adjoins the upswept canopy over an entrance to St John's Shopping Centre (*see* King Edward Street). Beyond is No. 103, jolly Jacobean of the later C19, its wooden pub front with skinny Ionic pilasters. Less fun is the flat-roofed brown brick block of Nos. 105–131 (by *James Parr & Partners*, 1969) straddling a broad pend (now a side entrance to St John's Shopping Centre). Artisan Mannerist pilastered shopfront on the late C19 Nos. 133–135. Then, the block at No. 137 South Street and Nos. 46–50 Scott Street, by *James Smart*, 1896–7. Free Renaissance with a slight French accent. On the corner, a projecting bow, its window mullions with attached columns, finished with a truncated conical slate roof, now deprived of cresting. Doorpiece to Scott Street with massive consoles under the balcony-topped cornice.

On the S side's W corner with Scott Street, No. 168, dourest mid-C19 commercial Georgian survival. Then the harled Nos. 170–178 of 1816. Shops and a pend at the ground floor. The space above originally contained a Methodist chapel whose tall pointed windows were partly blocked when an extra floor was inserted. Stripped Scots Renaissance of *c*. 1930 at Nos. 180–182. This is followed by a row of shops of the later C20 and Nos. 210–214, a bland five-storey tenement faced in concrete blockwork (by *Fraser, Gray Contracts*, 1995–6). On the corner of Canal Crescent, No. 220 by *Dunn & Findlay*, 1903–4. Large but plain free Scots Jacobean. Corbelled out from the canted corner, a turret which begins as a semi-octagonal two-storey oriel and is then corbelled out to a circular attic which rises through the eaves to a copper-clad flattened ogee dome.

W of Scott Street, South Street's N side continues with a Renaissance corner block (No. 143) by *David Smart*, 1897–9. It is faced with polished red sandstone ashlar. Giant Corinthian pilasters. Pediments, alternately triangular and segmental, over the first-floor windows. At the attic windows, swan-neck pediments containing swags and broken by cherubs' heads. The ground floor of the harled Nos. 151–157 of 1830 is occupied by shops and an elliptically arched pend entrance. On the upper floor, the former BAPTIST CHAPEL (now PERTH GOSPEL HALL), with three pointed windows, the outer two of two lights, the centre of three with intersecting tracery. Nondescript buildings to the W, a pend at No. 165 giving access to the former Old Light Antiburgher Chapel (*see* Churches, above). No. 175 is small-scale of the late C19, with round-arched first-floor windows; in the l. bay, a broad elliptically arched second-floor window under a gablet. The harled No. 177 of three storeys and two bays may be late C18. On the corner of South Methven Street, No. 189 by *McLaren & Mackay*, 1900–1. Four storeys of polished ashlar. Free Scots

Jacobean, the wallhead's segmental pediment broken by an obelisk-topped pedestal. Ground-floor pub front, its pilasters supporting cartouches. The canted corner is carried up into a console-buttressed octagonal low attic pierced by oval windows and crowned by a slated spired roof.

SOUTH METHVEN STREET was laid out in 1791 on the line of the medieval W wall of the burgh. At the N end's W side, on the corner with West Mill Street, a desperately plain late C19 two-storey building (Nos. 1–9) followed by the almost equally plain three-storey and attic CAMPBELL'S BUILDINGS (Nos. 11–21) dated 1888. Keeping the scale but showing a more aggressive spirit is the CLYDESDALE BANK by the *Cunningham Glass Partnership*, 1980–1. On the corner of High Street, the former TOWN AND COUNTY BANK (No. 25) by *D.N. Shaw*, 1888–9. Two storeys of Artisan Mannerist Baroque. At the ground floor, Ionic pilasters, the upper third of their shafts fluted; drapery swags hang from the volutes. Between them, three-light windows on the E front, their centre openings round-arched, and a single round-headed light in the S elevation, all with carved foliage in the spandrels. On the canted corner, a columned and open-pedimented Ionic aedicule framing the round-arched doorpiece whose spandrels are carved with relief portraits of two men whose moustaches extend into foliage. At the first floor, pilasters and, on the corner, a coat of arms.

The E side starts at the N with the former Sharp's Educational Institution set well back behind a forecourt (*see* Public Buildings, above). The street line is established by the red sandstone corner block, by *Peter Roy Jackson*, 1894. Restrained Jacobean Renaissance with a large octagonal cupola over the canted corner. On the front to High Street, a tall gablet topped by a broken segmental pediment.

S of High Street, the street's W side continues past the island site of St Paul's Church (*see* Churches, above) with plain tenements of the mid and later C19 at Nos. 37–59. More ambitious is the long three-storey block of *c.* 1840 at Nos. 61–71. Symmetrical polished ashlar frontage of eleven bays, the centre three slightly advanced with rusticated quoins and a pediment. Architraved and corniced first-floor windows, several pedimented. The scale drops to a low two-storey and attic at Nos. 73–79, a pair of three-bay early C19 buildings faced with broached ashlar.

On the E side, after the corner block with High Street (*see* above), the two-storey Nos. 20–28 of *c.* 1860, the diamond-panelled Ionic pilasters of the shopfronts surviving at the S end. The polished ashlar upper floor is divided into four four-bay sections by broad anta-pilasters, the centre section further divided in two by an empty image niche. Shouldered-arched corbelling under the parapet. Then, a two-storey and attic block of the later C19 (Nos. 34–44). Sixteen bays, with an off-centre pediment. Ground-floor shopfronts whose vermiculated ashlar piers and cornice have been badly cut into by later alterations. First-floor masonry of channelled ashlar. Lugged architraved windows, every other one and the two under the pediment flanked by mannerist console-topped pilasters. Humble early C19 tenement at Nos. 46–50. At Nos. 52–58 of *c.* 1800, a broad centre gablet, now bereft of its skews and chimney and beleaguered by box dormers. More box dormers and a central gablet (still skewed and chimneyed) on the contemporary Nos. 60–64. Nos. 66–68 of *c.* 1930 display tentative modernity. At each of the upper floors, a long horizontal window divided by mullions into five lights. Then the corner block with South Street (*see* above).

SOUTH ST JOHN'S PLACE formed the S side of the medieval square around the burgh church and was extended W at the beginning of the C20. The N side is filled by St John's Kirk of Perth and Perth City Hall (*see* Churches and Public Buildings, above). On the S side, after the corner block with St John Street (*see* above), No. 5, an office block by *James Parr & Partners*, *c.* 1985, built for the General Accident Fire & Life Assurance Corporation. Stepped arrangement of walls which are alternately of concrete blocks unbroken by openings and fully glazed with dark glass. A large metal relief of the company's coat of arms has gone. Across a small car park, to the W, No. 6 of *c.* 1905. Two-storey and attic in the Georgian survival manner of fifty years before, a consoled cornice over the ground-floor shopfront. The late C19 No. 7 is of red sandstone. Neo-Jacobean, with a Dutch gablet at the centre. Low wing, probably of the C19, to FLESHER'S VENNEL where its front wall contains a stone carved with the high relief of a thistle, the initials LR, MB, and the date 1766. Across Flesher's Vennel, a long two-storey block (No. 8). The E part with a central chimneyed gablet is by *John W. Smart*, 1910, its W continuation in the same manner by *Smart, Stewart & Mitchell*, 1926. Then a very plain early C20 building adjoining the corner block to King Edward Street (*see* above).

SOUTH WILLIAM STREET was laid out *c.* 1800 but the N side contains three large housing developments of the 1990s. The drydashed VICTORIA MEWS, is enlivened by shallowly projecting timber-clad oriels at the front gables and Roman Doric porticoes on the long W side. To the W, Nos. 21–23, by *James F. Stephen*, 1997, the walling of concrete block, hints of Mackintosh provided by the metal grilles in front of the large stair windows. KINGS COURT, by *Woodside & Parker*, 1998, is also drydashed, its prominent front gables giving it rather the look of model workers' housing of a century before. Across the street, an early C19 piend-roofed villa (No. 22) with a broad pilastered and corniced doorpiece; bowed projection at the rear.

SPEYGATE is short and its E side now a car park. On the W, Nos. 17–21, a three-storey and attic block of 1802. Droved ashlar front of six bays, the windows grouped 3:3; two-bay chimneyed gablet at the centre.

TAY STREET was opened in 1869, the buildings confined to the W side, the E open to the River Tay behind which rises Kinnoull Hill. What should be Perth's parade ground for the fashionable is curiously lifeless, characterised by worthiness rather than glitter. The E side is a tree-shaded promenade, its present appearance dating from 1999–2001 when it was repaved and furnished in connection with the Perth Flood Prevention Scheme. That scheme required that the railings which had topped the river embankment be replaced by a parapet. This is of stone, its E (river) side hammer-dressed like the earlier walling below, its W face of polished ashlar and punctuated by low pyramid-finialled piers of Late Georgian character, some with niches carved with reliefs and inscriptions. Openings for flood gates which are fronted by mild steel gates decorated with stylized motifs derived from the flora and fauna of the River Tay. On the axis of High Street the parapet breaks to give access to a rail-fronted elliptical viewing platform projecting above the river. Broad walkway on the landward side of the parapet, paved with Caithness stone slabs and setts, agreeably varied but refreshingly unfussy in design. Along the promenade are SCULPTURES. At the N end, the bronze 'Eagle of Perth' by *Shona Kinloch*, erected here in 2003. Near Queen's Bridge (*see* Public Buildings, above), 'Goldeneye on the Dark and Singing Tide', by *David Annand*, 2002. Near the S end, 'Salmon Run', by *Lee Brewster*, 2003, a sinuous metal bench, its curved undulating back pierced by figures of leaping salmon.

On Tay Street's W side, at the N end after the polite Late Georgian building on the corner of George Street (*see* above) No. 2, is a tall three-storey Thomsonesque Ægypto-Greek block of *c.* 1875, followed by the unexciting back of the Royal George Hotel (*see* George Street, above). The building line is established by the red sandstone bulk of the former Middle Free Church (*see* Churches, above). To its S, Nos. 8–10, a symmetrical Gothic double house by *Andrew Heiton Jun.*, 1878–9, its manner and stugged ashlar a prelude to the contemporary Old Council Chambers beyond (*see* Public Buildings, above).

On the S corner of High Street, the yellow-coloured Baroque edifice of the Council Buildings (*see* Public Buildings, above). Then the detached former Savings Bank (No. 26) by *Andrew Heiton Jun.*, 1874, villa-like, of two storeys and an attic. U-plan front of three broad bays, the advanced ends topped by French pavilion roofs (now bereft of cresting); on the wallhead of the centrepiece, a pedimented dormer. In this centrepiece, a ground-floor window of three round-headed and keystoned lights with Roman Doric column-mullions. At the ends, two-light first-floor windows with lugged architraves and cornices. At the ground floor of the S bay, a round-arched doorpiece under a balcony. The N bay has a two-light window but a N outshot contains a door of the same design as that at the S. After the steepled Gothic verticality of St Matthew's Church (*see* Churches, above), the long (twenty-one bay) three-storey gently convex frontage of Nos. 36–44, by *Andrew Heiton Jun.*, 1872. This is another polished ashlar essay in Thomsonesque Ægypto-Greek. GOWRIE HOUSE (Nos. 48–52) is by *John Young*, 1873, symmetrical stodgy Ruskinian Gothic but with bargeboarded dormers. On the N corner of South Street, the former County Buildings and, between South Street and Canal Street, the long temple front of Perth Sheriff Court, neither quite assertive enough of its importance (for these, see Public Buildings, above).

On the S corner of Canal Street, No. 60 Tay Street, by *Ian Burke Associates*, 1987–9, a large four-storey block of housing faced in rough-textured artificial stone. Some Neo-Victorian touches are provided by its gablets, roof cresting and a couple of perfunctory oriels but it remains unenjoyable. This occupies the site of the N end of a long range, by *John Young*, 1879–81, whose centre was originally the Perthshire Natural History Museum. The surviving two-thirds of the range is of two tall storeys and an attic, built of stugged ashlar. The style is polite but unexciting Flemish Renaissance. To the S, a large housing and office development, by *Woodside & Parker*, 1996–7, a crow-step-gabled parody of Victorian Scottish Baronial. At the end of Tay Street, a plate-girder span of the railway viaduct (see Public Buildings, above) cuts off the Fergusson Gallery (see Public Buildings, above) from the rest of the street.

VICTORIA STREET was formed at the beginning of the C19. At the E end, on the N side, a car park fronting a flat-roofed shed-like supermarket of the 1970s; on the S, 1990s development, for which see South William Street. Across Charles Street, on the N side, ST JOHNSTOUN'S BUILDINGS, working-class housing by *R. McKillop*, 1902–3. Two broad-eaved tenement blocks forming an L-shape. Harled, with half-timbering in the gables. Oriel windows and swan-neck-pedimented dormers. For the block beyond, see Scott Street. On the S side of Victoria Street and extending W to Scott Street, housing, by *R. Atkins*, 2003–4. On Victoria Street's N side, between Scott Street and James Street, is UNITY PLACE (Nos. 33–37) designed by *Charles S. Robertson* and built for the City of Perth Co-operative Society in 1895. Thrifty Scots Jacobean. W of James Street, Nos. 39–45, a terraced pair of mid-C19 double houses, each pair's pilastered entrances twinned under a Jacobean gabled centre.

WATERGATE was one of the streets of the medieval burgh but none of its present buildings are earlier than the C18. For the corner blocks at the N end, see High Street. On the W side, the former PERTH NIGHT SHELTER FOR FEMALES by *David Smart*, 1902, the title more exciting than the architecture. To its S, the former meeting place of the Wrights' Incorporation (Nos. 21–27), dated 1725 at the main entrance but now rendered and the roof altered. It is of three storeys and an attic, the narrow windows of the ten-bay frontage grouped in a not quite symmetrical 4:2:4 arrangement. At the off-centre main entrance, a Roman Doric pilastered and broken-pedimented doorpiece. Near the N end, a mid-C19 entrance, its round-arched and console-corniced door set in a Roman Doric pilastered and corniced frame, the frieze carved with emblems of the Masons' Guild which met here for a time. Further down, on the W, No. 41, by *James Smart*, 1898, a display of almost continuous mullioned glazing at the first floor; ground-floor pub front, its stumpy granite Ionic pilasters supporting tall consoles under the entablature. On the E side, a late C19 printing works (Nos. 60–66), the twin bargeboarded broad gables each containing a pair of tall elliptically arched cart openings. At the S end of the W side, Nos. 73–85, three-storey vernacular of *c.* 1800. For the end building, *see* South Street.

WEST MILL STREET. *See* Mill Street and Murray Street.

YORK PLACE, the W continuation of the line of South Street and County Place, was first developed as the site of the Perth City and County Infirmary (now A. K. Bell Library) in the 1830s and then for housing. The N side begins with Nos. 1–9 York Place and Nos. 43–47 New Row, a large four-storey tenement block of polished buff-coloured ashlar, by *G. P. K. Young*, 1907. Edwardian free Renaissance. Over the canted corner, a copper-roofed octagonal cupola. The corner's first- and second-floor windows are framed by broken-pedimented aedicules, the first-floor's segmental pediment containing a coat of arms, the second-floor pediment triangular and containing carved fruit. At the S front, the centre bay is given importance by channelled masonry. Under its second-floor window, a curved sill projected on consoles, the tall centre console stretching down to serve also as the keystone of the window below. The third-floor window is placed in an aedicule whose Corinthian columns carry an open segmental pediment; under the window sill, consoles whose fronts are carved with human heads. Ground-floor shopfronts whose glazing bars give the windows something of the appearance of Louis XV mirrors. Less exuberant Queen Anne-style block by *McLaren & Mackay*, 1908, at No. 13, again of polished ashlar. Beyond this are villas of the mid and later C19, mostly Jacobean in manner. Among them, Trinity Church of the Nazarene (*see* Churches, above). On the S side of York Place, set well back on a mound, is the commanding presence of the A. K. Bell Library (*see* Public Buildings, above).

W of Caledonian Road, more villas of the later C19. Nos. 18–20 form a double house, with Roman Doric column-mullions at the bay windows and piered doorpieces at the advanced centre. Another double house at No. 32, the bay windows and doorpieces with Ægypto-Greek ornament. At No. 35, a single-storey Jacobean rear wing added for the British Linen Co. Bank by *Peddie & Washington Browne* in 1898–9.

INDUSTRIAL BUILDINGS

CITY MILLS, West Mill Street. Informal rubble-built group on both sides of West Mill Street; they were served by the town's lade which brought water from the River Almond. On the S side of the street, the LOWER CITY MILLS, an oatmeal mill. It acquired its present shape and appearance in the rebuilding (after a fire) by *John Stewart*, wright in Perth, 1803, but probably incorporates earlier masonry. Three-storey main block, rectangular except for the canted SW corner, covered with three parallel piended roofs. At the W gable an elliptical arch at the entrance of the lade. S front of four bays. Short piend-roofed E wing. At the SE corner, a pyramid-roofed square kiln. Inside, a low-breast paddle wheel driving three pairs of stones. Across the street, to the N, a GRANARY of 1771. It is of four storeys, basement and attic. Six-bay E front; a stair-tower on the W. The building was cleaned in the late C20 when almost all the dressed stonework was renewed.

The granary is joined by a two-storey and attic harled wing of 1979–81 to the UPPER CITY MILLS (now, RAMADA JARVIS HOTEL). The mill (originally a grain mill) is an irregular U-shape, its ranges of three storeys or three storeys and an attic. Mid-C18 piend-roofed W range, its W front of five bays. The S and E ranges are of the later C18, the S probably added in 1788. The E courtyard was filled by a single-storey block and the windows given cement margins in 1970–1 when *T. M. Miller & Partners* converted the mill to a hotel.

DYE WORKS, St Catherine's Road. Now a shopping centre (HIGHLAND HOUSE) set in a retail park. By *Smart & Stewart*, 1919–21. Three-storey block, the rendered concrete frame containing panels of glazed red brick and glass. Segmental gable over the centre of the N front, shallow curvilinear gables at the front's E end and the bowed NW corner.

NORTH BRITISH DYE WORKS, Kinnoull Street, Mill Street, Skinnergate and Union Street. Now Perth and Kinross council offices. Remains of the biggest dye works in late C19 Scotland, built for the firm of J. Pullar & Sons which exploited Perth's position at the hub of Scotland's railway network for the speedy collection and dispatch of cloth.

The L-plan main block (now PULLAR HOUSE) on the corner of Kinnoull Street and Mill Street is dated 1865. Very large but unshowy Renaissance, built of stugged masonry; bracketed broad eaves to the piended roofs. Two storeys, the first-floor windows segmental-headed. At the twenty-nine-bay Mill Street front, a slightly advanced and pedimented three-bay centrepiece, its central window at both floors of three lights, the first-floor window's sidelights rectangular making a quasi-Venetian. Fifteen-bay elevation to Kinnoull Street with elliptically arched carriage entrances at the centre of the ground floor. Beside these, a bronze PLAQUE by *Singer & Sons*, 1899, commemorating Sir Robert Pullar's golden jubilee as a partner in the firm the previous year. It bears a relief depicting the works in 1848 and a portrait bust of Sir Robert by *John Tweed*. The building was converted to offices, given a glazed canopy over the front entrance and extended at the rear by *Keppie Design*, 1999–2000. At the E and N ends, crowstep-gabled additions by *J. Murray Robertson*, 1889–1901, also built of stugged masonry and with segment-headed windows at the upper floors. The E block, fronting Mill Street E of Curfew Row, is of three storeys and an attic. Thirty-one bays, with a slightly advanced centrepiece. Four-storey thirteen-bay N block (to Kinnoull Street), a hoist opening in the N gable. Further additions of the early and mid C20 at the SE corner and along Union Street.

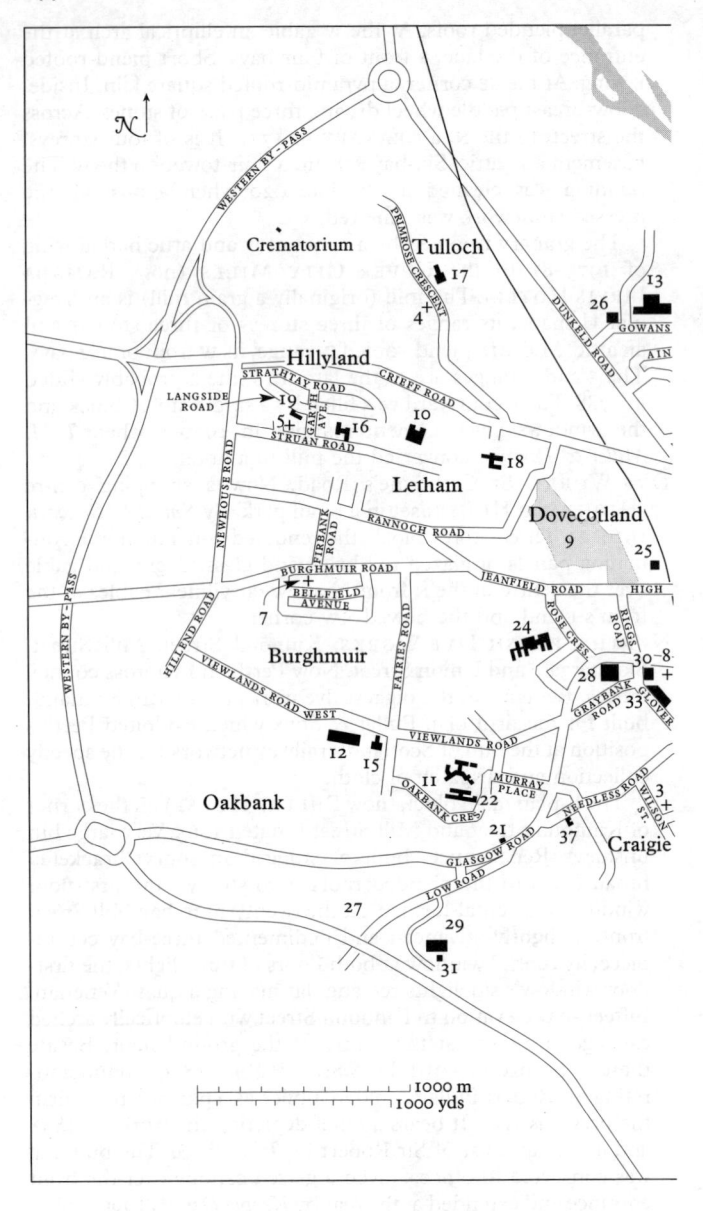

PERTH

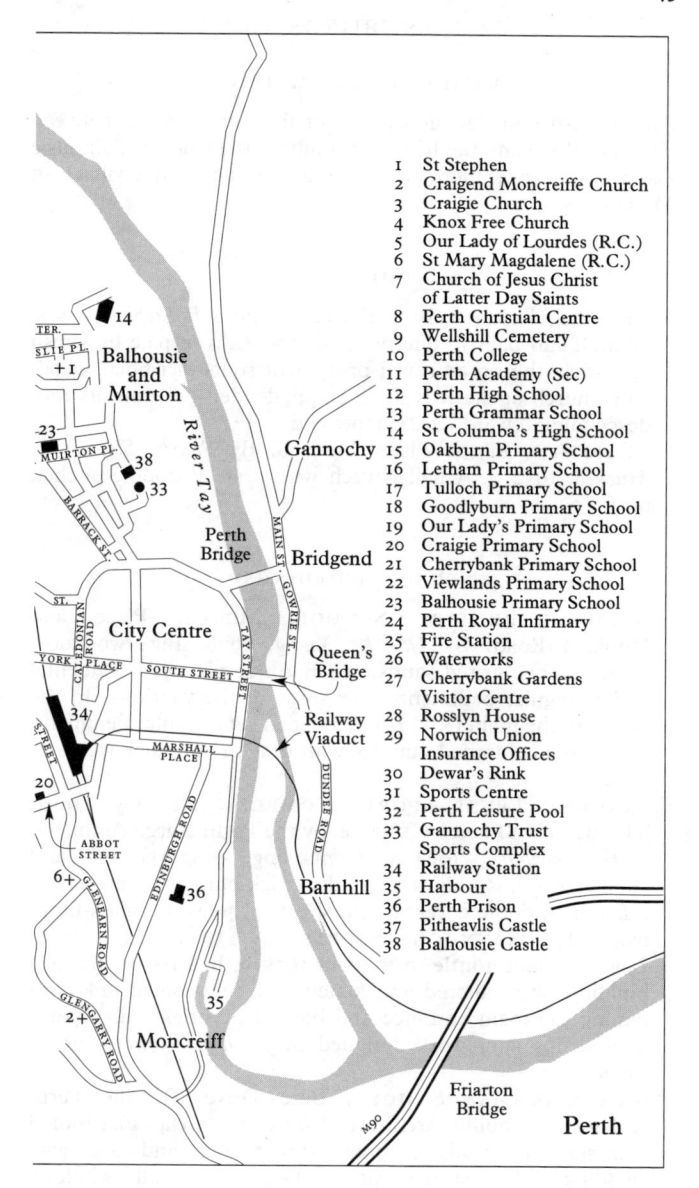

PERTH

1 St Stephen
2 Craigend Moncreiffe Church
3 Craigie Church
4 Knox Free Church
5 Our Lady of Lourdes (R.C.)
6 St Mary Magdalene (R.C.)
7 Church of Jesus Christ of Latter Day Saints
8 Perth Christian Centre
9 Wellshill Cemetery
10 Perth College
11 Perth Academy (Sec)
12 Perth High School
13 Perth Grammar School
14 St Columba's High School
15 Oakburn Primary School
16 Letham Primary School
17 Tulloch Primary School
18 Goodlyburn Primary School
19 Our Lady's Primary School
20 Craigie Primary School
21 Cherrybank Primary School
22 Viewlands Primary School
23 Balhousie Primary School
24 Perth Royal Infirmary
25 Fire Station
26 Waterworks
27 Cherrybank Gardens Visitor Centre
28 Rosslyn House
29 Norwich Union Insurance Offices
30 Dewar's Rink
31 Sports Centre
32 Perth Leisure Pool
33 Gannochy Trust Sports Complex
34 Railway Station
35 Harbour
36 Perth Prison
37 Pitheavlis Castle
38 Balhousie Castle

SUBURBS

BALHOUSIE AND MUIRTON

Area of C19 and C20 housing N of the City Centre, between Dunkeld Road and the River Tay, built on the lands of Balhousie Castle (*see* Description, below) and the site of the village of Muirton.

CHURCHES

RIVERSIDE CHURCH, Bute Drive. By *James F. Stephen*, 2002. Church and halls in one building, the walls of pale brownish red brick, the broad-eaved prominent roofs of ribbed metal. The church at the N is a tall stepped-sided polygon, its roof descending towards the narrow end.

ST STEPHEN, Ainslie Place. Disused. By *Smart, Stewart & Mitchell*, 1952–4. A hall church with a steep double-pitched roof.

PUBLIC BUILDINGS

BALHOUSIE PRIMARY SCHOOL, Muirton Place and Dunkeld Road. By *G. P. K. Young*, 1908. Big two-storey Wrenaissance in red sandstone. Baroque consoled segmental and triangular pediments over some of the windows. In the centre of the main (NW) front, an open semicircular pediment. Two Ionic columned cupolas with dragon and cock weathervanes.

GANNOCHY TRUST SPORTS COMPLEX, off Hay Street. The BELL'S SPORTS CENTRE, by the Perth Burgh Architect, *D. B. Cockburn*, 1964–8. Containing a sports hall and changing rooms, this is a circular brick-built structure under a flattened dome covered with sheets of polyester-glass-fibrenylon. The GANNOCHY SPORTS PAVILION, by *Gordon & Dey*, was built a little to the S in 1975–9. In 1989–91 the two buildings were altered and joined by a tent-roofed link containing the main entrance and backed by brick-built squash courts, this later work designed by *Perth & Kinross District Council*.

PERTH GRAMMAR SCHOOL, Bute Drive. By the Perth & Kinross County Architect, *John Nicol*, 1974. Flat-roofed complex, the walls covered with render and aggregate cladding. Three-storey main block, its small windows making it fortress-like but it lacks either excitement or civic presence.

ST COLUMBA'S HIGH SCHOOL, Malvina Place. By the Perth & Kinross County Architect, *Ian A. Moodie*, 1962. Flat-roofed main block with curtain-walled sides and brick gables, the S gable gripped by a narrow tower. Single-storey butterfly-roofed W addition of *c.* 1985.

ST NININAN'S PRIMARY SCHOOL, Barrack Street. By *John Young*, 1874–6. Single-storey; long, picturesquely gabled and broad-eaved.

WATERWORKS, Gowan Terrace. By *Crouch & Hogg*, 1962–5.

DESCRIPTION

The lands of Balhousie between Barossa Place and Low Street on the S and Muirton Bank on the N, and bounded by Dunkeld Road on the W and Hay Street on the E were laid out for housing in 1870 by *David Smart* who also produced elevations, adopted only for some houses in Balhousie Street. It is an area of Late Victorian and Edwardian villas, sparingly adorned with bargeboards; disappointingly few of the gardens contain monkey-puzzle trees. On the E side of HAY STREET is BAL-HOUSIE CASTLE, a large Baronial villa by *David Smart*, 1862–3, incorporating an L-plan house of 1631 whose rubble stonework is visible on the E side. NE addition of 1912, also Baronial and of three storeys but lower than the 1860s house.

N of Muirton Place, C20 local authority housing. The best, between Ainslie Place and Gowans Terrace, is by the Perth Burgh Surveyor, *Thomas McLaren*, with *John A. W. Grant* as consultant architect, 1937–8. Piend-roofed tenement blocks of two and three storeys, with red artificial stone dressings enlivening their harled walls. The style is early C18, the doorpieces corniced, some with segmental pediments; compromised but not unpleasantly by bay windows. The architectural dignity of these blocks was lost in the 1990s when the top floors and entrance bays of the three-storey blocks were picked out in a different colour from the rest and, at all the blocks, dressings were harled over and windows (formerly astragalled) replaced. In North Muirton, N of Gowans Terrace, housing by *James Miller & Partners Ltd.*, 1970.

On the E side of DUNKELD ROAD, between Florence Place and Ainslie Gardens, the ASDA shopping development by *Percy Johnson-Marshall & Partners*, 1989–90, clad in red brick with yellow brick bands for decoration. At the main entrance, a huge steep-pitched glass porch from which glazed verandas extend along the sides of the building.

BARNHILL, BRIDGEND AND GANNOCHY

Bridgend is on the E side of the Tay and in the parish of Kinnoull, much of which belonged to the Earls of Kinnoull from the early C17. Although it had become a burgh of barony in 1706, Bridgend was, until the opening of Perth Bridge in 1771, 'a poor paltry village, consisting of a few houses chiefly for the accommodation of the boatmen and their families'. Thereafter, it developed as a prosperous suburb of Perth, with villas along the bank of the River Tay and on the rising ground behind. Later C19 villa development extended to the lands of Barnhill to the S

PERTH

and along the A94 to the NE. Model housing for artisans was built on the farmland of Gannochy to the NE in the 1920s and 1930s.

CHURCHES

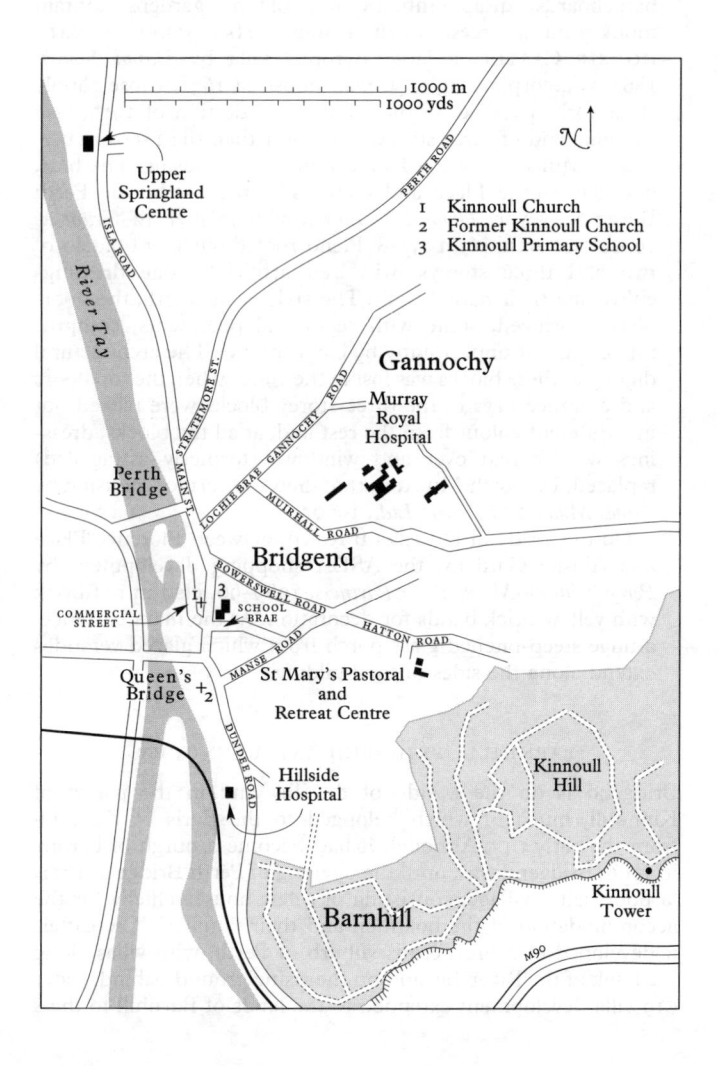

Former KINNOULL CHURCH, off Dundee Road. The church itself, of medieval origin but the body rebuilt in 1779, has been demolished except for a small transeptal N 'aisle' (the KINNOULL AISLE) built to house the burial vault and, presumably, the laird's seat of the Earls of Kinnoull. The date of 1635 on its NE skewputt is probably that of its erection but the masonry of the N gable suggests that it has been heightened and the roof pitch steepened, perhaps during construction, so as to accommodate the monument inside. Rubble-built, with a tall steeply pitched roof and crowstepped N gable, its top intaken. Cavetto eaves cornices at the sides, each of which is pierced by a pair of high-set rectangular windows. In the E side, between the windows, a door with a chamfered surround and surmounted by the moulded frame of a missing heraldic panel. The S gable must originally have contained an archway into the church but seems to have been rebuilt, probably in 1826 when the church was demolished. The Aisle was repaired by *Benjamin Tindall* in 1995 when a corrugated iron roof covering was replaced by slates.

Inside, the Aisle's N end is filled by the aedicular sandstone MONUMENT to George, first Earl of Kinnoull, Lord Chancellor and Keeper of the Great Seal of Scotland, †1634. This is an ostentatious display of Artisan Mannerism, originally painted. Tall corniced base or sarcophagus, its broad centre containing the strapwork frame for an inscription which has weathered away. At the corners the base breaks forward as pedestals, their fronts carved with trophies. The sides of the pedestals and the curvaceous panels which project laterally from the back of the base bear various motifs including a cartouche under an angel's head, a putto, foliage and mail-clad hands. Above the side panels are scroll-like panels decorated with rosettes under strapwork. The main superstructure of the monument is in the form of a portico. At its back, boldly projecting end pilasters, the l. carved with flowers and human and animal heads, the r. with strapwork. At the front, three skinny columns, their capitals of Corinthian aspiration, each standing on a pedestal whose front and sides are carved with cartouches, perhaps intended to be painted with heraldic motifs. The columns' design is inspired by Elstrack's frontispiece to Sir Walter Raleigh's *History of the World* (1614). As in the frontispiece, the shaft of each column is treated differently and probably intended to represent a virtue (as do the prototypes whose symbolism of the virtues of history is made explicit by identifying labels). The l. shaft is carved with upward-spiralling leafy oak branches, the centre shaft with strapwork. The r. shaft is of Solomonic barley-sugar form and crossed by two foliaged bands; at its upper half, a loosely draped cloth strip bearing an inscription from Virgil's *Aeneid*, DISCITE IUSTITIAM MONITE ('Be Warned, Learn Justice'). At the surmounting entablature, a boldly modelled fruit-covered frieze and mutuled cornice. On top, statues of unicorns (one now without its horn) supporting shields. These flank a large panel carved in high relief with the heraldic achievement of the Earl of Kinnoull. At the ends, small pedestals with spearhead finials.

The back of the 'portico' is carved in high relief with a scene depicting a life-size figure of the Earl closely modelled on his portrait by Daniel Mytens. He is richly dressed in an embroidered doublet and the Lord Chancellor's robe and with shoes decorated with huge pom-poms but his stockings slightly wrinkled. His l. hand rests on a table covered with a fringed cloth. On the table stands the purse containing the Great Seal of Scotland, its front bearing the royal arms. Beside this there used to be the carving of a human skull. Above the table hover the high reliefs of two chubby angels holding cloths. The walling above these figures was almost certainly painted, perhaps with clouds and a sunburst so that the whole scene may have signified Kinnoull's earthly glory ending in death from which his soul ascended to God.

GRAVEYARD. W of the Kinnoull Aisle, a TABLE STONE erected in 1782 by the shipmaster, John Turcan, to his son, David. The W upright is carved with the relief of a ship under full sail, the E with an anchor. – W of this, the HEADSTONE of John Duff and Mary Murray, also of 1782, its W face with the relief of a large angel floating above a ferryman. – Near the graveyard's SW corner, the much suaver HEADSTONE of 1805 commemorating Thomas Fyffe, the W face with drapery and a shield bearing the dividers, chisel and axe of a wright. – S of the Kinnoull Aisle, the HEADSTONE of Robert Knox, boatman, †1708, with a crudely carved angel's head (the soul) above a shield bearing a salmon.

KINNOULL CHURCH, Dundee Road. By *William Burn*, 1824–6. Late Georgian Perpendicular, built of broached Huntingtower ashlar, much patched with cement. The plan is basically a Greek cross but with a very short wing projecting from the W limb and, at the E limb, a façade which is stepped both on plan and in elevation. This is formed by a sizeable full-height wing projecting from the gable and a low porch protruding from this wing. The N and S limbs have pinnacled angle buttresses. At the corners of the main E and W limbs, diagonal buttresses whose tops slope into the walls. The E and W wings have octagonal buttresses, their pinnacles fatter than those of the N and S limbs. Octagonal clasping buttresses also at the porch but without pinnacles and with the cornice under the porch's parapet carried round them. At the top of the E wing's gable is corbelled out an octagonal spire-topped bellcote with gabled faces pierced by round-headed slits. Below the bellcote, a clock face erected in 1885. A five-light window in the gable of the W limb and four-light windows in the other gables, all with simple tracery and hoodmoulds. In the side walls of the limbs, two-light Y-traceried and hoodmoulded windows.

Inside, a plaster ceiling, with a saucer dome over the crossing, pointed tunnel vaults over the limbs. *Smart, Stewart & Mitchell* removed the galleries and refurnished the area in 1929–30. In the W limb, a COMMUNION TABLE of 1949 flanked by a simple Gothic oak PULPIT and FONT of 1930. – Oak PEWS of 1930. – In the NW corner of the W limb, the ORGAN by the *Electric Organ Co.*, 1895–6, its oak case also of 1930.

STAINED GLASS. Strongly coloured and realistic five-light main W window (Scenes from the Parables) designed by *J. E. Millais* and executed by *Lavers, Barraud & Westlake*, 1870. – In the W wall of the main W limb, and this limb's s side, a pair of two-light windows (Scenes from the Life of Our Lord) of 1945–6 by *Douglas Strachan*, well-coloured and restrained for that artist. – The s limb's garishly coloured w window (St Columba and St Ninian) is by *Roy D. Guild*, 1973. – The corresponding window in the N limb (Our Lord and Members of the Boys' Brigade) is by *John Blyth*, 1989. – Expressionist main E window (the Nativity of Our Lord; the Calling of St Andrew and St Peter; the Risen Lord by the Sea of Tiberias; the Risen Lord on the Emmaus Road) by *James Ballantine II*, 1933.

To the s, a HALL by *David Smart*, 1901–3. Gothic behind a Tudorish two-storey front block.

PUBLIC BUILDINGS

FRIARTON BRIDGE. Carrying the M90 over the River Tay, a gently curved and gently sloping concrete viaduct constructed as two parallel box girders, by *Freeman, Fox & Partners*, 1975–8. Principal elliptical-arched span over the river of 174 m. flanked by 114 m.-long approach spans and six further outer spans of 63 m. or 75 m. length, all supported on boxy piers.

HILLSIDE HOSPITAL, Dundee Road. By *J. Murray Robertson*, 1898–1901, in a sort of Georgian manner. At the E front, a boldly projecting porch, the entrance framed by Roman Doric columns. W front of eight bays, the two at either end under open pediments. The first-floor windows are set in round-headed recesses. Large but plain additions of 1928 (by *Heiton & McKay*) to the s and 1932 (by *Smart, Stewart & Mitchell*) to the N.

KINNOULL PRIMARY SCHOOL, Dundee Road. By *Andrew Heiton Jun.*, 1875–6. Single-storey, Italianate but with 'Greek' Thomson detail, built of stugged pinkish ashlar with polished yellow ashlar dressings. U-plan composed of three pitch-roofed ranges, the court filled with a flat-roofed block. The gables of the ranges are all pedimented and with acroteria. In each gable, a three-light window, that of the N plain, the others corniced and with classical pier-mullions. Two-light side windows at the N and s ranges, those of the N plain, those of the s again corniced and with pier-mullions.

KINNOULL TOWER, off Corsiehill Road. A folly erected by the Earl of Kinnoull and dramatically poised on the cliff-top edge of Kinnoull Hill overlooking the Carse of Gowrie, it is by *W. M. Mackenzie*, 1829. Rubble-built round tower, its parapet carried on small corbels; tall slit window in the s segment. The tower stands beside the ruin of a late C18 single-storey building which has been picturesquely dressed up with an arched E window (now fragmentary), a tall slit window to the w and a segmental-arched s window.

MURRAY ROYAL HOSPITAL, Muirhall Road and Gannochy Road. Founded as a lunatic asylum under the will of James Murray of Tarsappie, a native of Perth. *William Burn* was appointed architect in 1821 and the main block built in 1822–7.

This is large and stolid, of two storeys and a projecting basement which becomes a fully exposed ground floor in the fall of the ground at the back, the walls built of brown-coloured whinstone ashlar with dressings of polished sandstone. SE front of twenty-five bays, the first-floor windows joined by a sill course. The five centre bays and the two at each end are advanced and parapeted, their ground-floor windows corniced and aproned. Plain eight-bay links with a blocking course at the wallhead. At the advanced central bay of the centrepiece, a Roman Doric portico fronting the entrance; three-light window above. Rising one storey above the centrepiece is an octagonal tower, its cupola added in 1864. Rear wing, its broad NW gable with three-light windows in the end bays; the centre three bays of the upper floors contain elliptical arches, originally open to provide balcony/loggia spaces where the patients could enjoy the benefits of fresh air. Each side of this end, an L-plan single-storey wing added by Burn in 1833. At the front block's NE end, a flat-roofed single-storey extension of 1976, the harled walls broken by large areas of glazing.

Immediately NW of the main block, a pair of WARD BLOCKS by *Andrew Heiton Jun.*, 1889. Plain Renaissance, the masonry of buff-coloured stugged ashlar, with dressings of polished red sandstone. NW of this, the CHAPEL built in 1903–4 to a design by the hospital's Physician Superintendent, *Dr A. R. Urquhart*. Scots Late Gothic. Masonry of hammer-dressed red sandstone ashlar above a high base of crazy-paved whinstone. Crocketed pinnacled buttresses at the semi-octagonal apsed NW end. More buttresses at the corners of the crowstepped SE gable from which projects a whinstone-walled tower surmounted by an octagonal cupola. (Inside, STAINED GLASS apse windows (the Good Samaritan) by *Douglas Strachan*, 1913.) The chapel is flanked by a pair of two-storey identical harled VILLAS containing wards, by *McLaren & Mackay*, also of 1903–4. English Arts and Crafts, with half-timbering at the slightly jettied upper floors. At the centre of each front, a loggia, its columns of an idiosyncratic order. Battered chimneys give an Art Nouveau touch. To the SW, STAFF RESIDENCE by *Smart, Stewart & Mitchell*, 1937–9, a long three-storey harled building in a gentle Art Deco manner. At the SW corner of the site, an Italianate LODGE of *c.* 1865. Some way E of the main complex, GILGAL designed by *Smart, Stewart & Mitchell* to house voluntary patients and built in 1929–31. Squared-up Lorimerian Scotstyle in harling and artificial stone. Of one and two storeys, with a crowstepped centre gable, shaped dormerheads and bow windows under ogee-domed roofs.

ST MARY'S PASTORAL AND RETREAT CENTRE, Hatton Road. Built in 1867–70 for the Congregation of the Most Holy Redeemer (the Redemptorists), this was the first Roman Catholic religious house erected in Scotland since the Reformation. *Andrew Heiton Jun.* was the architect. The buildings originally formed an L, with the church at the N end of the living quarters. These are contained in an austere gabled and gableted range, built of hammer-dressed masonry. Asymmetrical U-plan W front. In its NW inner angle, a square tower under a fish-scale-slated truncated spire, with large lucarned dormer windows at its main faces; on top of the main spire, a spired cupola. A S range, containing quarters for novices, was added by *A. G. Heiton*, 1895–6. At this range's NE corner, a clock tower, its lower stages circular, its top octagonal and finished with a spired roof.

The CHURCH itself is tall, with an undercroft at the W (liturgical E) end where the ground slopes steeply. Four-bay nave with low aisles, the N buttressed, a NE porch and barely projecting SE chapel, transepts (the S a sacristy which joins to the living quarters) and semi-octagonal buttressed chancel. In the inner angle of the chancel and S transept, a round bell-tower, its top stage slightly intaken and pierced by tall pointed belfry openings; fish-scale-slated conical roof. The masonry is again hammer-dressed. Austere Gothic detail, with lancet windows to the aisles and, with bell capitals, at the nave's E gable and the N transept. Quatrefoil clearstorey openings placed in circular surrounds. Pointed doors with bell-capitalled shafts at the E end and, under an empty image niche, at the porch. At the chancel, much larger tabernacled niches filled. *c.* 1875, with statues of St Joseph, the Virgin and Child and St Alfonso de' Liguori, founder of the Redemptorist order.

Inside, the nave arcades have steeply pointed arches carried on columns, their shafts of Huntingtower sandstone, their bases and bell capitals of Dunmore stone. Vaulted plaster roofs, their ribs springing from bell-moulded corbels except at the E end where they are supported on foliage-capitalled attached columns, the shafts of polished granite. Pointed chancel arch carried on lobed piers which stand on squat foliage-capitalled columns supported by large corbels, each carved by *Thomas Earp* with the figure of an angel. Pointed dummy arch on the sacristy wall at the W end of the S aisle. To the chancel the sacristy presents a pointed door under a window of three trefoil-headed pointed lights. Pointed arches from the N aisle and the chancel into the N transept (the Chapel of St Alfonso de' Liguori).

Round the chancel's liturgical E end, pastrycutter blind arcading enlivened by figures of angels. This forms a backdrop for the HIGH ALTAR which is of Caen stone, the end panels containing marble-shafted attached columns, the centre panels decorated with metalwork. Above the altar, a tall steepled REREDOS. It is of Caen stone and alabaster, plentifully carved with angels (two of these designed by *George Goldie*) and bearing a painting of Our Lady of Perpetual Succour. – In the S transept, a gabled Gothic REREDOS with foliage-capitalled and marble shafted columns framing a large statue of St Alfonso de' Liguori above two reliefs of scenes from his life. – In the Chapel of the Sacred Heart at the (liturgical) E end of the (liturgical) S aisle, the REREDOS is painted with a depiction of the Sacred Heart flanked by statues of SS Peter and

Paul. – Victorian PEWS. – Late C19 ORGAN in the s transept, by *Henry Willis & Sons Ltd.*, its pipes stencilled. – STAINED GLASS. Liturgical w window (Scenes from the History of the Redemptorist Congregation), garishly coloured realism by *D. H. Didmann*, c. 1870. – In the (liturgical) N aisle, a mid-C20 two-light window (St Margaret of Scotland; St William of Rochester and Perth).

UPPER SPRINGLAND CENTRE, Isla Road. Residential complex for the handicapped, by *Gordon & Dey*, 1974–85. White dry-dashed low buildings, with concrete-tiled monopitch roofs and clearstorey glazing.

DESCRIPTION

DUNDEE ROAD, the former turnpike road, is the approach to Barnhill from the s. The first announcement of the approach of the city is given by the early C19 piend-roofed BARNHILL TOLL HOUSE. T-plan with the tail projecting towards the road. In the front of the tail, a recessed window framed by fluted Greek Doric columns. The next incident, also on the w side of the road, is HILLRISE, a tall white-harled house of c. 1930. Just to its N, BARNHILL LODGE at the entrance to the former policies of the now demolished Barnhill House. It was built in 1828 by *William Brough*, mason, and *Robert Smeaton*, wright, who also superintended the work but the design may be by *W. M. Mackenzie* who had been responsible for work at the mansion house two years before. Single-storey, of broached ashlar, with a semi-octagonal E end. Round-arched and hood-moulded windows.

Opposite, at the foot of the path to Kinnoull Hill, THE LOVER'S WELL, a Victorian drinking trough projecting from a stone slab carved with foliage; the slab is set between the tops of Late Georgian Gothick gatepiers. Further up the path is ST LEONARD'S MANSE (No. 112 Dundee Road) by *C. J. Menart*, 1905. Asymmetrical Edwardian domestic Baroque, the broad-eaved piended roof projected over a flattened mutule cornice, the eaves broken by a consoled open segmental pediment above a big bow window. On this window's parapet, panels carved with reliefs of grotesque heads and swags. The path continues uphill to the E past the s end of FAIRMOUNT TERRACE. Here is BALNACRAIG, a large red sandstone villa by *Dunn & Findlay*, 1895. Peaceful Baronial, with crowstepped gables and oriel windows; dormerheads with segmental or curvaceous pediments, some decorated with reliefs. Conical-roofed round tower and a round corner turret topped by a corbelled-out square caphouse. The other houses in Fairmount Terrace are prosperous but smaller bay-windowed and broad-eaved villas of the later C19.

In Dundee Road N of the path to Kinnoull Hill and St Leonard's Manse, more villas like those in Fairmount Terrace followed by a few vernacular buildings of the earlier C19, Nos. 66–68 with a chimneyed gablet at the centre of the wallhead. Opposite this but set below the road, Hillside Hospital (*see*

Public Buildings, above). To its N is RIVERSIDE PARK by *Oberlander Associates*, 1990. Two blocks of flats with tiered slated roofs, some cut into to form balconies. N of this, mid-C20 bungalows placed quite discreetly below the level of the road and screened from it by a stone wall. On the E side of Dundee Road, a couple of Victorian villas followed by the high garden wall of BELLWOOD HOUSE, a large early C19 harled villa with pedimented centrepieces at both its E and W fronts.

Further N, on the S corner of Dundee Road and MANSE ROAD is BEECHGROVE (originally Kinnoull Manse) by *W. M. Mackenzie*, 1829, a subdued *cottage orné*. Opposite, No. 41 Dundee Road, a piend-roofed Late Georgian house, stands beside the lane leading to the graveyard containing the remains of the former Kinnoull Church (*see* Churches, above).

N of Manse Road, the E side of Dundee Road is dominated by the ISLE OF SKYE HOTEL, formed by the late C20 linking of two villas of the earlier C19, the S with carved bargeboards, the N with hoodmoulds over the windows, and the erection of a tall N addition in indeterminate Georgian vernacular style, which faces down to the Queen's Bridge (for which, *see* City Centre: Public Buildings, above).

N of the Isle of Skye Hotel, on the corner of School Brae, RIO (No. 14 Dundee Road) by *David Smart*, c. 1860, Italianate with a pyramid-roofed tower. Across School Brae, Kinnoull Primary School (*see* Public Buildings, above) looking over to Kinnoull Church and its hall (*see* Churches, above). On the W side of the road, KINNOULL COTTAGE of c. 1840, a substantial but unexciting *cottage* not quite *orné*, still with some horizontal-paned glazing in the windows, followed by the small mid-C19 Jacobean No. 25 Dundee Road. Also Jacobean but much larger is the ruthlessly symmetrical and remorselessly crowstepped KNOWEHEAD HOUSE of 1852. These are overlooked by houses on the W side of KINNOULL TERRACE, their gardens sloping down to Dundee Road. Of these, No. 6 (by *David Smart*, c. 1860) has a French pavilion-roofed tower, and the mid-C19 No. 4 (GASKHILL) is faintly Italianate, with an anthemion-fronted cast-iron balcony and bracketed eaves; bracketed eaves again at No. 2 (LANGLANDS), also of the mid or later C19. On the E side of Kinnoull Terrace, at its N end, CRAIGIEVAR and DARNICK (Nos. 1–3) by *Andrew Heiton Jun.*, c. 1870, form a large rogue Ruskinian-Gothic double villa, with conical-roofed fat round towers at the corners of the front. Below, on the S corner of Dundee Road and Bowerswell Road, No. 2 Dundee Road, a Jacobean villa of c. 1840. Small harled house, also mid-C19 Jacobean, on the N corner.

Further up BOWERSWELL ROAD, more mid-C19 Jacobean villas at BANKHEAD on the N side and DUPPLIN PARK on the S. Also on the N (reached from BOWERSWELL LANE) is BOWERSWELL, a large house of 1848, its architecture accomplished Italianate, with a low pyramid-roofed tower. To its E, on the corner of Mount Tabor Road, BOWERSWELL LODGE, broad-eaved single-storey and attic, of c. 1860. On the E corner with MOUNT TABOR ROAD, the white painted MANDERLEY of

1938, designed by *Cecil Stewart* and *G. P. K. Young & Son*, the main block covered by a slated pyramidal roof topped by a red brick chimneystack, the windows tall and vertical; it succeeds in being modern-traditional without historicist references.

GOWRIE STREET continues the line of Dundee Road. Above it, on the hillside to the E, POTTERHILL FLATS (reached from EAST BRIDGE STREET) by *E. V. Collins* of *George Wimpey & Co. Ltd.*, 1961–2, and very similar to the same architect's flats in Pomarium Street (*see* City Centre: Streets). Long eight-storey harled block, the recessed picture windows to the living rooms fronted by partly glazed balconies. Off-centre service tower faced with concrete latticing.

Below Gowrie Street on the W is COMMERCIAL STREET, redeveloped in 1975–8 by *James Parr & Partners* (partner-in-charge: *Angus MacDonald*). Terraced housing broken by the irregular building line into small units, all covered with steeply pitched slated roofs. The consistent use of reddish concrete blockwork for the walls and the unfussy glazing keep it well clear of neo-vernacular tweeness. At the N end of Commercial Street, CROSS KEYS COURT, a plain former public house of *c.* 1800. To its W, fronting onto the end of Perth Bridge (for which, *see* City Centre: Public Buildings, above), No. 1 WEST BRIDGE STREET, a piend-roofed single-storey, basement and sub-basement former toll house of *c.* 1800 with an open pediment over the centre; the pilastered shopfront looks an addition of the later C19.

MAIN STREET provides a small urban centre for Bridgend and a reminder of its Georgian prosperity at the E end of Perth Bridge. On both sides, three-storey terraced tenements of the late C18 and early C19. The W side begins quite stylishly with a block (Nos. 2–12) of painted broached ashlar. At its corner to West Bridge Street, a shallowly bowed quadrant with three-light windows to the upper floors; round-arched shop windows on both fronts. This W terrace is ended by BRIDGEND COURT, a four-storey block of flats by *Alex Strang & Associates*, 1970–3, behind which the development continues with houses stepping down to the Tay. The terrace on the E side of Main Street is unambitious. At its N end, Nos. 27–31, perhaps late C18, with a chimneyed wallhead pediment. The adjoining near-contemporary building (Nos. 33–37) has a Venetian window with dummy sidelights in its wallhead gablet (most of the chimney now missing).

Villas resume on the W side of Main Street with INCHBANK HOUSE (No. 26). It was described as 'new' in 1795 when it belonged to *John Gregory*, mason, who probably built and may have designed it. It is a tall three storeys, basement and attic. Front of diagonally droved ashlar (now painted), with giant Roman Doric pilasters at the ends. The basement and ground floor are each of seven bays. At the centre of the ground floor, a console-corniced doorpiece, the frieze decorated with a husk-garlanded panel and rosettes; in the penultimate bays, narrow dummy doors. The first and second floors are three-bay, the second floor's centre window surmounted by a badly weathered segmental pediment. Above, an angle-pilastered and chimneyed gablet containing a Venetian window, its sidelights dummies. The piended dormers may be original. Rubble-built rear, with a semi-octagonal stair-tower. Fronting Main Street to the N of Inchbank are the late C20 BRIDGEND LEISURE CENTRE and a plain two-storey and attic early C19 terrace (Nos. 56–62). These hide from the street five early C19 piend-roofed villas sited behind, close to the bank of the Tay looking across to the North Inch. All are of two storeys and a basement with three-bay elevations to the E and W. They begin at the S with NEWLANDS HOUSE, its E porch containing a Roman Doric columned entrance and pointed side windows. At the white-painted W front, skinny giant Ionic columns framing the parapeted centre. INVERAVEN is a less expensive version, with pilasters instead of columns at both the porch and the W front. RIVERSDALE is plain except for a Victorian oriel window added to the N gable. The broad pedimented centrepiece on the E front of EARNOCH looks like an addition. At the back, three-light windows in the outer bays of the ground floor. SPRINGBANK has a bowed centre to the river. Its plain channelled gatepiers and broad-eaved Victorian lodge mark the end of Main Street.

STRATHMORE STREET leads uphill to the NE from the fork at Main Street's end. On the E side, at the entrance to Ardchoille Park, the late C19 ARDCHOILLE LODGE, small but fierce Baronial with crowstepped gables and large inverted-keyhole 'gunloops'. Its mansion house, ARDCHOILLE (originally, Rosemount), standing at the end of ARDCHOILLE PARK's late C20 housing, is a large but low-key Baronial villa of 1851. Just N of Ardchoille Park, on the E side of Strathmore Street, two blocks of flats (Nos. 27–83) of c. 1970, unremarkable architecture but on the 'Fyfestone' S gable of the N block are bronze SCULPTURES of four birds and, in front of the recessed three-storey S block, a bronze SCULPTURE of three human figures, one holding a bird, all these by *Frances Pelly*, 1976. The road then continues as PITCULLEN CRESCENT and SCONE ROAD, bordered by Late Victorian villas. Off Pitcullen Crescent to the W is KINCARRATHIE HOUSE, a plain two-storey and attic rubble-built mansion house of the later C18. SE wing of 1853–4, a Roman Doric portico at its NE end, a bow at its SW. Several additions for the house's present use as an old people's home, the most substantial at the SW of 1963. To the SW, an early C19 single-storey rubble-walled WASH HOUSE, its NE gable's windows and central door all primitivist Gothic, with boldly projecting stones at their margins and also at the quoined corners of this front. NE of this, a rubble-walled GARDEN, probably mid C19 but with late C20 housing along its NE side. N of the garden, a two-storey CRICKET PAVILION by *Smart, Stewart & Mitchell*, 1924–5. Rubble walls with much use of split-log boarding at the upper floors; a red pantiled roof with catslide and jerkin-head dormers. At the SE corner, a semi-octagonal projection surrounded by a two-storey veranda, its rustic log supports rising to the bellcast eaves of the domical roof. The effect is very English-looking, perhaps reinforcing the popular belief that cricket is an English import to Scotland. To the NW, a harled lectern DOOCOT, rather altered, the skews inscribed with the initials WSB and ISR and the date 1694; flight-holes in the gables. In the streets to the E of Pitcullen Crescent, the Gannochy housing development designed by *Smart, Stewart & Mitchell* and built in 1927–30 for the whisky blenders, Arthur Bell & Sons Ltd. It consists of model workers' cottages, all of red sandstone, with big broad-eaved and slated roofs.

ISLA ROAD provides the NW fork of the junction at the end of Main Street. On its W side, the TAYSIDE NURSING HOME by *James Parr & Partners*, 1966. Originally offices, it was converted to its present use in 1986–7. Of two storeys to the E and three in the sloping ground to the W. Long flat-roofed block, the horizontality emphasized on the E by the first-floor window being carried the length of the elevation, broken externally only by glazing bars. Opposite, No. 5 Isla Road, a surviving fragment of the Isla Distillery. It is of *c.* 1900. Two storeys of red and white brick with half-timbering in the gables. Depressed arch over the cart entrance; segmental-arched windows. Immediately to its N, set behind a front garden, is ROSE COTTAGE, mid-C19 piend-roofed Georgian survival, with a pilastered and corniced doorpiece and cornices over the ground-floor windows. Next door but now approached from KEIR STREET (its former front garden having become the site of a late C20 house) is the early C19 two-storey CROFT HOUSE, its roof now covered with concrete tiles. Front (now cement-rendered) of three bays, the ground-floor masonry channelled. The centre is advanced, with giant anta-pilasters supporting a pediment. Door and sidelights all under a segmental fanlight; first-floor window of three lights with column-mullions.

N of Keir Street, Isla Road is remarkable for the string of villas on its W side, most of them hidden or half-hidden behind garden walls but all looking over the Tay to the North Inch and readily seen from its riverside path. First, Nos. 1–4 MANSFIELD PLACE of *c.* 1840, a two-storey and attic terrace composed of two double houses, their W-facing fronts of polished ashlar, channelled at the ground floor. Each double house is of four bays with an open pediment over the two close-set centre bays at which are the paired entrances whose Roman Doric columned doorpieces share a single cornice. Pilastered and corniced windows in the outer bays of the ground floor. TAYFLETTS HOUSE is of *c.* 1800. Double-pile main block, a Venetian door at the centre of its E front; plain W elevation. Lateral wings and another to the SE. Then, DURN, a late C19 large but plain would-be *cottage orné* with bracketed eaves and a veranda across part of the W face. Piend-roofed and taller N addition of 1896 by *J. Murray Robertson*, an ogee-roofed tower on its E side. Plainer and still Georgian survival is GOWANBANK of the later C19, placed close to the road. Much more covetable and closer to the river is BRACO HOUSE of c. 1860, with a pyramid-roofed Italianate tower. Then, the late C19 EDENDALE and TAY PARK (originally a single house), the ogee-profiled French pavilion roof now deprived of its cresting. The white-harled SUMMERBANK is by *D. Y. Davies Associates*, 1994. Would-be traditional but eschewing scholarly revival. A trio of gables and a steeply pedimented doorpiece to the E. The W elevation has a central gablet but misses symmetry. It is looked down upon from the hill above by Kincarrathie House (*see* above).

The next of the riverside houses is MEADOWLAND, an example of what could be achieved by Scottish architects of the later C20. It is by *Morris & Steedman*, 1964–6, the s pavilion added by the same firm ten years later. Single-storey steel-framed construction, clad in light brown brick with a dark-stained wooden fascia. Main block at the N, the flat roof swept up at the s end to provide clearstorey lighting (and house the water tanks). The E side is austere. At the W front overlooking the river, the window sills step down from N to s where there is floor-to-ceiling glazing. Inside, these windows of differing depths help demarcate the three spaces of the wooden-ceilinged and brick-walled living room. Conservatory link (an unbroken wall on the E, fully glazed on the W) to the s pavilion, its W side almost fully glazed. Then, BOATLAND of the earlier C19, a big bow on its W front. Broad eaves and horizontal-paned glazing. WATERSIDE is small and boring of c. 1950. HOLMWOOD is another villa of the later C19, with broad eaves and gabled dormers.

Screened from the river and the North Inch by trees are KINNOULL HOUSE and MACMILLAN HOUSE, comprising a residential centre for the disabled, by *Gordon & Dey*, 1975, both drydashed, with steep monopitch roofs and clearstorey windows. Immediately to their N, SPRINGLAND HOUSE, a two-storey and basement classical villa of c. 1800. Three-bay s-facing front. At the centre, a portico with coupled Roman Doric columns; above, paired Ionic columns support an urn-topped pediment. More urns at the ends of the wallhead. To the W, beside the river, the contemporary BOATHOUSE, a two-storey battlemented rubble-built octagon. Pointed windows at the first floor; horizontal panes in the ground-floor windows. N of Springland, on the edge of the city, the Upper Springland Centre (*see* Public Buildings, above).

BURGHMUIR, DOVECOTLAND, HILLYLAND,
LETHAM AND OAKBANK

Large area between the railway line and the Western By-Pass, with Crieff Road the N boundary and Glasgow Road and Craigie Hill the s. Some Late Victorian housing, mostly small-scale, but this is predominantly a collection of C20 dormitories.

CHURCHES

CHURCH OF JESUS CHRIST OF LATTER DAY SAINTS, Burghmuir Road. By *The Church of Jesus Christ of Latter Day Saints' Church Building Department*, 1969. Sited on a slope. Brick-built with 'Fyfestone' (reconstituted granite) gables and a concrete-tiled roof which is swept down from the church to cover ancillary accommodation placed at a lower level.

OUR LADY OF LOURDES (R.C.), Struan Road. By *Peter Whiston*, 1958–9. Nave and chancel, both drydashed and with shallow double-pitched copper roofs, a broad bellcote at their junction.

WELLSHILL CEMETERY
Feus Road, Jeanfield Road and Rannoch Road

Opened, *c.* 1844. Large cemetery occupying the slopes of Wellshill; just N of the summit, a line of monkey-puzzle trees. At the top of the hill, a S-facing retaining wall. The best MONUMENTS are at its W end. James Macleish †1916, by *David Beveridge & Son*. Broad cross with minimally projecting arms, decorated with Celtic ornament. – To its W, a tripartite monument in the C17 manner to John Moncrieff †1899, by *James L. Thomson*. At the centre, an Ionic columned and segmental-pedimented aedicule. It is flanked by shellhead niches; Ionic pilasters at the ends. – To the W, Rufus Daniell Pullar, of the dyeing firm, †1917, a craggy granite slab carved with Celtic ornament and bearing a bronze cross. – Beside it, the monument erected by Sir Robert Pullar †1912 to his wife Ellen Mary Daniell †1904. Vaguely Byzantine inspiration. Octagonal leafy capitalled proto-classical columns supporting a shell-headed canopy. At the back of this recess, a polished granite slab on which are a pair of bronze plaques (one to the wife, the other to the husband), each with two panels displaying high reliefs of emblematic figures.

PUBLIC BUILDINGS

CHERRYBANK GARDENS VISITOR CENTRE, Necessity Brae. By *Fletcher Joseph*, 1999–2000. Two-storey rotunda of dark brown brick and glass; bowed stair-tower to the S. – In front, a large bronze SCULPTURE ('Pictish Dance') by *Diane Maclean*, the form inspired by an Early Christian hand bell in Forteviot Parish Church.

CHERRYBANK PRIMARY SCHOOL, Glasgow Road. By *James Ritchie*, 1864–5. Unassuming and quite plain.

FIRE STATION, Long Causeway. By *Williamson & Hubbard*, 1968.

GOODLYBURN PRIMARY SCHOOL, off Crieff Road. By the Perth & Kinross County Architect, *Ian A. Moodie*, 1957. Curtain-walled, with shallow double-pitched roofs.

LETHAM PRIMARY SCHOOL, Struan Road. By the Perth & Kinross County Architect, *Ian A. Moodie*, 1961. Mostly two-storey, with shallow double-pitch roofs and 'Fyfestone' walls.

OAKBANK PRIMARY SCHOOL, Viewlands Road West. By *Perth & Kinross County Council*, 1969. Two-storey block clad with concrete aggregate.

OUR LADY'S PRIMARY SCHOOL, Garth Avenue. By *Perth & Kinross County Council*, 1968. Curtain-walled two-storey block and a single-storey wing.

PERTH ACADEMY, Viewlands Road. By *T. Aikman Swan*, 1928–32. Polite and boring long Neo-Georgian block; over the centre, a tall copper-roofed stone cupola. Additions by *D. Harvey & A. Scott*, 1960, in the Modern Movement manner, and by *Tayside Regional Council*, 1986–9, in Postmodern style.

PERTH COLLEGE, off Crieff Road. The main block (BRAHAN BUILDING) is by *Boswell, Mitchell & Johnston*, 1968–71. Large but uninspiring, in red brick. – To the E, GOODLYBURN BUILDING (originally Goodlyburn Junior Secondary School) by *Alison & Hutchison & Partners*, 1957. Four storeys of curtain walling.

PERTH HIGH SCHOOL, Viewlands Road West. By *Bett-Bison* (chief architect: *J. M. Gillespie*), in association with *Perth & Kinross County Council*, 1968–71. Five five-storey blocks (the end ones of three bays, the others of five) joined at the back by a full-height corridor link gripped by stair-towers; low ancillary buildings. All flat-roofed and with aggregate cladding.

PERTH ROYAL INFIRMARY, Taymount Terrace and Western Avenue. Large complex which developed through the C20 in disorderly fashion from the carefully considered original buildings designed by *James Miller* in 1911 and opened in 1914.

Miller's LODGES on Taymount Terrace and Western Avenue are harled and pyramid-roofed squares, each with one corner cut out to serve as a porch. Only the Western Avenue lodge retains its diagonally set central chimney.

The HOSPITAL of 1911–14 stands at the SE of the site. Thrifty Neo-Georgian, harled with brick dressings. Pilaster strips at the corners of the buildings; mutuled cornices under the eaves. It consists of ward blocks (medical to the W, surgical to the E), each of two storeys with loggia/balconies at the front gables which are gripped by cupola-topped corner towers. Single-storey corridor links (much overlaid by later additions) join the wards to a lower two-storey and attic piend-roofed administration block (the upper floors originally containing accommodation for nurses). At the hospital's W end and placed on high ground, children's wards of one storey and an attic. The outpatients' and admission block at the E end was replaced by *Mackillop & McIntosh*, 1961–2, with a three-storey flat-roofed building (now, TRUST OFFICES), a glazed stair-tower its principal feature. In 1931 *James Miller* designed the two-storey ROBERT DOUGLAS MEMORIAL BLOCK W of the original hospital. Flat-roofed and harled, with pilasters at the advanced end bays.

The flat-roofed building containing the TAY AND EARN WARDS AND SIMPSON DAY CLINIC, by *Scott & McIntosh*, 1979–81, is built into the hillside to the W. To its N, the hospital's main EXTENSION, by *Scott & McIntosh*, 1988–93, is large but unexciting, faced with pale brown brickwork enlivened by horizontal bands of blue-painted ribbed metalwork.

NW of this, CORNHILL, a rubble-built two-storey villa of *c.* 1790. Piend-roofed main block, its three-bay front's slightly recessed centre containing a side-lit door under a segmental fanlight and a three-light window above. Plain rear wings.

At the NE corner of the Infirmary site, on the N side of Western Avenue, the single-storey WOMEN'S CLINIC (originally, MATERNITY BLOCK) by *James Miller*, 1926–7. Neo-Georgian, a Doric veranda along the S front. Behind, the larger but undistinguished late C20 MATERNITY AND GYNAECOLOGY UNIT.

S of the hospital complex, on the S side of Taymount Terrace, the NURSES' HOME, by *James Miller*, 1929–31, and again Neo-Georgian. Brick walls articulated by very broad harled giant pilasters, orderless except at the E front's three-bay centre where they are Ionic; console-corniced doorpiece. Piended platform roof studded with flat-topped dormer windows.

SPORTS CENTRE, off Necessity Brae. By *James Parr & Partners*, 1981. L-plan, both limbs with ribbed metal roofs of opposing slopes but unequal pitches which meet at the W part, their junction marked by a turret clearstorey.

VIEWLANDS PRIMARY SCHOOL, Oakbank Crescent. By *A. Watt Allison*, 1938–42. Single-storey, of brick, with a pitched slated roof.

OFFICES

BANK OF SCOTLAND, Necessity Brae. Designed by *J. & F. Johnston & Partners* as the headquarters of the whisky blenders, Arthur Bell & Sons, in 1980 and extended for United Distillers ten years later. Large and boxy.

NORWICH UNION INSURANCE OFFICES, off Necessity Brae. Originally the headquarters of the General Accident Fire & Life Insurance Corporation. By *James Parr & Partners*, 1986–8. Huge development built round nine courtyards but stepping down the N side of Craigie Hill as shelved terraces whose flat roofs' planting hangs over the corduroy-textured concrete of the walls. Tall and disappointingly routine entrance elevation to the S.

VILLAS AND HOUSING

HAMILTON HOUSE, Rosebank. By *Andrew Heiton Jun.*, *c.* 1865. Large but unexciting Italianate, with bracketed broad eaves and a pyramid-roofed tower. – Contemporary single-storey LODGE on Glasgow Road (No. 107) in the same manner, a Venetian window in the front gable.

PITHEAVLIS COTTAGES, Necessity Brae. English Picturesque, by *James Miller*, 1928. U-plan layout of single-storey houses, their harled walls enlivened by trimmings of red brick which is laid in herringbone pattern at the half-timbered porches; red Rosemary-tiled roofs. The main range's single-storey and attic centrepiece is marked by a tile-hung gable.

CRAIGIE AND MONCREIFFE

Area bounded by the railway line, Glasgow Road and the Western By-Pass. The N end was developed with respectable but unexciting tenements and villas from *c.* 1880, the rest is C20.

CHURCHES

CRAIGEND MONCREIFFE CHURCH, Glengarry Road. The roughcast and crowstep-gabled hall-church (now hall) is by *Erskine Thomson & Glass*, 1951. To its N, the church proper, by *Carvell & Partners*, 1974–5, octagonal, with a lead-covered octagonal spire rising from the roof.

CRAIGIE CHURCH, Abbot Street. By *G. P. K. Young*, 1894–6. Simple Gothic, the walls of hammer-dressed red Ballochmyle sandstone, the roofs covered with green Craiglea slates. Nave and low narrow aisles. Transepts and a SW steeple were intended but not built. In each gable, a stepped arrangement of three tall lancets under a circular light; parade of smaller lancets at the bottom of the W gable. At the sides, paired lancet windows to the aisles, Y-traceried two-light clearstorey windows. Tall octagonal-spired flèche. The session house with a three-bay loggia on its S side was added to the E end in 1908. It is also by *Young*.

ST MARY MAGDALENE (R.C.), Glenearn Road. By *Peter Whiston*, 1958–9. A-frame with a tall slated roof. Large triangular window in the N gable. Under the eaves, a strip of STAINED GLASS windows by *William Wilson*, 1959.

PUBLIC BUILDINGS

CRAIGIE PRIMARY SCHOOL, Abbot Street. By *Charles S. Robertson*, 1883. Free Renaissance single-storey, the polished buff ashlar looking over-cleaned.

DEWAR'S RINK, Glover Street. By *McLaren, Murdoch & Hamilton*, 1988–90. Respectable and stodgy venue for ice skaters, the walls patterned in dark red and pale brick.

PERTH CHRISTIAN CENTRE, No. 28 Glasgow Road. Originally an office for the distilling firm of John Dewar & Sons, it was designed by *Andrew Heiton Jun.*, 1893. Long asymmetrical block of one and two storeys, built of hammer-dressed red sandstone. The style is free Jacobean, with shaped and Dutch gables and mullioned and transomed windows; small octagonal cupola.

PERTH LEISURE POOL, Glover Street. By *Faulkner Browns*, 1985–8, the architecture promising enjoyment. Large irregularly shaped shed, its NE corner acutely pointed, covered by a huge monopitch roof sloping down to the E. Carried down the full length of the roof are two semicircular skylight projections, their W ends appearing as round porthole windows which cut down into and rise above the continuous glazing along the top of the front. At the S end of this W front, the entrance contained in a glazed bow.

ROSSLYN HOUSE, Glasgow Road. Originally the Perth Poorhouse and now housing. Large but very plain Jacobethan, by *Andrew Heiton Jun.*, 1859–61.

PITHEAVLIS CASTLE
Pitheavlis Castle Gardens

Harled three-storey laird's house of the late C16. L-plan with a SW jamb but also a conical-roofed round tower at the centre of the long N side; the two-storey NW wing is an addition, probably of the early C19. At the main block, crowstepped gables and a big off-centre chimney rising from the wallhead of the S front. The jamb is square; at its S corners, conical-roofed turrets flanking a crowstep-gabled dormer window. The main windows are C19, now with cement margins, but the S front's small ground floor windows with deeply splayed jambs look original.

TULLOCH

Triangular area N of Crieff Road, bounded on the NE by the railway line and on the NW by the Western By-Pass. A bleachfield was established here in the late C18 but the present buildings are predominantly late C20.

KNOX FREE CHURCH, Tulloch Terrace. By *Norris Hamilton Associates*, 1989. Of glazed yellow brick with concrete-tiled roofs. Square pyramid-roofed church; to its W, a piend-roofed hall.

CREMATORIUM, off Crieff Road. By the Perth Deputy Burgh Surveyor, *George Stewart*, 1959–62. Modern-traditional, faced in 'Fyfestone' and some Aberdeenshire granite, with a campanile-like chimney. In the entrance hall to the chapel, STAINED GLASS W window (Christ in Glory) by *Alexander L. Russell*, 1962. Clearstorey windows (Christian Symbols) also of 1962 and by Russell.

TULLOCH PRIMARY SCHOOL, School Close. By *Perth & Kinross County Council*, 1969. Of one and two storeys, with aggregate cladding.

DESCRIPTION. Tulloch is mostly filled by housing of the late C20. At the SE corner around HUNTER CRESCENT, some Neo-Georgian local authority housing of the type found also at Muirton (q.v.). It is by the Perth Burgh Surveyor, *Thomas McLaren*, with *John A. W. Grant* as consultant architect, 1934–6. Off Tulloch Road, the TULLOCH WORKS of the dyeing firm of J. Pullar & Sons, *c.* 1900, utilitarian in red brick. To their w, in TULLOCH TERRACE, associated two-storey workers' housing. At the E end, three terraces (Nos. 86–124) of 1882 with bracketed broad eaves and gablets. To their w, a fourth (Nos. 78–84), dated 1892, of the same design except that the roof is jerkin-headed. A fifth (Nos. 70–76) is dated 1897 and of a different design, with shallowly projecting oriel windows, their gablets half-timbered, and semicircular pedimented dormerheads breaking through the broad eaves of the piended roof.

PITCAIRNGREEN

Village founded by Thomas Graham of Balgowan (later Lord Lynedoch) *c.* 1785 to house workers at the nearby cotton mills. Unspecified designs, presumably for its layout and/or buildings, were provided by *James Playfair* in 1788 but much of the housing is C19 or C20 and only the central core of the village was developed.

DALCRUE BRIDGE, 2.2 km. WNW. By *W. H. Playfair*, 1832–6. Austerely elegant, built of ashlar, stugged at the sides, lightly droved at the parapet, polished and channelled at the soffit of the single segmental arch over the River Almond.

VILLAGE HALL. The altered two-storey rear block was built as Pitcairngreen Free Church School in 1845–6. Front block by *McLaren & Mackay*, 1902–3, when the building had become Pitcairngreen Public School. Single-storey with an ogee-domed cupola-ventilator. In the N gable, a three-light window, the centre opening tall and corniced.

DESCRIPTION. The village is built round a large roughly oblong green, its trees planted in 1953. At the E corner of the approach from the S, THE FEATHERS INN of *c.* 1790. Harled two-storey main block, the roof piended at the N gable. Three-bay front, the ground floor with C19 bay windows linked by a canopy over the central door. On the w side of the green, THE BIELD (originally Pitcairngreen Free Church Manse) by *A. & A. Heiton*, 1847. Georgian survival, of two storeys and three bays, the centre advanced under an open pediment. Pilastered porch flanked by large ground-floor windows with lugged architraves. Just NW of the green, on the N side of DALCRUE ROAD, the two-storey late C18 KNOCKERB HOUSE, its roof piended at the E gable, its flat-roofed dormer windows C20 additions. To its W, WESTEND COTTAGES of the later C19, with pedimented wooden dormers.

On the N side of the green, at the w end, a two-storey harled terrace of three plain Late Georgian houses followed by mid-C20 bungaloid double houses. Then THE OLD MANSE of *c.* 1790, two storeys and harled, the roof piended at the w gable; C20 porch. E of this, EAST END, a two-storey Late Georgian double house. At the N end of the green's E side, a plain rubble-built house, also Late Georgian, followed by a couple of late

C20 bungalows. On the s side of the green, the Village Hall (*see above*) and, immediately to its w, GREENVILLE of the earlier C19, its two-bay front facing s.

DALCRUE, 2.4 km. WNW. A farmhouse in the form of a suavely detailed Italianate villa, designed in 1832 by *W. H. Playfair* and built for Thomas Graham, Lord Lynedoch, owner of the Lynedoch estate. Agglomeration of broad-eaved and rubble-walled elements. At the w, the roughly T-plan two-storey main part, its w and s limbs with shallow-pitched gables. Tall ground-floor windows, both these and the windows above containing horizontal-paned glazing. In the sw inner angle, a square single-storey porch. At the s gable, a rectangular projection, also single-storey, with single-light windows in its sides and a two-light window to the front. In the SE inner angle, a tower finished with a low pyramid roof. Round-headed windows at the tower's lower stages; in each face of the top stage, a trio of round-headed louvred openings. Set well back on the main building's E side, a single-storey wing (originally a byre), its louvred openings replaced by windows when it was converted to a living room in the C20. – Contemporary STEADING to the NW, the s of its two rubble-built parallel ranges single-storey and plain. The N is of two storeys, with segmental-arched cartshed openings in its s face. On the N elevation, a 'bellcote' feature pierced by a round-headed arch; circular horsemill. – At the end of the short E drive, a harled and broad-eaved single-storey LODGE contemporary with the house but altered and extended in the C20. Segmental-arched windows survive.

LYNEDOCH COTTAGE, 2.5 km. NW. Built in 1789 as the gardener's house for the large villa (also known as Lynedoch Cottage and now demolished) which was constructed round an earlier farmhouse for Thomas Graham of Balgowan (later Lord Lynedoch) in the same year. Both were designed by *James Playfair*. Single-storey but very stylish. Piend-roofed main block, its front of droved ashlar with vermiculated strip quoins. Also vermiculated are the round-headed overarches which frame the door and flanking windows, these of two lights with slender stone mullions.

PITCUR CASTLE

2.4 km. SE of Kettins

On the edge of a mid-C19 farm steading, the roofless but largely intact tower house built for the Hallyburtons of Gask and Pitcur *c.* 1500.

The house is a rubble-walled T, the main block of three storeys, the w jamb of the same height but four-storey; rounded stair-tower in the sw inner angle. At the main block's s gable, a roughly central first-floor window with a rounded margin. The E wall has suffered the insertion of a large ground-floor opening (now built-up), probably in the C19. At this side's first floor, a pair of windows, their lintels at the same level but the

l. of horizontal proportions, the moulding of the deeper r. window's surround still evident. At the second floor, two decently sized windows and, between them, a pair of tiny garderobe openings. At the first floor of the N gable, a large circular gunloop and a smallish window. In the jamb's N side, windows to the first and second floors, the second-floor opening a slit. The jamb's W gable contains the tower's entrance, a moulded round-headed door under a corniced niche, originally filled by a heraldic panel, and a small window to the l. of the door. At each of the upper floors, a fair-sized window with a chamfered margin, these openings aligned vertically at the gable's N end. In the jamb's S side, a window to each floor, the ground-floor opening a slit, the second-floor window built up, the upper windows all with chamfered margins. At the stair-tower, two moulded string courses and slit windows.

Inside, the jamb's ground floor contained the kitchen, its stone vault now missing. Large elliptical-arched N fireplace, a salt-box in its E side. Above, a single room at each level, the joist holes showing that the floors were of wooden construction. In each W window, stone seats. Wall chambers in the gable.

The stair-tower contained a stone turnpike (now missing). Just above ground level, in the SW segment, a blocked circular gunloop.

On the ground floor of the main block, a pair of tunnel-vaulted stores which received light from keyhole gunloops (now blocked). The high first-floor hall has been vaulted. A wall chamber nudges into its NE corner. At the E side, the moulded jambs of a fireplace whose canopy is indicated by tusking. The second floor contained two rooms, each with a mural garderobe and a seated window in the E side.

PITFOUR CASTLE
0.6 km. SE of St Madoes

Powerfully composed essay in the Adam castellated manner, built in 1796 for John Richardson of Pitfour, a landowner and entrepeneur in the Tay salmon fishery.

The approach from the N leads to a solid-looking long and low stable range (now housing) joined originally by bowed screen walls (the W demolished) to the house itself whose upper part, visible from outside the forecourt, appears as a romantic towered keep. The single-storey and attic stables serve as an outer defence punctuated by round towers, their ground floors decorated with tall slit dummy windows, their parapets carried on moulded corbels. The E end tower was heightened with inconsequential effect in *William Burn*'s alterations of 1828–33. At the slightly taller three-bay centrepiece, a Venetian gateway (now windows) but with round-headed arches to the pedestrian side entrances as well as the central carriage pend; on the parapet above, a swagged coat of arms.

Inside the forecourt the house's entrance front is fully exposed. It is of three main bays, built of whinstone rubble with sandstone dressings. Three storeys over a low battered basement. Battlemented round corner towers are joined by parapeted one-bay linking sections to the crowstep-gabled centre from whose ends project narrow rectangular towers, also battlemented, all except the centre itself tied together by band and string courses. The hierarchy of the storeys they delineate is made clear by the size of the windows – small and almost square at the basement, tall at the ground-floor *piano nobile*, decently sized but smaller at the main bedroom floor above, smaller and almost square at the second floor. The corner towers are pierced by slit windows, round-headed and overarched at the ground floor, rectangular under dummy oculi and also framed by tall round-headed overarches at the first floor, small and without overarches at the second. More slit windows at the central towers, those of the ground floor repeats of the corner towers', but the first- and second-floor openings are rectangular combined in giant narrow overaches whose heads contain dummy oculi. At the centre itself, a straight flight of steps over the basement to the sidelit and semicircular-fanlit entrance. This and the floors above, each pierced by a Venetian window with round-headed sidelights, are all contained in a giant overarch, also round-headed; swagged coat of arms in the gable.

Projecting from the W corner of the front, an addition of 1828–33, comprising a tall single storey above a basement. The L-plan main block (library) has mullioned windows and a slender round tower at the inner angle from which projects a massive but low round tower (music room) finished with a corbelled parapet. The main block's SE wing partly overlays the side of the C18 house, whose only decorations are provided by a continuation of the front's band and string courses and its corbelled parapet. At the house's S corners, round towers like those at the N front. Corbelled parapet over the outer bays of the S elevation whose ground-floor windows, each now with three round-headed lights, were widened in 1828–33. Bowed centrepiece, its round-headed and overarched ground-floor windows alternating with tall crosslet dummy arrowslits. The first- and second-floor windows are contained in giant overarches whose ashlar pilasters are pierced by dummy slits. Extending from the SE corner, a screen wall ending at a battlemented round tower of 1828–33.

PITLOCHRY

Small town on the N of the River Tummel which achieved burgh status in 1947. It began as a village beside the military road from

Dunkeld to Inverness constructed by *General George Wade* in 1725–33. Major rebuilding and expansion stretching out to the nearby hamlet of Moulin followed the opening of the railway from Dunkeld and Perth in 1863 and its continuation N in the same year, the surrounding scenery and reputedly healthy climate attracting summer visitors as they continue to do.

CHURCHES

BAPTIST CHURCH, Atholl Road. By *David A. Crombie*, 1884. Dumpy Gothic, the walls of squared rubble. Nave with E and W transepts; at the W corner of the front (S) gable a low tower topped by an octagonal ashlar spire. Fish-scale slated flèche over the crossing. Inside, the pulpit has pride of place.

HOLY TRINITY (Episcopal), Perth Road. Simple rubble-built Dec in the manner of an English village church. The nave is by *Charles Buckeridge*, 1857–8; gableted bellcote on its E end, a porch on the S side. Slightly lower and narrower chancel, a vestry on its N side, added by *John Leonard*, 1889. This vestry was converted by Leonard to an organ chamber in 1902–3 when he added a hall-like new vestry to the N, a tall wooden ventilator on its roof.

Inside, scissor-truss roofs over the nave and chancel. The floors of the nave's central aisle and the choir are laid with black and red quarry tiles; encaustic tiles in the sanctuary. – Jacobean-inspired PULPIT of 1908. – REREDOS by *J. Ninian Comper*, 1893, richly coloured in red and gold. The outer panels are stencilled with fruit and flowers. Intermediate panels carved with shields bearing sacred emblems. At the centre Late Gothic tabernacle work over a high relief of the Risen Lord appearing to St Mary Magdalene. – ORGAN by *Hele & Co.*, 1902–3.

STAINED GLASS. Clearly drawn and coloured three-light E window (the Crucifixion, with Our Lady and St John) by *C. E. Kempe*, 1906. – On the N side of the sanctuary, one light (the Good Shepherd) by *A. Ballantine & Son*, 1911. – On the sanctuary's S side, a light (Our Lord Blessing) of 1896 by *Clayton & Bell*. – In the S window of the choir, a mid-C20 panel (St Andrew). – In the N wall of the nave, the E window (St Catharine and St Agnes) is of *c.* 1880. – Beside it, another Late Victorian window (the Adoration of the Magi). – Then a window (St George and St Denys) by *John Hardman & Co. Ltd.*, 1919. – In the nave's S wall, narrative E window (Our Lord with Martha and Mary) by *Mayer & Co.*, 1896. – Next, a repulsively sentimental window (Our Lord and Little Children) by *John Hardman & Co. Ltd.*, 1928. – Three-light W window (St Adamnan, St Luke and St Margaret of Scotland), Modernist realism by *Alexander L. Russell*, 1956.

At the entrance to the small churchyard, a buttressed rubble-built LYCHGATE of *c.* 1925. Steeply pitched roof, tunnel-vaulted inside.

MOULIN (PITLOCHRY) FREE CHURCH, Lower Oakfield. Now housing (JOHN STEWART COURT). Lancet-windowed large box, by *Campbell Douglas*, 1861–3. The front (S) gable is bisected by a central buttress supporting a tall stone-spired octagonal bellcote. The windows were altered and a glazed stair-tower added at the N end in 1994 on the building's conversion to flats.

MOULIN PARISH CHURCH, Moulin Square. Disused. By *Francis Farquharson*, 1829–31, but remodelled by *James C. Walker* in 1874–5 after a fire. Rubble-walled rectangle, a tower at the centre of the long N side, the corners of both church and tower diagonally buttressed. The church's elliptical-arched windows are of 1829–31. The stepped buttresses along its S side are probably additions of 1874–5 as are the jerkin-headed dormer windows.

The tower was originally of three stages. At the bottom, a pointed N door under a datestone of 1613 reused from the church's predecessor; rectangular window in the W face. At the second stage a depressed-arched louvred opening in each exposed face. The third stage has louvred circular openings which were given clock faces in 1874–5 when a new belfry was added, its two-light Gothic openings contained in gablets. Also of the 1870s are the slated pyramidal spire and weathercock.

INTERIOR of 1874–5. Queenpost truss roof, the posts treated as barley-sugar columns ending in Neo-Jacobean pendants. U-plan gallery round the ends and N side, its herringbone panels separated by attached columns with barley-sugar shafts. More barley-sugar columns at the COMMUNION TABLE and PULPIT (moved from the centre to one side of the S wall in the 1920s to make room for an organ, since removed). Simple PEWS. All this carpentry was executed by *Steven Bros* of Blairgowrie.

GRAVEYARD. W of the church, a HEADSTONE to James Ferguson †1743. On the W face two angels' heads (souls) at the top, a skeleton at the bottom; in the centre, a shield under a mantled helm. – S of the church, a HEADSTONE erected in 1818 by James Forbes, crudely incised with a smiling face. – SE of the church, a late medieval GRAVE-SLAB incised with a scabbarded sword with downward pointing quillons. – To its S, a HEADSTONE of 1789 to Finlay Robertson, the W face carved with an angel's head at the top, a shield charged with a sock and coulter at the centre, and a skull, crossbones and hourglass at the bottom. – Similar but taller and more weathered late C18 stone commemorating John McFarlan to its W. – S of that, another stone of the same type but aedicular with a swan-neck pediment; it is to John Stewart †1741 and his wife Margaret Macfarlane †1767.

PITLOCHRY PARISH CHURCH, Church Road. By *C. & L. Ower*, 1883–4. An energetically but mechanically detailed Romanesque compact cross. At the gable of each transept a large rose window above a low bowed projection. S clock tower with tall two-light windows. Cannon spouts at the chamfered corners, the NE surmounted by a spired octagonal caphouse. Broad-eaved and slated pyramidal spire, a steeply gabled belfry dormer at each face. Across the church's N end, a piend-roofed porch added by *Murdoch Architects*, 1995–6.

Inside, a terrific display of bracing at the roof over the crossing which was strengthened in 1901 by a pair of cast-iron columns. Simple Victorian PEWS. – COMMUNION TABLE of 1952.

S of the church, a detached low HALL by *Leonard & Morris*, 1910. Early Christian detail. Late C20 E extension.

E of the church, MONUMENT to the missionary and Pitlochry native, Alexander Duff, by *Thomas Beattie*, 1889. Large Celtic cross of polished Peterhead granite. At the base, a bronze portrait bust in relief.

PUBLIC BUILDINGS

ALDOUR BRIDGE, Bridge Road. By *Sir Alexander Gibb & Partners* as engineers, in collaboration with the architects *Tarbolton & Ochterlony*, 1949. Purposeful but not without elegance, of reinforced concrete. Three elliptical arches, the piers rising from keel-shaped cutwaters, crossing the River Tummel.

COUNCIL CHAMBERS AND PUBLIC LIBRARY, Atholl Road. Villa-like agglomeration. Tall and plain main range dated 1830. Later in the C19 was added a low front block with a battlemented porch and horizontal glazing in the windows. Utilitarian back wing. The main range's first-floor room has a Jacobean plaster ceiling.

PITLOCHRY DAM AND POWER STATION, Armoury Road. By *Sir Alexander Gibb & Partners* (chief architect: *T. H. Eley*), 1947–51. Massive concrete dam across the River Tummel forming Loch Faskally to its W; concrete bridge of two elliptical arches. At the S end, the flat-roofed generating station designed by *H. O. Tarbolton*, its walling of pre-cast slabs of reconstituted Aberdeen granite, the architecture modern-traditional in the manner of Sir Giles Gilbert Scott.

PITLOCHRY FESTIVAL THEATRE, Portnacraig. The theatre, founded by John Stewart in 1951, was housed first in a tent and then in a slightly less temporary structure. The present permanent building on the bank of the River Tummel is by *Law & Dunbar-Nasmith*, 1979–81. The bulk is of dark brown brick and utilitarian except for the glass-walled foyer wrapped round part of the E side and the N end where it is cantilevered out above a basement. Glass-fronted extension to the N, also with a cantilevered main floor and finished with a boldly projecting flat roof, N of that, a curtain-walled addition, by *Perth and Kinross Council*, 2000.

Inside, the foyer is unpompous, with a light stair at each end and boarded tent ceiling. Broad polygonal auditorium, the seating in an ellipse facing the stage, the ceiling filled with downward-pointing lights.

PITLOCHRY HIGH SCHOOL, East Moulin Road. By *Perth & Kinross County Council*, 1974–5, and extended later. Flat-roofed blocks of one and two storeys, red brick the dominant material.

PITLOCHRY TOWN HALL, West Moulin Road. By *Alexander Ness* of *John Bruce & Son*, 1898–1900. Small but punchily detailed Jacobean. Large corbels support a balustraded stone balcony under the front's mullioned and transomed central window, its cornice topped by strapwork, which rises into a gabled dormerhead. Ogee-roofed octagonal tower masking the obtuse angle formed by the join of the front block to the plain hall behind.

RAILWAY STATION, Station Road. By *Murdoch Paterson*, 1882. The main building is on the N platform. Single-storey, with crowstepped gables and mullioned and transomed windows. U-plan front to the platform, awning with a canted bay window, the centre covered by a valanced canopy supported on cast-iron columns and large circled brackets. On the S platform, a single-storey wooden building covered by bellcast piended roofs. – Lattice-sided iron FOOTBRIDGE (by *Hanna, Donald & Wilson*).

SUSPENSION BRIDGE over the River Tummel, Portnacraig. By *William Bell*, 1913. Lattice-sided steel bridge, ball finials on the skeletal pylons.

DESCRIPTION

PERTH ROAD leads in from the SE. The beginning of the town is announced by the Blair Atholl Distillery (*see* below) on the r. BRIDGE ROAD on the l. leads S to Aldour Bridge and, off Portnacraig, the Pitlochry Festival Theatre (*see* Public Buildings, above). In Portnacraig itself, formerly the site of a ferry across the River Tummel, a terrace of single-storey cottages and the two-storey FERRYMAN'S COTTAGE and PORTNACRAIG INN, all rubble-built early C19 vernacular. To the W, Pitlochry Dam and Power Station (*see* Public Buildings, above).

In Perth Road, after the junction with Bridge Street, on the l. the entrance to the drive of the FASGANEOIN HOTEL, a large villa of the later C19 with bracketed broad eaves and a Frenchy low tower containing the entrance. On the r. of Perth Road, Holy Trinity Episcopal Church (*see* Churches, above). Set well back from the road to its E, THE PARSONAGE of 1865, another large villa, with broad eaves and gableted dormerheads. Then, on the l. of Perth Road, DUNDARACH DRIVE leads up to the DUNDARACH HOTEL, an exceptionally large villa of the later C19 which was extended by *John Leonard* in 1902. Carved bargeboards at the gables and gablets; parsonical Gothic windows. Iron cresting on the roofs including that of a Frenchy tower. After Dundarach Drive Perth Road passes under a rubble-built segmental-arched RAILWAY VIADUCT of *c.* 1863.

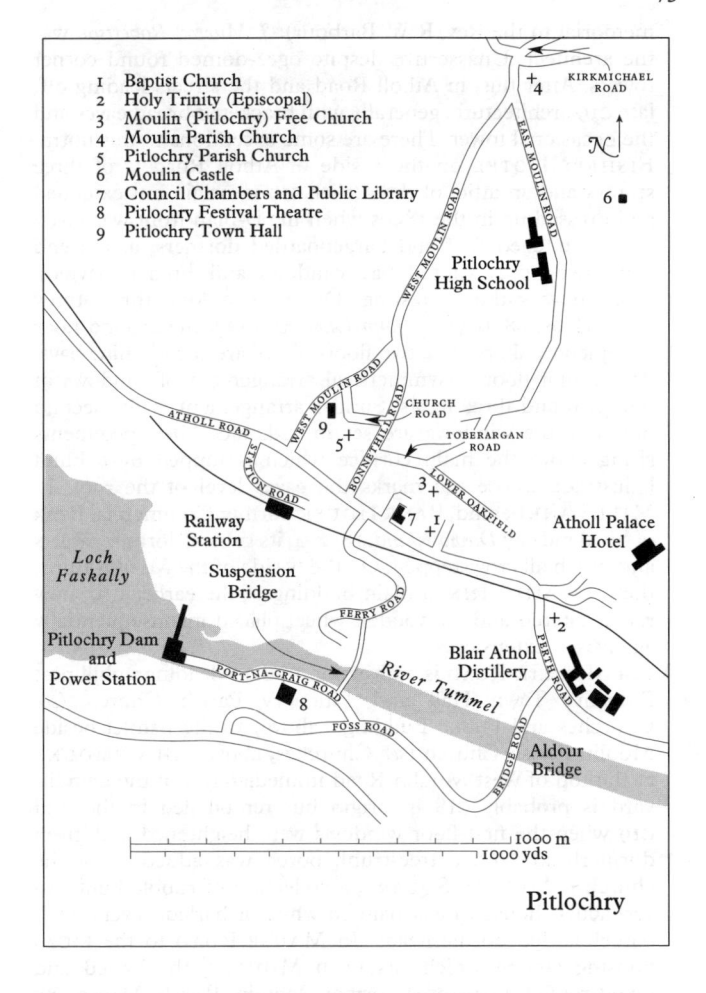

Pitlochry

1. Baptist Church
2. Holy Trinity (Episcopal)
3. Moulin (Pitlochry) Free Church
4. Moulin Parish Church
5. Pitlochry Parish Church
6. Moulin Castle
7. Council Chambers and Public Library
8. Pitlochry Festival Theatre
9. Pitlochry Town Hall

ATHOLL ROAD is Pitlochry's main street. At its start, on the N side, a lodge at the entrance to the drive to the Atholl Palace Hotel (*see* below). Beyond, on Atholl Road's N side and on the rising ground behind are bargeboarded late C19 villas, some with spire-topped low towers, several suffering from the addition of flat-roofed extensions in the later C20. Among them, a few houses of the later C20 and also the POLICE STATION, by *James C. Walker*, 1864–5, its piend-roofed Georgian survival manner an exception to Pitlochry's more picturesque Victorian norm. Beyond, the Baptist Church overlooked by the former Moulin (Pitlochry) Free Church (*see* Churches, above). Then the Council Chambers and Public Library (*see* Public Buildings, above).

The commercial centre of the town begins with No. 51 Atholl Road, built in 1894–5 as the BARBOUR INSTITUTE (a memorial to the Rev. R.W. Barbour); *J. Murray Robertson* was the architect. Unassertive despite ogee-domed round corner towers. After this, in Atholl Road and the streets leading off, late C19 architecture, generally with bracketed broad eaves and the occasional tower. There are some exceptions to this norm. FISHERS HOTEL on the S side of Atholl Road is of three storeys and an attic, of the earlier C19 in origin but extended and dressed up in the 1890s when the U-plan front was given a steep pitched roof and bargeboarded dormers; at the end bays, two-storey canted bay windows and French pavilion roofs, now without cresting. Opposite, a long three-storey block (Nos. 88–104) by *John Leonard*, 1897, the ground floor occupied by shops. The two floors above are each of nine bays. At the first floor, a symmetrical arrangement of windows of one, two and three lights. Similar arrangement at the second but here the windows are set in aedicules, their pediments rising above the main cornice which is topped by a blind balustrade whose rail marks the eaves level of the roof. In MILL LANE behind, BANK HOUSE (former Commercial Bank of Scotland) by *David Rhind*, 1852–4, its gables, dormer gablets and porch all crowstepped. On the W side of the Moulin Burn, the OLD MILL INN, a plain building of the earlier C19, now rather altered and its wooden wheel placed inconsequentially against an extension.

WEST MOULIN ROAD is a diversion to the N leading uphill past Pitlochry Town Hall and Pitlochry Parish Church (*see* Churches and Public Buildings, above) to the hamlet beside Moulin Parish Church (*see* Churches, above). BLAIRMOUNT at the top of West Moulin Road immediately S of the churchyard is probably C18 in origin but remodelled in the mid C19 when the first-floor windows were heightened and given dormerheads and a tree-trunk porch was added. N of the church is MOULIN SQUARE, a collection of rubble-built C19 vernacular houses, most painted white or harled, several with bargeboarded dormerheads. In MANSE ROAD to the E C20 housing among which sits OLD MOULIN, the harled and piend-roofed two-storey former Moulin Parish Manse, by *Alexander Strachan*, 1820. Front originally of three bays (the piend-roofed porch an addition of 1929) but extended W by *D. Mitchell* in 1882–3 when the back wing was heightened.

ATHOLL ROAD continues W of West Moulin Road with Nos. 120–134 on the N, a late C19 block with boldly carved bargeboards, gablets which are either jerkin-headed where they surmount oriel windows or have elaborate iron finials. Round turret at the corner to Birnam Place. Opposite STATION ROAD leads S from Atholl Road down to the Railway Station (*see* Public Buildings, above). Further W, Nos. 146–152 Atholl Road, a two-storey rubble-built cottage terrace of *c.* 1860. Picturesquely asymmetrical front, some sections advanced and gabled, others with gablets above the upper windows; bracketed broad eaves. On the S side, Nos. 127–133 of *c.* 1900, the ground floor occupied by shops, the upper floor harled with half-timbering in the gables. Flat-roofed round tower at the corner with Rie-achan Road. Dead plain mid-C19 single-storey terraced housing at Nos. 135–137 followed by late C19 villas and, on the S, a park. After Atholl Road's crossing of the railway, a single-storey and attic terrace (Nos. 141–157) of the later C19, the eaves less broad than usual in Pitlochry and the bargeboards mean. More ornate detailing at the contemporary cottages of Nos. 159–163 beyond.

ATHOLL PALACE HOTEL, off Atholl Road. Standing on a steeply sloping site, the hotel was built as a hydropathic spa in 1875 to a design by *Andrew Heiton Jun.* It is a massive H, constructed of hammer-dressed grey masonry. Main front to the N, the wings fronted by towers with French pavilion roofs finished with iron cresting; massive chimneys at the sides. Another massive chimney on the gable of the recessed centrepiece from which projects a long stone porch whose roof is continued over a porte cochère of stone and wood. Dormer windows with steeply pitched piended roofs. At the S elevation the wings are fronted by semi-octagonal towers finished with rounded attics surmounted by glazed circular garrets topped by conical roofs. Stretched across the recessed centre, a wood and iron conservatory, its columns with foliaged capitals; gabled centrepiece. Battlemented E and W retaining walls with round corner towers. To the E, a conference centre added *c.* 1975. – At the entrance to the drive, a pacific Baronial LODGE (also by *Heiton*, 1875). Conical-roofed fat round tower. Another conical roof over an octagonal dormer window.

BLAIR ATHOLL DISTILLERY, Perth Road. Rebuilt in 1949 and extended in 1973 and 1975. Pleasingly straightforward rubble-built complex, gablet ventilators on the roofs of the main two-storey buildings. Elliptical-arched pend at the gatehouse. At the W end, a two-storey double house, its upper windows rising into gablets.

MOULIN CASTLE (CAISTEAL DUBH), off East Moulin Road. Fragmentary remains of a C13 castle of enclosure built by the Earls of Atholl on a small island, the surrounding loch drained in the C18. Some of the rubble-built N and S walls stand to a fair height, as does a lower stub of the W wall. The rest has fallen to form grass-covered mounds. The castle has been a rough quadrangle, *c.* 33.5 m. by 25.9 m., with a round tower at each corner.

BALEDMUND. *See* p. 177.
BALNAKEILLY. *See* p. 184.
FASKALLY HOUSE. *See* p. 367.

PITNACREE HOUSE
1.7 km. NE of Strathtay

Small mansion house placed high above Strath Tay, probably C18 in origin but remodelled and extended in the early C19. Rubble-built, of two storeys. Front of five bays with full-height bay windows at the ends and a Roman Doric columned doorpiece to the pedimented centre. Extensive but plain outshots at the back. – Mid-C19 LODGE, with carved bargeboards on the W side facing the drive and a canted bay window to the S.

PRIORY ISLAND *see* ISLE OF LOCH TAY

RAIT

Small village, the houses mostly C19. At the W end, four reed-thatched cottages, probably of the early C19, their walls of painted rubble. At the E end, a large STEADING (now shops) of 1837, the piend-roofed main block with elliptical-arched cartshed openings.

RAIT PARISH CHURCH. Roofless ruin of the medieval church of a parish which was joined to Kilspindie at the beginning of the C17. Some of the N wall and almost all the E gable survive but so overgrown with ivy that no features are discernible.

In the surrounding GRAVEYARD, a few C17 GRAVE-SLABS carved with emblems of death but badly weathered.

RANNOCH STATION

Isolated at the W end of the road into Rannoch Moor, the small late C19 RANNOCH MOOR HOTEL and a railway station on the West Highland line from Glasgow to Fort William.

RANNOCH RAILWAY STATION. Buildings by *James Miller*, 1894. The main waiting room block is of wood above a brick base. Walls mostly clad in scalloped sheets and enlivened by half-timbering. The roof's broad bellcast eaves project to shelter the inner sides of the platform. A smaller building, in the same manner but with glass walls, to the N. – Lattice-girder FOOTBRIDGE, also of 1894, originally at Corrour Railway Station (Highland and Islands) and re-erected here in 1989.

REDGORTON

Church by itself.

REDGORTON PARISH CHURCH. Disused. Rubble-walled T-plan kirk, the body built in 1766, the N 'aisle' added by *Andrew Heiton Sen.*, 1839–40. On the W gable, a birdcage bellcote of 1766, with a flattened ogee-profile roof; each of its N and S sides is pierced by one semicircular and one round opening. In the S side of the main block, pointed windows in the two centre bays and shouldered-arched doors at the ends, the present form of all these openings perhaps dating from *John Macdonald*'s alterations of 1869–71. In the gables, sizeable rectangular area and gallery windows with chamfered margins. The lower windows were enlarged and the upper windows' sills lowered in 1869, probably the date they were filled with pointed lights.

The windows of the early C19 N 'aisle' are all rectangular with chamfered margins, the side windows' Gothic lights and the gable window's quatrefoil probably introduced in 1869–71. In the NE inner angle, a bowed projection of 1839–40 containing the gallery stair.

Inside, GALLERIES with plain panelled fronts at the E and W ends and filling the N 'aisle', all apparently of 1839–40. At the centre of the S wall, a Lorimerian PULPIT of *c.* 1950. – STAINED GLASS. Two windows flanking the pulpit, both of 1920. The one to the l. (Our Lord Blessing a Knight) is by *R. Anning Bell*, an accomplished example of stylized realism in good strong colours. The other (Our Lord as the Light of the World) is sadly routine.

GRAVEYARD. In the NW corner, a plain HEARSE HOUSE of 1832, a circular opening above the door. – S of the church, an early C19 piend-roofed SESSION HOUSE. Built into its SW corner, a stone SUNDIAL dated 1725. – Several C18 HEADSTONES displaying angels' heads (souls) at the top. Immediately S of the church's W end, Isoble Scott †1760. Aedicular with fluted Doric pilasters and a swan-neck pediment. Front carved with a mantled helm over a shield which bears a ploughshare. – E of this, the hogbacked GRAVE-SLAB of Thomas Jonstone †1680, its E end carved with a skull and crossbones, the top's N slope with the warning: REMBER [*sic*]. MAN.AS.THOV.GOS.BY.ASYOV.ART.NOV.SO.ONS.VAS.I.AS.I. AM.NOV SO.MOST.THOV.BE.REMBER.THAT.THOV.MAN.MOST.DEE. – To the S, a HEADSTONE of 1744 to Andreu [*sic*] Graham, its front carved with a weaver's loom, shuttle and stretchers and a tailor's iron and scissors. – Beside the graveyard's E wall, a C18 stone crudely decorated with a loom, shuttle, stretchers and a head, its mouth stuffed with another shuttle; skull and crossbones at the bottom.

RHYND

Church, manse and a handful of scattered Victorian cottages but no real village.

Former RHYND PARISH CHURCH, Easter Rhynd, 3.3 km SE. Roofless and ivy-covered remains of an early C17 church, some of the E gable and the N and S walls still standing. It has been a rubble-built oblong and had a bellcote at one end. A couple of mausolea, also covered in ivy, project to N and S.

GRAVEYARD. S of the church, a good number of carved HEADSTONES. Near the graveyard's E wall, a large stone of 1810 erected to the son of Gorge [*sic*] Brown, smith in Rhynd, the W face with a crude but spirited relief of two smiths working at an anvil, the scene surmounted by a crown. – Just to the W, a pair of identical stones, one of 1736 commemorating David Clark, the other of 1738 to William Clark, each with a pediment containing an angel's head (the soul) and with a shield bearing a shepherd's crook. – To the w, a half-buried small headstone of 1731 to Alexander Archibald, the w face carved with a weaver's loom and shuttle. – Another loom and shuttle to Andrew Paton †1743 to the s. – NW of this, the stone erected by Peter Robertson, boatman, to his grandmother, Elspit Ferrier †1784, a relief of a man in a boat on the w face. – N of this and now lying on the ground, the round-headed stone of 1729 commemorating John Lenox. Egg-and-dart border. Ploughshare carved in high relief above the inscription. – Just to the NW, an ogee-arched headstone erected in 1724 by William Cushney, gardener in Elcho, to his son, with a shield bearing a garden spade, rake, etc. – W of this the contemporary headstone to Andrew Blyth and Elizabeth Duncan whose initials appear on the w face under a pair of stars; below, an hourglass, crossbones and skull carved in exceptionally high relief. – To the w, a headstone of 1735 to JR and MI, with a shield bearing ploughshares; emblems of death below. – s of this, the headstone of 1734 to MI, incised with a skull and bones. – To the SW, the well-preserved stone of 1759 to William Scott, tenant in Kinmouth, again with emblems of death under a shield carved with a ploughshare. – To the NW, three C18 stones with reliefs of boats, the N (to David Imbrie and Katrine Sim) dated 1733 and showing fish in the boat, the middle stone (to Margaret Moncrief) with fish lying beside the boat.

RHYND PARISH CHURCH. Converted to a house (by *Calum MacCalman*, of *Davis Duncan Architects*, 2003–4). Built in 1839–42, probably to a design by *W. M. Mackenzie*. Georgian Gothic, the walls of mixed sandstone and whin, with sandstone dressings; overlapping skews. Cruciform, with a porch at the end of the s jamb and a tower providing the N limb. Tudor-arched porch door. The tower is of three stages, the top (belfry) stage marked off by a string course. The w label stop of its N door's hoodmould is carved with the cheerful head of a man, the E label stop is missing. Paired belfry openings. Pinnacles on the corners of the battlement.

Broad-eaved and bargeboarded MANSE (now RHYND HOUSE) of 1879 immediately to the SE.

EASTER ELCHO, 0.9 km. NE. Large but plain harled Tudor farmhouse, by *W. M. Mackenzie*, *c.* 1840.

ELCHO CASTLE. *See* p. 358.
KINMOUTH HOUSE. *See* p. 469.

ROHALLION LODGE
3 km. s of Birnam

Shooting lodge built in 1843 for Sir William George Drummond Stewart of Grandtully and probably designed by *James Gillespie Graham*, the architect responsible for Stewart's extensive building works at Murthly Castle in the 1830s and 1840s. Large and picturesque bargeboarded rubble-walled villa. Rising from the centre of the main (s) block, a conical-roofed round tower.

Slender octagonal tower, also conical-roofed, at the NE corner. Some Tudor detail and Gothic touches.

ROSSIE HOUSE
0.3 km. W of Forgandenny

0010

Sizeable but much altered harled laird's house of the early C18. The S-facing piend-roofed main block was originally of three storeys but the old first floor was lost, probably c. 1800, when the ground-floor rooms were heightened. Front of seven bays, formerly with a slightly advanced and pedimented centrepiece. This was removed c. 1950 and its place taken by a segmental-arched recess. Built into the sides of the recess are two stones dated 1657 and 1659, presumably from the house's predecessor. Both are carved with the impaled arms and initials of William Oliphant of Forgandenny and his wife, Isobel Drummond; the W bears the date 1657, the E 1659. E of the recess, a large canted bay window of the mid C19. The three first-floor windows above were probably lowered c. 1800 and those of the three W bays enlarged to match in the late C20.

The house was thickened to the N c. 1800, the back block of the same height but containing three storeys. The E part of this addition was removed in the mid C20. On the W side of the house, a late C20 bay window, its design taken from that on the S front.

Inside, behind the S (now garden) entrance, the staircase with a Late Georgian cast-iron balustrade. On either side, the drawing room and dining room, both very tall, their architectural character now of c. 1900, the drawing room classical and with pedimented doorcases, the dining room panelled and with a late C18 revival pine chimneypiece.

Immediately behind the house, the Late Georgian harled and piend-roofed STABLES OFFICES. – To the S, a rubble WALLED GARDEN, probably of c. 1800. The surviving greenhouse along part of its N side is by *Mackenzie & Moncur*, c. 1900; wrought-iron finials for decoration. – Just S of the garden, a ball-finialled half-domed WELL, perhaps C18. – In a field NW of the house, a Late Georgian DOOCOT. It is a tall, harled and crudely battlemented octagon with concave sides and a stilted round-headed arch at the entrance. – At the S end of the drive, classy GATEPIERS of c. 1800. V-jointed ashlar, with fluted tops under the mutuled cornices. Cast-iron urns surmount the two inner piers.

ROSSIE OCHIL
5.2 km. NW of Glenfarg

0010

Laird's house, the product of several stages of work. The earliest part is late C17, a crowstep-gabled two-storey and attic oblong. Its E front was overlaid c. 1850 by the addition of a pair of full-height wings, each with a broad crowstepped front gable containing three-light ground- and first-floor windows and with a shallow rectangular bay window on the outer side; at the N wing, a crowstepped gablet above the first-floor N window. Projecting between the wings, a narrow crowstep-gabled two-storey porch of 1989 which replaced a single-storey recessed porch. Its first-floor window's chamfered surround whose lintel bears the date 1691 seems to have been reused from the original house.

Badly altered W elevation. A SW wing, probably of the C19, joins to the S range of a courtyard steading, perhaps of the earlier C19. On this range's S side, late C20 segmental-arched windows evocative of cartshed openings. On its N side, the original rectangular cartshed doorways (now built up). Tall crowstep-gabled W range. Short piend-roofed N range. Single-storey and attic NE cottage wing.

Inside, at the S end of the ground floor of the original house, a simple moulded chimneypiece of the late C17. In the dining room on the ground floor of the NE wing, a wooden chimneypiece of *c.* 1900 carved with cherub musicians and, in the centre of the frieze, a courting couple in C18 dress.

ROSSIE PRIORY

1 km. NE of Baledgarno

Disappointing mid-C20 truncation and remodelling of the ecclesiastical Gothic mansion by *William Atkinson* which had been built for Charles, eighth Lord Kinnaird, in 1807–15. Atkinson's house was composed of two parts, each surrounding a courtyard, the E part containing the family's residence, the W the stables, coachhouses and riding school. In 1949 everything of the E part was demolished except for its back range whose rubble-built S elevation, quite plain except for a battlement and originally facing into the courtyard, was exposed to view. This elevation, now the house's principal front, was then remodelled by *Basil Spence* who added a two-storey canted bay window of Arts and Crafts derivation at its W end.

The W part (the C19 stables courtyard) survives. At its S front's E end, a gatehouse rebuilt in 1838–40 by *Andrew Heiton Sen.*, 1838–40. Tudor collegiate in manner, with a battlement and oriel window over the central arch (the arch itself by Atkinson) which opens onto a groin-vaulted pend. Built into the W wall of the courtyard behind (its N range demolished) is a convex-sided triangular stone, perhaps a dormerhead, bearing the Kinnaird coat of arms and the date 1664. W of the gatehouse, the buttressed tall S gable of Atkinson's riding school which was converted to a chapel by *Edward & Robertson* in 1865–6. Its Early Gothic five-light window is a replacement of the 1860s, the hoodmould with carved headstops; above, a cusped round window. Also of 1865–6 is the chapel's low semi-octagonal N apse, its two-light windows with cusped vesica heads. W of the chapel the S range continues the two-storey height and battlement of the gatehouse but the walling is broken only by a single tier of pointed dummy lights. At the W corner, a battlemented square tower. Behind this range, a coachhouse court, its ranges remodelled probably in the 1860s but with an original square tower in the NE corner.

Inside the house itself, now entered from a door in the E side of the stable gatehouse's pend, some C19 work survives. Atkinson's secondary (W) stair hall is covered by plaster vaulting. Off it, to the S, the present DRAWING ROOM formed in the 1950s but with a Frenchy marble chimneypiece of the earlier C19. N of the stair hall, the DINING ROOM (originally, family dining room) which was recast as the China Room by *Charles Edward* in 1863 when its walls were covered with display cupboards for china and 'bookshelves' with leather spines. At the room's N end, the lavishly carved woodwork of a low sideboard recess flanked by sliding doors opening onto food lifts from the basement. N of this, the PICTURE GALLERY, a tall but plain Gothic room formed *c.* 1865.

The interior of the CHAPEL is serious-minded Victorian Gothic of 1865–6 by *Edward & Robertson*, the walls clad in ashlar. Nave and passage aisles, the arcades' columns of quatrefoil section. Open roof, the arched braces pierced with quatrefoils and springing from stone corbels. Stone arch to the chancel, its panelled stone dado decorated with floral reliefs. Two Gothic recesses above elaborate corbels, the l. carved with a lamb, the r. with the Pelican in Piety. The chapel's floor is covered with encaustic tiles, their decoration richer in the chancel. – Bench PEWS. – In the chancel windows strongly coloured archaic STAINED GLASS (Scenes from the Life of Our Lord) of *c.* 1866.

WALLED GARDEN on the slope of Rossie Hill to the NW, its early C19 walls of brick.

MAUSOLEUM, 0.6 km. E. This is the medieval Rossie Church, disused after the union of that parish with Inchture in 1670 and reconstructed as a mausoleum by George, ninth Lord Kinnaird, *c.* 1863 to a design by *Charles Edward*. The church, perhaps built in the early C13, seems to have been a simple angle-buttressed oblong with no external differentiation between nave and chancel except for a buttress, probably an addition, on the S side. Walling of quite large blocks of roughly squared red sandstone rubble, that of the windowless N wall and E gable which is intaken at the level of the main wallhead largely medieval. On the W gable, an awkward conical-roofed bellcote of the 1860s, its design derived from the bellcote of *c.* 1600 on the former Alloway Parish Church (Ayrshire). Towards the W end of the N side, a simply moulded medieval pointed door. Victorian Gothic windows in the W gable and S side. The S door into the chancel and the S porch are both of *c.* 1863 but the roof slates of the porch were replaced by glass *c.* 1875 when it was converted to a mortuary chapel.

Inside, a stone pointed arch marks off the chancel, its floor laid with encaustic tiles. Hammerbeam and scissor-truss roof.

Rossie Priory,
Mausoleum, cross-slab

– Worn Tournai marble GRAVE-SLAB of *c.* 1260 in the chancel floor. Enough of its incised carving survives to show that it displayed a pair of cusped and crocketed arches enclosing figures of a knight (the lower part of his sword and shield discernible) and lady. It may have been made in a southern English workshop. – Near the E end of the nave, a CROSS-SLAB of the early C8 discovered in the adjacent graveyard. On the E face, a Greek cross, the inner ends of its limbs notched by hollow circles, the intersection carved with a roundel of interlaced work. More interlaced work on the panels of the limbs (the E arm badly weathered). Flanking the cross, a wondrously enjoyable assortment of fantastic beasts. On the W face, a border of interlaced work which extends into the panels of the head and arms of the central cross, also of Greek type but with semicircular notches instead of roundels at the inner ends of the limbs. More interlaced work on the central roundel. The shaft is divided into two panels, the lower an upside-down T-shape. These panels are carved with the reliefs of three horsemen. A pair of hounds and two more horsemen in the space to the r. of the shaft. In the space to the l., Pictish symbols (animals and a 'crescent-and-V-rod,' its upper end finished with volutes under a ball finial, the lower spearheaded). In the slab's top l. corner, the figure of a man holding two birds by their necks. In the top r. corner, an angel with outstretched wings and dangling feet.

Lots of late C19 and early C20 MONUMENTS to members of the Kinnaird family. In the S porch's mortuary chapel, illuminated by amber-tinted top-lighting, the Carrara marble life-size recumbent effigy of Olivia Barbara Kinnaird †1871, by

William Brodie. – At the w gable, a facsimile made in 1863 of the monument which had been erected *c.* 1840 in Malta to Graham Hay St Vincent de Ros Kinnaird, commander of HMS *Rapid*, †1838. Classical, with Roman Doric corner columns and an urn finial. – At the w end of the s wall, a high-relief marble depiction of Frederica Eliza Kinnaird †1856. – Further E, Catherine Kinnaird †1886, a roundel with the relief portrait of a child. – E of this, Douglas Arthur, Master of Kinnaird, †1914, a white marble bust. – At the w end of the N wall, a large white marble monument of *c.* 1863 to George, seventh Lord Kinnaird, and his wife, with the statue of an angel holding back drapery to disclose a pair of roundels carved in relief with heads of the deceased. These were copied from portraits by George Romney which hung in the later C19 in the dining room of Rossie Priory. – E of this, busts of Douglas Kinnaird †1830, Olivia, Lady Kinnaird, †1858 and Charles, eighth Lord Kinnaird, †1826 and, more appealing, of the youthful Charles Fox, Master of Kinnaird, †1860 at the age of nineteen. – Free-standing recumbent effigy of Victor Alexander, Master of Kinnaird, †1851 aged eleven. – Propped against the N wall, a heraldic stone of *c.* 1670 bearing the impaled arms and initials of Sir George Kinnaird of Rossie (later, first Lord Kinnaird) and his wife, Dame Margaret Crichton.

In the GRAVEYARD s of the mausoleum, several C17 and C18 TABLE STONES and HEADSTONES carved with emblems of death and angels' heads (souls).

A MARKET CROSS, on lower ground 100m. SE of the mausoleum, is the sole vestige of the village of Rossie that was removed at the end of the C18. Rising from a stepped base, a tall Corinthian shaft, its neck incised with the initials RH and KG and the date 1746, surmounted by four figures of lions and unicorns supporting a ball finial.

RUMBLING BRIDGE

Hamlet beside the narrow gorge of the River Devon. Informal small group of cottages, probably early C19 and partly pantiled. At the w end is the former inn (*see* below) beside the eponymous river crossing.

BRIDGES. Two bridges, one above the other, over the River Devon. The lower and earlier bridge was built by *William Gray*, *c.* 1713. Narrow round-arched ashlar span springing from the rocky sides of the gorge; no parapet. The taller and broader bridge above is of 1816 and also founded on rock. Segmental arch of hammer-dressed ashlar, the arch ring vermiculated, the spandrels pierced by narrow slits. The string courses at the base of the parapets are carried on small blocks and, at the projecting centre of each side, on moulded corbels.

INN. Now a nursing home. Early C19 harled and piend-roofed block beset by Victorian and C20 additions. On the s front, a panel, also early C19, carved with a depiction of the wooded gorge and the two bridges of Rumbling Bridge, its date of 1713 referring to the construction of the earlier bridge.

BRIGLANDS. See p. 246.
LENDRICK MUIR. See p. 500.

RUTHVENFIELD

Hamlet with a two-storey terrace of mid-C19 housing for workers at the (demolished) Ruthven calico printing and bleaching works.

RUTHVENFIELD PRIMARY SCHOOL. Dated 1868. Tall single-storey school, with mullioned windows, broad eaves and a bellcote. Two-storey schoolhouse in the same manner. Harled low E addition by *James Marshall*, 1912.

RUTHVEN HOUSE. Two-storey rubble-walled and piend-roofed house of *c.* 1800. Three-bay front with a pilastered doorpiece.

HUNTINGTOWER CASTLE. See p. 415.

ST FILLANS

Village strung out along a winding street overlooking the River Earn and the E end of Loch Earn. The houses are mostly of the later C19 with bracketed broad eaves and gabled dormers but some of the early C20.

CHURCHES

DUNDURN PARISH CHURCH. By *G. T. Ewing*, 1878–9. Broad-eaved and bargeboarded, the N end apsidal; porch at the S end. On the main S gable, a pyramid-roofed ventilator topped by a weathercock. Tudorish windows at the N and S ends; broad elliptical-arched windows at the side walls.

INTERIOR. In the chancel, oak PANELLING, COMMUNION TABLE and PULPIT of 1931 in a Neo-Celtic-cum-Romanesque manner. – FONT, a hollowed-out rounded boulder, perhaps originally in St Fillan's Chapel (*see* below), its wrought-iron stand provided in 1890. – At the N end of the E wall, a marble MONUMENT to Lieutenant William Stewart of Ardvorlich †1857, the inscription tablet topped by a draped urn and surmounting a coat of arms; it is signed by *S. Manning* of London (i.e. *Samuel Manning Jun.*). – STAINED GLASS. In the apse, two mid-C20 lights (Martha and Mary) by *J. & W. Guthrie & Andrew Wells Ltd.* – The W wall's N window (the Good Shepherd) is of *c.* 1910, an excruciatingly bad example of strongly coloured narrative art. – At the S end, two windows (St Peter and St John) by *R. Anning Bell*, 1931.

ST FILLAN'S CHAPEL, 1.2 km. ESE. The site is a drystone-walled circular graveyard. The now roofless chapel almost certainly occupies the site of a pre-Reformation chapel but was rebuilt

c. 1600 as the mausoleum of the Stewarts of Ardvorlich. Rubble-walled crowstep-gabled rectangle. The S skewputt at the E end is inscribed AS (presumably for Stewart of Ardvorlich), the W end's S skewputt with the monogram JC, the crossbar of the J lowered so as to form a cross. The only openings are in the S wall, a low rectangular door and, to its E, a small horizontally proportioned window checked internally for shutters. Inside, a scarcement at each gable. Aumbry between the door and window.

ST FILLANS FREE CHURCH. Now a house. Built in 1856. Rubble-walled rectangle. Shouldered-arch windows in the side elevations, pointed windows at the front (S) gable which is crowned with a tall gabled bellcote. Spiky Gothic porch.

PUBLIC BUILDINGS

RAILWAY STATION. Now in other use. By *Crouch & Hogg*, 1901. English picturesque in red brick and harling, with half-timbering and red tiled roofs. Over the platform, an awning carried on foliaged cast-iron brackets.

ST FILLANS BRIDGE over the River Earn. Humpbacked rubble bridge, probably of the C18. Segmental main arch; triangular cutwater at the W face.

ST FILLANS PRIMARY SCHOOL. School and schoolhouse of *c.* 1875. The school itself is of one tall storey with bracketed broad eaves. Straight-skewed roof at the main block, a jerkinhead gablet over one window; piend-roofed wing.

DRUMMOND ARMS HOTEL. Three-storey and attic main block by *Andrew Heiton Jun.*, *c.* 1875. Georgian survival but with bracketed broad eaves and two-light windows at the centre which is carried up as a pavilion-roofed tower, its top floor detailed in the manner of 'Greek' Thomson. A portico was replaced by a sun-lounge in 1967. The E wing is earlier in origin, perhaps of 1819 (the date on an oval panel, not *in situ*, which is inscribed ST FILLANS HIGHLAND SOCIETY HALL), but was heightened and given a canted bay window *c.* 1900.

CAIRN, Kindrochet, 3.2 km. SE. Large but untidy low mound in the upper valley of the River Earn, the original form obscured by the addition of stones cleared from neighbouring fields. It has been a long cairn, formed probably in the third millennium B.C. when it was *c.* 58 m. long, 11 m. broad at the E end tapering to perhaps *c.* 5 m. at the W. Excavation has shown that it contains three burial chambers, each originally a free-standing funerary monument constructed probably in the fourth millennium B.C., the E originally entered from that end, the other two from the S. Some slabs of their walls are visible.

FORT, Dundurn, 1.3 km SE. Occupying a craggy roughly oval hill, remains of a Pictish fort whose defences were formed and reconstructed during the C7 and C8 but seems to have been abandoned in the C10. The summit is surrounded on the W, S and E by a crescent-shaped natural terrace. A palisade was constructed around the outer edge of this terrace at the beginning of the C7. Probably later in the C7, the summit was fortified as an inner citadel surrounded by its own wooden rampart. The citadel's rampart, destroyed by fire, perhaps during an attack, was later replaced, perhaps in the C8, by a rubble-built rampart, *c.* 4m. wide, and, about the same time, the terrace's palisade by a massive second rampart, also of rubble possibly laced with wood, 8m. wide and at least 4m. high. Probably also in the C8, stone ramparts were constructed to enclose three lower terraces on the NE, NW and SW slopes of the hill. Roughly curved cultivation terraces have been formed at the foot of the hill's W side, their fronts revetted with stone blocks. They may be Pictish but could date from as late as the C18.

ARDVORLICH HOUSE. *See* p. 159.

ST MADOES

Village of C20 housing.

ST MADOES AND KINFAUNS PARISH CHURCH. Built in 1798–9, a rubble-walled T, the jamb projecting to the S and with the wallhead's moulded cornice returned at its chimneyed gable to suggest an open pediment. In the long N wall, four pointed windows. In each gable of the main block, a Venetian window lighting the gallery and a door below, the W door now contained in a porch and hall addition (by *Murdoch Architects*, 1996). On the W gable, a Tuscan columned birdcage bellcote, the ball finial of its flattened ogee-profile roof topped by a weathercock.

Inside, the laird's loft of the Richardsons of Pitfour in the jamb and galleries in the ends of the main block, all with simply panelled pine fronts. – Boxy PEWS. – Neo-Jacobean PULPIT, probably of 1923.

GRAVEYARD. Some C18 and early C19 HEADSTONES, those of the C18 carved variously with shields, angels' heads (souls) and emblems of death. S of the church, John Layell †1785, with two naked human figures reclining on the top, each holding a hand in front of his face. On the stone's W front, a weathered relief of Adam and Eve under a depiction of Father Time. – To the S, the large early C19 headstone of John Jackson, incised with the tools of a farmer (plough, hay rake, etc.) and with the relief of a man driving a horse and cart. – E of the church, the tall and narrow stone of William Todd, farmer, †1815, with the relief of a horse and plough.

MANSE (now KIRKWOOD) of 1804 in a wooded garden to the E. Harled two-storey and attic main block, with a segmental-arched entrance. Wings at the ends, both probably mid-C19 additions.

ST MADOES COMMUNITY CENTRE. Built as a school, by *David Smart*, 1892–3, and extended by *James Marshall* in 1912. Of red brick, with white brick trimmings.

PITFOUR CASTLE. *See* p. 667.

ST MARTINS

Little more than a place name, the church standing on a hill above the St Martins Burn.

ST MARTINS PARISH CHURCH. By *Andrew Heiton Sen.*, 1842. Unadorned Tudor Gothic T, built of purplish stugged ashlar. On the slightly projecting and gabled centre of the S side, a tall birdcage bellcote, its ogee-profiled roof rising into a large crocketed finial. Built into a retaining wall of the basement access to the boiler room at the NE corner is a MONUMENT to Isobel Rollo, the wife of George Hay, †1646. Fairly inept Ionic aedicule, the steep open pediment containing a coat of impaled arms.

Light and spacious interior, an elaborate boss at the centre of the ribbed plaster ceiling. In the N jamb and the ends of the main block, GALLERIES, their fronts decorated with long horizontal panels. – BOX PEWS. – Tall Gothic PULPIT, its body reached by a double stair. Octagonal canopy with crocketed finials round the edge and a much larger foliaged finial on top. – MONUMENTS. On the S wall, W of the pulpit, a carved and painted stone panel of *c.* 1600 proclaiming the CŒMETERIUM (burial place) of Henry Drummond of Gairdrum, his wife, Joanna Drummond of Blair, and their posterity. It is a would-be Corinthian aedicule, the open pediment containing the Drummond coat of arms; outside the pediment, depictions of the sun and moon. – On the W wall, a grey and white marble monument to William Macdonald of St Martins †1814. Aedicular, the pilasters with consoles instead of capitals, a coat of arms in the pediment. Within this frame, a bust of Macdonald perched on a tall pedestal.

GRAVEYARD. Simple Tudor GATEPIERS of 1842 at the N entrance. – Contemporary piend-roofed SESSION HOUSE SE of the church. – Just SW of the church, a GRAVE-SLAB to Patrick Coupar †1657. A pair of angels' heads (souls) at the top, in the centre, a shield bearing ploughshares; emblems of death at the bottom. – Another ploughshare on a shield below an angel's head is carved on the HEADSTONE of 1764 to members of the Miller family. – On the mid-C18 headstone of James Mitchel to the S, yet another shield displaying a ploughshare under an unusually stern angel's head; an hourglass, skull and crossbones at the base. – E of this and just SW of the church, the headstone of 1790 to James Tasker, its shield bearing the crowned hammer and anvil of a smith; an angel's head at the top, a skull, crossbones and hourglass at the base. – Similar headstone of 1811 to Thomas Allison, tenant in Rosefield, the shield with a pair of ploughshares. – N of this, the headstone of someone †1769, the E face with an angel's head at the top, the W with a pair of angels' heads in a swan-neck pediment and a shield bearing a sock and coulter. – Just E of this, the rather small ogee-arched headstone of 1744 commemorating John Blair, millwright, its E face carved with an oval frame containing a half-length figure, presumably a

portrait of Blair. The w face has leafily capitalled attached columns which frame an angel's head above a shield on which are the tools of a millwright. – To the s, a C18 headstone, weathered except for the crisply carved emblems of death at the base.
St Martins Public Hall. *See* Balbeggie.
description. Just NE of the Parish Church is Kirkstyle of St Martins, a small early C19 rubble-built house, the windows of its upper floor's outer bays heightened in the mid C19 to rise into bargeboarded dormerheads. To its N, a single-storey L-plan smithy, also of the early C19 and rubble-built. Immediately to the NW, a hump-backed rubble bridge of one segmental arch. It is dated 1782.

ST MARTIN'S ABBEY
0.6 km. E

Smart classical mansion house built for William Macdonald, an Edinburgh lawyer, in 1791–3. Three storeys, with small second-floor windows. The original s-facing five-bay entrance front is of ashlar with a string course above the ground floor of the outer bays and a first-floor sill course. Broad centre slightly advanced under a pediment, with a pilastered and corniced doorpiece and a first-floor Venetian window. At the centre of the N elevation, a full-height bow. A single-storey chapel with round-headed windows was added to the E end of the front in 1842–3. Extensive single-storey additions including a new entrance, all designed by *David Bryce*, were added at the NW in 1860–1. These were mostly removed by *A. G. Heiton* in 1921 but Bryce's Jacobean porch was rebuilt at the centre of the N elevation.

Rubble-built stables to the N. Bowed sw range, probably of 1785, the elliptical-arched entrance placed in a pilastered and open-pedimented aedicule. The NE range is early C18. At its centre, a tower containing a doocot. This was heightened in a Frenchy manner *c.* 1870, probably by *Peddie & Kinnear* who had produced unexecuted designs for remodelling the house as a château in 1869. – Brownie's Cottage E of the stables. Early C19, single-storey with a diagonally set chimney on the piended roof; diamond-paned glazing in the windows. – Walled Garden of *c.* 1800, of stone and brick. At the curved N wall, a battlemented tower. – At the NW entrance to the park, a single-storey rubble-built lodge of 1800. Three-light windows in the bowed ends. Contemporary corniced gatepiers. – On Dove Craig, N of the parkland, an ashlar obelisk commemorating Major-General Farquharson, Governor of St Lucia, †1834.

ST SERF'S PRIORY
2.9 km. sw of Kinnesswood

Near the N end of St Serf's Island in Loch Leven, the roofless medieval church of a house of Augustinian canons.

A convent of *Céli Dé*, said to have been established on St Serf's Island in 838, was replaced in 1145 by Augustinian canons (part of the establishment of St Andrews Cathedral) and the present church may have been built at about the same time. After the Reformation the church was abandoned for worship and its chancel demolished. *c*. 1834 the nave was lowered in height and converted to a shepherd's cottage, with a byre built against its N side. Later in the C19, this was unroofed and the byre partly removed.

The priory church consisted of a chancel, *c*. 4.6 m. by 3.7 m. (the dimensions revealed by C19 excavation), and nave, *c*. 8.5 m. by 6.1 m. The surviving nave walls, the S and E partly rebuilt in rubble, perhaps in the 1830s, seem originally to have been constructed of rough ashlar above a stepped base, the medieval stonework well preserved at the windowless N side. In the W gable, a blocked doorway, with the N impost and the springing of a round-headed arch surviving. This entrance is *c*. 2.1 m. broad and was perhaps intended to give access from the church to a tower. Towards the W end of the nave's S side, a rectangular door and, to the E of its inner side, remains of a stoup. Just E of the door, a blocked pointed window. Near the E end of this side where the walling seems to have been largely rebuilt, a plain rectangular window, probably of post-Reformation date and perhaps of *c*. 1834. In the E gable, the built-up chancel arch. Like the corresponding arch in the W end it has been round-headed but broader (*c*. 2.7 m.).

C19 excavation revealed evidence of an irregular T-plan building 0.2 km. to the W, probably the domestic quarters of the canons.

SCONE PALACE
2.4 km. W of New Scone

Standing beside the coronation place of the kings of Scots and within parkland from which the medieval village of Old Scone had been cleared, the huge but low-key castellated edifice built for David, eighth Viscount Stormont and third Earl of Mansfield,

Scone Palace.
East elevation by William Atkinson, 1803

in 1803–12. The architect was *William Atkinson* who displayed in this, his first major commission, his own rather stolid interpretation of the picturesque Gothic manner of his master, James Wyatt.

The site is within the grounds of the medieval Scone Abbey whose buildings were destroyed by Protestant reformers in 1559, a prelude to the formal dissolution of the monastery. In the 1580s these monastic lands were granted as a temporal lordship to the Earls of Gowrie and the erection of a major new house to the W of the site of the conventual buildings may have been begun in the late C16. The earldom of Gowrie was forfeited to the Crown in 1600 and four years later the lands of Scone were granted to David Murray of Gospetrie, cup-bearer to James VI, who was created Lord Scone and later Viscount Stormont. Murray seems to have completed a palace of Scone soon after.

The early C17 Scone Palace was built round two courtyards, the N fully enclosed, the S open to the W. In the rebuilding of 1803–12 parts of the existing S range and the W side of the E range were retained although re-cased in droved red sandstone like that of the new work, its crispness now eroded by weathering. The general shape of the earlier house was also kept but with the S courtyard's W side closed. Otherwise, the work is all new, a Late Georgian attempt to evoke the history of a great temporal lordship founded on abbey lands.

The S end of the Palace is an irregular U-shape and designed as a toy fort, its battlements for the most part sitting on a wallhead string course. At the outer corners of the five-bay E front of this part, square turrets with round-headed dummy slit windows. Two-storey outer bays, their hoodmoulded rectangular windows each containing two Gothic lights, the tall ground-floor windows denoting the principal storey. The second and fourth bays are three-storey towers with hoodmoulded pointed windows at the two lower floors and pointed slit windows at the top which is marked off by a string course. Recessed between these, the broad centre bay containing the hoodmoulded pointed entrance surmounted by a heraldic achievement which displays the impaled arms of David, third Earl of Mansfield, and Frederica Markham, his wife; above, a rectangular window of two Gothic lights under the stag's head crest of the Earls of Mansfield. Here, the battlement is projected on arcaded corbelling.

At the S and W elevations, the basement is fully exposed by the steeply falling ground. The long S front is of nine bays between the corner turrets. Slightly advanced broad centrepiece of three storeys above the basement, the top floor marked off by a string course. Its windows and basement door are all pointed, the tall window of the principal floor with a quatrefoiled head, the first-floor window smaller and the second-floor window very simple and without the hoodmould of the others. A turret rises above the NE corner to give a discreet touch of asymmetry. The outer bays are a storey lower. Hoodmoulded rectangular windows, each of two Gothic lights, very tall at the ground floor but small at the basement and first floor.

The W elevation of the 'fort' is of eight bays. Just asymmetrical, with one bay to the S and two to the N of its centrepiece and with a square bartizan instead of a full-height turret at the N corner. At the outer bays, two-light pointed and hoodmoulded windows to the basement and principal floor, the latter again very tall; at the first floor, small rectangular windows, also hoodmoulded, containing Gothic lights. Centrepiece of five bays, the outer two consisting of four-stage octagonal towers pierced by small pointed openings and Gothic blind arcading at the top stage. At the three two-storey and basement centre bays, their battlement projected on moulded corbels, rectangular windows with Gothic lights to the basement. The principal floor's tall windows are, like those of the outer bays, pointed and of two lights but with quatrefoiled heads; smaller Gothic windows at the top floor.

The E and W ranges N of the 'fort' are slightly recessed. Also battlemented but much more collegiate in feeling, probably intended to evoke the spirit of the vanished Abbey's claustral buildings. Both are of two storeys above a basement, partly hidden at the E, fully exposed at the W. E range of seven bays marked off by buttresses. Two-light pointed windows to the basement, tall hoodmoulded rectangular windows of two Gothic lights at the ground floor; tiny round-headed slit openings above. At the N end, a slightly advanced and sturdy two-storey and basement tower pierced by Gothic openings and with buttresses at the front. The W range, also ending with a tower, is almost identical but without the buttresses. N of these, single-storey service ranges, also battlemented, the E with hoodmoulded rectangular windows containing Gothic lights (the N now a door); at its N end, a two-storey square tower with a hoodmoulded Gothic window at the ground floor and a round-headed slit window above.

INTERIOR. The principal entrance's door knocker is of *c*. 1625, presumably reused from the previous house, and bears the initials of David, first Viscount Stormont, with the plate behind pierced by a star above a crescent. Oblong ENTRANCE HALL with a ribbed Gothic plaster ceiling. On the N and S sides, depressed-arched doors with Gothic panelled woodwork, as have all the doors of the principal rooms. At the entrance hall's W end, a tall pointed arch into the OCTAGON, a vestibule whose Gothic dress appears to have been inspired by James Wyatt's Fonthill Abbey. Attached columns in the corners, their capitals variously foliaged and one also displaying a grotesque head. From these spring plaster vaulting-ribs, the bosses at their intersections modelled with foliage, birds, a serpent, a coronet and the sacred 'IHS' initials, presumably in allusion to Scone Abbey. In the centre of the ceiling, the octagonal glazed cupola which lights the room. At the E, W and N sides, Gothic doorways, at the S a gilded mirror. At each of the other sides, a pointed niche, its back mirrored, its hoodmould's label stops

Scone Palace, Long Gallery.
Painting by Robert Gibb, c. 1827

modelled with the heads of a king and a monk in overt reference to Scone's historic position as an abbey and the coronation place of the Scottish kings.

The Octagon's N door opens into the LONG GALLERY, on the site and occupying most of the length of the early C17 house's gallery but with decoration suggestive of a medieval cloister. Its 44.8 m. nine-bay length is articulated by wall shafts with variously foliaged capitals from which spring the ribs of the plaster vaulted ceiling, its bosses also enriched with foliage. Two-thirds of the way up the shafts foliaged and battlemented corbels serve as lamp stands, those of the E side are original, the others are additions (perhaps of 1847 when gas lighting was introduced). In the heads of the windows of the E wall, stained glass with grisaille tracery; in the six northernmost of these, the coats of arms of the owners of Scone Palace from the first Viscount Stormont to the fifth Earl of Mansfield, the earliest probably part of the stained glass executed here by *Thomas Willement* in 1834, the latest of *c*. 1900 but in the same manner. At the gallery's N end, an ORGAN, by *Thomas Elliot*, 1813, its Gothick case enriched with carved foliage; human-head label stops at the ogee-arched hoodmould of the central compartment.

On the W side of the gallery, a pair of Gothic chimneypieces of veined black marble. Between them, a Gothic door into the SLIP GALLERY occupying a narrow range between the N and S courtyards, its design continuing the cloister theme. Rosetted and foliaged panels on its simple cornice. In the S wall, windows filled with obscured glass bordered by stained-glass Gothic tracery. Set into the N wall under rectangular hoodmoulds, their head stops modelled as identical pairs of male and female human faces, are five early C17 alabaster panels bearing the high-relief heraldic achievements of families connected to the first Viscount Stormont, the central panel displaying his coat of arms impaling that of his wife, Elizabeth Betoun.

A third and grander but more Baronial cloister-gallery is the INNER HALL on the S side of the S courtyard and entered from the Octagon. Heavily ribbed and compartmented plaster pitched ceiling, the transverse beams carried on corbels which are modelled as human heads (a king, monk, nun, etc.). In the N wall, three-light Gothic windows with coloured stained-glass tracery and grisaille oakleaves in the borders. On the S side, a pair of simply detailed early C19 Gothic stone chimneypieces, each set in an early C17 wooden surround, presumably from the previous house, their jambs carved with terminal caryatids and atlantes, the convex frieze of the E jamb decorated with strapwork and monstrous heads, that of the W also with heads and with stylized flowers. Between the fireplaces, a Gothic arched door; another Gothic door at the W end.

The doors from the Inner Hall open into the interconnecting state rooms which are arranged as an L along the S and W sides of the house's S end. The central S door gives access to the ANTE-ROOM. Delicate vaulted Gothic plaster ceiling, its ribs springing from pairs of attached columns, each pair's foliaged capitals linked by foliage-enriched bands. Gothic doorways on three sides, their hoodmoulds' head stops modelled as portraits of medieval characters including a king, queen and mitred abbot, the E and W doors flanked by elaborately tabernacled niches. In the S window, heraldic stained glass set among small panels of grisaille rosettes; borders of golden oakleaves.

E of the ante-room is the DINING ROOM. Cornice with foliaged panels; naturalistic ceiling rose. Simple grey marble Gothic chimneypiece. The DRAWING ROOM W of the ante-room is more elaborate. Compartmented plaster ceiling with foliaged bosses at the intersections of the ribs. In each square compartment, a diagonally set square, its inner sides cusped, the central cusp of each face having a foliaged finial. On the walls, panels of Empire-patterned damask, the original strong blue colour faded to a pale green. Liver-coloured Gothic marble chimneypiece. Over the E door, an elaborate painted and gilded Gothic plaster panel.

N of the drawing room, the LIBRARY occupies the three-bay centrepiece of the 'fort's' W range. Well but not extravagantly finished in a Gothic manner. Plaster ceiling with a foliaged cornice; central roundel enclosing a Star of David with foliage enrichment in the panels. Black marble and gilt chimneypiece. Battlemented oak bookcases. Doors set in rectangular surrounds with circled quatrefoils in the spandrels; the head stops of the hoodmoulds are modelled as portraits of kings and queens. In the windows, heraldic stained glass (the impaled arms of the third Earl of Mansfield and his wife flanked by the Royal Arms of Scotland and England). The library's cornice and ceiling roundel are repeated in the AMBASSADOR'S ROOM (originally the breakfast room) to the N but its Gothic chimneypiece is simpler and of grey marble.

The landscape of the surrounding PARK was laid out by J. C. Loudon in 1803 when the village of Scone which had stood c. 0.3 km. E of the house was removed, together with its Parish Church. This church had stood on the Moot or Boot Hill, an artificial mound on which had taken place the coronation of the Kings of Scots from the C9 to the C17, immediately E of the Palace's N end. All that survives of the church is a transeptal 'aisle' (now MAUSOLEUM) of sneck-harled rubble, probably erected in the C17 but heavily remodelled by Atkinson in 1807. At each corner, an early C19 octagonal clasping buttress finished with a crocketed spire rising above a band of quatrefoils. The E side, facing the Palace, is of three bays. At the centre, a hoodmoulded Gothic door of 1807. Above, a square heraldic panel (the coat of arms of the Earls of Mansfield), a late C20 replacement but whose chamfered surround looks like early C17 work reused in this position. High up, a rectangular window, perhaps of the C17 but with a hoodmould and simple Gothic lights of 1807. In the outer bays of the front, two-light windows, their heads and hoodmoulds of 1807 but their chamfered jambs may be C17. The N gable seems mostly of 1807. Cusped round window skied above the entrance to the mausoleum's burial vault. This is topped by a steep-sided triangular stone carved with strapwork surrounding a central panel which bears the initials of David, (first) Viscount Stormont, and is surmounted by a star (the heraldic device of the Murrays) and coronet. Presumably it dates from between 1621 when he was created a viscount and his death ten years later. High up in the S gable, a pointed window of 1807. It is of two lights with a quatrefoil in the head and a crocketed and foliage-finialled hoodmould.

p. 56

Inside, placed high on the E wall, are two stone PEDIMENTS, probably taken from the C17 Scone Palace. The l. bears the initials D^{L}S (for David, first Lord Scone, and so datable to between 1605 and 1621) and a crescent and star, the r. is carved with strapwork topped by a crescent and star and framing a panel bearing the DLS monogram and the date 1618. Between them, a square PANEL with a heraldic achievement identified by the inscription as that of DAVID VISCOUNT OF STORMONT (i.e. of between 1621 and 1631). Below these, the large and elegant Neoclassical MONUMENT in white and grey marble commemorating Henrica Frederica de Bunan, wife of David, seventh Viscount Stormont (later second Earl of Mansfield), †1766. It is a console-flanked rectangular niche containing a pedestal and urn. – On the S wall, another large but routine Gothic stone MONUMENT commemorates David William, third Earl of Mansfield, †1840. At the base, a pair of angels holding shields; above the inscription, the heraldic achievement of the Earls of Mansfield.

The mausoleum's N wall is filled with the magnificent MONUMENT commissioned by David, first Lord Scone (later first Viscount Stormont, †1631), from *Maximilian Colt* in 1618–19. It is almost a mirror image of the same sculptor's earlier monument to George Home, first Earl of Dunbar, in Dunbar Parish Church (Lothian). Executed in veined plum-coloured marble and black and white marbles, it takes the form of a triumphal arch framing a plum-coloured sarcophagus decorated with bands of white marble carved with lions' heads and feet. On this, the figure of Lord Scone dressed in part-armour and kneeling before a prayer desk in front of a background of plum and black marbles set in white marble borders studded with stars (the heraldic motif of the Murrays). Frieze enriched with small bow-ended panels. In the arch's tympanum, a black marble inscription panel framed by strapwork and drapery and surmounted by an angel's head (the soul); rosettes on the arch's soffit.

The framework is a display of sculptured allegory. At the sides, atlantes in the form of fully armoured C17 knights, the l. with his sword raised as if to smite wrongdoers and holding a shield which bears the arms of the Murrays of Tullibardine, the r. with his sword peacefully lowered behind his back and with a shield bearing the arms of the Earls Marischal. At their feet, a helmet and gauntlets; behind, reliefs of trophies. Above the entablature, Corinthian pilastered niches form backdrops to small statues of Justice and Peace. In the spandrels over the arch, large high-relief figures of angels, the l. holding a garland and quill, the r. a trumpet in each hand; between them, a foliaged keystone. Above, an upper entablature, its ends surmounted by strapwork-framed shields bearing the quartered arms of David, first Lord Scone, and Elizabeth Betoun, his wife. At the centre, a panel displaying the heraldic achievement of Lord Scone. It stands in a scroll-sided pilastered frame, the pilasters' faces carved with reliefs of pendant trophies dropping from lions' heads, surmounted by a miniature sarcophagus; on top, an angel's head flanked by pinnacled finials.

STABLES N of Moot Hill built in 1810 and also designed by *Atkinson*. Constructed of sneck-harled rubble, they form a courtyard, its NW side closed by a screen wall with corniced and pyramid-finialled gatepiers of droved ashlar. Two-storey piend-roofed NE and SW ranges. Single-storey SE range with elliptical-arched coachhouse doors.

SE of Moot Hill on the axis of the Palace's main entrance, an early C17 rubble-built GATEWAY. Elliptical arch flanked by round towers, both partly ruined and with oval gunloops. On the outer (NE) face of the archway, a badly weathered panel bearing the achievement of the royal arms of Scotland; in its frame's pediments, initials apparently CR (for *Carolus Rex*, i.e. Charles I). Two more heraldic achievements on the towers (the impaled arms of Murray and Betoun, i.e. of David, first Lord Scone and Viscount Stormont, and his wife, Elizabeth Betoun, on the N, and a weathered coat of arms above the Murray motto on the S), both in moulded frames. Another worn heraldic panel surmounted by a coronet and set in a round-headed pilastered frame on the gateway's inner face. The towers have had entrances placed some way above ground level on the SW side where part of a door jamb survives at the S tower which also had a first-floor entrance. The towers were linked at first-floor level by a passage-room above the archway. A rubble wall pierced by quatrefoil gunloops extends each side of the gateway.

S of the gateway, a rubble-walled GRAVEYARD which served the former village. Roughly in its NE corner, the GRAVE-SLAB of David Coupar †1644, carved with a shovel and pitchfork displayed saltire-wise. – To its WSW, a HEADSTONE now with an inscription to George McLagan †1863 but the W face is dated 1763 and crisply carved with an angel's head (the soul) above a shield bearing a weaver's shuttle and loom and with a grotesque head for crest; emblems of death at the bottom. – Further W, the curly-topped HEADSTONE of Elizabeth Taylor †1780. On the E face, an angel's head above the depiction of a jolly naked boy brandishing a hatchet and mason's mall and flanked by dividers and a setsquare. On top of the W face, a pudgy striding angel trumpeter. – Just W of this, RECUMBENT STONES, all probably C17, three of them hog-backed, one dated 1641 and carved with emblems of death. – W again, a HEADSTONE whose E face bears an inscription of 1879 to the parents of Alexander Gellatly but, on the W face, crude C18 carving of an angel's head above a grisly array of reminders of death and the dividers and setsquare of a wright. – To the N, a large stone of 1788, originally recumbent but now upright, to George Banks, with a shield bearing a peat cutter, spade and heart. – SW of this, an C18 stone, its W face with an angel's head above a shuttle and loom. – To the SW, a headstone of 1750 to IH and AB, with a crude angel's head above a shield bearing a ploughshare. – Beside it, an C18 aedicular stone, an angel's head in the open pediment; below, a heraldic achievement with naked human supporters. – To its E, an ogee-arched headstone, also C18, now with an inscription of 1881 to Ann Stewart. On the piecrust-bordered W face, an angel's head above a shield carved with a setsquare and dividers; reminders of death at the bottom.

On a small mound S of the gateway and at the head of the Lime Avenue, the MARKET CROSS of Old Scone, the only surviving structure from the village. It is probably late medieval. Rising from a crude octagonal base constructed of boulders is an octagonal shaft, its capital surmounted by a large rosette finial.

On the Queen's Drive, the approach to Scone Palace from the S, an early C19 BRIDGE. Small pointed arch of stugged ashlar over the Catmoor Burn; on each side, a cannon spout to drain the roadway. Droved ashlar battlement with a small turret at each corner. – At the S end of the drive, a mid-C19 single-storey LODGE. Plenty of crowstepped gables and a bay window overlooking the drive. Beside it, corniced and ball-finialled GATEPIERS of channelled ashlar, probably also of the mid C19.

SCOTLANDWELL

Small village, the name possibly but not certainly a reference to its well.

PORTMOAK FREE CHURCH, 0.6 km. NW. Now Portmoak Hall. Georgian survival rubble-walled box built in 1844 but recast in 1870. Round-headed windows and, in the top of each gable, a circular light. Gabled vestry at the centre of the N side. This side and the E end are overlaid by late C20 additions.

PORTMOAK PARISH CHURCH, 0.4 km. NW. By *Andrew Cumming*, 1831–2. Rough ashlar rectangle, a ball-finialled bellcote jettied out from a small pedestal on top of the W gable. In the N wall, square windows lighting the gallery; a rectangular door in each gable. Four-bay S front, the end bays each with a double tier of square windows. In the centre bays, tall pointed windows, the astragals of the upper sashes intersecting. To the N of the church and now joined to it by a glazed link, the single-storey piend-roofed SESSION HOUSE built in 1837, an octagonal chimney on each gable.

The INTERIOR of the church is well finished and very little altered. Lotus-flower ceiling rose. Semi-octagonal gallery carried on fluted columns with acanthus-leaf capitals. Boxy PEWS. In the centre of the S wall, the PULPIT, its canopy rising to an urn topped by a flame finial.

On the E wall, the PORTMOAK STONE, a fragment of a C10 or C11 cross-slab carved with interlaced decoration. It was unearthed at the site of the medieval Portmoak Parish Church, 1.6 km. SW of the present building. – Built into the W wall are three small square early C18 STONES, all with moulded borders and decorated with incised foliage. They bear the initials of Sir Robert Douglas of Kirkness, his wife, Dame Jean Balfour, and their son-in-law, the Rev. Mr Robert Douglas, Minister of Portmoak, and the dates of their respective deaths (1724, 1746 and 1742).

In the steeply sloping GRAVEYARD S of the church, a remarkable collection of well-preserved HEADSTONES of *c.* 1720–50. Most have semicircular or curvaceously pedimented tops; some also enjoy pilasters or attached columns. The fronts are decorated with reminders of death, angels' heads (souls) and trade symbols (e.g. the crowned hammer of the smiths, and masons' and tailors' tools). – Built into the W wall but half-buried are four larger aedicular MONUMENTS of 1731–46.

Well below the road to the W of the church is the harled PORTMOAK HOUSE, the former Portmoak Parish Manse, designed and built by *James Forbes*, 1827, its canted dormer windows additions of the late C19.

BURIAL GROUND, Friar Place. Unwalled lawn, the site of the vanished Hospital of St Mary which was founded here *c.* 1210. One GRAVE-SLAB may be C18. It is decorated with a panel carved with the relief of a skull and crossbones.

DESCRIPTION. The village is L-plan, with Leslie Road running E–W and Main Street going N from its W end. In LESLIE ROAD, late C20 housing and some vernacular buildings of the earlier C19, a few of their roofs pantiled. In MAIN STREET, opposite the T-junction with Leslie Road, BALMYRE, single-storey with a heavily stepped gable to the street. It was built as Portmoak Parish School in 1834 to a design by *Andrew Cumming*. A little to the N, a lane with pantile-roofed C19 cottages on its N side leads down to the WELL. This is covered by a wooden structure supporting a broad-eaved roof, the result like a *cottage orné* without walling; at the W end, a stone fountain and basin. All this is by *David Bryce*, 1858. S of the well, a WASHHOUSE of 1860, again like a broad-eaved *cottage orné* but stone-walled and with a ventilator on the roof.

Main Street is short, its general character C19 vernacular with a fair number of pantiled roofs. The rear part of the gable-ended No. 7 on the W has a crowstepped gable and windows with chamfered margins; it may be C17. N of this, a harled double house [?] (Nos. 3–5), its crowstepped gables and the margins of the windows (mostly enlarged) heavily restored in cement. At the S house (No. 5), a corniced door beside a small window whose lintel bears the date 1762.

VANE FARM, 3.6 km. SW. Rubble-built and pantile-roofed courtyard steading of the earlier C19. Piend-roofed L-plan main block of two storeys, tactfully altered for its present use as a reception centre for the Loch Leven Nature Reserve. At the back, a U of single-storey ranges.

ARNOT TOWER. *See* p. 159.

SOLSGIRTH HOUSE
1.3 km. S of Blairingone

A large villa built in three stages during the late C19 and early C20. It began *c.* 1870 as a straightforward two-storey oblong, the S front of five bays. In 1898 a sizeable extension was added to the E, with crowstepped gables and oriel windows to the two-storey S part and a single-storey billiard room wing, a mullioned and transomed four-light window in its gable, projecting boldly N. The original house was remodelled and thickened to the N *c.* 1910–13 by *J. Graham Fairley* who gave this W part bracketed broad eaves and bargeboarded dormer windows. He heightened the SW corner as a French pavilion-roofed low tower containing the principal entrance in a segmental-pedimented surround of Jacobean inspiration. A much taller and ogee-roofed tower, also Neo-Jacobean, was built on the W side. At the same time he erected a Tuscan-columned screen in front of the low 1890s service range at the house's E end. Interiors in a mixture of Jacobean and Frenchy manners but without panache, the principal room (the ballroom) apparently formed by Fairley throwing together two rooms of the 1890s.

SPITTAL OF GLENSHEE

Church and bridge standing at the point where Glen Lochsie and Gleann Beag debouch into Glen Shee.

GLENSHEE PARISH CHURCH. Built as a chapel of ease in 1831. Rubble-walled oblong, a ball-finialled birdcage bellcote on the W gable, a ball finial on the E. Round-headed door and windows, the E gable with a trio of narrow openings, the centre light a dummy. Inside, panel-fronted W gallery of 1831 on widely spaced marbled cast-iron Roman Doric columns *in antis*. *L. & J. Falconer* partitioned off the space below to form a vestibule, vestry and lavatory in 1889. – At the E end, PULPIT of 1831, with a panelled front and tall round-headed back. – PEWS of 1900. – STAINED GLASS. Two lights (the Maries at the Tomb) of *c.* 1900 in lush Glasgow style.

In the rubble-walled GRAVEYARD, immediately SW of the church, a curly-topped HEADSTONE of 1780 to John Robertson, its N face bearing an angel's head (the soul), the ploughshare and coulter of a farmer, and emblems of death. – On the graveyard's S side, an early C19 piend-roofed COTTAGE built of whitewashed rubble.

GLENSHEE BRIDGE. Constructed, *c.* 1755, to carry the military road from Blairgowrie to Braemar over the Lochsie Burn. Rubble-built and fearsomely humpbacked, of one broad segmental arch.

STANDING STONE, on a hillock immediately N of Glenshee Parish Church. Thin slab, *c.* 1.8 m. high, with a semicircular notch in each side, probably erected in the second or third millennium B.C.

STONE CIRCLE, 'Grave of Diarmid', 0.7 km. E. Surmounting a flat-topped glacial moraine overlooking the Shee Water, four standing stones erected probably in the second millennium B.C. They mark the corners of an oblong space, *c.* 2.5 m. by 3 m., their long faces aligned with the oblong's longer N and S sides. The two largest, *c.* 0.75 m. and 0.8 m. tall, stand at the W corners. The slimmer NE boulder is 0.7 m. tall but the SE only 0.3 m.

DALMUNZIE HOUSE. See p. 311.

SPITTALFIELD

Linen-weaving village laid out in the C18 round a green.

GLENDELVINE PRIMARY SCHOOL, 1.1 km. SW. By *A. Watt Allison*, 1926–7. Harled and piend-roofed single-storey on a U-plan; half-timbering in a gablet above the entrance. – Contemporary SCHOOLHOUSE to the E, with a jerkin-head roof; again, a half-timbered gablet.

SCHOOL, South Green. Converted to housing, 1937. By *D. Maclagan*, 1857. Single-storey, with a segmental-arched porch at the main entrance and carved bargeboards.

DESCRIPTION. Despite alterations of the later C19 and C20 a well-preserved grouping of Late Georgian workers' housing. In SOUTH GREEN, on the green's S side, the former School (*see above*) at the E end is followed by late C18 and early C19 vernacular, the harled walls of BEECHWOOD standing out from the village's prevalent sneck-harled rubble. On the green's W side (WEST GREEN), low two-storey houses of *c*. 1800, originally flatted with the upper floors entered from the back. On the N side (NORTH GREEN), two rows of cottages, perhaps early C19, a couple at each end (Nos. 2–3 and 10–12) with distinctive broad low windows. In the centre of this side, THE MUCKLE HOOSE, a piend-roofed two-storey and five-bay fronted former linen factory (now housing) of 1767, its windows very small. More single-storey cottages, also probably of the early C19, on the E side (EAST GREEN).

FORT, Inchtuthil, 1.7 km. S. W end of a promontory beside the River Tay which has been cut off by several lines of fortification, probably formed in stages during the first millennium B.C. and the early centuries of the first millennium A.D. Excavation has revealed that the tip of the promontory was first defended by a curved palisade, apparently later replaced by a ditch which enclosed a slightly larger area. This in turn was replaced by the present defences placed further E to enclose yet more ground. They consist of four straight ramparts with intervening narrow ditches. The two outer ramparts seem to be earlier than the inner pair and the massive innermost rampart incorporates blocks of dressed stone taken from the site of the late C1 Roman fortress which stood nearby and was destroyed by *c*. 90 A.D.

GLENDELVINE HOUSE. See p. 392.

STANLEY

Planned factory village to house workers at Stanley Mills to the E. It was laid out by *James Stobie* in 1785 after the fourth Duke of Atholl, owner of the Stanley estate, agreed to lease land for the village and mills to a partnership which included local lairds and Perth merchants, together with Richard Arkwright, the entrepeneur, textile industrialist, inventor and mill designer. The village's plan is a gridiron and its streets are broad, the housing now a mixture of Late Georgian and C20, agreeable but plain.

ST COLUMBA (Episcopal), Perth Road. A mission church, by *Speirs & Co.*, 1898. Wooden clad with touches of half-timbering and Gothic windows. Attached to the W end, a stone HALL of 1907. – Immediately N of the church, the village WAR MEMORIAL of *c.* 1920. Stone statue of a kilted soldier.

STANLEY FREE CHURCH, Perth Road. Now Stanley and District Public Hall. Plain Gothic of 1843–4, the centre of the W front advanced as if intended to support a tower.

STANLEY PARISH CHURCH, King Street. Built in 1828 by Deniston, Buchanan & Co., then owners of the Stanley Mills, for the spiritual welfare of their employees. Sizeable Georgian Gothic box, a tower at the N end, the walls of droved ashlar. At the N gable, corner pilasters surmounted by flat-topped pinnacles. Lattice glazing in the mullioned and transomed windows. Over the windows of the N gable and the doors in the N bay of each side are hoodmoulds whose label stops are carved as human heads. The tower is of three stages. At its bottom, a N door. At the second stage, a window of three lights, a quatrefoil in the head; hoodmould but with lateral returns in place of label stops. This stage is finished with a tall battlement, its corner merlons triangular; on the centre merlon, a clock face added *c.* 1860. Inside this battlement rises the tall conventionally battlemented belfry stage, its openings paired, its corners pilastered and with flat-topped pinnacles like those of the gable.

Inside, a large Perp ceiling rose. D-plan gallery on wooden bundle-shafted columns. The spaces under the gallery's S end were partitioned off to form a vestry and session house in 1960–1. The focal point is provided by the PULPIT, Georgian Gothick with a sounding-board. – Routine COMMUNION TABLE of *c.* 1920. – Plain mid-C19 PEWS brought here from the former Stanley Free Church in 1961. – In the vestibule, a large marble and alabaster Victorian Classical MONUMENT to Samuel Hood †1872, with an array of allegorical figures. – In the fanlight over the N entrance door, a pair of STAINED GLASS panels (the Resurrection; Daniel in the Lions' Den). They may be German work of the C17.

STANLEY PRIMARY SCHOOL, The Square. By *Thomas Lawson & Son*, 1877–8. Meanly bargeboarded single storey, the flèche of the central ventilator now missing.

STANLEY MILLS, off Mill Street. Large group of C18 and C19 cotton mills sited on a loop of the River Tay, from which water to power their wheels was diverted by a LADE designed by *James* Stobie in 1785. Originally tunnelled for 236.5 m. through Stanley Hill, it had a fall of *c.* 0.4 m. It was replaced *c.* 1825 by a new lade with a fall of *c.* 4.88 m. and which powered seven wheels. This lade was widened and floored in concrete *c.* 1925. At the mills, the main lade is above ground and is carried round the N and W sides of the complex with branches (largely underground) to serve individual buildings.

Construction of the first cotton mill was begun early in 1786 and probably completed by February 1787, when the Duke of

Atholl formally granted it in feu to the partnership, together with a corn mill which had been erected in 1729. The complex expanded spasmodically through the C19. The mills finally closed in 1989 and conversion to housing and a visitor centre began in 1997. The principal buildings surround a roughly rectangular courtyard. At the NW corner, an ogee-roofed circular GATEHOUSE of c. 1885, its late C17 revival manner reminiscent of that used at the pavilions of Kinross House (q.v.). On the W side of the courtyard, the BELL MILL of 1786–7, designed by *Richard Arkwright*. It is of five storeys and a basement, the two lowest floors of rubble and with rectangular windows, the upper floors of local red bricks laid in Flemish bond and with elliptically arched windows. W front of thirteen bays, the S covered by a shallowly projecting latrine tower (a later addition). Asymmetrically placed and slightly advanced 'centrepiece' of three bays under a chimneyed open pediment. At the four bays N of this the windows are grouped 1:3. Three-bay N gable, a round window at the top to light the roofspace. Crowning this gable is an octagonal birdcage bellcote, its weathervane in the shape of a ship. E elevation very like the W but without the 'centrepiece'. The S end also has a round window at the top but a bowed stair-tower overlays the E third of the gable. Inside, the ground and first floors were combined in the C19. The three floors above are original, the wooden beams and floors supported on cast-iron cruciform pillars, their tops slotted to receive transmission brackets. – W of the Bell Mill, an ashlar-walled SLUICE CHAMBER which served the demolished corn mill of 1729.

The courtyard's S range is provided by the MID MILL, its building history surprisingly complex. As first built c. 1825, it was of five or six storeys, the N front of fourteen bays with a bowed stair tower at the seventh bay from the l. In the 1830s it was extended by a further six bays to the W and four to the E. After a fire in 1848 it was partly rebuilt, the existing ground and first floor being retained but surmounted by new second, third and attic floors. Walls of red sandstone rubble; slated roof, piended at the E end. String course under the third floor whose windows are low and of horizontal proportion. Long roof-lights to the attic. At the S elevation, wooden balconies added in *Law & Dunbar-Nasmith*'s 1990s conversion of the building to housing. The ends are supported on ellipticalheaded arches which covered the tail races of the Bell Mill and East Mill, so they may be of the 1780s and 1790s. – In front, a tall and tapering square brick chimney of c. 1830 which served the gasworks that stood in the middle of the courtyard. Immediately N of the chimney, a round pit for the now missing gasholder.

The detached E range of the courtyard is the EAST MILL built c. 1805 on the site of a flax mill which had been built in 1796 but destroyed by fire three years later. This mill was reconstructed and enlarged c. 1825 and the top floors rebuilt after the fire of 1848. Again it is of red sandstone rubble. Five storeys and an attic, with a basement in the fall of the ground to the s. Plain rectangular openings. Segmental-headed arches under part of the E elevation. These mark the positions of the water wheels which were originally located at the sixth bay from the s and moved further N when the mill was enlarged in the 1820s. Across the N end, the piend-roofed stub of an intended but uncompleted N range of the 1820s. On its W side, a bowed lift tower added in 1997.

On the N side of the courtyard, a detached range. The main block is a two-storey mid-C19 WAREHOUSE, its s front of fifteen bays. At its W end, a contemporary single-storey STABLE. At the other end and extending E of the courtyard, a single-storey concrete OFFICE BLOCK of *c.* 1920. It ends against a piend-roofed single-storey HOUSE of the earlier C19, its two-light Gothick windows hoodmoulded.

E of the East Mill and parallel to it, a mid-C19 range, its N part a single-storey and attic WAREHOUSE, its doors round-headed. The s part, of two storeys and an attic, was a MILL, perhaps a hand-mule room or for handlooms. Behind, a BLEACH WORKS, originally of the 1820s but enlarged in the late C19 and early C20. Some way to the E, an ogee-roofed circular TURBINE HOUSE, its design similar to that of the NW lodge but it is of 1921 when a hydro-electric scheme was installed at the mills. Very plain contemporary ENGINE HOUSE adjoining.

TAYMOUNT HOUSE, 1.6 km. NE. Outsize harled *cottage orné* of 1829. Broad-eaved roofs which form gables at each face of the canted bay windows of the s front overlooking the River Tay.

STANLEY HOUSE. 0.8 km. E. On the wooded promontory in the River Tay E of Stanley Mill. The house, 2006–7, by *Harry Taylor & Co.*, in a Lorimerian Scots manner, is set immediately behind the site of its predecessor (a jointure house of *c.* 1700, enlarged in 1765 and rebuilt after a fire in 1887). This was partly demolished in the later C20 and in 2006 the remaining walls lowered to form garden enclosures. Behind is a rubble WALLED GARDEN, probably of the late C18 but much restored in 2003–4.

INCHBERVIS CASTLE, 0.4 km. E, occupies the E end of a promontory which has almost sheer drops to the N, s and E and whose W neck has been cut across by a ditch, perhaps formed in the C13. Set back from the ditch, remains of a rubble-built D-plan tower of *c.* 1500 which stands to the height of a single tall storey. Wide-mouthed gunloops in the W, NE and E segments. There may have been a fourth in the very thick but ruinous s wall. Inside, a tunnel-vaulted room which contained an entresol floor, its joists supported on rounded corbels. A hatch in the ceiling may have been the only access. On the room's W side, a recess whose tunnel vault rises above the level of the entresol, its outer face pierced by a gunloop. An embrasure, perhaps originally for a gunloop, in the very thick s wall. Just to the NE, a circular WELL with an ashlar parapet.

STOBHALL

3.2 km. SSE of Cargill

Informal grouping of manorial buildings on a promontory site overlooking the River Tay.

The lands of Cargill, held since the late C12 by the Montfiquets, were acquired *c.* 1345 by Malcolm Drummond, ancestor of the Lords Drummond (later Earls and titular Dukes of Perth), probably in consequence of his son's marriage to Mary Montfiquet. Perhaps soon after, the site of the principal residence of this barony was moved from the ringwork castle at Cargill to Stobhall where a house was certainly in existence by 1500 when John, first Lord Drummond, signed a charter there. However, by then the chief seat of the Drummonds was Drummond Castle (q.v.) and by the later C16 Stobhall seems to have become a jointure or dowry house and was used as such until the late C18. For much of the C19 it was occupied by the factor of this part of the Drummond estates and later by a gardener or caretaker. In 1953 Stobhall was acquired from the Earl of Ancaster, heir to the Drummond estates through a female line, by the seventeenth Earl of Perth, heir male of the Lords Drummond, who carried out tactful restoration and alterations over more than twenty years.

The irregularly shaped site occupies the S end of a ridge above the River Tay, with steep drops to the E, W and S. The approach from the N may formerly have been cut through by a ditch. The buildings are placed round and within a courtyard, with a sloping garden to the W, perhaps originally a secondary court. The main courtyard and the garden are enclosed by low rubble-built E, W and S walls, probably medieval in origin but much mended and rebuilt, the S wall containing datestones of 1721 and 1966 as evidence of two phases of such work. On the W wall, a ball-finialled SUNDIAL of C18 type but dated 1957.

The courtyard's N side is occupied by the DOWER HOUSE and adjoining and contemporary GATEHOUSE. Over the outer entrance to the gatehouse's pend, above the courtyard door to the Dower House and on a pedimented dormerhead of that house's rear elevation are coroneted shields. They bear the impaled arms of Drummond and Ker flanked by the initials I^{E}P and I^{C}P for John, second Earl of Perth, and Jean [Ker], Countess of Perth, and suggest a construction date of between 1613 when they married and 1622 when she died.* Both buildings are rubble-walled and crowstep-gabled. The two-storey gatehouse's N front is flush with the rear wall of the Dower House, its elevation to the courtyard set back from that of the

---

* But the same impaled arms and initials were erected on the gatehouse of Drummond Castle (q.v.) which is dated 1630. David MacGibbon and Thomas Ross, *The Castellated and Domestic Architecture of Scotland*, ii (1884), 363, recorded a date of 1671 on the building. This is no longer visible but may have referred to some alteration having been made in that year.

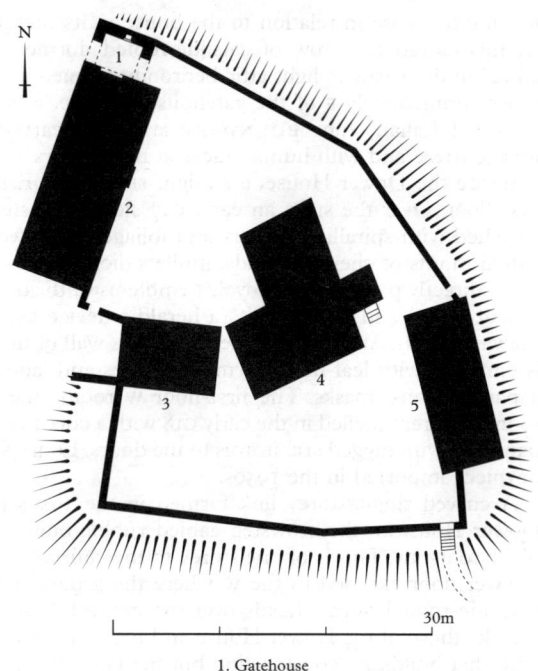

1. Gatehouse
2. Dower House
3. Kitchen
4. Chapel
5. Library

Stobhall.
Block-plan

Dower House. The provision of a pend high enough to allow a laden cart to pass through has pushed its upper floor and wallhead above those of the Dower House but its relative narrowness means that the roof ridge is lower. The openings to the flat-ceilinged pend are round-headed arches, the N with a roll-and-hollow moulding and springing from Doric-capitalled panelled pilasters and surmounted by a triangular-headed armorial panel. Similar panel over the Dower House's courtyard entrance whose roll-and-hollow moulding has been partly renewed in cement. This two-storey S elevation is of four bays, with catslide-roofed dormerheads over the first-floor windows. The two W of these are round-headed, as are the first-floor window of the W gable and the W window of the rear (N) elevation. They were perhaps altered in the early C18 when the room they light was remodelled. Roughly in the centre of the N elevation, a round Victorian tower, its conical roof covered with fish-scale slating. Near the E end of this elevation, a blocked window or door, its sill just below first-floor level, and making no sense in relation to the house in its present form. At this elevation, a row of catslide-roofed dormer windows added in the 1950s to light attic bedrooms formed in the roof-space. Immediately E of the gatehouse's N side, a large early medieval Italian stone BOUNDARY MARKER, carved with a foliage frieze and with human faces at the corners.

Inside the Dower House, a straight stone stair rises to the first floor. Over the stair, an early C17 sloping plaster ceiling enriched with spiralling flowers and foliage set between individual motifs of cherubs' heads, mullets, lions' masks and the more directly patriotic and royalist emblems of thistles, a rose, a fleur-de-lys and a portcullis (a heraldic device used by the Stewart kings). At the top of the stair, the S wall of the landing is enriched with leaf-tailed terminal figures and, above them, a pair of lions' masks. The first-floor W room (the drawing room) was remodelled in the early C18 with a coved ceiling and panelling with lugged architraves to the doors. Louis XV chimneypiece imported in the 1950s.

A curved single-storey link formed in the 1950s joins the Dower House to the crowstep-gabled rubble-built KITCHEN block to its SW. This is of one storey to the courtyard but with a lower floor exposed to the W where the ground falls away. Catslide-roofed dormerheads over the ground-floor windows are like those of the Dower House and perhaps contemporary with that building's construction but the kitchen block generally is likely to have been built to serve the Chapel block and to date from the 1570s. Large kitchen fireplace at the N end of the basement room. On the sloping garden ground W of the kitchen, a bronze SCULPTURE (the Stobhall Madonna) by *Janet Scrymgeour-Wedderburn,* an example of febrile stylized realism.

In the centre of the courtyard is the complex's strangest building, the CHAPEL. Despite its name and long ecclesiastical use it was probably built as a late C16 great hall with a small house at one end. The building consists of a cavetto-corniced S range, its E two-thirds of one tall storey, its W third of the same height but containing an upper floor. Projecting S from near its W end is a two-storey porch. On the other side, a three-storey NW jamb looking like a small tower house. The Chapel's walling is all of rubble, with intakes above the bases of the S block's gables. All the gables have crowsteps, those of the E gable of the S block renewed in the 1950s. Near the E end of this block's N side, a small window with chamfered jambs and a trefoil head. It may be C14 but is not necessarily *in situ* and of doubtful value as identifying the range as a medieval chapel rather than a late C16 hall block.* The Gothic windows of the block's S wall and E gable are Victorian insertions, the E window replac-

---

*If it had been a medieval chapel it would have been exceptionally large and it is hard to see why John, first Lord Drummond, should have founded a collegiate church at Innerpeffray in 1507 rather than endowing chaplainries here.

ing a late C16 or early C17 three-light rectangular window. Above the E window, a triangular panel containing the impaled arms of Drummond and Ruthven for David, second Lord Drummond, †1571 and his widow, Lilias Ruthven, and the date 1578, probably that of the building's completion. The same arms and date appear in another triangular panel over the entrance on the W side of the porch. W of the porch, a catslide-roofed dormerhead over the first-floor S window of the S block. At the join of the W gable of the S block and the NW jamb, a large stone rainwater spout.

The NW jamb is an oblong three-storey and basement tower. At the NW and SE corners are conical-roofed round turrets, the SE much fatter than the NW, carried on continuous corbelling. The top-floor window of the E side has a roll-and-hollow-moulded surround and rises through the eaves, its top part framed by short banded attached columns which carry a pediment (renewed in 2000), the tympanum carved with the Drummond coat of arms. Rounded margins to the other windows, the W second-floor window with a catslide-roofed dormerhead.

INTERIOR. The entrance from the S porch opens into a passage, its ceiling beams painted, probably in the late C16, with fruiting vines. E of the passage is the chapel fitted up for Roman Catholic worship in 1690. Before then it was clearly the great hall. Beamed wooden ceiling, the centre of its E end cut away to allow for the Victorian window. The ceiling is covered with early C17 painted tempera decoration. On the joists, stylized foliage. They divide the ceiling into five compartments, each containing four principal panels interspersed with panels bearing identical designs of stylized fruiting foliage. The principal panels at the ends of each compartment contain naturalistic depictions of animals and birds, each shown standing on or running along the ceiling's outer edge. In the centre panels, portraits of African and European monarchs (identified by Latin inscriptions) designed to be seen from the N side of the room where there may originally have been a fireplace. At the W end of the ceiling the panels depict a bird and bush, Prester John (the Emperor of Abyssinia), the King of Mauritania riding an elephant and accompanied by slaves, and a rearing horse. In the next compartment, a stag, the turbaned Emperor of Turkey, the King of Hungary, and a bird perched on a rock. Then, a boar, the King of Spain (a portrait of Philip IV), the King of Sweden, and an eagle. The compartment next to the E end contains a bird, the King of Poland, the King of Great Britain (a portrait of Charles I), and a pugilistic lion. The E compartment now has only the two outer panels painted with a hare and a peacock. Its two central panels depicting the Emperor of Germany (by mistake, a portrait of Henri IV) and the King of France have been re-erected on the chapel's W wall, probably in 1858 when the ceiling paintings were restored by *James Robertson Sen*. In this position they are flanked by panels of stylized foliage of the same design as the panels on the ceiling but larger, and in the centre is a panel painted with the heraldic achievement of the Earls of Perth, these panels all probably of 1858.

The ceiling's subject matter, all probably derived from woodcuts, is unique in Scotland although an early C17 ceiling at Nunraw (Lothian) displays the coats of arms of monarchs surrounding a shield which bears the initials of that house's owner and his wife. The Stobhall ceiling apparently places the kings in something like an order of precedence with the Africans at its bottom and the western Europeans at the top, and Charles I, King of Great Britain, at their centre. Was the ceiling painted in anticipation of his visit to Scotland in 1633, perhaps in the hope that he would dine at Stobhall? In the chapel's N wall, near its E end, an aumbry, its wooden door pierced with a wheel design and perhaps of the early C17.

Many if not all the chapel furnishings have been imported from elsewhere. Stone ALTAR, its slab probably medieval, the supports perhaps mid C19. – Early medieval stone FONT, the roughly hexagonal bowl carved with interlaced work and with a badly mutilated figure at one corner. – Stone STOUP incised with a cross, perhaps of the late C17.

In the Chapel building's S range, W of the passage, are a pair of small ground-floor rooms. The passage's N end opens onto the foot of the turnpike stair in the SE corner of the jamb. In the jamb's ground- and first-floor rooms W of the stair are ceilings whose beams are painted with flowers, fruiting vines, snakes and fish. The principal first-floor room occupies the W end of the S range. Rather narrow stone W fireplace of the late C16, its jambs carved with human faces from which rise spiralling flowers; on the lintel, more faces and oak boughs flanking the heraldic achievement of the Lords Drummond. In the second-floor room of the jamb, a stone fireplace whose lintel bears the initials and impaled arms of David, Lord Drummond, and Dame Lilias Ruthven above the date ANNO.D(OMI)NI.1578.

SW of the Chapel is the LIBRARY built in 1965 on the site of a very plain and altered C18 building. The Library, like the other buildings of the courtyard, is rubble-walled and crow-step-gabled. Tall ground floor. Attic with pedimented dormerheads, the centre one carved with the arms of the Earls of Perth, the other two with coronets and the initials of David, [seventeenth] Earl of Perth, and his wife, Nancy, Countess of Perth. Interior in the manner of the C18 High Drawing Room of Traquair House (Borders), with Corinthian pilastered bookcases and a prominent chimneypiece at the W end. Just behind the Library, a SCULPTURE (the Annunciation) by *Janet Scrymgeour-Wedderburn*, 1999, a bronze figure of a dancing (wingless) Archangel.

In the formal garden N of the courtyard, a SUNDIAL of the earlier C17. Doric column banded with a square stone, its faces incised with dials and one of its corners bearing the Drummond coat of arms under the coroneted initials I^{E}P for John, [second] Earl of Perth. The column is surmounted by a cubical stone with a round hollow dial in each face; ogee-arched top with a ball finial.

NE of the formal garden, a mid-C19 two-storey OFFICE RANGE, remodelled in the 1950s. Large gabled dormer windows to the upper floor, the centre one original, the others of the 1950s; in the W gable, the flight-holes of a doocot. – N of this, GATEPIERS surmounted by stone eagles. They may be early C19. In front of them, a horizontal SUNDIAL of the later C17, its badly weathered octagonal pedestal covered with a brass dial plate bearing the initials I^{E}P, probably for James, fourth Earl of Perth, and signed by *John Marke* of London.

Further N, THE FOLLY, by *Stewart Tod & Partners*, 1987–9, a single-storey and basement pink harled octagon. Gothic E door flanked by pointed niches containing concrete pineapples. Inside, the ground-floor room's walls and ceiling are covered with early C18 panelling imported from a garden pavilion at Polton House (Lothian) and restored and supplemented by *Brian Ingham*. The panels are painted in black and grey as faceted ashlar blocks, each decorated with a central 'O'; red coloured stiles. At the entrance to the room ceiling panels displaying the points of the compass and flanked by half-panels, one painted with the sky at dawn, the other at night. Chimneypiece with a pulvinated frieze.

STORMONTFIELD

Hamlet, formerly the site of a bleach works which was begun in 1788 but destroyed by fire in 1971.

ST DAVID'S CHURCH. Late Gothic, by *A. Marshall Mackenzie*, 1897. Very simple single-cell church, built of stugged and squared masonry, a ball finial on the W gable, a stone cross on the E. In the W gable, two tall cusped windows and a small circular opening at the apex. Hoodmoulded round-arched door at the W end of the S side whose windows are small with cusped heads. Three narrow pointed lights, the centre taller than the others, at the E gable; another circular opening at the apex. – Beside the door, a repoussé metal SUNDIAL, the border decorated with thistles and set with coloured glass; it was erected to commemorate Queen Victoria's Diamond Jubilee of 1897.

Inside, walls of stugged ashlar above a wooden dado; steeply pitched wagon roof. The E end is raised on three steps as a chancel. FURNISHINGS all of 1897. In the chancel, a red sandstone COMMUNION TABLE, the front with a relief of foliage. – Circular stone FONT at the W end. – LIGHT FITTINGS, originally for gas, and a brass SANCTUARY LAMP. – STAINED GLASS. Strongly coloured E window (the Light of the World) of 1897.

STRALOCH

Hamlet set in the hills at the confluence of the Allt Fearnach and Brerachan Waters.

STRALOCH CHURCH. Now a house. Opened as a chapel of ease in 1845. Small rubble-walled Gothic edifice, a gabled bellcote on its W end. In the nave's W gable, a four-light window with loop tracery in the head. Another loop-traceried four-light window in the slightly advanced and gabled transeptal centre of the S aisle.

STRALOCH PRIMARY SCHOOL. Rubble-built and broad-eaved single-storey school and two-storey schoolhouse of 1849.

STRALOCH HOUSE. 1 km. W. Shooting lodge, by *Edwin Lutyens*, 1912. Symmetrical Queen Anne, of two storeys and an attic, with no attempt at Scottishness but confidently at home in its Highland setting. Grey harled walling under a characteristically tall piended and slated roof. S front of seven bays, the centre three slightly recessed and with a pair of small hipped dormers. Large rear wing with slate-hung walls, small-paned mullioned windows and a jerkin-head gable.

STRATHALLAN CASTLE
2.4 km. W of Kinkell

Late Georgian castellated mansion house of the Drummonds of Machany taking its name from the attainted viscountcy of Strathallan which was restored to the family in 1824.

A fortified house or fortalice, then known as Auchtermachany, built *c.* 1600 for the Cunninghams of Glengarnock was acquired in 1615 by James Drummond, first Lord Maderty. By the late C18, if not originally, that house seems to have surrounded a courtyard. About 1800 General Andrew John Drummond (but for the attainder seventh Viscount of Strathallan) completely remodelled the existing building in Adam castle style, perhaps employing *John Paterson* who had produced an unexecuted design for a gamekeeper's house here in the 1790s. Further work, including the addition of a porte cochère, remodelling the W range and fitting out the interior, was carried out for General Drummond's cousin and heir, James Drummond, in 1817–18 by *Robert Smirke*.

To the approach from the NE the house presents two faces. The N range, mostly containing the offices, their utilitarian basement hidden behind a screen wall, is studiedly varied, partly the product of Smirke's alterations. At the W end, a battlemented round tower (*see* description of W range, below) and the S range's broad gable, a round bartizan on the E corner of its stepped parapet; windows of three round-headed lights under rectangular hoodmoulds. Gothic windowed link, its parapet (a replacement of *c.* 1900 for a battlement) carried on moulded corbels, to a boldly projecting square tower. The basement of the tower served as a porch, its exposed sides pierced by large Gothic openings. Above, a double tier of windows, each composed of two round-headed narrow lights, their rectangular hoodmoulds now missing. Then, a battlemented low two-storey and basement bow with, at the upper floors, round-headed windows to the N and Gothic lights to the NE. At the join of the bow to the E (entrance) range's N end, a battlemented tall and slender turret from which extends the wall screening the service court from the drive.

The E range, the house's grand public face, is dominated, not altogether to its advantage, by Smirke's porte cochère, its battlement perched on a string course. Broad Gothic arched openings in the exposed faces and octagonal clasping buttress-turrets at the outer corners. The E front of *c.* 1800 behind, its battlement projected on moulded corbels, is lighter-hearted. Seven bays, the three-bay centrepiece carried up as a three-storey tower; at the outer corners, square clasping buttress-turrets with tall pointed niches whose sill courses are carried across the front. In the two-storey outer bays, round-headed ground-floor windows linked by hoodmoulding. Hood-moulded rectangular first-floor windows. At the slightly advanced centre tower behind the porte cochère, a Gothic entrance, apparently remodelled in 1817–18. Above, at each of the tower's narrow outer bays, a tall and narrow pointed dummy window. The tower's broad centre, slightly further advanced, contains a first-floor window of Palladian form but with all its lights round-headed and another but with pointed lights at the second floor. Blind quatrefoil on the central merlon of the battlement.

This range's gable ends display two variations on a theme. At the N end, a canted bay. In each face, a Gothic two-light ground-floor window (the windows in the splayed sides dummies) with foliaged label stops to its pointed hoodmould. At the upper floor, broad pointed single lights under rectangular hoodmoulds. At the s end of the range, a bow with hood-moulded rectangular windows, those of the ground floor with Gothic woodwork in front of their top panes, an embellishment of 1817–18. On the bow's W side, a buttress-turret balancing that of the house's SE corner.

The S range's elevation between the bowed end of the E range and the end of the W range is of five bays, its battlement above a string course. Buttresses mark off the end bays. At each, an ogee-arched ground-floor window and a fairly small hoodmoulded rectangular window above, but the E bay's windows are of two lights and the W bay's of three; Gothic glazing of 1817–18. At the three centre bays, rectangular windows at both floors, the upper windows quite small, their Gothic glazing also by Smirke. The W part of the S front is provided by the slightly lower S end of the W range which was remodelled by Smirke. This end is of two bays. At the ground floor, a battlemented Gothic porch and a hoodmoulded narrow rectangular window. The first floor originally had a pair of one-light windows but the W of these was enlarged to three lights in the early C20. Boldly projecting three-storey SW circular corner tower, some of its pointed openings dummies, the battlement carried on a cavetto cornice.

The W elevation is all of 1817–18. Five bays between the corner towers, the upper floor marked off by a string course. Hoodmoulded rectangular windows, those of the ground floor alternately of three lights and two narrow lights (one of these windows a door), the upper windows alternating two-light and single openings but the latter of the same width as the two-light openings below. Round NW corner tower projecting less boldly than the SW tower and of only two storeys but with moulded corbels under its battlement; pointed windows again, some dummies.

The principal rooms of the INTERIOR are all of 1817–18. Plain entrance hall with a triple-arched glazed screen at the W, the heads of its Gothic arches filled with heraldic stained glass displaying crests and the achievement of the Drummonds, Viscounts of Strathallan. Ahead, a two-storey square inner hall with a very simple compartmented ceiling. Balcony across its E side; on the W, a window filled with stained glass quarries giving light from what remains of the house's internal courtyard. A short passage leads from the inner hall to the STAIR HALL which fills much of the former courtyard. Flying stair along three sides, a first-floor balcony on the S.

N of the inner hall, the entrance to the DINING ROOM in the house's NE corner, its N side a canted bay. Simple compartmented Jacobean ceiling; black marble chimneypiece. On the S side of the inner hall, the door into the LIBRARY which consists of an ante-room and the library proper to the E, the two spaces divided by a Tudor archway. The ante-room's plaster ceiling has diagonal ribs which meet at a roundel containing a quatrefoil. Gothic chimneypiece of veined grey-green marble. In the library proper, a shallow bow window on the S side. Compartmented ceiling with foliaged bosses at the intersections of its thin ribs. Black marble Gothic chimneypiece on the N side. DRAWING ROOM to the W, its division into two parts, the E of three bays, the W of one, formerly marked by a columned screen (removed in 1938). In both parts, plaster panelled walls, the stiles enriched with foliage, a heavy foliaged cornice and Gothic-panelled doors. At the N side of the E part, a white marble Gothic chimneypiece enriched with some carved foliage. The Corinthian-columned wooden chimneypiece at the end of the W part looks a replacement of *c.* 1900. Rosettes on the ends of its frieze whose principal section is carved with foliaged arabesques and a central panel depicting putti at play.

STABLES courtyard N of the house, probably of the 1790s. Front (E) range with pyramid-roofed end pavilions, their windows in tall segmental-headed overarches. Two-bay single-storey links to the pedimented centrepiece which contains a round-headed pend arch.

On each of the N and S drives, a rubble BRIDGE (the N over the Machany Water, the S now over the weir from the pond below the house) with projecting keystones to its elliptical arch. Each bears the date 1797 in Roman numerals and the inscription PIGNUS AMICIT[I]A[E] ('a pledge of friendship'). – Mid-C19 single-storey ashlar-walled NORTH LODGE, with broad eaves and carved bargeboards. – Rubble-built and picturesque SOUTH LODGE of the earlier C19, also with broad eaves.

STRATHALLAN SCHOOL
0.5 km. E of Forgandenny

0010

Originally Freeland House, built in 1827–32 for the sixth Lord Ruthven of Freeland incorporating a late C18 house. The architect was *William Burn* who executed and adapted a design by *Edward Blore*. It is a large, low-key, almost boring Elizabethan mansion, the architectural impact neither greatly helped nor hindered by additions made for a coal magnate, Collingwood Lindsay Wood, who bought the estate in 1873. More overpowering is the large E extension built *c.* 1925 after the house had become a school. Sizeable but undistinguished institutional buildings of the later C20 crowd round on the N and E.

The early C19 house, built of reddish stugged ashlar, faced S. This front is an asymmetrical two-storey composition. Repetitive Elizabethan detail, the windows mostly of two or three arched lights; rectangular hoodmoulds over the ground-floor openings except at the E bay window whose transomed openings denote the primacy of the first floor. At the E end, a slightly advanced broad gable with a two-storey canted bay window projecting from it. Lower two-bay link to the boldly advanced and higher single bay containing the former entrance, a stone-roofed octagonal turret in the inner angle. Then, a three-bay section of the same height as the entrance bay, its front wall on the line of the E bay window. At the W end, set back to the line of the E link, a further three bays, originally also of two storeys but lower than the rest; a third storey in the same manner was added *c.* 1885. The principal features of the E side, now smothered by the 1920s addition, were a full-height semi-octagonal projection fronted by a veranda and with an octagonal turret (still visible) in the inner angle.

W elevation also asymmetrical but its N part of three storeys and with a three-storey and attic gabled bay, its second floor projected on moulded corbels, at the join with the end of the front block. Detail like that of the front but with hoodmoulds over both the ground- and first-floor windows. Projecting from the N end of this side and overlaying its gable is a two-storey block of the same height, its tall ground floor containing the Great Hall, which was added by *Wardrop & Reid* in 1880, the masonry of a greyer stone than that of the early C19 work. Hoodmoulded Tudor windows at both floors. Slightly later conservatory-porch at the W end.

The higgledy-piggledy N elevation became the entrance front in the 1890s. At its W end, the side of the Great Hall. Projecting from the centre of Burn's house is a plain three-storey block added *c.* 1890 when the entrance was moved to this side, but is now as remodelled and heightened by *Anderson, Simon & Crawford* in 1899. It is fronted by a Tudor porch, with ogee-domed turret-buttresses at the outer corners, which was added to the house's S front *c.* 1885 and moved here *c.* 1890. To the E, a three-storey stretch of the rubble N wall of the late C18 house but with Tudor windows inserted in the early C19. Early C19 office wing at the NE, the windows of its upper floor breaking through the parapet into gablet heads. The wing combines with a contemporary single-storey block to the E to form a small court.

INTERIOR. The early C19 principal rooms are on the first floor, grouped round a central hall. Two approaches to them. One is from the original S entrance to the house. This opened into an entrance hall (now bursar's office) with a compartmented ceiling. Behind, a straight stair, the balustrade and dado of oak, rising under another compartmented ceiling to the central hall. The other approach is from the late C19 N entrance. Entrance hall of *c.* 1890 in rather thinly detailed Jacobean good taste with panelled walls and a compartmented ceiling. Behind, a contemporary stair rises to the W end of the early C19 central hall. This hall itself is double-height and top-lit. Heavy foliaged cornice on which sit rows of angels fronting curved brackets pierced with foliage designs which support the ends of the beams of the compartmented ceiling. At the outer bays, bosses at the beams' intersections. In the centre of the ceiling, a second tier of angels under a square cupola whose sides are pierced by Tudor windows. At the hall's E end, a late C19 Neo-Jacobean oak chimneypiece. Ionic attached columns flanking the fireplace, Corinthian columns at the overmantel which is topped by strapwork between obelisk finials. N of the hall, the dining room, its ceiling coffered. S of the hall, an ante-room and, to its E, the drawing room, again with a Neo-Jacobean ceiling.

The GREAT HALL at the house's NW corner has ashlar-faced walls above an oak dado. Panelled oak ceiling supported by braces pierced by Gothic arcading. Tudor arched doors, their hoodmoulds' label stops carved with foliage.

CHAPEL NW of the house, by *James Gillespie & Scott*, 1962. Cheap-looking traditional, the walls covered with a mixture of stone and drydash.

STABLES–COACHHOUSE COURT (now RILEY HOUSE) to the w. Plain Tudor, by *William Burn*, 1830–2. – To its N, late C19 brick-built OFFICES.

On the w side of the drive, the ivy-covered remains of the front of the demolished LADY WELL. It may be late C17. Elliptically arched narrow entrance set in a Roman Doric pilastered aedicule. – LODGE at the s end of the drive, by *Wardrop & Anderson*, 1891. Picturesque, the gambrel roof covered with red Rosemary tiles.

STRATHTAY

9050

Strung-out village, its villas and cottages mostly of the later C19, many with bracketed eaves and bargeboarded gables. On the N side of the main street, the gatepiers and lodge at the entrance to the drive to Pitcastle (*see* below).

ST ANDREW (Episcopal). Simple Gothic, begun in 1888 when a stone chancel was added to an iron church, the latter replaced by the present nave in 1919. The result is a buttressed rectangle, the nave and chancel, each of two bays, under a continuous roof. Single-light side windows, those of the nave with cusped heads and taller than the chancel's plain lancets. Three-light E window, cusped loop tracery in the head. At the w end, a porch added in 1982, its w wall pierced by a large circular window reused from the church's w gable.

Inside, an open roof over the nave, a panelled wooden tunnel vault over the chancel. – ENCAUSTIC TILES on the floors of the choir and sanctuary. – Simple Late Victorian Gothic pine PEWS. – Early C20 wooden eagle LECTERN. On its elaborate Gothic stem are tabernacled niches containing figures of the Four Evangelists. – Oak PULPIT of 1922 in a Late Gothic manner, with a thistle frieze and a canopied niche containing a figure of the Archangel Gabriel. – STAINED GLASS. Three-light E window (the Nativity, Crucifixion and Last Supper), by *Heaton, Butler & Bayne*, 1898. – In the side walls of the nave, brightly coloured mid-C19 lights (Scenes from the Life of Our Lord), like illustrations from a children's Bible, by *Thomas Willement* and brought here from Folkestone Parish Church. – In the porch's circular w window, the Nativity of Our Lord by *John Hardman & Co.*, 1913, and formerly in St Margaret's (Episcopal) Church at Aberfeldy.

STRATHTAY CHURCH. Built in 1899. Broad-eaved rectangle, the walls harled above a battered base of roughly dressed stonework. Small gableted bellcote at the w end; short low vestry at the E. NW porch, a touch of half-timbering in the gable. Rectangular side windows, each containing three lights with flattened cusped heads. In the w gable, a three-light window, the head of its depressed arch filled with large-scale loop tracery, its bottom with stone panels carved with cusping; small vesica light above.

Inside, pitch-pine PEWS and a heavy PULPIT of 1899. Pride of place is now given to the COMMUNION TABLE and MINISTER'S AND ELDERS' CHAIRS of *c.* 1965. On the walls, late Victorian OIL LAMPS (now electrified) with wrought-iron brackets, brought here from the demolished Grandtully Parish Church.

PITCASTLE, 0.5km. N. High on a hillside above the village, a harled shooting lodge of *c.* 1890. Crowstepped gables and a plain tower with a conical-roofed caphouse on one corner. – At the entrance to the drive, battlemented GATEPIERS of *c.* 1890 and a LODGE built, probably, in the mid C19, with broad eaves and hoodmoulded windows but its S gable given a battlemented bay window *c.* 1890.

CLOCHFOLDICH. *See* p. 271.
DERCULICH. *See* p. 312.
FINDYNATE HOUSE. *See* p. 368.
PITNACREE HOUSE. *See* p. 675.

STRATHTUMMEL

Tiny hamlet overlooking Loch Tummel.

LOCH TUMMEL INN. Picturesque gabled and gableted inn of the earlier C19. Horizontal-paned glazing and a tree-trunk porch. Rather altered coachhouse wing at the E, the carriage doors elliptically arched.

ALLEAN HOUSE, 0.2km. S. Large wacky Baronial villa of 1865, a conical-roofed round tower containing the entrance under a display of heraldry. Also Scots but more sober, the back wing of 1915. On the S front, a conservatory added *c.* 2000 to enjoy the view over the loch.

STRUAN

Dispersed scatter of houses beside the River Garry.

STRUAN CHURCH, Old Struan. Designed and built by *Charles Sim*, 1827–8. Sneck-harled rubble box with pointed windows; two-tier birdcage bellcote on the W gable.

The interior was subdivided in 1938 when a wall was built down the middle, the S (church) half being provided with a chancel. On the chancel's N side, a SYMBOL STONE, probably of the C6 or C7, incised with a 'double-disc-and-Z-rod'; a second symbol to the r. is now indecipherable.

STRUAN FREE CHURCH, Clachan of Struan. Now a house. Dumpy rubble-built oblong of 1878–9, with round-headed door and windows. Gableted bellcote on the S gable.

BRIDGES over the River Garry. The rubble-built single-span ROAD BRIDGE, is of 1862–3 by *Joseph Mitchell*, who also designed the contemporary RAILWAY VIADUCT, that crosses over it. This is of hammer-dressed masonry, in three spans, the elliptical centre arch flanked by round-headed arches; bartizans at the parapet. It was erected for the Inverness & Perth Junction Railway. Immediately to its E is a second RAILWAY VIADUCT of 1899, a steel-truss bridge supported on piers of hammer-dressed masonry.

AUCHLEEKS HOUSE. *See* p. 164.

TAYMOUTH CASTLE
1.4 km. NE of Kenmore

Huge castellated status symbol constructed by the first and second Marquesses of Breadalbane between 1801 and 1842, the exterior stodgy, the interior opulent.

In 1792 John Campbell of Carwhin succeeded a distant cousin as fourth Earl of Breadalbane and the owner of estates in Perthshire and Argyll covering over 167,000 ha. The principal seat which he inherited was Taymouth (formerly Balloch) Castle, a sizeable mid-C16 house which had been remodelled in the early C17 and again by *William Adam* in 1739 when two-storey quadrants and pavilions were added. Seven years after his succession, the fourth Earl commissioned *Robert Mylne* to prepare designs for additions and alterations to the house, and further designs for alterations were made by *John Paterson* in 1798 and *Alexander Trotter* and *James Elliot* in 1800. None of these were carried out. Instead, the Earl decided to rebuild the house 'in the Stile of a Castle' and in 1801 the C16 and C17 main block was demolished and work begun on a three-storey replacement designed by Paterson. Much of the exterior had been completed by December 1804, when Lord Breadalbane ordered a stop to the work, having decided to build the house, to a modified design and with another architect, on a new site further sw. He quickly changed his mind and resumed work on the existing building in February 1805 but now with *James & Archibald Elliot*. They increased the height of the main block from three to four storeys and also designed 'very elegant Wings to it which are to communicate with the main Body of the House by very handsome Cloisters'. These were never built but the main block was sufficiently complete in 1812 for its occupation; minor internal works continued for another two years.

In 1818–22 Breadalbane employed *William Atkinson* as architect for a new East* Wing, a very much larger replacement of Adam's E quadrant and pavilion and including extensive stables and coachhouses. In 1826–8 Atkinson replaced the w quadrant with a new link to the w pavilion which he remodelled in castellated dress and extended N.

---

*Really NE. For convenience I have described the house as if it faced due S. However, in the description of the parkland and its buildings the true compass orientations are given.

John, second Marquess of Breadalbane, succeeded his father (made a marquess at the coronation of William IV) in 1834. Three years later he employed *James Gillespie Graham* to carry out minor internal work and then, in 1838, to prepare designs for a complete remodelling and heightening of the W pavilion (the West Wing) and of Atkinson's link to it. Work on this and redecoration of several of the main block's principal rooms was completed in 1842 when Queen Victoria and the Prince Consort stayed for four days in the 'newly and exquisitely finished' Taymouth Castle.

Only relatively minor alterations have been made to the house since the mid C19. After the death of the eighth Earl of Breadalbane (the marquessate having previously become extinct) in 1923 Taymouth Castle and most of its contents were sold, the house opening as a hotel in 1929, with a golf course laid out on the adjoining parkland. During the Second World War the house was used as a military hospital and subsequently a Civil Defence Technical Training School and, briefly, a small private school. Since the 1970s it has been without either a domestic or institutional function. In 2004 planning permission was granted for the building's conversion to a hotel and leisure centre and for the addition of a large bedroom wing to the N. Work on repairs was begun by *LDN Architects*, 2005.

EXTERIOR

The general conception of the MAIN BLOCK, a battlemented square mass with round towers at the corners and an oblong tower rising from the centre, is Paterson's, presumably derived from Inveraray Castle (Argyll and Bute), but the top storey, the detail of the central tower and the 'cloister' wrapped round the ground floor belong to the Elliots' modification of his design. The walls are faced with broached local ashlar from Bolfracks quarry, its greeny grey colour unappealing although the 'cloister's' stonework has weathered to a more pronounced grey.

Paterson's three-storey design for the battlemented main block was thrifty, the walling rising from a battered ground floor at the S front to the battlement, with only a cavetto string course between the first and second floors for decoration. At the main elevations, rectangular windows, each containing a pair of Gothic lights (the ground floor's mostly now altered) and with hoodmoulds at the upper floors, the first-floor openings tall to denote the *piano nobile*. Narrow pointed lights, also hoodmoulded, at the corner towers. Flanking the entrance in the centre of the S front, a pair of Gothic niches.

The Elliots' remodelling alleviated the starkness with a battlemented Gothic 'cloister' round the ground floor, the regular procession of arched openings broken by turrets decorated with crosslets and 'arrow slits'. Gothic S porch framed by tall buttresses surmounted by concave-sided gablets. Inside the 'cloister', the S range is vaulted, with ribs springing from foliaged capitals. In their alterations the Elliots also inserted a three-light first-floor window in the S bay of the E side and one of five lights at the N end of the W side, both of these Gothic, the E window with uncusped lights and simple tracery, the W's narrower cusped lights surmounted by elaborate tracery and with a wheel of cusped loops in the head. At their third floor they provided hoodmoulded small pointed windows and round dummy windows at the attic storey of the corner towers. The wallheads' battlements projected on moulded corbels are all to Paterson's design and reused by the Elliots when they heightened the building.

The central tower makes an impact only from a distance where its detail, all provided by the Elliots, is hard to see. The corners are clasped by buttresses of two battlemented stages. At their lower stage, pointed slit dummy windows and stepped merlons; at the slenderer upper stage, rectangular slits under pointed ones and straightforward merlons. Each elevation of the tower is divided into two bays by a central buttress. Hoodmoulded tall Gothic windows, each of four lights with a thick central mullion, a diamond-patterned transom and delicate tracery. The crowning battlement has stepped merlons decorated with pointed dummy slits.

Atkinson's EAST WING of 1818–22 is set well back, tenuously attached to the main block's NE corner by an extension of the 'cloister'. Long and low ranges round a courtyard, the S front and E end of stugged ashlar, with polished dressings, the utilitarian courtyard and rear elevations harled. The front of the principal (S) range is divided into two parts. The fourteen-bay W part contained domestic accommodation including a suite of rooms for Lord Glenorchy, the Earl of Breadalbane's eldest son. It is in a Tudor collegiate-Gothic manner, with a sizeable off-centre three-stage tower. The E part, slightly taller but of only one storey, is quasi-ecclesiastical like the W end of a Gothic college chapel with a central gable flanked by two-bay transepts. Battlemented bartizans over the corner buttresses and the apex of the gable. The centre window is flanked by heraldic panels. On the weathered l. panel, the coat of arms of the Earls of Breadalbane, on the r. the arms of Campbell of Glenorchy under the inscription SIR:C.C./1440, the initials those of Sir Colin Campbell of Glenorchy, progenitor of the Breadalbanes. Above the window, a round clock face.

The east wing's E elevation is buttressed, the buttresses flanking its central courtyard entrance topped by bartizans. Two-light mullioned and transomed Gothic windows. Inside the courtyard, harled ranges, rather altered and partly overlaid by late C19 and C20 additions including a Late Victorian tall square chimney finished with a corbelled battlement. At the W end of the N range's outer side, a tower like that of the S range.

The WEST LINK on the site of William Adam's W quadrant between the main block and the West Wing is part of Gillespie Graham's work of 1838–42. Stonework of lightly droved ashlar. The S front is partly cut across by the main block's SW tower but this intrusion disguised by the treatment of the gable which contrives to pretend that the roof ridge (hidden from view) is to the W of its true position. Low ground floor serving as a sturdy base for the huge triangular-headed upper window lighting the Baronial Hall inside. This is of nine cusped-arched main lights under a display of tracery, mostly of English Perp character but including circles filled with spiralling loops to give a Scottish note. Under the transom, eighteen small lights, also with cusped arches. The gable's cavetto cornice is studded with reliefs of winged beasts, foliage and, at the apex, a grotesque head. Above, a double-pitch battlement pierced by cusped Gothic arches both at the merlons and under the crenelles; foliage-capitalled octagonal finial.

At the N corner of the link's battlemented W side a slender octagonal tower, its faces decorated with cusped-arched slit windows in rectangular frames arranged to suggest (falsely) the internal presence of a turnpike stair. Carried round the tower, at the level of the link's main wallhead, a cornice studded with reliefs of grotesque heads. Above this, the open top stage, its sides pierced by Gothic lights, finished with a battlement, the crenelles placed above lozenges, the central N merlon carved with foliage.

At the West Link's N gable, three Gothic first-floor windows, the outer two of three cusped lights (and six below the transom) with vertical mouchettes in their traceried heads and male and female headstops to the hoodmoulds. Tall and slender diagonally set buttresses with crocketed pinnacles divide the outer windows from the centre one. This is of six lights (and twelve under the transom), the tracery in their heads similar to that of the outer windows but with a vertical cusped loop in the middle. The gable's double pitch is finished in similar fashion to that of the S gable, its cornice bearing reliefs of monsters; cusped loops under the merlons of the battlement.

The WEST WING's main (S) part is formed by the W pavilion of 1739 as remodelled and heightened by Gillespie Graham in 1838–42, its appearance wholly Early Victorian. It is of five bays by four, faced, like the west link, with lightly droved ashlar. Three storeys, the ground floor with a bold batter, its shouldered-arched windows recessed in angular Gothic embrasures. Sloped string course under the first floor and a moulded string course under the second, these floors' hoodmoulded windows following the pattern of those of the main block but containing horizontal panes. Boldly modelled arcaded corbelling under the tall battlement whose merlons are alternately stepped and pierced by dummy slits. At the back of this part of the wing, a massive chimneystack rising behind the battlement's centre.

The West Wing's back part is Atkinson's work of 1826–8 and built of rendered brickwork. It is a battlemented and Gothicwindowed two-storey block with a three-storey tower, also battlemented and with Gothic windows, at the NW corner.

Fronting the principal first-floor W window, a cast-iron Gothic stair added by Gillespie Graham in 1840.

INTERIOR

The interior is the product of the house's successive architects, several rooms displaying superimposed layers of work but all combining in celebration of the lineage and wealth of the Breadalbanes.

ENTRANCE HALL* at the centre of the S front, the design by the Elliots, the Perpendicular Gothic plasterwork executed by *Allan Johnstone* in 1808. The room is low and divided into three bays by the bell-capitalled vaulting shafts of the ceiling. At the end bays, delicately detailed niches in the side walls and cusped ogee-arched panels on the ceiling. Over the square centre the ceiling is suggestive of a fan vault. To the W, the BILLIARD ROOM, its ceiling (also of 1808 and by Johnstone) with a large rosetted circle (the heavy foliaged rose at its centre a late C19 embellishment) from which radiate concentric circles of ogee and round-headed arched panels; cusped roundels in the corners. Rather small black marble Gothic chimneypiece.

A Tudor arch from the entrance hall opens into the STAIR HALL. This is entered under the wholly unadorned slab-like soffit of the stair's first-floor landing which precludes a visitor from gaining more than the most limited view of the soaring space until reaching the foot of the imperial stair to the first-floor. The stair's Gothic arcaded brass balustrade was made by *W. H. Abercrombie* in 1811; at the stair foot and on the landing, contemporary lamp standards, also Gothic and with foliaged capitals. Only at the half landing is revealed the full height (over 24 m.) and delicate lavishness of the Perpendicular plasterwork, all executed by *Francis Bernasconi* in 1809–11. From first-floor level the walls are divided by horizontal bands (the first enriched with quatrefoils, the second with rosetted bosses, the third with quatrefoils enclosing shields) into four stages. Each side of the two lower stages is divided vertically by slender foliage-finialled buttresses into three bays. At the first stage foliage-finialled attached shafts carry cusped blind arches, the spandrels filled with shields set among tracery. In the arches of the N side, the two N arches of the E and W and the outer arches of the S side, elaborately tabernacled niches (formerly containing suits of armour). In the other arches, doors onto the first-floor landing, their Gothic panelled woodwork (by Allan Johnstone) set in crocketed finialled ogee-arched surrounds with blind-traceried heads. The stair hall's upper stages are unencumbered by the stair. At the second stage each bay is pierced by a deep arch carried on orders of attached columns and containing a railing like that of the stair

---

* Room names at Taymouth Castle have changed many times. The names used here are those contained in an inventory drawn up in January 1863, immediately after the death of the second Marquess of Breadalbane.

Taymouth Castle. First-floor plan

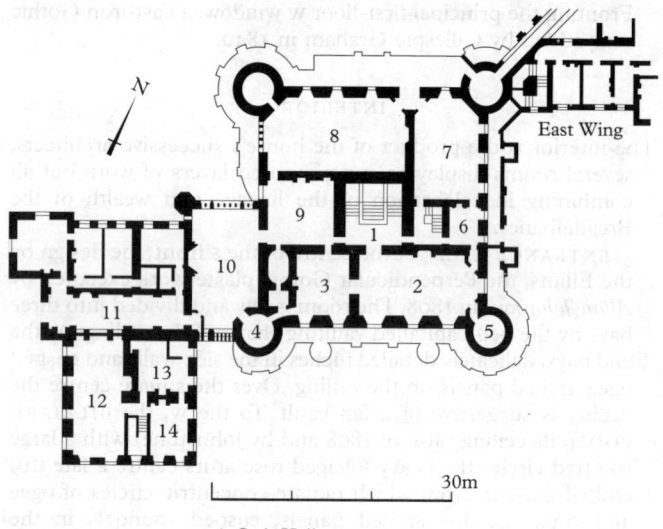

1. Stair Hall
2. Great Drawing Room
3. Small Drawing Room
4. Portrait Tower
5. Stuart Tower
6. Ante-Room
7. Breakfast Room
8. Dining Hall
9. Print Room
10. Baronial Hall
11. Long Gallery
12. Library
13. Tapestry Bedroom
14. Tapestry Dressing Room

balustrade. These arches open onto the second-floor bedroom corridors whose Late Gothic plaster vaulting and battlemented doorcases date from 1810. At the stair hall's third stage, blind arcading; at the fourth, pairs of hoodmoulded four-light windows, their glass originally painted. Rising from foliaged corbels at the corners of the band above the second stage and from plaster angels holding shields at the centre of the band's sides are slender shafts which support the wonderfully elaborate fan-vaulted ceiling, its central pendant surrounded by diagonally set shields and a ring of circles enclosing spiralling loops.

The door on the S side of the stair landing opens into the GREAT DRAWING ROOM, its general form the work of the Elliots in 1809–12, its decoration largely of 1842 by *Frederick Crace & Son* from designs by *Gillespie Graham* assisted by *A.*

W. N. Pugin. The room is of three bays with a lower apse entered through a Tudor arch at the E end and double doors into the Small Drawing Room at the W. Coved ceiling over the main part of the room; fan vaulting over the apse. Above the room's panelled dado, panels intended to be hung with silk, their stiles decorated with crossed ribbons and foliage. Gothic panelled doors and shutters. The doorcases were provided in 1842. At the N wall and in the apse these have flattened ogee arches adorned with crockets and foliaged finials; more carved foliage on their jambs and lintels, the centre of each bearing a coroneted B (for Breadalbane). At the sides of the wider and taller W doorcase slender octagonal piers are surmounted by stags (the Breadalbanes' armorial supporters) holding shields painted with the coats of arms of families related to the Breadalbanes; over the stags are crocketed canopies. Richly carved canopy surmounted by cresting above the W doorcase. At the S windows, gilded and crested pelmets, also of 1842 and richly carved in a Late Gothic manner. From them hang valances of silk brocade with velvet borders and silk tassels, the front of each bearing a coroneted letter B. Above the low and surprisingly plain Gothic white marble chimneypiece, of almost identical design to that in the Small Drawing Room (*see* below) and presumably of *c*. 1875, a huge overmantel mirror of 1842, its carved and gilded frame a replica of the W doorcase.

All this is grand enough but it is the Craces' painted decoration which makes the room sumptuous. In the spandrels of the arch to the apse, quatrefoils contain stencilled foliage and two coats of arms, the l. that of the Breadalbanes. On the panels of the apse's fan vault, stylized foliage. The ceiling of the main part of the room is richly decorated. The main cornice, of three bands, the lowest modelled with vine leaves, the centre with rosettes and the top crested, is of 1809–11 and by Bernasconi. Originally the flat of the ceiling was enriched only with three roses. These were removed in 1842 when the flat was given a border of foliaged rosettes. Inside the border, three lines of pendants with a much larger Tudor Gothic pendant at the centre. Painted decoration on both the coving and the flat. On the coving, above the cornice, two bands of green leaves on a gold ground. Between them, a broad band with a blue ground on which is set naturalistic foliage and face-to-face monsters; interrupting the band are quatrefoils containing half-length human figures. The flat is divided into foliage-bordered panels containing stylized foliage. Set among this, in the bow-ended panels linking the smaller pendants, are coats of arms of families connected to the Breadalbanes. In the panels circling the central pendant are depictions of mounted knights.

In the SMALL DRAWING ROOM to the W, the walls, doors, doorcases, pelmets and valances are treated like those of the Great Drawing Room, the work dating from the same time. Overmantel and chimneypiece of the same design but the chimneypiece bears the coats of arms of Breadalbane and Graham (for Gavin, seventh Earl (later, first Marquess of the second creation) of Breadalbane, and Lady Alma Graham, whom he married in 1872) providing a date for it of *c.* 1875 when *Peddie & Kinnear* carried out some alterations to the house. In the corners of the room, shafts carrying fan vaults. These, together with the ceiling's plasterwork (a foliaged cornice and central oval with rosettted and foliaged borders enclosing a Gothic pendant), are by Bernasconi, 1809–11, but the ceiling's painted decoration is of 1842 by Frederick Crace & Son. Outer border with stylized foliage. In the panels surrounding the pendant, lighter-coloured foliage together with depictions of monsters, the portraits of a man and woman and the coats of arms of Breadalbane and Baillie (for Eliza Baillie, wife of John, second Marquess of Breadalbane).

Off the Small Drawing Room, a circular room (the PORTRAIT TOWER) in the SW tower of the main block, its ceiling a truncated dome. Plasterwork of 1808 by *Allan Johnstone*, the cornice with acanthus-leaf and guilloche ornament, the ribs with guilloche. Small mirrored flat panel at the centre bearing the gilded head of Apollo in a sunburst. The corresponding room (STUART TOWER) in the SE tower off the Great Drawing Room originally had an identical ceiling (the head now missing) but its panels have been painted, probably in 1842 by Crace but perhaps a few years later by *Thomas Bonnar Jun.*, their Rococo decoration incorporating heraldry and coroneted panels bearing the initials of Eliza, [Marchioness of] Breadalbane.

On the E side of the main block, N of the Great Drawing Room, an ANTE-ROOM, its Gothic plaster ceiling with a central pendant provided in 1809–11 by Bernasconi. N of this, the apsidal-ended BREAKFAST ROOM (originally, Dining Room), its minimally arched ceiling enriched with cusped-arched Gothic panels, also of 1809–11 and by Bernasconi. Also Gothic the contemporary black marble chimneypiece but its oak surround and mirrored overmantel, together with the room's dado and sideboard, all date from Peddie & Kinnear's alterations of *c.* 1875. Their work is in a heavy Tudor manner. Dado with linenfold panels. Shields on the lintel of the fireplace surround. The oak sideboard recess takes the form of an altar, its front bearing shields, surmounted by a canopied reredos, its back a large mirror flanked by statues of St Margaret of Scotland and Sir William Wallace. The window shutters have late medieval carved panels, perhaps Flemish, introduced probably *c.* 1875 or perhaps in 1842.

W of the Breakfast Room and occupying the W two-thirds of the house's N side is the DINING HALL (or Baron's Hall), its E end a shallow splay-sided apse, its W end filled with a stained-glass window. The door surrounds, chimneypiece, stained glass and plasterwork are all of 1809–13 and designed by the Elliots, the ceiling's painted decoration and the dado of 1842 to designs by Gillespie Graham and Pugin. Ogee-arched and crocketed door surrounds with richly carved foliage (the doors themselves of the standard Gothic panelled design used elsewhere in the main block's principal rooms). Strawberry Hill Gothick chimneypiece executed by *Coade & Sealy* in 1813, its inspiration taken from medieval funerary monuments. Low fireplace opening flanked by arched niches and surmounted by a triple-arched splay-sided overmantel, all the arches cusped, crocketed and foliage-finialled, the niches flanked by pinnacled buttresses; more pinnacles between the arches of the overmantel which is painted with gold flowers on a blue ground and carved with the coat of arms and boar's-head crest of the Breadalbanes at the centre. The five-light W window's STAINED GLASS (some of the painted work now lost) is by *W. R. Eginton*, 1813. Its centrepiece is the large heraldic achievement of the Earls of Breadalbane. This is surrounded by full-length portraits of the first ten Campbells of Glenorchy, progenitors of the Earls and Marquesses of Breadalbane. Heraldic shields of families connected to the Breadalbanes by marriage in the tracery and the top panels of the outer lights. The ceiling's plasterwork, its elaborate heavily modelled and intricate late Gothic vaulting inspired by St George's Chapel, Windsor, is of 1809–11 and by Bernasconi. From its three foliaged pendants hang Gothic lanterns supplied by *W. R. Naish* in 1824, their glass sides painted with full-length figures. The panels beneath the vaulting ribs are covered with decoration, probably of 1842, with a latticed ground on which are superimposed painted devices of stylized foliage, heraldic shields and carved coronets. Dado of 1837, designed by Gillespie Graham and Pugin and executed by the firm of *The Heirs of William Trotter*, with elaborately carved Gothic panels containing reliefs of birds, animals and heraldic crests.

S of the Dining Hall, the PRINT ROOM (originally, Music Room). Plaster ceiling by Bernasconi, 1809–11. Thrifty vaulting with flattened fans at the corners. Small Gothic chimneypiece of the later C19. This serves as an ante-room to the BARONIAL HALL (known in the C20 as the Banner Hall) which occupies the whole upper floor of the west link of 1838–42. Gillespie Graham had suggested, unsuccessfully, that this be a chapel, and there is something of the ecclesiastical about it especially at the S end where he (again in association with Pugin) provided a 'sanctuary' housing a dais and flanked by richly carved full-height splay-sided screens, the E masking the intrusion of the main block's SW tower into this corner, the W serving as a lobby to the west wing. Covering the room, a richly painted Tudor-arched hammerbeam roof, the vaulting shafts of the coved sides springing from corbels. On these and on the pendants of the hammers are heraldic shields painted, like all the decoration of the room, by Frederick Crace & Son. The ceiling between the beams is compartmented, each panel's rounded corners filled with sprigs of gilded foliage, the centre of each panel painted with stencilled foliage which serves as the background for a shield, the possessor of its coat of arms identified by a scroll, the heraldic ensemble proclaiming 'the Descent of the House of Breadalbane through the Blood Royal of Scotland & England the Lords of the Isles & the Lords of Lorne'. Parquet floor, whose panels display the gyronny heraldic device of the Campbells. Elaborately carved and crested dado of late Gothic character. At the room's W side, a massive stone chimneypiece, its form that of a canopied medieval tomb, the fireplace opening a shouldered arch within a cusped frame flanked by columns, their shafts carved with downward-pointing foliage. Arcaded canopy surmounted by a crested and panelled parapet punctuated by crocketed pinnacled buttresses; tabernacled niches at the centre and splayed ends. In the N and S windows, patterned STAINED GLASS, two of the S window's main lights also filled with fragments of medieval figurative glass supplemented by 1840s glass supplied by *William Cooper*. Puginian Gothic brass lamp standards at the ends of the room.

Entered through the screen at the Baronial Hall's SW corner, a lobby dominated by the life-size figure of a man writhing under a pillar, possibly C16 German work. From this lobby is entered the GALLERY, contained in the 1820s part of the west wing, the entrance flanked by two more writhing figures. The Gallery's simple compartmented Jacobean ceiling is Atkinson's. Probably also of the 1820s are the heavy Jacobean dado, the bookcases and chimneypiece, all elaborately carved and apparently incorporating some genuine C17 work (e.g. the panels carved with cherubs' heads on the fireplace's overmantel). Contrasting with this is the much lighter Gothic screen provided by Gillespie Graham and Pugin in 1842 near the S wall's W end at the entrance to the library. This is tripartite, each compartment formed as a four-centred arch containing a basket-arched door, its lower panels carved with shields set among foliage, the upper panels pierced with rich tracery in which are set small figures of the progenitors of the Breadalbane family; beautifully detailed Gothic hinges by Frederick Crace & Son. Flanking the large central arch, pinnacled buttresses on which stand heraldic supporters holding shields painted with the coat of arms of the Marquesses of Breadalbane.

The LIBRARY was formed by Gillespie Graham and Pugin in 1839–42 from the three C18 first-floor rooms which occupied the W half of William Adam's W pavilion. It is considerably higher than the Gallery, the space above the arches of the N doors filled with blind arcading surrounding the doors' hoodmoulds which are here swept up to form crocketed and foliage-finialled ogee arches containing more foliage, the centre archway also flanked by buttresses surmounted by heraldic supporters holding painted shields. Set into the walls of the room under painted Latin labels denoting different branches of learning are crested Gothic bookcases divided by variously carved columns, each topped by tabernacle work containing a small martial figure. A pair of niches flank the E wall's curvaceously lintelled stone fireplace, its wooden overmantel filled with three traceried Gothic arched panels under a broad cusped arch whose centre is tweaked up to support a finial. At the room's s end, three arches with traceried blind heads. The l. of these contains a bookcase, the r. a deep window embrasure. Within the niche-flanked larger central arch, an inner arch like that of the overmantel contains a pair of doors, their bottom panels carved with linenfold, those above pierced by traceried arcading, the top panels bearing shields which display the initials JC and EB (for John Campbell, second Marquess of Breadalbane, and Eliza Baillie, his wife). Behind these doors, a small room, its N side containing a window whose splayed W ingo is covered with mirrored glass. At the library's W windows, their deep embrasures entered through cusped arches, shutters carved in Jacobean manner with foliage and fruits. Are these of 1842 or reused C17 work?

What both unifies the library and gives it especial richness is the roof, a broad Tudor arch with a pair of longitudinal beams from which hang pendants; joining the pendants both longitudinally and transversely are arched braces, their spandrels pierced by quatrefoils. The ceiling above this framework is divided into small compartments, each containing moulded cusping and painted in blue and gold, the effect a jewel box of encrustation.

A door disguised as a bookcase in the library's E wall opens onto the landing of the west wing's staircase. Off this, to the N, the TAPESTRY BEDROOM fitted up in 1842. Crace & Son provided the compartmented Jacobean plaster ceiling, panels decorated with stencilling and bearing coats of arms, the initials VR, AP and VA and the date 1842 in honour of Queen Victoria's and Prince Albert's visit. The basket-arched chimneypiece of veined white marble survives from Adam's finishing of the room, also as a bedroom, in 1739. In the doors are panels, perhaps reused work of *c.* 1600, carved with reliefs of classical scenes. TAPESTRY DRESSING ROOM to the S, also of 1842 with a Jacobean compartmented ceiling.

LANDSCAPE

The house sits on a flat roughly triangular promontory bounded on two sides by the River Tay. To the NW, across the Tay, rises the forested mass of Drummond Hill, its dense planting in place by the later C18.

SE and SW of the house, undulating PARKLAND studded with trees (now a golf course) rises into the steep and forested Braes of Taymouth. Formal planting of the parkland carried out in the earlier C18 was restricted to clumps of trees SW of the house and avenues along the steep banks of the Tay. Between *c.* 1760 and his death in 1782 the third Earl of Breadalbane constructed a number of buildings in stone or wood to serve as eyecatchers or vantage points from which to enjoy the views over and beyond the parkland, including a tower high up on the Braes of Taymouth and a fort lower down, temples standing on mounds inside the park and, beside the avenue along the W side of the Tay, Maxwell's Building and the Star Seat (or Battery). In the first half of the C19 these were partly replaced by more permanent structures, supplemented by new lodges and gateways. Since the 1920s the park's deer have been replaced by golfers and several of its buildings have been left to decay or been destroyed.

The PARK WALL along the road (A827) bordering the SE side of the landscape, was constructed in 1826–35. Rubble-built, its coping formed of edge-set slabs in rough approximation of a battlement. – NE LODGE AND GATEWAY of 1812, designed by *John, fourth Earl of Breadalbane*, and built of stugged ashlar. The main GATEWAY is a large moulded Gothic arch, its head flanked on the E side by two large panels bearing the heraldic achievement of the Campbells of Glenorchy (later, Earls and Marquesses of Breadalbane) and the impaled arms of Campbell of Glenorchy and Ruthven (for Colin Campbell, sixth of Glenorchy, and his wife, Katherine Ruthven); above the arch a third panel, carved with an angel's head under the date 1570, a possible date for all three. They were presumably taken from the former mansion house of Balloch (or Taymouth) Castle. Probably also of the same provenance are the two panels on the gateway's W side, one late C16 and carved with the achievement of the Campbells of Glenorchy flanked by the initials CC (for Colin Campbell, sixth of Glenorchy), the other with the royal arms of Great Britain and presumably early C17. Flanking the gateway, a pair of towers. The N is circular, and telescope-like, of two stages, both battlemented, and with round-headed dummy slit windows. The S tower is also battlemented, with square bartizans corbelled out at its E and W faces; dummy slit windows but they are rectangular. Extending from these, battlemented screen walls, the N ending at a slender octagonal tower, also battlemented. The S screen wall, pierced by a Gothic pedestrian gate, joins to the LODGE. This is a two-storey octagon, its rectangular windows hood-moulded, its battlement carried on heavily moulded arcaded corbelling. At the lodge's SE corner, a round tower of three stages, with hoodmoulded Gothic windows and a battlement, again on arcaded corbelling. Over the N door, a panel bearing the coat of arms of Campbell of Glenorchy flanked by the initials CC (for Colin Campbell, sixth of Glenorchy) and surmounted by the date 1556. The carving looks early C19, perhaps replicating a stone from Balloch Castle.

At the W entrance to the parkland S of the River Tay, the KENMORE GATE built in 1827, its design probably at least in part by *William Atkinson*. This is a crudely battlemented Gothick fantasy, its rubble construction curiously contributing to its air of impermanence. Tripartite, the gabled centrepiece marked off by octagonal turret-buttresses; rising inside their battlements, spired and cross-finialled pinnacles. Oculus above the hoodmoulded four-centred archway. At the lower outer bays, screen walls pierced by hoodmoulded pedestrian gates join to smallish octagonal towers at the outer corners

Outside the park walls but clearly visible from the mansion house and obviously intended as an eyecatcher from it is THE TOWER built probably c. 1765 by the third Earl of Breadalbane. Three-storey Gothick-windowed and harled round tower, its top slightly jettied. Battlemented lateral screen walls decorated with crosslet 'arrowslits' hide a cottage (rather altered) wrapped round the base of the tower. – N of The Tower, beside the A827, FORT LODGE, a single-storey *cottage orné* of c. 1840 with a steep pitched roof, tree-trunk hoodmoulds over the windows and a tree-trunk porch at the NE side. At the NW front, a tree-trunk veranda with wooden brackets and larch-twig decoration under its curvaceous eaves, the back wall panelled with saplings radiating from crosses. – NW of Fort Lodge and just inside the park wall, THE FORT of 1765 designed as both an eyecatcher (now hidden by trees) and a vantage point overlooking the park and mansion house. Battlemented harled screen wall, tall at the centre where it is pierced by a semicircular doorway under a Gothic window. Lower screens, also battlemented and pierced by round openings, join this to low drum towers, also with pointed windows.

The drive from the Kenmore Gate through the park to the mansion house passes a wooded mound. In the later C18 this was the site of the Temple of Venus which was replaced in 1830–1 by the DAIRY, designed by *William Atkinson*, the E side a prominent feature in the parkland, its visibility enhanced by the sparkle of its white quartz walls, originally with attached tree trunks rising to the eaves. It is composed of a two-storey chimney-topped piend-roofed tower, a bow projecting at the centre of its E front, round which are wrapped single-storey ranges with tree-trunk verandas to the N and S. At the centre of the piend-roofed E range, a broad bow. To its N, on a corniced ashlar pedestal, a Baroque stone URN, perhaps Italian of c. 1700. It is carved with foliage below swagged drapery. The lid's cornice is enriched with egg-and-dart, its finial with fruit and flowers. Spilling out from under this are fruit, flowers and a lion's head. – N of the Dairy a walk beside the River Tay is bounded by an early C19 rubble-built BATTLEMENT which breaks at intervals into tower-like embrasures, the retaining wall below the battlement constructed of rustic boulder masonry.

NW of Taymouth Castle, the CHINESE BRIDGE over the Tay, designed by *William Atkinson* and constructed in 1829–30. Despite the name, a memento of its C18 predecessor, the bridge's arched cast-iron structure (by the *Devon Iron Co.*) supported on a pair of keel-shaped ashlar piers is Tudor Gothic. Cast-iron balustrades, the arches grouped in threes, the spandrels containing arcading. Inside each arch a quatrefoil-finialled upright rises through the mid-rail. Three tall transverse arches across the walkway, the outer two with semi-octagonal heads, the centre round-headed. – N of the bridge, facing down the pathway which leads from it to the road at the foot of Drummond Hill, is the now roofless early C19 ROCK LODGE, its walls built of boulders. Single-storey main block, the wallhead topped by boulders, and a two-storey round tower at the E end, the door and windows all Gothic.

From the Chinese Bridge's N end walks lead SW and NE along the bank of the Tay. Beside the SW walk, 1.1 km. SW of the bridge, stands MAXWELL'S TEMPLE built in 1830 to replace the C18 Maxwell's Building. Working drawings were produced by *William Atkinson* but the decision to build a simplified large version of the late C13 Eleanor Cross at Northampton (illustrated in John Britton's *Architectural Antiquities*) was made by John, fourth Earl (later, first Marquess) of Breadalbane. Standing on a stepped base, a three-tier structure. The lowest stage is a buttressed octagon. The fronts of the buttresses, their pinnacles now mostly broken off, are decorated with cusped arched panels. At each side of the octagon, a crocketed gableted arch containing a two-light Y-traceried panel on which is placed a pair of shields, the SW face's panel a cast-iron door. This stage is finished with a corniced band studded with foliaged bosses, a much simpler version of the richly carved and crested band of the prototype. At the second stage's cardinal points, four thinly buttressed and crocketed gableted canopies projecting from a solid core. Unlike the Eleanor Cross where the canopies contain statues, the Maxwell Temple's canopies shelter nothing except a viewing platform. The set-back third stage is low and square with pinnacled corner buttresses. As at the Eleanor Cross, each gableted face contains a blind-arched four-light Y-traceried panel. The building is finished with a large but plain stone cross. Inside, a stone turnpike stair gives access to the viewing platform. – At the SW end of this walk, immediately N of Kenmore Bridge (*see* Kenmore), a mid-C19 two-storey LODGE (now, THE BEECHES). L-plan, each limb with a splay-sided triple-gabled end; porch in the inner angle.

The walk NE of the Chinese Bridge winds round to the promontory of Inchadney on which, 0.6 km. SE of the bridge, is the STAR BATTERY built in 1829 under *John Murray*'s direction and occupying a vantage point (the view now obscured by trees) looking over to Taymouth Castle and its parkland. It is a mock fortification constructed of stugged ashlar above a rock-faced retaining wall. The centre of the S side projects as a triangular bastion; semicircular tower at the SE corner. – From here the walk continues N to the derelict NEWHALL BRIDGE, by *Andrew Heiton Sen.*, 1838–9. Cast-iron structure with a single segmental arch over the Tay, the spandrels filled with lattice work. More lattice work at the sides of the walkway, the principal uprights rising from curvaceous bottoms. At the ends of the bridge, panelled and ball-finialled piers, probably of the later C19.

Across Newhall Bridge, set back above the E bank of the Tay, is NEWHALL designed by *John Paterson* in 1800 as a courtyard of stables and coachhouses to serve Taymouth Castle. Rubble-built ranges, formerly harled, all now roofless. Single-storey and attic Gothick E show front of eighteen bays, the ends and 'centrepiece' (bays 9-11) slightly advanced. At the s end bay, a round-headed niche. Pointed openings at the seven bays to its r. At the centrepiece, its truncated gable topped by a battlement, a broad segmental-arched pend entrance flanked by niches. At the outer bays of the attic, grotesquely large crosslet 'arrowslits' and, higher up, a central dummy oculus. N of the centrepiece, a quartet of elliptical-arched coachhouse entrances (their heads blind) set between pointed openings; remains of an oculus at the attic. In the N end bay, a tall Gothic door, its head blind. The other ranges are utilitarian. – On the pathway leading s from Newhall towards Taymouth Castle, a small BRIDGE over the Carmilton Burn designed by *John Paterson* in 1798. Single elliptical arch, the exaggeratedly rustic masonry constructed of boulders and with upright boulders forming the parapet. – 1.2 km. SE in woodland bordering the park, a BRIDGE over the Taymouth Burn, probably early C19, a single segmental arch with crenellated parapets. – Also in woodland, 0.2 km. W, the single-storey and attic DAIRY BYRE of 1853-4, with carved bargeboards for decoration.

TENANDRY

Just the church and manse on a wooded steep hillside.

TENANDRY PARISH CHURCH. Built as a chapel of ease in 1835-6, it is a rubble-walled T with a spiky birdcage bellcote on the E jamb. Tudor Gothic openings in the long W side facing the road and, at gallery level, in the N and S gables. The other windows are rectangular.

Inside, galleries at the N and S ends and filling the jamb, all with panelled fronts. PULPIT on the W side, also in a simple Late Georgian manner. PEWS of 1895.

Contemporary MANSE to the w. Quite plain except for bay windows and a late C20 glazed porch.

RAILWAY VIADUCT, Killiecrankie, 1.2 km. NNE. By *Joseph Mitchell*, 1863. Built of hammer-dressed squared rubble, ten segmental-headed 16.5 m.-high arches supporting parapets. At the centre and ends, full-height rounded cutwaters surmounted by battlements. Battlemented turrets along the parapet of the 631 m.-long retaining wall to the S. Battlemented entrances to the tunnel to the N.

HOUSE OF URRARD, 1.9 km. N. Two-storey main block by *William Burn*, 1831. Ashlar front of three bays, the centre advanced under a shaped gable and containing a hoodmoulded Tudor door and a first-floor two-light window. This block was added to an earlier house which was replaced in the 1860s by service quarters, themselves rebuilt in 1963 after a fire.

TIBBERMORE

Hamlet, the Parish Church and former manse by themselves 0.3 km. to the S.

PARISH CHURCH. Disused. T-plan kirk, the product of addition and subtraction. About 1500 George Brown, Bishop of Dunkeld (1484–1514), restored and built ('*restauravit et construxit*') the church here.* Brown's church, consisting of a nave and chancel, was apparently repaired or altered in 1632 (a datestone of that year is now built into the bellcote). In 1789 *Andrew Paterson*, mason, and *James Miller*, wright, removed the chancel and extended the nave to the E by *c.* 3m. A bellcote was added in 1808 and a N 'aisle' to accommodate workers at the Ruthven Printfield at Ruthvenfield in 1808–10.

The harled main block (i.e. the medieval nave as extended and reconstructed in 1789) is a fairly narrow rectangle, the W gable crowstepped, the E with straight skews. On the W gable, the birdcage bellcote added in 1808, with pinnacled corners and a pierced ball-finial on the pyramid roof. Simple rectangular windows, all apparently of 1789. The W porch and session house were added by *William Dawson* in 1814, the store at the E end later in the C19. The rubble-walled N 'aisle' has a forestair against its E side; a late C19 ventilator has been added to the piended roof. In the E inner angle with the main block, a heating chamber by *William McLaren*, 1874.

Inside, galleries at the E and W ends of the main block and in the N 'aisle'. The PEWS are replacements of 1874. – In the two tall S windows flanking the pulpit, STAINED GLASS (the Baptism of Our Lord; St Margaret of Scotland) by *Oscar Paterson*, 1920.

GRAVEYARD. On the W wall of the 'aisle', three MONUMENTS. One, to Major-General John Cunningham †1843, is classical, topped by an urn and ball finials. The second, commemorating James Ritchie, farmer at Cairney, †1840, is signed by *Cochran* of Perth. Flanking the inscription tablet are pedestals whose fronts are carved with dowsed tablets and surmounted by baskets of fruit. Above the inscription, the high-relief portrait of a cow. On top, a sarcophagus, its front decorated with the relief of a wheatsheaf. The third, a large pedimented Neoclassical monument, commemorates George Ritchie †1872. On the panels flanking the inscription, reliefs of dowsed torches. – Propped against the S wall of the church, the HEADSTONE dated 1727, erected by Andrew Guthrie to his son, David, the front carved with the initials AG and IS, a shield, and reliefs of a skull, crossbones and an hourglass. – S of the church, some C18 HEADSTONES. One, dated 1782, was erected by Robert McKillop to his wife, Jennet Douglas. Carved at the top is an angel's head (the soul); below, a shield

---

*According to the early C16 account of Alexander Myln, *Vitae Dunkeldensis Ecclesiæ Episcoporum*, ed. T. Thomson (Bannatyne Club, 1831). The church's bell (now in Perth Museum and Art Gallery) bears Brown's coat of arms.

bearing initials and, at the bottom, reminders of death. – In line with the w gable of the church, the stone to James Sprunt, mason, †1747. On one side, the inscription under an angel's head. On the other, a shield under a mantled helm; emblems of mortality at the bottom.

Former MANSE immediately s of the churchyard. The main block, by *William Stirling I*, 1823–4, is of two storeys and an attic. At its parapeted three-bay front, a corniced doorpiece with panelled pilasters flanked by three-light ground-floor windows. The rear wing was built by *Alexander Strachan* in 1803 as an addition to the previous manse of 1744.

SCHOOL. Broad-eaved and Venetian-windowed school and an adjoining schoolhouse, by *Andrew Heiton Jun.*, 1865, extending and remodelling a building of 1829.

NORTH BLACKRUTHVEN, 1.4km. NE. Piend-roofed laird's house of *c.* 1820. Three-bay s front, the fanlit central door in a Roman Doric columned surround with classical ornaments on its centre and ends. Canted bay windows were added later in the C19, as were rear additions.

TOWER OF LETHENDY
1.1 km. E of Lethendy

Scottish Baronial mansion by *Andrew Heiton Jun.*, 1884, with a laird's house of *c.* 1600 serving as an appendage at the sw, all built of red sandstone.

Heiton's work, designed for Colonel John Gammell, whose great-grandfather had acquired the estate in 1808, is mechanically detailed and of little charm. At the house's SE corner, a massive ashlar-clad four-storey tower, the first floor marked off by a string course, the second floor jettied and with its corners carried on continuous corbelling, the crowstep-gabled top floor set back within a corbelled battlement. At the corners of the battlement, conical-roofed fat round turrets, the NE rising from the second floor. Canted first-floor oriel window on continuous corbelling at the s face. Adjoining this tower, three-storey N and w blocks are tied to it by a continuation of the first-floor string course and second-floor jettying, the latter supported on corbels at the w range. The N range is short, its E front a crowstepped gable abutting a chimney; a corbelled-out and crowstepped gablet on the splayed NE corner. At this block's N end, a large conical-roofed round tower, also of three storeys and with a first-floor string course and jettied second floor. Another tower of the same design at the w end of the s range. This range's second-floor windows rise through the wallhead to ball-finialled segmental dormerheads.

The house built for the Herings of Glasclune *c.* 1600 at the sw is a rubble-walled L of three storeys and an attic but lower than the Victorian mansion. The crowstepped gable of the SE jamb was refaced in 1884 when the Victorian sw range's string

1040

course was continued across it, jumping up over the first-floor window. In this gable, a symmetrical disposition of windows, the first-floor opening centred and the two second-floor windows evenly spaced as are the smaller and closer-set attic windows. At the house's other elevations, the upper windows are placed above each other. The N and S sides of the main block have thick ground-floor walling under sloped offsets. Against the S side have been added a pair of sturdy sloping buttresses, perhaps constructed in the late C17. Unusually, the house's entrance was placed not in the inner angle but at the main block's E gable which now forms an internal wall of the (extended) mansion. The door is round-headed; above, a weathered heraldic panel said to have borne the date 1678, probably that of alterations to the house. There was a wide-mouthed gunloop to the l. of the door.

Inside, above the first flight of the dog-leg stair in the jamb of the house of *c.* 1600, two carved SLABS have been inserted as lintels. One (1.13m. long and 0.36m. wide), its top and sides partly missing, is probably C10 and was originally upright, its unsculptured base intended to be inserted in the ground. At the top, the lower part of an angel, his feet dangling just above the heads of two clerics, their figures portrayed frontally, both also with dangling feet. Below them, a relief of a harpist and piper shown in profile; between them, a dog. Of the other slab, less than half (1.19m. long and 0.25 m. wide) is visible. It is incised with the r. half, up to shoulder height, of the figure of a man dressed in a three-quarter-length gown, close-fitting hose and a broad-toed shoe, the style of dress suggesting a date of *c.* 1515. A small part of a marginal inscription can be seen and bears the letters NBUL, probably for Turnbull. Possibly this was the grave-slab of William Turnbull who was Procurator of the Perth Charterhouse in 1503 and may have been brought here from its chapel which was demolished after the Reformation.

TRINITY GASK

Church and manse in isolation.

PARISH CHURCH. Harled box of *c.* 1770. On the W gable, a plain birdcage bellcote rebuilt by *James Scobie* in 1814, its stone-slabbed roof of ogee profile. Rectangular windows, their lattice glazing an alteration of 1865, the date also of the W porch added by *James Stevenson*. At the E end, a flat-roofed session house of 1962.

The interior, now orientated to the E, was recast by Stevenson in 1865; boxy PEWS of that date. – STAINED GLASS E window (Our Lord and Little Children) by *Norman M. Macdougall*, *c.* 1910.

GRAVEYARD. Immediately outside the entrance to the church, a SLAB, perhaps C17, one end broken off, incised with a splay-ended hammer and a crossed setsquare and adze. Presumably it commemorated a wright. – Just s of the centre of the church, a couple of large HEADSTONES (now painted). One is to Thomas Cant †1826, late farmer in Cow Gask, the front carved with an oval panel bearing the relief of a plough under a hand-held hammer. The other, to Robert Cant †1875, is classical in the 'Greek' Thomson manner. – Further s, some C18 HEADSTONES decorated with reminders of death. Two display also the tools of a wright (setsquare, dividers and axe) and one a plough.

Former MANSE to the N, built in 1779 (the date on the skewputts). Plain rubble front of three bays, the bracketed cornice over the door an embellishment, perhaps of 1819–20 when *William Stirling I* made the house double-pile by the addition of a rear block.

BLAIRDAMS, 2.1 km. NE. Early C19 rubble-built two-storey farmhouse. Four-bay front, with an off-centre Roman Doric columned doorpiece and a gableted window above.

KIRKTON, 0.1 km. NW. Rubble-walled farmhouse, probably of the late C18, with a chimneyed gablet over the centre of the N front. It was extended E and the entrance moved to the S by *William Donaldson*, mason, and *James Miller*, wright, in 1835. Gablets of 1835 over the first-floor windows. Of the same year the small STEADING at the rear; its round brick chimney is late C19.

TULLIBARDINE

Hamlet, the housing mainly C20.

TULLIBARDINE CHURCH. Chantry chapel founded in 1446 by Sir David Murray of Tullibardine. His grandson, William Murray, endowed a further chaplainry in 1455. Work on the building, probably its enlargement from a single cell to a cruciform plan with a W tower, was carried out *c.* 1500, by William's younger son, Sir Andrew Murray.

The chapel is a sturdy crowstep-gabled cross, built of reddish sandstone rubble. The choir is of the 1440s. High up in its E gable, a rectangular window, the surround checked for shutters. In the S wall, a window of two ogee-arched lights (the mullion and heads renewed) and, to its W, a single light, its head a flattened ogee arch. In the N wall of the choir, a single ogee-arched light, its head incised with a fleur-de-lys finialled 'hoodmould'.

The transepts may have been added *c.* 1500. The N transept faces the approach from the site of Tullibardine Castle and its gable is a showpiece. Hoodmoulded window of two pointed lights, uncusped loop tracery in the heads. E of the window, a panel bearing the impaled arms of Murray and Colquhoun (for Sir David Murray and his wife, Margaret Colquhoun), probably re-set here when the transept was built. W of the window, a second panel carved with the Murray coat of arms and, below this panel, a simply moulded rectangular door. The gable's skewputts are each carved with a mullet (the armorial motif of the Murrays).

The S transept has a splay-topped base. In the gable, a hood-moulded window of the same size and shape as that of the N gable but it is of three lights, the tracery again of uncusped loops. Above, a rectangular niche designed for an armorial panel. The gable's W skewputt is carved with the coat of arms of Sir Andrew Murray, the E with those of his wife, Margaret Barclay.

Near the E end of the nave's S side is a round-arched simply moulded window, probably of c. 1500 and perhaps marking the position of the chapel's original W end. At the W end of this wall, a hoodmoulded round-arched door with heavy filleted roll mouldings and simplified imposts.

In the W gable of the nave, each side of the tower and placed just below the skew, is a window whose head follows the sloping line of the roof. The walling of the squat square tower rises unbroken by string courses to a jettied plain parapet. Low down in the tower's W face, a narrow rectangular window. Higher up, a round shot-hole under an economically canopied image niche.

INTERIOR. The open roofs are largely medieval, the rafters joined by two tiers of high-placed collars; at the wallheads, triangles formed by sole-pieces and wall posts. At the W end, a low rectangular door from the nave into the tower. Beside the S door, a mutilated stoup. Aligned with the nave's S window are two steps which, unusually, descend to the E parts of the chapel. Immediately E of this window, a small rectangular aumbry. The transepts are entered through broad segmental-headed arches springing from semi-octagonal responds, their capitals simply moulded. At the W face of the S transept's E respond, an ogee-headed niche, presumably intended for a statue. At the S end of this transept's E wall, a plain rectangular aumbry. Another aumbry in the N transept, placed quite high near the N end of its W wall.

The choir's walls all have intakes above the line of the heads of the side windows. At the E end of the S wall, an ogee-arched aumbry. Just W of the N window, a panel carved with the quartered coat of arms of Stewart of Innermeath and Murray (presumably for the founder's parents, Isobel Stewart and Sir David Murray of Tullibardine).

Stone-slabbed floors throughout. In the S transept, a GRAVE-SLAB, perhaps C17, carved with a skull, crossbones and hourglass.

The chapel sits in a small rubble-walled GRAVEYARD. Immediately S of the S transept, the well-preserved HEAD-STONE of David Malcolm, merchant, †1762, a merchant's mark (like a figure 4) carved above the inscription. On the other face, relief of an angel's head (the soul) above a coat of arms; skull, crossbones and hourglass at the bottom.

STRATHALLAN HALL. Built in 1924. Crowstepped gables and hoodmoulded windows.

TULLIEBOLE CASTLE
1.7 km. E of Crook of Devon

Harled and crowstep-gabled laird's house built in 1608 for John Halyday, an advocate, whose father had bought the estate ten years before. It is a determined assertion of baronial status (not formally achieved until 1615 when James VI created the barony of Tulliebole).

The E two-thirds constitute a T-plan house of three storeys, the W third a four-storey tower. Projecting S from the centre of the E part is the jamb, which rises to a massive chimney, its upper part probably rebuilt, together with the house's other chimneys, c. 1800. At the outer corners of the jamb's gable, ashlar-walled

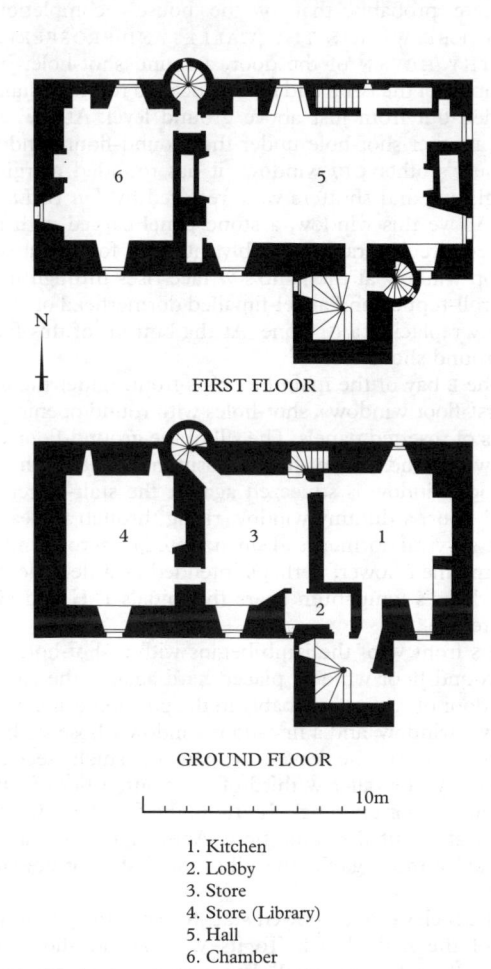

FIRST FLOOR

GROUND FLOOR

10m

1. Kitchen
2. Lobby
3. Store
4. Store (Library)
5. Hall
6. Chamber

Tulliebole Castle.
Plans

and conical-roofed round turrets projected on continuous corbelling. Across the E segment of the E turret, a stone gutter ending in a large spout. This drains a box machicolation supported on heavy moulded corbels at the top of the jamb's E face, the single large crenelle of the battlement now containing a bell. The machicolation defends, at least symbolically, the ground-floor entrance to the house. Roll-and-hollow moulding to the door surround. Above, a large panel, its frame studded with small bosses carved with individual motifs (a cross, a star, etc.). At the centre of the panel, the initials I^{M}H and HO for Mr John Halyday and Helen Oliphant, his wife, and a shield bearing their impaled coats of arms. Flanking the shield are two inscriptions. The l. reads THE.LORD.IS./ONLIE.MY./DEFENCE/ 2.APRIL.1608 (the date probably that of the house's completion), the r.|PEACE.BE./WITHIN.THY./WALLES.AND/PROSPERITIE./WITHIN.THY./HOVS.N of the door, a round shot-hole. In the E inner angle of the jamb and main block is a rounded stair-turret corbelled out from just above ground level. At the jamb's S gable, another shot-hole under the ground-floor window; like the house's other C17 windows it has rounded margins. The fixed glazing and shutters were restored by *Ian G. Lindsay* in 1959. Above this window, a stone panel carved with a rope-moulded circular frame, possibly intended for a coat of arms. The top window at the jamb's W face rises through the eaves to a scroll-topped and angel-finialled dormerhead of 1801, presumably replacing a C17 one. At the bottom of this face, two small round shot-holes.

At the E bay of the main block's S front, under the ground- and first-floor windows, shot-holes with round openings at the centres of rosetted panels. The sill of the ground-floor window was lowered and its shot-hole repositioned *c.* 1800; the narrow first-floor window is squeezed against the stair-turret. At the second floor, a dummy window rising through the eaves to a Gothic survival dormerhead surmounted by scrolls and a finial of a simplified flower, perhaps intended as a fleur-de-lys. The dormerhead's tympanum bears the initials I^{M}H and HO and the date 1608.

The S front W of the jamb begins with a shot-hole under a tiny ground-floor window placed hard against the jamb. W of this, a door of *c.* 1800, probably in the position originally occupied by a window, and a first-floor window whose sill has been lowered. Under the eaves, a pair of small second-floor windows. At the taller W third of the front, a tier of windows, the ground-floor opening of *c.* 1800, the first-floor window sill lowered at about the same time. Another tier of windows in the S half of the W gable, the sill of the first-floor opening also lowered.

At the N elevation, a bowed stair-tower at the join of the two parts of the main block. To its W, a ground-floor window which, although fairly small, has probably been enlarged. Tall first-floor window of *c.* 1800. At the second floor a small window, again probably enlarged and originally of the same size as the tiny garderobe light above. Immediately E of the stair-tower, a quite discreet crowstep-gabled three-storey bathroom addition of 1929. Filling its E inner angle with the main block, a lean-to single-storey kitchen extension by *Ian G. Lindsay*, 1959, its long windows taking advantage of the view to the wooded banks of the burn to the N. Above this extension, a first-floor window with a surround of *c.* 1800 but placed here in the late C19 when an earlier bathroom addition blocked its original position. To its E, a tiny early C17 window and, E of that and placed higher, another tiny window which lit a mezzanine. Two windows under the eaves, the W widened *c.* 1800.

In the E gable, two tall first-floor windows. The S is early C17, its sill perhaps lowered *c.* 1800 when the N was inserted. Above this N window, a blocked C17 mezzanine window. Pair of early C17 windows to the second floor.

INTERIOR. The entrance to the S jamb opens onto the foot of a comfortable turnpike stair which rises to the first floor. On the N side of the STAIR HALL, a pair of doors set awkwardly behind the front face of the main block's S wall, the walling supported on a corbel which projects from the top stone of the doors' shared central jamb. The r. door gives access to the C17 KITCHEN occupying the E third of the main block's ground floor. In its N wall, a slop-sink. In the E side, a large fireplace, the top of its round-headed arch now cut across by the ceiling, so presumably this part of the room was originally higher. The l. door from the stair hall opens into a small tunnel-vaulted lobby contained in the wall thickness. On the lobby's W side, in the wall thickness of the SE corner of the ground floor's central room, an inner lobby-cum-window embrasure, its vault at right angles to the first. The central room may originally have been divided by wooden partitions into stores and passages. At the NE corner, the entrance to a straight service stair contained in the house's N wall; at the NW corner, the entrance to a tight turnpike stair in the N stair tower. Rather broad and low doorway into the W room of the ground floor (now the library). This originally contained storage, its E fireplace (now built up) being an insertion of the C18 or C19, its flue carried up through part of the original opening of the fireplace of the first-floor hall.

The HALL occupies the E two-thirds of the main block. In its W wall, an immensely broad fireplace (later infillings removed in 1959) with a roll-and-hollow-moulded stone surround; salt-box in the S ingo. S of the fireplace, the chamfered N jamb and lintel of a tall opening, now into a wall recess but perhaps originally the doorway into the room to the W. N of the fireplace, a lower door into a lobby from the turnpike stair, this lobby's door into the W room perhaps an insertion. The E end of the hall must originally have been partitioned off. At the E end of the N wall, a door *c.* 2 m. above the floor level of the hall and formerly reached by a continuation of the service stair. At the same level a blocked window (above the Late Georgian inserted window) at the N end of the E wall and, to its r., an offset across the chimney-breast and a fireplace. Clearly there has been a mezzanine floor directly over the higher E end of the kitchen. But the E wall's C17 S window is at the same level as the hall's other windows, so the mezzanine cannot have extended the full width. Perhaps originally there was a screens passage running from the hall's entrance from the principal staircase to the doorway to the service stair and, E of the passage, a SE room at hall level and a larger room on the mezzanine. The house's other rooms, those of the second and third floors reached by a tight turnpike in the stair turret beside the S jamb and by the turnpike in the N stair-tower, are of plain Late Georgian or Victorian character. However, in the N wall of the second-floor W room and of a dressing room off the room above are recesses, each with a small window, and these were probably garderobes, the upper recess provided also with a wall recess in which to place a lamp.

W of the house and screened by planting, a STABLE COURTYARD of c. 1800. Rubble-walled single-storey buildings, the E range with a round-arched coach opening in the S gable and rope-moulded club skewputts, the N (cottage) range with a NE wing of c. 1840. – NE of the house, across the burn, a roofless lectern DOOCOT of 1751, its rubble (formerly harled) walls crossed by a single ratcourse. – E of the house, remains of a mid-C19 WASHHOUSE, a Venetian door in its front wall.

TULLIEMET HOUSE

2.3 km. NE of Ballinluig

Harled laird's house of c. 1800, high above Strath Tummel. Two-storey main block, its piended platform roof studded with round-headed dormer windows added in the late C19 or early C20. S front of three bays, the centre projecting as a rather crudely battlemented bow. Set back at the W end, a flat-roofed single-storey porch fronted by a pedimented Roman Doric portico. Low service wings altered in the mid C19 enclosing a courtyard at the back. – At the W end of the drive, early C19 Tudor Gothic cast-iron GATEPIERS.

TULLYBELTON HOUSE

3.9 km. SW of Bankfoot

Unpretentious rubble-built house of generally Late Georgian character but built in stages. The two-storey main block is probably late C18 in origin. Five-bay E front, the windows' architraves mid-C19 embellishments, the mutuled wallhead cornice and bellcast-eaved piended roof and central porch, with a Roman Doric columned doorpiece, all provided by *A. G. Heiton* in 1911–12 after a fire. Also of this date is the full-height bay window at this block's S end. Slightly recessed two-storey N addition, probably of 1821–2 but its windows dressed up in the mid C19. Projecting from this is the single-storey NE wing, again of 1911–12, with a canted bay window.

STABLES of 1823. Long thirteen-bay range, its outer bays single-storey. Slightly advanced piend-roofed three-bay centrepiece, the outer bays of two storeys, with segmental-arched coachhouse openings at the ground floor and small first-floor windows. The centre bay rises another storey as a low pyramid-roofed tower with bracketed broad eaves. The two lower floors are like those of the adjoining bays. The top stage is a doocot, its flight-holes contained in a lunette.

TUMMEL BRIDGE

Power stations and a handful of C19 and C20 houses at the crossing of the River Tummel.

ERROCHTY POWER STATION, 0.9km. E. Built in 1957. High rubble-walled and flat-roofed box, the corners rounded; tall rectangular windows.

OLD BRIDGE over the River Tummel. Constructed in 1733 as part of *General George Wade*'s military road from Crieff to Dalnacardoch. Rubble-built and hump-backed, with plain parapets. Tall segmental arch over the river and a smaller floodwater arch at the angled N approach.

TUMMEL BRIDGE POWER STATION. Built in 1933. Tall white-painted block of bull-nosed masonry with polished ashlar dressings. Two storeys, the immensely tall lower floor with keystoned segmental-arched windows; rectangular windows at the upper floor. Front of seven bays, the second and sixth recessed. Heavy wallhead cornice.

DALRIACH HOUSE, 2.1km. W. Sizeable black-and-white harled and half-timbered villa of *c.* 1900.

WEEM

Two churches, a farm, a hotel and a handful of late C19 and C20 houses.

DULL AND WEEM PARISH CHURCH. Built as St David's (Episcopal) Church in 1878. Spikily buttressed lancet-windowed cross. Gabled bellcote on the W end; SW porch. At the E end, a semi-octagonal apse, its windows gableted.

INTERIOR largely of the 1870s. Collar-braced kingpost truss roof, the timbers intersecting over the crossing. Steps up to the choir and again to the sanctuary, the floors of both laid with encaustic tiles, that of the choir with a centrepiece of Our Lord and men with snakes. – FURNISHINGS of pine except for the stone FONT at the W end. – ORGAN by *J. W. Walker & Sons*, 1875. – STAINED GLASS. The three windows of the apse (the Annunciation, Ascension, and Empty Tomb) were erected in 1908.

WAR MEMORIAL in the churchyard, by *Gibb Bros.*, *c.* 1920. A Celtic cross, the front carved with the relief of a sheathed sword.

Former WEEM PARISH CHURCH (MENZIES MAUSOLEUM). Rubble-walled T-plan kirk apparently built or reconstructed in 1609–14 and altered in 1753 when the side walls were heightened by *c.* 0.6 m. (2 ft). The building was re-roofed in 1936. On the W gable, a flat-roofed birdcage bellcote, probably early C17, topped by a weathercock. Pointed W window with a roll-and-hollow-moulded surround. The W gable's S skewputt is carved with a blank shield flanked by the initials AM (for Alexander Menzies of that Ilk) and the date 1614. Above the rectangular door at the W end of the S side, a heraldic achievement, again flanked by the initials of Alexander Menzies together with those of his third wife, Marjorie Campbell. A second door is placed a little to the E of the centre of this side. Above it, a concrete replica of a stone bearing the same initials and flanking a coat of arms (those of Menzies impaling Campbell), a weathered date said* to have read 1609, and the inscription VIL GOD. ISAL|CONTENDITE.INTRARE.PER.AVGUSTAM PORTAM SANCTIS MORS IANVA VITÆ.EST.MEMENTO MORI ('Strive to enter through the strait gate. To the saints death is the door of life. Remember you must die'). Between these doors, large windows. Like the doors the windows are rectangular and have roll-and-hollow mouldings but documentary evidence suggests they are insertions of 1753, perhaps reusing or replicating earlier work. At the S wall's E end another window, also rectangular and with a roll-and-hollow moulding but much smaller. In the E gable, a pointed window like that of the W gable.

In the E side of the N jamb a (now blocked) door inserted in 1753. In the jamb's W side, another rectangular window with a roll-and-hollow moulding, probably of the early C17. Attached to the jamb is a catslide-roofed NW outshot. In its W gable a small rectangular opening whose glazing grooves suggest a C17 date. Plain door in the N side of the outshot.

The INTERIOR has been stripped of plaster. The N jamb formerly contained a gallery whose end fireplace survives. In the church's S wall, beside the W door, an aumbry whose lintel bears the initials DM, presumably for Duncan Menzies of that Ilk (1600–56). Beside this wall's E door another and rougher aumbry, its lintel inscribed with the initials IMP. Two aumbries in the E gable, the N shelved.

On the N wall of the choir, a large and very ambitious full-height MONUMENT of 1616, its Latin main inscription explaining that it was erected by (Sir) Alexander Menzies of Weem or that Ilk, descendant in the maternal line of the families of Stewart of Atholl, Campbell of Lawers, Gordon of Huntly and Lindsay of Edzell, to commemorate himself and his (third) wife, Marjorie Campbell. It is an unabashed celebration of

---

*By *The Statistical Account of Scotland*, xii (1794), 810.

illustrious lineage, although not oblivious of human mortality and the Christian promise of redemption.

The general form of the monument, a sarcophagus contained in a segmental-arched recess, is Late medieval but the detail and outer frame are classical of Artisan Mannerist type, the inspiration probably culled from the frontispieces of books. The sarcophagus' front is divided into three compartments by foliage-capitalled pilasters, their tapering shafts also foliaged. In the compartments are weathered inscription panels, their borders strapworked but with human heads at the top of the l. border; more heads at the sides of the r. border and angels at its top. On the back of the recess a large strapwork-bordered panel containing the main inscription; its position makes it clear that no effigy was intended to lie on the sarcophagus. The inscription panel is flanked by small coats of arms – on the l., those of Christina Gordon and Margaret Lindsay (the great-grandmother and great-great-grandmother of Sir Alexander Menzies of that Ilk) and, on the r., those of Barbara Stewart and Christina Campbell (his mother and grandmother). Above the inscription panel, a roundel carved in fairly high relief with emblems of death, a skull at the centre. The roundel is flanked by the coats of arms of Sir Alexander Menzies's first two wives, Margaret Campbell †1598 and Elizabeth Forrester †1603. The moulded arch of the recess springs from attached columns, their capitals carved with thistles. Suspended from the top of the arch is a carved angel holding a panel which bears an elaborate monogram. Lower down the arch, two crested and mantled shields displaying the coats of arms of Menzies and Campbell.

The sarcophagus' recess is set in a rectangular frame. At the bottom of each end, a pedestal, its front and outer side decorated with round-headed panels whose arches spring from baluster-pilasters and which contain reliefs of flowers. Standing on the pedestals are full-size figures of Faith and Charity surmounted by tabernacle canopies under cubical blocks, the l. carved with the date 1616, the r. with Jan. 24, which support the ends of the cornice over the framework. Inside the framework the spandrels over the sarcophagus recess contain bay-leaf-bordered roundels bearing inscriptions (GLORIA. DEO.PAX.HOMINIBVS ('Glory to God, peace to men') on the l., TRIVNI.DEO.GLORIA ('Glory to the triune God') on the r.), each roundel accompanied by the relief of an angel. On top of the ends of the framework's cornice are figures, the l. a man, the r. a woman, kneeling at prayer-desks, the front of the l. carved with a trophy, that of the r. with an angel's head above a lozenge which contains the sacred IHS inscription. On the centre of the cornice, a broken pediment, trumpeting angels of the Resurrection perched precariously on its steeply sloped sides, the tympanum carved with a heraldic achievement (the impaled arms of Menzies and Campbell). Above the pediment, a round-headed panel bearing a relief of God the Father.

Immediately W of this C17 monument, an aedicular recess containing the white marble SCULPTURE of the half-length effigy of a woman; it looks to be of the mid or later C19. – In the N jamb and body of the church are two roughly hewn stone CROSSES, perhaps of the C8, one without its head, the other with narrow arms. They were brought here in the early C19 from Dull Parish Churchyard and may originally have marked the sanctuary boundary of the Celtic monastery of Dull. – Lying on the floor at the E end of the church is a GRAVE-SLAB, probably of the C16, the badly worn marginal inscription apparently commemorating one of the Campbells of Murthly. The face is compartmented. In the two tall panels at the top, half-length reliefs of a knight and a woman. Below, a horizontal panel containing smaller half-lengths of five men, one holding a sword. Under this, a second horizontal panel carved with the half-lengths of three men, and a tree. In the bottom panel a prone skeleton, an hourglass at his head. – Propped against the W end of the church's N wall is a worn GRAVE-SLAB, again probably C16. In its large vertically proportioned top panel, the relief of a half-length figure of a man flanked by the initials IB. Below, two horizontal panels, one bearing two coats of arms, the other two skulls and two bones. – On the walls, heavily restored HATCHMENTS of the C19 and early C20 displaying the heraldic achievement of the Menzies of that Ilk.

On the outside of the W gable, a MONUMENT to Captain James Carmichael †1750, with the inscription:

> Where now O Son of Mars is Honours aim.
> What once thou wast or wish'd no more's thy claim.
> Thy Tomb Carmichael tells thy Honours Rot
> And Man is born as thee to be forgot.
> But Virtue lives to Glaze thy Honours o'er
> And Heaven will Smile when brittle Stone's no more.

WEEM FARM. Late C19. Jerkin-head gables at the U-plan steading.

WEEM HOTEL. Harled main block of *c.* 1800. Three storeys and an attic, front of five bays. The two-storey E wing of two broad bays may be early C18. At both the main block and the wing are dormer windows of later C19 character.

CLUNY HOUSE, 3.5km. E. Villa of *c.* 1820 in a luxuriantly wooded garden above Strath Tay. Piend-roofed main block of two storeys. The centre of its three-bay front is carried up as a pyramid-roofed tower, the lowest stage containing the house's pointed entrance, the top a hoodmoulded window of four small Gothic lights. Gothic lights also in the minimally projecting rectangular bay window to the N. The full-height canted bay S of the tower is probably of 1880, as is the two-storey S wing. Single-storey piend-roofed N wing of *c.* 1820.

THE HOUSE OF MENZIES, 1.2 km. W. White-harled two-storey early C19 farmhouse, with single-storey piend-roofed wings. – STEADING (converted to a gallery by *Michael Gray Architects*, 1999) of the later C19, with a pyramid-roofed two-storey tower, its front openings Gothic, the side windows Romanesque; flight-holes for a doocot under the eaves.

KILLIECHASSIE, 2 km. E. Multi-gabled two-storey *cottage orné*, by *Brown & Wardrop*, 1864–5, with carved bargeboards at the main block. – STABLES to the N, also of the 1860s. – N of the stables, a Gothic DOOCOT, contemporary with the house. It is composed of a small single-storey block and, at its centre, a tower containing the flight-holes, its tall pyramidal roof with bellcast eaves and a weathercock.

CASTLE MENZIES. *See* p. 262.

WHITEFIELD CASTLE
1.8 km. NE of Kirkmichael

0060

Ruined late C16 laird's house standing on a hill high above Strath Ardle and commanding extensive views over the surrounding country.

Built of silvery grey rubble, the house has been of three storeys, perhaps with an attic, but the walls now stand only to the first floor. L-plan, the jamb projecting both N and W of the main block's NW corner. In the S inner angle of the main block and jamb, at the E end of the jamb's S face, the rectangular entrance with a roll-and-hollow-moulded margin, the lintel's carved date of 1577 very plausibly that of the house's construction.* Above the door and slightly W of its centre, a round-headed roll-and-hollow-moulded niche with a floriated finial; presumably it was intended to house a heraldic panel. Oval gunloops at the ground floor of every face of the main block and jamb. In the jamb's W front there is also a round shot-hole at the level of the half landing of the stair to the first floor. In the W side of the main block, two ground-floor windows. One, near the N end, is a chamfered-margined slit; the other, towards the S end, is larger and of horizontal proportions but robbed of dressings. At the W end of the main block's N gable, above the gunloop, a slit window, its margin rounded. At the first floor of the main block, a pair of decent-sized W windows, their margins plain, the S missing its top part. Two more windows but narrower and with chamfered margins in the S gable. The first-floor walling of the main block's E and N faces has been demolished. In the N and W faces of the jamb, windows at the half landing of the stair, the N a slit with a chamfered margin, the W robbed of dressings. Above and S of this W window, a first-floor opening which has been much altered and in which have been inserted fragments of moulded jambs, perhaps rescued from demolished stonework. Just above this, two large weathered corbels, perhaps for a bartizan entered from the second floor. In the N inner angle of the main block and jamb, continuous corbelling

---

*But it was described by David MacGibbon and Thomas Ross, *The Castellated and Domestic Architecture of Scotland*, v (1892), 226, as 'almost effaced' so perhaps it has been re-cut.

for a round turret which has contained the stair from the first floor to the floor or floors above.

What remains of the INTERIOR suggests the house was comfortable. The entrance opens onto a stone-vaulted stair hall in the jamb. On its S side, beside the door, a hole in the wall to allow the insertion of a wedge to hold the door's bar in place. Dog-leg stone stair to the first floor. The space under its upper flight serves as a guardroom with gunloops in the S, E and N sides, the lower part of the S side's walling recessed under a broad elliptical arch. Remains of a stone parapet at the stair's first-floor landing.

Along the W side of the ground floor of the main block a tunnel-vaulted passage lit by gunloops and a slit window. Off this, a cellar at the block's N end, its only lighting obtained from gunloops. Contained in the thickness of its N wall, a straight stair to the first floor. At the passage's S end and filling the full width of the block is the kitchen, also tunnel-vaulted and lit from gunloops and one window. Large S fireplace. To its E, an aumbry-like recess with a gunloop in its back. At the S end of the W wall, a stone basin with a drain to the outside. The first floor seems to have been occupied by the hall.

WOLFHILL

Village with some C19 cottages but most of the housing is late C20.

CARGILL FREE CHURCH, Old Church Road. Roofless but conserved as a garden feature, the church was built in 1843–4. Nave and aisles, the walls of sneck-harled rubble. Rectangular side windows. Tudor-arched window in the W gable which is crowned with a pinnacled bellcote. – Two-storey MANSE of 1852 (now WOLFHILL HOUSE) to the S.

DUNSINNAN HOUSE. *See* p. 355.

WOODEND

1 km. W of Madderty

Long and skinny harled laird's house of two storeys and an attic. Perhaps C17 in origin, it was rebuilt or remodelled in the mid C18 to produce a S front of seven bays with a central entrance. In the mid C19 it was extended W, the entrance was given a gabled doorpiece and a dormer window was added at the E end. Further W addition of 1928. Inside, mid-C18 work, the staircase with turned balusters. On the first floor, a panelled drawing room with a pedimented overmantel.

WOODSIDE *see* BURRELTON AND WOODSIDE

GLOSSARY

Numbers and letters refer to the illustrations (by John Sambrook) on pp. 758-65

ABACUS: flat slab forming the top of a capital (3a).
ACANTHUS: classical formalized leaf ornament (3b).
ACCUMULATOR TOWER: see Hydraulic power.
ACHIEVEMENT: a complete display of armorial bearings (i.e. coat of arms, crest, supporters and motto).
ACROTERION: plinth for a statue or ornament on the apex or ends of a pediment; more usually, both the plinth and what stands on it (4a).
ADDORSED: descriptive of two figures placed back to back.
AEDICULE (*lit.* little building): architectural surround, consisting usually of two columns or pilasters supporting a pediment.
AFFRONTED: descriptive of two figures placed face to face.
AGGREGATE: see Concrete, Harling.
AISLE: subsidiary space alongside the body of a building, separated from it by columns, piers or posts. Also (Scots) projecting wing of a church, often for special use, e.g. by a guild or by a landed family whose burial place it may contain.
AMBULATORY (*lit.* walkway): aisle around the sanctuary (q.v.).
ANGLE ROLL: roll moulding in the angle between two planes (1a).
ANSE DE PANIER: see Arch.
ANTAE: simplified pilasters (4a), usually applied to the ends of the enclosing walls of a portico (q.v.) *in antis*.
ANTEFIXAE: ornaments projecting at regular intervals above a Greek cornice, originally to conceal the ends of roof tiles (4a).
ANTHEMION: classical ornament like a honeysuckle flower (4b).
APRON: panel below a window or wall monument or tablet.
APSE: semicircular or polygonal end of an apartment, especially of a chancel or chapel. In classical architecture sometimes called an *exedra*.
ARABESQUE: non-figurative surface decoration consisting of flowing lines, foliage scrolls etc., based on geometrical patterns. Cf. Grotesque.
ARCADE: series of arches supported by piers or columns. *Blind arcade* or *arcading*: the same applied to the wall surface. *Wall arcade*: in medieval churches, a blind arcade forming a dado below windows. Also a covered shopping street.
ARCH: Shapes see 5c. *Basket arch* or *anse de panier* (basket handle): three-centred and depressed, or with a flat centre. *Nodding*: ogee arch curving forward from the wall face. *Parabolic*: shaped like a chain suspended from two level points, but inverted.
Special purposes. *Chancel*: dividing chancel from nave or crossing. *Crossing*: spanning piers at a crossing (q.v.). *Relieving* or *discharging*: incorporated in a wall to relieve superimposed weight (5c). *Skew*: spanning responds not diametrically opposed. *Strainer*: inserted in an opening to resist inward pressure. *Transverse*: spanning a main axis (e.g. of a vaulted space). See also Jack arch, Overarch, Triumphal arch.
ARCHITRAVE: formalized lintel, the lowest member of the classical entablature (3a). Also the moulded frame of a door or window (often borrowing the profile of a classical architrave). For *lugged* and *shouldered* architraves see 4b.
ARCUATED: dependent structurally on the arch principle. Cf. Trabeated.

GLOSSARY

ARK: chest or cupboard housing the tables of Jewish law in a synagogue.

ARRIS: sharp edge where two surfaces meet at an angle (3a).

ASHLAR: masonry of large blocks wrought to even faces and square edges (6d). *Broached ashlar* (Scots): scored with parallel lines made by a narrow-pointed chisel (broach). *Droved ashlar*: similar but with lines made by a broad chisel.

ASTRAGAL: classical moulding of semicircular section (3f). Also (Scots) glazing-bar between window panes.

ASTYLAR: with no columns or similar vertical features.

ATLANTES: see Caryatids.

ATRIUM (plural: atria): inner court of a Roman or C20 house; in a multi-storey building, a toplit covered court rising through all storeys. Also an open court in front of a church.

ATTACHED COLUMN: see Engaged column.

ATTIC: small top storey within a roof. Also the storey above the main entablature of a classical façade.

AUMBRY: recess or cupboard, especially one in a church, to hold sacred vessels used for the Mass.

BAILEY: see Motte-and-bailey.

BALANCE BEAM: see Canals.

BALDACCHINO: freestanding canopy, originally fabric, over an altar. Cf. Ciborium.

BALLFLOWER: globular flower of three petals enclosing a ball (1a). Typical of the Decorated style.

BALUSTER: pillar or pedestal of bellied form. *Balusters*: vertical supports of this or any other form, for a handrail or coping, the whole being called a *balustrade* (6c). *Blind balustrade*: the same applied to the wall surface.

BARBICAN: outwork defending the entrance to a castle.

BARGEBOARDS (corruption of 'vergeboards'): boards, often carved or fretted, fixed beneath the eaves of a gable to cover and protect the rafters.

BARMKIN (Scots): wall enclosing courtyard attached to a tower house.

BARONY: see Burgh.

BAROQUE: style originating in Rome c.1600 and current in England c.1680–1720, characterized by dramatic massing and silhouette and the use of the giant order.

BARROW: burial mound.

BARTIZAN: corbelled turret, square or round, frequently at an angle (8a).

BASCULE: hinged part of a lifting (or bascule) bridge.

BASE: moulded foot of a column or pilaster. For *Attic* base see 3b. For *Elided* base see Elided.

BASEMENT: lowest, subordinate storey; hence the lowest part of a classical elevation, below the piano nobile (q.v.).

BASILICA: a Roman public hall; hence an aisled building with a clerestory.

BASTION: one of a series of defensive semicircular or polygonal projections from the main wall of a fortress or city.

BATTER: intentional inward inclination of a wall face.

BATTLEMENT: defensive parapet, composed of *merlons* (solid) and *crenelles* (embrasures) through which archers could shoot (8a); sometimes called *crenellation*. Also used decoratively.

BAY: division of an elevation or interior space as defined by regular vertical features such as arches, columns, windows etc.

BAY LEAF: classical ornament of overlapping bay leaves (3f).

BAY WINDOW: window of one or more storeys projecting from the face of a building. *Canted*: with a straight front and angled sides. *Bow window*: curved. *Oriel*: rests on corbels or brackets and starts above ground level; also the bay window at the dais end of a medieval great hall.

BEAD-AND-REEL: see Enrichments.

BEAKHEAD: Norman ornament with a row of beaked bird or beast heads usually biting into a roll moulding (1a).

BEE-BOLL: wall recess to contain a beehive.

BELFRY: chamber or stage in a tower where bells are hung. Also belltower in a general sense.

BELL CAPITAL: see 1b.

BELLCAST: see Roof.

BELLCOTE: bell-turret set on a roof or gable. *Birdcage bellcote*: framed structure, usually of stone.

GLOSSARY

BERM: level area separating a ditch from a bank on a hillfort or barrow.

BILLET: Norman ornament of small half-cylindrical or rectangular blocks (1a).

BIVALLATE: of a hillfort: defended by two concentric banks and ditches.

BLIND: see Arcade, Baluster, Portico.

BLOCK CAPITAL: see 1a.

BLOCKED: columns etc. interrupted by regular projecting blocks (*blocking*), as on a Gibbs surround (4b).

BLOCKING COURSE: course of stones, or equivalent, on top of a cornice and crowning the wall.

BÖD: see Bü.

BOLECTION MOULDING: covering the joint between two different planes (6b).

BOND: the pattern of long sides (*stretchers*) and short ends (*headers*) produced on the face of a wall by laying bricks in a particular way (6e).

BOSS: knob or projection, e.g. at the intersection of ribs in a vault (2c).

BOW WINDOW: see Bay window.

BOX FRAME: timber-framed construction in which vertical and horizontal wall members support the roof. Also concrete construction where the loads are taken on cross walls; also called *cross-wall construction*.

BRACE: subsidiary member of a structural frame, curved or straight. *Bracing* is often arranged decoratively, e.g. quatrefoil, herringbone. See also Roofs.

BRATTISHING: ornamental crest, usually formed of leaves, Tudor flowers or miniature battlements.

BRESSUMER (*lit.* breast-beam): big horizontal beam supporting the wall above, especially in a jettied building.

BRETASCHE (*lit.* battlement): defensive wooden gallery on a wall.

BRICK: see Bond, Cogging, Engineering, Gauged, Tumbling.

BRIDGE: *Bowstring*: with arches rising above the roadway which is suspended from them. *Clapper*: one long stone forms the roadway. *Roving*: see Canal. *Suspension*: roadway suspended from cables or chains slung between towers or pylons. *Stay-suspension* or *stay-cantilever*: supported by diagonal stays from towers or pylons. See also Bascule.

BRISES-SOLEIL: projecting fins or canopies which deflect direct sunlight from windows.

BROACH: see Spire and 1c.

BROCH (Scots): circular tower-like structure, open in the middle, the double wall of dry-stone masonry linked by slabs forming internal galleries at varying levels; found in W and N Scotland and mostly dating from between 100 B.C. and A.D. 100.

BÜ or BÖD (Scots, esp. Shetland; *lit.* booth): combined house and store.

BUCRANIUM: ox skull used decoratively in classical friezes.

BULLSEYE WINDOW: small oval window, set horizontally (cf. Oculus). Also called *oeil de boeuf*.

BURGH: formally constituted town with trading privileges. *Royal Burghs*: monopolized foreign trade till the C17 and paid duty to the Crown. *Burghs of Barony*: founded by secular or ecclesiastical barons to whom they paid duty on their local trade. *Police Burghs*: instituted after 1850 for the administration of new centres of population and abolished in 1975. They controlled planning, building etc.

BUT-AND-BEN (Scots, *lit.* outer and inner rooms): two-room cottage.

BUTTRESS: vertical member projecting from a wall to stabilize it or to resist the lateral thrust of an arch, roof or vault (1c, 2c). A *flying buttress* transmits the thrust by means of an arch or half-arch (1c).

CABLE or ROPE MOULDING: originally Norman, like twisted strands of a rope.

CAMES: see Quarries.

CAMPANILE: freestanding bell-tower.

CANALS: *Flash lock*: removable weir or similar device through which boats pass on a flush of water. Predecessor of the *pound lock*: chamber with gates at each end allowing boats to float from one level to another. *Tidal gates*: single pair of lock gates allowing vessels to pass when the tide makes a level. *Balance beam*: beam projecting horizontally for opening

GLOSSARY

and closing lock gates. *Roving bridge*: carrying a towing path from one bank to the other.

CANDLE-SNUFFER ROOF: conical roof of a turret (8a).

CANNON SPOUT: see 8a.

CANTILEVER: horizontal projection (e.g. step, canopy) supported by a downward force behind the fulcrum.

CAPHOUSE (Scots): small chamber at the head of a turnpike stair, opening onto the parapet walk (8a). Also a chamber rising from within the parapet walk.

CAPITAL: head or crowning feature of a column or pilaster; for classical types see 3a; for medieval types see 1b.

CARREL: compartment designed for individual work or study, e.g. in a library.

CARTOUCHE: classical tablet with ornate frame (4b).

CARYATIDS: female figures supporting an entablature; their male counterparts are *Atlantes* (*lit.* Atlas figures).

CASEMATE: vaulted chamber, with embrasures for defence, within a castle wall or projecting from it.

CASEMENT: side-hinged window. Also a concave Gothic moulding framing a window.

CASTELLATED: with battlements (q.v.).

CAST IRON: iron containing at least 2.2 per cent of carbon, strong in compression but brittle in tension; cast in a mould to required shape, e.g. for columns or repetitive ornaments. *Wrought iron* is a purer form of iron, with no more than 0.3 per cent of carbon, ductile and strong in tension, forged and rolled into e.g. bars, joists, boiler plates; *mild steel* is its modern equivalent, similar but stronger.

CATSLIDE: see 7.

CAVETTO: concave classical moulding of quarter-round section (3f).

CELURE or CEILURE: enriched area of roof above rood or altar.

CEMENT: see Concrete.

CENOTAPH (*lit.* empty tomb): funerary monument which is not a burying place.

CENTRING: wooden support for the building of an arch or vault, removed after completion.

CHAMBERED TOMB: Neolithic burial mound with a stone-built chamber and entrance passage covered by an earthen barrow or stone cairn.

CHAMFER (*lit.* corner-break): surface formed by cutting off a square edge or corner. For types of chamfers and *chamfer stops* see 6a. See also Double chamfer.

CHANCEL: E end of the church containing the sanctuary; often used to include the choir.

CHANTRY CHAPEL: often attached to or within a church, endowed for the celebration of Masses principally for the soul of the founder.

CHECK (Scots): rebate.

CHERRY-CAULKING or CHERRY-COCKING (Scots): decorative masonry technique using lines of tiny stones (*pins* or *pinning*) in the mortar joints.

CHEVET (*lit.* head): French term for chancel with ambulatory and radiating chapels.

CHEVRON: V-shape used in series or double series (later) on a Norman moulding (1a). Also (especially when on a single plane) called *zigzag*.

CHOIR: the part of a church E of the nave, intended for the stalls of choir monks, choristers and clergy.

CIBORIUM: a fixed canopy over an altar, usually vaulted and supported on four columns; cf. Baldacchino.

CINQUEFOIL: see Foil.

CIST: stone-lined or slab-built grave.

CLACHAN (Scots): a hamlet or small village; also, a village inn.

CLADDING: external covering or skin applied to a structure, especially a framed one.

CLEARSTOREY: uppermost storey of the nave of a church, pierced by windows. Also high-level windows in secular buildings.

CLOSE (Scots): courtyard or passage giving access to a number of buildings.

CLOSER: a brick cut to complete a bond (6e).

CLUSTER BLOCK: see Multi-storey.

COADE STONE: ceramic artificial stone made in Lambeth 1769–c.1840 by Eleanor Coade (†1821) and her associates.

COB: walling material of clay mixed with straw.

COFFERING: arrangement of sunken panels (coffers), square or polygonal, decorating a ceiling, vault or arch.

GLOSSARY

COGGING: a decorative course of bricks laid diagonally (6e). Cf. Dentilation.

COLLAR: see Roofs and 7.

COLLEGIATE CHURCH: endowed for the support of a college of priests, especially for the saying of masses for the soul(s) of the founder(s).

COLONNADE: range of columns supporting an entablature. Cf. Arcade.

COLONNETTE: small column or shaft.

COLOSSAL ORDER: see Giant order.

COLUMBARIUM: shelved, niched structure to house multiple burials.

COLUMN: a classical, upright structural member of round section with a shaft, a capital and usually a base (3a, 4a).

COLUMN FIGURE: carved figure attached to a medieval column or shaft, usually flanking a doorway.

COMMENDATOR: receives the revenues of an abbey *in commendam* ('in trust') when the position of abbot is vacant.

COMMUNION TABLE: table used in Protestant churches for the celebration of Holy Communion.

COMPOSITE: see Orders.

COMPOUND PIER: grouped shafts (q.v.), or a solid core surrounded by shafts.

CONCRETE: composition of *cement* (calcined lime and clay), *aggregate* (small stones or rock chippings), sand and water. It can be poured into *formwork* or *shuttering* (temporary frame of timber or metal) on site (*in-situ* concrete), or *pre-cast* as components before construction. *Reinforced*: incorporating steel rods to take the tensile force. *Prestressed*: with tensioned steel rods. Finishes include the impression of boards left by formwork (*board-marked* or *shuttered*), and texturing with steel brushes (*brushed*) or hammers (*hammer-dressed*). See also Shell.

CONDUCTOR (Scots): down-pipe for rainwater; see also Rhone.

CONSOLE: bracket of curved outline (4b).

COPING: protective course of masonry or brickwork capping a wall (6d).

COOMB or COMB CEILING (Scots): with sloping sides corresponding to the roof pitch up to a flat centre.

CORBEL: projecting block supporting something above. *Corbel course:* continuous course of projecting stones or bricks fulfilling the same function. *Corbel table*: series of corbels to carry a parapet or a wall-plate or wall-post (7). *Corbelling*: brick or masonry courses built out beyond one another to support a chimneystack, window etc. For *continuous* and *chequer-set* corbelling see 8a.

CORINTHIAN: see Orders and 3d.

CORNICE: flat-topped ledge with moulded underside, projecting along the top of a building or feature, especially as the highest member of the classical entablature (3a). Also the decorative moulding in the angle between wall and ceiling.

CORPS-DE-LOGIS: the main building(s) as distinct from the wings or pavilions.

COTTAGE ORNÉ: an artfully rustic small house associated with the Picturesque movement.

COUNTERSCARP BANK: low bank on the downhill or outer side of a hillfort ditch.

COUR D'HONNEUR: formal entrance court before a house in the French manner, usually with flanking wings and a screen wall or gates.

COURSE: continuous layer of stones etc. in a wall (6e).

COVE: a broad concave moulding, e.g. to mask the eaves of a roof. *Coved ceiling*: with a pronounced cove joining the walls to a flat central panel smaller than the whole area of the ceiling.

CRADLE ROOF: see Wagon roof.

CREDENCE: shelved niche or table, usually beside a piscina (q.v.), for the sacramental elements and vessels.

CRENELLATION: parapet with crenelles (*see* Battlement).

CRINKLE-CRANKLE WALL: garden wall undulating in a series of serpentine curves.

CROCKETS: leafy hooks. *Crocketing* decorates the edges of Gothic features, such as pinnacles, canopies etc. *Crocket capital*: see 1b.

CROSSING: central space at the junction of the nave, chancel and transepts. *Crossing tower*: above a crossing.

CROSS-WINDOW: with one mullion and one transom (qq.v.).

CROWN-POST: *see* Roofs and 7.

CROWSTEPS: squared stones set like steps, especially on a crowstepped gable (7, 8a).

CRUCKS (*lit.* crooked): pairs of inclined timbers (*blades*), usually curved, set at bay-lengths; they support the roof timbers and, in timber buildings, also support the walls. *Base*: blades rise from ground level to a tie-or collar-beam which supports the roof timbers. *Full*: blades rise from ground level to the apex of the roof, serving as the main members of a roof truss. *Jointed*: blades formed from more than one timber; the lower member may act as a wall-post; it is usually elbowed at wall-plate level and jointed just above. *Middle*: blades rise from halfway up the walls to a tie-or collar-beam. *Raised*: blades rise from halfway up the walls to the apex. *Upper*: blades supported on a tie-beam and rising to the apex.

CRYPT: underground or half-underground area, usually below the E end of a church. *Ring crypt*: corridor crypt surrounding the apse of an early medieval church, often associated with chambers for relics. Cf. Undercroft.

CUPOLA (*lit.* dome): especially a small dome on a circular or polygonal base crowning a larger dome, roof or turret. Also (Scots) small dome or skylight as an internal feature, especially over a stairwell.

CURSUS: a long avenue defined by two parallel earthen banks with ditches outside.

CURTAIN WALL: a connecting wall between the towers of a castle. Also a non-load-bearing external wall applied to a C20 framed structure.

CUSP: *see* Tracery and 2b.

CYCLOPEAN MASONRY: large irregular polygonal stones, smooth and finely jointed.

CYMA RECTA and CYMA REVERSA: classical mouldings with double curves (3f). Cf. Ogee.

DADO: the finishing (often with panelling) of the lower part of a wall in a classical interior; in origin a formalized continuous pedestal. *Dado rail*: the moulding along the top of the dado.

DAGGER: *see* Tracery and 2b.

DEC (DECORATED): English Gothic architecture c. 1290 to c. 1350. The name is derived from the type of window tracery (q.v.) used during the period.

DEMI- or HALF-COLUMNS: engaged columns (q.v.) half of whose circumference projects from the wall.

DENTIL: small square block used in series in classical cornices (3c). *Dentilation* is produced by the projection of alternating headers along cornices or stringcourses.

DIAPER: repetitive surface decoration of lozenges or squares flat or in relief. Achieved in brickwork with bricks of two colours.

DIOCLETIAN or THERMAL WINDOW: semicircular with two mullions, as used in the Baths of Diocletian, Rome (4b).

DISTYLE: having two columns (4a).

DOGTOOTH: E.E. ornament, consisting of a series of small pyramids formed by four stylized canine teeth meeting at a point (1a).

DOOCOT (Scots): dovecot. When freestanding, usually *Lectern* (rectangular with single-pitch roof) or *Beehive* (circular, diminishing towards the top).

DORIC: *see* Orders and 3a, 3b.

DORMER: window projecting from the slope of a roof (7). *Dormer head*: gable above a dormer, often formed as a pediment (8a).

DOUBLE CHAMFER: a chamfer applied to each of two recessed arches (1a).

DOUBLE PILE: *see* Pile.

DRAGON BEAM: *see* Jetty.

DRESSINGS: the stone or brickwork worked to a finished face about an angle, opening or other feature.

DRIPSTONE: moulded stone projecting from a wall to protect the lower parts from water. Cf. Hoodmould, Weathering.

DRUM: circular or polygonal stage supporting a dome or cupola. Also one of the stones forming the shaft of a column (3a).

DRY-STONE: stone construction without mortar.

GLOSSARY

DUN (Scots): small stone-walled fort.
DUTCH or FLEMISH GABLE: *see* 7.

EASTER SEPULCHRE: tomb-chest, usually within or against the N wall of a chancel, used in Holy Week ceremonies for reservation (entombment) of the sacrament after the mass of Maundy Thursday.
EAVES: overhanging edge of a roof; hence *eaves cornice* in this position.
ECHINUS: ovolo moulding (q.v.) below the abacus of a Greek Doric capital (3a).
EDGE RAIL: *see* Railways.
EDGE-ROLL: moulding of semicircular section or more at the edge of an opening.
E.E. (EARLY ENGLISH): English Gothic architecture *c.* 1190–1250.
EGG-AND-DART: *see* Enrichments and 3f.
ELEVATION: any face of a building or side of a room. In a drawing, the same or any part of it, represented in two dimensions.
ELIDED: used to describe a compound feature, e.g. an entablature, with some parts omitted. Also, parts of, e.g., a base or capital, combined to form a larger one.
EMBATTLED: with battlements.
EMBRASURE: splayed opening in a wall or battlement (q.v.).
ENCAUSTIC TILES: earthenware tiles fired with a pattern and glaze.
EN DELIT: stone laid against the bed.
ENFILADE: reception rooms in a formal series, usually with all doorways on axis.
ENGAGED or ATTACHED COLUMN: one that partly merges into a wall or pier.
ENGINEERING BRICKS: dense bricks, originally used mostly for railway viaducts etc.
ENRICHMENTS: the carved decoration of certain classical mouldings, e.g. the ovolo with *egg-and-dart*, the cyma reversa with *waterleaf*, the astragal with *bead-and-reel* (3f).
ENTABLATURE: in classical architecture, collective name for the three horizontal members (architrave, frieze and cornice) carried by a wall or a column (3a).
ENTASIS: very slight convex deviation from a straight line, used to prevent an optical illusion of concavity.
ENTRESOL: mezzanine floor subdividing what is constructionally a single storey, e.g. a vault.
EPITAPH: inscription on a tomb or monument.
EXEDRA: *see* Apse.
EXTRADOS: outer curved face of an arch or vault.
EYECATCHER: decorative building terminating a vista.

FASCIA: plain horizontal band, e.g. in an architrave (3c, 3d) or on a shopfront.
FENESTRATION: the arrangement of windows in a façade.
FERETORY: site of the chief shrine of a church, behind the high altar.
FESTOON: ornamental garland, suspended from both ends. Cf. Swag.
FEU (Scots): land granted, e.g. by sale, by the *feudal superior* to the *vassal* or *feuar*, on conditions that usually include the annual payment of a fixed sum of *feu duty*. Any subsequent proprietor of the land becomes the feuar and is subject to the same obligations.
FIBREGLASS (or glass-reinforced polyester (GRP)): synthetic resin reinforced with glass fibre. GRC: glass-reinforced concrete.
FIELD: *see* Panelling and 6b.
FILLET: a narrow flat band running down a medieval shaft or along a roll moulding (1a). It separates larger curved mouldings in classical cornices, fluting or bases (3c).
FLAMBOYANT: the latest phase of French Gothic architecture, with flowing tracery.
FLASH LOCK: *see* Canals.
FLATTED: divided into apartments. Also with a colloquial (Scots) meaning: 'He stays on the first flat' means that he lives on the first floor.
FLÈCHE or SPIRELET (*lit.* arrow): slender spire on the centre of a roof.
FLEURON: medieval carved flower or leaf, often rectilinear (1a).
FLUSHWORK: knapped flint used with dressed stone to form patterns.
FLUTING: series of concave grooves (flutes), their common edges sharp (arris) or blunt (fillet) (3).

GLOSSARY

FOIL (*lit.* leaf): lobe formed by the cusping of a circular or other shape in tracery (2b). *Trefoil* (three), *quatrefoil* (four), *cinquefoil* (five) and *multifoil* express the number of lobes in a shape.

FOLIATE: decorated with leaves.

FORE-BUILDING: structure protecting an entrance.

FORESTAIR: external stair, usually unenclosed.

FORMWORK: see Concrete.

FRAMED BUILDING: where the structure is carried by a framework - e.g. of steel, reinforced concrete, timber - instead of by load-bearing walls.

FREESTONE: stone that is cut, or can be cut, in all directions.

FRESCO: *al fresco*: painting on wet plaster. *Fresco secco*: painting on dry plaster.

FRIEZE: the middle member of the classical entablature, sometimes ornamented (3a). *Pulvinated frieze* (*lit.* cushioned): of bold convex profile (3c). Also a horizontal band of ornament.

FRONTISPIECE: in C16 and C17 buildings the central feature of doorway and windows above linked in one composition.

GABLE: peaked external wall at end of double-pitch roof. For types see 7. Also (Scots): whole end wall of whatever shape. *Pedimental gable*: treated like a pediment.

GADROONING: classical ribbed ornament like inverted fluting that flows into a lobed edge.

GAIT or GATE (Scots): street, usually with a prefix indicating use, direction or destination.

GALILEE: chapel or vestibule usually at the W end of a church enclosing the main portal(s).

GALLERY: a long room or passage; an upper storey above the aisle of a church, looking through arches to the nave; a balcony or mezzanine overlooking the main interior space of a building; or an external walkway.

GALLETING: small stones set in a mortar course.

GAMBREL ROOF: see 7.

GARDEROBE: medieval privy.

GARGOYLE: projecting water spout, often carved into human or animal shape. For cannon spout see 8.

GAUGED or RUBBED BRICKWORK: soft brick sawn roughly, then rubbed to a precise (gauged) surface. Mostly used for door or window openings (5c).

GAZEBO (jocular Latin, 'I shall gaze'): ornamental lookout tower or raised summer house.

GEOMETRIC: English Gothic architecture *c.* 1250–1310. *See also* Tracery. For another meaning, see Stairs.

GIANT or COLOSSAL ORDER: classical order (q.v.) whose height is that of two or more storeys of the building to which it is applied.

GIBBS SURROUND: C18 treatment of an opening (4b), seen particularly in the work of James Gibbs (1682–1754).

GIRDER: a large beam. *Box*: of hollow-box section. *Bowed*: with its top rising in a curve. *Plate*: of I-section, made from iron or steel plates. *Lattice*: with braced framework.

GLACIS: artificial slope extending out and downwards from the parapet of a fort.

GLAZING-BARS: wooden or sometimes metal bars separating and supporting window panes.

GLAZING GROOVE: groove in a window surround into which the glass is fitted.

GNOMON: vane or indicator casting a shadow onto a sundial.

GRAFFITI: see Sgraffito.

GRANGE: farm owned and run by a religious order.

GRC: see Fibreglass.

GRISAILLE: monochrome painting on walls or glass.

GROIN: sharp edge at the meeting of two cells of a cross-vault; *see* Vault and 2b.

GROTESQUE (*lit.* grotto-esque): wall decoration adopted from Roman examples in the Renaissance. Its foliage scrolls incorporate figurative elements. Cf. Arabesque.

GROTTO: artificial cavern.

GRP: see Fibreglass.

GUILLOCHE: classical ornament of interlaced bands (4b).

GUNLOOP: opening for a firearm (8a).

GUSHET (Scots): a triangular or wedge-shaped piece of land or the corner building on such a site.

GUTTAE: stylized drops (3b).

GLOSSARY

HALF-TIMBERING: archaic term for timber-framing (q.v.). Sometimes used for non-structural decorative timberwork.

HALL CHURCH: medieval church with nave and aisles of approximately equal height. Also (Scots C20) building for use as both hall and church, the double function usually intended to be temporary until a separate church is built.

HAMMERBEAM: see Roofs and 7.

HARLING (Scots, *lit.* hurling): wet dash, i.e. a form of roughcasting in which the mixture of aggregate and binding material (e.g. lime) is dashed onto a wall.

HEADER: see Bond and 6e.

HEADSTOP: stop (q.v.) carved with a head (5b).

HELM ROOF: see 1c.

HENGE: ritual earthwork with a surrounding ditch and outer bank.

HERM (*lit.* the god Hermes): male head or bust on a pedestal.

HERRINGBONE WORK: see 6e (for brick bond). Cf. Pitched masonry.

HEXASTYLE: see Portico.

HILLFORT: Iron Age earthwork enclosed by a ditch and bank system.

HIPPED ROOF: see 7.

HOODMOULD: projecting moulding above an arch or lintel to throw off water (2b, 5b). When horizontal often called a *label*. For label stop see Stop.

HORIZONTAL GLAZING: with panes of horizontal proportions.

HORSEMILL: circular or polygonal farm building with a central shaft turned by a horse to drive agricultural machinery.

HUNGRY-JOINTED: *see* Pointing.

HUSK GARLAND: festoon of stylized nutshells (4b).

HYDRAULIC POWER: use of water under high pressure to work machinery. *Accumulator tower*: houses a hydraulic accumulator which accommodates fluctuations in the flow through hydraulic mains.

HYPOCAUST (*lit.* underburning): Roman underfloor heating system.

IMPOST: horizontal moulding at the springing of an arch (5c).

IMPOST BLOCK: block between abacus and capital (1b).

IN ANTIS: *see* Antae, Portico and 4a.

INDENT: shape chiselled out of a stone to receive a brass. Also, in restoration, new stone inserted as a patch.

INDUSTRIALIZED or SYSTEM BUILDING: system of manufactured units assembled on site.

INGLENOOK (*lit.* fire-corner): recess for a hearth with provision for seating.

INGO (Scots): the reveal of a door or window opening where the stone is at right angles to the wall.

INTERCOLUMNATION: interval between columns.

INTERLACE: decoration in relief simulating woven or entwined stems or bands.

INTRADOS: *see* Soffit.

IONIC: *see* Orders and 3c.

JACK ARCH: shallow segmental vault springing from beams, used for fireproof floors, bridge decks etc.

JAMB (*lit.* leg): one of the vertical sides of an opening. Also (Scots) wing or extension adjoining one side of a rectangular plan making it into an L-, T- or Z-plan.

JETTY: the projection of an upper storey beyond the storey below. In a stone building this is achieved by corbelling. In a timber-framed building it is made by the beams and joists of the lower storey oversailing the wall; on their outer ends is placed the sill of the walling for the storey above.

JOGGLE: the joining of two stones to prevent them slipping by a notch in one and a projection in the other.

KEEL MOULDING: moulding used from the late C12, in section like the keel of a ship (1a).

KEEP: principal tower of a castle.

KENTISH CUSP: *see* Tracery.

KEY PATTERN: *see* 4b.

KEYSTONE: central stone in an arch or vault (4b, 5c).

KINGPOST: *see* Roofs and 7.

KNEELER: horizontal projecting stone at the base of each side of a gable to support the inclined coping stones (7).

LABEL: *see* Hoodmould and 5b.

LABEL STOP: *see* Stop and 5b.

LACED BRICKWORK: vertical strips of brickwork, often in a contrasting colour, linking openings on different floors.
LACING COURSE: horizontal reinforcement in timber or brick to walls of flint, cobble etc.
LADE (Scots): channel formed to bring water to a mill; mill-race.
LADY CHAPEL: dedicated to the Virgin Mary (Our Lady).
LAIGH or LAICH (Scots): low.
LAIR (Scots): a burial space reserved in a graveyard
LAIRD (Scots): landowner.
LANCET: slender single-light, pointed-arched window (2a).
LANTERN: circular or polygonal windowed turret crowning a roof or a dome. Also the windowed stage of a crossing tower lighting the church interior.
LANTERN CROSS: churchyard cross with lantern-shaped top.
LAVATORIUM: in a religious house, a washing place adjacent to the refectory.
LEAN-TO: see Roofs.
LESENE (*lit.* a mean thing): pilaster without base or capital. Also called *pilaster strip*.
LIERNE: see Vault and 2c.
LIGHT: compartment of a window defined by the mullions.
LINENFOLD: Tudor panelling carved with simulations of folded linen.
LINTEL: horizontal beam or stone bridging an opening.
LOFT: gallery in a church. *Organ loft*: in which the organ, or sometimes only the console (keyboard), is placed. *Laird's loft, Trades loft* etc. (Scots): reserved for an individual or special group. See also Rood (loft).
LOGGIA: gallery, usually arcaded or colonnaded along one side; sometimes freestanding.
LONG-AND-SHORT WORK: quoins consisting of stones placed with the long side alternately upright and horizontal, especially in Saxon building.
LOUVRE: roof opening, often protected by a raised timber structure, to allow the smoke from a central hearth to escape. *Louvres*: overlapping boards to allow ventilation but keep the rain out.
LOWSIDE WINDOW: set lower than the others in a chancel side wall, usually towards its W end.
L-PLAN: *see* Tower house and 8b.
LUCARNE (*lit.* dormer): small gabled opening in a roof or spire.
LUCKENBOOTH (Scots): lock-up booth or shop.
LUGGED ARCHITRAVE: *see* 4b.
LUNETTE: semicircular window or blind panel.
LYCHGATE (*lit.* corpse-gate): roofed gateway entrance to a churchyard for the reception of a coffin.
LYNCHET: long terraced strip of soil on the downward side of prehistoric and medieval fields, accumulated because of continual ploughing along the contours.

MACHICOLATIONS (*lit.* mashing devices): series of openings between the corbels that support a projecting parapet through which missiles can be dropped (8a). Used decoratively in post-medieval buildings.
MAINS (Scots): home farm on an estate.
MANOMETER or STANDPIPE TOWER: containing a column of water to regulate pressure in water mains.
MANSARD: *see* 7.
MANSE: house of a minister of religion, especially in Scotland.
MARGINS (Scots): dressed stones at the edges of an opening. 'Back-set margins' (RCAHMS) are actually set forward from a rubble wall to act as a stop for harling (q.v.). Also called *rybats*.
MARRIAGE LINTEL (Scots): door or window lintel carved with the initials of the owner and his wife and the date of building work, only coincidentally of their marriage.
MATHEMATICAL TILES: facing tiles with the appearance of brick, most often applied to timber-framed walls.
MAUSOLEUM: monumental building or chamber usually intended for the burial of members of one family.
MEGALITHIC: the use of large stones, singly or together.
MEGALITHIC TOMB: massive stonebuilt Neolithic burial chamber covered by an earth or stone mound.
MERCAT (Scots): market. The *Mercat Cross* of a Scottish burgh

was the focus of market activity and local ceremonial. Most examples are post-Reformation with heraldic or other finials (not crosses).

MERLON: *see* Battlement.

MESOLITHIC: Middle Stone Age, in Britain *c.* 5000 to *c.* 3500 B.C.

METOPES: spaces between the triglyphs in a Doric frieze (3b).

MEZZANINE: low storey between two higher ones or within the height of a high one, not extending over its whole area.

MILD STEEL: *see* Cast iron.

MISERICORD (*lit.* mercy): shelf on a carved bracket placed on the underside of a hinged choir stall seat to support an occupant when standing.

MIXER-COURTS: forecourts to groups of houses shared by vehicles and pedestrians.

MODILLIONS: small consoles (q.v.) along the underside of a Corinthian or Composite cornice (3d). Often used along an eaves cornice.

MODULE: a predetermined standard size for co-ordinating the dimensions of components of a building.

MORT-SAFE (Scots): device to secure corpse(s): either an iron frame over a grave or a building where bodies were kept during decomposition.

MOTTE-AND-BAILEY: C11 and C12 type of castle consisting of an earthen mound (motte) topped by a wooden tower within or adjoining a bailey, an enclosure defended by a ditch and palisade, and also, sometimes, by an inner bank.

MOUCHETTE: *see* Tracery and 2b.

MOULDING: shaped ornamental strip of continuous section; *see* Cavetto, Cyma, Ovolo, Roll.

MULLION: vertical member between window lights (2b).

MULTI-STOREY: five or more storeys. Multi-storey flats may form a *cluster block*, with individual blocks of flats grouped round a service core; a *point block*, with flats fanning out from a service core; or a *slab block*, with flats approached by corridors or galleries from service cores at intervals or towers at the ends (plan also used for offices, hotels etc.). *Tower block* is a generic term for a high multi-storey building.

MULTIVALLATE: of a hillfort: defended by three or more concentric banks and ditches.

MUNTIN: *see* Panelling and 6b.

MUTULE: square block under the corona of a Doric cornice.

NAILHEAD: E.E. ornament consisting of small pyramids regularly repeated (1a).

NARTHEX: enclosed vestibule or covered porch at the main entrance to a church.

NAVE: the body of a church w of the crossing or chancel, often flanked by aisles (q.v.).

NEOLITHIC: New Stone Age in Britain, *c.* 3500 B.C. until the Bronze Age.

NEWEL: central or corner post of a staircase (6c). For Newel stair *see* Stairs.

NIGHT STAIR: stair by which religious entered the transept of their church from their dormitory to celebrate night offices.

NOGGING: *see* Timber-framing.

NOOK-SHAFT: shaft set in the angle of a wall or opening (1a).

NORMAN: *see* Romanesque.

NOSING: projection of the tread of a step (6c). *Bottle nosing*: half round in section.

NUTMEG: medieval ornament with a chain of tiny triangles placed obliquely.

OCULUS: circular opening.

OEIL DE BOEUF: *see* Bullseye window.

OGEE: double curve, bending first one way and then the other, as in an *ogee* or *ogival arch* (5c). Cf. Cyma recta and Cyma reversa.

OPUS SECTILE: decorative mosaic-like facing.

OPUS SIGNINUM: composition flooring of Roman origin.

ORATORY: a private chapel in a church or a house. Also a church of the Oratorian Order.

ORDER: one of a series of recessed arches and jambs forming a splayed medieval opening, e.g. a doorway or arcade arch (1a).

ORDERS: the formalized versions of the post-and-lintel system in classical architecture. The main orders are *Doric*, *Ionic* and *Corinthian*. They are Greek in origin

GLOSSARY

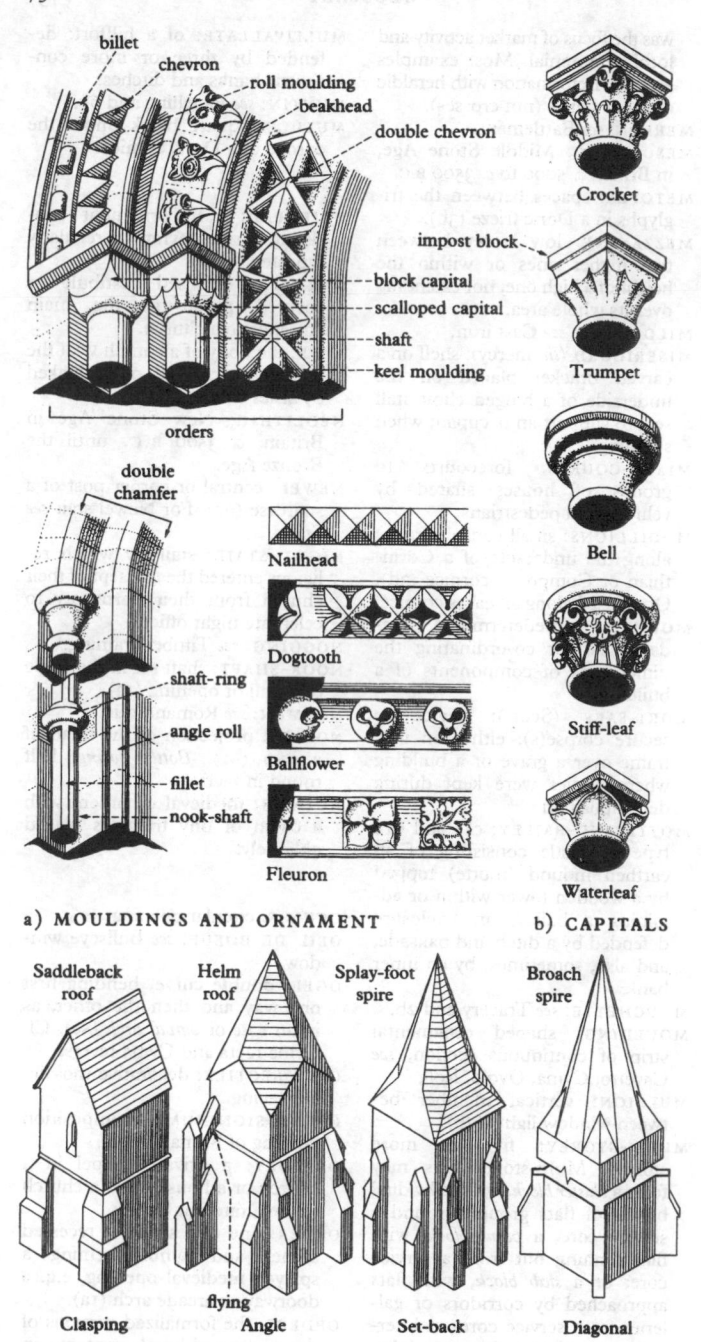

a) MOULDINGS AND ORNAMENT

- billet
- chevron
- roll moulding
- beakhead
- double chevron
- impost block
- block capital
- scalloped capital
- shaft
- keel moulding
- orders
- double chamfer
- shaft-ring
- angle roll
- fillet
- nook-shaft
- Nailhead
- Dogtooth
- Ballflower
- Fleuron

b) CAPITALS

- Crocket
- Trumpet
- Bell
- Stiff-leaf
- Waterleaf

c) BUTTRESSES, ROOFS AND SPIRES

- Saddleback roof
- Helm roof
- Splay-foot spire
- Broach spire
- Clasping
- Angle (flying)
- Set-back
- Diagonal

FIGURE 1: MEDIEVAL

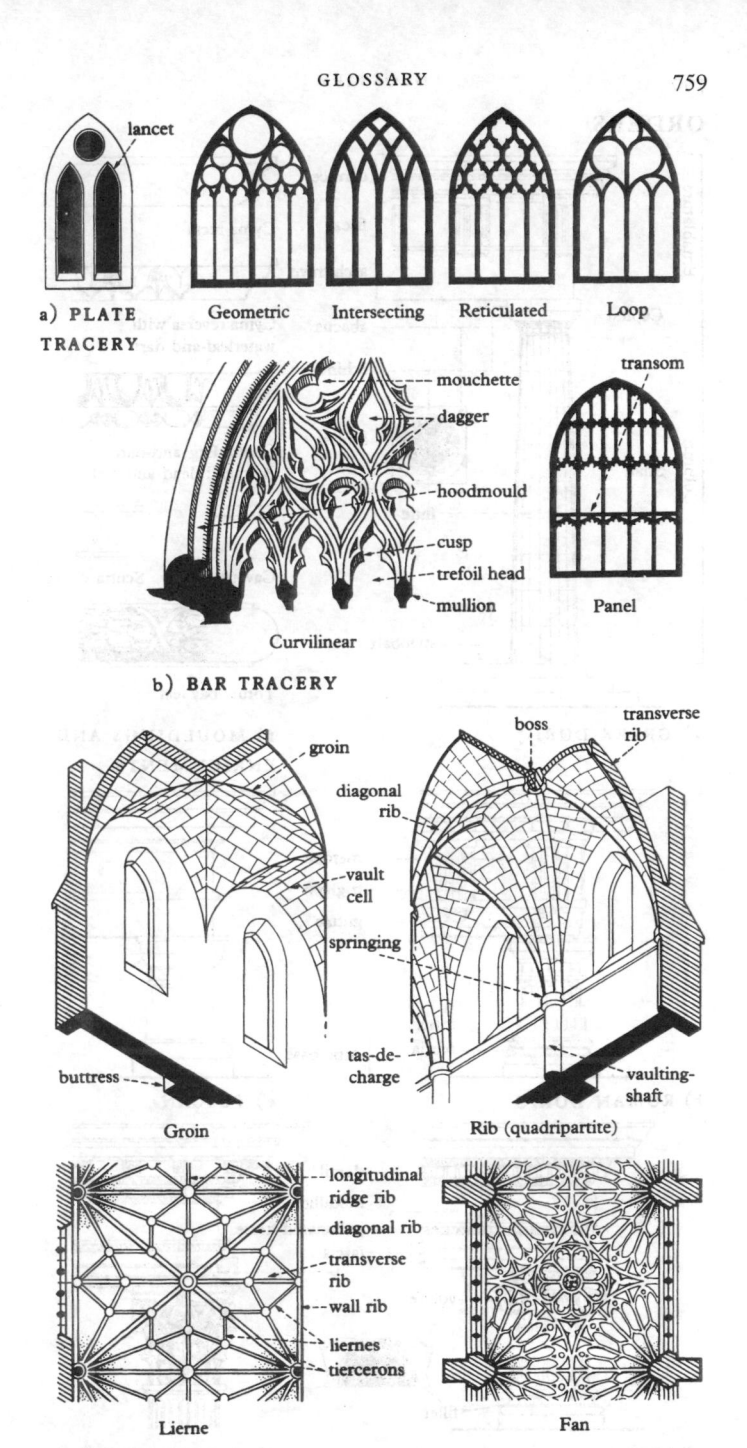

GLOSSARY

a) PLATE TRACERY — lancet; Geometric; Intersecting; Reticulated; Loop

b) BAR TRACERY — Curvilinear (mouchette, dagger, hoodmould, cusp, trefoil head, mullion); Panel (transom)

c) VAULTS — Groin (groin, vault cell, buttress); Rib (quadripartite) (boss, transverse rib, diagonal rib, springing, tas-de-charge, vaulting-shaft); Lierne (longitudinal ridge rib, diagonal rib, transverse rib, wall rib, liernes, tiercerons); Fan

FIGURE 2: MEDIEVAL

GLOSSARY

ORDERS

a) GREEK DORIC

- Entablature: cornice, frieze, architrave
- Capital: abacus, echinus
- Column: Shaft, arris, flute, drum
- stylobate

f) MOULDINGS AND ENRICHMENTS

- Cyma recta
- Cyma reversa with waterleaf-and-dart
- Ovolo: Egg-and-dart
- Astragal: Bead-and-reel
- Cavetto
- Scotia
- Torus: bay leaf

b) ROMAN DORIC

- metope
- triglyph
- guttae
- torus
- scotia
- Attic base

e) TUSCAN

c) IONIC

- dentil
- modillion
- pulvinated frieze
- fascia
- volute
- fillet

d) CORINTHIAN

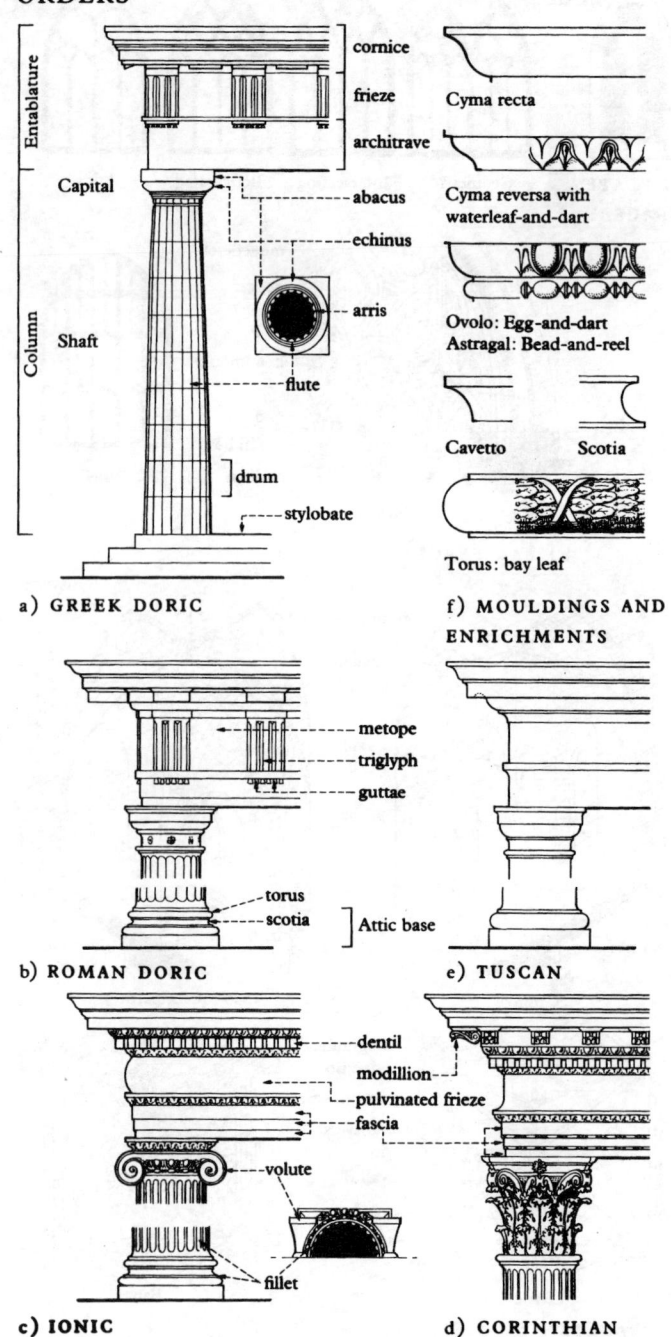

FIGURE 3: CLASSICAL

GLOSSARY

a) PORTICO

b) ORNAMENTS AND FEATURES

FIGURE 4: CLASSICAL

GLOSSARY

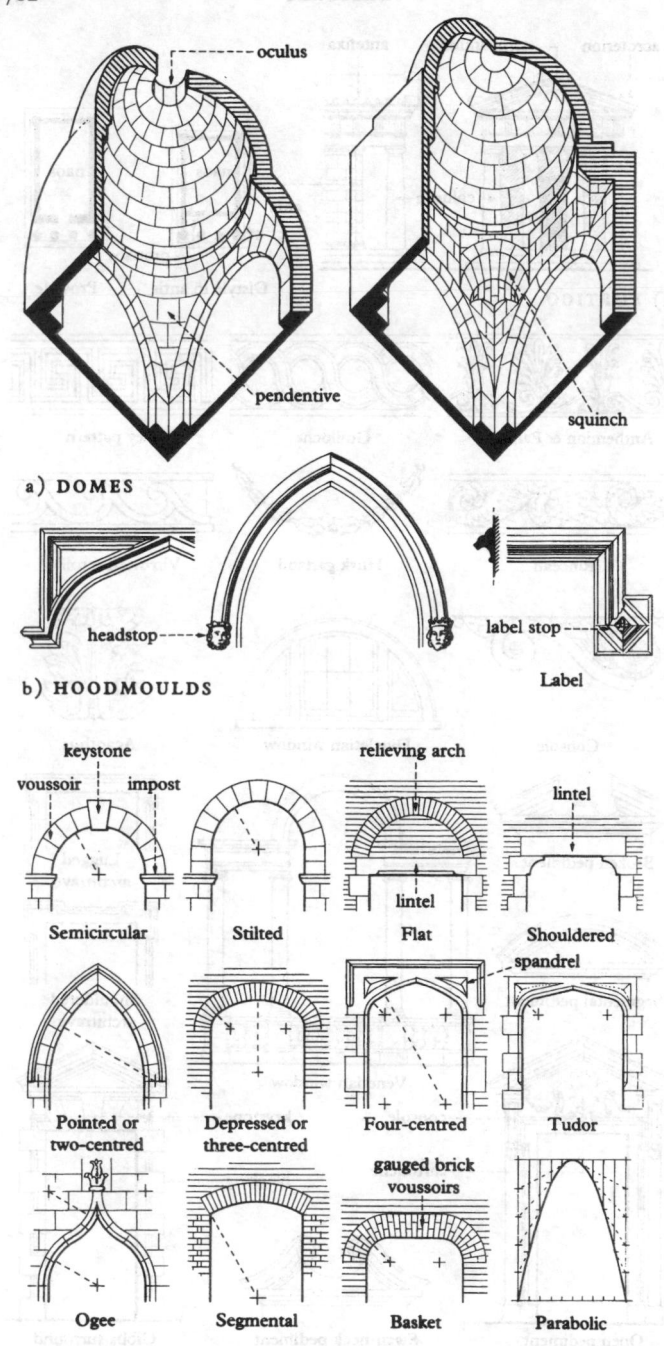

a) DOMES

- oculus
- pendentive
- squinch

b) HOODMOULDS

- headstop
- label stop
- Label

c) ARCHES

- Semicircular (voussoir, keystone, impost)
- Stilted
- Flat (relieving arch, lintel)
- Shouldered (lintel)
- Pointed or two-centred (spandrel)
- Depressed or three-centred
- Four-centred
- Tudor
- Ogee
- Segmental
- Basket (gauged brick voussoirs)
- Parabolic

FIGURE 5: CONSTRUCTION

GLOSSARY

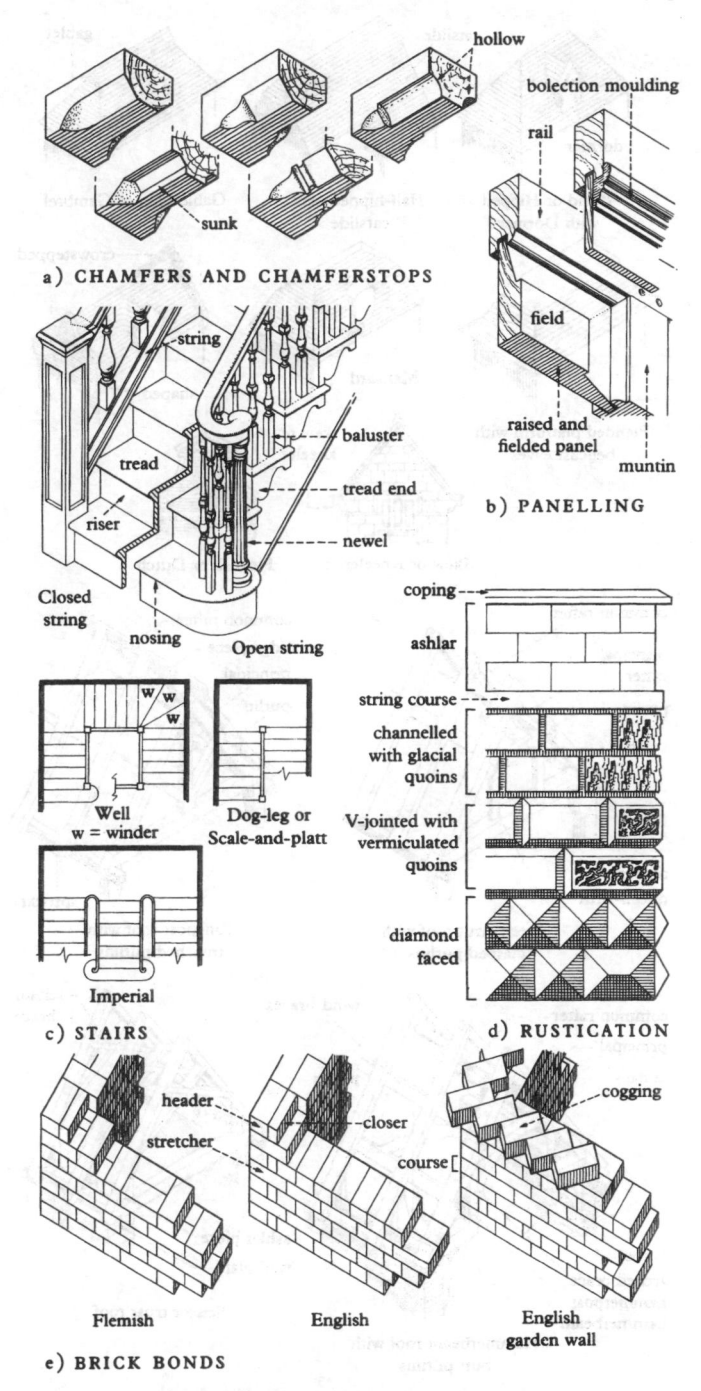

a) CHAMFERS AND CHAMFERSTOPS

hollow

sunk

b) PANELLING

bolection moulding
rail
field
raised and fielded panel
muntin

c) STAIRS

string
baluster
tread
tread end
riser
newel
Closed string
nosing
Open string

Well w = winder
Dog-leg or Scale-and-platt
Imperial

d) RUSTICATION

coping
ashlar
string course
channelled with glacial quoins
V-jointed with vermiculated quoins
diamond faced

e) BRICK BONDS

header
closer
stretcher
cogging
course

Flemish
English
English garden wall

FIGURE 6: CONSTRUCTION

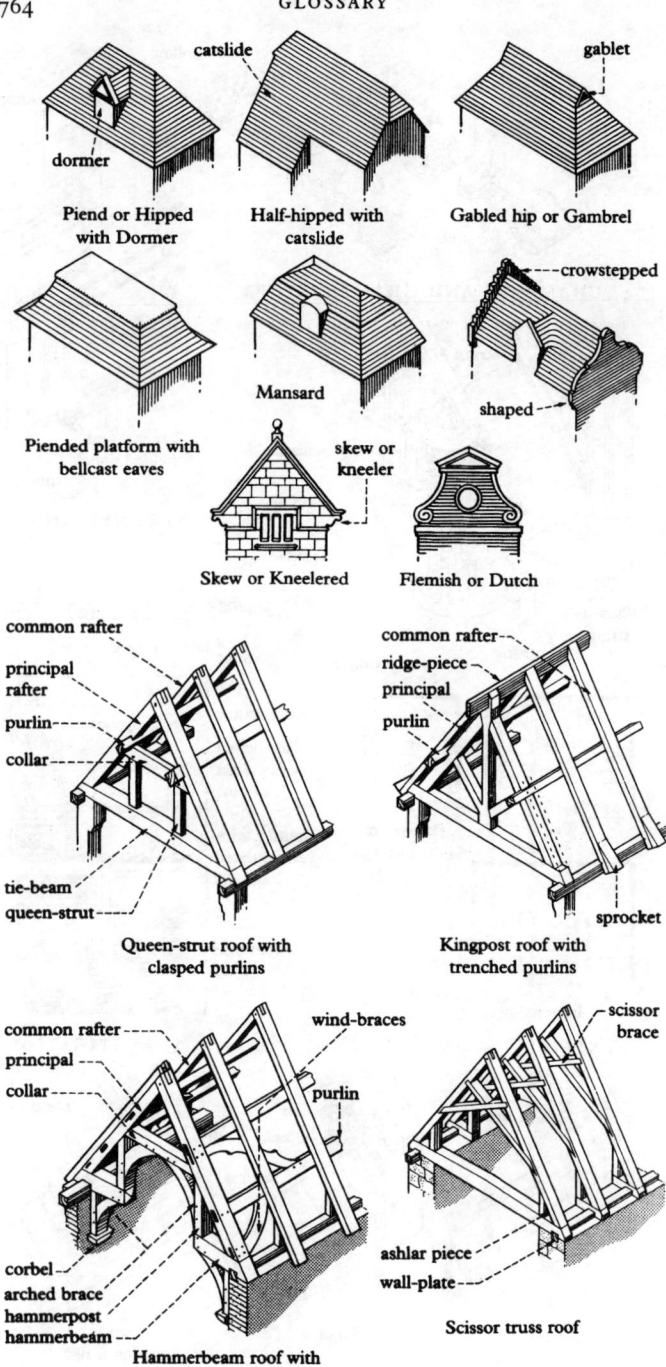

FIGURE 7: ROOFS AND GABLES

GLOSSARY

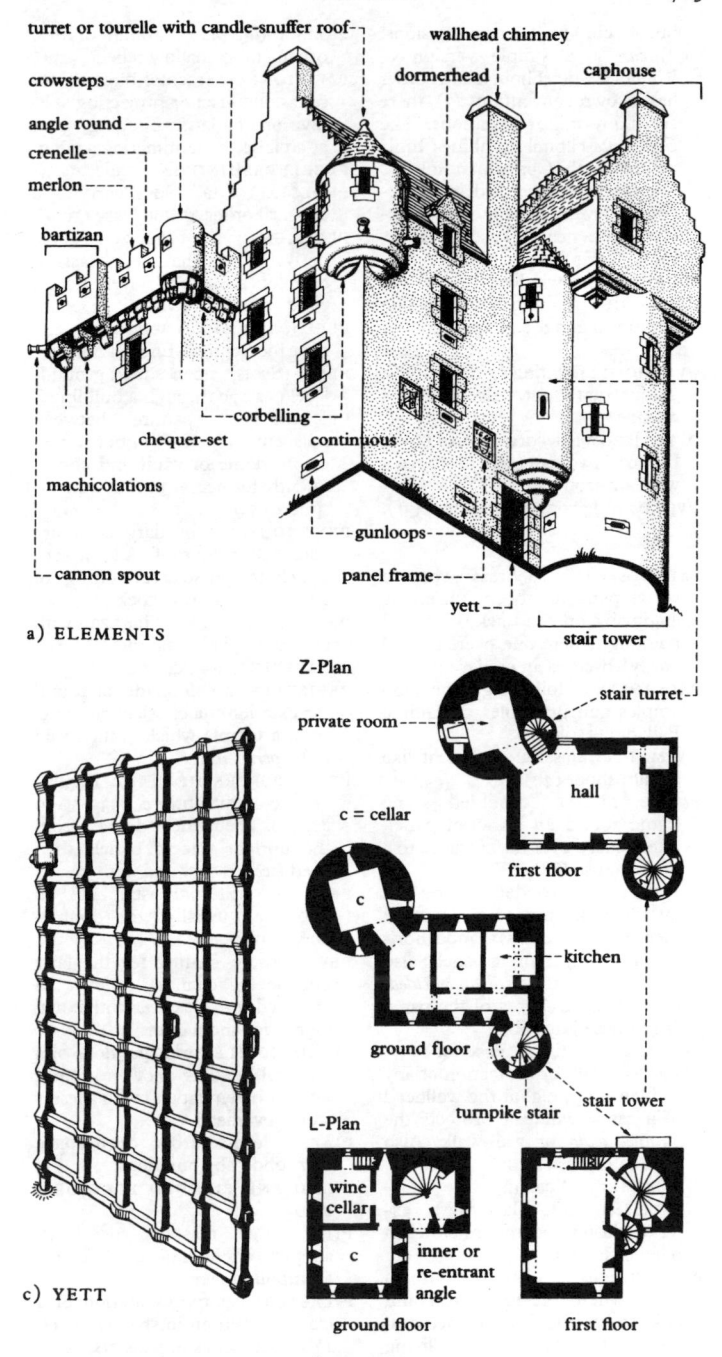

a) ELEMENTS

Labels: turret or tourelle with candle-snuffer roof; crowsteps; angle round; crenelle; merlon; bartizan; chequer-set; machicolations; cannon spout; corbelling; continuous; gunloops; panel frame; yett; wallhead chimney; dormerhead; caphouse; stair tower

b) FORMS

Z-Plan — private room; hall; first floor; c = cellar; kitchen; ground floor; turnpike stair; stair tower; stair turret

L-Plan — wine cellar; inner or re-entrant angle; c; ground floor; first floor

c) YETT

FIGURE 8: THE TOWER HOUSE

but occur in Roman versions. *Tuscan* is a simple version of Roman Doric. Though each order has its own conventions (3), there are many minor variations. The *Composite* capital combines Ionic volutes with Corinthian foliage. *Superimposed orders*: orders on successive levels, usually in the upward sequence of Tuscan, Doric, Ionic, Corinthian, Composite.

ORIEL: *see* Bay window.

OVERARCH: framing a wall which has an opening, e.g. a window or door.

OVERDOOR: painting or relief above an internal door. Also called a *sopraporta*.

OVERTHROW: decorative fixed arch between two gatepiers or above a wrought-iron gate.

OVOLO: wide convex moulding (3f).

PALIMPSEST: of a brass: where a metal plate has been reused by engraving on the back; of a wall painting: where one overlaps and partly obscures an earlier one.

PALLADIAN: following the examples and principles of Andrea Palladio (1508–80).

PALMETTE: classical ornament like a palm shoot (4b).

PANEL FRAME: moulded stone frame round an armorial panel, often placed over the entrance to a tower house (8a).

PANELLING: wooden lining to interior walls, made up of vertical members (*muntins*) and horizontals (*rails*) framing panels: also called *wainscot*. *Raised-and-fielded*: with the central area of the panel (*field*) raised up (6b).

PANTILE: roof tile of S section.

PARAPET: wall for protection at any sudden drop, e.g. at the wallhead of a castle where it protects the *parapet walk* or wall-walk. Also used to conceal a roof.

PARCLOSE: *see* Screen.

PARGETING (*lit.* plastering): exterior plaster decoration, either in relief or incised.

PARLOUR: in a religious house, a room where the religious could talk to visitors; in a medieval house, the semi-private living room below the solar (q.v.).

PARTERRE: level space in a garden laid out with low, formal beds.

PATERA (*lit.* plate): round or oval ornament in shallow relief.

PAVILION: ornamental building for occasional use; or projecting subdivision of a larger building, often at an angle or terminating a wing.

PEBBLEDASHING: *see* Rendering.

PEDESTAL: a tall block carrying a classical order, statue, vase etc.

PEDIMENT: a formalized gable derived from that of a classical temple; also used over doors, windows etc. For variations *see* 4b.

PEEL (*lit.* palisade): stone tower, e.g. near the Scottish-English border.

PEND (Scots): open-ended ground-level passage through a building.

PENDENTIVE: spandrel between adjacent arches, supporting a drum, dome or vault and consequently formed as part of a hemisphere (5a).

PENTHOUSE: subsidiary structure with a lean-to roof. Also a separately roofed structure on top of a C20 multi-storey block.

PEPPERPOT TURRET: bartizan with conical or pyramidal roof.

PERIPTERAL: *see* Peristyle.

PERISTYLE: a colonnade all round the exterior of a classical building, as in a temple which is then said to be *peripteral*.

PERP (PERPENDICULAR): English Gothic architecture c. 1335–50 to c. 1530. The name is derived from the upright tracery panels then used (*see* Tracery and 2a).

PERRON: external stair to a doorway, usually of double-curved plan.

PEW: loosely, seating for the laity outside the chancel; strictly, an enclosed seat. *Box pew*: with equal high sides and a door.

PIANO NOBILE: principal floor of a classical building above a ground floor or basement and with a lesser storey overhead.

PIAZZA: formal urban open space surrounded by buildings.

PIEND AND PIENDED PLATFORM ROOF: *see* 7.

PIER: large masonry or brick support, often for an arch. *See also* Compound pier.

PILASTER: flat representation of a classical column in shallow relief. *Pilastrade*: series of pilasters, equivalent to a colonnade.

PILE: row of rooms. *Double pile*: two rows thick.

PILLAR: freestanding upright member of any section, not conforming to one of the orders (q.v.).
PILLAR PISCINA: see Piscina.
PILOTIS: C20 French term for pillars or stilts that support a building above an open ground floor.
PINS OR PINNINGS (Scots): see Cherry-caulking.
PISCINA: basin for washing Mass vessels, provided with a drain; set in or against wall to S of an altar or freestanding (*pillar piscina*).
PITCHED MASONRY: laid on the diagonal, often alternately with opposing courses (*pitched and counterpitched* or herringbone).
PIT PRISON: sunk chamber with access from above through a hatch.
PLATE RAIL: see Railways.
PLATEWAY: see Railways.
PLATT (Scots): platform, doorstep or landing. *Scale-and-platt stair*: see Stairs and 6c.
PLEASANCE (Scots): close or walled garden.
PLINTH: projecting courses at the foot of a wall or column, generally chamfered or moulded at the top.
PODIUM: a continuous raised platform supporting a building; or a large block of two or three storeys beneath a multi-storey block of smaller area.
POINT BLOCK: see Multi-storey.
POINTING: exposed mortar jointing of masonry or brickwork. Types include *flush*, *recessed* and *tuck* (with a narrow channel filled with finer, whiter mortar). *Bag-rubbed*: flush at the edges and gently recessed in the middle. *Ribbon*: joints formed with a trowel so that they stand out. *Hungry-jointed*: either with no pointing or deeply recessed to show the outline of each stone.
POPPYHEAD: carved ornament of leaves and flowers as a finial for a bench end or stall.
PORTAL FRAME: C20 frame comprising two uprights rigidly connected to a beam or pair of rafters.
PORTCULLIS: gate constructed to rise and fall in vertical gooves at the entry to a castle.
PORTE COCHÈRE: porch large enough to admit wheeled vehicles.
PORTICO: a porch with the roof and frequently a pediment supported by a row of columns (4a). A portico *in antis* has columns on the same plane as the front of the building. A *prostyle* porch has columns standing free. Porticoes are described by the number of front columns, e.g. tetrastyle (four), hexastyle (six). The space within the temple is the *naos*, that within the portico the *pronaos*. *Blind portico*: the front features of a portico applied to a wall.
PORTICUS (plural: porticūs): subsidiary cell opening from the main body of a pre-Conquest church.
POST: upright support in a structure.
POSTERN: small gateway at the back of a building or to the side of a larger entrance door or gate.
POTENCE (Scots): rotating ladder for access to doocot nesting boxes.
POUND LOCK: see Canals.
PREDELLA: in an altarpiece, the horizontal strip below the main representation, often used for subsidiary representations.
PRESBYTERY: the part of a church lying E of the choir where the main altar is placed. Also a priest's residence.
PRESS (Scots): cupboard.
PRINCIPAL: see Roofs and 7.
PRONAOS: see Portico and 4a.
PROSTYLE: see Portico and 4a.
PULPIT: raised and enclosed platform for the preaching of sermons. *Three-decker*: with reading desk below and clerk's desk below that. *Two-decker*: as above, minus the clerk's desk.
PULPITUM: stone screen in a major church dividing choir from nave.
PULVINATED: see Frieze and 3c.
PURLIN: see Roofs and 7.
PUTHOLES or PUTLOG HOLES: in wall to receive putlogs, the horizontal timbers which support scaffolding boards; not always filled after construction is complete.
PUTTO (plural: putti): small naked boy.

QUARRIES: square (or diamond) panes of glass supported by lead strips (*cames*); square floor-slabs or tiles.
QUATREFOIL: see Foil.
QUEEN-STRUT: see Roofs and 7.
QUILLONS: the arms forming the cross-guard of a sword.

QUIRK: sharp groove to one side of a convex medieval moulding.

QUOINS: dressed stones at the angles of a building (6d).

RADBURN SYSTEM: pedestrian and vehicle segregation in residential developments, based on that used at Radburn, New Jersey, U.S.A., by Wright and Stein, 1928–30.

RADIATING CHAPELS: projecting radially from an ambulatory or an apse (see Chevet).

RAFTER: see Roofs and 7.

RAGGLE: groove cut in masonry, especially to receive the edge of a roof-covering.

RAIL: see Panelling and 6b.

RAILWAYS: *Edge rail*: on which flanged wheels can run. *Plate rail*: L-section rail for plain unflanged wheels. *Plateway*: early railway using plate rails.

RAISED AND FIELDED: see Panelling and 6b.

RAKE: slope or pitch.

RAMPART: defensive outer wall of stone or earth. *Rampart walk*: path along the inner face.

RATCOURSE: projecting stringcourse on a doocot to deter rats from climbing to the flight holes.

REBATE: rectangular section cut out of a masonry edge to receive a shutter, door, window etc.

REBUS: a heraldic pun, e.g. a fiery cock for Cockburn.

REEDING: series of convex mouldings, the reverse of fluting (q.v.). Cf. Gadrooning.

RENDERING: the covering of outside walls with a uniform surface or skin for protection from the weather. *Lime-washing*: thin layer of lime plaster. *Pebbledashing*: where aggregate is thrown at the wet plastered wall for a textured effect. *Roughcast*: plaster mixed with a coarse aggregate such as gravel. *Stucco*: fine lime plaster worked to a smooth surface. *Cement rendering*: a cheaper substitute for stucco, usually with a grainy texture.

REPOUSSÉ: relief designs in metalwork, formed by beating it from the back.

REREDORTER (*lit.* behind the dormitory): latrines in a medieval religious house.

REREDOS: painted and/or sculptured screen behind and above an altar. Cf. Retable.

RESPOND: half-pier or half-column bonded into a wall and carrying one end of an arch. It usually terminates an arcade.

RETABLE: painted or carved panel standing on or at the back of an altar, usually attached to it.

RETROCHOIR: in a major church, the area between the high altar and E chapel.

REVEAL: the plane of a jamb, between the wall and the frame of a door or window.

RHONE (Scots): gutter along the eaves for rainwater: see also Conductor.

RIB-VAULT: see Vault and 2c.

RIG (Scots): a strip of ploughed land raised in the middle and sloped to a furrow on each side; early cultivation method (runrig) usually surrounded by untilled grazing land.

RINCEAU: classical ornament of leafy scrolls (4b).

RISER: vertical face of a step (6c).

ROCK-FACED: masonry cleft to produce a rugged appearance.

ROCOCO: style current between c. 1720 and c. 1760, characterized by a serpentine line and playful, scrolled decoration.

ROLL MOULDING: medieval moulding of part-circular section (1a).

ROMANESQUE: style current in the C11 and C12. In England often called Norman. See also Saxo-Norman.

ROOD: crucifix flanked by representations of the Virgin and St John, usually over the entry into the chancel, painted on the wall, on a beam (*rood beam*) or on top of a *rood screen* or pulpitum (q.v.) which often had a walkway (*rood loft*) along the top, reached by a *rood stair* in the side wall. *Hanging rood*: cross or crucifix suspended from roof.

ROOFS: For the main external shapes (hipped, gambrel etc.) see 7. *Helm* and *Saddleback*: see 1c. *Lean-to*: single sloping roof built against a vertical wall; also applied to the part of the building beneath. *Bellcast*: sloping roof slightly swept out over the eaves. Construction. See 7. *Single-framed* roof: with no main trusses. The rafters may be fixed

to the wall-plate or ridge, or longitudinal timbers may be absent altogether.
Double-framed roof: with longitudinal members, such as purlins, and usually divided into bays by principals and principal rafters.
Other types are named after their main structural components, e.g. *hammerbeam*, *crown-post* (see Elements below and 7).
Elements. *See* 7.
Ashlar piece: a short vertical timber connecting an inner wall-plate or timber pad to a rafter.
Braces: subsidiary timbers set diagonally to strengthen the frame. *Arched braces*: curved pair forming an arch, connecting wall or post below with a tie- or collar-beam above. *Passing braces*: long straight braces passing across other members of the truss. *Scissor braces*: pair crossing diagonally between pairs of rafters or principals. *Wind-braces*: short, usually curved braces connecting side purlins with principals; sometimes decorated with cusping.
Collar or *collar-beam*: horizontal transverse timber connecting a pair of rafter or cruck blades (q.v.), set between apex and the wall-plate.
Crown-post: a vertical timber set centrally on a tie-beam and supporting a collar purlin braced to it longitudinally. In an open truss lateral braces may rise to the collar-beam; in a closed truss they may descend to the tie-beam.
Hammerbeams: horizontal brackets projecting at wall-plate level like an interrupted tie-beam; the inner ends carry *hammerposts*, vertical timbers which support a purlin and are braced to a collar-beam above.
Kingpost: vertical timber set centrally on a tie-or collar-beam, rising to the apex of the roof to support a ridge piece (cf. Strut).
Plate: longitudinal timber set square to the ground. *Wall-plate*: along the top of a wall to receive the ends of rafters; cf. Purlin.
Principals: pair of inclined lateral timbers of a truss. Usually they support side purlins and mark the main bay divisions.
Purlin: horizontal longitudinal timber. *Collar purlin* or *crown plate*: central timber which carries collar-beams and is supported by crown-posts. *Side purlins*: pairs of timbers placed some way up the slope of the roof, which carry common rafters. *Butt* or *tenoned purlins* are tenoned into either side of the principals. *Through purlins* pass through or past the principal; they include *clasped purlins*, which rest on queenposts or are carried in the angle between principals and collar, and *trenched purlins* trenched into the backs of principals.
Queen-strut: paired vertical, or near-vertical, timbers placed symmetrically on a tie-beam to support side purlins.
Rafters: inclined lateral timbers supporting the roof covering. *Common rafters*: regularly spaced uniform rafters placed along the length of a roof or between principals. *Principal rafters*: rafters which also act as principals.
Ridge, ridge piece: horizontal longitudinal timber at the apex supporting the ends of the rafters.
Sprocket: short timber placed on the back and at the foot of a rafter to form projecting eaves.
Strut: vertical or oblique timber between two members of a truss, not directly supporting longitudinal timbers.
Tie-beam: main horizontal transverse timber which carries the feet of the principals at wall level.
Truss: rigid framework of timbers at bay intervals, carrying the longitudinal roof timbers which support the common rafters. *Closed truss*: with the spaces between the timbers filled, to form an internal partition.
See also Cruck, Wagon roof.
ROPE MOULDING: *see* Cable moulding.
ROSE WINDOW: circular window with tracery radiating from the centre. Cf. Wheel window.
ROTUNDA: building or room circular in plan.
ROUGHCAST: *see* Rendering.
ROUND (Scots): bartizan, usually roofless.
ROVING BRIDGE: *see* Canals.
RUBBED BRICKWORK: *see* Gauged brickwork.
RUBBLE: masonry whose stones are wholly or partly in a rough state. *Coursed*: coursed stones with rough faces. *Random*: uncoursed

stones in a random pattern. *Snecked*: with courses broken by smaller stones (snecks).

RUSTICATION: see 6d. Exaggerated treatment of masonry to give an effect of strength. The joints are usually recessed by V-section chamfering or square-section channelling (*channelled rustication*). *Banded rustication* has only the horizontal joints emphasized. The faces may be flat, but can be *diamond-faced*, like shallow pyramids, *vermiculated*, with a stylized texture like worm-casts, and *glacial* (frost-work), like icicles or stalactites.

RYBATS (Scots): *see* Margins.

SACRAMENT HOUSE: safe cupboard in a side wall of the chancel of a church and not directly associated with an altar, for reservation of the sacrament.

SACRISTY: room in a church for sacred vessels and vestments.

SADDLEBACK ROOF: *see* 1c.

SALTIRE CROSS: with diagonal limbs.

SANCTUARY: part of church at E end containing high altar. Cf. Presbytery.

SANGHA: residence of Buddhist monks or nuns.

SARCOPHAGUS: coffin of stone or other durable material.

SARKING (Scots): boards laid on the rafters to support the roof covering.

SAXO-NORMAN: transitional Romanesque style combining Anglo-Saxon and Norman features, current *c.* 1060–1100.

SCAGLIOLA: composition imitating marble.

SCALE-AND-PLATT (*lit.* stair and landing): *see* Stair and 6c.

SCALLOPED CAPITAL: *see* 1a.

SCARCEMENT: extra thickness of the lower part of a wall, e.g. to carry a floor.

SCARP: artificial cutting away of the ground to form a steep slope.

SCOTIA: a hollow classical moulding, especially between tori (q.v.) on a column base (3b, 3f).

SCREEN: in a medieval church, usually at the entry to the chancel; see Rood (screen) and Pulpitum. A *parclose screen* separates a chapel from the rest of the church.

SCREENS or SCREENS PASSAGE: screened-off entrance passage between great hall and service rooms or between the hall of a tower house and the stair.

SCRIBE (Scots): to cut and mark timber against an irregular stone or plaster surface.

SCUNTION (Scots): reveal.

SECTION: two-dimensional representation of a building, moulding etc., revealed by cutting across it.

SEDILIA (singular: sedile): seats for clergy (usually for a priest, deacon and sub-deacon) on the S side of the chancel.

SEPTUM: dwarf wall between the nave and choir.

SESSION HOUSE (Scots): a room or separate building for meetings of the minister and elders who form a kirk session. Also a shelter by the church or churchyard entrance for an elder collecting for poor relief, built at expense of kirk session.

SET-OFF: *see* Weathering.

SGRAFFITO: decoration scratched, often in plaster, to reveal a pattern in another colour beneath. *Graffiti*: scratched drawing or writing.

SHAFT: vertical member of round or polygonal section (1a, 3a). *Shaft-ring*: at the junction of shafts set *en délit* (q.v.) or attached to a pier or wall (1a).

SHEILA-NA-GIG: female fertility figure, usually with legs apart.

SHELL: thin, self-supporting roofing membrane of timber or concrete.

SHEUGH (Scots): a trench or open drain; a street gutter.

SHOULDERED ARCH: *see* 5a.

SHOULDERED ARCHITRAVE: *see* 4b.

SHUTTERING: *see* Concrete.

SILL: horizontal member at the bottom of a window-or doorframe; or at the base of a timber-framed wall into which posts and studs are tenoned.

SKEW (Scots): sloping or shaped stones finishing a gable upstanding from the roof. *Skewputt*: bracket at the bottom end of a skew. *See* 7.

SLAB BLOCK: *see* Multi-storey.

SLATE-HANGING: covering of overlapping slates on a wall. *Tile-hanging* is similar.

SLYPE: covered way or passage leading E from the cloisters between transept and chapter house.

GLOSSARY

SNECKED: see Rubble.

SOFFIT (*lit.* ceiling): underside of an arch (also called *intrados*), lintel etc. *Soffit roll*: medieval roll moulding on a soffit.

SOLAR: private upper chamber in a medieval house, accessible from the high end of the great hall.

SOPRAPORTA: see Overdoor.

SOUNDING-BOARD: see Tester.

SOUTERRAIN: underground stone-lined passage and chamber.

SPANDRELS: roughly triangular spaces between an arch and its containing rectangle, or between adjacent arches (5c). Also non-structural panels under the windows in a curtain-walled building.

SPERE: a fixed structure screening the lower end of the great hall from the screens passage. *Speretruss*: roof truss incorporated in the spere.

SPIRE: tall pyramidal or conical feature crowning a tower or turret. *Broach*: starting from a square base, then carried into an octagonal section by means of triangular faces; *splayed-foot*: a variation of the broach form, found principally in the south-east of England, in which the four cardinal faces are splayed out near their base, to cover the corners, while oblique (or intermediate) faces taper away to a point (1c). *Needle spire*: thin spire rising from the centre of a tower roof, well inside the parapet: when of timber and lead often called a *spike*.

SPIRELET: see Flèche.

SPLAY: of an opening when it is wider on one face of a wall than the other.

SPRING OR SPRINGING: level at which an arch or vault rises from its supports. *Springers*: the first stones of an arch or vaulting-rib above the spring (2c).

SQUINCH: arch or series of arches thrown across an interior angle of a square or rectangular structure to support a circular or polygonal superstructure, especially a dome or spire (5a).

SQUINT: an aperture in a wall or through a pier, usually to allow a view of an altar.

STAIRS: see 6c. *Dog-leg stair* or (Scots) *Scale-and-platt stair*: parallel flights rising alternately in opposite directions, without an open well. *Flying stair*: cantilevered from the walls of a stairwell, without newels; sometimes called a *geometric* stair when the inner edge describes a curve. *Turnpike* or *newel stair*: ascending round a central supporting newel (8b); also called a *spiral stair* or *vice* when in a circular shaft, a *winder* when in a rectangular compartment. (Winder also applies to the steps on the turn.) *Well stair*: with flights round a square open well framed by newel posts. *See also* Perron.

STAIR TOWER: full-height projection from a main block (especially of a tower house) containing the principal stair from the ground floor (8a).

STAIR TURRET: turret corbelled out from above ground level and containing a stair from one of the upper floors of a building, especially a tower house (8a).

STALL: fixed seat in the choir or chancel for the clergy or choir (cf. Pew). Usually with arm rests, and often framed together.

STANCHION: upright structural member, of iron, steel or reinforced concrete.

STANDPIPE TOWER: see Manometer.

STEADING (Scots): farm building or buildings; generally used for the principal group of buildings on a farm.

STEAM ENGINES: *Atmospheric*: worked by the vacuum created when low-pressure steam is condensed in the cylinder, as developed by Thomas Newcomen. *Beam engine*: with a large pivoted beam moved in an oscillating fashion by the piston. It may drive a flywheel or be *non-rotative*. *Watt* and *Cornish*: single-cylinder; *compound*: two cylinders; *triple expansion*: three cylinders.

STEEPLE: tower together with a spire, lantern or belfry.

STIFFLEAF: type of E.E. foliage decoration. *Stiffleaf capital*: see 1b.

STOP: plain or decorated terminal to mouldings or chamfers, or at the end of hoodmoulds and labels (*label stop*), or stringcourses (5b, 6a); *see also* Headstop.

STOUP: vessel for holy water, usually near a door.

GLOSSARY

STRAINER: see Arch.

STRAPWORK: decoration like interlaced leather straps, late C16 and C17 in origin.

STRETCHER: see Bond and 6e.

STRING: see 6c. Sloping member holding the ends of the treads and risers of a staircase. *Closed string*: a broad string covering the ends of the treads and risers. *Open string*: cut into the shape of the treads and risers.

STRINGCOURSE: horizontal course or moulding projecting from the surface of a wall (6d).

STUCCO: decorative plasterwork. See also Rendering.

STUDS: subsidiary vertical timbers of a timber-framed wall or partition.

STUGGED (Scots): of masonry hacked or picked as a key for rendering; used as a surface finish in the C19.

STUPA: Buddhist shrine, circular in plan.

STYLOBATE: top of the solid platform on which a colonnade stands (3a).

SUSPENSION BRIDGE: see Bridge.

SWAG: like a festoon (q.v.), but representing cloth.

SYSTEM BUILDING: see Industrialized building.

TABERNACLE: safe cupboard above an altar to contain the reserved sacrament or a relic; or architectural frame for an image or statue.

TABLE STONE or TABLE TOMB: memorial slab raised on freestanding legs.

TAS-DE-CHARGE: the lower courses of a vault or arch which are laid horizontally (2c).

TENEMENT: holding of land, but also applied to a purpose-built flatted block.

TERM: pedestal or pilaster tapering downward, usually with the upper part of a human figure growing out of it.

TERRACOTTA: moulded and fired clay ornament or cladding.

TERREPLEIN: in a fort the level surface of a rampart behind a parapet for mounting guns.

TESSELLATED PAVEMENT: mosaic flooring, particularly Roman, made of *tesserae*, i.e. cubes of glass, stone or brick.

TESTER: flat canopy over a tomb or pulpit, where it is also called a *sounding-board*.

TESTER TOMB: tomb-chest with effigies beneath a tester, either freestanding (tester with four or more columns), or attached to a wall (*half-tester*) with columns on one side only.

TETRASTYLE: see Portico.

THERMAL WINDOW: see Diocletian window.

THREE-DECKER PULPIT: see Pulpit.

TIDAL GATES: see Canals.

TIE-BEAM: see Roofs and 7.

TIERCERON: see Vault and 2c.

TIFTING (Scots): mortar bed for verge slates laid over gable skew.

TILE-HANGING: see Slate-hanging.

TIMBER-FRAMING: method of construction where the structural frame is built of interlocking timbers. The spaces are filled with non-structural material, e.g. *infill* of wattle and daub, lath and plaster, brickwork (known as *nogging*) etc., and may be covered by plaster, weatherboarding (q.v.) or tiles.

TOLBOOTH (Scots; *lit.* tax booth): burgh council building containing council chamber and prison.

TOMB-CHEST: chest-shaped tomb, usually of stone. Cf. Table tomb, Tester tomb.

TORUS (plural: tori): large convex moulding, usually used on a column base (3b, 3f).

TOUCH: soft black marble quarried near Tournai.

TOURELLE: turret corbelled out from the wall (8a).

TOWER BLOCK: see Multi-storey.

TOWER HOUSE (Scots): for elements and forms see 8a, 8b. Compact fortified house with the main hall raised above the ground and at least one more storey above it. A medieval Scots type continuing well into the C17 in its modified forms: *L-plan* with a jamb at one corner; *Z-plan* with a jamb at each diagonally opposite corner.

TRABEATED: dependent structurally on the use of the post and lintel. Cf. Arcuated.

TRACERY: openwork pattern of masonry or timber in the upper part of an opening. *Blind* tracery is tracery applied to a solid wall.

Plate tracery, introduced c. 1200, is the earliest form, in which shapes are cut through solid masonry (2a).

Bar tracery was introduced into England *c.* 1250. The pattern is formed by intersecting moulded ribwork continued from the mullions. It was especially elaborate during the Decorated period (q.v.). Tracery shapes can include circles, *daggers* (elongated ogee-ended lozenges), *mouchettes* (like daggers but with curved sides) and upright rectangular *panels*. They often have *cusps*, projecting points defining lobes or *foils* (q.v.) within the main shape: *Kentish* or *split-cusps* are forked.

Types of bar tracery (*see* 2b) include *geometric(al)*: *c.* 1250–1310, chiefly circles, often foiled; *Y-tracery*: *c.* 1300, with mullions branching into a Y-shape; *intersecting*: *c.* 1300, formed by interlocking mullions; *reticulated*: early C14, net-like pattern of ogee-ended lozenges; *curvilinear*: C14, with uninterrupted flowing curves; *loop*: *c.* 1500–45, with large uncusped loop-like forms; *panel*: Perp, with straight-sided panels, often cusped at the top and bottom.

TRANSE (Scots): passage.

TRANSEPT: transverse portion of a cruciform church.

TRANSITIONAL: generally used for the phase between Romanesque and Early English (*c.* 1175–*c.* 1200).

TRANSOM: horizontal member separating window lights (2b).

TREAD: horizontal part of a step. The *tread end* may be carved on a staircase (6c).

TREFOIL: *see* Foil.

TRIFORIUM: middle storey of a church treated as an arcaded wall passage or blind arcade, its height corresponding to that of the aisle roof.

TRIGLYPHS (*lit.* three-grooved tablets): stylized beam-ends in the Doric frieze, with metopes between (3b).

TRIUMPHAL ARCH: influential type of Imperial Roman monument.

TROPHY: sculptured or painted group of arms or armour.

TRUMEAU: central stone mullion supporting the tympanum of a wide doorway. *Trumeau figure*: carved figure attached to it (cf. Column figure).

TRUMPET CAPITAL: *see* 1b.

TRUSS: braced framework, spanning between supports. *See also* Roofs.

TUMBLING or TUMBLING-IN: courses of brickwork laid at right angles to a slope, e.g. of a gable, forming triangles by tapering into horizontal courses.

TURNPIKE: *see* Stairs.

TUSCAN: *see* Orders and 3e.

TUSKING STONES (Scots): projecting end stones for bonding with an adjoining wall.

TWO-DECKER PULPIT: *see* Pulpit.

TYMPANUM: the surface between a lintel and the arch above it or within a pediment (4a).

UNDERCROFT: usually describes the vaulted room(s) beneath the main room(s) of a medieval house. Cf. Crypt.

UNIVALLATE: of a hillfort: defended by a single bank and ditch.

VAULT: arched stone roof (sometimes imitated in timber or plaster). For types *see* 2c.

Tunnel or *barrel vault*: continuous semicircular or pointed arch, often of rubble masonry.

Groin vault: tunnel vaults intersecting at right angles. *Groins* are the curved lines of the intersections.

Rib vault: masonry framework of intersecting arches (ribs) supporting *vault cells*, used in Gothic architecture. *Wall rib* or *wall arch*: between wall and vault cell. *Transverse rib*: spans between two walls to divide a vault into bays. *Quadripartite* rib vault: each bay has two pairs of diagonal ribs dividing the vault into four triangular cells. *Sexpartite* rib vault: most often used over paired bays, has an extra pair of ribs springing from between the bays. More elaborate vaults may include *ridge-ribs* along the crown of a vault or bisecting the bays; *tiercerons*: extra decorative ribs springing from the corners of a bay; and *liernes*: short decorative ribs in the crown of a vault, not linked to any springing point. A *stellar* or *star* vault has liernes in star formation.

Fan vault: form of barrel vault used in the Perp period, made up of halved concave masonry cones decorated with blind tracery.

VAULTING-SHAFT: shaft leading up to the spring or springing (q.v.) of a vault (2c).

VENETIAN or SERLIAN WINDOW: derived from Serlio (4b). The motif is used for other openings.

VERMICULATION: see Rustication and 6d.

VESICA: oval with pointed ends.

VICE: see Stair.

VILLA: originally a Roman country house or farm. The term was revived in England in the C18 under the influence of Palladio and used especially for smaller, compact country houses. In the later C19 it was debased to describe any suburban house.

VITRIFIED: bricks or tiles fired to a darkened glassy surface. *Vitrified fort*: built of timber-laced masonry, the timber having later been set on fire with consequent vitrification of the stonework.

VITRUVIAN SCROLL: classical running ornament of curly waves (4b).

VOLUTES: spiral scrolls. They occur on Ionic capitals (3c). *Angle volute*: pair of volutes, turned outwards to meet at the corner of a capital.

VOUSSOIRS: wedge-shaped stones forming an arch (5c).

WAGON ROOF: with the appearance of the inside of a wagon tilt; often ceiled. Also called *cradle roof*.

WAINSCOT: see Panelling.

WALLED GARDEN: in C18 and C19 Scotland, combined vegetable and flower garden, sometimes well away from the house.

WALLHEAD: straight top of a wall. *Wallhead chimney*: chimney rising from a wallhead (8a). *Wallhead gable*: gable rising from a wallhead.

WALL MONUMENT: attached to the wall and often standing on the floor. *Wall tablets* are smaller with the inscription as the major element.

WALL-PLATE: see Roofs and 7.

WALL-WALK: see Parapet.

WARMING ROOM: room in a religious house where a fire burned for comfort.

WATERHOLDING BASE: early Gothic base with upper and lower mouldings separated by a deep hollow.

WATERLEAF: see Enrichments and 3f.

WATERLEAF CAPITAL: Late Romanesque and Transitional type of capital (1b).

WATER WHEELS: described by the way water is fed on to the wheel. *Breastshot*: mid-height, falling and passing beneath. *Overshot*: over the top. *Pitchback*: on the top but falling backwards. *Undershot*: turned by the momentum of the water passing beneath. In a *water turbine*, water is fed under pressure through a vaned wheel within a casing.

WEALDEN HOUSE: type of medieval timber-framed house with a central open hall flanked by bays of two storeys, roofed in line; the end bays are jettied to the front, but the eaves are continuous.

WEATHERBOARDING: wall cladding of overlapping horizontal boards.

WEATHERING: or SET-OFF: inclined, projecting surface to keep water away from the wall below.

WEEPERS: figures in niches along the sides of some medieval tombs. Also called *mourners*.

WHEEL HOUSE: Late Iron Age circular stone dwelling; inside, partition walls radiating from the central hearth like wheel spokes.

WHEEL WINDOW: circular, with radiating shafts like spokes. Cf. Rose window.

WROUGHT IRON: see Cast iron.

WYND (Scots): subsidiary street or lane, often running into a main street or gait (q.v.).

YETT (Scots, *lit.* gate): hinged openwork gate at a main doorway, made of iron bars alternately penetrating and penetrated (8c).

Z-PLAN: see Tower house and 8b.

INDEX OF ARCHITECTS AND ARTISTS

Entries for partnerships and group practices are listed after entries for a single surname. Minor differences in title are disregarded.

Abbey Studio (glass-stainers), 167, 256, 293, 393, 443
Abbot & Smith (organ builders), 197
Abercrombie, W. H. (smith), 721
Adam, John (mason in Buchanan, fl. 1736), 148
Adam, John (of Blair Adam, 1721–92), 89, 203, 205, 206
Adam, Matthew (b. 1876), 116, 396
Adam, R. & J. (Robert Adam, q.v.; James Adam, 1730–94), 77, 391
Adam, Robert (1728–92), 101, 477, Pl. 105
Adam & Small (glass-stainers: Stephen Adam, q.v.; David Small, 1846–1927), 583
Adam, Stephen (glass-stainer, 1848–1910), 151, 447, 509
Adam (Stephen) & Co. (Stephen Adam, q.v.), 456
Adam (Stephen) & Son (glass-stainers: Stephen Adam, q.v.; Stephen Adam Jun., 1873–1960), 581
Adam, William (1689–1748), 55, 75, 93, 137, 147, 203, 497–9, 717, 719, 726–7, Pl. 95
Aiken, Emma Butler-Cole (glass-stainer), 509
Albion Foundry (founders), 295
Alexander, George, 114, 618, 630
Alexander, James (painter, fl. 1660–97), 493
Alexander, William (1841–1904), 109, 609
Alexandre Ltd. Architects' Department, 621
Alison & Hutchison & Partners, 661
Allan & Friskin (W. Allan, d. 1945; William Wallace Friskin, b. 1889), 193
Allan-Fraser, Patrick (1813–90), 83, 200
Allardice & Napier (sculptors), 430
Allison, A. Watt, 119, 198, 296, 372, 478, 556, 560, 611, 662, 700
Anderson, Adam (d. 1846), 130, 131, 602
Anderson Christie (Karen Anderson; David Christie; Adam Bell), 119, 168

Anderson, James (carver, fl. 1686), 487
Anderson, James (wright, fl. 1782), 526
Anderson, Simon & Crawford (Sir Robert Rowand Anderson, 1834–1921; Frank Lewis Worthington Simon, 1862–1933; Alexander Hunter Crawford, 1865–1945), 714
Anderson, William (sculptor, fl. 1845–65), 617
Angus, George (1792–1845), 43, 392, 475
Angus, Raymond, 191
Annan & Imrie (plasterers), 461
Annan (James) & Sons (plasterers), 190
Annand, David Andrew (sculptor, b. 1948), 62, 198, 621, 640
Arkwright, Sir Richard (engineer, 1732–92), 702, Pl. 125
Arrol's Bridge & Roof Co. Ltd., 372
Arrol (William) & Co. (engineers), 95
Arrol (Sir William) & Co. (engineers), 278
Arthur (George) & Son (John Maurice Arthur, 1877–1954), 210
Artios C.S. (glass-stainers), 585
Atholl, Anne Home Drummond, Duchess of (d. 1897), 112, 180
Atholl, John George Murray, 8th Duke of (1871–1942), 210
Atkins, R., 641
Atkins (W. S.) Health Care Ltd., 296
Atkinson, William (c. 1773–1839), 55, 80, 81, 88, 609n., 680, 690, 694–5, 717–20, 726, 728–30, Pls. 79–80, 85
Babtie, Shaw & Morton (engineers), 130, 245, 412
Bachop, John (mason), 442
Bachop, Tobias (mason, d. 1710), 483, 489
Baird (John) & James Thomson (James Thomson, 1835–1905), 193
Baker, William (1705–87), 55
Baldie, Robert (fl. 1862–91), 476
Ballantine (A.) & Gardiner (glass-stainers, 1892–1905: Alexander Ballantine, d. 1906), 54, 202, 350, 447–8, 513, 581, 601

INDEX OF ARCHITECTS AND ARTISTS

Ballantine (A.) & Son (glass-stainers, 1905–18: Alexander Ballantine, d. 1906; James Ballantine II, q.v.), 54, 151, 348, 350, 669
Ballantine & Allan (glass-stainers, 1828–60: James Ballantine, 1808–77; George Allan), 53, 552
Ballantine Bo'ness Iron Co. (founders), 594
Ballantine, James, II (glass-stainer, 1878–1940), 283, 313, 476, 581, 651
Ballantine (James) & Son (glass-stainers, 1860–92: James Ballantine, 1808–77; Alexander Ballantine, d. 1906), 54, 198, 343, 363, 447, 604
Ballingal, James (fl. 1791–1801), 142, 449
Ballingall (fl. 1829), 142
Ballingall, James (fl. 1839–47), 190, 191
Bardwell, Thomas (artist, 1704–67?), 221
Barry, Sir Charles (1795–1860), 319, 325
Baxter, Clark & Paul, 533
Baxter, John, Jun. (d. 1798), 93, 444
Beaton, Alexander K. (1874–1954), 100, 622, 623, 634
Beaton, Peter Campbell McIntyre, 277
Beattie, Thomas (sculptor, fl. 1889), 671
Beattie, Thomas (plasterer and modeller, c. 1861–1938), 86, 183, 541
Beckett, Sir Martyn Gervase (1918–2001), 422
Bell & Cameron (William Bell, q.v.; Rhoderic Cameron, 1860–1928), 136, 140, 180
Bell, H. J., 459
Bell-Ingram, 620
Bell Ingram Design, 390, 602
Bell, John (wright, fl. 1788), 534
Bell, John (fl. 1833–5), 112, 511
Bell, John, Jun. (fl. 1833), 558
Bell, Robert Anning (glass-stainer, 1863–1933), 228, 255, 677, 684
Bell, William (engineer and architect, 1856–1914), 110, 116, 137, 138, 281, 672
Bernasconi, Francis (plasterer, 1762–1841), 721, 723–4, Pls. 84, 88
Bett-Bison, 119, 661
Bett (Bison), 615
Beveridge, D. (marble cutter), 293
Beveridge (David) & Son (sculptors), 199, 613, 622, 623, 660
Beveridge, John (builder-architect), 530
Beveridge, Thomas (wright), 534
Bevington & Sons (organ builders: Lewis H. Bevington, c. 1859–1938), 341

Black (architect at Harviestoun, fl. 1805), 304
Black, James (d. 1841), 304
Black, William (decorator), 498
Blackadder, John (carver), 190; see also Trotter, The Heirs of William
Blanc, Hippolyte Jean (1844–1917), 52, 149, 428, 583
Blockley, Goodwin & Warner, 389
Blore, Edward (1787–1879), 713
Blyth, B. & E. (engineers: Benjamin Hall Blyth I, 1819–66; Edward L. I. Blyth), 611
Blyth, John W. (glass-stainer), 152, 456, 651
Blyth & Westland (engineers: Benjamin Hall Blyth II, 1849–1917; David Monro Westland, 1845–1926), 95, 98, 610, 611
Bone, Phyllis Mary (sculptor, 1896–1972), 575
Bonnar, Thomas, Jun. (decorator, d. 1899), 724
Bose, Fanindra Nath (sculptor, d. 1926), 580–1
Boswell, Mitchell & Johnston (Peter Mitchell; Ninian Rutherford Jamieson Johnston, 1912–90; Frank Campbell; Scott Noble; Eric Hardgreave), 119, 421, 661
Bowie, Alexander (builder), 349
Boys, Peter Paul (carver), 484
Braid, James (golf course designer, 1870–1950), 396
Breadalbane, Alma Imogen Leonora Carlotta Graham, Countess (later Marchioness) of (1854–1932), 444
Breadalbane, John Campbell, 4th Earl (later 1st Marquess) of (1762–1834), 728
Brewster, Lee (sculptor), 62, 640
Bridgeman (sculptor), 208
British Railways Board's Architects Office, 611
Brodie, William (sculptor, 1815–81), 61, 613, 683
Bromsgrove Guild (plasterers), 410
Brooks (Joseph) & Co. (organ builders), 431
Brough, William (mason), 654
Brown Bros. (cabinet makers), 348
Brown Construction, 453
Brown, Kellock (sculptor, 1856–1934), 153
Brown, Patrick (mason at Dryburgh, fl. 1798), 459
Brown, Patrick, Sen. (mason, fl. 1794), 457
Brown, Patrick, Jun. (mason-architect, fl. 1794), 457, Pl. 97
Brown, Peter (builder), 446
Brown, Thomas (of Uphall, d. 1833), 104, 206, 477

INDEX OF ARCHITECTS AND ARTISTS

Brown, Thomas, Jun. (d. c. 1872), 110, 607–8
Brown & Wardrop (Thomas Brown Jun., q.v.; James Maitland Wardrop, 1824–82), 745
Browne, Sir George Washington (1853–1939), 401
Bruce (John) & Son (John Bruce; James Prain Bruce, 1860–1935; Alexander Ness), 522, 672
Bruce, Sir William (c. 1630–1710), 74–5, 87, 477, 483–93, Pls. 69–72
Bryce, D. & J. (John Bryce, d. 1922), 83, 175, 215, 223
Bryce, David (1803–76), 51, 83, 84, 152, 204–5, 209, 212–4, 220, 223, 306, 308, 438–9, 523–5, 688, 698, Pl. 89
Bryceson, Son & Ellis (organ builders), 587
Bryson, William (modeller), 462
Buchan, James (mason), 378
Buckeridge, Charles (c. 1832–73), 51, 669
Building Design Centre, 191
Building Design Partnership, 120, 605, Pl. 122
Buist, Henry (surveyor), 567
Burke (Ian) Associates, 641
Burlison & Grylls (glass-stainers: John Burlison, 1843–91; Thomas John Grylls, 1845–1913; Thomas Henry Grylls, 1873–1953), 54, 341, 592
Burn, Robert (1752–1815), 433, 534
Burn, William (1789–1870), 43, 82, 84, 86, 107, 111, 123, 134, 173–4, 175–6, 189, 244, 263–4, 331, 355, 356, 367, 512, 594, 650, 651, 667, 713, 715, 731, Pl. 60
Burne-Jones, Sir Edward Coley (artist, 1833–98), 198, 277–8, 539
Burnet, Sir John James (1857–1938), 84, 173–5
Burnet (John), Son & Campbell (John Burnet, 1814–1901; Sir John James Burnet, q.v.; John Archibald Campbell, 1859–1909), 173, 175
Burnett (Watson) Design Partnership (Watson Burnett), 253
Burns Architects, 636
Butler, Vincent (sculptor, b.1933), 60, 511
Butterfield, William (1814–1900), 51, 54, 588–92, Pl. 46
Cairns & Barlass, 370
Caitcheon, John (carver), 220
Caledonian Railway Divisional Engineer's Office, 396–7, 625
Callander, John (smith), 487
Cameron, Duncan (d. 1899), 115, 138
Camm & Co. (glass-stainers: Thomas William Camm; C. H. D. Camm; Florence Camm, 1874–1960; James F. P. Camm, fl. 1892–1902), 293

Camm, Walter Herbert (glass-stainer, b. 1881), 86, 183
Campbell, Duncan (smith), 556
Carmichael, Holme (sculptor), 152
Carnegie & Son (sculptors), 429
Carrick, Alexander (sculptor, 1882–1966), 60, 232, 543
Carron Ironworks (founders), 204
Carter, Thomas (sculptor, d. 1756), 219, 221–2, Pl. 76
Carvell & Partners, 53, 663
Carver, John (1834–96), 47, 113, 152, 196, 229, 282, 446–7, 464, 516, 521, 522
Carver, John, Sen. (d. 1858), 85, 152, 177, 196
Cattanach, Alexander, Jun.(c. 1896–1977), 120, 627
Cattle, James, 326
Chalmers, Peter Macgregor (1859–1922), 48, 245, 363, 443, 473
Chatterton, R., 621
Cheere, John (sculptor, 1709–87), 223–4
Chessels, Archibald (wright), 215, 218, Pl. 75
Chilton, Margaret Isabel (glass-stainer, 1875–1962), 54, 151, 208, 509, 581
Christie, Alexander (artist, 1807–60), 549, 552
Church of Jesus Christ of Latter Day Saints Church Building Department (The), 660
City Glass Co. (glass-stainers), 272
Clark, Thomas (mason), 427
Clayton & Bell (glass-stainers: John Richard Clayton, 1824–1913; Alfred Bell, 1832–95; John Clement Bell, 1860–1944; Reginald Otto Bell, 1864–1950), 54, 152, 208, 284, 476, 509, 669
Clayton, Thomas (plasterer, fl. 1710–60), 75–6, 215, 218, 220–2, 395, Pls. 74–7
Clifford (H. E.) & Lunan (Henry Edward Clifford, 1852–1932; Thomas Melville Lunan, b. 1878), 109, 604
Clow, W. & A. (carvers: William Clow, 1851–1935; Alexander Clow, 1861–1946), 578–80
Coade & Sealy (marble cutters: Eleanor Coade, 1742–1821; John Sealy, d. 1813), 209, 725
Cochran (sculptors), 732
Cochrane Bros. (sculptors), 626
Cockburn, D. B., 120, 646
Cocker, Douglas (sculptor, b. 1945), 62, 625
Cole, E. (sculptor), 56, 256
Collins, E. V., 121, 628, 656

INDEX OF ARCHITECTS AND ARTISTS

Colt, Maximilian (sculptor, fl. 1600–18), 57, 695, Pl. 25
Comb, Alexander (wright), 372
Common Services Agency, 296
Comper, Sir John Ninian (1864–1960), 52, 54, 388, 591, 669, Pls. 46–7
Compton (John) Ltd. (organ builders: John Hayward Compton, 1876–1957), 509
Comrie, Peter (wright), 280
Conacher & Co. (organ builders), 580, 592
Cooper, William (glass-stainer), 726
Cottier, Daniel (glass-stainer, 1839–91), 118, 172, 726
Cousin & Gale (David Cousin, 1808–78; William Gale, d. 1858), 165
Cox & Buckley (church furnishers), 391
Cox & Sons (church furnishers), 284
Crace (Frederick) & Son (decorators: Frederick Crace, 1779–1859; John Gregory Crace, 1809–89), 722–7, Pls. 87–8
Cramb & Beveridge (sculptors), 391
Crawford, John (carver), 601
Crichton, Richard (?1771–1817), 77, 81, 367, 381, 497–8
Crombie, David Alexander (b. 1858), 669
Cross, John (wright), 146
Crouch & Hogg (engineers: William Crouch, 1840–1921; Charles Pullar Hogg, 1848–1927; Liston Carnie; Donal Mackenzie Hamilton; Thomas Todd; William Murray Cormie; Alexander Leslie), 647, 654, 685
Cullen (Alexander), Lochead & Brown (James Lochead, 1870–1942; William Brown, b. 1873), 625
Cumming, Andrew (fl. 1831–4), 697, 698, Pl. 30
Cumming, Andrew (fl. 1868), 479
Cunningham Glass Partnership, 120, 627, 638
Currey, Ada (artist, 1852–1913), 168
Dalgetty, Ian Roger, 151
Darling, Kenneth, 375
Davies (D.Y.) Associates, 615, 659
Davis Duncan Architects (Ray Davis; Greg Duncan; Calum MacCalman; Grant Robertson), 678
Davis, Louis (glass-stainer, 1861–1941), 54, 581
Davison, Thomas (mason), 268
Dawson, William (builder-architect), 732
Dean, Marcus, 269
Dearle, John Henry (artist and glass-stainer, 1860–1932), 539
Deas, Francis William (1862–1951), 368, 462–3

Denholm (James) Associates, 303
Denholm (James) Partnership, 278
Dent (E.) & Co. (clockmakers), 577
Derby, Charlotte de la Trémouille, Countess of (d. 1663), 219
Deuchars, Louis (sculptor, 1871–1927), 183
Devon Iron Co. (founders), 729
Dewar, James (builder), 523
Dick, John (sculptor), 343
Dickson, R. & R. (Richard Dickson, 1792–1857; Robert Dickson, c. 1794–1865), 45, 81, 112, 117, 133, 210, 343, 529, 555, Pl. 100
Didmann, D. H. (glass-stainer), 654
Doig, Charles Chree (1855–1918), 129, 141, Pl. 124
Donaldson & Burns (sculptors: William Donaldson, 1882–c. 1945; James Burns, 1888–1957), 575–6, 580
Donaldson, John, 202
Donaldson, P. R., 282
Donaldson, William (mason), 735
Donechy, T. J. (engineer), 256
Douglas, Campbell (1828–1910), 670
Douglas (Campbell) & Morrison (Campbell Douglas, q.v.; Alexander Barr Morrison, 1857–1937), 109, 612
Douglas, John (mason-architect, d. c. 1778), 75, 76, 155, 212, 218, 548, Pl. 73
Douglas, John (fl. 1851), 327
Dow (John S.) & Mills (Peter Ramsay Mills), 558
Dow, Thomas Millie (artist, 1848–1919), 256
Drummond, John Murray (artist, 1803–89), 54, 363
Duncan, Alexander, 196, 545, 547
Duncan, Robert, 111
Dundee Foundry Co. (founders), 602
Dunn & Findlay (James Bow Dunn, q.v.; James Leslie Findlay, 1868–1952), 118, 637, 654
Dunn, James Bow (1861–1930), 85, 403
Dunn (W.) & R. Watson (William Dunn, 1859–1934; Robert Watson, 1865–1916), 48, 49, 85, 115, 334, 341, 373, 374, 375, 404
Duthie, A. C., 506
Earp, Thomas (sculptor), 653
Edmonstone, A. F. (organ builder), 168, 226, 341, 372, 580, 592
Edward, Alexander (1651–1708), 57, 342, Pl. 27
Edward, Charles (1816–90), 681
Edward & Robertson (Charles Edward, q.v.; Thomas Saunders Robertson, q.v.), 111, 145, 680–1
Eginton, William Raphael (glass-stainer, 1778–1834), 725

INDEX OF ARCHITECTS AND ARTISTS

Electric Organ Co. (organ builders), 648
Eley, T. H., 671
Elliot, Archibald (1760–1823), 42, 79, 91, 206, 313, 334, 338, 347, 717–9, 721–2, 724, Pls. 85, 87
Elliot, James (1770–1810), 79, 717–9, 721–2, 724, Pls. 85, 87
Elliot, Thomas (organ builder, c. 1759–1832), 692
Evans & Barr Ltd. (organ builders), 268
Ewan, Robert (1828–1917), 116, 147, 279, 290, 296, 302
Ewing, Charles Turnbull (1880–1953), 280
Ewing, George Turnbull (1852–1925), 113, 253, 276, 277, 278, 280, 292, 300, 320, 323, 513, 684, Pl. 43
Faed, Thomas (artist, 1826–1900), 552, Pl. 42
Faichney, John (mason), 425
Fairley, James Graham (1846–1934), 698
Fairlie, Reginald Francis Joseph (1883–1952), 53, 60, 196, 197, 232, 399, 456, 543, 627
Falconer, L. & J. (Lake Falconer Sen., q.v.; James G. Falconer), 229, 253, 495, 699
Falconer, Lake, Sen. (d. 1922), 111, 227, 228, 233, 241, 371, 495
Falconer, Thomas (builder), 481
Farmer & Brindley (sculptors), 429, 430
Farquharson, Francis, 670
Farrelly, Martin (glass-stainer), 348
Faulkner Browns, 119, 663, Pl. 121
Fenton, David (mason), 147
Ferguson, Peter S., 389; see also Spence (Basil) & Partners
Ferguson, Robert (mason), 159
Fergusson, John (builder), 209
Fergusson, John Duncan (sculptor, 1874–1961), 62, 602
Fielding, William (artist), 274
Fife, James (builder), 272
Findlay (Alexander) & Co. (founders), 611
Findlay, James (d. 1943), 146, 511
Finlayson & Campbell, 378
Finlayson, William (b. 1865), 292
Fleming, John (mason), 227
Fletcher Joseph (James A. MacFadyen; Robert J. Adams), 660
Flockart, James (mason), 480
Foley, John Henry (sculptor, 1818–74), 311
Forbes, James (builder-architect), 698
Forfar, Alexander (builder-architect), 531
Forfar, Robert (wright), 534
Forster & Andrews (organ builders: James Alderson Forster, c. 1818–86; Joseph King Andrews, c. 1820–96), 197
Forsyth, Fiona (artist), 348
Forsyth & Maule (William Adam Forsyth, 1872–1951; Hugh Patrick Guarin Maule, 1873–1940), 473
Frame (Thomas) & Son (Adam Frame, d. 1901), 393
Frampton, Sir George James (sculptor, 1860–1928), 58, 592, Pl. 51
Fraser, Gray Contracts, 637
Frazer, John (builder), 349
Freebairn, Charles, 102, 425, Pl. 106
Freeman, Fox & Partners (engineers), 95, 651
Freeman & Ogilvy (Percy Benjamin Frank Freeman, b. 1859; Gilbert Francis Molyneux Ogilvy, 1868–1953), 430
Friskin, William W. (b. 1889), 476; see also Allan & Friskin
Gaffin, Thomas (sculptor), 350
Gaia Architects, 136
Galbraith, William Robert (engineer, 1829–94), 98, 133
Gamley, Henry Snell (sculptor, 1865–1928), 61, 441
Gauldie, William (1876–1945), 432
Ghein, Peter van den (bell founder), 582
Gibb (Sir Alexander) & Partners (engineers: Alistair Gibb; Michael Gibb; J. Guthrie Brown; Stewart Salmond), 95, 130, 671, Pl. 126
Gibb Bros. (sculptors), 742
Gibbs, Alexander (glass-stainer, 1832–86), 54, 198, 592, Pl. 49
Gibbs, Charles Alexander (glass-stainer, 1825–77), 54, 198, 592
Gibson, Frederick, 270
Gibson, W. L. (engineer), 243
Gilfillan, Alexander (glass-stainer, fl. 1951–76), 559, 588
Gillespie, J. M., 661
Gillespie, James (1777–1855) see Graham, James Gillespie
Gillespie (James) & Scott (James Scott, 1861–1944; Michael Scott), 312, 714
Gillespie, Kidd & Coia (Jack (J. Antonio) Coia, 1898–1981; Andy MacMillan, b. 1928; Isi Metzstein, b. 1928), 53, 452
Gillett & Johnston Ltd. (bell founders), 582
Glass Co. (glass-stainers), 469
Glass from Vitrics (glass etchers), 443
Glendinning, John, 293
Goldie, George (1828–87), 653
Goldsmith (R. C.) Ltd. (organ builders), 588

INDEX OF ARCHITECTS AND ARTISTS

Good, Thomas (sculptor), 489
Goold, Andrew (mason), 393
Gordon & Dey (Alexander Esmé Gordon, 1910–93; William Gordon Dey), 119, 120, 646, 654, 659
Goudie, Isobel Turner Maxwell (glass-stainer, b. 1903), 54, 582
Graham, James Gillespie (1777–1855), 43, 49, 51, 78, 80, 83, 86, 89, 114, 196, 201, 306, 308–9, 310, 344, 362, 382, 546, 548–50, 555, 564, 573, 678, 718–22, 724–6, Pls. 36, 41–2, 85–7
Graham, Lieutenant-General (later General) Sir Thomas (later Lord Lynedoch) (1748–1843), 43, 537
Grainger, Andrew Heiton *see* Heiton, Andrew Grainger
Grandison (L.) & Son (plasterers: Leonard S. Grandison), 221
Grant, Francis (d. 1818), 78, 450
Grant, John Alexander William (1885–1959), 121, 647, 664
Grant, Mary (sculptor, d. 1908), 585
Grant (W. J. Brewster) & Henderson, 116, 120, 229, 230, 23
Gray, Jane Campbell (glass-stainer, b. 1931), 585
Gray, Marshall & Associates (Alan Stuart Marshall, q.v.; Jocelyn M. Cunliffe), 478
Gray (Michael) Architects, 209, 744
Gray, William (mason), 683
Green, William Curtis (1875–1960), 374
Gregory, John (mason), 656
Greig, Caroline (sculptor), 391
Grieve, Nathaniel (joiner), 86, 184
Guild, Roy D. (glass-stainer), 649
Guthrie (J. & W.) & Andrew Wells Ltd. (glass-stainers: William Guthrie, 1852–1939; Archibald Wells; Charles Paine), 54, 228, 581, 684
Habershon, William Gilbee (c. 1818–91), 329–30
Habershon (William G.) & Pite (William Gilbee Habershon, c. 1818–91; Alfred Robert Pite, 1832–1911), 354
Hadden, Thomas (ornamental blacksmith, 1871–1940), 86, 182, 183, 540–1
Haggart, John (d. 1897), 151, 284
Hair, Alexander (superintendent of work), 295
Hall (John C.) & Co. (glass-stainers: John C. Hall, 1868–1955), 202
Halliburton, Thomas (wright), 548
Hamilton, D. & T. (organ builders), 372
Hamilton, Douglas (glass-stainer, 1895–1957), 476
Hamilton, John (carver, fl. 1686), 487
Hamilton, John (1851–1935), 636
Hamilton, Thomas (1754–1858), 43, 150, 151, Pl. 38
Handley & Moore (clockmakers), 337
Handyside, Archibald (mason), 415
Hanna, Donald & Wilson (founders), 672
Hardman (John) & Co. (glass-stainers: John Hardman Powell, 1828–95), 391, 715
Hardman (John) & Co. Ltd. (glass-stainers), 669
Hardman, Powell & Co. (church furnishers), 228
Hardman, Robert (mason), 393
Hardy & Wight (Henry Hardy, 1831–1908; John Rutherford Wight, 1829–1919), 268
Harrison & Harrison (organ builders: Thomas Hugh Harrison, 1839–1912; James Harrison), 151, 284, 388
Harvey (D.) & A. Scott, 661
Harvey, William John (engineer), 137, Pl. 98
Hay, J., W. H. & J. M. (John Hay, 1811–61; William Hardie Hay, 1813–1901; James Murdoch Hay, 1823–1915), 51, 112, 364, 584
Hay, William (1818–88), 284
Heaton, Butler & Bayne (glass-stainers: James Butler, 1830–1913; Robert Turville Bayne, 1837–1915; Clement James Butler, 1856–1929; Richard Cato Bayne, 1870–1940), 293, 495, 715
Heiton, A. & A. (Andrew Heiton Sen., q.v.; Andrew Heiton Jun., q.v.), 83, 98, 114, 115, 139, 154, 198, 203, 270, 328, 345, 367, 378, 584, 611, 618, 665, 687
Heiton, Andrew, Sen. (c. 1793–1858), 43, 112, 170, 297, 355, 372, 379, 528, 676, 680, 687, 730, Pls. 39–40
Heiton, Andrew, Jun. (1823–94), 48, 50, 83, 108, 113, 114, 115, 116, 118, 154, 172, 235, 236, 280, 288, 289, 294, 310, 368, 379, 408, 410, 438, 457, 468, 494, 524, 564, 573, 584, 593, 597, 599, 603, 617, 625, 640, 651, 652, 655, 662, 663, 664, 675, 685, 733, Pl. 114
Heiton, Andrew Grainger (c. 1862–1927), 109, 110, 254–5, 385, 388, 389, 395, 419, 585, 599, 604, 620, 622, 653, 688, 740
Heiton & Grainger (Andrew Heiton Jun., q.v.; Andrew Heiton Grainger, later Andrew Grainger Heiton, q.v.), 108, 152, 282, 573
Heiton & McKay (John Sibbald McKay, d. 1938), 651
Hele & Co. (organ builders), 669

INDEX OF ARCHITECTS AND ARTISTS

Henderson, George (1846–1905), 384
Henderson, J. B. (b. c. 1827), 51, 228
Henderson, John (1804–62), 50, 113, 384, 387, 514
Henderson, Peter Lyle Barclay (1848–1912), 109, 478
Henderson, William (1805–72), 47, 201
Hendrie, Herbert (glass-stainer, 1887–1947), 54, 443, 581–2
Henry, James Macintyre (1852–1929), 109, 209, 214–5, 347
Henry & Maclennan (James Macintyre Henry, q.v.; Thomas Forbes Maclennan, 1873–1957), 214–15, 564
Heriot, Alan B. (sculptor), 61, 613
Hill (William) & Son and Norman & Beard (organ builders: John Christie), 166–7
Hilsdon (H.) Ltd. (organ builders), 228, 293
Hislop, George, 297
Holiday, Henry (glass-stainer, 1839–1927), 54, 151
Honeyman, Jack & Robertson (William A. P. Jack; George Robertson, d. c. 1984; Charles Archibald Robertson, d. 1995; John M. Cochrane; Tom Rankin; Robert H. McEachern; Alan MacDonald), 389
Honeyman, John (1831–1914), 48, 527, 587
Honeyman & Keppie (John Honeyman, q.v.; John Keppie, 1862–1945), 588
Honeyman, Keppie & Mackintosh (John Honeyman, q.v.; John Keppie, 1862–1945; Charles Rennie Mackintosh, 1868–1928), 48, 116, 166, 279, Pl. 52
Hopper, Thomas (1776–1856), 82
Horne, James (smith), 488–9
Horsbrough, Adam (wright), 401
Hughes, Henry (glass-stainer), 53, 389
Hurd (Robert) & Partners (Robert Philip Andrew Hurd, 1905–63; Ian McKerron Begg, b. 1925; Lawrence Anderson Lyon Rolland, b. 1937), 164, 318
Hurd Rolland Partnership (The) (Lawrence Anderson Lyon Rolland, b. 1937; D. I. Pirie; H. M. Bunch; J. H. Shepherd; Alan Clyde; Mike Rolland; Brian Paul; Kenneth Williamson), 398–9
Hutcheson, Alexander (d. 1917), 508
Hutton, James (d. 1901), 118, 429, 432
Ibbeson, Graham (sculptor), 61, 619
Ingham, Brian (joiner), 709
Ingram & Co. (organ builders), 168, 202

Ingram, Eustace (organ builder), 592
Ingram, William (c. 1831–98), 47, 531
Inskip & Wilozynski, 636
Ireland & Maclaren (James Ireland, d. 1886; David Maclaren, 1848–87), 284
Ironhorse Studios (blacksmiths), 478
Ivory, James (clockmaker, fl. 1762–95), 447
Jack, Robert (builder), 527
Jackson, Peter Roy, 638
James, Richard Croft (1872–1949), 515
Jardine, James (engineer, 1776–1858), 243
Jebb, Sir Joshua (1793–1863), 607
Jennings, John (glass-stainer), 256
Johnson-Marshall (Percy) & Partners, 647
Johnston, Alexander (1839–1922), 158, 195, 230, 364, 365, 447
Johnston & Baxter (Alexander Johnston, q.v.; David William Baxter, 1874–1957; David Baxter Jun., b. 1907), 121, 154, 229, 365, 366
Johnston (J. & F.) & Partners, 662
Johnstone, Allan (plasterer), 721, 724
Jones, Gascoigne Hastings Fowler (b. 1850), 448
Jones, William, 349, 353
Jones & Willis (glass-stainers), 476, 586
Justice, John (founder), 241
Keates, Albert (organ builder), 228
Keay, J. (builder), 527
Keay, John (wright), 297
Keay, P., 527
Keillar, William (builder), 272
Keiller, Robert (wright, c. 1817–71), 467
Kemp, Marjorie (glass-stainer, fl. 1921–55), 54, 151, 293, 581–2
Kempe, Charles Eamer (glass-stainer, 1834–1907), 54, 168, 198, 669
Kennedy, Bruce, 605
Kennedy, George Penrose (1821–98), 319, 321–2, 325, Pl. 58
Kennedy, Lewis (landscape architect), 319, 325
Keppie Design, 615, 624, 643
Kerr, Alexander (glass-stainer), 167
Kerr, William (1867–1940), 148, 393
Kier, W. & J. J. (glass-stainers: William Kier, 1825–86; James Johnstone Kier, fl. 1830–1908), 293
Kininmonth, Sir William Hardie (1904–88), 535
Kinloch, George (c.1755–1833), 464
Kinloch, Shona (sculptor, b. 1962), 62, 640
Kippen, James (wright), 141
Kirkland Restoration Ltd., 143
Laidlaw (R.) & Son (founders), 604

INDEX OF ARCHITECTS AND ARTISTS

Laidlaw, William Carruthers (1859–1914), 348
Laing, James, 327
Lamond, Lorraine (glass-stainer), 476
Lavers, Barraud & Westlake (glass-stainers: Nathaniel Wood Lavers, 1828–1911; Francis Philip Barraud, 1824–1900; N. H. J. Westlake, d.1921), 54, 650
Law & Dunbar-Nasmith (Graham Cowper Law, 1923–96; Sir James Duncan Dunbar-Nasmith, b. 1927; Colin Ross; Maurice Batten), 120, 671, 702, Pl. 119
Lawson (Thomas) & Son, 701
LDN Architects (Colin Ross; Tom Duff; Sam Russell; Mark Hopton; Dermot Patterson; Mark Sidgwick), 718
Leadbetter, Thomas Greenshields (1859–1931), 83, 328, 407–8
Leiper, William (1839–1916), 118, 167, 169, 171, 172
Leonard, John, 669, 672, 674
Leonard & Morris, 671
Leslie, James (engineer, 1801–89), 229
Lessels, John (1808–83), 51, 269, 476, 531
Lewis, Thomas Christopher (organ builder, fl. c. 1861–c. 1900), 277
Lindsay (Ian G.) & Partners (Ian Gordon Lindsay, q.v.; George Hay, 1911–87), 183, 345, 346
Lindsay, Ian Gordon (1906–66), 413, 415, 738–9
Lindsay, William (wright), 454
Locke & Errington (engineers: Joseph Locke, 1805–60; John Edward Errington, 1806–62), 455
Loosley, David W. (organ builder), 151, 587
Lorimer, Hew (sculptor, 1907–93), 452
Lorimer & Matthew (Sir Robert Stodart Lorimer, q.v.; John Fraser Matthew, 1875–1955), 53, 86, 134, 249, 436–7, 459
Lorimer, Sir Robert Stodart (1864–1929), 52, 86, 91, 176, 182–4, 208, 246, 248–9, 255, 292, 308, 318, 408–10, 447, 508, 540–2, 573, 576–80
Loudon, John Claudius (landscape architect, 1783–1843), 694
Lough, John Graham (sculptor, 1798–1876), 341
Low, Joseph (builder), 401
Lowe, Robert William (b. 1899), 286
Lutyens, Sir Edwin Landseer (1869–1944), 86, 710
Lyle & Constable (George A. Lyle, 1845–1905; William Constable, b. 1863), 191
Lyon, Walter Fitzgerald Knox (1844–94), 368

MacCalman, Calum, 678
McCarthy & Stone, 624
McCulloch, Charles (mason), 372
Macdonald (A.) & Co. (sculptors), 483
MacDonald, Angus L. M., 656; *see also* Parr (James) & Partners
McDonald, Daniel (wright), 495
MacDonald (F. A.) & Partners (engineers), 610
Macdonald, Ian, 151
McDonald, John, 113, 558–9, 560, 676
MacDonald (Sir Murdoch) & Partners (engineers), 130
Macdougall, Norman M. (glass-stainer, 1852–1939), 734
McDowell, Steven & Co. (founders), 235
McEachern, MacDuff (Gordon J. McEachern; Alisdair MacDuff), 386
McEachern, Robert H., 389; *see also* Honeyman, Jack & Robertson
McEwan, J. (plumber), 353
Macfarlane (Walter) & Co. (founders), 139, 301
McGarva, Donald (cabinet-maker), 377
McGaw, William (mason), 536
MacGibbon, David (1831–1902), 47, 202
McGill, Alexander (d. 1734)
McGlashan (Stewart) & Son (sculptors: Stewart McGlashan, d. 1904), 477
MacGregor, Alexander (d. 1868), 172
McInnes, Shona (glass-stainer), 559
McIntosh, D., 267
McKellar, John Campbell (1859–1941), 513
Mackenzie, Alexander Marshall (1848–1933), 709
Mackenzie, David (c. 1799–c. 1860), 43, 421, 432
Mackenzie & Matthews (Thomas Mackenzie, 1814–54; James Matthews, 1819–98), 83, 136, 310, Pl. 90
Mackenzie & Moncur (founders), 83, 90, 679
Mackenzie, William Macdonald (1797–1856), 43, 105, 106, 107, 108, 110, 112, 123, 257, 271, 316, 344, 372, 459, 467, 471, 515, 526, 527, 528, 585, 599, 616, 618, 622, 626, 632, 651, 654, 655, 678, Pls. 33–4
McKillop, Edward (wright), 268
MacKillop & McIntosh (Angus MacIntyre MacKillop; Frederick Malgrine Dalgetty McIntosh), 661
McKillop, R., 118, 634, 641
Maclachlan Monaghan, 198
Maclagan, D., 700
Maclaren, James (1829–93), 185

INDEX OF ARCHITECTS AND ARTISTS 783

MacLaren, James Marjoribanks (1853–90), 108–9, 117, 137, 373, 374, 375, 404
McLaren & Mackay (William McLaren; Robert Mackay), 116, 593, 619, 621, 624, 633, 634, 637, 642, 652, 665
McLaren, Murdoch & Hamilton (John S. McLaren; Kenneth L. S. Murdoch; Douglas V. Hamilton; Andrew G. Beatson; William A Millar; David MacLeod Murdoch), 294, 602, 613, 625, 630, 634, 663
Maclaren, Soutar & Salmond (John Turnbull Maclaren, 1863–1948; Charles Geddes Soutar, 1878–1952; William Salmond, 1878–1956; Andrew Graham Patrick, 1863–1951), 439
McLaren, Thomas, 121, 647, 664
McLaren, William, 192, 367, 539, 636, 732
Maclean, Diane (sculptor, b. 1939), 660
McLellan, D., 625
McLeran, James, 77, 446n., 561
McMillan, D. & J. R. (Duncan McMillan, 1840–1928; John Ross McMillan, 1868–1959), 226, 229
McNab, J. & A. (clockmakers), 531
McNeil, Andrew (mason), 297
McOmish, Donald (landscape architect), 295
Malcolm, Thomas (mason), 142
Manning, Samuel, Jun. (sculptor, 1816–65), 580, 684
Manson, John Wellwood (1902–52), 245
Marke, John (sundial maker), 325, 709
Marshall, Alan Stuart, 119, 478
Marshall, James (mason, fl. 1816), 297
Marshall, James (d. 1918), 171, 635, 637, 684, 686
Marshall, John, 374
Martyn, H. H. (sculptor), 591, 620
Mason Gillibrand, 249
Matheson, Donald Alexander (engineer, 1860–1935), 611
Matheson, Robert (1808–77), 110, 607
Matthew, Sir Robert Hogg (1906–75), 130, 427
Mayer & Co. (glass-stainers), 391, 669
Meacher, Allan John (b. 1870), 467
Mears (George) & Co. (bell founders), 582
Meikle, John (bell founder), 342, 509
Meikle (William) & Sons (glass-stainers: William Meikle Jun., b. 1870; Jonathan Edward Charles Carr, b. 1863; John Tytler Stewart, 1858–1930; John Stark Melville, 1886–1946), 54, 253, 581
Melvin, John (1805–84), 277, 533
Melvin (John) & Son (William Kerr, q.v.; John Gray, c. 1878–1946), 148, 393, 534
Menart, Charles Jean, 118, 654
Menart & Jarvie (Charles Jean Menart, q.v.; John Stirling Jarvie, b. 1876), 621
Meredith Williams, Morris (artist and glass-stainer, b. 1881), 54, 578, 581
Merredew, Jenny (artist), 270
Millais, Sir John Everett (artist, 1829–96), 54, 650
Millar, David (wright-architect), 393
Millar, H. & R. (clockmakers), 349
Miller, James (wright, fl. 1789), 732
Miller, James (wright, fl. 1835), 735
Miller, James (1860–1947), 90, 98, 111, 116, 117, 168, 356, 372, 373, 396, 629, 661–2, 676, Pl. 118
Miller (James) & Partners Ltd. (builders), 647
Miller (James), Son & Manson (John Wellwood Manson, q.v.), 245–6
Miller, John R. (organ builder), 152, 197, 207, 242, 255, 363, 430, 453, 526, 583, 592
Miller, Simon, 270
Miller (T. M.) & Partners, 643
Mills & Shepherd (John Donald Mills, 1872–1958; Godfrey Daniel Bower Shepherd, q.v.), 144, 386, 389, 515, Pl. 99
Milne, James (fl. 1811–34), 45, 530
Milne, Oswald Partridge (1881–1968), 86, 210
Mitchell, D., 674
Mitchell, George Bennett (1865–1941), 86, 311
Mitchell (J.) & Co. (engineers: Joseph Mitchell, q.v.; William Paterson; Murdoch Paterson, q.v.), 98, 507
Mitchell, James, 393
Mitchell, John (mason and engineer, 1779–1824), 209
Mitchell, Joseph (engineer, 1803–83), 98, 209, 223, 428, 716, 731, Pl. 96
Mitchell, Robert Matthew (1874–1949), 166; see also Smart, Stewart & Mitchell
Mitchell (Sydney) & Wilson (Arthur George Sydney Mitchell, 1856–1930; George Wilson, 1845–1912), 48, 115, 139, 157, 385, 402, 557, Pl. 44
Mitchell, William (mason-architect), 446
Monro & Partners (Geoffrey James Monro, 1907–85; John Forbes, d. 1970; Ian Cruikshank; David Sampson; Alistair Anderson Taylor), 619, 621

INDEX OF ARCHITECTS AND ARTISTS

Moodie, Ian A., 119, 137, 228, 345, 346, 478, 559, 646, 660; *see also* Perth & Kinross County Council

Moore, Arthur L. & Charles E. (glass-stainers), 399

Morant, G. (decorator), 85, 439, Pl. 83

Morison, David (1792–1855), 104, 605, Pl. 110

Morison, James (mason), 530

Morison, Robert (mason), 530

Morris & Co. (glass-stainers), 54, 198, 277–8, 539, Pl. 48

Morris, David, 135

Morris, James (wright), 145

Morris & Steedman (James Shepherd Morris, 1931–2006; Robert Russell Steedman, b. 1929), 121, 193, 602, 659

Morrison, J., 603

Mossman, William (sculptor), 61, 300

Moxon & Carfrae (painters), 578

Muirhead, Andrew (d. 1907), 478

Multon, Fred, 453

Murdoch Architects (David MacLeod Murdoch; Kenneth L. S. Murdoch), 363, 671, 686

Murdoch, Kenneth L. S., 529; *see also* McLaren, Murdoch & Hamilton

Murray, John, 496, 730

Murray, Patrick (sculptor), 342

Murray MacGregor, Amelia Georgiana (1829–1917), 224

Mylne, John, Sen. (d. 1657), 87, 319, 321, 325, Pls. 58, 91

Mylne, John, Jun. (1611–67), 288

Mylne, Robert (1633–1710), 100

Mylne, Robert (1733–1811), 717

Nairne, Margaret Nairne, Lady (d. 1747), 87, 223

Naish, W. R. (lantern manufacturer), 725

Neaper, John (mason), 411

Neilson, Alexander (sculptor), 167, 365

Nerven, Cornelius van (carver), 484

Ness, Alexander, 108, 672; *see also* Bruce (John) & Son

Ness, David (marble cutter, *c.* 1786–1852), 462, 549

Ness, James (sculptor, 1870–1946), 623

Nicol, David (mason), 530, 534

Nicol, John, 119, 478, 646; *see also* Perth & Kinross County Council

Nicoll Russell Studios, 121, 299; Pl. 120

Nimmo (William) & Partners (William Nimmo; Jean Welsh; James Robertson; John Carswell), 120, 615, 621, 623

Norman & Beard Ltd. (organ builders: Ernest William Norman, 1852–1927; Herbert John Norman, 1861–1936; George Wales Beard), 226, 294, 476, 538, 584

Norman & Beddoe, 197

Norris Hamilton Associates, 664

Oberlander Associates, 655

O'Connor (glass-stainers: Michael O'Connor, 1801–67; Arthur O'Connor, 1826–73), 53, 152

Office of Works (H.M.) (1851–77: Robert Matheson, q.v.; 1877–1904: Walter Wood Robertson, q.v.; 1904–12: William Thomas Oldrieve, 1853–1923; 1914–22: C. J. W. Simpson; 1922–43: John Wilson Paterson, q.v.), 110, 297, 334

Ohyma (Dhyma?), Vanessa (glass-stainer), 584

Ower, C. & L. (Charles Ower Jun., *c.* 1849–1921; Leslie Ower, *c.* 1852–1916), 48, 670

Panton Sargent, 296

Panton, William (surveyor), 149

Paolozzi, Sir Eduardo Luigi (artist, 1924–2005), 269

Parkneuk Works (founders), 611

Parr (James) & Partners (James Reginald Parr; Alan F. Bell; Joseph F. Wynne; Gordon Farquharson; Angus L. M. MacDonald; Alan J. Duncan; Alfred D. Maloco; Daniel L. Carmichael; Iain G. Rennie; Victor Hamilton), 120, 121, 636, 637, 639, 656, 658, 662

Pask & Pask (James Pask; Susan Pask), 634

Pate, Anita (glass-etcher), 443, 508

Paterson (builder), 442

Paterson, Alexander Nisbet (1862–1947), 109, 402

Paterson, Andrew (mason), 732

Paterson, George (d. 1789), 442

Paterson, John (d. 1832), 41, 78, 79, 89, 125, 260, 479, 508, 540, 592, 710, 717–8, 730–1, Pls. 37, 85

Paterson, John Wilson (1887–1969), 224; *see also* Office of Works, H.M.

Paterson, Murdoch (engineer, 1826–98), 672; *see also* Mitchell (J.) & Co.

Paterson, Oscar (glass-stainer, 1863–1934), 513, 732

Paterson, William A. (engineer), 611

Paton, Waller Hubert (sculptor, fl. 1881–1932), 541

Paulin, George Henry (sculptor, 1888–1962), 393

Pearson (builder), 479

Pearson, Frank Loughborough (1864–1947), 51, 388, 589–92, Pls. 46, 49, 51

Pearson, John Loughborough (1817–97), 385, 589

Peatt, John (clockmaker), 443

Peddie & Forbes Smith (John More Dick Peddie, 1853–1923; James Forbes Smith, b. 1876), 257

INDEX OF ARCHITECTS AND ARTISTS

Peddie & Kinnear (John Dick Peddie, 1824–91; Charles George Hood Kinnear, 1830–94), 83, 112, 231, 296–7, 469, 534, 688, 724

Peddie & Washington Browne (John More Dick Peddie, 1853–1923; Sir George Washington Browne, 1853–1939), 115, 160, 301, 642, Pl. 113

Pelly, Frances (sculptor, b. 1947), 62, 630, 657

Perth & Kinross Council, 119, 143, 594, 671

Perth & Kinross County Council, 295, 532, 661, 664, 672

Perth & Kinross District Council Architectural Services Department, 119, 198, 478, 599, 602, 615, 624, 646

Petrie, Alexander, 584

Phillimore (Claud) & Jenkins (Claud Stephen Phillimore, q.v.; Aubrey Henry Herbert Jenkins), 381

Phillimore, Claud Stephen (b. 1911), 86, 133

Pilkington, Frederick Thomas (1832–98), 118, 303

Pilkington (Thomas) & Son (Thomas Pilkington, b. c. 1799; Frederick Thomas Pilkington, q.v.), 112, 296

Pinfold, Michael (artist), 414

Pirnie, James (mason, fl. 1675), 547

Pirnie, James (builder, fl. 1819), 523

Pirnie, John (mason, fl. c. 1670), 547

Playfair, James (1755–94), 55, 78, 94, 260 and n., 527, 665, 666, Pl. 31

Playfair, William Henry (1790–1857), 94, 126, 538, 665, 666

Positive Organ Co. Ltd. (organ builders), 313

Positive Organ Co. (1922) Ltd. (organ builders), 377

Potts, G. H. (tile-maker), 284

Powell (James) & Sons (glass-stainers and church furnishers: Arthur Powell; James Cotton Powell; Nathaniel Powell; James Hogan), 53, 168, 240, 388, 592

Pugin, Augustus Welby Northmore (1812–52), 80, 83, 549–50, 722–6, Pls. 86–7

Pugin, Edward Welby (1834–75), 228

Ramsay, James (clockmaker), 197

Ramsay, John, 410, 449, 500

Rattray, George (clockmaker), 363

Readdie, James (inspector of work, c. 1799–1863), 227

Readdie, John (wright), 227

Readie, Alexander (wright), 530

Reid, Robert (1774–1856), 106, 107, 109–10, 123, 495, 507, 606, 610 and n., 625, Pl. 108

Reid, Robert (fl. 1897–1901), 226, 229

Rhind, David (1808–83), 114, 115, 231, 299, 631, 632, 635, 674, Pl. 112

Rhind, John (sculptor, 1828–92), 61, 343, Pl. 100

Rhind, John Stevenson (sculptor, 1859–97), 481

Rhind, William Birnie (sculptor, 1853–1933), 61, 141, 167, 610

Richard, Robert (mason), 147

Riddel, James, 153

Ritchie, James (sculptor, fl. 1837), 594

Ritchie, James (fl. 1862–77), 201, 454, 660

Ritchie (James) & Son (clockmakers), 610, 611

Robert (master mason), 333

Robertson (fl. 1893), 268

Robertson, Charles (mason), 207

Robertson, Charles Sandeman (1838–97), 61, 108, 113, 114, 118, 143, 168, 198, 243, 343, 364, 629, 641, 663, Pl. 100

Robertson, Henry, 202

Robertson, James (mason, fl. 1675), 547

Robertson, James (builder, fl. 1833), 209

Robertson, James, Sen. (painter), 707

Robertson, John (1840–1925), 430

Robertson, John M. (fl. 1903–4), 402

Robertson, John Murray (1844–1901), 111, 128, 436–7, 643, 651, 658, 674

Robertson, Malcolm (sculptor), 627

Robertson, Robert (mason), 141

Robertson, Thomas Saunders (1835–1923), 55, 369–70; *see also* Edward & Robertson

Robertson, Walter Wood (1845–1907), 110; *see also* Office of Works (H.M.)

Robson, Joseph (organ builder), 592

Ross, Charles (carver), 219–20, 222, Pl. 76

Ross & Macbeth (Alexander Ross, 1834–1925; Robert John Macbeth, 1857–1912), 167

Ross, Thomas (1839–1930), 90, 484, 486, 493

Rothwell, Frederick (organ builder), 245, 580

Rowan, William Gardner (1846–1924), 559

Ruider, Hans Popen (bell founder), 448

Rushworth & Dreaper (organ builders), 580, 584

Russell, Alexander L. (glass-stainer), 284, 664, 669

Russell & Spence, 129, 202

Salisbury, James, 77, 497

Salvin, Harvey (glass-stainer), 54, 581

Santvoort, Jan van (carver), 493

INDEX OF ARCHITECTS AND ARTISTS

Saracen Foundry (founders), 139, 301

Scobie, James (builder), 734

Scott, George Gilbert, Jun. (1839–97), 293

Scott & McIntosh (John Malcolm McIntosh; Walter Scott; Robert Y. Fergus; David Stillie; Anne Y. Symons), 661–2

Scott Morton & Co. (decorators and joiners), 86, 184, 296, 437, 463

Scott Morton & Tynecastle Co. (cabinet makers), 583

Scott, Walter Schomberg (1910–88), 86, 356, 580

Scott, William (d. 1872), 422

Scottish Special Housing Association, 345

Scottish Urban Archaeological Trust, 594

Scrimgeour, John, 326

Scrymgeour-Wedderburn, Janet Mary (sculptor, b. 1941), 706, 708

Shaftoe, Alan (cabinet maker), 399

Shallis, Alfred Charles, 612

Shaw, D. N., 638

Shearer (James) & Annand (James David Shearer, 1919–74; Marcus Johnston), 480

Shepherd, Godfrey Daniel Bower (1874–1937), 385, 386, 389; *see also* Mills & Shepherd

Sheppard, Oliver (sculptor, 1865–1941), 296

Sherriff, William (carver), 174

Shillinglaw & Scott (marble cutters), 461

Shirreffs, William (carver), 600

Sim, Charles (builder-architect), 716

Sim, John (*c.* 1854–1919), 495

Simpson & Brown (James Walter Thorburn Simpson, b. 1944; Andrew Stewart Brown, b. 1945), 190, 203

Simpson, Ebenezer (1854–1934), 109, 257

Simpson, John (mason-architect), 478

Simpson, William (*c.* 1810–90), 168, 237

Singer & Sons (founders), 643

Skeen, Peter, 135, 513

Slater, William (1819–72), 51, 197

Smart, David (mason, fl. 1736–56), 145, 146

Smart, David (1824–1914), 108, 110, 112, 115, 117, 192, 227, 285, 297, 342, 372, 402, 451, 466, 482, 599, 601, 609, 612, 623, 624, 629, 634, 637, 641, 647, 651, 655, 686

Smart, James (1847–1903), 117, 253, 586, 621, 624, 633, 634, 637, 642

Smart (James) & Son (James Smart, q.v.; John Walker Smart, q.v.), 631

Smart, John Walker (1872–1941), 621, 639

Smart & Stewart (David Smart, q.v.; Donald Alexander Stewart, q.v.), 128, 229, 481, 615, 635, 643

Smart, Stewart & Mitchell (Donald Alexander Stewart, q.v.; Robert Matthew Mitchell, q.v.), 104, 116, 165, 277, 453, 522, 605, 623, 624–5, 632, 636, 639, 646, 650, 651, 652, 657, 658

Smeaton, John (engineer, 1724–92), 93, 604

Smeaton, Robert (wright), 654

Smirke, Sir Robert (1780–1867), 82, 104, 309, 460–3, 609, 710–2, Pl. 110

Smith, David (glass-stainer), 476

Smith (George) & Co. (founders), 295, 300, 611

Smith, James (*c.* 1645–1731), 75, 256, 487

Smith, James (*c.* 1779–1862), 115, 630

Smith, Ron (organ builder), 268

Soutar, Charles Geddes (1878–1952), 85, 467; *see also* Maclaren, Soutar & Salmond

Speir, Robert Thomas Napier (1841–1922), 277, 308, 556

Speirs & Co., 701

Spence, Sir Basil Urwin (1907–76), 411, 680

Spence (Basil) & Partners (Sir Basil Urwin Spence, q.v.; Bruce Robertson; John Hardie Glover; Peter S. Ferguson, q.v.), 385, 386, 388, 389

Spens, Michael Patrick, 269

Sprecht, Johannes (bell founder), 374

Sprunt, David (mason), 363

Steadman, Vincent (d. 1931), 515

Steel (James) & Co. (glass-stainers), 539

Steele (H. B. W.) & Balfour (Henry Bell Wesley Steele, *c.* 1852–1902; Andrew Balfour, 1863–1948), 49, 538, 584

Steell, John (carver, d. 1849), 549

Steell, Sir John (sculptor, 1804–91), 58, 209, 341, 609, Pl. 50

Stephen, James F., 53, 639, 646

Steuart, Charles (artist), 221

Steuart, George (artist), 412

Steven Bros. (joiners), 670

Steven, David, 500

Steven, John (mason-architect), 148, 319, 323

Stevens, 274

Stevenson, David Watson (sculptor, 1842–1904), 477

Stevenson, James (builder), 734

Stevenson, John James (1831–1908), 48, 290, 369, 586

INDEX OF ARCHITECTS AND ARTISTS

Stevenson (Robert) & Sons (engineers: Robert Stevenson, 1772–1850; Alan Stevenson, 1807–65; David Stevenson, 1815–85; Thomas Stevenson, 1818–87), 99, 602

Stevenson, William Grant (sculptor, 1849–1919), 293

Stewart, Allan Duncan (engineer, 1831–94), 604

Stewart, Cecil (b. 1911), 121, 656

Stewart, Donald Alexander (1876–1940), 453, 522; *see also* Smart & Stewart; Smart, Stewart & Mitchell

Stewart, Duncan D., 51, 113, 176, 390, 421, 431, Pl. 53

Stewart, George (fl. 1838), 162

Stewart, George (fl. 1959–62), 664

Stewart, John (wright-architect, fl. 1794–1819), 41, 191, 196, 207, 278, 506, 507, 548, 642, Pl. 29

Stewart, John (mason, fl. 1820), 401

Stewart, John (*c*. 1869–1954), 60, 166

Stewart & Paterson (John Stewart, 1870–1954, q.v.; George Andrew Paterson, 1876–1934), 111, 166, 169, 274

Stirling, William, I (1772–1838), 43, 91, 123, 201n., 227, 280, 316, 356, 372, 373, 536, 538, 542, 543, 544, 733, 735

Stobie, James (surveyor), 103, 700, 701

Strachan, Alexander (builder-architect, fl. 1803–20), 674, 733

Strachan, Alexander (glass-stainer, fl. 1929–46), 304

Strachan, Douglas (glass-stainer, 1875–1950), 54, 167, 292, 296, 456, 581, 651, 652

Strang (Alex.) & Associates (Alex. Strang, 1916–84), 121, 656

Sugden, Rev. Edward (1850–1901), 180, 197, 207, 391

Sun Foundry (founders), 98, 295, 300, 611

Swan, Abraham (fl. 1745–60), 76, 219–20, 222, 224

Swan, Thomas Aikman (1883–1945), 119, 661

Swift (Arthur) & Partners, 633

Tarbolton, Harold Ogle (1869–1947), 130, 671, Pl. 126

Tarbolton & Ochterlony (Harold Ogle Tarbolton, q.v.; Sir Matthew Montgomerie Ochterlony, 1880–1947), 95, 589–90, 671

Tatham, Charles Heathcote (1772–1842), 55, 91, 562

Taylor (Harry) & Co., 703

Taylor, Harry Ramsay (*c*. 1864–1922), 271

Taylor, John (mason), 526

Tayside Regional Council, 243, 256, 661

Telford, Thomas (engineer, 1757–1834), 94, 343

Ternouth, John (sculptor, 1795–1849), 58, 342, Pl. 27

Thoms & Wilkie (Patrick Hill Thoms, 1873–1946; William Fleming Wilkie, 1876–1961), 431, 511

Thomson (inspector), 145

Thomson (Erskine) & Glass (William Erskine Thomson, 1875–1962; John Guthrie Lornie Glass, d. 1980), 180, 582, 634, 663

Thomson, James (1835–1905), 84, 193, 194

Thomson, James L. (sculptor), 660

Thomson, John (builder), 523

Thomson, William, 427, 469

Thomson, William Erskine (1875–1962), 60, 139, 254

Tiffany Studios (glass-stainers), 544

Tindall, Benjamin Hemsley, 649

Tite, Sir William (1798–1873), 98, 610–11

Tod, Stewart (b. 1927), 587

Tod (Stewart) & Partners (Stewart Tod, q.v.; Vivienne Tod; Anthony C. S. Dixon; Roger Taylor; Rosalind Taylor), 709

Traquair, Ramsay R. (1874–1952), 403

Trotter, Alexander (1755–1842), 717

Trotter, The Heirs of William (carvers: John Blackadder), 725

Trotter, William (1772–1833), 85, 178–9

Troughton (Jamie) & Hugh Broughton, 213, 215

Turnbull, John, 624; *see also* Perth & Kinross District Council Architectural Services Department

Tweed, John (sculptor, 1869–1933), 643

University of Dundee Department of Civil Engineering (The), 137, Pl. 98

Urquhart, Dr A. R., 652

Victor & Sons (clockmakers), 494

Waddell (J. Jeffrey) & Young (John Jeffrey Waddell, q.v.; Thomas Peach Weir Young, b. 1892), 443

Waddell, John Jeffrey (1876–1941), 52, 376–7, 506

Wade, General (later Field-Marshal) George (1673–1748), 93, 137, 669, 741

Wadsworth & Bros. (organ builders), 556

Waghevens, Peter (bell founder), 38, 582

Wailes & Strang (glass-stainers: Thomas Rankine Strang, 1835–99), 294

INDEX OF ARCHITECTS AND ARTISTS

Walker (J.W.) & Son Ltd. (organ builders: James John Walker, 1846–1922), 741
Walker, James Campbell (1821–88), 49. 110, 215, 402, 495, 507, 670, 673
Walker, Joseph William (organ builder, 1802–70), 588
Wardrop & Anderson (Hew Montgomerie Wardrop, 1856–87; Sir Robert Rowand Anderson, 1834–1921), 91, 715
Wardrop & Reid (James Maitland Wardrop, 1824–82; Charles Reid, 1828–83), 83, 714
Watherston (John) & Sons (builders and architects: James Watherston, 1831–1907; Robert Henderson Watherston, 1869–1923), 84, 86, 184, 355, 410
Watson, Agnes (sculptor), 391
Watson, Thomas Lennox (1850–1920), 48, 294, 583, Pl. 45
Watson, William, 364
Watt (engineer and architect), 532
Watt, George (bell founder), 167
Watt, James (mason), 526
Waugh, Sep (glass-stainer), 421
Webster, Alfred A. (glass-stainer, 1884–1915), 151
Webster, Gordon MacWhirter (glass-stainer, 1908–87), 54, 256, 284, 294, 585
Westman's Pottery (tile-makers), 615
Whiston, Peter (b. 1912), 660, 663
Whitechapel Bell Foundry (bell founders), 582
Whyte, David A. (d. 1830), 85, 438, Pl. 82
Whytock & Reid (cabinet-makers), 86
Willement, Thomas (glass-stainer, 1786–1871), 692, 715
Williamson & Hubbard, 660
Williamson (James) & Partners (engineers: E. John K. Chapman, b. 1911; William Young, 1908–80), 130, 427
Willis (Henry) & Sons Ltd. (organ builders: Henry Willis, 1821–1901; Henry Willis II; Vincent Willis), 654
Wilson (fl. 1850), 500

Wilson, J. & E. (cabinet-makers), 350
Wilson (John C.) & Co. (bell founders), 582
Wilson, Peter, 209
Wilson, Roger, 375
Wilson, Samuel (plasterer), 86, 183–4, 248
Wilson, William (mason), 227
Wilson, William (glass-stainer, 1905–72), 54, 142, 151, 278, 293, 304, 443, 581, 663
Wimpey (George) & Co. Ltd., 121, 628, 656
Winter, James, 75–6, 212, 218, 223
Wippell (J.) & Co. Ltd. (glass-stainers), 585
Wood, Mary Isobel (glass-stainer, fl. 1925–44), 378
Woodside-Parker (Samuel Woodside; Philip Parker), 602
Woodside & Parker (Samuel Woodside; Philip Parker), 624, 639, 641
Woolworth (F.W.) & Co. Ltd. Construction Department, 621
Wright, Gordon Lorimer (b. 1876), 116, 301
Wright, Robert, 297
Wyatt, Benjamin Dean (1775–1855), 609n.
Wyatt, Jeffry *see* Wyatville, Sir Jeffry
Wyatville, Sir Jeffry (1766–1840), 609n.
Young, Frank (engineer), 610
Young (G. P. K.) & Son (George Penrose Kennedy Young, q.v.; Graham Conacher Young, b. 1892), 121, 601, 656
Young, George (glass-stainer), 294
Young, George Penrose Kennedy (1858–1933), 109, 114, 117, 176, 243, 527, 599, 617, 618, 642, 646, 663, Pl. 115
Young, J. & G. (John Young, q.v.; George Penrose Kennedy Young, q.v.), 628
Young, James (sculptor), 167
Young, John (1826–95), 135, 617, 640, 641, 647
Yuille, Robert (clerk of works), 326

INDEX OF PLACES

Principal references are in **bold** type; demolished buildings are shown in *italic*.

Aberargie **133**
  railway viaducts (Glen Farg and Kilnockiebank) 98, **133**
Abercairny 81–2, 86, **133**
Aberdalgie **133–5**
  Manse 123
  Milltown of Aberdalgie 126, **135**
  Parish Church 38, 40, 41, 53, **133–5**
Aberfeldy 93, 97, 108, **135–41**
  churches 46, **135–7**, 715
  Craig Formal stone circle 9
  industrial buildings **141**
    Aberfeldy Distillery 129, 138, **141**, Pl. 124
    gasworks 130, **139**
    Water Mill 129, **141**
  Margmore cairn 7
  Moness House **141**
  public buildings **137–8**
    Black Watch Memorial 61, **141**
    drinking fountain 61, **139**
    post office 110, **138**
    suspension bridge 95, **137**, Pl. 98
    Tay Bridge 93, **137–8**, Pl. 95
    Town Hall 108–9, **137**
    war memorial 60–1, **139–40**
  streets, commercial buildings and houses 116, **138–41**
    The Birks 120, **138–9**
    Palace Hotel 115, **138**
    Royal (former Commercial) Bank of Scotland 115, **139**
  Tyndrum, The Dun 15
Abernethy 24, 99, **141–5**
  Carey Roman camp 17
  Carpow Roman fortress 21–2
  Castle Law fort 15, **145**
  churches **142–3**
    Abernethy and Dron Parish Church 40, 54, **142**
    medieval church 35
    monastic house 26, 35, *141–2*
    Round Tower and symbol stone 26–7, 28, **142–3**
    United Presbyterian church 46, **143**
  public buildings **143**
    Abernethy Primary School 119, **143**
  War Memorial **144**, Pl.99
  streets and houses 106, **143–5**
  The Cross 100, **144**, Pl. 99
  manse 123
Abernyte *102*, **145–6**
  manse 122, **146**
  Parish Church 40, 59, **145–6**
Aberuchill Castle 70, **146–7**
Aberuthven **147–8**
  St Kattan's Church 33, 55, **147–8**
Acharn 117, **148**
  Callelochan 125–6
  Hermit's Cave 88, 129, **148**
  Old Mill 129, **148**
Achloa *see* Keltneyburn
Airleywight *see* Bankfoot
Airlich *see* Amulree
Aldie Castle *see* House of Aldie
Allean House *see* Strathtummel
Almondbank 47, **149**
Alyth 97, 99, 108, **149–55**
  Barry Hill fort 14–15, 16, **155**, Pl. 3
  Bruceton symbol stone 27, **155**
  churches **150–2**
    Alyth Free Church 46, **150**
    Alyth Parish Church 28, 43, 44, 54, **150–1**, Pl. 38
    Alyth Parish Church (former) 34, 36, 55, 149, **150**
    Alyth United Presbyterian Church 46, **151–2**
    St Ninian (Episcopal) 51, 53, 54, **152**
  public buildings 108, **152–3**
    Alyth High School 113, **152**
    Market Cross 100–1, **154**
    Old Pack Horse Bridge 92, **153**
    Town Hall 108, **152–3**
  streets, houses etc. 103, 121, 149, **153–5**
    corn mill 129, **154**
    Losset Inn 104, **153**
Amulree 93, **155–6**
  Airlich stone circle 9
  Clach na Tiompan tombs 6
  Meikle Findowie stone circle 9, **156**
  White Cairn 7
Ardblair Castle 64, 65, 68, 71, **156–8**, Pl. 65

INDEX OF PLACES

Ardler 46, **158**
Ardoch *see* Braco
Ardunie *see* Findo Gask
Ardvorlich House **159**
Arlary House 77, **159**
Arnbathie *see* New Scone
Arngask *see* Glenfarg
Arnot Tower 64, 65, **159–60**
Arthurstone 83–4, 89–90, **160–3**
  fragments from Coupar Angus 32, **162–3**
Ashintully Castle 68, 71, **163–4**
Auchleeks House **164–5**, 184
Auchnaguie *see* Ballinluig
Auchterarder 91, 94, 96, 97, 99, 108, 126n., **165–75**
  Auchterarder Castle 173
  Auchterarder House 82, 84, **173–5**
  Ben Effery fort 15
  Castle Mains **173**
  churches **165–8**, *350*
    Auchterarder Free Church 46, **165**
    Auchterarder Parish Church 47, 48, 54, **166–7**, Pl. 52
    Auchterarder Parish Church (former) 40, **166**, 167
    St Mackessog (Kirkton) 167, **168**
  industrial buildings **173**
  Ogle Hill fort 15
  public buildings **168–9**
    Auchterarder School (former) 113, **168**
    Aytoun Hall 108, **168**
    Community School of Auchterarder 119, **168**
    Gleneagles Railway Station 98, **168–9**
    St Margaret's Hospital 111, **169**
    War Memorial 60, **166**
  streets, commercial buildings and houses 106, **169–71**
    hotels 115, **169–70**
    villas 118, **171–2**
Ayton House **175–6**

Baird Monument *see* Monzievaird
Balbeggie 109, **176**
Balchrochan *see* Kirkmichael
Baledgarno **176–7**
Baledmund **177**
Balendoch **177**
Balhary 85, **177–8**
Balhousie *see* Perth suburbs
Ballathie House **178**
Ballechin *see* Strathtay
Ballindean House 85, **178–80**
Ballinluig 97, **180**
  Auchnaguie distillery 129
  Logierait Primary School 112, **180**
Ballintuim **180–1**
  Grey Cairn and standing stones, Balnabroich 7, **180–1**
  St Michael and All Angels 51–2, **180**

Balmanno Castle 69, 86, **181–4**
Balnabroich *see* Ballintuim
Balnacraig *see* Fortingall; Pitlochry
Balnakeilly **184**
Balthayock Castle and House 64, 65, 67, **185–6**
Balvaird Castle 64, 65, 67–8, 71, **186–9**, Pl. 56
Bamff **189–91**
Bankfoot 97, **191–2**
  Airleywight 85, **192**
  Auchtergaven Parish Church 41, **191–2**
  Auchtergaven United Presbyterian Church 46, **192**
Bardmony House **192**
Barnhill *see* Perth suburbs
Barry Hill *see* Alyth
Battleby **192–3**
Belmont Castle 84, **193–5**
  Macbeth's Stone 8, 11, **195**
Ben Effery *see* Auchterarder
Bendochy **195–6**
  Bendochy Parish Church 36, 40, **195–6**
  Bridge of Couttie 93, **196**
Bertha *see* Perth City Centre
Binn Hill *see* Kinfauns
Birnam 96, 97, 117, **196–200**
  churches **196–8**
    Little Dunkeld Kirk 40, 41, **196–7**
    St Columba (R.C.) 53, **197**
    St Mary (Episcopal) 51, 52, 54, **197–8**, Pl. 48
  public buildings **198**
    Birnam Institute and John Kinnaird Hall 101, 108, **198**
    Dalguise Pillar 101, **198**
    Dunkeld and Birnam Railway Station 98, **198**
    Royal High School of Dunkeld 119, **198**
  streets, commercial buildings and houses 117, 196, **199–200**
    Bee Cottage 126, **200**
    Birnam House Hotel 105, **199**
    Murthly Terrace 117, **199**
    St Mary's Tower 118
Blackcraig Castle 83, **200–1**
Blackford 62, **201–3**
  churches **201–2**
    Blackford Free Church 46, 47, **201**
    Blackford Parish Church (former) 40, 41, 47, 60, **201–2**
    Blackford Parish Church 47, **202**
  maltings 129, **202**
  Peterhead symbol stone 27, **203**
  public buildings **202**
  streets, houses etc. **202–3**
  Tullibardine Distillery 129
Blair Adam **203–6**
Blair Atholl 3, 93, **206–11**
  churches **206–9**

INDEX OF PLACES

St Adamnan-Kilmaveonaig
  Church 45, 52, 54, **207–8**
St Bride's Kirk (Old Blair) 40,
  208–9
Dalnacardoch 93
Monzie and Strathgroy cairns 7, **211**
public buildings **209–10**
  Bridge of Tilt **209**, 512
  Village Hall 109, **209–10**
  War Memorial 60, **210**
streets and houses 117, **210–11**
Tirinie 86, **210–11**
Blair Castle 63, 75–6, 77, 83–4,
  87–90, 91, 103, 206, 209, **211–24**,
  Pls. 74–78, 89
Blairgowrie 93, 94, 97, 99, 108,
  224–35
Castle of Rattray 62–3
churches **225–8**
  Blairgowrie Parish Church (for
    mer) 43, 151, **226**, Pl. 35
  Blairgowrie Parish (former St
    Andrew's United Free)
    Church 47, **226–7**
  Blairgowrie South Free Church
    46, **227**
  Rattray Parish Church 43, 44,
    227
  St Catherine (Episcopal) 51, **228**
industrial buildings 127, 225, **233**
  Ericht Works 127, **233**
  Keathbank Mill 127, **233**
  Meikle Mill 127
Milton of Rattray 5
Newton Castle **233–4**, Pl. 66
Old Mains of Rattray 12
public buildings **228–9**
  Blairgowrie Cottage Hospital
    111, **228**
  Bridge of Blairgowrie 94, **229**
  Picture House (former) 120, **230**
  St Stephen's Primary (formerly
    Blairgowrie Parish) School
    112, **229**
  school (1772) 105
  war memorial 60, **232**
streets, commercial buildings and
  houses 106, 225, **229–33**
  Clydesdale Bank 114, **232**
  Commercial Bank of Scotland
    120, **232**
  Dome Café 116, **232**
  manse 122
  Old Bank House (Commercial
    Bank) 115, **231**
  Perth Bank (former) 114, **232**
  Royal Bank of Scotland 114,
    231–2
  Royal Hotel 115, **231**
  Tulach 107, **231**
The Welton fort 15
Blairingone 94, 106, **235**
Bolfracks **235–6**

Bonhard House **236**
Bonskeid House **236–7**
'Bore Stone' *see* Moncreiffe House
Braco 91, **237–40**
  Ardoch Old Bridge 92, **237**
  Ardoch Roman fort 17, 18–21,
    238–9, 368, Pl.6
  Braco Free Church 46, **237**
  Glenbank Roman fortlet 18, 21
  Kaims Castle Roman fortlet 18,
    21, **239**
Braes of Rannoch *see* Bridge of Gaur
Bridge of Cally **240–1**
  bridges 95, **240–1**
  Middleton Muir cairns and hut
    circles 7, **241**
Bridge of Couttie *see* Bendochy
Bridge of Earn 95, 96, 97, 103, **241–5**
  Carnac fort 24
  churches and cemetery **241–3**, 329
  *Dunbarney round-houses and enclo-
    sure 25*
  public buildings **243**
    bridge 92, **243**
    Public Hall and Institute 109, **243**
    school 113, **243**
  streets and houses 103, 107, **243–5**
Bridge of Gaur **245–6**
  Braes of Rannoch Church 48, 49,
    245
  Gaur Project 130, **245–6**
Bridgend *see* Perth suburbs (Barnhill,
  Bridgend and Gannochy)
Briglands 86, 91, **246–9**
Bruar **249**
  House of Bruar, The 120, **249**
Bruceton *see* Alyth
Buchanty *see* Fowlis Wester
Burghmuir *see* Perth suburbs
Burleigh Castle 64, 65, **250–3**, 533,
  Pl. 55
Burrelton and Woodside 113, **253**

Cambusmichael 33, 36, **253–4**
Caputh **254–6**
  Caputh Church **254–6**
  Caputh Hall 109, **257**
  Caputh Parish Church (former)
    38, 55, 56, **256**
  East Cult standing stones 8, 10, **256**
  manse 122
  school (1724) 102
  Victoria Bridge and Caputh Bridge
    95, **256**
Cardean *see* Meigle
Cardney House **257**
Carey *see* Abernethy
Cargill 62, **257–8**
  Mains of Cargill ringwork 63, 64,
    258, 704
  Newbigging cup-and-ring-marked
    stone **258**
  Parish Church (former) 40, **257–8**

792   INDEX OF PLACES

Park 46
railway viaduct 96, 98, **258**
Roman fort 18, 20
Carnbane Castle **259**
Carpow *see* Abernethy
Cashlie *see* Innerwick
Castle Cluggy **259**
Castle Dow *see* Logierait
Castle Huntly 66–8, 73, 78, 90, **259–62**, 507, 511
Castle Law *see* Abernethy; Forgandenny
Castle Menzies 69, 70, 71, **262–7**, Pl. 60
Chapelhill **267**
Chesthill **267**
Clach na Tiompan *see* Amulree
Cleaven Dyke *see* Meikleour
Cleish **267–70**
  Cleish Castle **269–70**
  Dumglow fort 15
  Parish Church 47, **267–8**
  school 106, **268**
Cloan **270–1**
Clochfoldich **271**
Clunie **271–3**
  Clunie Castle 63, 91, **272**, 505
  Clunie Church 43, 44–5, **271–2**, Pl. 34
  Craigend prehistoric houses 11
  Snaigow House 86
Collace **273–4**
  Collace Free Church *see* Kinrossie
  Collace Parish Church 43, **273–4**, Pl. 14
  Dunsinane Hill fort and house sites 11, 15, 16, **274–5**
  Little Dunsinane (or Black) Hill round-houses 13
Colquhalzie **274–5**
Comrie 62, **276–81**
  churches **276–8**
    Comrie Free Church (now Hall) 46, **276**
    Comrie Parish Church (former Comrie Free Church) 47, **277–8**
    Comrie United Presbyterian Church 46, **277**
    St Serf (Episcopal) 54, **277–8**
    White Church 41, **278**, Pl. 29
  Dalginross 17, 18
  Melville Monument 61, **280–1**
  public buildings 130, **278**
    bridges 95, **278**, 281
    Parish School (former) 106, **280**
  streets, commercial buildings and houses 106, 116, **279–81**
  Tullybannocher standing stones 10
Comrie Castle 68, **281**
Coupar Angus 94, 95, 97, 99, 124, 126, **281–7**
  churches **282–4**
    Abbey Church and graveyard 30, 31–2, 36, 38, 39, 47, 60, **162–3, 281–4**
    Coupar Angus Free Church 46, **284**
    St Anne (Episcopal) 54, **284**
    St Mary (R.C.; former United Presbyterian Church) 46, **284**
  maltings 129, **287**
  public buildings **284–5**
    school and house 105, **286**
    Tolbooth Steeple 101, **285**
    Town Hall 108, **285**
  streets and houses 100, 281, **285–7**
Craig Formal *see* Aberfeldy
Craigend *see* Clunie
Craighall-Rattray **287–8**
Craigie *see* Perth suburbs
Cray **288–9**
  Lair cairn 7, **289**
Creag Bhreac *see* Spittal of Glenshee
Crieff 93, 94, 96, 97, 99, 108, **289–304**
  churches etc. **290–5**
    Crieff Free Church 47, **290–2**
    Crieff Parish Church 47, 54, **292–3**, Pl. 43
    Crieff Parish Church (former) 41, **292**
    Crieff Parish Church (medieval) 293
    St Columba (Episcopal) 278, **294**
    St Fillan (R.C.) 50, **294**
    United Presbyterian Churches 46, 47, 54, **293–4**, Pl. 45
    West Church (St Ninian) 43, 47, **295**
  public buildings **295–8**
    Crieff Hospital 119, **295–6**
    Crieff Junction (now Gleneagles) Station *see* Auchterarder
    Crieff Primary School 112, **296**
    Morrison's Academy 112, **296–7**
    Murray Fountain 61, **300**
    Police Station 110, **297**
    Post Office 110, **297**
    Taylor's Institution 112, **297**
    Tolbooth 108
    tolbooth tower 101
    Town Hall 108, **297–8**
    war memorial 60, **298**
  Rottenreoch cairn 6, **303–4**
  streets, commercial buildings and houses 103, 106, 118, 289–90, **298–303**
    banks 115, **299–301**, Pl. 113
    Crieff Hydro (former Strathearn House Hydropathic) 116, **302–3**
    gasworks 130, **303**
    High Street 100, 289, 290, **301**, Pl. 113
    Inchglas 118, **303**
    James Square 100, 289, **299–300**
    Servite House 121, **299**, Pl. 120
    tearoom (former) 116, **301**
Croftmoraig *see* Kenmore

Cromwellpark *see* Pitcairngreen
Crook of Devon 99, **304–5**
　Fossoway, St Serf's and Devonside Church 41, 60, **304–5**, 531
　mill 129, **305**
Crossmount House **306**
Culdaremore *see* Fortingall
Culdees Castle 78–9, 83, 89, **306–9**
Culteuchar Hill *see* Forgandenny
Cultoquhey House 82, **309**

Dalcrue Bridge *see* Pitcairngreen
Dalginross *see* Comrie
Dalguise House **310**
Dall House 83, **310–11**, Pl. 90
Dalmunzie House 86, **311**
Dalnaglar Castle 83, **311**
Dalpatrick *see* Innerpeffray
Denmarkfield *see* Luncarty
Derculich **312**
Dornock *see* Muthill
Dovecotland *see* Perth suburbs (Burghmuir etc.)
Dowally **312–13**
　St Anne's Church 41, 42, **312–13**
Dowhill **313**
Dowhill Castle 64, 65, 205, **314–16**
Dron **316–17**
　Abernethy and Dron Parish Church *see* Abernethy
　Dron Parish Church and manse 43–4, 122, **316–17**
Drumkilbo **318**
Drummond Castle 65, 67, 70, 87, 90, 96, **318–25**, 434, 704, Pls. 58, 91
Drummond Hill *see* Kenmore
Drummonie House **325–6**, Pl. 67
Dull **326–8**
　Carse stone circle 9
　Dull Parish Church 41, **326–7**, 744
　Dull and Weem Parish Church *see* Weem
　manses *122*, 123, **327**
　Nether Camserney 102, 124–5, 126, **327–8**
Dumglow *see* Cleish
Dun, The *see* Logierait
Dun Mac Tual fort *see* Kenmore (Drummond Hill)
Dunalastair 83, **328–9**
Dunbarney *see* Bridge of Earn
Dunbarney House **329**
Duncrub Park **329–30**
　Duncrub Castle 296
Dundurn *see* St Fillans
Dunfallandy 28–9, **330–1**, Pl.12
*Dunira 82–3, 89, 280, **331–2***
Dunkeld 3, 24, 93, 94, 96, 99, 101, **332–47**
　cathedral *26*, 32–3, 36–9, 40, 42, 49, 54, 55, 56, 57–8, 90, 313, 332, **333–42**, 346, Pls. 10, 17–19, 27, 50

　'Apostles' Stone' 29, **342**
　churches 45, **342–3**
　　Dunkeld Free Church 47, **342–3**
　Dunkeld House (*and* C17 *predecessor*) 73, 82, 88, 90, 91, 94, 209, *212*, 332, 342, **347**
　Dunkeld Palace 82, 112, 332
　King's Seat fort 15, 16
　public buildings **343–4**
　　bridges 92, 94, 332, **343**
　　Duchess Anne Halls 112, **343**, Pl. 100
　　The Ell House (C18 St George's Hospital) 101, **346**
　　fountain 61, **343–4**, Pl. 100
　　St George's Hospital 101, 346
　streets, commercial buildings and houses 101, 102–3, 105, 107, 332, **344–7**
　　Atholl Arms 105, **344**
　　Atholl Street 105, 107, 332, **347**
　　banks 114, 115, **344**, **345**
　　Bridge Street 105, 107, 332, **344**
　　Cathedral Street 100, 103, 332, **346–7**
　　The Cross 100, 103
　　High Street 100, 103, 332, **345–6**, Pl. 100
　　Old Rectory 102–3, **346–7**
　　Royal Dunkeld Hotel 105, **347**
Dunning 62, 99, **347–55**
　churches **348–52**
　　St Serf 34, 40, 41, 55, 347; Dupplin Cross 27, 29, **350–2**
　Newton of Pitcairns 112, **353–4**
　Pitcairns 82, **355**
　public buildings 112, **353**
　　Roman camp 17
　　Rossie Law fort 15
　streets and houses 348, **353–5**
　　Pitcairns 82, **355**
　　Tron Square 100, **354**
Dunsinane Hill *see* Collace
Dunsinnan House 85, **355–6**
Dupplin Castle 73, 75, 82, 86, 89, 90, 123, **356–7**
　manse 122
Dupplin Cross *see* Dunning

East Cult *see* Caputh
Ecclesiamagirdle House, chapel and graveyard 59, 65, 71, 72, 90, **357–8**
Edradour **358**
　Distillery 129, **358**, Pl. 123
Elcho Castle 64, 69–70, 71, 72, 90, **358–62**, Pl. 63
　nunnery 31
Errol 62, 126, **362–6**
　churches **362–4**
　　Errol Free Church 46, **362**
　　Errol Parish Church and grave yard 43, 44, 54, 58, **362–4**, Pl. 36

Errol Park 64, **365–6**
Law Knowe motte 62, 64, **365**
public buildings **364**
  Errol Community Centre (former Female Industrial School) 112, **364**
  Errol Primary School 114, **364**
  fountain 61, **365**
  streets and houses 100, 106, *122*, **364–5**
Evelick Castle 69, 71, **366–7**, Pl. 61
  Pole Hill fort and cairn 7, 11, 15, 16, **367**

Faskally House 82, **367**
Fearnan *see* Fortingall
Fendoch *see* Monzie
Findo Gask 41, **367–8**
  Roman watch towers (Ardunie, Kirkhill, Muir o'Fauld) **368**
Findynate House **368**
Fordel House **368**
Forgandenny **368–71**
  Castle Law fort 16
  churches **369–70**
    Forgandenny Free Church 47, **369**
    Forgandenny Parish Church 34, **369–70**
  Culteuchar Hill fort 15, **370–1**
  manse *122*
Forneth House **371**
Forteviot 117, **371–3**
  bridges 94, 95, **372**
  manses *122*, *123*, **373**
  Muckersie Church *see* Invermay
  Old School 112, **372**
  palacium of Kenneth mac Alpin 23, 24, 25, 26–7, 29
  Village Hall **372**, Pl. 118
Fortingall **373–6**
  Balnacraig dun 13
  churches **373–4**
    Fortingall Free Church 46, **373**
    Fortingall Parish Church 48, 49, **373–4**
  Culdaremore *125*, **375**
  Fearnan, Oakbank crannog site 13
  streets and houses 117, **374–5**
    Fortingall Hotel 115, **374**
    Kirkton Cottages **374**, Pl. 116
    manse *123*, **374**
Foss **376**
  Roromore, Ceann na Coille, dun 13
Fowlis Wester *124*, **376–9**
  Fowlis Wester Parish Church 28–9, 36, 52, 60, **376–8**
  St Bean's Chapel, Buchanty **377–8**
  Thorn standing stones and stone circles 9–10, **379**
Freeland House *see* Strathallan School

Gairney Bank *see* Kinross
Gannochy *see* Perth suburbs (Barnhill, Bridgend and Gannochy)
Garth Castle 65, **379**
Garth House **379–80**
Garvock House **380**
Gask House and Old House of Gask 51, 72, 77, 157, **381–2**, 535
Gellybanks *see* Luncarty
Gellyburn *see* Murthly
Gilmerton **382**
Glasclune Castle 69, 71, **382–3**
Glenalmond College 50, 52, 53, 54, 112–13, **383–90**
Glenalmond House 85, **390**
Glencarse 117, **390–2**
  All Saints (Episcopal) 51, **390–1**, Pl.53
  Glencarse House 77, **391–2**
  souterrain 12
Glendelvine House 7, **392**
Glendevon 94, **392–5**
  Glendevon Castle **394**
  Glendevon House 85, **394–5**
  Glentower House 118, **393**
Glendoick House 77, **395–6**
Gleneagles Castle *see* Gleneagles House
Gleneagles Hotel 98, 116, **396–7**
Gleneagles House 77, 90, **397–401**
  Gleneagles Chapel 64, 65, 70, **400–1**
Gleneagles Railway Station *see* Auchterarder
Glenearn House **401**
Glenfarg 95, **401–3**
  Arngask Library (former Corbett Institute) 109, **402**, Pl. 117
  Arngask School 105–6
  hotels 115, **402**
  railway viaducts *see* Aberargie
Glenfarg House 85, **403**
Glenfincastle **403**
Glenlyon Church *see* Innerwick
Glenlyon Free Church *see* Innerwick
Glenlyon House 85, **404–5**
Glenshee Parish Church *see* Spittal of Glenshee
Glenturret Distillery *see* Hosh
Gold Castle *see* Stormontfield
Grandtully 97, **405–8**
  distillery 129
  Grandtully Castle 69, 70, 83, **407–8**
  St Mary's Church 55, 59, **405–6**, Pls. 20, 23, 32

Hallyburton House 83, **408–11**
Hermitage, The 88, **411–12**
High Keillor *see* Kettins
Hillyland *see* Perth suburbs (Burghmuir etc.)
Hosh **412–13**
  Glenturret Distillery 129, **412**
  Loch Turret Water Works 130, **412–13**

INDEX OF PLACES

House of Aldie 68, 71, **413–15**
House of Urrard *see* Tenandry
Huntingtower Castle 64–5, 67, 70, 71, **415–19**, Pl. 57
Huntingtowerfield **419**
  bleach works 128, **419**
  Huntingtower Haugh *128*

Inchaffray Abbey 26, 30, 31, 33, **420**
Inchbervis Castle *see* Stanley
Inchmartin Church *see* Kinnaird
Inchmartine House **420**
Inchture 96, 97, 117, **421–2**
  harbour 99
  Inchture Hotel 105, **422**
  Inchture Parish Church 43, **421**
  Inchture Primary School 119, **421**
Inchtuthil *see* Spittalfield
Inchyra 99
Inchyra House 27, 78, **422–3**, Pl. 81
Innerpeffray **423–6**
  Church of the Blessed Virgin Mary 35, 36, 38, 58–9, **423–5**, 706n.
  Dalpatrick 25
  Innerpeffray Castle 69, 275, **426**
  Innerpeffray Library 102, **425–6**, Pl. 106
  Strageath 18, 20, 368
Innerwick **426–7**
  Cashlie and Lubreoch Power Stations 130, **427**
  Glenlyon and Glenlyon Free churches **427**
  Roromore 13
Inver **427–8**
  inn 104, **427**
  viaduct 98, **428**
  see also Hermitage, The
Invergowrie 99, **428–32**
  Bullionfield Mill 128, **428**, *432*
  churches **428–31**
    All Souls (Episcopal) 4, 52, **428–30**
    Invergowrie Parish Church (former) 33, **430**
  public buildings **431**
    Invergowrie Primary School 113, **431**
  streets and houses **432**
    Brantwood 118, **432**
Invermay 29, **433–4**
  Muckersie Parish Church 372, 434
Inverquiech Castle 63, 91, **434–5**
Isle of Loch Tay **435–6**

Jordanstone 86, **436–8**

Kaims Castle *see* Braco
Keillour Castle **438**
Keithick 85, 89, 91, **438–40**, Pls. 82, 83
Keltie Castle **440–1**
Keltneyburn **441**
  Achloa 126, **441**
  bridge 95, **441**

Dun Mac Tual fort 15, 16, **441**
Litigan 25
Stewart Monument 61, **441**
Keltybridge 106, **442**
Kenmore 97, **442–6**
  Croftmoraig stone circle 8–9, 10, 11, **446**, Pl.4
  Kenmore Parish Church 41, 42, 54, 60, **442–4**
  public buildings **444**
    bridges 92, 93, 104, **444**
    library 109, **444**
  streets, commercial buildings and houses 90, 103, 117, **444–6**
    Kenmore Hotel 104, **445**
    manse 122
    The Square 109, 117, **445**
Kettins **446–50**
  High Keillor symbol stone 27, **450**
  Kettins Parish Church 41, 47, 60, **446–9**
  Lintrose souterrain 12
  Pitcur souterrain 12, **449–50**
Kilgraston School 53, 78, 91, **450–3**, Pl. 94
Killiechassie *see* Weem
Kilnockiebank *see* Aberargie
Kilspindie **453–4**
  Kilspindie and Rait Church and manse 40, 41, 55, 60, 123, **453–4**
  Pitroddie Farm 12–13
Kincairney House **454**
Kincardine Castle 79, **454–5**
Kinclaven **455–7**
  Bridge of Isla **457**, Pl. 97
  Kinclaven Castle 63, 91, **457**, 565
  Kinclaven Church 54, 60, **455–7**
Kindrochet *see* St Fillans
Kinfauns **457–64**
  Kinfauns Castle 55, 81, **460–4**
  Kinfauns Parish Church and graveyard 33, 37, 41, 42, 47, 55, 59, **457–9**
  manse 122
  tower (Binn Hill) 61, **459**
Kingoodie 99
Kings of Kinloch **464–5**
King's Seat *see* Dunkeld
Kinkell **465–6**
  churches **465–6**
    Antiburgher church (former) 45, **465**
    St Bean 40, **465–6**
  Kinkell Bridge 94, **466**
  North Mains 7
Kinloch **466–8**
  Kinloch House 85, **467–8**
  Kinloch Parish Church **466–7**
  manse (C18) 122
  Manse (C19; now The Old Pastorie) 123, **467**
Kinloch Rannoch 93, 103, **468–9**
Kinmouth House 83, **469–70**

INDEX OF PLACES

Kinnaird 62, **470–2**
  Barton Hill motte 62, 64, **470**
  churches **470–1**
    Inchmartin Church, Westown 33, **470–1**
  Kinnaird Castle 64, 66–7, 70, 90, **471–2**, Pls. 59, 92
  Manse 123, **471**
Kinnaird House 85, **472–3**
Kinnesswood **473–4**
  Glenlomond Hospital 111, **474**
Kinnoull Tower 61, **651**, Pl. 1
Kinross 94, 95, 96, 97, 99, **474–94**
  churches and churchyard **474–7**
    Antiburgher Church 45, **474–5**
    Kinross Parish Church (medieval) 55, 60, **476–7**
    Kinross Parish Church (C18) 108, **476**, 478
    Kinross Parish Church 43, **475–6**
    St Paul (Episcopal) 51, 54, **476**
    West United Presbyterian Church 46, **476**
  Gairney Bank 8
  industrial buildings 127, 474, **479**
  Kinross House 74–5, 87, 89, 90, **483–94**, Pls. 69–72
  public buildings **477–9**
    bridge 92, **479**
    County Buildings 103–4, **477**
    County House 101, **477–8**, Pl. 105
    Leisure Centre 120, **478**
    Library 109, **478**
    market cross 100, **479–80**
    Rachel House 119, **478**
    Town Hall 108, **478–9**
  streets, commercial buildings and houses 474, **479–83**
    Bank of Scotland (former British Linen Co. Bank) 114, **482**
    manses 123, **480**, 481
    Sandport 100, **479–80**
Kinrossie **494**
  Collace Free Church 46, **494**
  Mercat Cross **494**, 522, Pl. 103
Kippen House **494**
Kirkhill *see* Findo Gask
Kirkmichael **495–6**
  Balchrochan cairn 7, **495–6**
  Duff Memorial Free Church 47, **495**
  Kirkmichael Parish Church 40, 41, **495**
  Pitcarmick 11
  school and house 105, **495**
Kirktown of Collace *see* Collace
Knapp **496**

Lair *see* Cray
Law Knowe *see* Errol
Lawers **496–7**
  Machuim stone circle 9, **497**
  toll house 94, **497**
Lawers House 75, 77–8, 89, **497–500**

Lendrick Muir **500**
Letham *see* Perth suburbs (Burghmuir etc.)
Lethendy 62, *122*, **500–1**
  Lethendy and Kinloch Free Church 46, **500**
  Upper Gothens 12, 25
Litigan *see* Keltneyburn
Little Dunkeld *see* Birnam
Little Dunsinane (or Black) Hill *see* Collace
Lochlane 77, **501**
Lochleven Castle 63, 64, 74, 483, 486, 489–90, **501**, Pl. 54
Loch of Clunie Castle 272, **505**
Logiealmond *see* Chapelhill
Logierait **506–7**
  Blackhill Distillery 129
  forts (Castle Dow and The Dun) 16
  court house 101
  Logierait Parish Church 41, 52, 59, 341n., **506–7**
  cross-slab 29, **507**
  Logierait House (former manse) 123, **507**
  public buildings **507–8**
    Logierait Primary School *see* Ballinluig
    poorhouse 110, **507**
    railway viaduct 98, **507**
    schools 102, 105
Longforgan 99, 262, 496, **507–12**
  churches **508–11**
    Free Church (former) *see* Invergowrie
    Longforgan Parish Church 37, 38, 40, 41, 49, 54, 57, 59, 60, **508–11**
  public buildings **511–12**
    Longforgan Primary School 112, **511**
    market cross 101, **511**
    war memorial 60, **512**
Lubreoch *see* Innerwick
Lude House 82, **512**
Luncarty 97, **512–13**
  Denmarkfield Station 98, **513**
  Gellybanks standing stones 10

Macbeth's Stone *see* Belmont Castle
Machuim *see* Lawers
Madderty 123, **513–14**
Margmore *see* Aberfeldy
Meggernie Castle 70, 404, **514–16**
Megginch Castle 91, **515–16**, Pl. 93
Megginch Castle *see* Meggernie Castle
Meigle 99, **516–22**
  Cardean Roman forts 18
  churches **516–18**
    Kinloch Mausoleum 55, **518**
    Meigle Parish Church 37, 47, 48, **516–18**

INDEX OF PLACES

Pictish 520
St Margaret (Episcopal) 152
Meigle stones 27, 28–9, 30, **518–21**, Pls. 7–9, 11
South West Fullarton fragments **522**
Meikle Findowie *see* Amulree
Meikleour 62, **522–5**
   Cleaven Dyke 5, **523**
   Meikleour Hotel 105, **523**
   Meikleour House 75, 84, **523–5**
   Mercat Cross 100, 494, **522**, Pl. 102
   motte 62, **525**
   Upper Gothens *see* Lethendy
Methven 96, **525–9**
   churches **526–7**
     Methven and Logiealmond Parish Church, Lynedoch Mausoleum and Methven Aisle 26, 35, 43, 44, 55, **526–7**, Pls. 16, 31, 33
     Methven United Presbyterian Church 46, **527**
   Methven Castle 73, 326, **528–9**, Pl. 68
   public buildings, streets and houses **527–8**
   Lynedoch House (former manse) 123, **528**
   see also Glenalmond College
Middleton Muir *see* Bridge of Cally
Millearne 81–2, 86, **529–30**
Milltown of Aberdalgie *see* Aberdalgie
Milnathort 95, 96, 97, 127, **530–5**
   churches **530–2**
     Burgher Church 45, **530–1**
     Milnathort United Presbyterian Church 46, 47, **531**
     Orwell Parish Church 60, 304, **531–2**
   Orwell standing stones 10, 11, **535**
   public buildings **532**
     Ochil Hills Sanatorium 111
     Town Hall 108, **532**
   streets, commercial buildings and houses **532–5**
     Orwell House (former manse) 123, **534**
Milton of Edradour *see* Edradour
Moncreiffe *see* Perth suburbs (Craigie and Moncreiffe)
Moncreiffe House 86, **535–6**
   'Bore Stone' 28–9, **535**
   stone circle 9, **536**
Moncur Castle 69, 71, **536–7**
Moness House *see* Aberfeldy
Moneydie **537–8**
   Moneydie Parish Church and Manse 43, 123, **537–8**
Monzie **538–42**
   Fendoch Roman watch tower 18, 20, **539**
   Monzie Castle 9, 10, 73, 78, 91, **539–42**

Monzie Free Church *see* Gilmerton
Monzie Parish Church 43, 49, 54, 59, **538–9**
Monzievaird **542–4**
   Baird Monument 61, **543**
   fort 24, **543**
   churches **543**
     Monzievaird and Strowan Parish Church 40, **543**
     Strowan Church **543**
   Monzievaird House (manse) 123, **544**
   school 111–12, **543**
Morenish **544–5**
Moulin *see* Pitlochry
Muckersie Church *see* Invermay
Muirton *see* Perth suburbs (Balhousie and Muirton)
Murrayshall **545**
Murthly **545–53**
   Chapel of St Anthony the Eremite 40, 42, 49–50, 51, 53, 57, **550–3**
   Gellyburn 28
   Murthly Castle 68, 73, 75, 83, 84, 86, 89, 96, 199, 407, **546–50**, Pls. 41, 42, 73
     chapel *see* Chapel of St Anthony the Eremite *above*
   Perthshire District Lunatic Asylum 111
   Stewart Tower 126, **545**
Muthill 62, 96, **553–7**
   churches 47, **553–6**
     Muthill Old Church 26, 34, 36, 39, **553–5**, Pl.13
     Muthill Parish Church 43, 44, 45, **555**
     St James (Episcopal) 45, **555–6**
   Dornock Roman camp 17
   streets and houses 103, 107, 123, **556–7**

Nether Camserney *see* Dull
New Scone 126, **557–61**
   Arnbathie 15
   churches **557–9**
     Scone New Church 47, 48, **557–8**, Pl. 44
     Scone Old Parish Church 40–1, 42, **558–9**, Pl. 24
     Scone Parish Church *see* Scone Palace
   Old Scone 100, 557, 689, 696
   public buildings **559–60**
     Robert Douglas Memorial Institute (former school) 113, **560**
     Robert Douglas Memorial School 119, **560**
   Shien Hill cairn 7, **560–1**
   stone circle 9, **561**
Newbigging *see* Cargill
Newton Castle *see* Blairgowrie

INDEX OF PLACES

Newton of Pitcairns *see* Dunning
Newtyle *see* Dunkeld

Oakbank *see* Fortingall; Perth suburbs (Burghmuir etc.)
Ochtertyre 55, 77, 91, **561–3**
Ogle Hill *see* Auchterarder
Old Blair *see* Blair Atholl
Old Fincastle 76–7, **563**
Old House of Gask *see* Gask House
Old Mains of Rattray *see* Blairgowrie
Old Scone see New Scone
Orchil House **564**
Orwell *see* Milnathort

Park *see* Cargill
Perth City Centre (*for the outer areas, see* Perth suburbs) 1, 3, 39, 94, 95, 96, 97, 99–100, 108, 126, **564–643**
Bertha 18, 19, 22, 91, 238, 368
castle **564–6**
churches etc.:
  Baptist Chapel (now Perth Gospel Hall) 45, **637**
  Blackfriars (Dominican) friary 31, 566, 615, 628
  Carmelite friary 31, 566
  Carthusian friary (Charterhouse) 31, 566, 575, 622
  Church of England chapel (*1796–1800*) 45
  Franciscan (Greyfriars) friary 31, 58, 566, 593
  Free Presbyterian Church (Fortviot Hall) **582–3**
  Glasite meeting house (Grant Miller Memorial Hall) **622**
  Greyfriars Burial Ground 58, 59–60, 99, **593–8**
  Kinnoull Churches *see* Perth suburbs (Barnhill, Bridgend and Gannochy)
  Methodist Chapel (former), South Street 45, **637**
  Middle Free Church (former), Blackfriars Street **583**
  Middle Free Church, Tay Street 4, **583**, **588**
  North Church (former North United Presbyterian Church) 46, 48, **583**
  Old Light Antiburgher Chapel 45, **584**
  Perth Congregational Church **584**
  Perth Methodist Church **584**
  St Andrew 47, **584**
  St John the Baptist (Episcopal) 51, 52, **584–5**
  St John the Baptist (R.C.) 45, **584**, 627
  St John's Kirk of Perth (burgh church) 31, 34–5, 36, 37, 38, 39–40, 42, 52–3, 54, 100, 565, 566, **570–82**, Pl. 15
  St Leonard 43, 53, **585–6**, 622
  St Leonard's-in-the-Fields and Trinity (originally St Leonard's Free) 48, **586–7**, 626
  St Mary's Chapel 101, 108, **603–4**
  St Matthew (originally West Free Church) 47, 48, 49, **587–8**
  St Ninian's Cathedral (Episcopal) 50–1, 52, 54, 58, **588–92**, Pl. 46, 49, 51
  St Paul 41–2, 241, **592–3**, 622, Pl. 37
  St Stephen's United Free Church **593**
  Salvation Army Halls **636**
  Tayside Christian Fellowship **593**
  Trinity Church of the Nazarene (former York Place United Presbyterian Church) 48, **593**
  Wilson United Presbyterian Church 4
  York Place United Presbyterian Church (former) 48, **593**
industrial buildings 126–31, 565, 567–9, **642–3**
  Arthur Bell & Sons (whisky) 568, 569, 658, **662**
  City Mills 128, **642–3**
  Dye Works, St Catherine's Road (Highland House shopping centre) 128, 630, **643**
  Isla Distillery 129, **658**
  Milne's Cold Storage and Ice Factory **634**
  North British Dye Works and Pullar House 128, 568, 569, 623, **643**
  J. Pullar & Sons *see* North British Dye Works *above*
  Upper City Mills (Ramada Jarvis Hotel) **643**
  Wallace Works (John Shields & Co.) *127*
public buildings 104–6, 108–14, 568, **599–612**, 641
  A. K. Bell Public Library 110–11, 119, **599**, 642
  Caledonian Road Primary School 114, **599**
  City Hall *see* Perth City Hall *below*
  Council Buildings (former General Accident, Fire & Life head office) 117, 119, **599–601**, Pl. 115
  County Buildings (formerly part of Sheriff Court) 104, 110, **601–2**, 641
  Cromwellian citadels 566–7
  Fergusson Gallery (former Perth Waterworks) 119, **602**, 625
  Fortviot Hall **582–3**

INDEX OF PLACES

gas works 130
Grant Miller Memorial Hall **622**
Guildhall *101*, 109, **620–1**
Harbour 99, **602**
King James VI Hospital 101–2, **603**, 622, Pl. 104
Market Cross 100
Murray Royal Hospital *see* Perth suburbs (Barnhill, Bridgend and Gannochy)
Old Council Chambers 108, **603–4**, Pl. 114
Perth Academy 610, **661**
Perth Barracks 568
Perth Bridge *92*, 93–4, 103, *565*, *566*, 567, **604**, 647
Perth City and County Infirmary 110–11, 119, **599**
Perth City Hall *108*, 109, 569, **604–5**
Perth Concert Hall 120, **605**, Pl. 122
Perth Grammar School *105*, 106, 119, 610, *635*, **646**
Perth Leisure Pool 119, **663**, Pl. 121
Perth Museum and Art Gallery 104, **605**, Pl. 111
Perth Prison 109–10, 568, **605–8**
Perth Royal Infirmary *see* Perth suburbs (Burghmuir etc.)
Perth Sheriff Court 108, **609**, 641, Pl. 110
Perth Theatre 104, 109, **609–10**
Perth Waterworks 131, **602**, 625, **647**
Playhouse Cinema 120, **627**
Police Headquarters *110*, 119, **610**
Public Baths and Washhouses 109, 627
Public Seminaries 106, 107, **610**, 630, Pl. 108
Queen's Bridge 95, **610**
Railway Station 98, **610–11**, 658
Railway Viaduct 96, 98, **611**, 625
St John's Primary School **611**
Sandeman Public Library 109, **612**
sculpture 61–2, 570, **602**, 610, **613**, 617, 619, 621, 627, 640, **643**; Prince Albert 61, **613**; King Edward VII Memorial 100, 568–9, **623**; *Fair Maid* 61, **619**; *Fish with a Boy* 62, **625**; 51st Highland Division Monument 61, **613**; *Nae Dae Sae Dark*, High Street 61, **621**; Sir Walter Scott 61, **626**; *Seasons, Time, and Place* 62, **630**; Tay Street 62, **640**; *Torse de Femme* 62, **602**
Sharp's Educational Institution 112, **612**
Sheriff Court *see* County Buildings *above*

swimming pool 109
Telephone Exchange **612**
Theatre Royal 104, **613**
Tolbooth 101, 108, 604
town walls, moat and gates 99–100, *565*, *566*, *567*, 615
Victoria Bridge 95
Wrights' Incorporation hall 101, **641**
streets, commercial buildings and houses 102–3, 106–7, 115–18, 117–18, 565–9, **612–42**
Atholl Crescent 107, *567*, **612**, Pl. 107
Atholl Place 107, *567*, **613**
Atholl Street **613–14**
banks 114, 120; Bank of Scotland, St John Street 115, **630**; British Linen Bank, George Street 114, **618**; Central Bank of Scotland, St John Street 114, **631–2**; Clydesdale Bank, South Methven Street 120, **638**; Perth Bank, George Street 114, **618**; Royal Bank of Scotland, Kinnoull Street 115, **624**
Barossa Place 107, **614–15**
Barossa Street **615**
Blackfriars House 107, **628**
Blackfriars Street 130, *566*, **615**
Caledonian Road **615**
Canal Crescent *565*, **615**
Canal Street 109, 130, *565*, 567, **615–16**
Charlotte House 106–7, **616**
Charlotte Street and Charlotte Place 106, *567*, **616–17**
Exchange Coffee Room 105, **618**
Fair Maid of Perth's House 102, **628**
Flesher's Vennel **639**
General Accident, Fire & Life Assurance Corporation 120, 568, **639**, *658*; *see also* public buildings (Council Buildings) *above*
George Street 103, 105, 114, *567*, **617–18**
Matthew Gloag & Son 116, 568, **624**
Gowrie House (dem. 1807) *102*, *566*, 609
Gowrie House (1873) **640–1**
Graham Place **622**
High Street 99, 100, 109, *565*, *567*, **618–22**, 624
hotels 105, 115; City Hotel 105, **635**; Quality (former Station) Hotel 115, **625**; Royal George Hotel 105, **617**, 640; Salutation Hotel 105, **635**, Pl. 109
James Street **622**

King Street 116, **622–3**, 626
King Edward Street 120, 568, **623**
King James Place and King's Place **625–6**
Kinnoull Street 116, 117, **623–5**, 643
Kirkgate 565, 632
Leonard Street **625**
Marshall Place 107, **625–6**
Meal Vennel 565
Melville Street 567, **626–7**
Mill Street 109, 565, **627**, 643
Mill Wynd **627**
Milne Street **615**
Murray Street **627**
New Row 117, 566, 567, **642**
North Methven Street **627–8**
North Port 102, 107, **628**
Pomarium and Pomarium Street 121, 567, **628**, 656
Princes Street 567, **628–30**
Rose Terrace 106, 107, 567, **630**
St Catherine's Road **630**
St John Street 103, 107, 114, 116, 567, **630–2**, Pl. 112
St John's Place 573, **632**
St Johnstoun's Buildings 118, **641**
St Leonard's Bank **632–3**
Scott Street 117, **633–4**, 637
shops and supermarkets 116, 120, **615**, **623**, **630**; St John Street 116, **632**; St John's Shopping Centre 120, **623**, 637
Shore Road 130, **634**
Skinnergate 565, **634**, 643
South Street 99, 100, 105, 120, 565, 567, 628–9, **634–8**
South Methven Street 565, **638–9**
South St John's Place **639**
South William Street **639**
Speygate 566, **639**
Tay Street 62, **639–41**
Unity Place 118, **641**
Victoria Street 118, **641**
Watergate 99, 101, 102, 565, 566, **641–2**
West Mill Street *see* Mill Street and Murray Street *above*
Whitefriars Street 566
York Place 117, **642**
Perth suburbs (*for the City Centre, see* Perth City Centre) 103, 105, **644–65**
 Balhousie and Muirton **646–7**
  churches **646**; Riverside Church 53, **646**
  public buildings **646–7**; Balhousie Primary 114, **646**; Gannochy Trust Sports Complex 119–20, **646**; Perth Grammar School 119, **646**
  streets and houses **647**; Muirton housing scheme 121, 569
 Barnhill, Bridgend and Gannochy **647–59**
  churches **648–51**; Kinnoull Church (former) 55, 57, **648–50**; Kinnoull Church 43, 44, 54, **650–1**
  public buildings **651–4**; Friarton Bridge 95, **651**; Hillside Hospital 111, **651**; Kinnoull Primary School 113, **651**; Kinnoull Tower 61, **651**, Pl. 1; Murray Royal Hospital 111, **651–2**; St Mary's Pastoral and Retreat Centre 50, **652–4**; toll house 94, **654**; Upper Springland Centre 119, **654**
  streets, houses and villas 118, 121, 567, 568, 647, **654–9**; Ardchoille 118, **657**; Balnacraig 118, **654**; Bowerswell 118, **655**; Braco House 118, **659**; Bridgend Court 121, **656**; Commercial Street 121, **656**; Craigievar and Darnick 118, **655**; Gannochy housing development 569, **658**; Inchbank House 107, **656–7**; Knowehead House 118, **655**; Manderley 121, **655–6**; Meadowland 121, **659**; Potterhill Flats 121, **656**; Rose Cottage 118, **658**; St Leonard's Manse 118, **654**; Tayside Nursing Home (former General Accident offices) 120, **658**
 Bridgend *see* Barnhill, Bridgend and Gannochy *above*
 Burghmuir, Dovecotland, Hillyland, Letham and Oakbank **659–63**
  churches and Wellshill cemetery **660**
  offices **662**; Norwich Union (former General Accident) 120, **662**
  public buildings **660–2**; Perth Academy 119, **661**; Perth High School 119, **661**; Perth Royal Infirmary 110–11, 119, **661–2**
  villas and housing 569, 659, **662–3**; Pitheavlis Cottages 117, **662**
 Craigie and Moncreiffe **663–4**
  churches **663**; Craigend Moncreiffe Church 53, **663**; Craigie Church 4, 46, 367, **663**
  public buildings **663–4**; Dewar's Rink 120, **663**; Perth Christian Centre (former Dewar & Sons office) 116–17, **663**; Perth Leisure Pool 119, **663**, Pl. 121; Rosslyn House

INDEX OF PLACES

(former Perth Poorhouse) 110, **664**
Dovecotland *see* Burghmuir, Dovecotland, Hillyland, Letham and Oakbank *above*
Gannochy *see* Barnhill, Bridgend and Gannochy *above*
Hillyland *see* Burghmuir, Dovecotland, Hillyland, Letham and Oakbank *above*
Kinnoull *see* Barnhill, Bridgend and Gannochy *above*
Letham *see* Burghmuir, Dovecotland, Hillyland, Letham and Oakbank *above*
Moncreiffe *see* Craigie and Moncreiffe *above*
Muirton *see* Balhousie and Muirton *above*
Oakbank *see* Burghmuir, Dovecotland, Hillyland, Letham and Oakbank *above*
Pitheavlis Castle **664**
Tulloch **664–5**
bleach works 127
Hunter Crescent 121, **664–5**
Tulloch Works and housing for Pullar & Sons 117, **664–5**
Tullochfield dyeworks 128
Peterford *see* Blackford
Pitcairngreen 47, 103, **665–6**
Cromwellpark mills and dyeworks 127, 128
Dalcrue farmhouse 94, 126, **666**
Dalcrue Bridge 94, **665**
Lynedoch Cottage 94, 126, **666**
Pitcairns *see* Dunning
Pitcarmick *see* Kirkmichael
Pitcastle *see* Strathtay
Pitcur (souterrain) *see* Kettins
Pitcur Castle 68, 71, **666–7**
Pitfour Castle 78, **667–8**
Pitheavlis Castle *see* Perth suburbs
Pitlochry **668–75**
Balnacraig distillery 129
churches **669–71**
Holy Trinity (Episcopal) 51, 52, 54, **669**, Pl. 47
Moulin Parish Church 42, 49, **670**
Moulin (Pitlochry) Free Church 46, **670**
Pitlochry Parish Church 46, 48, 49, **670–1**
Moulin 103, 669, **674**
public buildings **671–2**
Aldour Bridge 95, **671**
Pitlochry Dam and Power Station 130, **671**, Pl. 126
Pitlochry Festival Theatre 120, **671–2**, Pl. 119
Pitlochry Town Hall 108, **672**
Police Station 110, **673**
Railway Station 98, **672**
suspension bridge 95, **672**
streets, commercial buildings and houses 118, 669, **672–5**
Atholl Palace Hotel (former Atholl Hydropathic) 116, **675**
Bank House (former Commercial Bank) 115, **674**
Blair Atholl Distillery 129, **675**
Moulin Castle (Caisteal Dubh) 63, **675**
Pitnacree *see* Pitnacree House; Strathtay
Pitnacree House **675–6**
Pitroddie Farm *see* Kilspindie
Pole Hill *see* Evelick Castle
Portmoak *see* Scotlandwell
Priory Island *see* Isle of Loch Tay

Rait 41, **676**, Pl. 101
see also Kilspindie
Rannoch Station 97, 98, **676**
Rattray Parish Church *see* Blairgowrie
Redgorton 4, 60, **676–7**
Rhynd 42, 43, **677–8**
Rohallion Lodge **678–9**
Rosemount *see* St Martins
Rossie (village) 683
Rossie Church *see* Rossie Priory
Rossie House 90, **679**
Rossie Law *see* Dunning
Rossie Ochil **679–80**
Rossie Priory 13, 52, 53, 81, 89, 96, 113, 422, 428–30, **680–3**
Rossie Church (now mausoleum) 28–9, 33, 38, 101, **681–3**
Rottenreoch *see* Crieff
Rumbling Bridge 94, 97, 104, **683–4**
bridges 92, 94, 104, **683–4**
Ruthvenfield **684**, 732
dyeworks 128, **684**

St Fillans 117, 130, **684–6**
churches **684–5**
Dundurn Parish Church 46, **684**
Dundurn fort 24, **685–6**, Pl. 5
Kindrochet cairn 6, **685**
public buildings **685–6**
Drummond Arms Hotel 115, **685**
Railway Station 98, **685**
St Madoes 4, **686**
St Madoes and Kinfauns Parish Church 28–9, 41, 42, **686**
St Martins **687–8**
Rosemount 15, 16
St Martin's Abbey 77, 89, **688**
St Martins Parish Church 43, 45, 57, 60, **687–8**, Pls. 28, 39, 40
St Serf's Priory 26, 30, 31, **688–9**
Scone Abbey see Scone Palace
Scone Palace 72, 80–1, 89, 122, **689–97**, Pls. 25, 79–80

market cross 100, **696**
Mausoleum 56, 57, 58, **694–5**
Moot Hill mound 24, **694**
Scone Abbey/Priory 30, 31, 32, *690–2*
Scone Parish Church (former) 55, **694**
Scone Parish Church *see* Scone Palace
Scone Priory see Scone Palace
Scotlandwell 106, **697–8**
Portmoak Parish Church 59, **697–8**, Pl. 30
Shien Hill *see* New Scone
Snaigow House see Clunie
Solsgirth House **698–9**
South West Fullarton *see* Meigle
Spittal of Glenshee **699**
Creag Bhreac 11
Glenshee Bridge 93, **699**
Spittalfield 103, **700**
Inchtuthil enclosure and fort 8, 15, 18–20, **700**
Muckle Hoose 127, **700**
Stralochy 12
Wester Drumatherty 11
see also Glendelvine House
Stanley 103, **700–3**
Inchbervis Castle 63, **703**
Stanley House 124, **703**
Stanley Mills 103, 127, 130, **700**, **701–3**
Bell Mill 127, **702**, Pl. 125
streets and houses 103, **700**, **703**
Stobhall 64, 69, 71, 87, **704–9**
Chapel 71–2, **706–8**, Pls. 62, 64
Dower House and gatehouse 64, 65, 72, **704–6**
sundials 440, **704**, **708–9**
Stormontfield **709**
Blairhall 5
bleach works 128, **709**
Colen stone circle 8
Gold Castle 15
Strageath *see* Innerpeffray
Straloch **710**
Straloch House 86, **710**
Tulloch Field 11
Stralochy *see* Spittalfield
Strathallan Castle 78, 89, **710–13**
Strathallan School (former Freeland House) 82–3, 91, **713–15**
Strathgroy *see* Blair Atholl
Strathtay **715–16**

Ballechin distillery 129
Pitnacree 5, 6–7, 11
Strathtummel 105, **716**
Allean House 83, **716**
Struan **716–17**
road bridge and railway viaduct 98, **716–17**, Pl. 96

Taymouth Castle 9, 75, 79–80, 87–90, 91, 109, 129, 156, **717–31**, Pls. 84–6, 87, 88
garden (Mains of Taymouth) **445**
Kenmore Gate 445, **728–9**
Newhall 88–9, 441, **730–1**
Tenandry **731**
House of Urrard 82, **731**
Thorn *see* Fowlis Wester
Tibbermore **732–3**
Parish Church and manse 123, **732–3**, Pl. 21
Tirinie *see* Blair Atholl
Tower of Lethendy 68, 83, **733–4**
Trinity Gask **734–5**
Tullibardine **735–6**
Tullibardine Castle **735**
Tullibardine Church 35, 399, **735–6**
Tulliebole Castle 30, 68, 70, 90, **737–40**
Tulliemet House **740**
Tulloch *see* Perth suburbs
Tulloch Field *see* Straloch
Tullybannocher *see* Comrie
Tullybelton House 192, **740–1**
Tummel Bridge **741**
Bridge 93, **741**
Tyndrum *see* Aberfeldy

Upper Gothens *see* Lethendy

Weem **741–5**
Dull and Weem Parish Church **741–2**
Killiechassie 90, **745**
Weem Hotel 105, **744**
Weem Parish Church (former; Menzies Mausoleum) 40, 56–7, **742–4**, Pls. 22, 26
Welton, The *see* Blairgowrie
Wester Drumatherty *see* Spittalfield
Whitefield Castle 68, **745–6**
Wolfhill **746**
Woodend **746**
Woodside *see* Burrelton and Woodside